CCNP and CCIE Enterprise Core

ENCOR 350-401

Official Cert Guide, Second Edition

BRAD EDGEWORTH, CCIE No. 31574

RAMIRO GARZA RIOS, CCIE No. 15469

DAVID HUCABY, CCIE No. 4594

JASON GOOLEY, CCIE No. 38759

Cisco Press

CCNP and CCIE Enterprise Core ENCOR 350-401 Official Cert Guide, Second Edition

Brad Edgeworth, Ramiro Garza Rios, David Hucaby, Jason Gooley

Published by: Cisco Press

1 2023

ISBN-13: 978-0-13-821676-4

ISBN-10: 0-13-821676-2

Warning and Disclaimer

This book is designed to provide information about the CCNP and CCIE Enterprise Core Exam. Every effort has been made to make this book as complete and as accurate as possible, but no warranty or fitness is implied.

The information is provided on an "as is" basis. The authors, Cisco Press, and Cisco Systems, Inc. shall have neither liability nor responsibility to any person or entity with respect to any loss or damages arising from the information contained in this book or from the use of the discs or programs that may accompany it.

The opinions expressed in this book belong to the authors and are not necessarily those of Cisco Systems, Inc.

Trademark Acknowledgments

All terms mentioned in this book that are known to be trademarks or service marks have been appropriately capitalized. Cisco Press or Cisco Systems, Inc., cannot attest to the accuracy of this information. Use of a term in this book should not be regarded as affecting the validity of any trademark or service mark.

Special Sales

For information about buying this title in bulk quantities, or for special sales opportunities (which may include electronic versions; custom cover designs; and content particular to your business, training goals, marketing focus, or branding interests), please contact our corporate sales department at corpsales@pearsoned.com or (800) 382-3419.

For government sales inquiries, please contact governmentsales@pearsoned.com.

For questions about sales outside the U.S., please contact intlcs@pearson.com.

Feedback Information

At Cisco Press, our goal is to create in-depth technical books of the highest quality and value. Each book is crafted with care and precision, undergoing rigorous development that involves the unique expertise of members from the professional technical community.

Readers' feedback is a natural continuation of this process. If you have any comments regarding how we could improve the quality of this book, or otherwise alter it to better suit your needs, you can contact us through email at feedback@ciscopress.com. Please make sure to include the book title and ISBN in your message.

We greatly appreciate your assistance.

Vice President, IT Professional: Mark Taub

Alliances Managers, Cisco Press: Jaci Featherly, James Risler

Director, ITP Product Management: Brett Bartow

Executive Editor: Malobika Chakraborty

Managing Editor: Sandra Schroeder

Senior Project Editor: Tonya Simpson

Copy Editor: Chuck Hutchinson

Composition: codeMantra

Technical Editors: Richard Furr, Denise Fishburne, Dmitry Figol, Patrick Croak

Editorial Assistant: Cindy Teeters

Cover Designer: Chuti Prasertsith

Development Editor: Ellie Bru

Indexer: Timothy Wright

Proofreader: Donna E. Mulder

Americas Headquarters
Cisco Systems, Inc.
San Jose, CA

Asia Pacific Headquarters
Cisco Systems (USA) Pte. Ltd.
Singapore

Europe Headquarters
Cisco Systems International BV Amsterdam,
The Netherlands

Cisco has more than 200 offices worldwide. Addresses, phone numbers, and fax numbers are listed on the Cisco Website at **www.cisco.com/go/offices.**

About the Author(s)

Brad Edgeworth, CCIE No. 31574 (R&S and SP), is an SD-WAN technical solutions architect at Cisco Systems. Brad is a distinguished speaker at Cisco Live, where he has presented on various topics. Before joining Cisco, Brad worked as a network architect and consultant for various Fortune 500 companies. Brad's expertise is based on enterprise and service provider environments, with an emphasis on architectural and operational simplicity. Brad holds a bachelor of arts degree in computer systems management from St. Edward's University in Austin, Texas. Brad can be found on Twitter as @BradEdgeworth.

Ramiro Garza Rios, CCIE No. 15469 (R&S, SP, and Security), has over 20 years of experience in the networking industry and currently works as a solutions architect in the Cisco Customer Experience (CX) organization. His expertise is on enterprise and service provider network environments, with a focus on evolving architectures and next-generation technologies. He is also a Cisco Live distinguished speaker.

Before joining Cisco Systems in 2005, he was a network consulting and presales engineer for a Cisco Gold Partner in Mexico, where he planned, designed, and implemented both enterprise and service provider networks.

David Hucaby, CCIE No. 4594 (R&S), CWNE No. 292, is a technical education content engineer for Cisco Meraki, where he focuses on eLearning for the Meraki product lines. David holds bachelor's and master's degrees in electrical engineering from the University of Kentucky. He has been authoring Cisco Press titles for almost 25 years.

Jason Gooley, CCIEx2 (RS, SP) No. 38759, has over 30 years of experience in the industry and currently works as a technical evangelist for the Worldwide Enterprise Networking and Software Sales team at Cisco Systems. Jason is passionate about helping others in the industry succeed. In addition to being a public speaker, Jason is a published Cisco Press author, developer of CCIE exams, an online training instructor, and a blogger. Jason is also co-founder and organizer of the Chicago Network Operators Group (CHI-NOG). He is the founder and host of *MetalDevOps*, which is a YouTube video show about the intersection of metal music and technology.

About the Technical Reviewers

Richard Furr, CCIE No. 9173 (R&S and SP), is an technical leader in the Cisco Customer Experience (CX) organization, providing support for customers and TAC teams around the world. Richard has authored and acted as a technical editor for Cisco Press publications. During the past 19 years, Richard has provided support to service provider, enterprise, and data center environments, resolving complex problems with routing protocols, MPLS, IP Multicast, IPv6, and QoS.

Denise "Fish" Fishburne, CCDE No. 2009::0014, CCIE No. 2639 (R&S and SNA), is a solutions architect with Cisco Systems. Fish is a geek who absolutely adores learning and passing it on. Fish has been with Cisco since 1996 and has worn many varying "hats," such as TAC engineer, advanced services engineer, CPOC engineer, and now solutions architect. Fish is heavily involved with Cisco Live, which is a huge passion of hers. Outside of Cisco, you will find her actively sharing and "passing it on" on her blog site, YouTube channel, and Twitter. Look for Fish swimming in the bits and bytes all around you or just go to www.NetworkingWithFish.com.

Dmitry Figol, CCIE No. 53592 (R&S), is a systems engineer in Cisco Systems Enterprise Sales. He is in charge of design and implementation of software applications and automation systems for Cisco. His main expertise is network programmability and automation. Before joining Cisco Sales, Dmitry worked on the Cisco Technical Assistance Center (TAC) Core Architecture and VPN teams. Dmitry maintains several open-source projects and is a regular speaker at conferences. He also does live streams on Twitch about network programmability and Python. Dmitry holds a bachelor of science degree in telecommunications. Dmitry can be found on Twitter as @dmfigol.

Patrick Croak, CCIE No. 34712 (Wireless), is a systems engineer with a focus on wireless and mobility. He is responsible for designing, implementing, and optimizing enterprise wireless networks. He also works closely with the business unit and account teams for product development and innovation. Prior to this role, he spent several years working on the TAC Support Escalation team, troubleshooting complex wireless network issues. Patrick has been with Cisco since 2006.

Dedications

Brad Edgeworth:

This book is dedicated to my wife, Tanya. The successes and achievements I have today are because of Tanya. Whenever I failed an exam, she provided the support and encouragement to dust myself off and try again. She sacrificed years' worth of weekends while I studied for my CCIE certifications. Her motivation has allowed me to overcome a variety of obstacles with great success.

Ramiro Garza:

I would like to dedicate this book to my wonderful and beautiful wife, Mariana, and to my four children, Ramiro, Frinee, Felix, and Lucia, for their love, patience, and support as I worked on this project. And to my parents, Ramiro and Blanca D., and my in-laws, Juan A. and Marisela, for their continued support and encouragement. And most important of all, I would like to thank God for all His blessings in my life.

David Hucaby:

As always, my work is dedicated to my wife and my daughters, for their love and support, and to God, who has blessed me with opportunities to learn, write, and work with so many friends.

Jason Gooley:

This book is dedicated to my wife, Jamie, and my children, Kaleigh and Jaxon. Without their support, these books would not be possible. To my father and brother, thank you for always supporting me.

Acknowledgments

Brad Edgeworth:

A debt of gratitude goes to my co-authors, Ramiro, Jason, and David. I'm privileged to be able to write a book with all of you.

To Brett Bartow, thank you for giving me the privilege to write on such an esteemed book. I'm thankful to work with Ellie Bru and Tonya Simpson again, along with the rest of the Pearson team.

To the technical editors—Richard, Denise, Dmitry, and Patrick—thank you for your attention to detail.

Many people within Cisco have provided feedback and suggestions to make this a great book. And to all of those who share knowledge (wherever you are located), keep doing it. That is how we make this world a better place.

To the readers of this text, never give up. Failure is an opportunity to learn and grow yourself. You probably will not like it, it does not taste good, but after you learn and overcome, you will learn to embrace it (or at least that is what I keep telling myself).

Ramiro Garza Rios:

I'd like to give a special thank you to Brett Bartow for giving us the opportunity to work on this project and for being our guiding light. I'm also really grateful and honored to have worked with Brad, Jason, and David; they are amazing and great to work with. I'd like to give special recognition to Brad for providing the leadership for this project. A big thank you to the Cisco Press team for all your support, especially to Ellie Bru. I would also like to thank our technical editors—Denise, Richard, Patrick, and Dmitry—for their valuable feedback to ensure that the technical content of this book is top-notch. And most important of all, I would like to thank God for all His blessings in my life.

David Hucaby:

I am very grateful to Brett Bartow for giving me the opportunity to work on this project. Brad, Ramiro, and Jason have been great to work with. Many thanks to Ellie Bru for her hard work editing our many chapters!

Jason Gooley:

Thank you to the rest of the author team for having me on this book. It has been a blast! Thanks to Brett and the whole Cisco Press team for all the support and always being available. This project is near and dear to my heart, as I am extremely passionate about helping others on their certification journey.

Contents at a Glance

Reader Services

Register your copy at www.ciscopress.com/title/9780138216764 for convenient access to downloads, updates, and corrections as they become available. To start the registration process, go to www.ciscopress.com/register and log in or create an account.* Enter the product ISBN 9780138216764 and click Submit. When the process is complete, you will find any available bonus content under Registered Products.

*Be sure to check the box that you would like to hear from us to receive exclusive discounts on future editions of this product.

Contents

Icons Used in This Book

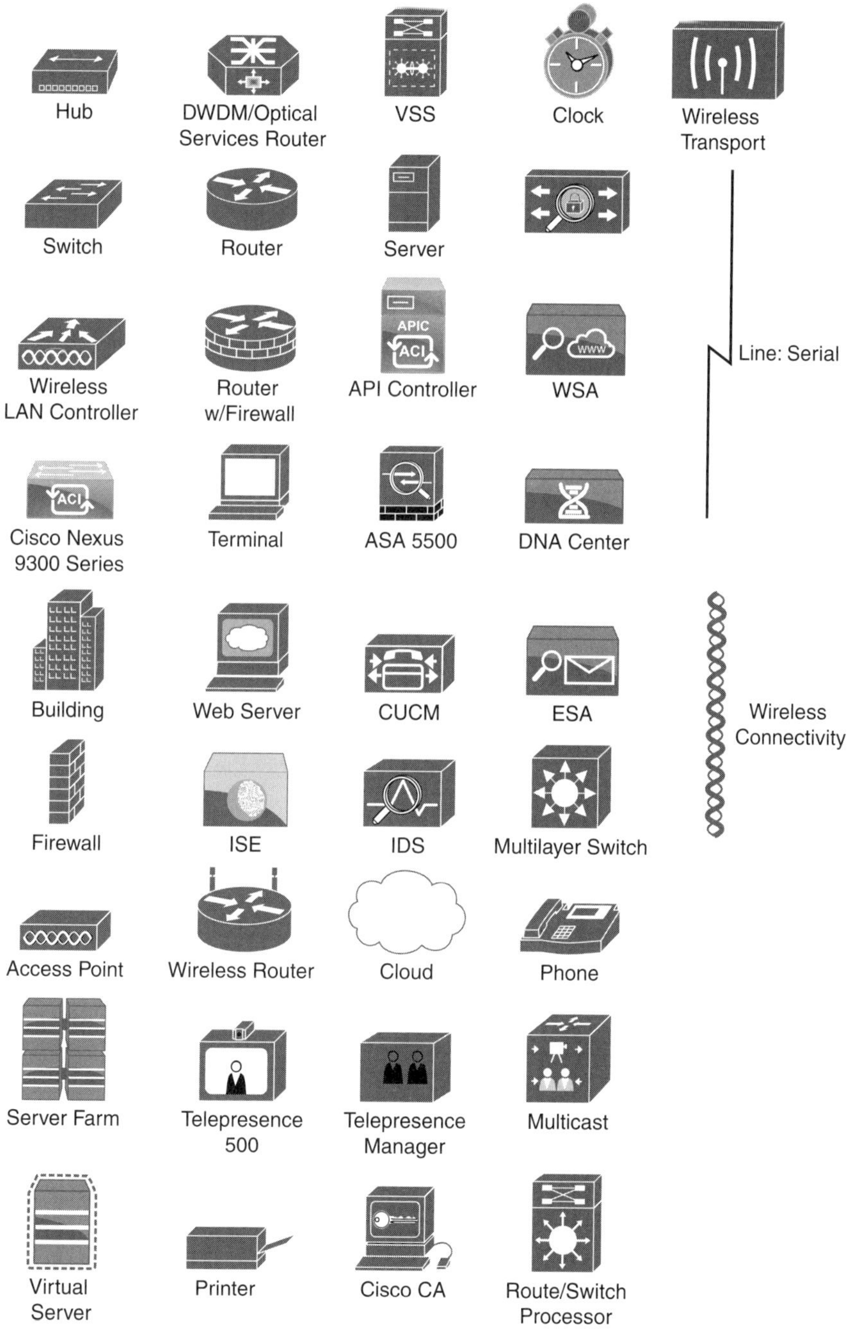

Command Syntax Conventions

The conventions used to present command syntax in this book are the same conventions used in the IOS Command Reference. The Command Reference describes these conventions as follows:

- **Boldface** indicates commands and keywords that are entered literally as shown. In actual configuration examples and output (not general command syntax), boldface indicates commands that are manually input by the user (such as a **show** command).
- *Italic* indicates arguments for which you supply actual values.
- Vertical bars (|) separate alternative, mutually exclusive elements.
- Square brackets ([ ]) indicate an optional element.
- Braces ({ }) indicate a required choice.
- Braces within brackets ([{ }]) indicate a required choice within an optional element.

Introduction

Congratulations! If you are reading this Introduction, then you have probably decided to obtain a Cisco certification. Obtaining a Cisco certification will ensure that you have a solid understanding of common industry protocols along with Cisco's device architecture and configuration. Cisco has a high market share of routers and switches, with a global footprint.

Professional certifications have been an important part of the computing industry for many years and will continue to become more important. Many reasons exist for these certifications, but the most popularly cited reason is credibility. All other factors being equal, a certified employee/consultant/job candidate is considered more valuable than one who is not certified.

Cisco provides three primary certifications: Cisco Certified Network Associate (CCNA), Cisco Certified Network Professional (CCNP), and Cisco Certified Internetwork Expert (CCIE). Cisco made the following changes to all three certifications in 2020. The following are the most notable of the many changes:

- The exams will include additional topics, such as programming.
- The CCNA certification is not a prerequisite for obtaining the CCNP certification. CCNA specializations will not be offered anymore.
- The exams will test a candidate's ability to configure and troubleshoot network devices in addition to answering multiple-choice questions.
- The CCNP is obtained by taking and passing a Core exam and a Concentration exam.
- The CCIE certification requires candidates to pass the Core written exam before the CCIE lab can be scheduled.

CCNP Enterprise candidates need to take and pass the CCNP and CCIE Enterprise Core ENCOR 350-401 examination. Then they need to take and pass one of the following Concentration exams to obtain their CCNP Enterprise:

- **300-410 ENARSI:** Implementing Cisco Enterprise Advanced Routing and Services (ENARSI)
- **300-415 ENSDWI:** Implementing Cisco SD-WAN Solutions (SDWAN300)
- **300-420 ENSLD:** Designing Cisco Enterprise Networks (ENSLD)
- **300-425 ENWLSD:** Designing Cisco Enterprise Wireless Networks (ENWLSD)
- **300-430 ENWLSI:** Implementing Cisco Enterprise Wireless Networks (ENWLSI)
- **300-435 ENAUTO:** Implementing Automation for Cisco Enterprise Solutions (ENAUI)
- **300-440 ENCC:** Designing and Implementing Cloud Connectivity (ENCC)

Be sure to visit www.cisco.com to find the latest information on CCNP Concentration requirements and to keep up to date on any new Concentration exams that are announced.

CCIE Enterprise candidates need to take and pass the CCNP and CCIE Enterprise Core ENCOR 350-401 examination. Then they need to take and pass the CCIE Enterprise Infrastructure or Enterprise Wireless lab exam.

Goals and Methods

The most important and somewhat obvious goal of this book is to help you pass the CCNP and CCIE Enterprise Core ENCOR 350-401 exam. In fact, if the primary objective of this book were different, then the book's title would be misleading; however, the methods used in this book to help you pass the exam are designed to also make you much more knowledgeable about how to do your job.

One key methodology used in this book is to help you discover the exam topics that you need to review in more depth, to help you fully understand and remember those details, and to help you prove to yourself that you have retained your knowledge of those topics. This book does not try to help you simply memorize; rather, it helps you truly learn and understand the topics. The CCNP and CCIE Enterprise Core exam is just one of the foundation topics in the CCNP certification, and the knowledge contained within is vitally important to being a truly skilled routing/switching engineer or specialist. This book would do you a disservice if it didn't attempt to help you learn the material. To that end, the book will help you pass the CCNP and CCIE Enterprise Core exam by using the following methods:

- Helping you discover which test topics you have not mastered
- Providing explanations and information to fill in your knowledge gaps
- Supplying exercises and scenarios that enhance your ability to recall and deduce the answers to test questions

Who Should Read This Book?

This book is not designed to be a general networking topics book, although it can be used for that purpose. This book is intended to tremendously increase your chances of passing the CCNP and CCIE Enterprise Core exam. Although other objectives can be achieved from using this book, the book is written with one goal in mind: to help you pass the exam.

So why should you want to pass the CCNP and CCIE Enterprise Core ENCOR 350-401 exam? Because it's one of the milestones toward getting the CCNP certification or to being able to schedule the CCIE lab—which is no small feat. What would getting the CCNP or CCIE mean to you? It might translate to a raise, a promotion, and recognition. It would certainly enhance your resume. It would demonstrate that you are serious about continuing the learning process and that you're not content to rest on your laurels. It might please your reseller-employer, who needs more certified employees for a higher discount from Cisco. Or you might have one of many other reasons.

Strategies for Exam Preparation

The strategy you use to prepare for the CCNP and CCIE Enterprise Core ENCOR 350-401 exam might be slightly different from strategies used by other readers, depending on the skills, knowledge, and experience you already have obtained. For instance, if you have attended the CCNP and CCIE Enterprise Core ENCOR 350-401 course, then you might take a different approach than someone who learned switching via on-the-job training.

Regardless of the strategy you use or the background you have, the book is designed to help you get to the point where you can pass the exam with the least amount of time required. For instance, there is no need for you to practice or read about IP addressing and subnetting if you fully understand it already. However, many people like to make sure that they truly know a topic and thus read over material that they already know. Several features of this book will help you gain the confidence that you need to be convinced that you know some material already and to also help you know what topics you need to study more.

The Companion Website for Online Content Review

All the electronic review elements, as well as other electronic components of the book, exist on this book's companion website.

How to Access the Companion Website

To access the companion website, which gives you access to the electronic content with this book, start by establishing a login at www.ciscopress.com and registering your book. To do so, simply go to www.ciscopress.com/register and enter the ISBN of the print book: 9780138216764. After you have registered your book, go to your account page and click the Registered Products tab. From there, click the Access Bonus Content link to get access to the book's companion website.

Note that if you buy the Premium Edition eBook and Practice Test version of this book from Cisco Press, your book will automatically be registered on your account page. Simply go to your account page, click the Registered Products tab, and select Access Bonus Content to access the book's companion website.

How to Access the Pearson Test Prep (PTP) App

You have two options for installing and using the Pearson Test Prep application: a web app and a desktop app. To use the Pearson Test Prep application, start by finding the registration code that comes with the book. You can find the code in these ways:

- **Print book or bookseller eBook versions:** You can get your access code by registering the print ISBN (9780138216764) on ciscopress.com/register. Make sure to use the print book ISBN regardless of whether you purchased an eBook or the print book. Once you register the book, your access code will be populated on your account page under the Registered Products tab. Instructions for how to redeem the code are available on the book's companion website by clicking the Access Bonus Content link.

- **Premium Edition:** If you purchase the Premium Edition eBook and Practice Test directly from the Cisco Press website, the code will be populated on your account page after purchase. Just log in at www.ciscopress.com, click Account to see details of your account, and click the digital purchases tab.

> **NOTE** After you register your book, your code can always be found in your account under the Registered Products tab.

Once you have the access code, to find instructions about both the PTP web app and the desktop app, follow these steps:

Step 1. Open this book's companion website, as shown earlier in this Introduction under the heading "How to Access the Companion Website."

Step 2. Click the Practice Exams button.

Step 3. Follow the instructions listed there both for installing the desktop app and for using the web app.

Note that if you want to use the web app only at this point, just navigate to www.pearsontestprep.com, establish a free login if you do not already have one, and register this book's practice tests using the registration code you just found. The process should take only a couple of minutes.

How This Book Is Organized

Although this book could be read cover to cover, it is designed to be flexible and allow you to easily move between chapters and sections of chapters to cover just the material that you need more work with. If you do intend to read them all, the order in the book is an excellent sequence to use.

The book includes the following chapters:

- **Chapter 1, "Packet Forwarding":** This chapter provides a review of basic network fundamentals and then dives deeper into technical concepts related to how network traffic is forwarded through a router or switch architecture.

- **Chapter 2, "Spanning Tree Protocol":** This chapter explains how switches prevent forwarding loops while allowing for redundant links with the use of Spanning Tree Protocol (STP) and Rapid Spanning Tree Protocol (RSTP).

- **Chapter 3, "Advanced STP Tuning":** This chapter reviews common techniques that are in Cisco Validated Design guides. Topics include root bridge placement and protection.

- **Chapter 4, "Multiple Spanning Tree Protocol":** This chapter completes the section of spanning tree by explaining Multiple Spanning Tree (MST) protocol.

- **Chapter 5, "VLAN Trunks and EtherChannel Bundles":** This chapter covers features such as VTP, DTP, and EtherChannel for switch-to-switch connectivity.
- **Chapter 6, "IP Routing Essentials":** This chapter revisits the fundamentals from Chapter 1 and examines some of the components of the operations of a router. It reinforces the logic of the programming of the Routing Information Base (RIB), reviews differences between common routing protocols, and explains common concepts related to static routes.
- **Chapter 7, "EIGRP":** This chapter explains the underlying mechanics of the EIGRP routing protocol, the path metric calculations, and the failure detection mechanisms and techniques for optimizing the operations of the routing protocol.
- **Chapter 8, "OSPF":** This chapter explains the core concepts of OSPF and the basics in establishing neighborships and exchanging routes with other OSPF routers.
- **Chapter 9, "Advanced OSPF":** This chapter expands on Chapter 8 and explains the functions and features found in larger enterprise networks. By the end of this chapter, you should have a solid understanding of the route advertisement within a multi-area OSPF domain, path selection, and techniques to optimize an OSPF environment.
- **Chapter 10, "OSPFv3":** This chapter explains how the OSPF protocol has changed to accommodate support of IPv6.
- **Chapter 11, "BGP":** This chapter explains the core concepts of BGP and its path attributes. This chapter explains configuration of BGP and advertisement and summarization of IPv4 and IPv6 network prefixes.
- **Chapter 12, "Advanced BGP":** This chapter expands on Chapter 11 and explains BGP's advanced features and concepts, such as BGP multihoming, route filtering, BGP communities, and the logic for identifying the best path for a specific network prefix.
- **Chapter 13, "Multicast":** This chapter describes the fundamental concepts related to multicast and how it operates. It also describes the protocols that are required to understand its operation in more detail, such as Internet Group Messaging Protocol (IGMP), IGMP snooping, Protocol Independent Multicast (PIM) Dense Mode/Sparse Mode, and rendezvous points (RPs).
- **Chapter 14, "Quality of Service (QoS)":** This chapter describes the different QoS models available: best effort, Integrated Services (IntServ), and Differentiated Services (DiffServ). It also describes tools and mechanisms used to implement QoS such as classification and marking, policing and shaping, and congestion management and avoidance, and it also explains how to configure them.
- **Chapter 15, "IP Services":** In addition to routing and switching network packets, a router can perform additional functions to enhance the network. This chapter covers time synchronization, virtual gateway technologies, and network address translation.

- **Chapter 16, "Overlay Tunnels":** This chapter explains Generic Routing Encapsulation (GRE) and IP Security (IPsec) fundamentals and how to configure them. It also explains Locator ID/Separation Protocol (LISP) and Virtual Extensible Local Area Network (VXLAN).
- **Chapter 17, "Wireless Signals and Modulation":** This chapter covers the basic theory behind radio frequency (RF) signals, measuring and comparing the power of RF signals, and basic methods and standards involved in carrying data wirelessly.
- **Chapter 18, "Wireless Infrastructure":** This chapter describes autonomous, cloud-based, centralized, embedded, and Mobility Express wireless architectures. It also explains the process that lightweight APs must go through to discover and bind to a wireless LAN controller. Various AP modes and antennas are also described.
- **Chapter 19, "Understanding Wireless Roaming and Location Services":** This chapter discusses client mobility from the AP and controller perspectives so that you can design and configure a wireless network properly as it grows over time. It also explains how components of a wireless network can be used to compute the physical locations of wireless devices.
- **Chapter 20, "Authenticating Wireless Clients":** This chapter covers several methods you can use to authenticate users and devices in order to secure a wireless network.
- **Chapter 21, "Troubleshooting Wireless Connectivity":** This chapter helps you get some perspective about problems wireless clients may have with their connections, develop a troubleshooting strategy, and become comfortable using a wireless LAN controller as a troubleshooting tool.
- **Chapter 22, "Enterprise Network Architecture":** This chapter provides a high-level overview of the enterprise campus architectures that can be used to scale from a small environment to a large campus-size network.
- **Chapter 23, "Fabric Technologies":** This chapter defines the benefits of Software-Defined Access (SD-Access) over traditional campus networks as well as the components and features of the Cisco SD-Access solution, including the nodes, fabric control plane, and data plane. It also defines the benefits of Software-Defined WAN (SD-WAN) over traditional WANs, as well as the components and features of the Cisco SD-WAN solution, including the orchestration plane, management plane, control plane, and data plane.
- **Chapter 24, "Network Assurance":** This chapter covers some of the tools most commonly used for operations and troubleshooting in the network environment. Cisco DNA Center with Assurance is also covered, to showcase how the tool can improve mean time to innocence (MTTI) and root cause analysis of issues.
- **Chapter 25, "Secure Network Access Control":** This chapter describes a Cisco security framework to protect networks from evolving cybersecurity threats as well as the security components that are part of the framework, such as next-generation firewalls, web security, email security, and much more. It also describes network access control (NAC) technologies such as 802.1x, Web Authentication (WebAuth), MAC Authentication Bypass (MAB), TrustSec, and MACsec.

- **Chapter 26, "Network Device Access Control and Infrastructure Security":** This chapter focuses on how to configure and verify network device access control through local authentication and authorization as well through AAA. It also explains how to configure and verify router security features, such as access control lists (ACLs), control plane policing (CoPP), and zone-based firewalls (ZBFWs), that are used to provide device and infrastructure security.
- **Chapter 27, "Virtualization":** This chapter describes server virtualization technologies such as virtual machines, containers, and virtual switching. It also describes the network functions virtualization (NFV) architecture and Cisco's enterprise NFV solution.
- **Chapter 28, "Foundational Network Programmability Concepts":** This chapter covers current network management methods and tools as well as key network programmability methods. It also covers how to use software application programming interfaces (APIs) and common data formats.
- **Chapter 29, "Introduction to Automation Tools":** This chapter discusses some of the most common automation tools that are available. It covers on-box, agent-based, and agentless tools and examples.
- **Chapter 30, "Final Preparation":** This chapter details a set of tools and a study plan to help you complete your preparation for the CCNP and CCIE Enterprise Core ENCOR 350-401 exam.

Certification Exam Topics and This Book

The questions for each certification exam are a closely guarded secret. However, we do know which topics you must know to *successfully* complete the CCNP and CCIE Enterprise Core ENCOR 350-401 exam. Cisco publishes them as an exam blueprint. Table I-1 lists each exam topic listed in the blueprint along with a reference to the book chapter that covers the topic. These are the same topics you should be proficient in when working with enterprise technologies in the real world.

Table I-1 CCNP and CCIE Enterprise Core ENCOR 350-401 Topics and Chapter References

CCNP and CCIE Enterprise Core ENCOR (350-401) Exam Topic	Chapter(s) in Which Topic Is Covered
1.0 Architecture	
1.1 Explain the different design principles used in an enterprise network	
1.1.a High-level enterprise network design such as 2-tier, 3-tier, fabric, and cloud	22
1.1.b High availability techniques such as redundancy, FHRP, and SSO	15, 22
1.2 Describe wireless network design principles	

CCNP and CCIE Enterprise Core ENCOR (350-401) Exam Topic	Chapter(s) in Which Topic Is Covered
1.2.a Wireless deployment models (centralized, distributed, controller-less, controller-based, cloud, remote branch)	18
1.2.b Location services in a WLAN design	19
1.2.c Client density	18
1.3 Explain the working principles of the Cisco SD-WAN solution	
1.3.a SD-WAN control and data planes elements	23
1.3.b Benefits and limitations of SD-WAN solutions	23
1.4 Explain the working principles of the Cisco SD-Access solution	
1.4.a SD-Access control and data planes elements	23
1.4.b Traditional campus interoperating with SD-Access	23
1.5 Interpret wired and wireless QoS configurations	
1.5.a QoS components	14
1.5.b QoS policy	14
1.6 Describe hardware and software switching mechanisms such as CEF, CAM, TCAM, FIB, RIB, and adjacency tables	1
2.0 Virtualization	
2.1 Describe device virtualization technologies	
2.1.a Hypervisor type 1 and 2	27
2.1.b Virtual machine	27
2.1.c Virtual switching	27
2.2 Configure and verify data path virtualization technologies	
2.2.a VRF	6
2.2.b GRE and IPsec tunneling	16
2.3 Describe network virtualization concepts	
2.3.a LISP	16
2.3.b VXLAN	16
3.0 Infrastructure	
3.1 Layer 2	
3.1.a Troubleshoot static and dynamic 802.1q trunking protocols	5
3.1.b Troubleshoot static and dynamic EtherChannels	5
3.1.c Configure and verify common Spanning Tree Protocols (RSTP, MST) and Spanning Tree enhancements such as root guard and BPDU guard	2, 3, 4
3.2 Layer 3	
3.2.a Compare routing concepts of EIGRP and OSPF (advanced distance vector vs. linked state, load balancing, path selection, path operations, metrics, and area types)	6, 7, 8, 9

CCNP and CCIE Enterprise Core ENCOR (350-401) Exam Topic	Chapter(s) in Which Topic Is Covered
3.2.b Configure simple OSPFv2/v3 environments, including multiple normal areas, summarization, and filtering (neighbor adjacency, point-to-point, and broadcast network types, and passive-interface)	8, 9, 10
3.2.c Configure and verify eBGP between directly connected neighbors (best path selection algorithm and neighbor relationships)	11, 12
3.2.d Describe policy-based routing	6
3.3 Wireless	
3.3.a Describe Layer 1 concepts, such as RF power, RSSI, SNR, interference, noise, bands, channels, and wireless client devices capabilities	17
3.3.b Describe AP modes and antenna types	18
3.3.c Describe access point discovery and join process (discovery algorithms, WLC selection process)	18
3.3.d Describe the main principles and use cases for Layer 2 and Layer 3 roaming	19
3.3.e Troubleshoot WLAN configuration and wireless client connectivity issues using GUI only	21
3.3.f Describe wireless segmentation with groups, profiles, and tags	18
3.4 IP Services	
3.4.a Interpret network time protocol configurations such as NTP and PTP	15
3.4.b Configure NAT/PAT	15
3.4.c Configure first hop redundancy protocols, such as HSRP, VRRP	15
3.4.d Describe multicast protocols, such as RPF check, PIM, and IGMP v2/v3	13
4.0 Network Assurance	24
4.1 Diagnose network problems using tools such as debugs, conditional debugs, traceroute, ping, SNMP, and syslog	24
4.2 Configure Flexible NetFlow	24
4.3 Configure and verify SPAN/RSPAN/ERSPAN	24
4.4 Configure and verify IPSLA	24
4.5 Describe Cisco DNA Center workflows to apply network configuration, monitoring, and management	24
4.6 Configure and verify NETCONF and RESTCONF	28
5.0 Security	
5.1 Configure and verify device access control	26

CCNP and CCIE Enterprise Core ENCOR (350-401) Exam Topic	Chapter(s) in Which Topic Is Covered
5.1.a Lines and local user authentication	26
5.1.b Authentication and authorization using AAA	26
5.2 Configure and verify infrastructure security features	26
5.2.a ACLs	26
5.2.b CoPP	26
5.3 Describe REST API security	28
5.4 Configure and verify wireless security features	
5.4.a 802.1X	20
5.4.b WebAuth	20
5.4.c PSK	20
5.4.d EAPOL (4-way handshake)	20
5.5 Describe the components of network security design	25
5.5.a Threat defense	25
5.5.b Endpoint security	25
5.5.c Next-generation firewall	25
5.5.d TrustSec and MACsec	25
5.5.e Network access control with 802.1X, MAB, and WebAuth	20, 25
6.0 Automation	
6.1 Interpret basic Python components and scripts	29
6.2 Construct valid JSON-encoded file	28
6.3 Describe the high-level principles and benefits of a data modeling language, such as YANG	28
6.4 Describe APIs for Cisco DNA Center and vManage	28
6.5 Interpret REST API response codes and results in payload using Cisco DNA Center and RESTCONF	28
6.6 Construct EEM applet to automate configuration, troubleshooting, or data collection	29
6.7 Compare agent vs. agentless orchestration tools, such as Chef, Puppet, Ansible, and SaltStack	29

Each version of the exam may emphasize different functions or features, and some topics are rather broad and generalized. The goal of this book is to provide the most comprehensive coverage to ensure that you are well prepared for the exam. Although some chapters might not address specific exam topics, they provide a foundation that is necessary for a clear understanding of important topics.

It is also important to understand that this book is a static reference, whereas the exam topics are dynamic. Cisco can and does change the topics covered on certification exams often.

This exam guide should not be your only reference when preparing for the certification exam. You can find a wealth of information available at Cisco.com that covers each topic in great detail. If you think that you need more detailed information on a specific topic, read the Cisco documentation that focuses on your chosen topic.

Note that as technologies continue to evolve, Cisco reserves the right to change the exam topics without notice. Although you can refer to the list of exam topics in Table I-1, always check Cisco.com to verify the actual list of topics to ensure that you are prepared before taking the exam. You can view the current exam topics on any current Cisco certification exam by visiting the Cisco.com website, hovering over Training & Events, and selecting from the Certifications list. Note also that, if needed, Cisco Press might post additional preparatory content on the web page associated with this book: http://www.ciscopress.com/title/9780138216764. It's a good idea to check the website a couple weeks before taking the exam to be sure that you have up-to-date content.

Figure Credits

Figure 28-2 through Figure 28-14: Postman, Inc

Figure 28-20 through Figure 28-23: GitHub, Inc

Figure 29-2, Figure 29-3: Perforce Software, Inc

Figure 29-4: Chef Software, Inc

Figure 29-5, Figure 29-6, Figure 29-7: VMware, Inc

Figure 29-14: Puppet

Figure 29-10 through Figure 29-13: YAML Lint

CHAPTER 1

Packet Forwarding

This chapter covers the following subjects:

- **Network Device Communication:** This section explains how switches forward traffic from a Layer 2 perspective and routers forward traffic from a Layer 3 perspective.
- **Forwarding Architectures:** This section examines the mechanisms used in routers and switches to forward network traffic.

This chapter provides a review of basic network fundamentals and then dives deeper into the technical concepts related to how network traffic is forwarded through a router or switch architecture.

"Do I Know This Already?" Quiz

The "Do I Know This Already?" quiz enables you to assess whether you should read the entire chapter. If you miss no more than one of these self-assessment questions, you might want to move ahead to the "Exam Preparation Tasks" section. Table 1-1 lists the major headings in this chapter and the "Do I Know This Already?" quiz questions covering the material in those headings so you can assess your knowledge of these specific areas. The answers to the "Do I Know This Already?" quiz appear in Appendix A, "Answers to the 'Do I Know This Already?' Questions."

Table 1-1 "Do I Know This Already?" Foundation Topics Section-to-Question Mapping

Foundation Topics Section	Questions
Network Device Communication	1–4
Forwarding Architectures	5–7

1. Forwarding of network traffic from a Layer 2 perspective uses what information?
   - **a.** Source IP address
   - **b.** Destination IP address
   - **c.** Source MAC address
   - **d.** Destination MAC address
   - **e.** Data protocol
2. What type of network device helps reduce the size of a collision domain?
   - **a.** Hub
   - **b.** Switch
   - **c.** Load balancer
   - **d.** Router

3. Forwarding of network traffic from a Layer 3 perspective uses what information?
   a. Source IP address
   b. Destination IP address
   c. Source MAC address
   d. Destination MAC address
   e. Data protocol
4. What type of network device helps reduce the size of a broadcast domain?
   a. Hub
   b. Switch
   c. Load balancer
   d. Router
5. The _________ can be directly correlated to the MAC address table.
   a. adjacency table
   b. CAM
   c. TCAM
   d. routing table
6. A ___________ forwarding architecture provides increased port density and forwarding scalability.
   a. centralized
   b. clustered
   c. software
   d. distributed
7. CEF is composed of which components? (Choose two.)
   a. Routing Information Base
   b. Forwarding Information Base
   c. Label Information Base
   d. Adjacency table
   e. MAC address table

Foundation Topics

Network Device Communication

The primary function of a network is to provide connectivity between devices. There used to be a variety of network protocols that were device specific or preferred; today, almost everything is based on *Transmission Control Protocol/Internet Protocol (TCP/IP)*. It is important to note that TCP/IP is based on the conceptual *Open Systems Interconnection (OSI)* model that is composed of seven layers. Each layer describes a specific function, and a layer can be modified or changed without requiring changes to the layer above or below it. The OSI model, which provides a structured approach for compatibility between vendors, is illustrated in Figure 1-1.

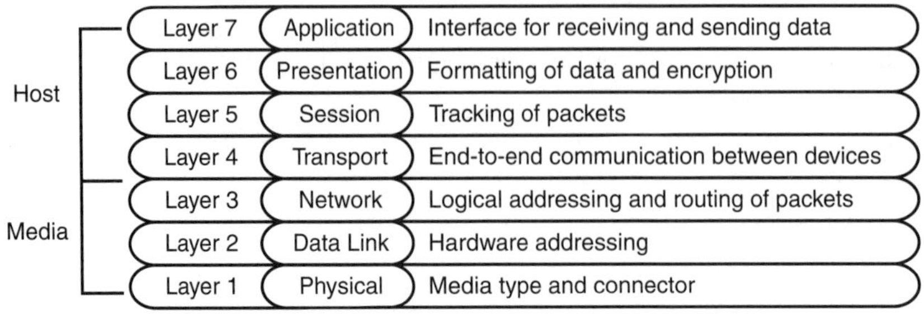

Figure 1-1 *OSI Model*

When you think about the flow of data, most network traffic involves communication of data between applications. The applications generate data at Layer 7, and the device/host sends data down the OSI model. As the data moves down the OSI model, it is encapsulated or modified as needed.

At Layer 3, the device/host decides whether the data needs to be sent to another application on the same device, and it would then start to move the data up the stack. Or, if the data needs to be sent to a different device, the device/host continues processing down the OSI model toward Layer 1. Layer 1 is responsible for transmitting the information on to the media (for example, cable, fiber, radio waves). On the receiving side, data starts at Layer 1, then moves to Layer 2, and so on, until it has moved completely up to Layer 7 and on to the receiving application.

This chapter reinforces concepts related to how a network device forwards traffic from either a Layer 2 or a Layer 3 perspective. The first Layer 2 network devices were bridges or switches, and Layer 3 devices were strictly routers. As technology advanced, the development of faster physical media required the ability to forward packets in hardware through application-specific integrated circuits (ASICs). As ASIC functionality continued to develop, multilayer switches (MLSs) were invented to forward Layer 2 traffic in hardware as if they were switches; however, they can also perform other functions, such as routing packets, from a Layer 3 perspective.

Layer 2 Forwarding

The second layer of the OSI model, the data link layer, handles addressing beneath the IP protocol stack so that communication is directed between hosts. Network packets include Layer 2 addressing with unique source and destination addresses for segments. Ethernet commonly uses *Media Access Control (MAC)* addresses, and other data link layer protocols such as Frame Relay use an entirely different method of Layer 2 addressing.

The focus of the Enterprise Core exam is on Ethernet and wireless technologies, both of which use MAC addresses for *Layer 2* addressing. This book focuses on the MAC address for **Layer 2 forwarding**.

Answers to the "Do I Know This Already?" quiz:

1 D **2** B **3** B **4** D **5** B **6** D **7** B, D

1

NOTE A MAC address is a 48-bit address that is split across six octets and notated in hexadecimal. The first three octets are assigned to a device manufacturer, known as the organizationally unique identifier (OUI), and the manufacturer is responsible for ensuring that the last three octets are unique. A device listens for network traffic that contains its MAC address as the packet's destination MAC address before moving the packet up the OSI stack to Layer 3 for processing.

Network broadcasts with MAC address FF:FF:FF:FF:FF:FF are the exception to the rule and will always be processed by all network devices on the same network segment. Broadcasts are not typically forwarded beyond a Layer 3 boundary.

Key Topic

Collision Domains

Ethernet is a shared communication medium. When two or more network devices tried to transmit data at the same time in the same network segment, the communication became garbled due to data collisions. To prevent data collisions, Ethernet includes *Carrier Sense Multiple Access/Collision Detect (CSMA/CD)*, which ensures that only one device transmits data at a time in a **collision domain**. A collision domain is a network segment where one device can detect if another device is transmitting data, regardless of the destination device. If a device detects that another device is transmitting data, it delays transmitting data until the cable is quiet. This means devices could perform only one action at a time, whether that is to transmit or to receive data (that is, operate at half-duplex).

When Ethernet became an Institute of Electrical and Electronic Engineers (IEEE) standard (802.3, CSMA/CD), it first used technologies like Thinnet (10BASE-2) and Thicknet (10BASE-5), which connected all the network devices using the same coaxial cable and T connectors.

With those technologies, as more devices were added to the same collision domain (same coaxial cable), the less efficient the network became, because devices would need to wait until the cable was quiet to be able to transmit data. Changing the medium to Category 3/4 cable and using network hubs proliferated the problem, because they add port density while repeating traffic, thereby increasing the size of the collision domain. Network hubs do not have any intelligence in them to direct network traffic; they simply repeat traffic out of every port.

Network switches enhance scalability and stability in a network through the creation of virtual channels. A switch maintains a table that associates a host's *Media Access Control (MAC)* Ethernet addresses to the port that sourced the network traffic. Instead of flooding all traffic out of every switch port, a switch uses the local **MAC address table** to forward network traffic only to the destination switch port associated with where the destination MAC is attached. This approach drastically reduces the size of the collision domain between the devices and enables the devices to transmit and receive data at the same time (that is, operate at full duplex).

Figure 1-2 demonstrates the collision domains on a hub versus on a switch. Both of these topologies show the same three PCs, as well as the same cabling. On the left, the PCs are connected to a network hub. Communication between PC-A and PC-B is received by PC-C too, because all three devices are in the same collision domain. PC-C must process the frame—in the process consuming resources—and then it discards the packet after determining that the destination MAC address does not belong to it. In addition, PC-C has to wait until the PC-A/PC-B conversation finishes before it can transmit data. On the right, the PCs are connected to a network switch. Communication between PC-A and PC-B is split into two collision domains. The switch can connect the two collision domains by using information from the MAC address table.

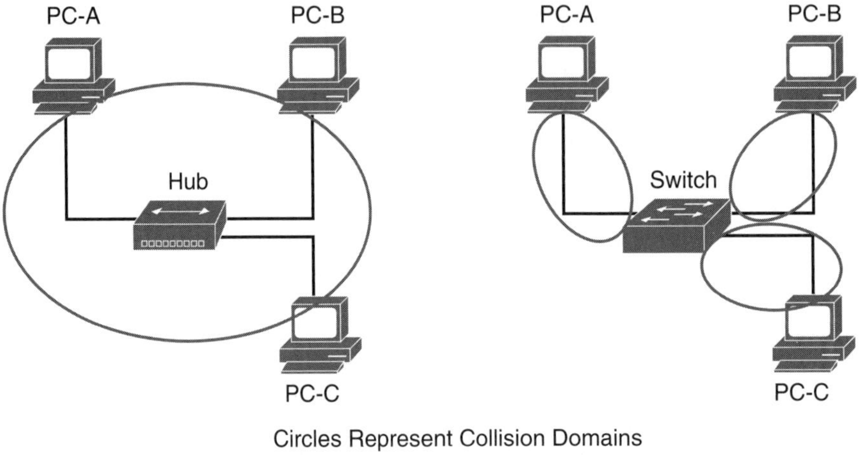

Figure 1-2 *Collision Domains on a Hub Versus a Switch*

When a switch receives a packet that contains a destination MAC address that is not in the switch's MAC address table, the switch forwards the packet out of every switch port, except the port that the packet was received on. This process is known as *unknown unicast flooding* because the destination MAC address is not known.

Broadcast traffic is network traffic intended for every host on the local area network (LAN) and is forwarded out of every switch port interface. Excessive broadcast traffic is undesirable: it diminishes the efficiencies of a network switch because it interrupts unicast communication between network devices. Network broadcasts do not cross Layer 3 boundaries (that is, from one subnet to another subnet). All devices that reside in the same Layer 2 segment are considered to be in the same **broadcast domain.**

Figure 1-3 illustrates four PCs connected to a switch (SW1) in the same Layer 2 segment. It also displays SW1's MAC address table, which correlates the PCs to the appropriate switch port. In the scenario on the left, PC-A is transmitting unicast traffic to PC-B. SW1 does not transmit data out of the Gi0/2 or Gi0/3 interface (which could potentially disrupt any network transmissions between those PCs). In the scenario on the right, SW1 is transmitting broadcast network traffic received from PC-A out of all active switch ports.

NOTE The terms *network device* and *host* are considered interchangeable in this text.

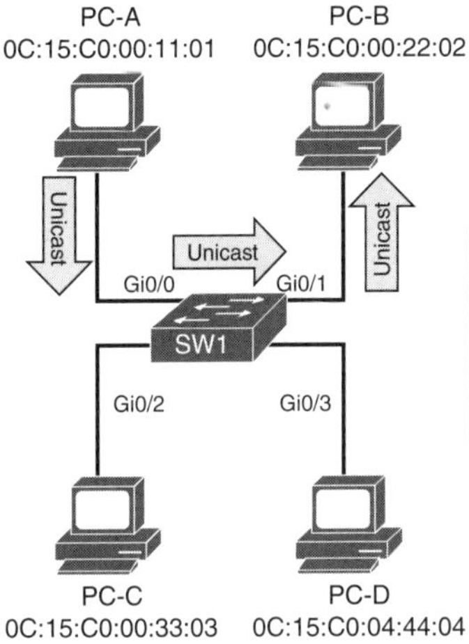

SW1 MAC Address Table

MAC Address	Interface
0C:15:C0:00:11:01	Gi0/0
0C:15:C0:00:22:02	Gi0/1
0C:15:C0:00:33:03	Gi0/2
0C:15:C0:04:44:04	Gi0/3

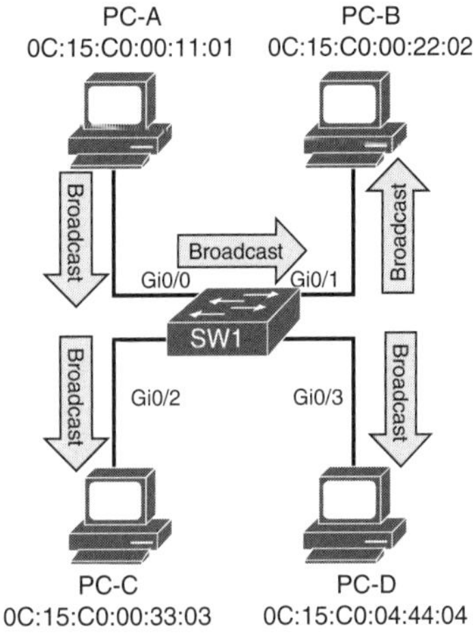

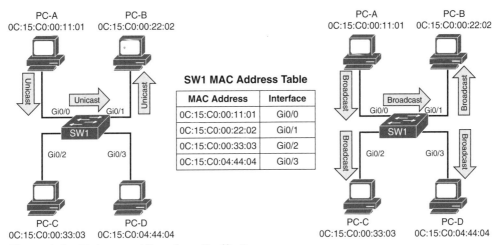

Figure 1-3 *Unicast and Broadcast Traffic Patterns*

Virtual LANs

Adding a router between LAN segments helps shrink broadcast domains and provides for optimal network communication. Host placement on a LAN segment varies because of network addressing. Poor host network assignment can lead to inefficient use of hardware because some switch ports could be unused.

Key Topic

Virtual LANs (VLANs) provide logical segmentation by creating multiple broadcast domains on the same network switch. VLANs provide higher utilization of switch ports because a port can be associated to the necessary broadcast domain, and multiple broadcast domains can reside on the same switch. Network devices in one VLAN cannot communicate with devices in a different VLAN without a router to interconnect the VLAN segments.

VLANs are defined in the IEEE 802.1Q standard, which states that 32 bits are added to the packet header in the following fields:

- **Tag protocol identifier (TPID):** This 16-bit field is set to 0x8100 to identify the packet as an 802.1Q packet.
- **Priority code point (PCP):** This 3-bit field indicates a class of service (CoS) as part of Layer 2 quality of service (QoS) between switches.
- **Drop eligible indicator (DEI):** This 1-bit field indicates whether the packet can be dropped when there is bandwidth contention.
- **VLAN identifier (VLAN ID):** This 12-bit field specifies the VLAN associated with a network packet.

Figure 1-4 displays the VLAN packet structure.

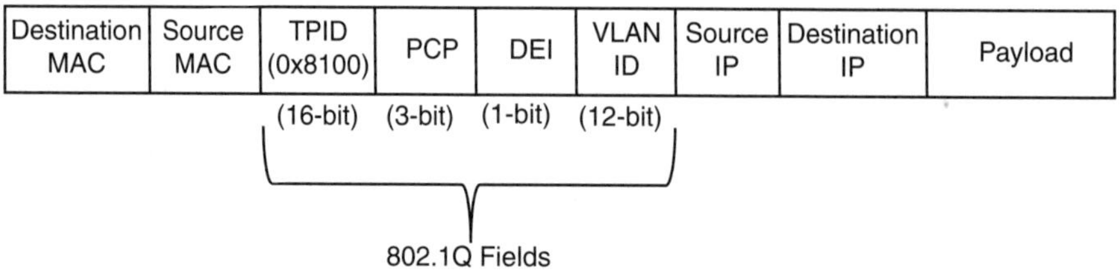

Figure 1-4 *VLAN Packet Structure*

> **NOTE** VLAN headers are not added to packets as they are forwarded locally in the switch. VLAN headers are added for packets that are sent across on trunk ports, which are covered later in this chapter.

The VLAN identifier has only 12 bits, which provide 4094 unique VLANs. Catalyst switches use the following logic for VLAN identifiers:

- VLAN 0 is reserved for 802.1p traffic and cannot be modified or deleted.
- VLAN 1 is the default VLAN and cannot be modified or deleted.
- VLANs 2 to 1001 are in the normal VLAN range and can be added, deleted, or modified as necessary.
- VLANs 1002 to 1005 are reserved and cannot be deleted.
- VLANs 1006 to 4094 are in the extended VLAN range and can be added, deleted, or modified as necessary.

VLANs are created by using the global configuration command **vlan** *vlan-id*. A friendly name (32 characters) is associated with a VLAN through the VLAN submode configuration command **name** *vlan-name*. The VLAN is not created until the command-line interface (CLI) has been moved back to the global configuration context or a different VLAN identifier.

Example 1-1 demonstrates the creation of VLAN 10 (PCs), VLAN 20 (Phones), and VLAN 99 (Guest) on SW1.

Example 1-1 *Creating a VLAN*

```
SW1# configure term
Enter configuration commands, one per line. End with CNTL/Z.
SW1(config)# vlan 10
SW1(config-vlan)# name PCs
SW1(config-vlan)# vlan 20
SW1(config-vlan)# name Phones
SW1(config-vlan)# vlan 99
SW1(config-vlan)# name Guest
```

VLANs and their port assignment are verified with the **show vlan** [{**brief** | **id** *vlan-id* | **name** *vlan-name* | **summary**}] command, as demonstrated in Example 1-2. Notice that the output is split into four main sections: VLAN-to-port assignments, system MTU, SPAN sessions, and private VLANs.

Example 1-2 *Viewing VLAN Assignments to Port Mapping*

```
SW1# show vlan
! Traditional and common VLANs will be listed in this section. The ports
! associated to these VLANs are displayed to the right.
VLAN Name                             Status    Ports
---- -------------------------------- --------- -------------------------------
1    default                          active    Gi1/0/1, Gi1/0/2, Gi1/0/3
                                                Gi1/0/4, Gi1/0/5, Gi1/0/6
                                                Gi1/0/10, Gi1/0/11, Gi1/0/17
                                                Gi1/0/18, Gi1/0/19, Gi1/0/20
                                                Gi1/0/21, Gi1/0/22, Gi1/0/23
                                                Gi1/1/1, Gi1/1/2, Te1/1/3
                                                Te1/1/4
10   PCs                              active    Gi1/0/7, Gi1/0/8, Gi1/0/9
                                                Gi1/0/12, Gi1/0/13
20   Phones                           active    Gi1/0/14
99   Guest                            active    Gi1/0/15, Gi1/0/1
1002 fddi-default                     act/unsup
1003 token-ring-default               act/unsup
1004 fddinet-default                  act/unsup
1005 trnet-default                    act/unsup
! This section displays the system wide MTU setting for all 1Gbps and faster
! interfaces

VLAN Type  SAID       MTU   Parent RingNo BridgeNo Stp  BrdgMode Trans1 Trans2
---- ----- ---------- ----- ------ ------ -------- ---- -------- ------ ------


VLAN Type  SAID       MTU   Parent RingNo BridgeNo Stp  BrdgMode Trans1 Trans2
---- ----- ---------- ----- ------ ------ -------- ---- -------- ------ ------
1    enet  100001     1500  -      -      -        -    -        0      0
10   enet  100010     1500  -      -      -        -    -        0      0
20   enet  100020     1500  -      -      -        -    -        0      0
99   enet  100099     1500  -      -      -        -    -        0      0
1002 fddi  101002     1500  -      -      -        -    -        0      0
1003 tr    101003     1500  -      -      -        -    -        0      0
1004 fdnet 101004     1500  -      -      -        ieee -        0      0
1005 trnet 101005     1500  -      -      -        ibm  -        0      0
```

```
! If a Remote SPAN VLAN is configured, it will be displayed in this section.
! Remote SPAN VLANs are explained in Chapter 24
Remote SPAN VLANs
------------------------------------------------------------------------------

! If Private VLANs are configured, they will be displayed in this section.
! Private VLANs are outside of the scope of this book, but more information
! can be found at http://www.cisco.com
Primary Secondary                      Type Ports
------- --------- ----------------- ------------------------------------------
```

The optional **show vlan** keywords provide the following benefits:

- **brief:** Displays only the relevant port-to-VLAN mappings.
- **summary:** Displays a count of VLANS, VLANs participating in VTP, and VLANs that are in the extended VLAN range.
- **id** *vlan-id*: Displays all the output from the original command but filtered to only the VLAN number that is specified.
- **name** *vlan-name*: Displays all the output from the original command but filtered to only the VLAN name that is specified.

Example 1-3 shows the use of the optional keywords. Notice that the output from the optional keywords **id** *vlan-id* is the same as the output from **name** *vlan-name*.

Example 1-3 *Using the Optional* **show vlan** *Keywords*

```
SW1# show vlan brief

VLAN Name                             Status    Ports
---- -------------------------------- --------- -------------------------------
1    default                          active    Gi1/0/1, Gi1/0/2, Gi1/0/3
                                                Gi1/0/4, Gi1/0/5, Gi1/0/6
                                                Gi1/0/10, Gi1/0/11, Gi1/0/17
                                                Gi1/0/18, Gi1/0/19, Gi1/0/20
                                                Gi1/0/21, Gi1/0/22, Gi1/0/23
                                                Gi1/1/1, Gi1/1/2, Te1/1/3
                                                Te1/1/4
10   PCs                              active    Gi1/0/7, Gi1/0/8, Gi1/0/9
                                                Gi1/0/12, Gi1/0/13
20   Phones                           active    Gi1/0/14
99   Guest                            active    Gi1/0/15, Gi1/0/16
1002 fddi-default                     act/unsup
1003 token-ring-default               act/unsup
1004 fddinet-default                  act/unsup
1005 trnet-default                    act/unsup
```

```
SW1# show vlan summary
Number of existing VLANs              : 8
 Number of existing VTP VLANs         : 8
 Number of existing extended VLANS    : 0
```

```
SW1# show vlan id 99


VLAN Name                             Status    Ports
---- -------------------------------- --------- -------------------------------
99   Guest                            active    Gi1/0/15, Gi1/0/16

VLAN Type  SAID       MTU   Parent RingNo BridgeNo Stp  BrdgMode Trans1 Trans2
---- ----- ---------- ----- ------ ------ -------- ---- -------- ------ ------
99   enet  100099     1500  -      -      -        -    -        0      0

Remote SPAN VLAN
----------------
Disabled

Primary Secondary Type              Ports
------- --------- ----------------- ------------------------------------------
```

```
SW1# show vlan name Guest

VLAN Name                             Status    Ports
---- -------------------------------- --------- -------------------------------
99   Guest                            active    Gi1/0/15, Gi1/0/16

VLAN Type  SAID       MTU   Parent RingNo BridgeNo Stp  BrdgMode Trans1 Trans2
---- ----- ---------- ----- ------ ------ -------- ---- -------- ------ ------
99   enet  100099     1500  -      -      -        -    -        0      0

Remote SPAN VLAN
----------------
Disabled

Primary Secondary Type              Ports
------- --------- ----------------- ------------------------------------------
```

Key Topic

Access Ports

Access ports are the fundamental building blocks of a switch. An access port is assigned to only one VLAN. It carries traffic from the specified VLAN to the device connected to it or from the device to other devices on the same VLAN on that switch. The 802.1Q tags are not included on packets transmitted or received on access ports.

Catalyst access switches place switch ports as Layer 2 access ports for VLAN 1 by default. The port can be manually configured as an access port with the command **switchport mode access**. A specific VLAN is associated to the port with the command **switchport access vlan** {*vlan-id* | **name** *vlan-name*}. The ability to set VLANs to an access port by name will still store the VLAN in numeric form in the configuration.

Example 1-4 demonstrates the configuration of switch ports Gi1/0/15 and Gi1/0/16 as access ports in VLAN 99 for Guests. Notice that the final configuration is stored as numbers for both ports, even though different commands are issued.

Example 1-4 *Configuring an Access Port*

```
SW1# configure terminal
Enter configuration commands, one per line. End with CNTL/Z.
SW1(config)# vlan 99
SW1(config-vlan)# name Guests
SW1(config-vlan)# interface gi1/0/15
SW1(config-if)# switchport mode access
SW1(config-if)# switchport access vlan 99
SW1(config-if)# interface gi1/0/16
SW1(config-if)# switchport mode access
SW1(config-if)# switchport access vlan name Guest
```

```
SW1# show running-config | begin interface GigabitEthernet1/0/15
interface GigabitEthernet1/0/15
 switchport access vlan 99
 switchport mode access
!
interface GigabitEthernet1/0/16
 switchport access vlan 99
 switchport mode access
```

Key Topic

Trunk Ports

Trunk ports can carry multiple VLANs. Trunk ports are typically used when multiple VLANs need connectivity between a switch and another switch, router, or firewall and use only one port. Upon receipt of the packet on the remote trunk link, the headers are examined, traffic is associated to the proper VLAN, then the 802.1Q headers are removed, and traffic is forwarded to the next port, based on the MAC address for that VLAN.

NOTE Thanks to the introduction of virtualization, some servers run a hypervisor for the operating system and contain a virtualized switch with different VLANs. These servers also provide connectivity via a trunk port.

Trunk ports are statically defined on Catalyst switches with the interface command **switchport mode trunk**. In Example 1-5, Gi1/0/2 and Gi1/0/3 are converted to a trunk port.

Example 1-5 *Configuring a Trunk Port*

```
SW1# configure terminal
Enter configuration commands, one per line. End with CNTL/Z.
SW1(config)# interface gi1/0/2
SW1(config-if)# switchport mode trunk
SW1(config-if)# interface gi1/0/3
SW1(config-if)# switchport mode trunk
```

Example 1-6 shows the output of the **show interfaces trunk** command. This command provides a lot of valuable information in several sections for troubleshooting connectivity between network devices:

- The first section lists all the interfaces that are trunk ports, the status, and which VLAN is the native VLAN for that trunk port. Native VLANs are explained in the next section. EtherChannel interfaces are explained in Chapter 5, "VLAN Trunks and EtherChannel Bundles."
- The second section of the output displays the list of VLANs that are allowed on the trunk port. Traffic can be minimized on trunk ports by restricting the allowed VLANs to specific switches, thereby restricting broadcast traffic too. Other use cases involve a form of load balancing between network links where select VLANs are allowed on one trunk link, while a different set of VLANs are allowed on a different trunk port.
- The third section displays the VLANs that are in a forwarding state on the switch. Ports that are in a blocking state are not listed in this section.

Example 1-6 *Verifying Trunk Port Status*

```
SW1# show interfaces trunk
! Section 1 displays the physical or EtherChannel interface status, encapsulation,
! and native VLAN associated to the interface

Port        Mode             Encapsulation  Status        Native vlan
Gi1/0/2     on               802.1q         trunking      1
Gi1/0/3     on               802.1q         trunking      1


! Section 2 displays all of the VLANs that are allowed to be transmitted across
! the trunk ports

Port        Vlans allowed on trunk
Gi1/0/2     1-4094
Gi1/0/3     1-4094

Port        Vlans allowed and active in management domain
Gi1/0/2     1,10,20,99
Gi1/0/3     1,10,20,99
```

```
! Section 3 displays all of the VLANs that are allowed across the trunk and are
! in a spanning tree forwarding state

Port        Vlans in spanning tree forwarding state and not pruned
Gi1/0/2     1,10,20,99
Gi1/0/3     1,10,20,99
```

Native VLANs

In the 802.1Q standard, any traffic that is transmitted or received on a trunk port without the 802.1Q VLAN tag is associated to the **native VLAN**. Any traffic associated to the native VLAN will flow across the trunk port untagged. The default native VLAN is VLAN 1.

A native VLAN is a port-specific configuration and is changed with the interface command **switchport trunk native vlan** *vlan-id*.

NOTE Two hosts on the same subnet could still communicate if one host was connected to an access port associated to VLAN10 and the other host connects to a trunk port configured with a native VLAN of 10. This is not a best practice but demonstrates how there is not an 802.1Q VLAN tag added to the packet on either of the two ports.

NOTE All switch control plane traffic is advertised using VLAN 1. The Cisco security hardening guidelines recommend changing the native VLAN to something other than VLAN 1. More specifically, it should be set to a VLAN that is not used at all (that is, has no hosts attached to it). The native VLAN should match on both ports for traffic to be transmitted for that VLAN across the trunk link.

Allowed VLANs

As stated earlier, VLANs can be restricted from certain trunk ports as a method of traffic engineering. This restriction can cause problems if traffic between two hosts is expected to traverse a trunk link and the VLAN is not allowed to traverse that trunk port. Restricting VLANs could limit MAC address flooding across switches that do not have hosts connected to restricted VLANs. The interface command **switchport trunk allowed vlan** *vlan-ids* specifies the VLANs that are allowed to traverse the link. Example 1-7 displays a sample configuration for limiting the VLANs that can cross the Gi1/0/2 trunk port for VLANs 1, 10, 20, and 99.

Example 1-7 *Viewing the VLANs That Are Allowed on a Trunk Link*

```
SW1# show run interface gi1/0/1
interface GigabitEthernet1/0/1
 switchport trunk allowed vlan 1,10,20,99
 switchport mode trunk
```

The full command syntax **switchport trunk allowed vlan** {*vlan-ids* | **all** | **none** | **add** *vlan-ids* | **remove** *vlan-ids* | **except** *vlan-ids*} provides a lot of power in a single command. The optional keyword **all** allows for all VLANs, while **none** removes all VLANs from the trunk link. The **add** keyword adds additional VLANs to those already listed, and the **remove** keyword removes the specified VLAN from the VLANs already identified for that trunk link.

NOTE When you are scripting configuration changes, it is best to use the **add** and **remove** keywords because they are more prescriptive. A common mistake is to use the **switchport trunk allowed vlan** *vlan-ids* command to list only the VLAN that is being added. This results in the current list being overwritten, causing traffic loss for the VLANs that were omitted.

Layer 2 Diagnostic Commands

The information in the "Layer 2 Forwarding" section, earlier in this chapter, provides a brief primer on the operations of a switch. The following sections provide some common diagnostic commands that are used in the daily administration, operation, and troubleshooting of a network.

MAC Address Table

The MAC address table is responsible for identifying the switch ports and VLANs with which a device is associated. A switch builds the MAC address table by examining the source MAC address for traffic that it receives. This information is then maintained to shrink the collision domain (point-to-point communication between devices and switches) by reducing the amount of unknown unicast flooding.

The MAC address table is displayed with the command **show mac address-table** [**address** *mac-address* | **dynamic** | **vlan** *vlan-id*]. The optional keywords with this command provide the following benefits:

- **address** *mac-address*: Displays entries that match the explicit MAC address. This command could be beneficial on switches with hundreds of ports.
- **dynamic**: Displays entries that are dynamically learned and are not statically set or burned in on the switch.
- **vlan** *vlan-id*: Displays entries that match the specified VLAN.

Example 1-8 shows the MAC address table on a Catalyst switch. The command in this example displays the VLAN, MAC address, type, and port associated to the connected network devices. Notice that port Gi1/0/3 has multiple entries, which indicates that this port is connected to a switch.

Example 1-8 *Viewing the MAC Address Table*

```
SW1# show mac address-table dynamic
          Mac Address Table

Vlan    Mac Address       Type        Ports
----    -----------       --------    -----
   1    0081.c4ff.8b01    DYNAMIC     Gi1/0/2
   1    189c.5d11.9981    DYNAMIC     Gi1/0/3
   1    189c.5d11.99c7    DYNAMIC     Gi1/0/3
   1    7070.8bcf.f828    DYNAMIC     Gi1/0/17
   1    70df.2f22.b882    DYNAMIC     Gi1/0/2
   1    70df.2f22.b883    DYNAMIC     Gi1/0/3
   1    bc67.1c5c.9304    DYNAMIC     Gi1/0/2
   1    bc67.1c5c.9347    DYNAMIC     Gi1/0/3
  99    189c.5d11.9981    DYNAMIC     Gi1/0/3
  99    7069.5ad4.c228    DYNAMIC     Gi1/0/15
  10    0087.31ba.3980    DYNAMIC     Gi1/0/9
  10    0087.31ba.3981    DYNAMIC     Gi1/0/9
  10    189c.5d11.9981    DYNAMIC     Gi1/0/3
  10    3462.8800.6921    DYNAMIC     Gi1/0/8
  10    5067.ae2f.6480    DYNAMIC     Gi1/0/7
  10    7069.5ad4.c220    DYNAMIC     Gi1/0/13
  10    e8ed.f3aa.7b98    DYNAMIC     Gi1/0/12
  20    189c.5d11.9981    DYNAMIC     Gi1/0/3
  20    7069.5ad4.c221    DYNAMIC     Gi1/0/14
Total Mac Addresses for this criterion: 19
```

NOTE Troubleshooting network traffic problems from a Layer 2 perspective involves locating the source and destination device and port; this task can be done by examining the MAC address table. If multiple MAC addresses appear on the same port, you know that a switch, hub, or server with a virtual switch is connected to that switch port. Connecting to downstream switches may be required to identify the port that a specific network device is attached to.

Some older technologies (such as load balancing) require a static MAC address entry in the MAC address table to prevent unknown unicast flooding. The global configuration command **mac address-table static** *mac-address* **vlan** *vlan-id* {**drop** | **interface** *interface-id*} adds a manual entry with the ability to associate it to a specific switch port or to drop traffic upon receipt.

The command **clear mac address-table dynamic** [{**address** *mac-address* | **interface** *interface-id* | **vlan** *vlan-id*}] flushes the MAC address table for the entire switch. Using the optional keywords can flush the MAC address table for a specific MAC address, switch port, or interface.

Key Topic

The MAC address table resides in **content addressable memory (CAM)**. The CAM uses high-speed memory that is faster than typical computer RAM due to its search techniques. The CAM table provides a binary result for any query of 0 for true or 1 for false. The CAM is used with other functions to analyze and forward packets very quickly. Switches are built with large CAM to accommodate all the Layer 2 hosts for which they must maintain forwarding tables.

Switch Port Status

Examining the configuration for a switch port can be useful; however, some commands that are stored elsewhere in the configuration preempt the configuration set on the interface. The command **show interfaces** *interface-id* **switchport** provides all the relevant information for a switch port's status. The command **show interfaces switchport** displays the same operational parameters for all ports on the switch.

Example 1-9 shows the output from the **show interfaces gi1/0/5 switchport** command on SW1. The key fields to examine at this time are the switch port state, operational mode, and access mode VLAN.

Example 1-9 *Viewing the Switch Port Status*

```
SW1# show interfaces gi1/0/5 switchport
Name: Gi1/0/5
! The following line indicates if the port is configured as an L2 switchport.
Switchport: Enabled
Administrative Mode: dynamic auto
! The following line indicates if the port is acting as static access port, trunk
! port, or if is down due to carrier detection (i.e. link down)
Operational Mode: down
Administrative Trunking Encapsulation: dot1q
Negotiation of Trunking: On
! The following line displays the VLAN assigned to the access port
Access Mode VLAN: 1 (default)
Trunking Native Mode VLAN: 1 (default)
Administrative Native VLAN tagging: enabled
Voice VLAN: none
Administrative private-vlan host-association: none
Administrative private-vlan mapping: none
Administrative private-vlan trunk native VLAN: none
Administrative private-vlan trunk Native VLAN tagging: enabled
Administrative private-vlan trunk encapsulation: dot1q
Administrative private-vlan trunk normal VLANs: none
Administrative private-vlan trunk associations: none
```

```
Administrative private-vlan trunk mappings: none
Operational private-vlan: none
Trunking VLANs Enabled: ALL
Pruning VLANs Enabled: 2-1001
Capture Mode Disabled
Capture VLANs Allowed: ALL

Protected: false
Unknown unicast blocked: disabled
Unknown multicast blocked: disabled
Appliance trust: none
```

Interface Status

The command **show interfaces status** is useful for viewing the status of switch ports in a condensed and simplified manner. Example 1-10 demonstrates the use of this command and includes the following fields in the output:

- **Port:** Displays the interface ID or port channel.
- **Name:** Displays the configured interface description.
- **Status:** Displays *connected* for links where a connection was detected and established to bring up the link. Displays *notconnect* when a link is not detected and *err-disabled* when an error has been detected and the switch has disabled the ability to forward traffic out of that port.
- **VLAN:** Displays the VLAN number assigned for access ports. Trunk links appear as *trunk*, and ports configured as Layer 3 interfaces display *routed*.
- **Duplex:** Displays the duplex of the port. If the duplex auto-negotiated, it is prefixed by *a-*.
- **Speed:** Displays the speed of the port. If the port speed was auto-negotiated, it is prefixed by *a-*.
- **Type:** Displays the type of interface for the switch port. If it is a fixed RJ-45 copper port, it includes TX in the description (for example, 10/100/1000BASE-TX). Small form-factor pluggable (SFP)–based ports are listed with the SFP model if there is a driver for it in the software; otherwise, it displays *unknown*.

Example 1-10 *Viewing Overall Interface Status*

```
SW1# show interface status

Port      Name               Status       Vlan       Duplex  Speed Type
Gi1/0/1                      notconnect   1            auto   auto 10/100/1000BaseTX
Gi1/0/2   SW-2 Gi1/0/1       connected    trunk      a-full a-1000 10/100/1000BaseTX
```

```
Gi1/0/3    SW-3 Gi1/0/1       connected     trunk       a-full a-1000 10/100/1000BaseTX
Gi1/0/4                       notconnect    1             auto   auto 10/100/1000BaseTX
Gi1/0/5                       notconnect    1             auto   auto 10/100/1000BaseTX
Gi1/0/6                       notconnect    1             auto   auto 10/100/1000BaseTX
Gi1/0/7    Cube13.C           connected     10          a-full a-1000 10/100/1000BaseTX
Gi1/0/8    Cube11.F           connected     10          a-full a-1000 10/100/1000BaseTX
Gi1/0/9    Cube10.A           connected     10          a-full  a-100 10/100/1000BaseTX
Gi1/0/10                      notconnect    1             auto   auto 10/100/1000BaseTX
Gi1/0/11                      notconnect    1             auto   auto 10/100/1000BaseTX
Gi1/0/12   Cube14.D Phone     connected     10          a-full a-1000 10/100/1000BaseTX
Gi1/0/13   R1-G0/0/0          connected     10          a-full a-1000 10/100/1000BaseTX
Gi1/0/14   R2-G0/0/1          connected     20          a-full a-1000 10/100/1000BaseTX
Gi1/0/15   R3-G0/1/0          connected     99          a-full a-1000 10/100/1000BaseTX
Gi1/0/16   R4-G0/1/1          connected     99          a-full a-1000 10/100/1000BaseTX
Gi1/0/17                      connected     1           a-full a-1000 10/100/1000BaseTX
Gi1/0/18                      notconnect    1             auto   auto 10/100/1000BaseTX
Gi1/0/19                      notconnect    1             auto   auto 10/100/1000BaseTX
Gi1/0/20                      notconnect    1             auto   auto 10/100/1000BaseTX
Gi1/0/21                      notconnect    1             auto   auto 10/100/1000BaseTX
Gi1/0/22                      notconnect    1             auto   auto 10/100/1000BaseTX
Gi1/0/23                      notconnect    routed        auto   auto 10/100/1000BaseTX
Gi1/0/24                      disabled      4011          auto   auto 10/100/1000BaseTX
Te1/1/1                       notconnect    1             full    10G SFP-10GBase-SR
Te1/1/2                       notconnect    1             auto   auto unknown
```

Layer 3 Forwarding

Now that we have looked at the mechanisms of a switch and how it forwards Layer 2 traffic, let's review the process for forwarding a packet from a Layer 3 perspective. Recall that all traffic starts at Layer 7 and works its way down to Layer 1 on the source device, so the **Layer 3 forwarding** logic occurs before Layer 2 forwarding. There are two main methodologies for Layer 3 forwarding:

- Forwarding traffic to devices on the same subnet
- Forwarding traffic to devices on a different subnet

The following sections explain these two methodologies.

Local Network Forwarding

Two devices that reside on the same subnet communicate locally. As the packet headers are built, the device detects that the destination is on the same network. However, the device still needs to add the Layer 2 information (that is, the source and destination MAC addresses) to the packet headers. It knows its own MAC address but does not initially know the destination's MAC address.

Key Topic

The **Address Resolution Protocol (ARP)** table provides a method of mapping Layer 3 IP addresses to Layer 2 MAC addresses by storing the IP address of a host and its corresponding MAC address. The device then uses the ARP table to add the appropriate Layer 2 headers to the data packet before sending it down the OSI model for processing and forwarding.

For example, if an IP host needs to communicate with another IP host in the same Layer 2 segment (same broadcast domain), and an ARP entry for the other host does not exist in the local ARP table, the IP host performs address resolution by broadcasting an ARP request to the entire Layer 2 switching segment. The ARP request strictly asks that whoever owns the IP address respond with an ARP reply. All hosts in the Layer 2 segment receive the request, but only the host with the matching IP address should reply to the request.

The responding host generates a unicast ARP reply that includes the IP and MAC address from the ARP request. The requesting host receives the ARP reply and then updates its local ARP table. Now, the host is able to add the appropriate Layer 2 headers and sends the original data packet for processing and forwarding.

The ARP table contains entries for hosts or network devices that the host has communicated with recently and that are on the same IP network segment. It does not contain entries for devices on a remote network but does contain the ARP entry for the IP address of the next hop to reach the remote network. If communication has not occurred with a host after a length of time, the entry becomes stale and is removed from the local ARP table.

NOTE The ARP table can be viewed with the command **show ip arp** [*mac-address* | *ip-address* | **vlan** *vlan-id* | *interface-id*]. The optional keywords make it possible to filter the information.

Packet Routing

Packets must be routed when two devices are on different networks. As the data is encapsulated with its IP address, a device detects that its destination is on a different network and must be routed. The device checks its local routing table to identify its next-hop IP address, which may be learned in one of several ways:

- From a static route entry, it can get the destination network, subnet mask, and next-hop IP address.
- A default-gateway is a simplified static default route that is used for all non-local traffic.
- Routes can be learned from routing protocols.

Key Topic

The source device must add the appropriate Layer 2 headers (source and destination MAC addresses), but the destination MAC address is needed for the next-hop IP address. The device looks for the next-hop IP addresses entry in the ARP table and uses the MAC address from the next-hop IP address's entry as the destination MAC address. The packet headers are added, and then the packet is sent down to Layer 1 for processing and forwarding.

The next router receives the packet based on the destination MAC address, analyzes the destination IP address, locates the appropriate network entry in its routing table, identifies the outbound interface, and then finds the MAC address for the destination device (or the MAC address for the next-hop address if it needs to be routed further). The router then modifies the source MAC address to the MAC address of the router's outbound interface and modifies the destination MAC address to the MAC address for the destination device (or next-hop router).

Figure 1-5 illustrates the concept, with PC-A sending a packet to PC-B through an Ethernet connection to R1. PC-A sends the packet to R1's MAC address, 00:C1:5C:00:00:A1. R1 receives the packet, removes the Layer 2 information, and looks for a route to the 192.168.2.2 address. R1 identifies that connectivity to the 192.168.2.2 IP address is through Gigabit Ethernet 0/1. R1 adds the Layer 2 source address by using its Gigabit Ethernet 0/1 MAC address 00:C1:5C:00:00:B1 and the destination address 00:00:00:BB:BB:BB for PC-B.

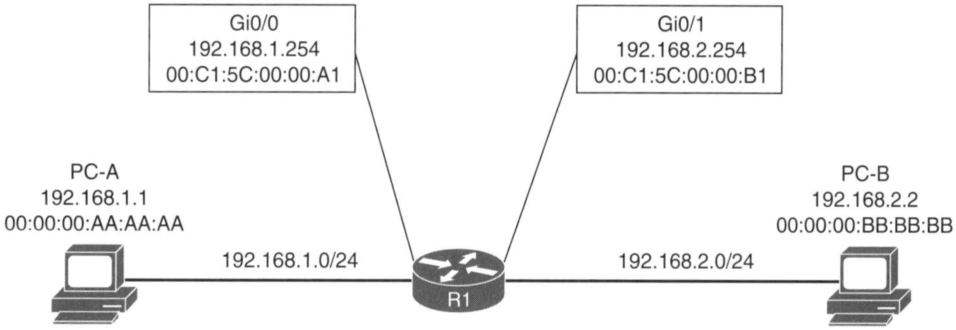

Destination MAC Address	Source MAC Address	Source IP Address	Destination IP Address
00:C1:5C:00:00:A1	00:00:00:AA:AA:AA	192.168.1.1	192.168.2.2

Destination MAC Address	Source MAC Address	Source IP Address	Destination IP Address
00:00:00:BB:BB:BB	00:C1:5C:00:00:B1	192.168.1.1	192.168.2.2

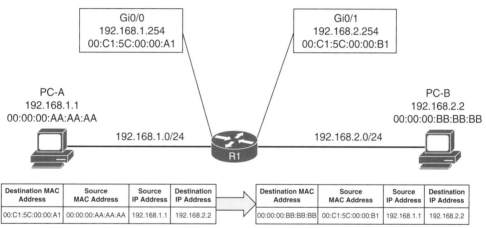

Figure 1-5 *Layer 2 Addressing Rewrite*

NOTE This process continues on and on as needed to get the packet from the source device to the destination device.

IP Address Assignment

TCP/IP has become the standard protocol for most networks. Initially, it was used with IPv4 and 32-bit network addresses. The number of devices using public IP addresses has increased at an exponential rate and depleted the number of publicly available IP addresses. To deal with the increase in the demand for public addresses, a second standard, called IPv6, was developed in 1998; it provides 128 bits for addressing. Technologies and mechanisms have been created to allow IPv4 and IPv6 networks to communicate with each other. With either version, an IP address must be assigned to an interface for a router or multilayer switch to route packets.

Key Topic

IPv4 addresses are assigned with the interface configuration command **ip address** *ip-address subnet-mask*. An interface with a configured IP address and that is in an operational "up" state injects the associated network into the router's routing table (**Routing Information Base [RIB]**). Connected networks or routes have an *administrative distance (AD)* of zero. It is not possible for any routing protocol or static route to preempt a connected route in the RIB.

It is possible to attach multiple IPv4 networks to the same interface by configuring a secondary IPv4 address to the same interface with the command **ip address** *ip-address subnet-mask* **secondary**.

IPv6 addresses are assigned with the interface configuration command **ipv6 address** *ipv6-address/prefix-length*. This command can be repeated multiple times to add multiple IPv6 addresses to the same interface.

Example 1-11 demonstrates the configuration of IP addresses on routed interfaces. A routed interface is basically any interface on a router. Notice that a second IPv4 address requires the use of the **secondary** keyword; the **ipv6 address** command can be used multiple times to configure multiple IPv6 addresses.

Example 1-11 *Assigning IP Addresses to Routed Interfaces*

```
R1# configure terminal
Enter configuration commands, one per line. End with CNTL/Z.
R1(config)# interface gi0/0/0
R1(config-if)# ip address 10.10.10.254 255.255.255.0
R1(config-if)# ip address 172.16.10.254 255.255.255.0 secondary
R1(config-if)# ipv6 address 2001:db8:10::254/64
R1(config-if)# ipv6 address 2001:db8:10:172::254/64
R1(config-if)# interface gi0/0/1
R1(config-if)# ip address 10.20.20.254 255.255.255.0
R1(config-if)# ip address 172.16.20.254 255.255.255.0 secondary
R1(config-if)# ipv6 address 2001:db8:20::254/64
R1(config-if)# ipv6 address 2001:db8:20:172::254/64
```

Routed Subinterfaces

A routed subinterface is required when there are multiple VLANs on a switch that require routing, and it is not desirable to use a dedicated physical routed interface per VLAN, or there are not enough physical router interfaces to accommodate all the VLANs. To overcome this issue, it is possible to create a trunk port on the switch and create a logical subinterface on the router. A subinterface is created by appending a period and a numeric value after the period. Then the VLAN needs to be associated with the subinterface with the command **encapsulation dot1q** *vlan-id*.

Example 1-12 demonstrates the configuration of two subinterfaces on R2. The subinterface number does not have to match the VLAN ID, but if it does, it helps with operational support.

Example 1-12 *Configuring Routed Subinterfaces*

```
R2# configure terminal
Enter configuration commands, one per line. End with CNTL/Z.
R2(config-if)# int g0/0/1.10
R2(config-subif)# encapsulation dot1Q 10
R2(config-subif)# ip address 10.10.10.2 255.255.255.0
R2(config-subif)# ipv6 address 2001:db8:10::2/64
R2(config-subif)# int g0/0/1.99
R2(config-subif)# encapsulation dot1Q 99
R2(config-subif)# ip address 10.20.20.2 255.255.255.0
R2(config-subif)# ipv6 address 2001:db8:20::2/64
```

Switched Virtual Interfaces

With Catalyst switches, it is possible to assign an IP address to a *switched virtual interface (SVI)*, also known as a *VLAN interface*. An SVI is configured by defining the VLAN on the switch and then defining the VLAN interface with the command **interface vlan** *vlan-id*. The switch must have an interface associated to that VLAN in an *up* state for the SVI to be in an *up* state. If the switch is a multilayer switch, the SVIs can be used for routing packets between VLANs without the need of an external router.

Example 1-13 demonstrates the configuration of the SVI for VLANs 10 and 99.

Example 1-13 *Creating a Switched Virtual Interface (SVI)*

```
SW1# configure terminal
Enter configuration commands, one per line. End with CNTL/Z.
SW1(config)# interface vlan 10
SW1(config-if)# ip address 10.10.10.1 255.255.255.0
SW1(config-if)# ipv6 address 2001:db8:10::1/64
SW1(config-if)# no shutdown
SW1(config-if)# interface vlan 99
SW1(config-if)# ip address 10.99.99.1 255.255.255.0
SW1(config-if)# ipv6 address 2001:db8:99::1/64
SW1(config-if)# no shutdown
```

Routed Switch Ports

Some network designs include a point-to-point link between switches for routing. For example, when a switch needs to connect to a router, some network engineers would build out a transit VLAN (for example, VLAN 2001), associate the port connecting to the router to VLAN 2001, and then build an SVI for VLAN 2001. There is always the potential that VLAN 2001 could exist elsewhere in the Layer 2 realm, or that a spanning tree could impact the topology.

Instead, the multilayer switch port can be converted from a Layer 2 switch port to a routed switch port with the interface configuration command **no switchport**. Then the IP address can be assigned to it. Example 1-14 demonstrates port Gi1/0/14 being converted from a Layer 2 switch port to a routed switch port and then having an IP address assigned to it.

Example 1-14 *Configuring a Routed Switch Port*

```
SW1# configure terminal
Enter configuration commands, one per line. End with CNTL/Z.
SW1(config)# int gi1/0/14
SW1(config-if)# no switchport
SW1(config-if)# ip address 10.20.20.1 255.255.255.0
SW1(config-if)# ipv6 address 2001:db8:20::1/64
SW1(config-if)# no shutdown
```

Verification of IP Addresses

IPv4 addresses can be viewed with the command **show ip interface [brief |** *interface-id* **| vlan** *vlan-id***]**. This command's output contains a lot of useful information, such as MTU, DHCP relay, ACLs, and the primary IP address. The optional **brief** keyword displays the output in a condensed format. However, on devices with large port counts, using the CLI parser and adding an additional **| exclude** field (for example, **unassigned**) yields a streamlined view of interfaces that are configured with IP addresses.

Example 1-15 shows the **show ip interface brief** command used with and without the CLI parser. Notice the drastic reduction in unnecessary data that is presented.

Example 1-15 *Viewing Device IPv4 Addresses*

```
SW1# show ip interface brief
Interface              IP-Address      OK? Method Status     Protocol
Vlan1                  unassigned      YES manual up         up
Vlan10                 10.10.10.1      YES manual up         up
Vlan99                 10.99.99.1      YES manual up         up
GigabitEthernet0/0     unassigned      YES unset  down       down
GigabitEthernet1/0/1   unassigned      YES unset  down       down
GigabitEthernet1/0/2   unassigned      YES unset  up         up
GigabitEthernet1/0/3   unassigned      YES unset  up         up
GigabitEthernet1/0/4   unassigned      YES unset  down       down
GigabitEthernet1/0/5   unassigned      YES unset  down       down
GigabitEthernet1/0/6   unassigned      YES unset  down       down
GigabitEthernet1/0/7   unassigned      YES unset  up         up
GigabitEthernet1/0/8   unassigned      YES unset  up         up
GigabitEthernet1/0/9   unassigned      YES unset  up         up
GigabitEthernet1/0/10  unassigned      YES unset  down       down
GigabitEthernet1/0/11  unassigned      YES unset  down       down
GigabitEthernet1/0/12  unassigned      YES unset  down       down
GigabitEthernet1/0/13  unassigned      YES unset  up         up
GigabitEthernet1/0/14  10.20.20.1      YES manual up         up
GigabitEthernet1/0/15  unassigned      YES unset  up         up
GigabitEthernet1/0/16  unassigned      YES unset  up         up
GigabitEthernet1/0/17  unassigned      YES unset  down       down
```

```
SW1# show ip interface brief | exclude unassigned
```

```
Interface              IP-Address     OK? Method Status     Protocol
Vlan10                 10.10.10.1     YES manual up         up
Vlan99                 10.99.99.1     YES manual up         up
GigabitEthernet1/0/14  10.20.20.1     YES manual up         up
GigabitEthernet1/0/23  192.168.1.1    YES manual down       down
```

The same information can be viewed for IPv6 addresses with the command **show ipv6 interface** [**brief** | *interface-id* | **vlan** *vlan-id*]. Just as with IPv4 addresses, a CLI parser can be used to reduce the information to what is relevant, as demonstrated in Example 1-16.

Example 1-16 *Viewing Device IPv6 Addresses*

```
SW1# show ipv6 interface brief
! Output omitted for brevity
Vlan1                  [up/up]
    FE80::262:ECFF:FE9D:C547
    2001:1::1
Vlan10                 [up/up]
    FE80::262:ECFF:FE9D:C546
    2001:DB8:10::1
Vlan99                 [up/up]
    FE80::262:ECFF:FE9D:C55D
    2001:DB8:99::1
GigabitEthernet0/0     [down/down]
    unassigned
GigabitEthernet1/0/1   [down/down]
    unassigned
GigabitEthernet1/0/2   [up/up]
    unassigned
GigabitEthernet1/0/3   [up/up]
    unassigned
GigabitEthernet1/0/4   [down/down]
    unassigned
GigabitEthernet1/0/5   [down/down]
    Unassigned
```

```
SW1# show ipv6 interface brief | exclude unassigned|GigabitEthernet
Vlan1                  [up/up]
    FE80::262:ECFF:FE9D:C547
    2001:1::1
Vlan10                 [up/up]
    FE80::262:ECFF:FE9D:C546
    2001:DB8:10::1
Vlan99                 [up/up]
    FE80::262:ECFF:FE9D:C55D
    2001:DB8:99::1
```

Forwarding Architectures

The first Cisco routers would receive a packet, remove the Layer 2 information, and verify that the route existed for the destination IP address. If a matching route could not be found, the packet was dropped. If a matching route was found, the router would identify and add new Layer 2 header information to the packet.

Advancements in technologies have streamlined the process so that routers do not remove and add the Layer 2 addressing but simply rewrite the addresses. IP packet switching or IP packet forwarding is a faster process for receiving an IP packet on an input interface and making a decision about whether to forward the packet to an output interface or drop it. This process is simple and streamlined so that a router can forward large numbers of packets.

When the first Cisco routers were developed, they used a mechanism called process switching to switch the packets through the routers. As network devices evolved, Cisco created *fast switching* and Cisco Express Forwarding (CEF) to optimize the switching process for the routers to be able to handle larger packet volumes.

Key Topic

Process Switching

Process switching, also referred to as *software switching* or *slow path*, is a switching mechanism in which the general-purpose CPU on a router is in charge of packet switching. In IOS, the *ip_input* process runs on the general-purpose CPU for processing incoming IP packets. Process switching is the fallback for CEF because it is dedicated to processing punted IP packets when they cannot be switched by CEF.

The types of packets that generally require software handling include the following:

- Packets sourced or destined to the router (using control traffic or routing protocols)
- Packets that are too complex for the hardware to handle (that is, IP packets with IP options)
- Packets that require extra information that is not currently known (for example, unresolved ARP entries)

> **NOTE** Software switching is significantly slower than switching done in hardware. The *ip_input* process is designed to handle a very small percentage of traffic handled by the system. Packets are hardware switched whenever possible.

Figure 1-6 illustrates how a packet that cannot be CEF switched is punted to the CPU for processing. The *ip_input* process consults the routing table and ARP table to obtain the next-hop router's IP address, outgoing interface, and MAC address. It then overwrites the destination MAC address of the packet with the next-hop router's MAC address, overwrites the source MAC address with the MAC address of the outgoing Layer 3 interface, decrements the IP time-to-live (TTL) field, recomputes the IP header checksum, and finally delivers the packet to the next-hop router.

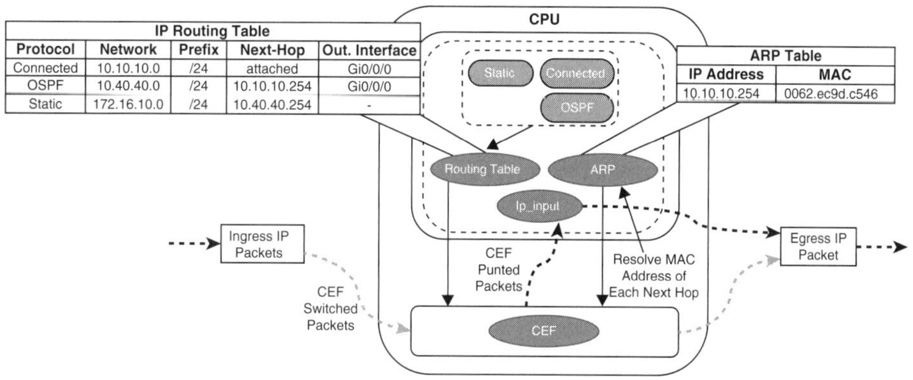

Figure 1-6 *Process Switching*

The routing table, also known as the *Routing Information Base (RIB)*, is built from information obtained from dynamic routing protocols and directly connected and static routes. The ARP table is built from information obtained from the ARP protocol.

Key Topic

Cisco Express Forwarding

Cisco Express Forwarding (CEF) is a Cisco proprietary switching mechanism developed to keep up with the demands of evolving network infrastructures. It has been the default switching mechanism on most Cisco platforms that do all their packet switching using the general-purpose CPU (software-based routers) since the 1990s, and it is the default switching mechanism used by all Cisco platforms that use specialized application-specific integrated circuits (ASICs) and network processing units (NPUs) for high packet throughput (hardware-based routers).

The general-purpose CPUs on software-based and hardware-based routers are similar and perform all the same functions; the difference is that on software-based routers, the general-purpose CPU is in charge of all operations, including CEF switching (software CEF), and the hardware-based routers do CEF switching using forwarding engines that are implemented in specialized ASICs, ternary content addressable memory (TCAM), and NPUs (hardware CEF). Forwarding engines provide the packet switching, forwarding, and route lookup capability to routers.

Key Topic

Ternary Content Addressable Memory

A switch's **ternary content addressable memory (TCAM)** allows for the matching and evaluation of a packet on more than one field. TCAM is an extension of the CAM architecture but enhanced to allow for upper-layer processing such as identifying the Layer 2/3 source/destination addresses, protocol, QoS markings, and so on. TCAM provides more flexibility in searching than does CAM, which is binary. A TCAM search provides three results: 0 for true, 1 false, and X for do not care, which is a ternary combination.

The TCAM entries are stored in Value, Mask, and Result (VMR) format. The value indicates the fields that should be searched, such as the IP address and protocol fields. The mask indicates the field that is of interest and that should be queried. The result indicates the action that should be taken with a match on the value and mask. Multiple actions can be selected besides allowing or dropping traffic, but tasks like redirecting a flow to a QoS policer or specifying a pointer to a different entry in the forwarding table are possible.

Most switches implement multiple TCAM entries so that inbound/outbound security, QoS, and Layer 2 and Layer 3 forwarding decisions occur all at once. TCAM operates in hardware, providing faster processing and scalability than process switching. This allows for some features like ACLs to process at the same speed regardless of whether there are 10 entries or 500. The TCAM is not an infinite resource, and balancing memory allocations between functions has trade-offs.

Centralized Forwarding

Given the low cost of general-purpose CPUs, the price of software-based routers is becoming more affordable, but at the expense of total packet throughput.

When a route processor (RP) engine is equipped with a forwarding engine so that it can make all the packet switching decisions, this is known as a *centralized forwarding architecture*. If the line cards are equipped with forwarding engines so that they can make packet switching decisions without intervention of the RP, this is known as a *distributed forwarding architecture*.

For a centralized forwarding architecture, when a packet is received on the ingress line card, it is transmitted to the forwarding engine on the RP. The forwarding engine examines the packet's headers and determines that the packet will be sent out a port on the egress line card and forwards the packet to the egress line card to be forwarded.

Distributed Forwarding

For a distributed forwarding architecture, when a packet is received on the ingress line card, it is transmitted to the line card's local forwarding engine. The forwarding engine performs a packet lookup, and if it determines that the outbound interface is local, it forwards the packet out a local interface. If the outbound interface is located on a different line card, the packet is sent across the switch fabric, also known as the backplane, directly to the egress line card, bypassing the RP.

Figure 1-7 shows the difference between centralized and distributed forwarding architectures.

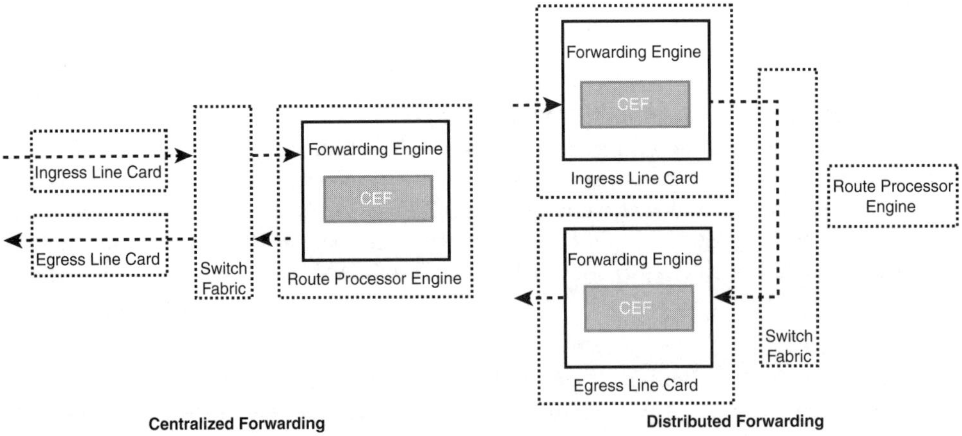

Figure 1-7 *Centralized Versus Distributed Forwarding Architectures*

Key Topic

Software CEF

Software CEF, also known as the *software* **Forwarding Information Base (FIB)**, consists of the following components:

- **Forwarding Information Base:** The FIB is built directly from the routing table and contains the next-hop IP address for each destination in the network. It keeps a mirror image of the forwarding information contained in the IP routing table. When a routing or topology change occurs in the network, the IP routing table is updated, and these changes are reflected in the FIB. CEF uses the FIB to make IP destination prefix-based switching decisions.
- **Adjacency table:** The adjacency table, also known as the Adjacency Information Base (AIB), contains the directly connected next-hop IP addresses and their corresponding next-hop MAC addresses, as well as the egress interface's MAC address. The adjacency table is populated with data from the ARP table or other Layer 2 protocol tables.

Figure 1-8 illustrates how the CEF table is built from the routing table. First, the FIB is built from the routing table. The 172.16.10.0/24 prefix is a static route with a next hop of 10.40.40.254, which is dependent upon the 10.40.40.0/24 prefix learned via OSPF. The adjacency pointer in the FIB for the 172.16.10.0/24 entry is exactly the same IP address that OSPF uses for the 10.40.40.0/24 prefix (10.10.10.254). The adjacency table is then built using the ARP table and cross-referencing the MAC address with the MAC address table to identify the outbound interface.

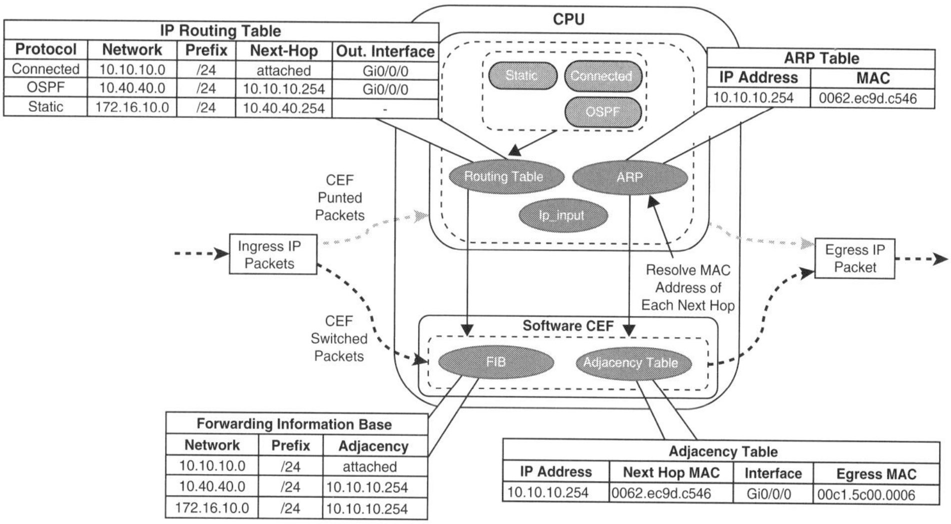

Figure 1-8 *CEF Switching*

Upon receipt of an IP packet, the FIB is checked for a valid entry. If an entry is missing, it is a "glean" adjacency in CEF, which means the packet should go to the CPU because CEF is unable to handle it. Valid FIB entries continue processing by looking for the appropriate adjacency entry based on that FIB record. Missing adjacency entries invoke the ARP process. After ARP is resolved, the complete CEF entry can be created.

As part of the packet forwarding process, the packet's headers are rewritten. The router overwrites the destination MAC address of a packet with the next-hop router's MAC address from the adjacency table, overwrites the source MAC address with the MAC address of the outgoing Layer 3 interface, decrements the IP time-to-live (TTL) field, recomputes the IP header checksum, and finally delivers the packet to the next-hop router.

NOTE Packets processed by the CPU are typically subject to a rate limiter when an invalid or incomplete adjacency exists to prevent the starving of CPU cycles from other essential processes.

NOTE The TTL is a Layer 3 loop prevention mechanism that reduces a packet's TTL field by 1 for every Layer 3 hop. If a router receives a packet with a TTL of 0, the packet is discarded.

Hardware CEF

The ASICs in hardware-based routers are expensive to design, produce, and troubleshoot. ASICs allow for very high packet rates, but the trade-off is that they are limited in their functionality because they are hardwired to perform specific tasks. The routers are equipped with NPUs that are designed to overcome the inflexibility of ASICs. Unlike ASICs, NPUs are programmable, and their firmware can be changed with relative ease.

The main advantage of the distributed forwarding architectures is that the packet throughput performance is greatly improved by offloading the packet switching responsibilities to the line cards. Packet switching in distributed architecture platforms is done via distributed CEF (dCEF), which is a mechanism in which the CEF data structures are downloaded to forwarding ASICs and the CPUs of all line cards so that they can participate in packet switching; this allows for the switching to be done at the distributed level, thus increasing the packet throughput of the router.

NOTE Software CEF in hardware-based platforms is not used to do packet switching as in software-based platforms; instead, it is used to program the hardware CEF.

Key Topic

SDM Templates

The capacity of MAC addresses that a switch needs compared to the number of routes that it holds depends on where it is deployed in the network. The memory used for TCAM tables is limited and statically allocated during the bootup sequence of the switch. When a section of a hardware resource is full, all processing overflow is sent to the CPU, which seriously impacts the performance of the switch.

The allocation ratios between the various TCAM tables are stored and can be modified with Switching Database Manager (SDM) templates. Multiple Cisco switches exist, and the SDM template varies by model. SDM templates can be configured on Catalyst 9300 switches with the global configuration command **sdm prefer** {**vlan** | **advanced**}. The switch must then be restarted with the **reload** command.

NOTE Every switch in a switch stack must be configured with the same SDM template.

Table 1-2 shows the approximate number of resources available per template. This number could vary based on the switch platform or software version in use. These numbers are typical for Layer 2 and IPv4 features. Some features, such as IPv6, use twice the entry size, which means only half as many entries can be created.

Table 1-2 Approximate Number of Feature Resources Allowed by Templates

Resource	Advanced	VLAN
Number of VLANs	4094	4094
Unicast MAC addresses	32,768	32,768
Overflow unicast MAC addresses	512	512
IGMP groups and multicast routes	4096	4096
Overflow IGMP groups and multicast routes	512	512
Directly connected routes	16,384	16,384
Indirect routes	7168	7168
Policy-based routing access control entries (ACEs)	1024	0
QoS classification ACEs	3000	3000
Security ACEs	3000	3000
NetFlow ACEs	768	768
Input Microflow policer ACEs	256,000	0
Output Microflow policer ACEs	256,000	0
Flow Span (FSPAN) ACEs	256	256
Control plane entries	512	512

The current SDM template can viewed with the command **show sdm prefer**, as demonstrated in Example 1-17.

Example 1-17 *Viewing the Current SDM Template*

```
SW1# show sdm prefer
Showing SDM Template Info

This is the Advanced (high scale) template.
  Number of VLANs:                                         4094
  Unicast MAC addresses:                                   32768
  Overflow Unicast MAC addresses:                          512
  IGMP and Multicast groups:                               4096
  Overflow IGMP and Multicast groups:                      512
  Directly connected routes:                               16384
  Indirect routes:                                         7168
```

```
  Security Access Control Entries:              3072
  QoS Access Control Entries:                   2560
  Policy Based Routing ACEs:                    1024
  Netflow ACEs:                                 768
  Wireless Input Microflow policer ACEs:        256
  Wireless Output Microflow policer ACEs:       256
  Flow SPAN ACEs:                               256
  Tunnels:                                      256
  Control Plane Entries:                        512
  Input Netflow flows:                          8192
  Output Netflow flows:                         16384
  SGT/DGT and MPLS VPN entries:                 3840
  SGT/DGT and MPLS VPN Overflow entries:        512
These numbers are typical for L2 and IPv4 features.
Some features such as IPv6, use up double the entry size;
so only half as many entries can be created.
```

Exam Preparation Tasks

You have a couple of choices for exam preparation: the exercises here, Chapter 30, “Final Preparation,” and the exam simulation questions in the Pearson Test Prep Software Online.

Review All Key Topics

Review the most important topics in the chapter, noted with the Key Topic icon in the outer margin of the page. Table 1-3 lists these key topics and the page number on which each is found.

Key Topic

Table 1-3 Key Topics for Chapter 1

Key Topic Element	Description	Page
Section	Collision Domains	5
Paragraph	Virtual LANs (VLANs)	7
Section	Access Ports	11
Section	Trunk Ports	12
Paragraph	Content addressable memory	17
Paragraph	Address Resolution Protocol (ARP)	20
Paragraph	Packet routing	20
Paragraph	IP address assignment	22
Section	Process switching	26
Section	Cisco Express Forwarding (CEF)	27
Section	Ternary Content Addressable Memory	27
Section	Software CEF	29
Section	SDM Templates	30

Complete Tables and Lists from Memory

There are no memory tables in this chapter.

Define Key Terms

Define the following key terms from this chapter and check your answers in the Glossary:

access port, Address Resolution Protocol (ARP), broadcast domain, Cisco Express Forwarding (CEF), collision domain, content addressable memory (CAM), Layer 2 forwarding, Layer 3 forwarding, Forwarding Information Base (FIB), MAC address table, native VLAN, process switching, Routing Information Base (RIB), trunk port, ternary content addressable memory (TCAM), virtual LAN (VLAN)

Use the Command Reference to Check Your Memory

Table 1-4 lists the important commands from this chapter. To test your memory, cover the right side of the table with a piece of paper, read the description on the left side, and see how much of the command you can remember.

Table 1-4 Command Reference

Task	Command Syntax
Define a VLAN	**vlan** *vlan-id* **name** *vlan-name*
Configure an interface as a trunk port	**switchport mode trunk**
Configure an interface as an access port assigned to a specific VLAN	**switchport mode access** **switchport access vlan** {*vlan-id* | **name** *name*}
Configure a static MAC address entry	**mac address-table static mac-address vlan** *vlan-id* **interface** *interface-id*
Clear MAC addresses from the MAC address table	**clear mac address-table dynamic** [{**address** *mac-address* | **interface** *interface-id* | **vlan** *vlan-id*}]
Assign an IPv4 address to an interface	**ip address** *ip-address subnet-mask*
Assign a secondary IPv4 address to an interface	**ip address** *ip-address subnet-mask* **secondary**
Assign an IPv6 address to an interface	**ipv6 address** *ipv6-address/prefix-length*
Modify the SDM database	**sdm prefer** {**vlan** | **advanced**}
Display the interfaces that are configured as a trunk port and all the VLANs that they permit	**show interfaces trunk**
Display the list of VLANs and their associated ports	**show vlan** [{**brief** | **id** *vlan-id* | **name** *vlan-name* | **summary**}]
Display the MAC address table for a switch	**show mac address-table** [**address** *mac-address* | **dynamic** | **vlan** *vlan-id*]
Display the current interface state, including duplex, speed, and link state	**show interfaces status**
Display the Layer 2 configuration information for a specific switch port	**show interfaces** *interface-id* **switchport**

Task	Command Syntax
Display the ARP table	**show ip arp** [*mac-address* | *ip-address* | **vlan** *vlan-id* | *interface-id*]
Display the IP interface table	**show ip interface** [**brief** | *interface-id* | **vlan** *vlan-id*]
Display the IPv6 interface table	**show ipv6 interface** [**brief** | *interface-id* | **vlan** *vlan-id*]

References in This Chapter

Bollapragada, Vijay, Russ White, and Curtis Murphy. *Inside Cisco IOS Software Architecture*. (ISBN-13: 9781587058165).

Stringfield, Nakia, Russ White, and Stacia McKee. *Cisco Express Forwarding*. (ISBN-13: 9780133433340).

CHAPTER 2

Spanning Tree Protocol

This chapter covers the following subjects:

- **Spanning Tree Protocol Fundamentals:** This section provides an overview of how switches become aware of other switches and prevent forwarding loops.
- **Rapid Spanning Tree Protocol:** This section examines the improvements made to STP for faster convergence.

A good network design provides redundancy in devices and network links (that is, paths). The simplest solution involves adding a second link between switches to overcome a network link failure or ensuring that a switch is connected to at least two other switches in a topology. However, such topologies cause problems when a switch must forward broadcasts or when unknown unicast flooding occurs. Network broadcasts forward in a continuous loop until the link becomes saturated, and the switch is forced to drop packets. In addition, the MAC address table must constantly change ports as the packets make loops. The packets continue to loop around the topology because there is not a time-to-live (TTL) mechanism for Layer 2 forwarding. The switch CPU utilization increases, as does memory consumption, which could result in the crashing of the switch.

This chapter explains how switches prevent forwarding loops while allowing for redundant links with the use of Spanning Tree Protocol (STP) and Rapid Spanning Tree Protocol (RSTP). Two other chapters also explain STP-related topics:

- **Chapter 3, "Advanced STP Tuning":** Covers advanced STP topics such as BPDU guard and BPDU filter.
- **Chapter 4, "Multiple Spanning Tree Protocol":** Covers Multiple Spanning Tree Protocol.

"Do I Know This Already?" Quiz

The "Do I Know This Already?" quiz enables you to assess whether you should read the entire chapter. If you miss no more than one of these self-assessment questions, you might want to move ahead to the "Exam Preparation Tasks" section. Table 2-1 lists the major headings in this chapter and the "Do I Know This Already?" quiz questions covering the material in those headings so you can assess your knowledge of these specific areas. The answers to the "Do I Know This Already?" quiz appear in Appendix A, "Answers to the 'Do I Know This Already?' Questions."

Table 2-1 "Do I Know This Already?" Foundation Topics Section-to-Question Mapping

Foundation Topics Section	Questions
Spanning Tree Protocol Fundamentals	1–6
Rapid Spanning Tree Protocol	7–9

1. How many different BPDU types are there?
   a. One
   b. Two
   c. Three
   d. Four
2. What primary attribute is used to elect a root bridge?
   a. Switch port priority
   b. Bridge priority
   c. Switch serial number
   d. Path cost
3. The original 802.1D specification assigns what port cost value to a 1 Gbps interface?
   a. 1
   b. 2
   c. 4
   d. 19
4. All of the ports on a root bridge are assigned what role?
   a. Root port
   b. Designated port
   c. Superior port
   d. Master port
5. Using default settings, how long does a port stay in the listening state?
   a. 2 seconds
   b. 5 seconds
   c. 10 seconds
   d. 15 seconds
6. Upon receipt of a configuration BPDU with the topology change flag set, how do the downstream switches react?
   a. By moving all ports to a blocking state on all switches
   b. By flushing out all MAC addresses from the MAC address table
   c. By temporarily moving all non-root ports to a listening state
   d. By flushing out all old MAC addresses from the MAC address table
   e. By updating the Topology Change version flag on the local switch database

7. Which of the following are not RSTP port states?
   a. Blocking
   b. Listening
   c. Learning
   d. Forwarding
8. True or false: When 802.1D is compared to RSTP, the number of port states is reduced from five to four.
   a. True
   b. False
9. True or false: In a large Layer 2 switch topology that is running RSTP, the infrastructure must fully converge before any packets can be forwarded.
   a. True
   b. False

Foundation Topics

Spanning Tree Protocol Fundamentals

Spanning Tree Protocol (STP) enables switches to become aware of other switches through the advertisement and receipt of **bridge protocol data units (BPDUs)**. STP builds a Layer 2 loop-free topology in an environment by temporarily blocking traffic on redundant ports. STP operates by selecting a specific switch as the best switch and running a tree-based algorithm to identify which redundant ports should not forward traffic.

STP has multiple iterations:

- 802.1D, which is the original specification
- Per-VLAN Spanning Tree (PVST)
- Per-VLAN Spanning Tree Plus (PVST+)
- 802.1W Rapid Spanning Tree Protocol (RSTP)
- 802.1S Multiple Spanning Tree Protocol (MST)

Catalyst switches now operate in PVST+, RSTP, and MST modes. All three of these modes are backward compatible with 802.1D.

IEEE 802.1D STP

The original version of STP comes from the IEEE 802.1D standards and provides support for ensuring a loop-free topology for one VLAN. This topic is vital to understand as a foundation for Rapid Spanning Tree Protocol (RSTP) and Multiple Spanning Tree Protocol (MST).

802.1D Port States

In 802.1D STP, every port transitions through the following states:

- **Disabled:** The port is in an administratively off position (that is, shut down).
- **Blocking:** The switch port is enabled, but the port is not forwarding any traffic to ensure that a loop is not created. The switch does not modify the MAC address table. It can only receive BPDUs from other switches.
- **Listening:** The switch port has transitioned from a blocking state and can now send or receive BPDUs. It cannot forward any other network traffic. The duration of the state correlates to the STP forwarding time. The next port state is learning.
- **Learning:** The switch port can now modify the MAC address table with any network traffic that it receives. The switch still does not forward any other network traffic besides BPDUs. The duration of the state correlates to the STP forwarding time. The next port state is forwarding.
- **Forwarding:** The switch port can forward all network traffic and can update the MAC address table as expected. This is the final state for a switch port to forward network traffic.
- **Broken:** The switch has detected a configuration or an operational problem on a port that can have major effects. The port discards packets as long as the problem continues to exist.

NOTE The entire 802.1D STP initialization time takes about 30 seconds for a port to transition from a blocking to a forwarding state using default timers after a switch port transitions to a carrier up state.

802.1D Port Types

The 802.1D STP standard defines the following three port types:

Key Topic

- **Root port (RP):** A network port that connects to the root bridge or an upstream switch in the spanning-tree topology. There should be only one root port per VLAN on a switch.
- **Designated port (DP):** A network port that receives and forwards BPDU frames to other switches. Designated ports provide connectivity to downstream devices and switches. There should be only one active designated port on a link.
- **Blocking port:** A network port that is not forwarding traffic because of STP calculations.

Key Topic

STP Key Terminology

Several key terms are related to STP:

- **Root bridge:** The root bridge is the most important switch in the Layer 2 topology. All ports are in a forwarding state. This switch is considered the top of the spanning tree for all path calculations by other switches. All ports on the root bridge are categorized as designated ports.

- **Bridge protocol data unit (BPDU):** This network packet is used for network switches to identify a hierarchy and notify of changes in the topology. A BPDU uses the destination MAC address 01:80:c2:00:00:00. There are two types of BPDUs:
  - **Configuration BPDU:** This type of BPDU is used to identify the root bridge, root ports, designated ports, and blocking ports. The configuration BPDU consists of the following fields: STP type, root path cost, root bridge identifier, local bridge identifier, max age, hello time, and forward delay.
  - **Topology change notification (TCN) BPDU:** This type of BPDU is used to communicate changes in the Layer 2 topology to other switches. It is explained in greater detail later in the chapter.
- **Root path cost:** This is the combined cost for a specific path toward the root switch.
- **System priority:** This 4-bit value indicates the preference for a switch to be root bridge. The default value is 32,768.
- **System ID extension:** This 12-bit value indicates the VLAN that the BPDU correlates to. The system priority and system ID extension are combined as part of the switch's identification of a bridge.
- **Root bridge identifier:** This is a combination of the root bridge system MAC address, system ID extension, and system priority of the root bridge.
- **Local bridge identifier:** This is a combination of the local switch's bridge system MAC address, system ID extension, and system priority of the local bridge.
- **Max age:** This is the maximum length of time that a bridge port stores its BPDU information. The default value is 20 seconds, but the value can be configured with the command **spanning-tree vlan** *vlan-id* **max-age** *maxage*. If a switch loses contact with the BPDU's source, it assumes that the BPDU information is still valid for the duration of the Max Age timer.
- **Hello time:** This is the time interval that a BPDU is advertised out of a port. The default value is 2 seconds, but the value can be configured to 1 to 10 seconds with the command **spanning-tree vlan** *vlan-id* **hello-time** *hello-time*.
- **Forward delay:** This is the amount of time that a port stays in a listening and learning state. The default value is 15 seconds, but the value can be changed to a value of 4 to 30 seconds with the command **spanning-tree vlan** *vlan-id* **forward-time** *forward-time*.

NOTE STP was defined before modern switches existed. The devices that originally used STP were known as bridges. Switches perform the same role at a higher speed and scale while essentially bridging Layer 2 traffic. The terms *bridge* and *switch* are interchangeable in this context.

Answers to the "Do I Know This Already?" quiz:

1 B **2** B **3** C **4** B **5** D **6** D **7** A, B **8** B **9** B

Spanning Tree Path Cost

The interface STP cost is an essential component for root path calculation because the root path is found based on the cumulative interface STP cost to reach the root bridge. The interface STP cost was originally stored as a 16-bit value with a reference value of 20 Gbps. As switches have developed with higher-speed interfaces, 10 Gbps might not be enough. Another method, called *long mode*, uses a 32-bit value and uses a reference speed of 20 Tbps. The original method, known as *short mode*, has been the default for most switches, but has been transitioning to long mode based on specific platform and OS versions.

Table 2-2 displays a list of interface speeds and the correlating interface STP costs.

Table 2-2 Default Interface STP Port Costs

Link Speed	Short-Mode STP Cost	Long-Mode STP Cost
10 Mbps	100	2,000,000
100 Mbps	19	200,000
1 Gbps	4	20,000
10 Gbps	2	2000
20 Gbps	1	1000
100 Gbps	1	200
1 Tbps	1	20
10 Tbps	1	2

Devices can be configured with the long-mode interface cost with the command **spanning-tree pathcost method long**. The entire Layer 2 topology should use the same setting for every device in the environment to ensure a consistent topology. Before you enable this setting in an environment, it is important to conduct an audit to ensure that the setting will work.

Building the STP Topology

This section focuses on the logic switches use to build an STP topology. Figure 2-1 shows the simple topology used here to demonstrate some important spanning tree concepts. The configurations on all the switches do not include any customizations for STP, and the focus is primarily on VLAN 1, but VLANs 10, 20, and 99 also exist in the topology. SW1 has been identified as the root bridge, and the RP, DP, and blocking ports have been identified visually to assist in the following sections.

Key Topic

Root Bridge Election

The first step with STP is to identify the root bridge. As a switch initializes, it assumes that it is the root bridge and uses the local bridge identifier as the root bridge identifier. It then listens to its neighbor's configuration BPDU and does the following:

- If the neighbor's configuration BPDU is inferior to its own BPDU, the switch ignores that BPDU.
- If the neighbor's configuration BPDU is preferred to its own BPDU, the switch updates its BPDUs to include the new root bridge identifier along with a new root path cost that correlates to the total path cost to reach the new root bridge. This process continues until all switches in a topology have identified the root bridge switch.

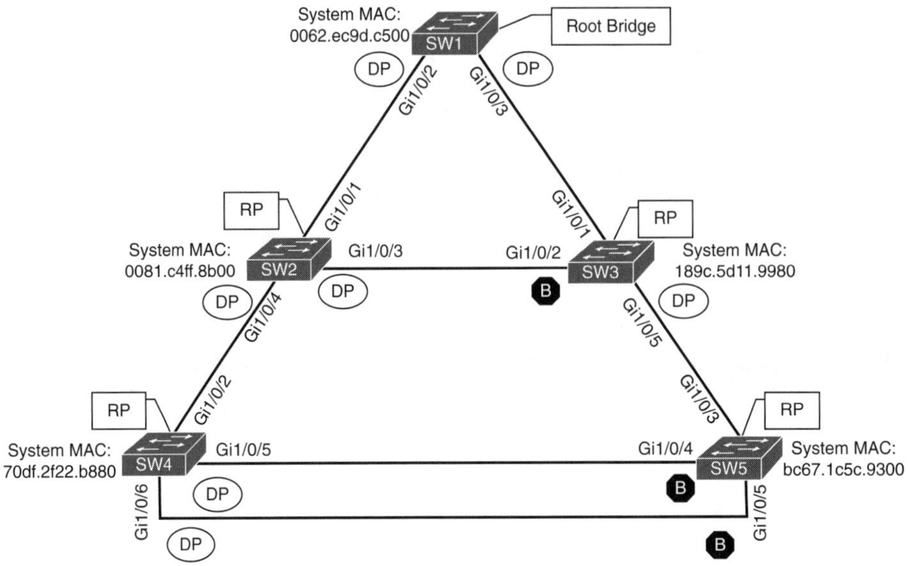

Figure 2-1 *Basic STP Topology*

STP deems a switch more preferable if the priority in the bridge identifier is lower than the priority of the other switch's configuration BPDUs. If the priority is the same, then the switch prefers the BPDU with the lower system MAC.

NOTE Generally, older switches have a lower MAC address and are considered more preferable. Configuration changes can be made for optimizing placement of the root bridge in a Layer 2 topology to prevent the insertion of an older switch from becoming the new root bridge.

In Figure 2-1, SW1 can be identified as the root bridge because its system MAC address (0062.ec9d.c500) is the lowest in the topology. This is further verified by using the command **show spanning-tree root** to display the root bridge. Example 2-1 demonstrates this command being executed on SW1. The output includes the VLAN number, root bridge identifier, root path cost, hello time, max age time, and forwarding delay. Because SW1 is the root bridge, all ports are designated ports, so the Root Port field is empty. Using this command is one way to verify that the connected switch is the root bridge for the VLAN.

Example 2-1 *Verifying the STP Root Bridge*

```
SW1# show spanning-tree root
                                        Root    Hello Max Fwd
Vlan                   Root ID          Cost    Time  Age Dly  Root Port
---------------- -------------------- --------- ----- --- ---  ------------
VLAN0001         32769 0062.ec9d.c500        0     2   20  15
VLAN0010         32778 0062.ec9d.c500        0     2   20  15
VLAN0020         32788 0062.ec9d.c500        0     2   20  15
VLAN0099         32867 0062.ec9d.c500        0     2   20  15
```

In Example 2-1, notice that the root bridge priority on SW1 for VLAN 1 is 32,769 and not 32,768. The priority in the configuration BPDU packets is actually the priority plus the value of the *sys-id-ext* (which is the VLAN number). You can confirm this by looking at VLAN 10, which has a priority of 32,778, which is 10 higher than 32,768.

When a switch generates the BPDUs, the root path cost includes only the calculated metric to the root and does not include the cost of the port that the BPDU is advertised out of. The receiving switch adds the port cost for its interface on which the BPDU was received in conjunction with the value of the root path cost in the BPDU. The root path cost is always zero on the root bridge. Figure 2-2 illustrates the root path cost as SW1 advertises the configuration BPDUs toward SW3 and then SW3's configuration BPDUs toward SW5.

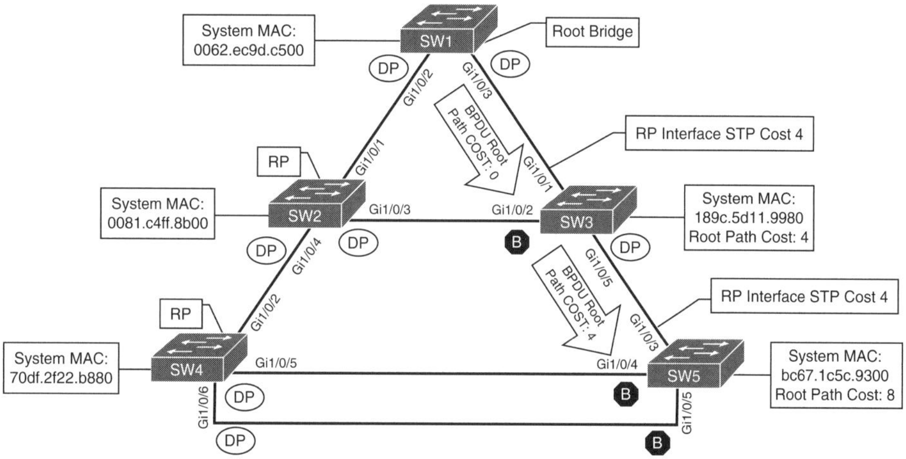

Figure 2-2 *STP Path Cost Advertisements*

Example 2-2 shows the output of the **show spanning-tree root** command run on SW2 and SW3. The Root ID field is exactly the same as for SW1, but the root path cost has changed to 4 because both switches must use the 1 Gbps link to reach SW1. Gi1/0/1 has been identified on both switches as the root port.

Example 2-2 *Identifying the Root Ports*

```
SW2# show spanning-tree root
                                        Root    Hello Max Fwd
Vlan                   Root ID          Cost    Time  Age Dly  Root Port
---------------- -------------------- --------- ----- --- ---  ------------
VLAN0001         32769 0062.ec9d.c500         4    2   20  15  Gi1/0/1
VLAN0010         32778 0062.ec9d.c500         4    2   20  15  Gi1/0/1
VLAN0020         32788 0062.ec9d.c500         4    2   20  15  Gi1/0/1
VLAN0099         32867 0062.ec9d.c500         4    2   20  15  Gi1/0/1
```

```
SW3# show spanning-tree root
                                        Root    Hello Max Fwd
Vlan                   Root ID          Cost    Time  Age Dly  Root Port
---------------- -------------------- --------- ----- --- ---  ------------
```

```
VLAN0001         32769 0062.ec9d.c500          4    2   20  15  Gi1/0/1
VLAN0010         32778 0062.ec9d.c500          4    2   20  15  Gi1/0/1
VLAN0020         32788 0062.ec9d.c500          4    2   20  15  Gi1/0/1
VLAN0099         32867 0062.ec9d.c500          4    2   20  15  Gi1/0/1
```

Key Topic

Locating Root Ports

After the switches have identified the root bridge, they must determine their root port (RP). The root bridge continues to advertise configuration BPDUs out all of its ports. The switch compares the BPDU information received on its port to identify the RP. The RP is selected using the following logic (where the next criterion is used in the event of a tie):

1. The interface associated to lowest path cost is more preferred.
2. The interface associated to the lowest system priority of the advertising switch is preferred next.
3. The interface associated to the lowest system MAC address of the advertising switch is preferred next.
4. When multiple links are associated to the same switch, the lowest port priority from the advertising switch is preferred.
5. When multiple links are associated to the same switch, the lower port number from the advertising switch is preferred.

Example 2-3 shows the output of running the command **show spanning-tree root** on SW4 and SW5. The Root ID field is exactly the same as on SW1, SW2, and SW3 in Examples 2-1 and 2-2. However, the root path cost has changed to 8 on SW4 and SW5 because both switches must traverse two 1 Gbps links to reach SW1. Gi1/0/2 was identified as the RP for SW4, and Gi1/0/3 was identified as the RP for SW5.

Example 2-3 *Identifying the Root Ports on SW4 and SW5*

```
SW4# show spanning-tree root

                                          Root    Hello Max Fwd
Vlan                   Root ID            Cost    Time  Age Dly  Root Port
---------------- -------------------- --------- ----- --- ---  ------------
VLAN0001          32769 0062.ec9d.c500         8    2   20  15   Gi1/0/2
VLAN0010          32778 0062.ec9d.c500         8    2   20  15   Gi1/0/2
VLAN0020          32788 0062.ec9d.c500         8    2   20  15   Gi1/0/2
VLAN0099          32867 0062.ec9d.c500         8    2   20  15   Gi1/0/2
```

```
SW5# show spanning-tree root
                                          Root    Hello Max Fwd
Vlan                   Root ID            Cost    Time  Age Dly  Root Port
---------------- -------------------- --------- ----- --- ---  ------------
VLAN0001          32769 0062.ec9d.c500         8    2   20  15   Gi1/0/3
VLAN0010          32778 0062.ec9d.c500         8    2   20  15   Gi1/0/3
VLAN0020          32788 0062.ec9d.c500         8    2   20  15   Gi1/0/3
VLAN0099          32867 0062.ec9d.c500         8    2   20  15   Gi1/0/3
```

The root bridge can be identified for a specific VLAN through the use of the command **show spanning-tree root** and examination of the CDP or LLDP neighbor information to identify the host name of the RP switch. The process can be repeated until the root bridge is located.

Locating Blocked Designated Switch Ports

Now that the root bridge and RPs have been identified, all other ports are considered designated ports. However, if two non-root switches are connected to each other on their designated ports, one of those switch ports must be set to a blocking state to prevent a forwarding loop. In our sample topology, this would apply to the following links:

SW2 Gi1/0/3 ←→ SW3 Gi1/0/2

SW4 Gi1/0/5 ←→ SW5 Gi1/0/4

SW4 Gi1/0/6 ←→ SW5 Gi1/0/5

The logic to calculate which ports should be blocked between two non-root switches is as follows:

1. The interface is a designated port and must not be considered an RP.
2. The switch with the lower path cost to the root bridge forwards packets, and the one with the higher path cost blocks. If they tie, they move on to the next step.
3. The system priority of the local switch is compared to the system priority of the remote switch. The local port is moved to a blocking state if the remote system priority is lower than that of the local switch. If they tie, they move on to the next step.
4. The system MAC address of the local switch is compared to the system MAC address of the remote switch. The local designated port is moved to a blocking state if the remote system MAC address is lower than that of the local switch.

All three links (SW2 Gi1/0/3 ←→ SW3 Gi1/0/2, SW4 Gi1/0/5 ←→ SW5 Gi1/0/4, and SW4 Gi1/0/6 ←→ SW5 Gi1/0/5) would use step 4 of the process just listed to identify which port moves to a blocking state. SW3's Gi1/0/2, SW5's Gi1/0/4, and SW5's Gi1/0/5 ports would all transition to a blocking state because the MAC addresses are lower for SW2 and SW4. SW5 does not need to examine port numbers or priorities for the Gi1/0/4 and Gi1/0/5 interface because SW4 is not in the root path.

The command **show spanning-tree** [**vlan** *vlan-id*] provides useful information for locating a port's STP state. In Example 2-4, this command is being used to show SW1's STP information for VLAN 1. The first portion of the output displays the relevant root bridge's information, which is followed by the local bridge's information. The associated interface's STP port cost, port priority, and port type also are displayed. All of SW1's ports are designated ports (Desg) because SW1 is the root bridge.

These port types are expected on Catalyst switches:

- **Point-to-point (P2P):** This port type connects with another network device (PC or RSTP switch).
- **P2P edge:** This port type specifies that portfast is enabled on this port.

Example 2-4 *Viewing SW1's STP Information*

```
SW1# show spanning-tree vlan 1

VLAN0001
  Spanning tree enabled protocol rstp
! This section displays the relevant information for the STP root bridge
  Root ID    Priority    32769
             Address     0062.ec9d.c500
             This bridge is the root
             Hello Time   2 sec  Max Age 20 sec  Forward Delay 15 sec
! This section displays the relevant information for the Local STP bridge
  Bridge ID  Priority    32769  (priority 32768 sys-id-ext 1)
             Address     0062.ec9d.c500
             Hello Time   2 sec  Max Age 20 sec  Forward Delay 15 sec
             Aging Time  300 sec

Interface           Role Sts Cost      Prio.Nbr Type
------------------- ---- --- --------- -------- --------------------------------
Gi1/0/2             Desg FWD 4          128.2    P2p
Gi1/0/3             Desg FWD 4          128.3    P2p
Gi1/0/14            Desg FWD 4          128.14   P2p Edge
```

NOTE If the Type field includes *TYPE_Inc -, this indicates a port configuration mismatch between this Catalyst switch and the switch it is connected to. Common issues are the port type being incorrect and the port mode (access versus trunk) being misconfigured.

Example 2-5 shows the STP topology for SW2 and SW3. Notice that in the first root bridge section, the output provides the total root path cost and the port on the switch that is identified as the RP.

All the ports on SW2 are in a forwarding state, but port Gi1/0/2 on SW3 is in a blocking (BLK) state. Specifically, SW3's Gi1/0/2 port has been designated as an alternate port to reach the root in the event that the Gi1/0/1 connection fails.

The reason that SW3's Gi1/0/2 port rather than SW2's Gi1/0/3 port was placed into a blocking state is that SW2's system MAC address (0081.c4ff.8b00) is lower than SW3's system MAC address (189c.5d11.9980). This can be deduced by looking at the system MAC addresses in the output and confirmed by the topology in Figure 2-1.

Example 2-5 *Verifying the Root and Blocking Ports for a VLAN*

```
SW2# show spanning-tree vlan 1


VLAN0001
  Spanning tree enabled protocol rstp
  Root ID    Priority    32769
              Address     0062.ec9d.c500
              Cost        4
              Port        1 (GigabitEthernet1/0/1)
              Hello Time   2 sec  Max Age 20 sec  Forward Delay 15 sec

  Bridge ID  Priority    32769  (priority 32768 sys-id-ext 1)
              Address     0081.c4ff.8b00
              Hello Time   2 sec  Max Age 20 sec  Forward Delay 15 sec
              Aging Time  300 sec

Interface           Role Sts Cost      Prio.Nbr Type
------------------- ---- --- --------- -------- --------------------------------
Gi1/0/1             Root FWD 4          128.1    P2p
Gi1/0/3             Desg FWD 4          128.3    P2p
Gi1/0/4             Desg FWD 4          128.4    P2p
```

```
SW3# show spanning-tree vlan 1

VLAN0001
  Spanning tree enabled protocol rstp
! This section displays the relevant information for the STP root bridge
  Root ID    Priority    32769
              Address     0062.ec9d.c500
              Cost        4
              Port        1 (GigabitEthernet1/0/1)
              Hello Time   2 sec  Max Age 20 sec  Forward Delay 15 se

! This section displays the relevant information for the Local STP bridge
  Bridge ID  Priority    32769  (priority 32768 sys-id-ext 1)
              Address     189c.5d11.9980
              Hello Time   2 sec  Max Age 20 sec  Forward Delay 15 sec
              Aging Time  300 sec

Interface           Role Sts Cost      Prio.Nbr Type
------------------- ---- --- --------- -------- --------------------------------
Gi1/0/1             Root FWD 4          128.1    P2p
Gi1/0/2             Altn BLK 4          128.2    P2p
Gi1/0/5             Desg FWD 4          128.5    P2
```

Verification of VLANs on Trunk Links

All the interfaces that participate in a VLAN are listed in the output of the command **show spanning-tree**. Using this command can be a daunting task for trunk ports that carry multiple VLANs. The output includes the STP state for every VLAN on an interface for every switch interface. The command **show spanning-tree interface** *interface-id* [**detail**] drastically reduces the output to the STP state for only the specified interface. The optional **detail** keyword provides information on port cost, port priority, number of transitions, link type, and count of BPDUs sent or received for every VLAN supported on that interface. Example 2-6 demonstrates the use of both iterations of the command.

If a VLAN is missing on a trunk port, you can check the trunk port configuration for accuracy. Trunk port configuration is covered in more detail in Chapter 5, "VLAN Trunks and EtherChannel Bundles." A common problem is that a VLAN may be missing from the allowed VLANs list for that trunk interface.

Example 2-6 *Viewing VLANs Participating with STP on an Interface*

```
SW3# show spanning-tree interface gi1/0/1

Vlan                Role Sts Cost      Prio.Nbr Type
------------------- ---- --- --------- -------- --------------------------------
VLAN0001            Root FWD 4         128.1    P2p
VLAN0010            Root FWD 4         128.1    P2p
VLAN0020            Root FWD 4         128.1    P2p
VLAN0099            Root FWD 4         128.1    P2p
```

```
SW3# show spanning-tree interface gi1/0/1 detail
! Output omitted for brevity
Port 1 (GigabitEthernet1/0/1) of VLAN0001 is root forwarding
   Port path cost 4, Port priority 128, Port Identifier 128.1.
   Designated root has priority 32769, address 0062.ec9d.c500
   Designated bridge has priority 32769, address 0062.ec9d.c500
   Designated port id is 128.3, designated path cost 0
   Timers: message age 16, forward delay 0, hold 0
   Number of transitions to forwarding state: 1
   Link type is point-to-point by default

   BPDU: sent 15, received 45908

 Port 1 (GigabitEthernet1/0/1) of VLAN0010 is root forwarding
   Port path cost 4, Port priority 128, Port Identifier 128.1.
   Designated root has priority 32778, address 0062.ec9d.c500
   Designated bridge has priority 32778, address 0062.ec9d.c500
   Designated port id is 128.3, designated path cost 0
   Timers: message age 15, forward delay 0, hold 0
   Number of transitions to forwarding state: 1
   Link type is point-to-point by default
 MAC  BPDU: sent 15, received 22957
..
```

Key Topic

STP Topology Changes

In a stable Layer 2 topology, configuration BPDUs always flow from the root bridge toward the edge switches. However, changes in the topology (for example, switch failure, link failure, or links becoming active) have an impact on all the switches in the Layer 2 topology.

The switch that detects a link status change sends a topology change notification (TCN) BPDU toward the root bridge, out its RP. If an upstream switch receives the TCN, it sends out an acknowledgment and forwards the TCN out its RP to the root bridge.

Upon receipt of the TCN, the root bridge creates a new configuration BPDU with the Topology Change flag set, and it is then flooded to all the switches. When a switch receives a configuration BPDU with the Topology Change flag set, all switches change their MAC address timer to the forwarding delay timer (with a default of 15 seconds). This flushes out MAC addresses for devices that have not communicated in that 15-second window but maintains MAC addresses for devices that are actively communicating.

Flushing the MAC address table prevents a switch from sending traffic to a host that is no longer reachable by that port. However, a side effect of flushing the MAC address table is that it temporarily increases the unknown unicast flooding while it is rebuilt. Remember that this can impact hosts because of their CSMA/CD behavior. The MAC address timer is then reset to normal (300 seconds by default) after the second configuration BPDU is received.

TCNs are generated on a VLAN basis, so the impact of TCNs directly correlates to the number of hosts in a VLAN. As the number of hosts increases, the more likely TCN generation is to occur and the more hosts that are impacted by the broadcasts. Topology changes should be checked as part of the troubleshooting process. Chapter 3 describes mechanisms such as portfast that modify this behavior and reduce the generation of TCNs.

Topology changes are seen with the command **show spanning-tree** [**vlan** *vlan-id*] **detail** on a switch bridge. The output of this command shows the topology change count and time since the last change has occurred. A sudden or continuous increase in TCNs indicates a potential problem and should be investigated further for flapping ports or events on a connected switch.

Example 2-7 displays the output of the **show spanning-tree vlan 10 detail** command. Notice that it includes the time since the last TCN was detected and the interface from which the TCN originated.

Example 2-7 *Viewing a Detailed Version of Spanning Tree State*

```
SW1# show spanning-tree vlan 10 detail

 VLAN0010 is executing the rstp compatible Spanning Tree protocol
 Bridge Identifier has priority 32768, sysid 10, address 0062.ec9d.c500
 Configured hello time 2, max age 20, forward delay 15, transmit hold-count 6
 We are the root of the spanning tree
 Topology change flag not set, detected flag not set
 Number of topology changes 42 last change occurred 01:02:09 ago
           from GigabitEthernet1/0/2
 Times: hold 1, topology change 35, notification 2
        hello 2, max age 20, forward delay 15
 Timers: hello 0, topology change 0, notification 0, aging 300
```

The process of determining why TCNs are occurring involves checking a port to see whether it is connected to a host or to another switch. If it is connected to another switch, you need to connect to that switch and repeat the process of examining the STP details. You might need to examine CDP tables or your network documentation. You can execute the **show spanning-tree** [**vlan** *vlan-id*] **detail** command again to find the last switch in the topology to identify the problematic port.

Converging with Direct Link Failures

When a switch loses power or reboots, or when a cable is removed from a port, the Layer 1 signaling places the port into a down state, which can notify other processes, such as STP. STP considers such an event a direct link failure and can react in one of three ways, depending on the topology. This section explains each of these three possible scenarios with a simple three-switch topology where SW1 is the root switch.

Direct Link Failure Scenario 1

In the first scenario, the link between SW2 and SW3 fails. SW2's Gi1/0/3 port is the DP, and SW3's Gi1/0/2 port is in a blocking state. Because SW3's Gi1/0/2 port is already in a blocking state, there is no impact to traffic between the two switches as they both transmit data through SW1. Both SW2 and SW3 will advertise a TCN toward the root switch, which results in the Layer 2 topology flushing its MAC address table.

Direct Link Failure Scenario 2

In the second scenario, the link between SW1 and SW3 fails. Network traffic from SW1 or SW2 toward SW3 is impacted because SW3's Gi1/0/2 port is in a blocking state. Figure 2-3 illustrates the failure scenario and events that occur to stabilize the STP topology:

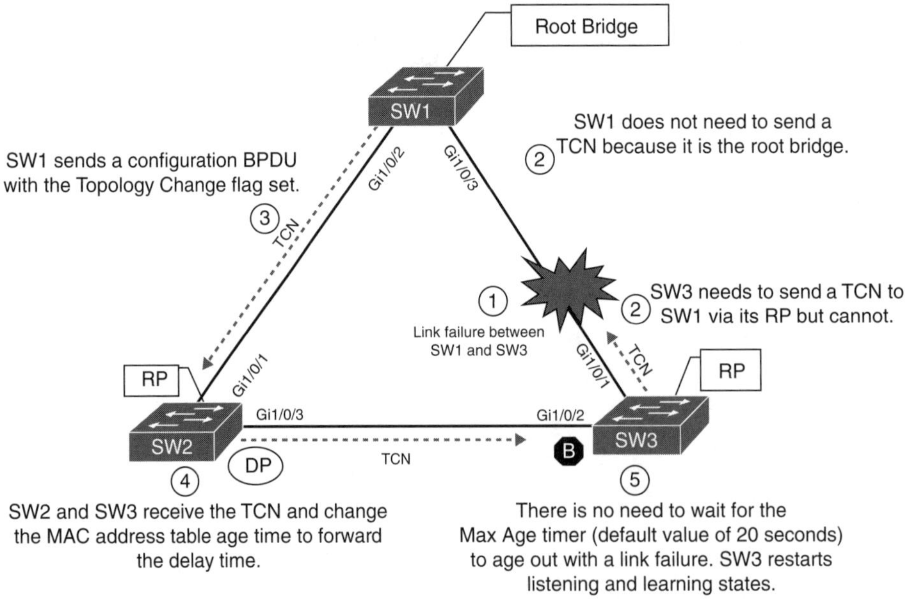

Figure 2-3 *Convergence with Direct Link Failure Between SW1 and SW3*

Phase 1. SW1 detects a link failure on its Gi1/0/3 interface. SW3 detects a link failure on its Gi1/0/1 interface.

Phase 2. Normally, SW1 would generate a TCN flag out its root port, but it is the root bridge, so it does not. SW1 would advertise a TCN if it were not the root bridge.

SW3 removes its best BPDU received from SW1 on its Gi1/0/1 interface because it is now in a down state. At this point, SW3 would attempt to send a TCN toward the root switch to notify it of a topology change; however, its root port is down.

Phase 3. SW1 advertises a configuration BPDU with the Topology Change flag out of all its ports. This BPDU is received and relayed to all switches in the environment.

NOTE If other switches were connected to SW1, they would receive a configuration BPDU with the Topology Change flag set also. These packets have an impact for all switches in the same Layer 2 domain.

Phase 4. SW2 and SW3 receive the configuration BPDU with the Topology Change flag. These switches then reduce the MAC address age timer to the forward delay timer to flush out older MAC entries. In this phase, SW2 does not know what changed in the topology.

Phase 5. There is no need to wait for the Max Age timer (default value of 20 seconds) to age out with a link failure. SW3 restarts the STP listening and learning states to learn about the root bridge on the Gi1/0/2 interface (which was in the blocking state previously).

The total convergence time for SW3 is 30 seconds: 15 seconds for the listening state and 15 seconds for the learning state before SW3's Gi1/0/2 can be made the RP.

Direct Link Failure Scenario 3

In the third scenario, the link between SW1 and SW2 fails. Network traffic from SW1 or SW3 toward SW2 is impacted because SW3's Gi1/0/2 port is in a blocking state. Figure 2-4 illustrates the failure scenario and events that occur to stabilize the STP topology:

Phase 1. SW1 detects a link failure on its Gi1/0/2 interface. SW2 detects a link failure on its Gi1/0/1 interface.

Phase 2. Normally SW1 would generate a TCN flag out its root port, but it is the root bridge, so it does not. SW1 would advertise a TCN if it were not the root bridge.

SW2 removes its best BPDU received from SW1 on its Gi1/0/1 interface because it is now in a down state. At this point, SW2 would attempt to send a TCN toward the root switch to notify it of a topology change; however, its root port is down.

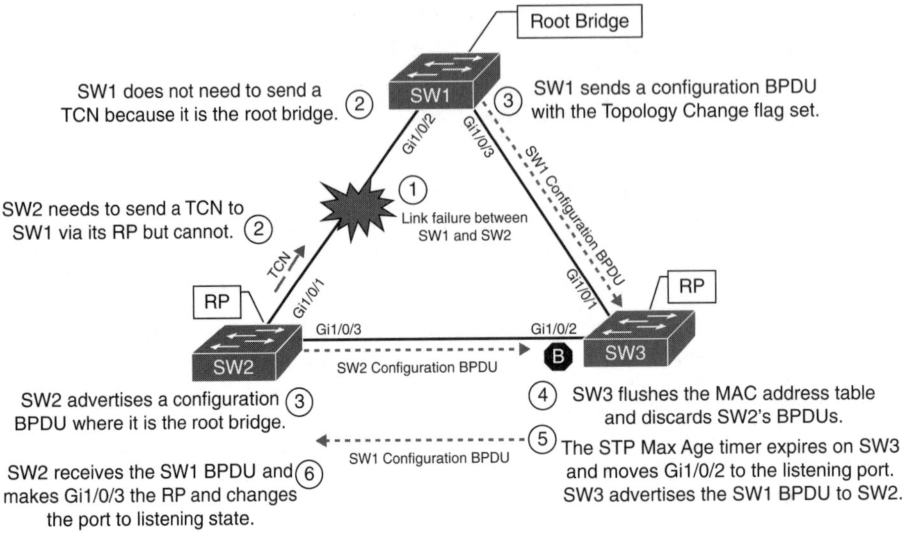

Figure 2-4 *Convergence with Direct Link Failure Between SW1 and SW2*

Phase 3. SW1 advertises a configuration BPDU with the Topology Change flag out of all its ports. This BPDU is then received and relayed to SW3. SW3 cannot relay this to SW2 because its Gi1/0/2 port is still in a blocking state.

SW2 assumes that it is now the root bridge and advertises configuration BPDUs with itself as the root bridge.

Phase 4. SW3 receives the configuration BPDU with the Topology Change flag from SW1. SW3 reduces the MAC address age timer to the forward delay timer to flush out older MAC entries. SW3 receives SW2's inferior BPDUs and discards them as it is still receiving superior BPDUs from SW1.

Phase 5. The Max Age timer on SW3 expires, and now SW3's Gi1/0/2 port transitions from blocking to listening state. SW3 can now forward the next configuration BPDU it receives from SW1 to SW2.

Phase 6. SW2 receives SW1's configuration BPDU via SW3 and recognizes it as superior. It marks its Gi1/0/3 interface as the root port and transitions it to the listening state.

The total convergence time for SW2 is 50 seconds: 20 seconds for the Max Age timer on SW3, 15 seconds for the listening state on SW2, and 15 seconds for the learning state.

Indirect Failures

In some failure scenarios, STP communication between switches is impaired or filtered while the network link remains up. This situation is known as an *indirect link failure*, and timers are required to detect and remediate the topology. Figure 2-5 illustrates an impediment or data corruption on the link between SW1 and SW3 along with the logic to resolve the loss of network traffic:

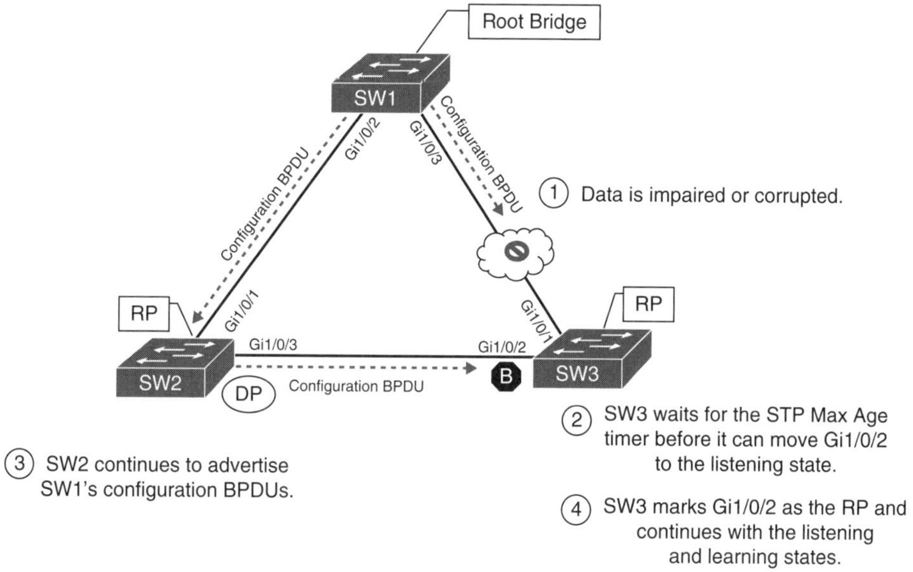

Figure 2-5 *Convergence with Indirect Link Failure*

Phase 1. An event occurs that impairs or corrupts data on the link. SW1 and SW3 still report a link up condition.

Phase 2. SW3 stops receiving configuration BPDUs on its RP. It keeps a cached entry for the RP on Gi1/0/1. SW1's configuration BPDUs that are being transmitted via SW2 are discarded because SW3's Gi1/0/2 port is in a blocking state.

After SW3's Max Age timer expires and flushes the RP's cached entry, SW3 transitions Gi1/0/2 from blocking to listening state.

Phase 3. SW2 continues to advertise SW1's configuration BPDUs toward SW3.

Phase 4. SW3 receives SW1's configuration BPDU via SW2 on its Gi1/0/2 interface. This port is now marked as the RP and continues to transition through the listening and learning states.

The total time for reconvergence on SW3 is 50 seconds: 20 seconds for the Max Age timer on SW3, 15 seconds for the listening state on SW3, and 15 seconds for the learning state on SW3.

Key Topic

Rapid Spanning Tree Protocol

Although 802.1D did a decent job of preventing Layer 2 forwarding loops, it used only one topology tree, which introduced scalability issues. Some larger environments with multiple VLANs need different STP topologies for traffic engineering purposes (for example, load-balancing, traffic steering). Cisco created Per-VLAN Spanning Tree (PVST) and Per-VLAN Spanning Tree Plus (PVST+) to allow more flexibility.

PVST and PVST+ were proprietary spanning protocols. The concepts in these protocols were incorporated with other enhancements to provide faster convergence into the IEEE 802.1W specification, known as Rapid Spanning Tree Protocol (RSTP).

Key Topic

RSTP (802.1W) Port States

RSTP reduces the number of port states to three:

- **Discarding:** The switch port is enabled, but the port is not forwarding any traffic to ensure that a loop is not created. This state combines the traditional STP states disabled, blocking, and listening.
- **Learning:** The switch port modifies the MAC address table with any network traffic it receives. The switch still does not forward any other network traffic besides BPDUs.
- **Forwarding:** The switch port forwards all network traffic and updates the MAC address table as expected. This is the final state for a switch port to forward network traffic.

NOTE A switch tries to establish an RSTP handshake with the device connected to the other end of the cable. If a handshake does not occur, the other device is assumed to be non-RSTP compatible, and the port defaults to regular 802.1D behavior. This means that host devices such as computers, printers, and so on still encounter a significant transmission delay (around 30 seconds) after the network link is established.

RSTP (802.1W) Port Roles

RSTP defines the following port roles:

- **Root port (RP):** A network port that connects to the root switch or an upstream switch in the spanning-tree topology. There should be only one root port per VLAN on a switch.
- **Designated port (DP):** A network port that receives and forwards frames to other switches. Designated ports provide connectivity to downstream devices and switches. There should be only one active designated port on a link.
- **Alternate port:** A network port that provides alternate connectivity toward the root switch through a different switch.
- **Backup port:** A network port that provides link redundancy toward the shared segment within the same collision domain, which is typically a network hub.

RSTP (802.1W) Port Types

RSTP defines three types of ports that are used for building the STP topology:

- **Edge port:** A port at the edge of the network where hosts connect to the Layer 2 topology with one interface and cannot form a loop. These ports directly correlate to ports that have the STP portfast feature enabled. STP portfast is explained in Chapter 3.
- **Non-Edge port:** A port that has received a BPDU.
- **Point-to-point port:** Any port that connects to another RSTP switch with full duplex. Full-duplex links do not permit more than two devices on a network segment, so determining whether a link is full duplex is the fastest way to check the feasibility of being connected to a switch.

NOTE Multi-access Layer 2 devices such as hubs can connect only at half duplex. If a port can connect only via half duplex, it must operate under traditional 802.1D forwarding states.

Key Topic

Building the RSTP Topology

With RSTP, switches exchange handshakes with other RSTP switches to transition through the following STP states faster. When two switches first connect, they establish a bidirectional handshake across the shared link to identify the root bridge. This is straightforward for an environment with only two switches; however, large environments require greater care to avoid creating a forwarding loop. RSTP uses a synchronization process to add a switch to the RSTP topology without introducing a forwarding loop. The synchronization process starts when two switches (such as SW1 and SW2) are first connected. The process proceeds as follows:

1. As the first two switches connect to each other, they verify that they are connected with a point-to-point link by checking the full-duplex status.
2. They establish a handshake with each other to advertise a proposal (in configuration BPDUs) that their interface should be the DP for that segment.
3. There can be only one DP per segment, so each switch identifies whether it is the superior or inferior switch, using the same logic as in 802.1D for the system identifier (that is, the lowest priority and then the lowest MAC address). Using the MAC addresses from Figure 2-1, SW1 (0062.ec9d.c500) is the superior switch to SW2 (0081.c4ff.8b00).
4. The inferior switch (SW2) recognizes that it is inferior and marks its local port (Gi1/0/1) as the RP. At that same time, it moves all non-edge ports to a discarding state. At this point in time, the switch has stopped all local switching for non-edge ports.
5. The inferior switch (SW2) sends an agreement (configuration BPDU) to the root bridge (SW1), which signifies to the root bridge that synchronization is occurring on that switch.
6. The inferior switch (SW2) moves its RP (Gi1/0/1) to a forwarding state. The superior switch moves its DP (Gi1/0/2) to a forwarding state too.
7. The inferior switch (SW2) repeats the process for any downstream switches connected to it.

RSTP Convergence

The RSTP convergence process can occur quickly. RSTP ages out the port information after it has not received hellos in three consecutive cycles. Using default timers, the Max Age would take 20 seconds, but RSTP requires only 6 seconds. And thanks to the new synchronization, ports can transition from discarding to forwarding in an extremely low amount of time.

If a downstream switch fails to acknowledge the proposal, the RSTP switch must default to 802.1D behaviors to prevent a forwarding loop.

Exam Preparation Tasks

You have a couple of choices for exam preparation: the exercises here, Chapter 30, "Final Preparation," and the exam simulation questions in the Pearson Test Prep Software Online.

Review All Key Topics

Review the most important topics in the chapter, noted with the Key Topic icon in the outer margin of the page. Table 2-3 lists these key topics and the page number on which each is found.

Key Topic

Table 2-3 Key Topics for Chapter 2

Key Topic Element	Description	Page
List	802.1D port types	39
Section	STP Key Terminology	39
Section	Root Bridge Election	41
Section	Locating Root Ports	44
Section	STP Topology Changes	49
Section	Rapid Spanning Tree Protocol	53
Section	RSTP (802.1W) Port States	54
Section	Building the RSTP Topology	55

Complete Tables and Lists from Memory

There are no memory tables in this chapter.

Define Key Terms

Define the following key terms from this chapter and check your answers in the Glossary:

bridge protocol data unit (BPDU), configuration BPDU, designated port (DP), forward delay, hello time, local bridge identifier, Max Age, root bridge, root bridge identifier, root path cost, root port, system priority, system ID extension, topology change notification (TCN)

Use the Command Reference to Check Your Memory

Table 2-4 lists the important commands from this chapter. To test your memory, cover the right side of the table with a piece of paper, read the description on the left side, and see how much of the command you can remember.

Table 2-4 Command Reference

Task	Command Syntax
Set the STP max age	**spanning-tree vlan** *vlan-id* **max-age**
Set the STP hello interval	**spanning-tree vlan** *vlan-id* **hello-time** *hello-time*
Set the STP forwarding delay	**spanning-tree vlan** *vlan-id* **forward-time** *forward-time*

Task	Command Syntax
Display the STP root bridge and cost	**show spanning-tree root**
Display the STP information (root bridge, local bridge, and interfaces) for one or more VLANs	**show spanning-tree** [**vlan** *vlan-id*]
Identify when the last TCN occurred and which port was the reason for it	**show spanning-tree** [**vlan** *vlan-id*] **detail**

CHAPTER 3

Advanced STP Tuning

This chapter covers the following subjects:

- **STP Topology Tuning:** This section explains some of the options for modifying the root bridge location or moving blocking ports to designated ports.
- **Additional STP Protection Mechanisms:** This section examines protection mechanisms such as root guard, BPDU guard, and STP loop guard.

This chapter reviews techniques for configuring a switch to be guaranteed as the root bridge or as a backup root bridge for a Layer 2 topology. In addition, this chapter explains features that prevent other switches from unintentionally taking over the root bridge role. The chapter also explains other common features that are used in Cisco's enterprise campus validated design guides.

"Do I Know This Already?" Quiz

The "Do I Know This Already?" quiz enables you to assess whether you should read the entire chapter. If you miss no more than one of these self-assessment questions, you might want to move ahead to the "Exam Preparation Tasks" section. Table 3-1 lists the major headings in this chapter and the "Do I Know This Already?" quiz questions covering the material in those headings so you can assess your knowledge of these specific areas. The answers to the "Do I Know This Already?" quiz appear in Appendix A, "Answers to the 'Do I Know This Already?' Questions."

Table 3-1 "Do I Know This Already?" Foundation Topics Section-to-Question Mapping

Foundation Topics Section	Questions
STP Topology Tuning	1–3
Additional STP Protection Mechanisms	4–6

1. A switch's STP priority can be configured in increments of ______.
   a. 1
   b. 256
   c. 2048
   d. 4096

2. True or false: The advertised path cost includes the advertising link's port cost as part of the configuration BPDU advertisement.
   a. True
   b. False
3. True or false: The switch port with the lower STP port priority is more preferred.
   a. True
   b. False
4. What happens to a switch port when a BPDU is received on it when BPDU guard is enabled on that port?
   a. A message syslog is generated, and the BPDU is filtered.
   b. A syslog message is not generated, and the BPDU is filtered.
   c. A syslog message is generated, and the port is sent back to a listening state.
   d. A syslog message is generated, and the port is placed into an err-disabled state.
5. Enabling root guard on a switch port does what?
   a. Upon receipt of an inferior BPDU, the port is shut down.
   b. Upon receipt of a superior BPDU, the port is placed into a root inconsistent state.
   c. Upon receipt of an inferior BPDU, the BPDU is filtered.
   d. When the root port is shut down, only authorized designated ports can become root ports.
6. UDLD solves the problem of ______.
   a. time for Layer 2 convergence
   b. a cable that sends traffic in only one direction
   c. corrupt BPDU packets
   d. flapping network links

Foundation Topics

STP Topology Tuning

A properly designed network strategically places the root bridge on a specific switch and modifies which ports should be designated ports (that is, forwarding state) and which ports should be alternate ports (that is, discarding/blocking state). Design considerations factor in hardware platform, resiliency, and network topology. This chapter uses the same reference topology from Chapter 2, "Spanning Tree Protocol," as shown in Figure 3-1.

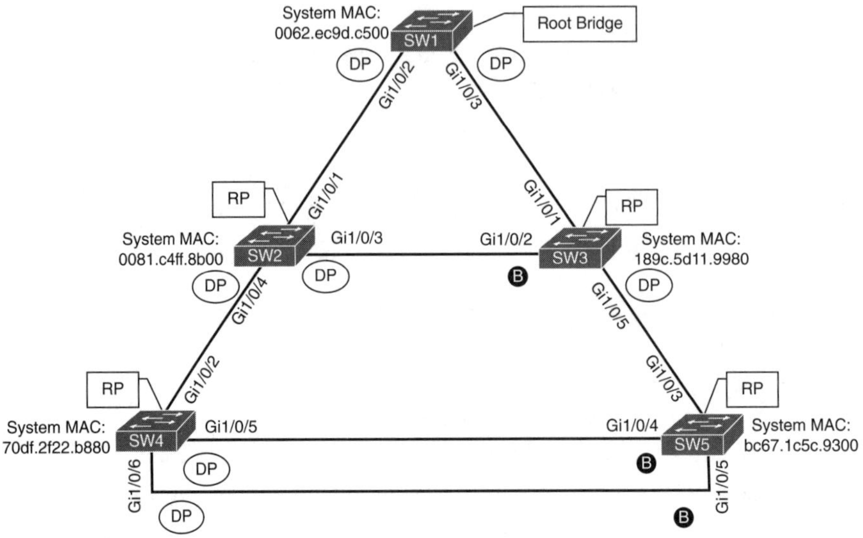

Figure 3-1 *STP Topology for Tuning*

Key Topic

Placing the Root Bridge

Ideally, the root bridge is placed on a core switch, and a secondary root bridge is designated to minimize changes to the overall spanning tree. Root bridge placement is accomplished by lowering the system priority on the root bridge to the lowest value possible, raising the secondary root bridge to a value slightly higher than that of the root bridge, and (ideally) increasing the system priority on all other switches. This effort ensures consistent placement of the root bridge. The priority is set with either of the following commands:

- **spanning-tree vlan** *vlan-id* **priority** *priority*: The priority is a value between 0 and 61,440, in increments of 4096.
- **spanning-tree vlan** *vlan-id* **root {primary | secondary} [diameter** *diameter***]**: This command executes a script that sets the priority numerically, along with the potential for timers if the **diameter** keyword is used. The **primary** keyword sets the priority to 24,576, and the **secondary** keyword sets the priority to 28,672.

NOTE If a different switch has a priority of 24,576 (or lower) and is more preferred when the command **spanning-tree vlan** *vlan-id* **root** {**primary** | **secondary**} is executed, the script has logic to lower the priority to a lower value in an attempt to make it the root bridge.

The optional **diameter** command makes it possible to tune the Spanning Tree Protocol (STP) convergence and modifies the timers; it should reference the maximum number of Layer 2 hops between a switch and the root bridge. The timers do not need to be modified on other switches because they are carried throughout the topology through the root bridge's bridge protocol data units (BPDUs).

Answers to the "Do I Know This Already?" quiz:

1 D **2** B **3** A **4** D **5** B **6** B

Example 3-1 verifies the initial priority for VLAN 1 on SW1 and then checks how the change is made. Afterward, the priority is checked again to ensure that the priority is lowered.

Example 3-1 *Changing the STP System Priority on SW1*

```
! Verification of SW1 Priority before modifying the priority
SW1# show spanning-tree vlan 1
VLAN0001
  Spanning tree enabled protocol rstp
  Root ID    Priority    32769
               Address     0062.ec9d.c500
               This bridge is the root
               Hello Time   2 sec  Max Age 20 sec  Forward Delay 15 sec

  Bridge ID  Priority    32769  (priority 32768 sys-id-ext 1)
               Address     0062.ec9d.c500
               Hello Time   2 sec  Max Age 20 sec  Forward Delay 15 sec
               Aging Time  300 sec
```

```
! Configuring the SW1 priority as primary root for VLAN 1
SW1(config)# spanning-tree vlan 1 root primary
```

```
! Verification of SW1 Priority after modifying the priority
SW1# show spanning-tree vlan 1

VLAN0001
  Spanning tree enabled protocol rstp
  Root ID    Priority    24577
             Address     0062.ec9d.c500
             This bridge is the root
             Hello Time   2 sec  Max Age 20 sec  Forward Delay 15 sec

  Bridge ID  Priority    24577  (priority 24576 sys-id-ext 1)
             Address     0062.ec9d.c500
             Hello Time   2 sec  Max Age 20 sec  Forward Delay 15 sec
             Aging Time  300 sec

Interface           Role Sts Cost      Prio.Nbr Type
------------------- ---- --- --------- -------- --------------------------------
Gi1/0/2             Desg FWD 4          128.2    P2p
Gi1/0/3             Desg FWD 4          128.3    P2p
Gi1/0/14            Desg FWD 4          128.14   P2p
```

Example 3-2 verifies the priority for VLAN 1 on SW2 before changing its priority so that it will be the backup root bridge in the event of a failure with SW1. Notice that the root bridge priority is now 24,577, and the local switch's priority is initially set to 32,769 (the default). Then the command **spanning-tree vlan 1 root secondary** is executed to modify SW2's priority, setting it to 28,673.

Example 3-2 *Changing the STP System Priority on SW2*

```
! Verification of SW2 Priority before modifying the priority
SW2# show spanning-tree vlan 1
! Output omitted for brevity

VLAN0001
  Spanning tree enabled protocol rstp
  Root ID    Priority    24577
             Address     0062.ec9d.c500
             Cost        4
             Port        1 (GigabitEthernet1/0/1)
             Hello Time   2 sec  Max Age 20 sec  Forward Delay 15 sec

  Bridge ID  Priority    32769  (priority 32768 sys-id-ext 1)
             Address     0081.c4ff.8b00
             Hello Time   2 sec  Max Age 20 sec  Forward Delay 15 sec
             Aging Time  300 sec

Interface           Role Sts Cost      Prio.Nbr Type
------------------- ---- --- --------- -------- --------------------------------
Gi1/0/1             Root FWD 4          128.1    P2p
Gi1/0/3             Desg FWD 4          128.3    P2p
Gi1/0/4             Desg FWD 4          128.4    P2p
```

```
! Configuring the SW2 priority as root secondary for VLAN 1
SW2(config)# spanning-tree vlan 1 root secondary
```

```
SW2# show spanning-tree vlan 1

VLAN0001
  Spanning tree enabled protocol rstp
  Root ID    Priority    24577
             Address     0062.ec9d.c500
             Cost        4
             Port        1 (GigabitEthernet1/0/1)
             Hello Time   2 sec  Max Age 20 sec  Forward Delay 15 sec

  Bridge ID  Priority    28673  (priority 28672 sys-id-ext 1)
             Address     0081.c4ff.8b00
             Hello Time   2 sec  Max Age 20 sec  Forward Delay 15 sec
             Aging Time  300 sec

Interface           Role Sts Cost      Prio.Nbr Type
------------------- ---- --- --------- -------- --------------------------------
Gi1/0/1             Root FWD 4          128.1    P2p
Gi1/0/3             Desg FWD 4          128.3    P2p
Gi1/0/4             Desg FWD 4          128.4    P2p
```

The placement of the root bridge is an important decision and often should be chosen to minimize the number of hops to the furthest switch in the topology. The design should consider where redundant connections exist, connections that will be blocked, and the ability (performance) for the root switch to handle cross-switch traffic. Generally, root switches are at Layer 2/Layer 3 boundaries.

Key Topic

The best way to prevent erroneous devices from taking over the STP root role is to set the priority to 0 for the primary root switch and to 4096 for the secondary root switch. In addition, root guard should be used (as discussed later in this chapter).

Modifying STP Root Port and Blocked Switch Port Locations

The STP port cost is used in calculating the STP tree. When a switch generates the BPDUs, the root path cost includes only the calculated metric to the root and does not include the cost of the port out which the BPDU is advertised. The receiving switch adds the port cost for the interface on which the BPDU was received in conjunction with the value of the root path cost in the BPDU.

In Figure 3-2, SW1 advertises its BPDUs to SW3 with a root path cost of 0. SW3 receives the BPDU and adds its STP port cost of 4 to the root path cost in the BPDU (0), resulting in a value of 4. SW3 then advertises the BPDU toward SW5 with a root path cost of 4, to which SW5 then adds its STP port cost of 4. SW5 therefore reports a root path cost of 8 to reach the root bridge via SW3.

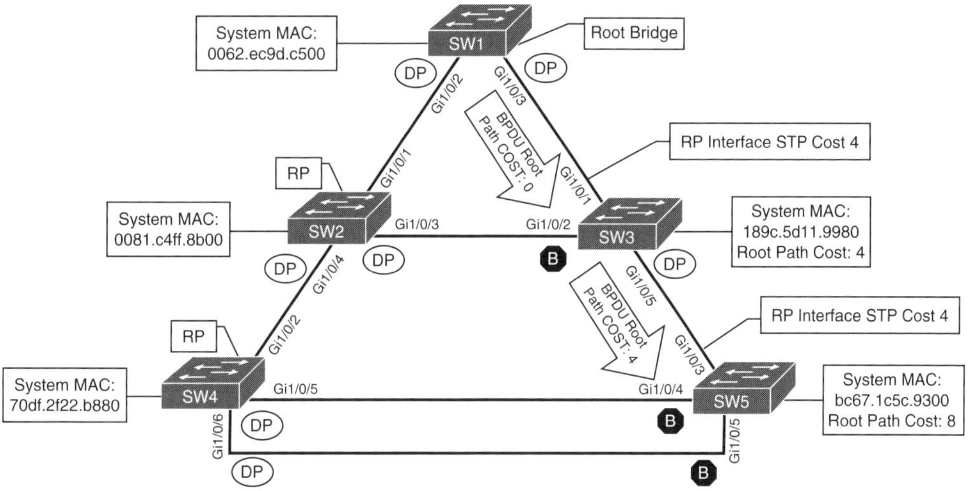

Figure 3-2 *STP Path Cost Calculation*

The logic is confirmed in the output of Example 3-3. Notice that there is not a root path cost in SW1's output.

Example 3-3 *Verifying the Total Path Cost*

```
SW1# show spanning-tree vlan 1
! Output omitted for brevity
VLAN0001
  Root ID    Priority    32769
             Address     0062.ec9d.c500
             This bridge is the root
..
Interface           Role Sts Cost      Prio.Nbr Type
------------------- ---- --- --------- -------- --------------------------------
Gi1/0/2             Desg FWD 4         128.2    P2p
Gi1/0/3             Desg FWD 4         128.3    P2p
```

```
SW3# show spanning-tree vlan 1
! Output omitted for brevity
VLAN0001
  Root ID    Priority    32769
             Address     0062.ec9d.c500
             Cost        4
             Port        1 (GigabitEthernet1/0/1)
..
Interface           Role Sts Cost      Prio.Nbr Type
------------------- ---- --- --------- -------- --------------------------------
Gi1/0/1             Root FWD 4          128.1    P2p
Gi1/0/2             Altn BLK 4          128.2    P2p
Gi1/0/5             Desg FWD 4          128.5    P2p
```

```
SW5# show spanning-tree vlan 1
! Output omitted for brevity
VLAN0001
  Root ID    Priority    32769
             Address     0062.ec9d.c500
             Cost        8
             Port        3 (GigabitEthernet1/0/3)
..
Interface           Role Sts Cost      Prio.Nbr Type
------------------- ---- --- --------- -------- --------------------------------
Gi1/0/3             Root FWD 4          128.3    P2p
Gi1/0/4             Altn BLK 4          128.4    P2p
Gi1/0/5             Altn BLK 4          128.5    P2p
```

Key Topic

By changing the STP port costs with the command **spanning-tree** [**vlan** *vlan-id*] **cost** *cost*, you can modify the STP forwarding path. You can lower a path that is currently an alternate port while making it designated, or you can raise the cost on a port that is designated to turn it into a blocking port. The **spanning-tree** command modifies the cost for all VLANs unless the optional **vlan** keyword is used to specify a VLAN.

Example 3-4 demonstrates the modification of SW3's port cost for Gi1/0/1 to a cost of 1, which impacts the port state between SW2 and SW3. SW2 receives a BPDU from SW3 with a cost of 5, and SW3 receives a BPDU from SW2 with a cost of 8. SW3's Gi1/0/2 is no longer an alternate port but is now a designated port. SW2's Gi1/0/3 port has changed from a designated port to an alternate port.

3

Example 3-4 *Modifying STP Port Cost*

```
SW3# conf t
SW3(config)# interface gi1/0/1
SW3(config-if)# spanning-tree cost 1
```

```
SW3# show spanning-tree vlan 1
! Output omitted for brevity
VLAN0001
  Root ID    Priority    32769
               Address     0062.ec9d.c500
               Cost        1
               Port        1 (GigabitEthernet1/0/1)

  Bridge ID  Priority    32769  (priority 32768 sys-id-ext 1)
               Address     189c.5d11.9980
..
Interface           Role Sts Cost      Prio.Nbr Type
------------------- ---- --- --------- -------- --------------------------------
Gi1/0/1             Root FWD 1          128.1    P2p
Gi1/0/2             Desg FWD 4          128.2    P2p
Gi1/0/5             Desg FWD 4          128.5    P2p
```

```
SW2# show spanning-tree vlan 1
! Output omitted for brevity
VLAN0001
  Root ID    Priority    32769
               Address     0062.ec9d.c500
               Cost        4
               Port        1 (GigabitEthernet1/0/1)

  Bridge ID  Priority    32769  (priority 32768 sys-id-ext 1)
               Address     0081.c4ff.8b00
..
```

```
Interface           Role Sts Cost      Prio.Nbr Type
------------------- ---- --- --------- -------- --------------------------------
Gi1/0/1             Root FWD 4          128.1    P2p
Gi1/0/3             Altn BLK 4          128.3    P2p
Gi1/0/4             Desg FWD 4          128.4    P2p
```

Modifying STP Port Priority

The STP port priority impacts which port is an alternate port when multiple links are used between switches. In our test topology, shutting down the link between SW3 and SW5 forces SW5 to choose one of the links connected to SW4 as a root port.

Example 3-5 verifies that this change makes SW5's Gi1/0/4 the root port (RP) toward SW4. Remember that system ID and port cost are the same, so the next check is port priority, followed by the port number. Both the port priority and port number are controlled by the upstream switch, because it is closer to the root bridge.

Example 3-5 *Viewing STP Port Priority*

```
SW5# show spanning-tree vlan 1
! Output omitted for brevity
VLAN0001
  Spanning tree enabled protocol rstp
  Root ID     Priority    32769
              Address     0062.ec9d.c500
              Cost        12
              Port        4 (GigabitEthernet1/0/4)

  Bridge ID  Priority    32769  (priority 32768 sys-id-ext 1)
              Address     bc67.1c5c.9300
..
Interface           Role Sts Cost      Prio.Nbr Type
------------------- ---- --- --------- -------- --------------------------------
Gi1/0/4             Root FWD 4          128.4    P2p
Gi1/0/5             Altn BLK 4          128.5    P2p
```

You can modify the port priority on SW4's Gi1/0/6 (toward SW5's Gi1/0/5 interface) with the command **spanning-tree** [**vlan** *vlan-id*] **port-priority** *priority*. The optional **vlan** keyword allows you to change the priority on a VLAN-by-VLAN basis. Example 3-6 shows how to change the port priority on SW4's Gi1/0/6 port to 64.

Example 3-6 *Verifying Port Priority Impact on an STP Topology*

```
SW4# configure terminal
Enter configuration commands, one per line. End with CNTL/Z.
SW4(config)# interface gi1/0/6
SW4(config-if)# spanning-tree port-priority 64
```

Now SW4's Gi1/0/6 port has a value of 64, which is lower than the value of its Gi1/0/5 port, which is using a default value of 128. SW4's Gi1/0/6 interface is now preferred and will change the RP on SW5, as displayed in Example 3-7.

Example 3-7 *Determining the Impact of Port Priority on a Topology*

```
SW4# show spanning-tree vlan 1
! Output omitted for brevity
Interface           Role Sts Cost      Prio.Nbr Type
------------------- ---- --- --------- -------- --------------------------------
Gi1/0/2             Root FWD 4          128.2    P2p
Gi1/0/5             Desg FWD 4          128.5    P2p
Gi1/0/6             Desg FWD 4           64.6    P2p
```

```
SW5# show spanning-tree vlan 1
! Output omitted for brevity
Interface           Role Sts Cost      Prio.Nbr Type
------------------- ---- --- --------- -------- --------------------------------
Gi1/0/4             Altn BLK 4          128.4    P2p
Gi1/0/5             Root FWD 4          128.5    P2p
```

Additional STP Protection Mechanisms

Network packets do not decrement the time-to-live portion of the header as a packet is forwarded in a Layer 2 topology. A network forwarding loop occurs when the logical topology allows for multiple active paths between two devices. Broadcast and multicast traffic wreak havoc as they are forwarded out of every switch port and continue the forwarding loop. High CPU consumption and low free memory space are common symptoms of a Layer 2 forwarding loop. In Layer 2 forwarding loops, in addition to constantly consuming switch bandwidth, the CPU spikes. Because the packet is received on a different interface, the switch must move the Media Access Control (MAC) address from one interface to the next. The network throughput is impacted drastically; users are likely to notice a slowdown on their network applications, and the switches might crash due to exhausted CPU and memory resources.

The following scenarios are common for Layer 2 forwarding loops:

- STP disabled on a switch
- A misconfigured load balancer that transmits traffic out multiple ports with the same MAC address
- A misconfigured virtual switch that bridges two physical ports (Virtual switches typically do not participate in STP.)
- End users using a dumb network switch or hub

Catalyst switches detect a MAC address that is flapping between interfaces and notify via syslog with the MAC address of the host, VLAN, and ports between which the MAC address is flapping. These messages should be investigated to ensure that a forwarding loop does not exist. Example 3-8 shows a sample syslog message for a flapping MAC address where STP has been removed from the topology.

Example 3-8 *Syslog Message for a Flapping MAC Address*

```
12:40:30.044: %SW_MATM-4-MACFLAP_NOTIF: Host 70df.2f22.b8c7 in vlan 1 is flapping
 between port Gi1/0/3 and port Gi1/0/2
```

In this scenario, you should check STP for all the switches hosting the VLAN mentioned in the syslog message to ensure that spanning tree is enabled and working properly.

Key Topic

Root Guard

Root guard is an STP feature that is enabled on a port-by-port basis; it prevents a configured port from becoming a root port. Root guard prevents a downstream switch (often misconfigured or rogue) from becoming a root bridge in a topology. Root guard functions by placing a port in a root inconsistent state for any VLANs with a superior BPDU that is received on a configured port. While in this state, the port acts like it is in a listening state and cannot forward traffic across this port. This prevents the configured DP with root guard from becoming an RP.

Root guard is enabled with the interface command **spanning-tree guard root**. Root guard is placed on designated ports toward other switches that should never become root bridges.

In the sample topology shown in Figure 3-1, root guard should be placed on SW2's Gi1/0/4 port toward SW4 and on SW3's Gi1/0/5 port toward SW5. This placement prevents SW4 and SW5 from ever becoming root bridges but still allows SW2 to maintain connectivity to SW1 via SW3 if the link connecting SW1 to SW2 fails.

Key Topic

STP Portfast

The generation of topology change notification (TCN) for hosts does not make sense because a host generally has only one connection to the network. Restricting TCN creation to only ports that connect with other switches and network devices increases the L2 network's stability and efficiency. The **STP portfast** feature disables TCN generation for access ports.

Another major benefit of the STP portfast feature is that the access ports bypass the earlier 802.1D STP states (learning and listening) and forward traffic immediately. This is beneficial in environments where computers use Dynamic Host Configuration Protocol (DHCP) or Preboot Execution Environment (PXE). If a BPDU is received on a portfast-enabled port, the portfast functionality is removed from that port, and it progresses through the learning and listening states.

The portfast feature is enabled on a specific access port with the command **spanning-tree portfast** or globally on all access ports with the command **spanning-tree portfast default.** If portfast needs to be disabled on a specific port when portfast is enabled globally, you can use the interface configuration command **spanning-tree portfast disable** to remove portfast on that port.

Portfast can be enabled on trunk links with the command **spanning-tree portfast trunk.** However, this command should be used only with ports that are connecting to a single host (such as a server with only one NIC that is running a hypervisor with VMs on different VLANs).

NOTE Remember that enabling portfast changes the RSTP port type to an Edge port.

Example 3-9 shows how to enable portfast for SW1's Gi1/0/13 port. Then the configuration is verified by examining the STP for VLAN 10 or examining the STP interface. Notice that the portfast ports are displayed with P2P Edge. The last section of output demonstrates how portfast is enabled globally for all access ports.

Example 3-9 *Enabling STP Portfast on Specific Interfaces*

```
SW1(config)# interface gigabitEthernet 1/0/13
SW1(config-if)# switchport mode access
SW1(config-if)# switchport access vlan 10
SW1(config-if)# spanning-tree portfast
```

```
SW1# show spanning-tree vlan 10
! Output omitted for brevity
VLAN0010
Interface           Role Sts Cost      Prio.Nbr Type
------------------- ---- --- --------- -------- --------------------------------
Gi1/0/2             Desg FWD 4          128.2     P2p
Gi1/0/3             Desg FWD 4          128.3     P2p
Gi1/0/13            Desg FWD 4          128.13    P2p Edge
```

```
SW1# show spanning-tree interface gi1/0/13 detail
 Port 13 (GigabitEthernet1/0/13) of VLAN0010 is designated forwarding
 Port path cost 4, Port priority 128, Port Identifier 128.13.
 Designated root has priority 32778, address 0062.ec9d.c500
 Designated bridge has priority 32778, address 0062.ec9d.c500
 Designated port id is 128.13, designated path cost 0
 Timers: message age 0, forward delay 0, hold 0
 Number of transitions to forwarding state: 1
 The port is in the portfast mode
 Link type is point-to-point by default
 BPDU: sent 23103, received 0
```

Example 3-10 shows how to enable portfast globally for all access ports on SW2 and then disable it for Gi1/0/8.

Example 3-10 *Enabling STP Portfast Globally*

```
SW2# conf t
Enter configuration commands, one per line. End with CNTL/Z.
SW2(config)# spanning-tree portfast default
%Warning: this command enables portfast by default on all interfaces. You
 should now disable portfast explicitly on switched ports leading to hubs,
 switches and bridges as they may create temporary bridging loops.
SW2(config)# interface gi1/0/8
SW2(config-if)# spanning-tree portfast disable
```

Key Topic

BPDU Guard

BPDU guard is a safety mechanism that places ports configured with STP portfast into an ErrDisabled state upon receipt of a BPDU. While in an ErrDisabled state, a port does not process any network traffic. Assuming that all access ports have portfast enabled, this ensures that a loop cannot accidentally be created if an unauthorized switch is added to a topology.

BPDU guard is enabled globally on all STP portfast ports with the command **spanning-tree portfast bpduguard default**. BPDU guard can be enabled or disabled on a specific interface with the command **spanning-tree bpduguard** {**enable** | **disable**}.

Example 3-11 shows how to configure BPDU guard globally on SW1 for all access ports but with the exception of disabling BPDU guard on Gi1/0/8. The **show spanning-tree interface** *interface-id* **detail** command displays whether BPDU guard is enabled for the specified port.

Example 3-11 *Configuring BPDU Guard*

```
SW1# configure terminal
Enter configuration commands, one per line. End with CNTL/Z.
SW1(config)# spanning-tree portfast bpduguard default
SW1(config)# interface gi1/0/8
SW1(config-if)# spanning-tree bpduguard disable
```

```
SW1# show spanning-tree interface gi1/0/7 detail
 Port 7 (GigabitEthernet1/0/7) of VLAN0010 is designated forwarding
   Port path cost 4, Port priority 128, Port Identifier 128.7.
   Designated root has priority 32778, address 0062.ec9d.c500
   Designated bridge has priority 32778, address 0062.ec9d.c500
   Designated port id is 128.7, designated path cost 0
   Timers: message age 0, forward delay 0, hold 0
   Number of transitions to forwarding state: 1
   The port is in the portfast mode
   Link type is point-to-point by default
   Bpdu guard is enabled by default
   BPDU: sent 23386, received 0
SW1# show spanning-tree interface gi1/0/8 detail
   Port 8 (GigabitEthernet1/0/8) of VLAN0010 is designated forwarding
   Port path cost 4, Port priority 128, Port Identifier 128.8.
   Designated root has priority 32778, address 0062.ec9d.c500
   Designated bridge has priority 32778, address 0062.ec9d.c500
   Designated port id is 128.8, designated path cost 0
   Timers: message age 0, forward delay 0, hold 0
   Number of transitions to forwarding state: 1
   The port is in the portfast mode by default
   Link type is point-to-point by default
   BPDU: sent 23388, received 0
```

NOTE BPDU guard is typically configured with all host-facing ports that are enabled with portfast.

Example 3-12 shows the syslog messages that appear when a BPDU is received on a BPDU guard–enabled port. The port is then placed into an ErrDisabled state, as shown with the command **show interfaces status.**

Example 3-12 *Detecting a BPDU on a BPDU Guard–Enabled Port*

```
12:47:02.069: %SPANTREE-2-BLOCK_BPDUGUARD: Received BPDU on port Gigabit
    Ethernet1/0/2 with BPDU Guard enabled. Disabling port.
12:47:02.076: %PM-4-ERR_DISABLE: bpduguard error detected on Gi1/0/2,
    putting Gi1/0/2 in err-disable state
12:47:03.079: %LINEPROTO-5-UPDOWN: Line protocol on Interface Gigabit
    Ethernet1/0/2, changed state to down
12:47:04.082: %LINK-3-UPDOWN: Interface GigabitEthernet1/0/2, changed
    state to down
```

```
SW1# show interfaces status

Port      Name          Status        Vlan     Duplex  Speed  Type
Gi1/0/1                 notconnect    1        auto    auto   10/100/1000BaseTX
Gi1/0/2   SW2 Gi1/0/1   err-disabled  1        auto    auto   10/100/1000BaseTX
Gi1/0/3   SW3 Gi1/0/1   connected     trunk    a-full  a-1000 10/100/1000BaseTX
```

By default, ports that are put in the ErrDisabled state because of BPDU guard do not automatically restore themselves. The Error Recovery service can be used to reactivate ports that are shut down for a specific problem, thereby reducing administrative overhead. To use Error Recovery to recover ports that were shut down from BPDU guard, use the command **errdisable recovery cause bpduguard**. The period that the Error Recovery checks for ports is configured with the command **errdisable recovery interval** *time-seconds*.

Example 3-13 demonstrates the configuration of the Error Recovery service for BPDU guard, verification of the Error Recovery service for BPDU guard, and the syslog messages from the process.

Example 3-13 *Configuring Error Recovery Service*

```
SW1# configure terminal
Enter configuration commands, one per line. End with CNTL/Z.
SW1(config)# errdisable recovery cause bpduguard
```

```
SW1# show errdisable recovery
! Output omitted for brevity
ErrDisable Reason            Timer Status
-----------------            --------------
```

```
arp-inspection              Disabled
bpduguard                   Enabled
..
Recovery command: "clear    Disabled

Timer interval: 300 seconds

Interfaces that will be enabled at the next timeout:

Interface       Errdisable reason       Time left(sec)
---------       -----------------       --------------
Gi1/0/2               bpduguard            295
```

```
! Syslog output from BPDU recovery. The port will be recovered, and then
! triggered again because the port is still receiving BPDUs.
SW1#
01:02:08.122: %PM-4-ERR_RECOVER: Attempting to recover from bpduguard err-disable
    state on Gi1/0/2
01:02:10.699: %SPANTREE-2-BLOCK_BPDUGUARD: Received BPDU on port Gigabit
    Ethernet1/0/2 with BPDU Guard enabled. Disabling port.
01:02:10.699: %PM-4-ERR_DISABLE: bpduguard error detected on Gi1/0/2, putting
    Gi1/0/2 in err-disable state
```

NOTE The Error Recovery service operates every 300 seconds (5 minutes). This can be changed to a value of 30 to 86,400 seconds with the global configuration command **errdisable recovery interval** *time*.

Key Topic

BPDU Filter

BPDU filter simply blocks BPDUs from being transmitted out a port. BPDU filter can be enabled globally or on a specific interface. The global BPDU filter configuration uses the command **spanning-tree portfast bpdufilter default.** The interface-specific BPDU filter is enabled with the interface configuration command **spanning-tree bpdufilter enable**.

If BPDU filter is enabled on a portfast enabled port, the behavior changes depending on the configuration:

- If BPDU filter is enabled globally, the port sends a series of 10 to 12 BPDUs on a portfast enabled port. If the switch receives any BPDUs, it checks to identify which switch is more preferred.
  - The preferred switch does not process any BPDUs that it receives, but it still transmits BPDUs to inferior downstream switches.
  - A non-preferred switch processes BPDUs that are received from a superior switch, but it does not transmit BPDUs to the superior switch.

- If BPDU filter is enabled on a specific portfast enabled port, the port does not send any BPDUs on an ongoing basis. If the remote port has BPDU guard on it, that generally places the port into an ErrDisabled state as a loop prevention mechanism.

NOTE Be careful with the deployment of BPDU filter because it could cause problems. Most network designs do not require BPDU filter, which adds an unnecessary level of complexity and also introduces risk.

Example 3-14 shows SW1's Gi1/0/2 statistics after BPDU filter is enabled on the Gi1/0/2 interface. In the first set of output, BPDU filter is enabled specifically on the Gi1/0/2 interface (thereby prohibiting any BPDUs from being sent or received). The second set of output enables BPDU filtering globally so that BPDUs are transmitted when the port first becomes active; the filtering is verified by the number of BPDUs sent changing from 56 to 58.

Example 3-14 *Verifying a BPDU Filter*

```
! SW1 was enabled with BPDU filter only on port Gi1/0/2
SW1# show spanning-tree interface gi1/0/2 detail | in BPDU|Bpdu|Ethernet
 Port 2 (GigabitEthernet1/0/2) of VLAN0001 is designated forwarding
    Bpdu filter is enabled
    BPDU: sent 113, received 84
SW1# show spanning-tree interface gi1/0/2 detail | in BPDU|Bpdu|Ethernet
 Port 2 (GigabitEthernet1/0/2) of VLAN0001 is designated forwarding
    Bpdu filter is enabled
 BPDU: sent 113, received 84
```

```
!   SW2 was enabled with BPDU filter globally
SW2# show spanning-tree interface gi1/0/2 detail | in BPDU|Bpdu|Ethernet
 Port 1 (GigabitEthernet1/0/2) of VLAN0001 is designated forwarding
   BPDU: sent 56, received 5
SW2# show spanning-tree interface gi1/0/2 detail | in BPDU|Bpdu|Ethernet
 Port 1 (GigabitEthernet1/0/2) of VLAN0001 is designated forwarding
   BPDU: sent 58, received 5
```

Problems with Unidirectional Links

Fiber-optic cables consist of strands of glass/plastic that transmit light. A cable typically consists of one strand for sending data and another strand for receiving data on one side; the order is directly opposite at the remote site. Network devices that use fiber for connectivity can encounter unidirectional traffic flows if one strand is broken. In such scenarios, the interface still shows a line-protocol up state; however, BPDUs are not able to be transmitted, and the downstream switch eventually times out the existing root port and identifies a different port as the root port. Traffic is then received on the new root port and forwarded out the strand that is still working, thereby creating a forwarding loop.

A couple solutions can resolve this scenario:

- STP loop guard
- Unidirectional Link Detection

STP Loop Guard

STP loop guard prevents any alternative or root ports from becoming designated ports (ports toward downstream switches) due to loss of BPDUs on the root port. Loop guard places the original port in a loop inconsistent state while BPDUs are not being received. When BPDU transmission starts again on that interface, the port recovers and begins to transition through the STP states again.

Loop guard is enabled globally by using the command **spanning-tree loopguard default**, or it can be enabled on an interface basis with the interface command **spanning-tree guard loop**. It is important to note that loop guard should not be enabled on portfast-enabled ports (because it directly conflicts with the root/alternate port logic).

Example 3-15 demonstrates the configuration of loop guard on SW2's Gi1/0/1 port.

Example 3-15 *Configuring Loop Guard*

```
SW2# config t
SW2(config)# interface gi1/0/1
SW2(config-if)# spanning-tree guard loop
! Placing BPDU filter on SW2's RP (Gi1/0/1) triggers loop guard.
SW2(config-if)# interface gi1/0/1
SW2(config-if)# spanning-tree bpdufilter enable
01:42:35.051: %SPANTREE-2-LOOPGUARD_BLOCK: Loop guard blocking port Gigabit
    Ethernet1/0/1 on VLAN0001
```

```
SW2# show spanning-tree vlan 1 | b Interface
Interface           Role Sts Cost      Prio.Nbr Type
------------------- ---- --- --------- -------- --------------------
Gi1/0/1             Root BKN*4         128.1    P2p *LOOP_Inc
Gi1/0/3             Root FWD 4         128.3    P2p
Gi1/0/4             Desg FWD 4         128.4    P2p
```

At this point, the port is considered to be in an inconsistent state and does not forward any traffic. Inconsistent ports are viewed with the command **show spanning-tree inconsistentports**, as shown in Example 3-16. Notice that an entry exists for all the VLANs carried across the Gi1/0/1 port.

Example 3-16 *Viewing the Inconsistent STP Ports*

```
SW2# show spanning-tree inconsistentports

Name                 Interface                Inconsistency
-------------------- ------------------------ ------------------
VLAN0001             GigabitEthernet1/0/1     Loop Inconsistent
VLAN0010             GigabitEthernet1/0/1     Loop Inconsistent
VLAN0020             GigabitEthernet1/0/1     Loop Inconsistent
VLAN0099             GigabitEthernet1/0/1     Loop Inconsistent

Number of inconsistent ports (segments) in the system : 4
```

Unidirectional Link Detection

Unidirectional Link Detection (UDLD) allows for the bidirectional monitoring of fiber-optic cables. UDLD operates by transmitting UDLD packets to a neighbor device that includes the system ID and port ID of the interface transmitting the UDLD packet. The receiving device then repeats that information, including its system ID and port ID, back to the originating device. The process continues indefinitely. UDLD operates in two different modes:

- **Normal:** In normal mode, if a frame is not acknowledged, the link is considered undetermined and the port remains active.
- **Aggressive:** In aggressive mode, when a frame is not acknowledged, the switch sends another eight packets in 1-second intervals. If those packets are not acknowledged, the port is placed into an error state.

UDLD is enabled globally with the command **udld enable** [**aggressive**]. This command enables UDLD on any small form-factor pluggable (SFP)–based port. UDLD can be disabled on a specific port with the interface configuration command **udld port disable.** UDLD recovery can be enabled with the command **udld recovery** [**interval** *time*], where the optional **interval** keyword allows for the timer to be modified from the default value of 5 minutes. UDLD can be enabled on a port-by-port basis with the interface configuration command **udld port** [**aggressive**], where the optional **aggressive** keyword places the ports in UDLD aggressive mode.

Example 3-17 shows how to enable UDLD normal mode on SW1.

Example 3-17 *Configuring UDLD*

```
SW1# conf t
Enter configuration commands, one per line. End with CNTL/Z.
SW1(config)# udld enable
```

UDLD must be enabled on the remote switch as well. After it is configured, the status of UDLD neighborship can be verified with the command **show udld neighbors.** You can view more detailed information with the command **show udld** *interface-id*.

Example 3-18 displays the verification of SW1's neighborship with SW2. The link is operating in a bidirectional state. More information is obtained with the **show udld Te1/1/3** command, which includes the current state, device IDs (that is, serial numbers), originating interface IDs, and return interface IDs.

Example 3-18 *Verifying UDLD Neighbors and Switch Port Status*

```
SW1# show udld neighbors
Port     Device Name   Device ID     Port ID    Neighbor State
----     -----------   ---------     -------    --------------
Te1/1/3  081C4FF8B0      1            Te1/1/3    Bidirectional
```

```
SW1# show udld Te1/1/3

Interface Te1/1/3
---
```

```
Port enable administrative configuration setting: Follows device default
Port enable operational state: Enabled
Current bidirectional state: Bidirectional
Current operational state: Advertisement - Single neighbor detected
Message interval: 15000 ms
Time out interval: 5000 ms

Port fast-hello configuration setting: Disabled
Port fast-hello interval: 0 ms
Port fast-hello operational state: Disabled
Neighbor fast-hello configuration setting: Disabled
Neighbor fast-hello interval: Unknown


    Entry 1
    ---
    Expiration time: 41300 ms
    Cache Device index: 1
    Current neighbor state: Bidirectional
    Device ID: 081C4FF8B0
    Port ID: Te1/1/3
    Neighbor echo 1 device: 062EC9DC50
    Neighbor echo 1 port: Te1/1/3

    TLV Message interval: 15 sec
    No TLV fast-hello interval
    TLV Time out interval: 5
    TLV CDP Device name: SW2
```

Exam Preparation Tasks

You have a couple of choices for exam preparation: the exercises here, Chapter 30, "Final Preparation," and the exam simulation questions in the Pearson Test Prep Software Online.

Review All Key Topics

Review the most important topics in the chapter, noted with the Key Topic icon in the outer margin of the page. Table 3-2 lists these key topics and the page number on which each is found.

Key Topic

Table 3-2 Key Topics for Chapter 3

Key Topic Element	Description	Page
Section	Placing the Root Bridge	60
Paragraph	Root bridge values	63

Key Topic Element	Description	Page
Paragraph	Spanning tree port cost	65
Section	Root Guard	68
Section	STP Portfast	68
Section	BPDU Guard	70
Section	BPDU Filter	72

3

Complete Tables and Lists from Memory

There are no memory tables in this chapter.

Define Key Terms

Define the following key terms from this chapter and check your answers in the Glossary:

BPDU filter, BPDU guard, root guard, STP portfast, STP loop guard, Unidirectional Link Detection (UDLD)

Use the Command Reference to Check Your Memory

Table 3-3 lists the important commands from this chapter. To test your memory, cover the right side of the table with a piece of paper, read the description on the left side, and see how much of the command you can remember.

Table 3-3 Command Reference

Task	Command Syntax
Configure the STP priority for a switch so that it is a root bridge or a backup root bridge	**spanning-tree vlan** *vlan-id* **root** {**primary** | **secondary**} [**diameter** *diameter*] OR **spanning-tree vlan** *vlan-id* **priority** *priority*
Configure the STP port cost	**spanning tree** [**vlan** *vlan-id*] **cost** *cost*
Configure the STP port priority on the downstream port	**spanning-tree** [**vlan** *vlan-id*] **port-priority** *priority*
Enable root guard on an interface	**spanning-tree guard root**
Enable STP portfast globally, for a specific port, or for a trunk port	**spanning-tree portfast default** OR **spanning-tree portfast** OR **spanning-tree portfast trunk**
Enable BPDU guard globally or for a specific switch port	**spanning-tree portfast bpduguard default** OR **spanning-tree bpduguard** {**enable** | **disable**}

Task	Command Syntax
Enable BPDU filter globally or for a specific interface	**spanning-tree portfast bpdufilter default** OR **spanning-tree bpdufilter enable**
Enable STP loop guard globally or for a specific interface	**spanning-tree loopguard default** OR **spanning-tree guard loop**
Enable automatic error recovery for BPDU guard	**errdisable recovery cause bpduguard**
Change the automatic error recovery time	**errdisable recovery interval** *time-seconds*
Enable UDLD globally or for a specific port	**udld enable [aggressive]** OR **udld port [aggressive]**
Display the list of STP ports in an inconsistent state	**show spanning-tree inconsistentports**
Display the list of neighbor devices running UDLD	**show udld neighbors**

CHAPTER 4

Multiple Spanning Tree Protocol

This chapter covers the following subject:

- **Multiple Spanning Tree Protocol:** This section examines the benefits and operations of MST.

This chapter completes the section on spanning tree by explaining Multiple Spanning Tree Protocol (MST). MST is the one of three STP modes supported on Catalyst switches.

"Do I Know This Already?" Quiz

The "Do I Know This Already?" quiz enables you to assess whether you should read the entire chapter. If you miss no more than one of these self-assessment questions, you might want to move ahead to the "Exam Preparation Tasks" section. Table 4-1 lists the major headings in this chapter and the "Do I Know This Already?" quiz questions covering the material in those headings so you can assess your knowledge of these specific areas. The answers to the "Do I Know This Already?" quiz appear in Appendix A, "Answers to the 'Do I Know This Already?' Questions."

Table 4-1 "Do I Know This Already?" Foundation Topics Section-to-Question Mapping

Foundation Topics Section	Questions
Multiple Spanning Tree Protocol	1–7

1. Which of the following issues does MST solve? (Choose two.)
    - **a.** Enables traffic load balancing for specific VLANs
    - **b.** Reduces the CPU and memory resources needed for environments with large numbers of VLANs
    - **c.** Overcomes MAC address table scaling limitations for environments with large numbers of devices
    - **d.** Detects issues with cabling that transmits data in one direction
    - **e.** Prevents unauthorized switches from attaching to the Layer 2 domain
2. With MST, VLANs are directly associated with ______.
    - **a.** areas
    - **b.** regions
    - **c.** instances
    - **d.** switches

3. What do CST and 802.1D have in common?
   a. They support only one topology.
   b. They support multiple topologies.
   c. They allow for load balancing of traffic across different VLANs.
   d. They provide switch authentication so that inter-switch connectivity can occur.
4. True or false: The MST root bridge advertises the VLAN-to-instance mappings to all other MST switches.
   a. True
   b. False
5. True or false: The MST configuration version is locally significant.
   a. True
   b. False
6. True or false: The MST topology can be tuned for root bridge placement, just like PVST+ and RSTP.
   a. True
   b. False
7. MST regions can interact with PVST+/RSTP in which of the following ways? (Choose two.)
   a. The MST region is the root bridge for all VLANs.
   b. The MST region is the root bridge for some VLANs.
   c. The PVST+/RSTP topology is the root bridge for all VLANs.
   d. The PVST+/RSTP topology is the root bridge for some VLANs.

Foundation Topics

Multiple Spanning Tree Protocol

Key Topic

The original 802.1D standard supported only one STP instance for an entire switch network. In this situation, referred to as **Common Spanning Tree (CST)**, all VLANs used the same topology, which meant it was not possible to load share traffic across links by blocking for specific VLANs on one link and then blocking for other VLANs on alternate links.

Figure 4-1 shows four VLANs sharing the same topology. All network traffic from SW2 toward SW3 must traverse through SW1. If VLAN 4 contained devices only on SW2 and SW3, the topology could not be tuned with traffic going directly between the two switches.

Cisco developed the Per-VLAN Spanning Tree (PVST) protocol to allow for an STP topology for each VLAN. With PVST, the root bridge can be placed on a different switch or can cost ports differently, on a VLAN-by-VLAN basis. This allows for a link to be blocked for one VLAN and forwarding for another.

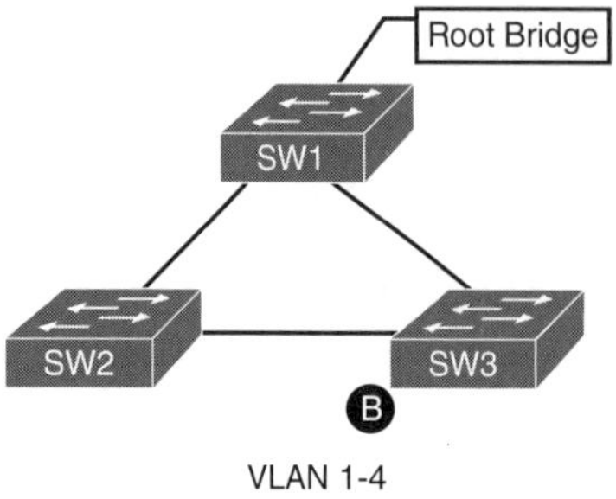

Figure 4-1 *Common Spanning Tree Instance (CST) Topology*

Figure 4-2 demonstrates how all three switches maintain an STP topology for each of the 4 VLANs. If 10 more VLANs were added to this environment, the switches would have to maintain 14 STP topologies. With the third STP instance for VLAN 3, the blocking port moves to the SW1 ←→ SW3 link due to STP tuning to address the needs of the traffic between SW2 (where servers attach) and SW3 (where clients attach). On the fourth STP instance, devices on VLAN 4 reside only on SW2 and SW3, so moving the blocking port to the SW2 ←→ SW1 link allows for optimal traffic flow.

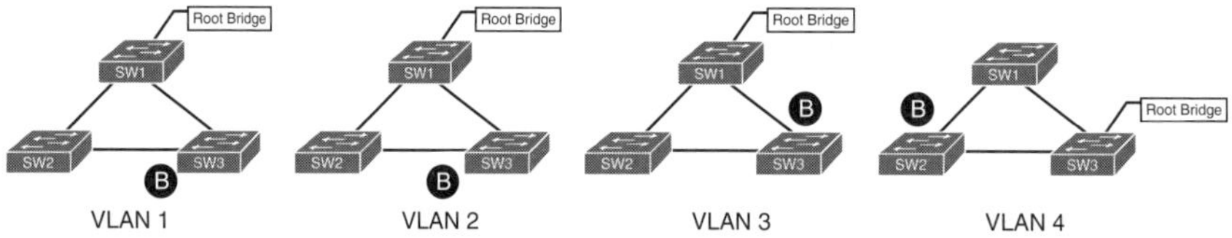

Figure 4-2 *Per-VLAN Spanning Tree (PVST) Topologies*

Key Topic

Now, in environments with thousands of VLANs, maintaining an STP state for all the VLANs can become a burden to the switch's processors. The switches must process BPDUs for every VLAN, and when a major trunk link fails, they must compute multiple STP operations to converge the network. MST provides a blended approach by mapping one or multiple VLANs onto a single STP tree, called an **MST instance (MSTI)**.

Figure 4-3 shows how all three switches maintain three STP topologies for 4 VLANs. If 10 more VLANs were added to this environment, then the switches would maintain three STP topologies if they aligned to one of the three existing MSTIs. VLANs 1 and 2 correlate to one MSTI, VLAN 3 to a second MSTI, and VLAN 4 to a third MSTI.

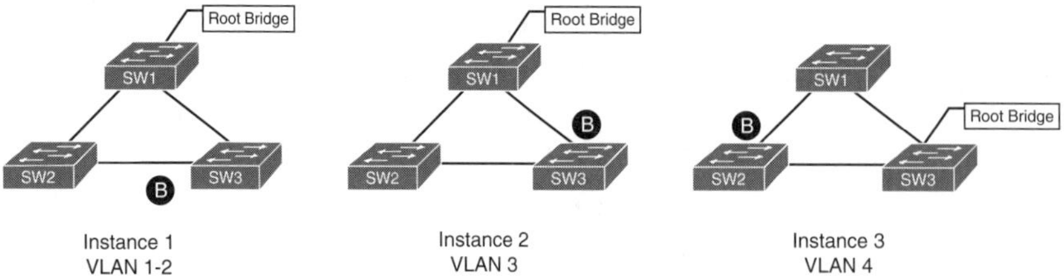

Figure 4-3 *MST Topologies*

Answers to the "Do I Know This Already?" quiz:

1 A, B **2** C **3** A **4** B **5** B **6** A **7** A, C

Key Topic

A grouping of MST switches with the same high-level configuration is known as an **MST region**. MST incorporates mechanisms that make an MST region appear as a single virtual switch to external switches as part of a compatibility mechanism.

Figure 4-4 demonstrates the concept further, showing the actual STP topology beside the topology perceived by devices outside the MST region. Normal STP operations would calculate SW5 blocking the port toward SW3 by using the operations explained in Chapter 2, "Spanning Tree Protocol." But special notice should go toward SW3 blocking the port toward SW1. Normally, SW3 would mark that port as an RP, but because it sees the topology from a larger collective, it is blocking that port rather than blocking the port between SW2 and SW3. In addition, SW7 is blocking the port toward the MST region. SW7 and SW5 are two physical hops away from the root bridge, but SW5 is part of the MST region virtual switch and appears to be one hop away, from SW7's perspective. That is why SW7 places its port into a blocking state.

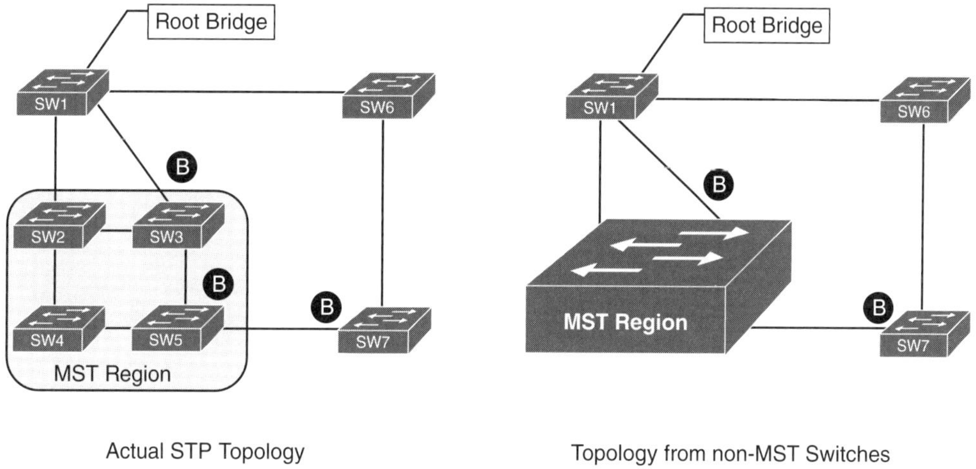

Figure 4-4 *Operating Functions Within an MST Region*

MST Instances (MSTIs)

Key Topic

MST uses a special STP instance called the **internal spanning tree (IST)**, which is always the first instance, instance 0. The IST runs on all switch port interfaces for switches in the MST region, regardless of the VLANs associated with the ports. Additional information about other MSTIs is included (nested) in the IST BPDU that is transmitted throughout the MST region. This enables the MST to advertise only one set of BPDUs, minimizing STP traffic regardless of the number of instances while providing the necessary information to calculate the STP for other MSTIs.

NOTE The number of MST instances varies by platform, and should have at least 16 instances. The IST is always instance 0, so instances 1 to 15 can support other VLANs. There is not a special name for instances 1 to 15; they are simply known as MSTIs.

MST Configuration

MST is configured using the following process:

Step 1. Define MST as the spanning tree protocol with the command **spanning-tree mode mst**.

Step 2. (Optional) Define the MST instance priority, using one of two methods:

- **spanning-tree mst** *instance-number* **priority** *priority*

  The priority is a value between 0 and 61,440, in increments of 4096.

- **spanning-tree mst** *instance-number* **root {primary | secondary}[diameter** *diameter*]

  The **primary** keyword sets the priority to 24,576, and the **secondary** keyword sets the priority to 28,672.

Step 3. Associate VLANs to an MST instance. By default, all VLANs are associated to the MST 0 instance. The MST configuration submode must be entered with the command **spanning-tree mst configuration.** Then the VLANs are assigned to a different MST instance with the command **instance** *instance-number* **vlan** *vlan-id*.

Step 4. Specify the MST version number. The MST version number must match for all switches in the same MST region. The MST version number is configured with the submode configuration command **revision** *version*.

Step 5. (Optional) Define the MST region name. MST regions are recognized by switches that share a common name. By default, a region name is an empty string. The MST region name is set with the command **name** *mst-region-name*.

Example 4-1 demonstrates the MST configuration on SW1. MST instance 2 contains VLAN 99, MST instance 1 contains VLANs 10 and 20, and MST instance 0 contains all the other VLANs.

Example 4-1 *Configuring MST on SW1*

```
SW1(config)# spanning-tree mode mst
SW1(config)# spanning-tree mst 0 root primary
SW1(config)# spanning-tree mst 1 root primary
SW1(config)# spanning-tree mst 2 root primary
SW1(config)# spanning-tree mst configuration
SW1(config-mst)# name ENTERPRISE_CORE
SW1(config-mst)# revision 2
SW1(config-mst)# instance 1 vlan 10,20
SW1(config-mst)# instance 2 vlan 99
```

The command **show spanning-tree mst configuration** provides a quick verification of the MST configuration on a switch. Example 4-2 shows the output. Notice that MST instance 0 contains all the VLANs except for VLANs 10, 20, and 99, regardless of whether those VLANs are configured on the switch. MST instance 1 contains VLAN 10 and 20, and MST instance 2 contains only VLAN 99.

Example 4-2 *Verifying the MST Configuration*

```
SW2# show spanning-tree mst configuration
Name      [ENTERPRISE_CORE]
Revision  2     Instances configured 3

Instance  Vlans mapped
--------  ---------------------------------------------------------------
0         1-9,11-19,21-98,100-4094
1         10,20
2         99
```

MST Verification

The relevant spanning tree information can be obtained with the command **show spanning-tree.** However, the VLAN numbers are not shown, and the MST instance is provided instead. In addition, the priority value for a switch is the MST instance plus the switch priority. Example 4-3 shows the output of this command.

Example 4-3 *Brief Review of MST Status*

```
SW1# show spanning-tree
! Output omitted for brevity
! Spanning Tree information for Instance 0 (All VLANs but 10,20, and 99)
MST0
  Spanning tree enabled protocol mstp
  Root ID    Priority    24576
               Address     0062.ec9d.c500
               This bridge is the root
               Hello Time   2 sec  Max Age 20 sec  Forward Delay 15 sec

  Bridge ID  Priority    24576  (priority 24576 sys-id-ext 0)
               Address     0062.ec9d.c500
               Hello Time   2 sec  Max Age 20 sec  Forward Delay 15 sec

Interface           Role Sts Cost      Prio.Nbr Type
------------------- ---- --- --------- -------- --------------------------------
Gi1/0/2             Desg FWD 20000     128.2    P2p
Gi1/0/3             Desg FWD 20000     128.3    P2p

! Spanning Tree information for Instance 1 (VLANs 10 and 20)
MST1
  Spanning tree enabled protocol mstp
  Root ID Priority 24577
            Address     0062.ec9d.c500
            This bridge is the root
            Hello Time   2 sec  Max Age 20 sec  Forward Delay 15 sec
```

```
  Bridge ID  Priority    24577  (priority 24576 sys-id-ext 1)
             Address     0062.ec9d.c500
             Hello Time   2 sec  Max Age 20 sec  Forward Delay 15 sec

Interface           Role Sts Cost      Prio.Nbr Type
------------------- ---- --- --------- -------- --------------------------------
Gi1/0/2             Desg FWD 20000      128.2    P2p
Gi1/0/3             Desg FWD 20000      128.3    P2p

! Spanning Tree information for Instance 2 (VLAN 99)
MST2
  Spanning tree enabled protocol mstp
  Root ID    Priority    24578
             Address     0062.ec9d.c500
             This bridge is the root
             Hello Time   2 sec  Max Age 20 sec  Forward Delay 15 sec

  Bridge ID  Priority    24578  (priority 24576 sys-id-ext 2)
             Address     0062.ec9d.c500
             Hello Time   2 sec  Max Age 20 sec  Forward Delay 15 sec

Interface           Role Sts Cost      Prio.Nbr Type
------------------- ---- --- --------- -------- --------------------------------
Gi1/0/2             Desg FWD 20000      128.2    P2p
Gi1/0/3             Desg FWD 20000      128.3    P2p
```

A consolidated view of the MST topology table is displayed with the command **show spanning-tree mst** [*instance-number*]. The optional *instance-number* can be included to restrict the output to a specific instance. The command is shown in Example 4-4. Notice that the VLANs are displayed next to the MST instance, which simplifies troubleshooting.

Example 4-4 *Granular View of MST Topology*

```
SW1# show spanning-tree mst
! Output omitted for brevity

##### MST0    vlans mapped:   1-9,11-19,21-98,100-4094
Bridge         address 0062.ec9d.c500  priority      0     (24576 sysid 0)
Root           this switch for the CIST
Operational   hello time 2 , forward delay 15, max age 20, txholdcount 6
Configured    hello time 2 , forward delay 15, max age 20, max hops    20

Interface                        Role Sts Cost      Prio.Nbr Type
----------------                 ---- --- --------- -------- ------------------------
Gi1/0/2                          Desg FWD 20000     128.2    P2p
Gi1/0/3                          Desg FWD 20000     128.3    P2p
```

```
##### MST1    vlans mapped:   10,20
Bridge        address 0062.ec9d.c500  priority      24577 (24576 sysid 1)
Root           this switch for MST1

Interface                        Role Sts Cost      Prio.Nbr Type
----------------                 ---- --- --------- -------- ------------------------
Gi1/0/2                          Desg FWD 20000     128.2    P2p
Gi1/0/3                          Desg FWD 20000     128.3    P2p

##### MST2    vlans mapped:   99
Bridge        address 0062.ec9d.c500  priority      24578 (24576 sysid 2)
Root          this switch for MST2

Interface                        Role Sts Cost      Prio.Nbr Type
----------------                 ---- --- --------- -------- ------------------------
Gi1/0/2                          Desg FWD 20000     128.2     P2p
Gi1/0/3                          Desg FWD 20000     128.3     P2p
```

The specific MST settings are viewed for a specific interface with the command **show spanning-tree mst interface** *interface-id*, as shown in Example 4-5. Notice that the output in this example includes additional information about optional STP features such as BPDU filter and BPDU guard.

Example 4-5 *Viewing Interface-Specific MST Settings*

```
SW2# show spanning-tree mst interface gigabitEthernet 1/0/1

GigabitEthernet1/0/1 of MST0 is root forwarding
Edge port: no              (default)        port guard : none        (default)
Link type: point-to-point (auto)          bpdu filter: disable     (default)
Boundary : internal                          bpdu guard : disable     (default)
Bpdus sent 17, received 217

Instance Role Sts Cost      Prio.Nbr Vlans mapped
-------- ---- --- --------- -------- -------------------------------
0        Root FWD 20000      128.1    1-9,11-19,21-98,100-4094
1        Root FWD 20000      128.1    10,20
2        Root FWD 20000      128.1    99
```

MST Tuning

MST supports the tuning of port cost and port priority. The interface configuration command **spanning-tree mst** *instance-number* **cost** *cost* sets the interface cost. Example 4-6 demonstrates the configuration of SW3's Gi1/0/1 port being modified to a cost of 1 and verification of the interface cost before and after the change.

Example 4-6 *Changing the MST Interface Cost*

```
SW3# show spanning-tree mst 0
! Output omitted for brevity
Interface                         Role Sts Cost      Prio.Nbr Type
----------------                  ---- --- --------- -------- --------------------
Gi1/0/1                           Root FWD 20000      128.1    P2p
Gi1/0/2                           Altn BLK 20000      128.2    P2p
Gi1/0/5                           Desg FWD 20000      128.5    P2p
```

```
SW3# configure term
Enter configuration commands, one per line. End with CNTL/Z.
SW3(config)# interface gi1/0/1
SW3(config-if)# spanning-tree mst 0 cost 1
```

```
SW3# show spanning-tree mst 0
! Output omitted for brevity
Interface                         Role Sts Cost      Prio.Nbr Type
----------------                  ---- --- --------- -------- --------------------
Gi1/0/1                           Root FWD 1         128.1    P2p
Gi1/0/2                           Desg FWD 20000     128.2    P2p
Gi1/0/5                           Desg FWD 20000     128.5    P2p
```

The interface configuration command **spanning-tree mst** *instance-number* **port-priority** *priority* sets the interface priority. Example 4-7 demonstrates the configuration of SW4's Gi1/0/5 port being modified to a priority of 64 and verification of the interface priority before and after the change.

Example 4-7 *Changing the MST Interface Priority*

```
SW4# show spanning-tree mst 0
! Output omitted for brevity
##### MST0    vlans mapped:   1-9,11-19,21-98,100-4094
Interface                         Role Sts Cost      Prio.Nbr Type
----------------                  ---- --- --------- -------- --------------------
Gi1/0/2                           Root FWD 20000     128.2    P2p
Gi1/0/5                           Desg FWD 20000     128.5    P2p
Gi1/0/6                           Desg FWD 20000     128.6    P2p
```

```
SW4# configure term
Enter configuration commands, one per line. End with CNTL/Z.
SW4(config)# interface gi1/0/5
SW4(config-if)# spanning-tree mst 0 port-priority 64
```

```
SW4# show spanning-tree mst 0
! Output omitted for brevity
##### MST0 vlans mapped: 1-9,11-19,21-98,100-4094
```

```
Interface                       Role Sts Cost      Prio.Nbr Type
----------------                ---- --- --------- -------- --------------------
Gi1/0/2                         Root FWD 20000     128.2     P2p
Gi1/0/5                         Desg FWD 20000      64.5     P2p
Gi1/0/6                         Desg FWD 20000     128.6     P2p
```

Common MST Misconfigurations

Network engineers should be aware of two common misconfigurations within the MST region:

- VLAN assignment to the IST
- Trunk link pruning

These scenarios are explained in the following sections.

VLAN Assignment to the IST

Remember that the IST operates across all links in the MST region, regardless of the VLAN assigned to the actual port. The IST topology may not correlate to the access layer and might introduce a blocking port that was not intentional.

Figure 4-5 presents a sample topology in which VLAN 10 is assigned to the IST, and VLAN 20 is assigned to MSTI 1. SW1 and SW2 contain two network links between them, with VLAN 10 and VLAN 20. It appears as if traffic between PC-A and PC-B would flow across the Gi1/0/2 interface, as it is an access port assigned to VLAN 10. However, all interfaces belong to the IST instance. SW1 is the root bridge, and all of its ports are designated ports (DPs), so SW2 must block either Gi1/0/1 or Gi1/0/2. SW2 blocks Gi1/0/2, based on the port identifier from SW1, which is Gi1/0/2. So now SW2 is blocking the Gi1/0/2 for the IST instance, which is the instance that VLAN 10 is mapped to.

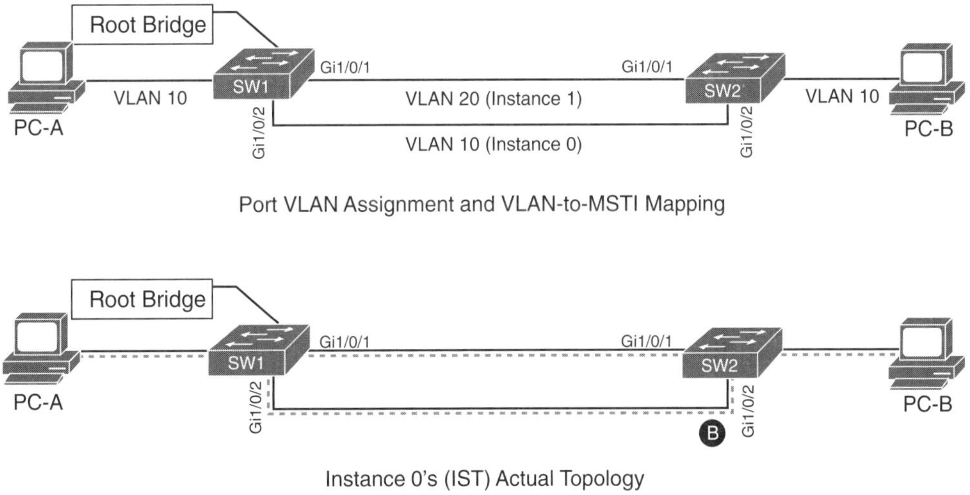

Figure 4-5 *Understanding the IST Topology*

There are two solutions for this scenario:

- Move VLAN 10 to an MSTI instance other than the IST. If you do this, the switches will build a topology based on the links in use by that MSTI.
- Allow the VLANs associated with the IST on all interswitch (trunk) links.

Trunk Link Pruning

Pruning of VLANs on a trunk link is a common practice for load balancing. However, it is important that pruning of VLANs does not occur for VLANs in the same MST on different network links.

Figure 4-6 presents a sample topology in which VLAN 10 and VLAN 20 are throughout the entire topology. A junior network engineer has pruned VLANs on the trunk links between SW1 to SW2 and SW1 to SW3 to help load balance traffic. Shortly after implementing the change, users attached to SW1 and SW3 cannot talk to the servers on SW2. The reason is that although the VLANs on the trunk links have changed, the MSTI topology has not.

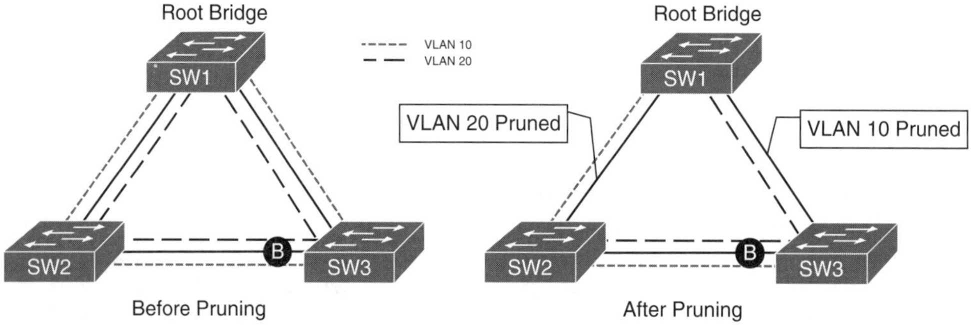

Figure 4-6 *Trunk Link Pruning*

A simple rule to follow is to prune all the VLANs in the same MSTI for a trunk link.

Key Topic

MST Region Boundary

The topology for all the MST instances is contained within the IST, which operates internally to the MST region. An **MST region boundary** is any port that connects to a switch that is in a different MST region or that connects to 802.1D or 802.1W BPDUs.

MSTIs never interact outside the region. MST switches can detect PVST+ neighbors at MST region boundaries. Propagating the CST (derived from the IST) at the MST region boundary involves a feature called the *PVST simulation mechanism*.

The PVST simulation mechanism sends out PVST+ (and also includes RPVST) BPDUs (one for each VLAN), using the information from the IST. To be very explicit, this requires a mapping of one topology (IST) to multiple VLANs (VLANs toward the PVST link). The PVST simulation mechanism is required because PVST+/RPVST topologies do not understand the IST BPDU structure.

When the MST boundary receives PVST+ BPDUs, it does not map the VLANs to the appropriate MSTIs. Instead, the MST boundary maps only the PVST+ BPDU from VLAN 1 to the IST instance. The MST boundary engages the PVST simulation mechanism only when it receives a PVST BPDU on a port.

There are two design considerations when integrating an MST region with a PVST+/RPVST environment: The MST region is the root bridge, or the MST region is not a root bridge for any VLAN. These scenarios are explained in the following sections.

MST Region as the Root Bridge

Making the MST region the root bridge ensures that all region boundary ports flood the same IST instance BPDU to all the VLANs in the PVST topology. Making the IST instance more preferable than any other switch in the PVST+ topology enables this design. The MST region appears as a single entity, and the PVST+ switches detect the alternate link and place it into a blocking state.

Figure 4-7 shows the IST instance as the root bridge for all VLANs. SW1 and SW2 advertise multiple superior BPDUs for each VLAN toward SW3, which is operating as a PVST+ switch. SW3 is responsible for blocking ports.

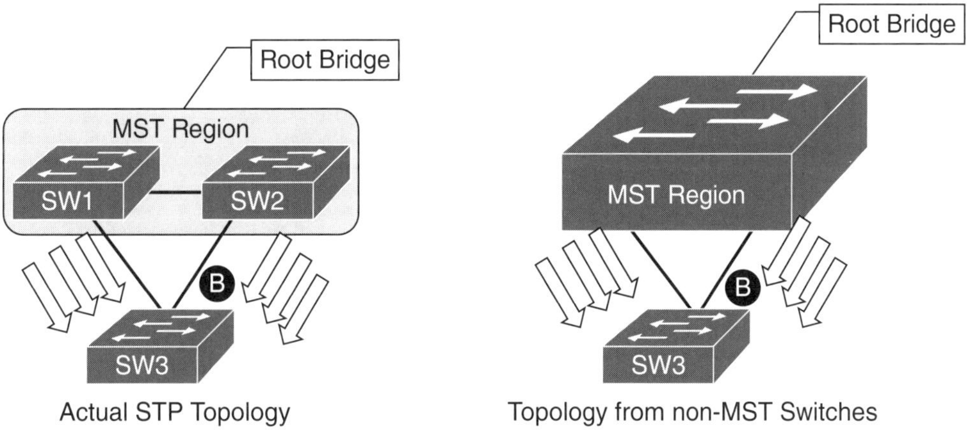

Figure 4-7 *MST Region as the Root*

NOTE SW3 could load balance traffic between the VLANs by setting the STP port cost on a VLAN-by-VLAN basis on each uplink.

MST Region Not a Root Bridge for Any VLAN

In this scenario, the MST region boundary ports can only block or forward for all VLANs. Remember that only the VLAN 1 PVST BPDU is used for the IST and that the IST BPDU is a one-to-many translation of IST BPDUs to all PVST BPDUs. There is not an option to load balance traffic because the IST instance must remain consistent.

If an MST switch detects a better BPDU for a specific VLAN on a boundary port, the switch will use BPDU guard to block this port. The port will then be placed into a root inconsistent state. Although this may isolate downstream switches, it is done to ensure a loop-free topology; this is called the **PVST simulation check**.

Exam Preparation Tasks

You have a couple of choices for exam preparation: the exercises here, Chapter 30, "Final Preparation," and the exam simulation questions in the Pearson Test Prep Software Online.

Review All Key Topics

Review the most important topics in the chapter, noted with the Key Topic icon in the outer margin of the page. Table 4-2 lists these key topics and the page number on which each is found.

Key Topic

Table 4-2 Key Topics for Chapter 4

Key Topic Element	Description	Page
Section	Multiple Spanning Tree Protocol	81
Paragraph	MST instance	82
Paragraph	MST region	83
Paragraph	Internal spanning tree (IST)	83
Section	MST Region Boundary	90

Complete Tables and Lists from Memory

There are no memory tables in this chapter.

Define Key Terms

Define the following key terms from this chapter and check your answers in the Glossary:

Common Spanning Tree (CST), internal spanning tree (IST), MST instance (MSTI), MST region, MST region boundary, PVST simulation check

Use the Command Reference to Check Your Memory

Table 4-3 lists the important commands from this chapter. To test your memory, cover the right side of the table with a piece of paper, read the description on the left side, and see how much of the command you can remember.

Table 4-3 Command Reference

Task	Command Syntax
Configure the switch for a basic MST region that includes all VLANS and the version number 1	**spanning-tree mode mst** **spanning-tree mst configuration** **instance** 0 **vlan** 1-4094 **revision** 1
Modify a switch's MSTI priority or make it the root bridge for the MSTI	**spanning-tree mst** *instance-number* **priority** *priority* OR **spanning-tree mst** *instance-number* **root** {**primary** | **secondary**}[**diameter** *diameter*]

Task	Command Syntax
Specify additional VLANs to an MSTI	**spanning-tree mst configuration** **instance** *instance-number* **vlan** *vlan-id*
Change the MST version number	**spanning-tree mst configuration** **revision** *version*
Change the port cost for a specific MSTI	**spanning-tree mst** *instance-number* **cost** *cost*
Change the port priority for a specific MSTI	**spanning-tree mst** *instance-number* **port-priority** *priority*
Display the MST configuration	**show spanning-tree mst configuration**
Verify the MST switch status	**show spanning-tree mst** [*instance-number*]
View the STP topology for the MST	**show spanning-tree mst interface** *interface-id*

4

CHAPTER 5

VLAN Trunks and EtherChannel Bundles

This chapter covers the following subjects:

- **VLAN Trunking Protocol (VTP):** This section provides an overview of how VLANs can be provisioned on switches systematically.
- **Dynamic Trunking Protocol (DTP):** This section explains how trunk links can be established dynamically between switches.
- **EtherChannel Bundle:** This section explains how multiple physical interfaces can be combined to form a logical interface to increase throughput and provide seamless resiliency.

This chapter covers multiple features for switch-to-switch connectivity. The chapter starts off by explaining VLAN Trunking Protocol (VTP) and Dynamic Trunking Protocol (DTP) to assist with provisioning of VLANs and ensuring that switch-to-switch connectivity can carry multiple VLANs. Finally, the chapter explains using EtherChannel bundles as a method of adding bandwidth and suppressing topology changes from link failures.

"Do I Know This Already?" Quiz

The "Do I Know This Already?" quiz enables you to assess whether you should read the entire chapter. If you miss no more than one of these self-assessment questions, you might want to move ahead to the "Exam Preparation Tasks" section. Table 5-1 lists the major headings in this chapter and the "Do I Know This Already?" quiz questions covering the material in those headings so you can assess your knowledge of these specific areas. The answers to the "Do I Know This Already?" quiz appear in Appendix A, "Answers to the 'Do I Know This Already?' Questions."

Table 5-1 "Do I Know This Already?" Foundation Topics Section-to-Question Mapping

Foundation Topics Section	Questions
VLAN Trunking Protocol	1–4
Dynamic Trunking Protocol	5–6
EtherChannels	7–11

1. Which of the following is not a switch role for VTP?
   a. Client
   b. Server
   c. Proxy
   d. Transparent
   e. Off
2. True or false: The VTP summary advertisement includes the VLANs that were recently added, deleted, or modified.
   a. True
   b. False
3. True or false: There can be only one switch in a VTP domain that has the server role.
   a. True
   b. False
4. Which of the following is a common disastrous VTP problem with moving a switch from one location to another?
   a. The domain certificate must be deleted and re-installed on the VTP server.
   b. The moved switch sends an update to the VTP server and deletes VLANs.
   c. The moved switch interrupts the VTP.
   d. The moved switch causes an STP forwarding loop.
5. True or false: If two switches are connected and configured with the command **switchport mode dynamic auto**, the switches will establish a trunk link.
   a. True
   b. False
6. The command ________ prevents DTP from communicating and agreeing upon a link being a trunk port.
   a. **switchport dtp disable**
   b. **switchport disable dtp**
   c. **switchport nonegotiate**
   d. **no switchport mode trunk handshake**
   e. **server**
7. True or false: PAgP is an industry standard dynamic link aggregation protocol.
   a. True
   b. False
8. An EtherChannel bundle allows for link aggregation for which types of ports? (Choose all that apply.)
   a. Access
   b. Trunk
   c. Routed
   d. Loopback

9. What are the benefits of using an EtherChannel? (Choose two.)

- **a.** Increased bandwidth between devices
- **b.** Reduction of topology changes/convergence
- **c.** Smaller configuration
- **d.** Per-packet load balancing

10. One switch has EtherChannel configured as auto. What options on the other switch can be configured to establish an EtherChannel bundle?

- **a.** Auto
- **b.** Active
- **c.** Desirable
- **d.** Passive

11. True or false: LACP and PAgP allow you to set the maximum number of member links in an EtherChannel bundle.

- **a.** True
- **b.** False

Foundation Topics

Key Topic

VLAN Trunking Protocol

Before APIs were available on Cisco platforms, configuring a switch was a manual process. Cisco created the proprietary protocol called **VLAN Trunking Protocol (VTP)** to reduce the burden of provisioning VLANs on switches. Adding a VLAN might seem like a simple task, but in an environment with 100 switches, adding a VLAN required logging in to 100 switches to provision one VLAN. Thanks to VTP, switches that participate in the same VTP domain can have a VLAN created once on a VTP server and propagated to other VTP client switches in the same VTP domain.

There are four roles in the VTP architecture:

- **Server:** The server switch is responsible for the creation, modification, and deletion of VLANs within the VTP domain.
- **Client:** The client switch receives VTP advertisements and modifies the VLANs on that switch. VLANs cannot be configured locally on a VTP client.
- **Transparent:** VTP transparent switches receive and forward VTP advertisements but do not modify the local VLAN database. VLANs are configured only locally.
- **Off:** A switch does not participate in VTP advertisements and does not forward them out of any ports either. VLANs are configured only locally.

Figure 5-1 shows a simple topology in which SW1 is the VTP server, and SW2, SW4, SW5, and SW6 are VTP clients. SW3 is in transparent mode and does not update its VLAN database as changes are propagated through the VTP domain. SW3 forwards VTP changes to SW6.

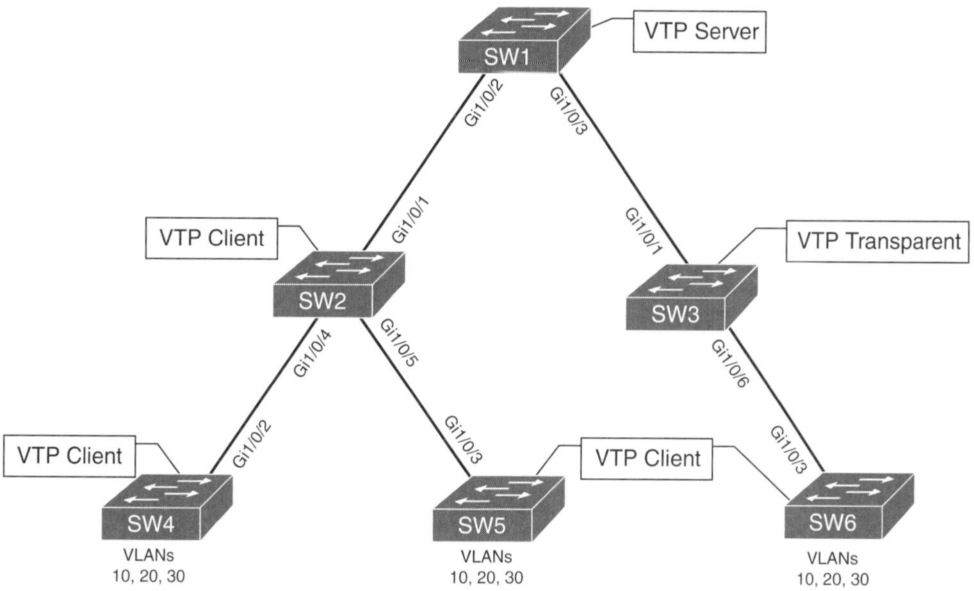

Figure 5-1 *Sample Topology for VTP*

There are three versions of VTP, and Version 1 is the default. At its simplest, VTP Versions 1 and 2 limited propagation to VLANs numbered 1 to 1005. VTP Version 3 allows for the full range of VLANs 1 to 4094. At the time of this writing, most switches should be capable of running VTP Version 3.

VTP supports having multiple VTP servers in a domain. These servers process updates from other VTP servers just as a client does. If a VTP domain is Version 3, the primary VTP server must be set with the executive command **vtp primary**.

VTP Communication

VTP advertises updates by using a multicast address across the trunk links for advertising updates to all the switches in the VTP domain. There are three main types of advertisements:

- **Summary:** This advertisement occurs every 300 seconds or when a VLAN is added, removed, or changed. It includes the VTP version, domain, configuration revision number, and time stamp.
- **Subset:** This advertisement occurs after a VLAN configuration change occurs. It contains all the relevant information for the switches to make changes to the VLANs on them.
- **Client requests:** This advertisement is a request by a client to receive the more detailed subset advertisement. Typically, this occurs when a switch with a lower revision number joins the VTP domain and observes a summary advertisement with a higher revision than it has stored locally.

VTP Configuration

The steps for configuring VTP are as follows:

Step 1. Define the VTP version with the command **vtp version** {**1** | **2** | **3**}.

Step 2. Define the VTP domain with the command **vtp domain** *domain-name*. Changing the VTP domain resets the local switch's VTP database revision to 0.

Step 3. Define the VTP switch role with the command **vtp mode** { **server** | **client** | **transparent** | **off** }.

Step 4. (Optional) Secure the VTP domain with the command **vtp password** *password*. (This step is optional but recommended because it helps prevent unauthorized switches from joining the VTP domain.)

Step 5. (For VTP Version 3 only) Designate a VTP server as primary server. Only the primary VTP server can add or remove VLANs—unlike earlier VTP versions where you could have multiple VTP servers make changes. A VTP server is made the VTP primary with the executive command **vtp primary**.

Example 5-1 demonstrates the VTP configuration on SW1, SW2, SW3, and SW6 from Figure 5-1. It shows sample configurations for three of the VTP roles: SW1 as a server, SW3 as transparent, and the other switches as VTP clients.

Example 5-1 *Configuring the VTP Domain*

```
SW1(config)# vtp version 3
09:08:11.965: %SW_VLAN-6-OLD_CONFIG_FILE_READ: Old version 2 VLAN configuration
  file detected and read OK. Version 3 files will be written in the future.
SW1(config)# vtp domain CISCO
09:08:12.085: %SW_VLAN-6-VTP_DOMAIN_NAME_CHG: VTP domain name changed to CiscoPress.
Changing VTP domain name from CCNP to CISCO
SW1(config)# vtp mode server
Setting device to VTP Server mode for VLANS.
SW1(config)# vtp password PASSWORD
Setting device VTP password to PASSWORD
SW1(config)# exit
SW1# vtp primary
This system is becoming primary server for feature vlan
No conflicting VTP3 devices found.
Do you want to continue? [confirm]
09:25:02.038: %SW_VLAN-4-VTP_PRIMARY_SERVER_CHG: 0062.ec9d.c500 has become the
    primary server for the VLAN VTP feature
```

```
SW2(config)# vtp version 3
SW2(config)# vtp domain CISCO
SW2(config)# vtp mode client
SW2(config)# vtp password PASSWORD
Setting device VTP password to PASSWORD
```

Answers to the "Do I Know This Already?" quiz:

1 C **2** B **3** B **4** B **5** B **6** C **7** B **8** A, B, and C **9** A, B **10** C **11** B

```
SW3(config)# vtp version 3
SW3(config)# vtp domain CISCO
SW3(config)# vtp mode transparent
SW3(config)# vtp password PASSWORD
```

```
SW6(config)# vtp version 3
SW6(config)# vtp domain CISCO
SW6(config)# vtp mode client
SW6(config)# vtp password PASSWORD
```

VTP Verification

The VTP status is verified with the command **show vtp status**. The most important information displayed is the VTP version, VTP domain name, VTP mode, the number of VLANs (standard and extended), and the configuration version.

Example 5-2 shows the output for SW1, SW2, SW3, and SW4. Notice the highlighted operating mode for SW2, SW3, and SW4. The last two VTP Operating Mode entries are not relevant because they are used for other functions.

5

Example 5-2 *Verifying VTP*

```
SW1# show vtp status
VTP Version capable              : 1 to 3
VTP version running              : 3
VTP Domain Name                  : CISCO
VTP Pruning Mode                 : Disabled
VTP Traps Generation             : Disabled
Device ID                        : 0062.ec9d.c500

Feature VLAN:
--------------
VTP Operating Mode               : Primary Server
Number of existing VLANs         : 5
Number of existing extended VLANs : 0
Maximum VLANs supported locally  : 4096
Configuration Revision           : 1
Primary ID                       : 0062.ec9d.c500
Primary Description              : SW1
MD5 digest                       : 0x9D 0xE3 0xCD 0x04 0x22 0x70 0xED 0x73
                                   0x96 0xDE 0x0B 0x7A 0x15 0x65 0xE2 0x65
! The following information is used for other functions not covered in the Enterprise
! Core exam and are not directly relevant and will not be explained
Feature MST:
--------------
VTP Operating Mode               : Transparent
```

```
Feature UNKNOWN:
--------------
VTP Operating Mode                : Transparent
```

```
SW2# show vtp status | i version run|Operating|VLANS|Revision
VTP version running              : 3
VTP Operating Mode                : Client
Configuration Revision           : 1
VTP Operating Mode                : Transparent
VTP Operating Mode                : Transparent
```

```
SW3# show vtp status | i version run|Operating|VLANS|Revision
VTP version running              : 3
VTP Operating Mode                : Transparent
VTP Operating Mode                : Transparent
VTP Operating Mode                : Transparent
```

```
SW6# show vtp status | i version run|Operating|VLANS|Revision
VTP version running              : 3
VTP Operating Mode                : Client
Configuration Revision           : 1
VTP Operating Mode                : Transparent
VTP Operating Mode                : Transparent
```

Now that the VTP domain has been initialized, let's look at how VTP works; Example 5-3 shows the creation of VLANS 10, 20, and 30 on SW1. After the VLANs are created on the VTP server, examining the VTP status provides a method to verify that the revision number has incremented (from 1 to 4 because three VLANs were added).

Example 5-3 *Creating VLANs on the VTP Domain Server*

```
SW1(config)# vlan 10
SW1(config-vlan)# name PCs
SW1(config-vlan)# vlan 20
SW1(config-vlan)# name VoIP
SW1(config-vlan)# vlan 30
SW1(config-vlan)# name Guest
```

```
SW1# show vtp status | i version run|Operating|VLANS|Revision
VTP version running              : 3
VTP Operating Mode                : Primary Server
Configuration Revision           : 4
VTP Operating Mode                : Transparent
VTP Operating Mode                : Transparent
```

Example 5-4 confirms that SW6 has received the VTP update messages from SW3, which is operating in transparent mode. Notice that SW6 shows a configuration revision of 4, which matches the configuration revision number from SW1. The VLAN database confirms that all three VLANs were created on this switch without needing to be configured through the CLI.

Example 5-4 *Verifying VTP with a Transparent Switch*

```
SW6# show vtp status | i version run|Operating|VLANS|Revision
VTP version running             : 3
VTP Operating Mode              : Client
Configuration Revision          : 4
VTP Operating Mode              : Transparent
VTP Operating Mode              : Transparent
SW6# show vlan

VLAN Name                             Status    Ports
---- -------------------------------- --------- -------------------------------
1    default                          active    Gi1/0/1, Gi1/0/2, Gi1/0/4
                                                   Gi1/0/5, Gi1/0/6, Gi1/0/7
                                                   Gi1/0/8, Gi1/0/9, Gi1/0/10
                                                   Gi1/0/11, Gi1/0/12, Gi1/0/13
                                                   Gi1/0/14, Gi1/0/15, Gi1/0/16
                                                   Gi1/0/17, Gi1/0/18, Gi1/0/19
                                                   Gi1/0/20, Gi1/0/21, Gi1/0/22
                                                   Gi1/0/23, Gi1/0/24
10   PCs                                active
20   VoIP                               active
30   Guest                              active
1002 fddi-default                     act/unsup
1003 trcrf-default                    act/unsup
1004 fddinet-default                  act/unsup
1005 trbrf-default                    act/unsup
```

Key Topic

It is very important that every switch that connects to a VTP domain has the VTP revision number reset to 0. Failing to reset the revision number on a switch could result in the switch providing an update to the VTP server. This is not an issue if VLANs are added but is catastrophic if VLANs are removed because those VLANs will be removed throughout the domain.

Dynamic Trunking Protocol

Chapter 1, "Packet Forwarding," describes how trunk switch ports connect a switch to another device (for example, a switch or a firewall) while carrying multiple VLANs across them. The most common format involves statically setting the switch port to a trunk port, but Cisco provides a mechanism for switch ports to dynamically form a trunk port.

Key Topic

Dynamic trunk ports are established by the switch port sending **Dynamic Trunking Protocol (DTP)** packets to negotiate whether the other end can be a trunk port. If both ports can successfully negotiate an agreement, the port will become a trunk switch port. DTP advertises itself every 30 seconds to neighbors so that they are kept aware of its status. DTP requires that the VTP domain match between the two switches.

There are three modes to use in setting a switch port to trunk:

- **Trunk:** This mode statically places the switch port as a trunk and advertises DTP packets to the other end to establish a dynamic trunk. Place a switch port in this mode with the command **switchport mode trunk**.
- **Dynamic desirable:** In this mode, the switch port acts as an access port, but it listens for and advertises DTP packets to the other end to establish a dynamic trunk. If it is successful in negotiation, the port becomes a trunk port. Place a switch port in this mode with the command **switchport mode dynamic desirable**.
- **Dynamic auto:** In this mode, the switch port acts as an access port, but it listens for DTP packets. It responds to DTP packets and, upon successful negotiation, the port becomes a trunk port. Place a switch port in this mode with the command **switchport mode dynamic auto**. This is the default mode on Catalyst switches.

A trunk link can successfully form in almost any combination of these modes unless both ends are configured as dynamic auto. Table 5-2 shows a matrix for successfully establishing a dynamic trunk link.

Table 5-2 Matrix for Establishing a Dynamic Trunk Link

		Switch 2		
		Trunk	**Dynamic Desirable**	**Dynamic Auto**
Switch 1	Trunk	✓	✓	✓
	Dynamic desirable	✓	✓	✓
	Dynamic auto	✓	✓	X

Example 5-5 shows the configuration of DTP on SW1's Gi1/0/2 as a dynamic auto switch port and SW2's Gi1/0/1 as a dynamic desirable switch port.

Example 5-5 *Configuring DTP on SW1 and SW2*

```
SW1# configure terminal
Enter configuration commands, one per line. End with CNTL/Z.
SW1(config)# interface gi1/0/2
SW1(config-if)# switchport mode dynamic auto
```

```
SW2# configure terminal
Enter configuration commands, one per line. End with CNTL/Z.
SW2(config)# interface gi1/0/1
SW2(config-if)# switchport mode dynamic desirable
```

The trunk port status is verified with the command **show interface** [*interface-id*] **trunk**, as shown in Example 5-6. Under the Mode column, there are three options: *auto* for dynamic auto, *desirable* for dynamic desirable, and *on* for a static trunk port. Notice that SW1 shows the mode *auto*, and SW2 shows the mode *desirable*.

Example 5-6 *Verifying Dynamic Trunk Port Status*

```
SW1# show interfaces trunk
! Output omitted for brevity

Port        Mode            Encapsulation  Status        Native vlan
Gi1/0/2     auto            802.1q         trunking      1

Port        Vlans allowed on trunk
Gi1/0/2     1-4094
```

```
SW2# show interfaces trunk
! Output omitted for brevity

Port        Mode            Encapsulation  Status        Native vlan
Gi1/0/1     desirable       802.1q         trunking      1

Port        Vlans allowed on trunk
Gi1/0/1     1-4094
```

Key Topic

A static trunk port attempts to establish and negotiate a trunk port with a neighbor by default. However, the interface configuration command **switchport nonegotiate** prevents that port from forming a trunk port with a dynamic desirable or dynamic auto switch port. Example 5-7 demonstrates the use of this command on SW1's Gi1/0/2 interface. The setting is then verified by looking at the switch port status. Notice that *Negotiation of Trunking* now displays as Off.

Example 5-7 *Disabling Trunk Port Negotiation*

```
SW1# show run interface gi1/0/2
Building configuration...
!
interface GigabitEthernet1/0/2
 switchport mode trunk
 switchport nonegotiate
end
```

```
SW1# show interfaces gi1/0/2 switchport | i Trunk
Administrative Trunking Encapsulation: dot1q
Operational Trunking Encapsulation: dot1q
Negotiation of Trunking: Off
Trunking Native Mode VLAN: 1 (default)
Trunking VLANs Enabled: ALL
```

NOTE As a best practice, configure both ends of a link as a fixed port type (using **switchport mode access** or **switchport mode trunk**) to remove any uncertainty about the port's operations.

EtherChannel Bundle

Ethernet network speeds are based on powers of 10 (10 Mbps, 100 Mbps, 1 Gbps, 10 Gbps, 100 Gbps). When a link between switches becomes saturated, how can more bandwidth be added to that link to prevent packet loss?

If both switches have available ports with faster throughput than the current link (for example, 10 Gbps versus 1 Gbps), then changing the link to higher-speed interfaces solves the bandwidth contingency problem. However, in most cases, this change is not feasible.

Ideally, it would be nice to plug in a second cable and double the bandwidth between the switches. However, Spanning Tree Protocol (STP) will place one of the ports into a blocking state to prevent forwarding loops, as shown in Figure 5-2.

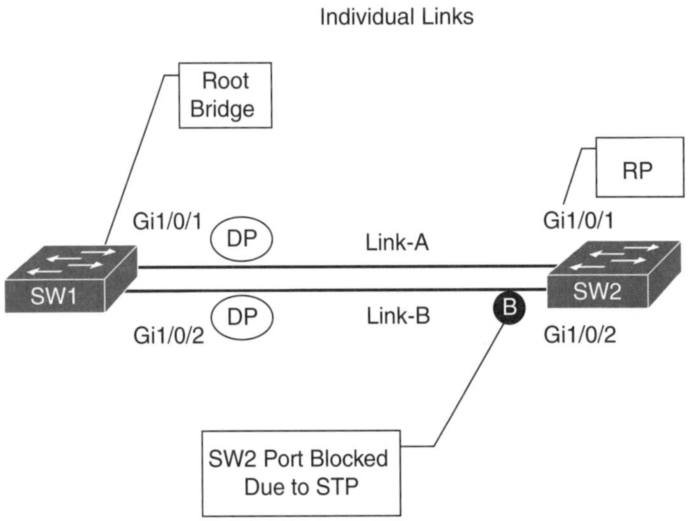

Figure 5-2 *Multiple Links with STP*

Fortunately, the physical links can be aggregated into a logical link called an **EtherChannel bundle**. The industry-based term for an EtherChannel bundle is *EtherChannel* (for short), or *port channel*, which is defined in the IEEE 802.3AD link aggregation specification. The physical interfaces that are used to assemble the logical EtherChannel are called *member interfaces*. STP operates on a logical link and not on a physical link. The logical link would then have the bandwidth of any active member interfaces, and it would be load balanced across all the links. EtherChannels can be used for either Layer 2 (access or trunk) or Layer 3 (routed) forwarding.

Figure 5-3 shows some of the key components of an EtherChannel bundle between SW1 and SW2, with their Gi1/0/1 and Gi1/0/2 interfaces.

> **NOTE** The terms *EtherChannel*, *EtherChannel bundle*, and *port channel* are interchanged frequently on the Catalyst platform, but other Cisco platforms only use the term *port channel* exclusively.

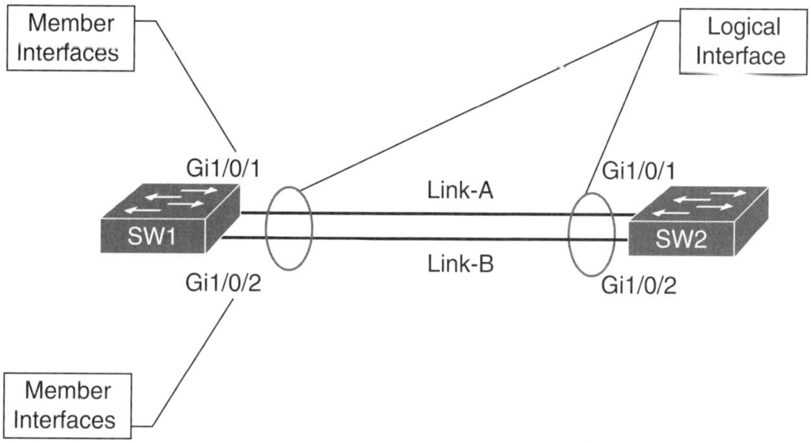

Figure 5-3 *EtherChannel Components*

A primary advantage of using port channels is a reduction in topology changes when a member link line protocol goes up or down. In a traditional model, a link status change may trigger a Layer 2 STP tree calculation or a Layer 3 route calculation. A member link failure in an EtherChannel does not impact those processes, as long as one active member still remains up.

A switch can successfully form an EtherChannel by statically setting member interfaces to an on state or by using a dynamic link aggregation protocol to detect connectivity between devices. Most network engineers prefer to use a dynamic method because it provides a way to ensure end-to-end connectivity between devices across all network links.

A significant downfall of statically setting an EtherChannel to an on state is that there is no health integrity check. If the physical medium degrades and keeps the line protocol in an up state, the port channel will reflect that link as viable for transferring data, which may not be accurate and would result in sporadic packet loss.

A common scenario involves the use of intermediary devices and technologies (for example, powered network taps, IPSs, Layer 2 firewalls, DWDM) between devices. It is critical for the link state to be propagated to the other side.

Figure 5-4 illustrates a scenario in which SW1 and SW2 have combined their Gi1/0/1 and Gi1/0/2 interfaces into a static EtherChannel across optical transport DWDM infrastructure. A failure on Link-A between the DWDM-1 and DWDM-2 is not propagated to SW1 or to SW2's Gi1/0/1 interface. The switches continue to forward traffic out the Gi1/0/1 interface because those ports still maintain physical state to DWDM-1 or DWDM-2. Both SW1 and SW2 load balance traffic across the Gi1/0/1 interface, resulting in packet loss for the traffic that is sent out of the Gi1/0/1 interface.

There is not a health-check mechanism with the EtherChannel ports being statically set to on. However, if a dynamic link aggregation protocol were used between SW1 and SW2, the link failure would be detected, and the Gi1/0/1 interfaces would be made inactive for the EtherChannel.

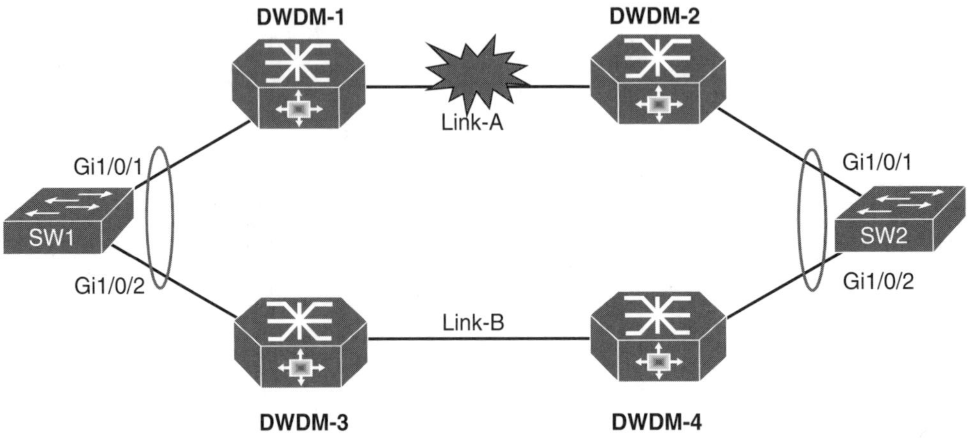

Figure 5-4 *EtherChannel Link-State Propagation and Detection*

Dynamic Link Aggregation Protocols

Two common link aggregation protocols are Link Aggregation Control Protocol (LACP) and Port Aggregation Protocol (PAgP). PAgP is Cisco proprietary and was developed first, and then LACP was created as an open industry standard. All the **member links** must participate in the same protocol on the local and remote switches.

Key Topic

PAgP Port Modes

PAgP advertises messages with the multicast MAC address 0100:0CCC:CCCC and the protocol code 0x0104. PAgP can operate in two modes:

- **Auto:** In this PAgP mode, the interface does not initiate an EtherChannel to be established and does not transmit PAgP packets out of it. If a PAgP packet is received from the remote switch, this interface responds and then can establish a PAgP adjacency. If both devices are PAgP auto, a PAgP adjacency does not form.
- **Desirable:** In this PAgP mode, an interface tries to establish an EtherChannel and transmit PAgP packets out of it. Desirable PAgP interfaces can establish a PAgP adjacency only if the remote interface is configured to auto or desirable.

Key Topic

LACP Port Modes

LACP advertises messages with the multicast MAC address 0180:C200:0002. LACP can operate in two modes:

- **Passive:** In this LACP mode, an interface does not initiate an EtherChannel to be established and does not transmit LACP packets out of it. If an LACP packet is received from the remote switch, this interface responds and then can establish an LACP adjacency. If both devices are LACP passive, an LACP adjacency does not form.
- **Active:** In this LACP mode, an interface tries to establish an EtherChannel and transmit LACP packets out of it. Active LACP interfaces can establish an LACP adjacency only if the remote interface is configured to active or passive.

Key Topic

EtherChannel Configuration

It is possible to configure EtherChannels by going into the interface configuration mode for the member interfaces and assigning them to an EtherChannel ID and configuring the appropriate mode:

- **Static EtherChannel:** A static EtherChannel is configured with the interface parameter command **channel-group** *etherchannel-id* **mode on**.
- **LACP EtherChannel:** An LACP EtherChannel is configured with the interface parameter command **channel-group** *etherchannel-id* **mode** {**active** | **passive**}.
- **PAgP EtherChannel:** A PAgP EtherChannel is configured with the interface parameter command **channel-group** *etherchannel-id* **mode** {**auto** | **desirable**} [**non-silent**].

By default, PAgP ports operate in silent mode, which allows a port to establish an EtherChannel with a device that is not PAgP capable and rarely sends packets. Using the optional **non-silent** keyword requires a port to receive PAgP packets before adding it to the EtherChannel. The **non-silent** keyword is recommended when connecting PAgP-compliant switches together; the **non-silent** option results in a link being established more quickly than if this keyword were not used.

The following additional factors need to be considered with EtherChannel configuration:

- Configuration settings for the EtherChannel are placed in the port-channel interface.
- Member interfaces need to be in the appropriate Layer 2 or Layer 3 mode (that is, **no switchport**) before being associated with the port channel. The member interface type dictates whether the EtherChannel operates at Layer 2 or Layer 3.

Example 5-8 shows the configuration for EtherChannel 1, using the member interfaces Gi1/0/1 and Gi1/0/2. SW1 uses LACP active (which accepts and initiates a request), and SW2 uses LACP passive (which only responds to an LACP initiation). The EtherChannel will be used as a trunk port, which is configured on each switch after the EtherChannel is created.

Example 5-8 *Configuring EtherChannel Bundles*

```
SW1# configure terminal
Enter configuration commands, one per line. End with CNTL/Z.
SW1(config)# interface range gi1/0/1-2
SW1(config-if-range)# channel-group 1 mode active
Creating a port-channel interface Port-channel 1
SW1(config-if-range)# interface port-channel 1
SW1(config-if)# switchport mode trunk
13:56:20.210: %LINEPROTO-5-UPDOWN: Line protocol on Interface
  GigabitEthernet1/0/1, changed state to down
13:56:20.216: %LINEPROTO-5-UPDOWN: Line protocol on Interface
GigabitEthernet1/0/2, changed state to down
13:56:32.214: %ETC-5-L3DONTBNDL2: Gi1/0/2 suspended: LACP currently not enabled
  on the remote port.
13:56:32.420: %ETC-5-L3DONTBNDL2: Gi1/0/1 suspended: LACP currently not enabled
  on the remote port.
```

```
SW2# configure terminal
Enter configuration commands, one per line. End with CNTL/Z.
SW2(config)# interface range gi1/0/1-2
SW2(config-if-range)# channel-group 1 mode passive
Creating a port-channel interface Port-channel 1
SW2(config-if-range)# interface port-channel 1
SW2(config-if)# switchport mode trunk
*13:57:05.434: %LINEPROTO-5-UPDOWN: Line protocol on Interface
  GigabitEthernet1/0/1, changed state to down
*13:57:05.446: %LINEPROTO-5-UPDOWN: Line protocol on Interface
  GigabitEthernet1/0/2, changed state to down
*13:57:12.722: %ETC-5-L3DONTBNDL2: Gi1/0/1 suspended: LACP currently not enabled
  on the remote port.
*13:57:13.072: %ETC-5-L3DONTBNDL2: Gi1/0/2 suspended: LACP currently not enabled
  on the remote port.
*13:57:24.124: %LINEPROTO-5-UPDOWN: Line protocol on Interface
 GigabitEthernet1/0/2, changed state to up
*13:57:24.160: %LINEPROTO-5-UPDOWN: Line protocol on Interface
  GigabitEthernet1/0/1, changed state to up
*13:57:25.103: %LINK-3-UPDOWN: Interface Port-channel1, changed state to up
*13:57:26.104: %LINEPROTO-5-UPDOWN: Line protocol on Interface Port-channel1,
  changed state to up
```

Verifying EtherChannel Status

After an EtherChannel has been configured, it is essential to verify that the EtherChannel has been established. As shown in Example 5-9, the command **show etherchannel summary** provides an overview of all the configured EtherChannels, along with the status and dynamic aggregation protocol for each one. A second EtherChannel using PAgP was configured on the topology to differentiate between LACP and PAgP interfaces.

Example 5-9 *Viewing EtherChannel Summary Status*

```
SW1# show etherchannel summary
Flags:  D - down        P - bundled in port-channel
        I - stand-alone s - suspended
        H - Hot-standby (LACP only)
        R - Layer3      S - Layer2
        U - in use      f - failed to allocate aggregator

        M - not in use, minimum links not met
        u - unsuitable for bundling

       w - waiting to be aggregated
        d - default port
        A - formed by Auto LAG
```

```
Number of channel-groups in use: 1
Number of aggregators:           1

Group  Port-channel  Protocol    Ports
------+-------------+-----------+-----------------------------------------------
1      Po1(SU)         LACP        Gi1/0/1(P)  Gi1/0/2(P)
2      Po2(SU)         PAgP        Gi1/0/3(P)  Gi1/0/4(P)
```

When you're viewing the output of the **show etherchannel summary** command, the first thing you should check is the EtherChannel status, which is listed in the Port-channel column. The status should be SU, as highlighted in Example 5-9.

NOTE The status codes are case sensitive, so please pay attention to the case of the field.

Table 5-3 provides a brief explanation of other key fields for the logical EtherChannel interface.

5

Table 5-3 Logical EtherChannel Interface Status Fields

Field	Description
U	The EtherChannel interface is working properly.
D	The EtherChannel interface is down.
M	The EtherChannel interface has successfully established at least one LACP adjacency; however, the EtherChannel is configured with a minimum number of active interfaces that exceeds the number of active participating member interfaces. Traffic will not be forwarded across this port channel. The command **port-channel min-links** *min-member-interfaces* is configured on the port-channel interface.
S	The EtherChannel interface is configured for Layer 2 switching.
R	The EtherChannel interface is configured for Layer 3 routing.

Table 5-4 provides a brief explanation of the fields that are related to the member interfaces.

Table 5-4 EtherChannel Member Interface Status Fields

Field	Description
P	The interface is actively participating and forwarding traffic for this EtherChannel.
H	The EtherChannel is configured with the maximum number of active interfaces. This interface is participating in LACP with the remote peer, but the interface is acting as a hot standby and does not forward traffic. The command **lacp max-bundle** *number-member-interfaces* is configured on the EtherChannel interface.
I	The member interface has not detected any LACP activity on this interface and is treated as an individual.
w	There is time left to receive a packet from this neighbor to ensure that it is still alive.
s	The member interface is in a suspended state.
r	The switch module associated with this interface has been removed from the chassis.

The logical interface can be viewed with the command **show interface port-channel** *port-channel-id*. The output includes traditional interface statistics and lists the member interfaces and indicates that the bandwidth reflects the combined throughput of all active member interfaces. As the bandwidth changes, systems that reference the bandwidth (such as QoS policies and interface costs for routing protocols) adjust accordingly.

Example 5-10 shows the use of the **show interface port-channel** *port-channel-id* command on SW1. Notice that the bandwidth is 2 Gbps and correlates to the two 1 Gbps interfaces in the **show etherchannel summary** command.

Example 5-10 *Viewing EtherChannel Interface Status*

```
SW1# show interfaces port-channel 1
Port-channel1 is up, line protocol is up (connected)
   Hardware is EtherChannel, address is 0062.ec9d.c501 (bia 0062.ec9d.c501)
   MTU 1500 bytes, BW 2000000 Kbit/sec, DLY 10 usec,
       reliability 255/255, txload 1/255, rxload 1/255
   Encapsulation ARPA, loopback not set
   Keepalive set (10 sec)
   Full-duplex, 1000Mb/s, link type is auto, media type is
   input flow-control is off, output flow-control is unsupported
   Members in this channel: Gi1/0/1 Gi1/0/2
..
```

Viewing EtherChannel Neighbors

The LACP and PAgP packets include a lot of useful information that can help identify inconsistencies in configuration. The command **show etherchannel port** displays detailed instances of the local configuration and information from the packets. Example 5-11 shows the output of this command and explains key points in the output for LACP and PAgP.

Example 5-11 *Viewing* show etherchannel port *Output*

```
SW1# show etherchannel port
! Output omitted for brevity
                Channel-group listing:
                ----------------------
! This is the header that indicates all the ports that are for the first
! EtherChannel interface. Every member link interface will be listed
Group: 1
----------
                Ports in the group:
                -------------------

! This is the first member interface for interface Po1. This interface
! is configured for LACP active
Port: Gi1/0/1
------------
```

```
Port state     = Up Mstr Assoc In-Bndl
Channel group = 1           Mode = Active          Gcchange = -
Port-channel  = Po1         GC   =     -             Pseudo port-channel = Po1
Port index     = 0           Load = 0x00             Protocol =   LACP

! This interface is configured with LACP fast packets, has a port priority
! of 32,768 and is active in the bundle.

Flags:  S - Device is sending Slow LACPDUs   F - Device is sending fast LACPDUs.
        A - Device is in active mode.  P - Device is in passive mode.

Local information:
                                  LACP port     Admin     Oper    Port        Port
Port       Flags    State      Priority        Key       Key     Number      State
Gi1/0/1    FA       bndl       32768            0x1       0x1     0x102       0x3F

! This interface's partner is configured with LACP fast packets, has a system-id
! of 0081.c4ff.8b00, a port priority of 32,768, and is active in the bundle
! for 0d:00h:03m:38s.

 Partner's information:
                    LACP port                          Admin  Oper    Port     Port
Port       Flags    Priority  Dev ID           Age     key     Key     Number  State
Gi1/0/1    FA       32768     0081.c4ff.8b00   0s      0x0     0x1     0x102   0x3F

Age of the port in the current state: 0d:00h:03m:38s

..
! This is the header that indicates all the ports that are for the second
! EtherChannel interface. Every member link interface will be listed.

Group: 2
----------
                Ports in the group:
                -------------------
! This is the first member interface for interface Po2. This interface
! is configured for PAgP desirable

Port: Gi1/0/3
------------

Port state     = Up Mstr In-Bndl
Channel group = 2           Mode = Desirable-Sl    Gcchange = 0
Port-channel  = Po2         GC   = 0x00020001        Pseudo port-channel = Po2
Port index     = 0           Load = 0x00             Protocol =   PAgP
```

```
! This interface is in a consistent state, has a neighbor with the
! 0081.c4ff.8b00 address and has been in the current state for 54m:45s

Flags:  S - Device is sending Slow hello. C - Device is in Consistent state.
        A - Device is in Auto mode. P - Device learns on physical port.
        d - PAgP is down.
Timers: H - Hello timer is running. Q - Quit timer is running.
         S - Switching timer is running. I - Interface timer is running.

Local information:
                                Hello    Partner  PAgP     Learning  Group
Port      Flags State   Timers  Interval Count   Priority   Method  Ifindex
Gi1/0/3   SC    U6/S7   H       30s      1        128        Any      51

Partner's information:
           Partner              Partner          Partner         Partner Group
Port      Name                  Device ID        Port       Age  Flags   Cap.
Gi1/0/3  SW2                   0081.c4ff.8b00   Gi1/0/3     1s SC      20001

Age of the port in the current state: 0d:00h:54m:45s
..
```

The output from the **show etherchannel port** command can provide too much information and slow down troubleshooting when a smaller amount of information is needed. The following sections provide some commands for each protocol that provide more succinct information.

LACP

The command **show lacp neighbor** [**detail**] displays additional information about the LACP neighbor and includes the neighbor's system ID, system priority, and whether it is using fast or slow LACP packet intervals as part of the output.

The LACP system identifier is used to verify that the member interfaces are connected to the same device and not split between devices. The local LACP system ID can be viewed by using the command **show lacp sys-id.** Example 5-12 shows the use of the command **show lacp neighbor.**

Example 5-12 *Viewing LACP Neighbor Information*

```
SW#1 show lacp neighbor
Flags:  S - Device is requesting Slow LACPDUs
         F - Device is requesting Fast LACPDUs
        A - Device is in Active mode       P - Device is in Passive mode

Channel group 1 neighbors
```

```
                   LACP port                          Admin   Oper    Port     Port
Port      Flags    Priority  Dev ID          Age     key     Key     Number   State
Gi1/0/1   SA       32768     0081.c4ff.8b00   1s     0x0     0x1     0x102    0x3D
Gi1/0/2   SA       32768     0081.c4ff.8b00  26s     0x0     0x1     0x103    0x3
```

```
SW2# show lacp sys-id
32678,  0081.c4ff.8b00
```

PAgP

The command **show pagp neighbor** displays additional information about the PAgP neighbor and includes the neighbor's system ID, remote port number, and whether it is using fast or slow PAgP packet intervals as part of the output. Example 5-13 shows the use of this command.

Example 5-13 *Viewing PAgP Neighbor Information*

```
SW1# show pagp neighbor
Flags:  S - Device is sending Slow hello.  C - Device is in Consistent state.
         A - Device is in Auto mode.  P - Device learns on physical port.

Channel group 2 neighbors
          Partner                  Partner           Partner          Partner Group
Port      Name                     Device ID         Port        Age  Flags   Cap.
Gi1/0/3   SW2                      0081.c4ff.8b00    Gi1/0/3     11s  SC      20001
Gi1/0/4   SW2                      0081.c4ff.8b00    Gi1/0/4      5s  SC      20001
```

Verifying EtherChannel Packets

A vital step in troubleshooting the establishment of port channels is to verify that LACP or PAgP packets are being transmitted between devices. The first troubleshooting step that can be taken is to verify the EtherChannel counters for the appropriate protocol.

LACP

The LACP counters are viewed with the command **show lacp counters**. The output includes a list of the EtherChannel interfaces, their associated member interfaces, counters for LACP packets sent/received, and any errors. An interface should see the sent and received columns increment over a time interval. The failure of the counters to increment indicates a problem. The problem could be related to a physical link, or it might have to do with an incomplete or incompatible configuration with the remote device. Check the LACP counters on the remote device to see if it is transmitting LACP packets.

Example 5-14 demonstrates the **show lacp counters** command on SW2. Notice that the Received column does not increment on Gi1/0/2 for port-channel 1, but the Sent column does increment. This indicates a problem that should be investigated further.

Example 5-14 *Viewing LACP Packet Counters*

```
SW2# show lacp counters
             LACPDUs         Marker       Marker Response    LACPDUs
Port         Sent   Recv     Sent   Recv    Sent   Recv      Pkts Err
---------------------------------------------------------------------
Channel group: 1
Gi1/0/1       23     23       0      0       0      0         0
Gi1/0/2       22      0       0      0       0      0         0
```

```
SW2# show lacp counters
             LACPDUs        Marker       Marker Response    LACPDUs
Port         Sent   Recv     Sent   Recv    Sent   Recv      Pkts Err
---------------------------------------------------------------------
Channel group: 1
Gi1/0/1       28     28       0      0       0      0         0
Gi1/0/2       27      0       0      0       0      0         0
```

NOTE The LACP counters can be cleared with the command **clear lacp counters.**

PAgP

The output of the PAgP command **show pagp counters** includes a list of the EtherChannel interfaces, their associated member interfaces, counters for PAgP packets sent/received, and any errors. The PAgP counters can be cleared with the command **clear pagp counters.**

Example 5-15 shows the command **show pagp counters** on SW2 for the second EtherChannel interface that was created on SW1.

Example 5-15 *Viewing PAgP Packet Counters*

```
SW1# show pagp counters
          Information       Flush        PAgP
Port      Sent    Recv     Sent   Recv    Err Pkts
---------------------------------------------------
Channel group: 2
Gi1/0/3   31      51        0      0       0
Gi1/0/4   44      38        0      0       0
```

Advanced LACP Configuration Options

LACP provides some additional tuning that is not available with PAgP. The following sections explain some of the advanced LACP configuration options and the behavioral impact they have on member interface selection for a port channel.

LACP Fast

The original LACP standards sent out LACP packets every 30 seconds. A link is deemed unusable if an LACP packet is not received after three intervals, which results in a potential 90 seconds of packet loss for a link before that member interface is removed from a port channel.

An amendment to the standards was made so that LACP packets are advertised every 1 second. This is known as *LACP fast* because a link can be identified and removed in 3 seconds compared to the 90 seconds specified in the initial LACP standard. LACP fast is enabled on the member interfaces with the interface configuration command **lacp rate fast**.

NOTE All the interfaces on both switches need to be configured the same—either using LACP fast or LACP slow—for the EtherChannel to successfully come up.

Example 5-16 shows how the current LACP state can be identified on the local and neighbor interfaces, along with how an interface can be converted to LACP fast.

Example 5-16 *Configuring LACP Fast and Verifying LACP Speed State*

```
SW1(config)# interface range gi1/0/1-2
SW1(config-if-range)# lacp rate fast
```

```
SW1# show lacp internal
Flags:  S - Device is requesting Slow LACPDUs
         F - Device is requesting Fast LACPDUs
         A - Device is in Active mode       P - Device is in Passive mode

Channel group 1

                               LACP port     Admin     Oper    Port        Port
Port      Flags   State      Priority        Key       Key    Number      State
Gi1/0/1   FA      bndl       32768           0x1       0x1    0x102       0x3F
Gi1/0/2   FA      bndl       32768           0x1       0x1    0x103       0xF
```

Key Topic

Minimum Number of EtherChannel Member Interfaces

An EtherChannel interface becomes active and up when only one member interface successfully forms an adjacency with a remote device. In some design scenarios using LACP, a minimum number of adjacencies is required before an EtherChannel interface becomes active. This option can be configured with the EtherChannel interface command **port-channel min-links** *min-links*.

Example 5-17 shows how to set the minimum number of EtherChannel interfaces to two and then shut down one of the member interfaces on SW1. Doing so prevents the EtherChannel from meeting the required minimum links and shuts it down. Notice that the EtherChannel status is *not in use* in the new state.

Example 5-17 *Configuring the Minimum Number of EtherChannel Member Interfaces*

```
SW1(config)# interface port-channel 1
SW1(config-if)# port-channel min-links 2
SW1(config-if)# interface gi1/0/1
SW1(config-if)# shutdown
10:44:46.516: %ETC-5-MINLINKS_NOTMET: Port-channel Po1 is down bundled ports (1)
   doesn't meet min-links
10:44:47.506: %LINEPROTO-5-UPDOWN: Line protocol on Interface Gigabit
   Ethernet1/0/2, changed state to down
10:44:47.508: %LINEPROTO-5-UPDOWN: Line protocol on Interface Port-channel1,
   changed state to down
10:44:48.499: %LINK-5-CHANGED: Interface GigabitEthernet1/0/1, changed state to
   administratively down
10:44:48.515: %LINK-3-UPDOWN: Interface Port-channel1, changed state to down
```

```
SW1# show etherchannel summary
! Output Omitted for Brevity
Flags:  D - down        P - bundled in port-channel
        I - stand-alone s - suspended
         H - Hot-standby (LACP only)
         R - Layer3      S - Layer2
         U - in use      f - failed to allocate aggregator
         M - not in use, minimum links not met
..
Group  Port-channel  Protocol    Ports
------+-------------+-----------+-----------------------------------------------
1      Po1(SM)         LACP      Gi1/0/1(D)  Gi1/0/2(P)
```

> **NOTE** The minimum number of EtherChannel member interfaces does not need to be configured on both devices to work properly. However, configuring it on both switches is recommended to accelerate troubleshooting and assist operational staff.

Key Topic

Maximum Number of EtherChannel Member Interfaces

An EtherChannel can be configured to have a specific maximum number of member interfaces in a port channel. This may be done to ensure that the active member interface count proceeds with powers of two (for example, 2, 4, 8) to accommodate load-balancing hashes. The maximum number of member interfaces in an EtherChannel can be configured with the port-channel interface command **lacp max-bundle** *max-links*.

Example 5-18 shows the configuration of the maximum number of active member interfaces for a port channel; you can see that those interfaces now show as Hot-standby.

Example 5-18 *Configuring and Verifying the Maximum Links*

```
SW1(config)# interface port-channel1
SW1(config-if)# lacp max-bundle 1
11:01:11.972: %LINEPROTO-5-UPDOWN: Line protocol on Interface Gigabit
   Ethernet1/0/1, changed state to down
11:01:11.979: %LINEPROTO-5-UPDOWN: Line protocol on Interface Gigabit
   Ethernet1/0/2, changed state to down
11:01:11.982: %LINEPROTO-5-UPDOWN: Line protocol on Interface Port-channel1,
   changed state to down
11:01:13.850: %LINEPROTO-5-UPDOWN: Line protocol on Interface Gigabit
   Ethernet1/0/1, changed state to up
11:01:13.989: %LINEPROTO-5-UPDOWN: Line protocol on Interface Port-channel1,
   changed state to up
```

```
SW1# show etherchannel summary
! Output omitted for brevity
Flags:  D - down        P - bundled in port-channel
         I - stand-alone s - suspended
         H - Hot-standby (LACP only)
         R - Layer3      S - Layer2
         U - in use      f - failed to allocate aggregator

         M - not in use, minimum links not met
         u - unsuitable for bundling
         w - waiting to be aggregated
         d - default port

         A - formed by Auto LAG
..
Group  Port-channel  Protocol    Ports
------+-------------+-----------+-----------------------------------------------
1      Po1(SU)         LACP      Gi1/0/1(P)  Gi1/0/2(H)
```

The maximum number of EtherChannel member interfaces needs to be configured only on the primary switch for that port channel; however, configuring it on both switches is recommended to accelerate troubleshooting and assist operational staff.

The EtherChannel primary switch controls which member interfaces (and associated links) are active by examining the LACP port priority. A lower port priority is preferred. If the port priority is the same, then the lower interface number is preferred.

Key Topic

LACP System Priority

The **LACP system priority** identifies which switch is the primary switch for an EtherChannel. The primary switch on an EtherChannel is responsible for choosing which member interfaces are active in a port channel when there are more member interfaces than the maximum number of member interfaces associated with a port-channel interface. The switch with the lower system priority is preferred. The LACP system priority can be changed with the command **lacp system-priority** *priority*.

Example 5-19 shows how the LACP system priority can be viewed and changed.

Example 5-19 *Viewing and Changing the LACP System Priority*

```
SW1# show lacp sys-id
32768, 0062.ec9d.c500
```

```
SW1# configure terminal
Enter configuration commands, one per line. End with CNTL/Z.
SW1(config)# lacp system-priority 1
```

```
SW1# show lacp sys-id
1, 0062.ec9d.c500
```

Key Topic

LACP Interface Priority

LACP interface priority enables the primary switch to choose which member interfaces are active in an EtherChannel when there are more member interfaces than the maximum number of member interfaces for an EtherChannel. A port with a lower port priority is preferred. The interface configuration command **lacp port-priority** *priority* sets the interface priority.

Example 5-20 changes the port priority on SW1 for Gi1/0/2 so that it is the most preferred interface when the LACP maximum link has been set to 1. SW1 is the primary switch for port channel 1, the Gi1/0/2 interface becomes active, and port Gi1/0/1 becomes Hot-standby.

Example 5-20 *Changing the LACP Port Priority*

```
SW1# show etherchannel summary | b Group
Group  Port-channel  Protocol    Ports
------+-------------+-----------+-----------------------------------------------
1       Po1(SU)          LACP       Gi1/0/1(P)  Gi1/0/2(H)
```

```
SW1(config)# interface gi1/0/2
SW1(config-if)# lacp port-priority 1
```

```
SW1# show etherchannel summary | b Group
Group  Port-channel  Protocol      Ports
------+-------------+-----------+-----------------------------------------------
1       Po1(SU)            LACP        Gi1/0/1(H)        Gi1/0/2(P)
```

Key Topic

Troubleshooting EtherChannel Bundles

It is important to remember that an EtherChannel is a logical interface, so all the member interfaces must have the same characteristics. If they do not, problems will occur.

As a general rule, when you're configuring EtherChannels on a switch, place each member interface in the appropriate switch port type (Layer 2 or Layer 3) and then associate the interfaces to a port channel. All other port-channel configuration is done via the port-channel interface.

The following configuration settings must match on the member interfaces:

- **Port type:** Every port in the interface must be consistently configured to be a Layer 2 switch port or a Layer 3 routed port.
- **Port mode:** All Layer 2 port channels must be configured as either access ports or trunk ports. They cannot be mixed.
- **Native VLAN:** The member interfaces on a Layer 2 trunk port channel must be configured with the same native VLAN, using the command **switchport trunk native vlan** *vlan-id*.
- **Allowed VLAN:** The member interfaces on a Layer 2 trunk port channel must be configured to support the same VLANs, using the command **switchport trunk allowed** *vlan-ids*.
- **Speed:** All member interfaces must be the same speed.
- **Duplex:** The duplex must be the same for all member interfaces.
- **MTU:** All Layer 3 member interfaces must have the same MTU configured. The interface cannot be added to the port channel if the MTU does not match the MTU of the other member interfaces.
- **Load interval:** The load interval must be configured the same on all member interfaces.
- **Storm control:** The member ports must be configured with the same storm control settings on all member interfaces.

In addition to paying attention to the preceding configuration settings, check the following when troubleshooting the establishment of an EtherChannel bundle:

- Ensure that a member link is between only two devices.
- Ensure that the member ports are all active.
- Ensure that both end links are statically set to *on* and that either LACP is enabled with at least one side set to *active* or PAgP is enabled with at least one side set to *desirable*.
- Ensure that all member interface ports are consistently configured (except for LACP port priority).
- Verify the LACP or PAgP packet transmission and receipt on both devices.

Key Topic

Load Balancing Traffic with EtherChannel Bundles

Traffic that flows across a port-channel interface is not forwarded out member links on a round-robin basis per packet. Instead, a hash is calculated, and packets are consistently forwarded across a link based on that hash, which runs on the various packet header fields. The **load-balancing hash** is a systemwide configuration that uses the global command **port-channel load-balance** *hash*. A common list of *hash* options follows (some of the newer IOS XE software versions include the VLAN number as part of the hash):

- **dst-ip:** Destination IP address
- **dst-mac:** Destination MAC address

- **dst-mixed-ip-port:** Destination IP address and destination TCP/UDP port
- **dst-port:** Destination TCP/UDP port
- **src-dst-ip:** Source and destination IP addresses
- **src-dest-ip-only:** Source and destination IP addresses only
- **src-dst-mac:** Source and destination MAC addresses
- **src-dst-mixed-ip-port:** Source and destination IP addresses and source and destination TCP/UDP ports
- **src-dst-port:** Source and destination TCP/UDP ports only
- **src-ip:** Source IP address
- **src-mac:** Source MAC address
- **src-mixed-ip-port:** Source IP address and source TCP/UDP port
- **src-port:** Source TCP/UDP port

If the links are unevenly distributed, changing the hash value may provide a different distribution ratio across member links. For example, if a port channel is established with a router, using a MAC address as part of the hash could impact the traffic flow because the router's MAC address does not change (as the MAC address for the source or destination will always be the router's MAC address). A better choice would be to use the source/destination IP address or base the hash on TCP/UDP session ports.

The command **show etherchannel load-balance** displays how a switch will load balance network traffic based on its type: non-IP, IPv4, or IPv6. Example 5-21 shows the command being executed on SW1.

Example 5-21 *Viewing the Port-Channel Hash Algorithm*

```
SW1# show etherchannel load-balance
EtherChannel Load-Balancing Configuration:
        src-dst-mixed-ip-port

EtherChannel Load-Balancing Addresses Used Per-Protocol:
Non-IP: Source XOR Destination MAC address
   IPv4: Source XOR Destination IP address and TCP/UDP (layer-4) port number
   IPv6: Source XOR Destination IP address and TCP/UDP (layer-4) port number
```

Another critical point is that a hash is a binary function, so links should be in powers of two (for example, 2, 4, 8) to be consistent. A three-port EtherChannel will not load balance as effectively as a two- or four-port EtherChannel. The best way to view the load of each member link is with the command **show etherchannel port**. The link utilization is displayed in hex under Load and is used to identify the distribution of traffic.

Exam Preparation Tasks

You have a couple of choices for exam preparation: the exercises here, Chapter 30, "Final Preparation," and the exam simulation questions in the Pearson Test Prep Software Online.

Review All Key Topics

Review the most important topics in the chapter, noted with the Key Topic icon in the outer margin of the page. Table 5-5 lists these key topics and the page number on which each is found.

Key Topic

Table 5-5 Key Topics for Chapter 5

Key Topic Element	Description	Page
Section	VLAN Trunking Protocol (VTP)	96
Paragraph	VTP revision reset	101
Paragraph	Dynamic Trunking Protocol (DTP)	101
Paragraph	Disabling DTP	103
Section	PAgP Port Modes	106
Section	LACP Port Modes	106
Section	EtherChannel Configuration	107
Section	Minimum Number of EtherChannel Member Interfaces	115
Section	Maximum Number of EtherChannel Member Interfaces	116
Section	LACP System Priority	117
Section	LACP Interface Priority	118
Section	Troubleshooting EtherChannel Bundles	118
Section	Load Balancing Traffic with EtherChannel Bundles	119

Complete Tables and Lists from Memory

There are no memory tables in this chapter.

Define Key Terms

Define the following key terms from this chapter and check your answers in the Glossary:

Dynamic Trunking Protocol (DTP), EtherChannel bundle, LACP interface priority, LACP system priority, load-balancing hash, member links, VLAN Trunking Protocol (VTP)

Use the Command Reference to Check Your Memory

Table 5-6 lists the important commands from this chapter. To test your memory, cover the right side of the table with a piece of paper, read the description on the left side, and see how much of the command you can remember.

Table 5-6 Command Reference

Task	Command Syntax
Configure the VTP version	**vtp version** {**1** | **2** | **3**}
Configure the VTP domain name	**vtp domain** *domain-name*
Configure the VTP mode for a switch	**vtp mode** { **server** | **client** | **transparent** | **off**} (required for the VTP v3 server) **vtp primary**
Configure a switch port to actively attempt to establish a trunk link	**switchport mode dynamic desirable**
Configure a switch port to respond to remote attempts to establish a trunk link	**switchport mode dynamic auto**
Configure the member ports for a static EtherChannel	**channel-group** *etherchannel-id* **mode on**
Configure the member ports for an LACP EtherChannel	**channel-group** *etherchannel-id* **mode** {**active** | **passive**}
Configure the member ports for a PAgP EtherChannel	**channel-group** *etherchannel-id* **mode** {**auto** | **desirable**} [**non-silent**]
Configure the LACP packet rate	**lacp rate** {**fast** | **slow**}
Configure the minimum number of member links for the LACP EtherChannel to become active	**port-channel min-links** *min-links*
Configure the maximum number of member links in an LACP EtherChannel	**lacp max-bundle** *max-links*
Configure a switch's LACP system priority	**lacp system-priority** *priority*
Configure a switch's LACP port priority	**lacp port-priority** *priority*
Configure the EtherChannel load-balancing hash algorithm	**port-channel load-balance** *hash*
Display the VTP system settings	**show vtp status**
Display the switch port DTP settings, native VLANs, and allowed VLANs	**show interface** [*interface-id*] **trunk**
Display a brief summary update on EtherChannel interfaces	**show etherchannel summary**
Display detailed information for the local EtherChannel interfaces	**show interface port-channel**
Display information about LACP neighbors	**show lacp neighbor** [**detail**]
Display the local LACP system identifier and priority	**show lacp** *system-id*
Display the LACP counters for configure interfaces	**show lacp counters**
Display information about PAgP neighbors	**show pagp neighbor**
Display the PAgP counters for configured interfaces	**show pagp counters**
Display the algorithm for load balancing network traffic based on the traffic type	**show etherchannel load-balance**

CHAPTER 6

IP Routing Essentials

This chapter covers the following subjects:

- **Routing Protocol Overview:** This section explains how different routing protocols advertise and identify routes.
- **Path Selection:** This section explains the logic a router uses to identify the best route and install it in the routing table.
- **Static Routing:** This section provides a brief overview of fundamental static route concepts.
- **Policy-based Routing:** This section explains how packets can be forwarded dynamically based on packet characteristics.
- **Virtual Routing and Forwarding:** This section explains the creation of logical routers on a physical router.

This chapter revisits the fundamentals from Chapter 1, "Packet Forwarding," as well as some of the components of the operations of a router. It reinforces the logic of the programming of the Routing Information Base (RIB), reviews differences between common routing protocols, and explains common concepts related to static routes.

"Do I Know This Already?" Quiz

The "Do I Know This Already?" quiz enables you to assess whether you should read the entire chapter. If you miss no more than one of these self-assessment questions, you might want to move ahead to the "Exam Preparation Tasks" section. Table 6-1 lists the major headings in this chapter and the "Do I Know This Already?" quiz questions covering the material in those headings so you can assess your knowledge of these specific areas. The answers to the "Do I Know This Already?" quiz appear in Appendix A, "Answers to the 'Do I Know This Already?' Questions."

Table 6-1 "Do I Know This Already?" Foundation Topics Section-to-Question Mapping

Foundation Topics Section	Questions
Routing Protocol Overview	1–5
Path Selection	6–8
Static Routing	9
Virtual Routing and Forwarding	10

1. Which of the following routing protocols is classified as an EGP?
   a. RIPv2
   b. EIGRP
   c. OSPF
   d. IS-IS
   e. BGP
2. Which of the following routing protocols are classified as IGPs? (Choose all that apply.)
   a. RIPv2
   b. EIGRP
   c. OSPF
   d. IS-IS
   e. BGP
3. A path vector routing protocol finds the best loop-free path by using ______.
   a. hop count
   b. bandwidth
   c. delay
   d. interface cost
   e. path attributes
4. A distance vector routing protocol finds the best loop-free path by using ______.
   a. hop count
   b. bandwidth
   c. delay
   d. interface cost
   e. path attributes
5. A link-state routing protocol finds the best loop-free path by using ______.
   a. hop count
   b. bandwidth
   c. delay
   d. interface cost
   e. path attributes
6. A router uses _________ as the first criterion for forwarding packets.
   a. path metric
   b. administrative distance
   c. longest match
   d. hop count

7. A router uses ________ as the second criterion for forwarding packets.
   a. path metric
   b. administrative distance
   c. longest match
   d. hop count
8. The ability to install multiple paths from the same routing protocol with the same path metric into the RIB is known as ______.
   a. per-packet load balancing
   b. round-robin load balancing
   c. equal-cost multipathing
   d. parallel link forwarding
9. Which static route should be used to avoid unintentional forwarding paths with an Ethernet link failure?
   a. A directly attached static route
   b. A recursive static route
   c. A fully specified static route
   d. A static null route
10. Virtual routing and forwarding (VRF) is useful with _____ addresses.
   a. MAC
   b. IPv4
   c. IPv6
   d. IPv4 and IPv6

Foundation Topics

As described in the previous chapters, a router is necessary to transmit packets between network segments. This chapter explains the process a router uses to insert routes into the routing table from routing protocol databases and the methodology for selecting a path. A brief overview of static routing also is provided. By the end of this chapter, you should have a solid understanding of the routing processes on a router.

Routing Protocol Overview

A router's primary function is to move an IP packet from one network to a different network. A router learns about nonattached networks through configuration of static routes or through dynamic IP routing protocols.

Dynamic IP routing protocols distribute network topology information between routers and provide updates without intervention when a topology change in the network occurs. Design requirements or hardware limitations may restrict IP routing to static routes, which do not accommodate topology changes very well and can burden network engineers, depending on the size of the network. With dynamic routing protocols, routers try to select the best loop-free path on which to forward a packet to its destination IP address.

Some network engineers might interchange the terms *network*, *subnet*, *network prefix*, and *path*. Depending on the context, they may be correct. The following delineations should provide a better reference point:

- A *subnet*, *network prefix*, or *prefix* refers to a specific location on a network.
- A *path* is a series of network links between two network prefixes. Often there are multiple paths, but not all of them may be efficient.
- A *route* is a path designated by static routes or dynamic routing protocol to reach a destination network. A route can exist in a local routing process such as OSPF and BGP, or a route can exist in a router's routing table.

A system of interconnected routers and related components managed under a common network administration is known as an *autonomous system (AS)*, or a *routing domain*. The Internet is composed of thousands of autonomous systems spanning the globe.

The common dynamic routing protocols found on most routing platforms today are as follows:

- Routing Information Protocol Version 2 (RIPv2)
- Enhanced Interior Gateway Routing Protocol (EIGRP)
- Open Shortest Path First (OSPF)
- Intermediate System-to-Intermediate System (IS-IS)
- Border Gateway Protocol (BGP)

With the exception of BGP, the protocols in this list are designed and optimized for routing within an autonomous system and are known as Interior Gateway Protocols (IGPs). Exterior Gateway Protocols (EGPs) route between autonomous systems. BGP is an EGP but can also be used within an autonomous system. If BGP exchanges routes within an autonomous system, it is known as an *interior BGP (iBGP) session*. If it exchanges routes between different autonomous systems, it is known as an *exterior BGP (eBGP) session*.

Figure 6-1 shows an illustration of how one or many IGPs as well as iBGP can be running within an autonomous system and how eBGP sessions interconnect the various autonomous systems together.

EGPs and IGPs use different algorithms for path selection and are discussed in the following sections.

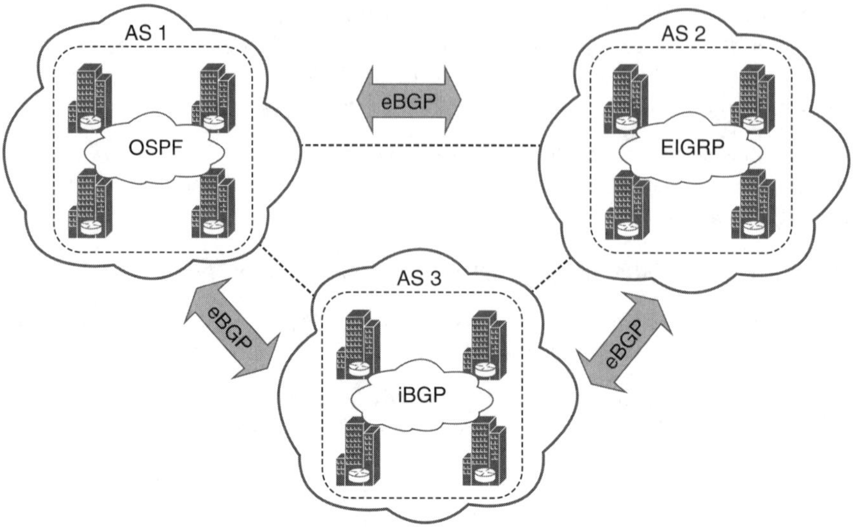

Figure 6-1 *BGP Autonomous Systems and How They Interconnect*

Distance Vector Algorithms

Distance vector routing protocols, such as RIPv2, advertise routes as vectors, where distance is a metric (or cost) such as hop count, and vector is the next-hop router's IP used to reach a destination network:

- **Distance:** The distance is the route metric to reach the network.
- **Vector:** The vector is the interface or direction to reach the network.

When a router receives routing information from a neighbor, it stores that information in a local routing database as it is received, and the distance vector algorithm (such as the Bellman-Ford and Ford-Fulkerson algorithms) is used to determine which paths are the best loop-free paths to each reachable destination. When the best paths are determined, they are installed into the routing table and are advertised to each neighbor router.

Routers running distance vector protocols advertise the routing information to their neighbors from their own perspective, modified from the original route received. Therefore, a distance vector protocol does not have a complete map of the whole network; instead, its database reflects that a neighbor router knows how to reach the destination network and how far the neighbor router is from the destination network. The advantage of distance vector protocols is that they require less CPU and memory and can run on low-end routers.

An analogy commonly used to describe distance vector protocols is a road sign at an intersection indicating that the destination is 2 miles to the west; drivers trust and blindly follow this information, without really knowing whether there is a shorter or better way to the destination or whether the sign is even correct. Figure 6-2 illustrates how a router using a distance vector protocol views the network and the direction that R3 needs to go to reach the 192.168.1.0/24 network.

Answers to the "Do I Know This Already?" quiz:

1 E **2** A, B, C, D **3** E **4** A **5** D **6** C **7** B **8** C **9** C **10** D

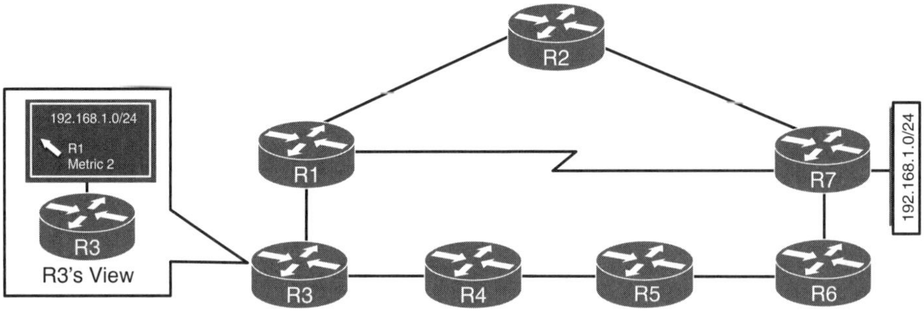

Figure 6-2 *Distance Vector Protocol View of a Network*

A distance vector protocol selects a path purely based on distance. It does not account for link speeds or other factors. In Figure 6-2, the link between R1 and R7 is a serial link with only 64 Kbps of bandwidth, and all of the other links are 1 Gbps Ethernet links. RIPv2 does not take this into consideration and forwards traffic across the serial link, which will result in packet loss when that link is oversubscribed.

Key Topic

Enhanced Distance Vector Algorithms

The diffusing update algorithm (DUAL) is an enhanced distance vector algorithm that EIGRP uses to calculate the shortest path to a destination network within a routing domain. EIGRP advertises network information to its neighbors as other distance vector protocols do, but it has some enhancements, as its name suggests. The following are some of the enhancements introduced into this algorithm compared to other distance vector algorithms:

- It offers rapid convergence time for changes in the network topology.
- It sends updates only when there is a change in the topology. It does not send full routing table updates in a periodic fashion, as distance vector protocols typically do.
- It uses hellos and forms neighbor relationships just as link-state protocols do.
- It can use bandwidth, delay, reliability, load, and maximum transmission unit (MTU) size instead of hop count for path calculations.
- It has the option to load balance traffic across equal- or unequal-cost paths.

Key Topic

EIGRP is sometimes referred to as a *hybrid routing protocol* because it has characteristics of both distance vector and link-state protocols, as shown in the preceding list. EIGRP relies on more advanced metrics other than hop count (for example, bandwidth) for its best-path calculations. By default, EIGRP advertises the total path delay and minimum bandwidth for a route. This information is advertised out every direction, as happens with a distance vector routing protocol; however, each router can calculate the best path based on the information provided by its direct neighbors.

Figure 6-3 shows the previous topology but now includes EIGRP's metric calculations for each of the links, where the lower metric value is preferred. R3 is trying to forward packets to the 192.168.1.0/24 destination network. If the routing domain used a distance vector routing protocol, such as RIPv2, it would select the R3→R1→R7 path, which is the shortest path to the destination based on hop count (two hops away), but cannot support traffic over 64 Kbps, while EIGRP would select the R3→R1→R2→R7 path, which is a longer path (three hops away), but provides more bandwidth and does not have as much delay (because of the serialization process on lower-speed interfaces).

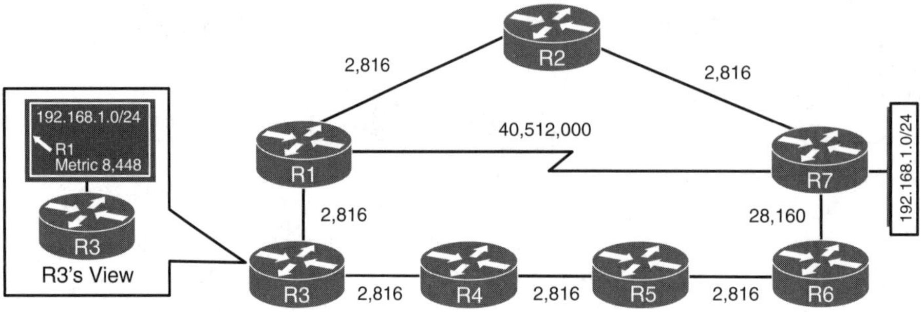

Figure 6-3 *Distance Vector Protocol Versus Enhanced Distance Vector*

Key Topic

Link-State Algorithms

A link-state dynamic IP routing protocol advertises the link state and link metric for each of its connected links and directly connected routers to every router in the network. OSPF and IS-IS are two **link-state routing protocols** commonly used in enterprise and service provider networks. OSPF advertisements are called *link-state advertisements (LSAs)*, and IS-IS uses *link-state packets (LSPs)* for its advertisements.

As a router receives an advertisement from a neighbor, it stores the information in a local database called the *link-state database (LSDB)* and advertises the link-state information on to each of its neighbor routers exactly as it was received. The link-state information is essentially flooded throughout the network, unchanged, from router to router, just as the originating router advertised it. This allows all the routers in the network to have a synchronized and identical map of the network.

Using the complete map of the network, every router in the network then runs the Dijkstra shortest path first (SPF) algorithm to calculate the best shortest loop-free paths. The link-state algorithm then populates the routing table with this information.

Because they have the complete map of the network, link-state protocols usually require more CPU and memory than distance vector protocols, but they are less prone to routing loops and make better path decisions. In addition, link-state protocols are equipped with extended capabilities such as opaque LSAs for OSPF and TLVs (type/length/value) for IS-IS that allow them to support features commonly used by service providers, such as MPLS traffic engineering.

An analogy for link-state protocols is a GPS navigation system. The GPS navigation system has a complete map and can make the best decision about which way is the shortest and best path to reach a destination. Figure 6-4 illustrates how R3 would view the routing domain and use this information to calculate the best shortest loop-free path to reach the 192.168.1.0/24 destination network, which would be the R3→R1→R4 path, based on the lowest metric value.

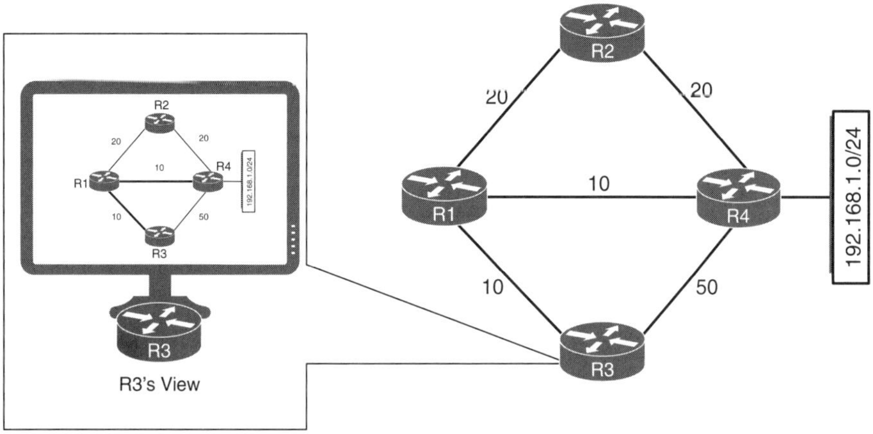

Figure 6-4 *Link-State Protocol View of a Network*

Key Topic

Path Vector Algorithm

A path vector protocol such as BGP is similar to a distance vector protocol; the difference is that instead of looking at the distance to determine the best loop-free path, it looks at various BGP path attributes. BGP path attributes include autonomous system path (AS_Path), multi-exit discriminator (MED), origin, next hop, local preference, atomic aggregate, and aggregator. BGP path attributes are covered in Chapter 11, "BGP," and Chapter 12, "Advanced BGP."

A path vector protocol guarantees loop-free paths by keeping a record of each autonomous system that the routing advertisement traverses. Any time a router receives an advertisement in which it is already part of the AS_Path, the advertisement is rejected because accepting the AS_Path would effectively result in a routing loop.

Figure 6-5 illustrates the loop prevention concept over the following steps:

1. R1 (AS 1) advertises the 10.1.1.0/24 prefix to R2 (AS 2). R1 adds AS 1 to the AS_Path during the route advertisement to R2.
2. R2 advertises the 10.1.1.0/24 prefix to R4 and adds AS 2 to the AS_Path during the route advertisement to R4.
3. R4 advertises the 10.1.1.0/24 prefix to R3 and adds AS 4 to the AS_Path during the route advertisement to R3.
4. R3 advertises the 10.1.1.0/24 prefix back to R1 and R2 after adding AS 3 to the AS_Path during the route advertisement.
5. As R1 receives the route advertisement from R3, it ignores the advertisement because R1 detects its AS (AS 1) in the AS_Path "3 4 2 1" and considers the advertisement as a loop. R2 also ignores the route advertisement from R3 as it detects its AS (AS 2) in the AS_Path "3 4 2 1" and considers it a loop too.

NOTE Figure 6-5 does not depict the advertisement of the 10.1.1.0/24 prefix from R1 toward R3 to make it easier to visualize, but the process happens in the other direction as well. R3 attempts to advertise the 10.1.1.0/24 prefix to R2 (and R4) and R2 will advertise the prefix to R1 as well. R1 ignores the route advertisement because it detects its AS (AS 1) in the AS_Path and considers it a loop as well.

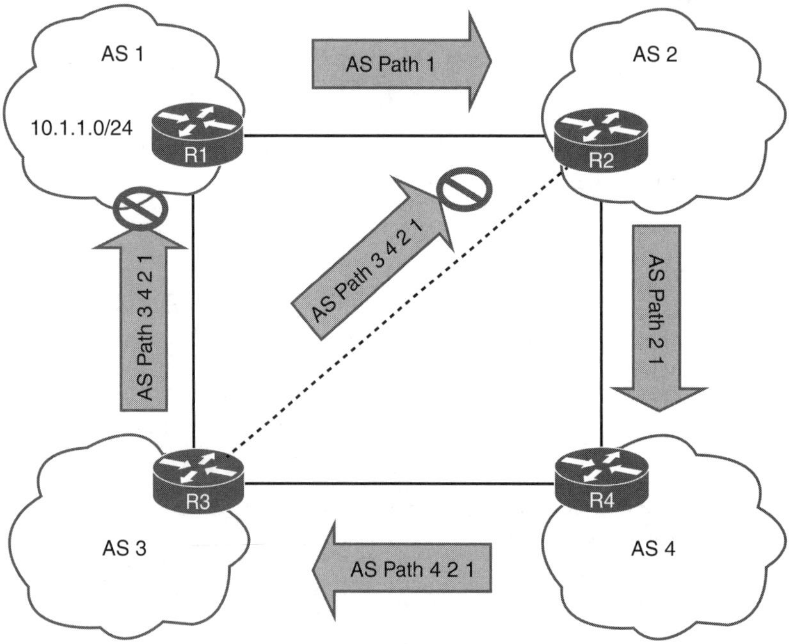

Figure 6-5 *Path Vector Loop Avoidance*

Key Topic

Path Selection

A router identifies the path that a packet should take by evaluating the prefix length that is programmed in the *Forwarding Information Base (FIB)*. The FIB is programmed through the routing table, which is also known as the *Routing Information Base (RIB)*. The RIB is composed of routes presented from the routing protocol processes. Path selection has three main components:

- **Prefix length:** The **prefix length** represents the number of leading binary bits in the subnet mask that are in the on position.
- **Administrative distance:** **Administrative distance (AD)** is a rating of the trustworthiness of a routing information source. If a router learns about a route to a destination from more than one routing protocol, and all the routes have the same prefix length, then the AD is compared.
- **Metrics:** A metric is a unit of measure used by a routing protocol in the best-path calculation. The metrics vary from one routing protocol to another.

Prefix Length

Let's look at a scenario in which a router selects a route when the packet destination is within the network range for multiple routes. Assume that a router has the following routes with various prefix lengths in the routing table:

- 10.0.3.0/28
- 10.0.3.0/26
- 10.0.3.0/24

Each of these routes, also known as *prefix routes* or simply *prefixes*, has a different prefix length (subnet mask). The routes are considered to be different destinations, and they will all be installed into the RIB, also known as the routing table. The routing table also includes the outgoing interface and the next-hop IP address (unless the prefix is a connected network). Table 6-2 shows this routing table. The applicable IP address range has been provided to help illustrate the concept.

Table 6-2 Representation of Routing Table

Prefix	IP Address Range	Next Hop	Outgoing Interface
10.0.3.0/28	10.0.3.0–10.0.3.15	10.1.1.1	GigabitEthernet 1/1
10.0.3.0/26	10.0.3.0–10.0.3.63	10.2.2.2	GigabitEthernet 2/2
10.0.3.0/24	10.0.3.0–10.0.3.255	10.3.3.3	GigabitEthernet 3/3

Key Topic

If a packet needs to be forwarded, the route chosen depends on the prefix length, where the longest prefix length is always preferred. For example, /28 is preferred over /26, and /26 is preferred over /24. The following is an example, using Table 6-2 as a reference:

- If a packet needs to be forwarded to 10.0.3.14, the router matches all three routes as it fits into all three IP address ranges. But the packet is forwarded to next hop 10.1.1.1 with the outgoing interface GigabitEthernet 1/1 because 10.0.3.0/28 has the longest prefix match.
- If a packet needs to be forwarded to 10.0.3.42, the router matches the 10.0.3.0/24 and 10.0.3.0/26 prefixes. But the packet is forwarded to 10.2.2.2 with the outgoing interface GigabitEthernet 2/2 because 10.0.3.0/26 has the longest prefix match.
- If a packet needs to be forwarded to 10.0.3.100, the router matches only the 10.0.3.0/24 prefix. The packet is forwarded to 10.3.3.3 with the outgoing interface GigabitEthernet 3/3.

The forwarding decision is a function of the FIB and results from the calculations performed in the RIB. The RIB is calculated through the combination of routing protocol metrics and administrative distance.

Administrative Distance

When a router is running multiple routing protocols, as each routing protocol receives routing updates and other routing information, each routing protocol chooses the best path to any given destination, and they each attempt to install this path into the routing table. Table 6-3 provides the default ADs for a variety of routing protocols.

Table 6-3 Routing Protocol Default Administrative Distances

Route Origin	Default Administrative Distance
Directly connected interface	0
Static route	1
EIGRP summary route	5
External BGP (eBGP) route	20
EIGRP (internal) route	90
OSPF route	110
IS-IS route	115
RIPv2 route	120
EIGRP (external) route	170
Internal BGP (iBGP) route	200

NOTE When a static route points to an outbound directly connected interface to reach the next hop instead of using the next-hop IP address, it is assigned the same default administrative value of 0 as a directly connected interface. This topic is covered in the "Directly Attached Static Routes" section in this chapter.

Key Topic

The RIB is programmed from the various routing protocol processes. Every routing protocol presents the same information to the RIB for insertion: the destination network, the next-hop IP address, the AD, and metric values. The RIB accepts or rejects a route based on the following logic:

- If the route does not exist in the RIB, the route is accepted.
- If the route exists in the RIB, the AD must be compared. If the AD of the route already in the RIB is lower than the new route being submitted, the new route is rejected and the routing process submitting the new route is notified.
- If the route exists in the RIB, the AD must be compared. If the AD of the route already in the RIB is higher than the new route being submitted, the route is accepted and installed, and the current source protocol is notified of the removal of the entry from the RIB.

Consider another example on this topic. Say that a router has OSPF, IS-IS, and EIGRP running, and all three protocols learn a route to the destination network 10.3.3.0/24 with a different best path and metric.

Each of these three protocols attempts to install the route to 10.3.3.0/24 into the routing table. Because the prefix length is the same, the next decision point is the AD, where the routing protocol with the lowest AD installs the route into the routing table.

Because the EIGRP internal route has the best AD, it is the one installed into the routing table, as demonstrated in Table 6-4.

Table 6-4 Route Selection for the RIB

Routing Protocol	AD	Network	Installs in the RIB
EIGRP	90	10.3.3.0/24	✓
OSPF	110	10.3.3.0/24	X
IS-IS	115	10.3.3.0/24	X

The routing protocol or protocols that failed to install their route into the table (in this example, OSPF and IS-IS) hang on to the route and tell the routing table process to report to them if the best path fails so that they can try to reinstall this route.

For example, if the EIGRP route 10.3.3.0/24 installed in the routing table fails for some reason, the routing table process calls OSPF and IS-IS and requests that they reinstall the route in the routing table. Out of these two protocols, the preferred route is chosen based on AD, which would be OSPF because of its lower AD.

Key Topic

Understanding the order of processing from a router is critical because in some scenarios the path with the lowest AD may not always be installed in the RIB. For example, BGP's path selection process could choose an iBGP path over an eBGP path. So BGP would present the path with an AD of 200, not 20, to the RIB, which might not preempt a route learned via OSPF that has an AD of 110. These situations are almost never seen; but remember that it is the best route from the routing protocol presented to the RIB when AD is then compared.

6

NOTE The default AD might not always be suitable for a network; for instance, there might be a requirement to adjust it so that OSPF routes are preferred over EIGRP routes. However, changing the AD on routing protocols can have severe consequences, such as routing loops and other odd behavior, in a network. It is recommended that the AD be changed only with extreme caution and only after what needs to be accomplished has been thoroughly thought out.

Metrics

The logic for selecting the best path for a routing protocol can vary. Most IGPs prefer internally learned routes over external routes and further prioritize the path with the lowest metric.

Key Topic

Equal-Cost Multipathing

If a routing protocol identifies multiple paths as a best path and supports multiple path entries, the router installs the maximum number of paths allowed per destination. This is known as **equal-cost multipathing (ECMP)** and provides load sharing across all links. RIPv2, EIGRP, OSPF, and IS-IS all support ECMP. ECMP provides a mechanism to increase bandwidth across multiple paths by splitting traffic equally across the links.

Figure 6-6 illustrates four routers running OSPF. All four routers belong to the same area and use the same interface metric cost. R1 has two paths with equal cost to reach R3's 10.3.3.0/24 network. R1 installs both routes in the routing table and forwards traffic across the R1→R2→R3 and R1→R4→R3 paths to reach the 10.3.3.0/24 network.

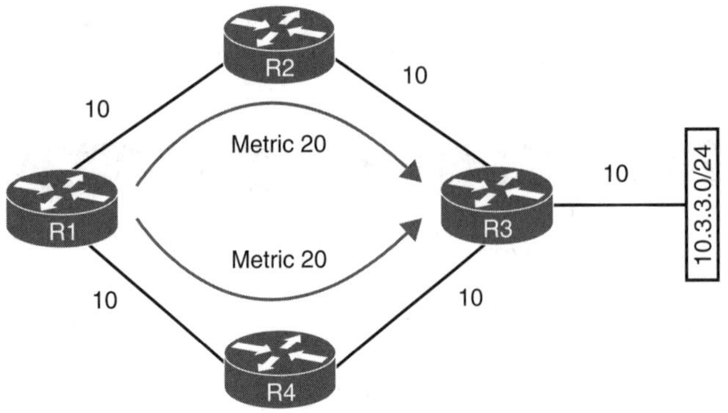

Figure 6-6 *OSPF ECMP Technology*

The output in Example 6-1 confirms that both paths have been installed into the RIB and, because the metrics are identical, that the router is using ECMP.

Example 6-1 *R1's Routing Table, Showing the ECMP Paths to 10.3.3.0/24*

```
R1# show ip route
! Output omitted for brevity
O     10.3.3.0/24 [110/30] via 10.12.1.2, 00:49:12, GigabitEthernet0/2
                  [110/30] via 10.14.1.4, 00:49:51, GigabitEthernet0/4
```

Key Topic

Unequal-Cost Load Balancing

By default, routing protocols install only routes with the lowest path metric. However, EIGRP can be configured (not enabled by default) to install multiple routes with different path metrics. This configuration allows for **unequal-cost load balancing** across multiple paths. Traffic is transmitted out the router's interfaces in a ratio to the path metric associated with that interface.

Figure 6-7 shows a topology with four routers running EIGRP. The delay has been incremented on R1's Gi0/2 interface from 1 μ to 10 μ. R1 sees the two paths with different metrics. The path from R1 to R3 via R1→R2→R3 has been assigned a path metric of 5632, and the path via R1→R4→R3 has been assigned a path metric of 3328.

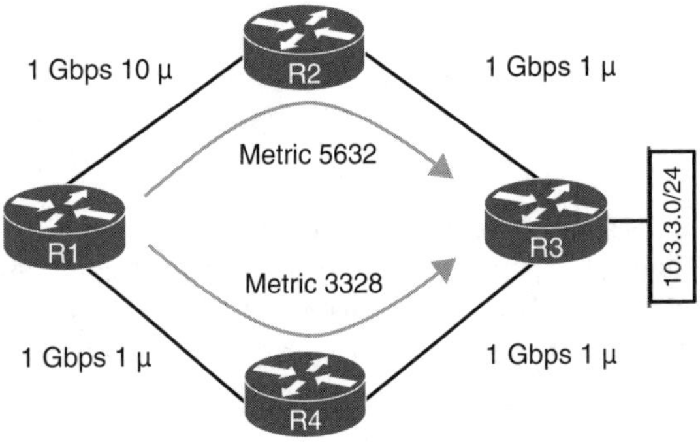

Figure 6-7 *EIGRP Unequal-Cost Load Balancing*

Example 6-2 shows the routing table of R1. Notice that the metrics are different for each path to the 10.3.3.0/24 network.

Example 6-2 *R1's Routing Table, Showing the Unequal-Cost Load Balancing*

```
R1# show ip route eigrp
! Output omitted for brevity
Gateway of last resort is not set

       10.0.0.0/8 is variably subnetted, 7 subnets, 2 masks
D         10.3.3.0/24 [90/3328] via 10.14.1.4, 00:00:02, GigabitEthernet0/4
                      [90/5632] via 10.12.1.2, 00:00:02, GigabitEthernet0/2
```

The explicit path must be viewed to see the traffic ratios with unequal-cost load balancing. In Example 6-3, R1 forwards 71 packets toward R2 for every 120 packets that are forwarded toward R4.

Example 6-3 *Viewing the Unequal-Cost Load Balancing Ratio*

```
R1# show ip route 10.3.3.0
Routing entry for 10.3.3.0/24
  Known via "eigrp 100", distance 90, metric 3328, type internal
  Redistributing via eigrp 100
  Last update from 10.14.1.4 on GigabitEthernet0/4, 00:00:53 ago
  Routing Descriptor Blocks:
  * 10.14.1.4, from 10.14.1.4, 00:00:53 ago, via GigabitEthernet0/4
       Route metric is 3328, traffic share count is 120
       Total delay is 30 microseconds, minimum bandwidth is 1000000 Kbit
       Reliability 255/255, minimum MTU 1500 bytes
       Loading 1/255, Hops 2
    10.12.1.2, from 10.12.1.2, 00:00:53 ago, via GigabitEthernet0/2
      Route metric is 5632, traffic share count is 71
      Total delay is 120 microseconds, minimum bandwidth is 1000000 Kbit
      Reliability 255/255, minimum MTU 1500 bytes
      Loading 1/255, Hops 2
```

Static Routing

Static routes provide precise control over routing but may create an administrative burden as the number of routers and network segments grows. Using static routing requires zero network bandwidth because implementing manual route entries does not require communication with other routers.

Unfortunately, because the routers are not communicating, there is no network intelligence. If a link goes down, other routers will not be aware that the network path is no longer valid. Static routes are useful when

- Dynamic routing protocols cannot be used on a router because of limited router CPU or memory
- Routes learned from dynamic routing protocols need to be superseded

Static Route Types

Static routes can be classified as one of the following:

- Directly attached static routes
- Recursive static routes
- Fully specified static routes

Directly Attached Static Routes

Key Topic

Point-to-point (P2P) serial interfaces do not have to worry about maintaining an adjacency table and do not use Address Resolution Protocol (ARP), so static routes can directly reference the outbound interface of a router. A static route that uses only the outbound next-hop interface is known as a **directly attached static route**, and it requires that the outbound interface be in an up state for the route to be installed into the RIB.

Directly attached static routes are configured with the command **ip route** *network subnet-mask next-hop-interface-id*.

Figure 6-8 illustrates R1 connecting to R2 using a serial connection. R1 uses a directly attached static route to the 10.22.22.0/24 network, and R2 uses a directly attached static route to the 10.11.11.0/24 network to allow connectivity between the two remote networks. Static routes are required on both routers so that return traffic will have a path back.

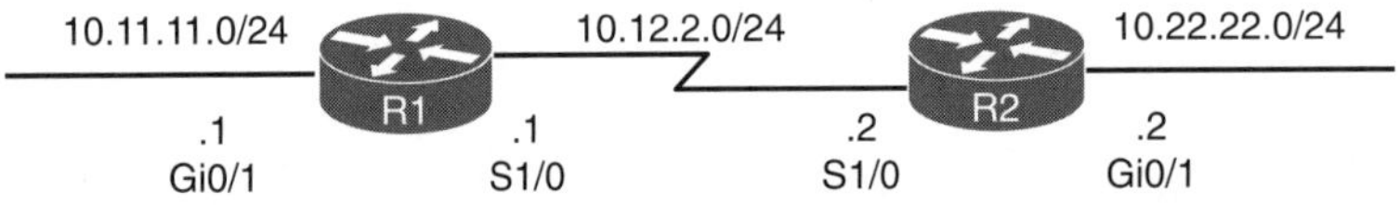

Figure 6-8 *R1 and R2 Connected with a Serial Connection*

Example 6-4 shows the configuration of R1 and R2 using static routes with serial 1/0 interfaces. R1 indicates that the 10.22.22.0/24 network is reachable via the S1/0 interface, and R2 indicates that the 10.11.11.0/24 network is reachable via the S1/0 interface.

Example 6-4 *Configuring Directly Attached Static Routes*

```
R1# configure term
Enter configuration commands, one per line. End with CNTL/Z.
R1(config)# ip route 10.22.22.0 255.255.255.0 Serial 1/0
```

```
R2# configure term
Enter configuration commands, one per line. End with CNTL/Z.
R2(config)# ip route 10.11.11.0 255.255.255.0 Serial 1/0
```

Example 6-5 shows the routing table with the static route configured. A directly attached static route does not display [AD/Metric] information when looking at the routing table. Notice that the static route displays *directly connected* with the outbound interface.

Example 6-5 *R1 and R2 Routing Table*

```
R1# show ip route
! Output omitted for brevity
Gateway of last resort is not set

       10.0.0.0/8 is variably subnetted, 5 subnets, 2 masks
C         10.11.11.0/24 is directly connected, GigabitEthernet0/1
C         10.12.2.0/24 is directly connected, Serial1/0
S         10.22.22.0/24 is directly connected, Serial1/0
```

```
R2# show ip route
! Output omitted for brevity
Gateway of last resort is not set

       10.0.0.0/8 is variably subnetted, 5 subnets, 2 masks
S         10.11.11.0/24 is directly connected, Serial1/0
C         10.12.2.0/24 is directly connected, Serial1/0
C         10.22.22.0/24 is directly connected, GigabitEthernet0/1
```

NOTE Configuring a directly attached static route to an interface that uses ARP (that is, Ethernet) causes problems and is not recommended. The router must repeat the ARP process for every destination that matches the static route, which consumes CPU and memory. Depending on the size of the prefix of the static route and the number of lookups, the configuration can cause system instability.

Key Topic

Recursive Static Routes

The forwarding engine on Cisco devices needs to know which interface an outbound packet should use. A **recursive static route** specifies the IP address of the next-hop address. The recursive lookup occurs when the router queries the RIB to locate the route toward the next-hop IP address (connected, static, or dynamic) and then cross-references the adjacency table.

Recursive static routes are configured with the command **ip route** *network subnet-mask next-hop-ip*. Recursive static routes require the route's next-hop address to exist in the routing table to install the static route into the RIB. A recursive static route may not resolve the next-hop forwarding address using the default route (0.0.0.0/0) entry. The static route will fail next-hop reachability requirements and will not be inserted into the RIB.

Figure 6-9 shows a topology with R1 and R2 connected using the Gi0/0 port. R1 uses a recursive static route to the 10.22.22.0/24 network, and R2 uses a recursive static route to the 10.11.11.0/24 network to allow connectivity between these networks.

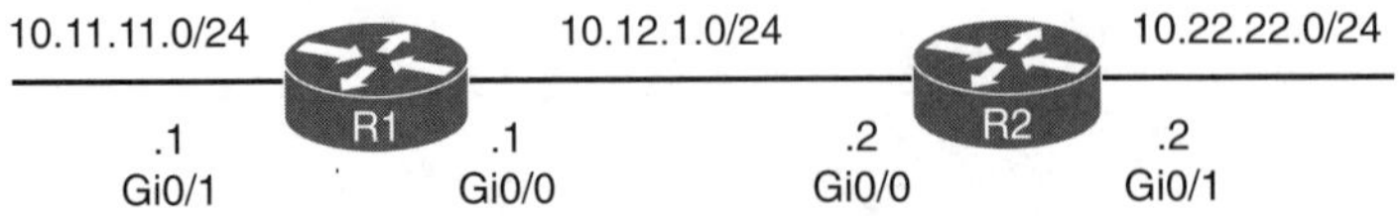

Figure 6-9 *R1 and R2 Connected by Ethernet*

In Example 6-6, R1's configuration states that the 10.22.22.0/24 network is reachable via the 10.12.1.2 IP address, and R2's configuration states that the 10.11.11.0/24 network is reachable via the 10.12.1.1 IP address.

Example 6-6 *Configuring Recursive Static Routes*

```
R1# configure term
Enter configuration commands, one per line. End with CNTL/Z.
R1(config)# ip route 10.22.22.0 255.255.255.0 10.12.1.2
```

```
R2# configure term
Enter configuration commands, one per line. End with CNTL/Z.
R2(config)# ip route 10.11.11.0 255.255.255.0 10.12.1.1
```

The output in Example 6-7 verifies that the static route was configured on R1 for the 10.22.22.0/24 network with the next-hop IP address 10.12.1.2. Notice that the [AD/Metric] information is present in the output and that the next-hop IP address is displayed.

Example 6-7 *IP Routing Table for R1*

```
R1# show ip route
! Output omitted for brevity

       10.0.0.0/8 is variably subnetted, 5 subnets, 2 masks
C         10.11.11.0/24 is directly connected, GigabitEthernet0/1
C         10.12.1.0/24 is directly connected, GigabitEthernet0/0
S         10.23.1.0/24  [1/0] via 10.12.1.2
S         10.22.22.0/24 [1/0] via 10.12.1.2
```

Cisco supports the configuration of multiple recursive static routes. In Figure 6-10, R1 needs connectivity to the 10.23.1.0/24 network and to the 10.33.33.0/24 network.

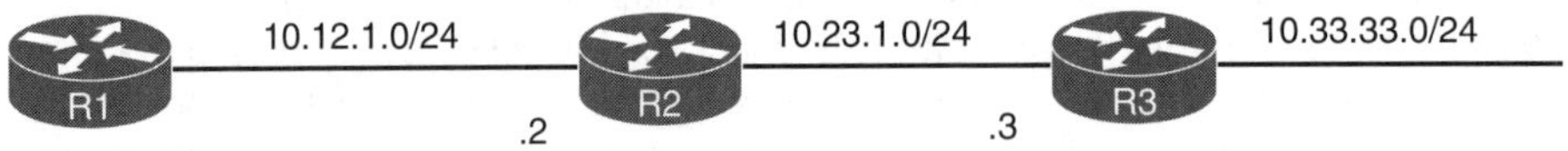

Figure 6-10 *Multi-Hop Topology*

R1 could configure the static route for the 10.33.33.0/24 network with a next-hop IP address as either 10.12.1.2 or 10.23.1.3. If R1 configured the static route with the 10.23.1.3 next-hop IP address, the router performs a second lookup when building the CEF entry for the 10.33.33.0/24 network.

Key Topic

Fully Specified Static Routes

Static route recursion can simplify topologies if a link fails because it may allow the static route to stay installed while it changes to a different outbound interface in the same direction as the destination. However, problems arise if the recursive lookup resolves to a different interface pointed in the opposite direction.

To correct this issue, the static route configuration should use the outbound interface and the next-hop IP address. A static route with both an interface and a next-hop IP address is known as a **fully specified static route**. If the interface listed is not in an up state, the router removes the static route from the RIB. Specifying the next-hop address along with the physical interface removes the recursive lookup and does not involve the ARP processing problems that occur when using only the outbound interface.

Fully specified static routes are configured with the command **ip route** *network subnet-mask interface-id next-hop-ip*.

Revisiting Figure 6-9, R1 and R2 use fully specified static routes to connect to the 10.11.11.0/24 and 10.22.22.0/24 networks using the Gi0/0 interface. The configuration is demonstrated in Example 6-8.

Example 6-8 *Configuring Fully Specified Static Routes*

```
R1# configure term
Enter configuration commands, one per line. End with CNTL/Z.
R1(config)# ip route 10.22.22.0 255.255.255.0 GigabitEthernet0/0 10.12.1.2
```

```
R2# configure term
Enter configuration commands, one per line. End with CNTL/Z.
R2(config)# ip route 10.11.11.0 255.255.255.0 GigabitEthernet0/0 10.12.1.1
```

6

The output in Example 6-9 verifies that R1 can only reach the 10.22.22.0/24 network via 10.12.1.2 from the Gi0/0 interface.

Example 6-9 *Verifying the Fully Specified Static Route*

```
R1# show ip route
! Output omitted for brevity

       10.0.0.0/8 is variably subnetted, 5 subnets, 2 masks
C         10.11.11.0/24 is directly connected, GigabitEthernet0/1
C         10.12.1.0/24 is directly connected, GigabitEthernet0/0
S         10.22.22.0/24 [1/0] via 10.12.1.2, GigabitEthernet0/0
```

Key Topic

Floating Static Routing

The default AD on a static route is 1, but a static route can be configured with an AD value of 1 to 255 for a specific route. The AD is set on a static route by appending the AD as part of the command structure.

Using a **floating static route** is a common technique for providing backup connectivity for prefixes learned via dynamic routing protocols. A floating static route is configured with an AD higher than that of the primary route. Because the AD is higher than that of the primary route, it is installed in the RIB only when the primary route is withdrawn.

In Figure 6-11, R1 and R2 are configured with two links. The 10.12.1.0/24 transit network is preferred over the 10.12.2.0/24 network.

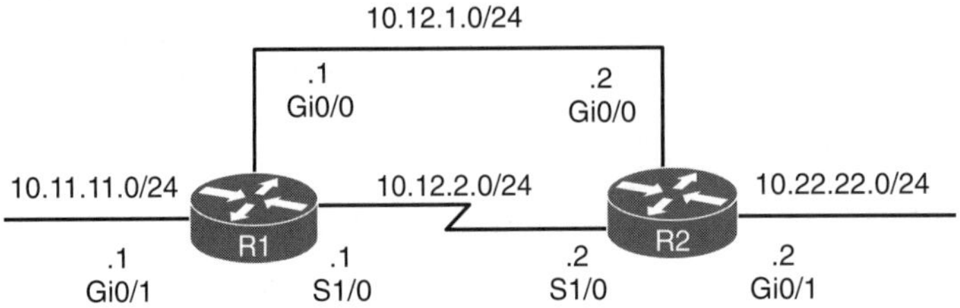

Figure 6-11 *Floating Static Route Topology*

Example 6-10 shows the configuration of the floating static route on R1, and R2 would be configured similarly. The static route using the Ethernet link (10.12.1.0/24) has an AD of 10, and the serial link (10.12.2.0/24) has an AD set to 210.

Example 6-10 *Configuring the Floating Static Route for R1*

```
R1# configure terminal
Enter configuration commands, one per line. End with CNTL/Z.
R1(config)# ip route 10.22.22.0 255.255.255.0 10.12.1.2 10
R1(config)# ip route 10.22.22.0 255.255.255.0 Serial 1/0 210
```

Example 6-11 shows the routing tables of R1. Notice that the static route across the serial link is not installed into the RIB. Only the static route for the Ethernet link (10.12.1.0/24) with an AD of 10 is installed into the RIB.

Example 6-11 *Routing Table of R1 with a Floating Static Route*

```
R1# show ip route
! Output omitted for brevity

Gateway of last resort is not set

       10.0.0.0/8 is variably subnetted, 5 subnets, 2 masks
C         10.11.11.0/24 is directly connected, GigabitEthernet0/1
C         10.12.1.0/24 is directly connected, GigabitEthernet0/0
C         10.12.2.0/24 is directly connected, Serial1/0
S         10.22.22.0/24 [10/0] via 10.12.1.2
```

Example 6-12 shows the routing table for R1 after shutting down the Gi0/0 Ethernet link to simulate a link failure. The 10.12.1.0/24 network (R1's Gi0/0) is removed from the RIB. The floating static route through the 10.12.2.0/24 network (R1's S1/0) is now the best path and is installed into the RIB. Notice that the AD is not shown for that static route.

Example 6-12 *Routing Table After Ethernet Link Failure*

```
R1# configure terminal
Enter configuration commands, one per line. End with CNTL/Z.
R1(config)# interface GigabitEthernet0/0
R1(config-if)# shutdown
```

```
R1# show ip route
! Output omitted for brevity

Gateway of last resort is not set

       10.0.0.0/8 is variably subnetted, 5 subnets, 2 masks
C         10.11.11.0/24 is directly connected, GigabitEthernet0/1
C         10.12.2.0/24 is directly connected, Serial1/0
S         10.22.22.0/24 is directly connected, Serial1/0
```

Even though the static route's AD is not shown, it is still programmed in the RIB. Example 6-13 shows the explicit network entry. The output confirms that the floating static route with AD 210 is currently active in the routing table.

Example 6-13 *Verifying the AD for the Floating Static Route*

```
R1# show ip route 10.22.22.0
Routing entry for 10.22.22.0/24
  Known via "static", distance 210, metric 0 (connected)
  Routing Descriptor Blocks:
  * directly connected, via Serial1/0
      Route metric is 0, traffic share count is 1
```

Key Topic

Static Routes to Null Interfaces

The null interface is a virtual interface that is always in an up state. Null interfaces do not forward or receive network traffic; instead, they drop all traffic destined toward them without adding overhead to a router's CPU.

Configuring a static route to a null interface provides a method of dropping network traffic without requiring the configuration of an access list. Creating a static route to the Null0 interface is a common technique to prevent routing loops. The static route to the Null0 interface uses a summarized network range, and routes that are more specific point toward the actual destination.

Figure 6-12 shows a common topology in which company ABC has acquired the 172.16.0.0/20 network range from its service provider. ABC uses only a portion of the given addresses but keeps the large network block in anticipation of future growth.

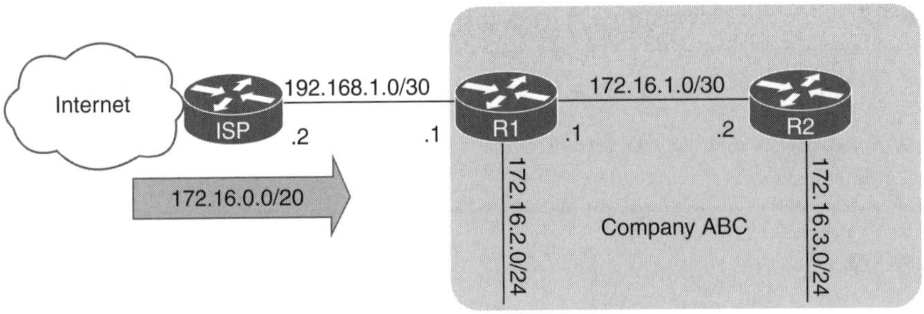

Figure 6-12 *Routing Loop Topology*

The service provider places a static route for the 172.16.0.0/20 network to R1's interface (192.168.1.1). R1 uses a static default route pointed toward the service provider (192.168.1.2) and a static route to the 172.16.3.0/24 network via R2 (172.16.1.2). Because R2 accesses all other networks through R1, a static default route points toward R1's interface (172.16.1.1).

If packets are sent to any address in the 172.16.0.0/20 range that is not used by company ABC, the packet gets stuck in a loop between R1 and the ISP, consuming additional bandwidth until the packet's TTL expires.

For example, a computer on the Internet sends a packet to 172.16.5.5, and the 172.16.5.0/24 network is not allocated on R1 or R2. The ISP sends the packet to R1 because of the 172.16.0.0/20 static route; R1 looks into the RIB, and the longest match for that prefix is the default route back to the ISP, so R1 sends the packet back to the ISP, creating the routing loop.

Example 6-14 shows the routing loop when packets originate from R2. Notice how the IP address in the traceroute alternates between the ISP router (192.168.1.2) and R1 (192.168.1.1).

Example 6-14 *Packet Traces Demonstrating the Routing Loop*

```
R2# trace 172.16.5.5 source GigabitEthernet 0/2

Type escape sequence to abort.
Tracing the route to 172.16.5.5

  1 172.16.1.1 0 msec 0 msec 0 msec
  2 192.168.1.1 0 msec 0 msec 0 msec
  3 192.168.1.2 0 msec 4 msec 0 msec
  4 192.168.1.1 0 msec 0 msec 0 msec
  5 192.168.1.2 0 msec 0 msec 0 msec
! Output omitted for brevity
```

To prevent the routing loop, a static route is added for 172.16.0.0/20, pointed to the Null0 interface on R1. Any packets matching the 172.16.0.0/20 network range that do not have a longer match in R1's RIB are dropped. Example 6-15 shows the static route configuration for R1 with the newly added null static route.

Example 6-15 *R1 Static Route for 172.16.0.0/20 to Null0*

```
R1
ip route 0.0.0.0 0.0.0.0 Gi0/0 192.168.1.2
ip route 172.16.3.0 255.255.255.0 Gi0/2 172.16.1.2
ip route 172.16.0.0 255.255.240.0 Null0
```

The output in Example 6-16 confirms that the null static route has removed the routing loop as intended.

Example 6-16 *Packet Traces Demonstrating Loop Prevention*

```
R2# trace 172.16.5.5 source GigabitEthernet 0/2
Type escape sequence to abort.
Tracing the route to 172.16.5.5

   1 172.16.1.1 * * *
   2 172.16.1.1 * * *
! Output omitted for brevity
```

Key Topic

IPv6 Static Routes

The static routing principles for IPv4 routes are exactly the same for IPv6. It is important to ensure that IPv6 routing is enabled by using the configuration command **ipv6 unicast routing**. IPv6 static routes are configured with the command **ipv6 route** *network/ prefix-length* { *next-hop-interface-id* | [*next-hop-interface-id*] *next-ip-address*}.

6

Figure 6-13 shows R1 and R2 with IPv6 addressing to demonstrate static routing.

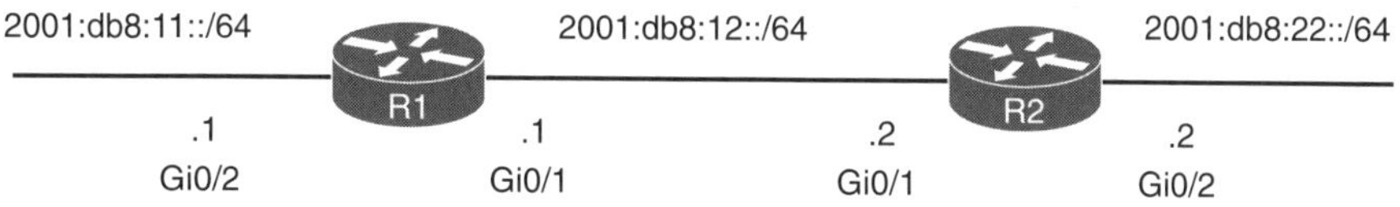

Figure 6-13 *IPv6 Static Route Topology*

R1 needs a static route to R2's 2001:db8:22::/64 network, and R2 needs a static route to R1's 2001:db8:11::/64 network. Example 6-17 demonstrates the IPv6 static route configuration for R1 and R2.

Example 6-17 *Configuring the IPv6 Static Route*

```
R1# configure terminal
Enter configuration commands, one per line. End with CNTL/Z.
R1(config)# ipv6 unicast-routing
R1(config)# ipv6 route 2001:db8:22::/64 2001:db8:12::2
```

```
R2# configure terminal
Enter configuration commands, one per line. End with CNTL/Z.
R2(config)# ipv6 unicast-routing
R2(config)# ipv6 route 2001:db8:11::/64 2001:db8:12::1
```

NOTE If the next-hop address is an IPv6 link-local address, the static route must be a fully specified static route.

The IPv6 routing table is displayed with the command **show ipv6 route**, as demonstrated in Example 6-18. The format is almost identical to that of the IPv4 routing table.

Example 6-18 *Displaying IPv6 Routing Table*

```
R1# show ipv6 route
! Output omitted for brevity
IPv6 Routing Table - default - 6 entries
Codes: C - Connected, L - Local, S - Static, U - Per-user Static route
       B - BGP, HA - Home Agent, MR - Mobile Router, R - RIP
       H - NHRP, I1 - ISIS L1, I2 - ISIS L2, IA - ISIS interarea
       IS - ISIS summary, D - EIGRP, EX - EIGRP external, NM - NEMO
       ND - ND Default, NDp - ND Prefix, DCE - Destination, NDr - Redirect
       RL - RPL, O - OSPF Intra, OI - OSPF Inter, OE1 - OSPF ext 1
       OE2 - OSPF ext 2, ON1 - OSPF NSSA ext 1, ON2 - OSPF NSSA ext 2
       la - LISP alt, lr - LISP site-registrations, ld - LISP dyn-eid
       lA - LISP away, a - Application
C   2001:DB8:11::/64 [0/0]
     via GigabitEthernet0/2, directly connected
C   2001:DB8:12::/64 [0/0]
     via GigabitEthernet0/1, directly connected
S   2001:DB8:22::/64 [1/0]
     via 2001:DB8:12::2
```

Connectivity can be verified with the **traceroute** or **ping** command. Example 6-19 shows R1 pinging R2's 2001:db8:22::2 interface IP address.

Example 6-19 *Verifying IPv6 Routing*

```
R1# ping 2001:db8:22::2
Type escape sequence to abort.
Sending 5, 100-byte ICMP Echos to 2001:DB8:22::2, timeout is 2 seconds:
!!!!!
Success rate is 100 percent (5/5), round-trip min/avg/max = 1/1/4 ms
```

Key Topic

Policy-based Routing

A router makes forwarding decisions based on the destination addresses in IP packets. Some scenarios accommodate other factors, such as packet length or source address, when deciding where the router should forward a packet.

Policy-based routing (PBR) allows for conditional forwarding of packets based on packet characteristics besides the destination IP address.

PBR provides the following capabilities:

- Routing by protocol type (ICMP, TCP, UDP, and so on)
- Routing by source IP address, destination IP address, or both
- Manual assignment of different network paths to the same destination, based on tolerance for latency, link speed, or utilization for specific transient traffic

Some of the drawbacks of conditional routing include the following:

- Administrative burden in scalability
- Lack of network intelligence
- Troubleshooting complexity
- Not all configuration options are supported by all hardware platforms

Packets are examined for PBR processing as they are received on the router interface. Local PBR policies can also identify traffic originating from the router.

PBR verifies the existence of the next-hop IP address and then forwards packets using the specified next-hop address. Additional next-hop addresses can be configured so that if the first next-hop address is not in the Routing Information Base (RIB), the secondary next-hop addresses can be used. If none of the specified next-hop addresses exist in the routing table, the packets are not conditionally forwarded.

6

NOTE PBR policies do not modify the RIB because the policies are not universal for all packets. Because PBR does not change the RIB, troubleshooting can become complicated as the routing table displays the next-hop address learned from the routing protocol but does not display a different next-hop address for the conditional traffic.

Figure 6-14 provides a sample topology for illustrating PBR concepts. R1, R2, R3, R4, and R5 are all configured with OSPF. Traffic between R2 and R5 flows across the 10.24.1.0/24 network because sending traffic to R3 results in a larger cost to the destination and has an additional cost for the second link.

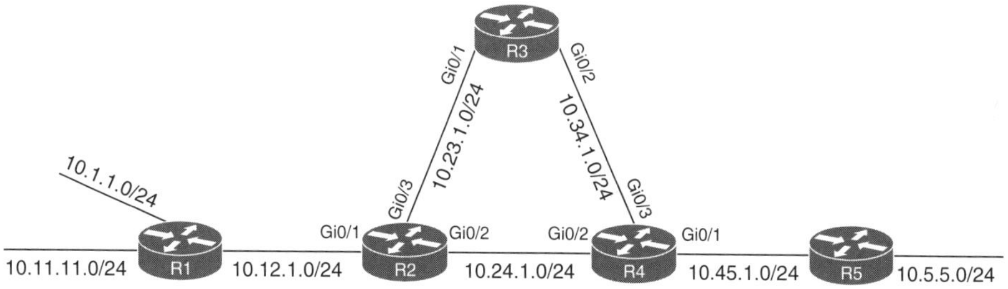

Figure 6-14 *PBR Next-Hop Topology*

Example 6-20 demonstrates the normal traffic path using **traceroute** between the 10.1.1.0/24 and 10.5.5.0/24 networks without PBR configured.

Example 6-20 traceroute *for Normal Traffic Flow*

```
R1# traceroute 10.5.5.5 source 10.1.1.1
Type escape sequence to abort.
Tracing the route to 10.5.5.5
  1 10.12.1.2 5 msec 7 msec 3 msec
  2 10.24.1.4 3 msec 5 msec 13 msec
  3 10.45.1.5 5 msec *  4 msec
```

Example 6-21 demonstrates that after a PBR policy has been configured on R2 to set the next hop to 10.23.1.3 for traffic sourced from R1's 10.1.1.0/24 network, the path taken from the 10.1.1.0/24 network does not flow across the 10.24.1.0/24 network and forwards across the longer path through R3 instead. The traffic sourced from R1's 10.11.11.0/24 network does not meet the criteria of the PBR policy and uses the routing table. This traffic follows the path shown earlier in Example 6-20.

Example 6-21 *R1 to R5 Paths Demonstrating PBR Selective Engagement*

```
R1# trace 10.5.5.5 source 10.1.1.1
Type escape sequence to abort.
Tracing the route to 10.5.5.5
  1 10.12.1.2 3 msec 3 msec 7 msec
  2 10.23.1.3 4 msec 6 msec 14 msec
  3 10.34.1.4 4 msec 1 msec 4 msec
  4 10.45.1.5 11 msec *  6 msec
```

```
R1# traceroute 10.5.5.5 source 10.11.11.11
Type escape sequence to abort.
Tracing the route to 10.5.5.5
  1 10.12.1.2 3 msec 3 msec 3 msec
  2 10.24.1.4 10 msec 4 msec 4 msec
  3 10.45.1.5 3 msec *  3 msec
```

Example 6-22 shows that applying a PBR configuration does not modify the routing table. Conditional packet forwarding is outside the view of the RIB and does not appear when you use the command **show ip route**.

Example 6-22 *R2 Routing Table for the 10.5.5.0/24 Network*

```
R2# show ip route 10.5.5.5
Routing entry for 10.5.5.0/24
  Known via "ospf 1", distance 110, metric 3, type intra area
  Last update from 10.24.1.4 on GigabitEthernet0/2, 00:12:37 ago
  Routing Descriptor Blocks:
  * 10.24.1.4, from 10.45.1.5, 00:12:37 ago, via GigabitEthernet0/2
      Route metric is 3, traffic share count is 1
```

Key Topic

Virtual Routing and Forwarding

Virtual routing and forwarding (VRF) is a technology that creates separate virtual routers on a physical router. Router interfaces, routing tables, and forwarding tables are completely isolated between VRFs, preventing traffic from one VRF from forwarding into another VRF. All router interfaces belong to the global VRF until they are specifically assigned to a user-defined VRF. The global VRF is synonymous to the regular routing table of non-VRF routers.

Every router's VRF maintains a separate routing table, so it is possible to allow for overlapping IP address ranges. VRF creates segmentation between network interfaces, network subinterfaces, IP addresses, and routing tables. Configuring VRF on a router ensures that the paths of each VRF are isolated, network security is increased through segmentation, and encrypting traffic on the network is not needed to maintain privacy between VRF instances.

Figure 6-15 shows two routers to help visualize the VRF routing table concept. One of the routers has no VRFs configured, and the other one has a management VRF instance named MGMT. This figure can be used as a reference for the following examples.

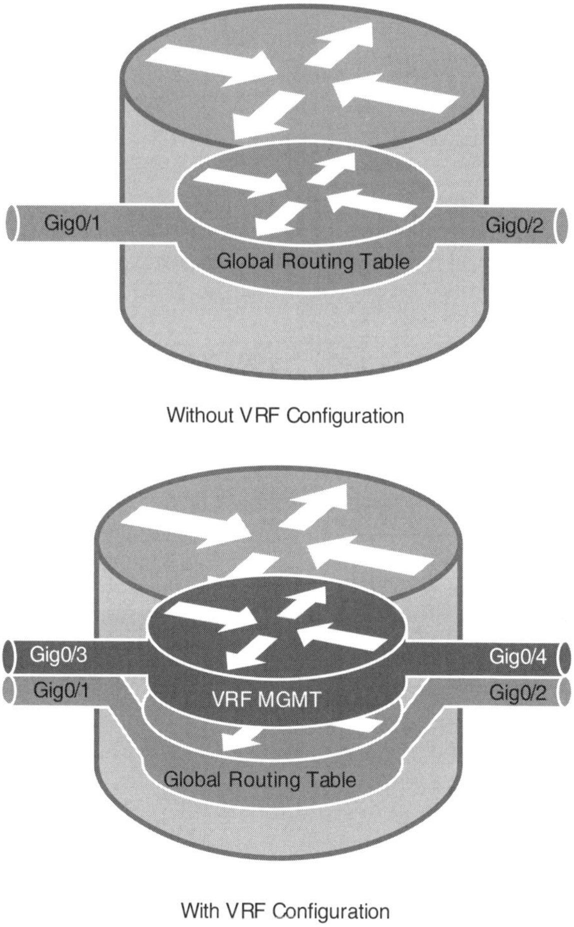

Figure 6-15 *Comparison of a Router with No VRF Instances and a Router with a VRF Instance*

The creation of multiprotocol VRF instances requires the global configuration command **vrf definition** *vrf-name*. Under the VRF definition submode, the command **address-family** {**ipv4** | **ipv6**} is required to specify the appropriate address family. The VRF instance is then associated to the interface with the command **vrf forwarding** *vrf-name* under the interface configuration submode.

The following steps are required to create a VRF and assign it to an interface:

Step 1. Create a multiprotocol VRF routing table by using the command **vrf definition** *vrf-name*.

Step 2. Initialize the appropriate address family by using the command **address-family** {**ipv4** | **ipv6**}. The address family can be IPv4, IPv6, or both.

Step 3. Enter interface configuration submode and specify the interface to be associated with the VRF instance by using the command **interface** *interface-id*.

Step 4. Associate the VRF instance to the interface or subinterface by entering the command **vrf forwarding** *vrf-name* under interface configuration submode.

Step 5. Configure an IP address (IPv4, IPv6, or both) on the interface or subinterface by entering either or both of the following commands:

IPv4:

```
ip address ip-address subnet-mask [secondary]
```

IPv6:

```
ipv6 address ipv6-address/prefix-length
```

Table 6-5 provides a set of interfaces and IP addresses that overlap between the global routing table and the VRF instance. This information is used in the following examples.

Table 6-5 Sample Interfaces and IP Addresses

Interface	IP Address	VRF	Global
Gigabit Ethernet 0/1	10.0.3.1/24	—	✓
Gigabit Ethernet 0/2	10.0.4.1/24	—	✓
Gigabit Ethernet 0/3	10.0.3.1/24	MGMT	—
Gigabit Ethernet 0/4	10.0.4.1/24	MGMT	—

Example 6-23 shows how the IP addresses are assigned to the interfaces in the global routing table, along with the creation of the VRF instance named MGMT and two interfaces associated with it (refer to Table 6-5). The IP addresses in the MGMT VRF instance overlap with the ones configured in the global table, but there is no conflict because they are in a different routing table.

Example 6-23 *IP Address Configuration in the Global Routing Table*

```
R1(config)# interface GigabitEthernet0/1
R1(config-if)# ip address 10.0.3.1 255.255.255.0
R1(config)# interface GigabitEthernet0/2
R1(config-if)# ip address 10.0.4.1 255.255.255.0
R1(config)# vrf definition MGMT
```

```
R1(config-vrf)# address-family ipv4
R1(config)# interface GigabitEthernet0/3
R1(config-if)# vrf forwarding MGMT
R1(config-if)# ip address 10.0.3.1 255.255.255.0
R1(config)# interface GigabitEthernet0/4
R1(config-if)# vrf forwarding MGMT
R1(config-if)# ip address 10.0.4.1 255.255.255.0
```

Example 6-24 shows the global routing table with the command **show ip route** to highlight the IP addresses configured in Example 6-23. Notice that the interfaces in the VRF MGMT routing table do not appear with this command.

Example 6-24 *Output of the Global Routing Table*

```
R1# show ip route
! Output omitted for brevity
       10.0.0.0/8 is variably subnetted, 4 subnets, 2 masks
C         10.0.3.0/24 is directly connected, GigabitEthernet0/1
L         10.0.3.1/32 is directly connected, GigabitEthernet0/1
C         10.0.4.0/24 is directly connected, GigabitEthernet0/2
L         10.0.4.1/32 is directly connected, GigabitEthernet0/2
```

Example 6-25 shows how the VRF MGMT IP addresses and routes configured in Example 6-23 are displayed with the command **show ip route vrf** *vrf-name*.

Example 6-25 *Output of the VRF Routing Table*

```
R1# show ip route vrf MGMT
! Output omitted for brevity
       10.0.0.0/8 is variably subnetted, 4 subnets, 2 masks
C         10.0.3.0/24 is directly connected, GigabitEthernet0/3
L         10.0.3.1/32 is directly connected, GigabitEthernet0/3
C         10.0.4.0/24 is directly connected, GigabitEthernet0/4
L         10.0.4.1/32 is directly connected, GigabitEthernet0/4
```

VRF instances on a router can be compared to that of virtual local area networks (VLANs) on a switch. However, instead of relying on Layer 2 technologies such as 802.1Q for separation, VRF instances allow for interaction and segmentation with Layer 3 dynamic routing protocols.

Exam Preparation Tasks

You have a couple of choices for exam preparation: the exercises here, Chapter 30, "Final Preparation," and the exam simulation questions in the Pearson Test Prep Software Online.

Review All Key Topics

Review the most important topics in the chapter, noted with the Key Topic icon in the outer margin of the page. Table 6-6 lists these key topics and the page number on which each is found.

Key Topic

Table 6-6 Key Topics for Chapter 6

Key Topic Element	Description	Page
Section	Distance Vector Algorithms	128
Paragraph	Distance vector perspective	128
Section	Enhanced Distance Vector Algorithm	129
Paragraph	Hybrid routing protocol	129
Section	Link-State Algorithms	130
Section	Path Vector Algorithm	131
Section	Path Selection	132
Paragraph	Longest match	133
Paragraph	RIB route installation	134
Paragraph	Order of processing from a router	135
Section	Equal-Cost Multipathing	135
Section	Unequal-Cost Load Balancing	136
Section	Directly Attached Static Routes	138
Section	Recursive Static Routes	139
Section	Fully Specified Static Routes	141
Section	Floating Static Routing	141
Section	Static Routes to Null Interfaces	143
Section	IPv6 Static Routes	145
Section	Policy-based Routing	146
Section	Virtual Routing and Forwarding	149

Complete Tables and Lists from Memory

There are no memory tables in this chapter.

Define Key Terms

Define the following key terms from this chapter and check your answers in the Glossary:

administrative distance, directly attached static route, distance vector routing protocol, equal-cost multipathing, floating static route, fully specified static route, link-state routing protocol, policy-based routing, prefix length, recursive static route, unequal-cost load balancing

Use the Command Reference to Check Your Memory

Table 6-7 lists the important commands from this chapter. To test your memory, cover the right side of the table with a piece of paper, read the description on the left side, and see how much of the command you can remember.

Table 6-7 Command Reference

Task	Command Syntax
Configure a directly attached IPv4 static route	**ip route network** *subnet-mask next-hop-interface-id*
Configure a recursive IPv4 static route	**ip route** *network subnet-mask next-hop-ip*
Configure a fully specified IPv4 static route	**ip route network** *subnet-mask interface-id next-hop-ip*

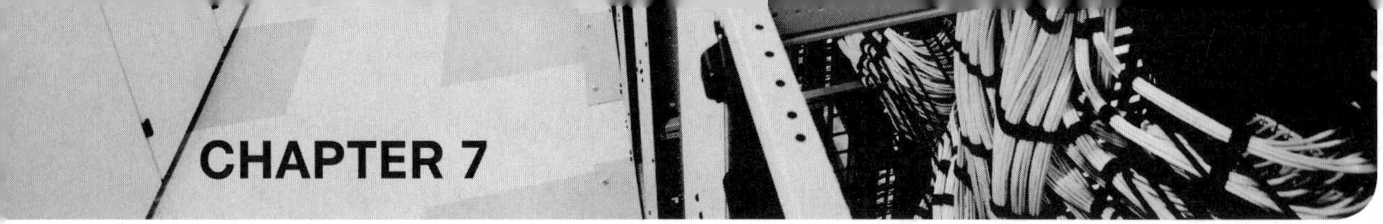

CHAPTER 7

EIGRP

This chapter covers the following subjects:

- **EIGRP Fundamentals:** This section explains how EIGRP establishes a neighbor adjacency with other routers and how routes are exchanged with other routers.
- **Path Metric Calculation:** This section explains how EIGRP calculates the path metric to identify the best and alternate loop-free paths.
- **Failure Detection and Timers:** This section explains how EIGRP detects the absence of a neighbor and the convergence process.
- **Route Summarization:** This section explains the logic and configuration related to summarizing routes on a router.

Enhanced Interior Gateway Routing Protocol (EIGRP) is an enhanced distance vector routing protocol commonly used in enterprise networks. Initially, it was a Cisco proprietary protocol, but it was released to the Internet Engineering Task Force (IETF) through RFC 7868, which was ratified in May 2016.

This chapter explains the underlying mechanics of the EIGRP routing protocol, the path metric calculations, and the failure detection mechanisms and techniques to optimize the operations of the routing protocol.

"Do I Know This Already?" Quiz

The "Do I Know This Already?" quiz enables you to assess whether you should read the entire chapter. If you miss no more than one of these self-assessment questions, you might want to move ahead to the "Exam Preparation Tasks" section. Table 7-1 lists the major headings in this chapter and the "Do I Know This Already?" quiz questions covering the material in those headings so you can assess your knowledge of these specific areas. The answers to the "Do I Know This Already?" quiz appear in Appendix A, "Answers to the 'Do I Know This Already?' Questions."

Table 7-1 "Do I Know This Already?" Foundation Topics Section-to-Question Mapping

Foundation Topics Section	Questions
EIGRP Fundamentals	1–5
Path Metric Calculation	6–7
Failure Detection and Timers	8–10
EIGRP Route Summarization	11

1. EIGRP uses the protocol number _______ to identify its packets.
   a. 87
   b. 88
   c. 89
   d. 90
2. EIGRP uses _______ packet types for inter-router communication.
   a. three
   b. four
   c. five
   d. six
   e. seven
3. What is an EIGRP successor?
   a. The next-hop router for the path with the lowest path metric for a destination prefix
   b. The path with the lowest metric for a destination prefix
   c. The router selected to maintain the EIGRP adjacencies for a broadcast network
   d. A route that satisfies the feasibility condition where the reported distance is less than the feasible distance
4. Which of the following attributes does the EIGRP topology table contain? (Choose all that apply.)
   a. Destination network prefix
   b. Hop count
   c. Total path delay
   d. Maximum path bandwidth
   e. List of EIGRP neighbors
5. Which of the following destination addresses does EIGRP use when feasible? (Choose two.)
   a. IP address 224.0.0.9
   b. IP address 224.0.0.10
   c. IP address 224.0.0.8
   d. MAC address 01:00:5E:00:00:0A
   e. MAC address 0C:15:C0:00:00:01
6. Which value can be modified on a router to manipulate the path taken by EIGRP but avoid having impacts on other routing protocols, such as OSPF?
   a. Interface bandwidth
   b. Interface MTU
   c. Interface delay
   d. Interface priority

7. EIGRP uses a reference bandwidth of ________ with the default metrics.
   a. 100 Mbps
   b. 1 Gbps
   c. 10 Gbps
   d. 40 Gbps
8. The default EIGRP hello timer for a high-speed interface is ______.
   a. 1 second
   b. 5 seconds
   c. 10 seconds
   d. 20 seconds
   e. 30 seconds
   f. 60 seconds
9. When a path has been identified using EIGRP and in a stable fashion, the route is considered ______.
   a. passive
   b. dead
   c. active
   d. alive
10. How does an EIGRP router indicate that a path computation is required for a specific route?
    a. EIGRP sends out an EIGRP update packet with the topology change notification flag set.
    b. EIGRP sends out an EIGRP update packet with a metric value of zero.
    c. EIGRP sends out an EIGRP query with the delay set to infinity.
    d. EIGRP sends a route withdrawal, notifying other neighbors to remove the route from the topology table.
11. True or false: EIGRP summarization occurs for network prefixes as it crosses all network interfaces.
    a. True
    b. False

Foundation Topics

EIGRP Fundamentals

EIGRP overcomes the deficiencies of other distance vector routing protocols like RIPv2 with features such as unequal-cost load balancing, support for networks 255 hops away, and rapid convergence features. EIGRP uses a *diffusing update algorithm (DUAL)* to identify network paths and enable fast convergence using precalculated loop-free backup paths. Most distance vector routing protocols use hop count as the metric for routing decisions. However, using hop count for path selection does not take into account link speed and total delay. EIGRP adds to the route selection algorithm logic that uses factors other than hop count alone.

Autonomous Systems

A router can run multiple EIGRP processes. Each process operates under the context of an **autonomous system**, which represents a common routing domain. Routers within the same domain use the same metric calculation formula and exchange routes only with members of the same autonomous system. An EIGRP autonomous system should not be confused with a Border Gateway Protocol (BGP) autonomous system.

In Figure 7-1, EIGRP autonomous system (AS) 100 consists of R1, R2, R3, and R4, and EIGRP AS 200 consists of R3, R5, and R6. Each EIGRP process correlates to a specific autonomous system and maintains an independent EIGRP topology table. R1 does not have knowledge of routes from AS 200 because it is different from its own autonomous system, AS 100. R3 is able to participate in both autonomous systems and by default does not transfer routes learned from one autonomous system into a different autonomous system.

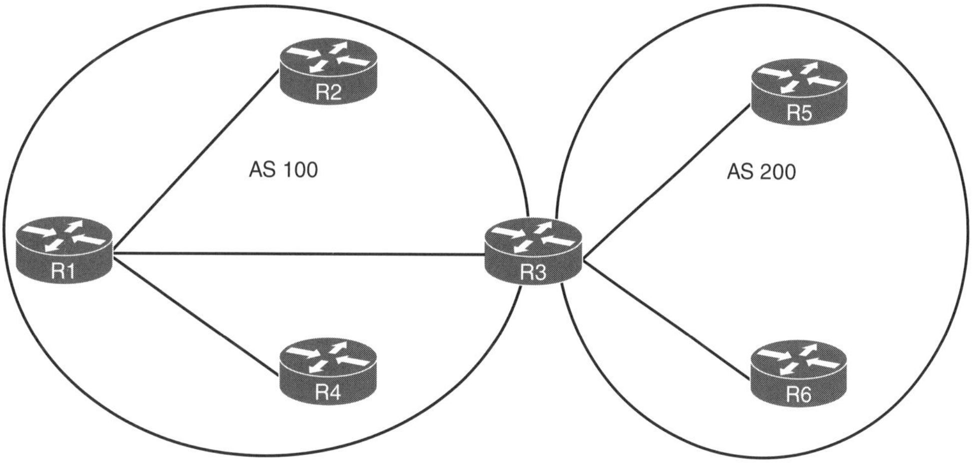

Figure 7-1 *EIGRP Autonomous Systems*

EIGRP Terminology

This section explains some of the core concepts of EIGRP and the path selection process in EIGRP. Figure 7-2 is the reference topology for this section; it shows R1 calculating the best path and alternative loop-free paths to the 10.4.4.0/24 network. Each value in parentheses represents a particular link's calculated metric for a segment, based on bandwidth and delay.

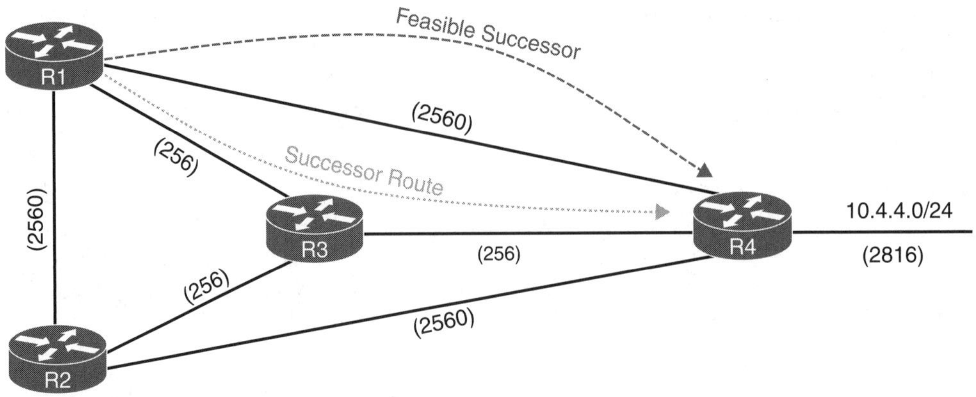

Figure 7-2 *EIGRP Reference Topology*

Table 7-2 lists some key terms, definitions, and their correlation to Figure 7-2.

Key Topic

Table 7-2 EIGRP Terminology

Term	Definition
Successor route	The route with the lowest path metric to reach a destination. The successor route for R1 to reach 10.4.4.0/24 on R4 is R1→R3→R4.
Successor	The first next-hop router for the successor route. R1's successor for 10.4.4.0/24 is R3.
Feasible distance (FD)	The metric value for the lowest-metric path to reach a destination. The feasible distance is calculated locally using the formula shown in the "Path Metric Calculation" section, later in this chapter. The FD calculated by R1 for the 10.4.4.0/24 destination network is 3328 (that is, 256+256+2816).
Reported distance (RD)	The distance reported by a router to reach a destination. The reported distance value is the feasible distance for the advertising router. R3 advertises the 10.4.4.0/24 destination network to R1 and R2 with an RD of 3072. R4 advertises the 10.4.4.0/24 destination network to R1, R2, and R3 with an RD of 2816.
Feasibility condition	A condition under which, for a route to be considered a backup route, the reported distance received for that route must be less than the feasible distance calculated locally. This logic guarantees a loop-free path.
Feasible successor	A route that satisfies the feasibility condition and is maintained as a backup route. The feasibility condition ensures that the backup route is loop free. The route R1→R4 is the feasible successor because the RD 2816 is lower than the FD 3328 for the R1→R3→R4 path.

Answers to the "Do I Know This Already?" quiz:

1 B **2** C **3** A **4** A, B, C, E **5** B, D **6** C **7** C **8** B **9** A **10** C **11** B

Topology Table

EIGRP contains a **topology table** that makes it different from a "true" distance vector routing protocol. EIGRP's topology table is a vital component to DUAL and contains information to identify loop-free backup routes. The topology table contains all the network prefixes advertised within an EIGRP autonomous system. Each entry in the table contains the following:

- Network prefix
- EIGRP neighbors that have advertised that prefix
- Metrics from each neighbor (for example, reported distance, hop count)
- Values used for calculating the metric (for example, load, reliability, total delay, minimum bandwidth)

Figure 7-3 shows the topology table for R1 in Figure 7-2. This section focuses on the 10.4.4.0/24 network in explaining the topology table.

```
R1#show ip eigrp topology
EIGRP-IPv4 Topology Table for AS(100)/ID(192.168.1.1)
Codes: P - Passive, A - Active, U - Update, Q - Query, R - Reply,
       r - reply Status, s - sia Status

P 10.12.1.0/24, 1 successors, FD is 2816
        via Connected, GigabitEthernet0/3
P 10.13.1.0/24, 1 successors, FD is 2816
        via Connected, GigabitEthernet0/1
P 10.14.1.0/24, 1 successors, FD is 5120
        via Connected, GigabitEthernet0/2
P 10.23.1.0/24, 2 successors, FD is 3072
        via 10.12.1.2 (3072/2816), GigabitEthernet0/3
        via 10.13.1.3 (3072/2816), GigabitEthernet0/1
P 10.34.1.0/24, 1 successors, FD is 3072
        via 10.13.1.3 (3072/2816), GigabitEthernet0/1
        via 10.14.1.4 (5376/2816), GigabitEthernet0/2
P 10.24.1.0/24, 1 successors, FD is 5376
        via 10.12.1.2 (5376/5120), GigabitEthernet0/3
        via 10.14.1.4 (7680/5120), GigabitEthernet0/2
P 10.4.4.0/24, 1 successors, FD is 3328
        via 10.13.1.3 (3328/3072), GigabitEthernet0/1
        via 10.14.1.4 (5376/2816), GigabitEthernet0/2
```


Figure 7-3 *EIGRP Topology Output*

Upon examining the route entry for the 10.4.4.0/24 destination network, notice that R1 calculates an FD of 3328 for the successor route. The successor (upstream router) advertises the successor route with an RD of 3072. The second path entry has a metric of 5376 and has an RD of 2816. Because 2816 is less than 3328, the second entry passes the feasibility condition, which means the second entry is classified as the feasible successor for the 10.4.4.0/24 network.

The 10.4.4.0/24 route is passive (P), which means the topology is stable. During a topology change, routes go into an active (A) state when computing a new path.

EIGRP Neighbors

EIGRP neighbors exchange the entire routing table when forming an adjacency, and they advertise only incremental updates as topology changes occur within a network. The neighbor adjacency table is vital for tracking neighbor status and the updates sent to each neighbor.

EIGRP uses five different packet types to communicate with other routers, as shown in Table 7-3. EIGRP uses IP protocol number 88 in the IP header, and it uses multicast packets where possible and unicast packets when necessary. Communication between routers is done with multicast, using the group address 224.0.0.10 when possible.

Key Topic

Table 7-3 EIGRP Packet Types

Opcode Value	Packet Type	Function
1	Update	Used to transmit routing and reachability information with other EIGRP neighbors
2	Request	Used to get specific information from one or more neighbors
3	Query	Sent out to search for another path during convergence
4	Reply	Sent in response to a query packet
5	Hello	Used for discovery of EIGRP neighbors and for detecting when a neighbor is no longer available

Path Metric Calculation

Metric calculation is a critical component for any routing protocol. EIGRP uses multiple factors to calculate the metric for a path. Metric calculation uses *bandwidth* and *delay* by default, but it can include interface load and reliability too. The formula shown in Figure 7-4 illustrates the EIGRP classic metric formula.

$$\text{Metric} = 256 * \left[\left(K_1 * \text{BW} + \frac{K_2 * \text{BW}}{256 - \text{Load}} + K_3 * \text{Delay}\right) * \frac{K_5}{K_4 + \text{Reliability}}\right]$$

Figure 7-4 *EIGRP Classic Metric Formula*

EIGRP uses **K values** to define which factors the formula uses and the associated impact of a factor when calculating the metric. A common misconception is that K values directly apply to bandwidth, load, delay, or reliability; this is not accurate. For example, K_1 and K_2 both reference bandwidth (BW).

BW represents the slowest link in the path scaled to a 10 Gbps link (10^7). Link speed correlates to the configured interface bandwidth on an interface and is measured in kilobits per second. Delay is the total measure of delay in the path, measured in tens of microseconds (μs).

Taking these definitions into consideration, the formula for Classic EIGRP Metrics is shown in Figure 7-5.

$$\text{Metric} = 256 * \left[\left(K_1 * \frac{10^7}{\text{Min. Bandwidth}} + \frac{\frac{10^7}{K_2 * \text{Min. Bandwidth}}}{256 - \text{Load}} + \frac{K_3 * \text{Total Delay}}{10}\right) * \frac{K_5}{K_4 + \text{Reliability}}\right]$$

Figure 7-5 *EIGRP Classic Metric Formula with Definitions*

> **NOTE** RFC 7868 states that if the K_5=0, then the reliability quotient is defined to be 1. This step is not demonstrated in the top portion of Figure 7-6 but is in the lower simpler formula of Figure 7-6.

By default, K_1 and K_3 have the value 1, and K_2, K_4, and K_5 are set to 0. Figure 7-6 places default K values into the formula and then shows a streamlined version of the formula.

$$\text{Metric} = 256 * \left[\left(1 * \frac{10^7}{\text{Min. Bandwidth}} + \frac{\frac{10^7}{0 * \text{Min. Bandwidth}}}{256 - \text{Load}} + \frac{1 * \text{Total Delay}}{10}\right) * \frac{0}{0 + \text{Reliability}}\right]$$

Equals

$$\text{Metric} = 256 * \left(\frac{10^7}{\text{Min. Bandwidth}} + \frac{\text{Total Delay}}{10}\right)$$

Figure 7-6 *EIGRP Classic Metric Formula with Default K Values*

The EIGRP update packet includes path attributes associated with each prefix. The EIGRP path attributes can include hop count, cumulative delay, minimum bandwidth link speed, and RD. The attributes are updated each hop along the way, allowing each router to independently identify the shortest path.

Figure 7-7 displays the information in the EIGRP update packets for the 10.1.1.0/24 network propagating through the autonomous system. Notice that the hop count increments, minimum bandwidth decreases, total delay increases, and RD changes with each router in the AS.

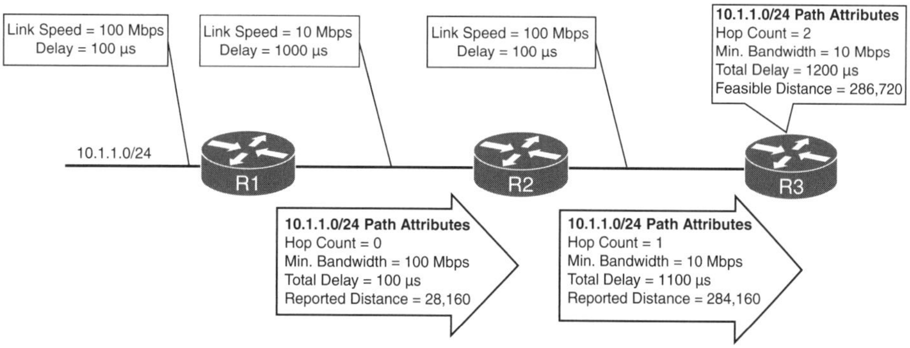

Figure 7-7 *EIGRP Attribute Propagation*

7

Table 7-4 shows some of the common network types, link speeds, delay, and EIGRP metrics, using the streamlined formula from Figure 7-6.

Table 7-4 Default EIGRP Interface Metrics for Classic Metrics

Interface Type	Link Speed (kbps)	Delay	Metric
Serial	64	20,000 μs	40,512,000
T1	1544	20,000 μs	2,170,031
Ethernet	10,000	1000 μs	281,600
FastEthernet	100,000	100 μs	28,160
GigabitEthernet	1,000,000	10 μs	2816
10 GigabitEthernet	10,000,000	10 μs	512

Using the topology from Figure 7-2, the metric from R1 and R2 for the 10.4.4.0/24 network can be calculated using the formula in Figure 7-8. The link speed for both routers is 1 Gbps, and the total delay is 30 μs (10 μs for the 10.4.4.0/24 link, 10 μs for the 10.34.1.0/24 link, and 10 μs for the 10.13.1.0/24 link).

$$\text{Metric} = 256 * \left(\frac{10^7}{1{,}000{,}000} + \frac{30}{10}\right) = 3{,}328$$

Figure 7-8 *EIGRP Classic Metric Formula with Default K Values*

Wide Metrics

The original EIGRP specifications measured delay in 10 μs units and bandwidth in kilobits per second, which did not scale well with higher-speed interfaces. In fact, EIGRP classic metrics do not differentiate between an 11 Gbps link and a 50 Gbps link.

EIGRP includes support for a second set of metrics, known as **wide metrics**, that addresses the issue of scalability with higher-capacity interfaces. Just as EIGRP scaled by 256 to accommodate IGRP, EIGRP wide metrics scale by 65,536 to accommodate higher-speed links. This provides support for interface speeds up to 655 Tbps (65,536 × 10^7) without any scalability issues. Figure 7-9 shows the explicit EIGRP wide metrics formula. Notice that an additional K value (K_6) is included; it adds an extended attribute to measure jitter, energy, or other future attributes.

Key Topic

$$\text{Wide Metric} = 65{,}536 * \left[\left(K_1 * \text{BW} + \frac{K_2 * \text{BW}}{256 - \text{Load}} + K_3 * \text{Latency} + K_6 * \text{Extended}\right) * \frac{K_5}{K_4 + \text{Reliability}}\right]$$

Figure 7-9 *EIGRP Wide Metrics Formula*

Latency is the total interface delay measured in picoseconds (10^{-12}) instead of measuring in microseconds (10^{-6}). Figure 7-10 displays the updated EIGRP wide metric formula that takes into account the conversions in latency and scalability.

$$\text{Wide Metric} = 65{,}536 * \left[\left(\frac{K_1 * 10^7}{\text{Min. Bandwidth}} + \frac{\frac{K_2 * 10^7}{\text{Min. Bandwidth}}}{256 - \text{Load}} + \frac{K_3 * \text{Latency}}{10^{-6}} + K_6 * \text{Extended}\right) * \frac{K_5}{K_4 + \text{Reliability}}\right]$$

Figure 7-10 *EIGRP Wide Metrics Formula with Definitions*

Metric Backward Compatibility

EIGRP wide metrics were designed with backward compatibility in mind. With EIGRP wide metrics, K_1 and K_3 are set to a value of 1, and K_2, K_4, K_5, and K_6 are set to 0, which allows backward compatibility because the K value metrics match with classic metrics. As long as K_1 through K_5 are the same and K_6 is not set, the two metrics styles allow adjacency between routers. EIGRP is able to detect when peering with a router using classic metrics, and it *unscales* the metric.

Load Balancing

EIGRP allows multiple successor routes (using the same metric) to be installed into the RIB. Installing multiple paths into the RIB for the same prefix is called *equal-cost multipathing (ECMP)*.

Key Topic

EIGRP supports unequal-cost load balancing, which allows installation of both successor routes and feasible successors into the EIGRP RIB. EIGRP supports unequal-cost load balancing by changing EIGRP's *variance multiplier*. The EIGRP **variance value** is the feasible distance (FD) for a route multiplied by the EIGRP variance multiplier. Any feasible successor's FD with a metric below the EIGRP variance value is installed into the RIB. EIGRP installs multiple routes where the FD for the routes is less than the EIGRP variance value up to the maximum number of ECMP routes, as discussed earlier.

Dividing the feasible successor metric by the successor route metric provides the variance multiplier. The variance multiplier is a whole number, so any remainders should always round up.

Example 7-1 provides a brief verification that both paths have been installed into the RIB. Notice that the metrics for the paths are different. One path metric is 3328, and the other path metric is 5376. The *traffic share count* setting correlates to the ratio of traffic sent across each path.

7

Example 7-1 *Verifying Unequal-Cost Load Balancing*

```
R1# show ip route 10.4.4.0
Routing entry for 10.4.4.0/24
   Known via "eigrp 100", distance 90, metric 3328, type internal
   Redistributing via eigrp 100
   Last update from 10.13.1.3 on GigabitEthernet0/1, 00:00:35 ago
   Routing Descriptor Blocks:
   * 10.14.1.4, from 10.14.1.4, 00:00:35 ago, via GigabitEthernet0/2
        Route metric is 5376, traffic share count is 149
        Total delay is 110 microseconds, minimum bandwidth is 1000000 Kbit
        Reliability 255/255, minimum MTU 1500 bytes
        Loading 1/255, Hops 1
     10.13.1.3, from 10.13.1.3, 00:00:35 ago, via GigabitEthernet0/1
        Route metric is 3328, traffic share count is 240
        Total delay is 30 microseconds, minimum bandwidth is 1000000 Kbit
        Reliability 254/255, minimum MTU 1500 bytes
        Loading 1/255, Hops 2
```

Failure Detection and Timers

A secondary function for the EIGRP **hello packets** is to ensure that EIGRP neighbors are still healthy and available. EIGRP hello packets are sent out in intervals determined by the **hello timer**. The default EIGRP hello timer is 5 seconds, but it is 60 seconds on slow-speed interfaces (T1 or lower).

EIGRP uses a second timer for the *hold time*, which is the amount of time EIGRP deems the router reachable and functioning. The hold time value defaults to 3 times the hello interval. The default value is 15 seconds, and it is 180 seconds for slow-speed interfaces (T1 or lower). The hold time decrements, and upon receipt of a hello packet, the hold time resets and restarts the countdown. If the hold time reaches 0, EIGRP declares the neighbor unreachable and notifies DUAL of a topology change.

Key Topic

Convergence

When a link fails, and the interface protocol moves to a down state, any neighbor attached to that interface moves to a down state too. When an EIGRP neighbor moves to a down state, path recomputation must occur for any prefix where that EIGRP neighbor was a successor (upstream router).

When EIGRP detects that it has lost its successor for a path, the feasible successor, if one exists, instantly becomes the successor route, providing a backup route. The router sends out an update packet for that path because of the new EIGRP path metrics. Downstream routers run their own DUAL for any impacted prefixes to account for the new EIGRP metrics. It is possible that a change of the successor route or feasible successor may occur upon receipt of new EIGRP metrics from a successor router for a prefix.

Figure 7-11 demonstrates such a scenario, where the link between R1 and R3 fails. When the link fails, R3 installs the feasible successor path advertised from R2 as the successor route. R3 sends an update packet with a new RD of 19 for the 10.1.1.0/24 prefix. R5 receives the update packet from R3 and calculates an FD of 29 for the R3→R2→R1 path to 10.1.1.0/24. R5 compares that path to the one received from R4, which has a path metric of 25. R5 chooses the path via R4 as the successor route.

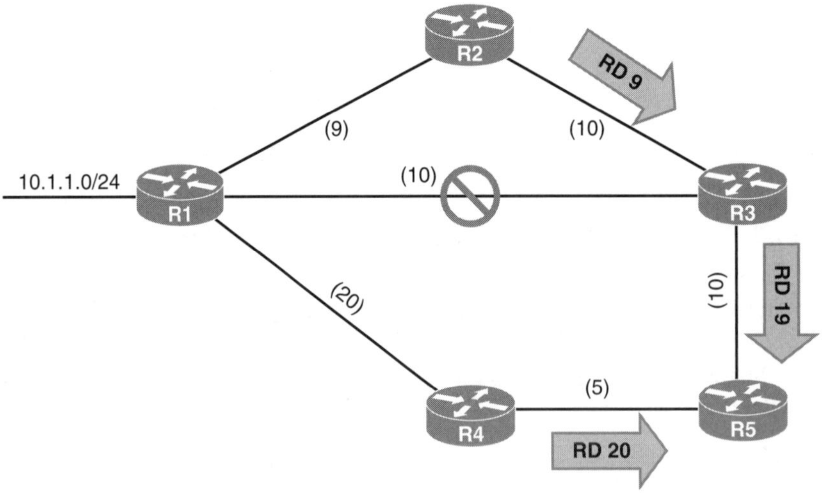

Figure 7-11 *EIGRP Topology with Link Failure*

Key Topic

If a feasible successor is not available for a prefix, DUAL must perform a new route calculation. The route state changes from passive (P) to active (A) in the EIGRP topology table.

The router detecting the topology change sends out query packets to EIGRP neighbors for the route. The query packet includes the prefix with the delay set to infinity so that other routers are aware that it has gone active. When the router sends the EIGRP query packets, it sets the reply status flag set for each neighbor on a per prefix basis. The router tracks the reply status for each of the EIGRP query packets on a prefix basis.

Upon receipt of a query packet, an EIGRP router does one of the following:

- It might reply to the query that the router does not have a route to the prefix.
- If the query did not come from the successor for that route, it detects the delay set for infinity, but ignores it because it did not come from the successor. The receiving router replies with the EIGRP attributes for that route.
- If the query came from the successor for the route, the receiving router detects the delay set for infinity, sets the prefix as active in the EIGRP topology, and sends out a query packet to all downstream EIGRP neighbors for that route.

The query process continues from router to router until a query reaches a query boundary. A query boundary is established when a router does not mark the prefix as active, meaning that it responds to a query as follows:

- It says it does not have a route to the prefix.
- It replies with EIGRP attributes because the query did not come from the successor.

When a router receives a reply for every downstream query that was sent out, it completes the DUAL, changes the route to passive, and sends a reply packet to any upstream routers that sent a query packet to it. Upon receiving the reply packet for a prefix, the reply packet is notated for that neighbor and prefix. The reply process continues upstream for the queries until the first router's queries are received.

Figure 7-12 shows a topology where the link between R1 and R2 has failed and R2 has generated queries for the 10.1.1.0/24 network.

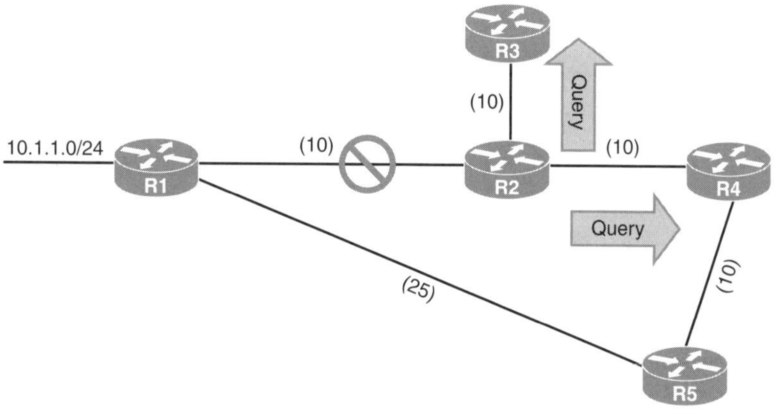

Figure 7-12 *Generation of Query Packets on R2*

The following steps are processed in order from the perspective of R2 calculating a new route to the 10.1.1.0/24 network:

Step 1. R2 detects the link failure. R2 does not have a feasible successor for the route, sets the route entry for 10.1.1.0/24 as active, and sends queries to R3 and R4.

Step 2. R3 receives the query from R2 and processes the Delay field that is set to infinity. R3 does not have any other EIGRP neighbors and sends a reply to R2 saying that a route does not exist.

R4 receives the query from R2 and processes the Delay field that is set to infinity. Because the query was received by the successor, and a feasible successor for the prefix does not exist, R4 marks the route as active and sends a query to R5.

Step 3. R5 receives the query from R4 and detects that the Delay field is set to infinity. Because the query was received by a non-successor and a successor exists on a different interface, R5 sends a reply for the 10.1.1.0/24 network to R4 with the appropriate EIGRP attributes.

Step 4. R4 receives R5's reply, acknowledges the packet, and computes a new path. Because this is the last outstanding query packet on R4, R4 sets the prefix as passive. With all queries satisfied, R4 responds to R2's query with the new EIGRP metrics.

Step 5. R2 receives R4's reply, acknowledges the packet, and computes a new path. Because this is the last outstanding query packet on R2, R2 sets the prefix as passive.

Route Summarization

EIGRP works well with minimal optimizations. Scalability of an EIGRP autonomous system depends on **summarization**. As the size of an EIGRP autonomous system increases, convergence may take longer. Scaling an EIGRP topology requires summarizing routes in a hierarchical fashion.

EIGRP summarizes routes on a per-interface basis and not under the routing process. Summarization is enabled by configuring a summary address range under an EIGRP interface, where all the routes that fall within the summary address range are referred to as component routes. With summarization enabled, the component routes are suppressed (not advertised), and only the summary route is advertised. The summary route is not advertised until one of the component routes matches it. Interface-specific summarization can be performed in any portion of the network topology. In addition to shrinking the routing tables of all the routers, summarization creates a query boundary and shrinks the query domain when a route goes active during convergence.

Figure 7-13 illustrates the concept of EIGRP summarization. Without summarization, R2 advertises the routes 172.16.1.0/24, 172.16.3.0/24, 172.16.12.0/24, and 172.16.23.0/24 toward R4. R2 can summarize these routes to the summary route 172.16.0.0/16 so that only one advertisement is sent to R4.

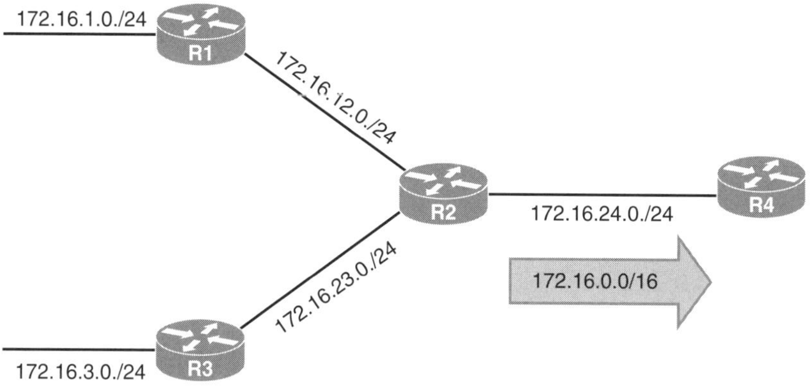

Figure 7-13 *EIGRP Summarization*

Exam Preparation Tasks

You have a couple of choices for exam preparation: the exercises here, Chapter 30, "Final Preparation," and the exam simulation questions in the Pearson Test Prep Software Online.

Review All Key Topics

Review the most important topics in the chapter, noted with the Key Topic icon in the outer margin of the page. Table 7-5 lists these key topics and the page number on which each is found.

Key Topic

Table 7-5 Key Topics for Chapter 7

Key Topic Element	Description	Page
Table 7-2	EIGRP Terminology	158
Section	Topology Table	159
Table 7-3	EIGRP Packet Types	160
Figure 7-9	EIGRP Wide Metrics Formula	162
Paragraph	EIGRP unequal-cost load balancing	163
Section	Convergence	164
Paragraph	Active route state	165

Complete Tables and Lists from Memory

Print a copy of Appendix B, "Memory Tables" (found on the companion website), or at least the section for this chapter, and complete the tables and lists from memory. Appendix C, "Memory Tables Answer Key," also on the companion website, includes completed tables and lists you can use to check your work.

Define Key Terms

Define the following key terms from this chapter, and check your answers in the glossary:

autonomous system, feasible distance, feasibility condition, feasible successor, hello packets, hello timer, K values, reported distance, successor, successor route, summarization, topology table, variance value, wide metric

References in This Chapter

Edgeworth, Brad, Aaron Foss, and Ramiro Garza Rios. *IP Routing on Cisco IOS, IOS XE, and IOS XR*. Indianapolis: Cisco Press: 2014.

RFC 7868, *Cisco's Enhanced Interior Gateway Routing Protocol (EIGRP)*, D. Savage, J. Ng, S. Moore, D. Slice, P. Paluch, and R. White. http://tools.ietf.org/html/rfc7868, May 2016.

Cisco IOS Software Configuration Guides. http://www.cisco.com.

CHAPTER 8

OSPF

This chapter covers the following subjects:

- **OSPF Fundamentals:** This section provides an overview of communication between OSPF routers.
- **OSPF Configuration:** This section describes the OSPF configuration techniques and commands that can be executed to verify the exchange of routes.
- **Default Route Advertisement:** This section explains how default routes are advertised in OSPF.
- **Common OSPF Optimizations:** This section reviews common OSPF settings for optimizing the operation of the protocol.

The Open Shortest Path First (OSPF) protocol is the first link-state routing protocol covered in this book. OSPF is a nonproprietary Interior Gateway Protocol (IGP) that overcomes the deficiencies of other distance vector routing protocols and distributes routing information within a single OSPF routing domain. OSPF introduced the concept of variable-length subnet masking (VLSM), which supports classless routing, summarization, authentication, and external route tagging. There are two main versions of OSPF in production networks today:

- **OSPF Version 2 (OSPFv2):** Defined in RFC 2328 and supports IPv4
- **OSPF Version 3 (OSPFv3):** Defined in RFC 5340 and modifies the original structure to support IPv6

This chapter explains the core concepts of OSPF and the basics of establishing neighborships and exchanging routes with other OSPF routers. Two other chapters in this book also cover OSPF-related topics. Here is an overview of them:

- **Chapter 9, "Advanced OSPF":** Explains the function of segmenting the OSPF domain into smaller areas to support larger topologies.
- **Chapter 10, "OSPFv3":** Explains how OSPF can be used for routing IPv6 packets.

"Do I Know This Already?" Quiz

The "Do I Know This Already?" quiz enables you to assess whether you should read the entire chapter. If you miss no more than one of these self-assessment questions, you might want to move ahead to the "Exam Preparation Tasks" section. Table 8-1 lists the major headings in this chapter and the "Do I Know This Already?" quiz questions covering the material in those headings so you can assess your knowledge of these specific areas. The answers to the "Do I Know This Already?" quiz appear in Appendix A, "Answers to the 'Do I Know This Already?' Questions."

Table 8-1 "Do I Know This Already?" Foundation Topics Section-to-Question Mapping

Foundation Topics Section	Questions
OSPF Fundamentals	1–3
OSPF Configuration	4–5
Default Route Advertisement	6
Common OSPF Optimizations	7–10

1. OSPF uses the protocol number __________ for its inter-router communication.

a. 87

b. 88

c. 89

d. 90

2. OSPF uses __________ packet types for inter-router communication.

a. three

b. four

c. five

d. six

e. seven

3. What destination addresses does OSPF use, when feasible? (Choose two.)

a. IP address 224.0.0.5

b. IP address 224.0.0.10

c. IP address 224.0.0.8

d. MAC address 01:00:5E:00:00:05

e. MAC address 01:00:5E:00:00:0A

4. True or false: OSPF is only enabled on a router interface by using the command **network** *ip-address wildcard-mask* **area** *area-id* under the OSPF router process.

a. True

b. False

5. True or false: The OSPF process ID must match for routers to establish a neighbor adjacency.

a. True

b. False

6. True or false: A default route advertised with the command **default information-originate** in OSPF will always appear as an OSPF inter-area route.

a. True

b. False

7. True or false: The router with the highest IP address is the designated router when using a serial point-to-point link.

a. True

b. False

8. OSPF automatically assigns a link cost to an interface based on a reference bandwidth of __________.
   a. 100 Mbps
   b. 1 Gbps
   c. 10 Gbps
   d. 40 Gbps
9. What command is configured to prevent a router from becoming the designated router for a network segment?
   a. The interface command **ip ospf priority 0**
   b. The interface command **ip ospf priority 255**
   c. The command **dr-disable** *interface-id* under the OSPF process
   d. The command **passive interface** *interface-id* under the OSPF process
   e. The command **dr-priority** *interface-id* **255** under the OSPF process
10. What is the advertised network for the loopback interface with IP address 10.123.4.1/30?
   a. 10.123.4.1/24
   b. 10.123.4.0/30
   c. 10.123.4.1/32
   d. 10.123.4.0/24

Foundation Topics

OSPF Fundamentals

OSPF sends to neighboring routers link-state advertisements (LSAs) that contain the link state and link metric. The received LSAs are stored in a local database called the link-state database (LSDB), and they are flooded throughout the OSPF routing domain, just as the advertising router advertised them. All OSPF routers maintain a synchronized identical copy of the LSDB for the same area.

The LSDB provides the topology of the network, in essence providing for the router a complete map of the network. All OSPF routers run the Dijkstra shortest path first (SPF) algorithm to construct a loop-free topology of shortest paths. OSPF dynamically detects topology changes within the network and calculates loop-free paths in a short amount of time with minimal routing protocol traffic.

Each router sees itself as the root or top of the SPF tree, and the **shortest path tree (SPT)** contains all destination networks within the OSPF domain. The SPT differs for each OSPF router, but the LSDB used to calculate the SPT is identical for all OSPF routers.

Figure 8-1 shows a simple OSPF topology and the SPT from R1's and R4's perspective. Notice that the local router's perspective will always be the root (top of the tree). There is a difference in connectivity to the 10.3.3.0/24 network from R1's SPT and R4's SPT. From R1's perspective, the serial link between R3 and R4 is missing; from R4's perspective, the Ethernet link between R1 and R3 is missing.

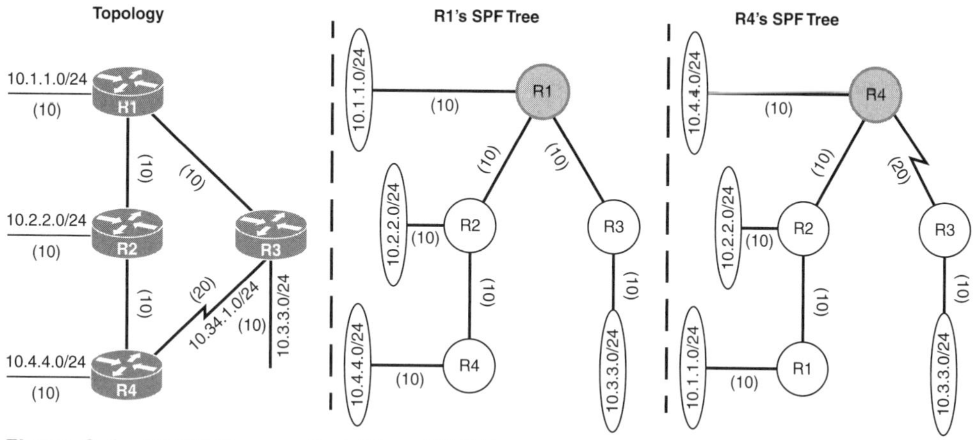

Figure 8-1 *OSPF Shortest Path First (SPF) Tree*

The SPTs give the illusion that no redundancy exists to the networks, but remember that the SPT shows the shortest path to reach a network and is built from the LSDB, which contains all the links for an area. During a topology change, the SPT is rebuilt and may change.

Key Topic

OSPF provides scalability for the routing table by using multiple OSPF areas within the routing domain. Each OSPF area provides a collection of connected networks and hosts that are grouped together. OSPF uses a two-tier hierarchical architecture, where Area 0 is a special area known as the *backbone*, to which all other areas must connect. In other words, Area 0 provides transit connectivity between non-backbone areas. Non-backbone areas advertise routes into the backbone, and the backbone then advertises routes into other non-backbone areas.

Figure 8-2 shows route advertisement into other areas. Area 12 routes are advertised to Area 0 and then into Area 34. Area 34 routes are advertised to Area 0 and then into Area 12. Area 0 routes are advertised into all other OSPF areas.

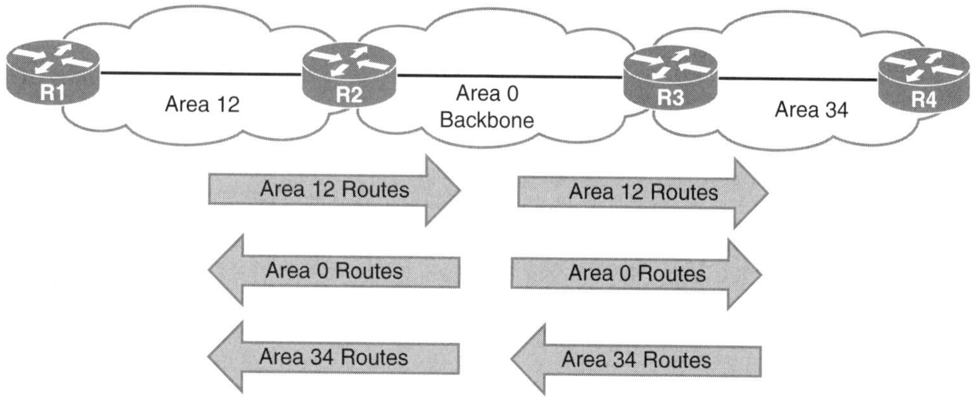

Figure 8-2 *Two-Tier Hierarchical Area Structure*

The exact topology of the area is invisible from outside the area while still providing connectivity to routers outside the area. This means that routers outside the area do not have a complete topological map for that area, which reduces OSPF traffic in that area.

When you segment an OSPF routing domain into multiple areas, it is no longer true that all OSPF routers will have identical LSDBs; however, all routers within the same area will have identical area LSDBs.

The reduction in routing traffic uses less router memory and resources and therefore provides scalability. Chapter 9 explains areas in greater depth; this chapter focuses on the core OSPF concepts. For the remainder of this chapter, OSPF Area 0 is used as a reference area.

A router can run multiple OSPF processes. Each process maintains its own unique database, and routes learned in one OSPF process are not available to a different OSPF process without redistribution of routes between processes. The OSPF process numbers are locally significant and do not have to match among routers. Running OSPF process number 1 on one router and running OSPF process number 1234 will still allow the two routers to become neighbors.

Key Topic

Inter-Router Communication

OSPF runs directly over IPv4, using protocol number 89 in the IP header, which is reserved for OSPF by the Internet Assigned Numbers Authority (IANA). OSPF uses multicast where possible to reduce unnecessary traffic. The two OSPF multicast addresses are as follows:

- **AllSPFRouters:** IPv4 address 224.0.0.5 or MAC address 01:00:5E:00:00:05. All routers running OSPF should be able to receive these packets.
- **AllDRouters:** IPv4 address 224.0.0.6 or MAC address 01:00:5E:00:00:06. Communication with designated routers (DRs) uses this address.

Within the OSPF protocol, five types of packets are communicated. Table 8-2 briefly describes these OSPF packet types.

Key Topic

Table 8-2 OSPF Packet Types

Type	Packet Name	Functional Overview
1	Hello	These packets are for discovering and maintaining neighbors. Packets are sent out periodically on all OSPF interfaces to discover new neighbors while ensuring that other adjacent neighbors are still online.
2	Database description (DBD) or (DDP)	These packets are for summarizing database contents. Packets are exchanged when an OSPF adjacency is first being formed. These packets are used to describe the contents of the LSDB.
3	Link-state request (LSR)	These packets are for database downloads. When a router thinks that part of its LSDB is stale, it may request a portion of a neighbor's database by using this packet type.
4	Link-state update (LSU)	These packets are for database updates. This is an explicit LSA for a specific network link and normally is sent in direct response to an LSR.
5	Link-state ack	These packets are for flooding acknowledgments. These packets are sent in response to the flooding of LSAs, thus making flooding a reliable transport feature.

Answers to the "Do I Know This Already?" quiz:

1 C **2** C **3** A, D **4** B **5** B **6** B **7** B **8** A **9** A **10** C

OSPF Hello Packets

OSPF **hello packets** are responsible for discovering and maintaining neighbors. In most instances, a router sends hello packets to the AllSPFRouters address (224.0.0.5). Table 8-3 lists some of the data contained within an OSPF hello packet.

Table 8-3 OSPF Hello Packet Fields

Data Field	Description
Router ID (RID)	A unique 32-bit ID within an OSPF domain used to build a topology.
Authentication options	A field that allows secure communication between OSPF routers to prevent malicious activity. Options are none, clear text, or Message Digest 5 (MD5) authentication.
Area ID	The OSPF area that the OSPF interface belongs to. It is a 32-bit number that can be written in dotted-decimal format (0.0.1.0) or decimal (256).
Interface address mask	The network mask for the primary IP address for the interface out which the hello is sent.
Interface priority	The router interface priority for DR elections.
Hello interval	The time span, in seconds, that a router sends out hello packets on the interface.
Dead interval	The time span, in seconds, that a router waits to hear a hello from a neighbor router before it declares that router down.
Designated router and backup designated router	The IP address of the DR and backup DR (BDR) for the network link.
Active neighbor	A list of OSPF neighbors seen on the network segment. A router must have received a hello from the neighbor within the dead interval.

Router ID

The OSPF router ID (RID) is a 32-bit number that uniquely identifies an OSPF router, and is an essential component for building an OSPF topology. In some OSPF output commands, *neighbor ID* refers to the RID; the terms are synonymous. The RID must be unique for each OSPF process in an OSPF domain and must be unique between OSPF processes on a router.

Neighbors

An OSPF neighbor is a router that shares a common OSPF-enabled network link. OSPF routers discover other neighbors via the OSPF hello packets. An adjacent OSPF neighbor is an OSPF neighbor that shares a synchronized OSPF database between the two neighbors.

Each OSPF process maintains a table for adjacent OSPF neighbors and the state of each router. Table 8-4 briefly describes the OSPF neighbor states.

Key Topic

Table 8-4 OSPF Neighbor States

State	Description
Down	This is the initial state of a neighbor relationship. It indicates that the router has not received any OSPF hello packets.
Attempt	This state is relevant to NBMA networks that do not support broadcast and require explicit neighbor configuration. This state indicates that no information has been received recently, but the router is still attempting communication.
Init	This state indicates that a hello packet has been received from another router, but bidirectional communication has not been established.
2-Way	Bidirectional communication has been established. If a DR or BDR is needed, the election occurs during this state.
ExStart	This is the first state in forming an adjacency. Routers identify which router will be the primary or secondary for the LSDB synchronization.
Exchange	During this state, routers are exchanging link states by using DBD packets.
Loading	LSR packets are sent to the neighbor, asking for the more recent LSAs that have been discovered (but not received) in the Exchange state.
Full	Neighboring routers are fully adjacent.

Designated Router and Backup Designated Router

Multi-access networks such as Ethernet (LANs) and Frame Relay allow more than two routers to exist on a network segment. Such a setup could cause scalability problems with OSPF as the number of routers on a segment increases. Additional routers flood more LSAs on the segment, and OSPF traffic becomes excessive as OSPF neighbor adjacencies increase. If four routers share the same multi-access network, six OSPF adjacencies form, along with six occurrences of database flooding on a network. Figure 8-3 shows a simple four-router physical topology and the adjacencies established.

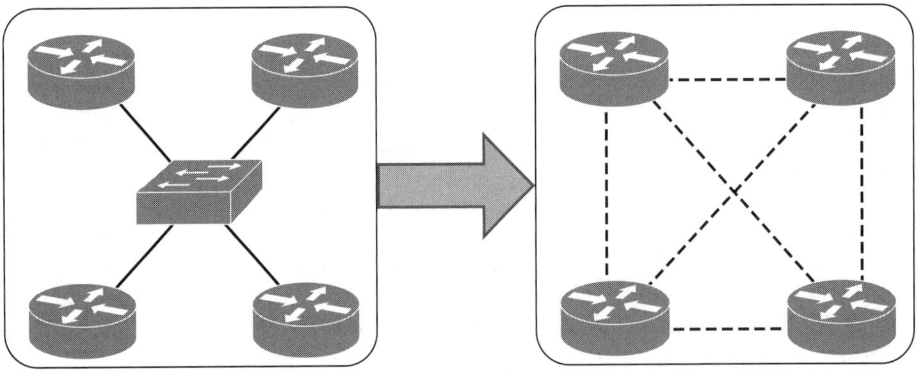

Figure 8-3 *Multi-Access Physical Topology Versus Logical Topology*

The number of edges formula, $n(n - 1) / 2$, where n represents the number of routers, is used to identify the number of sessions in a full mesh topology. If 5 routers were present on a segment, $5(5 - 1) / 2 = 10$, then 10 OSPF adjacencies would exist for that segment. Continuing the logic, adding 1 additional router would make 15 OSPF adjacencies on a network segment. Having so many adjacencies per segment consumes more bandwidth, more CPU processing, and more memory to maintain each of the neighbor states.

Figure 8-4 illustrates the exponential rate of OSPF adjacencies needed as routers on a network segment increase.

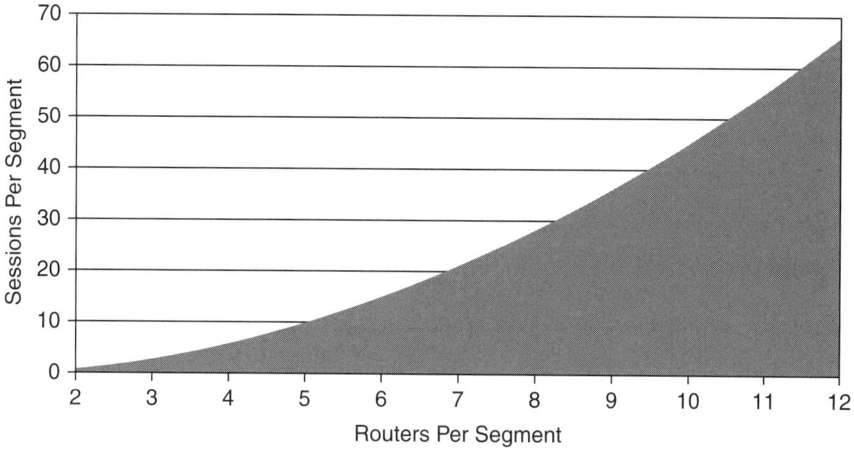

Figure 8-4 *Exponential LSA Sessions for Routers on the Same Segment*

Key Topic

OSPF overcomes this inefficiency by creating a pseudonode (virtual router) to manage the adjacency state with all the other routers on that broadcast network segment. A router on the broadcast segment, known as the **designated router (DR)**, assumes the role of the pseudonode. The DR reduces the number of OSPF adjacencies on a multi-access network segment because routers form a full OSPF adjacency only with the DR and not each other. The DR is responsible for flooding updates to all OSPF routers on that segment as the updates occur. Figure 8-5 demonstrates how using a DR simplifies a four-router topology with only three neighbor adjacencies.

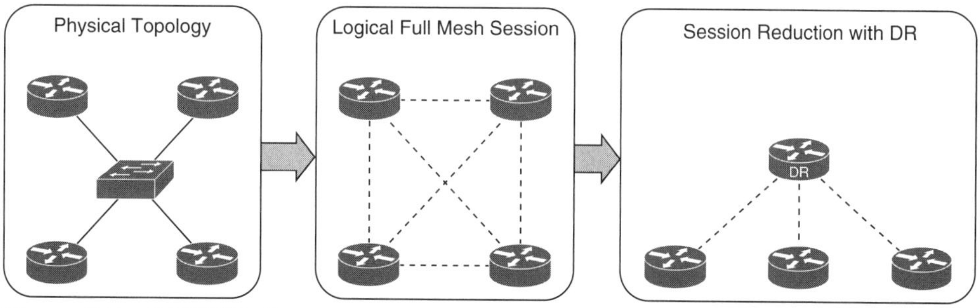

Figure 8-5 *OSPF DR Concept*

If the DR were to fail, OSPF would need to form new adjacencies, invoking all new LSAs, and could potentially cause a temporary loss of routes. In the event of DR failure, a **backup designated router (BDR)** becomes the new DR; then an election occurs to replace the BDR. To minimize transition time, the BDR also forms full OSPF adjacencies with all OSPF routers on that segment.

The DR/BDR process distributes LSAs in the following manner, assuming that all OSPF routers (DR, BDR, and DROTHER) on a segment form a full OSPF adjacency with the DR and BDR:

1. As an OSPF router learns of a new route, it sends the updated LSA to the AllDRouters (224.0.0.6) address, which only the DR and BDR accept and process, as illustrated in step 1 of Figure 8-6.
2. The DR sends a unicast acknowledgment to the router that sent the initial LSA update, as illustrated in step 2 of Figure 8-6.
3. The DR floods the LSA to all the routers on the segment via the AllSPFRouters (224.0.0.5) address, as shown in step 3 of Figure 8-6.

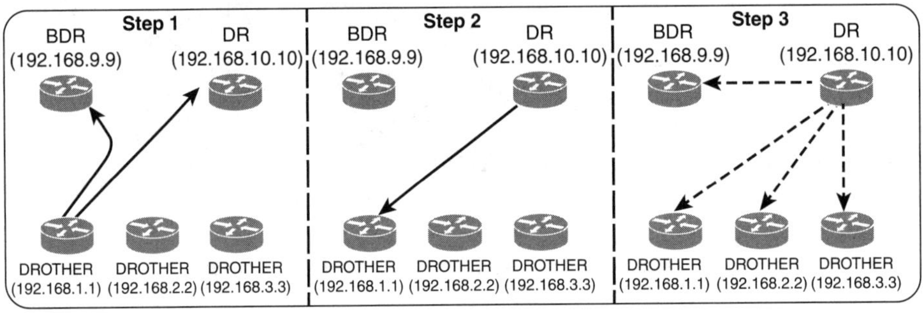

Figure 8-6 *LSA Flooding with DR Segments*

OSPF Configuration

The configuration process for OSPF resides mostly under the OSPF process, but some OSPF options go directly on the interface configuration submode. The command **router ospf** *process-id* defines and initializes the OSPF process. The OSPF process ID is locally significant but is generally kept the same for operational consistency. OSPF is enabled on an interface using two methods:

- An OSPF network statement
- Interface-specific configuration

The following section describes these techniques.

Key Topic

OSPF Network Statement

The OSPF network statement identifies the interfaces that the OSPF process will use and the area that those interfaces participate in. The network statements match against the primary IPv4 address and netmask associated with an interface.

A common misconception is that the network statement advertises the networks into OSPF; in reality, though, the network statement is selecting and enabling OSPF on the interface. The interface is then advertised in OSPF through the LSA. The network statement uses a wildcard mask, which allows the configuration to be as specific or vague as necessary. The selection of interfaces within the OSPF process is accomplished by using the command **network** *ip-address wildcard-mask* **area** *area-id*.

The concept is similar to the configuration of Enhanced Interior Gateway Routing Protocol (EIGRP), except that the OSPF area is specified. If the IP address for an interface matches two network statements with different areas, the most explicit network statement (that is, the longest match) preempts the other network statements for area allocation.

The connected network for the OSPF-enabled interface is added to the OSPF LSDB under the corresponding OSPF area in which the interface participates. Secondary connected networks are added to the LSDB only if the secondary IP address matches a network statement associated with the same area.

To help illustrate the concept, the following scenarios explain potential use cases of the network statement for a router with four interfaces. Table 8-5 provides IP addresses and interfaces.

Table 8-5 Sample Interfaces and IP Addresses

Router Interface	IP Address
GigabitEthernet0/0	10.0.0.10/24
GigabitEthernet0/1	10.0.10.10/24
GigabitEthernet0/2	192.0.0.10/24
GigabitEthernet0/3	192.10.0.10/24

The configuration in Example 8-1 enables OSPF for Area 0 only on the interfaces that explicitly match the IP addresses in Table 8-5.

Example 8-1 *Configuring OSPF with Explicit IP Addresses*

```
router ospf 1
     network 10.0.0.10 0.0.0.0 area 0
     network 10.0.10.10 0.0.0.0 area 0
     network 192.0.0.10 0.0.0.0 area 0
     network 192.10.0.10 0.0.0.0 area 0
```

Example 8-2 displays the OSPF configuration for Area 0, using network statements that match the subnets used in Table 8-5. If you set the last octet of the IP address to 0 and change the wildcard mask to 255, the network statements match all IP addresses within the /24 network.

Example 8-2 *Configuring OSPF with Explicit Subnet*

```
router ospf 1
     network 10.0.0.0 0.0.0.255 area 0
     network 10.0.10.0 0.0.0.255 area 0
     network 192.0.0.0 0.0.0.255 area 0
     network 192.10.0.0 0.0.0.255 area 0
```

Example 8-3 displays the OSPF configuration for Area 0, using network statements for interfaces that are within the 10.0.0.0/8 or 192.0.0.0/8 network ranges, and will result in OSPF being enabled on all four interfaces, as in the previous two examples.

Example 8-3 *Configuring OSPF with Large Subnet Ranges*

```
router ospf 1
     network 10.0.0.0 0.255.255.255 area 0
     network 192.0.0.0 0.255.255.255 area 0
```

Example 8-4 displays the OSPF configuration for Area 0 to enable OSPF on all interfaces.

Example 8-4 *Configuring OSPF for All Interfaces*

```
router ospf 1
    network 0.0.0.0 255.255.255.255 area 0
```

NOTE For simplicity, this chapter focuses on OSPF operation from a single area, Area 0. Chapter 9 explains multi-area OSPF behavior in detail.

Key Topic

Interface-Specific Configuration

The second method for enabling OSPF on an interface for IOS XE is to configure it specifically on an interface with the command **ip ospf** *process-id* **area** *area-id* [**secondaries none**]. This method also adds secondary connected networks to the LSDB unless the **secondaries none** option is used.

This method provides explicit control for enabling OSPF; however, the configuration is not centralized and increases in complexity as the number of interfaces on the routers increases. If a hybrid configuration exists on a router, interface-specific settings take precedence over the network statement with the assignment of the areas.

Example 8-5 provides a sample interface-specific configuration.

Example 8-5 *Configuring OSPF on IOS for a Specific Interface*

```
interface GigabitEthernet 0/0
    ip address 10.0.0.1 255.255.255.0
    ip ospf 1 area 0
```

Statically Setting the Router ID

By default, the RID is dynamically allocated using the highest IP address of any *up* loopback interfaces. If there are no *up* loopback interfaces, the highest IP address of any active *up* physical interfaces becomes the RID when the OSPF process initializes.

The OSPF process selects the RID when the OSPF process initializes, and it does not change until the process restarts. Interface changes (such as the addition or removal of IP addresses) on a router are detected when the OSPF process restarts, and the RID changes accordingly.

The OSPF topology is built on the RID. Setting a static RID helps with troubleshooting and reduces LSAs when an RID changes in an OSPF environment. The RID is four octets in length and generally represents an IPv4 address that resides on the router for operational simplicity; however, this is not a requirement. The command **router-id** *router-id* statically assigns the OSPF RID under the OSPF process.

The EXEC command **clear ip ospf process** restarts the OSPF process on a router so that OSPF can use the new RID.

Key Topic

Passive Interfaces

Enabling an interface with OSPF is the quickest way to advertise a network segment to other OSPF routers. However, it might be easy for someone to plug in an unauthorized OSPF router on an OSPF-enabled network segment and introduce false routes, thus causing havoc in the network. Making the network interface passive still adds the network segment into the LSDB but prohibits the interface from forming OSPF adjacencies. A **passive interface** does not send out OSPF hellos and does not process any received OSPF packets.

The command **passive-interface** *interface-id* under the OSPF process makes the interface passive, and the command **passive-interface default** makes all interfaces passive. To allow for an interface to process OSPF packets, the command **no passive-interface** *interface-id* is used.

Key Topic

Requirements for Neighbor Adjacency

The following list of requirements must be met for an OSPF adjacency to be formed:

- RIDs must be unique between the two devices. They should be unique across all areas of the entire OSPF routing domain to prevent errors.
- The interfaces must share a common subnet. OSPF uses the interface's primary IP address when sending out OSPF hellos. The network mask (netmask) in the hello packet is used to extract the network ID of the hello packet. Network masks on the interfaces must match, except for OSPF point-to-point network type interfaces or virtual links.
- The maximum transmission units (MTUs) on the interfaces must match. The OSPF protocol does not support fragmentation, so the MTUs on the interfaces should match.
- The area ID must match for the segment.
- The DR enablement must match for the segment.
- OSPF hello and dead timers must match for the segment.
- Authentication type and credentials (if any) must match for the segment.
- Area type flags must match for the segment (for example, Stub, NSSA). (These are not discussed in this book.)

Sample Topology and Configuration

Figure 8-7 shows a topology example of a basic OSPF configuration. All four routers have loopback IP addresses that match their RIDs (R1 equals 192.168.1.1, R2 equals 192.168.2.2, and so on).

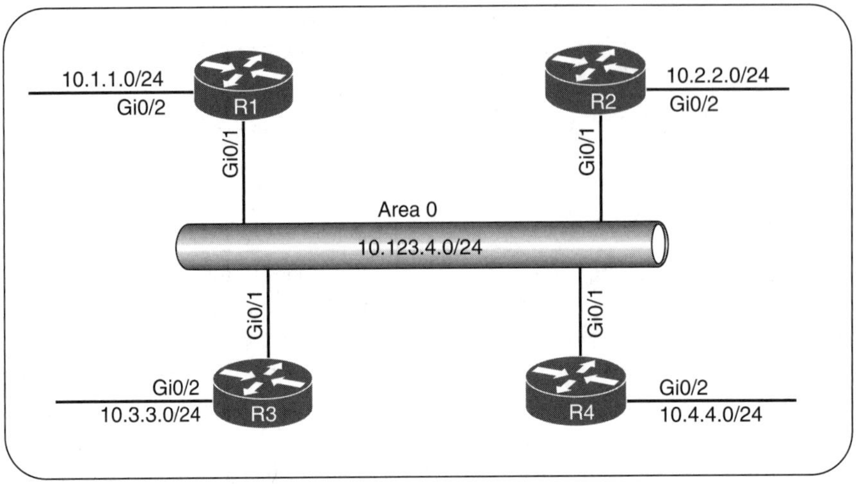

Figure 8-7 *Sample OSPF Topology*

On R1 and R2, OSPF is enabled on all interfaces with one command, R3 uses specific network-based statements, and R4 uses interface-specific commands. R1 and R2 set the Gi0/2 interface as passive, and R3 and R4 make all interfaces passive by default but make Gi0/1 active.

Example 8-6 provides a sample configuration for all four routers.

Example 8-6 *Configuring OSPF for the Topology Example*

```
! OSPF is enabled with a single command, and the passive interface is
! set individually
R1# configure terminal
Enter configuration commands, one per line. End with CNTL/Z.
R1(config)# interface Loopback0
R1(config-if)# ip address 192.168.1.1 255.255.255.255
R1(config-if)# interface GigabitEthernet0/1
R1(config-if)# ip address 10.123.4.1 255.255.255.0
R1(config-if)# interface GigabitEthernet0/2
R1(config-if)# ip address 10.1.1.1 255.255.255.0
R1(config-if)#
R1(config-if)# router ospf 1
R1(config-router)# router-id 192.168.1.1
R1(config-router)# passive-interface GigabitEthernet0/2
R1(config-router)# network 0.0.0.0 255.255.255.255 area 0
```

```
! OSPF is enabled with a single command, and the passive interface is
! set individually
R2(config)# interface Loopback0
R2(config-if)# ip address 192.168.2.2 255.255.255.255
```

```
R2(config-if)# interface GigabitEthernet0/1
R2(config-if)# ip address 10.123.4.2 255.255.255.0
R2(config-if)# interface GigabitEthernet0/2
R2(config-if)# ip address 10.2.2.2 255.255.255.0
R2(config-if)#
R2(config-if)# router ospf 1
R2(config-router)# router-id 192.168.2.2
R2(config-router)# passive-interface GigabitEthernet0/2
R2(config-router)# network 0.0.0.0 255.255.255.255 area 0
```

```
! OSPF is enabled with a network command per interface, and the passive interface
! is enabled globally while the Gi0/1 interface is reset to active state
R3(config)# interface Loopback0
R3(config-if)# ip address 192.168.3.3 255.255.255.255
R3(config-if)# interface GigabitEthernet0/1
R3(config-if)# ip address 10.123.4.3 255.255.255.0
R3(config-if)# interface GigabitEthernet0/2
R3(config-if)# ip address 10.3.3.3 255.255.255.0
R3(config-if)#
R3(config-if)# router ospf 1
R3(config-router)# router-id 192.168.3.3
R3(config-router)# passive-interface default
R3(config-router)# no passive-interface GigabitEthernet0/1
R3(config-router)# network 10.3.3.3 0.0.0.0 area 0
R3(config-router)# network 10.123.4.3 0.0.0.0 area 0
R3(config-router)# network 192.168.3.3 0.0.0.0 area 0
```

```
! OSPF is enabled with a single command under each interface, and the
! passive interface is enabled globally while the Gi0/1 interface is made active.
R4(config-router)# interface Loopback0
R4(config-if)# ip address 192.168.4.4 255.255.255.255
R4(config-if)# ip ospf 1 area 0
R4(config-if)# interface GigabitEthernet0/1
R4(config-if)# ip address 10.123.4.4 255.255.255.0
R4(config-if)# ip ospf 1 area 0
R4(config-if)# interface GigabitEthernet0/2
R4(config-if)# ip address 10.4.4.4 255.255.255.0
R4(config-if)# ip ospf 1 area 0
R4(config-if)#
R4(config-if)# router ospf 1
R4(config-router)# router-id 192.168.4.4
R4(config-router)# passive-interface default
R4(config-router)# no passive-interface GigabitEthernet0/1
```

8

Confirmation of Interfaces

It is a good practice to verify that the correct interfaces are running OSPF after making changes to the OSPF configuration. The command **show ip ospf interface** [**brief** | *interface-id*] displays the OSPF-enabled interfaces.

Example 8-7 displays a snippet of the output from R1. The output lists all the OSPF-enabled interfaces, the IP address associated with each interface, the RID for the DR and BDR (and their associated interface IP addresses for that segment), and the OSPF timers for that interface.

Example 8-7 *OSPF Interface Output in Detailed Format*

```
R1# show ip ospf interface
! Output omitted for brevity
Loopback0 is up, line protocol is up
  Internet Address 192.168.1.1/32, Area 0, Attached via Network Statement
  Process ID 1, Router ID 192.168.1.1, Network Type LOOPBACK, Cost: 1
  Topology-MTID    Cost    Disabled    Shutdown      Topology Name
        0           1         no          no            Base
  Loopback interface is treated as a stub Host
GigabitEthernet0/1 is up, line protocol is up
  Internet Address 10.123.4.1/24, Area 0, Attached via Network Statement
  Process ID 1, Router ID 192.168.1.1, Network Type BROADCAST, Cost: 1
  Topology-MTID    Cost    Disabled    Shutdown      Topology Name
        0           1         no          no            Base
  Transmit Delay is 1 sec, State DROTHER, Priority 1
  Designated Router (ID) 192.168.4.4, Interface address 10.123.4.4
  Backup Designated router (ID) 192.168.3.3, Interface address 10.123.4.3
  Timer intervals configured, Hello 10, Dead 40, Wait 40, Retransmit 5
..
  Neighbor Count is 3, Adjacent neighbor count is 2
    Adjacent with neighbor 192.168.3.3  (Backup Designated Router)
    Adjacent with neighbor 192.168.4.4  (Designated Router)
  Suppress hello for 0 neighbor(s)
```

Example 8-8 shows the **show ip ospf interface** command with the **brief** keyword.

Example 8-8 *OSPF Interface Output in Brief Format*

```
R1# show ip ospf interface brief
Interface    PID   Area            IP Address/Mask    Cost  State Nbrs F/C
Lo0           1     0               192.168.1.1/32     1     LOOP  0/0
Gi0/2         1     0               10.1.1.1/24        1     DR     0/0
Gi0/1         1     0               10.123.4.1/24      1     DROTH 2/3
```

```
R2# show ip ospf interface brief
Interface    PID   Area            IP Address/Mask    Cost  State Nbrs F/C
Lo0           1     0               192.168.2.2/32     1     LOOP  0/0
Gi0/2         1     0               10.2.2.2/24        1     DR     0/0
```

```
Gi0/1          1     0               10.123.4.2/24      1    DROTH 2/3
```

```
R3# show ip ospf interface brief
Interface    PID   Area              IP Address/Mask    Cost  State Nbrs F/C
Lo0           1     0                 192.168.3.3/32     1     LOOP  0/0
Gi0/1         1     0                 10.123.4.3/24      1     BDR   3/3
Gi0/2         1     0                 10.3.3.3/24        1     DR     0/0
```

```
R4# show ip ospf interface brief
Interface    PID   Area              IP Address/Mask    Cost  State Nbrs F/C
Lo0           1     0                 192.168.4.4/32     1     LOOP  0/0
Gi0/1         1     0                 10.123.4.4/24      1     DR    3/3
Gi0/2         1     0                 10.4.4.4/24        1     DR    0/0
```

Table 8-6 provides an overview of the fields in the output in Example 8-8.

Key Topic

Table 8-6 OSPF Interface Columns

Field	Description
Interface	Interfaces with OSPF enabled
PID	The OSPF process ID associated with this interface
Area	The area that this interface is associated with
IP Address/Mask	The IP address and subnet mask (network mask) for the interface
Cost	The cost metric assigned to an interface that is used to calculate a path metric
State	The current interface state, which could be DR, BDR, DROTHER, LOOP, or Down
Nbrs F	The number of neighbor OSPF routers for a segment that are fully adjacent
Nbrs C	The number of neighbor OSPF routers for a segment that have been detected and are in a 2-Way state

NOTE The DROTHER is a router on the DR-enabled segment that is not the DR or the BDR; it is simply the other router. DROTHERs do not establish full adjacency with other DROTHERs.

Verification of OSPF Neighbor Adjacencies

The command **show ip ospf neighbor** [**detail**] provides the OSPF neighbor table. Example 8-9 shows sample output on R1, R2, R3, and R4.

Example 8-9 *OSPF Neighbor Output*

```
R1# show ip ospf neighbor
Neighbor ID     Pri   State           Dead Time   Address         Interface
192.168.2.2       1   2WAY/DROTHER    00:00:37    10.123.4.2      GigabitEthernet0/1
192.168.3.3       1   FULL/BDR        00:00:35    10.123.4.3      GigabitEthernet0/1
192.168.4.4       1   FULL/DR         00:00:33    10.123.4.4      GigabitEthernet0/1
```

```
R2# show ip ospf neighbor
Neighbor ID     Pri   State           Dead Time   Address         Interface
192.168.1.1       1   2WAY/DROTHER    00:00:30    10.123.4.1      GigabitEthernet0/1
192.168.3.3       1   FULL/BDR        00:00:32    10.123.4.3      GigabitEthernet0/1
192.168.4.4       1   FULL/DR         00:00:31    10.123.4.4      GigabitEthernet0/1
```

```
R3# show ip ospf neighbor
Neighbor ID     Pri   State           Dead Time   Address         Interface
192.168.1.1       1   FULL/DROTHER    00:00:35    10.123.4.1      GigabitEthernet0/1
192.168.2.2       1   FULL/DROTHER    00:00:34    10.123.4.2      GigabitEthernet0/1
192.168.4.4       1   FULL/DR         00:00:31    10.123.4.4      GigabitEthernet0/1
```

```
R4# show ip ospf neighbor
Neighbor ID     Pri   State           Dead Time   Address         Interface
192.168.1.1       1   FULL/DROTHER    00:00:36    10.123.4.1      GigabitEthernet0/1
192.168.2.2       1   FULL/DROTHER    00:00:34    10.123.4.2      GigabitEthernet0/1
192.168.3.3       1   FULL/BDR        00:00:35    10.123.4.3      GigabitEthernet0/1
```

Table 8-7 provides a brief overview of the fields shown in Example 8-9. The neighbor states on R1 identify R3 as the BDR and R4 as the DR. R3 and R4 identify R1 and R2 as DROTHER in the output.

Key Topic

Table 8-7 OSPF Neighbor State Fields

Field	Description
Neighbor ID	The router ID (RID) of the neighboring router.
PRI	The priority for the neighbor's interface, which is used for DR/BDR elections.
State	The first field is the neighbor state, as described in Table 8-4. The second field is the DR, BDR, or DROTHER role if the interface requires a DR. For non-DR network links, the second field shows just a hyphen (-).
Dead Time	The time left until the router is declared unreachable.
Address	The primary IP address for the OSPF neighbor.
Interface	The local interface to which the OSPF neighbor is attached.

Verification of OSPF Routes

The next step is to verify the OSPF routes installed in the IP routing table. OSPF routes that install into the Routing Information Base (RIB) are shown with the command **show ip route ospf**.

Example 8-10 provides sample output of the OSPF routing table for R1. In the output, where two sets of numbers are in the brackets (for example, [110/2], the first number is the administrative distance (AD), which is 110 by default for OSPF, and the second number is the metric of the path used for that network. The output for R2, R3, and R4 would be similar to the output in Example 8-10.

Example 8-10 *OSPF Routes Installed in the RIB*

```
R1# show ip route ospf
! Output omitted for brevity
Codes: L - local, C - connected, S - static, R - RIP, M - mobile, B - BGP
       D - EIGRP, EX - EIGRP external, O - OSPF, IA - OSPF inter area
       N1 - OSPF NSSA external type 1, N2 - OSPF NSSA external type 2
       E1 - OSPF external type 1, E2 - OSPF external type 2
Gateway of last resort is not set

      10.0.0.0/8 is variably subnetted, 7 subnets, 2 masks
O        10.2.2.0/24 [110/2] via 10.123.4.2, 00:35:03, GigabitEthernet0/1
O        10.3.3.0/24 [110/2] via 10.123.4.3, 00:35:03, GigabitEthernet0/1
O        10.4.4.0/24 [110/2] via 10.123.4.4, 00:35:03, GigabitEthernet0/1
      192.168.2.0/32 is subnetted, 1 subnets
O        192.168.2.2 [110/2] via 10.123.4.2, 00:35:03, GigabitEthernet0/1
      192.168.3.0/32 is subnetted, 1 subnets
O        192.168.3.3 [110/2] via 10.123.4.3, 00:35:03, GigabitEthernet0/1
      192.168.4.0/32 is subnetted, 1 subnets
O        192.168.4.4 [110/2] via 10.123.4.4, 00:35:03, GigabitEthernet0/1
```

NOTE The terms *path cost* and *path metric* are synonymous from OSPF's perspective.

Key Topic

Default Route Advertisement

OSPF supports advertising the default route into the OSPF domain. The default route is advertised by using the command **default-information originate** [**always**] [**metric** *metric-value*] [**metric-type** *type-value*] underneath the OSPF process.

If a default route does not exist in a routing table, the **always** optional keyword advertises a default route regardless of whether a default route exists in the RIB or not. In addition, the route metric can be changed with the **metric** *metric-value* option, and the metric type can be changed with the **metric-type** *type-value* option.

Figure 8-8 illustrates a common scenario, where R1 has a static default route to a firewall that is connected to the Internet. To provide connectivity to other parts of the network (for example, R2 and R3), R1 advertises a default route into OSPF.

8

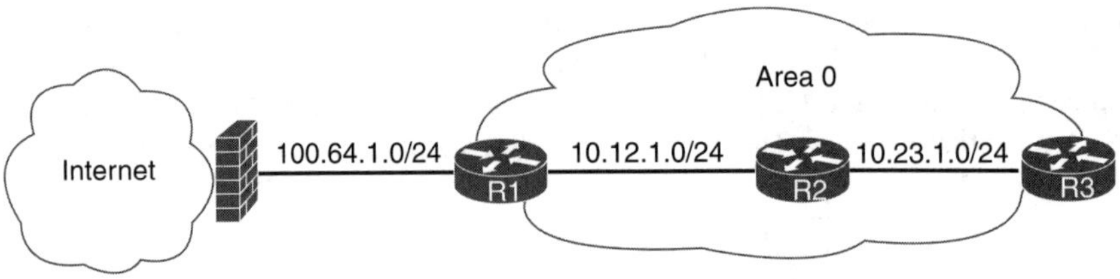

Figure 8-8 *Default Route Topology*

Example 8-11 provides the relevant configuration on R1. Notice that R1 has a static default route to the firewall (100.64.1.2) to satisfy the requirement of having the default route in the RIB, so the **always** keyword is not required.

Example 8-11 *OSPF Default Information Origination Configuration*

```
R1
ip route 0.0.0.0 0.0.0.0 100.64.1.2
!
router ospf 1
 network 10.0.0.0 0.255.255.255 area 0
 default-information originate
```

Example 8-12 provides the routing tables for R2 and R3. Notice that OSPF advertises the default route as an external OSPF route.

Example 8-12 *Routing Tables for R2 and R3*

```
R2# show ip route | begin Gateway
Gateway of last resort is 10.12.1.1 to network 0.0.0.0
O*E2   0.0.0.0/0 [110/1] via 10.12.1.1, 00:02:56, GigabitEthernet0/1
        10.0.0.0/8 is variably subnetted, 4 subnets, 2 masks
C             10.12.1.0/24 is directly connected, GigabitEthernet0/1
C             10.23.1.0/24 is directly connected, GigabitEthernet0/2
```

```
R3# show ip route | begin Gateway
Gateway of last resort is 10.23.1.2 to network 0.0.0.0
O*E2  0.0.0.0/0 [110/1] via 10.23.1.2, 00:01:47, GigabitEthernet0/1
       10.0.0.0/8 is variably subnetted, 3 subnets, 2 masks
O         10.12.1.0/24 [110/2] via 10.23.1.2, 00:05:20, GigabitEthernet0/1
C         10.23.1.0/24 is directly connected, GigabitEthernet0/1
```

Common OSPF Optimizations

Almost every network requires tuning based on the equipment, technical requirements, or a variety of other factors. The following sections explain common concepts involved with the tuning of an OSPF network.

Key Topic

Link Costs

Interface cost is an essential component of Dijkstra's SPF calculation because the shortest path metric is based on the cumulative interface cost (that is, metric) from the router to the destination. OSPF assigns the OSPF link cost (that is, metric) for an interface by using the formula in Figure 8-9.

$$\text{Cost} = \frac{\text{Reference Bandwidth}}{\text{Interface Bandwidth}}$$

Figure 8-9 *OSPF Interface Cost Formula*

The default reference bandwidth is 100 Mbps. Table 8-8 provides the OSPF cost for common network interface types using the default reference bandwidth.

Table 8-8 OSPF Interface Costs Using Default Settings

Interface Type	OSPF Cost
T1	64
Ethernet	10
FastEthernet	1
GigabitEthernet	1
10 GigabitEthernet	1

Notice in Table 8-8 that there is no differentiation in the link cost associated with a FastEthernet interface and a 10 GigabitEthernet interface. Changing the reference bandwidth to a higher value allows for a differentiation of cost between higher-speed interfaces. Making the value too high could cause issues because low-bandwidth interfaces would not be distinguishable. The OSPF LSA metric field is 16 bits, and the interface cost cannot exceed 65,535.

Under the OSPF process, the command **auto-cost reference-bandwidth** *bandwidth-in-mbps* changes the reference bandwidth for all OSPF interfaces associated with that process. If the reference bandwidth is changed on one router, the reference bandwidth should be changed on all OSPF routers to ensure that SPF uses the same logic to prevent routing loops. It is a best practice to set the same reference bandwidth for all OSPF routers.

8

NOTE NX-OS uses a default reference cost of 40,000 Mbps. To align with other routers and incorporate higher-speed interfaces, setting the reference bandwidth to 40,000 Mbps could standardize the reference bandwidth across multiple platforms.

The OSPF cost can be set manually with the command **ip ospf cost** *1–65535* under the interface configuration submode. While the interface cost is limited to 65,535 because of LSA field limitations, the path metric can exceed a 16-bit value (65,535) because all the link metrics are calculated locally.

Key Topic

Failure Detection

A secondary function of the OSPF hello packets is to ensure that adjacent OSPF neighbors are still healthy and available. OSPF sends hello packets at set intervals, based on the hello timer. OSPF uses a second timer called the *OSPF dead interval timer*, which defaults to four times the hello timer. Upon receipt of a hello packet from a neighboring router, the OSPF dead timer resets to the initial value and then starts to decrement again.

If a router does not receive a hello before the OSPF dead interval timer reaches 0, the neighbor state is changed to down. The OSPF router immediately sends out the appropriate LSA, reflecting the topology change, and the SPF algorithm processes on all routers within the area.

Hello Timer

The default OSPF hello timer interval varies based on the OSPF network type. OSPF allows modification to the hello timer interval with values between 1 and 65,535 seconds. Changing the hello timer interval modifies the default dead interval too. The OSPF hello timer is modified with the interface configuration submode command **ip ospf hello-interval** *1–65535*.

Dead Interval Timer

The dead interval timer can be changed to a value between 1 and 65,535 seconds. The OSPF dead interval timer can be changed with the command **ip ospf dead-interval** *1–65535* under the interface configuration submode.

NOTE Always make sure that the dead interval timer setting is greater than the hello timer setting to ensure that the dead interval timer does not reach 0 in between hello packets.

OSPF Timers

The timers for an OSPF interface are shown with the command **show ip ospf interface**, as demonstrated in Example 8-13. Notice the highlighted hello and dead timers.

Example 8-13 *OSPF Interface Timers*

```
R1# show ip ospf interface | i Timer|line
Loopback0 is up, line protocol is up
GigabitEthernet0/2 is up, line protocol is up
  Timer intervals configured, Hello 10, Dead 40, Wait 40, Retransmit 5
GigabitEthernet0/1 is up, line protocol is up
  Timer intervals configured, Hello 10, Dead 40, Wait 40, Retransmit 5
```

NOTE Hello and dead interval timers must match for OSPF neighbors to become adjacent.

DR Placement

The DR and BDR roles for a broadcast network consume CPU and memory on the host routers in order to maintain states with all the other routers for that segment. Placing the DR and BDR roles on routers with adequate resources is recommended.

The following sections explain the DR election process and how the DR role can be assigned to specific hardware.

Key Topic

Designated Router Elections

The DR/BDR election occurs during OSPF adjacency—specifically during the last phase of 2-Way neighbor state and just before the ExStart state. When a router enters the 2-Way state, it has already received a hello from the neighbor. If the hello packet includes an RID other than 0.0.0.0 for the DR or BDR, the new router assumes that the current routers are the actual DR and BDR.

Any router with an OSPF priority of 1 to 255 on its OSPF interface attempts to become the DR. By default, all OSPF interfaces use a priority of 1. The routers place their RID and OSPF priorities in their OSPF hellos for that segment.

Routers then receive and examine OSPF hellos from neighboring routers. If a router identifies itself as being a more favorable router than the OSPF hellos it receives, it continues to send out hellos with its RID and priority listed. If the hello received is more favorable, the router updates its OSPF hello packet to use the more preferable RID in the DR field. OSPF deems a router more preferable if the priority for the interface is the highest for that segment. If the OSPF priority is the same, the higher RID is more favorable.

After all the routers have agreed on the same DR, all routers for that segment become adjacent with the DR. Then the election for the BDR takes place. The election follows the same logic for the DR election, except that the DR does not add its RID to the BDR field of the hello packet.

The OSPF DR and BDR roles cannot be preempted after the DR/BDR election. Only upon the failure (or process restart of the DR or BDR) does the election start to replace the role that is missing.

NOTE To ensure that all routers on a segment have fully initialized, OSPF initiates a wait timer when OSPF hello packets do not contain a DR/BDR router for a segment. The default value for the wait timer is the dead interval timer. After the wait timer has expired, a router participates in the DR election. The wait timer starts when OSPF first starts on an interface; so that a router can still elect itself as the DR for a segment without other OSPF routers, it waits until the wait timer expires.

The easiest way to determine the interface role is by viewing the OSPF interface with the command **show ip ospf interface brief**. Example 8-14 shows this command executed on R1 and R3 of the sample topology. Notice that R1's Gi0/2 interface is the DR for the 10.1.1.0/24 network (because no other router is present), and R1's Gi0/1 interface is DROTHER for the 10.123.4.0/24 segment. R3's Gi0/1 interface is the BDR for the 10.123.4.0/24 network segment.

8

Example 8-14 *OSPF Interface State*

```
R1# show ip ospf interface brief
Interface    PID   Area            IP Address/Mask    Cost  State Nbrs F/C
Lo0            1     0               192.168.1.1/32      1      LOOP  0/0
Gi0/2          1     0               10.1.1.1/24         1      DR      0/0
Gi0/1          1     0               10.123.4.1/24       1      DROTH 2/3
```

```
R3# show ip ospf interface brief
Interface    PID   Area            IP Address/Mask    Cost  State Nbrs F/C
Lo0            1     0               192.168.3.3/32      1      LOOP   0/0
Gi0/1          1     0               10.123.4.3/24       1      BDR    3/3
Gi0/2          1     0               10.3.3.3/24         1      DR       0/0
```

The neighbor's full adjacency field reflects the number of routers that have become adjacent on that network segment; the neighbors count field is the number of other OSPF routers on that segment. You might assume that all routers will become adjacent with each other, but that would defeat the purpose of using a DR. Only the DR and BDR become adjacent with routers on a network segment.

DR and BDR Placement

In Example 8-14, R4 won the DR election, and R3 won the BDR election because all the OSPF routers had the same OSPF priority, so the next decision point was the higher RID. The RIDs matched the Loopback 0 interface IP addresses, and R4's loopback address is the highest on that segment; R3's is the second highest.

Modifying a router's RID for DR placement is a bad design strategy. A better technique involves modifying the interface priority to a higher value than the existing DR has. In our current topology, the DR role for the segment (10.123.4.0/24) requires that the priority change to a higher value than 1 (the existing DR's priority) on the desired node. Remember that OSPF does not preempt the DR or BDR roles, and the OSPF process might need to be restarted on the current DR/BDR for the changes to take effect.

The priority can be set manually under the interface configuration with the command **ip ospf priority** *0–255*. Setting an interface priority to 0 removes that interface from the DR/BDR election immediately. Raising the priority above the default value (1) makes that interface more favorable compared to interfaces with the default value.

Figure 8-10 provides a topology example to illustrate modification of DR/BDR placement in a network segment. R4 should never become the DR/BDR for the 10.123.4.0/24 segment, and R1 should always become the DR for the 10.123.4.0/24 segment.

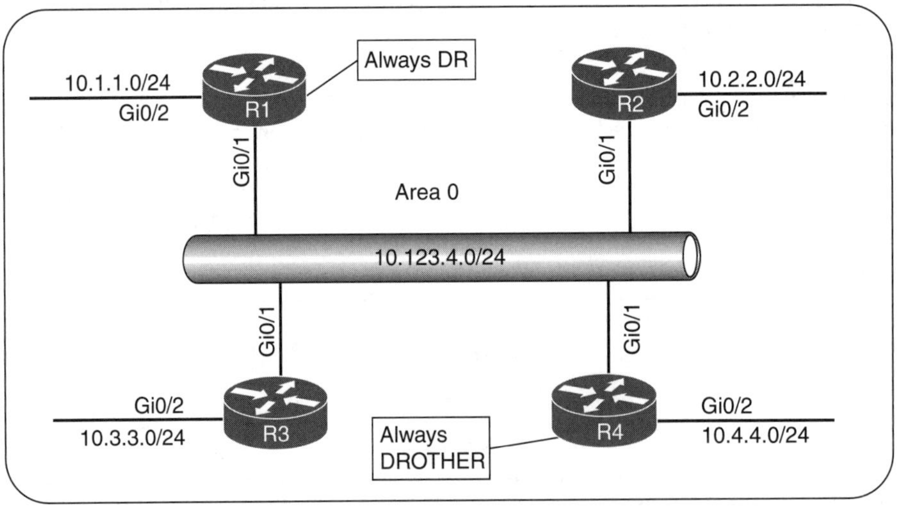

Figure 8-10 *OSPF Topology for DR/BDR Placement*

To prevent R4 from entering into the DR/BDR election, the OSPF priority is changed to 0. R1's interface priority needs to be changed to a value higher than 1 to ensure that it always wins the DR election.

Example 8-15 provides the relevant configuration for R1 and R4. No configuration changes have occurred on R2 and R3.

Example 8-15 *Configuring OSPF with DR Manipulation*

```
R1# configure terminal
Enter configuration commands, one per line. End with CNTL/Z.
R1(config)# interface GigabitEthernet 0/1
R1(config-if)# ip ospf priority 100
```

```
R4# configure terminal
Enter configuration commands, one per line. End with CNTL/Z.
R4(config)# interface GigabitEthernet 0/1
R4(config-if)# ip ospf priority 0
21:52:54.479: %OSPF-5-ADJCHG: Process 1, Nbr 192.168.1.1 on GigabitEthernet0/1 from
LOADING to FULL, Loading Done
```

Notice that upon configuring the interface priority to 0 on R4, the neighbor state with R1 changed. When the interface DR priority changed to zero, R4 removed itself as DR, R3 was promoted from the BDR to the DR, and then R1 was elected to the BDR. Because R1 is now a BDR, any DROTHER adjacencies were allowed to progress with establishing a complete adjacency with other routers.

Example 8-16 checks the status of the topology. R1 shows a priority of 100, and R4 shows a priority of 0. However, R1 is in the BDR position and not the DR role, as intended.

Example 8-16 *Verifying DR Manipulation*

```
R2# show ip ospf neighbor

Neighbor ID     Pri   State           Dead Time   Address         Interface
192.168.1.1     100   FULL/BDR        00:00:31    10.123.4.1      GigabitEthernet0/1
192.168.3.3       1   FULL/DR         00:00:33    10.123.4.3      GigabitEthernet0/1
192.168.4.4       0   2WAY/DROTHER    00:00:31    10.123.4.4      GigabitEthernet0/1
```

This example shows normal operation because the DR/BDR role does not support preemption. If all routers started as the same type, R1 would be the DR because of the wait timer in the initial OSPF DR election process. To complete the migration of the DR to R1, the OSPF process must be restarted on R3, as demonstrated in Example 8-17. After the process is restarted, the OSPF adjacency is checked again, and now R1 is the DR for the 10.123.4.0/24 network segment.

Example 8-17 *Clearing the DR OSPF Process*

```
R3# clear ip ospf process
Reset ALL OSPF processes? [no]: y
21:55:09.054: %OSPF-5-ADJCHG: Process 1, Nbr 192.168.1.1 on GigabitEthernet0/1
  from FULL to DOWN, Neighbor Down: Interface down or detached
21:55:09.055: %OSPF-5-ADJCHG: Process 1, Nbr 192.168.2.2 on GigabitEthernet0/1
  from FULL to DOWN, Neighbor Down: Interface down or detached
21:55:09.055: %OSPF-5-ADJCHG: Process 1, Nbr 192.168.4.4 on GigabitEthernet0/1
 from FULL to DOWN, Neighbor Down: Interface down or detached
```

```
R3# show ip ospf neighbor
Neighbor ID     Pri   State           Dead Time   Address         Interface
192.168.1.1     100   FULL/DR         00:00:37    10.123.4.1      GigabitEthernet0/1
192.168.2.2       1   FULL/DROTHER    00:00:34    10.123.4.2      GigabitEthernet0/1
192.168.4.4       0   FULL/DROTHER    00:00:35    10.123.4.4      GigabitEthernet0/1
```

OSPF Network Types

Different media can provide different characteristics or might limit the number of nodes allowed on a segment. Frame Relay and Ethernet are common multi-access media, and because they support more than two nodes on a network segment, the need for a DR exists. Other network circuits, such as serial links (with HDLC or PPP encapsulation), do not require a DR, and having one would just waste router CPU cycles.

The default OSPF network type is set based on the media used for the connection and can be changed independently of the actual media type used. Cisco's implementation of OSPF considers the various media and provides five OSPF network types, as listed in Table 8-9.

Key Topic

Table 8-9 OSPF Network Types

Type	Description	DR/BDR Field in OSPF Hellos	Timers
Broadcast	Default setting on OSPF-enabled Ethernet links.	Yes	Hello: 10 Wait: 40 Dead: 40
Non-broadcast	Default setting on OSPF-enabled Frame Relay main interface or Frame Relay multipoint subinterfaces.	Yes	Hello: 30 Wait: 120 Dead: 120
Point-to-point	Default setting on OSPF-enabled Frame Relay point-to-point subinterfaces.	No	Hello: 10 Wait: 40 Dead: 40
Point-to-multipoint	Not enabled by default on any interface type. Interface is advertised as a host route (/32) and sets the next-hop address to the outbound interface. Primarily used for hub-and-spoke topologies.	No	Hello: 30 Wait: 120 Dead: 120
Loopback	Default setting on OSPF-enabled loopback interfaces. Interface is advertised as a host route (/32).	N/A	N/A

The non-broadcast or point-to-multipoint network types are beyond the scope of the Enterprise Core exam, but the other OSPF network types are explained in the following sections.

Broadcast

Broadcast media such as Ethernet are better defined as broadcast multi-access to distinguish them from non-broadcast multi-access (NBMA) networks. Broadcast networks are multi-access in that they are capable of connecting more than two devices, and broadcasts sent out one interface are capable of reaching all interfaces attached to that segment.

The OSPF network type is set to broadcast by default for Ethernet interfaces. A DR is required for this OSPF network type because of the possibility that multiple nodes can exist on a segment, and LSA flooding needs to be controlled. The hello timer defaults to 10 seconds, as defined in RFC 2328.

The interface parameter command **ip ospf network broadcast** overrides the automatically configured setting and statically sets an interface as an OSPF broadcast network type.

Point-to-Point Networks

A network circuit that allows only two devices to communicate is considered a point-to-point (P2P) network. Because of the nature of the medium, point-to-point networks do not use Address Resolution Protocol (ARP), and broadcast traffic does not become the limiting factor.

The OSPF network type is set to point-to-point by default for serial interfaces (HDLC or PPP encapsulation), generic routing encapsulation (GRE) tunnels, and point-to-point Frame Relay subinterfaces. Only two nodes can exist on this type of network medium, so OSPF does not waste CPU cycles on DR functionality. The hello timer is set to 10 seconds on OSPF point-to-point network types.

Figure 8-11 shows a serial connection between R1 and R2.

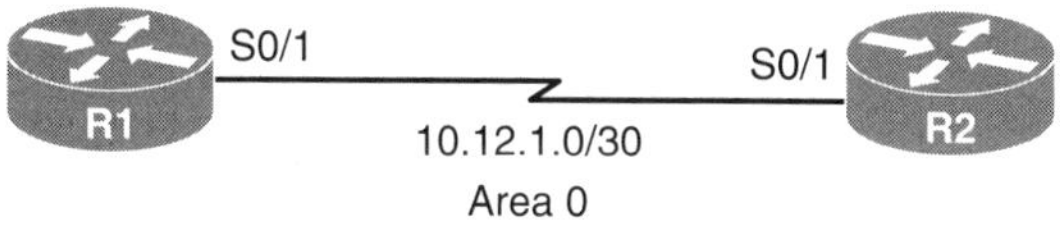

Figure 8-11 *OSPF Topology with Serial Interfaces*

Example 8-18 shows the relevant serial interface and OSPF configuration for R1 and R2. Notice that there are not any special commands placed in the configuration.

Example 8-18 *Configuring R1 and R2 Serial Interfaces and OSPF*

```
R1
interface serial 0/1
  ip address 10.12.1.1 255.255.255.252
!
router ospf 1
   router-id 192.168.1.1
   network 0.0.0.0 255.255.255.255 area 0
```

```
R2
interface serial 0/1
  ip address 10.12.1.2 255.255.255.252
!
router ospf 1
   router-id 192.168.2.2
   network 0.0.0.0 255.255.255.255 area 0
```

Example 8-19 verifies that the OSPF network type is set to POINT_TO_POINT, indicating the OSPF point-to-point network type.

Example 8-19 *Verifying the OSPF P2P Interfaces*

```
R1# show ip ospf interface s0/1 | include Type
  Process ID 1, Router ID 192.168.1.1, Network Type POINT_TO_POINT, Cost: 64
```

```
R2# show ip ospf interface s0/1 | include Type
  Process ID 1, Router ID 192.168.2.2, Network Type POINT_TO_POINT, Cost: 64
```

Example 8-20 shows that point-to-point OSPF network types do not use a DR. Notice the hyphen (-) in the State field.

Example 8-20 *Verifying OSPF Neighbors on P2P Interfaces*

```
R1# show ip ospf neighbor

Neighbor ID     Pri   State           Dead Time   Address         Interface
192.168.2.2       0   FULL/  -        00:00:36    10.12.1.2      Serial0/1
```

Interfaces using an OSPF P2P network type form an OSPF adjacency more quickly because the DR election is bypassed, and there is no wait timer. Ethernet interfaces that are directly connected with only two OSPF speakers in the subnet could be changed to the OSPF point-to-point network type to form adjacencies faster and to simplify the SPF computation. The interface parameter command **ip ospf network point-to-point** sets an interface as an OSPF point-to-point network type.

Loopback Networks

The OSPF network type loopback is enabled by default for loopback interfaces and can be used only on loopback interfaces. The OSPF loopback network type states that the IP address is always advertised with a /32 prefix length, even if the IP address configured on the loopback interface does not have a /32 prefix length. It is possible to demonstrate this behavior by reusing Figure 8-11 and advertising a Loopback 0 interface. Example 8-21 provides the updated configuration. Notice that the network type for R2's loopback interface is set to the OSPF point-to-point network type to ensure that R2's loopback interface advertises the network prefix of 192.168.2.0/24 and not 192.168.2.2/32.

Example 8-21 *OSPF Loopback Network Type*

```
R1
interface Loopback0
    ip address 192.168.1.1 255.255.255.0
interface Serial 0/1
    ip address 10.12.1.1 255.255.255.252
!
router ospf 1
    router-id 192.168.1.1
    network 0.0.0.0 255.255.255.255 area 0
```

```
R2
interface Loopback0
     ip address 192.168.2.2 255.255.255.0
```

```
     ip ospf network point-to-point
interface Serial 0/0
     ip address 10.12.1.2 255.255.255.252
!
router ospf 1
    router-id 192.168.2.2
    network 0.0.0.0 255.255.255.255 area 0
```

The network types for the R1 and R2 loopback interfaces are checked to verify that they changed and are different, as demonstrated in Example 8-22.

Example 8-22 *Displaying OSPF Network Type for Loopback Interfaces*

```
R1# show ip ospf interface Loopback 0 | include Type
  Process ID 1, Router ID 192.168.1.1, Network Type LOOPBACK, Cost: 1
```

```
R2# show ip ospf interface Loopback 0 | include Type
Process ID 1, Router ID 192.168.2.2, Network Type POINT_TO_POINT, Cost: 1
```

Two methods of verification of the subnet mask are included in the loopback interface advertisement. The first method requires examining the route from a different router. Example 8-23 shows the routing table for R1 and R2. Notice that R1's loopback address is a /32 network prefix in R2's routing table, which is the expected behavior for a loopback with the default OSPF network type of loopback. R2's loopback appears as a /24 network prefix in R1's routing table because the OSPF network type was changed to point-to-point. R1's and R2's loopbacks were configured with a /24 prefix; however, because R1's Lo0 is an OSPF network type of loopback, it is advertised as a /32 network.

Example 8-23 *OSPF Route Table for OSPF Loopback Network Types*

```
R1# show ip route ospf
! Output omitted for brevity
Gateway of last resort is not set


192.168.2.0/24 [110/65] via 10.12.1.2, 00:02:49, Serial0/0
```

```
R2# show ip route ospf
! Output omitted for brevity
Gateway of last resort is not set
      192.168.1.0/32 is subnetted, 1 subnets
O        192.168.1.1 [110/65] via 10.12.1.1, 00:37:15, Serial0/0
```

The second method of verification involves examining the OSPF database as shown in Example 8-24.

Example 8-24 *OSPF Database Entries for OSPF Loopback Network Types*

```
R1# show ip ospf database router | I Advertising|Network|Mask
  Advertising Router: 192.168.1.1
    Link connected to: a Stub Network
     (Link ID) Network/subnet number: 192.168.1.1
     (Link Data) Network Mask: 255.255.255.255
    Link connected to: a Stub Network
     (Link ID) Network/subnet number: 10.12.1.0
     (Link Data) Network Mask: 255.255.255.0
  Advertising Router: 192.168.2.2
    Link connected to: a Stub Network
     (Link ID) Network/subnet number: 192.168.2.0
     (Link Data) Network Mask: 255.255.255.0
    Link connected to: a Stub Network
     (Link ID) Network/subnet number: 10.12.1.0
     (Link Data) Network Mask: 255.255.255.0
```

Exam Preparation Tasks

You have a couple of choices for exam preparation: the exercises here, Chapter 30, "Final Preparation," and the exam simulation questions in the Pearson Test Prep Software Online.

Review All Key Topics

Review the most important topics in the chapter, noted with the Key Topic icon in the outer margin of the page. Table 8-10 lists these key topics and the page number on which each is found.

Key Topic

Table 8-10 Key Topics for Chapter 8

Key Topic Element	Description	Page
Paragraph	OSPF backbone	173
Section	Inter-Router Communication	174
Table 8-2	OSPF Packet Types	174
Table 8-4	OSPF Neighbor States	176
Paragraph	Designated router	177
Section	OSPF Network Statement	178
Section	Interface-Specific Enablement	180
Section	Passive Interfaces	181
Section	Requirements for Neighbor Adjacency	181
Table 8-6	OSPF Interface Columns	185
Table 8-7	OSPF Neighbor State Fields	186
Section	Default Route Advertisement	187
Section	Link Costs	189

Key Topic Element	Description	Page
Section	Failure Detection	189
Section	Designated Router Elections	190
Table 8-9	OSPF Network Types	194

Complete Tables and Lists from Memory

Print a copy of Appendix B, "Memory Tables" (found on the companion website), or at least the section for this chapter, and complete the tables and lists from memory. Appendix C, "Memory Tables Answer Key," also on the companion website, includes completed tables and lists you can use to check your work.

Define Key Terms

Define the following key terms from this chapter and check your answers in the Glossary:

backup designated router (BDR), dead interval, designated router (DR), hello interval, hello packets, interface priority, passive interface, router ID (RID), shortest path tree (SPT)

Use the Command Reference to Check Your Memory

Table 8-11 lists the important commands from this chapter. To test your memory, cover the right side of the table with a piece of paper, read the description on the left side, and see how much of the command you can remember.

Table 8-11 Command Reference

Task	Command Syntax
Initialize the OSPF process	**router ospf** *process-id*
Enable OSPF on network interfaces matching a specified network range for a specific OSPF area	**network** *ip-address wildcard-mask* **area** *area-id*
Enable OSPF on an explicit specific network interface for a specific OSPF area	**ip ospf** *process-id* **area** *area-id*
Configure a specific interface as passive	**passive-interface** *interface-id*
Configure all interfaces as passive	**Passive-interface default**
Advertise a default route into OSPF	**default-information originate** [**always**] [**metric** *metric-value*] [**metric-type** *type-value*]
Modify the OSPF reference bandwidth for dynamic interface metric costing	**auto-cost reference-bandwidth** *bandwidth-in-mbps*
Statically set the OSPF metric for an interface	**ip ospf cost** *1–65535*
Configure the OSPF priority for a DR/BDR election	**ip ospf priority** *0–255*
Statically configure an interface as a broadcast OSPF network type	**ip ospf network broadcast**
Statically configure an interface as a point-to-point OSPF network type	**ip ospf network point-to-point**

Task	Command Syntax
Restart the OSPF process	**clear ip ospf process**
Display the OSPF interfaces on a router	**show ip ospf interface** [**brief** | *interface-id*]
Display the OSPF neighbors and their current states	**show ip ospf neighbor** [**detail**]
Display the OSPF routes that are installed in the RIB	**show ip route ospf**

References in This Chapter

RFC 2328, *OSPF Version 2*, John Moy, http://www.ietf.org/rfc/rfc2328.txt, April 1998.

Edgeworth, Brad, Aaron Foss, and Ramiro Garza Rios. *IP Routing on Cisco IOS, IOS XE, and IOS XR*. Indianapolis: Cisco Press: 2014.

Cisco IOS Software Configuration Guides. http://www.cisco.com.

CHAPTER 9

Advanced OSPF

This chapter covers the following subjects:

- **Areas:** This section describes the benefits and functions of areas within an OSPF routing domain.
- **Link-State Advertisements:** This section explains how OSPF stores, communicates, and builds a topology from the link-state advertisements (LSAs).
- **Discontiguous Networks:** This section demonstrates a discontiguous network and explains why such a network cannot distribute routes to all areas properly.
- **OSPF Path Selection:** This section explains how OSPF makes path selection choices for routes learned within the OSPF routing domain.
- **Summarization of Routes:** This section explains how network summarization works with OSPF.
- **Route Filtering:** This section explains how OSPF routes can be filtered on a router.

The Open Shortest Path First (OSPF) protocol scales well with proper network planning. IP addressing schemes, area segmentation, address summarization, and hardware capabilities for each area should all be taken into consideration for a network design.

This chapter expands on Chapter 8, "OSPF," and explains the functions and features found in larger enterprise networks. By the end of this chapter, you should have a solid understanding of the route advertisement within a multi-area OSPF domain, path selection, and techniques to optimize an OSPF environment.

"Do I Know This Already?" Quiz

The "Do I Know This Already?" quiz enables you to assess whether you should read the entire chapter. If you miss no more than one of these self-assessment questions, you might want to move ahead to the "Exam Preparation Tasks" section. Table 9-1 lists the major headings in this chapter and the "Do I Know This Already?" quiz questions covering the material in those headings so you can assess your knowledge of these specific areas. The answers to the "Do I Know This Already?" quiz appear in Appendix A, "Answers to the 'Do I Know This Already?' Questions."

Table 9-1 "Do I Know This Already?" Foundation Topics Section-to-Question Mapping

Foundation Topics Section	Questions
Areas	1–2
Link-State Advertisements	3–6
Discontiguous Networks	7
OSPF Path Selection	8
Summarization of Routes	9–10

1. True or false: A router with an interface associated with Area 1 and Area 2 will be able to inject routes learned from one area into another area.
   a. True
   b. False
2. True or false: A member router contains a complete copy of the LSDBs for every area in the routing domain.
   a. True
   b. False
3. How many OSPF link-state advertisement (LSA) types are used for routing traditional IPv4 packets?
   a. Two
   b. Three
   c. Five
   d. Six
   e. Seven
4. What is the LSA age field in the LSDB used for?
   a. For version control—to ensure that the most recent LSA is present
   b. To age out old LSAs by removing an LSA when its age reaches zero
   c. For troubleshooting—to identify exactly when the LSA was advertised
   d. To age out old LSAs by removing an LSA when it reaches 3600 seconds
5. Which LSA type exists in all OSPF areas?
   a. Network
   b. Summary
   c. Router
   d. AS external
6. True or false: When an ABR receives a network LSA, the ABR forwards the network LSA to the other connected areas.
   a. True
   b. False
7. When a type 3 LSA is received in a non-backbone area, what does the ABR do?
   a. Discards the type 3 LSA and does not process it
   b. Installs the type 3 LSA for only the area where it was received

   c. Advertises the type 3 LSA to the backbone area and displays an error
   d. Advertises the type 3 LSA to the backbone area

8. True or false: OSPF uses the shortest total path metric to identify the best path for every internal OSPF route (intra-area and inter-area).
   a. True
   b. False

9. True or false: Breaking a large OSPF topology into smaller OSPF areas can be considered a form of summarization.
   a. True
   b. False

10. How is the process of summarizing internal routes on an OSPF router accomplished?
    a. By using the interface configuration command **summary-address** *network prefix-length*
    b. By using the OSPF process configuration command **summary-address** *network prefix-length*
    c. By using the OSPF process configuration command **area** *area-id* **range** *network subnet-mask*
    d. By using the interface configuration command **area** *area-id* **summary-address** *network subnet-mask*

Foundation Topics

Areas

An OSPF area is a logical grouping of routers or, more specifically, a logical grouping of router interfaces. Area membership is set at the interface level, and the area ID is included in the OSPF hello packet. An interface can belong to only one area. All routers within the same OSPF area maintain an identical copy of the link-state database (LSDB).

An OSPF area grows in size as network links and the number of routers increase in the area. While using a single area simplifies the topology, there are trade-offs:

- A full shortest path first (SPF) tree calculation runs when a link flaps within the area.
- The LSDB increases in size and becomes unmanageable if the network grows because the LSDB will consume more memory, and take longer during the SPF calculation process.
- No summarization of route information occurs.

Proper design addresses each of these issues by segmenting the OSPF routing domain into multiple OSPF areas, thereby keeping the LSDB to a manageable size. Sizing and design of OSPF networks should account for the hardware constraints of the smallest router in that area.

If a router has interfaces in multiple areas, the router has multiple LSDBs (one for each area). The internal topology of one area is invisible from outside that area. If a topology change occurs (such as a link flap or an additional network being added) within an area, all routers in the same OSPF area calculate the SPF tree again. Routers outside that area do not calculate the full SPF tree again but perform a partial SPF calculation if the metrics have changed or a prefix is removed.

In essence, an OSPF area hides the topology from another area but enables the networks to be visible in other areas within the OSPF domain. Segmenting the OSPF domain into multiple areas reduces the size of the LSDB for each area, making SPF tree calculations faster, and decreasing LSDB flooding between routers when a link flaps.

Just because a router connects to multiple OSPF areas does not mean the routes from one area will be injected into another area. Figure 9-1 shows router R1 connected to Area 1 and Area 2. Routes from Area 1 will not advertise into Area 2 and vice versa.

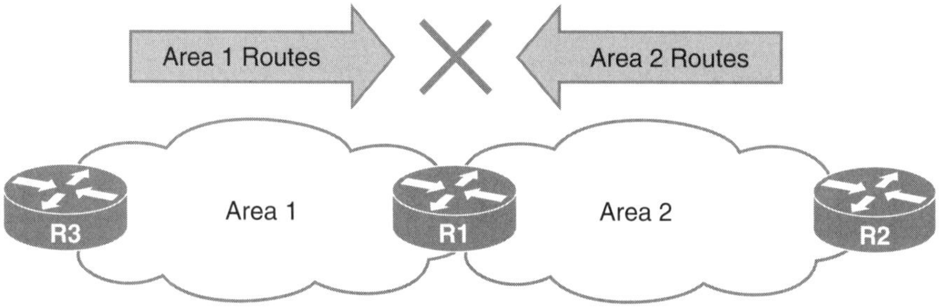

Figure 9-1 *Failed Route Advertisement Between Areas*

Key Topic

Area 0 is a special area called the *backbone*. By design, all areas must connect to Area 0 because OSPF expects all areas to inject routing information into the backbone, and Area 0 advertises the routes into other areas. The backbone design is crucial to preventing routing loops.

Key Topic

Area border routers (ABRs) are OSPF routers connected to Area 0 and another OSPF area, per Cisco definition and according to RFC 3509. ABRs are responsible for advertising routes from one area and injecting them into a different OSPF area. Every ABR needs to participate in Area 0; otherwise, routes will not advertise into another area. ABRs compute an SPF tree for every area that they participate in.

9

Figure 9-2 shows that R1 is connected to Area 0, Area 1, and Area 2. R1 is a proper ABR because it now participates in Area 0. The following occurs on R1:

- Routes from Area 1 advertise into Area 0.
- Routes from Area 2 advertise into Area 0.
- Routes from Area 0 advertise into Area 1 and 2. This includes the local Area 0 routes, in addition to the routes that were advertised into Area 0 from Area 1 and Area 2.

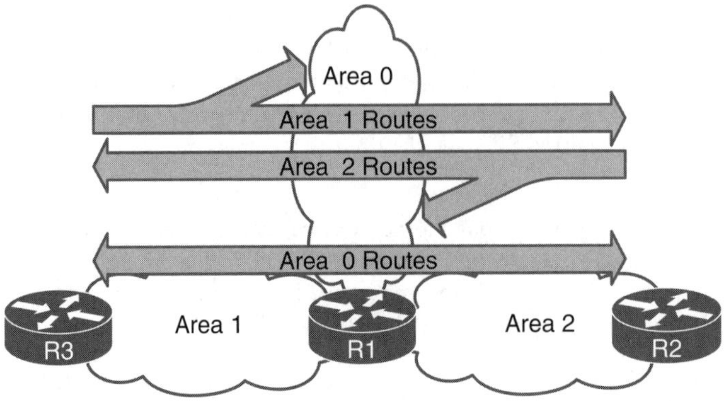

Figure 9-2 *Successful Route Advertisement Between Areas*

Figure 9-3 shows a larger-scale OSPF multi-area topology that is used throughout this chapter to describe various OSPF concepts.

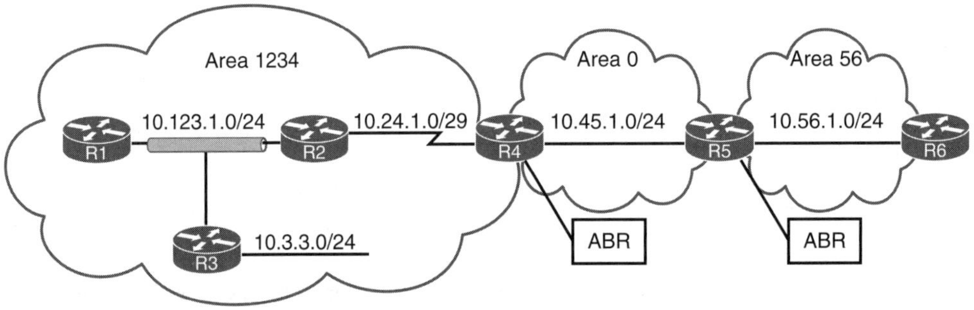

Figure 9-3 *OSPF Multi-Area Topology*

In the topology:

- R1, R2, R3, and R4 belong to Area 1234.
- R4 and R5 belong to Area 0.
- R5 and R6 belong to Area 56.
- R4 and R5 are ABRs.
- Area 1234 connects to Area 0, and Area 56 connects to Area 0.
- Routers in Area 1234 can see routes from routers in Area 0 and Area 56 and vice versa.

Example 9-1 shows the OSPF configuration for the ABRs R4 and R5. Notice that R4 and R5 have an interface in Area 0 and a non-backbone area. In addition, R4's OSPF network statement for the serial link does not need to match the 10.24.1.0/29 network exactly, as long as it falls within the configured range.

Answers to the "Do I Know This Already?" quiz:

1 B **2** B **3** D **4** D **5** C **6** B **7** B **8** B **9** A **10** C

Example 9-1 *Sample Multi-Area OSPF Configuration*

```
R4
router ospf 1
 router-id 192.168.4.4
 network 10.24.1.0 0.0.0.255 area 1234
 network 10.45.1.0 0.0.0.255 area 0
```

```
R5
router ospf 1
 router-id 192.168.5.5
 network 10.45.1.0 0.0.0.255 area 0
 network 10.0.0.0 0.255.255.255 area 56
```

Example 9-2 verifies that interfaces on R4 belong to Area 1234 and Area 0 and that interfaces on R5 belong to Area 0 and Area 56.

Example 9-2 *Verifying Interfaces for ABRs*

```
R4# show ip ospf interface brief
Interface    PID   Area            IP Address/Mask    Cost  State Nbrs F/C
Gi0/0        1     0               10.45.1.4/24       1     BDR    1/1
Se1/0        1     1234            10.24.1.4/29       64   P2P    1/1
```

```
R5# show ip ospf interface brief
Interface    PID   Area            IP Address/Mask    Cost  State Nbrs F/C
Gi0/0        1     0               10.45.1.5/24       1     DR    1/1
Gi0/1        1     56              10.56.1.5/24       1     BDR   1/1
```

Key Topic

Area ID

The area ID is a 32-bit field and can be formatted in simple decimal (0 through 4,294,967,295) or dotted decimal (0.0.0.0 through 255.255.255.255). During router configuration, the area can use decimal format on one router and dotted-decimal format on a different router, and the routers can still form an adjacency. OSPF advertises the area ID in dotted-decimal format in the OSPF hello packet.

OSPF Route Types

OSPF routes to destination networks within the same area are known as **intra-area routes**. In Figure 9-3, the serial link between R2 and R4 (10.24.1.0/29) is an intra-area route to R1. The IP routing table displays OSPF intra-area routes with an *O*.

OSPF routes to destination networks from a different area using an ABR are known as **inter-area routes**. In Figure 9-3, the Ethernet link between R4 and R5 (10.45.1.0/24) is an inter-area route to R1. The IP routing table displays OSPF inter-area routers with *O IA*.

Example 9-3 provides the routing table for R1 from Figure 9-3. Notice that R1's OSPF routing table shows routes from within Area 1234 as intra-area (*O* routes) and routes from Area 0 and Area 56 as inter-area (*O IA* routes).

Example 9-3 *OSPF Routing Tables for Sample Multi-Area OSPF Topology*

```
R1# show ip route | begin Gateway
Gateway of last resort is not set

      10.0.0.0/8 is variably subnetted, 6 subnets, 3 masks
! The following two routes are OSPF intra-area routes as they all come from
! Area 1234
O        10.3.3.0/24 [110/2] via 10.123.1.3, 00:12:07, GigabitEthernet0/0
O        10.24.1.0/29 [110/65] via 10.123.1.2, 00:12:07, GigabitEthernet0/0
! The following two routes are OSPF inter-area routes as they all come from
! outside of Area 1234
O IA     10.45.1.0/24 [110/66] via 10.123.1.2, 00:12:07, GigabitEthernet0/0
O IA     10.56.1.0/24 [110/67] via 10.123.1.2, 00:12:07, GigabitEthernet0/0
C         10.123.1.0/24 is directly connected, GigabitEthernet0/0
```

Example 9-4 provides the routing table for R4 from Figure 9-3. Notice that R4's routing table shows the routes from within Area 1234 and Area 0 as intra-area and routes from Area 56 as inter-area because R4 does not connect to Area 56.

Notice that the metric for the 10.3.3.0/24 and 10.123.1.0/24 routes has drastically increased compared to the metric for the 10.56.1.0/24 route. The reason is that it must cross the slow serial link, which has an interface cost of 64.

Example 9-4 *OSPF Routing Table for ABR R4*

```
R4# show ip route | begin Gateway
Gateway of last resort is not set

      10.0.0.0/8 is variably subnetted, 7 subnets, 3 masks
O        10.3.3.0/24 [110/66] via 10.24.1.2, 00:03:45, Serial1/0
C        10.24.1.0/29 is directly connected, Serial1/0
C        10.45.1.0/24 is directly connected, GigabitEthernet0/0
O IA     10.56.1.0/24 [110/2] via 10.45.1.5, 00:04:56, GigabitEthernet0/0
O        10.123.1.0/24 [110/65] via 10.24.1.2, 00:13:19, Serial1/0
```

Example 9-5 provides the OSPF routing tables (with CLI output filtering) for R5 and R6 from Figure 9-3. R5 and R6 contain only inter-area routes in the OSPF routing table because intra-area routes are directly connected.

Example 9-5 *OSPF Routing Tables for R5 and R6*

```
R5# show ip route ospf | begin Gateway
Gateway of last resort is not set

      10.0.0.0/8 is variably subnetted, 7 subnets, 3 masks
O IA     10.3.3.0/24 [110/67] via 10.45.1.4, 00:04:13, GigabitEthernet0/0
O IA     10.24.1.0/29 [110/65] via 10.45.1.4, 00:04:13, GigabitEthernet0/0
O IA     10.123.1.0/24 [110/66] via 10.45.1.4, 00:04:13, GigabitEthernet0/0
```

```
R6# show ip route ospf | begin Gateway
Gateway of last resort is not set

      10.0.0.0/8 is variably subnetted, 6 subnets, 3 masks
O IA     10.3.3.0/24 [110/68] via 10.56.1.5, 00:07:04, GigabitEthernet0/0
O IA     10.24.1.0/24 [110/66] via 10.56.1.5, 00:08:19, GigabitEthernet0/0
O IA     10.45.1.0/24 [110/2] via 10.56.1.5, 00:08:18, GigabitEthernet0/0
O IA     10.123.1.0/24 [110/67] via 10.56.1.5, 00:08:19, GigabitEthernet0/0
```

OSPF routes to destination networks from outside the OSPF domain that are injected into the OSPF domain through redistribution are known as *external routes*. External OSPF routes can come from a different OSPF domain or from a different routing protocol. External OSPF routes are beyond the scope of the CCNP and CCIE Enterprise Core ENCOR 350-401 exam and are not covered in this book.

Key Topic

Link-State Advertisements

When OSPF neighbors become adjacent, the LSDBs synchronize between the OSPF routers. As an OSPF router adds or removes a directly connected network link to or from its database, the router floods the link-state advertisement (LSA) out all active OSPF interfaces. The OSPF LSA contains a complete list of networks advertised from that router.

OSPF uses six LSA types for IPv4 routing:

- **Type 1, router LSA:** Advertises the LSAs that originate within an area
- **Type 2, network LSA:** Advertises a multi-access network segment attached to a DR
- **Type 3, summary LSA:** Advertises network prefixes that originated from a different area
- **Type 4, ASBR summary LSA:** Advertises a summary LSA for a specific ASBR
- **Type 5, AS external LSA:** Advertises LSAs for routes that have been redistributed
- **Type 7, NSSA external LSA:** Advertises redistributed routes in NSSAs

LSA types 1, 2, and 3, which are used for building the SPF tree for intra-area and inter-area routes, are explained in this section.

Figure 9-4 shows a packet capture of an OSPF update LSA and outlines the important components of the LSA: the LSA type, LSA age, sequence number, and advertising router. Because this is a type 1 LSA, the link IDs add relevance because they list the attached networks and the associated OSPF cost for each interface.

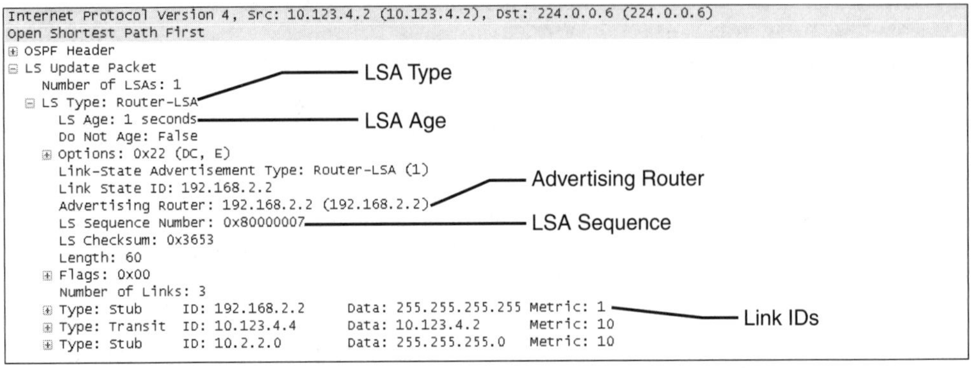

Figure 9-4 *Packet Capture of an LSA Update for the Second Interface*

LSA Sequences

OSPF uses the sequence number to overcome problems caused by delays in LSA propagation in a network. The LSA sequence number is a 32-bit number for controlling versioning. When the originating router sends out LSAs, the LSA sequence number is incremented. If a router receives an LSA sequence that is greater than the one in the LSDB, it processes the LSA. If the LSA sequence number is lower than the one in the LSDB, the router deems the LSA old and discards the LSA.

LSA Age and Flooding

Every OSPF LSA includes an age that is entered into the local LSDB and that will increment by 1 every second. When a router's OSPF LSA age exceeds 1800 seconds (30 minutes) for its networks, the originating router advertises a new LSA with the LSA age set to 0. As each router forwards the LSA, the LSA age is incremented with a calculated (minimal) delay that reflects the link. If the LSA age reaches 3600, the LSA is deemed invalid and is purged from the LSDB. The repetitive flooding of LSAs is a secondary safety mechanism to ensure that all routers maintain a consistent LSDB within an area.

LSA Types

All routers within an OSPF area have an identical set of LSAs for that area. The ABRs maintain a separate set of LSAs for each OSPF area. Most LSAs in one area will be different from the LSAs in another area. Generic **router LSA** output is shown with the command **show ip ospf database.**

LSA Type 1: Router Link

Every OSPF router advertises a type 1 LSA. Type 1 LSAs are the essential building blocks within the LSDB. A type 1 LSA entry exists for each OSPF-enabled link (that is, every interface and its attached networks). Figure 9-5 shows that in this example, the type 1 LSAs are not advertised outside Area 1234, which means the underlying topology in an area is invisible to other areas.

> **NOTE** Type 1 LSAs for an area are shown with the command **show ip ospf database router.**

Key Topic

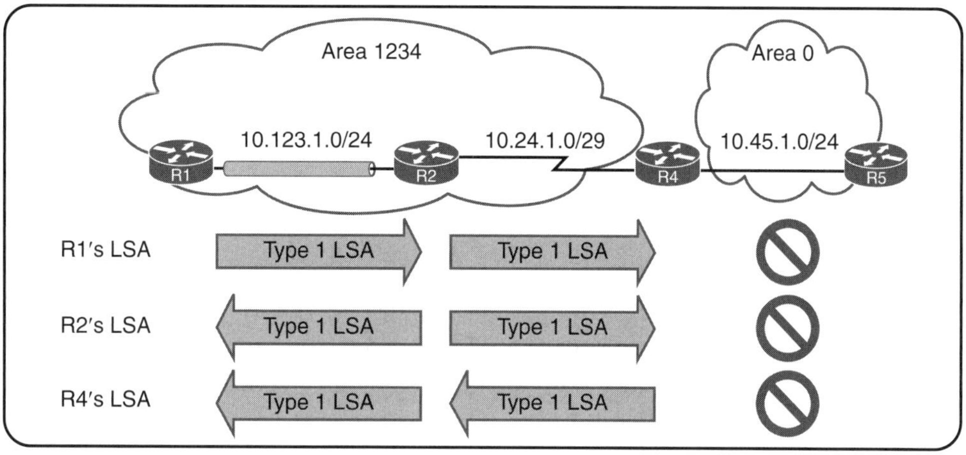

Figure 9-5 *Type 1 LSA Flooding in an Area*

The initial fields of each type 1 LSA indicate the RID for the LSA's advertising router, age, sequence, link count, and link ID. Every OSPF-enabled interface is listed under the number of links for each router. Each network link on a router contains the link type, correlating information for neighbor router identification, and interface metric.

The correlating information for neighbor router identification is often the neighbor RID, with the exception of multi-access network segments that contain designated routers (DRs). In those scenarios, the interface address of the DR identifies the neighbor router.

Figure 9-6 is a reference subsection of Area 1234 taken from the original Figure 9-3.

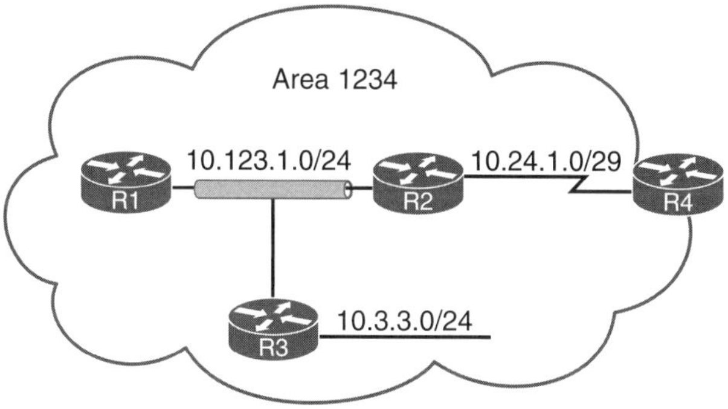

Figure 9-6 *Type 1 LSA Flooding Reference Topology*

If we correlate just type 1 LSAs from the reference topology of Figure 9-6, then Figure 9-7 demonstrates the topology built by all routers in Area 1234 using the LSA attributes for Area 1234 from all four routers. Using only type 1 LSAs, a connection is made between R2 and R4 because they point to each other's RID in the point-to-point LSA. Notice that the three router links on R1, R2, and R3 (10.123.1.0) have not been directly connected yet.

9

Key Topic

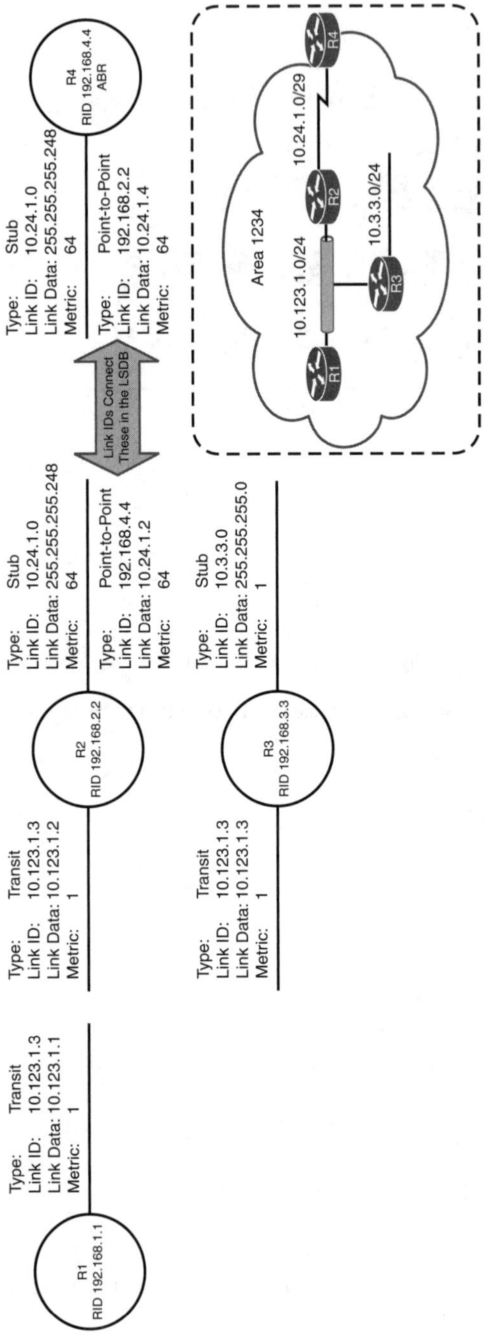

Figure 9-7 *Visualization of Type 1 LSAs*

Key Topic

LSA Type 2: Network Link

A type 2 LSA represents a multi-access network segment that uses a DR. The DR always advertises the type 2 LSA and identifies all the routers attached to that network segment. If a DR has not been elected, a type 2 LSA is not present in the LSDB because the corresponding type 1 transit link type LSA is a stub. Like type 1 LSAs, type 2 LSAs are not flooded outside the originating OSPF area.

Area 1234 has only one DR segment that connects R1, R2, and R3 because R3 has not formed an OSPF adjacency on the 10.3.3.0/24 network segment. On the 10.123.1.0/24 network segment, R3 is elected as the DR, and R2 is elected as the BDR based on their RIDs.

> **NOTE** Detailed type 2 LSA information is shown with the command **show ip ospf database network.**

Now that we have the type 2 LSA for Area 1234, all the network links are connected. Figure 9-8 provides a visualization of the type 1 and type 2 LSAs, which correspond with Area 1234 perfectly.

> **NOTE** When the DR changes for a network segment, a new type 2 LSA is created, causing SPF to run again within the OSPF area.

Key Topic

LSA Type 3: Summary Link

Type 3 LSAs represent networks from other areas. The role of the ABRs is to participate in multiple OSPF areas and ensure that the networks associated with type 1 LSAs are reachable in the non-originating OSPF areas.

As explained earlier, ABRs do not forward type 1 or type 2 LSAs into other areas. When an ABR receives a type 1 LSA, it creates a type 3 LSA referencing the network in the original type 1 LSA; the type 2 LSA is used to determine the network mask of the multi-access network. The ABR then advertises the type 3 LSA into other areas. If an ABR receives a type 3 LSA from Area 0 (the backbone), it regenerates a new type 3 LSA for the non-backbone area and lists itself as the advertising router, with the additional cost metric.

Figure 9-9 demonstrates the concept of a type 3 LSA interaction with type 1 LSAs.

Key Topic

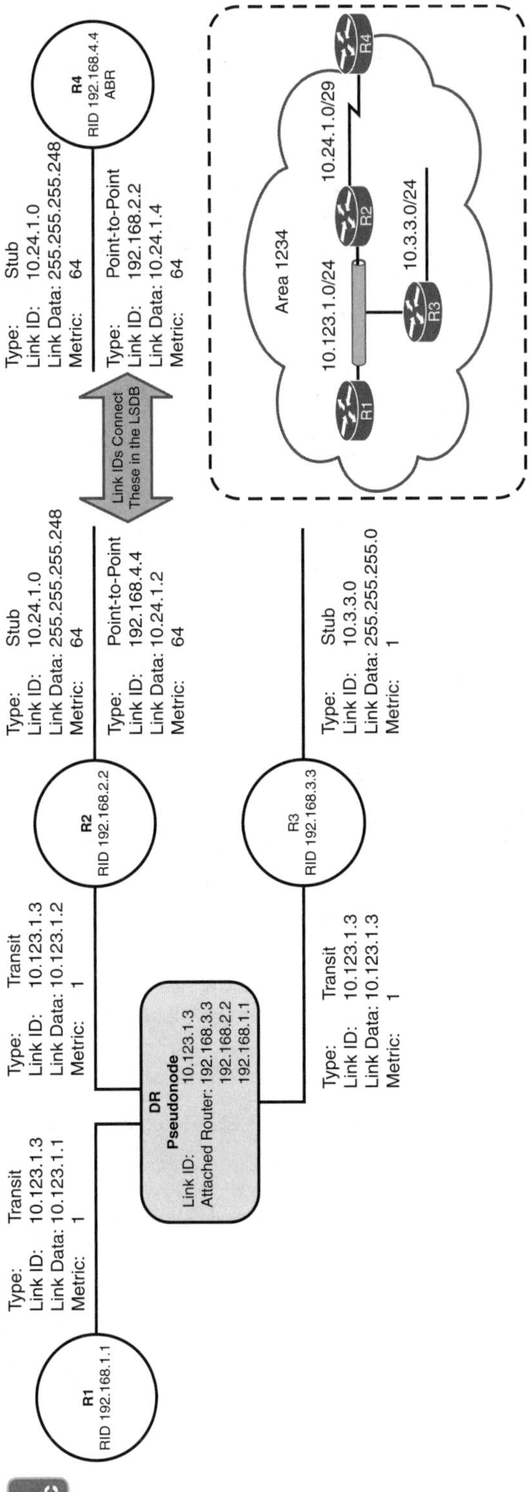

Figure 9-8 *Visualization of Area 1234 with Type 1 and Type 2 LSAs*

Key Topic

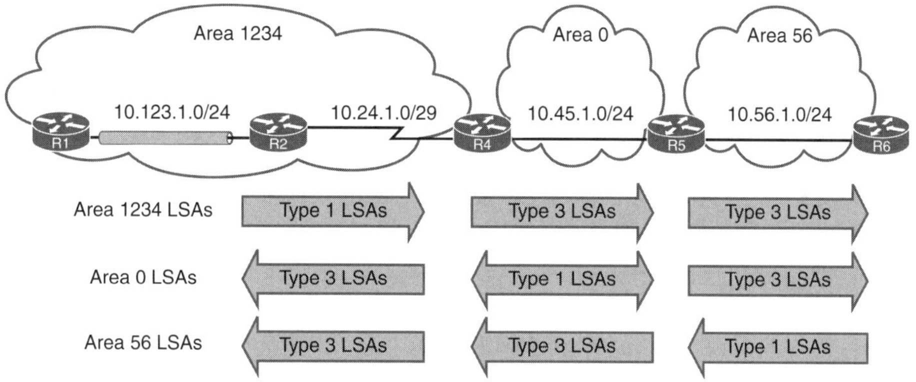

Figure 9-9 *Type 3 LSA Conceptual Overview*

The type 3 LSAs show up under the appropriate areas where they exist in the OSPF domain. For example, the 10.56.1.0 type 3 LSA is in Area 0 and Area 1234 on R4; however, on R5 the type 3 LSA exists only in Area 0 because the 10.56.1.0 network is a type 1 LSA in Area 56.

Detailed type 3 LSA information is shown with the command **show ip ospf database summary**. The output can be restricted to a specific LSA by appending the network prefix to the end of the command.

The advertising router for type 3 LSAs is the last ABR that advertises the prefix. The metric within the type 3 LSA uses the following logic:

- If the type 3 LSA is created from a type 1 LSA, it is the total path metric to reach the originating router in the type 1 LSA.
- If the type 3 LSA is created from a type 3 LSA from Area 0, it is the total path metric to the ABR plus the metric in the original type 3 LSA.

For example, from Figure 9-9, as R2 advertises the 10.123.1.0/24 network, the following happens:

- R4 receives R2's type 1 LSA and creates a new type 3 LSA by using the metric 65: the cost of 1 for R2's LAN interface and 64 for the serial link between R2 and R4.
- R4 advertises the type 3 LSA with the metric 65 into Area 0.
- R5 receives the type 3 LSA and creates a new type 3 LSA for Area 56, using the metric 66: the cost of 1 for the link between R4 and R5 plus the original type 3 LSA metric 65.
- R6 receives the type 3 LSA. Part of R6's calculation is the metric to reach the ABR (R5), which is 1 plus the metric in the type 3 LSA (66). R6 therefore calculates the metric 67 to reach 10.123.1.0/24.

The type 3 LSA contains the link-state ID (network number), the subnet mask, the IP address of the advertising ABR, and the metric for the network prefix.

Figure 9-10 provides R4's perspective of the type 3 LSA created by ABR (R5) for the 10.56.1.0/24 network. R4 does not know if the 10.56.1.0/24 network is directly attached to the ABR (R5) or multiple hops away. R4 knows that its metric to the ABR (R5) is 1 and that the type 3 LSA already has a metric of 1, so its total path metric to reach the 10.56.1.0/24 network is 2.

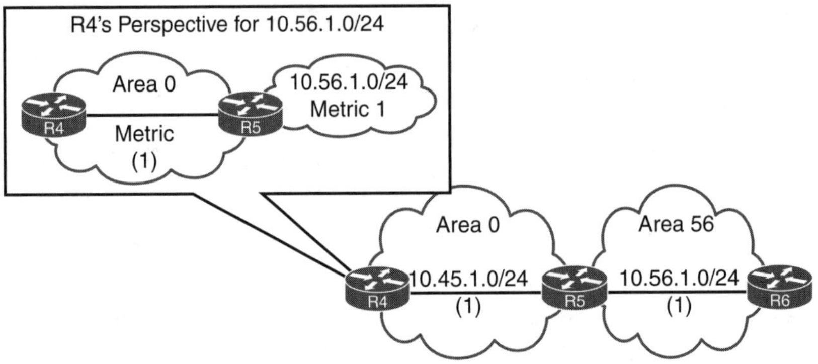

Figure 9-10 *Visualization of the 10.56.1.0/24 Type 3 LSA from Area 0*

Figure 9-11 provides R3's perspective of the type 3 LSA created by ABR (R4) for the 10.56.1.0/24 network. R3 does not know if the 10.56.1.0/24 network is directly attached to the ABR (R4) or multiple hops away. R3 knows that its metric to the ABR (R4) is 65 and that the type 3 LSA already has a metric of 2, so its total path metric to reach the 10.56.1.0/24 network is 67.

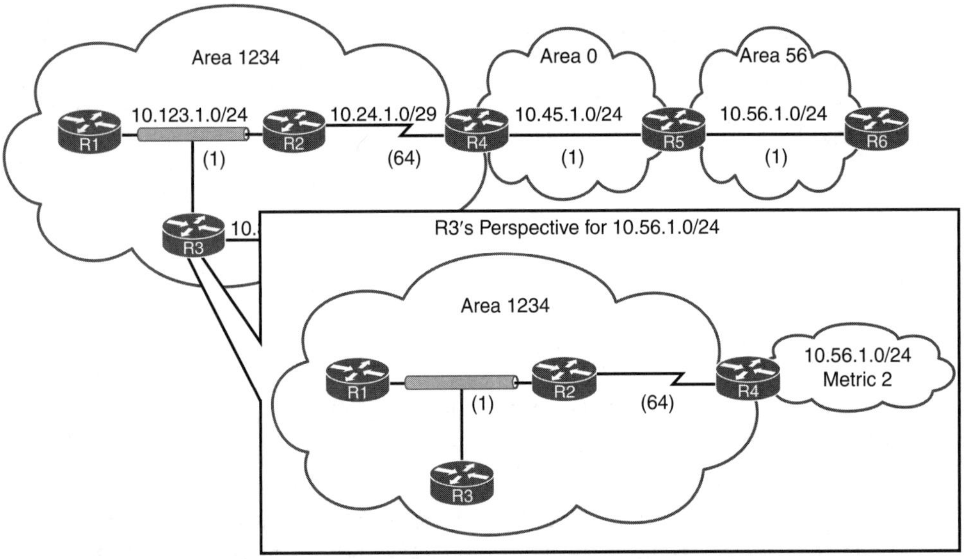

Figure 9-11 *Visualization of 10.56.1.0/24 Type 3 LSA from Area 1234*

NOTE An ABR advertises only one type 3 LSA for a prefix, even if it is aware of multiple paths from within its area (type 1 LSAs) or from outside its area (type 3 LSAs). The metric for the best path will be used when the LSA is advertised into a different area.

NOTE OSPF contains functionality to optimize or summarize routes as an ABR advertises routes between areas. OSPF Stubby or Not-So-Stubby Areas (NSSAs) provide a method to block external routes from entering an area and are replaced with a default route. These area types can be further enhanced to a Totally Stubby or Totally NSSAs to prevent external routes and inter-area routes from entering an area by the ABR and are replaced with a default route as well.

Discontiguous Networks

Network engineers who do not fully understand OSPF design may create a topology such as the one illustrated in Figure 9-12. While R2 and R3 have OSPF interfaces in Area 0, traffic from Area 12 must cross Area 23 to reach Area 34. An OSPF network with this design is discontiguous because inter-area traffic is trying to cross a non-backbone area.

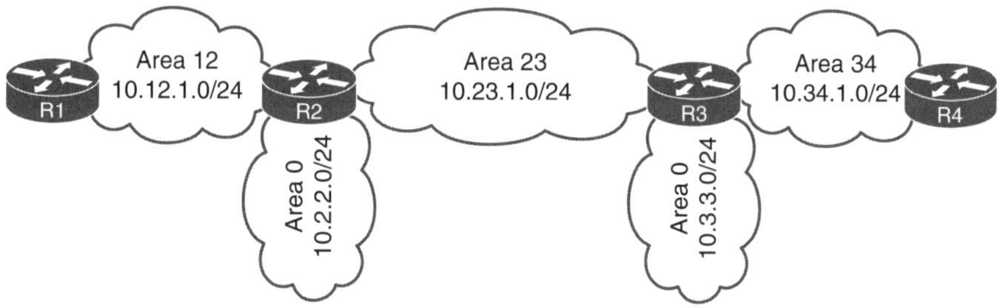

Figure 9-12 *Discontiguous Network*

At first glance, it looks like routes in the routing tables on R2 and R3 in Figure 9-13 are being advertised across Area 23; however, that is not the case. The 10.34.1.0/24 network is advertised into OSPF by R3 and R4 as a type 1 LSA. R3 is an ABR and converts Area 34's 10.34.1.0/24 type 1 LSA into a type 3 LSA in Area 0. R3 uses the type 3 LSA from Area 0 to generate the type 3 LSA for Area 23. R2 is able to install the type 3 LSA from Area 23 into its routing table.

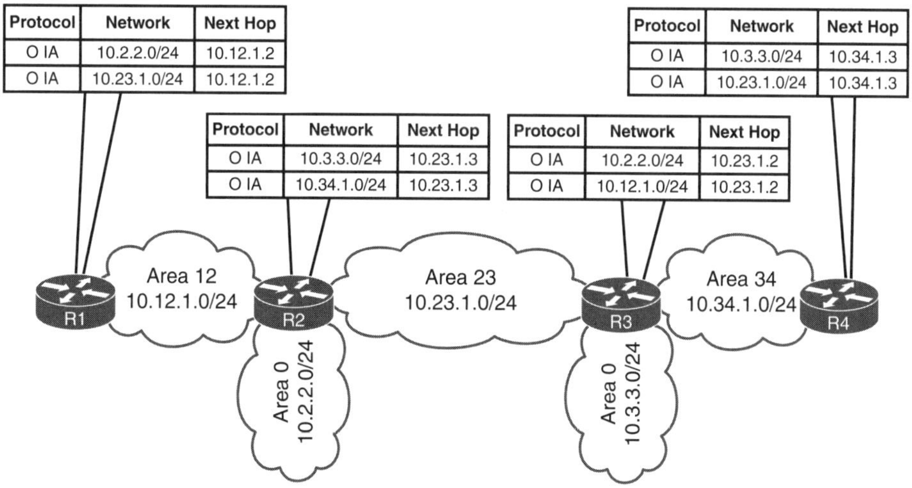

Figure 9-13 *OSPF Routes for Discontiguous Network*

Most people would assume that the 10.34.1.0/24 route learned by Area 23 would then advertise into R2's Area 0 and then propagate to Area 12. However, they would be wrong. There are three fundamental rules ABRs use for creating type 3 LSAs:

Key Topic

- Type 1 LSAs received from an area create type 3 LSAs into the **backbone area** and non-backbone areas.
- Type 3 LSAs received from Area 0 are created for the non-backbone area.
- Type 3 LSAs received from a non-backbone area only insert into the LSDB for the source area. ABRs do not create a type 3 LSA for the other areas (including a segmented Area 0).

The simplest fix for a **discontiguous network** is to ensure that Area 0 is contiguous. There are other functions, like virtual links or usage of GRE tunnels, that can be used as well; however, they are beyond the scope of this book and complicate the operational environment.

NOTE Real-life scenarios of discontiguous networks involve Area 0 becoming partitioned due to hardware failures. Ensuring that multiple paths exist to keep the backbone contiguous is an important factor in network design.

Key Topic

OSPF Path Selection

OSPF executes Dijkstra's shortest path first (SPF) algorithm to create a loop-free topology of shortest paths. All routers use the same logic to calculate the shortest path for each network. Path selection prioritizes paths by using the following logic:

1. Intra-area
2. Inter-area
3. External routes (which involve additional logic not covered in this book)

Intra-Area Routes

OSPF intra-area routes are always preferred over inter-area routes. If multiple intra-area routes exist for the same destination network, the route with the lowest total path metric is installed in the OSPF Routing Information Base (RIB), which is then presented to the router's global RIB. If there is a tie in metric, both routes are installed into the OSPF RIB.

In Figure 9-14, R1 is calculating the route to 10.4.4.0/24. Instead of taking the faster Ethernet connection (R1→R2→R4), R1 takes the path across the slower serial link (R1→R3→R4) to R4 because intra-area routes are preferred over inter-area routes.

Example 9-6 shows R1's routing table entry for the 10.4.4.0/24 network. Notice that the metric is 111 and that the intra-area route was selected over the inter-area route, even though the inter-area route has a lower total path metric.

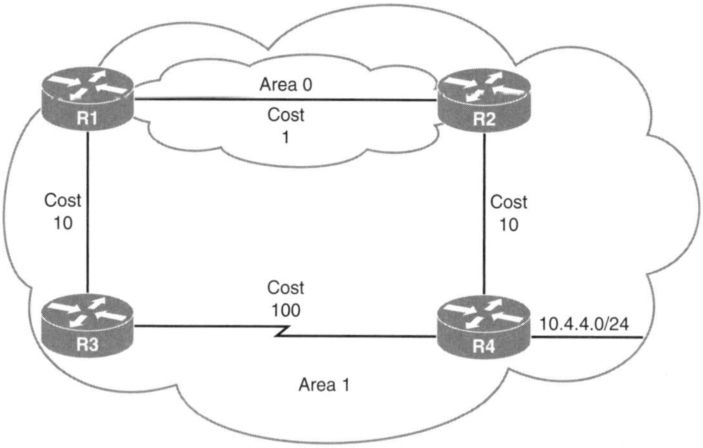

Figure 9-14 *Intra-Area Routes over Inter-Area Routes*

Example 9-6 *R1's Routing Table for the 10.4.4.0/24 Network*

```
R1# show ip route 10.4.4.0
Routing entry for 10.4.4.0/24
  Known via "ospf 1", distance 110, metric 111, type intra area
  Last update from 10.13.1.3 on GigabitEthernet0/1, 00:00:42 ago
  Routing Descriptor Blocks:
 * 10.13.1.3, from 10.34.1.4, 00:00:42 ago, via GigabitEthernet0/1
      Route metric is 111, traffic share count is 1
```

Inter-Area Routes

The next priority for selecting a path to a network in a different area is selecting the path with the lowest total path metric to the destination. If there is a tie in the metric, both paths install into the OSPF RIB. All inter-area paths for a route must go through Area 0 to be considered.

In Figure 9-15, R1 is computing the path to R6. R1 uses the path R1→R3→R5→R6 because its total path metric is 35 versus the R1→R2→R4→R6 path, with a metric of 40.

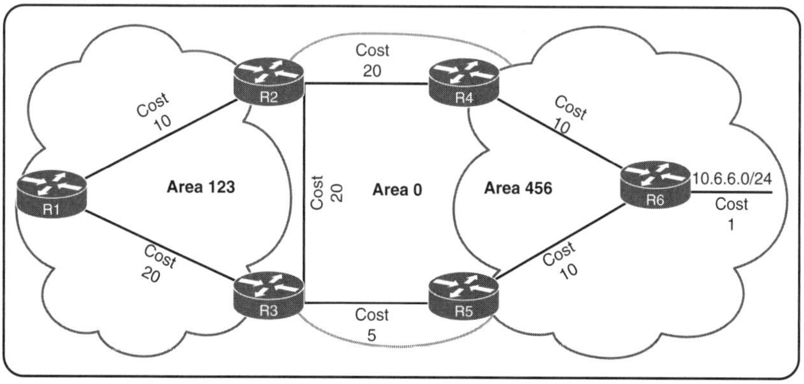

Figure 9-15 *Inter-Area Route Selection*

Equal-Cost Multipathing

If OSPF identifies multiple paths in the path selection algorithms, those routes are installed into the routing table as equal-cost multipathing (ECMP) routes. The default maximum number of ECMP paths is four paths. The default ECMP setting can be overwritten with the command **maximum-paths** *maximum-paths* under the OSPF process to modify the default setting.

Key Topic

Summarization of Routes

Route scalability is a large factor for the IGP routing protocols used by service providers because there can be thousands of routers running in a network. Splitting up an OSPF routing domain into multiple areas reduces the size of the LSDB for each area. While the number of routers and networks remains the same within the OSPF routing domain, the detailed type 1 and type 2 LSAs are exchanged for simpler type 3 LSAs.

For example, referencing our topology for LSAs, in Figure 9-16 for Area 1234, there are three type 1 LSAs and one type 2 LSA for the 10.123.1.0/24 network. Those four LSAs become one type 3 LSA outside of Area 1234. Figure 9-16 illustrates the reduction of LSAs through area segmentation for the 10.123.1.0/24 network.

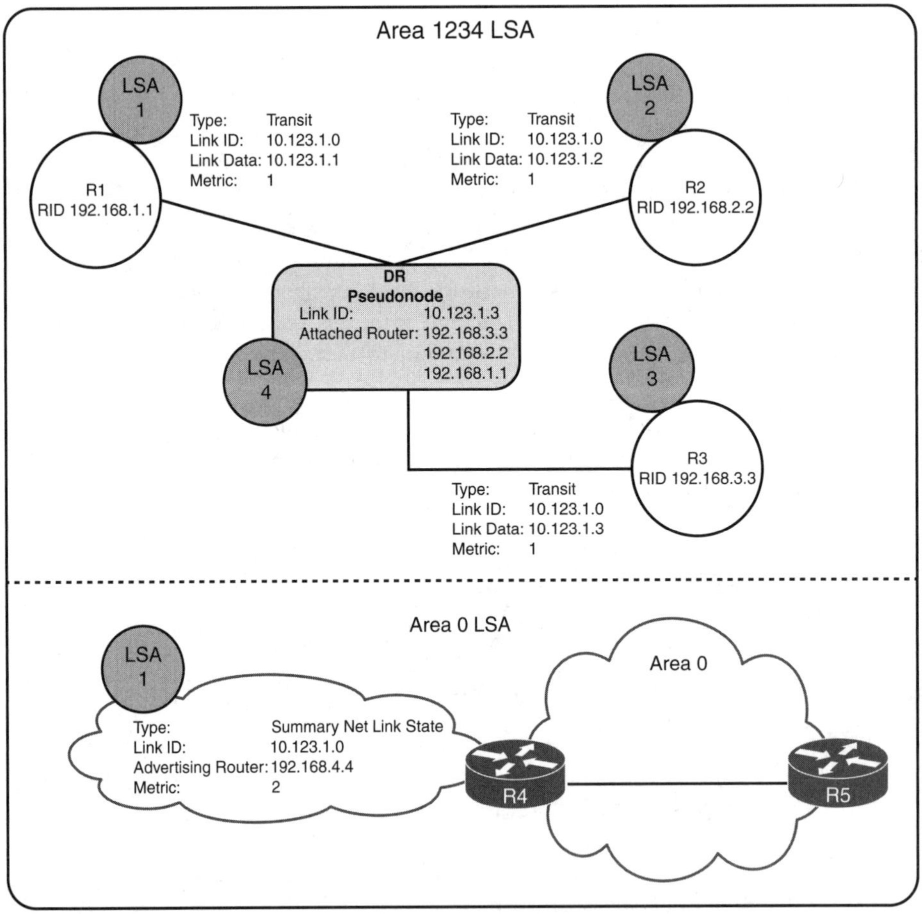

Figure 9-16 *LSA Reduction Through Area Segmentation*

Summarization Fundamentals

Another method of shrinking the LSDB involves summarizing network prefixes. Newer routers have more memory and faster processors than those in the past, but because all routers have an identical copy of the LSDB, an OSPF area needs to accommodate the smallest and slowest router in that area.

Summarization of routes also helps SPF calculations run faster. A router that has 10,000 network routes will take longer to run the SPF calculation than a router with 500 network routes. Because all routers within an area must maintain an identical copy of the LSDB, summarization occurs between areas on the ABRs.

Summarization can eliminate the SPF calculation outside the area for the summarized prefixes because the smaller prefixes are hidden. Figure 9-17 provides a simple network topology where the serial link between R3 and R4 has a higher path metric, and R1, R2, and R3 all use the path via 10.1.24.0/24 to reach the 172.16.46.0/24 network. If the 10.1.24.0/24 link fails, all routers in Area 1 have to run SPF calculations. R4 would identify that the 10.1.12.0/24 and 10.1.13.0/24 networks would change their next hop through the serial link. Both of the type 3 LSAs for these networks need to be updated with new path metrics and advertised into Area 0. The routers in Area 0 run an SPF calculation only on those two prefixes.

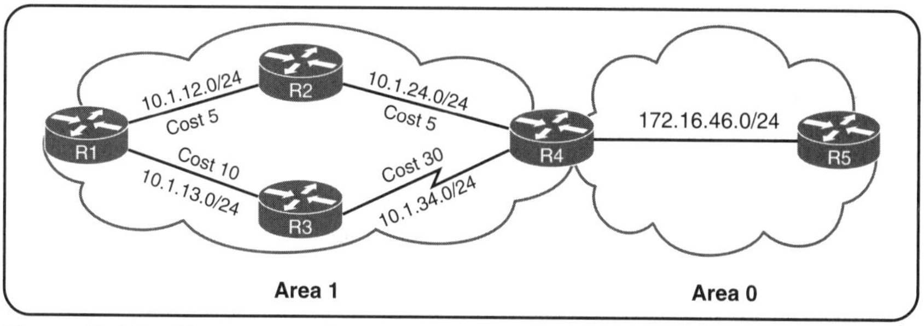

Figure 9-17 *The Impact of Summarization on SPF Topology Calculation*

Figure 9-18 shows the networks in Area 1 being summarized at the ABR into the aggregate 10.1.0.0/18 prefix. If the 10.1.12.0/24 link fails, all the routers in Area 1 still run the SPF calculation, but routers in Area 0 are not impacted because the 10.1.13.0/24 and 10.1.34.0/24 networks are not known outside Area 1.

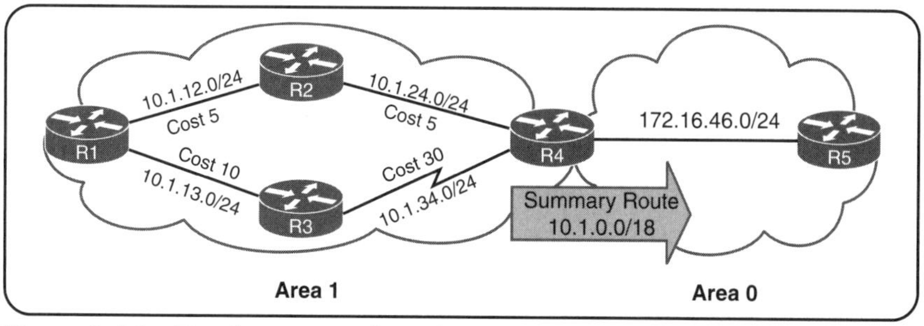

Figure 9-18 *Topology Example with Summarization*

This concept applies to networks of various sizes but is beneficial for networks with a carefully developed IP addressing scheme and proper summarization. The following sections explain summarization in more detail.

Key Topic

Inter-Area Summarization

Inter-area summarization reduces the number of type 3 LSAs that an ABR advertises into an area when it receives type 1 LSAs. The network summarization range is associated with a specific source area for type 1 LSAs.

When a type 1 LSA within the summarization range reaches the ABR from the source area, the ABR creates a type 3 LSA for the summarized network range. The ABR suppresses the more specific type 3 LSAs from being generated and advertised in the neighboring areas. Inter-area summarization does not impact the type 1 LSAs in the source area.

Figure 9-19 shows 15 type 1 LSAs (172.16.1.0/24 through 172.16.15.0/24) being summarized into one type 3 LSA (the 172.16.0.0/20 network).

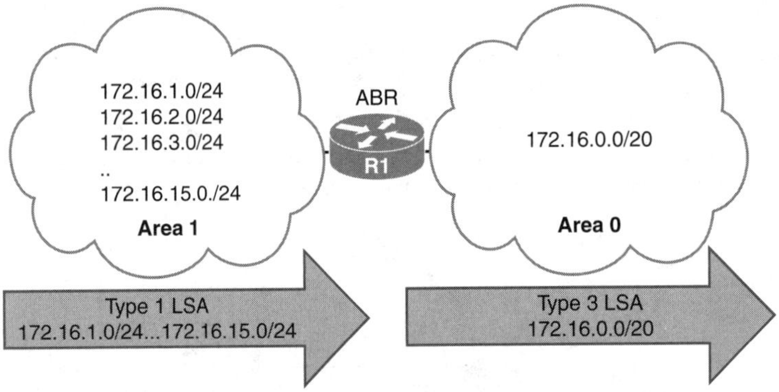

Figure 9-19 *OSPF Inter-Area Summarization*

Summarization works only on type 1 LSAs and is normally configured (or designed) so that summarization occurs as routes enter the backbone from non-backbone areas.

Summarization Metrics

At the time of the writing, IOS XE routers set the default metric for the *summary LSA* to be the lowest metric associated with an LSA based on RFC 1583 guidelines. However, the summary metric can statically be set as part of the configuration. In Figure 9-20, R1 summarizes three prefixes with various path costs. The 172.16.3.0/24 prefix has the lowest metric, so that metric is used for the summarized route.

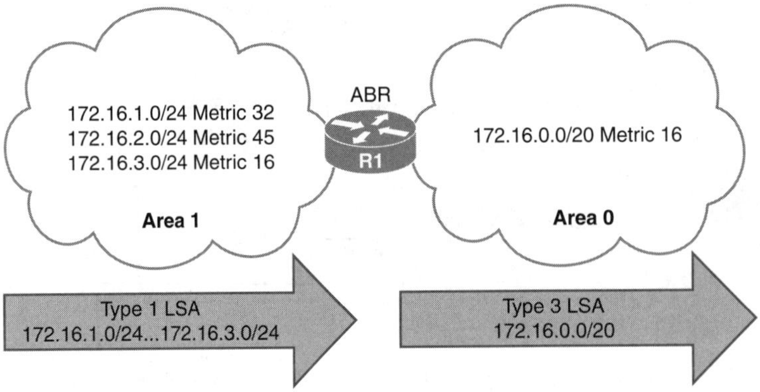

Figure 9-20 *Inter-Area Summarization Metric*

OSPF behaves similarly to Enhanced Interior Gateway Routing Protocol (EIGRP) and checks every prefix within the summarization range when a matching type 1 LSA is added or removed. If a lower metric is available, the summary LSA is advertised with the newer metric; if the lowest metric is removed, a newer and higher metric is identified, and a new summary LSA is advertised with the higher metric.

Key Topic

Configuration of Inter-Area Summarization

To define the summarization range and associated area, use the command **area** *area-id* **range** *network subnet-mask* [**advertise** | **not-advertise**] [**cost** *metric*] under the OSPF process on the ABR. The default behavior is to advertise the summary prefix, so the keyword **advertise** is not necessary. Appending the **cost** *metric* keyword to the command statically sets the metric on the summary route.

Figure 9-21 provides a topology example in which R1 is advertising the 172.16.1.0/24, 172.16.2.0/24, and 172.16.3.0/24 networks.

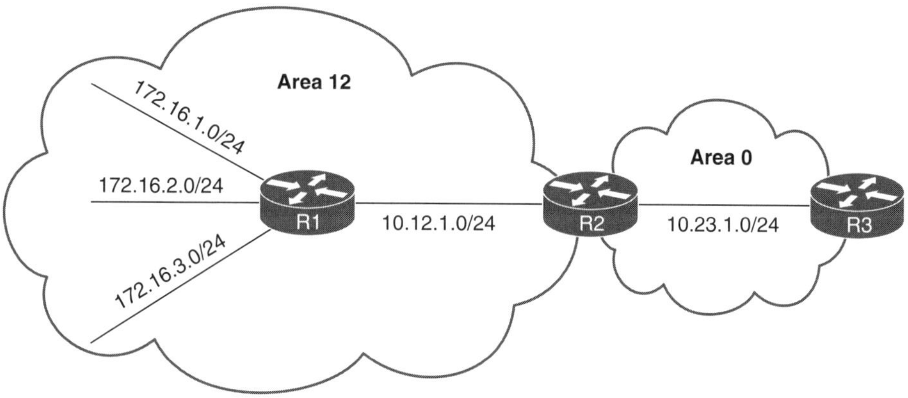

Figure 9-21 *OSPF Inter-Area Summarization Example*

Example 9-7 displays the routing table on R3 before summarization. Notice that the 172.16.1.0/24, 172.16.2.0/24, and 172.16.3.0/24 routes are all present.

Example 9-7 *Routing Table Before OSPF Inter-Area Route Summarization*

```
R3# show ip route ospf | begin Gateway
Gateway of last resort is not set

      10.0.0.0/8 is variably subnetted, 5 subnets, 2 masks
O IA     10.12.1.0/24 [110/2] via 10.23.1.2, 00:02:22, GigabitEthernet0/1
      172.16.0.0/24 is subnetted, 3 subnets
O IA     172.16.1.0 [110/3] via 10.23.1.2, 00:02:12, GigabitEthernet0/1
O IA     172.16.2.0 [110/3] via 10.23.1.2, 00:02:12, GigabitEthernet0/1
O IA     172.16.3.0 [110/3] via 10.23.1.2, 00:02:12, GigabitEthernet0/1
```

As the component routes 172.16.1.0/24, 172.16.2.0/24, and 172.16.3.0/24 are being advertised into Area 0, R2 summarizes them into a single summary route, 172.16.0.0/16. Example 9-8 provides R2's configuration for inter-area summarization into an aggregate route of 172.16.0.0/16. A static cost of 45 is added to the summary route to reduce CPU load if any of the three networks flap.

9

Example 9-8 *R2's Inter-Area Route Summarization Configuration*

```
router ospf 1
 router-id 192.168.2.2
 area 12 range 172.16.0.0 255.255.0.0 cost 45
 network 10.12.0.0 0.0.255.255 area 12
 network 10.23.0.0 0.0.255.255 area 0
```

Example 9-9 displays R3's routing table for verification that the smaller component routes were suppressed while the summary route was aggregated. Notice that the path metric is 46, whereas previously the metric for the 172.16.1.0/24 network was 3.

Example 9-9 *Routing Table After OSPF Inter-Area Route Summarization*

```
R3# show ip route ospf | begin Gateway
Gateway of last resort is not set

      10.0.0.0/8 is variably subnetted, 3 subnets, 2 masks
O IA     10.12.1.0/24 [110/2] via 10.23.1.2, 00:02:04, GigabitEthernet0/1
O IA  172.16.0.0/16 [110/46] via 10.23.1.2, 00:00:22, GigabitEthernet0/1
```

The ABR performing inter-area summarization installs a discard route—that is, a route to the Null0 interface that matches the summarized network range. Discard routes prevent routing loops where portions of the summarized network range do not have a more specific route in the RIB. The AD for the OSPF summary discard route for internal networks is 110, and it is 254 for external networks.

Example 9-10 shows the discard route on R2 for the 172.16.0.0/16 prefix.

Example 9-10 *Discarding a Route for Loop Prevention*

```
R2# show ip route ospf | begin Gateway
Gateway of last resort is not set

      172.16.0.0/16 is variably subnetted, 4 subnets, 2 masks
O        172.16.0.0/16 is a summary, 00:03:11, Null0
O        172.16.1.0/24 [110/2] via 10.12.1.1, 00:01:26, GigabitEthernet0/0
O        172.16.2.0/24 [110/2] via 10.12.1.1, 00:01:26, GigabitEthernet0/0
O        172.16.3.0/24 [110/2] via 10.12.1.1, 00:01:26, GigabitEthernet0/0
```

Route Filtering

Route filtering is a method for selectively identifying routes that are advertised or received from neighbor routers. Route filtering may be used to manipulate traffic flows, reduce memory utilization, or improve security.

Filtering of routes with vector-based routing protocols is straightforward because the routes are filtered as routing updates are advertised to downstream neighbors. However, with link-state routing protocols such as OSPF, every router in an area shares a complete copy of the link-state database. Therefore, filtering of routes generally occurs as routes enter the area on the ABR.

The following sections describe three techniques for filtering routes with OSPF.

Filtering with Summarization

One of the easiest methodologies for filtering routes is to use the **not-advertise** keyword during prefix summarization. Using this keyword prevents creation of any type 3 LSAs for any networks in that range, thus making the smaller component routes visible only within the area where they originate.

The full command structure is **area** *area-id* **range** *network subnet-mask* **not-advertise** under the OSPF process.

If we revisit Figure 9-21, where R1 is advertising the 172.16.1.0/24, 172.16.2.0/24, and 172.16.3.0/24 routes, we see that R2 can filter out any of the type 1 LSAs that are generated in Area 12 from being advertised into Area 0. The configuration is displayed in Example 9-11.

Example 9-11 *R2's Configuration for Filtering via Summarization*

```
R2# configure terminal
Enter configuration commands, one per line. End with CNTL/Z.
R2(config)# router ospf 1
R2(config-router)# area 12 range 172.16.2.0 255.255.255.0 not-advertise
```

Example 9-12 shows R3's routing table after the area filtering configuration has been placed on R2. The 172.16.2.0/24 route is filtered and removed from Area 0. If a larger network range were configured, then more of the component routes would be filtered.

Example 9-12 *Verifying Removal of 172.16.2.0 from Area 0*

```
R3# show ip route ospf | begin Gateway
Gateway of last resort is not set

       10.0.0.0/8 is variably subnetted, 3 subnets, 2 masks
O IA      10.12.1.0/24 [110/3] via 10.23.1.2, 00:02:24, GigabitEthernet0/0
       172.16.0.0/24 is subnetted, 2 subnets
O IA      172.16.1.0 [110/4] via 10.23.1.2, 00:00:17, GigabitEthernet0/0
O IA      172.16.3.0 [110/4] via 10.23.1.2, 00:00:17, GigabitEthernet0/0
```

Area Filtering

Although filtering via summarization is easy, it is limited in its ability. For example, in Figure 9-22, if the 172.16.1.0/24 route needs to be present in Area 0 but removed in Area 34, it is not possible to filter the route using summarization.

Other network designs require filtering of OSPF routes based on other criteria. OSPF supports filtering when type 3 LSA generation occurs. This allows for the original route to be installed in the LSDB for the source area so that the route can be installed in the RIB of the ABR. Filtering can occur in either direction on the ABR. Figure 9-23 demonstrates the concept.

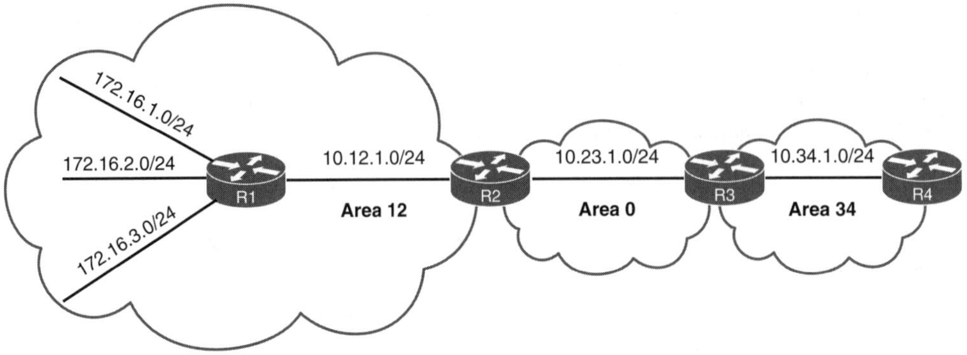

Key Topic

Figure 9-22 *Expanded Topology for Filtering Routes*

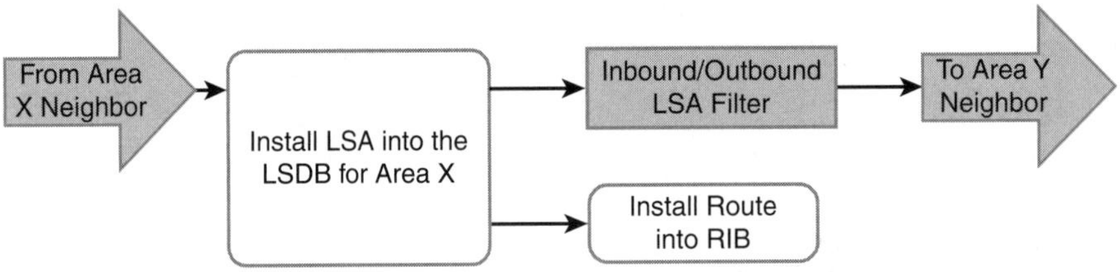

Figure 9-23 *OSPF Area Filtering*

Figure 9-24 expands on the sample topology and demonstrates that the ABR can filter routes as they advertise out of an area or into an area. R2 is able to filter routes (LSAs) outbound as they leave Area 12 or inbound as they enter Area 0. In addition, R3 can filter routes as they leave Area 0 or enter Area 34. The same logic applies with routes advertised in the opposite direction.

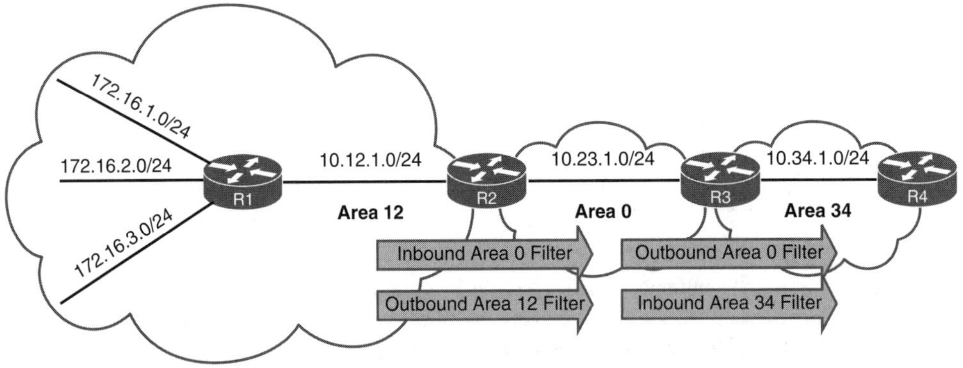

Figure 9-24 *OSPF Area Filtering Topology*

OSPF area filtering is accomplished by using the command **area** *area-id* **filter-list prefix** *prefix-list-name* {**in** | **out**} on the ABR. Say that R1 is advertising the 172.16.1.0/24, 172.16.2.0/24, and 172.16.3.0/24 routes. R2 is configured to filter the 172.16.1.0/24 route as it enters Area 0, and R3 is configured to filter the 172.16.2.0/24 route as it leaves Area 0. Example 9-13 provides the necessary configuration for R2 and R3.

Example 9-13 *Configuring OSPF Area Filtering*

```
R2
ip prefix-list PREFIX-FILTER seq 5 deny 172.16.1.0/24
ip prefix-list PREFIX-FILTER seq 10 permit 0.0.0.0/0 le 32
!
router ospf 1
 router-id 192.168.2.2
 network 10.12.1.0 0.0.0.255 area 12
 network 10.23.1.0 0.0.0.255 area 0
 area 0 filter-list prefix PREFIX-FILTER in
```

```
R3
ip prefix-list PREFIX-FILTER seq 5 deny 172.16.2.0/24
ip prefix-list PREFIX-FILTER seq 10 permit 0.0.0.0/0 le 32
!
router ospf 1
 router-id 192.168.3.3
 network 10.23.1.0 0.0.0.255 area 0
 network 10.34.1.0 0.0.0.255 area 34
 area 0 filter-list prefix PREFIX-FILTER out
```

Example 9-14 shows the routing table on R3 where the 172.16.1.0/24 route has been filtered from all the routers in Area 0. The 172.16.2.0/24 route has been filtered from all the routers in Area 34. This verifies that the area filtering was successful for routes entering the backbone and leaving the backbone.

Example 9-14 *Verifying OSPF Area Filtering*

```
R3# show ip route ospf | begin Gateway
Gateway of last resort is not set

       10.0.0.0/8 is variably subnetted, 5 subnets, 2 masks
O IA      10.12.1.0/24 [110/2] via 10.23.1.2, 00:17:39, GigabitEthernet0/1
       172.16.0.0/24 is subnetted, 2 subnets
O IA      172.16.2.0 [110/3] via 10.23.1.2, 00:16:30, GigabitEthernet0/1
O IA      172.16.3.0 [110/3] via 10.23.1.2, 00:16:30, GigabitEthernet0/1
```

```
R4# show ip route ospf | begin Gateway
Gateway of last resort is not set

       10.0.0.0/8 is variably subnetted, 4 subnets, 2 masks
O IA      10.12.1.0/24 [110/3] via 10.34.1.3, 00:19:41, GigabitEthernet0/0
O IA      10.23.1.0/24 [110/2] via 10.34.1.3, 00:19:41, GigabitEthernet0/0
       172.16.0.0/24 is subnetted, 1 subnets
O IA      172.16.3.0 [110/4] via 10.34.1.3, 00:17:07, GigabitEthernet0/0
```

Exam Preparation Tasks

You have a couple of choices for exam preparation: the exercises here, Chapter 30, "Final Preparation," and the exam simulation questions in the Pearson Test Prep Software Online.

Review All Key Topics

Review the most important topics in the chapter, noted with the Key Topic icon in the outer margin of the page. Table 9-2 lists these key topics and the page number on which each is found.

Key Topic

Table 9-2 Key Topics for Chapter 9

Key Topic Element	Description	Page
Paragraph	Area 0 backbone	205
Paragraph	Area border routers	205
Section	Area ID	207
Section	Link-State Advertisements	209
Figure 9-5	Type 1 LSA Flooding in an Area	211
Figure 9-7	Visualization of Type 1 LSAs	212
Section	LSA Type 2: Network Link	213
Figure 9-8	Visualization of Area 1234 with Type 1 and Type 2 LSAs	214
Section	LSA Type 3 Summary Link	213
Figure 9-9	Type 3 LSA Conceptual Overview	215
List	ABR rules for type 3 LSAs	218
Section	OSPF Path Selection	218
Section	Summarization of Routes	220
Section	Inter-Area Summarization	222
Section	Configuration of Inter-Area Summarization	223
Figure 9-23	OSPF Area Filtering	226

Complete Tables and Lists from Memory

There are no memory tables in this chapter.

Define Key Terms

Define the following key terms from this chapter and check your answers in the Glossary:

area border router (ABR), backbone, discontiguous network, inter-area route, intra-area route, router LSA, summary LSA

Use the Command Reference to Check Your Memory

Table 9-3 lists the important commands from this chapter. To test your memory, cover the right side of the table with a piece of paper, read the description on the left side, and see how much of the command you can remember.

Table 9-3 Command Reference

Task	Command Syntax
Initialize the OSPF process	**router ospf** *process-id*
Summarize routes as they are crossing an OSPF ABR	**area** *area-id* **range network subnet-mask** [**advertise** | **not-advertise**] [**cost** *metric*]
Filter routes as they are crossing an OSPF ABR	**area** *area-id* **filter-list prefix** *prefix-list-name* {**in** | **out**}
Display the LSAs in the LSDB	**show ip ospf database** [**router** | **network** | **summary**]

References in This Chapter

RFC 2328, *OSPF Version 2*, John Moy. http://www.ietf.org/rfc/rfc2328.txt, April 1998.

RFC 3509, *Alternative Implementations of OSPF Area Border Routers*, Alex Zinin, Acee Lindem, and Derek Yeung. https://tools.ietf.org/html/rfc3509, April 2003.

Edgeworth, Brad, Aaron Foss, and Ramiro Garza Rios, *IP Routing on Cisco IOS, IOS XE, and IOS XR*. Indianapolis: Cisco Press, 2014.

Cisco IOS Software Configuration Guides. http://www.cisco.com.

CHAPTER 10

OSPFv3

This chapter covers the following subjects:

- **OSPFv3 Fundamentals:** This section provides an overview of the OSPFv3 routing protocol and the similarities to OSPFv2.
- **OSPFv3 Configuration:** This section demonstrates the configuration and verification of an OSPFv3 environment.
- **IPv4 Support in OSPFv3:** This section explains and demonstrates how OSPFv3 can be used for exchanging IPv4 routes.

OSPF Version 3 (OSPFv3), which is the latest version of the OSPF protocol, includes support for both the IPv4 and IPv6 address families. The OSPFv3 protocol is not backward compatible with OSPFv2, but the protocol mechanisms described in Chapters 8, "OSPF," and 9, "Advanced OSPF," are essentially the same for OSPFv3. This chapter expands on Chapter 9 and discusses OSPFv3 and its support of IPv6.

"Do I Know This Already?" Quiz

The "Do I Know This Already?" quiz enables you to assess whether you should read the entire chapter. If you miss no more than one of these self-assessment questions, you might want to move ahead to the "Exam Preparation Tasks" section. Table 10-1 lists the major headings in this chapter and the "Do I Know This Already?" quiz questions covering the material in those headings so you can assess your knowledge of these specific areas. The answers to the "Do I Know This Already?" quiz appear in Appendix A, "Answers to the 'Do I Know This Already?' Questions."

Table 10-1 "Do I Know This Already?" Foundation Topics Section-to-Question Mapping

Foundation Topics Section	Questions
OSPFv3 Fundamentals	1–2
OSPFv3 Configuration	3–4
IPv4 Support in OSPFv3	5

1. OSPFv3 uses __________ packet types for inter-router communication.

   a. three
   b. four
   c. five
   d. six
   e. seven

2. The OSPFv3 hello packet uses the __________ for the destination address.
   a. MAC addrcss 00:C1:00:5C:00:FF
   b. MAC address E0:00:00:06:00:AA
   c. IP address 224.0.0.8
   d. IP address 224.0.0.10
   e. IPv6 address FF02::A
   f. IPv6 address FF02::5
3. How do you enable OSPFv3 on an interface?
   a. Use the command **network** *prefix/prefix-length* under the OSPF process.
   b. Use the command **network** *interface-id* under the OSPF process.
   c. Use the command **ospfv3** *process-id* **ipv6 area** *area-id* under the interface.
   d. Nothing. OSPFv3 is enabled on all IPv6 interfaces upon initialization of the OSPF process.
4. True or false: On a brand-new router installation, OSPFv3 requires only that an IPv6 link-local address be configured and that OSPFv3 be enabled on that interface to form an OSPFv3 neighborship with another router.
   a. True
   b. False
5. True or false: OSPFv3 support for IPv4 networks only requires that an IPv4 address be assigned to the interface and that the OSPFv3 process be initialized for IPv4.
   a. True
   b. False

Foundation Topics

Key Topic

OSPFv3 Fundamentals

OSPFv3 is different from OSPFv2 in the following ways:

- **Support for multiple address families:** OSPFv3 supports IPv4 and IPv6 address families.
- **New LSA types:** New LSA types have been created to carry IPv6 prefixes.
- **Removal of addressing semantics:** The IP prefix information is no longer present in the OSPF packet headers. Instead, it is carried as LSA payload information, making the protocol essentially address family independent, much like IS-IS. OSPFv3 uses the term *link* instead of *network* because the SPT calculations are per link instead of per subnet.
- **LSA flooding:** OSPFv3 includes a new link-state type field that is used to determine the flooding scope of LSA, as well as the handling of unknown LSA types.
- **Packet format:** OSPFv3 runs directly over IPv6, and the number of fields in the packet header has been reduced.

- **Router ID:** The router ID is used to identify neighbors, regardless of the network type in OSPFv3. When you're configuring OSPFv3 on IOS routers, the ID must always be manually assigned in the routing process.
- **Authentication:** Neighbor authentication has been removed from the OSPF protocol and is now performed through IPsec extension headers in the IPv6 packet.
- **Neighbor adjacencies:** OSPFv3 inter-router communication is handled by IPv6 link-local addressing. Neighbors are not automatically detected over non-broadcast multiple access (NBMA) interfaces. A neighbor must be manually specified using the link-local address. IPv6 allows for multiple subnets to be assigned to a single interface, and OSPFv3 allows for neighbor adjacency to form even if the two routers do not share a common subnet.
- **Multiple instances:** OSPFv3 packets include an instance ID field that may be used to manipulate which routers on a network segment are allowed to form adjacencies.

NOTE RFC 5340 provides in-depth coverage of all the differences between OSPFv2 and OSPFv3.

OSPFv3 Link-State Advertisement

The OSPF link-state database information is organized and advertised differently in Version 3 than in Version 2. OSPFv3 modifies the structure of the router LSA (type 1), renames the network summary LSA to inter-area prefix LSA, and renames the ASBR summary LSA to inter-area router LSA. The principal difference is that the router LSA is only responsible for announcing interface parameters such as the interface type (point-to-point, broadcast, NBMA, point-to-multipoint, and virtual links) and metric (cost).

IP address information is advertised independently by two new LSA types:

- Intra-area prefix LSA
- Link LSA

The OSPF Dijkstra calculation used to determine the shortest path tree (SPT) only examines the router and network LSAs. Advertising the IP prefix information using new LSA types eliminates the need for OSPF to perform full shortest path first (SPF) tree calculations every time a new IP address (prefix) is added or changed on an interface. The OSPFv3 link-state database (LSDB) creates a shortest path topology tree based on links instead of networks.

OSPFv3 Communication

OSPFv3 packets use protocol number 89 in the IPv6 header, and routers communicate with each other using the local interface's IPv6 link-local address as the source. It also uses the

---

Answers to the "Do I Know This Already?" quiz:

1 C **2** F **3** C **4** B **5** B

same five packet types and logic as OSPFv2. Depending on the packet type, the destination address is either a unicast link-local address or a multicast link-local scoped address:

- **FF02::05:** OSPFv3 AllSPFRouters
- **FF02::06:** OSPFv3 AllDRouters

Every router uses the AllSPFRouters multicast address FF02::5 to send OSPF hello messages to routers on the same link. The hello messages are used for neighbor discovery and detecting whether a neighbor relationship is down. The DR and BDR routers also use this address to send link-state update and flooding acknowledgment messages to all routers.

Non-DR/BDR routers send an update or link-state acknowledgment message to the DR and BDR by using the AllDRouters address FF02::6.

OSPFv3 Configuration

The process of configuring OSPFv3 involves the following steps:

Step 1. Initialize the routing process. As a prerequisite, **ipv6 unicast-routing** must be enabled on the router. Afterward, the OSPFv3 process is configured with the command **router ospfv3** [*process-id*].

Step 2. Define the router ID. The command **router-id** *router-id* assigns a router ID to the OSPF process. The router ID is a 32-bit value that does not need to match an IPv4 address. It may be any number in IPv4 address format (for example, 0.1.2.3), as long as the value is unique within the OSPF domain.

OSPFv3 uses the same algorithm as OSPFv2 for dynamically locating the RID. If there are not any IPv4 interfaces available, the RID is set to 0.0.0.0 and does not allow adjacencies to form.

Step 3. (Optional) Initialize the address family. The address family is initialized within the routing process with the command **address-family** {**ipv6** | **ipv4**} **unicast**. The appropriate address family is enabled automatically when OSPFv3 is enabled on an interface.

Step 4. Enable OSPFv3 on an interface. The interface command **ospfv3** *process-id* **ipv6 area** *area-id* enables the protocol and assigns the interface to an area.

NOTE OSPFv3 does not use the network statement for initializing interfaces.

Figure 10-1 displays a simple four-router topology to demonstrate OSPFv3 configuration. Area 0 consists of R1, R2, and R3, and Area 34 contains R3 and R4. R3 is the ABR.

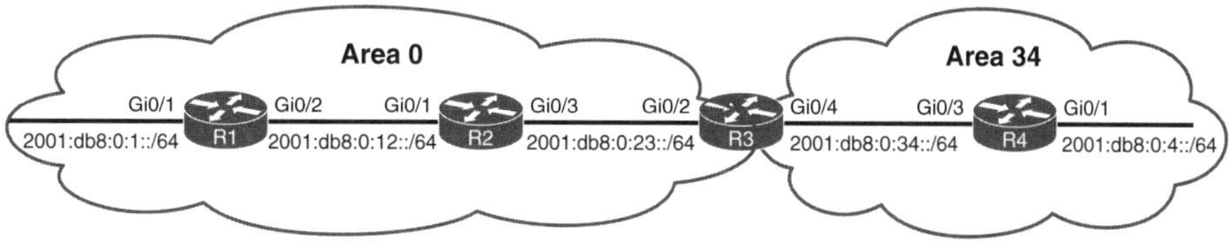

Figure 10-1 *OSPFv3 Topology*

Example 10-1 provides the OSPFv3 and IPv6 address configurations for R1, R2, R3, and R4. IPv6 link-local addressing has been configured so that all router interfaces reflect their local numbers (for example, R1's interfaces are set to FE80::1) in addition to traditional IPv6 addressing. The link-local addressing is statically configured to assist with any diagnostic output in this chapter. The OSPFv3 configuration has been highlighted in this example.

Example 10-1 *IPv6 Addressing and OSPFv3 Configuration*

```
R1
interface Loopback0
 ipv6 address 2001:DB8::1/128
 ospfv3 1 ipv6 area 0
!
interface GigabitEthernet0/1
 ipv6 address FE80::1 link-local
 ipv6 address 2001:DB8:0:1::1/64
 ospfv3 1 ipv6 area 0
!
interface GigabitEthernet0/2
 ipv6 address FE80::1 link-local
 ipv6 address 2001:DB8:0:12::1/64
 ospfv3 1 ipv6 area 0
!
router ospfv3 1
 router-id 192.168.1.1
```

```
R2
interface Loopback0
 ipv6 address 2001:DB8::2/128
 ospfv3 1 ipv6 area 0
!
interface GigabitEthernet0/1
 ipv6 address FE80::2 link-local
 ipv6 address 2001:DB8:0:12::2/64
ospfv3 1 ipv6 area 0
!
interface GigabitEthernet0/3
 ipv6 address FE80::2 link-local
 ospfv3 1 ipv6 area 0
!
router ospfv3 1
 router-id 192.168.2.2
```

```
R3
interface Loopback0
 ipv6 address 2001:DB8::3/128
```

```
 ospfv3 1 ipv6 area 0
!
interface GigabitEthernet0/2
 ipv6 address FE80::3 link-local
 ipv6 address 2001:DB8:0:23::3/64
 ospfv3 1 ipv6 area 0
!
interface GigabitEthernet0/4
 ipv6 address FE80::3 link-local
 ipv6 address 2001:DB8:0:34::3/64
 ospfv3 1 ipv6 area 34
!
router ospfv3 1
 router-id 192.168.3.3
```

```
R4
interface Loopback0
ipv6 address 2001:DB8::4/128
 ospfv3 1 ipv6 area 34
!
interface GigabitEthernet0/1
 ipv6 address FE80::4 link-local
 ipv6 address 2001:DB8:0:4::4/64
 ospfv3 1 ipv6 area 34
!
interface GigabitEthernet0/3
 ipv6 address FE80::4 link-local
 ipv6 address 2001:DB8:0:34::4/64
 ospfv3 1 ipv6 area 34
!
router ospfv3 1
 router-id 192.168.4.4
```

NOTE Earlier versions of IOS used the commands **ipv6 router ospf** for initialization of the OSPF process and **ipv6 ospf** *process-id* **area** *area-id* for identification of the interface. These commands are considered legacy and should be migrated to the ones used in this book.

10

Key Topic

OSPFv3 Verification

The commands for viewing OSPFv3 settings and statuses are similar to those used in OSPFv2; they essentially replace **ip ospf** with **ospfv3 ipv6.** Supporting OSPFv3 requires verifying the OSPFv3 interfaces, neighborship, and the routing table.

For example, to view the neighbor adjacency for OSPFv2, the command **show ip ospf neighbor** is executed, and for OSPFv3, the command **show ospfv3 ipv6 neighbor** is used. Example 10-2 shows this command executed on R3.

Example 10-2 *Identifying R3's OSPFv3 Neighbors*

```
R3# show ospfv3 ipv6 neighbor

         OSPFv3 1 address-family ipv6 (router-id 192.168.3.3)

Neighbor ID  Pri   State        Dead Time    Interface ID    Interface
192.168.2.2   1   FULL/DR      00:00:32     5                 GigabitEthernet0/2
192.168.4.4   1   FULL/BDR     00:00:33     5                 GigabitEthernet0/4
```

Example 10-3 shows R1's GigabitEthernet0/2 OSPFv3-enabled interface status with the command **show ospfv3 interface** [*interface-id*]. Notice that address semantics have been removed compared to OSPFv2. The interface maps to the interface ID value 3 rather than an IP address value, as in OSPFv2. In addition, some helpful topology information describes the link. The local router is the DR (192.168.1.1), and the adjacent neighbor router is the BDR (192.168.2.2).

Example 10-3 *Viewing the OSPFv3 Interface Configuration*

```
R1# show ospfv3 interface GigabitEthernet0/2
GigabitEthernet0/2 is up, line protocol is up
  Link Local Address FE80::1, Interface ID 3
  Area 0, Process ID 1, Instance ID 0, Router ID 192.168.1.1
  Network Type BROADCAST, Cost: 1
  Transmit Delay is 1 sec, State DR, Priority 1
  Designated Router (ID) 192.168.1.1, local address FE80::1
  Backup Designated router (ID) 192.168.2.2, local address FE80::2
  Timer intervals configured, Hello 10, Dead 40, Wait 40, Retransmit 5
    Hello due in 00:00:01
  Graceful restart helper support enabled
  Index 1/1/1, flood queue length 0
  Next 0x0(0)/0x0(0)/0x0(0)
  Last flood scan length is 0, maximum is 4
  Last flood scan time is 0 msec, maximum is 0 msec
  Neighbor Count is 1, Adjacent neighbor count is 1
    Adjacent with neighbor 192.168.2.2 (Backup Designated Router)
  Suppress hello for 0 neighbor(s)
```

A brief version of the OSPFv3 interface settings can be viewed with the command **show ospfv3 interface brief**. The associated process ID, area, address family (IPv4 or IPv6), interface state, and neighbor count are provided in the output.

Example 10-4 demonstrates this command being executed on the ABR, R3. Notice that some interfaces reside in Area 0, and others reside in Area 34.

Example 10-4 *Viewing a Brief Version of OSPFv3 Interfaces*

```
R3# show ospfv3 interface brief
Interface     PID    Area             AF         Cost   State Nbrs F/C
Lo0            1     0                 ipv6        1       LOOP  0/0
Gi0/2          1     0                 ipv6        1       BDR    1/1
Gi0/4          1     34                ipv6        1       DR     1/1
```

The OSPFv3 IPv6 routing table is viewed with the command **show ipv6 route ospf**. Intra-area routes are indicated with *O*, and inter-area routes are indicated with *OI*.

Example 10-5 shows this command being executed on R1. The forwarding address for the routes is the link-local address of the neighboring router.

Example 10-5 *Viewing the OSPFv3 Routes in the IPv6 Routing Table*

```
R1# show ipv6 route ospf
! Output omitted for brevity
IPv6 Routing Table - default - 11 entries
       RL - RPL, O - OSPF Intra, OI - OSPF Inter, OE1 - OSPF ext 1
       OE2 - OSPF ext 2, ON1 - OSPF NSSA ext 1, ON2 - OSPF NSSA ext 2
..
O   2001:DB8::2/128 [110/1]
     via FE80::2, GigabitEthernet0/2
O   2001:DB8::3/128 [110/2]
     via FE80::2, GigabitEthernet0/2
OI  2001:DB8::4/128 [110/3]
     via FE80::2, GigabitEthernet0/2
OI  2001:DB8:0:4::/64 [110/4]
     via FE80::2, GigabitEthernet0/2
O   2001:DB8:0:23::/64 [110/2]
     via FE80::2, GigabitEthernet0/2
OI  2001:DB8:0:34::/64 [110/3]
     via FE80::2, GigabitEthernet0/2
```

Passive Interface

OSPFv3 supports the ability to mark an interface as passive. The command is placed under the OSPFv3 process or under the specific address family. Placing the command under the global process cascades the setting to both address families. An interface is marked as being passive with the command **passive-interface** *interface-id* or globally with **passive-interface default**, and then the interface is marked as active with the command **no passive-interface** *interface-id*.

Example 10-6 shows how to make the LAN interface on R1 explicitly passive and how to make all interfaces passive on R4 while marking the Gi0/3 interface as active.

Example 10-6 *Configuring OSPFv3 Passive Interfaces*

```
R1(config)# router ospfv3 1
R1(config-router)# passive-interface GigabitEthernet0/1
```

```
R4(config)# router ospfv3 1
R4(config-router)# passive-interface default
22:10:46.838: %OSPFv3-5-ADJCHG: Process 1, IPv6, Nbr 192.168.3.3 on
GigabitEthernet0/3 from FULL to DOWN, Neighbor Down: Interface down or detached
R4(config-router)# no passive-interface GigabitEthernet 0/3
```

The active/passive state of an interface is verified by examining the OSPFv3 interface status using the command **show ospfv3 interface** [*interface-id*] and searching for the *Passive* keyword. In Example 10-7, R1 confirms that the Gi0/3 interface is passive.

Example 10-7 *Viewing an OSPFv3 Interface State*

```
R1# show ospfv3 interface GigabitEthernet 0/1 | include Passive
    No Hellos (Passive interface)
```

Summarization

The ability to summarize IPv6 networks is as important as summarizing routes in IPv4 (and it may even be more important, due to hardware scale limitations). Example 10-8 shows the IPv6 routing table on R4 before summarization is applied on R3.

Example 10-8 *R4's IPv6 Routing Table Before Summarization*

```
R4# show ipv6 route ospf | begin Application
       lA - LISP away, a - Application
OI   2001:DB8::1/128 [110/3]
      via FE80::3, GigabitEthernet0/3
OI   2001:DB8::2/128 [110/2]
      via FE80::3, GigabitEthernet0/3
OI   2001:DB8::3/128 [110/1]
      via FE80::3, GigabitEthernet0/3
OI   2001:DB8:0:1::/64 [110/4]
      via FE80::3, GigabitEthernet0/3
OI   2001:DB8:0:12::/64 [110/3]
      via FE80::3, GigabitEthernet0/3
OI   2001:DB8:0:23::/64 [110/2]
      via FE80::3, GigabitEthernet0/3
```

Summarizing the Area 0 router's loopback interfaces (2001:db8:0::1/128, 2001:db8:0::2/128, and 2001:db8:0::3/128) removes three routes from the routing table.

NOTE A common mistake with summarization of IPv6 addresses is to confuse hex with decimal. We typically perform summarization logic in decimal, and the first and third digits in a hextet should not be confused as decimal values. For example, the first hextet of the IPv6 address 2001::1/128 is 2001. When we separate those values further, it is not 20 and 1 in decimal format. The decimal values in that hextet are 32 (20 in hex) and 1 (1 in hex).

Key Topic

Summarization of internal OSPFv3 routes follows the same rules as in OSPFv2 and must occur on ABRs. In our topology, R3 summarizes the three loopback addresses into the 2001:db8:0:0::/65 network. Summarization involves the command **area** *area-id* **range** *prefix/prefix-length*, which resides under the address family in the OSPFv3 process.

Example 10-9 shows R3's configuration for summarizing these prefixes.

Example 10-9 *IPv6 Summarization*

```
R3# configure terminal
Enter configuration commands, one per line. End with CNTL/Z.
R3(config)# router ospfv3 1
R3(config-router)# address-family ipv6 unicast
R3(config-router-af)# area 0 range 2001:db8:0:0::/65
```

Example 10-10 shows R4's IPv6 routing table after configuring R3 to summarize the Area 0 loopback interfaces. The summary route is highlighted in this example.

Example 10-10 *R4's IPv6 Routing Table After Summarization*

```
R4# show ipv6 route ospf | begin Application
       lA - LISP away, a - Application
OI  2001:DB8::/65 [110/4]
     via FE80::3, GigabitEthernet0/3
OI  2001:DB8:0:1::/64 [110/4]
     via FE80::3, GigabitEthernet0/3
OI  2001:DB8:0:12::/64 [110/3]
     via FE80::3, GigabitEthernet0/3
OI  2001:DB8:0:23::/64 [110/2]
     via FE80::3, GigabitEthernet0/3
```

Network Type

OSPFv3 supports the same OSPF network types as OSPFv2. Example 10-11 shows that R2's Gi0/3 interface is set as a broadcast OSPF network type and is confirmed as being in a DR state.

Example 10-11 *Viewing the Dynamic Configured OSPFv3 Network Type*

```
R2# show ospfv3 interface GigabitEthernet 0/3 | include Network
  Network Type BROADCAST, Cost: 1
R2# show ospfv3 interface brief
Interface    PID   Area            AF         Cost  State Nbrs F/C
Lo0            1     0               ipv6       1      LOOP  0/0
Gi0/3          1     0               ipv6       1      DR    1/1
Gi0/1          1     0               ipv6       1      BDR   1/1
```

The OSPFv3 network type is changed with the interface parameter command **ospfv3 network** {**point-to-point** | **broadcast**}. Example 10-12 shows the interfaces associated with the 2001:DB8:0:23::/64 network being changed to point-to-point.

Example 10-12 *Changing the OSPFv3 Network Type*

```
R2# configure terminal
Enter configuration commands, one per line. End with CNTL/Z.
R2(config)# interface GigabitEthernet 0/3
R2(config-if)# ospfv3 network point-to-point
```

```
R3(config)# interface GigabitEthernet 0/2
R3(config-if)# ospfv3 network point-to-point
```

After the changes are typed in, the new settings are verified in Example 10-13. The network is now a point-to-point link, and the interface state shows as P2P for confirmation.

Example 10-13 *Viewing the Statically Configured OSPFv3 Network Type*

```
R2# show ospfv3 interface GigabitEthernet 0/3 | include Network
  Network Type POINT_TO_POINT, Cost: 1
R2# show ospfv3 interface brief
Interface     PID   Area            AF          Cost  State Nbrs F/C
Lo0            1     0               ipv6         1      LOOP  0/0
Gi0/3          1     0               ipv6         1      P2P   1/1
Gi0/1          1     0               ipv6         1      BDR   1/1
```

IPv4 Support in OSPFv3

RFC 5838 specifies that OSPFv3 should support multiple address families by setting the instance ID value from the IPv6 reserved range to the IPv4 reserved range (64 to 95) in the link LSAs.

Enabling IPv4 support for OSPFv3 is straightforward:

Key Topic

Step 1. Ensure that the IPv4 interface has an IPv6 address (global or link local) configured. Remember that configuring a global address also places a link-local address; alternatively, a link-local address can statically be configured.

Step 2. Enable the OSPFv3 process for IPv4 on the interface with the command **ospfv3** *process-id* **ipv4 area** *area-id*.

Using the topology shown in Figure 10-1, IPv4 addressing has been placed onto R1, R2, R3, and R4 using the conventions outlined earlier. Example 10-14 demonstrates the deployment of IPv4 using the existing OSPFv3 deployment.

Example 10-14 *Configuration Changes for IPv4 Support*

```
R1(config)# interface Loopback 0
R1(config-if)# ospfv3 1 ipv4 area 0
R1(config-if)# interface GigabitEthernet0/1
R1(config-if)# ospfv3 1 ipv4 area 0
R1(config-if)# interface GigabitEthernet0/2
R1(config-if)# ospfv3 1 ipv4 area 0
```

```
R2(config)# interface Loopback 0
R2(config-if)# ospfv3 1 ipv4 area 0
R2(config-if)# interface GigabitEthernet0/1
R2(config-if)# ospfv3 1 ipv4 area 0
R2(config-if)# interface GigabitEthernet0/3
R2(config-if)# ospfv3 1 ipv4 area 0
```

```
R3(config)# interface Loopback 0
R3(config-if)# ospfv3 1 ipv4 area 0
R3(config-if)# interface GigabitEthernet0/2
R3(config-if)# ospfv3 1 ipv4 area 0
```

```
R3(config-if)# interface GigabitEthernet0/4
R3(config-if)# ospfv3 1 ipv4 area 34
```

```
R4(config)# interface Loopback 0
R4(config-if)# ospfv3 1 ipv4 area 34
R4(config-if)# interface GigabitEthernet0/1
R4(config-if)# ospfv3 1 ipv4 area 34
R4(config-if)# interface GigabitEthernet0/3
R4(config-if)# ospfv3 1 ipv4 area 34
```

Example 10-15 verifies that the routes were exchanged and installed into the IPv4 RIB.

Example 10-15 *Verifying IPv4 Route Exchange with OSPFv3*

```
R4# show ip route ospfv3 | begin Gateway
Gateway of last resort is not set


      10.0.0.0/8 is variably subnetted, 5 subnets, 2 masks
O IA     10.1.1.0/24 [110/4] via 10.34.1.3, 00:00:39, GigabitEthernet0/3
O IA     10.12.1.0/24 [110/3] via 10.34.1.3, 00:00:39, GigabitEthernet0/3
O IA     10.23.1.0/24 [110/2] via 10.34.1.3, 00:00:39, GigabitEthernet0/3
      192.168.1.0/32 is subnetted, 1 subnets
O IA     192.168.1.1 [110/3] via 10.34.1.3, 00:00:39, GigabitEthernet0/3
      192.168.2.0/32 is subnetted, 1 subnets
O IA     192.168.2.2 [110/2] via 10.34.1.3, 00:00:39, GigabitEthernet0/3
      192.168.3.0/32 is subnetted, 1 subnets
O IA     192.168.3.3 [110/1] via 10.34.1.3, 00:00:39, GigabitEthernet0/3
```

The command **show ospfv3 interface** [**brief**] displays the address families enabled on an interface. When IPv4 and IPv6 are both configured on an interface, an entry appears for each address family. Example 10-16 lists the interfaces and associated address families.

Example 10-16 *Listing of OSPFv3 Interfaces and Their Address Families*

```
R4# show ospfv3 interface brief
Interface    PID   Area            AF         Cost  State Nbrs F/C
Lo0           1     34               ipv4        1     LOOP  0/0
Gi0/1         1     34               ipv4        1     DR    1/1
Gi0/3         1     34               ipv4        1     DR    1/1
Lo0           1     34               ipv6        1     LOOP  0/0
Gi0/1         1     34               ipv6        1     DR    0/0
Gi0/3         1     34               ipv6        1     BDR   1/1
```

Example 10-17 shows how to view the OSPFv3 neighbors to display the neighbors enabled for IPv4 and IPv6 as separate entities.

Example 10-17 *Verifying OSPFv3 IPv4 Neighbors*

```
R4# show ospfv3 neighbor

          OSPFv3 1 address-family ipv4 (router-id 192.168.4.4)

Neighbor ID     Pri   State           Dead Time   Interface ID    Interface
192.168.3.3       1   FULL/BDR        00:00:30    6               GigabitEthernet0/3

          OSPFv3 1 address-family ipv6 (router-id 192.168.4.4)

Neighbor ID     Pri   State           Dead Time   Interface ID    Interface
192.168.3.3       1   FULL/DR         00:00:31    6               GigabitEthernet0/3
192.168.3.3 1 FULL/DR 00:00:31 6 GigabitEthernet0/3
```

Exam Preparation Tasks

You have a couple of choices for exam preparation: the exercises here, Chapter 30, "Final Preparation," and the exam simulation questions in the Pearson Test Prep Software Online.

Review All Key Topics

Review the most important topics in the chapter, noted with the Key Topic icon in the outer margin of the page. Table 10-2 lists these key topics and the page number on which each is found.

Key Topic

Table 10-2 Key Topics for Chapter 10

Key Topic Element	Description	Page
Section	OSPFv3 Fundamentals	231
Section	OSPFv3 Verification	235
Paragraph	OSPFv3 summarization	238
List	IPv4 support on OSPFv3	240

Complete Tables and Lists from Memory

There are no memory tables in this chapter.

Define Key Terms

There are no key terms in this chapter.

Use the Command Reference to Check Your Memory

Table 10-3 lists the important commands from this chapter. To test your memory, cover the right side of the table with a piece of paper, read the description on the left side, and see how much of the command you can remember.

Table 10-3 Command Reference

Task	Command Syntax
Configure OSPFv3 on a router and enable it on an interface	**router ospfv3** [*process-id*] **interface** *interface-id* **ospfv3** *process-id* {**ipv4** | **ipv6**} **area** *area-id*
Configure a specific OSPFv3 interface as passive	**passive-interface** *interface-id*
Configure all OSPFv3 interfaces as passive	**passive-interface default**
Summarize an IPv6 network range on an ABR	**area** *area-id* **range** *prefix/prefix-length*
Configure an OSPFv3 interface as a point-to-point or broadcast network type	**ospfv3 network** {**point-to-point** | **broadcast**}
Display OSPFv3 interface settings	**show ospfv3 interface** [*interface-id*]
Display OSPFv3 IPv6 neighbors	**show ospfv3 ipv6 neighbor**

References in This Chapter

RFC 5340, *OSPF for IPv6*, R. Coltun, D. Ferguson, J. Moy, A. Lindem, and IETF. http://www.ietf.org/rfc/rfc5340.txt, July 2008.

RFC 5838, *Support of Address Families in OSPFv3*, A. Lindem, S. Mirtorabi, A. Roy, M. Barnes, R. Aggarwal, and IETF. http://www.ietf.org/rfc/rfc5838.txt, April 2010.

Edgeworth, Brad, Aaron Foss, and Ramiro Garza Rios, *IP Routing on Cisco IOS, IOS XE, and IOS XR*. Indianapolis: Cisco Press, 2014.

Cisco IOS Software Configuration Guides. http://www.cisco.com.

CHAPTER 11

BGP

This chapter covers the following subjects:

- **BGP Fundamentals:** This section provides an overview of the fundamentals of the BGP routing protocol.
- **Basic BGP Configuration:** This section walks through the process of configuring BGP to establish a neighbor session and how routes are exchanged between peers.
- **IPv4 Route Summarization:** This section provides an overview of how route summarization works with BGP and some of the design considerations with summarization.
- **Multiprotocol BGP for IPv6:** This section explains how BGP provides support for IPv6 routing and configuration.

RFC 1654 defines *Border Gateway Protocol (BGP)* as an EGP standardized routing protocol that provides scalability, flexibility, and network stability. When BGP was created, the primary design consideration was for IPv4 inter-organization connectivity on public networks like the Internet and on private dedicated networks. BGP is the only protocol used to exchange networks on the Internet, which, at the time of this writing, has more than 940,000 IPv4 network prefixes and more than 180,000 IPv6 network prefixes and continues to grow. Due to the large size of the BGP tables, BGP does not advertise incremental updates or refresh network advertisements as OSPF and IS-IS do. BGP prefers stability within the network, as a link flap could result in route computation for thousands of routes.

This chapter covers the fundamentals of BGP (path attributes, address families, and inter-router communication), BGP configuration, route summarization, and support for IPv6. Chapter 12, "Advanced BGP," explains common scenarios in enterprise environments for BGP, route filtering and manipulation, BGP communities, and the logic BGP uses for identifying a route as the best path.

"Do I Know This Already?" Quiz

The "Do I Know This Already?" quiz enables you to assess whether you should read the entire chapter. If you miss no more than one of these self-assessment questions, you might want to move ahead to the "Exam Preparation Tasks" section. Table 11-1 lists the major headings in this chapter and the "Do I Know This Already?" quiz questions covering the material in those headings so you can assess your knowledge of these specific areas. The answers to the "Do I Know This Already?" quiz appear in Appendix A, "Answers to the 'Do I Know This Already?' Questions."

Table 11-1 "Do I Know This Already?" Foundation Topics Section-to-Question Mapping

Foundation Topics Section	Questions
BGP Fundamentals	1–4
Basic BGP Configuration	5–8
IPv4 Route Summarization	9
Multiprotocol BGP for IPv6	10

1. Which of the following autonomous systems are private? (Choose two.)
   a. 64,512–65,534
   b. 65,000–65,534
   c. 4,200,000,000–4,294,967,294
   d. 4,265,000–4,265,535,016
2. Which BGP attribute must be recognized by all BGP implementations and advertised to other autonomous systems?
   a. Well-known mandatory
   b. Well-known discretionary
   c. Optional transitive
   d. Optional non-transitive
3. True or false: BGP supports dynamic neighbor discovery by both routers.
   a. True
   b. False
4. True or false: A BGP session is always one hop away from a neighbor.
   a. True
   b. False
5. True or false: The IPv4 address family must be initialized to establish a BGP session with a peer using IPv4 addressing.
   a. True
   b. False
6. Which command is used to view the BGP neighbors and their hello intervals?
   a. **show bgp neighbors**
   b. **show bgp** *afi safi* **neighbors**
   c. **show bgp** *afi safi* **summary**
   d. **show** *afi* **bgp interface brief**
7. How many tables does BGP use for storing prefixes?
   a. One
   b. Two
   c. Three
   d. Four

8. True or false: BGP advertises all its paths for every prefix so that every neighbor can build its own topology table.
   a. True
   b. False
9. Which BGP command advertises a summary route to prevent link-flap processing by downstream BGP routers?
   a. **aggregate-address** *network subnet-mask* **as-set**
   b. **aggregate-address** *network subnet-mask* **summary-only**
   c. **summary-address** *network subnet-mask*
   d. **summary-address** *network* **mask** *subnet-mask*
10. True or false: The IPv6 address family must be initialized to establish a BGP session with a peer using IPv6 addressing.
   a. True
   b. False

Foundation Topics

BGP Fundamentals

From the perspective of BGP, an **autonomous system (AS)** is a collection of routers under a single organization's control, using one or more IGPs and common metrics to route packets within the AS. If multiple IGPs or metrics are used within an AS, the AS must appear consistent to external ASs in routing policy. An IGP is not required within an AS; an AS could use BGP as the only routing protocol.

Key Topic

Autonomous System Numbers

An organization requiring connectivity to the Internet must obtain an autonomous system number (ASN). ASNs were originally 2 bytes (16-bit range), which made 65,535 ASNs possible. Due to ASN exhaustion, RFC 4893 expanded the ASN field to accommodate 4 bytes (32-bit range). This allows for 4,294,967,295 unique ASNs, providing quite an increase from the original 65,535 ASNs.

Two blocks of private ASNs are available for any organization to use, as long as they are never exchanged publicly on the Internet. ASNs 64,512–65,534 are private ASNs in the 16-bit ASN range, and 4,200,000,000–4,294,967,294 are private ASNs within the extended 32-bit range.

NOTE RFC 1930 defined the private ASN range as 64,512–65,635, but RFC 6996 changed the 16-bit private ASN range to 64,512–65,534. RFC 7300 defines the reason why the ASNs at the end of the 16-bit and 32-bit ASN range, 65,535 and 4,294,967,295 respectively, should not be used.

The *Internet Assigned Numbers Authority (IANA)* is responsible for assigning all public ASNs to ensure that they are globally unique. IANA requires the following items when requesting a public ASN:

- Proof of a publicly allocated network range
- Proof that Internet connectivity is provided through multiple connections
- Need for a unique routing policy from providers

If an organization cannot provide this information, it should use the ASN provided by its service provider.

NOTE It is imperative to use only the ASN assigned by IANA, the ASN assigned by your service provider, or a private ASN. Using another organization's ASN without permission could result in traffic loss and cause havoc on the Internet.

Key Topic

Path Attributes

BGP uses path attributes (PAs) associated with each network path. The PAs provide BGP with granularity and control of routing policies within BGP. The BGP prefix PAs are classified as follows:

- **Well-known mandatory**
- **Well-known discretionary**
- **Optional transitive**
- **Optional non-transitive**

Per RFC 4271, well-known attributes must be recognized by all BGP implementations. Well-known mandatory attributes must be included with every prefix advertisement; well-known discretionary attributes may or may not be included with a prefix advertisement.

Optional attributes do not have to be recognized by all BGP implementations. Optional attributes can be set so that they are transitive and stay with the route advertisement from AS to AS. Other PAs are *non-transitive* and cannot be shared from AS to AS.

Loop Prevention

BGP is a **path vector routing protocol** and does not contain a complete topology of the network, as link-state routing protocols do. BGP behaves like distance vector protocols, ensuring that a path is loop free.

Key Topic

The BGP attribute **AS_Path** is a well-known mandatory attribute and includes a complete list of all the ASNs that the prefix advertisement has traversed from its source AS. AS_Path is used as a loop-prevention mechanism in BGP. If a BGP router receives a prefix advertisement with its AS listed in the AS_Path attribute, it discards the prefix because the router thinks the advertisement forms a loop.

Figure 11-1 shows the loop-prevention mechanism:

- AS 100 advertises the 172.16.1.0/24 route to AS 200.
- AS 200 advertises the route to AS 400, which then advertises the route to AS 300.
- AS 300 advertises the route back to AS 100 with an AS_Path of 300 400 200 100. AS 100 sees itself in the AS_Path and discards the route.

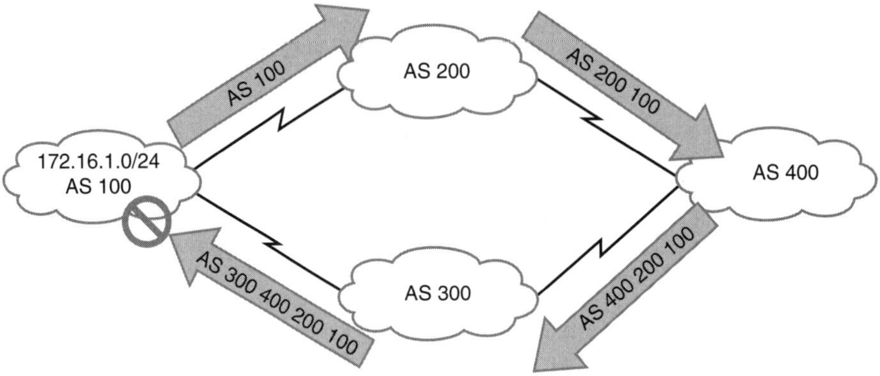

Figure 11-1 *Path Vector Loop Prevention*

Address Families

Originally, BGP was intended for routing of IPv4 prefixes between organizations, but RFC 2858 added Multiprotocol BGP (MP-BGP) capability by adding an extension called the address family identifier (AFI). An **address family** correlates to a specific network protocol, such as IPv4 or IPv6, and additional granularity is provided through a subsequent address-family identifier (SAFI) such as unicast or multicast. In BGP, the *Network Layer Reachability Information (NLRI)* is the prefix length and the prefix.

> **NOTE** Some network engineers refer to Multiprotocol BGP as MP-BGP, and other network engineers use the term MBGP. Both terms refer to the same thing.

Key Topic

Every address family maintains a separate database and configuration for each protocol (address family + sub-address family) in BGP. This allows for a routing policy in one address family to be different from a routing policy in a different address family, even though the router uses the same BGP session with the other router. BGP includes an AFI and SAFI with every route advertisement to differentiate between the AFI and SAFI databases.

Key Topic

Inter-Router Communication

BGP does not use hello packets to discover neighbors, as do IGP protocols, and two BGP neighbors cannot discover each other dynamically like OSPF. BGP was designed as an inter-autonomous routing protocol, implying that neighbor adjacencies should not change frequently and are coordinated. BGP neighbors are defined by IP address.

Answers to the "Do I Know This Already?" quiz:

1 A, C **2** A **3** B **4** B **5** B **6** B **7** C **8** B **9** B **10** A

BGP uses TCP port 179 to communicate with other routers. TCP allows for handling of fragmentation, sequencing, and reliability (acknowledgment and retransmission) of communication packets. Most recent implementations of BGP set the do-not-fragment (DF) bit to prevent fragmentation and rely on path MTU discovery.

IGPs follow the physical topology because the sessions are formed with hellos that cannot cross network boundaries (that is, single hop only). BGP uses TCP, which is capable of crossing network boundaries (that is, multi-hop capable). While BGP can form neighbor adjacencies that are directly connected, it can also form adjacencies that are multiple hops away.

A BGP session refers to the established adjacency between two BGP routers. Multi-hop sessions require that the router use an underlying route installed in the RIB (static or from any routing protocol) to establish the TCP session with the remote endpoint.

In Figure 11-2, R1 is able to establish a direct BGP session with R2. In addition, R2 is able to establish a BGP session with R4, even though it passes through R3. R1 and R2 use a directly connected route to locate each other. R2 uses a static route to reach the 10.34.1.0/24 network, and R4 has a static route to reach the 10.23.1.0/24 network. R3 is unaware that R2 and R4 have established a BGP session even though the packets flow through R3.

Key Topic

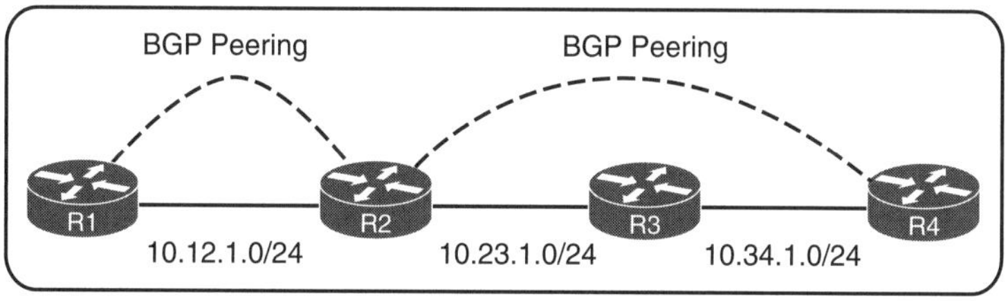

Figure 11-2 *BGP Single- and Multi-Hop Sessions*

> **NOTE** BGP neighbors connected to the same network use the ARP table to locate the IP address of the peer. Multi-hop BGP sessions require routing table information for finding the IP address of the peer. It is common to have a static route or an IGP running between iBGP neighbors for providing the topology path information to establish the BGP TCP session. A default route is not sufficient to establish a multi-hop BGP session.

BGP can be thought of as a control plane routing protocol or as an application because it allows for the exchange of routes with a peer that is multiple hops away. In Figure 11-2, R2 has established a multi-hop BGP session with R4. R3 does not require a BGP session with R2 or R4 but does need to know all the routes that will be forwarded through them to provide connectivity between R2 and R4.

Key Topic

BGP Session Types

BGP sessions are categorized into two types:

- **Internal BGP (iBGP):** Sessions established with an iBGP router that are in the same AS or that participate in the same BGP confederation. iBGP prefixes are assigned an administrative distance (AD) of 200 upon installation in the router's RIB.
- **External BGP (eBGP):** Sessions established with a BGP router that are in a different AS. eBGP prefixes are assigned an AD of 20 upon installation in the router's RIB.

11

The following sections review these two types of BGP sessions.

iBGP

The need for BGP within an AS typically occurs when multiple routing policies are required or when transit connectivity is provided between autonomous systems. In Figure 11-3, AS 65200 provides transit connectivity to AS 65100 and AS 65300. AS 65100 connects at R2, and AS 65300 connects at R4.

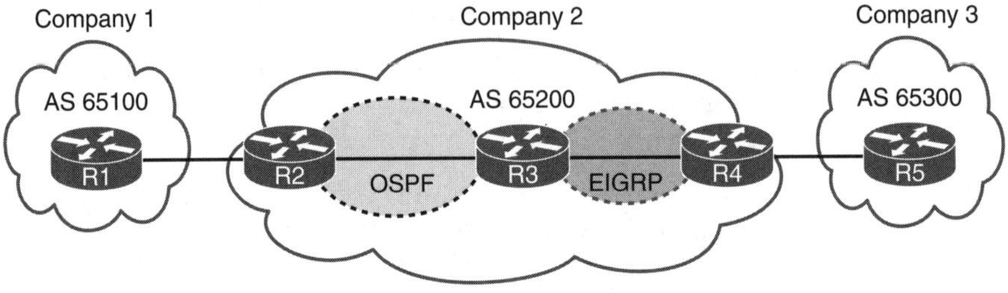

Figure 11-3 *AS 65200 Providing Transit Connectivity*

R2 could form an iBGP session directly with R4, but R3 would not know where to forward traffic to reach AS 65100 or AS 65300 when traffic from either AS reaches R3, as shown in Figure 11-4, because R3 would not have the appropriate route forwarding information for the destination traffic.

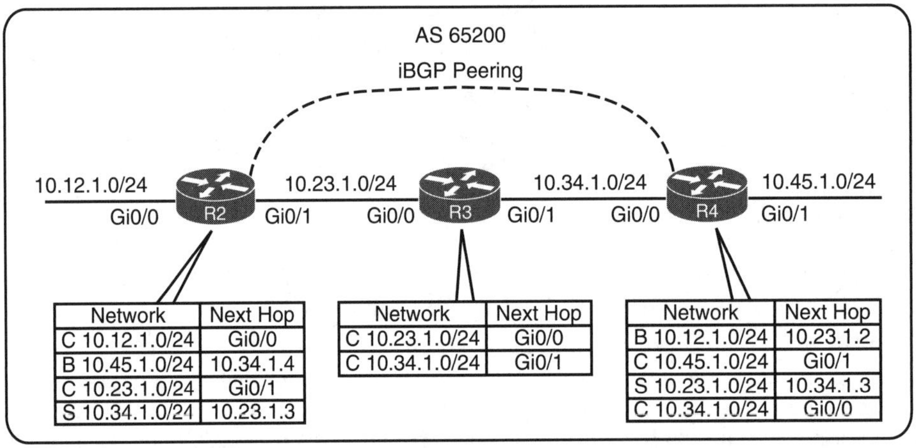

Figure 11-4 *iBGP Prefix Advertisement Behavior*

You might assume that redistributing the BGP table into an IGP overcomes the problem, but this not a viable solution for several reasons:

- **Scalability:** The Internet at the time of this writing has 940,000+ IPv4 network prefixes and continues to increase in size. IGPs cannot scale to that level of routes.
- **Custom routing:** Link-state protocols and distance vector routing protocols use metric as the primary method for route selection. IGP protocols always use this routing pattern for path selection. BGP uses multiple steps to identify the best path and allows for

BGP path attributes to manipulate a prefix's path. The path could be longer, and that would normally be deemed suboptimal from an IGP's perspective.

- **Path attributes:** All the BGP path attributes cannot be maintained within IGP protocols. Only BGP is capable of maintaining the path attribute as the prefix is advertised from one edge of the AS to the other edge.

Using Figure 11-3 as a reference, establishing iBGP sessions in AS 65200 between all routers (R2, R3, and R4) in a full mesh allows for proper forwarding between AS 65100 and AS 65300.

NOTE Service providers provide transit connectivity. Enterprise organizations are consumers and should not provide transit connectivity between autonomous systems across the Internet.

Key Topic

eBGP

eBGP peerings are the core component of BGP on the Internet. eBGP involves the exchange of network prefixes between autonomous systems. The following behaviors are different on **eBGP sessions** than on **iBGP sessions**:

- Time-to-live (TTL) on eBGP packets is set to 1 by default. eBGP packets drop in transit if a multi-hop BGP session is attempted. (TTL on iBGP packets is set to 255, which allows for multi-hop sessions.)
- The advertising router modifies the BGP next-hop address to the IP address sourcing the BGP connection.
- The advertising router prepends its ASN to the existing AS_Path attribute.
- The receiving router verifies that the AS_Path attribute does not contain an ASN that matches the local ASN. BGP discards the route if it fails the AS_Path loop prevention check.

The configurations for eBGP and iBGP sessions are fundamentally the same except that the ASN in the **remote-as** statement is different from the ASN defined in the BGP process.

Figure 11-5 shows the eBGP and iBGP sessions that would be needed between the routers to allow reachability between AS 65100 and AS 65300. Notice that all routers in AS 65200 establish iBGP sessions in a full mesh to allow for proper forwarding between AS 65100 and AS 65300.

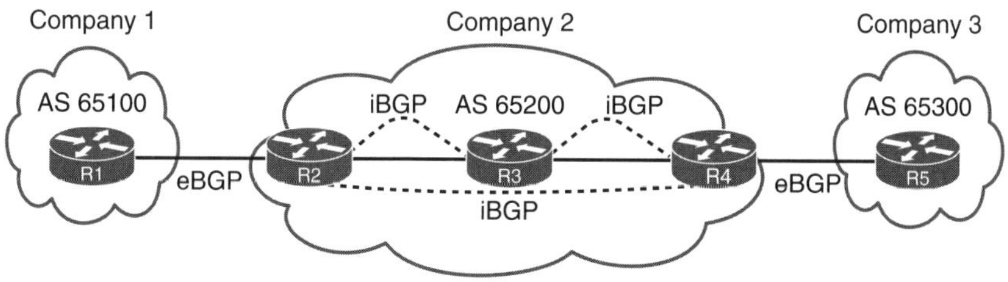

Figure 11-5 *eBGP and iBGP Sessions*

BGP Messages

BGP communication uses four message types, as shown in Table 11-2.

Table 11-2 BGP Packet Types

Type	Name	Functional Overview
1	OPEN	Sets up and establishes BGP adjacency
2	UPDATE	Advertises, updates, or withdraws routes
3	NOTIFICATION	Indicates an error condition to a BGP neighbor
4	KEEPALIVE	Ensures that BGP neighbors are still alive

- **OPEN:** An OPEN message is used to establish a BGP adjacency. Both sides negotiate session capabilities before BGP peering is established. The OPEN message contains the BGP version number, the ASN of the originating router, the hold time, the BGP identifier, and other optional parameters that establish the session capabilities.
  - **Hold time:** The hold time field in the OPEN message sets the proposed value for the hold timer in seconds, for each BGP neighbor. The hold timer in conjunction with keepalive messages is a heartbeat mechanism for BGP neighbors to ensure that a neighbor is healthy and alive.When establishing a BGP session, the routers use the smaller hold time value contained in the two routers' OPEN messages. The hold time value must be at least 3 seconds, or set to 0 to disable keepalive messages. For Cisco routers, the default hold timer is 180 seconds.
  - **BGP identifier:** The *BGP router ID (RID)* is a 32-bit unique number that identifies the BGP router in the advertised prefixes. The RID can be used as a loop-prevention mechanism for routers advertised within an autonomous system. The RID can be set manually or dynamically for BGP. A nonzero value must be set in order for routers to become neighbors.
- **KEEPALIVE:** BGP does not rely on the TCP connection state to ensure that the neighbors are still alive. KEEPALIVE messages are exchanged every one-third of the hold timer agreed upon between the two BGP routers. Cisco devices have a default hold time of 180 seconds, so the default keepalive interval is 60 seconds. If the hold time is set to 0, then no keepalive messages are sent between the BGP neighbors.
- **UPDATE:** An UPDATE message advertises any feasible routes, withdraws previously advertised routes, or can do both. An UPDATE message includes the advertised prefixes in the Network Layer Reachability Information (NLRI) PA, as well as other associated BGP PAs. Prefixes that need to be withdrawn are advertised in the WITHDRAWN ROUTES field of the UPDATE message. An UPDATE message can act as a keepalive to reduce unnecessary traffic. Upon receipt of an UPDATE, the hold timer resets to the initial value. If the hold timer reaches zero, the BGP session is torn down, routes from that neighbor are removed, and an UPDATE message is sent to other BGP neighbors to withdraw the affected prefixes.
- **NOTIFICATION:** A NOTIFICATION message is sent when an error is detected with the BGP session, such as a hold timer expiring, neighbor capabilities changing, or a BGP session reset being requested. This causes the BGP connection to close.

BGP Neighbor States

BGP forms a TCP session with neighbor routers called *peers*. BGP uses the finite-state machine (FSM) to maintain a table of all BGP peers and their operational status. The BGP session may report the following states:

- Idle
- Connect
- Active
- OpenSent
- OpenConfirm
- Established

Figure 11-6 shows the BGP FSM and the states, listed in the order used in establishing a BGP session.

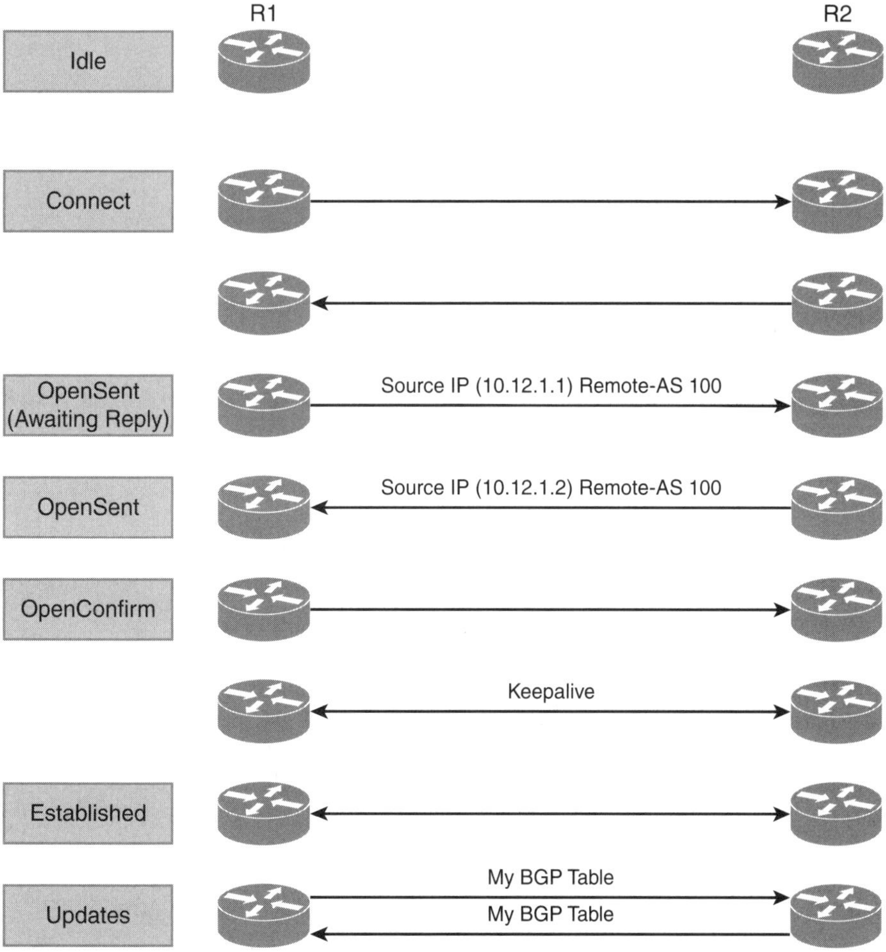

Figure 11-6 *BGP Neighbor States with Session Establishment*

Idle

Idle is the first stage of the BGP FSM. BGP detects a start event and tries to initiate a TCP connection to the BGP peer and also listens for a new connection from a peer router.

If an error causes BGP to go back to the Idle state for a second time, the ConnectRetryTimer is set to 60 seconds and must decrement to zero before the connection can be initiated again. Further failures to leave the Idle state result in the ConnectRetryTimer doubling in length from the previous time.

Connect

In the Connect state, BGP initiates the TCP connection. If the three-way TCP handshake is completed, the established BGP session process resets the ConnectRetryTimer and sends an Open message to the neighbor; it then changes to the OpenSent state.

If the ConnectRetryTimer depletes before this stage is complete, a new TCP connection is attempted, the ConnectRetryTimer is reset, and the state stays in Connect. If the TCP connection fails, the state changes to Active. For any other events, the state is changed to Idle.

BGP routers use TCP port 179 to listen for incoming connections and as the destination port to connect to BGP peers. The router initiating the outgoing TCP connection uses a random source port and the destination port 179.

Example 11-1 shows an established BGP session using the command **show tcp brief** to display the TCP sessions between the routers. Notice that for R2, the TCP source port is 59884 and the destination port is 179; this means R2 initiated the TCP connection.

Example 11-1 *An Established BGP Session*

```
R1# show tcp brief
TCB         Local Address          Foreign Address          (state)
F6F84258    10.12.1.1.179         10.12.1.2.59884           ESTAB
```

```
R2# show tcp brief
TCB         Local Address          Foreign Address          (state)
EF153B88    10.12.1.2.59884       10.12.1.1.179             ESTAB
```

Active

In the Active state, BGP starts a new three-way TCP handshake. If a connection is established, an Open message is sent, the hold timer is set to 4 minutes, and the state moves to OpenSent. If this attempt for TCP connection fails, the state moves back to the Connect state, and the ConnectRetryTimer is reset.

OpenSent

In the OpenSent state, an Open message has been sent from the originating router and is awaiting an Open message from the other router. Once the originating router receives the OPEN message from the other router, both OPEN messages are checked for errors. The following items are examined:

- BGP versions must match.
- The source IP address of the OPEN message must match the IP address that is configured for the neighbor.

- The AS number in the OPEN message must match what is configured for the neighbor.
- BGP identifiers (RIDs) must be unique. If an RID does not exist, this condition is not met.
- Security parameters (such as password and TTL) must be set appropriately.

If the OPEN messages do not have any errors, the hold time is negotiated (using the lower value), and a KEEPALIVE message is sent (assuming that the value is not set to 0). The connection state is then moved to OpenConfirm. If an error is found in the OPEN message, a NOTIFICATION message is sent, and the state is moved back to Idle.

If TCP receives a disconnect message, BGP closes the connection, resets the ConnectRetryTimer, and sets the state to Active. Any other events in this process result in the state moving to Idle.

OpenConfirm

In the OpenConfirm state, BGP waits for a KEEPALIVE or NOTIFICATION message. Upon receipt of a neighbor's KEEPALIVE message, the state is moved to Established. If the hold timer expires, a stop event occurs, or if a NOTIFICATION message is received, the state is moved to Idle.

Established

In the Established state, the BGP session is established. BGP neighbors exchange routes using UPDATE messages. As UPDATE and KEEPALIVE messages are received, the hold timer is reset. If the hold timer expires, an error is detected, and BGP moves the neighbor back to the Idle state.

Key Topic

Basic BGP Configuration

When you're configuring BGP, it is best to think of the configuration from a modular perspective. BGP router configuration requires the following components:

- **BGP session parameters:** BGP session parameters provide settings that involve establishing communication to the remote BGP neighbor. Session settings include the ASN of the BGP peer, authentication, and keepalive timers.
- **Address family initialization:** The address family is initialized under the BGP router configuration mode. Network advertisement and summarization occur within the address family.
- **Activate the address family on the BGP peer:** For a session to initiate, one address family for a neighbor must be activated. The router's IP address is added to the neighbor table, and BGP attempts to establish a BGP session or accepts a BGP session initiated from the peer router.

The following steps show how to configure BGP:

Step 1. Initialize the BGP routing process with the global command **router bgp** *as-number*.

Step 2. (Optional) Statically define the BGP router ID (RID). The dynamic RID allocation logic uses the highest IP address of any *up* loopback interfaces. If there is not an *up* loopback interface, then the highest IP address of any active *up* interfaces becomes the RID when the BGP process initializes.

To ensure that the RID does not change, a static RID is assigned (typically representing an IPv4 address that resides on the router, such as a loopback address). Any IPv4 address can be used, including IP addresses not configured on the router. Statically configuring the BGP RID is a best practice and involves using the command **bgp router-id** *router-id*.

When the router ID changes, all BGP sessions reset and need to be reestablished.

Step 3. Identify the BGP neighbor's IP address and autonomous system number with the BGP router configuration command **neighbor** *ip-address* **remote-as** *as-number*. It is important to understand the traffic flow of BGP packets between peers. The source IP address of the BGP packets still reflects the IP address of the outbound interface. When a BGP packet is received, the router correlates the source IP address of the packet to the IP address configured for that neighbor. If the BGP packet source does not match an entry in the neighbor table, the packet cannot be associated to a neighbor and is discarded.

NOTE IOS XE activates the IPv4 address family by default. This can simplify the configuration in an IPv4 environment because steps 4 and 5 are optional but may cause confusion when working with other address families. The BGP router configuration command **no bgp default ipv4-unicast** disables the automatic activation of the IPv4 AFI so that steps 4 and 5 are required.

Step 4. Initialize the address family with the BGP router configuration command **address-family** *afi safi*. Examples of *afi* values are IPv4 and IPv6, and examples of *safi* values are unicast and multicast.

Step 5. Activate the address family for the BGP neighbor with the BGP address family configuration command **neighbor** *ip-address* **activate**.

NOTE On IOS XE devices, the default subsequent address family identifier (SAFI) for the IPv4 and IPv6 address families is unicast and is optional.

Figure 11-7 shows a topology for a simple BGP configuration.

Example 11-2 shows how to configure R1 and R2 using the default and optional IPv4 AFI modifier CLI syntax. R1 is configured with the default IPv4 address family enabled, and R2 disables IOS's default IPv4 address family and manually activates it for the specific neighbor

10.12.1.1. The command **no bgp default ipv4-unicast** is not necessary on R2, and BGP will work properly for IPv4 prefixes, but standardizing behavior is easier when you're working with other address families like IPv6.

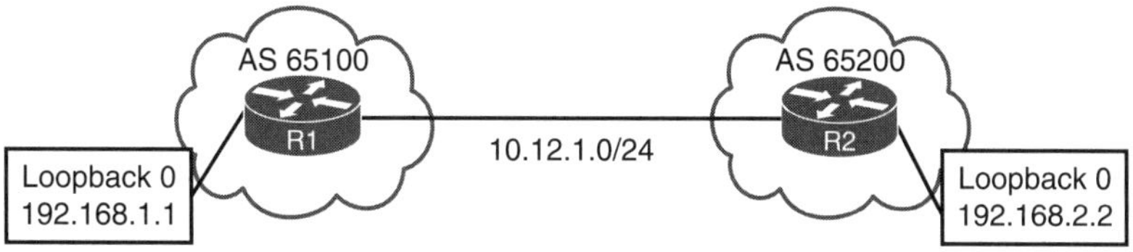

Figure 11-7 *Simple BGP Topology*

Example 11-2 *Configuring Basic BGP on IOS XE*

```
R1 (Default IPv4 Address-Family Enabled)
router bgp 65100
 neighbor 10.12.1.2 remote-as 65200
```

```
R2 (Default IPv4 Address-Family Disabled)
router bgp 65200
 no bgp default ipv4-unicast
 neighbor 10.12.1.1 remote-as 65100
 !
 address-family ipv4
  neighbor 10.12.1.1 activate
```

Key Topic

Verification of BGP Sessions

The BGP session is verified with the command **show bgp** *afi safi* **summary**. Example 11-3 shows the IPv4 BGP unicast summary. Notice that the BGP RID and table version are the first components shown. The Up/Down column indicates that the BGP session is up for over 5 minutes.

NOTE Earlier commands like **show ip bgp summary** came out before MBGP and do not provide a structure for the current multiprotocol capabilities within BGP. Using the AFI and SAFI syntax ensures consistency for the commands, regardless of information exchanged by BGP. This will become more apparent as engineers work with address families like IPv6, VPNv4, and VPNv6.

Example 11-3 *Verifying the BGP IPv4 Session Summary*

```
R1# show bgp ipv4 unicast summary
BGP router identifier 192.168.1.1, local AS number 65100
BGP table version is 1, main routing table version 1

Neighbor        V       AS MsgRcvd MsgSent   TblVer  InQ OutQ Up/Down  State/PfxRcd
10.12.1.2       4    65200       8       9        1    0    0 00:05:23        0
```

Table 11-3 explains the fields of output displayed in a BGP table (as in Example 11-3).

Table 11-3 BGP Summary Fields

Field	Description
Neighbor	IP address of the BGP peer
V	BGP version spoken by the BGP peer
AS	Autonomous system number of the BGP peer
MsgRcvd	Count of messages received from the BGP peer
MsgSent	Count of messages sent to the BGP peer
TblVer	Last version of the BGP database sent to the peer
InQ	Number of messages received from the peer and queued to be processed
OutQ	Number of messages queued to be sent to the peer
Up/Down	Length of time the BGP session is established or the current status if the session is not in an established state
State/PfxRcd	Current BGP peer state or the number of prefixes received from the peer

BGP neighbor session state, timers, and other essential peering information is available with the command **show bgp** *afi safi* **neighbors** *ip-address*, as shown in Example 11-4.

Example 11-4 *BGP IPv4 Neighbor Output*

```
R2# show bgp ipv4 unicast neighbors 10.12.1.1
! Output ommitted for brevity

! The first section provides the neighbor's IP address, remote-as, indicates if
! the neighbor is 'internal' or 'external', the neighbor's BGP version, RID,
! session state, and timers.

BGP neighbor is 10.12.1.1, remote AS65100, external link
  BGP version 4, remote router ID 192.168.1.1
  BGP state = Established, up for 00:01:04
  Last read 00:00:10, last write 00:00:09, hold is 180, keepalive is 60 seconds
  Neighbor sessions:
    1 active, is not multisession capable (disabled)
! This second section indicates the capabilities of the BGP neighbor and
! address-families configured on the neighbor.
  Neighbor capabilities:
    Route refresh: advertised and received(new)
    Four-octets ASN Capability: advertised and received
    Address family IPv4 Unicast: advertised and received
    Enhanced Refresh Capability: advertised
    Multisession Capability:
    Stateful switchover support enabled: NO for session 1
```

```
  Message statistics:
    InQ depth is 0
    OutQ depth is 0

! This section provides a list of the BGP packet types that have been received
! or sent to the neighbor router.
                         Sent         Rcvd
    Opens:               1            1
    Notifications:       0            0
    Updates:             0            0
    Keepalives:          2            2
    Route Refresh:       0            0
    Total:               3            3
  Default minimum time between advertisement runs is 0 seconds

! This section provides the BGP table version of the IPv4 Unicast address-
! family. The table version is not a 1-to-1 correlation with routes as multiple
! route change can occur during a revision change. Notice the Prefix Activity
! columns in this section.

For address family: IPv4 Unicast
  Session: 10.12.1.1
  BGP table version 1, neighbor version 1/0
  Output queue size : 0
  Index 1, Advertise bit 0
                                 Sent       Rcvd
  Prefix activity:               ----       ----
    Prefixes Current:              0          0
    Prefixes Total:                0          0
    Implicit Withdraw:             0          0
    Explicit Withdraw:             0          0
    Used as bestpath:            n/a          0
    Used as multipath:           n/a          0

                                 Outbound    Inbound
  Local Policy Denied Prefixes:  --------    -------
    Total:                             0           0

 Number of NLRIs in the update sent: max 0, min 0

! This section indicates that a valid route exists in the RIB to the BGP peer IP
! address, provides the number of times that the connection has established and
! time dropped, since the last reset, the reason for the reset, if path-mtu-
! discovery is enabled, and ports used for the BGP session.
```

```
  Address tracking is enabled, the RIB does have a route to 10.12.1.1
   Connections established 2; dropped 1
   Last reset 00:01:40, due to Peer closed the session
   Transport(tcp) path-mtu-discovery is enabled
Connection state is ESTAB, I/O status: 1, unread input bytes: 0
Minimum incoming TTL 0, Outgoing TTL 255
Local host: 10.12.1.2, Local port: 179
Foreign host: 10.12.1.1, Foreign port: 56824
```

Key Topic

Route Advertisement

BGP **network** statements do not enable BGP for a specific interface; instead, they identify specific network prefixes to be installed into the BGP table, known as the **Loc-RIB**.

After configuring a BGP **network** statement, the BGP process searches the RIB routes for an exact network prefix match. The route can be from a connected network, a secondary connected network, or any route from a routing protocol. After verifying that the **network** statement matches a route in the RIB, the following BGP PAs are set, depending on the route type:

- **Connected network:** The next-hop BGP attribute is set to 0.0.0.0, the BGP origin attribute is set to i (IGP), and the BGP weight is set to 32,768.
- **Static route or routing protocol:** The next-hop BGP attribute is set to the next-hop IP address in the RIB, the BGP origin attribute is set to i (IGP), the BGP weight is set to 32,768, and the MED is set to the IGP metric.

After the BGP PAs are set, the route is installed into the Loc-RIB (the BGP table). Not every route in the Loc-RIB is advertised to a BGP peer. All routes in the Loc-RIB use the following process for advertisement to BGP peers:

Step 1. Pass a validity check. Verify that the NLRI is valid and that the next-hop address is resolvable in the RIB. If the NLRI fails, the NLRI remains but does not process further.

Step 2. Process outbound neighbor route policies. After processing, if a route was not denied by the outbound policies, the route is maintained in the Adj-RIB-Out for later reference.

Step 3. Advertise the routes to BGP peers. If the next-hop BGP PA is 0.0.0.0 for the prefixes in the NLRI PA, then the next-hop address is changed to the IP address of the BGP session.

Figure 11-8 illustrates the concept of installing routes from the RIB via network statement and then advertising them to BGP peers.

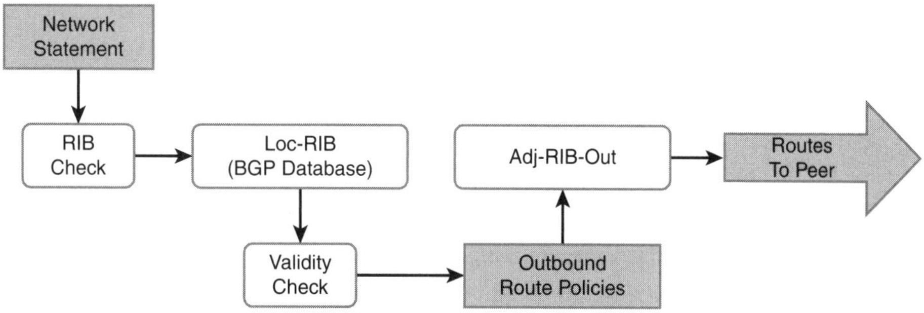

Figure 11-8 *BGP Database Processing of Local Route Advertisements*

NOTE BGP only advertises the best path by default to other BGP peers, regardless of the number of routes in the Loc-RIB.

The **network** statement resides under the appropriate address family within the BGP router configuration. The command **network** *network* **mask** *subnet-mask* [**route-map** *route-map-name*] is used for advertising IPv4 networks. The optional **route-map** provides a method of setting specific BGP PAs when the route installs into the Loc-RIB. Route maps are discussed in more detail in Chapter 12.

Figure 11-7 illustrates R1 and R2 connected through the 10.12.1.0/24 network. Example 11-5 demonstrates the configuration where both routers will advertise the Loopback 0 interfaces (192.168.1.1/32 and 192.168.2.2/32, respectively) and the 10.12.1.0/24 network into BGP. Notice that R1 uses the default IPv4 address family, and R2 explicitly specifies the IPv4 address family.

Example 11-5 *Configuring BGP Network Advertisement*

```
R1
router bgp 65100
 neighbor 10.12.1.2 remote-as 65200
 network 10.12.1.0 mask 255.255.255.0
 network 192.168.1.1 mask 255.255.255.255
```

```
R2
router bgp 65200
 no bgp default ipv4-unicast
 neighbor 10.12.1.1 remote-as 65100
 !
 address-family ipv4
network 10.12.1.0 mask 255.255.255.0
network 192.168.2.2 mask 255.255.255.255
  neighbor 10.12.1.1 activate
```

Receiving and Viewing Routes

BGP uses three tables for maintaining the network prefix and path attributes (PAs) for a route:

- **Adj-RIB-In:** Contains the routes in original form (that is, from before inbound route policies are processed). To save memory, the table is purged after all route policies are processed.
- **Loc-RIB:** Contains all the routes that originated locally or were received from other BGP peers. After the routes pass the validity and next-hop reachability check, the BGP best-path algorithm selects the best route for a specific prefix. The Loc-RIB, also known as the BGP table, is used for presenting routes to the IP routing table (RIB).
- **Adj-RIB-Out:** Contains the routes after outbound route policies have been processed.

Not every route in the Loc-RIB is advertised to a BGP peer or installed into the RIB when received from a BGP peer. BGP performs the following route processing steps:

Step 1. Store the route in the Adj-RIB-In in the original state and apply the inbound route policy based on the neighbor on which the route was received.

Step 2. Update the Loc-RIB with the latest entry. The Adj-RIB-In is cleared to save memory.

Step 3. Pass a validity check to verify that the route is valid and that the next-hop address is resolvable in the RIB. If the route fails, the route remains in the Loc-RIB but is not processed further.

Step 4. Identify the BGP best path and pass only the best path and its path attributes to step 5. The BGP best path selection process is covered in Chapter 12.

Step 5. Install the best-path route into the RIB, process the outbound route policy, store the non-discarded routes in the Adj-RIB-Out, and advertise to BGP peers.

Figure 11-9 shows the complete BGP route processing logic. It includes the receipt of a route from a BGP peer and the BGP best-path algorithm.

Key Topic

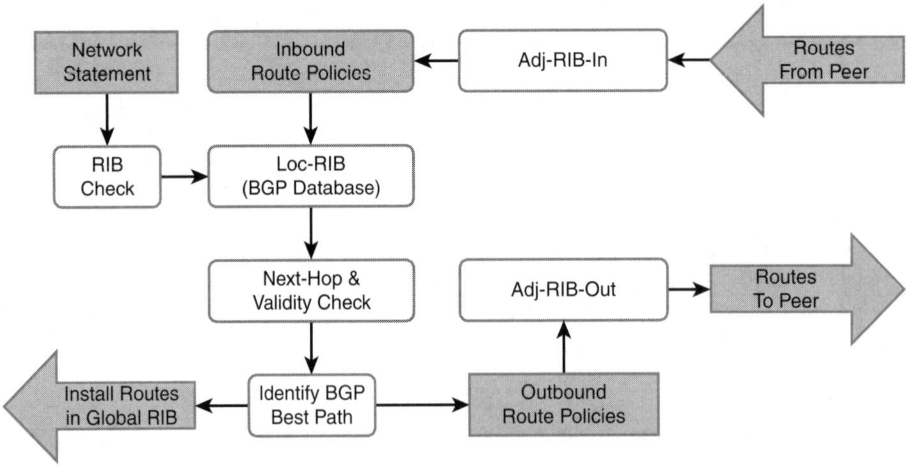

Figure 11-9 *BGP Decision Process*

The command **show bgp** *afi safi* displays the contents of the BGP table (Loc-RIB) on the router. Every entry in the Loc-RIB contains at least one path but could contain multiple paths for the same network prefix. Example 11-6 displays the BGP table on R1, which contains received routes and locally generated routes.

Example 11-6 *Displaying the BGP Table (Loc-RIB)*

```
R1# show bgp ipv4 unicast
BGP table version is 4, local router ID is 192.168.1.1
Status codes: s suppressed, d damped, h history, * valid, > best, i - internal,
              r RIB-failure, S Stale, m multipath, b backup-path, f RT-Filter,
              x best-external, a additional-path, c RIB-compressed,
Origin codes: i - IGP, e - EGP, ? - incomplete
RPKI validation codes: V valid, I invalid, N Not found
      Network          Next Hop            Metric LocPrf Weight Path
 *    10.12.1.0/24     10.12.1.2                0             0 65200 i
 *>                    0.0.0.0                  0         32768 i
 *>   192.168.1.1/32   0.0.0.0                  0         32768 i
 *>   192.168.2.2/32   10.12.1.2                0             0 65200 i
```

```
R2# show bgp ipv4 unicast | begin Network
      Network          Next Hop            Metric LocPrf Weight Path
 *    10.12.1.0/24     10.12.1.1                0             0 65100 i
 *>                    0.0.0.0                  0         32768 i
 *>   192.168.1.1/32   10.12.1.1                0             0 65100 i
 *>   192.168.2.2/32   0.0.0.0                  0         32768 i
```

Table 11-4 explains the fields of output when displaying the BGP table.

Key Topic

Table 11-4 BGP Table Fields

Field	Description
Network	A list of the prefixes installed in BGP. If multiple paths exist for the same prefix, only the first prefix is listed, and other paths leave an empty space in the output. Valid paths are indicated by the *. The path selected as the best path is indicated by an angle bracket (>).
Next Hop	A well-known mandatory BGP path attribute that defines the IP address for the next hop for that specific path.
Metric	*Multiple-exit discriminator (MED)*: An optional non-transitive BGP path attribute used in BGP for the specific path.
LocPrf	*Local Preference*: A well-known discretionary BGP path attribute used in the BGP best-path algorithm for the specific path.
Weight	A locally significant Cisco-defined attribute used in the BGP best-path algorithm for the specific path.

11

Field	Description
Path and Origin	*AS_Path*: A well-known mandatory BGP path attribute used for loop prevention and in the BGP best-path algorithm for the specific path. *Origin*: A well-known mandatory BGP path attribute used in the BGP best-path algorithm. A value of ***i*** represents an IGP, ***e*** indicates EGP, and ***?*** indicates a route that was redistributed into BGP.

The command **show bgp** *afi safi network* displays all the paths for a specific prefix and the BGP path attributes for that prefix. Example 11-7 shows the paths for the 10.12.1.0/24 prefix. The output includes the number of paths and which path is the best path.

Example 11-7 *Viewing Explicit BGP Routes and Path Attributes*

```
R1# show bgp ipv4 unicast 10.12.1.0
BGP routing table entry for 10.12.1.0/24, version 2
Paths: (2 available, best #2, table default)
  Advertised to update-groups:
     2
  Refresh Epoch 1
  65200
    10.12.1.2 from 10.12.1.2 (192.168.2.2)
      Origin IGP, metric 0, localpref 100, valid, external
      rx pathid: 0, tx pathid: 0
  Refresh Epoch 1
  Local
    0.0.0.0 from 0.0.0.0 (192.168.1.1)
      Origin IGP, metric 0, localpref 100, weight 32768, valid, sourced, local, best
      rx pathid: 0, tx pathid: 0x0
```

NOTE The command **show bgp** *afi safi* **detail** displays the entire BGP table with all the path attributes, such as those shown in Example 11-7.

The Adj-RIB-Out is a unique table maintained for each BGP peer. It enables a network engineer to view routes advertised to a specific router. The command **show bgp** *afi safi* **neighbor** *ip-address* **advertised routes** displays the contents of the Adj-RIB-Out for a specific neighbor.

Example 11-8 shows the Adj-RIB-Out entries specific to each neighbor. Notice that the next-hop address reflects the local router and will be changed as the route advertises to the peer.

Example 11-8 *Neighbor-Specific View of the Adj-RIB-Out*

```
R1# show bgp ipv4 unicast neighbors 10.12.1.2 advertised-routes
! Output omitted for brevity
     Network          Next Hop            Metric LocPrf Weight Path
*>  10.12.1.0/24      0.0.0.0                  0         32768 i
*>  192.168.1.1/32    0.0.0.0                  0         32768 i

Total number of prefixes 2
```

```
R2# show bgp ipv4 unicast neighbors 10.12.1.1 advertised-routes
! Output omitted for brevity
     Network          Next Hop            Metric LocPrf Weight Path
*>  10.12.1.0/24      0.0.0.0                  0         32768 i
*>  192.168.2.2/32    0.0.0.0                  0         32768 i

Total number of prefixes 2
```

The **show bgp ipv4 unicast summary** command can also be used to verify the exchange of routes between nodes, as shown in Example 11-9.

Example 11-9 *BGP Summary with Prefixes*

```
R1# show bgp ipv4 unicast summary
! Output omitted for brevity
Neighbor        V       AS MsgRcvd MsgSent   TblVer  InQ OutQ Up/Down  State/PfxRcd
10.12.1.2       4      65200        11        10       9    0    0 00:04:56        2
```

The BGP routes in the global IP routing table (RIB) are displayed with the command **show ip route bgp**. Example 11-10 shows these commands in the sample topology. The prefixes are from an eBGP session and have an AD of 20, and no metric is present.

Example 11-10 *Displaying BGP Routes in an IP Routing Table*

```
R1# show ip route bgp | begin Gateway
Gateway of last resort is not set

      192.168.2.0/32 is subnetted, 1 subnets
B        192.168.2.2 [20/0] via 10.12.1.2, 00:06:12
```

BGP Route Advertisements from Indirect Sources

As stated earlier, BGP should be thought of as a routing application as the BGP session and route advertisement are two separate components. Figure 11-10 demonstrates a topology where R1 installs multiple routes learned from static routes, EIGRP, and OSPF. R1 can advertise these routes to R2.

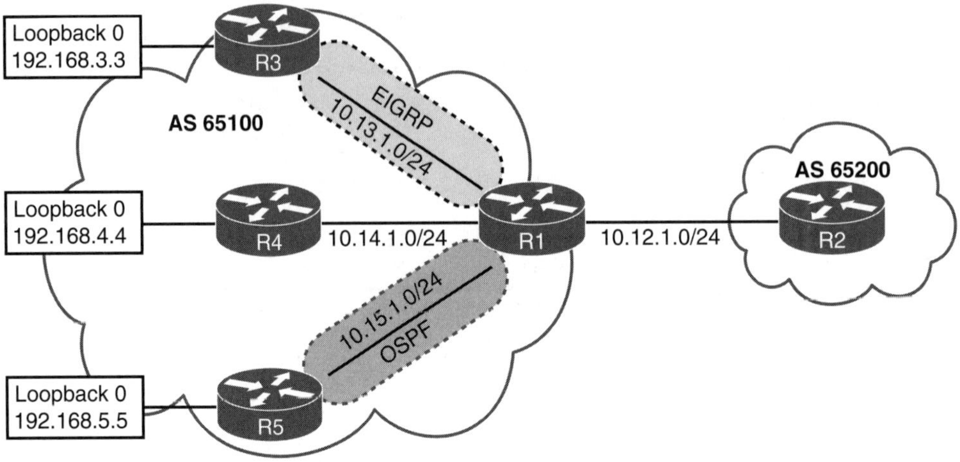

Figure 11-10 *Multiple BGP Route Sources*

Example 11-11 shows the routing table for R1. Notice that R3's loopback is learned via EIGRP, R4's loopback is reached using a static route, and R5's loopback is learned from OSPF.

Example 11-11 *R1's Routing Table with Loopbacks for R3, R4, and R5*

```
R1# show ip route
! Output omitted for brevity
Codes: L - local, C - connected, S - static, R - RIP, M - mobile, B - BGP
       D - EIGRP, EX - EIGRP external, O - OSPF, IA - OSPF inter area
..
Gateway of last resort is not set


       10.0.0.0/8 is variably subnetted, 8 subnets, 2 masks
C          10.12.1.0/24 is directly connected, GigabitEthernet0/0
C          10.13.1.0/24 is directly connected, GigabitEthernet0/1
C          10.14.1.0/24 is directly connected, GigabitEthernet0/2
C          10.15.1.0/24 is directly connected, GigabitEthernet0/3
C          192.168.1.1 is directly connected, Loopback0
B          192.168.2.2 [20/0] via 10.12.1.2, 00:01:17
D          192.168.3.3 [90/3584] via 10.13.1.3, 00:02:10, GigabitEthernet0/1
S          192.168.4.4 [1/0] via 10.14.1.4
O          192.168.5.5 [110/11] via 10.15.1.5, 00:00:08, GigabitEthernet0/3
```

Example 11-12 shows the installation of R3's and R4's loopback using a **network** statement. R5's loopback is learned by redistributing OSPF straight into BGP.

Example 11-12 *Configuring Advertising Routes for Non-Connected Routes*

```
R1
router bgp 65100
 network 10.12.1.0 mask 255.255.255.0
 network 192.168.1.1 mask 255.255.255.255
 network 192.168.3.3 mask 255.255.255.255
 network 192.168.4.4 mask 255.255.255.255
 redistribute ospf 1
 neighbor 10.12.1.2 remote-as 65200
```

NOTE Redistributing routes learned from an IGP into BGP is completely safe; however, BGP learned routes should be redistributed into an IGP with caution. BGP is designed for large scale and can handle a routing table the size of the Internet (940,000+ prefixes), whereas IGPs could have stability problems with fewer than 20,000 routes.

Example 11-13 shows the BGP routing tables on R1 and R2. Notice that on R1, the next hop matches the next hop learned from the RIB, the AS_Path is blank, and the origin code is *IGP* (for routes learned from network statement) or *incomplete* (redistributed). The metric is carried over from R3's and R5's IGP routing protocols and is reflected as the MED. R2 learns the routes strictly from eBGP and sees only the MED and the origin codes.

Example 11-13 *BGP Table for Routes from Multiple Sources*

```
R1# show bgp ipv4 unicast
BGP table version is 9, local router ID is 192.168.1.1
Status codes: s suppressed, d damped, h history, * valid, > best, i - internal,
              r RIB-failure, S Stale, m multipath, b backup-path, f RT-Filter,
              x best-external, a additional-path, c RIB-compressed,
Origin codes: i - IGP, e - EGP, ? - incomplete
RPKI validation codes: V valid, I invalid, N Not found

     Network          Next Hop            Metric LocPrf Weight Path
 *>  10.12.1.0/24     0.0.0.0                  0         32768 i
 *                    10.12.1.2                0             0 65200 i
 *>  10.15.1.0/24     0.0.0.0                  0         32768 ?
 *>  192.168.1.1/32   0.0.0.0                  0         32768 i
 *>  192.168.2.2/32   10.12.1.2                0             0 65200 i
 ! The following route comes from EIGRP and uses a network statement
 *>  192.168.3.3/32   10.13.1.3             3584         32768 i
! The following route comes from a static route and uses a network statement
 *>  192.168.4.4/32   10.14.1.4                0         32768 i
! The following route was redistributed from OSPF
*>  192.168.5.5/32   10.15.1.5              11         32768 ?
```

```
R2# show bgp ipv4 unicast | begin Network
      Network          Next Hop            Metric LocPrf Weight Path
 *    10.12.1.0/24     10.12.1.1                0             0 65100 i
 *>                      0.0.0.0                0         32768 i
 *>   10.15.1.0/24     10.12.1.1                0             0 65100 ?
 *>   192.168.1.1/32   10.12.1.1                0             0 65100 i
 *>   192.168.2.2/32   0.0.0.0                  0         32768 i
 *>   192.168.3.3/32   10.12.1.1             3584             0 65100 i
 *>   192.168.4.4/32   10.12.1.1                0             0 65100 i
 *>   192.168.5.5/32   10.12.1.1               11             0 65100 ?
```

IPv4 Route Summarization

Route summarization, also referred to as route aggregation, conserves router resources and accelerates best-path calculation by reducing the size of the table. Summarization also provides the benefit of stability by hiding route flaps from downstream routers, thereby reducing routing churn. While most service providers do not accept prefixes larger than /24 for IPv4 (/25 through /32), the Internet, at the time of this writing, still has more than 940,000 routes and continues to grow. Route summarization is required to reduce the size of the BGP table for Internet routers.

BGP route summarization on BGP edge routers reduces route computation on routers in the core for received routes or for advertised routes. In Figure 11-11, R3 summarizes all the eBGP routes received from AS 65100 and AS 65200 to reduce route computation on R4 during link flaps. In the event of a link flap on the 10.13.1.0/24 network, R3 removes all the AS 65100 routes learned directly from R1 and identifies the same network prefixes via R2 with different path attributes (a longer AS_Path). R3 has to advertise new routes to R4 because of these flaps, which is a waste of CPU cycles because R4 receives connectivity only from R3. If R3 summarized the network prefix range, R4 would execute the best-path algorithm once and not need to run during link flaps of the 10.13.1.0/24 link.

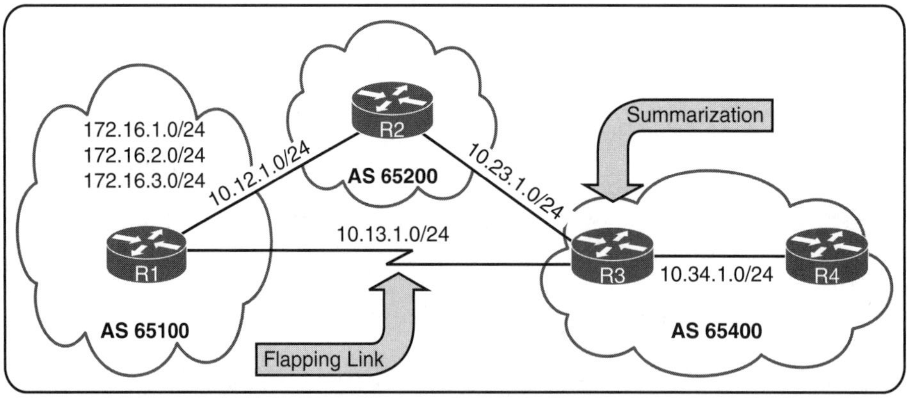

Figure 11-11 *BGP Route Summarization Hiding Link Flaps*

There are two techniques for BGP summarization:

Key Topic

- **Static:** Create a static route to Null0 for the summary network prefix and then advertise the prefix with a **network** statement. The downfall of this technique is that the summary route is always advertised, even if the networks are not available.
- **Dynamic:** Configure an aggregation network prefix. When viable component routes that match the aggregate network prefix enter the BGP table, then the aggregate prefix is created. The originating router sets the next hop to Null0 as a discard route for the aggregated prefix for loop prevention.

In both methods of route aggregation, a new network prefix with a shorter prefix length is advertised into BGP. Because the aggregated prefix is a new route, the summarizing router is the originator for the new aggregate route.

Key Topic

Aggregate Address

Dynamic route summarization is accomplished with the BGP address family configuration command **aggregate-address** *network subnet-mask* [**summary-only**] [**as-set**].

Figure 11-12 removes the flapping serial link between R1 and R3 to demonstrate BGP route summarization and the effects of the **aggregate-address** command.

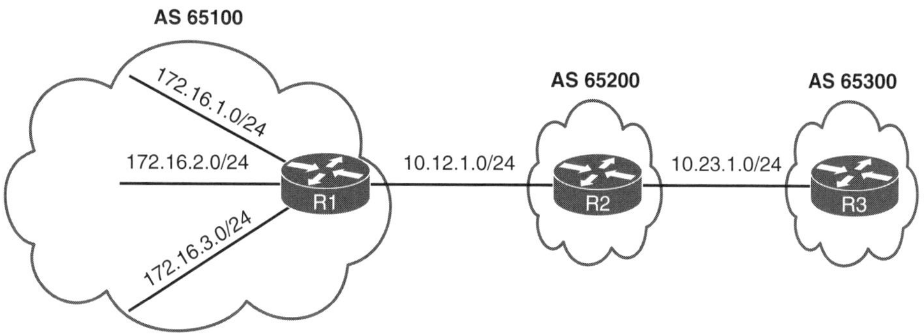

Figure 11-12 *BGP Summarization Topology*

Example 11-14 shows the BGP tables for R1, R2, and R3 before route summarization is performed. R1's stub networks (172.16.1.0/24, 172.16.2.0/24, and 172.16.3.0/24) are advertised through all the autonomous systems, along with the loopback addresses of R1, R2, and R3 (192.168.1.1/32, 192.168.2.2/32, and 192.168.3.3/32) and the peering links (10.12.1.0/24 and 10.23.1.0/24).

Example 11-14 *BGP Tables for R1, R2, and R3 Without Summarization*

```
R1# show bgp ipv4 unicast | begin Network
     Network          Next Hop            Metric LocPrf Weight Path
 *   10.12.1.0/24     10.12.1.2                0             0 65200 ?
 *>                   0.0.0.0                  0         32768 ?
 *>  10.23.1.0/24     10.12.1.2                0             0 65200 ?
```

11

```
*>  172.16.1.0/24     0.0.0.0                  0         32768 ?
*>  172.16.2.0/24     0.0.0.0                  0         32768 ?
*>  172.16.3.0/24     0.0.0.0                  0         32768 ?
*>  192.168.1.1/32    0.0.0.0                  0         32768 ?
*>  192.168.2.2/32    10.12.1.2                0             0 65200 ?
*>  192.168.3.3/32    10.12.1.2                              0 65200 65300 ?
```

```
R2# show bgp ipv4 unicast | begin Network
     Network          Next Hop            Metric LocPrf Weight Path
 *   10.12.1.0/24     10.12.1.1                0             0 65100 ?
 *>                   0.0.0.0                  0         32768 ?
 *   10.23.1.0/24     10.23.1.3                0             0 65300 ?
 *>                   0.0.0.0                  0         32768 ?
 *>  172.16.1.0/24    10.12.1.1                0             0 65100 ?
 *>  172.16.2.0/24    10.12.1.1                0             0 65100 ?
 *>  172.16.3.0/24    10.12.1.1                0             0 65100 ?
 *>  192.168.1.1/32   10.12.1.1                0             0 65100 ?
 *>  192.168.2.2/32   0.0.0.0                  0         32768 ?
 *>  192.168.3.3/32   10.23.1.3                0             0 65300 ?
```

```
R3# show bgp ipv4 unicast | begin Network
     Network          Next Hop            Metric LocPrf Weight Path
 *>  10.12.1.0/24     10.23.1.2                0             0 65200 ?
 *   10.23.1.0/24     10.23.1.2                0             0 65200 ?
 *>                   0.0.0.0                  0         32768 ?
 *>  172.16.1.0/24    10.23.1.2                              0 65200 65100 ?
 *>  172.16.2.0/24    10.23.1.2                              0 65200 65100 ?
 *>  172.16.3.0/24    10.23.1.2                              0 65200 65100 ?
 *>  192.168.1.1/32   10.23.1.2                              0 65200 65100 ?
 *>  192.168.2.2/32   10.23.1.2                0             0 65200 ?
 *>  192.168.3.3/32   0.0.0.0                  0         32768 ?
```

R1 aggregates all the stub networks (172.16.1.0/24, 172.16.2.0/24, and 172.16.3.0/24) into a 172.16.0.0/20 summary route. R2 summarizes all of the router's loopback addresses into a 192.168.0.0/16 summary route. Example 11-15 shows the configuration for R1 using the default IPv4 address family and R2 with the default IPv4 address family disabled.

Example 11-15 *Configuring BGP Route Summarization*

```
R1# show running-config | section router bgp
router bgp 65100
 aggregate-address 172.16.0.0 255.255.240.0
 redistribute connected
 neighbor 10.12.1.2 remote-as 65200
```

```
R2# show running-config | section router bgp
router bgp 65200
```

```
no bgp default ipv4-unicast
neighbor 10.12.1.1 remote-as 65100
neighbor 10.23.1.3 remote-as 65300
!
address-family ipv4
aggregate-address 192.168.0.0 255.255.0.0
redistribute connected
neighbor 10.12.1.1 activate
neighbor 10.23.1.3 activate
```

Example 11-16 shows the BGP tables for R1, R2, and R3 after summarization is configured on R1 and R2.

Example 11-16 *BGP Tables for R1, R2, and R3 with Summarization*

```
R1# show bgp ipv4 unicast | begin Network
      Network          Next Hop            Metric LocPrf Weight Path
 *    10.12.1.0/24     10.12.1.2                0             0 65200 ?
 *>                    0.0.0.0                  0         32768 ?
 *>   10.23.1.0/24     10.12.1.2                0             0 65200 ?
 *>   172.16.0.0/20    0.0.0.0                            32768 i
 *>   172.16.1.0/24    0.0.0.0                  0         32768 ?
 *>   172.16.2.0/24    0.0.0.0                  0         32768 ?
 *>   172.16.3.0/24    0.0.0.0                  0         32768 ?
 *>   192.168.0.0/16   10.12.1.2                0             0 65200 i
 *>   192.168.1.1/32   0.0.0.0                  0         32768 ?
 *>   192.168.2.2/32   10.12.1.2                0             0 65200 ?
 *>   192.168.3.3/32   10.12.1.2                              0 65200 65300 ?
```

```
R2# show bgp ipv4 unicast | begin Network
      Network          Next Hop            Metric LocPrf Weight Path
 *    10.12.1.0/24     10.12.1.1                0             0 65100 ?
 *>                    0.0.0.0                  0         32768 ?
 *    10.23.1.0/24     10.23.1.3                0             0 65300 ?
 *>                    0.0.0.0                  0         32768 ?
 *>   172.16.0.0/20    10.12.1.1                0             0 65100 i
 *>   172.16.1.0/24    10.12.1.1                0             0 65100 ?
 *>   172.16.2.0/24    10.12.1.1                0             0 65100 ?
 *>   172.16.3.0/24    10.12.1.1                0             0 65100 ?
 *>   192.168.0.0/16   0.0.0.0                            32768 i
 *>   192.168.1.1/32   10.12.1.1                0             0 65100 ?
 *>   192.168.2.2/32   0.0.0.0                  0         32768 ?
 *>   192.168.3.3/32   10.23.1.3                0             0 65300 ?
```

```
R3# show bgp ipv4 unicast | begin Network
     Network          Next Hop            Metric LocPrf Weight Path
 *>  10.12.1.0/24     10.23.1.2                0             0 65200 ?
 *   10.23.1.0/24     10.23.1.2                0             0 65200 ?
 *>                   0.0.0.0                  0         32768 ?
 *>  172.16.0.0/20    10.23.1.2                              0 65200 65100 i
 *>  172.16.1.0/24    10.23.1.2                              0 65200 65100 ?
 *>  172.16.2.0/24    10.23.1.2                              0 65200 65100 ?
*>  172.16.3.0/24     10.23.1.2                              0 65200 65100 ?
 *>  192.168.0.0/16   10.23.1.2                0             0 65200 i
*>   192.168.1.1/32   10.23.1.2                              0 65200 65100 ?
 *>  192.168.2.2/32   10.23.1.2                0             0 65200 ?
 *>  192.168.3.3/32   0.0.0.0                  0         32768 ?
```

Key Topic

Notice that the 172.16.0.0/20 and 192.168.0.0/16 summary routes are visible, but the smaller component routes still exist on all the routers. The **aggregate-address** command advertises the summary route in addition to the original component routes. Using the optional **summary-only** keyword suppresses the component routes, and only the summary route is advertised. Example 11-17 shows the configuration with the **summary-only** keyword.

Example 11-17 *BGP Route Summarization Configuration with Suppression*

```
R1# show running-config | section router bgp
router bgp 65100
aggregate-address 172.16.0.0 255.255.240.0 summary-only
 redistribute connected
 neighbor 10.12.1.2 remote-as 65200
```

```
R2# show running-config | section router bgp
router bgp 65200
 no bgp default ipv4-unicast
 neighbor 10.12.1.1 remote-as 65100
 neighbor 10.23.1.3 remote-as 65300
 !
 address-family ipv4
  aggregate-address 192.168.0.0 255.255.0.0 summary-only
  redistribute connected
  neighbor 10.12.1.1 activate
  neighbor 10.23.1.3 activate
```

Example 11-18 shows the BGP table for R3 after the **summary-only** keyword is added to the **aggregate-address** command on R1 and R2. Notice that the 172.16.0.0/20 and 192.168.0.0/16 summary routes are visible, but the smaller component routes are no longer present.

Example 11-18 *BGP Tables for R3 with Aggregation and Suppression*

```
R3# show bgp ipv4 unicast | begin Network
      Network          Next Hop            Metric LocPrf Weight Path
 *>   10.12.1.0/24     10.23.1.2                0             0 65200 ?
 *    10.23.1.0/24     10.23.1.2                0             0 65200 ?
 *>                    0.0.0.0                  0         32768 ?
 *>   172.16.0.0/20    10.23.1.2                              0 65200 65100 i
 *>   192.168.0.0/16   10.23.1.2                0             0 65200 i
 *>   192.168.3.3/32   0.0.0.0                  0         32768 ?
```

Example 11-19 shows the BGP table and RIB for R2. Notice that the component loopback networks have been suppressed by BGP and are not advertised by R2. In addition, a summary discard route has been installed to Null0 as a loop-prevention mechanism.

Example 11-19 *R2's BGP and RIB After Aggregation with Suppression*

```
R2# show bgp ipv4 unicast
BGP table version is 10, local router ID is 192.168.2.2
Status codes: s suppressed, d damped, h history, * valid, > best, i - internal,
              r RIB-failure, S Stale, m multipath, b backup-path, f RT-Filter,
              x best-external, a additional-path, c RIB-compressed,
Origin codes: i - IGP, e - EGP, ? - incomplete
RPKI validation codes: V valid, I invalid, N Not found
      Network          Next Hop            Metric LocPrf Weight Path
 *    10.12.1.0/24     10.12.1.1                0             0 65100 ?
 *>                    0.0.0.0                  0         32768 ?
 *    10.23.1.0/24     10.23.1.3                0             0 65300 ?
 *>                    0.0.0.0                  0         32768 ?
 *>   172.16.0.0/20    10.12.1.1                0             0 65100 i
 *>   192.168.0.0/16   0.0.0.0                            32768 i
 s>   192.168.1.1/32   10.12.1.1                0             0 65100 ?
 s>   192.168.2.2/32   0.0.0.0                  0         32768 ?
 s>   192.168.3.3/32   10.23.1.3                0             0 65300 ?
```

```
R2# show ip route bgp | begin Gateway
Gateway of last resort is not set
      172.16.0.0/20 is subnetted, 1 subnets
B        172.16.0.0 [20/0] via 10.12.1.1, 00:06:18
B     192.168.0.0/16 [200/0], 00:05:37, Null0
      192.168.1.0/32 is subnetted, 1 subnets
B        192.168.1.1 [20/0] via 10.12.1.1, 00:02:15
      192.168.3.0/32 is subnetted, 1 subnets
B        192.168.3.3 [20/0] via 10.23.1.3, 00:02:15
```

Example 11-20 shows that R1's stub networks have been suppressed, and the summary discard route for the 172.16.0.0/20 network has been installed in the RIB as well.

Example 11-20 *R1's BGP and RIB After Aggregation with Suppression*

```
R1# show bgp ipv4 unicast | begin Network
     Network          Next Hop            Metric LocPrf Weight Path
 *   10.12.1.0/24     10.12.1.2                0             0 65200 ?
 *>                   0.0.0.0                  0         32768 ?
 *>  10.23.1.0/24     10.12.1.2                0             0 65200 ?
 *>  172.16.0.0/20    0.0.0.0                            32768 i
 s>  172.16.1.0/24    0.0.0.0                  0         32768 ?
 s>  172.16.2.0/24    0.0.0.0                  0         32768 ?
 s>  172.16.3.0/24    0.0.0.0                  0         32768 ?
 *>  192.168.0.0/16   10.12.1.2                0             0 65200 i
 *>  192.168.1.1/32   0.0.0.0                  0         32768 ?
```

```
R1# show ip route bgp | begin Gateway
Gateway of last resort is not set

      10.0.0.0/8 is variably subnetted, 3 subnets, 2 masks
B        10.23.1.0/24 [20/0] via 10.12.1.2, 00:12:50
      172.16.0.0/16 is variably subnetted, 7 subnets, 3 masks
B        172.16.0.0/20 [200/0], 00:06:51, Null0
B     192.168.0.0/16 [20/0] via 10.12.1.2, 00:06:10
```

Key Topic

Atomic Aggregate

Summarized routes act like new BGP routes with a shorter prefix length. When a BGP router summarizes a route, it does not advertise the AS_Path information from before the route was summarized. BGP path attributes like AS_Path, MED, and BGP communities are not included in the new BGP advertisement.

The **atomic aggregate** attribute indicates that a loss of path information has occurred. To demonstrate this best, the previous BGP route summarization on R1 has been removed and added to R2 so that R2 is now summarizing the 172.16.0.0/20 and 192.168.0.0/16 networks with specific route suppression using the **summary-only** keyword. Example 11-21 shows the configuration on R2.

Example 11-21 *Configuring Aggregation for 172.16.0.0/20 and 192.168.0.0/16*

```
R2# show running-config | section router bgp
router bgp 65200
 no bgp default ipv4-unicast
 neighbor 10.12.1.1 remote-as 65100
 neighbor 10.23.1.3 remote-as 65300
 !
```

```
address-family ipv4
 aggregate-address 192.168.0.0 255.255.0.0 summary-only
 aggregate-address 172.16.0.0 255.255.240.0 summary-only
 redistribute connected
 neighbor 10.12.1.1 activate
 neighbor 10.23.1.3 activate
```

Example 11-22 shows R2's and R3's BGP tables. R2 is summarizing and suppressing R1's stub networks (172.16.1.0/24, 172.16.2.0/24, and 172.16.3.0/24) into the 172.16.0.0/20 summary route. The component routes maintain an AS_Path of 65100 on R2, while the 172.16.0.0/20 summary route appears locally generated on R2.

From R3's perspective, R2 does not advertise R1's stub networks; instead, it advertises the 172.16.0.0/20 summary route as its own. The AS_Path for the 172.16.0.0/20 summary route on R3 is simply AS 65200 and does not include AS 65100.

Example 11-22 *R2's and R3's BGP Tables with Path Attribute Loss*

```
R2# show bgp ipv4 unicast | begin Network
     Network          Next Hop            Metric LocPrf Weight Path
 *   10.12.1.0/24     10.12.1.1                0             0 65100 ?
 *>                   0.0.0.0                  0         32768 ?
 *   10.23.1.0/24     10.23.1.3                0             0 65300 ?
 *>                   0.0.0.0                  0         32768 ?
 *>  172.16.0.0/20    0.0.0.0                            32768 i
 s>  172.16.1.0/24    10.12.1.1                0             0 65100 ?
 s>  172.16.2.0/24    10.12.1.1                0             0 65100 ?
 s>  172.16.3.0/24    10.12.1.1                0             0 65100 ?
 *>  192.168.0.0/16   0.0.0.0                            32768 i
 s>  192.168.1.1/32   10.12.1.1                0             0 65100 ?
 s>  192.168.2.2/32   0.0.0.0                  0         32768 ?
 s>  192.168.3.3/32   10.23.1.3                0             0 65300 ?
```

```
R3# show bgp ipv4 unicast | begin Network
     Network          Next Hop            Metric LocPrf Weight Path
 *>  10.12.1.0/24     10.23.1.2                0             0 65200 ?
 *   10.23.1.0/24     10.23.1.2                0             0 65200 ?
 *>                   0.0.0.0                  0         32768 ?
 *>  172.16.0.0/20    10.23.1.2                0             0 65200 i
 *>  192.168.0.0/16   10.23.1.2                0             0 65200 i
 *>  192.168.3.3/32   0.0.0.0                  0         32768 ?
```

Example 11-23 shows the explicit 172.16.0.0/20 prefix entry on R3. The route's information indicates that the routes were summarized (aggregated) in AS 65200 by the router with the RID 192.168.2.2. In addition, the atomic aggregate attribute has been set to indicate a loss of path attributes, such as AS_Path in this scenario.

11

Example 11-23 *Examining the BGP Attribute for the Atomic Aggregate Attribute*

```
R3# show bgp ipv4 unicast 172.16.0.0
BGP routing table entry for 172.16.0.0/20, version 25
Paths: (1 available, best #1, table default)
  Not advertised to any peer
  Refresh Epoch 2
  65200, (aggregated by 65200 192.168.2.2)
    10.23.1.2 from 10.23.1.2 (192.168.2.2)
      Origin IGP, metric 0, localpref 100, valid, external, atomic-aggregate, best
      rx pathid: 0, tx pathid: 0x0
```

Key Topic

Route Aggregation with AS_SET

To keep the BGP path information history, the optional **as-set** keyword may be used with the **aggregate-address** command. As the router generates the summary route, BGP path information from the component routes is copied over to it. The AS_Path settings from the original component routes are stored in the AS_SET portion of the AS_Path. The AS_SET, which is displayed within brackets, counts as only one hop, even if multiple ASs are listed.

Example 11-24 shows R2's updated BGP configuration for summarizing both networks with the **as-set** keyword.

Example 11-24 *Configuring Aggregation While Preserving BGP Attributes*

```
R2# show running-config | section router bgp
router bgp 65200
 no bgp default ipv4-unicast
 neighbor 10.12.1.1 remote-as 65100
 neighbor 10.23.1.3 remote-as 65300
 !
 address-family ipv4
  aggregate-address 192.168.0.0 255.255.0.0 as-set summary-only
  aggregate-address 172.16.0.0 255.255.240.0 as-set summary-only
  redistribute connected
  neighbor 10.12.1.1 activate
  neighbor 10.23.1.3 activate
```

Example 11-25 shows the 172.16.0.0/20 summary route again, including the BGP path information copied into it. Notice that the AS_Path information now contains AS 65100.

Example 11-25 *Verifying That Path Attributes Are Injected into the BGP Aggregate*

```
R3# show bgp ipv4 unicast 172.16.0.0
BGP routing table entry for 172.16.0.0/20, version 30
Paths: (1 available, best #1, table default)
  Not advertised to any peer
```

```
  Refresh Epoch 2
  65200 65100, (aggregated by 65200 192.168.2.2)
    10.23.1.2 from 10.23.1.2 (192.168.2.2)
      Origin incomplete, metric 0, localpref 100, valid, external, best
      rx pathid: 0, tx pathid: 0x0
```

```
R3# show bgp ipv4 unicast | begin Network
     Network          Next Hop            Metric LocPrf Weight Path
 *>  10.12.1.0/24     10.23.1.2                0             0 65200 ?
 *   10.23.1.0/24     10.23.1.2                0             0 65200 ?
 *>                   0.0.0.0                  0         32768 ?
 *>  172.16.0.0/20    10.23.1.2                0             0 65200 65100 ?
 *>  192.168.3.3/32   0.0.0.0                  0         32768 ?
```

Did you notice that the 192.168.0.0/16 summary route is no longer present in R3's BGP table? The reason for this is that on R2, R2 is summarizing all of the loopback networks from R1 (AS 65100), R2 (AS 65200), and R3 (AS 65300). And now that R2 is copying all component routes' BGP path attributes into the AS_SET information, the AS_Path for the 192.168.0.0/16 summary route contains AS 65300. When the aggregate is advertised to R3, R3 discards that route because it sees its own AS_Path in the advertisement and thinks that it is a loop.

Example 11-26 shows R2's BGP table and the path attributes for the 192.168.0.0/16 route entry.

Example 11-26 *Viewing the Aggregated Properties of 192.168.0.0/16*

```
R2# show bgp ipv4 unicast | begin Network
     Network          Next Hop            Metric LocPrf Weight Path
 *   10.12.1.0/24     10.12.1.1                0             0 65100 ?
 *>                   0.0.0.0                  0         32768 ?
 *   10.23.1.0/24     10.23.1.3                0             0 65300 ?
 *>                   0.0.0.0                  0         32768 ?
 *>  172.16.0.0/20    0.0.0.0                       100  32768 65100 ?
 s>  172.16.1.0/24    10.12.1.1                0             0 65100 ?
 s>  172.16.2.0/24    10.12.1.1                0             0 65100 ?
 s>  172.16.3.0/24    10.12.1.1                0             0 65100 ?
 *>  192.168.0.0/16   0.0.0.0                       100  32768 {65100,65300} ?
 s>  192.168.1.1/32   10.12.1.1                0             0 65100 ?
 s>  192.168.2.2/32   0.0.0.0                  0         32768 ?
 s>  192.168.3.3/32   10.23.1.3                0             0 65300 ?
```

```
R2# show bgp ipv4 unicast 192.168.0.0
BGP routing table entry for 192.168.0.0/16, version 28
Paths: (1 available, best #1, table default)
```

```
Advertised to update-groups:
   1
Refresh Epoch 1
{65100,65300}, (aggregated by 65200 192.168.2.2)
  0.0.0.0 from 0.0.0.0 (192.168.2.2)
    Origin incomplete, localpref 100, weight 32768, valid, aggregated, local, best
    rx pathid: 0, tx pathid: 0x0
```

R1 does not install the 192.168.0.0/16 summary route for the same reasons that R3 does not install the 192.168.0.0/16 network. R1 thinks that the advertisement is a loop because it detects AS 65100 in the advertisement. You can confirm this by examining R1's BGP table, as shown in Example 11-27.

Example 11-27 *R1's BGP Table, with 192.168.0.0/16 Discarded*

```
R1# show bgp ipv4 unicast | begin Network
     Network          Next Hop            Metric LocPrf Weight Path
 *    10.12.1.0/24     10.12.1.2                0             0 65200 ?
 *>                    0.0.0.0                  0         32768 ?
 *>   10.23.1.0/24     10.12.1.2                0             0 65200 ?
 *>   172.16.1.0/24    0.0.0.0                  0         32768 ?
 *>   172.16.2.0/24    0.0.0.0                  0         32768 ?
 *>   172.16.3.0/24    0.0.0.0                  0         32768 ?
 *>   192.168.1.1/32   0.0.0.0                  0         32768 ?
```

Key Topic

Multiprotocol BGP for IPv6

Multiprotocol BGP (MP-BGP) enables BGP to carry routes for multiple protocols, such as IPv4, IPv6, and Multiprotocol Label Switching (MPLS) Layer 3 virtual private networks (L3VPNs).

RFC 4760 defines the following new features:

- A new address family identifier (AFI) model
- New BGPv4 optional and non-transitive attributes:
  - Multiprotocol reachable NLRI
  - Multiprotocol unreachable NLRI

The new multiprotocol reachable NLRI path attribute describes IPv6 route information, and the multiprotocol unreachable NLRI attribute withdraws the IPv6 route from service. The attributes are optional and non-transitive, so if an older router does not understand the attributes, the information can just be ignored.

All the same underlying IPv4 path vector routing protocol features and rules also apply to MP-BGP for IPv6. MP-BGP for IPv6 continues to use the same well-known TCP port 179 for session peering as BGP uses for IPv4. During the initial open message negotiation, the BGP peer routers exchange capabilities. The MP-BGP extensions include an address family identifier (AFI) that describes the supported protocols, along with subsequent address family identifier (SAFI) attribute fields that describe whether the prefix applies to the unicast or multicast routing table:

- **IPv4 unicast:** AFI: 1, SAFI: 1
- **IPv6 unicast:** AFI: 2, SAFI: 1

Figure 11-13 demonstrates a simple topology with three different ASs and R2 forming an eBGP session with R1 and R3. The link-local addresses have been configured from the defined link-local range FE80::/10. All of R1's links are configured to FE80::1, all of R2's links are set to FE80::2, and all of R3's links are configured for FE80::3. This topology is used throughout this section.

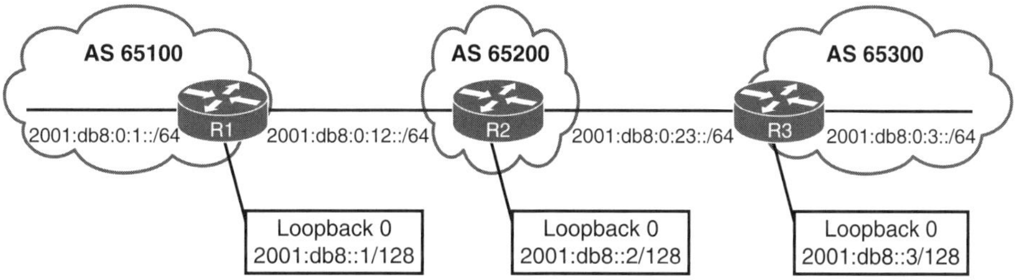

Figure 11-13 *IPv6 Sample Topology*

Key Topic

IPv6 Configuration

All the BGP configuration rules demonstrated earlier apply with IPv6, except that the IPv6 address family must be initialized, and the neighbor is activated. Routers with only IPv6 addressing must statically define the BGP RID to allow sessions to form.

The protocol used to establish the BGP session is independent of the AFI/SAFI route advertisements. The TCP session used by BGP is a Layer 4 protocol, and it can use either an IPv4 or IPv6 address to form a session adjacency and exchange routes. Advertising IPv6 prefixes over an IPv4 BGP session is feasible but beyond the scope of this book because additional configuration is required.

NOTE Unique global unicast addressing is the recommended method for BGP peering to avoid operational complexity. BGP peering using the link-local address may introduce risk if the address is not manually assigned to an interface. A hardware failure or cabling move will change the MAC address, resulting in a new link-local address. This will cause the session to fail because the stateless address autoconfiguration will generate a new IP address.

Example 11-28 shows the IPv6 BGP configuration for R1, R2, and R3. The peering uses global unicast addressing for establishing the session. The BGP RID has been set to the IPv4 loopback format used throughout this book. R1 advertises all its networks through redistribution, and R2 and R3 use the **network** statement to advertise all their connected networks.

11

Example 11-28 *Configuring IPv6 BGP*

```
R1
router bgp 65100
 bgp router-id 192.168.1.1
 no bgp default ipv4-unicast
 neighbor 2001:DB8:0:12::2 remote-as 65200
 !
address-family ipv6
  neighbor 2001:DB8:0:12::2 activate
  redistribute connected
```

```
R2
router bgp 65200
 bgp router-id 192.168.2.2
 no bgp default ipv4-unicast
 neighbor 2001:DB8:0:12::1 remote-as 65100
 neighbor 2001:DB8:0:23::3 remote-as 65300
!
 address-family ipv6
  neighbor 2001:DB8:0:12::1 activate
  neighbor 2001:DB8:0:23::3 activate
  network 2001:DB8::2/128
  network 2001:DB8:0:12::/64
  network 2001:DB8:0:23::/64
```

```
R3
router bgp 65300
 bgp router-id 192.168.3.3
 no bgp default ipv4-unicast
 neighbor 2001:DB8:0:23::2 remote-as 65200
 !
 address-family ipv6
  neighbor 2001:DB8:0:23::2 activate
  network 2001:DB8::3/128
  network 2001:DB8:0:3::/64
  network 2001:DB8:0:23::/64
```

NOTE IPv4 unicast routing capability is advertised by default in IOS XE unless the neighbor is specifically shut down within the IPv4 address family or globally within the BGP process with the command **no bgp default ipv4-unicast**.

Routers exchange AFI capabilities during the initial BGP session negotiation. The command **show bgp ipv6 unicast neighbors** *ip-address* [**detail**] displays detailed information on whether the IPv6 capabilities were negotiated successfully. Example 11-29 shows the fields that should be examined for IPv6 session establishment and route advertisement.

Example 11-29 *Viewing BGP Neighbors for IPv6 Capabilities*

```
R1# show bgp ipv6 unicast neighbors 2001:DB8:0:12::2
! Output omitted for brevity
BGP neighbor is 2001:DB8:0:12::2, remote AS 65200, external link
  BGP version 4, remote router ID 192.168.2.2
  BGP state = Established, up for 00:28:25
  Last read 00:00:54, last write 00:00:34, hold time is 180, keepalive interval is
60 seconds
  Neighbor sessions:
    1 active, is not multisession capable (disabled)
 Neighbor capabilities:
   Route refresh: advertised and received(new)
   Four-octets ASN Capability: advertised and received
   Address family IPv6 Unicast: advertised and received
   Enhanced Refresh Capability: advertised and received
 ..
For address family: IPv6 Unicast
 Session: 2001:DB8:0:12::2
 BGP table version 13, neighbor version 13/0
 Output queue size : 0
Index 1, Advertise bit 0
 1 update-group member
 Slow-peer detection is disabled
 Slow-peer split-update-group dynamic is disabled
 Sent Rcvd
                                   Sent       Rcvd
  Prefix activity:               ----       ----
    Prefixes Current:               3          5 (Consumes 520 bytes)
    Prefixes Total:                 6         10
```

The command **show bgp ipv6 unicast summary** displays a status summary of the sessions, including the number of prefixes that have been exchanged and the session uptime.

Example 11-30 highlights the IPv6 AFI neighbor status for R2. Notice that the two neighbor adjacencies have been up for about 25 minutes. Neighbor 2001:db8:0:12::1 is advertising three prefixes, and neighbor 2001:db8:0:23::3 is advertising three prefixes.

11

Example 11-30 *Verifying an IPv6 BGP Session*

```
R2# show bgp ipv6 unicast summary
BGP router identifier 192.168.2.2, local AS number 65200
BGP table version is 19, main routing table version 19
7 network entries using 1176 bytes of memory
8 path entries using 832 bytes of memory
3/3 BGP path/bestpath attribute entries using 456 bytes of memory
2 BGP AS-PATH entries using 48 bytes of memory
0 BGP route-map cache entries using 0 bytes of memory
0 BGP filter-list cache entries using 0 bytes of memory
BGP using 2512 total bytes of memory
BGP activity 7/0 prefixes, 8/0 paths, scan interval 60 secs

Neighbor          V      AS MsgRcvd MsgSent TblVer InQ OutQ Up/Down  State/PfxRcd
2001:DB8:0:12::1 4   65100      35      37     19   0    0 00:25:08         3
2001:DB8:0:23::3 4   65300      32      37     19   0    0 00:25:11         3
```

Example 11-31 shows the IPv6 unicast BGP tables for R1, R2, and R3. Notice that some of the routes include an unspecified address (::) as the next hop. An unspecified address indicates that the local router is generating the prefix for the BGP table. The weight value 32,768 also indicates that the prefix is locally originated by the router.

Example 11-31 *Viewing the IPv6 BGP Tables*

```
R1# show bgp ipv6 unicast
BGP table version is 13, local router ID is 192.168.1.1
Status codes: s suppressed, d damped, h history, * valid, > best, i - internal,
              r RIB-failure, S Stale, m multipath, b backup-path, f RT-Filter,
              x best-external, a additional-path, c RIB-compressed,
Origin codes: i - IGP, e - EGP, ? - incomplete
RPKI validation codes: V valid, I invalid, N Not found
     Network          Next Hop            Metric LocPrf Weight Path
 *>  2001:DB8::1/128  ::                       0         32768 ?
 *>  2001:DB8::2/128  2001:DB8:0:12::2         0             0 65200 i
 *>  2001:DB8::3/128  2001:DB8:0:12::2                       0 65200 65300 i
 *>  2001:DB8:0:1::/64  ::                     0         32768 ?
 *>  2001:DB8:0:3::/64  2001:DB8:0:12::2                     0 65200 65300 i
 *   2001:DB8:0:12::/64 2001:DB8:0:12::2       0             0 65200 i
 *>                   ::                       0         32768 ?
 *>  2001:DB8:0:23::/64 2001:DB8:0:12::2                     0 65200 i
```

```
R2# show bgp ipv6 unicast | begin Network
     Network          Next Hop            Metric LocPrf Weight Path
 *>  2001:DB8::1/128  2001:DB8:0:12::1         0             0 65100 ?
 *>  2001:DB8::2/128  ::                       0         32768 i
 *>  2001:DB8::3/128  2001:DB8:0:23::3         0             0 65300 i
 *>  2001:DB8:0:1::/64  2001:DB8:0:12::1       0             0 65100 ?
```

```
 *>  2001:DB8:0:3::/64  2001:DB8:0:23::3        0             0 65300 i
 *>  2001:DB8:0:12::/64 ::                      0         32768 i
 *                      2001:DB8:0:12::1        0             0 65100 ?
 *>  2001:DB8:0:23::/64 ::                      0         32768 i
                        2001:DB8:0:23::3        0             0 65300 i
```

```
R3# show bgp ipv6 unicast | begin Network
     Network            Next Hop            Metric LocPrf Weight Path
 *>  2001:DB8::1/128    2001:DB8:0:23::2                      0 65200 65100 ?
 *>  2001:DB8::2/128    2001:DB8:0:23::2        0             0 65200 i
 *>  2001:DB8::3/128    ::                      0         32768 i
 *>  2001:DB8:0:1::/64  2001:DB8:0:23::2                      0 65200 65100 ?
 *>  2001:DB8:0:3::/64  ::                      0         32768 i
 *>  2001:DB8:0:12::/64 2001:DB8:0:23::2        0             0 65200 i
 *>  2001:DB8:0:23::/64 ::                      0         32768 i
```

The BGP path attributes for an IPv6 route are displayed with the command **show bgp ipv6 unicast** *prefix/prefix-length*. Example 11-32 shows R3 examining R1's loopback address. Some of the common attributes, such as AS_Path, origin, and local preference, are identical to those for IPv4 routes.

Example 11-32 *Viewing the BGP Path Attributes for an IPv6 Route*

```
R3# show bgp ipv6 unicast 2001:DB8::1/128
BGP routing table entry for 2001:DB8::1/128, version 9
Paths: (1 available, best #1, table default)
  Not advertised to any peer
  Refresh Epoch 2
  65200 65100
    2001:DB8:0:23::2 (FE80::2) from 2001:DB8:0:23::2 (192.168.2.2)
      Origin incomplete, localpref 100, valid, external, best
      rx pathid: 0, tx pathid: 0x0
```

Example 11-33 shows the IPv6 BGP route entries for R2. Notice that the next-hop address is the link-local address for the next-hop forwarding address, which is resolved through a recursive lookup.

Example 11-33 *RIB Route Entries for BGP Learned IPv6 Routes*

```
R2# show ipv6 route bgp | begin Application
       a - Application
B    2001:DB8::1/128 [20/0]
      via FE80::1, GigabitEthernet0/0
B    2001:DB8::3/128 [20/0]
      via FE80::3, GigabitEthernet0/1
B    2001:DB8:0:1::/64 [20/0]
      via FE80::1, GigabitEthernet0/0
B    2001:DB8:0:3::/64 [20/0]
      via FE80::3, GigabitEthernet0/1
```

11

Key Topic

IPv6 Route Summarization

The same process of summarization/route aggregation for IPv4 routes occurs with IPv6 routes, and the format is identical except that the configuration is placed under the IPv6 address family using the command **aggregate-address** *prefix/prefix-length* [**summary-only**] [**as-set**].

Let's revisit the previous IPv6 deployment, but now we want to summarize all the loopback addresses (2001:db8:0:1/128, 2001:db8:0:2/128, and 2001:db8:0:3/128) along with the peering link between R1 and R2 (2001:db8:0:12/64) on R2. The configuration would look as shown in Example 11-34.

Example 11-34 *Configuring IPv6 BGP Aggregation on R2*

```
router bgp 65200
 bgp router-id 192.168.2.2
 neighbor 2001:DB8:0:12::1 remote-as 65100
 neighbor 2001:DB8:0:23::3 remote-as 65300
 !
 address-family ipv4
  no neighbor 2001:DB8:0:12::1 activate
  no neighbor 2001:DB8:0:23::3 activate
!
address-family ipv6
 network 2001:DB8::2/128
 network 2001:DB8:0:12::/64
 network 2001:DB8:0:23::/64
 aggregate-address 2001:DB8::/58 summary-only
 neighbor 2001:DB8:0:12::1 activate
 neighbor 2001:DB8:0:23::3 activate
```

Example 11-35 shows the BGP tables on R1 and R3. You can see that all the smaller component routes have been suppressed and aggregated into the 2001:db8::/58 summary route, as expected.

Example 11-35 *Verifying IPv6 Route Aggregation*

```
R3# show bgp ipv6 unicast | b Network
     Network            Next Hop            Metric LocPrf Weight Path
 *>  2001:DB8::/59      2001:DB8:0:23::2         0             0 65200 i
 *>  2001:DB8::3/128    ::                       0         32768 i
 *>  2001:DB8:0:3::/64  ::                       0         32768 i
 *>  2001:DB8:0:23::/64 ::                       0         32768 i
```

```
R1# show bgp ipv6 unicast | b Network
     Network            Next Hop            Metric LocPrf Weight Path
 *>  2001:DB8::/59      2001:DB8:0:12::2         0             0 65200 i
 *>  2001:DB8::1/128    ::                       0         32768 ?
 *>  2001:DB8:0:1::/64  ::                       0         32768 ?
 *>  2001:DB8:0:12::/64 ::                       0         32768 ?
```

The summarization of the IPv6 loopback addresses (2001:db8::1/128, 2001:db8::2/128, and 2001:db8::3/128) and R1/R3's stub networks (2001:db8:0:1::/64 and 2001:db8:0:3::/64) is fairly simple because they all fall into the base IPv6 summary range 2001:db8:0:0::/64. The fourth hextet beginning with a decimal value of 1, 2, or 3 would consume only 2 bits; the range could be summarized easily into the 2001:db8:0:0::/62 (or 2001:db8::/62) network range.

The peering link between R2 and R3 (2001:db8:0:23::/64) requires thinking in hex first, rather than in decimal values. The fourth hextet carries a decimal value of 35 (not 23), which requires 6 bits minimum. Table 11-5 lists the bits needed for summarization, the IPv6 summary address, and the component networks in the summary range.

Table 11-5 IPv6 Summarization Table

Bits Needed	Summary Address	Component Networks
2	2001:db8:0:0::/62	2001:db8:0:0::/64 through 2001:db8:0:3::/64
3	2001:db8:0:0::/61	2001:db8:0:0::/64 through 2001:db8:0:7::/64
4	2001:db8:0:0::/60	2001:db8:0:0::/64 through 2001:db8:0:F::/64
5	2001:db8:0:0::/59	2001:db8:0:0::/64 through 2001:db8:0:1F::/64
6	2001:db8:0:0::/58	2001:db8:0:0::/64 through 2001:db8:0:3F::/64

Exam Preparation Tasks

You have a couple of choices for exam preparation: the exercises here, Chapter 30, "Final Preparation," and the exam simulation questions in the Pearson Test Prep Software Online.

Review All Key Topics

Review the most important topics in the chapter, noted with the Key Topic icon in the outer margin of the page. Table 11-6 lists these key topics and the page number on which each is found.

Key Topic

Table 11-6 Key Topics for Chapter 11

Key Topic Element	Description	Page
Section	Autonomous System Numbers	246
Section	Path Attributes	247
Paragraph	BGP attribute AS_Path	247
Paragraph	Address family databases and configuration	248
Section	Inter-Router Communication	248
Figure 11-2	BGP Single- and Multi-Hop Sessions	249
Section	BGP Session Types	249
Section	eBGP	251
Section	Basic BGP Configuration	255
Section	Verification of BGP Sessions	257
Section	Route Advertisement	260
Figure 11-9	BGP Decision Process	262

Key Topic Element	Description	Page
Table 11-4	BGP Table Fields	263
List	BGP summarization techniques	269
Section	Aggregate Address	269
Paragraph	Aggregate address with **summary-only**	272
Section	Atomic Aggregate	274
Section	Route Aggregation with AS_SET	276
Section	Multiprotocol BGP for IPv6	278
Section	IPv6 Configuration	279
Section	IPv6 Route Summarization	284

Complete Tables and Lists from Memory

There are no memory tables in this chapter.

Define Key Terms

Define the following key terms from this chapter, and check your answers in the Glossary:

address family, AS_Path, atomic aggregate, autonomous system (AS), eBGP session, iBGP session, Loc-RIB, optional non-transitive, optional transitive, path vector routing protocol, well-known discretionary, well-known mandatory

Use the Command Reference to Check Your Memory

Table 11-7 lists the important commands from this chapter. To test your memory, cover the right side of the table with a piece of paper, read the description on the left side, and see how much of the command you can remember.

Table 11-7 Command Reference

Task	Command Syntax
Initialize the BGP router process	**router bgp** *as-number*
Identify a BGP peer to establish a session with	**neighbor** *ip-address* **remote-as** *as-number*
Disable the automatic IPv4 address family configuration mode	**no bgp default ipv4-unicast**
Initialize a specific address family and sub-address family	**address-family** *afi safi*
Activate a BGP neighbor for a specific address family	**neighbor** *ip-address* **activate**
Advertise a network in BGP	**network** *network* **mask** *subnet-mask* [**route-map** *route-map-name*]
Configure a BGP summary IPv4 route	**aggregate-address** *network subnet-mask* [**summary-only**] [**as-set**]
Configure a BGP summary IPv6 route	**aggregate-address** *prefix/prefix-length* [**summary-only**] [**as-set**]

Task	Command Syntax
Display the contents of the Loc-RIB	**show bgp** *afi safi* [**network**] [**detailed**]
Display a summary of the BGP table and neighbor peering sessions	**show bgp** *afi safi* **summary**
Display the negotiated BGP settings with a specific peer and the number of prefixes exchanged with that peer	**show bgp** *afi safi* **neighbors** *ip-address*
Display the Adj-RIB-Out for a specific BGP neighbor	**show bgp** *afi safi* **neighbor** *ip-address* **advertised routes**

References in This Chapter

RFC 1654, *A Border Gateway Protocol 4 (BGP-4)*, Yakov Rekhter and Tony Li. https://www.ietf.org/rfc/rfc1654.txt, July 1994.

RFC 1930, *Guidelines for Creation, Selection, and Registration of an Autonomous System (AS)*, J. Hawkinson and T. Bates. https://www.ietf.org/rfc/rfc1930.txt, March 1996.

RFC 2858, *Multiprotocol Extensions for BGP-4*, Yakov Rekhter, Tony Bates, Ravi Chandra, and Dave Katz. https://www.ietf.org/rfc/rfc2858.txt, June 2000.

RFC 4271, *A Border Gateway Protocol 4 (BGP-4)*, Yakov Rekhter, Tony Li, and Susan Hares. https://www.ietf.org/rfc/rfc4271.txt, January 2006.

RFC 4760, *Multiprotocol Extensions for BGP-4*, Yakov Rekhter, Tony Bates, Ravi Chandra, and Dave Katz. https://www.ietf.org/rfc/rfc4760.txt, January 2007.

RFC 4893, *BGP Support for Four-octet AS Number Space*, Quaizar Vohra and Enke Chen. https://www.ietf.org/rfc/rfc4893.txt, May 2007.

RFC 6996, *Autonomous System (AS) Reservation for Private Use*, J. Mitchell. https://www.ietf.org/rfc/rfc6996.txt, July 2013.

RFC 7300, *Reservation of Last Autonomous System (AS) Numbers*, J. Haas and J. Mitchell. https://www.ietf.org/rfc/rfc7300.txt, July 2014.

Edgeworth, Brad, Aaron Foss, and Ramiro Garza Rios, *IP Routing on Cisco IOS, IOS XE, and IOS XR.* Indianapolis: Cisco Press, 2014.

11

CHAPTER 12

Advanced BGP

This chapter covers the following subjects:

- **BGP Multihoming:** This section reviews the methods of providing resiliency through redundant BGP connections, along with desired and undesired design considerations for Internet and MPLS connections (branch and data center).
- **Conditional Matching:** This section provides an overview of how network prefixes can be conditionally matched with ACLs, prefix lists, and regular expressions.
- **Route Maps:** This section explains the structure of a route map and how conditional matching and conditional actions can be combined to filter or manipulate routes.
- **BGP Route Filtering and Manipulation:** This section expands on how conditional matching and route maps work by applying real-world use cases to demonstrate the filtering or manipulation of BGP routes.
- **BGP Communities:** This section explains the BGP well-known mandatory path attributes and how they can be used to tag a prefix to have route policies applied by routers in the same autonomous system or in an external autonomous system.
- **Understanding BGP Path Selection:** This section describes the logic used by BGP to identify the best path when multiple routes are installed in the BGP table.

Border Gateway Protocol (BGP) can support hundreds of thousands of routes, making it the ideal choice for the Internet. Organizations also use BGP for its flexibility and traffic engineering properties. This chapter expands on Chapter 11, "BGP," explaining BGP's advanced features and concepts involved with the BGP routing protocol, such as BGP multihoming, route filtering, BGP communities, and the logic for identifying the best path for a specific destination network.

"Do I Know This Already?" Quiz

The "Do I Know This Already?" quiz enables you to assess whether you should read the entire chapter. If you miss no more than one of these self-assessment questions, you might want to move ahead to the "Exam Preparation Tasks" section. Table 12-1 lists the major headings in this chapter and the "Do I Know This Already?" quiz questions covering the material in those headings so you can assess your knowledge of these specific areas. The answers to the "Do I Know This Already?" quiz appear in Appendix A, "Answers to the 'Do I Know This Already?' Questions."

Table 12-1 "Do I Know This Already?" Foundation Topics Section-to-Question Mapping

Foundation Topics Section	Questions
BGP Multihoming	1
Conditional Matching	2–4
Route Maps	5–6
BGP Route Filtering and Manipulation	7
BGP Communities	8
Understanding BGP Path Selection	9–10

1. Transit routing between a multihomed enterprise network and a service provider is generally not recommend in which scenarios? (Choose all that apply.)
   - **a.** Internet connections at data centers
   - **b.** Internet connections at branch locations
   - **c.** MPLS data centers
   - **d.** MPLS branch locations
2. True or false: An extended ACL used to match routes changes behavior if the routing protocol is an IGP rather than BGP.
   - **a.** True
   - **b.** False
3. Which network prefixes match the prefix match pattern 10.168.0.0/13 ge 24? (Choose two.)
   - **a.** 10.168.0.0/13
   - **b.** 10.168.0.0/24
   - **c.** 10.173.1.0/28
   - **d.** 10.104.0.0/24
4. What is the correct regular expression syntax for matching a route that originated in AS 300?
   - **a.** ^300_
   - **b.** $300!
   - **c.** _300_
   - **d.** _300$
5. What happens when the route map **route-map QUESTION permit 20** does not contain a conditional match statement?
   - **a.** The routes are discarded, and a syslog message is logged.
   - **b.** All routes are discarded.
   - **c.** All routes are accepted.
   - **d.** An error is assigned when linking the route map to a BGP peer.

6. What happens to a route that does not match the PrefixRFC1918 prefix list when using the following route map?

```
route-map QUESTION deny 10
 match ip address prefix-list PrefixRFC1918
route-map QUESTION permit 20
 set metric 200
```

   a. The route is allowed, and the metric is set to 200.
   b. The route is denied.
   c. The route is allowed.
   d. The route is allowed, and the default metric is set to 100.

7. True or false: A BGP AS_Path ACL and a prefix list can be applied to a neighbor at the same time.
   a. True
   b. False

8. Which of the following is not a well-known BGP community?
   a. No_Advertise
   b. Internet
   c. No_Export
   d. Private_Route

9. Which of the following techniques is the second selection criterion for the BGP best path?
   a. Weight
   b. Local preference
   c. Origin
   d. MED

10. True or false: For MED to be used as a selection criterion, the routes must come from different autonomous systems.
   a. True
   b. False

Foundation Topics

The Internet has become a vital component for businesses today. Internet connectivity is required for email and research at a minimum. In addition, some organizations host e-commerce servers, use Voice over IP (VoIP) telephony, or terminate VPN tunnels through private MPLS connections. An organization must incorporate redundancies in the network architecture to ensure that there are not any single points of failure (SPOF) with network connectivity to support the needs of the business.

A company can connect to the Internet with a simple default route using a single connection. However, if a company wants to use multiple service providers (SPs) for redundancy or additional throughput, BGP is required. BGP is the routing protocol used on the Internet.

A company's use of BGP is not limited to Internet connectivity. If the company uses MPLS L3VPN from a service provider, it is probably using BGP to exchange the LAN networks with the service provider. Routes are typically redistributed between BGP and the LAN-based routing protocol. In both of these scenarios, BGP is used at the edge of the network (Internet or WAN) and has redundant connections to ensure a reliable network. It provides advanced path selection and connectivity for an organization.

BGP Multihoming

The simplest method of providing redundancy is to provide a second circuit. Adding a second circuit and establishing a second BGP session across that peering link is known as **BGP multihoming** because there are multiple sessions to learn routes and establish connectivity. BGP's default behavior is to advertise only the best path to the RIB, which means that only one path for a network prefix is used when forwarding network traffic to a destination.

Key Topic

Resiliency in Service Providers

Routing failures can occur within a service provider network, and some organizations choose to use a different SP for each circuit. A second service provider could be selected for a variety of reasons, but the choice typically comes down to cost, circuit availability for remote locations, or separation of the control plane.

If a different SP is used, if one SP has problems in its network, network traffic can still flow across the other SP. In addition, adding more SPs means traffic can select an optimal path between devices due to the BGP best-path algorithm, discussed later in this chapter.

Figure 12-1 illustrates four common multihoming scenarios:

- **Scenario 1:** R1 connects to R3 with the same SP. This design accounts for link failures; however, a failure on either router or within SP1's network results in a network failure.
- **Scenario 2:** R1 connects to R3 and R4 with the same SP. This design accounts for link failures; however, a failure on R1 or within SP1's network results in a network failure.
- **Scenario 3:** R1 connects to R3 and R4 with the different SPs. This design accounts for link failures and failures in either SP's network, and it can optimize routing traffic. However, a failure on R1 results in a network failure.
- **Scenario 4:** R1 and R2 form an iBGP session with each other. R3 connects to SP1, and R4 connects to SP2. This design accounts for link failures and failures in either SP's network, and it can optimize routing traffic.

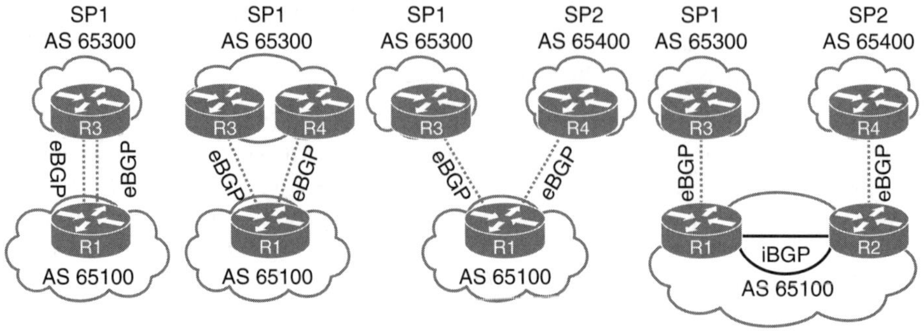

Figure 12-1 *Common BGP Multihoming Scenarios*

Key Topic

Internet Transit Routing

If an enterprise uses BGP to connect with more than one service provider, it runs the risk of its autonomous system (AS) becoming a transit AS. In Figure 12-2, AS 500 is connecting to two different service providers (SP3 and SP4) for resiliency.

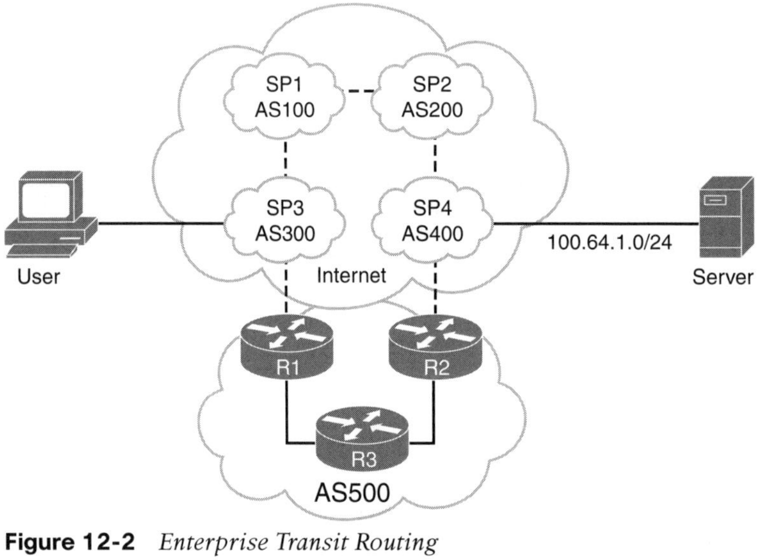

Figure 12-2 *Enterprise Transit Routing*

If R1 and R2 use the default BGP routing policy, SP3 receives the 100.64.1.0/24 prefix from AS 100 and AS 500. SP3 selects the path through AS 500 because the AS_Path is much shorter than going through SP1 and SP2's networks. A user who connects to SP3 (AS 300) routes through the enterprise network (AS 500) to reach a server that attaches to SP4 (AS 400).

The AS 500 network is providing **transit routing** to everyone on the Internet, which can saturate AS 500's peering links. In addition to causing problems for the users in AS 500, this situation has an impact on traffic from the users who are trying to traverse AS 500.

Answers to the "Do I Know This Already?" quiz:

1 A, B, D **2** A **3** B, C **4** D **5** C **6** A **7** A **8** D **9** B **10** B

Transit routing can be avoided by applying outbound BGP route policies that only allow for local BGP routes to be advertised to other autonomous systems. This topic is discussed later in this chapter, in the section "BGP Route Filtering and Manipulation."

Branch Transit Routing

Proper network design should take traffic patterns into account to prevent suboptimal routing or routing loops. Figure 12-3 shows a multihomed design using multiple transports for all the sites. All the routers are configured so that they prefer the MPLS SP2 transport over the MPLS SP1 transport (active/passive). All the branch routers peer and advertise all the routes via eBGP to the SP routers. The branch routers do not filter any of the prefixes, and all the branch routers set the local preference for MPLS SP2 to a higher value to route traffic through it.

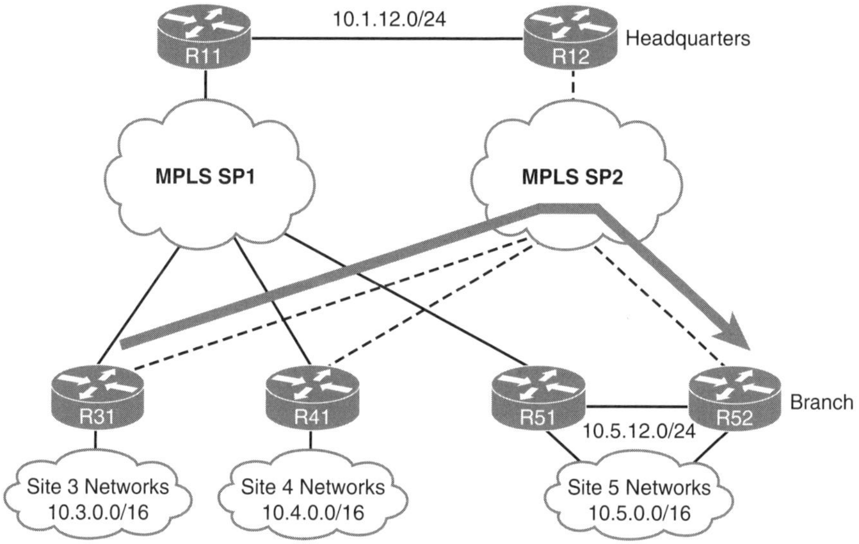

Figure 12-3 *Deterministic Routing*

When the network is working as intended, traffic between the sites uses the preferred SP network (MPLS SP2) in both directions. This simplifies troubleshooting when the traffic flow is symmetric (the same path in both directions) as opposed to asymmetric forwarding (a different path for each direction) because the full path has to be discovered in both directions. The path is considered *deterministic* when the flow between sites is predetermined and predictable.

During a link failure within the SP network, there is a possibility of a branch router connecting to the destination branch router through an intermediary branch router. Figure 12-4 shows the failure scenario with R41 providing transit connectivity between Site 3 and Site 5.

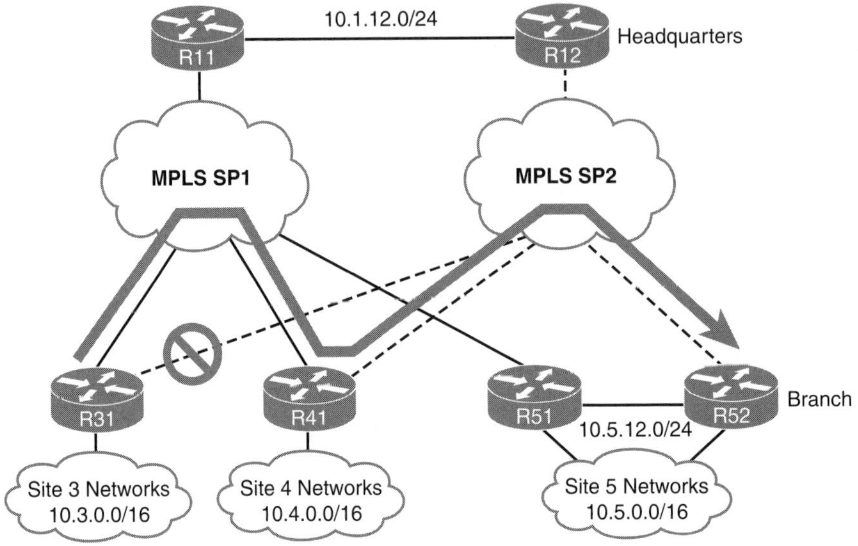

Figure 12-4 *Nondeterministic Routing During Failover*

Unplanned transit connectivity presents the following issues:

- The transit router's circuits can become oversaturated because they were sized only for that site's traffic and not the traffic crossing through them.
- The routing patterns can become unpredictable and nondeterministic. In this scenario, traffic from R31 flows through R41, but the return traffic may take a different return path. The path might be very different if the traffic were sourced from a different router. This prevents deterministic routing, complicates troubleshooting, and can make your NOC staff feel as if they are playing whack-a-mole when troubleshooting network issues.

Multihomed environments should be configured so that branch routers cannot act as transit routers. In most designs, transit routing of traffic from another branch is undesirable, because WAN bandwidth may not be sized accordingly. Transit routing can be avoided by configuring outbound route filtering at each branch site. In essence, the branch sites do not advertise what they learn from the WAN but advertise only networks that face the LAN. If transit behavior is required, it is restricted to the data centers or specific locations as follows:

- Proper routing design can accommodate outages.
- Bandwidth can be sized accordingly.
- The routing pattern is bidirectional and predictable.

NOTE Transit routing at the data center or other planned locations is normal in enterprise designs because they have accounted for the bandwidth. Typically, this is done when some branches are available only with one SP, and the other branches connect with a different SP.

Conditional Matching

This section reviews some of the common techniques used to conditionally match a route—using access control lists (ACLs), prefix lists, regular expressions (regex), and AS path ACLs.

Access Control Lists

Originally, access control lists (ACLs) were intended to provide filtering of packets flowing into or out of a network interface, similar to the functionality of a basic firewall. Today, in addition to their original function, ACLs provide packet classification for a variety of features, such as quality of service (QoS), or for identifying networks within routing protocols.

ACLs are composed of *access control entries (ACEs)*, which are entries in the ACL that identify the action to be taken (permit or deny) and the relevant packet classification. Packet classification starts at the top (lowest sequence) and proceeds down (higher sequence) until a matching pattern is identified. When a match is found, the appropriate action (permit or deny) is taken, and processing stops. At the end of every ACL is an implicit deny ACE, which denies all packets that did not match earlier in the ACL.

NOTE ACE placement within an ACL is important, and unintended consequences may result from ACEs being out of order.

ACLs are classified into two categories:

- **Standard ACLs:** Define packets based solely on the source network.
- **Extended ACLs:** Define packets based on source, destination, protocol, port, or a combination of other packet attributes. This book is concerned with routing and limits the scope of ACLs to source, destination, and protocol.

Standard ACLs use a numbered entry 1–99, 1300–1999, or a named ACL. Extended ACLs use a numbered entry 100–199, 2000–2699, or a named ACL. Named ACLs provide relevance to the functionality of the ACL, can be used with standard or extended ACLs, and are generally preferred.

Standard ACLs

The following is the process for defining a standard ACL:

Step 1. Define the ACL by using the command **ip access-list standard** {*acl-number* | *acl-name*} and placing the CLI in ACL configuration mode.

Step 2. Configure the specific ACE entry with the command [*sequence*] {**permit** | **deny** } *source source-wildcard*. In lieu of using *source source-wildcard*, the keyword **any** replaces 0.0.0.0 255.255.255.255, and use of the **host** keyword refers to a /32 IP address so that the *source-wildcard* can be omitted.

Table 12-2 provides sample ACL entries from within the ACL configuration mode and specifies the networks that would match with a standard ACL.

Table 12-2 Standard ACL-to-Network Entries

ACE Entry	Networks
permit any	Permits all networks
permit 172.16.0.0 0.0.255.255	Permits all networks in the 172.16.0.0/16 network range
permit host 192.168.1.1	Permits only the 192.168.1.1/32 network

Extended ACLs

The following is the process for defining an extended ACL:

Step 1. Define the ACL by using the command **ip access-list extended** {*acl-number* | *acl-name*} and placing the CLI in ACL configuration mode.

Step 2. Configure the specific ACE entry with the command [*sequence*] {**permit** | **deny**} *protocol source source-wildcard destination destination-wildcard*. The behavior for selecting a network prefix with an extended ACL varies depending on whether the protocol is an IGP (EIGRP, OSPF, or IS-IS) or BGP.

Key Topic

BGP Network Selection

Extended ACLs react differently when matching BGP routes than when matching IGP routes. The source fields match against the network portion of the route, and the destination fields match against the network mask, as shown in Figure 12-5. Until the introduction of prefix lists, extended ACLs were the only match criteria used with BGP.

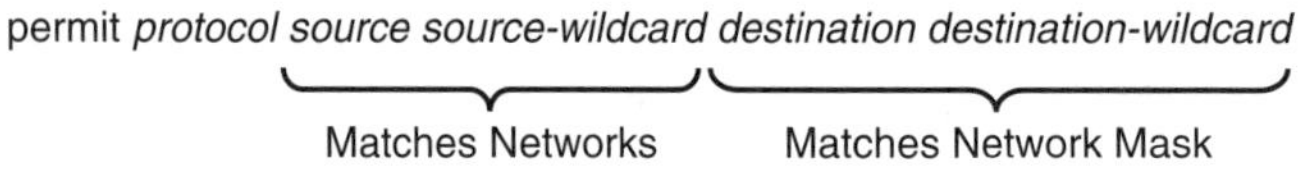

Figure 12-5 *BGP Extended ACL Matches*

Table 12-3 demonstrates the concept of the wildcard for the network and subnet mask.

Table 12-3 Extended ACL for BGP Route Selection

Extended ACL	Matches These Networks
permit ip 10.0.0.0 0.0.0.0 255.255.0.0 0.0.0.0	Permits only the 10.0.0.0/16 network
permit ip 10.0.0.0 0.0.255.0 255.255.255.0 0.0.0.0	Permits any 10.0.x.0 network with a /24 prefix length
permit ip 172.16.0.0 0.0.255.255 255.255.255.0 0.0.0.255	Permits any 172.16.x.x network with a /24 to /32 prefix length
permit ip 172.16.0.0 0.0.255.255 255.255.255.128 0.0.0.127	Permits any 172.16.x.x network with a /25 to /32 prefix length

Prefix Matching

Prefix lists provide another method of identifying networks in a routing protocol. A prefix list identifies a specific IP address, network prefix, or network range and allows for the selection of multiple networks with a variety of prefix lengths by using a prefix match specification. Many network engineers prefer this over the ACL network selection method.

Key Topic

A prefix match specification contains two parts: a high-order bit pattern and a high-order bit count, which determines the high-order bits in the bit pattern that are to be matched. Some documentation refers to the high-order bit pattern as the address or network and the high-order bit count as the prefix length or mask length.

In Figure 12-6, the prefix match specification has the high-order bit pattern 192.168.0.0 and the high-order bit count 16. The high-order bit pattern has been converted to binary to demonstrate where the high-order bit count lies. Because there are not additional matching length parameters included, the high-order bit count is an exact match.

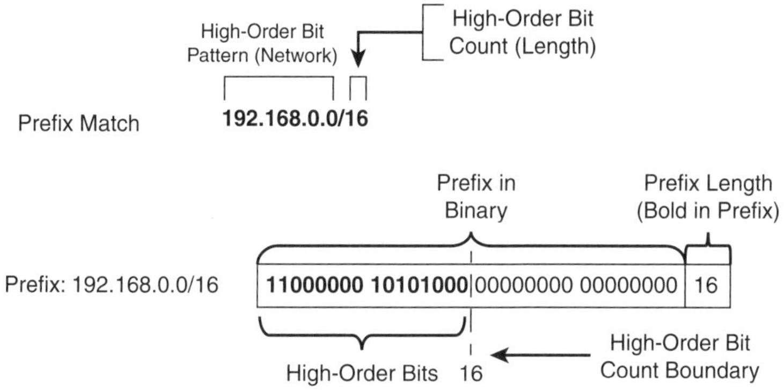

Figure 12-6 *Basic Prefix Match Pattern*

Key Topic

At this point, the prefix match specification logic looks identical to the functionality of an access list. The true power and flexibility comes in using matching length parameters to identify multiple networks with specific prefix lengths with one statement. The matching length parameter options are

- **le:** Less than or equal to, <=
- **ge:** Greater than or equal to, >=

Figure 12-7 demonstrates the prefix match specification with the high-order bit pattern 10.168.0.0 and high-order bit count 13; the matching length of the prefix must be greater than or equal to 24.

The 10.168.0.0/13 prefix does not meet the matching length parameter because the prefix length is less than the minimum of 24 bits, whereas the 10.168.0.0/24 prefix does meet the matching length parameter. The 10.173.1.0/28 prefix qualifies because the first 13 bits match the high-order bit pattern, and the prefix length is within the matching length parameter. The 10.104.0.0/24 prefix does not qualify because the high-order bit pattern does not match within the high-order bit count.

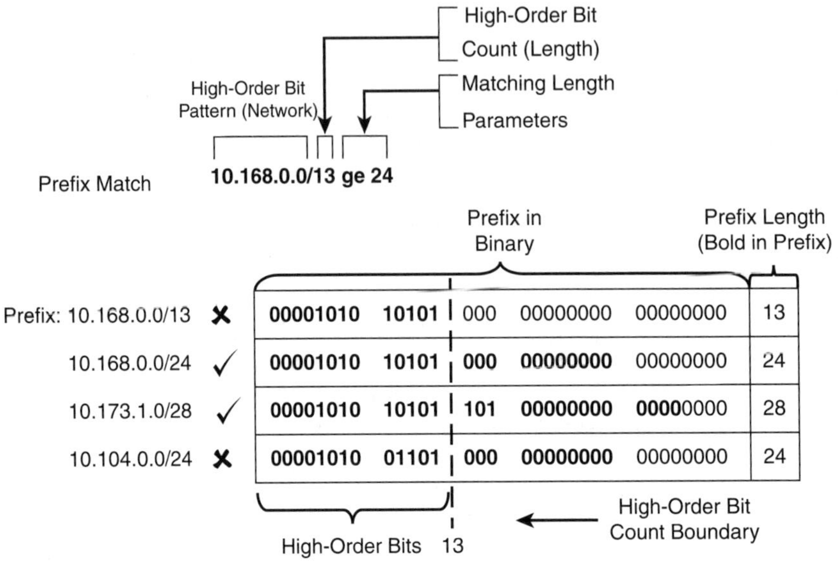

Figure 12-7 *Prefix Match Pattern with Matching Length Parameters*

Figure 12-8 demonstrates a prefix match specification with the high-order bit pattern 10.0.0.0, high-order bit count 8, and matching length between 22 and 26.

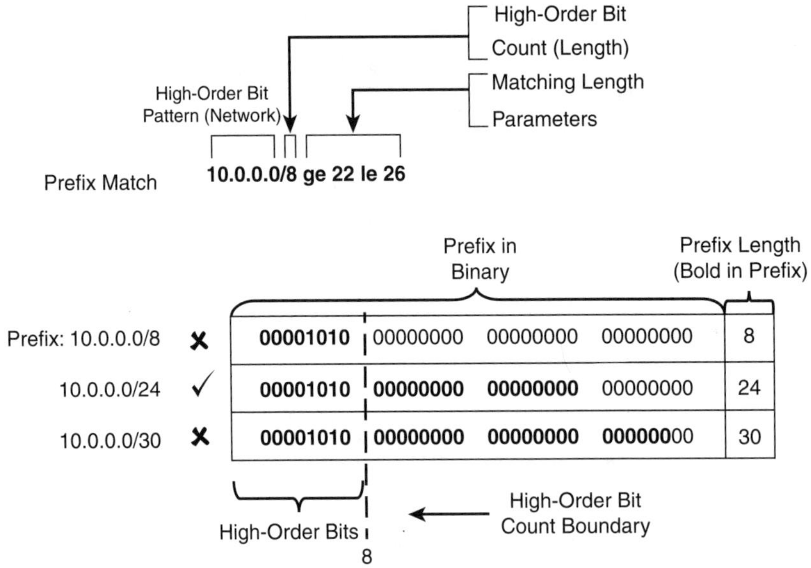

Figure 12-8 *Prefix Match with Ineligible Matched Prefixes*

The 10.0.0.0/8 prefix does not match because the prefix length is too short. The 10.0.0.0/24 network qualifies because the bit pattern matches, and the prefix length is between 22 and 26. The 10.0.0.0/30 prefix does not match because the prefix length is too long. Any prefix that starts with 10 in the first octet and has a prefix length between 22 and 26 will match.

NOTE Matching to a specific prefix length that is higher than the high-order bit count requires that the *ge-value* and *le-value* match.

Key Topic

Prefix Lists

Prefix lists can contain multiple prefix matching specification entries that contain a permit or deny action. Prefix lists process in sequential order in a top-down fashion, and the first prefix match processes with the appropriate permit or deny action.

Prefix lists are configured with the global configuration command **ip prefix-list** *prefix-list-name* [**seq** *sequence-number*] {**permit** | **deny**} *high-order-bit-pattern/high-order-bit-count* [**ge** *ge-value*] [**le** *le-value*].

If a sequence is not provided, the sequence number auto-increments by 5, based on the highest sequence number. The first entry is 5. Sequencing enables the deletion of a specific entry. Because prefix lists cannot be resequenced, it is advisable to leave enough space for insertion of sequence numbers at a later time.

IOS XE requires that the *ge-value* be greater than the high-order bit count and that the *le-value* be greater than or equal to the *ge-value*:

high-order bit count < ge-value <= le-value

Example 12-1 provides a sample prefix list named RFC1918 for all of the networks in the RFC 1918 address range. The prefix list allows only /32 prefixes to exist in the 192.168.0.0 network range and not exist in any other network range in the prefix list.

Notice that sequence 5 permits all /32 prefixes in the 192.168.0.0/16 bit pattern, and sequence 10 denies all /32 prefixes in any bit pattern, and sequences 15, 20, and 25 permit routes in the appropriate network ranges. The sequence order is important for the first two entries to ensure that only /32 prefixes exist in the 192.168.0.0 network in the prefix list.

Example 12-1 *Sample Prefix List*

```
ip prefix-list RFC1918 seq 5 permit 192.168.0.0/16 ge 32
ip prefix-list RFC1918 seq 10 deny 0.0.0.0/0 ge 32
ip prefix-list RFC1918 seq 15 permit 10.0.0.0/8 le 32
ip prefix-list RFC1918 seq 20 permit 172.16.0.0/12 le 32
ip prefix-list RFC1918 seq 25 permit 192.168.0.0/16 le 32
```

IPv6 Prefix Lists

The prefix matching logic works exactly the same for IPv6 networks as for IPv4 networks. The most important point to remember is that IPv6 networks are notated in hex and not in decimal when identifying ranges. Ultimately, however, everything functions at the binary level.

IPv6 prefix lists are configured with the global configuration command **ipv6 prefix-list** *prefix-list-name* [**seq** *sequence-number*] {**permit** | **deny**} *high-order-bit-pattern/high-order-bit-count* [**ge** *ge-value*] [**le** *le-value*].

Example 12-2 provides a sample prefix list named PRIVATE-IPV6 for all the networks in the documentation and benchmarking IPv6 space.

Example 12-2 *Sample IPv6 Prefix List*

```
ipv6 prefix-list PRIVATE-IPV6 seq 5 permit 2001:2::/48 le 128
ipv6 prefix-list PRIVATE-IPV6 seq 10 permit 2001:db8::/32 le 128
```

Key Topic

Regular Expressions (regex)

There may be times when conditionally matching on network prefixes may be too complicated, and identifying all routes from a specific organization is preferred. In such a case, path selection can be made by using a BGP AS_Path.

Regular expressions (regex) are used to parse through the large number of available ASNs (4,294,967,295). Regular expressions are based on query modifiers used to select the appropriate content. The BGP table can be parsed with regex by using the command **show bgp** *afi safi* **regexp** *regex-pattern*.

Table 12-4 provides a brief list and description of the common regex query modifiers.

Table 12-4 RegEx Query Modifiers

Modifier	Description
_ (underscore)	Matches a space
^ (caret)	Indicates the start of a string
$ (dollar sign)	Indicates the end of a string
[] (brackets)	Matches a single character or nesting within a range
- (hyphen)	Indicates a range of numbers in brackets
[^] (caret in brackets)	Excludes the characters listed in brackets
() (parentheses)	Used for nesting of search patterns
| (pipe)	Provides OR functionality to the query
. (period)	Matches a single character, including a space
* (asterisk)	Matches zero or more characters or patterns
+ (plus sign)	Matches one or more instances of the character or pattern
? (question mark)	Matches one or no instances of the character or pattern

Learning regex can take time, but the most common ones used in BGP involve the ^, $, and _. Table 12-5 displays some common BGP regex.

Table 12-5 Common BGP Regular Expressions

Regular Expression	Meaning
^$	Local originating routes
permit ^200_	Only routes from neighbor AS 200
permit _200$	Only routes originating from AS 200
permit _200_	Only routes that pass through AS 200
permit ^[0-9]+ [0-9]+ [0-9]+?	Routes with three or fewer AS_Path entries

NOTE Hands-on experience is helpful when learning technologies such as regex. Public servers called *looking glasses* allow users to log in and view BGP tables. Most of these devices are Cisco routers, but some are from other vendors. These servers allow network engineers to see if they are advertising their routes to the Internet as they had intended and provide a great method to try out regular expressions on the Internet BGP table.

A quick search on the Internet will provide website listings of looking glass and route servers. We suggest www.bgp4.as.

Route Maps

Route maps provide many different features to a variety of routing protocols. At the simplest level, route maps can filter networks much the same way as ACLs, but they also provide additional capability through the addition or modification of network attributes. To influence a routing protocol, a route map must be referenced from the routing protocol. Route maps are critical to BGP because they are the main component in modifying a unique routing policy on a neighbor-by-neighbor basis.

A route map has four components:

Key Topic

- **Sequence number:** Dictates the processing order of the route map.
- **Conditional matching criteria:** Identifies prefix characteristics (the prefix itself, BGP path attribute, next hop, and so on) for a specific sequence.
- **Processing action:** Permits or denies the prefix.
- **Optional action:** Allows for manipulations, depending on how the route map is referenced on the router. Actions can include modification, addition, or removal of route characteristics.

A route map uses the command syntax **route-map** *route-map-name* [**permit** | **deny**] [*sequence-number*]. The following rules apply to route map statements:

Key Topic

- If a processing action is not provided, the default value **permit** is used.
- If a sequence number is not provided, the sequence number is incremented by 10 automatically.
- If a matching statement is not included, an implied match *all prefixes* is associated with the statement.
- Processing within a route map stops after all optional actions have processed (if configured) after matching a conditional matching criterion.
- An implicit deny or drop is associated for prefixes that are not associated with a **permit** action.

Example 12-3 provides a sample route map to demonstrate the four components of a route map shown earlier. The conditional matching criterion is based on network ranges specified in an ACL. Comments have been added to this example to explain the behavior of the route map in each sequence.

Example 12-3 *Sample Route Map*

```
route-map EXAMPLE permit 10
 match ip address ACL-ONE
! Prefixes that match ACL-ONE are permitted. Route-map completes processing
! upon a match

route-map EXAMPLE deny 20
 match ip address ACL-TWO
! Prefixes that match ACL-TWO are denied. Route-map completes processing upon
! a match

route-map EXAMPLE permit 30
 match ip address ACL-THREE
 set metric 20
! Prefixes that match ACL-THREE are permitted and their metric is modified.
! Route-map completes processing upon a match

route-map EXAMPLE permit 40
! Because matching criteria were not specified, all other prefixes are permitted
! If this sequence was not configured, all other prefixes would drop because of the
! implicit deny with route-maps
```

NOTE When you're deleting a specific route-map statement, include the sequence number to prevent deleting the entire route map.

Key Topic

Conditional Matching

Now that the components and processing order of a route map have been explained, this section expands on how a prefix can be matched. Table 12-6 provides the command syntax for the most common methods for conditionally matching prefixes and describes their usage. As you can see, a number of options are available.

Table 12-6 Conditional Match Options

match Command	Description
match as-path *acl-number*	Selects prefixes based on a regex query to isolate the ASN in the BGP path attribute (PA) AS path. The AS path ACLs are numbered 1 to 500. This command allows for multiple match variables.
match ip address {*acl-number* | *acl-name*}	Selects prefixes based on network selection criteria defined in the ACL. This command allows for multiple match variables.

match Command	Description
match ip address prefix-list *prefix-list-name*	Selects prefixes based on prefix selection criteria. This command allows for multiple match variables.
match local-preference *local-preference*	Selects prefixes based on the BGP attribute local preference. This command allows for multiple match variables.
match metric {*1-4294967295* | **external** *1-4294967295*} [**+-** *deviation*]	Selects prefixes based on a metric that can be exact, a range, or within an acceptable deviation.
match tag *tag-value*	Selects prefixes based on a numeric tag (0 to 4294967295) that was set by another router. This command allows for multiple match variables.
match community {*1-500* | *community-list-name* [**exact**]}	Selects prefixes based on a community list ACL. The community list ACLs are numbered 1 to 500. This command allows for multiple match variables.

Key Topic

Multiple Conditional Match Conditions

If multiple variables (ACLs, prefix lists, tags, and so on) are configured for a specific route map sequence, only one variable must match for the prefix to qualify. The Boolean logic uses an OR operator for this configuration.

In Example 12-4, sequence 10 requires that a prefix pass ACL-ONE or ACL-TWO. Notice that sequence 20 does not have a match statement, so all prefixes that are not passed in sequence 10 will qualify and are denied.

Example 12-4 *Multiple Match Variables Route Map Example*

```
route-map EXAMPLE permit 10
 match ip address ACL-ONE ACL-TWO
!
route-map EXAMPLE deny 20
```

NOTE In Example 12-4, sequence 20 is redundant because of the implicit deny for any prefixes that are not matched in sequence 10.

If multiple match options are configured for a specific route map sequence, both match options must be met for the prefix to qualify for that sequence. The Boolean logic uses an AND operator for this configuration.

In Example 12-5, sequence 10 requires that the prefix match ACL-ONE and that the metric be a value between 500 and 600. If the prefix does not qualify for both match options, the prefix does not qualify for sequence 10 and is denied because another sequence does not exist with a permit action.

Example 12-5 *Multiple Match Options Route Map Example*

```
route-map EXAMPLE permit 10
 match ip address ACL-ONE
 match metric 550 +- 50
```

Complex Matching

Some network engineers find route maps too complex if the conditional matching criteria (i.e., ACL, an AS path ACL, or a prefix list) contain a **deny** statement. Example 12-6 shows a configuration where the ACL uses a **deny** statement for the 172.16.1.0/24 network range.

Reading configurations like this should follow the sequence order first and conditional matching criteria second, and only after a match occurs should the processing action and optional action be used. Matching a **deny** statement in the conditional match criteria excludes the route from that sequence in the route map.

The prefix 172.16.1.0/24 is denied by ACL-ONE, which implies that there is not a match in sequences 10 and 20; therefore, the processing action (**permit** or **deny**) is not needed. Sequence 30 does not contain a match clause, so any remaining routes are permitted. The prefix 172.16.1.0/24 would pass on sequence 30 with the metric set to 20. The prefix 172.16.2.0/24 would match ACL-ONE and would pass in sequence 10.

Example 12-6 *Complex Matching Route Maps*

```
ip access-list standard ACL-ONE
 deny 172.16.1.0 0.0.0.255
 permit 172.16.0.0 0.0.255.255

route-map EXAMPLE permit 10
 match ip address ACL-ONE
!
route-map EXAMPLE deny 20
 match ip address ACL-ONE
!
route-map EXAMPLE permit 30
 set metric 20
```

NOTE Route maps process using a particular order of evaluation: the sequence, conditional match criteria, processing action, and optional action in that order. Any **deny** statements in the match component are isolated from the route map sequence action.

Key Topic

Optional Actions

In addition to permitting the prefix to pass, route maps can modify route attributes. Table 12-7 provides a brief overview of the most popular attribute modifications.

Table 12-7 Route Map Set Actions

Set Action	Description
set as-path prepend {*as-number-pattern* | **last-as** *1-10*}	Prepends the AS path for the network prefix with the pattern specified or from multiple iterations from a neighboring AS.
set ip next-hop {*ip-address* | **peer-address** | **self**}	Sets the next-hop IP address for any matching prefix. BGP dynamic manipulation uses the **peer-address** or **self** keywords.
set local-preference *0-4294967295*	Sets the BGP PA local preference.
set metric {+*value* | -*value* | *value*} (where value parameters are 0–4294967295)	Modifies the existing metric or sets the metric for a route.
set origin {**igp** | **incomplete**}	Sets the BGP PA origin.
set tag *tag-value*	Sets a numeric tag (0–4294967295) for identification of networks by other routers.
set weight *0–65535*	Sets the BGP PA weight.
set community *bgp-community* [**additive**]	Sets the BGP PA communities.

The continue Keyword

Default route map behavior processes the route map sequences in order, and upon the first match, it executes the processing action, performs any optional action (if feasible), and stops processing. This prevents multiple route map sequences from processing.

Adding the keyword **continue** to a route map allows the route map to continue processing other route map sequences. Example 12-7 provides a basic configuration. The network prefix 192.168.1.1 matches in sequences 10, 20, and 30. Because the keyword **continue** was added to sequence 10, sequence 20 processes, but sequence 30 does not because a **continue** command was not present in sequence 20. The 192.168.1.1 prefix is permitted, and it is modified so that the metric is 20, with the next-hop address 10.12.1.1.

Example 12-7 *Route Map with the* **continue** *Keyword*

```
ip access-list standard ACL-ONE
 permit 192.168.1.1 0.0.0.0
 permit 172.16.0.0 0.0.255.255
 !
ip access-list standard ACL-TWO
 permit 192.168.1.1 0.0.0.0
 permit 172.31.0.0 0.0.255.255
!
route-map EXAMPLE permit 10
 match ip address ACL-ONE
 set metric 20
 continue
!
```

```
route-map EXAMPLE permit 20
 match ip address ACL-TWO
 set ip next-hop 10.12.1.1
!
route-map EXAMPLE permit 30
 set ip next-hop 10.13.1.3
```

NOTE The **continue** command is not commonly used because it adds complexity when troubleshooting route maps.

BGP Route Filtering and Manipulation

Route filtering is a method of selectively identifying routes that are advertised or received from neighbor routers. Route filtering may be used to manipulate traffic flows, reduce memory utilization, or improve security. For example, it is common for ISPs to deploy route filters on BGP peerings to customers. Ensuring that only the customer routes are allowed over the peering link prevents the customer from accidentally becoming a transit AS on the Internet.

Figure 12-9 shows the complete BGP route processing logic. Notice that the routing policies occur on inbound route receipt and outbound route advertisement.

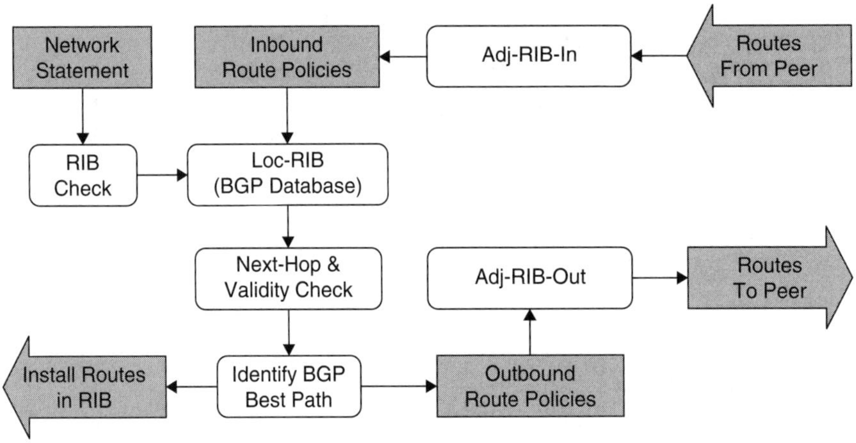

Figure 12-9 *BGP Route Policy Processing*

IOS XE provides four methods of filtering routes inbound or outbound for a specific BGP peer. These methods can be used individually or simultaneously with other methods:

- **Distribute list:** A distribute list involves the filtering of network prefixes based on a standard or extended ACL. An implicit deny is associated with any prefix that is not permitted.

- **Prefix list:** Prefix-matching specifications in a list permit or deny network prefixes in a top-down fashion, similar to an ACL. An implicit deny is associated with any prefix that is not permitted.
- **AS path ACL/filtering:** Regex commands in a list allow for the permit or deny of a network prefix based on the current AS path values. An implicit deny is associated with any prefix that is not permitted.
- **Route maps:** Route maps provide a method of conditional matching on a variety of prefix attributes and taking a variety of actions. Actions could be a simple permit or deny, or could include the modification of BGP path attributes. An implicit deny is associated with any prefix that is not permitted.

NOTE A BGP neighbor cannot use a distribute list and prefix list at the same time in the same direction (inbound or outbound).

The following sections explain each of these filtering techniques in more detail. Imagine a simple scenario with R1 (AS 65100) that has a single eBGP peering with R2 (AS 65200), which then may peer with other autonomous systems (such as AS 65300). The relevant portion of the topology is that R1 peers with R2 and focuses on R1's BGP table, as shown in Example 12-8, with an emphasis on the network prefix and the AS path.

Example 12-8 *Reference BGP Table*

```
R1# show bgp ipv4 unicast | begin Network
     Network          Next Hop            Metric LocPrf Weight Path
 *>  10.3.3.0/24      10.12.1.2               33             0 65200 65300 3003 ?
 *   10.12.1.0/24     10.12.1.2               22             0 65200 ?
 *>                     0.0.0.0                0         32768 ?
 *>  10.23.1.0/24     10.12.1.2              333             0 65200 ?
 *>  100.64.2.0/25    10.12.1.2               22             0 65200 ?
 *>  100.64.2.192/26  10.12.1.2               22             0 65200 ?
 *>  100.64.3.0/25    10.12.1.2               22             0 65200 65300 300 ?
 *>  192.168.1.1/32   0.0.0.0                  0         32768 ?
 *>  192.168.2.2/32   10.12.1.2               22             0 65200 ?
 *>  192.168.3.3/32   10.12.1.2             3333             0 65200 65300 ?
```

Key Topic

Distribute List Filtering

Distribute lists perform route filtering on a neighbor-by-neighbor basis, using standard or extended ACLs. Configuring a distribute list requires using the BGP address-family configuration command **neighbor** *ip-address* **distribute-list** {*acl-number* | *acl-name*} {**in**|**out**}. Remember that extended ACLs for BGP use the source fields to match the network portion and the destination fields to match against the network mask.

Example 12-9 provides R1's BGP configuration, which demonstrates filtering with distribute lists. The configuration uses an extended ACL named ACL-ALLOW that contains two entries. The first entry allows for any prefix that starts in the 192.168.0.0 to 192.168.255.255

range with only a /32 prefix length. The second entry allows for prefixes that contain the 100.64.x.0 pattern with a prefix length of /25 to demonstrate the wildcard abilities of an extended ACL with BGP. The distribute list is then associated with R2's BGP session.

Example 12-9 *BGP Distribute List Configuration*

```
R1
ip access-list extended ACL-ALLOW
 permit ip 192.168.0.0 0.0.255.255 host 255.255.255.255
 permit ip 100.64.0.0 0.0.255.0 host 255.255.255.128
!
router bgp 65100
 neighbor 10.12.1.2 remote-as 65200
 address-family ipv4
  neighbor 10.12.1.2 activate
  neighbor 10.12.1.2 distribute-list ACL-ALLOW in
```

Example 12-10 displays the BGP table of R1. Two local routes are injected into the BGP table by R1 (10.12.1.0/24 and 192.168.1.1/32). The two loopback routes from R2 (AS 65200) and R3 (AS 65300) are allowed because they are within the first ACL-ALLOW entry, and two of the routes matching the 100.64.x.0 pattern (100.64.2.0/25 and 100.64.3.0/25) are accepted. The 100.64.2.192/26 route is rejected because the prefix length does not match the second ACL-ALLOW entry. Example 12-8 can be referenced to identify the routes before the BGP distribute list was applied.

Example 12-10 *Viewing Routes Filtered by BGP Distribute List*

```
R1# show bgp ipv4 unicast | begin Network
     Network          Next Hop            Metric LocPrf Weight Path
 *>  10.12.1.0/24     0.0.0.0                  0         32768 ?
 *>  100.64.2.0/25    10.12.1.2               22             0 65200 ?
 *>  100.64.3.0/25    10.12.1.2               22             0 65200 65300 300 ?
 *>  192.168.1.1/32   0.0.0.0                  0         32768 ?
 *>  192.168.2.2/32   10.12.1.2               22             0 65200 ?
 *>  192.168.3.3/32   10.12.1.2             3333             0 65200 65300 ?
```

Key Topic

Prefix List Filtering

Prefix lists perform route filtering on a neighbor-by-neighbor basis, using a prefix list. Configuring a prefix list involves using the BGP address family configuration command **neighbor** *ip-address* **prefix-list** *prefix-list-name* {**in** | **out**}.

To demonstrate the use of a prefix list, we can use the same initial BGP table from Example 12-8 and filter it to allow only routes within the RFC 1918 space. The same prefix list from Example 12-1 is used and will be applied on R1's peering to R2 (AS 65200). Example 12-11 shows the configuration of the prefix list and application to R2.

Example 12-11 *Prefix List Filtering Configuration*

```
R1# configure terminal
Enter configuration commands, one per line. End with CNTL/Z.
R1(config)# ip prefix-list RFC1918 seq 5 permit 192.168.0.0/16 ge 32
R1(config)# ip prefix-list RFC1918 seq 10 deny 0.0.0.0/0 ge 32
R1(config)# ip prefix-list RFC1918 seq 15 permit 10.0.0.0/8 le 32
R1(config)# ip prefix-list RFC1918 seq 20 permit 172.16.0.0/12 le 32
R1(config)# ip prefix-list RFC1918 seq 25 permit 192.168.0.0/16 le 32
R1(config)# router bgp 65100
R1(config-router)# address-family ipv4 unicast
R1(config-router-af)# neighbor 10.12.1.2 prefix-list RFC1918 in
```

Now that the prefix list has been applied, the BGP table can be examined on R1, as shown in Example 12-12. Notice that the 100.64.2.0/25, 100.64.2.192/26, and 100.64.3.0/25 routes were filtered because they did not fall within the prefix list matching criteria. Example 12-8 can be referenced to identify the routes before the BGP prefix list was applied.

Example 12-12 *Verification of Filtering with a BGP Prefix List*

```
R1# show bgp ipv4 unicast | begin Network
     Network          Next Hop            Metric LocPrf Weight Path
 *>  10.3.3.0/24      10.12.1.2               33             0 65200 65300 3003 ?
 *   10.12.1.0/24     10.12.1.2               22             0 65200 ?
 *>                     0.0.0.0                0         32768 ?
 *>  10.23.1.0/24     10.12.1.2              333             0 65200 ?
 *>  192.168.1.1/32   0.0.0.0                  0         32768 ?
 *>  192.168.2.2/32   10.12.1.2               22             0 65200 ?
 *>  192.168.3.3/32   10.12.1.2             3333             0 65200 65300 ?
```

AS_Path ACL Filtering

Selecting routes from a BGP neighbor by using the AS_Path requires the definition of an **AS_Path access control list (AS_Path ACL).** Regular expressions, introduced earlier in this chapter, are a component of AS_Path filtering.

Example 12-13 shows the routes that R2 (AS 65200) is advertising to R1 (AS 65100).

Example 12-13 *Advertised Routes from R2 to R1*

```
R2# show bgp ipv4 unicast neighbors 10.12.1.1 advertised-routes | begin Network
     Network          Next Hop            Metric LocPrf Weight Path
 *>  10.3.3.0/24      10.23.1.3               33             0 65300 3003 ?
 *>  10.12.1.0/24     0.0.0.0                  0         32768 ?
 *>  10.23.1.0/24     0.0.0.0                  0         32768 ?
 *>  100.64.2.0/25    0.0.0.0                  0         32768 ?
 *>  100.64.2.192/26  0.0.0.0                  0         32768 ?
 *>  100.64.3.0/25    10.23.1.3                3             0 65300 300 ?
 *>  192.168.2.2/32   0.0.0.0                  0         32768 ?
 *>  192.168.3.3/32   10.23.1.3              333             0 65300 ?

Total number of prefixes 8
```

R2 is advertising the routes learned from R3 (AS 65300) to R1. In essence, R2 provides transit connectivity between the autonomous systems. If this were an Internet connection and R2 were an enterprise, it would not want to advertise routes learned from other ASs. Using an AS_Path access list to restrict the advertisement of only AS 65200 routes would be recommended.

Key Topic

Processing is performed in a sequential top-down order, and the first qualifying match processes against the appropriate **permit** or **deny** action. An implicit deny exists at the end of the AS_Path ACL. IOS supports up to 500 AS_Path ACLs and uses the command **ip as-path access-list** *acl-number* {**deny** | **permit**} *regex-query* for creating an AS_Path ACL. The ACL is then applied with the command **neighbor** *ip-address* **filter-list** *acl-number* {**in**|**out**}.

Example 12-14 shows the configuration on R2 using an AS_Path ACL to restrict traffic to only locally originated traffic, using the regex pattern ^$ (refer to Table 12-4). To ensure completeness, the AS_Path ACL is applied on all eBGP neighborships.

Example 12-14 *AS Path Access List Configuration*

```
R2
ip as-path access-list 1 permit ^$
!
router bgp 65200
 neighbor 10.12.1.1 remote-as 65100
 neighbor 10.23.1.3 remote-as 65300
 address-family ipv4 unicast
  neighbor 10.12.1.1 activate
  neighbor 10.23.1.3 activate
  neighbor 10.12.1.1 filter-list 1 out
  neighbor 10.23.1.3 filter-list 1 out
```

Now that the AS_Path ACL has been applied, the advertised routes can be checked again. Example 12-15 displays the routes being advertised to R1. Notice that all the routes do not have an AS_Path, confirming that only locally originating routes are being advertised externally. Example 12-13 can be referenced to identify the routes before the BGP AS_Path ACL was applied.

Example 12-15 *Verification of Local Route Advertisements with an AS_Path ACL*

```
R2# show bgp ipv4 unicast neighbors 10.12.1.1 advertised-routes | begin Network
     Network          Next Hop            Metric LocPrf Weight Path
 *>  10.12.1.0/24     0.0.0.0                  0         32768 ?
 *>  10.23.1.0/24     0.0.0.0                  0         32768 ?
 *>  100.64.2.0/25    0.0.0.0                  0         32768 ?
 *>  100.64.2.192/26  0.0.0.0                  0         32768 ?
 *>  192.168.2.2/32   0.0.0.0                  0         32768 ?

Total number of prefixes 5
```

Key Topic

Route Maps

As explained earlier, route maps provide additional functionality over pure filtering. Route maps provide a method to manipulate BGP path attributes as well. Route maps are applied on a per-BGP neighbor basis for routes that are advertised or received. A different route map can be used for each direction. The route map is associated with a BGP neighbor with the command **neighbor** *ip-address* **route-map** *route-map-name* {**in**|**out**} under the specific address family.

Example 12-16 shows the BGP table of R1, which is used here to demonstrate the power of a route map.

Example 12-16 *BGP Table Before Applying a Route Map*

```
R1# show bgp ipv4 unicast | begin Network
      Network          Next Hop            Metric LocPrf Weight Path
 *>  10.1.1.0/24      0.0.0.0                  0         32768 ?
 *>  10.3.3.0/24      10.12.1.2               33             0 65200 65300 3003 ?
 *   10.12.1.0/24     10.12.1.2               22             0 65200 ?
 *>                    0.0.0.0                 0         32768 ?
 *>  10.23.1.0/24     10.12.1.2              333             0 65200 ?
 *>  100.64.2.0/25    10.12.1.2               22             0 65200 ?
 *>  100.64.2.192/26  10.12.1.2               22             0 65200 ?
 *>  100.64.3.0/25    10.12.1.2               22             0 65200 65300 300 ?
 *>  192.168.1.1/32   0.0.0.0                  0         32768 ?
 *>  192.168.2.2/32   10.12.1.2               22             0 65200 ?
 *>  192.168.3.3/32   10.12.1.2             3333             0 65200 65300 ?
```

Route maps allow for multiple steps in processing as well. To demonstrate this concept, our route map will consist of four steps:

1. Deny any routes that are in the 192.168.0.0/16 network range by using a prefix list.
2. Match any routes originating from AS 65200 that are within the 100.64.0.0/10 network range and set the BGP local preference to 222.
3. Match any routes originating from AS 65200 that did not match step 2 and set the BGP weight to 23456.
4. Permit all other routes to process.

Example 12-17 demonstrates R1's configuration, where multiple prefix lists are referenced along with an AS path ACL.

Example 12-17 *R1's Route Map Configuration for Inbound AS 65200 Routes*

```
R1
ip prefix-list FIRST-RFC1918 permit 192.168.0.0/16 le 32
ip as-path access-list 1 permit _65200$
ip prefix-list SECOND-CGNAT permit 100.64.0.0/10 le 32
!
```

```
route-map AS65200IN deny 10
 description Deny RFC1918 192.168.0.0/16 routes via Prefix List Matching
 match ip address prefix-list FIRST-RFC1918
!
route-map AS65200IN permit 20
 description Change local preference for AS65200 originated route in 100.64.x.x/10
 match ip address prefix-list SECOND-CGNAT
 match as-path 1
 set local-preference 222
!
route-map AS65200IN permit 30
 description Change the weight for AS65200 originated routes
 match as-path 1
 set weight 23456
!
route-map AS65200IN permit 40
 description Permit all other routes un-modified
!
router bgp 65100
 neighbor 10.12.1.2 remote-as 65200
 address-family ipv4 unicast
  neighbor 10.12.1.2 activate
  neighbor 10.12.1.2 route-map AS65200IN in
```

Example 12-18 displays R1's BGP table. The following actions have occurred:

- The 192.168.2.2/32 and 192.168.3.3/32 routes were discarded. The 192.168.1.1/32 route is a locally generated route.
- The 100.64.2.0/25 and 100.64.2.192/26 routes had the local preference modified to 222 because they originated from AS 65200 and are within the 100.64.0.0/10 network range.
- The 10.12.1.0/24 and 10.23.1.0/24 routes from R2 were assigned the locally significant BGP attribute weight 23456.
- All other routes were accepted and not modified.

Example 12-18 *Verifying Changes from R1's Route Map to AS 65200*

```
R1# show bgp ipv4 unicast | b Network
     Network          Next Hop            Metric LocPrf Weight Path
 *>  10.1.1.0/24      0.0.0.0                  0         32768 ?
 *>  10.3.3.0/24      10.12.1.2               33             0 65200 65300 3003 ?
  >  10.12.1.0/24     10.12.1.2               22         23456 65200 ?
 *>                     0.0.0.0                0         32768 ?
```

```
*>  10.23.1.0/24       10.12.1.2         333              23456 65200 ?
*>  100.64.2.0/25      10.12.1.2          22       222        0 65200 ?
*>  100.64.2.192/26    10.12.1.2          22       222        0 65200 ?
*>  100.64.3.0/25      10.12.1.2          22                  0 65200 65300 300 ?
*>  192.168.1.1/32     0.0.0.0             0              32768 ?
```

NOTE It is considered a best practice to use a different route policy for inbound and outbound prefixes for each BGP neighbor.

Clearing BGP Connections

Depending on the change to the BGP route manipulation technique, a BGP session may need to be refreshed in order to take effect. BGP supports two methods of clearing a BGP session. The first method is a *hard reset*, which tears down the BGP session, removes BGP routes from the peer, and is the most disruptive. The second method is a *soft reset*, which invalidates the BGP cache and requests a full advertisement from its BGP peer.

Routers initiate a hard reset with the command **clear ip bgp** *ip-address* [**soft**] and a soft reset by using the optional **soft** keyword. All the active BGP sessions can be cleared by using an asterisk * in lieu of the peer's IP address.

When a BGP policy changes, the BGP table must be processed again so that the neighbors can be notified accordingly. Routes received by a BGP peer must be processed again. If the BGP session supports *route refresh* capability, the peer re-advertises (refreshes) the prefixes to the requesting router, allowing for the inbound policy to process using the new policy changes. The route refresh capability is negotiated for each address family when the session is established.

Performing a soft reset on sessions that support route refresh capability actually initiates a route refresh. Soft resets can be performed for a specific address family with the command **clear bgp** *afi safi* {*ip-address*|*} **soft** [**in** | **out**]. Soft resets reduce the number of routes that must be exchanged if multiple address families are configured with a single BGP peer. Changes to the outbound routing policies use the optional **out** keyword, and changes to inbound routing policies use the optional **in** keyword. You can use an * in lieu of specifying a peer's IP address to perform that action for all BGP peers.

Key Topic

BGP Communities

BGP communities provide additional capability for tagging routes and for modifying BGP routing policy on upstream and downstream routers. BGP communities can be appended, removed, or modified selectively on each attribute as a route travels from router to router.

BGP communities are an optional transitive BGP path attribute that can traverse from AS to AS. A **BGP community** is a 32-bit number that can be included with a route. A BGP community can be displayed as a full 32-bit number (0–4,294,967,295) or as two 16-bit numbers (0–65535):(0–65535), commonly referred to as *new format*.

Private BGP communities follow a particular convention where the first 16 bits represent the AS of the community origination, and the second 16 bits represent a pattern defined by the originating AS. A private BGP community pattern can vary from organization to organization, does not need to be registered, and can signify geographic locations for one AS while signifying a method of route advertisement in another AS. Some organizations publish their private BGP community patterns on websites such as www.onesc.net/communities/.

In 2006, RFC 4360 expanded BGP communities' capabilities by providing an extended format. *Extended BGP communities* provide structure for various classes of information and are commonly used for VPN services. RFC 8092 provides support for communities larger than 32 bits (which are beyond the scope of this book).

Well-Known Communities

RFC 1997 defines a set of global communities (known as *well-known communities*) that are within the community range 4,294,901,760 (0xFFFF0000) to 4,294,967,295 (0xFFFFFFFF). All routers that are capable of sending/receiving BGP communities must implement well-known communities. Following are four common well-known communities:

- **Internet:** This is a standardized community for identifying routes that should be advertised on the Internet. In larger networks that deploy BGP into the core, advertised routes should be advertised to the Internet and should have this community set. This allows for the edge BGP routers to only allow the advertisement of BGP routes with the Internet community to the Internet. Filtering is not automatic but can be done with an outbound route map.

- **No_Advertise:** Routes with this community will not be advertised to any BGP peer (iBGP or eBGP).

- **Local-AS:** Routes with this community are not advertised to an eBGP peer but can be advertised to BGP confederation peers. BGP confederation peers are considered outside the scope of the exam.

- **No_Export:** When a route with this community is received, the route is not advertised to any eBGP peer. Routes with this community can be advertised to iBGP peers.

Key Topic

Enabling BGP Community Support

IOS XE routers do not advertise BGP communities to peers by default. Communities are enabled on a neighbor-by-neighbor basis with the BGP address family configuration command **neighbor** *ip-address* **send-community** [**standard** | **extended** | **both**] under the neighbor's address family configuration. If a keyword is not specified, standard communities are sent by default.

IOS XE routers can display communities in new format, which is easier to read, with the global configuration command **ip bgp-community new-format**. Example 12-19 displays the BGP community in decimal format first, followed by the new format.

Example 12-19 *BGP Community Formats*

```
! Decimal Format
R3# show bgp 192.168.1.1
! Output omitted for brevity
BGP routing table entry for 192.168.1.1/32, version 6
Community: 6553602 6577023
```

```
! New-Format
R3# show bgp 192.168.1.1
! Output omitted for brevity
BGP routing table entry for 192.168.1.1/32, version 6
Community: 100:2 100:23423
```

Conditionally Matching BGP Communities

Conditionally matching BGP communities allows for selection of routes based on the BGP communities within the route's path attributes so that selective processing can occur in route maps. Example 12-20 demonstrates the BGP table for R1, which has received multiple routes from R2 (AS 65200).

Example 12-20 *BGP Routes from R2 (AS 65200)*

```
R1# show bgp ipv4 unicast | begin Network
     Network          Next Hop            Metric LocPrf Weight Path
 *>  10.1.1.0/24      0.0.0.0                  0         32768 ?
 *   10.12.1.0/24     10.12.1.2               22             0 65200 ?
 *>                   0.0.0.0                  0         32768 ?
 *>  10.23.1.0/24     10.12.1.2              333             0 65200 ?
 *>  192.168.1.1/32   0.0.0.0                  0         32768 ?
 *>  192.168.2.2/32   10.12.1.2               22             0 65200 ?
 *>  192.168.3.3/32   10.12.1.2             3333             0 65200 65300 ?
```

In this example, say that you want to conditionally match for a specific community. The entire BGP table can be displayed with the command **show bgp** *afi safi* **detail** and then you can manually select a route with a specific community. However, if the BGP community is known, all the routes matching the community can be displayed with the command **show bgp** *afi safi* **community** *community*, as shown in Example 12-21.

Example 12-21 *Displaying the BGP Routes with a Specific Community*

```
R1# show bgp ipv4 unicast community 333:333 | begin Network
     Network          Next Hop            Metric LocPrf Weight Path
 *>  10.23.1.0/24     10.12.1.2              333             0 65200 ?
```

Example 12-22 displays the explicit path entry for the 10.23.1.0/24 network and all the BGP path attributes. Notice that two BGP communities (333:333 and 65300:333) are added to the path.

Example 12-22 *Viewing BGP Path Attributes for the 10.23.1.0/24 Network*

```
R1# show ip bgp 10.23.1.0/24
BGP routing table entry for 10.23.1.0/24, version 15
Paths: (1 available, best #1, table default)
  Not advertised to any peer
  Refresh Epoch 3
  65200
    10.12.1.2 from 10.12.1.2 (192.168.2.2)
      Origin incomplete, metric 333, localpref 100, valid, external, best
      Community: 333:333 65300:333
      rx pathid: 0, tx pathid: 0x0
```

Key Topic

Conditionally matching requires the creation of a community list that shares a similar structure to an ACL, can be standard or expanded, and can be referenced by number or name. Standard community lists are numbered 1 to 99 and match either well-known communities or a private community number (*as-number:16-bit-number*). Expanded community lists are numbered 100 to 500 and use regex patterns.

The configuration syntax for a community list is **ip community-list** {*1-500* | **standard** *list-name* | **expanded** *list-name*} {**permit** | **deny**} *community-pattern*. After defining the community list, the community list is referenced in the route map with the command **match community** {*1-500* | *community-list-name* [**exact**]}.

> **NOTE** When multiple communities are on the same **ip community list** statement, all communities for that statement must exist in the route. If only one out of many communities is required, you can use multiple **ip community list** statements.

Example 12-23 demonstrates the creation of a BGP community list that matches on the community 333:333. The BGP community list is then used in the first sequence of *route-map COMMUNITY-CHECK*, which denies any routes with that community. The second route map sequence allows all other BGP routes and sets the BGP weight (locally significant) to 111. The route map is then applied inbound on routes advertised from R2 to R1.

Example 12-23 *Conditionally Matching BGP Communities*

```
R1
ip community-list 100 permit 333:333
!
route-map COMMUNITY-CHECK deny 10
 description Block Routes with Community 333:333 in it
 match community 100
route-map COMMUNITY-CHECK permit 20
 description Allow routes with either community in it
```

```
 set weight 111
!
router bgp 65100
 address-family ipv4 unicast
  neighbor 10.12.1.2 route-map COMMUNITY-CHECK in
```

Example 12-24 shows the BGP table after the route map has been applied to the neighbor. The 10.23.1.0/24 route was discarded, and all the other routes learned from AS 65200 had the BGP weight set to 111.

Example 12-24 *R1's BGP Table After Applying the Route Map*

```
R1# show bgp ipv4 unicast | begin Network
     Network          Next Hop            Metric LocPrf Weight Path
 *>  10.1.1.0/24      0.0.0.0                  0         32768 ?
 *   10.12.1.0/24     10.12.1.2               22           111 65200 ?
 *>                   0.0.0.0                  0         32768 ?
 *>  192.168.1.1/32   0.0.0.0                  0         32768 ?
 *>  192.168.2.2/32   10.12.1.2               22           111 65200 ?
 *>  192.168.3.3/32   10.12.1.2             3333           111 65200 65300 ?
```

Key Topic

Setting Private BGP Communities

A private BGP community is set in a route map with the command **set community** *bgp-community* [**additive**]. By default, when you are setting a community, any existing communities are overwritten but can be preserved by using the optional **additive** keyword.

Example 12-25 shows the BGP table entries for the 10.23.1.0/24 route, which has the 333:333 and 65300:333 BGP communities. The 10.3.3.0/24 route has the 65300:300 community.

Example 12-25 *Viewing the BGP Communities for Two Network Prefixes*

```
R1# show bgp ipv4 unicast 10.23.1.0/24
! Output omitted for brevity
BGP routing table entry for 10.23.1.0/24, version 15
  65200
     10.12.1.2 from 10.12.1.2 (192.168.2.2)
       Origin incomplete, metric 333, localpref 100, valid, external, best
       Community: 333:333 65300:333
```

```
R1# show bgp ipv4 unicast 10.3.3.0/24
! Output omitted for brevity
BGP routing table entry for 10.3.3.0/24, version 12
  65200 65300 3003
     10.12.1.2 from 10.12.1.2 (192.168.2.2)
       Origin incomplete, metric 33, localpref 100, valid, external, best
       Community: 65300:300
```

Example 12-26 shows the configuration where the BGP community is set to 10:23 for the 10.23.1.0/24 route. The **additive** keyword is not used, so the previous community values 333:333 and 65300:333 are overwritten with the 10:23 community. The 10.3.3.0/24 route has the communities 3:0, 3:3, and 10:10 added to the existing communities. The route map is then associated to R2 (AS 65200).

Example 12-26 *Setting Private BGP Community Configuration*

```
ip prefix-list PREFIX10.23.1.0 seq 5 permit 10.23.1.0/24
ip prefix-list PREFIX10.3.3.0 seq 5 permit 10.3.3.0/24
!
route-map SET-COMMUNITY permit 10
 match ip address prefix-list PREFIX10.23.1.0
 set community 10:23
route-map SET-COMMUNITY permit 20
  match ip address prefix-list PREFIX10.3.3.0
 set community 3:0 3:3 10:10 additive
route-map SET-COMMUNITY permit 30
!
router bgp 65100
 address-family ipv4
  neighbor 10.12.1.2 route-map SET-COMMUNITY in
```

Now that the route map has been applied and the routes have been refreshed, the path attributes can be examined, as demonstrated in Example 12-27. As anticipated, the previous BGP communities were removed for the 10.23.1.0/24 network but were maintained for the 10.3.3.0/24 network.

Example 12-27 *Verifying BGP Community Changes*

```
R1# show bgp ipv4 unicast 10.23.1.0/24
! Output omitted for brevity
BGP routing table entry for 10.23.1.0/24, version 22
  65200
    10.12.1.2 from 10.12.1.2 (192.168.2.2)
      Origin incomplete, metric 333, localpref 100, valid, external, best
      Community: 10:23
```

```
R1# show bgp ipv4 unicast 10.3.3.0/24
BGP routing table entry for 10.3.3.0/24, version 20
  65200 65300 3003
    10.12.1.2 from 10.12.1.2 (192.168.2.2)
      Origin incomplete, metric 33, localpref 100, valid, external, best
      Community: 3:0 3:3 10:10 65300:300
```

Understanding BGP Path Selection

The BGP best-path selection algorithm influences how traffic enters or leaves an AS. Some router configurations modify the BGP attributes to influence inbound traffic, outbound traffic, or inbound and outbound traffic, depending on the network design requirements. A lot of network engineers do not understand BGP best-path selection, which can often result in suboptimal routing. This section explains the logic used by a router that uses BGP when forwarding packets.

Key Topic

Routing Path Selection Using Longest Match

Routers always select the path a packet should take by examining the prefix length of a network entry. The path selected for a packet is chosen based on the prefix length, where the longest prefix length is always preferred. For example, /28 is preferred over /26, and /26 is preferred over /24.

This logic can be used to influence path selection in BGP. Assume that an organization owns the 100.64.0.0/16 network range but only needs to advertise two subnets (100.64.1.0/24 and 100.64.2.0/24). It could advertise both prefixes (100.64.1.0/24 and 100.64.2.0/24) from all its routers, but how can it distribute the load for each subnet if all traffic comes in on one router (such as R1)?

The organization could modify various BGP path attributes (PAs) that are advertised externally, but an SP could have a BGP routing policy that ignores those path attributes, resulting in random receipt of network traffic.

A more elegant way that guarantees that paths are selected deterministically outside the organization is to advertise a summary prefix (100.64.0.0/16) out both routers. Then the organization can advertise a longer matching prefix out the router that should receive network traffic for that prefix. Figure 12-10 shows the concept, with R1 advertising the 100.64.1.0/24 prefix, R2 advertising the 100.64.2.0/24 prefix, and both routers advertising the 100.64.0.0/16 summary network prefix.

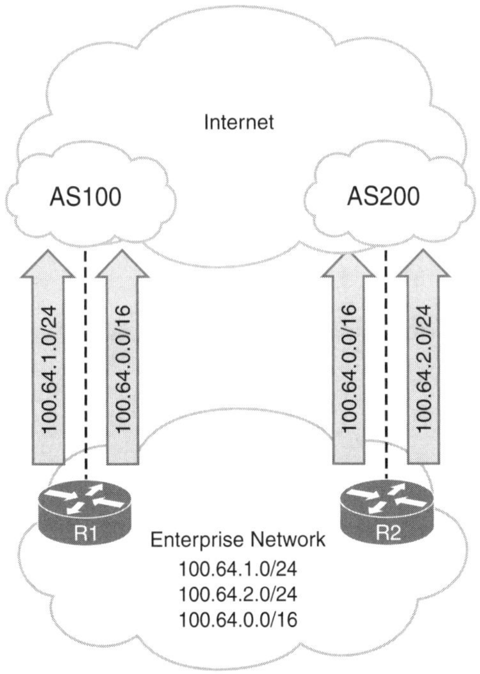

Figure 12-10 *BGP Path Selection Using Longest Match*

Regardless of an SP's routing policy, the more specific prefixes are advertised out only one router. Redundancy is provided by advertising the summary address. If R1 crashes, devices use R2's route advertisement of 100.64.0.0/16 to reach the 100.64.1.0/24 network.

NOTE Ensure that the network summaries that are being advertised from your organization are within only your network range. In addition, service providers typically do not accept IPv4 routes longer than /24 (for example, /25 or /26) or IPv6 routes longer than /48. Routes are restricted to control the size of the Internet routing table.

BGP Best Path Overview

In BGP, route advertisements consist of BGP update packets containing Network Layer Reachability Information (NLRI). The NLRI consists of the prefix length and the prefix. A BGP route may contain multiple paths to the same destination network. Every path's attributes impact the desirability of the route when a router selects the best path. By default, a BGP router advertises only the best path to the neighboring routers.

Inside the Loc-RIB, all the routes and their path attributes are maintained with the best path calculated. The best path is then installed in the RIB of the router. If the best path is no longer available, the router can use the existing paths to quickly identify a new best path. BGP recalculates the best path for a prefix upon four possible events:

- BGP next-hop reachability change
- Failure of an interface connected to an eBGP peer
- Redistribution change
- Reception of new or removed paths for a route

BGP automatically installs the first received path as the best path. When additional paths are received for the same network prefix length, the newer paths are compared against the current best path. If there is a tie, processing continues until a best-path winner is identified.

The BGP best-path algorithm uses the following attributes, in the order shown, for the best-path selection:

Key Topic

1. Weight
2. Local preference
3. Locally originated (network statement, redistribution, or aggregation)
4. AIGP
5. Shortest AS_Path
6. Origin type
7. Lowest MED
8. eBGP over iBGP
9. Lowest IGP metric to next hop
10. Prefer the path from the *oldest* eBGP session

11. Prefer the route that comes from the BGP peer with the lower RID
12. Prefer the route with the minimum cluster list length
13. Prefer the path that comes from the lowest neighbor address

The BGP routing policy can vary from organization to organization, based on the manipulation of the BGP PAs. Because some PAs carry from one AS to another AS, those changes could impact downstream routing for other SPs too. Other PAs only influence the routing policy within the organization. Network prefixes are conditionally matched on a variety of factors, such as AS_Path length, specific ASN, BGP communities, or other attributes.

The best-path algorithm is explained in the following sections.

Weight

BGP weight is a Cisco-defined attribute and the first step for selecting the BGP best path. Weight is a 16-bit value (0 to 65,535) assigned locally on the router; it is not advertised to other routers. The path with the higher weight is preferred. Weight can be set for specific routes with an inbound route map or for all routes learned from a specific neighbor. Weight only influences outbound traffic from a router or an AS. Because it is the first step in the best-path algorithm, it should be used when other attributes should not influence the best path for a specific network.

Examining a network prefix with the command **show bgp** *afi safi network* will display all of the paths and the associated path attributes as well as the best path selected. Identifying the best path may take time for people that are new to BGP, and newer versions of IOS XE provide commands to identify the best path quickly with the command **show bgp** *afi safi network* **bestpath**. The command **show bgp** *afi safi network* **best-path-reason** will display all paths and describe why a path is preferred or not preferred.

Example 12-28 displays the BGP table for the 172.16.0.0/24 network prefix on R5. On the fourth line of the output, the router indicates that two paths exist, and the second path is the best path. By examining the output of each path, the path learned through AS 200 has a weight of 123. The path through AS 300 does not have the weight, which equates to a value of 0; therefore, the route through AS 200 is the best path. Notice that the second set of output uses the **bestpath** optional keyword and only displays the best path. The third set of output includes the **best-path-reason** optional keyword. That output indicates that the first path has a lower weight than the selected best-path.

Example 12-28 *An Example of a BGP Best-Path Choice Based on Weight*

```
R5# show bgp ipv4 unicast 172.16.0.0/24
! Output omitted for brevity
BGP routing table entry for 172.16.0.0/24, version 5
Paths: (2 available, best #2, table default)
  Not advertised to any peer
  300 100
    192.168.6.6 (metric 130816) from 192.168.6.6 (192.168.6.6)
      Origin IGP, metric 0, localpref 100, valid, internal
  200 100
```

```
    192.168.4.4 (metric 130816) from 192.168.4.4 (192.168.4.4)
      Origin IGP, metric 0, localpref 100, weight 123, valid, internal, best
```

```
R5# show bgp ipv4 unicast 172.16.0.0/24 bestpath
! Output omitted for brevity
BGP routing table entry for 172.16.0.0/24, version 5
Paths: (2 available, best #2, table default)
  200 100
    192.168.4.4 (metric 130816) from 192.168.4.4 (192.168.4.4)
      Origin IGP, metric 0, localpref 100, weight 123, valid, internal, best
```

```
R5# show bgp ipv4 unicast 172.16.0.0/24 best-path-reason
! Output omitted for brevity
BGP routing table entry for 172.16.0.0/24, version 5
Paths: (2 available, best #2, table default)
  300 100
    192.168.6.6 (metric 130816) from 192.168.6.6 (192.168.6.6)
      Origin IGP, metric 0, localpref 100, valid, internal
      Best Path Evaluation: Lower weight
  200 100
    192.168.4.4 (metric 130816) from 192.168.4.4 (192.168.4.4)
      Origin IGP, metric 0, localpref 100, weight 123, valid, internal, best
      Best Path Evaluation: Overall best path
```

Local Preference

Local preference (LOCAL_PREF) is a well-known path attribute and is included with path advertisements throughout an AS. The local preference attribute is a 32-bit value (0 to 4,294,967,295) that indicates the preference for exiting the AS to the destination network. The local preference is not advertised between eBGP peers and is typically used to influence the next-hop address for outbound traffic (that is, leaving an autonomous system). Local preference can be set for specific routes by using a route map or for all routes received from a specific neighbor.

A higher value is preferred over a lower value. If an edge BGP router does not define the local preference upon receipt of a prefix, the default local preference value of 100 is used during best-path calculation, and it is included in advertisements to other iBGP peers. Modifying the local preference can influence the path selection on other iBGP peers without impacting eBGP peers because local preference is not advertised outside the autonomous system.

Example 12-29 shows the BGP table for the 172.16.1.0/24 network prefix on R4. On the third line of the output, the router indicates that two paths exist, and the first path is the best path. The BGP weight does not exist, so the local preference is used to select the best path. The path learned through AS 300 is the best path because it has a local preference of 333, while the path through AS 200 has a local preference of 111.

Example 12-29 *An Example of a BGP Best-Path Choice Based on Local Preference*

```
R4# show bgp ipv4 unicast 172.16.1.0/24 best-path-reason
! Output omitted for brevity
 BGP routing table entry for 172.16.1.0/24, version 6
Paths: (2 available, best #1, table default)
  300 100
    192.168.6.6 (metric 131072) from 192.168.6.6 (192.168.6.6)
      Origin IGP, metric 0, localpref 333, valid, internal, best
      Best Path Evaluation: Overall best path
  200 100
    100.64.24.2 from 100.64.24.2 (192.168.2.2)
      Origin IGP, localpref 111, valid, external
      Best Path Evaluation: Lower local preference
```

Locally Originated via Network or Aggregate Advertisement

The third decision point in the best-path algorithm is to determine whether the route originated locally. Preference is given in the following order:

- Routes that were advertised locally
- Networks that have been aggregated locally
- Routes received by BGP peers

Accumulated Interior Gateway Protocol Metric

Accumulated Interior Gateway Protocol (AIGP) is an optional nontransitive path attribute that is included with advertisements throughout an AS. IGPs typically use the lowest-path metric to identify the shortest path to a destination but cannot provide the scalability of BGP. BGP uses an AS to identify a single domain of control for a routing policy. BGP does not use path metric due to scalability issues combined with the notion that each AS may use a different routing policy to calculate metrics.

AIGP provides the ability for BGP to maintain and calculate a conceptual path metric in environments that use multiple ASs with unique IGP routing domains in each AS. The ability for BGP to make routing decisions based on a path metric is a viable option because all the ASs are under the control of a single domain, with consistent routing policies for BGP and IGPs.

In Figure 12-11, AS 100, AS 200, and AS 300 are all under the control of the same service provider. AIGP has been enabled on the BGP sessions between all the routers, and the IGPs are redistributed into BGP. The AIGP metric is advertised between AS 100, AS 200, and AS 300, allowing BGP to use the AIGP metric for best-path calculations between the autonomous systems.

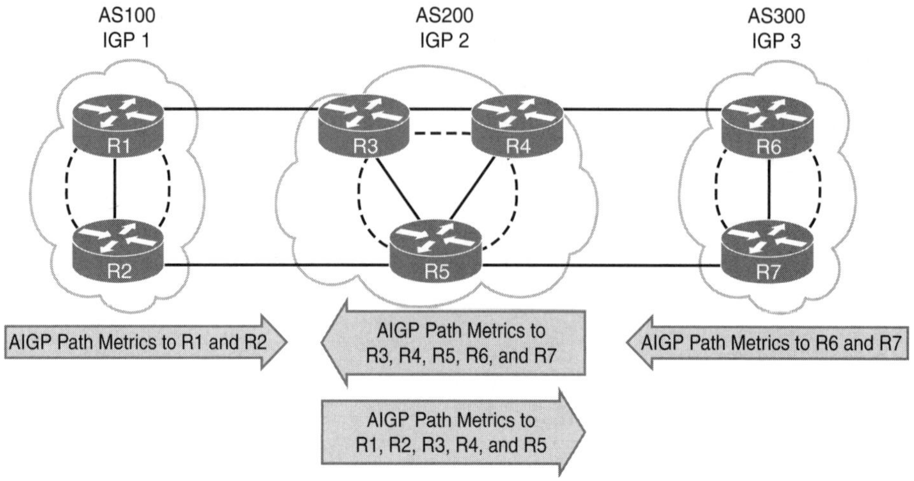

Figure 12-11 *AIGP Path Attribute Exchange Between Autonomous Systems*

The following guidelines apply to AIGP metrics:

- A path with an AIGP metric is preferred to a path without an AIGP metric.
- If the next-hop address requires a recursive lookup, the AIGP path needs to calculate a derived metric to include the distance to the next-hop address. This ensures that the cost to the BGP edge router is included. The formula is

  Derived AIGP metric = (Original AIGP metric + Next-hop AIGP metric)

  - If multiple AIGP paths exist and one next-hop address contains an AIGP metric and the other does not, the non-AIGP path is not used.
  - The next-hop AIGP metric is recursively added if multiple lookups are performed.
- AIGP paths are compared based on the derived AIGP metric (with recursive next hops) or the actual AIGP metric (non-recursive next hop). The path with the lower AIGP metric is preferred.
- When R2 advertises an AIGP-enabled path that was learned from R1, if the next-hop address changes to an R2 address, R2 increments the AIGP metric to reflect the distance (the IGP path metric) between R1 and R2.

Shortest AS Path

The next decision factor for the BGP best-path algorithm is the AS path length. The path length typically correlates to the AS hop count. A shorter AS path is preferred over a longer AS path.

Prepending ASNs to the AS path makes it longer, thereby making that path less desirable compared to other paths. Typically, the AS path is prepended with the network owner's ASN.

In general, a path that has had the AS path prepended is not selected as the BGP best path because the AS path is longer than the non-prepended path advertisement. Inbound traffic is influenced by prepending AS path length in advertisements to other ASs, and outbound traffic is influenced by prepending advertisements received from other ASs.

Example 12-30 shows the BGP table for the 172.24.0.0/16 route on R4. There is no weight set on either route, and the local preference is identical. The first route has an AS path length of 2 (300 100), while the second route has an AS path length of 4 (200 200 200 100). The first route learned through AS 300 is selected as the best path because it has a shorter AS path length.

Example 12-30 *An Example of a BGP Best-Path Choice Based on AS Path Length*

```
R4# show bgp ipv4 unicast 172.24.0.0/16 best-path-reason
! Output omitted for brevity
BGP routing table entry for 172.24.0.0/16, version 18
Paths: (2 available, best #1, table default)
  300 100
    192.168.6.6 (metric 131072) from 192.168.6.6 (192.168.6.6)
      Origin IGP, metric 0, localpref 100, valid, internal, best
      Best Path Evaluation: Overall best path
  200 200 200 100
    100.64.24.2 from 100.64.24.2 (192.168.2.2)
      Origin IGP, localpref 100, valid, external
      rx pathid: 0, tx pathid: 0
      Best Path Evaluation: Longer AS path
```

NOTE The ASNs are repeated for the second route, which indicates that AS 200 prepended its BGP advertisement to steer network traffic.

NOTE Peering with different Internet providers provides optimal routing to most companies because one SP may be one AS path hop away (or provide connectivity to other tier 2/3 SPs), while a different SP may have a shorter AS path to other customers.

Origin Type

The next BGP best-path decision factor is the well-known mandatory BGP attribute named *origin*. By default, networks that are advertised through the **network** statement are set with the IGP or i origin, and redistributed networks are assigned the Incomplete or ? origin attribute. The origin preference order is

1. IGP origin (most)
2. EGP origin
3. Incomplete origin (least)

Example 12-31 displays R4's BGP table. Notice that the 172.24.0.0/24 route has two paths. The path from AS 300 was selected as the best path because it was advertised from an IGP, while the path from AS 200 has an incomplete origin and is deemed inferior to the path via AS 300.

Example 12-31 *An Example of a BGP Best-Path Choice Based on Origin Type*

```
R4# show bgp ipv4 unicast
BGP table version is 21, local router ID is 192.168.4.4
Status codes: s suppressed, d damped, h history, * valid, > best, i - internal,
              r RIB-failure, S Stale, m multipath, b backup-path, f RT-Filter,
              x best-external, a additional-path, c RIB-compressed,
              t secondary path, L long-lived-stale,
Origin codes: i - IGP, e - EGP, ? - incomplete
RPKI validation codes: V valid, I invalid, N Not found

      Network          Next Hop            Metric LocPrf Weight Path
 *>   172.16.0.0/24    10.24.1.2                              0 200 100 i
 * i  172.20.0.0/24    192.168.6.6              0    100      0 300 100 i
 *>                    10.24.1.2                              0 200 100 i
 *>i  172.24.0.0/24    192.168.6.6              0    100      0 300 100 i
 *                     10.24.1.2                              0 200 100 ?
```

Multi-Exit Discriminator

The next BGP best-path decision factor is the non-transitive BGP path attribute named *multiple-exit discriminator (MED)*. MED uses a 32-bit value (0 to 4,294,967,295) called a *metric*. BGP sets the MED automatically to the IGP path metric during network advertisement or redistribution. If the MED is received from an eBGP session, it can be advertised to other iBGP peers, but it should not be sent outside the AS that received it. MED's purpose is to influence traffic flows inbound from a different AS. A lower MED is preferred over a higher MED.

NOTE For MED to be an effective decision factor, the paths being decided upon must come from the same ASN.

RFC 4451 guidelines state that a prefix without a MED value should be given priority and, in essence, should be compared with a value of 0. Some organizations require that a MED be set to a specific value for all the prefixes and declare that paths without the MED should be treated as the least preferred. By default, if the MED is missing from a prefix learned from an eBGP peer, devices use a MED of 0 for the best-path calculation. IOS XE routers advertise a MED of 0 to iBGP peers for eBGP routes that do not have a MED.

Example 12-32 shows the BGP table for the 172.16.1.0/24 route on R2. Notice that R2 is peering only with AS 300 for MED to be eligible for the best-path selection process. The first path has a MED of 0, and the second path has a MED of 33. The first path is preferred because the MED is lower.

Example 12-32 *An Example of a BGP Best-Path Choice Based on MED*

```
R2# show bgp ipv4 unicast 172.16.1.0
BGP routing table entry for 172.16.1.0/24, version 9
Paths: (2 available, best #1, table default)
  Advertised to update-groups:
     2
  Refresh Epoch 4
  300
    10.12.1.1 from 10.12.1.1 (192.168.1.1)
       Origin IGP, metric 0, localpref 100, valid, external, best
  Refresh Epoch 14
  300
    10.23.1.3 from 10.23.1.3 (192.168.3.3)
      Origin IGP, metric 33, localpref 100, valid, external
```

NOTE It is possible for the SP to forget to advertise the MED from both peers and configure only one. This situation might have unintended consequences and can be easily fixed.

eBGP over iBGP

The next BGP best-path decision factor is whether the route comes from an iBGP, eBGP, or confederation member AS (sub-AS) peering. The best-path selection order is

1. eBGP peers (most desirable)
2. Confederation member AS peers
3. iBGP peers (least desirable)

NOTE BGP confederations are beyond the scope of the CCNP and CCIE Enterprise Core ENCOR 350-401 exam and are not discussed in this book.

Lowest IGP Metric

The next decision step is to use the lowest IGP cost to the BGP next-hop address. Figure 12-12 illustrates a topology where R2, R3, R4, and R5 are in AS 400, and the focus is going to be on R3 and R5. AS 400 peers in a full mesh and establishes BGP sessions using Loopback 0 interfaces. R2 and R4 advertise network prefixes with the next-hop-self feature. R1 advertises the 172.16.0.0/24 network prefix to R2 and R4.

R3 prefers the path from R2 compared to the iBGP path from R4 because the metric to reach the next-hop address is lower. R5 prefers the path from R4 compared to the iBGP path from R2 because the metric to reach the next-hop address is lower.

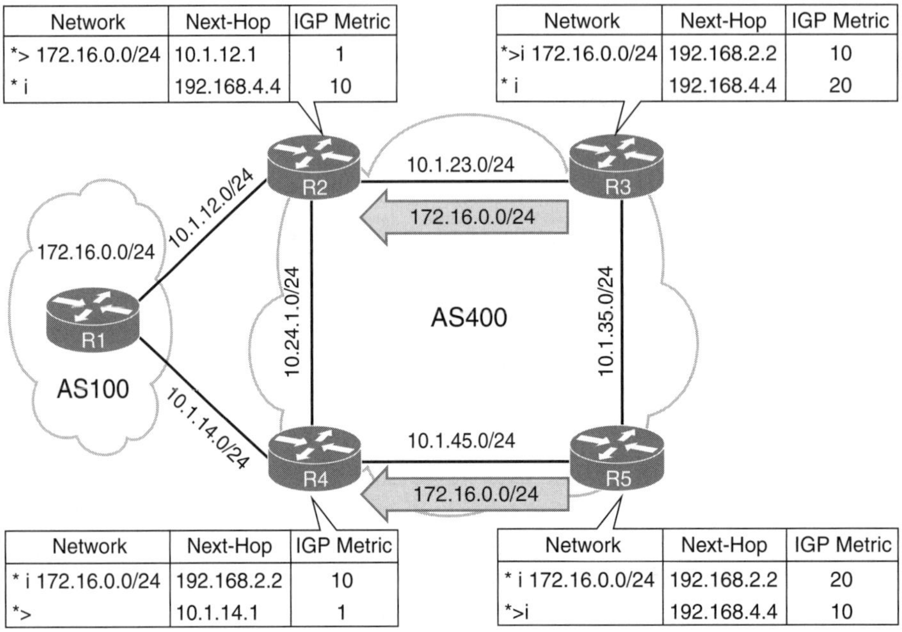

Figure 12-12 *Lowest IGP Metric Topology*

Prefer the Path from the Oldest eBGP Session

BGP can maintain large routing tables, and unstable sessions result in the BGP best-path calculation executing frequently. BGP maintains stability in a network by preferring the path from the oldest (established) eBGP session.

The downside of this technique is that it does not lead to a deterministic method of identifying the BGP best path from a design perspective.

Router ID

The next step for the BGP best-path algorithm is to select the best path using the lowest router ID of the advertising BGP router. If the route was received by a route reflector, then the originator ID is substituted for the router ID. Example 12-33 demonstrates a scenario where R5 chooses the path through R6 over R4 because of the higher router ID.

Example 12-33 *BGP Best-Path Choice Based on Router ID*

```
R5# show bgp ipv4 unicast 172.16.0.0/16 best-path-reason
! Output omitted for brevity
BGP routing table entry for 172.16.0.0/16, version 8
Paths: (2 available, best #2, table default)
  300 100
    192.168.6.6 (metric 130816) from 192.168.6.6 (192.168.6.6)
      Origin IGP, metric 0, localpref 100, valid, internal
      Best Path Evaluation: Higher router ID
```

```
200 100
  192.168.4.4 (metric 130816) from 192.168.4.4 (192.168.4.4)
    Origin IGP, metric 0, localpref 100, valid, internal, best
    Best Path Evaluation: Overall best path
```

Minimum Cluster List Length

The next step in the BGP best-path algorithm is to select the best path using the lowest cluster list length. The *cluster list* is a non-transitive BGP attribute that is appended (not overwritten) by a route reflector with its cluster ID. Route reflectors use the cluster ID attribute as a loop-prevention mechanism. The cluster ID is not advertised between ASs and is locally significant. In simplest terms, this step locates the path that has traveled the lowest number of iBGP advertisement hops.

NOTE BGP route reflectors are beyond the scope of the CCNP and CCIE Enterprise Core ENCOR 350-401 exam and are not discussed in this book.

Lowest Neighbor Address

The last step of the BGP best-path algorithm is to select the path that comes from the lowest BGP neighbor address. This step is limited to iBGP peerings because eBGP peerings used the oldest received path as the tie breaker.

Figure 12-13 demonstrates the concept of choosing the router with the lowest neighbor address. R1 is advertising the 172.16.0.0/24 network prefix to R2. R1 and R2 have established two BGP sessions using the 10.12.1.0/24 and 10.12.2.0/24 networks. R2 selects the path advertised from 10.12.1.1 because it is the lower IP address.

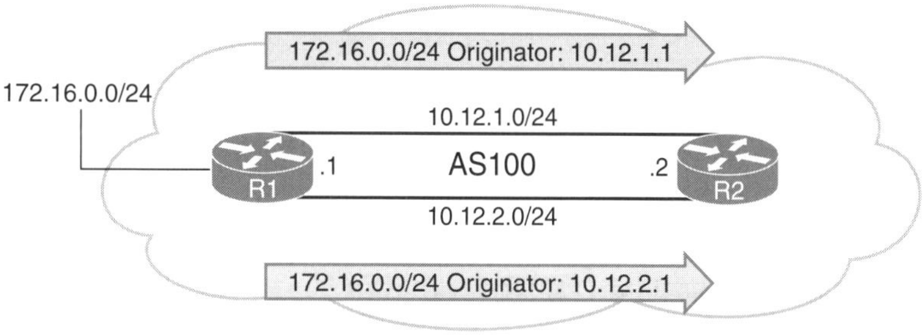

Figure 12-13 *Lowest IP Address*

Exam Preparation Tasks

You have a couple of choices for exam preparation: the exercises here, Chapter 30, "Final Preparation," and the exam simulation questions in the Pearson Test Prep Software Online.

Review All Key Topics

Review the most important topics in the chapter, noted with the Key Topic icon in the outer margin of the page. Table 12-8 lists these key topics and the page number on which each is found.

Key Topic

Table 12-8 Key Topics for Chapter 12

Key Topic Element	Description	Page
Section	Resiliency in Service Providers	291
Section	Internet Transit Routing	292
Section	BGP Network Selection	296
Paragraph	Prefix match specifications	297
Paragraph	Prefix matching with length parameters	297
Section	Prefix Lists	299
Section	Regular Expressions (regex)	300
List	Route map components	301
List	Route map syntax and processing	301
Section	Conditional Matching	302
Section	Multiple Conditional Match Conditions	303
Section	Optional Actions	304
Section	Distribute List Filtering	307
Section	Prefix List Filtering	308
Paragraph	BGP AS path ACL	310
Section	Route Maps	311
Section	BGP Communities	313
Section	Enabling BGP Community Support	314
Paragraph	BGP community list	316
Section	Setting Private BGP Communities	317
Section	Routing Path Selection Using Longest Match	319
List	BGP best-path algorithm	320

Complete Tables and Lists from Memory

There are no memory tables in this chapter.

Define Key Terms

Define the following key terms from this chapter and check your answers in the Glossary:

AS_Path access control list (AS_Path ACL), BGP community, BGP multihoming, distribute list, prefix list, regular expression (regex), route map, transit routing

Use the Command Reference to Check Your Memory

Table 12-9 lists the important commands from this chapter. To test your memory, cover the right side of the table with a piece of paper, read the description on the left side, and see how much of the command you can remember.

Table 12-9 Command Reference

Task	Command Syntax
Configure a prefix list	{**ip** | **ipv6**} **prefix-list** *prefix-list-name* [**seq** *sequence-number*] {**permit** | **deny**} *high-order-bit-pattern/high-order-bit-count* [**ge** *ge-value*] [**le** *le-value*]
Create a route map entry	**route-map** *route-map-name* [**permit** | **deny**] [*sequence-number*]
Conditionally match in a route map by using the AS path	**match as-path** *acl-number*
Conditionally match in a route map by using an ACL	**match ip address** {*acl-number* | *acl-name*}
Conditionally match in a route map by using a prefix list	**match ip address prefix-list** *prefix-list-name*
Conditionally match in a route map by using a local preference	**match local-preference** *local-preference*
Filter routes to a BGP neighbor by using an ACL	**neighbor** *ip-address* **distribute-list** {*acl-number* | *acl-name*} {**in**|**out**}
Filter routes to a BGP neighbor by using a prefix list	**neighbor** *ip-address* **prefix-list** *prefix-list-name* {**in** | **out**}
Create an ACL based on the BGP AS path	**ip as-path access-list** *acl-number* {**deny** | **permit**} *regex-query*
Filter routes to a BGP neighbor by using an AS path ACL	**neighbor** *ip-address* **filter-list** *acl-number* {**in**|**out**}
Associate an inbound or outbound route map with a specific BGP neighbor	**neighbor** *ip-address* **route-map** *route-map-name* {**in**|**out**}
Configure IOS-based routers to display the community in new format for easier readability of BGP communities	**ip bgp-community new-format**
Create a BGP community list for conditional route matching	**ip community-list** {*1-500* | **standard** *list-name* | **expanded** *list-name*} {**permit** | **deny**} *community-pattern*
Set BGP communities in a route map	**set community** *bgp-community* [**additive**]
Initiate a route refresh for a specific BGP peer	**clear bgp** *afi safi* {*ip-address*|*} **soft** [**in** | **out**]
Display the current BGP table, based on routes that meet a specified AS path regex pattern	**show bgp** *afi safi* **regexp** *regex-pattern*

Task	Command Syntax
Display the current BGP table, based on routes that meet a specified BGP community	**show bgp** *afi safi* **community** *community*

References in This Chapter

RFC 4360, *BGP Extended Communities Attribute*, Yakov Rekhter, Dan Tappan, and Srihari R. Sangli. https://www.ietf.org/rfc/rfc4360.txt, February 2006.

RFC 8092, *BGP Large Communities Attribute*, John Heasley et al. https://www.ietf.org/rfc/rfc2858.txt, February 2017.

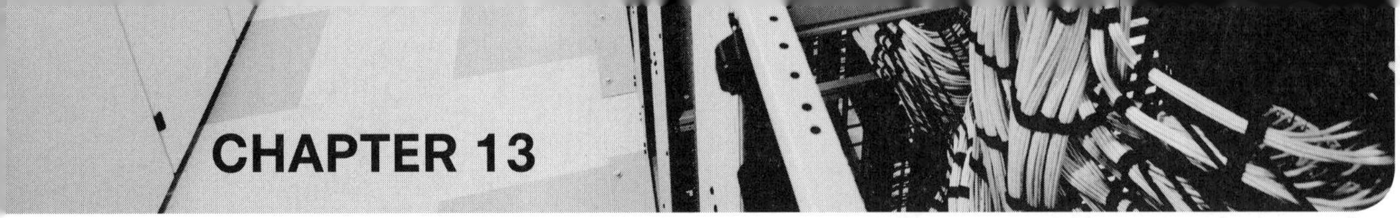

CHAPTER 13

Multicast

This chapter covers the following subjects:

- **Multicast Fundamentals:** This section describes multicast concepts as well as the need for multicast.
- **Multicast Addressing:** This section describes the multicast address scopes used by multicast to operate at Layer 2 and Layer 3.
- **Internet Group Management Protocol:** This section explains how multicast receivers join multicast groups to start receiving multicast traffic using IGMPv2 or IGMPv3. It also describes how multicast flooding on Layer 2 switches is prevented using a feature called IGMP snooping.
- **Protocol Independent Multicast:** This section describes the concepts, operation, and features of PIM. PIM is the protocol used to route multicast traffic across network segments from a multicast source to a group of receivers.
- **Rendezvous Points:** This section describes the purpose, function, and operation of rendezvous points in a multicast network.

Multicast is deployed on almost every type of network. It allows a source host to send data packets to a group of destination hosts (receivers) in an efficient manner that conserves bandwidth and system resources. This chapter describes the need for multicast as well as the fundamental protocols that are required to understand its operation, such as IGMP, PIM dense mode/sparse mode, and rendezvous points (RPs).

"Do I Know This Already?" Quiz

The "Do I Know This Already?" quiz enables you to assess whether you should read the entire chapter. If you miss no more than one of these self-assessment questions, you might want to move ahead to the "Exam Preparation Tasks" section. Table 13-1 lists the major headings in this chapter and the "Do I Know This Already?" quiz questions covering the material in those headings so you can assess your knowledge of these specific areas. The answers to the "Do I Know This Already?" quiz appear in Appendix A, "Answers to the 'Do I Know This Already?' Questions."

Table 13-1 "Do I Know This Already?" Foundation Topics Section-to-Question Mapping

Foundation Topics Section	Questions
Multicast Fundamentals	1–2
Multicast Addressing	3–4

Foundation Topics Section	Questions
Internet Group Management Protocol	5–8
Protocol Independent Multicast	9–11
Rendezvous Points	12–13

1. Which of the following transmission methods is multicast known for?
   a. One-to-one
   b. One-to-all
   c. One-for-all
   d. All-for-one
   e. One-to-many
2. Which protocols are essential to multicast operation? (Choose two.)
   a. Open Shortest Path First (OSPF)
   b. Protocol Independent Multicast (PIM)
   c. Internet Group Management Protocol (IGMP)
   d. Auto-RP and BSR
3. Which of the following multicast address ranges match the administratively scoped block? (Choose two.)
   a. 239.0.0.0 to 239.255.255.255
   b. 232.0.0.0 to 232.255.255.255
   c. 224.0.0.0 to 224.0.0.255
   d. 239.0.0.0/8
   e. 224.0.1.0/24
4. The first 24 bits of a multicast MAC address always start with ______.
   a. 01:5E:00
   b. 01:00:53
   c. 01:00:5E
   d. 01:05:E0
   e. None of these answers are correct.
5. What should a host do to start receiving multicast traffic? (Choose two.)
   a. Send an IGMP join
   b. Send an unsolicited membership report
   c. Send an unsolicited membership query
   d. Send an unsolicited group specific query

6. What is the main difference between IGMPv2 and IGMPv3?
   a. IGMPv3's max response time is 10 seconds by default.
   b. IGMPv3 sends periodic IGMP membership queries.
   c. IGMPv3 introduced a new IGMP membership report with source filtering support.
   d. IGMPv3 can work only with SSM, whereas IGMPv2 can work only with PIM-SM/DM.
7. True or false: IGMPv3 was designed to work exclusively with SSM and is not backward compatible with IGMPv2.
   a. True
   b. False
8. How can you avoid flooding of multicast frames in a Layer 2 network?
   a. Disable unknown multicast flooding
   b. Enable multicast storm control
   c. Enable IGMP snooping
   d. Enable control plane policing
9. Which of the following best describe SPT and RPT? (Choose two.)
   a. RPT is a source tree where the rendezvous point is the root of the tree.
   b. SPT is a source tree where the source is the root of the tree.
   c. RPT is a shared tree where the rendezvous point is the root of the tree.
   d. SPT is a shared tree where the source is the root of the tree.
10. What does an LHR do after it receives an IGMP join from a receiver?
    a. It sends a PIM register message toward the RP.
    b. It sends a PIM join toward the RP.
    c. It sends a PIM register message toward the source.
    d. It sends a PIM join message toward the source.
11. What does an FHR do when an attached source becomes active and there are no interested receivers?
    a. It encapsulates PIM register messages and unicasts them to the RP. It stops after receiving a register stop from the RP.
    b. It encapsulates multicast data in PIM register messages and unicasts the register messages to the RP. It stops after receiving a register stop from the RP.
    c. It waits for the RP to send a register message indicating that there are interested receivers.
    d. It multicasts encapsulated register messages to the RP and stops after a register stop from the RP.
    e. It unicasts encapsulated register messages to the RP until there are interested receivers.

12. Which of the following is a group-to-RP mapping mechanism developed by Cisco?
    a. BSR
    b. Static RP
    c. Auto-RP
    d. Phantom RP
    e. Anycast-RP
13. True or false: When PIM is configured in dense mode, it is mandatory to choose one or more routers to operate as rendezvous points (RPs).
    a. True
    b. False

Foundation Topics

Multicast Fundamentals

Traditional IP communication between network hosts typically uses one of the following transmission methods:

- Unicast (one-to-one)
- Broadcast (one-to-all)
- Multicast (one-to-many)

Multicast communication is a technology that optimizes network bandwidth utilization and conserves system resources. It relies on **Internet Group Management Protocol (IGMP)** for its operation in Layer 2 networks and **Protocol Independent Multicast (PIM)** for its operation in Layer 3 networks.

Figure 13-1 illustrates how IGMP operates between the receivers and the local multicast router and how PIM operates between routers. These two technologies work hand-in-hand to allow multicast traffic to flow from the source to the receivers, and they are explained in this chapter.

Figure 13-2 shows an example where five workstations are watching the same video that is advertised by a server using unicast traffic (one-to-one). Each arrow represents a data stream of the same video going to five different hosts. If each stream is 10 Mbps, the network link between R1 and R2 needs 50 Mbps of bandwidth. The network path between R2 and R4 requires 30 Mbps of bandwidth, and the link between R2 and R5 requires 20 Mbps of bandwidth. The server must maintain session state information for all the sessions between the hosts. The bandwidth and load on the server increase as more receivers request the same video feed.

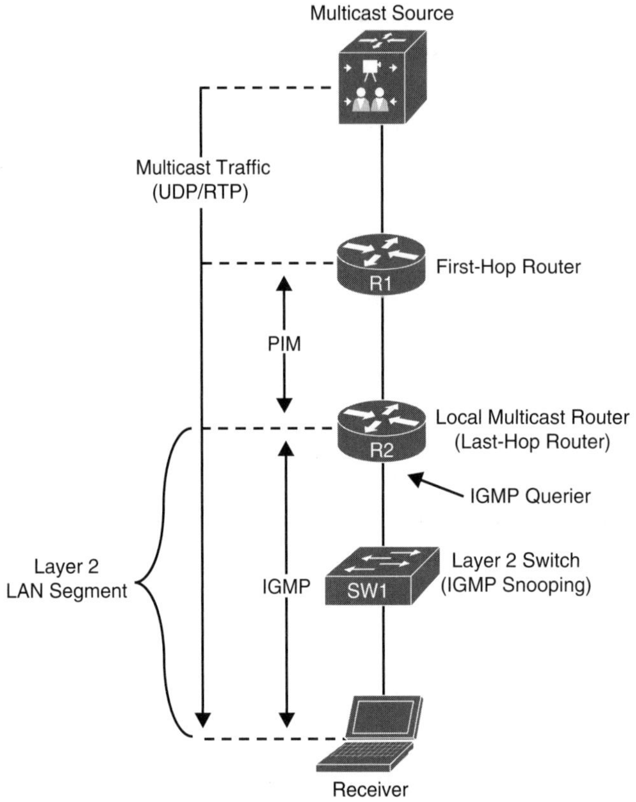

Figure 13-1 *Multicast Architecture*

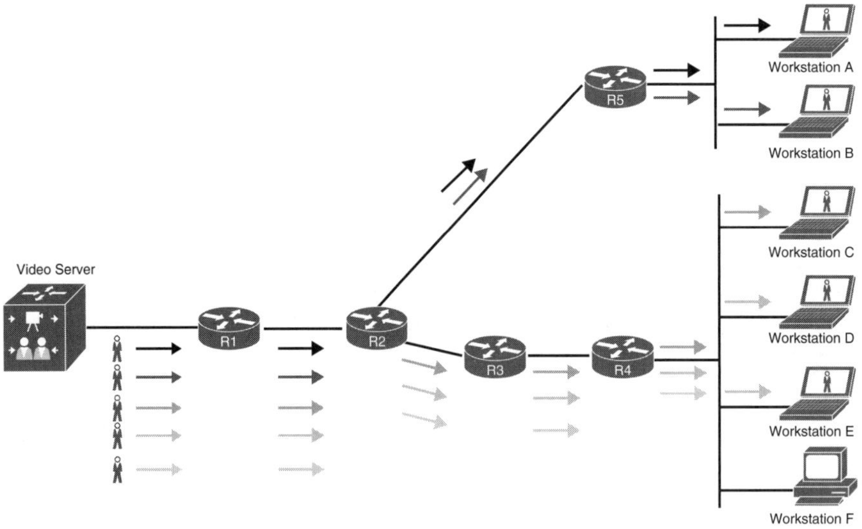

Figure 13-2 *Unicast Video Feed*

Answers to the "Do I Know This Already?" quiz:

1 E **2** B, C **3** A, D **4** C **5** A, B **6** C **7** B **8** C **9** B, C **10** B **11** B **12** C **13** B

An alternative method for all five workstations to receive the video is to send it from the server using broadcast traffic (one-to-all). Figure 13-3 shows an example of how the same video stream is transmitted using IP directed broadcasts. The load on the server is reduced because it needs to maintain only one session state rather than many. The same video stream consumes only 10 Mbps of bandwidth on all network links. However, this approach does have disadvantages:

- IP directed broadcast functionality is not enabled by default on Cisco routers, and enabling it exposes the router to distributed denial-of-service (DDoS) attacks.
- The network interface cards (NICs) of uninterested workstations must still process the broadcast packets and send them on to the workstation's CPU, which wastes processor resources. In Figure 13-3, Workstation F is processing unwanted packets.

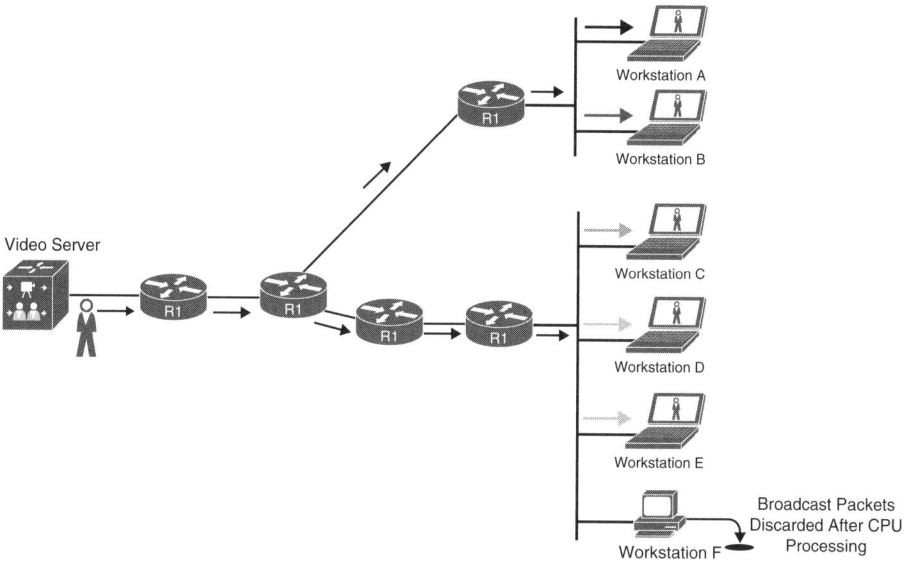

Figure 13-3 *Broadcast Video Feed*

For these reasons, broadcast traffic is generally not recommended.

Key Topic

Multicast traffic provides one-to-many communication, where only one data packet is sent on a link as needed and then is replicated between links as the data forks (splits) on a network device along the multicast distribution tree (MDT). The data packets are known as a *stream* that uses a special destination IP address, known as a *group address*. A server for a stream still manages only one session, and network devices selectively request to receive the stream. Recipient devices of a multicast stream are known as *receivers*. Common applications that take advantage of multicast traffic include Cisco TelePresence, real-time video, IPTV, stock tickers, distance learning, video/audio conferencing, music on hold, and gaming.

Figure 13-4 shows an example of the same video feed using multicast. Each of the network links consumes only 10 Mbps of bandwidth, as much as with broadcast traffic, but only receivers that are interested in the video stream process the multicast traffic. For example,

Workstation F would drop the multicast traffic at the NIC level because it would not be programmed to accept the multicast traffic.

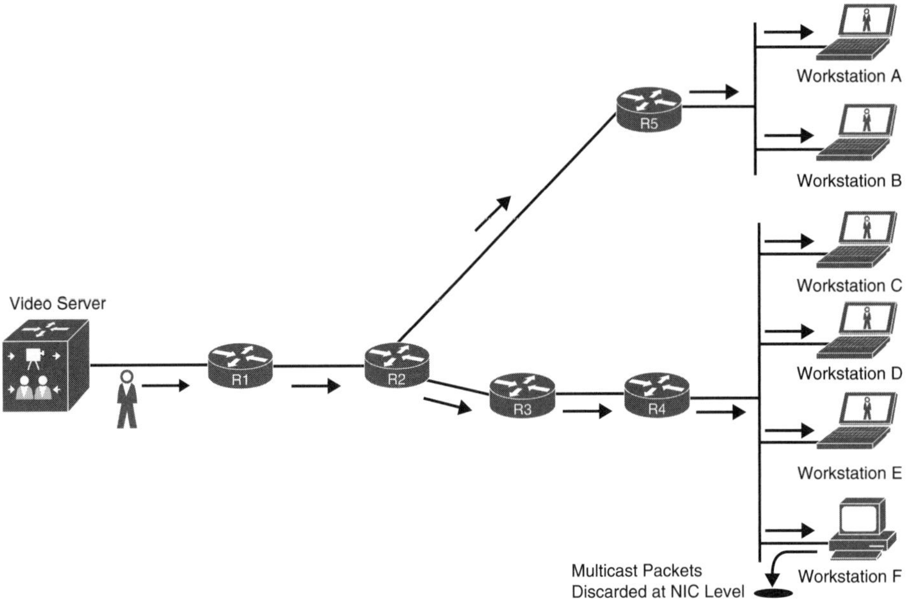

Figure 13-4 *Multicast Video Feed*

> **NOTE** Workstation F would not receive any multicast traffic if the switch for that network segment enabled Internet Group Management Protocol (IGMP) snooping. IGMP and IGMP snooping are covered in the next section.

Multicast Addressing

The Internet Assigned Numbers Authority (IANA) assigned the IP Class D address space 224.0.0.0/4 for multicast addressing; it includes addresses ranging from 224.0.0.0 to 239.255.255.255. The first 4 bits of this whole range start with 1110.

In the multicast address space, multiple blocks of addressing are reserved for specific purposes, as shown in Table 13-2.

Key Topic

Table 13-2 IP Multicast Addresses Assigned by IANA

Designation	Multicast Address Range
Local network control block	224.0.0.0 to 224.0.0.255
Internetwork control block	224.0.1.0 to 224.0.1.255
Ad hoc block I	224.0.2.0 to 224.0.255.255
Reserved	224.1.0.0 to 224.1.255.255
SDP/SAP block	224.2.0.0 to 224.2.255.255
Ad hoc block II	224.3.0.0 to 224.4.255.255

Designation	Multicast Address Range
Reserved	224.5.0.0 to 224.251.255.255
DIS transient groups	224.252.0.0 to 224.255.255.255
Reserved	225.0.0.0 to 231.255.255.255
Source Specific Multicast (SSM) block	232.0.0.0 to 232.255.255.255
GLOP block	233.0.0.0 to 233.251.255.255
Ad hoc block III	233.252.0.0 to 233.255.255.255
Unicast-Prefix-based IPv4 multicast addresses	234.0.0.0 to 234.255.255.255
Reserved	235.0.0.0 to 238.255.255.255
Organization-local scope (commonly known as the Administratively scoped block)	239.0.0.0 to 239.255.255.255

Out of the multicast blocks mentioned in Table 13-2, the most important are as follows:

- **Local network control block (224.0.0.0/24):** Addresses in the local network control block are used for protocol control traffic that is not forwarded outside of a broadcast domain. Examples of this type of multicast control traffic are all hosts in this subnet (224.0.0.1), all routers in this subnet (224.0.0.2), and all PIM routers (224.0.0.13).
- **Internetwork control block (224.0.1.0/24):** Addresses in the internetwork control block are used for protocol control traffic that may be forwarded through the Internet. Examples include Network Time Protocol (NTP) (224.0.1.1), Cisco-RP-Announce (224.0.1.39), and Cisco-RP-Discovery (224.0.1.40).

  Table 13-3 lists some of the well-known local network control block and internetwork control block multicast addresses.

Key Topic

Table 13-3 Well-Known Reserved Multicast Addresses

IP Multicast Address	Description
224.0.0.0	Base address (reserved)
224.0.0.1	All hosts in this subnet (all-hosts group)
224.0.0.2	All routers in this subnet
224.0.0.5	All OSPF routers (AllSPFRouters)
224.0.0.6	All OSPF DRs (AllDRouters)
224.0.0.9	All RIPv2 routers
224.0.0.10	All EIGRP routers
224.0.0.13	All PIM routers
224.0.0.18	VRRP
224.0.0.22	IGMPv3
224.0.0.102	HSRPv2 and GLBP
224.0.1.1	NTP
224.0.1.39	Cisco-RP-Announce (Auto-RP)
224.0.1.40	Cisco-RP-Discovery (Auto-RP)

- **Source Specific Multicast (SSM) block (232.0.0.0/8):** This is the default range used by SSM. SSM is a PIM extension described in RFC 4607. SSM forwards traffic to receivers from only those multicast sources for which the receivers have explicitly expressed interest; it is primarily targeted to one-to-many applications.
- **GLOP block (233.0.0.0/8):** Addresses in the GLOP block are globally scoped statically assigned addresses. The assignment is made for domains with a 16-bit autonomous system number (ASN) by mapping the domain's ASN, expressed in octets as X.Y, into the middle two octets of the GLOP block, yielding an assignment of 233.X.Y.0/24. The mapping and assignment are defined in RFC 3180. Domains with a 32-bit ASN may apply for space in ad-hoc block III or can consider using IPv6 multicast addresses.
- **Organization-Local Scope (239.0.0.0/8):** These addresses, described in RFC 2365, are limited to a local group or organization. These addresses are similar to the reserved IP unicast ranges (such as 10.0.0.0/8) defined in RFC 1918 and will not be assigned by the IANA to any other group or protocol. In other words, network administrators are free to use multicast addresses in this range inside of their domain without worrying about conflicting with others elsewhere on the Internet.

Key Topic

Layer 2 Multicast Addresses

Historically, NICs on a LAN segment could receive only packets destined for their burned-in MAC address or the broadcast MAC address. Using this logic can cause a burden on routing resources during packet replication for LAN segments. Another method for multicast traffic was created so that replication of multicast traffic did not require packet manipulation, and a method of using a standardized destination MAC address was created.

A MAC address is a unique value associated with a NIC that is used to uniquely identify the NIC on a LAN segment. MAC addresses are 12-digit hexadecimal numbers (48 bits in length), and they are typically stored in 8-bit segments separated by hyphens (-) or colons (:) (for example, 00-12-34-56-78-00 or 00:12:34:56:78:00).

Every multicast group address (IP address) is mapped to a special MAC address that allows Ethernet interfaces to identify multicast packets to a specific group. A LAN segment can have multiple streams, and a receiver knows which traffic to send to the CPU for processing based on the MAC address assigned to the multicast traffic.

The first 24 bits of a multicast MAC address always start with 01:00:5E. The low-order bit of the first byte is the *individual/group bit (I/G)* bit, also known as the unicast/multicast bit, and when it is set to 1, it indicates that the frame is a multicast frame, and the 25th bit is always 0. The low-order 23 bits of the multicast MAC address are copied from the low-order 23 bits of the IP multicast group address.

Figure 13-5 shows an example of mapping the multicast IP address 239.255.1.1 into the multicast MAC address 01:00:5E:7F:01:01. The high-order 25 bits are always fixed, and the low-order 23 bits are copied directly from the low-order 23 bits of the IP multicast group address.

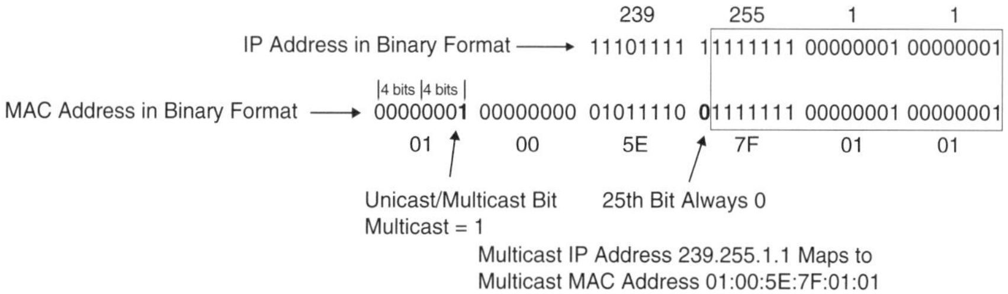

Figure 13-5 *Multicast IP Address to Multicast MAC Address Mapping*

Out of the 9 bits from the multicast IP address that are not copied into the multicast MAC address, the high-order bits 1110 are fixed; that leaves 5 bits that are variable that are not transferred into the MAC address. Because of this, there are 32 (2^5) multicast IP addresses that are not universally unique and could correspond to a single MAC address; in other words, they overlap. Figure 13-6 shows an example of two multicast IP addresses that overlap because they map to the same multicast MAC address.

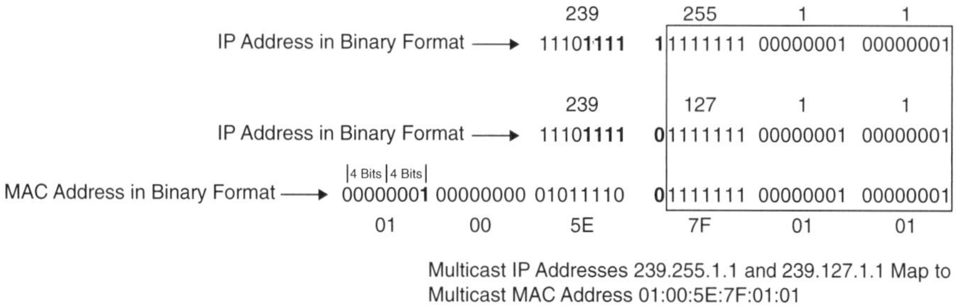

Figure 13-6 *Multicast IP Address to Multicast MAC Address Mapping Overlap*

When a receiver wants to receive a specific multicast feed, it sends an IGMP join using the multicast IP group address for that feed. The receiver reprograms its interface to accept the multicast MAC group address that correlates to the group address. For example, a PC could send an IGMP join to 239.255.1.1 and would reprogram its NIC to receive 01:00:5E:7F:01:01. If the PC were to receive an OSPF update sent to 224.0.0.5 and its corresponding multicast MAC 01:00:5E:00:00:05, it would ignore that update and eliminate wasted CPU cycles by avoiding the processing of undesired multicast traffic.

Internet Group Management Protocol

Key Topic

Internet Group Management Protocol (IGMP) is the protocol that receivers use to join multicast groups and start receiving traffic from those groups. IGMP must be supported by receivers and the router interfaces facing the receivers. When a receiver wants to receive multicast traffic from a source, it sends an IGMP join to its router. If the router does not have IGMP enabled on the interface, the request is ignored.

Three versions of IGMP exist. RFC 1112 defines IGMPv1, which is old and rarely used. RFC 2236 defines IGMPv2, which is common in most multicast networks, and RFC 3376 defines IGMPv3, which is used by SSM. Only IGMPv2 and IGMPv3 are described in this chapter.

IGMPv2

IGMPv2 uses the message format shown in Figure 13-7. This message is encapsulated in an IP packet with a protocol number of 2. Messages are sent with the IP router alert option set, which indicates that the packets should be examined more closely, and a time-to-live (TTL) of 1. TTL is an 8-bit field in an IP packet header that is set by the sender of the IP packet and decremented by every router on the route to its destination. If the TTL reaches 0 before reaching the destination, the packet is discarded. IGMP packets should not be forwarded beyond the local network segment, and for this reason, they are sent with a TTL of 1. This ensures the IGMP packets are processed only by the local router(s) and not forwarded to any other routers.

32 Bits		
8 Bits	8 Bits	16 Bits
Type	Max Response Time	Checksum
Group Address		

Figure 13-7 *IGMP Message Format*

The IGMP message format fields are defined as follows:

- **Type:** This field describes five different types of IGMP messages used by routers and receivers:
  - **Version 2 membership report** (type value 0x16) is a message type also commonly referred to as an IGMP join; it is used by receivers to join a multicast group or to respond to a local router's membership query message.
  - **Version 1 membership report** (type value 0x12) is used by receivers for backward compatibility with IGMPv1.
  - **Version 2 leave group** (type value 0x17) is used by receivers to indicate they want to stop receiving multicast traffic for a group they joined.
  - **General membership query** (type value 0x11) is periodically sent to the all-hosts group address 224.0.0.1 to see whether there are any receivers in the attached subnet. It sets the group address field to 0.0.0.0.
  - **Group specific query** (type value 0x11) is sent in response to a leave group message to the group address the receiver requested to leave. The group address is the destination IP address of the IP packet and the group address field.
- **Max response time:** This field is set only in general and group-specific membership query messages (type value 0x11); it specifies the maximum allowed time before sending a responding report in units of one-tenth of a second. In all other messages, it is set to 0x00 by the sender and ignored by receivers.
- **Checksum:** This field is the 16-bit 1s complement of the 1s complement sum of the IGMP message. This is the standard checksum algorithm used by TCP/IP.

- **Group address:** This field is set to 0.0.0.0 in general query messages and is set to the group address in group-specific messages. Membership report messages carry the address of the group being reported in this field; group leave messages carry the address of the group being left in this field.

Key Topic

When a receiver wants to receive a multicast stream, it sends an unsolicited membership report, commonly referred to as an IGMP join, to the local router for the group it wants to join (for example, 239.1.1.1). The local router then sends a PIM join message upstream toward the source to request the multicast stream. When the local router starts receiving the multicast stream, it forwards it downstream to the subnet where the receiver that requested it resides.

NOTE *IGMP join* is not a valid message type in the IGMP RFC specifications, but the term is commonly used in the field in place of *IGMP membership report* because it is easier to say and write.

The router then starts periodically sending general membership query messages into the subnet, to the all-hosts group address 224.0.0.1, to see whether any members are in the attached subnet. The general query message contains a max response time field that is set to 10 seconds by default.

In response to this query, receivers set an internal random timer between 0 and 10 seconds (which can change if the max response time is using a non-default value). When the timer expires, receivers send membership reports for each group they belong to. If a receiver receives another receiver's report for one of the groups it belongs to while it has a timer running, it stops its timer for the specified group and does not send a report; this is meant to suppress duplicate reports.

When a receiver wants to leave a group, if it was the last receiver to respond to a query, it sends a leave group message to the all-routers group address 224.0.0.2. Otherwise, it can leave quietly because there must be another receiver in the subnet.

When the leave group message is received by the router, it follows with a group-specific membership query to the group multicast address to determine whether there are any receivers interested in the group remaining in the subnet. If there are none, the router removes the IGMP state for that group.

If there is more than one router in a LAN segment, an IGMP querier election takes place to determine which router will be the querier. IGMPv2 routers send general membership query messages with their interface address as the source IP address and destined to the 224.0.0.1 multicast address. When an IGMPv2 router receives such a message, it checks the source IP address and compares it to its own interface IP address. The router with the lowest interface IP address in the LAN subnet is elected as the IGMP querier. At this point, all the non-querier routers start a timer that resets each time they receive a membership query report from the querier router.

If the querier router stops sending membership queries for some reason (for instance, if it is powered down), a new querier election takes place. A non-querier router waits twice the query interval, which is by default 60 seconds, and if it has heard no queries from the IGMP querier, it triggers IGMP querier election.

IGMPv3

Key Topic

In IGMPv2, when a receiver sends a membership report to join a multicast group, it does not specify which source it would like to receive multicast traffic from. *IGMPv3* is an extension of IGMPv2 that adds support for multicast source filtering, which gives the receivers the capability to pick the source they wish to accept multicast traffic from.

IGMPv3 is designed to coexist with IGMPv1 and IGMPv2.

IGMPv3 supports all IGMPv2's IGMP message types and is backward compatible with IGMPv2. The differences between the two are that IGMPv3 added new fields to the IGMP membership query and introduced a new IGMP message type called Version 3 membership report to support source filtering.

IGMPv3 supports applications that explicitly signal sources from which they want to receive traffic. With IGMPv3, receivers signal membership to a multicast group address using a membership report in the following two modes:

- **Include mode:** In this mode, the receiver announces membership to a multicast group address and provides a list of source addresses (the *include list*) from which it wants to receive traffic.
- **Exclude mode:** In this mode, the receiver announces membership to a multicast group address and provides a list of source addresses (the *exclude list*) from which it does not want to receive traffic. The receiver then receives traffic only from sources whose IP addresses are not listed on the exclude list. To receive traffic from all sources, which is the behavior of IGMPv2, a receiver uses exclude mode membership with an empty exclude list.

NOTE IGMPv3 is used to provide source filtering for Source Specific Multicast (SSM).

IGMP Snooping

To optimize forwarding and minimize flooding, switches need a method of sending traffic only to interested receivers. In the case of unicast traffic, Cisco switches learn about Layer 2 MAC addresses and what ports they are attached to by inspecting the Layer 2 MAC address source; they store this information in the MAC address table. If they receive a Layer 2 frame with a destination MAC address that is not in this table, they treat it as an unknown unicast frame and flood it out all the ports within the same VLAN except the interface the frame was received on. Uninterested workstations will notice that the destination MAC address in the frame is not theirs and will discard the packet.

In Figure 13-8, SW1 starts with an empty MAC address table. When Workstation A sends a frame, it stores its source MAC address and interface in the MAC address table and floods the frame it received out all ports (except the port it received the frame on).

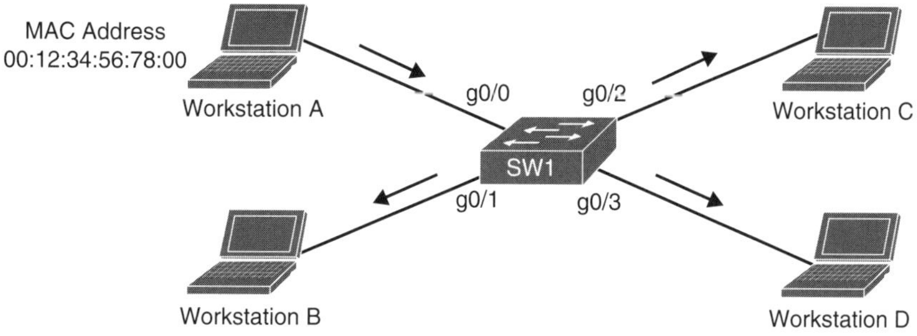

Switch MAC Address Table	
MAC Address	**Interface**
00:12:34:56:78:00	g0/0

Figure 13-8 *Unknown Frame Flooding*

If any other workstation sends a frame destined to the MAC address of Workstation A, the frame is not flooded anymore because it's already in the MAC address table, and it is sent only to Workstation A, as shown in Figure 13-9.

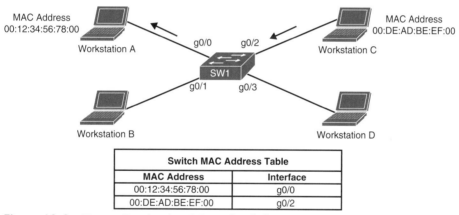

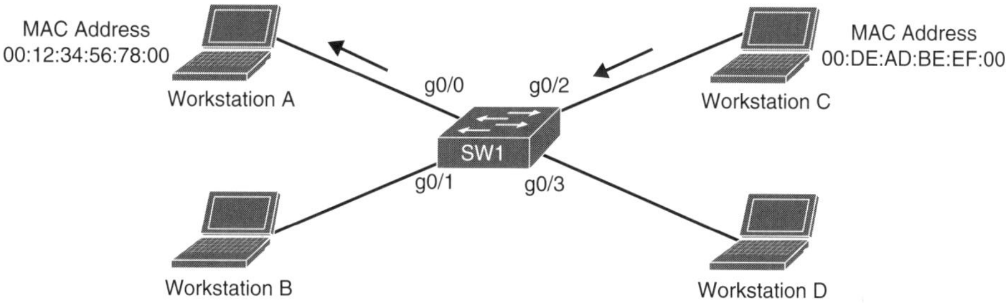

Switch MAC Address Table	
MAC Address	**Interface**
00:12:34:56:78:00	g0/0
00:DE:AD:BE:EF:00	g0/2

Figure 13-9 *Known Destination Is Not Flooded*

In the case of multicast traffic, a multicast MAC address is never used as a source MAC address. By default, switches treat multicast MAC addresses as unknown multicast frames and flood them out all ports. It is then up to the workstations to select which frames to process and which to discard. Uninterested workstations discard the multicast traffic at the NIC level because they would not be programmed to accept the multicast traffic. The flooding of multicast traffic on a switch wastes bandwidth utilization on each LAN segment.

Cisco switches support two methods to reduce multicast flooding on a LAN segment:

- IGMP snooping
- Static MAC address entries

Key Topic

IGMP snooping, defined in RFC 4541, is the most widely used method and works by examining IGMP joins sent by receivers and maintaining a table of interfaces to IGMP joins. When the switch receives a multicast frame destined for a multicast group, it forwards the packet only out the ports where IGMP joins were received for that specific multicast group.

Figure 13-10 illustrates Workstation A and Workstation C sending IGMP joins to 239.255.1.1, which maps to the multicast MAC address 01:00:5E:7F:01:01 (see Figure 13-5 for an example of multicast IP address to MAC address mapping). Switch 1 has IGMP snooping enabled and populates the MAC address table with this information.

NOTE Even with IGMP snooping enabled, some multicast groups are still flooded on all ports (for example, 224.0.0.0/24 reserved addresses).

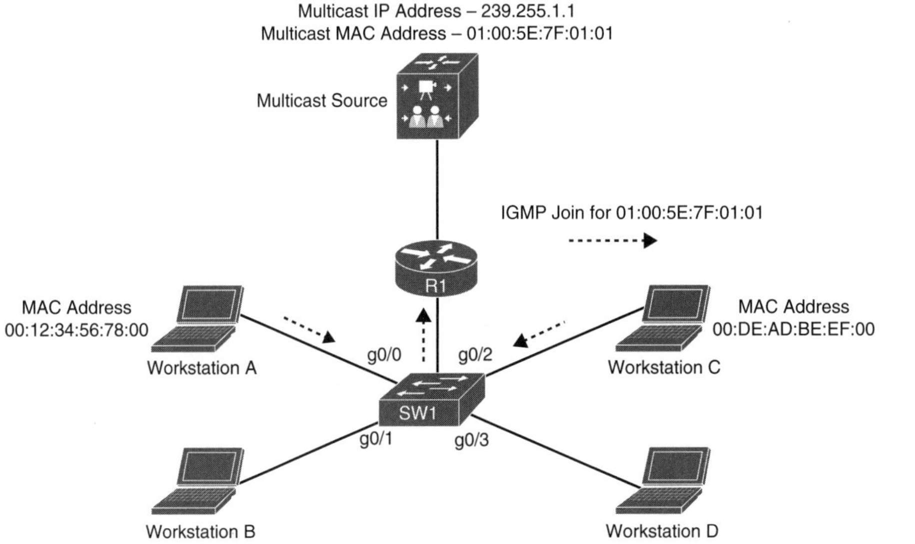

Switch MAC Address Table	
MAC Address	**Interface**
00:12:34:56:78:00	g0/0
00:DE:AD:BE:EF:00	g0/2
01:00:5E:7F:01:01	g0/0, g0/2

← Multicast MAC Address

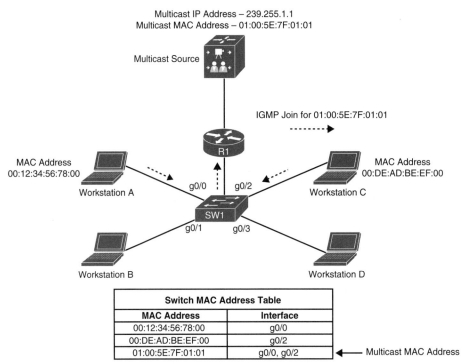

Figure 13-10 *IGMP Snooping Example*

Figure 13-11 illustrates the source sending traffic to 239.255.1.1 (01:00:5E:7F:01:01). Switch 1 receives this traffic, and it forwards it out only the g0/0 and g0/2 interfaces because those are the only ports that received IGMP joins for that group.

A multicast static entry can also be manually programmed into the MAC address table, but this is not a scalable solution because it cannot react dynamically to changes; for this reason, it is not a recommended approach.

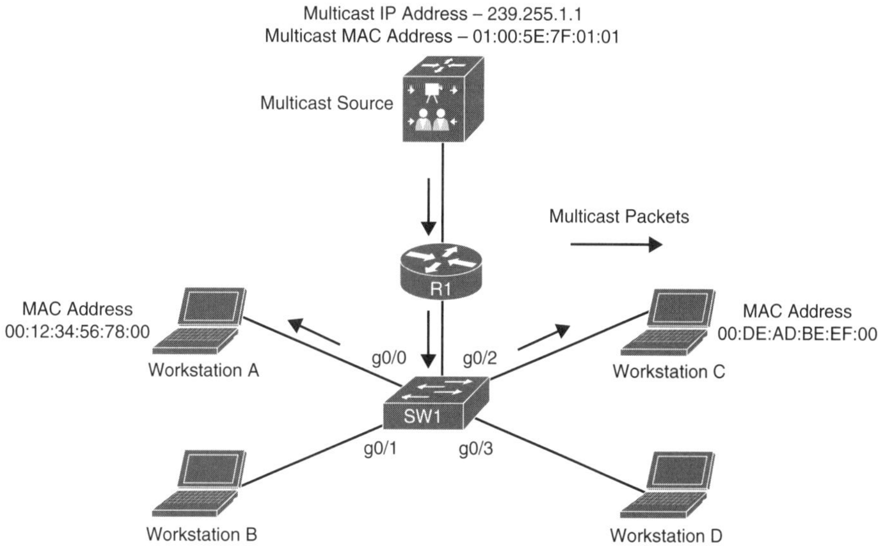

Switch MAC Address Table	
MAC Address	**Interface**
00:12:34:56:78:00	g0/0
00:DE:AD:BE:EF:00	g0/2
01:00:5E:7F:01:01	g0/0, g0/2

← Multicast MAC Address

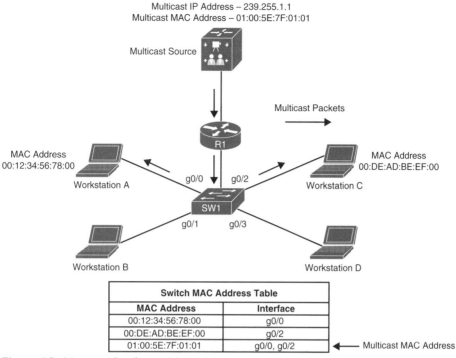

Figure 13-11 *No Flooding with IGMP Snooping*

Protocol Independent Multicast

Key Topic

Receivers use IGMP to join a multicast group, which is sufficient if the group's source connects to the same router to which the receiver is attached. A multicast routing protocol is necessary to route the multicast traffic throughout the network so that routers can locate and request multicast streams from other routers. Multiple multicast routing protocols exist, but Cisco fully supports only Protocol Independent Multicast (PIM), which is the most popular and is an industry standard protocol defined in RFC 4601.

PIM is a multicast routing protocol that routes multicast traffic between network segments. PIM can use any of the unicast routing protocols to identify the path between the source and receivers.

PIM Distribution Trees

Multicast routers create distribution trees that define the path that IP multicast traffic follows through the network to reach the receivers. The two basic types of multicast distribution trees are source trees, also known as **shortest path trees (SPTs)**, and shared trees.

Source Trees

Key Topic

A *source tree* is a multicast distribution tree where the source is the root of the tree, and branches form a distribution tree through the network all the way down to the receivers.

When this tree is built, it uses the shortest path through the network from the source to the leaves of the tree; for this reason, it is also referred to as a shortest path tree (SPT).

The forwarding state of the SPT is known by the notation (S,G), pronounced "S comma G," where S is the source of the multicast stream (server), and G is the multicast group address. Using this notation, the SPT state for the example shown in Figure 13-12 is (10.1.1.2, 239.1.1.1), where the multicast source S is 10.1.1.2, and the multicast group G is 239.1.1.1, joined by Receivers A and B.

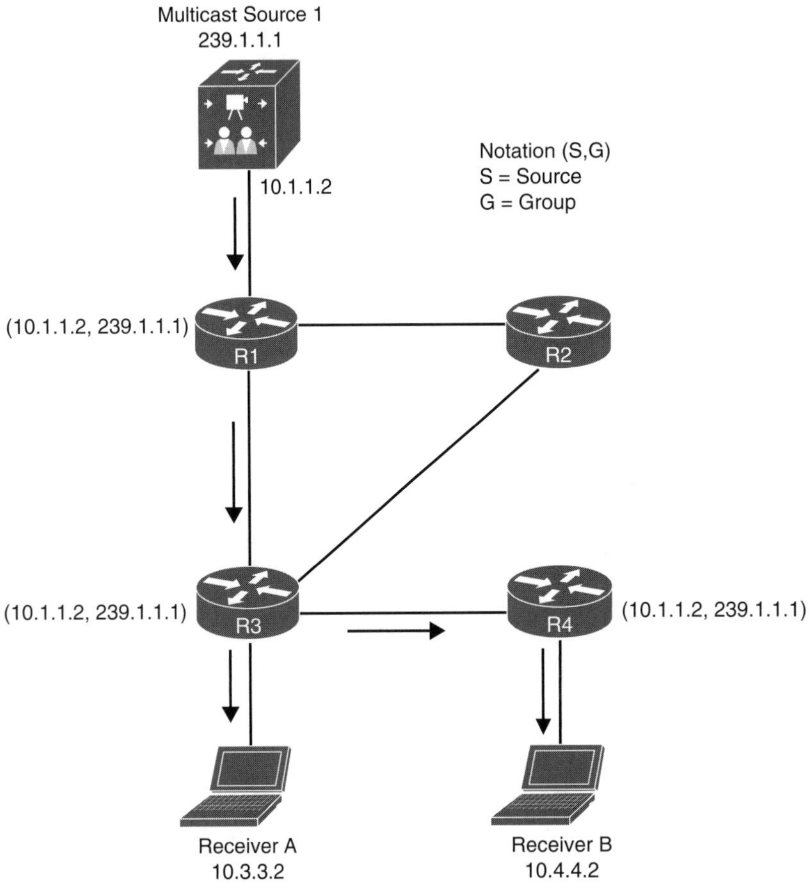

Figure 13-12 *Source Tree Example*

Because every SPT is rooted at the source S, every source sending to a multicast group requires an SPT.

Shared Trees

Key Topic

A shared tree is a multicast distribution tree where the root of the shared tree is not the source but a router designated as the **rendezvous point (RP)**. For this reason, shared trees are also referred to as **rendezvous point trees (RPTs)**. Multicast traffic is forwarded down the shared tree according to the group address G that the packets are addressed to, regardless of the source address. For this reason, the forwarding state on the shared tree is referred to by the notation (*,G), pronounced "star comma G." Figure 13-13 illustrates a shared tree where R2 is the RP, and the (*,G) is (*,239.1.1.1).

NOTE In any-source multicast (ASM), the (S,G) state requires a parent (*,G). For this reason, Figure 13-13 illustrates R1 and R2 as having (*,G) state. And R3 and R4 have not yet joined the source tree, indicated by the lack of (S,G) in their multicast routing table.

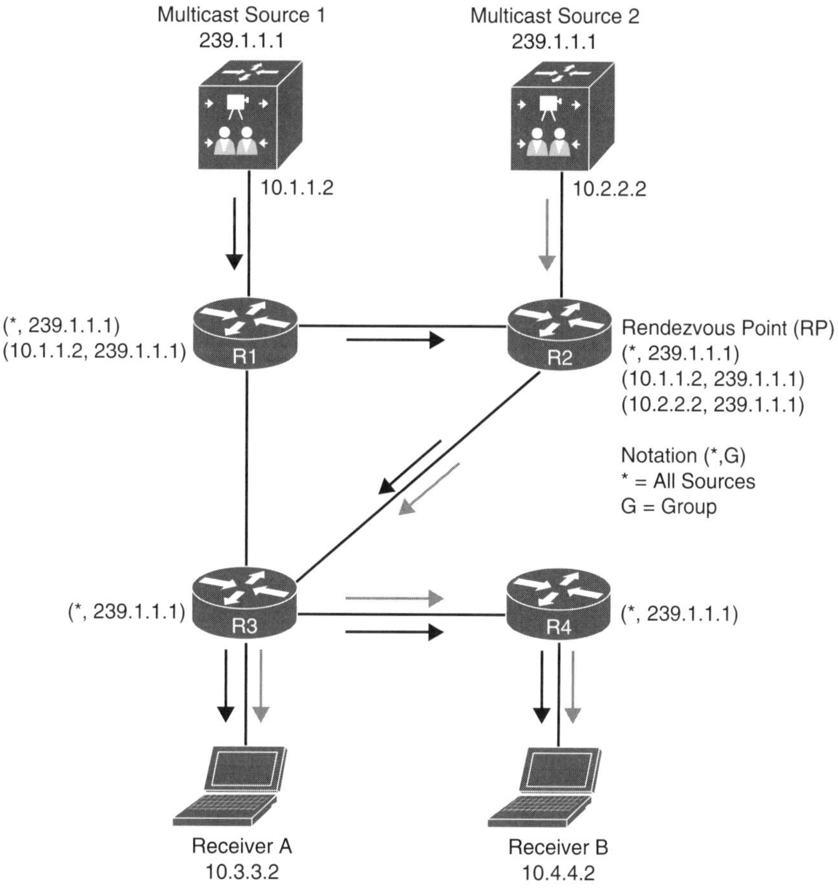

Figure 13-13 *Shared Tree Between RP and LHRs*

One of the benefits of shared trees over source trees is that they require fewer multicast entries (for example, S,G and *,G). For instance, as more sources are introduced into the network, sending traffic to the same multicast group, the number of multicast entries for R3 and R4 always remains the same: (*,239.1.1.1).

The major drawback of shared trees is that the receivers receive traffic from all the sources sending traffic to the same multicast group. Even though the receivers' applications can filter out the unwanted traffic, this situation still generates a lot of unwanted network traffic, wasting bandwidth. In addition, because shared trees can allow multiple sources in an IP multicast group, there is a potential network security issue because unintended sources could send unwanted packets to receivers.

PIM Terminology

Figure 13-14 provides a reference topology for some multicast routing terminology.

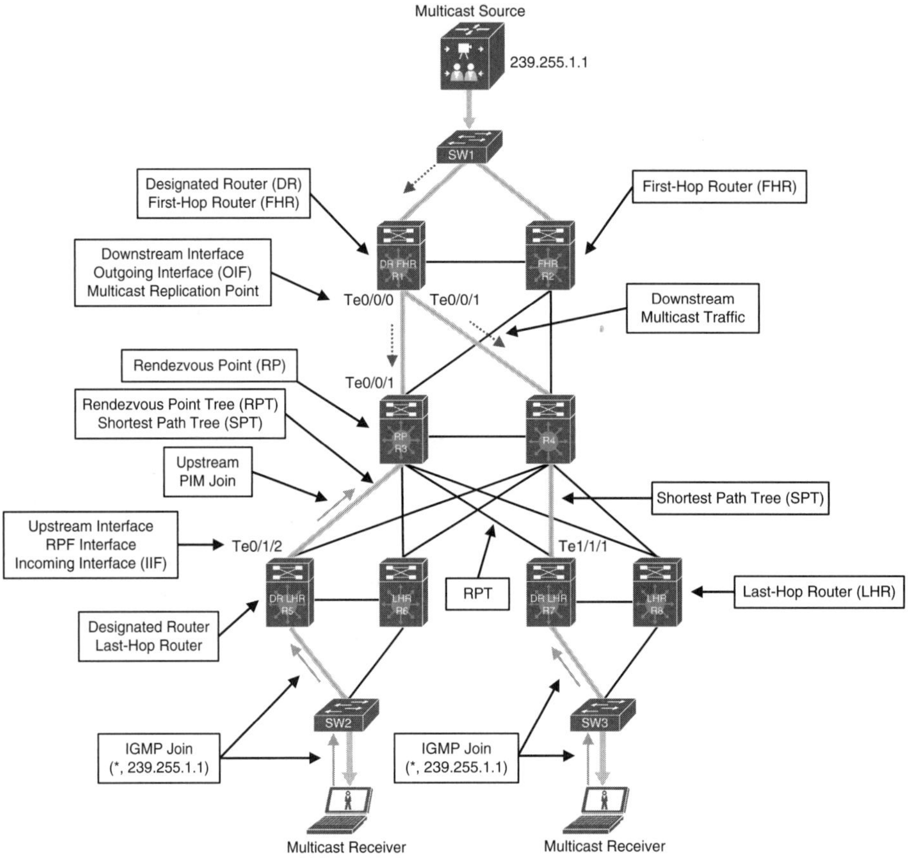

Figure 13-14 *PIM Terminology Illustration*

The following list defines the common PIM terminology illustrated in Figure 13-14:

Key Topic

- **Reverse Path Forwarding (RPF) interface:** The interface with the lowest-cost path (based on administrative distance [AD] and metric) to the IP address of the source (SPT) or the RP, in the case of shared trees. If multiple interfaces have the same cost, the interface with the highest IP address is chosen as the tiebreaker. An example of this type of interface is Te0/1/2 on R5 because it is the shortest path to the source. Another example is Te1/1/1 on R7 because the shortest path to the source was determined to be through R4.

- **RPF neighbor:** The PIM neighbor on the RPF interface. For example, if R7 is using the RPT shared tree, the RPF neighbor would be R3, which is the lowest-cost path to the RP. If it is using the SPT, R4 would be its RPF neighbor because it offers the lowest cost to the source.
- **Upstream:** Toward the source of the tree, which could be the actual source in source-based trees or the RP in shared trees. A PIM join travels upstream toward the source.
- **Upstream interface:** The interface toward the source of the tree. It is also known as the RPF interface or the incoming interface (IIF). An example of an upstream interface is R5's Te0/1/2 interface, which can send PIM joins upstream to its RPF neighbor.
- **Downstream:** Away from the source of the tree and toward the receivers.
- **Downstream interface:** Any interface that is used to forward multicast traffic down the tree, also known as an outgoing interface (OIF). An example of a downstream interface is R1's Te0/0/0 interface, which forwards multicast traffic to R3's Te0/0/1 interface.
- **Incoming interface (IIF):** The only type of interface that can accept multicast traffic coming from the source, which is the same as the RPF interface. An example of this type of interface is Te0/0/1 on R3 because the shortest path to the source is known through this interface.
- **Outgoing interface (OIF):** Any interface that is used to forward multicast traffic down the tree, also known as the downstream interface.
- **Outgoing interface list (OIL):** A group of OIFs that are forwarding multicast traffic to the same group. An example of this is R1's Te0/0/0 and Te0/0/1 interfaces sending multicast traffic downstream to R3 and R4 for the same multicast group.
- **Last-hop router (LHR):** A router that is directly attached to the receivers, also known as a leaf router. It is responsible for sending PIM joins upstream toward the RP or to the source.
- **First-hop router (FHR):** A router that is directly attached to the source, also known as a root router. It is responsible for sending register messages to the RP.
- **Multicast Routing Information Base (MRIB):** A topology table that is also known as the multicast route table (mroute). It is built based on information from the unicast routing table and PIM. MRIB contains the source S, group G, incoming interfaces (IIF), outgoing interfaces (OIFs), and RPF neighbor information for each multicast route as well as other multicast-related information.
- **Multicast Forwarding Information Base (MFIB):** A forwarding table that uses the MRIB to program multicast forwarding information in hardware for faster forwarding.
- **Multicast state:** The multicast traffic forwarding state that is used by a router to forward multicast traffic. The multicast state is composed of the entries found in the mroute table (S, G, IIF, OIF, and so on).

There are currently five PIM operating modes:

Key Topic

- PIM Dense Mode (PIM-DM)
- PIM Sparse Mode (PIM-SM)
- PIM Sparse Dense Mode
- PIM Source Specific Multicast (PIM-SSM)
- PIM Bidirectional Mode (Bidir-PIM)

NOTE PIM-DM and PIM-SM are also commonly referred to as any-source multicast (ASM).

All PIM control messages use the IP protocol number 103; they are either unicast (that is, register and register stop messages sent with a TTL greater than 1) or multicast, with a TTL of 1 to the all PIM routers address 224.0.0.13.

Table 13-4 lists the PIM control messages.

Key Topic

Table 13-4 PIM Control Message Types

Type	Message Type	Destination	PIM Protocol
0	Hello	224.0.0.13 (all PIM routers)	PIM-SM, PIM-DM, Bidir-PIM, and SSM
1	Register	RP address (unicast)	PIM-SM
2	Register stop	First-hop router (unicast)	PIM SM
3	Join/prune	224.0.0.13 (all PIM routers)	PIM-SM, Bidir-PIM, and SSM
4	Bootstrap	224.0.0.13 (all PIM routers)	PIM-SM and Bidir-PIM
5	Assert	224.0.0.13 (all PIM routers)	PIM-SM, PIM-DM, and Bidir-PIM
8	Candidate RP advertisement	Bootstrap router (BSR) address (unicast to BSR)	PIM-SM and Bidir-PIM
9	State refresh	224.0.0.13 (all PIM routers)	PIM-DM
10	DF election	224.0.0.13 (all PIM routers)	Bidir-PIM

PIM hello messages are sent by default every 30 seconds out each PIM-enabled interface to learn about the neighboring PIM routers on each interface to the *all PIM routers* address shown in Table 13-4. Hello messages are also the mechanism used to elect a **designated router (DR)**, as described later in this chapter, and to negotiate additional capabilities. All PIM routers must record the hello information received from each PIM neighbor.

PIM Dense Mode

Key Topic

PIM routers can be configured for PIM Dense Mode (PIM-DM) when it is safe to assume that the receivers of a multicast group are located on every subnet within the network—in other words, when the multicast receivers of a multicast group are densely populated across the network.

For PIM-DM, the multicast tree is built by flooding traffic out every interface from the source to every Dense Mode router in the network. The tree is grown from the root toward the leaves. As each router receives traffic for the multicast group, it must decide whether it already has active receivers wanting to receive the multicast traffic. If so, the router remains quiet and lets the multicast flow continue. If no receivers have requested the multicast stream for the multicast group on the LHR, the router sends a prune message toward the source. That branch of the tree is then pruned off so that the unnecessary traffic does not continue. The resulting tree is a source tree because it is unique from the source to the receivers.

Figure 13-15 shows the flood and prune operation of Dense Mode. The multicast traffic from the source is flooding throughout the entire network. As each router receives the multicast traffic from its upstream neighbor via its RPF interface, it forwards the multicast traffic to all its PIM-DM neighbors. This results in some traffic arriving via a non-RPF interface, as in the case of R3 receiving traffic from R2 on its non-RPF interface. Packets arriving via the non-RPF interface are discarded.

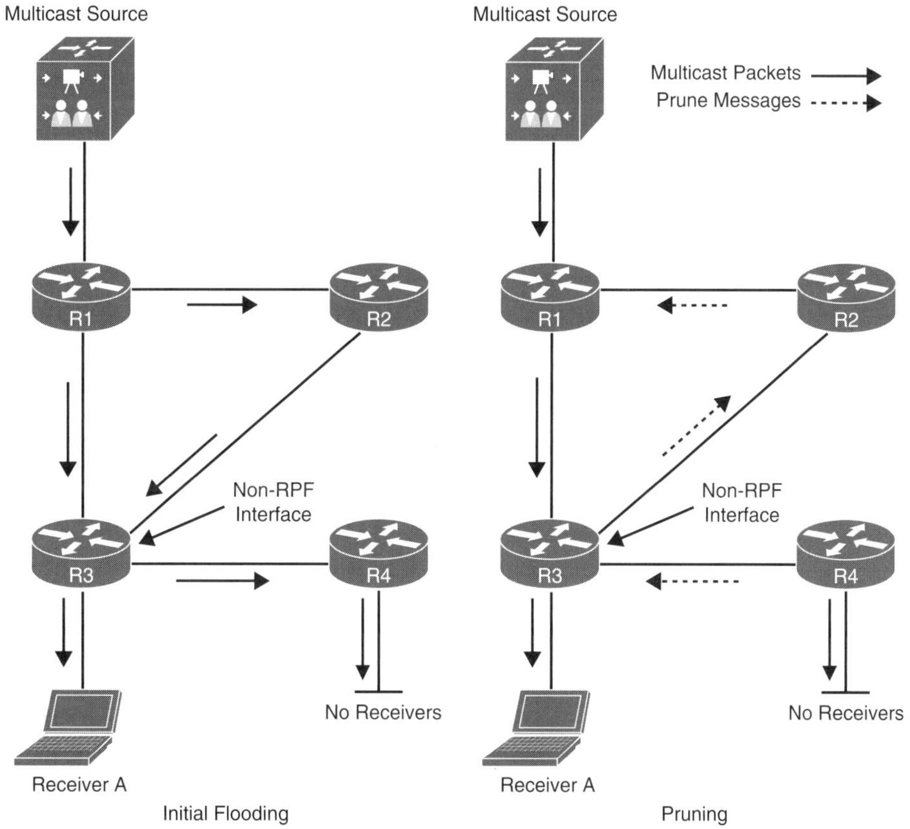

Figure 13-15 *PIM-DM Flood and Prune Operation*

These non-RPF multicast flows are normal for the initial flooding of multicast traffic and are corrected by the normal PIM-DM pruning mechanism. The pruning mechanism is used to stop the flow of unwanted traffic. Prunes (denoted by the dashed arrows) are sent out the RPF interface when the router has no downstream members that need the multicast traffic, as is the case for R4, which has no interested receivers, and they are also sent out non-RPF interfaces to stop the flow of multicast traffic that is arriving through the non-RPF interface, as is the case for R3, where multicast traffic is arriving through a non-RPF interface from R2, which results in a prune message.

Figure 13-16 illustrates the resulting topology after all unnecessary links have been pruned off. This results in an SPT from the source to the receiver. Even though the flow of multicast traffic is no longer reaching most of the routers in the network, the (S,G) state still remains in all routers in the network. This (S,G) state remains until the source stops transmitting.

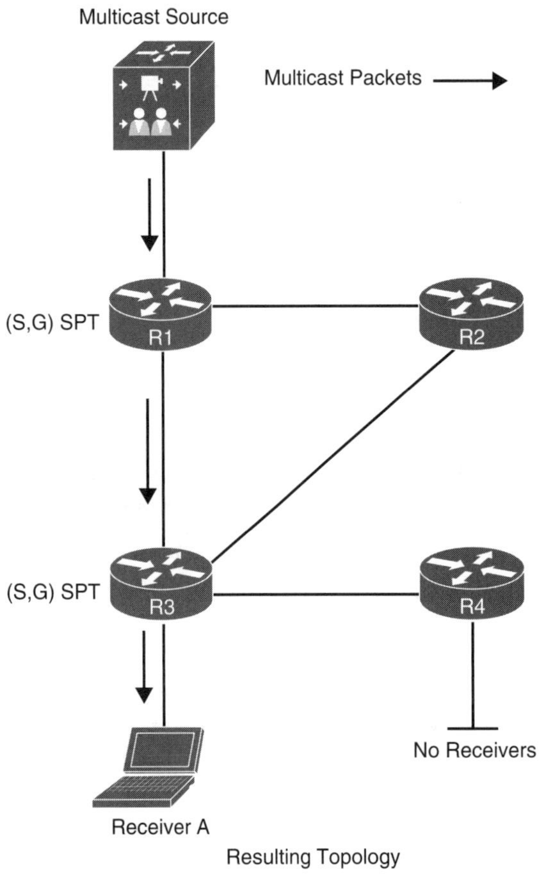

Figure 13-16 *PIM-DM Resulting Topology After Pruning*

In PIM-DM, prunes expire after three minutes. This causes the multicast traffic to be reflooded to all routers just as was done during the initial flooding. This periodic (every three minutes) flood and prune behavior is normal and must be taken into account when a network is designed to use PIM-DM.

PIM-DM is applicable to small networks where there are active receivers on every subnet of the network. Because this is rarely the case, PIM-DM is not widely deployed and not recommended for production environments.

PIM Sparse Mode

Key Topic

PIM Sparse Mode (PIM-SM) was designed for networks with multicast application receivers scattered throughout the network—in other words, when the multicast receivers of a multicast group are sparsely populated across the network. However, PIM-SM also works well in densely populated networks. It also assumes that no receivers are interested in multicast traffic unless they explicitly request it.

Just like PIM-DM, PIM-SM uses the unicast routing table to perform RPF checks, and it does not care which routing protocol (including static routes) populates the unicast routing table; therefore, it is protocol independent.

PIM Shared and Source Path Trees

PIM-SM uses an explicit join model where the receivers send an IGMP join to their locally connected router, which is also known as the *last-hop router (LHR)*, and this join causes the LHR to send a PIM join in the direction of the root of the tree, which is either the RP in the case of a shared tree (RPT) or the first-hop router (FHR) where the source transmitting the multicast streams is connected in the case of an SPT.

A multicast forwarding state is created as the result of these explicit joins; it is very different from the flood and prune or implicit join behavior of PIM-DM, where the multicast packet arriving on the router dictates the forwarding state.

Figure 13-17 illustrates a multicast source sending multicast traffic to the FHR. The FHR then sends this multicast traffic to the RP, which makes the multicast source known to the RP. It also illustrates a receiver sending an IGMP join to the LHR to join the multicast group. The LHR then sends a PIM join (*,G) to the RP, and this forms a shared tree from the RP to the LHR. The RP then sends a PIM join (S,G) to the FHR, forming a source tree between the source and the RP. In essence, two trees are created: an SPT from the FHR to the RP (S,G) and a shared tree from the RP to the LHR (*,G).

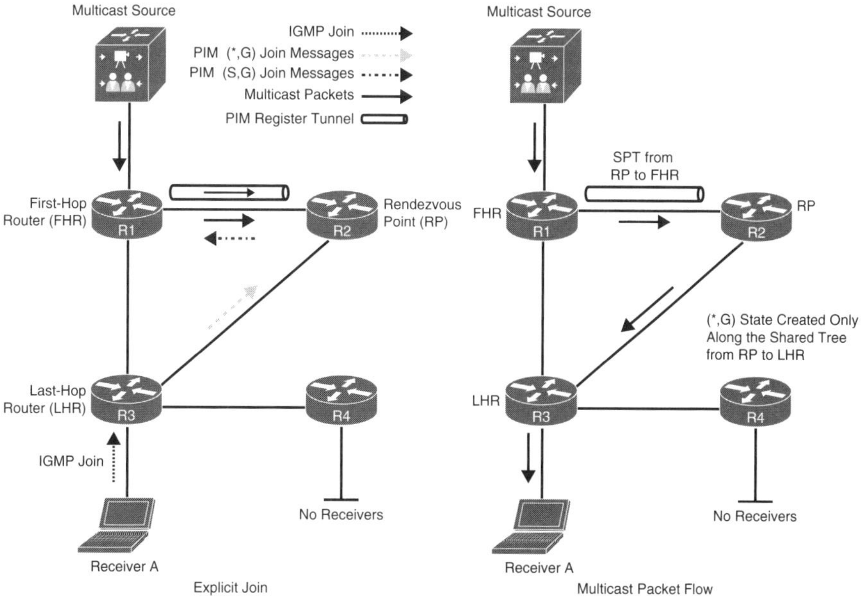

Figure 13-17 *PIM-SM Multicast Distribution Tree Building*

At this point, multicast starts flowing down from the source to the RP and from the RP to the LHR and then finally to the receiver. This is an oversimplified view of how PIM-SM achieves multicast forwarding. The following sections explain it in more detail.

Shared Tree Join

Key Topic

Figure 13-17 shows Receiver A attached to the LHR joining multicast group G. The LHR knows the IP address of the RP for group G, and it then sends a (*,G) PIM join for this group to the RP. If the RP were not directly connected, this (*,G) PIM join would travel hop-by-hop to the RP, building a branch of the shared tree that would extend from the RP to the LHR. At this point, group G multicast traffic arriving at the RP can flow down the shared tree to the receiver.

Source Registration

Key Topic

In Figure 13-17, as soon as the source for a group G sends a packet, the FHR that is attached to this source is responsible for registering this source with the RP and requesting the RP to build a tree back to that router.

The FHR creates a unidirectional PIM register tunnel interface that encapsulates the multicast data received from the source in a special PIM-SM message called the *register message*. The encapsulated multicast data is then unicast to the RP using the PIM register tunnel.

When the RP receives a register message, it decapsulates the multicast data packet inside the register message, and if there is no active shared tree because there are no interested receivers, the RP unicasts a register stop message directly to the registering FHR, without traversing the PIM register tunnel, instructing it to stop sending the register messages.

If there is an active shared tree for the group, it forwards the multicast packet down the shared tree, and it sends an (S,G) join back toward the source network S to create an (S,G) SPT. If there are multiple hops (routers) between the RP and the source, this results in an (S,G) state being created in all the routers along the SPT, including the RP. There will also be a (*,G) in R1 and all of the routers between the FHR and the RP.

As soon as the SPT is built from the source router to the RP, multicast traffic begins to flow natively from the source S to the RP.

Once the RP begins receiving data natively (that is, down the SPT) from source S, it sends a register stop message to the source's FHR to inform it that it can stop sending the unicast register messages. At this point, multicast traffic from the source is flowing down the SPT to the RP and, from there, down the shared tree (RPT) to the receiver.

The PIM register tunnel from the FHR to the RP remains in an active up/up state even when there are no active multicast streams, and it remains active as long as there is a valid RPF path for the RP.

PIM SPT Switchover

Key Topic

PIM-SM allows the LHR to switch from the RPT (shared tree) to an SPT for a specific source. In Cisco routers, this is the default behavior, and it happens immediately after the first multicast packet is received from the RP via the RPT, even if the shortest path to the source is through the RP. Figure 13-18 illustrates the SPT switchover concept. When the LHR receives the first multicast packet from the RP, it becomes aware of the IP address of the multicast source. At this point, the LHR checks its unicast routing table to see which is the shortest path to the source, and it sends an (S,G) PIM join toward the source hop-by-hop until it reaches the FHR to form an SPT. When the LHR receives a multicast packet from the source through the SPT, if the SPT RPF interface differs from the RPT RPF interface, the LHR will start receiving duplicate multicast traffic from the source; at this moment, it will switch the RPF interface to be the SPT RPF interface and send an (S,G) PIM prune message to the RP to shut off the duplicate multicast traffic coming through the RPT. In Figure 13-18, the shortest path to the source is between R1 and R3; if that link were shut down or not present, the shortest path would be through the RP, in which case an SPT switchover would still take place, even though the path used by the SPT is the same as the RPT.

NOTE The PIM SPT switchover mechanism can be disabled for all groups or for specific groups.

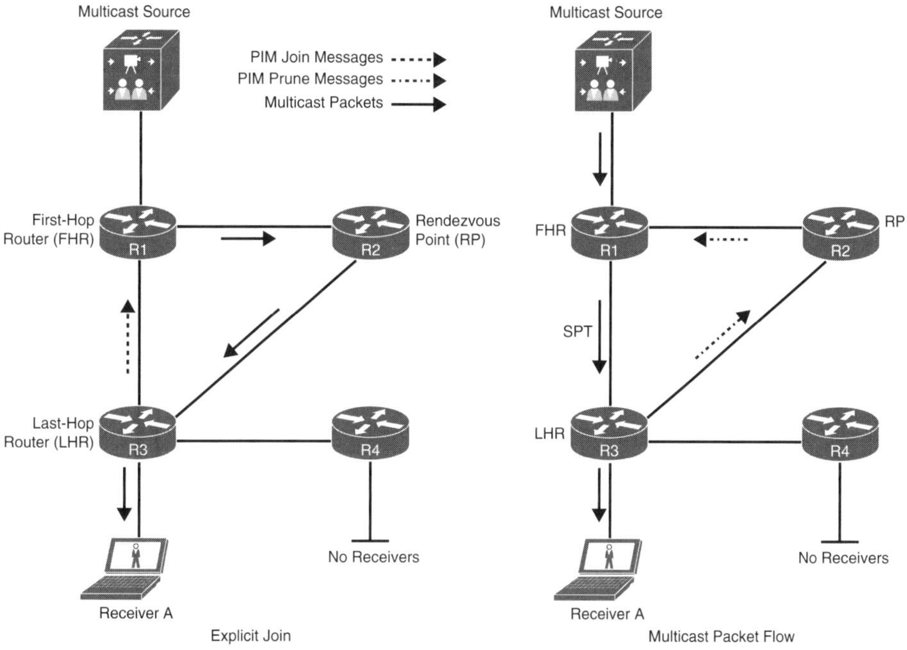

Figure 13-18 *PIM-SM SPT Switchover Example*

If the RP has no other interfaces that are interested in the multicast traffic, it sends a PIM prune message in the direction of the FHR. If there are any routers between the RP and the FHR, this prune message would travel hop-by-hop until it reaches the FHR.

Designated Routers

Key Topic

When multiple PIM-SM routers exist on a LAN segment, PIM hello messages are used to elect a designated router (DR) to avoid sending duplicate multicast traffic into the LAN or the RP. By default, the DR priority value of all PIM routers is 1, and it can be changed to force a particular router to become the DR during the DR election process, where a higher

DR priority is preferred. If a router in the subnet does not support the DR priority option or if all routers have the same DR priority, the highest IP address in the subnet is used as a tiebreaker.

On an FHR, the designated router is responsible for encapsulating in unicast register messages any multicast packets originated by a source that are destined to the RP. On an LHR, the designated router is responsible for sending PIM join and prune messages toward the RP to inform it about host group membership, and it is also responsible for performing a PIM SPT switchover.

Without DRs, all LHRs on the same LAN segment would be capable of sending PIM joins upstream, which could result in duplicate multicast traffic arriving on the LAN. On the source side, if multiple FHRs exist on the LAN, they all send register messages to the RP at the same time.

The default DR hold time is 3.5 times the hello interval, or 105 seconds. If there are no hellos after this interval, a new DR is elected. To reduce DR failover time, the hello query interval can be reduced to speed up failover with a trade-off of more control plane traffic and CPU resource utilization of the router.

Reverse Path Forwarding

Key Topic

Reverse Path Forwarding (RPF) is an algorithm used to prevent loops and ensure that multicast traffic is arriving on the correct interface. RPF functions as follows:

- If a router receives a multicast packet on an interface it uses to send unicast packets to the source, the packet has arrived on the RPF interface.
- If the packet arrives on the RPF interface, a router forwards the packet out the interfaces present in the outgoing interface list (OIL) of a multicast routing table entry.
- If the packet does not arrive on the RPF interface, the packet is discarded to prevent loops.

PIM uses multicast source trees between the source and the LHR and between the source and the RP. It also uses multicast shared trees between the RP and the LHRs. The RPF check is performed differently for each, as follows:

- If a PIM router has an (S,G) entry present in the multicast routing table (an SPT state), the router performs the RPF check against the IP address of the source for the multicast packet.
- If a PIM router has no explicit source-tree state, this is considered a shared-tree state. The router performs the RPF check on the address of the RP, which is known when members join the group.

PIM-SM uses the RPF lookup function to determine where it needs to send joins and prunes. (S,G) joins (which are SPT states) are sent toward the source. (*,G) joins (which are shared tree states) are sent toward the RP.

The topology on the left side of Figure 13-19 illustrates a failed RPF check on R3 for the (S,G) entry because the packet is arriving via a non-RPF interface. The topology on the right shows the multicast traffic arriving on the correct interface on R3; it is then forwarded out all the OIFs.

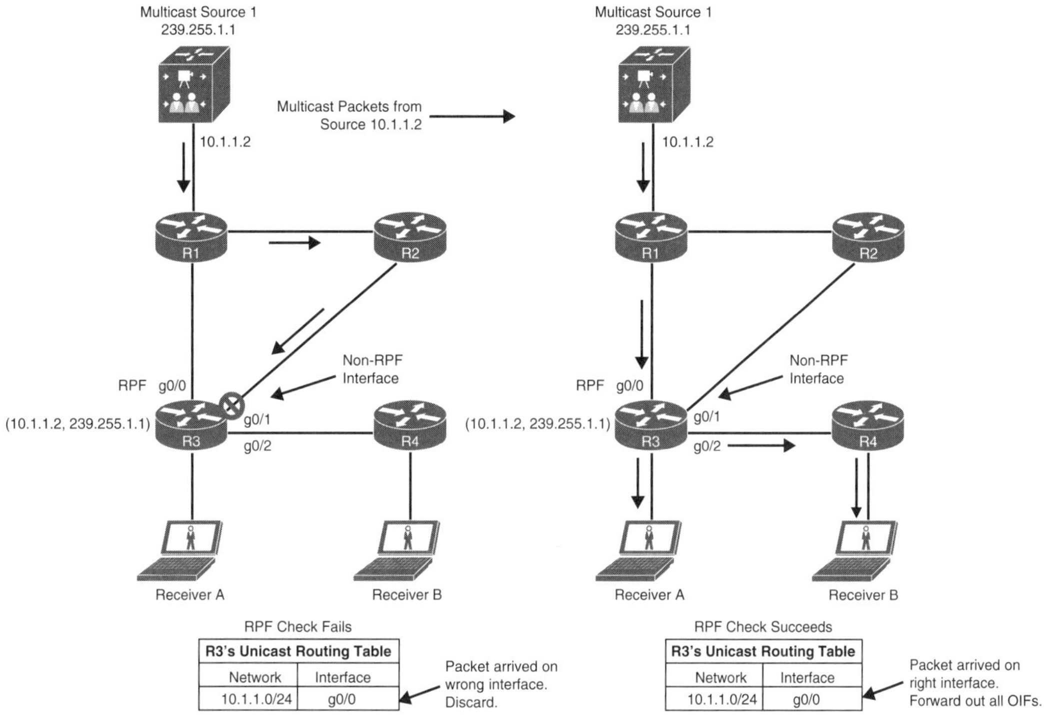

Figure 13-19 *RPF Check*

13

Key Topic

PIM Forwarder

In certain scenarios duplicate multicast packets could flow onto a multi-access network. The PIM assert mechanism stops these duplicate flows.

Figure 13-20 illustrates R2 and R3 both receiving the same (S,G) traffic via their RPF interfaces and forwarding the packets on to the LAN segment. R2 and R3 therefore receive an (S,G) packet via their downstream OIF that is in the OIF of their (S,G) entry. In other words, they detect a multicast packet for a specific (S,G) coming into their OIF that is also going out the same OIF for the same (S,G). This triggers the assert mechanism.

R2 and R3 both send PIM assert messages into the LAN. These assert messages send their administrative distance (AD) and route metric back to the source to determine which router should forward the multicast traffic to that network segment.

Each router compares its own values with the received values. Preference is given to the PIM message with the lowest AD to the source. If a tie exists, the lowest route metric for the protocol wins; and as a final tiebreaker, the highest IP address is used.

The losing router prunes its interface just as if it had received a prune on this interface, and the winning router is the PIM forwarder for the LAN.

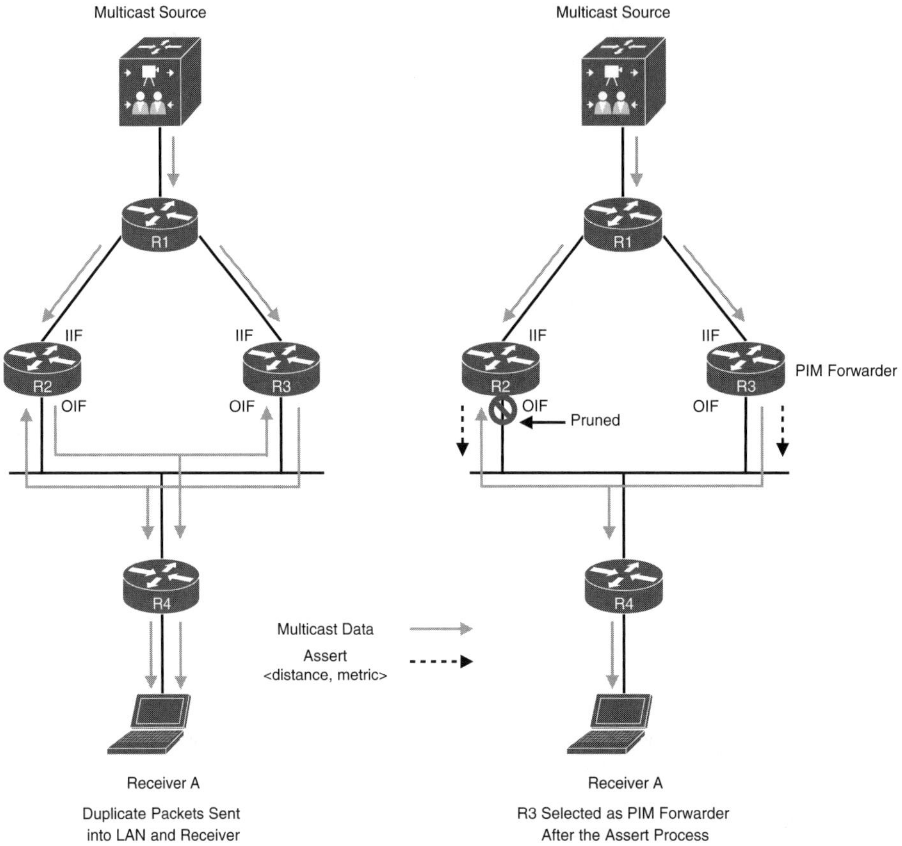

Figure 13-20 *PIM Forwarder Example*

NOTE The prune times out after three minutes on the losing router and causes it to begin forwarding on the interface again. This triggers the assert process to repeat. If the winning router were to go offline, the loser would take over the job of forwarding on to this LAN segment after its prune timed out.

The PIM forwarder concept applies to PIM-DM and PIM-SM. It is commonly used by PIM-DM but rarely required by PIM-SM because duplicate packets can end up in a LAN only if there is some sort of routing inconsistency.

With the topology shown in Figure 13-20, PIM-SM would not send duplicate flows into the LAN as PIM-DM would because of the way PIM-SM operates. For example, assuming that R1 is the RP, when R4 sends a PIM join message upstream toward it, it sends the message to the all PIM routers address 224.0.0.13, and R2 and R3 receive it. One of the fields of the PIM join message includes the IP address of the upstream neighbor, also known as the RPF neighbor. Assuming that R3 is the RPF neighbor, R3 is the only one that will send a PIM join to R1. R2 will not because the PIM join was not meant for it. At this point, a shared tree exists between R1, R3, and R4, and no traffic duplication exists.

Figure 13-21 illustrates how duplicate flows could exist in a LAN using PIM-SM. On the topology on the left side, R2 and R4 are running the Open Shortest Path First (OSPF) protocol, and R3 and R5 are running Enhanced Interior Gateway Routing Protocol (EIGRP). R4 learns about the RP (R1) through R2, and R5 learns about the RP through R3. R4's RPF neighbor is R2, and R5's RPF neighbor is R3. Assuming that Receiver A and Receiver B join the same group, R4 would send a PIM join to its upstream neighbor R2, which would in turn send a PIM join to R1. R5 would send a PIM join to its upstream neighbor R3, which would send a PIM join to R1. At this point, traffic starts flowing downstream from R1 into R2 and R3, and duplicate packets are then sent out into the LAN and to the receivers. At this point, the PIM assert mechanism kicks in, R3 is elected as the PIM forwarder, and R2's OIF interface is pruned, as illustrated in the topology on the right side.

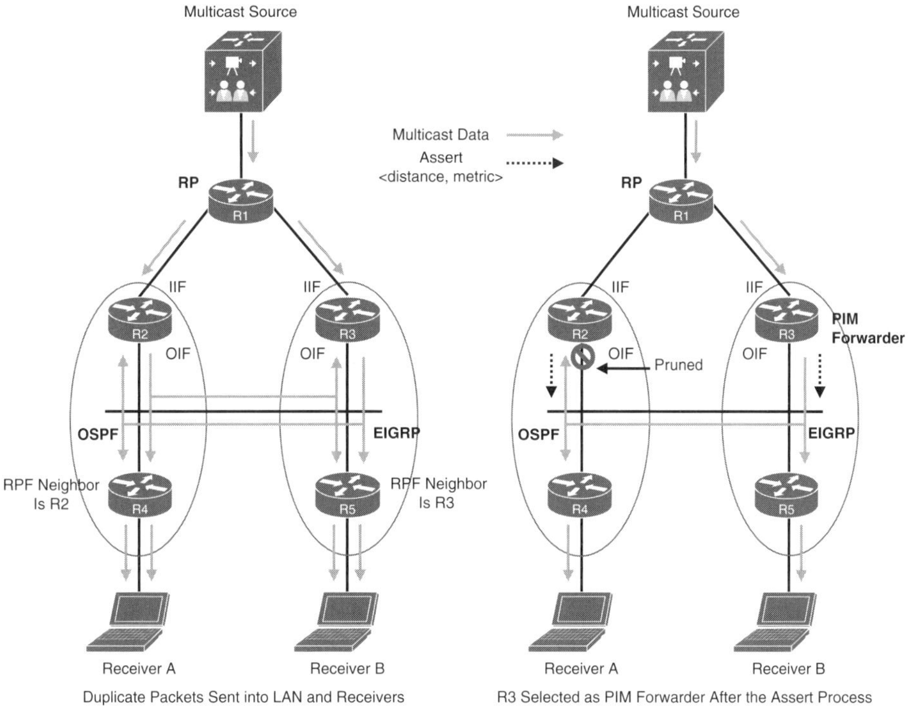

Figure 13-21 *PIM-SM PIM Forwarder Example*

Rendezvous Points

Key Topic

In PIM-SM, it is mandatory to choose one or more routers to operate as *rendezvous points (RPs)*. An RP is a single common root placed at a chosen point of a shared distribution tree, as described earlier in this chapter. An RP can be either configured statically in each router or learned through a dynamic mechanism. A PIM router can be configured to function as an RP either statically in each router in the multicast domain or dynamically by configuring Auto-RP or a PIM bootstrap router (BSR), as described in the following sections.

NOTE BSR and Auto-RP were not designed to work together and may introduce unnecessary complexities when deployed in the same network. The recommendation is not to use them concurrently.

Static RP

Key Topic

It is possible to statically configure RP for a multicast group range by configuring the address of the RP on every router in the multicast domain. Configuring static RPs is relatively simple and can be achieved with one or two lines of configuration on each router. If the network does not have many different RPs defined or if the RPs do not change very often, this could be the simplest method for defining RPs. It can also be an attractive option if the network is small.

However, static configuration can increase administrative overhead in a large and complex network. Every router must have the same RP address. This means changing the RP address requires reconfiguring every router. If several RPs are active for different groups, information about which RP is handling which multicast group must be known by all routers. To ensure this information is complete, multiple configuration commands may be required. If a manually configured RP fails, there is no failover procedure for another router to take over the function performed by the failed RP, and this method by itself does not provide any kind of load splitting.

Auto-RP

Key Topic

Auto-RP is a Cisco proprietary mechanism that automates the distribution of group-to-RP mappings in a PIM network. Auto-RP has the following benefits:

- It is easy to use multiple RPs within a network to serve different group ranges.
- It allows load splitting among different RPs.
- It simplifies RP placement according to the locations of group participants.
- It prevents inconsistent manual static RP configurations that might cause connectivity problems.
- Multiple RPs can be used to serve different group ranges or to serve as backups for each other.
- The Auto-RP mechanism operates using two basic components: candidate RPs (C-RPs) and RP mapping agents (MAs).

Candidate RPs

Key Topic

A C-RP advertises its willingness to be an RP via RP announcement messages. These messages are sent by default every RP announce interval, which is 60 seconds by default, to the reserved well-known multicast group 224.0.1.39 (Cisco-RP-Announce). The RP announcements contain the default group range 224.0.0.0/4, the C-RP's address, and the hold time, which is three times the RP announce interval. If there are multiple C-RPs, the C-RP with the highest IP address is preferred.

NOTE The RP announcement can be configured to announce specific multicast groups instead of the default group range 224.0.0.0/4. This allows for having multiple RPs in the network serving different multicast groups, which is useful for RP design.

RP Mapping Agents

Key Topic

RP MAs join group 224.0.1.39 to receive the RP announcements. They store the information contained in the announcements in a group-to-RP mapping cache, along with hold times. If multiple RPs advertise the same group range, the C-RP with the highest IP address is elected.

The RP MAs advertise the RP mappings to another well-known multicast group address, 224.0.1.40 (Cisco-RP-Discovery). These messages are advertised by default every 60 seconds or when changes are detected. The MA announcements contain the elected RPs and the group-to-RP mappings. All PIM-enabled routers join 224.0.1.40 and store the RP mappings in their private cache.

Multiple RP MAs can be configured in the same network to provide redundancy in case of failure. There is no election mechanism between them, and they act independently of each other; they all advertise identical group-to-RP mapping information to all routers in the PIM domain.

Figure 13-22 illustrates the Auto-RP mechanism where the MA periodically receives the C-RP Cisco RP announcements to build a group-to-RP mapping cache and then periodically multicasts this information to all PIM routers in the network using Cisco RP discovery messages.

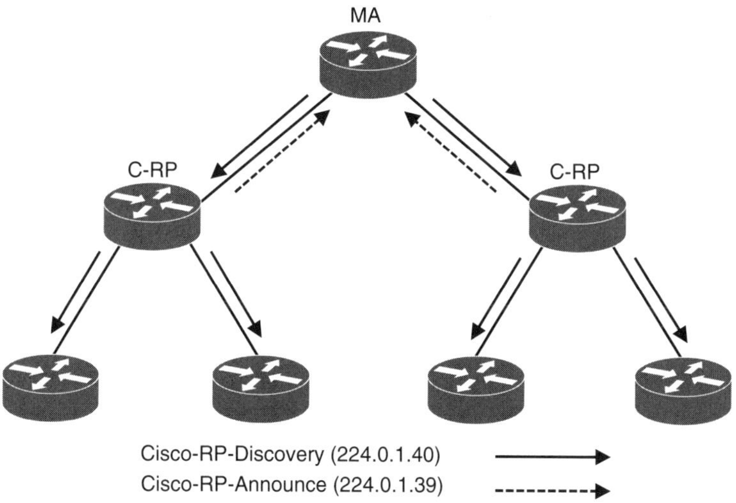

Figure 13-22 *Auto-RP Mechanism*

With Auto-RP, all routers automatically learn the RP information, which makes it easier to administer and update RP information. Auto-RP permits backup RPs to be configured, thus enabling an RP failover mechanism.

PIM Bootstrap Router

Key Topic

The *bootstrap router (BSR)* mechanism, described in RFC 5059, is a nonproprietary mechanism that provides a fault-tolerant, automated RP discovery and distribution mechanism.

PIM uses the BSR to discover and announce RP set information for each group prefix to all the routers in a PIM domain. This is the same function accomplished by Auto-RP, but BSR is implemented in a different way and is not compatible with Auto-RP. BSR is an IETF standard that is part of the PIM Version 2 specification, which is defined in RFC 4601.

The RP set is a group-to-RP mapping that contains the following components:

- Multicast group range
- RP priority
- RP address
- Hash mask length
- SM/Bidir flag

Bootstrap messages (BSMs) originate on the BSR, and they are flooded hop-by-hop by intermediate routers. When a Bootstrap message is forwarded, it is forwarded out of every PIM-enabled interface that has PIM neighbors (including the one over which the message was received). Bootstrap messages use the all PIM routers address 224.0.0.13 with a TTL of 1.

To avoid a single point of failure, multiple candidate BSRs (C-BSRs) can be deployed in a PIM domain. All C-BSRs participate in the BSR election process by sending PIM Bootstrap messages containing their BSR priority out all interfaces.

The C-BSR with the highest priority is elected as the BSR and sends Bootstrap messages to all PIM routers in the PIM domain. If the BSR priorities are equal or if the BSR priority is not configured, the C-BSR with the highest IP address is elected as the BSR.

Candidate RPs

Key Topic

A router that is configured as a candidate RP (C-RP) receives the Bootstrap messages, which contain the IP address of the currently active BSR. Because it knows the IP address of the BSR, the C-RP can unicast candidate RP advertisement (C-RP-Adv) messages directly to it. A C-RP-Adv message carries a list of group address and group mask field pairs. This enables a C-RP to specify the group ranges for which it is willing to be the RP.

The active BSR stores all incoming C-RP advertisements in its group-to-RP mapping cache. The BSR then sends the entire list of C-RPs from its group-to-RP mapping cache in Bootstrap messages every 60 seconds by default to all PIM routers in the entire network. As the routers receive copies of these Bootstrap messages, they update the information in their local group-to-RP mapping caches, and this allows them to have full visibility into the IP addresses of all C-RPs in the network.

Unlike with Auto-RP, where the mapping agent elects the active RP for a group range and announces the election results to the network, the BSR does not elect the active RP for a group. Instead, it leaves this task to each individual router in the network.

Each router in the network uses a well-known hashing algorithm to elect the currently active RP for a particular group range. Because each router is running the same algorithm against the same list of C-RPs, they will all select the same RP for a particular group range. C RPs with a lower priority are preferred. If the priorities are the same, the C-RP with the highest IP address is elected as the RP for the particular group range.

Figure 13-23 illustrates the BSR mechanism, where the elected BSR receives candidate RP advertisement messages from all candidate RPs in the domain, and it then sends Bootstrap messages with RP set information out all PIM-enabled interfaces, which are flooded hop-by-hop to all routers in the network.

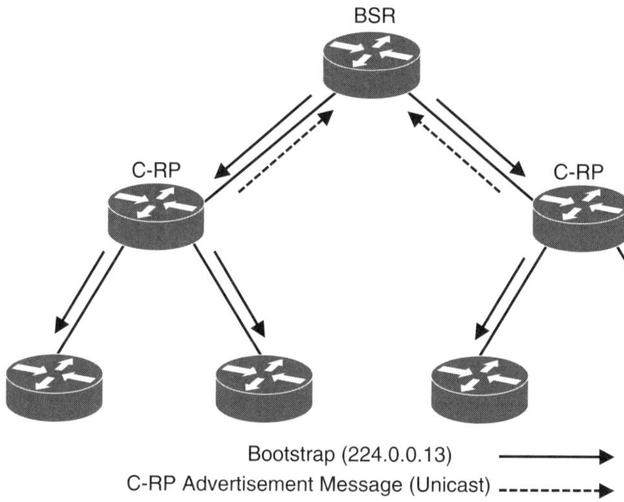

Figure 13-23 *BSR Mechanism*

Exam Preparation Tasks

You have a couple of choices for exam preparation: the exercises here, Chapter 30, "Final Preparation," and the exam simulation questions in the Pearson Test Prep Software Online.

Review All Key Topics

Review the most important topics in the chapter, noted with the Key Topic icon in the outer margin of the page. Table 13-5 lists these key topics and the page number on which each is found.

Key Topic

Table 13-5 Key Topics for Chapter 13

Key Topic Element	Description	Page
Paragraph	Multicast fundamentals	339
Table 13-2	IP Multicast Addresses Assigned by IANA	340
Table 13-3	Well-Known Reserved Multicast Addresses	341
Section	Layer 2 multicast addresses	342

Key Topic Element	Description	Page
Paragraph	IGMP description	343
Section	IGMPv2	344
List	IGMP message format field definitions	344
Paragraph	IGMPv2 operation	345
Paragraph	IGMPv3 definition	346
Paragraph	IGMP snooping	348
Paragraph	PIM definition	349
Paragraph	PIM source tree definition	349
Paragraph	PIM shared tree definition	350
List	PIM terminology	352
List	PIM operating modes	354
Table 13-4	PIM Control Message Types	354
Paragraph	PIM-DM definition	354
Paragraph	PIM-SM definition	357
Paragraph	PIM-SM shared tree operation	358
Paragraph	PIM-SM source registration	358
Paragraph	PIM-SM SPT switchover	358
Paragraph	PIM-SM designated routers	359
Paragraph	RPF definition	360
Section	PIM Forwarder	361
Paragraph	Rendezvous point definition	363
Paragraph	Static RP definition	364
Paragraph	Auto-RP definition	364
Paragraph	Auto-RP C-RP definition	364
Paragraph	Auto-RP mapping agent definition	365
Paragraph	PIM BSR definition	366
Paragraph	PIM BSR C-RP definition	366

Complete Tables and Lists from Memory

Print a copy of Appendix B, "Memory Tables" (found on the companion website), or at least the section for this chapter, and complete the tables and lists from memory. Appendix C, "Memory Tables Answer Key," also on the companion website, includes completed tables and lists you can use to check your work.

Define Key Terms

Define the following key terms from this chapter and check your answers in the Glossary:

designated router (DR), downstream, downstream interface, first-hop router (FHR), incoming interface (IIF), IGMP snooping, Internet Group Management Protocol (IGMP), last-hop router (LHR), Multicast Forwarding Information Base (MFIB), Multicast Routing Information Base (MRIB), multicast state, outgoing interface (OIF), outgoing interface list (OIL),

Protocol Independent Multicast (PIM), rendezvous point (RP), rendezvous point tree (RPT), Reverse Path Forwarding (RPF) interface, RPF neighbor, shortest path tree (SPT), upstream, upstream interface

Reference in This Chapter

Edgeworth, Brad, Aaron Foss, and Ramiro Garza Rios, *IP Routing on Cisco IOS, IOS XE and IOS XR*. Indianapolis: Cisco Press, 2014.

CHAPTER 14

Quality of Service (QoS)

This chapter covers the following subjects:

- **The Need for QoS:** This section describes the leading causes of poor quality of service and how they can be alleviated by using QoS tools and mechanisms.
- **QoS Models:** This section describes the three different models available for implementing QoS in a network: best effort, Integrated Services (IntServ), and Differentiated Services (DiffServ).
- **Modular QoS CLI:** This section describes the main components of Cisco's MQC and how it can be used to implement QoS in a network.
- **Classification and Marking:** This section describes classification, which is used to identify and assign IP traffic into different traffic classes, and marking, which is used to mark packets with a specified priority based on classification or traffic conditioning policies. This section also explains class-based classification and class-based marking configuration.
- **Policing and Shaping:** This section describes how policing is used to enforce rate limiting, where IP traffic is either dropped or re-marked, and how traffic shaping is used to buffer and delay traffic that momentarily peaks above the desired maximum rate. This section also explains class-based policing configuration.
- **Congestion Management and Avoidance:** This section describes congestion management, which is a queuing mechanism used to prioritize and protect IP traffic. It also describes congestion avoidance, which involves discarding IP traffic to avoid network congestion. This section also explains class-based weighted fair queuing (CBWFQ) and class-based shaping configuration.

QoS is a network infrastructure technology that relies on a set of tools and mechanisms to assign different levels of priority to different IP traffic flows and provides special treatment to higher-priority IP traffic flows. For higher-priority IP traffic flows, it reduces packet loss during times of network congestion and also helps control delay (latency) and delay variation (jitter); for low-priority IP traffic flows, it provides a best-effort delivery service. This is analogous to how a high-occupancy vehicle (HOV) lane, also referred to as a carpool lane, works: A special high-priority lane is reserved for use of carpools (high-priority traffic), and those who carpool can flow freely by bypassing the heavy traffic congestion in the adjacent general-purpose lanes.

These are the primary goals of implementing QoS on a network:

- Expediting delivery for real-time applications
- Ensuring business continuance for business-critical applications
- Providing fairness for non-business-critical applications when congestion occurs
- Establishing a trust boundary across the network edge to either accept or reject traffic markings injected by the endpoints

QoS uses the following tools and mechanisms to achieve its goals:

- Classification and marking
- Policing and shaping
- Congestion management and avoidance

All of these QoS mechanisms are described in this chapter.

"Do I Know This Already?" Quiz

The "Do I Know This Already?" quiz enables you to assess whether you should read the entire chapter. If you miss no more than one of these self-assessment questions, you might want to move ahead to the "Exam Preparation Tasks" section. Table 14-1 lists the major headings in this chapter and the "Do I Know This Already?" quiz questions covering the material in those headings so you can assess your knowledge of these specific areas. The answers to the "Do I Know This Already?" quiz appear in Appendix A, "Answers to the 'Do I Know This Already?' Questions."

Table 14-1 "Do I Know This Already?" Foundation Topics Section-to-Question Mapping

Foundation Topics Section	Questions
The Need for QoS	1–2
QoS Models	3–5
Modular QoS CLI	6–7
Classification and Marking	8–10
Policing and Shaping	11–12
Congestion Management and Avoidance	13–15

1. Which of the following are the leading causes of quality of service issues? (Choose all that apply.)
   a. Bad hardware
   b. Lack of bandwidth
   c. Latency and jitter
   d. Copper cables
   e. Packet loss

2. Network latency can be broken down into which of the following types? (Choose all that apply.)

   a. Propagation delay (fixed)

   b. Time delay (variable)

   c. Serialization delay (fixed)

   d. Processing delay (fixed)

   e. Packet delay (fixed)

   f. Delay variation (variable)

3. Which of the following is *not* a QoS implementation model?

   a. IntServ

   b. Expedited forwarding

   c. Best effort

   d. DiffServ

4. Which of the following is the QoS implementation model that requires a signaling protocol?

   a. IntServ

   b. Best effort

   c. DiffServ

   d. RSVP

5. Which of the following is the most popular QoS implementation model?

   a. IntServ

   b. Best effort

   c. DiffServ

   d. RSVP

6. Which of the following commands is used to configure a traffic class under policy-map configuration mode?

   a. **class-map [match-any | match-all]** *class-map-name*

   b. **class [match-any | match-all]** *class-map-name*

   c. **class-map** *class-map-name*

   d. **class** *class-map-name*

7. Which command is used to apply a policy map to an interface?

   a. **policy-map [input|output]** *policy-map-name*

   b. **policy-map [inbound|outbound]** *policy-map-name*

   c. **service-policy** *policy-map-name*

   d. **service-policy [input|output]** *policy-map-name*

   e. **service-policy [inbound|outbound]** *policy-map-name*

8. True or false: Traffic classification should always be performed in the core of the network.

   a. True

   b. False

9. True or false: The DiffServ field is an 8-bit Differentiated Services Code Point (DSCP) field that allows for classification of up to 64 values (0 to 63).
   a. True
   b. False
10. Which of the following configurations can be used to mark VOIP-TELEPHONY classified traffic with a DSCP EF value? (Choose two.)
    a.
    ```
    policy-map INBOUND-MARKING-POLICY
     class VOIP-TELEPHONY
      mark dscp ef
    ```
    b.
    ```
    policy-map INBOUND-MARKING-POLICY
     class VOIP-TELEPHONY
      set ip dscp ef
    ```
    c.
    ```
    policy-map INBOUND-MARKING-POLICY
     class VOIP-TELEPHONY
      set dscp ef
    ```
11. Which traffic conditioning tool can be used to drop or mark down traffic that goes beyond a desired traffic rate?
    a. Policers
    b. Shapers
    c. WRR
    d. None of these answers are correct.
12. What does Tc stand for? (Choose two.)
    a. Committed time interval
    b. Token credits
    c. Bc bucket token count
    d. Traffic control
13. Which of the following are the recommended congestion management mechanisms for modern rich-media networks? (Choose two.)
    a. Class-based weighted fair queuing (CBWFQ)
    b. Priority queuing (PQ)
    c. Weighted RED (WRED)
    d. Low-latency queuing (LLQ)
14. Which of the following is a recommended congestion-avoidance mechanism for modern rich-media networks?
    a. Weighted RED (WRED)
    b. Tail drop
    c. FIFO
    d. RED

15. Examine the following configuration. What does percent 30 mean? (Choose two.)

```
policy-map QUEUING
     class VOIP
     priority level 1 percent 30
```

a. Priority traffic will always be policed to 30% of the interface bandwidth.

b. Priority traffic will be policed to 30% of the interface bandwidth only if there is congestion on the interface.

c. The priority traffic can never use more than 30% of the interface bandwidth.

d. The priority traffic can go over 30% of the interface traffic if there is enough bandwidth available.

Foundation Topics

The Need for QoS

Modern real-time multimedia applications such as IP telephony, telepresence, broadcast video, Cisco Webex, and IP video surveillance are extremely sensitive to delivery delays and create unique quality of service (QoS) demands on a network. When packets are delivered using a best-effort delivery model, they may not arrive in order or in a timely manner, and they may be dropped. For video, this can result in pixelization of the image, pausing, choppy video, audio and video being out of sync, or no video at all. For audio, it could cause echo, talker overlap (a walkie-talkie effect where only one person can speak at a time), unintelligible and distorted speech, voice breakups, long silence gaps, and call drops. The following are the leading causes of quality issues:

- Lack of bandwidth
- Latency and jitter
- Packet loss

Lack of Bandwidth

The available bandwidth on the data path from a source to a destination equals the capacity of the lowest-bandwidth link. When the maximum capacity of the lowest-bandwidth link is surpassed, link congestion takes place, resulting in traffic drops. The obvious solution to this type of problem is to increase the link bandwidth capacity, but this is not always possible, due to budgetary or technological constraints. Another option is to implement QoS mechanisms such as policing and queuing to prioritize traffic according to level of importance. Voice, video, and business-critical traffic should get prioritized forwarding and sufficient bandwidth to support their application requirements, and the least important traffic should be allocated the remaining bandwidth.

Latency and Jitter

One-way end-to-end delay, also referred to as *network latency*, is the time it takes for packets to travel across a network from a source to a destination. ITU Recommendation G.114 recommends that, regardless of the application type, a network latency of 400 ms should not be exceeded, and for real-time traffic, network latency should be less than 150 ms; however, ITU and Cisco have demonstrated that real-time traffic quality does not begin to significantly degrade until network latency exceeds 200 ms. To be able to implement these recommendations, it is important to understand what causes network latency. Network latency can be broken down into fixed and variable latency:

- Propagation delay (fixed)
- Serialization delay (fixed)
- Processing delay (fixed)
- Delay variation (variable)

Propagation Delay

Propagation delay is the time it takes for a packet to travel from the source to a destination at the speed of light over a medium such as fiber-optic cables or copper wires. The speed of light is 299,792,458 meters per second in a vacuum. The lack of vacuum conditions in a fiber-optic cable or a copper wire slows down the speed of light by a ratio known as the *refractive index*; the larger the refractive index value, the slower light travels.

The average speed of light through a fiber-optic cable with a refractive index of 1.5 is approximately 200,000,000 meters per second (that is, 300,000,000 / 1.5). If a single fiber-optic cable with a refractive index of 1.5 were laid out around the equatorial circumference of Earth, which is about 40,075 km, the propagation delay would be approximately 200 ms, which would be an acceptable value even for real-time traffic.

Keep in mind that optical fibers are not always physically placed over the shortest path between two points. Fiber-optic cables may be hundreds or even thousands of miles longer than expected. In addition, other components required by fiber-optic cables, such as repeaters and amplifiers, may introduce additional delay. A provider's service-level agreement (SLA) can be reviewed to estimate and plan for the minimum, maximum, and average latency for a circuit.

NOTE Sometimes it is necessary to use satellite communication for hard-to-reach locations. The propagation delay for satellite circuits is the time it takes a radio wave traveling at the speed of light from the Earth's surface to a satellite (which could mean multiple satellite hops) and back to the Earth's surface; depending on the number of hops, this may surpass the recommended maximum 400 ms. For cases like this, nothing can be done to reduce the delay other than to try to find a satellite provider that offers lower propagation delays.

Serialization Delay

Serialization delay is the time it takes to place all the bits of a packet onto a link. It is a fixed value that depends on the link speed; the higher the link speed, the lower the delay. The serialization delay s is equal to the packet size in bits divided by the line speed in bits per second. For example, the serialization delay for a 1500-byte packet over a 1 Gbps interface is 12 μs and can be calculated as follows:

s = packet size in bits / line speed in bps

s = (1500 bytes × 8) / 1 Gbps

s = 12,000 bits / 1,000,000,000 bps = 0.000012 s × 1000 = .012 ms × 1000 = 12 μs

Processing Delay

Processing delay is the fixed amount of time it takes for a networking device to take the packet from an input interface and place the packet onto the output queue of the output interface. The processing delay depends on factors such as the following:

- CPU speed (for software-based platforms)
- CPU utilization (load)
- IP packet switching mode (process switching, software CEF, or hardware CEF)
- Router architecture (centralized or distributed)
- Configured features on both input and output interfaces

Delay Variation

Delay variation, also referred to as *jitter*, is the difference in the latency between packets in a single flow. For example, if one packet takes 50 ms to traverse the network from the source to destination, and the following packet takes 70 ms, the jitter is 20 ms. The major factors affecting variable delays are queuing delay, dejitter buffers, and variable packet sizes.

Jitter is experienced due to the queuing delay experienced by packets during periods of network congestion. Queuing delay depends on the number and sizes of packets already in the queue, the link speed, and the queuing mechanism. Queuing introduces unequal delays for packets of the same flow, thus producing jitter.

Voice and video endpoints typically come equipped with dejitter buffers that can help smooth out changes in packet arrival times due to jitter. A dejitter buffer is often dynamic and can adjust for approximately 30 ms changes in arrival times of packets. If a packet is not received within the 30 ms window allowed for by the dejitter buffer, the packet is dropped, and this affects the overall voice or video quality.

To prevent jitter for high-priority real-time traffic, it is recommended to use queuing mechanisms such as low-latency queuing (LLQ) that allow matching packets to be forwarded prior to any other low-priority traffic during periods of network congestion.

Packet Loss

Packet loss can be caused by various network-related problems—for instance, faulty hardware or even cable or circuit errors in the physical layer. Another common source of drops is due to congestion, which can be prevented by implementing one of the following approaches:

- Increase link speed.
- Implement QoS congestion-avoidance and congestion-management mechanisms.

Answers to the "Do I Know This Already?" quiz:

1 B, C, E **2** A, C, D, F **3** B **4** A **5** C **6** D **7** D **8** B **9** B **10** B, C **11** A **12** A, C **13** A, D **14** A **15** B, D

- Implement traffic policing to drop low-priority packets and allow high-priority traffic through.
- Implement traffic shaping to delay packets instead of dropping them because traffic may burst and exceed the capacity of an interface buffer. Traffic shaping is not recommended for real-time traffic because it relies on queuing that can cause jitter.

NOTE Standard traffic shaping is unable to handle data bursts that occur on a microsecond time interval (that is, micro-bursts). Microsecond or low-burst shaping is required for cases where micro-bursts need to be smoothed out by a shaper.

QoS Models

There are three different QoS implementation models:

Key Topic

- **Best effort:** QoS is not enabled for this model. It is used for traffic that does not require any special treatment.
- **Integrated Services (IntServ):** Applications signal the network to make a bandwidth reservation and to indicate that they require special QoS treatment.
- **Differentiated Services (DiffServ):** The network identifies classes that require special QoS treatment.

Key Topic

The IntServ model was created for real-time applications such as voice and video that require bandwidth, delay, and packet-loss guarantees to ensure both predictable and guaranteed service levels. In this model, applications signal their requirements to the network to reserve the end-to-end resources (such as bandwidth) they require to provide an acceptable user experience. IntServ uses Resource Reservation Protocol (RSVP) to reserve resources throughout a network for a specific application and to provide call admission control (CAC) to guarantee that no other IP traffic can use the reserved bandwidth. The bandwidth reserved by an application that is not being used is wasted.

To be able to provide end-to-end QoS, all nodes, including the endpoints running the applications, need to support, build, and maintain RSVP path state for every single flow. This is the biggest drawback of IntServ because it means it cannot scale well on large networks that might have thousands or millions of flows due to the large number of RSVP flows that would need to be maintained.

Figure 14-1 illustrates how RSVP hosts issue bandwidth reservations.

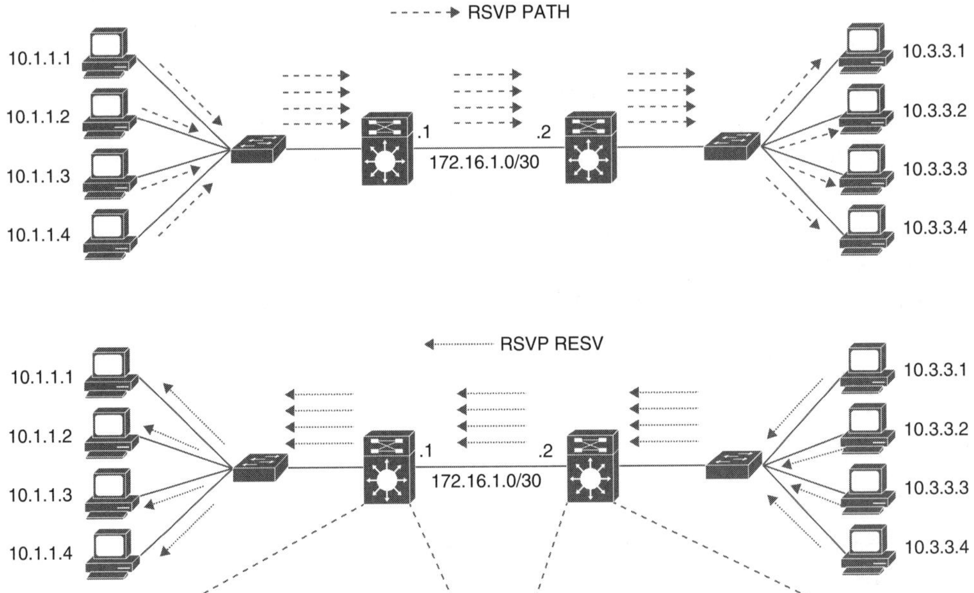

RSVP Path State

From	To	Protocol	Dest Port	Src Port	Previous Hop	Resv bps
10.1.1.1	10.3.3.1	TCP	23	12345	10.1.1.1	64k
10.1.1.2	10.3.3.2	TCP	53	32143	10.1.1.2	128k
10.1.1.3	10.3.3.3	TCP	25	15243	10.1.1.3	256k
10.1.1.4	10.3.3.4	TCP	23	54321	10.1.1.4	128k

RSVP Path State

From	To	Protocol	Dest Port	Src Port	Previous Hop	Resv bps
10.1.1.1	10.3.3.1	TCP	23	12345	172.16.1.1	64k
10.1.1.2	10.3.3.2	TCP	53	32143	172.16.11	128k
10.1.1.3	10.3.3.3	TCP	25	15243	172.16.1.1	256k
10.1.1.4	10.3.3.4	TCP	23	54321	172.16.1.1	128k

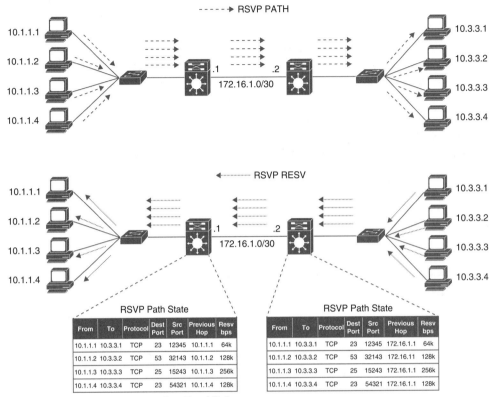

Figure 14-1 *RSVP Reservation Establishment*

In Figure 14-1, each host on the left side (senders) attempts to establish a one-to-one bandwidth reservation to each host on the right side (receivers). The senders start by sending RSVP PATH messages to the receivers along the same path used by regular data packets. RSVP PATH messages carry the sender's source address, the receiver's destination address, and the bandwidth they wish to reserve. This information is stored in the RSVP path state of each node. After the RSVP PATH messages reach the receivers, each receiver sends RSVP reservation request (RESV) messages in the reverse path of the data flow toward the receivers, hop-by-hop. At each hop, the IP destination address of a RESV message is the IP address of the previous-hop node, obtained from the RSVP path state of each node. As RSVP RESV messages cross each hop, they reserve bandwidth on each of the links for the traffic flowing from the receiver hosts to the sender hosts.

If bandwidth reservations are required from the hosts on the right side to the hosts on the left side, the hosts on the right side need to follow the same procedure of sending RSVP PATH messages, which doubles the RSVP state on each networking device in the data path. This demonstrates how RSVP state can increase quickly as more hosts reserve bandwidth. Apart from the scalability issues, long distances between hosts could also trigger long bandwidth reservation delays.

Key Topic

DiffServ was designed to address the limitations of the best-effort and IntServ models. With this model, there is no need for a signaling protocol, and there is no RSVP flow state to maintain on every single node, which makes it highly scalable; QoS characteristics (such as bandwidth and delay) are managed on a hop-by-hop basis with QoS policies that are defined independently at each device in the network. DiffServ is not considered an end-to-end QoS solution because end-to-end QoS guarantees cannot be enforced.

DiffServ divides IP traffic into classes and marks it based on business requirements so that each of the classes can be assigned a different level of service. As IP traffic traverses a network, each network device identifies the packet class by its marking and services the packets according to this class. Many levels of service can be chosen with DiffServ. For example, IP phone voice traffic is very sensitive to latency and jitter, so it should always be given preferential treatment over all other application traffic. Email, on the other hand, can withstand a great deal of delay and could be given best-effort service, and non-business, non-critical scavenger traffic (such as from YouTube) can either be heavily rate limited or blocked entirely. The DiffServ model is the most popular and most widely deployed QoS model and is covered in detail in this chapter.

Modular QoS CLI

Modular QoS CLI (MQC) is Cisco's approach to implementing QoS on Cisco routers. MQC provides a modular CLI framework to create QoS policies that are used to perform traffic classification and QoS actions such as marking, policing, shaping, congestion management, and congestion avoidance.

MQC policies are implemented by using the following three MQC components:

Key Topic

- **Class maps:** These maps define the traffic classification criteria by identifying the type of traffic that needs QoS treatment (for example, matching voice traffic). Multiple class maps are usually required to identify all the different types of traffic that need to be classified. Class maps are defined using the **class-map [match-any | match-all]** *class-map-name* command, and each class map can include one or more **match** command statements within it for traffic classification.

- **Policy maps:** These maps provide QoS actions for each traffic class defined by the class maps. Each policy map can include one or more traffic classes, and each traffic class can have one or more QoS actions. Policy maps are configured using **policy-map** *policy-map-name*.

- **Service policies:** These policies are used to apply policy maps to interfaces in an inbound and/or outbound direction. Service policies are applied with the **service-policy {input | output}** *policy-map-name* command, and the same policies can be reused on multiple interfaces.

A policy map consists of two main elements:

- A traffic class to classify traffic, identified with the **class** *class-map-name* command
- The QoS action(s) to apply to the traffic that matches the traffic class

Because policy maps use traffic classes to apply QoS actions, QoS actions applied using MQC are referred to as *class-based* QoS actions.

The following class-based QoS actions supported by MQC can be applied to traffic matching a traffic class:

- Class-based weighted fair queuing (CBWFQ)
- Class-based policing
- Class-based shaping
- Class-based marking

Key Topic

All traffic that is not matched by any of the user-defined traffic classes within the policy map is referred to as unclassified traffic. Unclassified traffic is matched by an implicitly configured default class called *class-default*. Unclassified traffic is typically best-effort traffic that requires no QoS guarantees; however, class-based QoS actions can also be applied to the default class if necessary.

Key Topic

Policy maps have no effect until they are applied to an interface in an inbound or outbound direction using the **service-policy {input | output}** *policy-map-name* command.

Key Topic

Service policies can be used to apply the same policy map to multiple interfaces. They can also be used to apply a single inbound and/or a single outbound policy map to a single interface.

Figure 14-2 illustrates an example of the MQC framework. The command syntax and the syntax description for each of the commands are covered in later sections of this chapter.

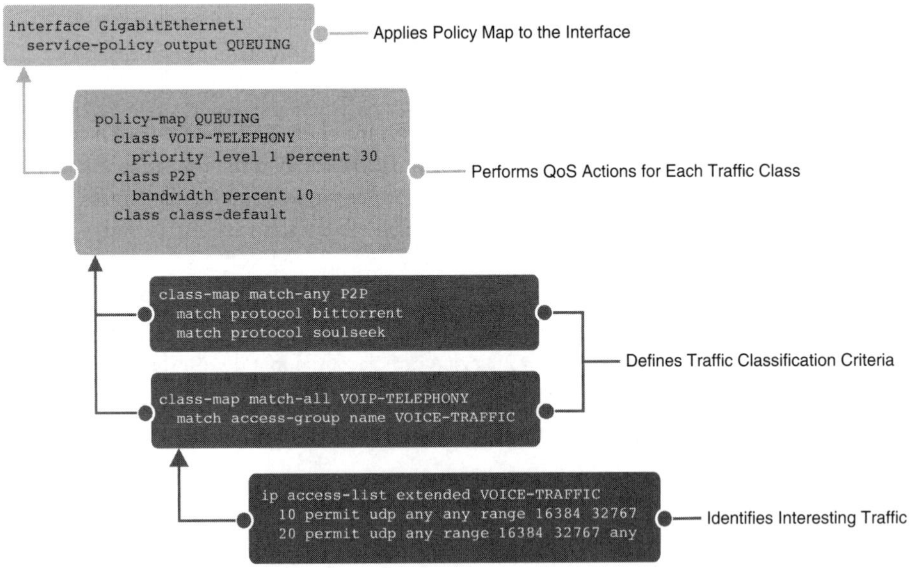

Figure 14-2 *MQC Framework Example*

NOTE The class map and policy map names are case sensitive. Making the name all uppercase characters is a best practice and makes it easier to read in the configuration.

Key Topic

Figure 14-2 shows the policy map applied to an interface, but policy maps can also be applied to other policies (also referred to as *parent policies*) to create hierarchical QoS policy maps (also referred to as *nested policy maps*). The **service-policy** *policy-map-name* command is used to apply a child policy map inside a parent policy map.

Figure 14-3 shows a policy map called CHILD-POLICY that is applied to the default class of another policy map called PARENT-POLICY using the **service-policy** *policy-map-name*. The PARENT-POLICY is the one that is applied to the interface.

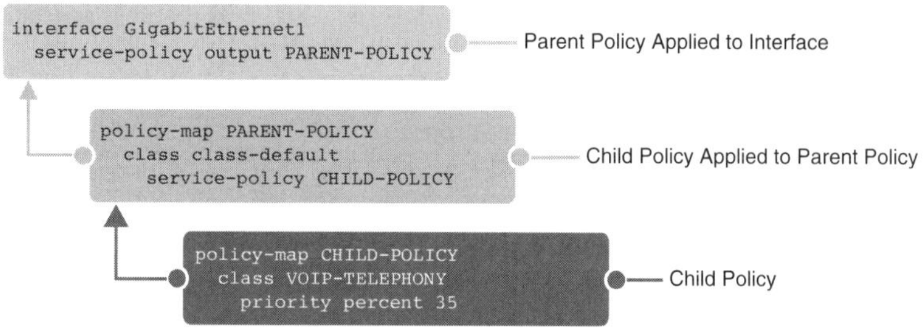

Figure 14-3 *MQC Hierarchical QoS Policy Map Example*

Classification and Marking

Before any QoS mechanism can be applied, IP traffic must first be identified and categorized into different classes, based on business requirements. Network devices use classification to identify IP traffic as belonging to a specific class. After the IP traffic is classified, marking can be used to mark or color individual packets so that other network devices can apply QoS mechanisms to those packets as they traverse the network.

This section introduces the concepts of classification and marking, explains the different marking options that are available for Layer 2 frames and Layer 3 packets, and explains where classification and marking tools should be used in a network.

Key Topic

Classification

Packet classification is a QoS mechanism responsible for distinguishing between different traffic streams. It uses traffic descriptors to categorize an IP packet within a specific class. Packet classification should take place at the network edge, as close to the source of the traffic as possible. After an IP packet is classified, packets can then be marked/re-marked, queued, policed, shaped, or any combination of these and other actions.

The following traffic descriptors are typically used for classification:

Key Topic

- **Internal:** QoS groups (locally significant to a router)
- **Layer 1:** Physical interface, subinterface, or port
- **Layer 2:** MAC address and 802.1Q/p class of service (CoS) bits

- **Layer 2.5:** MPLS experimental (EXP) bits
- **Layer 3:** **Differentiated Services Code Points (DSCP)**, IP Precedence (IPP), and source/destination IP address
- **Layer 4:** TCP or UDP ports
- **Layer 7:** Next-Generation Network-Based Application Recognition (NBAR2)

For enterprise networks, the most commonly used traffic descriptors used for classification include the Layer 2, Layer 3, Layer 4, and Layer 7 traffic descriptors listed here.

Key Topic

Layer 7 Classification

NBAR2 is a deep packet inspection engine that can classify and identify a wide variety of protocols and applications using Layer 3 to Layer 7 data, including difficult-to-classify applications that dynamically assign Transmission Control Protocol (TCP) or User Datagram Protocol (UDP) port numbers.

NBAR2 can recognize close to 1500 applications, and monthly protocol packs are provided for recognition of new and emerging applications, without requiring an IOS upgrade or router reload.

NBAR2 has two modes of operation that are independent of each other:

- **Protocol Discovery:** Protocol Discovery enables NBAR2 to discover and get real-time statistics on applications currently running in the network.
- **Modular QoS CLI (MQC):** Using MQC, the **match protocol** command under class map configuration mode is used to perform NBAR2 traffic classification. NBAR2 classifies traffic not just by TCP/UDP port numbers, but by performing subport classification, which is traffic classification based on the contents of the TCP/UDP payload. Examples include a URL string, a Multipurpose Internet Mail Extension (MIME) type, an HTTP request method, peer-to-peer traffic, DNS snooping, behavior analysis, and so on.

Key Topic

MQC Classification Configuration

Traffic classification using MQC is performed by using the **match** command within **class-map** configuration mode. If the traffic being classified matches the condition specified by the **match** command, then the condition returns a match result, and a no match result if it doesn't match.

Key Topic

The **match** command within a class map has the following characteristics:

- It matches on packet characteristics such as CoS, DSCP, or ACLs (source/destination networks or ports).
- If no **match** command is specified within the class map, **match none** is the default value.
- The **match any** command within a class map matches all packets.
- The **match protocol** command within a class map is used for NBAR traffic classification.

Key Topic

When there is more than one **match** command within a class map, the two matching options in the **class-map [match-any | match-all]** *class-map-name* command are used to determine the matching criteria:

- **Match any (logical OR operation):** At least one of the match conditions within the class map must be met. This option is configured with the **class-map match-any** command.
- **Match all (logical AND operation):** All match conditions within the class map must be met. Match all is the default matching behavior when the **class-map match-any** command is not specified. It can also be explicitly configured with the **class-map match-all** command.

Table 14-2 lists the most popular **match** commands used with MQC for traffic classification.

Key Topic

Table 14-2 Most-Used MQC **match** Commands and Descriptions

Command	Description
match access-group {*access-list-number* | **name** *access-list name*}	Matches an ACL by number or name.
match any	Matches any packet.
match cos *cos-value-list*	Matches one of the specified Layer 2 CoS values in a frame. Up to eight different CoS values can be specified in the list.
match [ip] dscp *dscp-value-list*	With the optional **ip** keyword, it matches one of the specified DSCP values in IPv4 packets. Without the optional **ip** keyword, it matches one of the specified DSCP values in IPv4 and IPv6 packets. Up to eight different DSCP values can be specified in the list.
match [ip] precedence *precedence-value-list*	With the optional **ip** keyword, it matches one of the specified IP Precedence values in IPv4 packets. Without the optional **ip** keyword, it matches one of specified Precedence values in IPv4 and IPv6 packets. Up to four different IP Precedence values can be specified in the list.
match ip rtp *starting-port-number port-number-range*	Matches any RTP port number in the specified range.
match protocol *protocol-name*	Matches the specified NBAR protocol name.
match qos-group *qos-group-value*	Matches the specified QoS group value. Only one QoS group value can be specified.

Table 14-3 lists the most used NBAR2 **match protocol** commands.

Table 14-3 NBAR2 **match protocol** Commands and Descriptions

Command	Description
match protocol http [**url** *url-string* | **host** *hostname-string* | **mime** *MIME-type*]	Matches HTTP traffic by URL, hostname, or MIME type
match protocol rtp [**audio** | **video** | **payload-type** *payload-string*]	Matches RTP based on audio or video payload type or a more granular payload type
match protocol *peer-to-peer-application*	Matches peer-to-peer (P2P) applications such as Soulseek, BitTorrent, and Skype

Example 14-1 shows multiple class maps, each with different **match** commands. The VOIP-TELEPHONY class map is configured with match-all (logical AND operation) and the CONTROL class map with match-any (logical OR operation). For the VOIP-TELEPHONY class map to be matched, the packet being evaluated should include a DSCP marking of EF and should also be permitted by the VOICE-TRAFFIC ACL. For the CONTROL class map to be matched, the packet being evaluated should match any of the specified DSCP values in the list or be permitted by the CALL-CONTROL ACL. The class maps with the **match protocol** command show how traffic can be classified using NBAR2.

Example 14-1 *Class Map Example*

```
ip access-list extended VOICE-TRAFFIC
  10 permit udp any any range 16384 32767
  20 permit udp any range 16384 32767 any

ip access-list extended CALL-CONTROL
  10 permit tcp any any eq 1719
  20 permit tcp any eq 1719 any

class-map match-all VOIP-TELEPHONY
  match dscp ef
  match access-group name VOICE-TRAFFIC

class-map match-any CONTROL
  match dscp cs3 af31 af32 af33
  match access-group name CALL-CONTROL

class-map match-any HTTP-VIDEO
  match protocol http mime "video/*"

class-map match-any P2P
  match protocol bittorrent
  match protocol soulseek


class-map match-all RTP-AUDIO
  match protocol rtp audio

class-map match-all HTTP-WEB-IMAGES
  match protocol http url "*.jpeg|*.jpg"
```

Key Topic

Marking

Packet *marking* is a QoS mechanism that colors a packet by changing a field within a packet or a frame header with a traffic descriptor so it is distinguished from other packets during the application of other QoS mechanisms (such as re-marking, policing, queuing, or congestion avoidance).

The following traffic descriptors are used for marking traffic:

Key Topic

- **Internal:** QoS groups
- **Layer 2:** 802.1Q/p class of service (CoS) bits
- **Layer 2.5:** MPLS experimental (EXP) bits
- **Layer 3:** Differentiated Services Code Points (DSCP) and IP Precedence (IPP)

NOTE QoS groups are used to mark packets as they are received and processed internally within the router and are automatically removed when packets egress the router. They are used only in special cases in which traffic descriptors marked or received on an ingress interface would not be visible for packet classification on egress interfaces due to encapsulation or de-encapsulation.

For enterprise networks, the most commonly used traffic descriptors for marking traffic include the Layer 2 and Layer 3 traffic descriptors mentioned in the previous list. Both of them are described in the following sections.

Layer 2 Marking

Key Topic

The **802.1Q** standard is an IEEE specification for implementing VLANs in Layer 2 switched networks. The 802.1Q specification defines two 2-byte fields: Tag Protocol Identifier (TPID) and Tag Control Information (TCI), which are inserted within an Ethernet frame following the Source Address field, as illustrated in Figure 14-4.

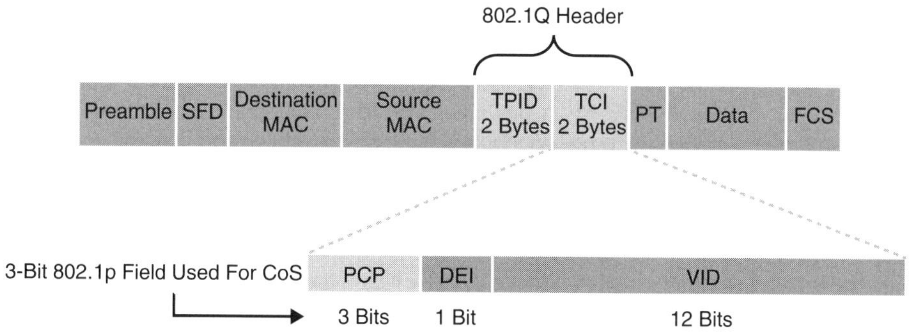

Figure 14-4 *802.1Q Layer 2 QoS Using 802.1p CoS*

The TPID value is a 16-bit field assigned the value 0x8100 that identifies it as an 802.1Q tagged frame.

The TCI field is a 16-bit field composed of the following three fields:

- Priority Code Point (PCP) field (3 bits)
- Drop Eligible Indicator (DEI) field (1 bit)
- VLAN Identifier (VLAN ID) field (12 bits)

Priority Code Point (PCP)

The specifications of the 3-bit PCP field are defined by the IEEE **802.1p** specification. This field is used to mark packets as belonging to a specific CoS. The CoS marking allows a Layer 2 Ethernet frame to be marked with eight different levels of priority values, 0 to 7, where 0 is the lowest priority and 7 is the highest. Table 14-4 includes the IEEE 802.1p specification standard definition for each CoS.

Table 14-4 IEEE 802.1p CoS Definitions

PCP Value/Priority	Acronym	Traffic Type
0 (lowest)	BK	Background
1 (default)	BE	Best effort
2	EE	Excellent effort
3	CA	Critical applications
4	VI	Video with < 100 ms latency and jitter
5	VO	Voice with < 10 ms latency and jitter
6	IC	Internetwork control
7 (highest)	NC	Network control

One drawback of using CoS markings is that frames lose their CoS markings when traversing a non-802.1Q link or a Layer 3 network. For this reason, packets should be marked with other higher-layer markings whenever possible so the marking values can be preserved end-to-end. This is typically accomplished by mapping a CoS marking into another marking. For example, the CoS priority levels correspond directly to IPv4's IP Precedence **type of service (ToS)** values so they can be mapped directly to each other.

Drop Eligible Indicator (DEI)

The DEI field is a 1-bit field that can be used independently or in conjunction with PCP to indicate frames that are eligible to be dropped during times of congestion. The default value for this field is 0, and it indicates that this frame is not drop eligible; it can be set to 1 to indicate that the frame is drop eligible.

VLAN Identifier (VLAN ID)

The VLAN ID field is a 12-bit field that defines the VLAN used by 802.1Q. Because this field is 12 bits, it restricts the number of VLANs supported by 802.1Q to 4096, which may not be sufficient for large enterprise or service provider networks.

Layer 3 Marking

As a packet travels from its source to its destination, it might traverse non-802.1Q trunked, or non-Ethernet links that do not support the CoS field. Using marking at Layer 3 provides a more persistent marker that is preserved end-to-end.

Figure 14-5 illustrates the ToS/DiffServ field within an IPv4 header.

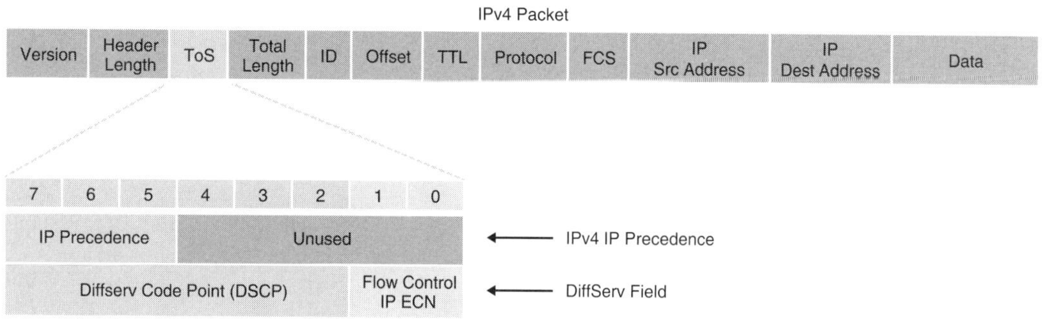

Figure 14-5 *IPv4 ToS/DiffServ Field*

The ToS field, defined in RFC 791, is an 8-bit field where only the first 3 bits of the ToS field, referred to as *IP Precedence (IPP)*, are used for marking, and the rest of the bits are unused. IPP values, which range from 0 to 7, allow the traffic to be partitioned in up to six usable classes of service; IPP 6 and 7 are reserved for internal network use.

RFC 2474 redefined the IPv4 ToS and the IPv6 Traffic Class fields as an 8-bit DiffServ field (DS field). The DS field uses the same 8 bits that were previously used for the IPv4 ToS and the IPv6 Traffic Class fields, and this allows it to be backward compatible with IP Precedence. The DS field is composed of a 6-bit Differentiated Services Code Point (DSCP) field that allows for classification of up to 64 values (0 to 63) and a 2-bit Explicit Congestion Notification (ECN) field.

DSCP Per-Hop Behaviors

Packets are classified and marked to receive a particular per-hop forwarding behavior (that is, expedited, delayed, or dropped) on network nodes along their path to the destination. The DS field is used to mark packets according to their classification into DiffServ Behavior Aggregates (BAs). A DiffServ BA is a collection of packets with the same DiffServ value crossing a link in a particular direction. **Per-hop behavior (PHB)** is the externally observable forwarding behavior (forwarding treatment) applied at a DiffServ-compliant node to a collection of packets with the same DiffServ value crossing a link in a particular direction (DiffServ BA).

In other words, PHB is expediting, delaying, or dropping a collection of packets by one or multiple QoS mechanisms on a per-hop basis, based on the DSCP value. A DiffServ BA could be multiple applications—for example, SSH, Telnet, and SNMP all aggregated together and marked with the same DSCP value. This way, the core of the network performs only simple PHB, based on DiffServ BAs, while the network edge performs classification, marking, policing, and shaping operations. This makes the DiffServ QoS model very scalable.

Four PHBs have been defined and characterized for general use:

- **Class Selector (CS) PHB:** The first 3 bits of the DSCP field are used as CS bits. The CS bits make DSCP backward compatible with IP Precedence because IP Precedence uses the same 3 bits to determine class.
- **Default Forwarding (DF) PHB:** Used for best-effort service.
- **Assured Forwarding (AF) PHB:** Used for guaranteed bandwidth service.
- **Expedited Forwarding (EF) PHB:** Used for low-delay service.

Class Selector (CS) PHB

RFC 2474 made the ToS field obsolete by introducing the DS field, and the Class Selector (CS) PHB was defined to provide backward compatibility for DSCP with IP Precedence. Figure 14-6 illustrates the CS PHB.

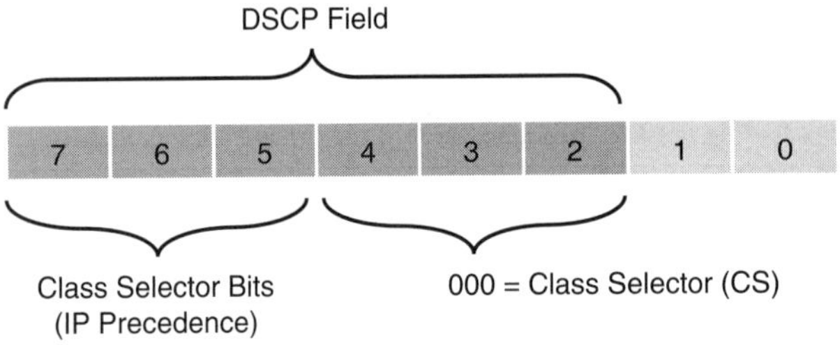

Figure 14-6 *Class Selector (CS) PHB*

Packets with higher IP Precedence should be forwarded in less time than packets with lower IP Precedence.

The last 3 bits of the DSCP (bits 2 to 4), when set to 0, identify a Class Selector PHB, but the Class Selector bits 5 to 7 are the ones where IP Precedence is set. Bits 2 to 4 are ignored by non-DiffServ-compliant devices performing classification based on IP Precedence.

There are eight CS classes, ranging from CS0 to CS7, that correspond directly with the eight IP Precedence values.

Default Forwarding (DF) PHB

Default Forwarding (DF) and Class Selector 0 (CS0) provide best-effort behavior and use the DS value 000000. Figure 14-7 illustrates the DF PHB.

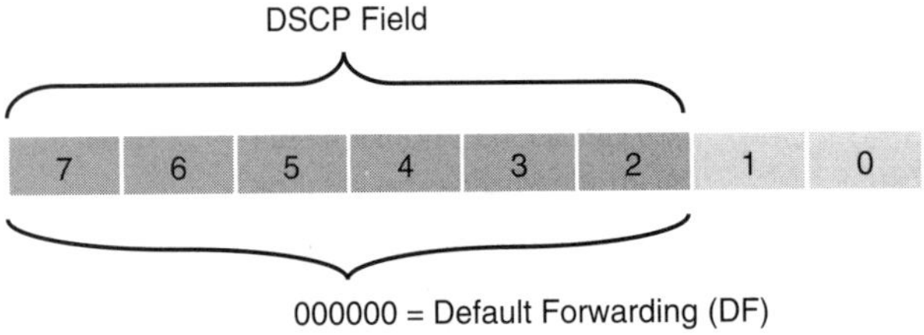

Figure 14-7 *Default Forwarding (DF) PHB*

Default best-effort forwarding is also applied to packets that cannot be classified by a QoS mechanism such as queuing, shaping, or policing. This usually happens when a QoS policy on the node is incomplete or when DSCP values are outside the ones that have been defined for the CS, AF, and EF PHBs.

Assured Forwarding (AF) PHB

The AF PHB guarantees a certain amount of bandwidth to an AF class and allows access to extra bandwidth, if available. Packets requiring AF PHB have a DSCP structure of aaadd0, where aaa is the binary value of the AF class (bits 5, 6, and 7), and dd (bits 2, 3, and 4) is the drop probability where bit 2 is unused and always set to 0. Figure 14-8 illustrates the AF PHB.

There are four standard-defined AF classes: AF1, AF2, AF3, and AF4. The AF class number does not represent precedence; for example, AF4 does not get any preferential treatment over AF1. Each class should be treated independently and placed into different queues.

Table 14-5 illustrates how each AF class is assigned an IP Precedence (under AF Class Value Bin) and has three drop probabilities: low, medium, and high.

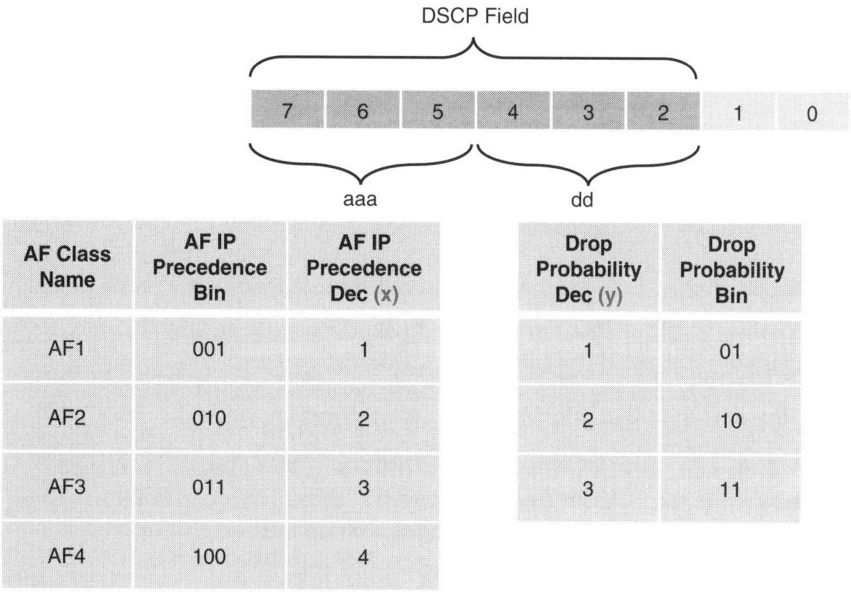

Figure 14-8 *Assured Forwarding (AF) PHB*

The AF Name (AF*xy*) is composed of the AF IP Precedence value in decimal (*x*) and the Drop Probability value in decimal (*y*). For example, AF41 is a combination of IP Precedence 4 and Drop Probability 1.

To quickly convert the AF Name into a DSCP value in decimal, use the formula $8x + 2y$. For example, the DSCP value for AF41 is $8(4) + 2(1) = 34$.

Table 14-5 AF PHBs with Decimal and Binary Equivalents

AF Class Name	AF IP Precedence Dec (*x*)	AF IP Precedence Bin	Drop Probability	Drop Probability Value Bin	Drop Probability Value Dec (*y*)	AF Name (AF*xy*)	DSCP Value Bin	DSCP Value Dec
AF1	1	001	Low	01	1	**AF11**	001010	10
AF1	1	001	Medium	10	2	**AF12**	001100	12
AF1	1	001	High	11	3	**AF13**	001110	14
AF2	2	010	Low	01	1	**AF21**	010010	18
AF2	2	010	Medium	10	2	**AF22**	010100	20
AF2	2	010	High	11	3	**AF23**	010110	22
AF3	3	011	Low	01	1	**AF31**	011010	26

AF Class Name	AF IP Precedence Dec (*x*)	AF IP Precedence Bin	Drop Probability	Drop Probability Value Bin	Drop Probability Value Dec (*y*)	AF Name (AF*xy*)	DSCP Value Bin	DSCP Value Dec
AF3	3	011	Medium	10	2	**AF32**	011100	28
AF3	3	011	High	11	3	**AF33**	011110	30
AF4	4	100	Low	01	1	**AF41**	100010	34
AF4	4	100	Medium	10	2	**AF42**	100100	36
AF4	4	100	High	11	3	**AF43**	100110	38

NOTE In RFC 2597, *drop probability* is referred to as *drop precedence.*

An AF implementation must detect and respond to long-term congestion within each class by dropping packets using a congestion-avoidance algorithm such as weighted random early detection (WRED). WRED uses the AF Drop Probability value within each class—where 1 is the lowest possible value, and 3 is the highest possible—to determine which packets should be dropped first during periods of congestion. It should also be able to handle short-term congestion resulting from bursts if each class is placed in a separate queue, using a queuing algorithm such as class-based weighted fair queuing (CBWFQ). The AF specification does not define the use of any particular algorithms to use for queuing and congestion avoidance, but it does specify the requirements and properties of such algorithms.

Expedited Forwarding (EF) PHB

The EF PHB can be used to build a low-loss, low-latency, low-jitter, assured bandwidth, end-to-end service. The EF PHB guarantees bandwidth by ensuring a minimum departure rate and provides the lowest possible delay to delay-sensitive applications by implementing low-latency queuing. It also prevents starvation of other applications or classes that are not using the EF PHB by policing EF traffic when congestion occurs.

Packets requiring EF should be marked with DSCP binary value 101110 (46 in decimal). Bits 5 to 7 (101) of the EF DSCP value map directly to IP Precedence 5 for backward compatibility with non-DiffServ-compliant devices. IP Precedence 5 is the highest user-definable IP Precedence value and is used for real-time delay-sensitive traffic (such as VoIP).

Table 14-6 includes all the DSCP PHBs (DF, CS, AF, and EF) with their decimal and binary equivalents. This table can also be used to see which IP Precedence value corresponds to each PHB.

Table 14-6 DSCP PHBs with Decimal and Binary Equivalents and IPP

DSCP Class	DSCP Value Bin	Decimal Value Dec	Drop Probability	Equivalent IP Precedence Value
DF (CS0)	000 000	0		0
CS1	001 000	8		1
AF11	001 010	10	Low	1
AF12	001 100	12	Medium	1

DSCP Class	DSCP Value Bin	Decimal Value Dec	Drop Probability	Equivalent IP Precedence Value
AF13	001 110	14	High	1
CS2	010 000	16		2
AF21	010 010	18	Low	2
AF22	010 100	20	Medium	2
AF23	010 110	22	High	2
CS3	011 000	24		3
AF31	011 010	26	Low	3
AF32	011 100	28	Medium	3
AF33	011 110	30	High	3
CS4	100 000	32		4
AF41	100 010	34	Low	4
AF42	100 100	36	Medium	4
AF43	100 110	38	High	4
CS5	101 000	40		5
EF	101 110	46		5
CS6	110 000	48		6
CS7	111 000	56		7

Scavenger Class

The scavenger class is intended to provide less than best-effort services. Applications assigned to the scavenger class have little or no contribution to the business objectives of an organization and are typically entertainment-related applications. These include peer-to-peer applications (such as Torrent), gaming applications (for example, Minecraft, Fortnite), and entertainment video applications (for example, YouTube, Vimeo, Netflix). These types of applications are usually heavily rate limited or blocked entirely.

Something very peculiar about the scavenger class is that it is intended to be lower in priority than a best-effort service. Best-effort traffic uses a DF PHB with a DSCP value of 000000 (CS0). Because there are no negative DSCP values, it was decided to use CS1 as the marking for scavenger traffic. This use is defined in RFC 4594.

Key Topic

Trust Boundary

To provide an end-to-end and scalable QoS experience, packets should be marked by the endpoint or as close to the endpoint as possible. When an endpoint marks a frame or a packet with a CoS or DSCP value, the switch port it is attached to can be configured to accept or reject the CoS or DSCP values. If the switch accepts the values, it means it trusts the endpoint and does not need to do any packet reclassification and re-marking for the received endpoint's packets. If the switch does not trust the endpoint, it rejects the markings and reclassifies and re-marks the received packets with the appropriate CoS or DSCP value.

For example, consider a campus network with IP telephony and host endpoints; the IP phones by default mark voice traffic with a CoS value of 5 and a DSCP value of 46 (EF), while incoming traffic from an endpoint (such as a PC) attached to the IP phone's switch port is re-marked to a CoS value of 0 and a DSCP value of 0. Even if the endpoint is sending tagged frames with a specific CoS or DSCP value, the default behavior for Cisco IP phones is to not trust the endpoint and zero out the CoS and DSCP values before sending the frames to the switch. When the IP phone sends voice and data traffic to the switch, the switch can classify voice traffic as higher priority than the data traffic, thanks to the high-priority CoS and DSCP markings for voice traffic.

For scalability, trust boundary classification should be done as close to the endpoint as possible. Figure 14-9 illustrates trust boundaries at different points in a campus network, where 1 and 2 are optimal, and 3 is acceptable only when the access switch is not capable of performing classification.

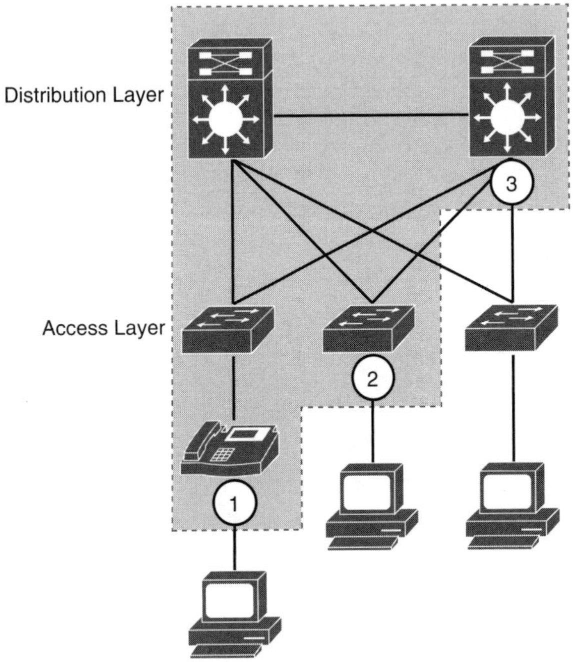

Figure 14-9 *Trust Boundaries*

Key Topic

Class-Based Marking Configuration

Class-based marking using the MQC can be achieved in two ways:

1. Using the **set** command under a traffic class of a policy map
2. Marking traffic that has exceeded a configured threshold with the **police** command in a policy map

In this section, we cover only the **set** command option. Marking with a policer is covered in the section "Policing and Shaping."

Table 14-7 lists the **set** commands that are used for class-based marking configuration. Multiple **set** commands are supported under a single traffic class.

Table 14-7 Class-Based Marking **set** Commands and Descriptions

Command	Description
set qos-group *qos-group-id*	Marks the classified traffic with an internal QoS group ID
set cos *cos-value*	Marks the Layer 2 CoS value
set [ip] precedence *ip-precedence-value*	Marks the Precedence value for IPv4 and IPv6 packets
set [ip] dscp *ip-dscp-value*	Marks the DSCP value for IPv4 and IPv6 packets

Example 14-2 shows an inbound policy map using the **set** command to perform ingress traffic marking.

Example 14-2 *Inbound Marking Policy Example*

```
policy-map INBOUND-MARKING-POLICY
  class VOIP-TELEPHONY
    set dscp ef
  class VIDEO
    set dscp af31
  class CONFERENCING
    set dscp af41
    set cos 4
  class class-default
    set dscp default
    set cos 0
```

A Practical Example: Wireless QoS

A wireless network can be configured to leverage the QoS mechanisms described in this chapter. For example, a wireless LAN controller (WLC) sits at the boundary between wireless and wired networks, so it becomes a natural location for a QoS trust boundary. Traffic entering and exiting the WLC can be classified and marked so that it can be handled appropriately as it is transmitted over the air and onto the wired network.

Wireless QoS can be uniquely defined on each wireless LAN (WLAN), using the four traffic categories listed in Table 14-8. Notice that the category names are human-readable words that translate to specific 802.1p and DSCP values.

Table 14-8 Wireless QoS Policy Categories and Markings

QoS Category	Traffic Type	802.1p Tag	DSCP Value
Platinum	Voice	5	46 (EF)
Gold	Video	4	34 (AF41)
Silver	Best effort (default)	0	0
Bronze	Background	1	10 (AF11)

When you create a new WLAN, its QoS policy defaults to Silver, or best-effort handling. In Figure 14-10, a WLAN named voice has been created to carry voice traffic, so its QoS policy has been set to Platinum. Wireless voice traffic will then be classified for low latency and low jitter and marked with an 802.1p CoS value of 5 and a DSCP value of 46 (EF).

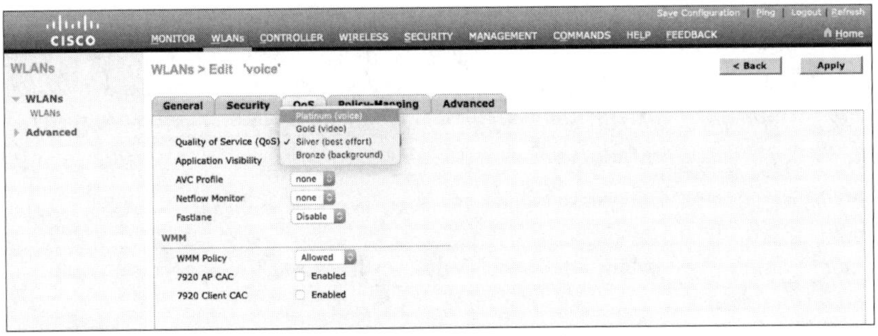

Figure 14-10 *Setting the QoS Policy for a Wireless LAN*

Policing and Shaping

Key Topic

Traffic policers and shapers are traffic-conditioning QoS mechanisms used to control the flow of traffic, but they differ in their implementation:

- **Policers:** Transmit or re-mark incoming or outgoing traffic that conforms to the desired traffic rate, and drop or mark down incoming or outgoing traffic that goes beyond the desired traffic rate.
- **Shapers:** Buffer and delay egress traffic rates that momentarily peak above the desired rate until the egress traffic rate drops below the defined traffic rate. If the egress traffic rate is below the desired rate, the traffic is sent immediately.

Figure 14-11 illustrates the difference between traffic policing and shaping. Policers drop or re-mark excess traffic, while shapers buffer and delay excess traffic.

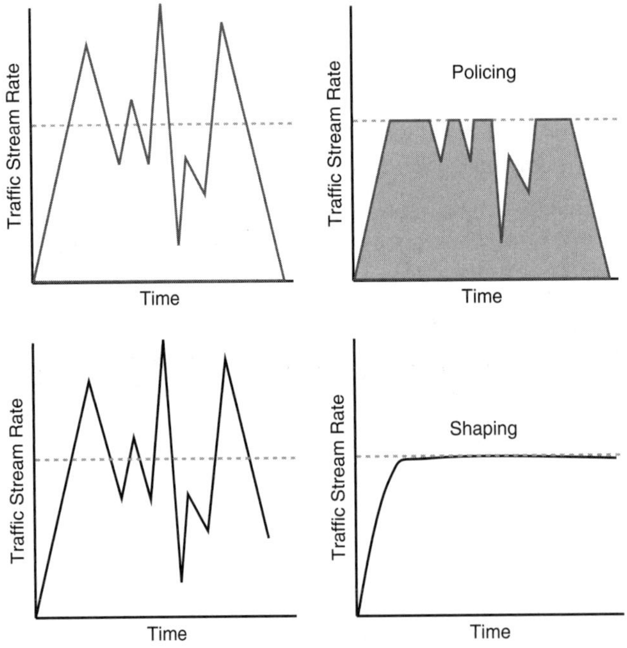

Figure 14-11 *Policing Versus Shaping*

Placing Policers and Shapers in the Network

Policers for incoming traffic are most optimally deployed at the edge of the network to keep traffic from wasting valuable bandwidth in the core of the network. Policers for outbound traffic are most optimally deployed at the edge of the network or core-facing interfaces on network edge devices. A downside of policing is that it causes TCP retransmissions when it drops traffic.

Shapers are used for egress traffic and typically deployed by enterprise networks on service provider (SP)–facing interfaces. Shaping is useful in cases where SPs are policing incoming traffic or when SPs are not policing traffic but do have a maximum traffic rate SLA, which, if violated, could incur monetary penalties. Shaping buffers and delays traffic rather than dropping it, and this causes fewer TCP retransmissions compared to policing.

14

Key Topic

Markdown

When a desired traffic rate is exceeded, a policer can take one of the following actions:

- Drop the traffic.
- Mark down the excess traffic with a lower priority.

Marking down excess traffic involves re-marking the packets with a lower-priority class value; for example, excess traffic marked with AFx1 should be marked down to AFx2 (or AFx3 if using two-rate policing). After marking down the traffic, congestion-avoidance mechanisms, such as DSCP-based weighted random early detection (WRED), should be configured throughout the network to drop AFx3 more aggressively than AFx2 and drop AFx2 more aggressively than AFx1.

Token Bucket Algorithms

Cisco IOS policers and shapers are based on token bucket algorithms. The following definitions are used to explain how token bucket algorithms operate:

Key Topic

- **Committed Information Rate (CIR):** The policed traffic rate, in bits per second (bps), defined in the traffic contract.
- **Committed Time Interval (Tc):** The time interval, in milliseconds (ms), over which the committed burst (Bc) is sent. Tc can be calculated with the formula Tc = (Bc [bits] / CIR [bps]) × 1000.
- **Committed Burst Size (Bc):** The maximum size of the CIR token bucket, measured in bytes, and the maximum amount of traffic that can be sent within a Tc. Bc can be calculated with the formula Bc = CIR (Tc / 1000).
- **Token:** A single token represents 1 byte or 8 bits.
- **Token bucket:** A bucket that accumulates tokens until a maximum predefined number of tokens is reached (such as the Bc when using a single token bucket); these tokens are added into the bucket at a fixed rate (the CIR). Each packet is checked for conformance to the defined rate and takes tokens from the bucket equal to its packet size; for example, if the packet size is 1500 bytes, it takes 12,000 bits (1500 × 8) from the

bucket. If there are not enough tokens in the token bucket to send the packet, the traffic conditioning mechanism can take one of the following actions:

- Buffer the packets while waiting for enough tokens to accumulate in the token bucket (traffic shaping)
- Drop the packets (traffic policing)
- Mark down the packets (traffic markdown)

It is recommended for the Bc value to be larger than or equal to the size of the largest possible IP packet in a traffic stream. Otherwise, there will never be enough tokens in the token bucket for larger packets, and they will always exceed the defined rate. If the bucket fills up to the maximum capacity, newly added tokens are discarded. Discarded tokens are not available for use in future packets.

Token bucket algorithms may use one or multiple token buckets. For single token bucket algorithms, the measured traffic rate can conform to or exceed the defined traffic rate. The measured traffic rate is conforming if there are enough tokens in the token bucket to transmit the traffic. The measured traffic rate is exceeding if there are not enough tokens in the token bucket to transmit the traffic.

Figure 14-12 illustrates the concept of the single token bucket algorithm.

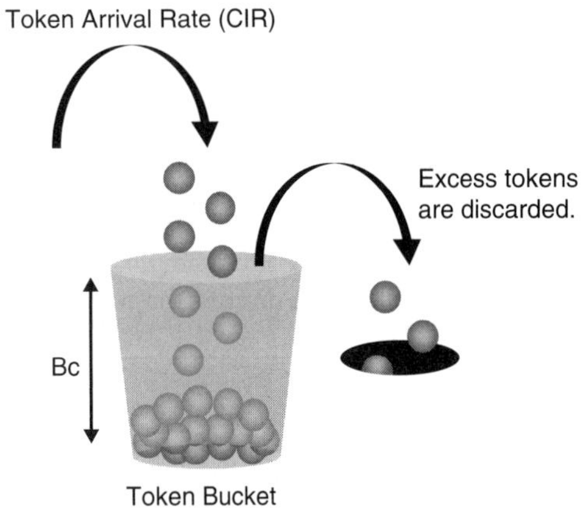

Figure 14-12 *Single Token Bucket Algorithm*

To understand how the single token bucket algorithms operate in more detail, assume that a 1 Gbps interface is configured with a policer defined with a CIR of 120 Mbps and a Bc of 12 Mb. The Tc value cannot be explicitly defined in IOS, but it can be calculated as follows:

Tc = (Bc [bits] / CIR [bps]) × 1000

Tc = (12 Mb / 120 Mbps) × 1000

Tc = (12,000,000 bits / 120,000,000 bps) × 1000 = 100 ms

When the Tc value is known, the number of Tcs within a second can be calculated as follows:

Tcs per second = 1000 / Tc

Tcs per second = 1000 ms / 100 ms = 10 Tcs

If a continuous stream of 1500-byte (12,000-bit) packets is processed by the token algorithm, only a Bc of 12 Mb can be taken by the packets within each Tc (100 ms). The number of packets that conform to the traffic rate and are allowed to be transmitted can be calculated as follows:

Number of packets that conform within each Tc = Bc / packet size in bits (rounded down)

Number of packets that conform within each Tc = 12,000,000 bits / 12,000 bits = 1000 packets

Any additional packets beyond 1000 will either be dropped or marked down.

To figure out how many packets would be sent in one second, the following formula can be used:

Packets per second = Number of packets that conform within each Tc × Tcs per second

Packets per second = 1000 packets × 10 intervals = 10,000 packets

To calculate the CIR for the 10,000, the following formula can be used:

CIR = Packets per second × Packet size in bits

CIR = 10,000 packets per second × 12,000 bits = 120,000,000 bps = 120 Mbps

To calculate the time interval it would take for the 1000 packets to be sent at interface line rate, the following formula can be used:

Time interval at line rate = (Bc [bits] / Interface speed [bps]) × 1000

Time interval at line rate = (12 Mb / 1 Gbps) × 1000

Time interval at line rate = (12,000,000 bits / 1,000,000,000 bps) × 1000 = 12 ms

Figure 14-13 illustrates how the Bc (1000 packets at 1500 bytes each, or 12 Mb) is sent every Tc interval. After the Bc is sent, there is an interpacket delay of 88 ms (100 ms minus 12 ms) within the Tc where there is no data transmitted.

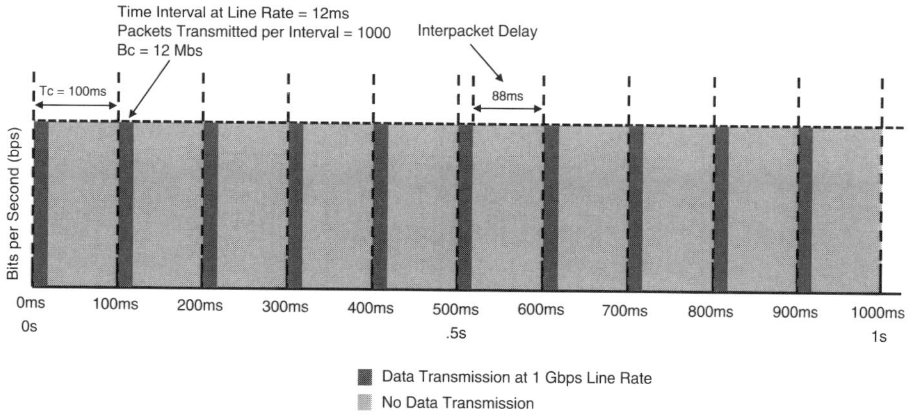

Figure 14-13 *Token Bucket Operation*

The recommended values for Tc range from 8 ms to 125 ms. Shorter Tcs, such as 8 ms to 10 ms, are necessary to reduce interpacket delay for real-time traffic such as voice. Tcs longer than 125 ms are not recommended for most networks because the interpacket delay becomes too large.

Class-Based Policing Configuration

The **police** command under a traffic class of a policy map is used for class-based policing. With class-based policing, the classified input or output traffic can be rate-limited, marked, or dropped. The **police** command syntax is as follows:

police [**cir**] *cir-in-bps* [**bc**] *committed-burst-size-in-bytes*
[**be**] *excess-burst-size-in-bytes* [**conform-action**
action] [**exceed-action** *action*] [**violate-action** *action*]

Table 14-9 lists the **police** command keywords and their description.

Key Topic

Table 14-9 police Command Keywords and Keyword Descriptions

Keyword	Description
cir	Optional keyword to explicitly specify the average CIR rate.
cir-in-bps	Average CIR rate in bits per second. The CIR can be configured with the postfix values **k** (Kbps), **m** (Mbps), and **g** (Gbps). The postfix values support decimal points.
bc	Optional keyword to explicitly specify the committed burst size.
committed-burst-size-in-bytes	Optional Bc size in bytes. The default is 1500 bytes or the configured CIR rate divided by 32 (CIR/32); whichever number is higher is chosen as the Bc size.
be	Optional keyword to explicitly specify the excess burst (Be) size.
excess-burst-size-in-bytes	Optional Be size in bytes. The default is the value of Bc.
conform-action	Optional keyword to specify the action to take on packets that conform to the CIR. The default action is to transmit.
exceed-action	Optional keyword to specify the action to take on packets that exceed the CIR. The default action is to drop.
violate-action	Optional keyword to specify the action to take on packets that violate the normal and maximum burst sizes. The default action is to drop.
action	The action to take on packets; some examples include **drop:** Drops the packet (default for exceed and violate actions). **transmit:** Transmits the packet (default for conform action). **set-dscp-transmit** *dscp-value*: Marks and transmits the packet with the specified DSCP value. **set-prec-transmit** *precedence-value*: Marks and transmits the packet with the specified Precedence value. **set-cos-transmit** *cos-value*: Marks and transmits the packet with the specified CoS value. **set-qos-transmit** *qos-group-value*: Marks the packet with the specified internal qos-group value. This option is valid only on inbound policy maps.

Types of Policers

There are different policing algorithms, including the following:

Key Topic

- Single-rate two-color marker/policer
- Single-rate three-color marker/policer (srTCM)
- Two-rate three-color marker/policer (trTCM)

Single-Rate Two-Color Markers/Policers

The first policers implemented use a single-rate two-color model based on the single token bucket algorithm. For this type of policer, traffic can be either conforming to or exceeding the CIR. Marking down or dropping actions can be performed for each of the two states.

Figure 14-14 illustrates different actions that the single-rate two-color policer can take. The section above the dotted line on the left side of the figure represents traffic that exceeded the CIR and was marked down. The section above the dotted line on the right side of the figure represents traffic that exceeded the CIR and was dropped.

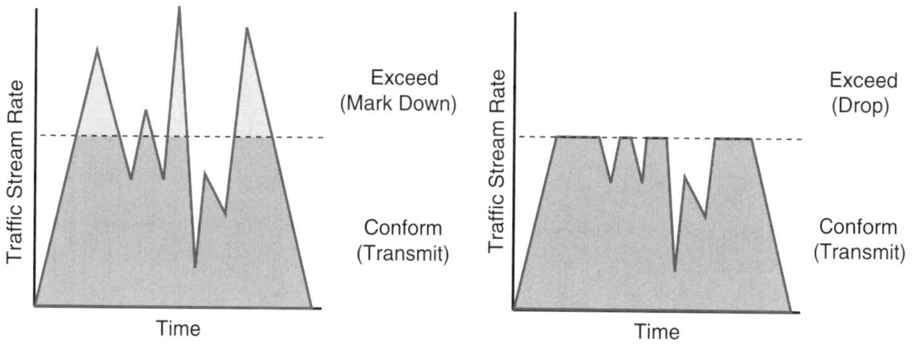

Figure 14-14 *Single-Rate Two-Color Marker/Policer*

Example 14-3 shows the configuration of a single-rate two-color policy map with two traffic classes. Traffic matching the VOIP-TELEPHONY traffic class is being policed to a CIR of 50 Mbps, and traffic matching the VIDEO traffic class is being policed to 25 Mbps. Traffic for both classes that conforms to the CIR is transmitted, exceeding traffic for the VOIP-TELEPHONY traffic class is dropped, and exceeding traffic for the VIDEO traffic class is marked down and transmitted with the DSCP value AF21.

Example 14-3 *Single-Rate Two-Color Marker/Policer Example*

```
policy-map OUTBOUND-POLICY
  class VOIP-TELEPHONY
    police 50000000 conform-action transmit exceed-action drop
  class VIDEO
    police 25000000 conform-action transmit exceed-action set-dscp-transmit af21

interface GigabitEthernet1
  service-policy output OUTBOUND-POLICY
```

In Example 14-3, the **cir**, **bc**, and **be** optional keywords were not specified for the **police** commands. To see the default values, the **show policy-map** *policy-map-name* command is used. Example 14-4 shows the output of the **show policy-map** *policy-map-name* command for the OUTBOUND-POLICY. For the VOIP-TELEPHONY class, the Bc default value is 50,000,000/32 (1,562,500 bytes), and for the VIDEO class, the default Bc value is 25,000,000/32 (781,250). There is no Be, because single-rate two-color markers/policers (single token bucket algorithms) do not allow excess bursting. Excess bursting is explained in the section "Single-Rate Three-Color Markers/Policers (srTCM)" in this chapter.

Example 14-4 *Verifying CIR, Bc, and Be Default Values*

```
router# show policy-map OUTBOUND-POLICY
  Policy Map OUTBOUND-POLICY
    Class VOIP-TELEPHONY
     police cir 50000000 bc 1562500
       conform-action transmit
       exceed-action drop
    Class VIDEO
     police cir 25000000 bc 781250
       conform-action transmit
       exceed-action set-dscp-transmit af21
router#
```

Single-Rate Three-Color Markers/Policers (srTCM)

Single-rate three-color policer algorithms are based on RFC 2697. This type of policer uses two token buckets, and the traffic can be classified as either conforming to, exceeding, or violating the CIR. Marking down or dropping actions are performed for each of the three states of traffic.

The first token bucket operates similarly to the single-rate two-color system; the difference is that if there are any tokens left over in the bucket after each time period due to low or no activity, instead of discarding the excess tokens (overflow), the algorithm places them in a second bucket to be used later for temporary bursts that might exceed the CIR. Tokens placed in this second bucket are referred to as the *excess burst (Be)*, and Be is the maximum number of bits that can exceed the Bc burst size.

With the two token-bucket mechanism, traffic can be classified in three colors or states, as follows:

- **Conform:** Traffic under Bc is classified as conforming and green. Conforming traffic is usually transmitted and can be optionally re-marked.
- **Exceed:** Traffic over Bc but under Be is classified as exceeding and yellow. Exceeding traffic can be dropped or marked down and transmitted.
- **Violate:** Traffic over Be is classified as violating and red. This type of traffic is usually dropped but can be optionally marked down and transmitted.

Figure 14-15 illustrates different actions that a single-rate three-color policer can take. The section below the straight dotted line on the left side of the figure represents the traffic that conformed to the CIR, the section right above the straight dotted line represents the exceed ing traffic that was marked down, and the top section represents the violating traffic that was also marked down. The exceeding and violating traffic rates vary because they rely on random tokens spilling over from the Bc bucket into the Be. The section right above the straight dotted line on the right side of the figure represents traffic that exceeded the CIR and was marked down, and the top section represents traffic that violated the CIR and was dropped.

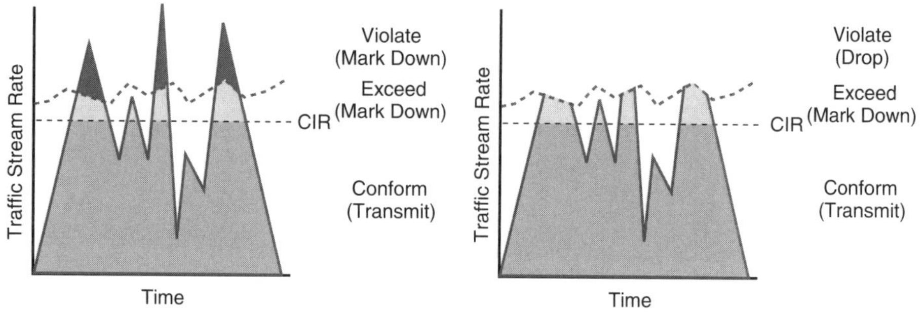

Figure 14-15 *Single-Rate Three-Color Marker/Policer*

The single-rate three-color marker/policer uses the following parameters to meter the traffic stream:

- **Committed Information Rate (CIR):** The policed rate.
- **Committed Burst Size (Bc):** The maximum size of the CIR token bucket, measured in bytes. Referred to as *Committed Burst Size (CBS)* in RFC 2697.
- **Excess Burst Size (Be):** The maximum size of the excess token bucket, measured in bytes. Referred to as *Excess Burst Size (EBS)* in RFC 2697.
- **Bc Bucket Token Count (Tc):** The number of tokens in the Bc bucket. Not to be confused with the committed time interval Tc.
- **Be Bucket Token Count (Te):** The number of tokens in the Be bucket.
- **Incoming Packet Length (B):** The packet length of the incoming packet, in bits.

Figure 14-16 illustrates the logical flow of the single-rate three-color marker/policer two-token-bucket algorithm.

The single-rate three-color policer's two bucket algorithm causes fewer TCP retransmissions and is more efficient for bandwidth utilization. It is the perfect policer to be used with AF classes (AFx1, AFx2, and AFx3). Using a three-color policer makes sense only if the actions taken for each color differ. If the actions for two or more colors are the same—for example, conform and exceed both transmit without re-marking—the single-rate two-color policer is recommended to keep things simpler.

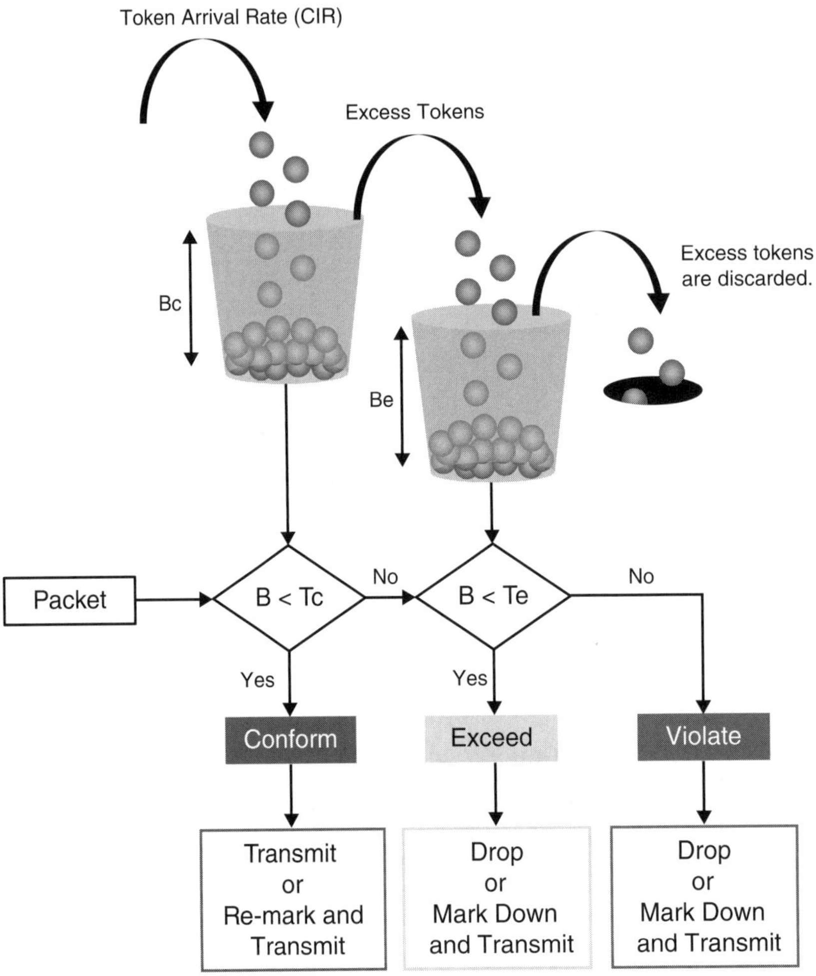

Figure 14-16 *Single-Rate Three-Color Marker/Policer Token Bucket Algorithm*

Example 14-5 shows the configuration of a single-rate three-color policy map with one traffic class. Traffic matching the VOIP-TELEPHONY traffic class is policed to a CIR of 50 Mbps; traffic that conforms to the CIR is re-marked and transmitted with DSCP AF31; exceeding traffic is marked down and transmitted with DSCP AF32, and all violating traffic is dropped.

Example 14-5 *Single-Rate Three-Color Marker/Policer Example*

```
policy-map OUTBOUND-POLICY
  class VOIP-TELEPHONY
    police 50000000 conform-action set-dscp-transmit af31 exceed-action
set-dscp-transmit af32 violate-action drop


interface GigabitEthernet1
  service-policy output OUTBOUND-POLICY
```

Example 14-6 shows the output of the **show policy-map** *policy-map-name* command for the OUTBOUND-POLICY. For the VOIP-TELEPHONY class, the Bc and Be values were not specified; therefore, the default Bc value is 50,000,000/32 (1,562,500 bytes), and the Be value defaults to the Bc value.

Example 14-6 *Verifying Be and Bc Default Values*

```
router# show policy-map OUTBOUND-POLICY
  Policy Map OUTBOUND-POLICY
    Class VOIP-TELEPHONY
     police cir 50000000 bc 1562500 be 1562500
       conform-action set-dscp-transmit af31
       exceed-action set-dscp-transmit af32
       violate-action drop
```


Two-Rate Three-Color Markers/Policers (trTCM)

The two-rate three-color marker/policer is based on RFC 2698 and is similar to the single-rate three-color policer. The difference is that single-rate three-color policers rely on excess tokens from the Bc bucket, which introduces a certain level of variability and unpredictability in traffic flows; the two-rate three-color marker/policers address this issue by using two distinct rates—the CIR and the Peak Information Rate (PIR). The two-rate three-color marker/policer allows for a sustained excess rate based on the PIR that allows for different actions for the traffic exceeding the different burst values; for example, violating traffic can be dropped at a defined rate, and this is something that is not possible with the single-rate three-color policer.

Figure 14-17 illustrates how violating traffic that exceeds the PIR can either be marked down (on the left side of the figure) or dropped (on the right side of the figure). Compare Figure 14-17 to Figure 14-16 to see the difference between the two-rate three-color policer and the single-rate three-color policer.

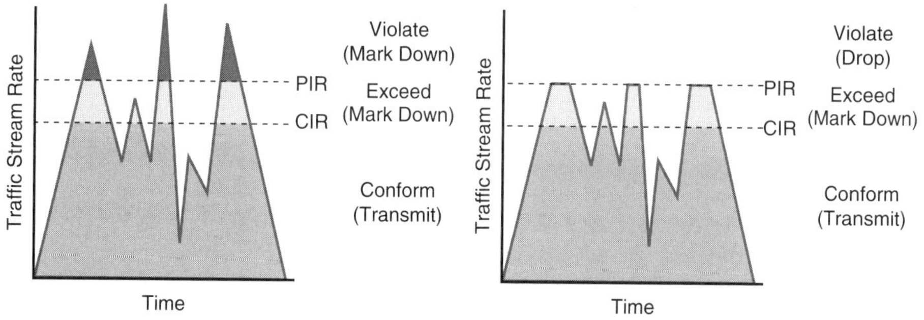

Figure 14-17 *Two-Rate Three-Color Marker/Policer Token Bucket Algorithm*

The two-rate three-color marker/policer uses the following parameters to meter the traffic stream:

- **Committed Information Rate (CIR):** The policed rate.
- **Peak Information Rate (PIR):** The maximum rate of traffic allowed. PIR should be equal to or greater than the CIR.

- **Committed Burst Size (Bc):** The maximum size of the second token bucket, measured in bytes. Referred to as *Committed Burst Size (CBS)* in RFC 2698.
- **Peak Burst Size (Be):** The maximum size of the PIR token bucket, measured in bytes. Referred to as *Peak Burst Size (PBS)* in RFC 2698. Be should be equal to or greater than Bc.
- **Bc Bucket Token Count (Tc):** The number of tokens in the Bc bucket. Not to be confused with the committed time interval Tc.
- **Bp Bucket Token Count (Tp):** The number of tokens in the Bp bucket.
- **Incoming Packet Length (B):** The packet length of the incoming packet, in bits.

The two-rate three-color policer also uses two token buckets, but the logic varies from that of the single-rate three-color policer. Instead of transferring unused tokens from the Bc bucket to the Be bucket, this policer has two separate buckets that are filled with two separate token rates. The Be bucket is filled with the PIR tokens, and the Bc bucket is filled with the CIR tokens. In this model, the Be represents the peak limit of traffic that can be sent during a subsecond interval.

The logic varies further in that the initial check is to see whether the traffic is within the PIR. Only then is the traffic compared against the CIR. In other words, a violate condition is checked first, then an exceed condition, and finally a conform condition, which is the reverse of the logic of the single-rate three-color policer. Figure 14-18 illustrates the token bucket algorithm for the two-rate three-color marker/policer. Compare it to the token bucket algorithm of the single-rate three-color marker/policer in Figure 14-16 to see the differences between the two.

Key Topic

To configure the two-rate policer, in addition to the CIR, the PIR needs to be specified. The PIR is configured with the **pir** keyword in the **police** command as follows:

police [cir] *cir-in-bps* **[bc]** *committed-burst-size-in-bytes* **pir** *pir-in-bps*
[be] *excess-burst-size-in-bytes* **[conform-action** *action***] [exceed-action** *action***] [violate-action** *action***]**

If Bc is not specified in the **police** command, the default is 1500 bytes or the configured CIR rate divided by 32 (CIR/32); whichever number is higher is chosen as the Bc size. If Be is not specified, the default is 1500 bytes or the configured PIR rate divided by 32 (PIR/32); whichever number is higher is chosen as the Be size.

Example 14-7 shows the configuration of a Two-Rate Three-Color (trTCM) policy map with one traffic class. For trTCM policies, the violate condition is checked first; therefore, traffic matching the VOIP-TELEPHONY class that violates the PIR of 100 Mbps will be dropped, traffic that exceeds the CIR of 50 Mbps is marked down and transmitted with DSCP AF31, and traffic that conforms to the CIR is transmitted as is.

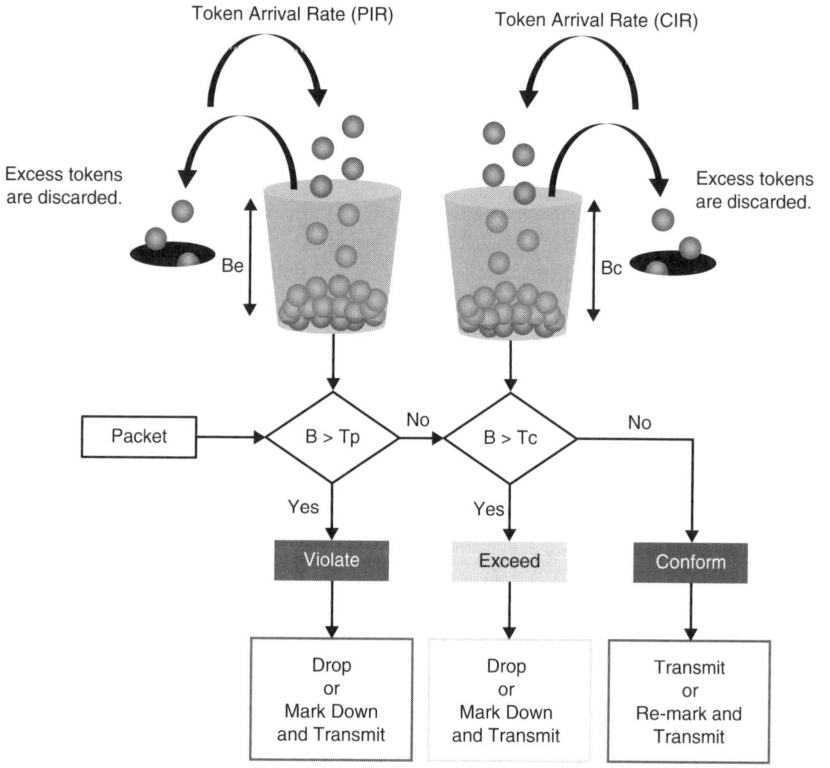

Figure 14-18 *Two-Rate Three-Color Marker/Policer Token Bucket Algorithm*

Example 14-7 *Two-Rate Three-Color Marker/Policer Example*

```
policy-map OUTBOUND-POLICY
  class VOIP-TELEPHONY
    police cir 50000000 pir 100000000 conform-action transmit exceed-action
set-dscp-transmit af31 violate-action drop
```

Example 14-8 shows the output of the **show policy-map** *policy-map-name* command for the OUTBOUND-POLICY. For the VOIP-TELEPHONY class, the Bc value was not specified; therefore, the default value is 50,000,000/32 (1,562,500 bytes). The Be value was also not specified; therefore, the default Be value is 100,000,000/32 (3,125,000).

Example 14-8 *Verifying Bc and Be Default Values*

```
router# show policy-map OUTBOUND-POLICY
  Policy Map OUTBOUND-POLICY
    Class VOIP-TELEPHONY
     police cir 50000000 bc 1562500 pir 100000000 be 3125000
       conform-action transmit
       exceed-action set-dscp-transmit af31
       violate-action drop
router#
```

Congestion Management and Avoidance

This section explores the queuing algorithms used for congestion management as well as packet drop techniques that can be used for congestion avoidance. These tools provide a way of managing excessive traffic during periods of congestion.

Congestion Management

Congestion management involves a combination of queuing and scheduling. Queuing (also known as *buffering*) is the temporary storage of excess packets. Queuing is activated when an output interface is experiencing congestion and deactivated when congestion clears. Congestion is detected by the queuing algorithm when a Layer 1 hardware queue present on physical interfaces, known as the *transmit ring (Tx-ring or TxQ)*, is full. When the Tx-ring is not full anymore, this indicates that there is no congestion on the interface, and queuing is deactivated. Congestion can occur for one of these two reasons:

- The input or ingress interface is a higher speed than the output or egress interface—for example, when packets are received on a 100 Gbps input interface and transmitted out of a 10 Gbps egress interface.
- Multiple input or ingress interfaces forwarding packets to a single output or egress interface that is a lower speed than the sum of the speeds of the input or ingress interfaces—for example, when packets are received on twenty 10 Gbps input interfaces simultaneously (summing up to 200 Gbps) and transmitted out of a single 100 Gbps egress interface.

When congestion is taking place, the queues fill up, and packets can be reordered by some of the queuing algorithms so that higher-priority packets exit the output interface sooner than lower-priority ones. At this point, a scheduling algorithm decides which packet to transmit next. Scheduling is always active, regardless of whether the interface is experiencing congestion.

Many queuing algorithms are available, but most of them are not adequate for modern rich-media networks carrying voice and high-definition video traffic because they were designed before these traffic types came to be. The legacy queuing algorithms that predate the MQC architecture include the following:

Key Topic

- **First-in, first-out queuing (FIFO):** FIFO involves a single queue where the first packet to be placed on the output interface queue is the first packet to leave the interface (first come, first served). In FIFO queuing, all traffic belongs to the same class.
- **Round robin:** With round robin, queues are serviced in sequence one after the other, and each queue processes one packet only. No queues starve with round robin because every queue gets an opportunity to send one packet every round. No queue has priority over others, and if the packet sizes from all queues are about the same, the interface bandwidth is shared equally across the round robin queues. A limitation of round robin is that it does not include a mechanism to prioritize traffic.
- **Weighted round robin (WRR):** WRR was developed to provide prioritization capabilities for round robin. It allows a weight to be assigned to each queue, and based on that weight, each queue effectively receives a portion of the interface bandwidth that is not necessarily equal to the other queues' portions.

- **Custom queuing (CQ):** CQ is a Cisco implementation of WRR that involves a set of 16 queues with a round-robin scheduler and FIFO queuing within each queue. Each queue can be customized with a portion of the link bandwidth for each selected traffic type. If a particular type of traffic is not using the bandwidth reserved for it, other traffic types may use the unused bandwidth. CQ causes long delays and also suffers from all the same problems as FIFO within each of the 16 queues that it uses for traffic classification.
- **Priority queuing (PQ):** With PQ, four queues in a set (high, medium, normal, and low) are served in strict-priority order, with FIFO queuing within each queue. The high-priority queue is always serviced first, and lower-priority queues are serviced only when all higher-priority queues are empty. For example, the medium queue is serviced only when the high-priority queue is empty. The normal queue is serviced only when the high and medium queues are empty; finally, the low queue is serviced only when all the other queues are empty. At any point in time, if a packet arrives for a higher queue, the packet from the higher queue is processed before any packets in lower-level queues. For this reason, if the higher-priority queues are continuously being serviced, the lower-priority queues are starved.
- **Weighted fair queuing (WFQ):** The WFQ algorithm automatically divides the interface bandwidth by the number of flows (weighted by IP Precedence) to allocate bandwidth fairly among all flows. This method provides better service for high-priority real-time flows but can't provide a fixed-bandwidth guarantee for any particular flow.

14

The current queuing algorithms recommended for rich-media networks (and supported by MQC) combine the best features of the legacy algorithms. These algorithms provide real-time, delay-sensitive traffic bandwidth and delay guarantees while not starving other types of traffic. The recommended queuing algorithms include the following:

Key Topic

- **Class-based weighted fair queuing (CBWFQ):** CBWFQ enables the creation of up to 256 queues, serving up to 256 traffic classes. Each queue is serviced based on the bandwidth assigned to that class. It extends WFQ functionality to provide support for user-defined traffic classes. With CBWFQ, packet classification is done based on traffic descriptors such as QoS markings, protocols, ACLs, and input interfaces. After a packet is classified as belonging to a specific class, it is possible to assign bandwidth, weight, queue limit, and maximum packet limit to it. The bandwidth assigned to a class is the minimum bandwidth delivered to the class during congestion. The queue limit for that class is the maximum number of packets allowed to be buffered in the class queue. After a queue has reached the configured queue limit, excess packets are dropped. CBWFQ by itself does not provide a latency guarantee and is only suitable for non-real-time data traffic.
- **Low-latency queuing (LLQ):** LLQ is CBWFQ combined with priority queuing (PQ), and it was developed to meet the requirements of real-time traffic, such as voice. Traffic assigned to the strict-priority queue is serviced up to its assigned bandwidth before other CBWFQ queues are serviced. All real-time traffic should be configured to be serviced by the priority queue. Multiple classes of real-time traffic can be defined, and separate bandwidth guarantees can be given to each, but a single priority queue

schedules all the combined traffic. If a traffic class is not using the bandwidth assigned to it, it is shared among the other classes.

This algorithm is suitable for combinations of real-time and non-real-time traffic. It provides both latency and bandwidth guarantees to high-priority real-time traffic. In the event of congestion, real-time traffic that goes beyond the assigned bandwidth guarantee is policed by a congestion-aware policer to ensure that the non-priority traffic is not starved.

Figure 14-19 illustrates the architecture of CBWFQ in combination with LLQ.

CBWFQ in combination with LLQ create queues into which traffic classes are classified. The CBWFQ queues are scheduled with a CBWFQ scheduler that guarantees bandwidth to each class. LLQ creates a high-priority queue that is always serviced first. During times of congestion, LLQ priority classes are policed to prevent the PQ from starving the CBWFQ non-priority classes (as legacy PQ does). When LLQ is configured, the policing rate must be specified as either a fixed amount of bandwidth or as a percentage of the interface bandwidth.

LLQ allows for two different traffic classes to be assigned to it so that different policing rates can be applied to different types of high-priority traffic. For example, voice traffic could be policed during times of congestion to 10 Mbps, while video could be policed to 100 Mbps. This would not be possible with only one traffic class and a single policer.

Congestion-Avoidance Tools

Congestion-avoidance techniques monitor network traffic loads to anticipate and avoid congestion by dropping packets. The default packet dropping mechanism is *tail drop*. Tail drop treats all traffic equally and does not differentiate between classes of service. With tail drop, when the output queue buffers are full, all packets trying to enter the queue are dropped, regardless of their priority, until congestion clears up and the queue is no longer full. Tail drop should be avoided for TCP traffic because it can cause TCP global synchronization. *TCP global synchronization* refers to the event that occurs when multiple TCP sessions that are sharing the same link back off their transmission rate simultaneously when the link becomes congested. When this happens, the link becomes underutilized and all the affected TCP sessions increase their transmission rate simultaneously, which causes the link to become congested again, and the cycle repeats over and over.

A better approach is to use a mechanism known as *random early detection (RED)*. RED provides congestion avoidance by randomly dropping packets before the queue buffers are full. Randomly dropping packets instead of dropping them all at once, as with tail drop, avoids global synchronization of TCP sessions. RED monitors the buffer depth and performs early drops on random packets when the minimum defined queue threshold is exceeded.

Key Topic

The Cisco implementation of RED is known as weighted RED (WRED). The difference between RED and WRED is that the randomness of packet drops can be manipulated by traffic weights denoted by either IP Precedence (IPP) or DSCP. Packets with a lower IPP value are dropped more aggressively than are higher IPP values; for example, IPP 3 would be dropped more aggressively than IPP 5 or DSCP, AFx3 would be dropped more aggressively than AFx2, and AFx2 would be dropped more aggressively than AFx1.

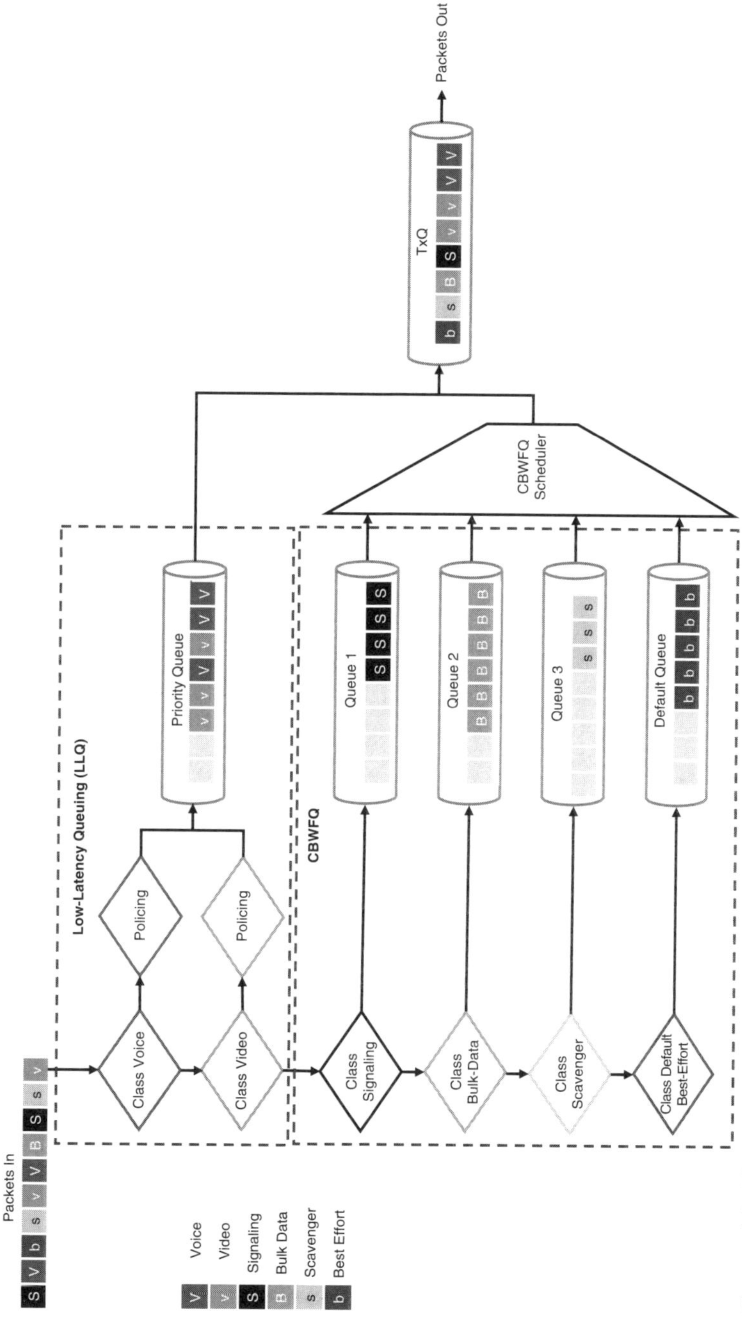

Figure 14-19 *CBWFQ with LLQ*

WRED can also be used to set the IP Explicit Congestion Notification (ECN) bits to indicate that congestion was experienced in transit. ECN is an extension to WRED that allows for signaling to be sent to ECN-enabled endpoints, instructing them to reduce their packet transmission rates.

CBWFQ Configuration

With CBWFQ, each traffic class in a policy map can perform queuing actions; therefore, a traffic class with queuing actions is functionally behaving as a queue. The **priority**, **bandwidth**, and **shape** commands are queuing (congestion management) actions that enable queuing for a class. The **bandwidth** and **shape** commands can be used together in the same class to provide a minimum bandwidth guarantee using the **bandwidth** command, and a maximum bandwidth based on the mean rate of the **shape** command. Table 14-10 lists the CBWFQ queuing commands and their syntax description.

> **NOTE** The commands discussed in this section may differ or may not be supported depending on the Cisco platform being used. Please visit www.cisco.com for specific command information relating to your platform.

Key Topic

Table 14-10 CBWFQ Queuing Commands and Descriptions

Command	Description
priority	Enables LLQ strict priority queuing. With this method, it is recommended to configure an explicit policer with the **police** command to rate-limit the priority traffic; otherwise, the other queues can be starved of bandwidth.
priority *police-rate-in-kbps* [*burst-in-bytes*]	Enables LLQ strict priority queuing with a conditional policing rate in kbps. Policing is in effect only during times of congestion.
priority percent *police-rate-in-percentage* [*burst-in-bytes*]	Enables LLQ strict priority queuing with a conditional policing rate calculated as a percentage of the interface bandwidth, or the shaping rate in a hierarchical policy. Policing is in effect only during times of congestion.
priority level {**1** | **2**}	Multilevel strict priority. With this method, it is recommended to configure an explicit policer with the **police** command to rate-limit the priority traffic; otherwise, the other queues can be starved of bandwidth.
priority level {**1** | **2**} *police-rate-in-kbps* [*burst-in-bytes*]	Multilevel strict priority with policing rate in kbps. Policing is in effect only during times of congestion.
priority level {**1** | **2**} **percent** *police-rate-in-percentage* [*burst-in-bytes*]	Multilevel strict priority with the policing rate calculated as a percentage of the interface bandwidth or the shaping rate in a hierarchical policy. Policing is in effect only during times of congestion.
bandwidth *bandwidth-kbps*	Minimum bandwidth guarantee, in kilobits per second (kbps), assigned to the class.
bandwidth remaining percent *percentage*	Minimum bandwidth guarantee based on a relative percent of the available bandwidth.

Command	Description
bandwidth remaining ratio *ratio*	Minimum bandwidth guarantee based on a relative ratio of the available bandwidth.
bandwidth percent *percentage*	Minimum bandwidth guarantee based on an absolute percent of the interface bandwidth, or the shaping rate in a hierarchical policy.
fair-queue	Enables flow-based queuing to manage multiple flows contending for a single queue.
shape {average | peak} *mean-rate-in-bps* [[*committed-burst-size*] [*excess-burst-size*]]	Enables class-based traffic shaping. **Average** shaping is used to forward packets at the configured mean rate and allows bursting up to the Bc at every Tc, and up to Be when extra tokens are available. This is the most-used shaping method. **Peak** shaping is used to forward packets at the mean rate multiplied by (1 + Be/Bc) at every Tc. This method is not commonly used. The mean rate can be configured with the postfix values **k** (Kbps), **m** (Mbps), and **g** (Gbps). The postfix values support decimal points. It is recommended to use the Bc and Be default values.

The **queue-limit** and **random-detect** commands are used for CBWFQ congestion avoidance (queue management) actions. Table 14-11 lists their syntax and command description.

Key Topic

Table 14-11 CBWFQ Queue Management Commands and Descriptions

Command	Description
queue-limit *queue-limit-size* **{cos cos-value | dscp dscp-value | precedence-value} percent** *percentage-of-packets*	Tail drop is the default packet dropping mechanism for every class. The **queue-limit** command is used in case there is a need to change the default tail drop values.
random-detect [dscp-based|precedence-based|cos-based]	This command enables WRED. The precedence-based option is the default. It is recommended to use **dscp-based** when using DSCP for classification. It is also recommended to use the default minimum threshold, maximum threshold, and drop probability values.

The following guidelines should be considered when configuring queuing policies:

Key Topic

- The **random-detect** and **fair-queue** commands require the **bandwidth** or **shape** commands to be present in the same user-defined class. This is not applicable to the default class.

- The **queue-limit** command requires the **bandwidth**, **shape**, or **priority** commands to be present in the same user-defined class. This is not applicable to the default class.

- The **random-detect**, **shape**, **fair-queue**, and **bandwidth** commands cannot coexist with the **priority** command in the same class.
- The **bandwidth** *bandwidth-kbps* or **bandwidth percent** commands cannot coexist in the same policy map with strict priority queues configured with the **priority** or **priority level** {1 | 2} commands, unless the strict-priority queues are being policed with the **police** command.
- The **bandwidth remaining percent** command can coexist with the **priority** or **priority level** {1 | 2} commands in the same policy map.
- Mixed **bandwidth** commands types are not supported in a policy map. They all need to be consistent across all the classes in the policy map.
- The **priority percent** *police-rate-in-percentage* or **priority level** {1 | 2} **percent** *police-rate-in-percentage* commands do not support an explicit policer configured with the **police** command.
- The sum total of all class bandwidths should not exceed 100%.
- Class-based traffic shaping is supported only in an outbound direction.

Example 14-9 shows a policy with multiple queuing classes configured. The VOIP and VIDEO classes are using multilevel priority policing, where they are each guaranteed a minimum bandwidth of 30% of the interface bandwidth. The CRITICAL and class-default classes are guaranteed a minimum bandwidth of 10%, the TRANSACTIONAL class a bandwidth of 15%, and for the SCAVENGER class, a bandwidth of 5%. For example, if the available bandwidth for the interface where the policy is applied is 1 Gbps, under congestion, the VOIP and VIDEO classes would each get a guaranteed minimum bandwidth of 300 Mbps (30% each), the CRITICAL and class-default classes would each get 100 Mbps (10% each), the TRANSACTIONAL class would get 150 Mbps (15%), and the SCAVENGER class would get 50 Mbps (5%).

Example 14-9 *Queuing Policy with Conditionally Policed Multilevel Priority Queues Example*

```
! The VOIP and VIDEO classes are conditionally policed.
! This means that the LLQ queues can use more than their configured
! policing rate if there is enough bandwidth available to use
policy-map QUEUING
  class VOIP
    priority level 1 percent 30
  class VIDEO
    priority level 2 percent 30
  class CRITICAL
    bandwidth percent 10
  class SCAVENGER
    bandwidth percent 5
  class TRANSACTIONAL
    bandwidth percent 15
 class class-default
    bandwidth percent 10
    fair-queue
```

```
    random-detect dscp-based
    queue-limit 64

interface GigabitEthernet1
  service-policy output QUEUING
```

Example 14-10 shows a similar policy as the one in Example 14-9. The difference is that in this new policy, the strict priority queues are not being policed (they are unconstrained). When strict priority queues are unconstrained, the rest of the classes/queues cannot be guaranteed a specific minimum bandwidth, and for this reason, the **bandwidth** *bandwidth-kbps* or **bandwidth percent** commands cannot coexist in the same policy map because they require specific minimum bandwidth guarantees.

The **bandwidth remaining** {**percent** *percentage* | **ratio** *ratio*} command can be used for this use case since it automatically adjusts to the relative percentage or ratio of the remaining bandwidth. For example, let's assume the VOIP and VIDEO classes are using 800 Mbps out of the available 1 Gbps for the interface. That would leave 200 Mbps available for the remaining classes. The CRITICAL class would get 80 Mbps (40% of 200 Mbps), and the rest of the classes would get 40 Mbps each (20% of 200 Mbps).

Example 14-10 *Queuing Policy with Unconstrained Multilevel Priority Queues Example*

```
! The VOIP and VIDEO classes do not have a policer (unconstrained).
! They can take up all of the available bandwidth, leaving
! no bandwidth remaining for the rest of the classes in the policy
policy-map QUEUING
  class VOIP
    priority level 1
  class VIDEO
    priority level 2
  class CRITICAL
    bandwidth remaining percent 40
! Each of the following classes can use up to 20 percent
! of the remaining bandwidth left by the strict priority queues
  class SCAVENGER
    bandwidth remaining percent 20
  class TRANSACTIONAL
    bandwidth remaining percent 20
  class class-default
    bandwidth remaining percent 20
    fair-queue
    random-detect dscp-based
    queue-limit 64

interface GigabitEthernet1
  service-policy output QUEUING
```

14

Let's assume outbound traffic of the 1 Gbps interface in Example 14-10 needs to be shaped to 100 Mbps to conform to the SLA of the SP, while keeping all the configuration of the QUEUING policy map intact. This can be achieved with class-based shaping in a hierarchical QoS policy.

Example 14-11 shows the policy from Example 14-10 applied as a child policy under the SHAPING parent policy. The SHAPING parent policy shapes all traffic to 100 Mbps. For this case, the QUEUING policy does not use the interface bandwidth of 1 Gbps as a reference for its queue bandwidth calculations; instead, it uses the mean rate of the traffic shaping policy, which is 100 Mbps. For example, let's assume the VOIP and VIDEO classes are using 80 Mbps out of the available 100 Mbps. That would leave 20 Mbps available for the remaining classes. The CRITICAL class would get 8 Mbps (40% of 20 Mbps), and the remaining three classes would each get 4 Mbps (20% of 20 Mbps).

Example 14-11 *Hierarchical Class-Based Shaping with Nested Queuing Example*

```
! Policy map SHAPING is the parent policy
policy-map SHAPING
  class class-default
     shape average 100000000
! Policy map QUEUING is the child policy
     service-policy QUEUING
! The parent policy SHAPING is the one applied to the interface
interface GigabitEthernet1
  service-policy output SHAPING
```

Exam Preparation Tasks

You have a couple of choices for exam preparation: the exercises here, Chapter 30, "Final Preparation," and the exam simulation questions in the Pearson Test Prep Software Online.

Review All Key Topics

Review the most important topics in the chapter, noted with the Key Topic icon in the outer margin of the page. Table 14-12 lists these key topics and the page number on which each is found.

Key Topic

Table 14-12 Key Topics for Chapter 14

Key Topic Element	Description	Page
List	QoS models	377
Paragraph	Integrated Services (IntServ)	377
Paragraph	Differentiated Services (DiffServ)	379
List	MQC components	379
Paragraph	Unclassified traffic	380
Paragraph	Policy maps	380

Key Topic Element	Description	Page
Paragraph	Service policies	380
Paragraph	Policy maps applied to policies	381
Section	Classification	381
List	Classification traffic descriptors	381
Section	Layer 7 Classification	382
Section	MQC Classification Configuration	382
Paragraph	**match** command	382
Paragraph	Matching criteria	383
Table 14-2	Most-Used MQC **match** Commands and Descriptions	383
Section	Marking	385
List	Marking traffic descriptors	385
Paragraph	802.1Q/p	385
List	802.1Q Tag Control Information (TCI) field	386
Section	Priority Code Point (PCP)	386
Paragraph	Type of Service (ToS) field	387
Paragraph	Differentiated Services Code Point (DSCP) field	387
Paragraph	Per-hop behavior (PHB) definition	387
List	Available PHBs	387
Section	Trust Boundary	391
Section	Class-Based Marking Configuration	392
Paragraph	Policing and shaping definition	394
Section	Markdown	395
List	Token bucket algorithm key definitions	395
Table 14-9	**police** Command Keywords and Keyword Descriptions	398
List	Policing algorithms	399
Paragraph	Two-rate policer	404
List	Legacy queuing algorithms	406
List	Current queuing algorithms	407
Paragraph	Weighted random early detection (WRED)	408
Table 14-10	CBWFQ Queuing Commands and Descriptions	410
Table 14-11	CBWFQ Queue Management Commands and Descriptions	411
List	Queuing policy guidelines	411

Complete Tables and Lists from Memory

Print a copy of Appendix B, "Memory Tables" (found on the companion website), or at least the section for this chapter, and complete the tables and lists from memory. Appendix C, "Memory Tables Answer Key," also on the companion website, includes completed tables and lists you can use to check your work.

Define Key Terms

Define the following key terms from this chapter and check your answers in the Glossary:

802.1Q, 802.1p, Differentiated Services (DiffServ), Differentiated Services Code Point (DSCP), per-hop behavior (PHB), type of service (ToS)

Use the Command Reference to Check Your Memory

Table 14-13 lists the important commands from this chapter. To test your memory, cover the right side of the table with a piece of paper, read the description on the left side, and see how much of the command you can remember.

Table 14-13 Command Reference

Task	Command Syntax
Apply an inbound policy map to an interface	**service-policy input** *policy-map-name*
Mark the DSCP value for IPv4 and IPv6 packets	**set [ip] dscp** *ip-dscp-value*
Apply a policy map under class-default	**class class-default** **service-policy** *policy-map-name*
LLQ with a 100 Mbps conditional policer	**priority 100000** Command syntax: **priority** *police-rate-in-kbps* [*burst-in-bytes*]
Configure an explicit class-based policer with a cir of 100 Mbps and a Bc of 312,500 bytes	**police 100000000 bc 3125000** or **police 100 m bc 3125000** or **police cir 100000000 bc 3125000** or **police cir 100 m bc 3125000** Command syntax: **police [cir]** *cir-in-bps* **[bc]** *committed-burst-size-in-bytes* **[be]** *excess-burst-size-in-bytes* **[conform-action** *action*] **[exceed-action** *action*] **[violate-action** *action*]
Enable WRED for IP Precedence	**random-detect** IP Precedence is the default option
Configure a class-based shaper with an average mean rate of 100 Mbps and the recommended Bc and Be values	**shape average 100 m** or **shape average 100000000** Default Bc and Be values are recommended
Configure a policy map named TEST with a class called TEST	**policy-map TEST** **class TEST**

Task	Command Syntax
Configure a class map where all match conditions within the class-map must be met	**class-map** *class-map-name* or **class-map match-all** *class-map-name* **match-all** is the default action
Configure the default class with a minimum bandwidth guarantee of 100 Kbps and a maximum average bandwidth of 100 Mbps	**class class-default** **bandwidth 100** **shape average 100 m** or **class class-default** **bandwidth 100** **shape average 100000000**

References in This Chapter

RFC 1633, *Integrated Services in the Internet Architecture: An Overview*, R. Braden, D. Clark, and S. Shenker. https://tools.ietf.org/html/rfc1633, June 1994.

RFC 2474, *Definition of the Differentiated Services Field (DS Field) in the IPv4 and IPv6 Headers*, K. Nichols, S. Blake, F. Baker, and D. Black. https://tools.ietf.org/html/rfc2474, December 1998.

RFC 2475, *An Architecture for Differentiated Services*, S. Blake, D. Black, M. Carlson, E. Davies, Z. Wang, and W. Weiss. https://tools.ietf.org/html/rfc2475, December 1998.

RFC 2597, *Assured Forwarding PHB Group*, J. Heinanen, Telia Finland, F. Baker, W. Weiss, and J. Wroclawski. https://tools.ietf.org/html/rfc2597, June 1999.

RFC 2697, *A Single Rate Three Color Marker*, J. Heinanen, Telia Finland, R. Guerin, and IETF. https://tools.ietf.org/html/rfc2697, September 1999.

RFC 2698, *A Two Rate Three Color Marker*, J. Heinanen, Telia Finland, R. Guerin, and IETF. https://tools.ietf.org/html/rfc2698, September 1999.

RFC 3140, *Per Hop Behavior Identification Codes*, D. Black, S. Brim, B. Carpenter, F. Le Faucheur, and IETF. https://tools.ietf.org/html/rfc3140, June 2001.

RFC 3246, *An Expedited Forwarding PHB (Per-Hop Behavior)*, B. Davie, A. Charny, J.C.R. Bennett, K. Benson, J.Y. Le Boudec, W. Courtney, S. Davari, V. Firoiu, and D. Stiliadis. https://tools.ietf.org/html/rfc3246, March 2002.

RFC 3260, *New Terminology and Clarifications for Diffserv*, D. Grossman and IETF. https://tools.ietf.org/html/rfc3260, April 2002.

RFC 4594, *Configuration Guidelines for DiffServ Service Classes*, J. Babiarz, K. Chan, F. Baker, and IETF. https://tools.ietf.org/html/rfc4594, August 2006.

CHAPTER 15

IP Services

This chapter covers the following subjects:

- **Time Synchronization:** This section describes the need for synchronizing time in an environment and covers Network Time Protocol and its operations to keep time consistent across devices.
- **Precision Time Protocol (PTP):** This section describes a newer high-precision distributed time synchronization protocol that is used to synchronize clocks across an Ethernet network.
- **First-Hop Redundancy Protocol:** This section gives details on how multiple routers can provide resilient gateway functionality to hosts at the Layer 2/Layer 3 boundaries.
- **Network Address Translation (NAT):** This section explains how a router can translate IP addresses from one network realm to another.

In addition to routing and switching network packets, a router can perform additional functions to enhance a network. This chapter covers time synchronization, virtual gateway technologies, and Network Address Translation.

"Do I Know This Already?" Quiz

The "Do I Know This Already?" quiz enables you to assess whether you should read the entire chapter. If you miss no more than one of these self-assessment questions, you might want to move ahead to the "Exam Preparation Tasks" section. Table 15-1 lists the major headings in this chapter and the "Do I Know This Already?" quiz questions covering the material in those headings so you can assess your knowledge of these specific areas. The answers to the "Do I Know This Already?" quiz appear in Appendix A, "Answers to the 'Do I Know This Already?' Questions."

Table 15-1 "Do I Know This Already?" Foundation Topics Section-to-Question Mapping

Foundation Topics Section	Questions
Time Synchronization	1–2
Precision Time Protocol (PTP)	3
First-Hop Redundancy Protocol	4–7
Network Address Translation (NAT)	8–10

1. NTP uses the concept of _______ to calculate the accuracy of the time source.
   a. administrative distance
   b. stratum
   c. atomic half-life
   d. deviation time
2. True or false: An NTP client can be configured with multiple NTP servers and can synchronize its local clock with all the servers.
   a. True
   b. False
3. True or false: PTPv2 is backward compatible with PTP.
   a. True
   b. False
4. In a resilient network topology, first-hop redundancy protocols (FHRPs) overcome the limitations of which of the following? (Choose two.)
   a. Static default routes
   b. Link-state routing protocols
   c. Vector-based routing protocols
   d. A computer with only one default gateway
5. Which of the following FHRPs are considered Cisco proprietary? (Choose two.)
   a. VRRP
   b. HSRP
   c. GLBP
   d. ODR
6. Which of the following commands defines the HSRP instance 1 VIP gateway instance 10.1.1.1?
   a. **standby 1 ip 10.1.1.1**
   b. **hsrp 1 ip 10.1.1.1**
   c. **hsrp 1 vip 10.1.1.1**
   d. **hsrp 1 10.1.1.1**
7. Which of the following FHRPs supports load balancing?
   a. ODR
   b. VRRP
   c. HSRP
   d. GLBP
8. Which command displays the translation table on a router?
   a. **show ip translations**
   b. **show ip xlate**
   c. **show xlate**
   d. **show ip nat translations**

9. A router connects multiple private networks in the 10.0.0.0/8 network range to the Internet. A user's IP address of 10.1.1.1 is considered the __________ IP address.
   a. inside local
   b. inside global
   c. outside local
   d. outside global
10. The IP translation table times out and clears dynamic TCP connection entries from the translation table after how long?
   a. 1 hour
   b. 4 hours
   c. 12 hours
   d. 24 hours

Foundation Topics

Time Synchronization

A device's system time is used to measure periods of idle state or computation. Ensuring that the time is consistent on a system is important because applications often use the system time to tune internal processes. From the perspective of managing a network, it is important that the time be synchronized between network devices for several reasons:

- Managing passwords that change at specific time intervals
- Handling encryption key exchanges
- Checking validity of certificates based on expiration date and time
- Correlating security-based events across multiple devices (routers, switches, firewalls, network access control systems, and so on)
- Troubleshooting network devices and correlating events to identify the root cause of an event

Without a method of synchronization, time can deviate from device to device. Even if the time was accurately set on all the devices, the time intervals could be faster on one device than on another device. Eventually, the times would start to drift away from each other. Some devices use only a software clock, which is reset when the power is reset. Other devices use a hardware clock, which can maintain time when the power is reset.

Key Topic

Network Time Protocol

RFC 958 introduced Network Time Protocol (NTP), which is used to synchronize a set of network clocks in a distributed client/server architecture. NTP is a UDP-based protocol that connects with servers on port 123. The client source port is dynamic.

NTP is based on a hierarchical concept of communication. At the top of the hierarchy are authoritative devices that operate as an **NTP server** with an atomic clock. The **NTP client** then queries the NTP server for its time and updates its time based on the response. Because NTP is considered an application, the query can occur over multiple hops, requiring NTP clients to identify the time accuracy based on messages with other routers.

The NTP synchronization process is not fast. In general, an NTP client can synchronize a large time discrepancy to within a couple seconds of accuracy with a few cycles of polling an NTP server. However, gaining accuracy of tens of milliseconds requires hours or days of comparisons. In some ways, the time of the NTP clients drifts toward the time of the NTP server.

Key Topic

NTP uses the concept of **stratums** to identify the accuracy of the time clock source. NTP servers that are directly attached to an authoritative time source are stratum 1 servers. An NTP client that queries a stratum 1 server is considered a stratum 2 client. The higher the stratum, the greater the chance of deviation in time from the authoritative time source due to the number of time drifts between the NTP stratums.

Figure 15-1 demonstrates the concept of stratums, with R1 attached to an atomic clock and considered a stratum 1 server. R2 is configured to query R1, so it is considered a stratum 2 client. R3 is configured to query R2, so it is considered a stratum 3 client. This could continue until stratum 15. Notice that R4 is configured to query R1 over multiple hops, and it is therefore considered a stratum 2 client.

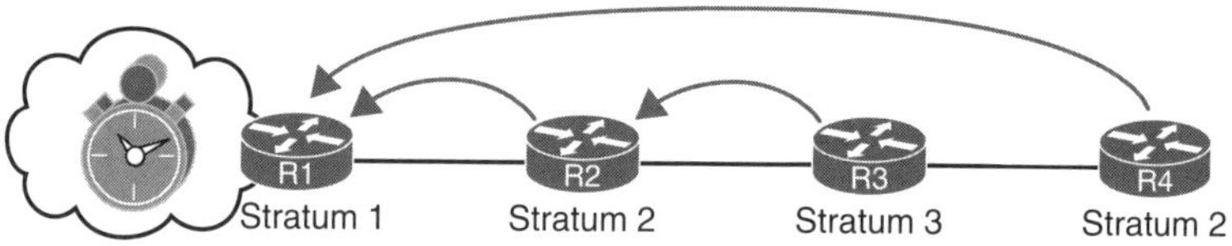

Figure 15-1 *NTP Stratums*

NTP Configuration

The configuration of an NTP client is pretty straightforward. The client configuration uses the global configuration command **ntp server** *ip-address* [**prefer**] [**source** *interface-id*]. The source interface, which is optional, is used to stipulate the source IP address for queries for that server. Multiple NTP servers can be configured for redundancy, and adding the optional **prefer** keyword indicates which NTP server time synchronization should come from.

Cisco devices can act as a server after they have been able to query an NTP server. For example, in Figure 15-1, once R2 has synchronized time with R1 (a stratum 1 time source), R2 can act as a server to R3. Configuration of external clocks is beyond the scope of this book. However, you should know that you can use the command **ntp master** *stratum-number* to statically set the stratum for a device when it acts as an NTP server.

Example 15-1 demonstrates the configuration of R1, R2, R3, and R4 from Figure 15-1.

Example 15-1 *Simple Multi-Stratum NTP Configuration*

```
R1# configure terminal
Enter configuration commands, one per line. End with CNTL/Z.
R1(config)# ntp master 1
```

```
R2# configure terminal
Enter configuration commands, one per line. End with CNTL/Z.
R2(config)# ntp server 192.168.1.1
```

```
R3# configure terminal
Enter configuration commands, one per line. End with CNTL/Z.
R3(config)# ntp server 192.168.2.2 source loopback 0
```

```
R4# configure terminal
Enter configuration commands, one per line. End with CNTL/Z.
R4(config)# ntp server 192.168.1.1
```

To view the status of NTP service, use the command **show ntp status**, which has the following output:

1. Whether the hardware clock is synchronized to the software clock (that is, whether the clock resets during power reset), the stratum reference of the local device, and the reference clock identifier (local or IP address)
2. The frequency and precision of the clock
3. The NTP uptime and granularity
4. The reference time
5. The clock offset and delay between the client and the lower-level stratum server
6. Root dispersion (that is, the calculated error of the actual clock attached to the atomic clock) and peer dispersion (that is, the root dispersion plus the estimated time to reach the root NTP server)
7. NTP loopfilter (which is beyond the scope of this book)
8. Polling interval and time since last update

Example 15-2 displays the output of the NTP status from R1, R2, and R3. Notice that the stratum has incremented, along with the reference clock.

Example 15-2 *Viewing NTP Status*

```
R1# show ntp status
Clock is synchronized, stratum 1, reference is .LOCL.
nominal freq is 250.0000 Hz, actual freq is 250.0000 Hz, precision is 2**10
ntp uptime is 2893800 (1/100 of seconds), resolution is 4000
reference time is E0E2D211.E353FA40 (07:48:17.888 EST Wed Jul 24 2019)
clock offset is 0.0000 msec, root delay is 0.00 msec
root dispersion is 2.24 msec, peer dispersion is 1.20 msec
```

Answers to the "Do I Know This Already?" quiz:

1 B **2** B **3** B **4** A, D **5** B, C **6** A **7** D **8** D **9** A **10** D

```
loopfilter state is 'CTRL' (Normal Controlled Loop), drift is 0.000000000 s/s
system poll interval is 16, last update was 4 sec ago.
```

```
R2# show ntp status
Clock is synchronized, stratum 2, reference is 192.168.1.1
nominal freq is 250.0000 Hz, actual freq is 249.8750 Hz, precision is 2**10
ntp uptime is 2890200 (1/100 of seconds), resolution is 4016
reference time is E0E2CD87.28B45C3E (07:28:55.159 EST Wed Jul 24 2019)
clock offset is 1192351.4980 msec, root delay is 1.00 msec
root dispersion is 1200293.33 msec, peer dispersion is 7938.47 msec
loopfilter state is 'SPIK' (Spike), drift is 0.000499999 s/s
system poll interval is 64, last update was 1 sec ago.
```

```
R3# show ntp status
Clock is synchronized, stratum 3, reference is 192.168.2.2
nominal freq is 250.0000 Hz, actual freq is 250.0030 Hz, precision is 2**10
ntp uptime is 28974300 (1/100 of seconds), resolution is 4000
reference time is E0E2CED8.E147B080 (07:34:32.880 EST Wed Jul 24 2019)
clock offset is 0.5000 msec, root delay is 2.90 msec
root dispersion is 4384.26 msec, peer dispersion is 3939.33 msec
loopfilter state is 'CTRL' (Normal Controlled Loop), drift is -0.000012120 s/s
system poll interval is 64, last update was 36 sec ago.
```

A streamlined version of the NTP server status and delay is provided with the command **show ntp associations.** The address 127.127.1.1 reflects to the local device when configured with the **ntp master** *stratum-number* command. Example 15-3 shows the NTP associations for R1, R2, and R3.

Example 15-3 *Viewing the NTP Associations*

```
R1# show ntp associations

  address         ref clock       st   when   poll reach  delay  offset   disp
*~127.127.1.1     .LOCL.  0        0     16    377  0.000  0.000  1.204
 * sys.peer, # selected, + candidate, - outlyer, x falseticker, ~ configured
```

```
R2# show ntp associations

  address         ref clock       st   when   poll reach  delay  offset   disp
*~192.168.1.1     127.127.1.1      1    115   1024     1  1.914   0.613 191.13
 * sys.peer, # selected, + candidate, - outlyer, x falseticker, ~ configured
```

```
R3# show ntp associations

  address         ref clock       st   when   poll reach  delay  offset   disp
*~192.168.2.2     192.168.1.1      2     24     64     1  1.000   0.500 440.16
 * sys.peer, # selected, + candidate, - outlyer, x falseticker, ~ configured
```

Key Topic

Stratum Preference

An NTP client can be configured with multiple NTP servers. The device will use only the NTP server with the lowest stratum. The top portion of Figure 15-2 shows R4 with two NTP sessions: one session with R1 and another with R3.

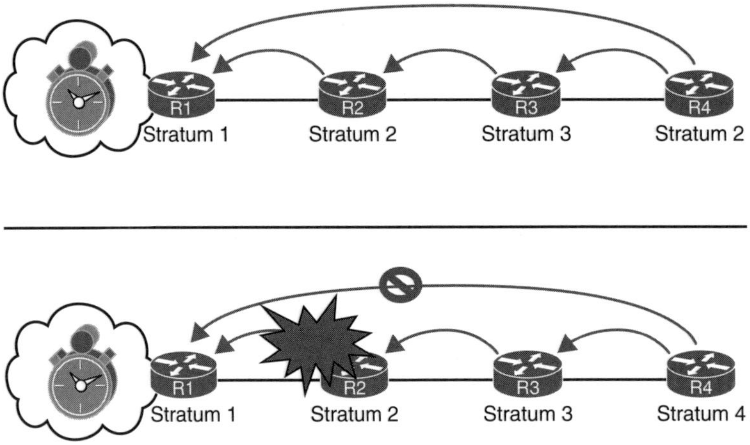

Figure 15-2 *NTP Stratum Preferences*

In the topology shown in Figure 15-2, R4 will always use R1 for synchronizing its time because it is a stratum 1 server. If R2 crashes, as shown at the bottom of Figure 15-2, preventing R4 from reaching R1, it synchronizes with R3's time (which may or may not be different due to time drift) and turns into a stratum 4 time device. When R2 recovers, R4 synchronizes with R1 and becomes a stratum 2 device again.

Key Topic

NTP Peers

Within the NTP client architecture, the NTP client changes its time to the time of the NTP server. The NTP server does not change its time to reflect the clients. Most enterprise organizations (such as universities, governments, and pool.ntp.org) use an external NTP server. A common scenario is to designate two devices to query a different external NTP source and then to peer their local stratum 2 NTP devices.

NTP peers act as clients and servers to each other, in the sense that they try to blend their time to each other. The NTP peer model is intended for designs where other devices can act as backup devices for each other and use different primary reference sources.

Figure 15-3 shows a scenario where R1 is an NTP client to 100.64.1.1, and R2 is an NTP client to 100.64.2.2. R1 and R2 are NTP peers with each other, so they query each other and move their time toward each other.

NOTE An NTP peer that is configured with an authoritative time source treats its peer as an equal and shifts its clock to synchronize with the peer. The peers adjust at a maximum rate of two minutes per query, so large discrepancies take some time to correct.

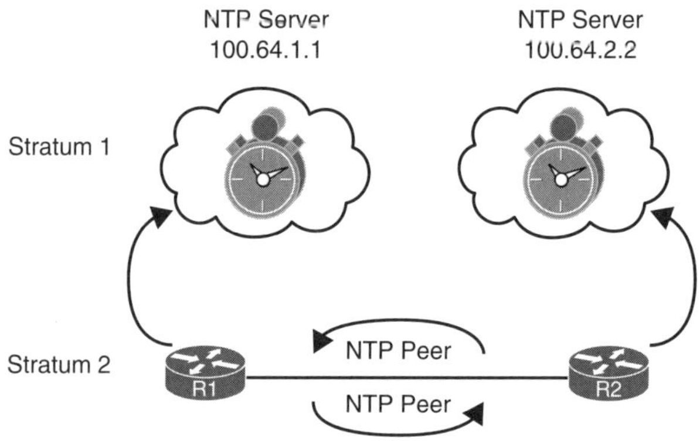

Figure 15-3 *NTP Stratums*

NTP peers are configured with the command **ntp peer** *ip-address*. Example 15-4 shows the sample NTP peer configuration for R1 and R2 (refer to Figure 15-3) peering with their loopback interfaces.

Example 15-4 *NTP Peer Configuration*

```
R1# configure terminal
Enter configuration commands, one per line. End with CNTL/Z.
R1(config)# ntp peer 192.168.2.2
```

```
R2# configure terminal
Enter configuration commands, one per line. End with CNTL/Z.
R2(config)# ntp peer 192.168.1.1
```

Key Topic

Precision Time Protocol (PTP)

IEEE 1588-2002 defined **Precision Time Protocol (PTP)** as a mechanism to provide clock synchronization for networked measurement and control systems. This mechanism was designed to synchronize network clocks on devices that are distributed throughout the network. PTP was updated in IEEE 1588-2008 (known as PTPv2) and is not backward-compatible with regular PTP.

Industrial networks are extremely sensitive to time drift and justified the creation of PTP. PTP is also an attractive feature because it requires minimal bandwidth and overhead to function. PTP offers more precise and accurate time, which is crucial for some of the new devices that work on packet-based networks. An example of this could be energy providers. They need to provide accurate usage measurement for peak and off-peak billing rates.

PTP can dynamically adjust device clocks in the network. This capability allows the distributed devices to stay synchronized with one another in the event of packet delay. This packet delay can arise due to intermittent moments of congestion and interface buffering as well as any kind of memory delay. Memory delay can impact packets and cause latency when a device such as a switch looks up MAC addresses in the MAC address table while verifying CRC fields in the packet. Packets coming out of the local memory of the device could potentially be forwarded with varying latency impacting network time.

PTP can address these concerns by adjusting the distributed clocks on the devices to accommodate for these scenarios. This adjustment is achieved through a series of PTPv2 message exchanges between other devices. These messages are then measured to look at the delay received in each direction between devices. This delay is an average that is run on all the received and transmitted messages to come up with the calculation. Transparent clocks are the mechanism used to make these calculations. Transparent clocks connect the PTP Server and PTP Client clocks. Other devices point to these clocks to reduce the latency of getting time from the PTP Server clock.

The two PTPv2 message types are *Event* and *General* messages. The General Events are not timestamped and are used to build the client/server topology.

The General message types are

- **Announce:** Used to determine which Grand Master is selected Best Master
- **Follow_Up:** Used to convey a captured timestamp of a transmitted SYNC message
- **Delay_Response:** Used to measure delay between IEEE 1588 devices
- **Pdelay_Response_Follow_Up:** Used between IEEE 1588 devices to measure the delay on an incoming link
- **Management:** Used between management devices and clocks
- **Signaling:** Used by clocks to deliver how messages are sent

The Announce message is used to set up the server/client topology or hierarchy, similar to hello packets; whereas Follow_Up and Delay_Response messages are used to synchronize ordinary and boundary clocks. A boundary clock is a device that is between areas of the network that can exchange these messages with other devices that are closer to them, like a geographic hierarchy.

The Event message types consist of

- **Sync:** Used to convey time
- **Delay_Request:** Used to measure delay from downstream devices
- **Pdelay_Request:** Used to initiate and measure delay
- **Pdelay_Response:** Used to respond and measure delay

These message types are critical because they contain the timestamps indicating when the data packets are passing through the ingress or egress of an interface. These timestamps are used to calculate the delay seen between the messages. Sync and Delay_Request messages are used to synchronize ordinary and boundary clocks as well; whereas Pdelay_Request, Pdelay_Response, and Pdelay_Response_Follow_Up messages are used to measure the link delay between the devices.

Similar to NTP, there is the concept of a server and client along with redundancy capabilities. If the primary server is down, the clients will redirect to the secondary server. Figure 15-4 illustrates a high-level view of a network running PTP.

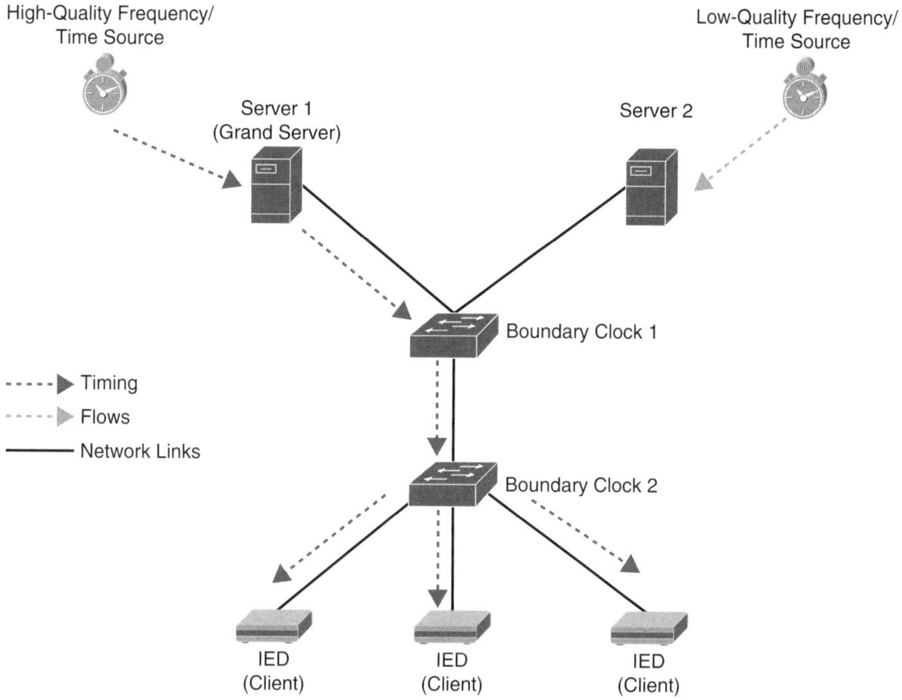

Figure 15-4 *PTP Hierarchy*

PTP Configuration

The configuration of PTP is slightly different than that of NTP. There are multiple options. You can configure PTP globally to pass the PTPv2 packets as multicast traffic in *Forward* mode, which will synchronize all switch ports with the Grand Server, which is the most accurate clock in the environment. However, as an alternative, PTP can be configured to be in *Boundary* mode. A requirement for per port PTP, the switch must be in Boundary mode. By default, after PTP is enabled, it is enabled on all fast Ethernet and gigabit Ethernet switch ports on a switch. Table 15-2 highlights the default settings on a Cisco IE2000 switch.

Table 15-2 Default PTP Parameters on a Cisco IE2000 Switch

Feature	Default Setting
PTP Boundary Mode	Disabled
PTP Forward Mode	Disabled
PTP Transparent Mode	Enabled
PTP Priority1 and PTP Priority2	Default Priority is 128
PTP Announce Interval	2 Seconds
PTP Announce Timeout	8 Seconds
PTP Delay Request Interval	32 Seconds
PTP Sync Interval	1 Second
PTP Sync Limit	50,000 Nanoseconds

Now that we've covered the basics on what PTP is and is used for, Example 15-5 lists the configuration of PTP Boundary mode on SW1 and End-to-End Transparent mode on SW2. Keep in mind that after PTP is enabled in Boundary mode, all enabled ports on connecting switches will automatically have PTP enabled. This is evident by the **Port State FAULTY: FALSE** line of the output on SW2. In contrast, if the Port State reads Port State FAULTY: TRUE, then there is an issue with SW2 communicating with SW1.

Example 15-5 *PTP Configuration Example on Cisco IE2000 Switch*

```
SW1# configure terminal
Enter configuration commands, one per line. End with CNTL/Z.
SW1(config)# ptp mode boundary
```

```
SW1# show ptp clock
 PTP CLOCK INFO
  PTP Device Type: Boundary clock
  PTP Device Profile: Default Profile
  Clock Identity: 0x00:60:5C:FF:FE:18:8C:00
  Clock Domain: 0
  Number of PTP ports: 10
  Priority1: 128
  Priority2: 128
  Clock Quality:
        Class: 248
        Accuracy: Unknown
        Offset (log variance): N/A
  Offset From Master(ns): 0
  Mean Path Delay(ns): 0
  Steps Removed: 0
  Local clock time: 01:40:15 UTC March 15 2023
```

```
SW2# show ptp clock
 PTP CLOCK INFO
  PTP Device Type: End to End transparent clock
  PTP Device Profile: Default Profile
  Clock Identity: 0x00:0A:F3:FF:FE:15:A8:00
  Clock Domain: 0
  Number of PTP ports: 10
  Delay Mechanism: End to End
  Local clock time: 01:36:55 UTC March 15 2023
```

```
SW2# show ptp port fa1/1
 PTP PORT DATASET: FastEthernet1/1
  Port identity: clock identity: 0x00:0A:F3:FF:FE:15:A8:00
```

```
Port identity: port number: 1
PTP version: 2
Port state FAULTY: FALSE
Sync fault limit: 500000000
```

NOTE The PTP features and configuration options vary depending on the device type and product family. Review the configuration guides to validate the configuration options for your device. PTP has many options; this section is designed to give a high-level nonexhaustive understanding of PTP.

First-Hop Redundancy Protocol

Network resiliency is a key component of network design. Resiliency with Layer 2 forwarding is accomplished by adding multiple Layer 2 switches into a topology. Resiliency with Layer 3 forwarding is accomplished by adding multiple Layer 3 paths or routers.

Figure 15-5 shows the concept of adding resiliency by using multiple Layer 2 switches and routers on the left or by adding resiliency with multiple multilayer switches on the right. In both scenarios:

- Two devices (172.16.1.2 and 172.16.1.3) can be the PC's gateway.
- There are two resilient Layer 2 links that connect SW6 to a switch that can connect the PC to either gateway.

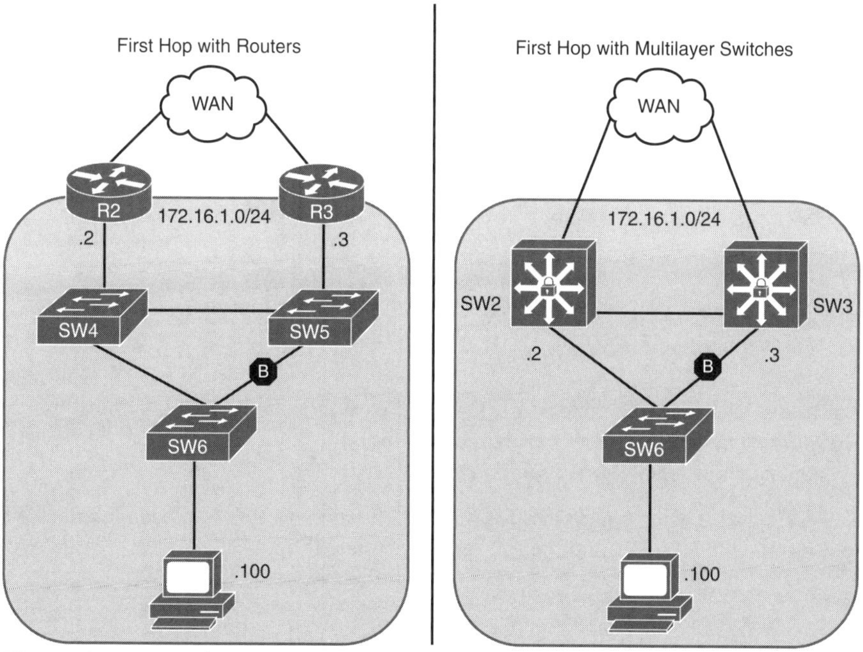

Figure 15-5 *Resiliency with Redundancy with Layer 2 and Layer 3 Devices*

NOTE STP is blocking traffic between SW6 and SW5 on the left and between SW6 and SW3 on the right in Figure 15-5.

The PC could configure its gateway as 172.16.1.2, but what happens when that device fails? The same problem occurs if the other gateway was configured. How can a host be configured with more than one gateway? Some operating systems support the configuration of multiple gateways, and others do not. Providing gateway accessibility to all devices is very important.

Key Topic

The deployment of **first-hop redundancy protocols** (FHRPs) solves the problem of hosts configuring multiple gateways. FHRPs work by creating a virtual IP (VIP) gateway instance that is shared between the Layer 3 devices. This book covers the following FHRPs:

- Hot Standby Router Protocol (HSRP)
- Virtual Router Redundancy Protocol (VRRP)
- Gateway Load Balancing Protocol (GLBP)

Object Tracking

FHRPs are deployed in a network for reliability and high availability to ensure load balancing and failover capability in case of a router failover. To ensure optimal traffic flow when a WAN link goes down, it would be nice to be able to determine the availability of routes or the interface state to which FHRP route traffic is directed.

Object tracking offers a flexible and customizable mechanism for linking with FHRPs and other routing components (for example, conditional installation of a static route). With this feature, users can track specific objects in the network and take necessary action when any object's state change affects network traffic.

Figure 15-6 shows a simple topology with three routers exchanging routes with EIGRP and advertising their loopback interfaces to EIGRP.

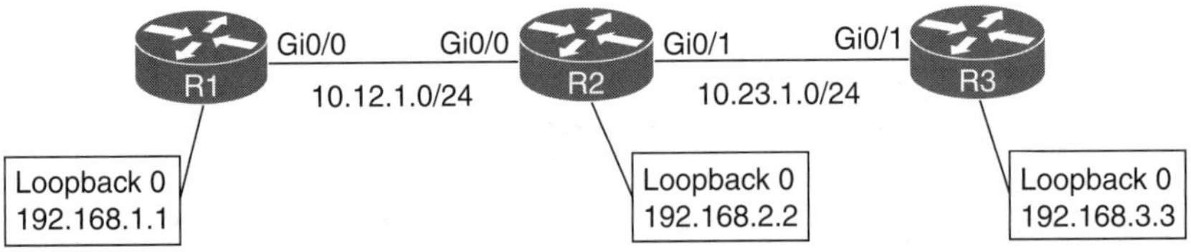

Figure 15-6 *Object Tracking*

Tracking of routes in the routing table is accomplished with the command **track** *object-number* **ip route** *route/prefix-length* **reachability**. The status object tracking can be viewed with the command **show track** [*object-number*].

Example 15-6 shows R1 being configured for tracking the route to R3's loopback interface. The route is installed in R1's RIB, and the tracked object state is up.

Example 15-6 *Tracking R3's Loopback Interface*

```
R1# configure terminal
Enter configuration commands, one per line. End with CNTL/Z.
R1(config)# track 1 ip route 192.168.3.3/32 reachability
```

```
R1# show track
Track 1
  IP route 192.168.3.3 255.255.255.255 reachability
  Reachability is Up (EIGRP)
    1 change, last change 00:00:32
  First-hop interface is GigabitEthernet0/0
```

Tracking of an interface's line protocol state is accomplished with the command **track** *object-number* **interface** *interface-id* **line-protocol**.

Example 15-7 shows R2 being configured for tracking the Gi0/1 interface toward R3. The line protocol for the interface is up.

Example 15-7 *Tracking R2's Gi0/1 Interface Line Protocol State*

```
R2# configure terminal
Enter configuration commands, one per line. End with CNTL/Z.
R2(config)# track 2 interface GigabitEthernet0/1 line-protocol
```

```
R2# show track
Track 2
  Interface GigabitEthernet0/1 line-protocol
  Line protocol is Up
    1 change, last change 00:00:37
```

Shutting down R2's Gi0/1 interface should change the tracked object state on R1 and R2 to a down state. Example 15-8 shows the shutdown of R2's Gi0/1 interface. Notice that the tracked state for R2 and R1 changed shortly after the interface was shut down.

Example 15-8 *Demonstrating a Change of Tracked State*

```
R2# configure terminal
Enter configuration commands, one per line. End with CNTL/Z.
R2(config)# interface GigabitEthernet0/1
R2(config-if)# shutdown
*03:04:18.975: %TRACK-6-STATE: 2 interface Gi0/1 line-protocol Up -> Down
*03:04:18.980: %DUAL-5-NBRCHANGE: EIGRP-IPv4 100: Neighbor 10.23.1.3 (GigabitEther-
net0/1) is * 03:04:20.976: %LINK-5-CHANGED: Interface GigabitEthernet0/1, changed
state to administratively down
* 03:04:21.980: %LINEPROTO-5-UPDOWN: Line protocol on Interface GigabitEthernet0/1,
changed state to down
```

```
R1#
03:04:24.007: %TRACK-6-STATE: 1 ip route 192.168.3.3/32 reachability Up -> Down
```

Example 15-9 shows the current track state for R1 and R2. R1 no longer has the 192.168.3.3/32 network in the RIB, and R2's Gi0/1 interface is in shutdown state.

Example 15-9 *Viewing the Track State After a Change*

```
R1# show track
Track 1
  IP route 192.168.3.3 255.255.255.255 reachability
  Reachability is Down (no ip route)
    2 changes, last change 00:02:09
 First-hop interface is unknown
```

```
R2# show track
Track 2
  Interface GigabitEthernet0/1 line-protocol
  Line protocol is Down ((hw admin-down))
    2 changes, last change 00:01:58
```

Object tracking works with protocols such as Hot Standby Router Protocol (HSRP), Virtual Router Redundancy Protocol (VRRP), and Gateway Load Balancing Protocol (GLBP) so that they take action when the state of an object changes. FHRP commonly tracks the availability of the WAN interface or the existence of a route learned via that next hop.

Key Topic

Hot Standby Router Protocol

Hot Standby Router Protocol (HSRP) is a Cisco proprietary protocol that provides transparent failover of the first-hop device, which typically acts as a gateway to the hosts.

HSRP provides routing redundancy for IP hosts on an Ethernet network configured with a default gateway IP address. A minimum of two devices is required to enable HSRP: One device acts as the active device and takes care of forwarding the packets, and the other acts as a standby that is ready to take over the role of active device in the event of a failure.

On a network segment, a virtual IP address is configured on each HSRP-enabled interface that belongs to the same HSRP group. HSRP selects one of the interfaces to act as the HSRP active router. Along with the virtual IP address, a virtual MAC address is assigned for the group. The active router receives and routes the packets destined for the virtual MAC address of the group.

When the HSRP active router fails, the HSRP standby router assumes control of the virtual IP address and virtual MAC address of the group. The HSRP election selects the router with the highest priority (which defaults to 100). In the event of a tie in priority, the router with the highest IP address for the network segment is preferred.

NOTE HSRP does not support preemption by default, so when a router with lower priority becomes active, it does not automatically transfer its active status to a superior router.

HSRP-enabled interfaces send and receive multicast UDP-based hello messages to detect any failure and designate active and standby routers. If a standby device does not receive a hello message or the active device fails to send a hello message, the standby device with the second highest priority becomes HSRP active. The transition of HSRP active between the devices is transparent to all hosts on the segment because the MAC address moves with the virtual IP address.

HSRP has two versions: Version 1 and Version 2. Table 15-3 shows some of the differences between HSRPv1 and HSRPv2.

Table 15-3 HSRP Versions

	HSRPv1	HSRPv2
Timers	Does not support millisecond timer values	Supports millisecond timer values
Group range	0 to 255	0 to 4095
Multicast address	224.0.0.2	224.0.0.102
MAC address range	0000.0C07.AC*xy*, where *xy* is a hex value representing the HSRP group number	0000.0C9F.F000 to 0000.0C9F.FFFF

Figure 15-7 shows a sample topology where SW2 and SW3 are the current gateway devices for VLAN 10. VLAN 1 provides transit routing to the WAN routers.

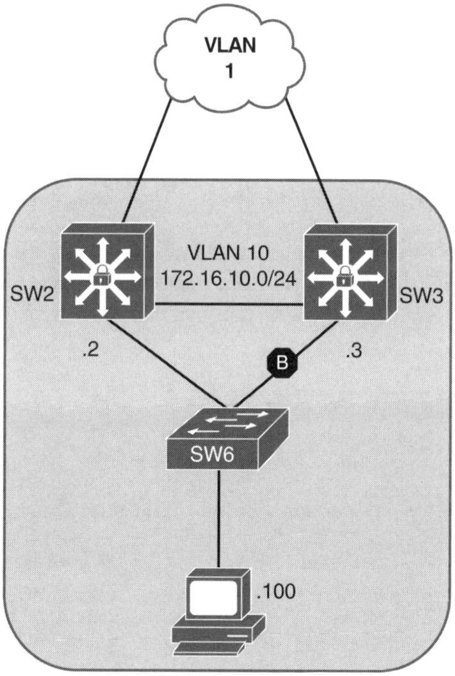

Figure 15-7 *Sample HSRP Topology*

The following steps show how to configure an HSRP virtual IP (VIP) gateway instance:

Key Topic

Step 1. Define the HSRP instance by using the command **standby** *instance-id* **ip** *vip-address*.

Step 2. (Optional) Configure HSRP router preemption to allow a more preferred router to take the active router status from an inferior active HSRP router. Enable preemption with the command **standby** *instance-id* **preempt**.

Step 3. (Optional) Define the HSRP priority by using the command **standby** *instance-id* **priority** *priority*. The priority is a value between 0 and 255.

Step 4. **(Optional)** Define the HSRP MAC Address.

The MAC address can be set with the command **standby** *instance-id* **mac-address** *mac-address*. Most organizations accept the automatically generated MAC address, but in some migration scenarios, the MAC address needs to be statically set to ease transitions when the hosts may have a different MAC address in their ARP table.

Step 5. (Optional) Define the HSRP timers by using the command **standby** *instance-id* **timers** {*seconds* | **msec** *milliseconds*}. HSRP can poll in intervals of 1 to 254 seconds or 15 to 999 milliseconds.

Step 6. (Optional) Establish HSRP authentication by using the command **standby** *instance-id* **authentication** {*text-password* | **text** *text-password* | **md5** {**key-chain** *key-chain* | **key-string** *key-string*}}.

NOTE It is possible to create multiple HSRP instances for the same interface. Some network architects configure half of the hosts for one instance and the other half of the hosts for a second instance. Setting different priorities for each instance makes it possible to load balance the traffic across multiple routers.

Example 15-10 shows a basic HSRP configuration for VLAN 10 on SW2 and SW3, using the HSRP instance 10 and the VIP gateway instance 172.16.10.1. Notice that once preemption was enabled, SW3 became the active speaker and SW2 became the standby speaker.

Example 15-10 *Simple HSRP Configuration*

```
SW2# configure terminal
Enter configuration commands, one per line. End with CNTL/Z.
SW2(config)# interface vlan 10
03:55:35.148: %LINEPROTO-5-UPDOWN: Line protocol on Interface Vlan10, changed state
to down
SW2(config-if)# ip address 172.16.10.2 255.255.255.0
SW2(config-if)# standby 10 ip 172.16.10.1
03:56:00.097: %HSRP-5-STATECHANGE: Vlan10 Grp 10 state Speak -> Standby
SW2(config-if)# standby 10 preempt
```

```
SW3(config)# interface vlan 10
```

```
03:56:04.478: %LINEPROTO-5-UPDOWN: Line protocol on Interface Vlan10, changed state
to down
SW3(config-if)# ip address 172.16.10.3 255.255.255.0
SW3(config-if)# standby 10 ip 172.16.10.1
SW3(config-if)# standby 10 preempt
03:58:22.113: %HSRP-5-STATECHANGE: Vlan10 Grp 10 state Standby -> Active
```

The HSRP status can be viewed with the command **show standby** [*interface-id*] [**brief**]. Specifying an interface restricts the output to a specific interface; this restriction can be useful when troubleshooting large amounts of information.

Example 15-11 shows the command **show standby brief** being run on SW2 and SW3, which includes the interfaces and the associated groups that are running HSRP. The output also includes the local interface's priority, whether preemption is enabled, the current state, the active speaker's address, the standby speaker's address, and the VIP gateway instance for that standby group.

15

Example 15-11 *Viewing the Summarized HSRP State*

```
SW2# show standby brief
                     P indicates configured to preempt.
                     |
Interface   Grp  Pri P State   Active          Standby         Virtual IP
Vl10        10   100 P Standby 172.16.10.3     local           172.16.10.1
```

```
SW3# show standby brief
                     P indicates configured to preempt.
                     |
Interface   Grp  Pri P State   Active          Standby         Virtual IP
Vl10        10   100 P Active  local           172.16.10.2     172.16.10.1
```

The non-brief iteration of the **show standby** command also includes the number of state changes for the HSRP instance, along with the time since the last state change, the timers, and a group name, as shown in Example 15-12.

Example 15-12 *Viewing the HSRP State*

```
SW2# show standby
Vlan10 - Group 10
  State is Standby
    9 state changes, last state change 00:13:12
 Virtual IP address is 172.16.10.1
  Active virtual MAC address is 0000.0c07.ac0a (MAC Not In Use)
    Local virtual MAC address is 0000.0c07.ac0a (v1 default)
  Hello time 3 sec, hold time 10 sec
    Next hello sent in 0.736 secs
```

```
  Preemption enabled
  Active router is 172.16.10.3, priority 100 (expires in 10.032 sec)
  Standby router is local
  Priority 100 (default 100)
  Group name is "hsrp-Vl10-10" (default)
```

```
SW3# show standby
Vlan10 - Group 10
  State is Active
    5 state changes, last state change 00:20:01
  Virtual IP address is 172.16.10.1
  Active virtual MAC address is 0000.0c07.ac0a (MAC In Use)
    Local virtual MAC address is 0000.0c07.ac0a (v1 default)
  Hello time 3 sec, hold time 10 sec
    Next hello sent in 1.024 secs
  Preemption enabled
  Active router is local
  Standby router is 172.16.10.2, priority 100 (expires in 11.296 sec)
  Priority 100 (default 100)
  Group name is "hsrp-Vl10-10" (default)
```

Key Topic

HSRP provides the capability to link object tracking to priority. For example, assume that traffic should flow through SW2's WAN connection whenever feasible. Traffic can be routed by SW3 to SW2 and then on to SW2's WAN connection; however, making SW2 the VIP gateway streamlines the process. But when SW2 loses its link to the WAN, it should move the HSRP active speaker role to SW3.

This configuration is accomplished as follows:

- Configure a tracked object to SW2's WAN link (in this example, VLAN 1).
- Change SW2's priority to a value higher than SW3 (in this case, 110).
- Configure SW2 to lower the priority if the tracked object state changes to down. This is accomplished with the command **standby** *instance-id* **track** *object-id* **decrement** *decrement-value*. The decrement value should be high enough so that when it is removed from the priority, the value is lower than that of the other HSRP router.

Example 15-13 shows the configuration of SW2 where a tracked object is created against VLAN 1's interface line protocol, increasing the HSRP priority to 110, and linking HSRP to the tracked object so that the priority decrements by 20 if interface VLAN 1 goes down.

Example 15-13 *Correlating HSRP to Tracked Objects*

```
SW2(config)# track 1 interface vlan 1 line-protocol
SW2(config-track)# interface vlan 10
SW2(config-if)# standby 10 priority 110
04:44:16.973: %HSRP-5-STATECHANGE: Vlan10 Grp 10 state Standby -> Active
SW2(config-if)# standby 10 track 1 decrement 20
```

Example 15-14 shows that the HSRP group on VLAN 10 on SW2 correlates the status of the tracked object for the VLAN 1 interface.

Example 15-14 *Verifying the Linkage of HSRP to Tracked Objects*

```
SW2# show standby
! Output omitted for brevity
Vlan10 - Group 10
  State is Active
    10 state changes, last state change 00:06:12
  Virtual IP address is 172.16.10.1
..
  Preemption enabled
  Active router is local
  Standby router is 172.16.10.3, priority 100 (expires in 9.856 sec)
  Priority 110 (configured 110)
    Track object 1 state Up decrement 20
```


Example 15-15 verifies the anticipated behavior by shutting down the VLAN 1 interface on SW2. The syslog messages indicate that the object track state changed immediately after the interface was shut down, and shortly thereafter, the HSRP role changed to a standby state. The priority was modified to 90 because of the failure in object tracking, making SW2's interface less preferred to SW3's interface of 100.

Example 15-15 *Verifying the Change of HSRP State with Object Tracking*

```
SW2# configure terminal
Enter configuration commands, one per line. End with CNTL/Z.
SW2(config)# interface vlan 1
SW2(config-if)# shut
04:53:16.490: %TRACK-6-STATE: 1 interface Vl1 line-protocol Up -> Down
04:53:17.077: %HSRP-5-STATECHANGE: Vlan10 Grp 10 state Active -> Speak
04:53:18.486: %LINK-5-CHANGED: Interface Vlan1, changed state to administratively
down
04:53:19.488: %LINEPROTO-5-UPDOWN: Line protocol on Interface Vlan1, changed state
to down
04:53:28.267: %HSRP-5-STATECHANGE: Vlan10 Grp 10 state Speak -> Standby
```

```
SW2# show standby
! Output omitted for brevity
Vlan10 - Group 10
  State is Standby
    12 state changes, last state change 00:00:39
..
  Active router is 172.16.10.3, priority 100 (expires in 9.488 sec)
  Standby router is local
  Priority 90 (configured 110)
    Track object 1 state Down decrement 20
  Group name is "hsrp-Vl10-10" (default)
```

Key Topic

Virtual Router Redundancy Protocol

Virtual Router Redundancy Protocol (VRRP) is an industry standard and operates similarly to HSRP. The behavior of VRRP is so close to that of HSRP that the following differences should be noted:

- The preferred active router controlling the VIP gateway is called the *master router*. All other VRRP routers are known as *backup routers*.
- VRRP enables preemption by default.
- The MAC address of the VIP gateway uses the structure 0000.5e00.01*xx*, where *xx* reflects the group ID in hex.
- VRRP uses the multicast address 224.0.0.18 for communication.

There are currently two versions of VRRP:

- **VRRPv2:** Supports IPv4
- **VRRPv3:** Supports IPv4 and IPv6

The following sections review these versions.

VRRPv2 Configuration

Early VRRPv2 configuration supported only IPv4 and was non-hierarchical in its configuration. The following steps are used for configuring VRRPv2:

Key Topic

Step 1. Define the VRRP instance by using the command **vrrp** *instance-id* **ip** *vip-address*.

Step 2. (Optional) Define the VRRP priority by using the command **vrrp** *instance-id* **priority** *priority*. The priority is a value between 1 and 255.

Step 3. (Optional) Enable object tracking so that the priority is decremented when the object is down. Do so by using the command **vrrp** *instance-id* **track** *object-id* **decrement** *decrement-value*. The decrement value should be high enough so that when it is removed from the priority, the value is lower than that of the other VRRP router.

Step 4. (Optional) Establish VRRP authentication by using the command **vrrp** *instance-id* **authentication** {*text-password* | **text** *text-password* | **md5** {**key-chain** *key-chain* | **key-string** *key-string*}}.

R2 and R3 are two routers that share a connection to a Layer 2 switch with their Gi0/0 interfaces, which both are on the 172.16.20.0/24 network. R2 and R3 use VRRP to create the VIP gateway 172.16.20.1.

Example 15-16 shows the configuration. Notice that after the VIP is assigned to R3, R3 preempts R2 and becomes the master.

Example 15-16 *Legacy VRRP Configuration*

```
R2# configure term
Enter configuration commands, one per line. End with CNTL/Z.
R2(config)# interface GigabitEthernet 0/0
R2(config-if)# ip address 172.16.20.2 255.255.255.0
R2(config-if)# vrrp 20 ip 172.16.20.1
04:32:14.109: %VRRP-6-STATECHANGE: Gi0/0 Grp 20 state Init -> Backup
04:32:14.113: %VRRP-6-STATECHANGE: Gi0/0 Grp 20 state Init -> Backup
04:32:17.728: %VRRP-6-STATECHANGE: Gi0/0 Grp 20 state Backup -> Master
04:32:47.170: %VRRP-6-STATECHANGE: Gi0/0 Grp 20 state Master -> Backup
```

```
R3# configure term
Enter configuration commands, one per line. End with CNTL/Z.
R3(config)# interface GigabitEthernet0/0
R3(config-if)# ip add 172.16.20.3 255.255.255.0
R3(config-if)# vrrp 20 ip 172.16.20.1
04:32:43.550: %VRRP-6-STATECHANGE: Gi0/0 Grp 20 state Init -> Backup
04:32:43.554: %VRRP-6-STATECHANGE: Gi0/0 Grp 20 state Init -> Backup
04:32:47.170: %VRRP-6-STATECHANGE: Gi0/0 Grp 20 state Backup -> Master
```

The command **show vrrp** [**brief**] provides a summary on the VRRP group, along with other relevant information for troubleshooting. Example 15-17 demonstrates the brief iteration of the command. All the output is similar to output with HSRP.

Example 15-17 *Viewing the Summarized VRRP State*

```
R2# show vrrp brief
Interface          Grp Pri Time  Own Pre State   Master addr     Group addr
Gi0/0              20  100 3609       Y  Backup  172.16.20.3     172.16.20.1
```

```
R3# show vrrp brief
Interface          Grp Pri Time  Own Pre State   Master addr     Group addr
Gi0/0              20  100 3609       Y  Master  172.16.20.3     172.16.20.1
```

Example 15-18 examines the detailed state of VRRP running on R2.

Example 15-18 *Viewing the Detailed VRRP State*

```
R2# show vrrp
GigabitEthernet0/0 - Group 20
  State is Backup
  Virtual IP address is 172.16.20.1
  Virtual MAC address is 0000.5e00.0114
  Advertisement interval is 1.000 sec
  Preemption enabled
  Priority is 100
  Master Router is 172.16.20.3, priority is 100
  Master Advertisement interval is 1.000 sec
  Master Down interval is 3.609 sec (expires in 2.904 sec)
```

VRRPv3 Configuration

IOS XE software supports configuration of VRRPv3 in a multi-address format that is hierarchical. The steps for configuring hierarchical VRRP are as follows:

Key Topic

Step 1. Enable VRRPv3 on the router by using the command **fhrp version vrrp v3**.

Step 2. Define the VRRP instance by using the command **vrrp** *instance-id* **address-family** {**ipv4** | **ipv6**}. This places the configuration prompt into the VRRP group for additional configuration.

Step 3. (Optional) Configure VRRPv2 compatibility mode by using the command **vrrpv2**. VRRPv2 and VRRPv3 are not compatible.

Step 4. Define the gateway VIP by using the command **address** *ip-address*.

Step 5. (Optional) Define the VRRP priority by using the command **priority** *priority*. The priority is a value between 1 and 255.

Step 6. (Optional) Enable object tracking so that the priority is decremented when the object is false. Do so by using the command **track** *object-id* **decrement** *decrement-value*. The decrement value should be high enough so that when it is removed from the priority, the value is lower than that of the other VRRP router.

Example 15-19 shows the VRRP configuration on a pair of switches running IOS XE 16.9.2 for VLAN 22 (172.16.22.0/24). The configuration looks similar to the previous VRRP configuration except that it is hierarchical. Associating parameters like priority and tracking are nested under the VRRP instance.

Example 15-19 *Configuring Hierarchical VRRP Configuration*

```
SW2# configure terminal
Enter configuration commands, one per line. End with CNTL/Z.
SW2(config)# fhrp version vrrp v3
SW2(config)# interface vlan 22
 19:45:37.385: %LINEPROTO-5-UPDOWN: Line protocol on Interface Vlan22, changed
 state to up
SW2(config-if)# ip address 172.16.22.2 255.255.255.0
SW2(config-if)# vrrp 22 address-family ipv4
SW2(config-if-vrrp)# address 172.16.22.1
SW2(config-if-vrrp)# track 1 decrement 20
SW2(config-if-vrrp)# priority 110
SW2(config-if-vrrp)# track 1 decrement 20
 19:48:00.338: %VRRP-6-STATE: Vlan22 IPv4 group 22 state INIT -> BACKUP
 19:48:03.948: %VRRP-6-STATE: Vlan22 IPv4 group 22 state BACKUP -> MASTER
```

```
SW3# configure terminal
Enter configuration commands, one per line. End with CNTL/Z.
SW3(config)# fhrp version vrrp v3
```

```
SW3(config)# interface vlan 22
 19:46:13.798: %LINEPROTO-5-UPDOWN: Line protocol on Interface Vlan22, changed state
to up
SW3(config-if)# ip address 172.16.22.3 255.255.255.0
SW3(config-if)# vrrp 22 address-family ipv4
SW3(config-if-vrrp)# address 172.16.22.1
 19:48:08.415: %VRRP-6-STATE: Vlan22 IPv4 group 22 state INIT -> BACKUP
```

The status of the VRRP routers can be viewed with the command **show vrrp** [**brief**]. The output is identical to that of the legacy VRRP configuration, as shown in Example 15-20.

Example 15-20 *Viewing Hierarchical VRRP State*

```
SW2# show vrrp brief
  Interface          Grp  A-F Pri  Time Own Pre State   Master addr/Group addr
  Vl22                22 IPv4 110     0  N   Y  MASTER  172.16.22.2(local)
172.16.22.1
```

```
SW2# show vrrp

Vlan22 - Group 22 - Address-Family IPv4
  State is MASTER
  State duration 51.640 secs
  Virtual IP address is 172.16.22.1
  Virtual MAC address is 0000.5E00.0116
  Advertisement interval is 1000 msec
  Preemption enabled
  Priority is 110
    Track object 1 state UP decrement 20
  Master Router is 172.16.22.2 (local), priority is 110
  Master Advertisement interval is 1000 msec (expires in 564 msec)
  Master Down interval is unknown
  FLAGS: 1/1
```

Key Topic

Gateway Load Balancing Protocol

As the name suggests, Gateway Load Balancing Protocol (GLBP) provides gateway redundancy and load-balancing capability to a network segment. It provides redundancy with an active/standby gateway, and it provides load-balancing capability by ensuring that each member of the GLBP group takes care of forwarding the traffic to the appropriate gateway.

The GLBP contains two roles:

- **Active virtual gateway (AVG):** The participating routers elect one AVG per GLBP group to respond to initial ARP requests for the VIP. For example, when a local PC sends an ARP request for the VIP, the AVG is responsible for replying to the ARP request with the virtual MAC address of the AVF.

- **Active virtual forwarder (AVF):** The AVF routes traffic received from assigned hosts. A unique virtual MAC address is created and assigned by the AVG to the AVFs. The AVF is assigned to a host when the AVG replies to the ARP request with the assigned AVF's virtual MAC address. ARP replies are unicast and are not heard by other hosts on that broadcast segment. When a host sends traffic to its default gateway address, which resolves to the virtual AVF MAC, the current router is responsible for routing it to the appropriate network. The AVFs are also recognized as *Fwd* instances on the routers.

GLBP supports four active AVFs and one AVG per GLBP group. A router can be an AVG and an AVF at the same time. In the event of a failure of the AVG, there is not a disruption of traffic due to the AVG role transferring to a standby AVG device. In the event of a failure of an AVF, another router takes over the forwarding responsibilities for that AVF, which includes the virtual MAC address for that instance.

The following steps detail how to configure GLBP under the interface configuration mode:

Key Topic

Step 1. Define the GLBP instance by using the command **glbp** *instance-id* **ip** *vip-address*.

Step 2. (Optional) Configure GLBP preemption to allow for a more preferred router to take the active virtual gateway status from an inferior active GLBP router. Preemption is enabled with the command **glbp** *instance-id* **preempt**.

Step 3. (Optional) Define the GLBP priority by using the command **glbp** *instance-id* **priority** *priority*. The priority is a value between 1 and 255.

Step 4. (Optional) Define the GLBP timers by using the command **glbp** *instance-id* **timers** {*hello-seconds* | **msec** *hello-milliseconds*} {*hold-seconds* | **msec** *hold-milliseconds*}.

Step 5. (Optional) Establish GLBP authentication by using the command **glbp** *instance-id* **authentication** {**text** *text-password* | **md5** {**key-chain** *key-chain* | **key-string** *key-string*}}.

SW2 and SW3 configure GLBP for VLAN 30 (172.16.30.0/24), with 172.16.30.1 as the VIP gateway. Example 15-21 demonstrates the configuration of both switches. Notice that the first syslog message on SW2 is for the AVG, and the second syslog message is for the first AVF (Fwd 1) for the GLBP pair. The first syslog message on SW3 is the second AVF (Fwd 2) for the GLBP pair.

Example 15-21 *Basic GLBP Configuration*

```
SW2# configure terminal
Enter configuration commands, one per line. End with CNTL/Z.
SW2(config)# interface vlan 30
SW2(config-if)# ip address 172.16.30.2 255.255.255.0
SW2(config-if)# glbp 30 ip 172.16.30.1
  05:41:15.802: %GLBP-6-STATECHANGE: Vlan30 Grp 30 state Speak -> Active
```

```
SW2(config-if)#
  05:41:25.938: %GLBP-6-FWDSTATECHANGE: Vlan30 Grp 30 Fwd 1 state Listen -> Active
SW2(config-if)# glbp 30 preempt
```

```
SW3# configure terminal
Enter configuration commands, one per line. End with CNTL/Z.
SW3(config)# interface vlan 30
SW3(config-if)# ip address 172.16.30.3 255.255.255.0
SW3(config-if)# glbp 30 ip 172.16.30.1
  05:41:32.239: %GLBP-6-FWDSTATECHANGE: Vlan30 Grp 30 Fwd 2 state Listen -> Active
SW3(config-if)# glbp 30 preempt
```


The command **show glbp brief** shows high-level details of the GLBP group, including the interface, group, active AVG, standby AVG, and statuses of the AVFs.

Example 15-22 demonstrates the commands run on SW2 and SW3. The first entry contains a hyphen (-) for the Fwd state, which means that it is the entry for the AVG. The following two entries are for the AVF instances; they identify which device is active for each AVF.

Example 15-22 *Viewing the Brief GLBP Status*

```
SW2# show glbp brief
Interface   Grp  Fwd Pri State    Address         Active router   Standby router
Vl30        30   -   100 Active   172.16.30.1     local           172.16.30.3
Vl30        30   1   -   Active   0007.b400.1e01  local           -
Vl30        30   2   -   Listen   0007.b400.1e02  172.16.30.3     -
```

```
SW3# show glbp brief
Interface   Grp  Fwd Pri State    Address         Active router   Standby router
Vl30        30   -   100 Standby  172.16.30.1     172.16.30.2     local
Vl30        30   1   -   Listen   0007.b400.1e01  172.16.30.2     -
Vl30        30   2   -   Active   0007.b400.1e02  local           -
```

The command **show glbp** displays additional information, including the timers, preemption settings, and statuses for the AVG and AVFs for the GLBP group. Example 15-23 shows the command **show glbp** run on SW2. Notice that the MAC addresses and interface IP addresses are listed under the group members, which can be used to correlate MAC address identities in other portions of the output.

Example 15-23 *Viewing the Detailed GLBP Status*

```
SW2# show glbp
Vlan30 - Group 30
  State is Active
    1 state change, last state change 00:01:26
  Virtual IP address is 172.16.30.1
```

```
Hello time 3 sec, hold time 10 sec
Next hello sent in 1.664 secs
Redirect time 600 sec, forwarder time-out 14400 sec
Preemption enabled, min delay 0 sec
Active is local
Standby is 172.16.30.3, priority 100 (expires in 7.648 sec)
Priority 100 (default)
Weighting 100 (default 100), thresholds: lower 1, upper 100
Load balancing: round-robin
Group members:
  70b3.17a7.7b65 (172.16.30.3)
  70b3.17e3.cb65 (172.16.30.2) local
```

```
There are 2 forwarders (1 active)
Forwarder 1
  State is Active
    1 state change, last state change 00:01:16
  MAC address is 0007.b400.1e01 (default)
  Owner ID is 70b3.17e3.cb65
  Redirection enabled
  Preemption enabled, min delay 30 sec
  Active is local, weighting 100
Forwarder 2
  State is Listen
  MAC address is 0007.b400.1e02 (learnt)
  Owner ID is 70b3.17a7.7b65
  Redirection enabled, 597.664 sec remaining (maximum 600 sec)
  Time to live: 14397.664 sec (maximum 14400 sec)
  Preemption enabled, min delay 30 sec
  Active is 172.16.30.3 (primary), weighting 100 (expires in 8.160 sec)
```

By default, GLBP balances the load of traffic in a round-robin fashion, as highlighted in Example 15-23. However, GLBP supports three methods of load-balancing traffic:

Key Topic

- **Round robin:** Uses each virtual forwarder MAC address to sequentially reply for the virtual IP address.
- **Weighted:** Defines weights to each device in the GLBP group to define the ratio of load balancing between the devices. This allows for a larger weight to be assigned to bigger routers that can handle more traffic.
- **Host dependent:** Uses the host MAC address to decide to which virtual forwarder MAC to redirect the packet. This method ensures that the host uses the same virtual MAC address as long as the number of virtual forwarders does not change within the group.

The load-balancing method can be changed with the command **glbp** *instance-id* **load-balancing** {**host-dependent** | **round-robin** | **weighted**}. The weighted load-balancing method has the AVG direct traffic to the AVFs based on the percentage of weight a router has over the total weight of all GLBP routers. Increasing the weight on more capable, bigger routers allows them to take more traffic than smaller devices. The weight can be set for a router with the command **glbp** *instance-id* **weighting** *weight*.

Example 15-24 shows how to change the load balancing to weighted and setting the weight to 20 on SW2 and 80 on SW3 so that SW2 receives 20% of the traffic and SW3 receives 80% of the traffic.

Example 15-24 *Changing the GLBP Load Balancing to Weighted*

```
SW2(config)# interface vlan 30
SW2(config-if)# glbp 30 load-balancing weighted
SW2(config-if)# glbp 30 weighting 20
```

```
SW3(config)# interface vlan 30
SW3(config-if)# glbp 30 load-balancing weighted
SW3(config-if)# glbp 30 weighting 80
```


Example 15-25 shows that the load-balancing method has been changed to weighted and that the appropriate weight has been set for each AVF.

Example 15-25 *Verifying GLBP Weighted Load Balancing*

```
SW2# show glbp
Vlan30 - Group 30
  State is Active
    1 state change, last state change 00:04:55
  Virtual IP address is 172.16.30.1
  Hello time 3 sec, hold time 10 sec
    Next hello sent in 0.160 secs
  Redirect time 600 sec, forwarder time-out 14400 sec
  Preemption enabled, min delay 0 sec
  Active is local
  Standby is 172.16.30.3, priority 100 (expires in 9.216 sec)
  Priority 100 (default)
  Weighting 20 (configured 20), thresholds: lower 1, upper 20
  Load balancing: weighted
  Group members:
    70b3.17a7.7b65 (172.16.30.3)
    70b3.17e3.cb65 (172.16.30.2) local
 There are 2 forwarders (1 active)
  Forwarder 1
    State is Active
```

```
    1 state change, last state change 00:04:44
   MAC address is 0007.b400.1e01 (default)
   Owner ID is 70b3.17e3.cb65
   Redirection enabled
   Preemption enabled, min delay 30 sec
   Active is local, weighting 20
 Forwarder 2
   State is Listen
   MAC address is 0007.b400.1e02 (learnt)
   Owner ID is 70b3.17a7.7b65
   Redirection enabled, 599.232 sec remaining (maximum 600 sec)
   Time to live: 14399.232 sec (maximum 14400 sec)
   Preemption enabled, min delay 30 sec
   Active is 172.16.30.3 (primary), weighting 80 (expires in 9.408 sec)
```

Network Address Translation

In the early stages of the Internet, large network blocks were assigned to organizations (for example, universities, companies). Network engineers started to realize that as more people connected to the Internet, the IP address space would become exhausted. RFC 1918 established common network blocks that should never be seen on the Internet (that is, they are non-globally routed networks):

- 10.0.0.0/8 accommodates 16,777,216 hosts.
- 172.16.0.0/12 accommodates 1,048,576 hosts.
- 192.168.0.0/16 accommodates 65,536 hosts.

These address blocks provide large private network blocks for companies to connect their devices together, but how can devices with private network addressing reach servers that are on the public Internet? If a packet is sourced from a 192.168.1.1 IP address and reaches the server with a 100.64.1.1 IP address, the server will not have a route back to the 192.168.1.1 network—because it does not exist on the Internet.

Key Topic

Connectivity is established with **Network Address Translation (NAT)**. Basically, NAT enables the internal IP network to appear as a publicly routed external network. A NAT device (typically a router or firewall) modifies the source or destination IP addresses in a packet's header as the packet is received on the outside or inside interface.

NAT can be used in use cases other than just providing Internet connectivity to private networks. It can also be used to provide connectivity when a company buys another company, and the two companies have overlapping networks (that is, the same network ranges are in use).

NOTE Most routers and switches perform NAT translation only with the IP header addressing and do not translate IP addresses within the payload (for example, DNS requests). Some firewalls have the ability to perform NAT within the payload for certain types of traffic.

Four important terms are related to NAT:

Key Topic

- **Inside local:** The actual private IP address assigned to a device on the inside network(s).
- **Inside global:** The public IP address that represents one or more inside local IP addresses to the outside.
- **Outside local:** The IP address of an outside host as it appears to the inside network. The IP address does not have to be reachable by the outside but is considered private and must be reachable by the inside network.
- **Outside global:** The public IP address assigned to a host on the outside network. This IP address must be reachable by the outside network.

Three types of NAT are commonly used today:

Key Topic

- **Static NAT:** Provides a static one-to-one mapping of a local IP address to a global IP address.
- **Pooled NAT:** Provides a dynamic one-to-one mapping of a local IP address to a global IP address. The global IP address is temporarily assigned to a local IP address. After a certain amount of idle NAT time, the global IP address is returned to the pool.
- **Port Address Translation (PAT):** Provides a dynamic many-to-one mapping of many local IP addresses to one global IP address. The NAT device needs a mechanism to identify the specific private IP address for the return network traffic. The NAT device translates the private IP address and port to a different global IP address and port. The port is unique from any other ports, which enables the NAT device to track the global IP address to local IP addresses based on the unique port mapping.

The following sections explain these types of NAT.

NAT Topology

Figure 15-8 is used throughout this section to illustrate NAT. R5 performs the translation; its Gi0/0 interface (10.45.1.5) is the outside interface, and its Gi0/1 (10.56.1.5) interface is the inside interface. R1, R2, R3, R7, R8, and R9 all act as either clients or servers to demonstrate how NAT functions.

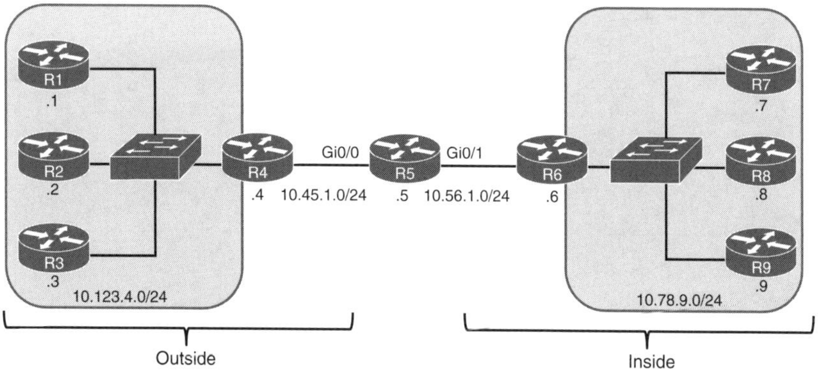

Figure 15-8 *NAT Topology*

R1, R2, and R3 all have a static default route toward R4, and R4 has a static default route toward R5. R7, R8, and R9 all have a static default route toward R6, and R6 has a static default route to R5. R5 contains a static route to the 10.123.4.0/24 network through R4, and a second static route to the 10.78.9.0/24 network through R6. Example 15-26 shows the routing tables of R1, R5, and R7.

Example 15-26 *Routing Tables of R1, R5, and R7*

```
R1# show ip route | begin Gateway
Gateway of last resort is 10.123.4.4 to network 0.0.0.0

S*    0.0.0.0/0 [1/0] via 10.123.4.4
      10.0.0.0/8 is variably subnetted, 2 subnets, 2 masks
C        10.123.4.0/24 is directly connected, GigabitEthernet0/0
```

```
R5# show ip route | begin Gateway
Gateway of last resort is not set

      10.0.0.0/8 is variably subnetted, 6 subnets, 2 masks
C        10.45.1.0/24 is directly connected, GigabitEthernet0/0
C        10.56.1.0/24 is directly connected, GigabitEthernet0/1
S        10.78.9.0/24 [1/0] via 10.56.1.6
S        10.123.4.0/24 [1/0] via 10.45.1.4
```

```
R7# show ip route | begin Gateway
Gateway of last resort is 10.78.9.6 to network 0.0.0.0

S*    0.0.0.0/0 [1/0] via 10.78.9.6
      10.0.0.0/8 is variably subnetted, 2 subnets, 2 masks
C        10.78.9.0/24 is directly connected, GigabitEthernet0/0
```

The topology provides full connectivity between the outside hosts (R1, R2, and R3) and the inside hosts (R7, R8, and R9). Example 15-27 shows a traceroute from R1 to R7.

Example 15-27 *Traceroute from R1 to R7*

```
R1# traceroute 10.78.9.7
Type escape sequence to abort.
Tracing the route to 10.78.9.7
VRF info: (vrf in name/id, vrf out name/id)
  1 10.123.4.4 1 msec 0 msec 0 msec
  2 10.45.1.5 1 msec 0 msec 0 msec
  3 10.56.1.6 1 msec 0 msec 0 msec
  4 10.78.9.7 1 msec * 1 msec
```

Using an IOS XE router for hosts (R1, R2, R3, R7, R8, and R9) enables you to log in using Telnet and identify the source and destination IP addresses by examining the TCP session details. In Example 15-28, R7 (10.78.9.7) initiates a Telnet connection to R1 (10.123.4.1). When you are logged in, the command **show tcp brief** displays the source IP address and port, along with the destination IP address and port.

The local IP address reflects R1 (10.123.4.1), and the remote address is R7 (10.78.9.7). These IP addresses appear as they are configured on the source and destination hosts, and therefore no NAT has occurred on R5 for this Telnet session.

Example 15-28 *Viewing the Source IP Address*

```
R7# telnet 10.123.4.1
Trying 10.123.4.1 ... Open
*************************************************************
* You have remotely connected to R1 on line 2
*************************************************************
User Access Verification
Password:

R1# show tcp brief
TCB       Local Address           Foreign Address          (state)
F69CE570  10.123.4.1.23           10.78.9.7.49024           ESTAB
```

15

Static NAT

Static NAT involves the translation of a global IP address to a local IP address, based on a static mapping of the global IP address to the local IP address. There are two types of static NAT, as described in the following sections:

- Inside static NAT
- Outside static NAT

Inside Static NAT

Inside static NAT involves the mapping of an inside local (private) IP address to an inside global (public) IP address. In this scenario, the private IP addresses are being hidden from the outside hosts.

The steps for configuring inside static NAT are as follows:

Key Topic

Step 1. Configure the outside interfaces by using the command **ip nat outside**.

Step 2. Configure the inside interface with the command **ip nat inside**.

Step 3. Configure the inside static NAT by using the command **ip nat inside source static** *inside-local-ip inside-global-ip*.

Example 15-29 shows the inside static NAT configuration on R5, where packets sourced from R7 (10.78.9.7) appear as if they came from 10.45.1.7.

Example 15-29 *Configuring Inside Static NAT*

```
R5# configure terminal
Enter configuration commands, one per line. End with CNTL/Z.
R5(config)# interface GigabitEthernet0/0
R5(config-if)# ip nat outside
R5(config-if)# interface GigabitEthernet0/1
R5(config-if)# ip nat inside
R5(config-if)# exit
R5(config)# ip nat inside source static 10.78.9.7 10.45.1.7
```

NOTE Most network engineers assume that the *inside-global-ip* must reside on the outside network. In this scenario, that would be an IP address on the 10.45.1.0/24 network. First, the *inside-global-ip* address should not be associated with the outside interface. Second, the *inside-global-ip* address could be an address for a network that does not exist on the NAT router (for example, 10.77.77.77). However, all outside routers must have a route for forwarding packets toward the router performing the NAT for that IP address (that is, 10.77.77.77).

Now that the NAT has been configured on R5, R7 initiates a Telnet session with R1, as demonstrated in Example 15-30. Upon viewing the TCP session on R1, the local address remains 10.123.4.1 as expected, but the remote address now reflects 10.45.1.7. This is a different source IP address than the baseline example in Example 15-28, where the remote address is 10.78.9.7.

Example 15-30 *Identification of the Source with Inside Static NAT*

```
R7# telnet 10.123.4.1
Trying 10.123.4.1 ... Open
*************************************************************
* You have remotely connected to R1 on line 3
*************************************************************
User Access Verification
Password:

R1# show tcp brief
TCB        Local Address              Foreign Address    (state)
F6D25D08 10.123.4.1.23              10.45.1.7.56708     ESTAB
```

The NAT translation table consists of static and dynamic entries. The NAT translation table is displayed with the command **show ip nat translations**. Example 15-31 shows R5's NAT translation table after R7 initiated a Telnet session to R1. There are two entries:

- The first entry is the dynamic entry correlating to the Telnet session. The inside global, inside local, outside local, and outside global fields all contain values. Notice that the ports in this entry correlate with the ports in Example 15-30.
- The second entry is the inside static NAT entry that was configured.

Example 15-31 *NAT Translation Table for Inside Static NAT*

```
R5# show ip nat translations
Pro Inside global         Inside local        Outside local       Outside global
tcp 10.45.1.7:56708       10.78.9.7:56708     10.123.4.1:23       10.123.4.1:23
--- 10.45.1.7             10.78.9.7           ---                 ---
```

Figure 15-9 displays the current topology with R5's translation table. The NAT translation follows these steps:

Key Topic

1. As traffic enters on R5's Gi0/1 interface, R5 performs a route lookup for the destination IP address, which points out of its Gi0/0 interface. R5 is aware that the Gi0/0 interface is an outside NAT interface and that the Gi0/1 interface is an inside NAT interface and therefore checks the NAT table for an entry.
2. Only the inside static NAT entry exists, so R5 creates a dynamic inside NAT entry with the packet's destination (10.123.4.1) for the outside local and outside global address.
3. R5 translates (that is, changes) the packet's source IP address from 10.78.9.7 to 10.45.1.7.
4. R1 registers the session as coming from 10.45.1.7 and then transmits a return packet. The packet is forwarded to R4 using the static default route, and R4 forwards the packet using the static default route.
5. As the packet enters on R5's Gi0/0 interface, R5 is aware that the Gi0/0 interface is an outside NAT interface and checks the NAT table for an entry.
6. R5 correlates the packet's source and destination ports with the first NAT entry, as shown in Example 15-31, and knows to modify the packet's destination IP address from 10.45.1.7 to 10.78.9.7.
7. R5 routes the packet out the Gi0/1 interface toward R6.

Inside Global	Inside Local	Outside Local	Outside Global
10.45.1.7	10.78.9.7	10.123.4.1	10.123.4.1
10.45.1.7	10.78.9.7	-	-

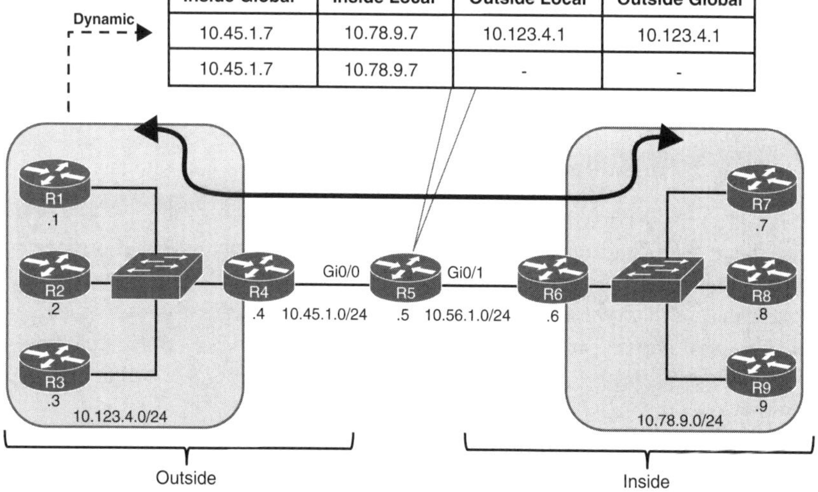

Figure 15-9 *Inside Static NAT Topology for R7 as 10.45.1.7*

Remember that a static NAT entry is a one-to-one mapping between the inside global and the inside local address. As long as the outside devices can route traffic to the inside global IP address, they can use it to reach the inside local device as well.

In Example 15-32, R2, with no sessions to any device in the topology, establishes a Telnet session with R7, using the inside global IP address 10.45.1.7. R5 simply creates a second dynamic entry for this new session. From R7's perspective, it has connected with R2 (10.123.4.2).

Example 15-32 *Connectivity from External Devices to the Inside Global IP Address*

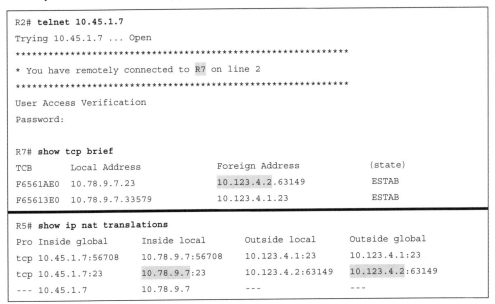

```
R2# telnet 10.45.1.7
Trying 10.45.1.7 ... Open
*************************************************************
* You have remotely connected to R7 on line 2
*************************************************************
User Access Verification
Password:

R7# show tcp brief
TCB         Local Address              Foreign Address             (state)
F6561AE0    10.78.9.7.23               10.123.4.2.63149            ESTAB
F65613E0    10.78.9.7.33579            10.123.4.1.23               ESTAB
```

```
R5# show ip nat translations
Pro Inside global        Inside local          Outside local          Outside global
tcp 10.45.1.7:56708      10.78.9.7:56708       10.123.4.1:23          10.123.4.1:23
tcp 10.45.1.7:23         10.78.9.7:23          10.123.4.2:63149       10.123.4.2:63149
--- 10.45.1.7            10.78.9.7             ---                    ---
```

Outside Static NAT

Outside static NAT involves the mapping of an outside global (public) IP address to an outside local (private) IP address. In this scenario, the real external IP addresses are being hidden from the inside hosts.

The steps for configuring outside static NAT are as follows:

Key Topic

Step 1. Configure the outside interfaces by using the command **ip nat outside**.

Step 2. Configure the inside interface by using the command **ip nat inside**.

Step 3. Configure the outside static NAT entry by using the command **ip nat outside source static** *outside-global-ip outside-local-ip* [**add-route**]. The router performs a route lookup first for the *outside-local-ip* address, and a route must exist for that network to forward packets out of the outside interface before NAT occurs. The optional **add-route** keyword adds the appropriate static route entry automatically.

Example 15-33 shows the outside static NAT configuration on R5, where packets sent from R6, R7, R8, or R9 to 10.123.4.222 will be sent to R2 (10.123.4.2). R5 already has a static route to the 10.123.4.0/24 network, so the **add-route** keyword is not necessary.

Example 15-33 *Configuring Outside Static NAT*

```
R5# configure terminal
Enter configuration commands, one per line. End with CNTL/Z.
R5(config)# interface GigabitEthernet0/0
R5(config-if)# ip nat outside
R5(config-if)# interface GigabitEthernet0/1
R5(config-if)# ip nat inside
R5(config-if)# exit
R5(config)# ip nat outside source static 10.123.4.2 10.123.4.222
```


R6, R7, R8, or R9 could initiate a Telnet session directly with R2's IP address (10.123.4.2), and no NAT translation would occur. The same routers could initiate a Telnet session with the R2's outside local IP address 10.123.4.222; or R2 could initiate a session with any of the inside hosts (R6, R7, R8, or R9) to demonstrate the outside static NAT entry.

Example 15-34 shows R2 establishing a Telnet session with R9 (10.78.9.9). From R9's perspective, the connection came from 10.123.4.222. At the same time, R8 initiated a Telnet session with the outside static NAT outside local IP address (10.123.4.222), but from R2's perspective, the source address is R8's 10.78.9.8 IP address.

Example 15-34 *Generating Network Traffic with Outside Static NAT*

```
R2# telnet 10.78.9.9
Trying 10.78.9.9 ... Open
*************************************************************
* You have remotely connected to R9 on line 2
*************************************************************
User Access Verification
Password:

R9#show tcp brief
TCB       Local Address            Foreign Address          (state)
F6A23AF0  10.78.9.9.23             10.123.4.222.57126       ESTAB
```

```
R8# telnet 10.123.4.222
Trying 10.123.4.222 ... Open
*************************************************************
* You have remotely connected to R2 on line 2
*************************************************************
User Access Verification
Password:
```

```
R2# show tcp brief
TCB        Local Address              Foreign Address          (state)
F64C9460   10.123.4.2.57126           10.78.9.9.23             ESTAB
F64C9B60   10.123.4.2.23              10.78.9.8.11339          ESTAB
```

Figure 15-10 shows R5's translation table for R2's outside static NAT entry for 10.123.4.222. Notice that there is a static mapping, and there are two dynamic entries for the two sessions on R2.

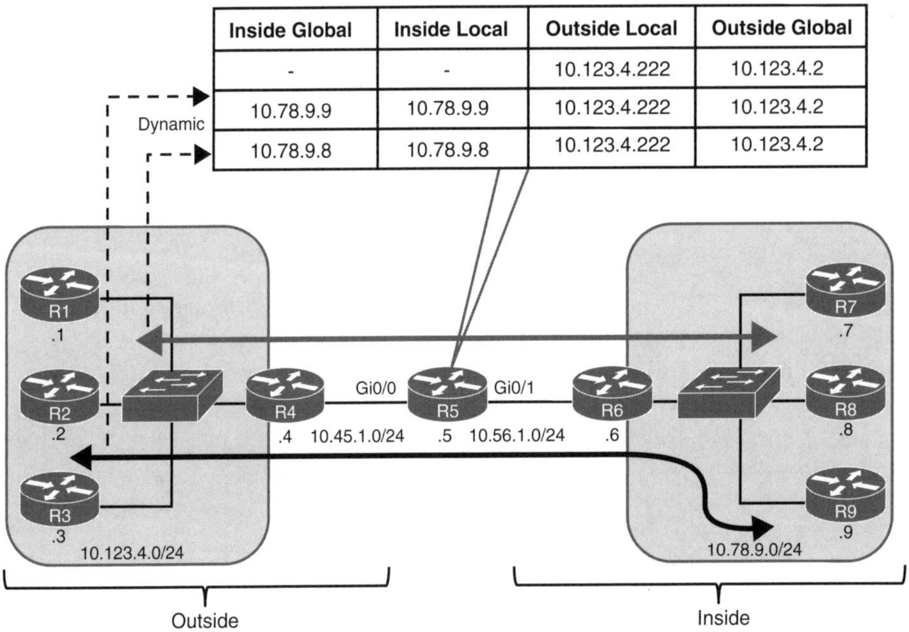

Figure 15-10 *Outside Static NAT Topology for R2 as 10.123.4.222*

Example 15-35 shows R5's NAT translation table. There are three entries:

- The first entry is the outside static NAT entry that was configured.
- The second entry is the Telnet session launched from R8 to the 10.123.4.222 IP address.
- The third entry is the Telnet session launched from R2 to R9's IP address (10.78.9.9).

Example 15-35 *NAT Translation Table for Outside Static NAT*

```
R5# show ip nat translations
Pro Inside global         Inside local          Outside local        Outside global
--- ---                   ---                   10.123.4.222         10.123.4.2
tcp 10.78.9.8:11339       10.78.9.8:11339       10.123.4.222:23      10.123.4.2:23
tcp 10.78.9.9:23          10.78.9.9:23          10.123.4.222:57126 10.123.4.2:57126
```

NOTE Outside static NAT configuration is not very common and is typically used to overcome the problems caused by duplicate IP/network addresses in a network.

Pooled NAT

Static NAT provides a simple method of translating addresses. A major downfall to the use of static NAT is the number of configuration entries that must be created on the NAT device; in addition, the number of global IP addresses must match the number of local IP addresses.

Pooled NAT provides a more dynamic method of providing a one-to-one IP address mapping—but on a dynamic, as-needed basis. The dynamic NAT translation stays in the translation table until traffic flow from the local address to the global address has stopped and the timeout period (24 hours by default) has expired. The unused global IP address is then returned to the pool to be used again.

Pooled NAT can operate as inside NAT or outside NAT. In this section, we focus on inside pooled NAT. The steps for configuring inside pooled NAT are as follows:

Key Topic

Step 1. Configure the outside interfaces by using the command **ip nat outside**.

Step 2. Configure the inside interface by using the command **ip nat inside**.

Step 3. Specify which by using a standard or extended ACL referenced by number or name. Using a standard ACL specifies the source IP addresses that could be translated, while using an extended ACL allows for the conditional translation based on protocol, port, or source or destination IP addresses. Using a user-friendly name may be simplest from an operational support perspective.

Step 4. Define the global pool of IP addresses by using the command **ip nat pool** *nat-pool-name starting-ip ending-ip* **prefix-length** *prefix-length*.

Step 5. Configure the inside pooled NAT by using the command **ip nat inside source list** *acl* **pool** *nat-pool-name*.

Example 15-36 shows a sample configuration for inside pooled NAT. This example uses a NAT pool with the IP addresses 10.45.1.10 and 10.45.1.11. A named ACL, ACL-NAT-CAPABLE, allows only packets sourced from the 10.78.9.0/24 network to be eligible for pooled NAT.

Example 15-36 *Configuring Inside Pooled NAT*

```
R5# configure terminal
Enter configuration commands, one per line. End with CNTL/Z.
R5(config)# ip access-list standard ACL-NAT-CAPABLE
R5(config-std-nacl)# permit 10.78.9.0 0.0.0.255
R5(config-std-nacl)# exit
R5(config)# interface GigabitEthernet0/0
```

```
R5(config-if)# ip nat outside
R5(config-if)# interface GigabitEthernet0/1
R5(config-if)# ip nat inside
R5(config-if)# exit
R5(config)# ip nat pool R5-OUTSIDE-POOL 10.45.1.10 10.45.1.11 prefix-length 24
R5(config)# ip nat inside source list ACL-NAT-CAPABLE pool R5-OUTSIDE-POOL
```

To quickly generate some traffic and build the dynamic inside NAT translations, R7 (10.78.9.7) and R8 (10.78.9.8), ping R1 (10.123.4.1), as demonstrated in Example 15-37. This could easily be another type of traffic (such as Telnet).

Example 15-37 *Initial Traffic for Pooled NAT*

```
R7# ping 10.123.4.1
Type escape sequence to abort.
Sending 5, 100-byte ICMP Echos to 10.123.4.1, timeout is 2 seconds:
!!!!!
Success rate is 100 percent (5/5), round-trip min/avg/max = 1/1/1 ms
```

```
R8# ping 10.123.4.1
Type escape sequence to abort.
Sending 5, 100-byte ICMP Echos to 10.123.4.1, timeout is 2 seconds:
!!!!!
Success rate is 100 percent (5/5), round-trip min/avg/max = 1/1/1 ms
```

In this case, the pings should have created a dynamic inside NAT translation and removed the 10.45.1.10 and 10.45.1.11 binding. Example 15-38 confirms this assumption. There are a total of four translations in R5's translation table. Two of them are for the full flow and specify the protocol, inside global, inside local, outside local, and outside global IP addresses.

Example 15-38 *Viewing the Pooled NAT Table for R5*

```
R5# show ip nat translations
Pro Inside global       Inside local       Outside local      Outside global
icmp 10.45.1.10:0       10.78.9.7:0        10.123.4.1:0       10.123.4.1:0
--- 10.45.1.10          10.78.9.7          ---                ---
icmp 10.45.1.11:0       10.78.9.8:0        10.123.4.1:0       10.123.4.1:0
--- 10.45.1.11          10.78.9.8          ---                ---
```

The other two translations are dynamic one-to-one mappings that could be used as R7 or R8 to create additional dynamic flows and maintain the existing global IP address. Based on the mapping before the flow, the additional flows from R8 (10.78.9.8) should be mapped to the global IP address 10.45.1.11.

In Example 15-39, R8 establishes a Telnet session with R2. R2 detects that the remote IP address of the session is 10.45.1.11. A second method of confirmation is to examine the NAT translation on R5, where there is a second dynamic translation entry for the full Telnet session.

Example 15-39 *Using the Dynamic One-to-One Mappings for Address Consistency*

```
R8# telnet 10.123.4.2
Trying 10.123.4.2 ... Open
*************************************************************
* You have remotely connected to R2 on line 2
*************************************************************
User Access Verification
Password:

R2# show tcp brief
TCB        Local Address             Foreign Address          (state)
F3B64440   10.123.4.2.23             10.45.1.11.34115         ESTAB
```

```
R5# show ip nat translations
Pro Inside global        Inside local        Outside local       Outside global
icmp 10.45.1.10:1        10.78.9.7:1         10.123.4.1:1        10.123.4.1:1
--- 10.45.1.10           10.78.9.7           ---                 ---
icmp 10.45.1.11:1        10.78.9.8:1         10.123.4.1:1        10.123.4.1:1
tcp 10.45.1.11:34115     10.78.9.8:34115     10.123.4.2:23       10.123.4.2:23
--- 10.45.1.11           10.78.9.8           ---                 ---
```

A downfall to using pooled NAT is that when the pool is exhausted, no additional translation can occur until the global IP address is returned to the pool. To demonstrate this concept, R5 has enabled debugging for NAT, and R9 tries to establish a Telnet session with R1. Example 15-40 demonstrates the concept, with the NAT translation failing on R5 and the packet being dropped.

Example 15-40 *Failed NAT Pool Allocation*

```
R9# telnet 10.123.4.1
Trying 10.123.4.1 ...
% Destination unreachable; gateway or host down
```

```
R5# debug ip nat detailed
IP NAT detailed debugging is on
R5#
 02:22:58.685: NAT: failed to allocate address for 10.78.9.9, list/map
ACL-NAT-CAPABLE
 02:22:58.685:  mapping pointer available mapping:0
 02:22:58.685: NAT*: Can't create new inside entry - forced_punt_flags: 0
 02:22:58.685: NAT: failed to allocate address for 10.78.9.9, list/map
ACL-NAT-CAPABLE
 02:22:58.685:  mapping pointer available mapping:0
 02:22:58.685: NAT: translation failed (A), dropping packet s=10.78.9.9 d=10.123.4.1
```

Key Topic

The default timeout for NAT translations is 24 hours, but this can be changed with the command **ip nat translation timeout** *seconds*. The dynamic NAT translations can be cleared out with the command **clear ip nat translation** {*ip-address* | *}, which removes all existing translations and could interrupt traffic flow on active sessions as they might be assigned new global IP addresses.

Example 15-41 demonstrates the reset of the NAT translations on R5 for all IP addresses and then on R9, which is successfully able to gain access to R1 through the newly allocated (reset) global IP address.

Example 15-41 *Clearing NAT Translation to Reset the NAT Pool*

```
R5# clear ip nat translation *
```

```
R9# telnet 10.123.4.1
Trying 10.123.4.1 ... Open
*************************************************************
* You have remotely connected to R1 on line 2
*************************************************************
User Access Verification
Password:

R1#
```

Port Address Translation

Pooled NAT translation simplifies the management of maintaining the one-to-one mapping for NAT (compared to static NAT). But pooled NAT translation still faces the limitation of ensuring that the number of global IP addresses is adequate to meet the needs of the local IP addresses.

Key Topic

Port Address Translation (PAT) is an iteration of NAT that allows for a mapping of many local IP addresses to one global IP address. The NAT device maintains the state of translations by dynamically changing the source ports as a packet leaves the outside interface. Another term for PAT is *NAT overload*.

Configuring PAT involves the following steps:

Key Topic

Step 1. Configure the outside interface by using the command **ip nat outside**.

Step 2. Configure the inside interface by using the command **ip nat inside**.

Step 3. Specify which traffic can be translated by using a standard or extended ACL referenced by number or name. Using a user-friendly name may be simplest from an operational support perspective.

Step 4. Configure Port Address Translation by using the command **ip nat inside source list** *acl* {**interface** *interface-id* | **pool** *nat-pool-name*} **overload**. Specifying an interface involves using the primary IP address assigned to that interface. Specifying a NAT pool requires the creation of the NAT pool, as demonstrated earlier, and involves using those IP addresses as the global address.

Example 15-42 demonstrates R5's PAT configuration, which allows network traffic sourced from the 10.78.9.0/24 network to be translated to R5's Gi0/0 interface (10.45.1.5) IP address.

Example 15-42 *Configuring PAT on R5*

```
R5# configure terminal
Enter configuration commands, one per line. End with CNTL/Z.
R5(config)# ip access-list standard ACL-NAT-CAPABLE
R5(config-std-nacl)# permit 10.78.9.0 0.0.0.255
R5(config-std-nacl)# exit
R5(config)# interface GigabitEthernet0/0
R5(config-if)# ip nat outside
R5(config-if)# interface GigabitEthernet0/1
R5(config-if)# ip nat inside
R5(config)# ip nat inside source list ACL-NAT-CAPABLE interface GigabitEthernet0/0
overload
```

15

Now that PAT has been configured on R5, traffic can be generated for testing. R7, R8, and R9 ping R1 (10.123.4.1), and R7 and R8 establish a Telnet session. Based on the TCP sessions in Example 15-43, you can see that both Telnet sessions are coming from R5's Gi0/0 (10.45.1.5) IP address. R7 has a remote port of 51,576, while R8 has a remote port of 31,515.

Example 15-43 *Generating Network Traffic for PAT*

```
R7# ping 10.123.4.1
Type escape sequence to abort.
Sending 5, 100-byte ICMP Echos to 10.123.4.1, timeout is 2 seconds:
!!!!!
Success rate is 100 percent (5/5), round-trip min/avg/max = 1/1/1 ms
```

```
R8# ping 10.123.4.1
Type escape sequence to abort.
Sending 5, 100-byte ICMP Echos to 10.123.4.1, timeout is 2 seconds:
!!!!!
Success rate is 100 percent (5/5), round-trip min/avg/max = 1/1/1 ms
```

```
R9# ping 10.123.4.1
Type escape sequence to abort.
Sending 5, 100-byte ICMP Echos to 10.123.4.1, timeout is 2 seconds:
!!!!!
Success rate is 100 percent (5/5), round-trip min/avg/max = 1/1/1 ms
```

```
R7# telnet 10.123.4.2
Trying 10.123.4.2 ... Open
************************************************************
* You have remotely connected to R2 on line 2
************************************************************
User Access Verification
```

```
Password:

R2# show tcp brief
TCB Local Address Foreign Address (state)
F3B64440 10.123.4.2.23 10.45.1.5.51576 ESTAB
```

```
R8# telnet 10.123.4.2
Trying 10.123.4.2 ... Open
*************************************************************
* You have remotely connected to R2 on line 3
*************************************************************
User Access Verification
Password:

R2# show tcp brief
TCB         Local Address             Foreign Address           (state)
F3B64440    10.123.4.2.23             10.45.1.5.51576           ESTAB
F3B65560    10.123.4.2.23             10.45.1.5.31515           ESTAB
```

Figure 15-11 shows R5's translation table after all the various flows have established. Notice that the inside global IP address is R5's Gi0/0 (10.45.1.5) IP address, while the inside local IP addresses are different. In addition, notice that the ports for the inside global entries are all unique—especially for the first two entries, which have an outside local entry for 10.123.4.1:3. PAT must make the inside global ports unique to maintain the one-to-many mapping for any return traffic.

Inside Global	Inside Local	Outside Local	Outside Global
10.45.1.5:4	10.78.9.7:4	10.123.4.1:4	10.123.4.1:4
10.45.1.5:3	10.78.9.8:3	10.123.4.1:3	10.123.4.1:3
10.45.1.5:1	10.78.9.9:1	10.123.4.1:1	10.123.4.1:1
10.45.1.5:51576	10.78.9.7:51576	10.123.4.2:23	10.123.4.2:23
10.45.1.5:31515	10.78.9.8:31515	10.123.4.2:23	10.123.4.2:23

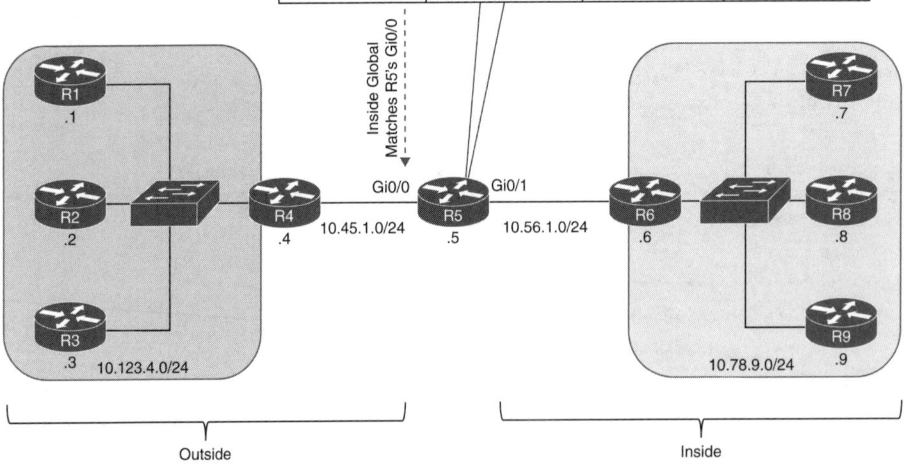

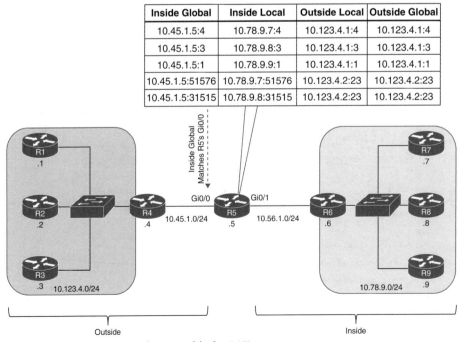

Figure 15-11 *R5's Translation Table for PAT*

Example 15-44 shows R5's NAT translation table. By taking the ports from the TCP brief sessions on R2 and correlating them to R5's NAT translation table, you can identify which TCP session belongs to R7 or R8.

Example 15-44 *R5's NAT Translation Table with PAT*

```
R5# show ip nat translations
Pro Inside global        Inside local          Outside local         Outside global
icmp 10.45.1.5:4         10.78.9.7:4           10.123.4.1:4          10.123.4.1:4
icmp 10.45.1.5:3         10.78.9.8:3           10.123.4.1:3          10.123.4.1:3
icmp 10.45.1.5:1         10.78.9.9:1           10.123.4.1:1          10.123.4.1:1
tcp 10.45.1.5:51576      10.78.9.7:51576       10.123.4.2:23         10.123.4.2:23
tcp 10.45.1.5:31515      10.78.9.8:31515       10.123.4.2:23         10.123.4.2:23
```


Exam Preparation Tasks

You have a couple of choices for exam preparation: the exercises here, Chapter 30, "Final Preparation," and the exam simulation questions in the Pearson Test Prep Software Online.

Review All Key Topics

Review the most important topics in the chapter, noted with the Key Topic icon in the outer margin of the page. Table 15-4 lists these key topics and the page number on which each is found.

Key Topic

Table 15-4 Key Topics for Chapter 15

Key Topic Element	Description	Page
Section	Network Time Protocol	420
Paragraph	NTP stratums	421
Section	Stratum Preferences	424
Section	NTP Peers	424
Section	Precision Time Protocol (PTP)	425
Paragraph	First-Hop Redundancy Protocol (FHRP)	430
Section	Hot Standby Router Protocol	432
List	HSRP configuration	434
Paragraph	HSRP object tracking	436
Section	Virtual Router Redundancy Protocol	438
List	Legacy VRRP configuration	438
List	Hierarchical VRRP configuration	440
Section	Gateway Load Balancing Protocol	441
List	GLBP configuration	442
List	GLBP load-balancing options	444
Paragraph	Network Address Translation (NAT)	446
List	NAT terms	447

Key Topic Element	Description	Page
List	Common NAT types	447
List	Inside static NAT configuration	449
Paragraph	Viewing the NAT translation table	451
List	NAT processing	452
List	Outside static NAT configuration	455
List	Pooled NAT configuration	455
Paragraph	NAT timeout	458
Paragraph	Port Address Translation (PAT)	458
List	PAT configuration	458

Complete Tables and Lists from Memory

There are no memory tables in this chapter.

Define Key Terms

Define the following key terms from this chapter, and check your answers in the Glossary:

first-hop redundancy protocol, inside global, inside local, Network Address Translation (NAT), NTP client, NTP peer, NTP server, outside local, outside global, pooled NAT, Port Address Translation (PAT), Precision Time Protocol, static NAT, stratum

Use the Command Reference to Check Your Memory

Table 15-5 lists the important commands from this chapter. To test your memory, cover the right side of the table with a piece of paper, read the description on the left side, and see how much of the command you can remember.

Table 15-5 Command Reference

Task	Command Syntax
Configure a device as an NTP client with the IP address of the NTP server	**ntp server** *ip-address* [**prefer**] [**source** *interface-id*]
Configure a device so that it can respond authoritatively to NTP requests when it does not have access to an atomic clock or an upstream NTP server	**ntp master** *stratum-number*
Configure the peering with another device with NTP	**ntp peer** *ip-address*
Configure the tracking of an interface's line protocol state	**track** *object-number* **interface** *interface-id* **line-protocol**
Configure a device to track the installation of a route in the routing table	**track** *object-number* **ip route** *route/prefix-length* **reachability**

Task	Command Syntax
Configure the VIP for the HSRP instance	**standby** *instance-id* **ip** *vip-address*
Enable preemption for the HSRP instance	**standby** *instance-id* **preempt**
Specify the MAC address for the HSRP VIP	**standby** *instance-id* **mac-address** *mac-address*
Configure the HSRP timers for neighbor health checks	**standby** *instance-id* **timers** {**seconds** | **msec milliseconds**}
Link object tracking to a decrease in priority upon failure of the HSRP	**standby** *instance-id* **track** *object-id* **decrement** *decrement-value*
Configure the VIP gateway for the VRRP instance	**vrrp** *instance-id* **ip** *vip-address*
Configure the priority for the VRRP instance	**vrrp** *instance-id* **priority** *priority*
Link object tracking to a decrease in priority upon failure with VRRP	**vrrp** *instance-id* **track** *object-id* **decrement** *decrement-value*
Configure the VIP gateway for a GLBP instance	**glbp** *instance-id* **ip** *vip-address*
Enable preemption for a GLBP instance	**glbp** *instance-id* **preempt**
Configure the priority for a GLBP instance	**glbp** *instance-id* **priority** *priority*
Configure GLBP timers for neighbor health checks	**glbp** *instance-id* **timers** {*hello-seconds* | **msec** *hello-milliseconds*} {*hold-seconds* | **msec** *hold-milliseconds*}
Configure the GLBP load-balancing algorithm	**glbp** *instance-id* **load-balancing** {**host-dependent** | **round-robin** | **weighted**}.
Configure the devices GLBP weight for traffic load balancing	**glbp** *instance-id* **weighting** *weight*
Configure an interface as an outside interface for NAT	**ip nat outside**
Configure an interface as an inside interface for NAT	**ip nat inside**
Configure static inside NAT	**ip nat inside source static** *inside-local-ip inside-global-ip*
Configure static outside NAT	**ip nat outside source static** *outside-global-ip outside-local-ip* [**add-route**]
Configure pooled NAT	**ip nat pool** *nat-pool-name starting-ip ending-ip* **prefix-length** *prefix-length*
Define the NAT pool for global IP addresses	**ip nat inside source list** *acl* **pool** *nat-pool-name*
Configure a device for PAT	**ip nat inside source list** *acl* {**interface** *interface-id* | **pool** *nat-pool-name*} **overload**
Modify the NAT timeout period	**ip nat translation timeout** *seconds*
Clear a dynamic NAT entry	**clear ip nat translation** {*ip-address* | *}

15

Task	Command Syntax
Display the status of the NTP service, hardware clock synchronization status, reference time, and time since last polling cycle	**show ntp status**
Display the list of configured NTP servers and peers and their time offset from the local device	**show ntp associations**
Display the status of a tracked object	**show track** [*object-number*]
Display the status of an HSRP VIP	**show standby** [*interface-id*] [**brief**]
Display the status of a VRRP VIP	**show vrrp** [**brief**]
Display the status of a GLBP VIP	**show glbp** [**brief**]
Display the translation table on a NAT device	**show ip nat translations**

CHAPTER 16

Overlay Tunnels

This chapter covers the following subjects:

- **Generic Routing Encapsulation (GRE) Tunnels:** This section explains GRE and how to configure and verify GRE tunnels.
- **IPsec Fundamentals:** This section explains IPsec fundamentals and how to configure and verify IPsec.
- **Cisco Locator/ID Separation Protocol (LISP):** This section describes the architecture, protocols, and operation of LISP.
- **Virtual Extensible Local Area Network (VXLAN):** This section describes VXLAN as a data plane protocol that is open to operate with any control plane protocol.

An **overlay network** is a logical or virtual network built over a physical transport network referred to as an **underlay network**. Overlay networks are used to overcome shortcomings of traditional networks by enabling network virtualization, **segmentation**, and security to make traditional networks more manageable, flexible, secure (by means of encryption), and scalable. Examples of overlay tunneling technologies include the following:

- Generic Routing Encapsulation (GRE)
- IP Security (IPsec)
- Locator ID/Separation Protocol (LISP)
- Virtual Extensible LAN (VXLAN)
- Multiprotocol Label Switching (MPLS)

A **virtual private network (VPN)** is an overlay network that enables private networks to communicate with each other across an untrusted network such as the Internet. VPN data sent across an unsecure network needs to be encrypted to ensure that an attacker does not view or tamper with data. The most common VPN encryption algorithm used is **Internet Protocol Security (IPsec)**.

Private networks typically use RFC 1918 address space (10.0.0.0/8, 172.16.0.0/12, and 192.168.0.0/16), which is not routable across the Internet. To be able to create VPNs between private networks, a tunneling overlay technology is necessary, and the most commonly used one is GRE.

NOTE MPLS tunneling is not supported across the Internet unless it is tunneled within another tunneling protocol, such as GRE, which can then be encrypted with IPsec (MPLS over GRE over IPsec). A key takeaway from this is that an overlay tunnel can be built over another overlay tunnel.

Different combinations of overlay tunneling and encryption technologies opened the door to next-generation overlay fabric networks such as

- Software-Defined WAN (SD-WAN)
- Software-Defined Access (SD-Access)
- Application Centric Infrastructure (ACI)
- Cisco Virtual Topology System (VTS)

This chapter covers GRE, IPsec, LISP, and VXLAN. These technologies are essential to understanding the operation of SD-Access and SD-WAN, which are covered in Chapter 23, "Fabric Technologies."

"Do I Know This Already?" Quiz

The "Do I Know This Already?" quiz enables you to assess whether you should read the entire chapter. If you miss no more than one of these self-assessment questions, you might want to move ahead to the "Exam Preparation Tasks" section. Table 16-1 lists the major headings in this chapter and the "Do I Know This Already?" quiz questions covering the material in those headings so you can assess your knowledge of these specific areas. The answers to the "Do I Know This Already?" quiz appear in Appendix A, "Answers to the 'Do I Know This Already?' Questions."

Table 16-1 "Do I Know This Already?" Foundation Topics Section-to-Question Mapping

Foundation Topics Section	Questions
Generic Routing Encapsulation (GRE) Tunnels	1–3
IPsec Fundamentals	4–6
Cisco Locator/ID Separation Protocol (LISP)	7–9
Virtual Extensible Local Area Network (VXLAN)	10–11

1. Which of the following commands are optional for GRE configuration? (Choose two.)

   a. **tunnel source** {*ip-address* | *interface-id*}

   b. **tunnel destination** *ip-address*

   c. **tunnel mode gre** {**ip** | **ipv6**}

   d. **keepalive**

2. True or false: GRE was originally created to provide transport for non-routable legacy protocols.
   a. True
   b. False
3. Which of the following should not be dynamically advertised via an IGP into a GRE tunnel?
   a. Loopback interfaces
   b. The GRE tunnel source interface or source IP address
   c. Connected interfaces
   d. The GRE tunnel IP address
4. Which of the following are modes of packet transport supported by IPsec? (Choose two.)
   a. Tunnel mode
   b. Transparent mode
   c. Transport mode
   d. Crypto mode
5. Which of the following are encryption protocols that should be avoided? (Choose two.)
   a. DES
   b. 3DES
   c. AES
   d. GCM
6. Which of the following is the message exchange mode used to establish an IKEv1 IPsec SA?
   a. Main mode
   b. Aggressive mode
   c. Quick mode
   d. CREATE_CHILD_SA
7. LISP separates IP addresses into which of the following? (Choose two.)
   a. RLOCs
   b. LISP entities
   c. Subnets and hosts
   d. EIDs
8. What is the destination UDP port used by the LISP data plane?
   a. 4341
   b. 4143
   c. 4342
   d. 4142

9. True or false: ETRs are the only devices responsible for responding to map requests originated by ITRs.

- **a.** True
- **b.** False

10. Which of the following UDP ports is the UDP port officially assigned by the IANA for VXLAN?

- **a.** 8947
- **b.** 4789
- **c.** 8472
- **d.** 4987

11. True or false: The VXLAN specification defines a data plane and a control plane for VXLAN.

- **a.** True
- **b.** False

Foundation Topics

Generic Routing Encapsulation (GRE) Tunnels

Key Topic

GRE is a tunneling protocol that provides connectivity to a wide variety of network-layer protocols by encapsulating and forwarding packets over an IP-based network. GRE was originally created to provide transport for non-routable legacy protocols such as *Internetwork Packet Exchange (IPX)* across an IP network and is now more commonly used as an overlay for IPv4 and IPv6. GRE tunnels have many uses. For example, they can be used to tunnel traffic through a firewall or an ACL or to connect discontiguous networks, and they can even be used as networking duct tape for bad routing designs. Their most important application is that they can be used to create VPNs.

When a router encapsulates a packet for a GRE tunnel, it adds new header information (known as *encapsulation*) to the packet, which contains the remote endpoint IP address as the destination. The new IP header information allows the packet to be routed between the two tunnel endpoints without inspection of the packet's payload. After the packet reaches the remote endpoint, the GRE headers are removed (known as *de-encapsulation*), and the packet is forwarded out the remote router. Figure 16-1 illustrates an IP packet before and after GRE encapsulation.

> **NOTE** GRE tunnels support IPv4 or IPv6 addresses as an underlay or overlay network.

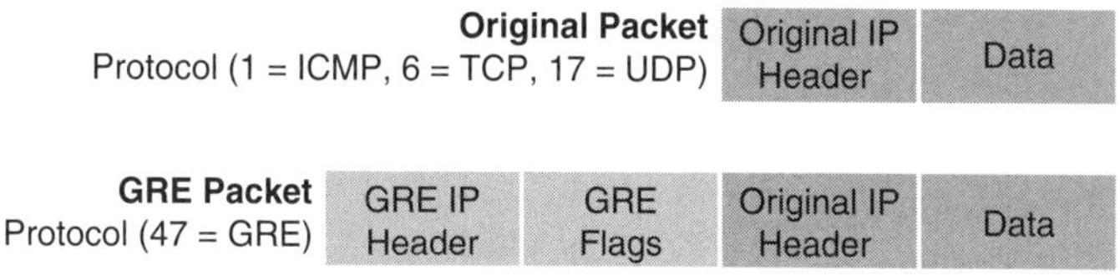

Figure 16-1 *IP Packet Before and After GRE Headers*

The following sections explain the fundamentals of GRE tunnels as well as the process for configuring them.

GRE Tunnel Configuration

Figure 16-2 illustrates a topology where R1 and R2 are using their respective ISP routers as their default gateways to reach the Internet. This allows R1 and R2 to reach each other's Internet-facing interfaces (Gi0/1 on both) to form a GRE tunnel over the Internet. For this case, the Internet, represented by 100.64.0.0/16, is the transport (underlay) network, and 192.168.100.0/24 is the GRE tunnel (overlay network).

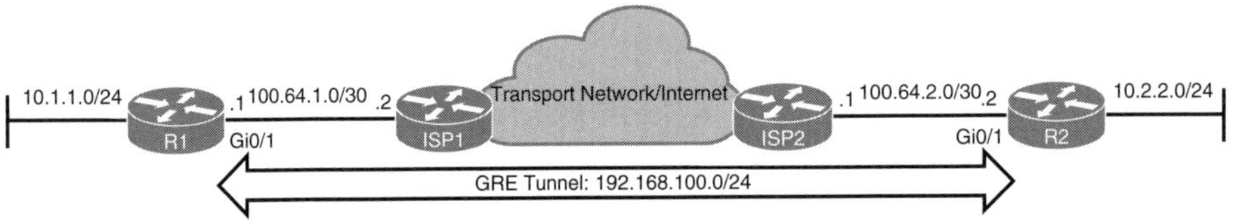

Figure 16-2 *GRE Tunnel Topology*

Example 16-1 shows the routing table of R1 before the GRE tunnels is created. Notice that there is a default route pointing to ISP1.

Example 16-1 *R1's Routing Table Without the GRE Tunnel*

```
R1# show ip route
! Output omitted for brevity
Codes: L - local, C - connected, S - static, R - RIP, M - mobile, B - BGP
..
       ia - IS-IS inter area, * - candidate default, U - per-user static route

Gateway of last resort is 100.64.1.2 to network 0.0.0.0

S* 0.0.0.0/0 [1/0] via 100.64.1.2
..
```

```
! A traceroute to R2's LAN interface is sent to the ISP1 router which is unable to
! forward it since it has no reachability into R2's LAN networks.

R1# trace 10.2.2.2
Tracing the route to 10.2.2.2
  1 100.64.1.2 2 msec 2 msec 3 msec
  2 100.64.1.2 !H !H *
```

```
! R2's Internet facing interface is reachable from R1's Internet facing interface.
```

Answers to the "Do I Know This Already?" quiz:

1 C, D **2** A **3** B **4** A, C **5** A, B **6** C **7** A, D **8** A **9** B **10** B **11** B

```
! These Internet facing addresses will be used as endpoints for the GRE tunnels

R1# ping 100.64.2.2 source 100.64.1.1
Sending 5, 100-byte ICMP Echos to 100.64.2.2, timeout is 2 seconds:
!!!!!
Success rate is 100 percent (5/5), round-trip min/avg/max = 2/3/5 ms
```

The steps for configuring GRE tunnels are as follows:

Key Topic

Step 1. Create the tunnel interface by using the global configuration command **interface tunnel** *tunnel-number*.

Step 2. Identify the local source of the tunnel by using the interface parameter command **tunnel source** {*ip-address* | *interface-id*}. The tunnel source interface indicates the interface that will be used for encapsulation and de-encapsulation of the GRE tunnel. The tunnel source can be a physical interface or a loopback interface. A loopback interface can provide reachability if one of the transport interfaces fails.

Step 3. Identify the remote destination IP address by using the interface parameter command **tunnel destination** *ip-address*. The tunnel destination is the remote router's underlay IP address toward which the local router sends GRE packets.

Step 4. Allocate an IP address to the tunnel interface to the interface by using the command **ip address** *ip-address subnet-mask*.

Step 5. (Optional) Define the tunnel bandwidth. Virtual interfaces do not have the concept of latency and need to have a reference bandwidth configured so that routing protocols that use bandwidth for best-path calculation can make an intelligent decision. Bandwidth is also used for *quality of service (QoS)* configuration on the interface. Bandwidth is defined with the interface parameter command **bandwidth** [*1-10000000*], which is measured in kilobits per second.

Step 6. (Optional) Specify a GRE tunnel keepalive. Tunnel interfaces are GRE *point-to-point (P2P)* by default, and the line protocol enters an up state when the router detects that a route to the tunnel destination exists in the routing table. If the tunnel destination is not in the routing table, the tunnel interface (line protocol) enters a down state.

Tunnel keepalives ensure that bidirectional communication exists between tunnel endpoints to keep the line protocol up. Otherwise, the router must rely on routing protocol timers to detect a dead remote endpoint.

Keepalives are configured with the interface parameter command **keepalive** [*seconds* [*retries*]]. The default timer is 10 seconds, with three retries.

Step 7. (Optional) Define the IP *maximum transmission unit (MTU)* for the tunnel interface. The GRE tunnel adds a minimum of 24 bytes to the packet size to accommodate the headers that are added to the packet. Specifying the IP MTU on the tunnel interface has the router perform the fragmentation in advance of the host having to detect and specify the packet MTU. IP MTU is configured with the interface parameter command **ip mtu** *mtu*.

Table 16-2 shows the encapsulation overhead for various tunnel techniques. The header size may change depending on the configuration options used. For all the examples in this chapter, the IP MTU is set to 1400.

Table 16-2 Encapsulation Overhead for Tunnels

Tunnel Type	Tunnel Header Size
GRE without IPsec	24 bytes
DES/3DES IPsec (transport mode)	18–25 bytes
DES/3DES IPsec (tunnel mode)	38–45 bytes
GRE + DES/3DES	42–49 bytes
GRE + AES + SHA-1	62–77 bytes

GRE Configuration Example

Example 16-2 provides a GRE tunnel configuration for R1 and R2, following the steps for GRE configuration listed earlier in this section. OSPF is enabled on the LAN (10.0.0.0/8) and GRE tunnel (192.168.100.0/24) networks. With this configuration, R1 and R2 become direct OSPF neighbors over the GRE tunnel and learn each other's routes. The default static routes are pointing to their respective ISP routers.

Example 16-2 *Configuring GRE*

```
R1
interface Tunnel100
 bandwidth 4000
 ip address 192.168.100.1 255.255.255.0
 ip mtu 1400
 keepalive 5 3
 tunnel source GigabitEthernet0/1
 tunnel destination 100.64.2.2
!
router ospf 1
 router-id 1.1.1.1
 network 10.1.1.1 0.0.0.0 area 1
 network 192.168.100.1 0.0.0.0 area 0
!
ip route 0.0.0.0 0.0.0.0 100.64.1.2
```

```
R2
interface Tunnel100
 bandwidth 4000
 ip address 192.168.100.2 255.255.255.0
 ip mtu 1400
 keepalive 5 3
 tunnel source GigabitEthernet0/1
 tunnel destination 100.64.1.1
!
```

```
router ospf 1
 router-id 2.2.2.2
 network 10.2.2.0 0.0.0.255 area 2
 network 192.168.100.2 0.0.0.0 area 0

ip route 0.0.0.0 0.0.0.0 100.64.2.1
```

Now that the GRE tunnel is configured, the state of the tunnel can be verified with the command **show interfaces tunnel** *number*. Example 16-3 shows output from this command. Notice that the output includes the tunnel source and destination addresses, keepalive values (if any), the tunnel line protocol state, and the fact that the tunnel is a GRE/IP tunnel.

Example 16-3 *Displaying GRE Tunnel Parameters*

```
R1# show interfaces tunnel 100 | include Tunnel.*is|Keepalive|Tunnel s|Tunnel p
Tunnel100 is up, line protocol is up
  Keepalive set (5 sec), retries 3
  Tunnel source 100.64.1.1 (GigabitEthernet0/1), destination 100.64.2.2
  Tunnel protocol/transport GRE/IP
```


Example 16-4 shows the routing table of R1 after forming an OSPF adjacency with R2 over the GRE tunnel. Notice that R1 learns the 10.2.2.0/24 network directly from R2 via tunnel 100, and it is installed as an OSPF inter-area (IA) route.

Example 16-4 *R1 Routing Table with GRE*

```
R1# show ip route
Codes: L - local, C - connected, S - static, R - RIP, M - mobile, B - BGP
       D - EIGRP, EX - EIGRP external, O - OSPF, IA - OSPF inter area

! Output omitted for brevity

Gateway of last resort is 100.64.1.2 to network 0.0.0.0

S*    0.0.0.0/0 [1/0] via 100.64.1.2
      1.0.0.0/32 is subnetted, 1 subnets
C        1.1.1.1 is directly connected, Loopback0
      10.0.0.0/8 is variably subnetted, 3 subnets, 2 masks
C        10.1.1.0/24 is directly connected, GigabitEthernet0/3
L        10.1.1.1/32 is directly connected, GigabitEthernet0/3
O IA     10.2.2.0/24 [110/26] via 192.168.100.2, 00:17:37, Tunnel100
      100.0.0.0/8 is variably subnetted, 2 subnets, 2 masks
C        100.64.1.0/30 is directly connected, GigabitEthernet0/1
L        100.64.1.1/32 is directly connected, GigabitEthernet0/1
      192.168.100.0/24 is variably subnetted, 2 subnets, 2 masks
C        192.168.100.0/24 is directly connected, Tunnel100
L        192.168.100.1/32 is directly connected, Tunnel100
```

Example 16-5 verifies that traffic from 10.1.1.1 takes tunnel 100 (192.168.100.0/24) to reach the 10.2.2.2 network.

Example 16-5 *Verifying the Tunnel*

```
R1# traceroute 10.2.2.2 source 10.1.1.1
Tracing the route to 10.2.2.2
  1 192.168.100.2 3 msec 5 msec *
```

Notice that from R1's perspective, the network is only one hop away. The traceroute does not display all the hops in the underlay. In the same fashion, the packet's *time-to-live (TTL)* is encapsulated as part of the payload. The original TTL decreases by only one for the GRE tunnel, regardless of the number of hops in the transport network. During GRE encapsulation, the default GRE TTL value is 255. The interface parameter command **tunnel ttl** *ttl-value* is used to change the GRE TTL value.

Problems with Overlay Networks: Recursive Routing

Recursive routing and outbound interface selection are two common problems with tunnel or overlay networks. This section explains these problems and describes a solution.

Explicit care must be taken when using a routing protocol on a network tunnel. If a router tries to reach the remote router's encapsulating interface (transport IP address) via the tunnel (overlay network), problems will occur. This is a common issue when the transport network is advertised into the same routing protocol that runs on the overlay network.

For example, say that a network administrator accidentally adds the 100.64.0.0/16 Internet-facing interfaces to OSPF on R1 and R2. The ISP routers are not running OSPF, so an adjacency does not form, but R1 and R2 advertise the Internet-facing IP addresses to each other over the GRE tunnel via OSPF, and since they would be more specific than the configured default static routes, they would be preferred and installed on the routing table. The routers would then try to use the tunnel to reach the tunnel endpoint address, which is not possible. This scenario is known as *recursive routing*.

A router detects recursive routing and generates a syslog message, as shown in Example 16-6. The tunnel is brought down, which terminates the OSPF adjacencies, and then R1 and R2 find each other by using the default route again. The tunnel is re-established, OSPF forms an adjacency, and the problem repeats over and over again.

Example 16-6 *Recursive Routing Syslogs*

```
! Internet interface added to OSPF on R1

R1(config)# router ospf 1
R1(config-router)# network 100.64.1.1 0.0.0.0 area 1
```

```
! Internet interface added to OSPF on R2
R2(config)# router ospf 1
R2(config-router)# network 100.64.2.2 0.0.0.0 area 2

! Once the tunnel source interface or source IP address is advertised into OSPF, the
! recursive routing issue starts and syslogs alerting on a recursive routing issue are
! generated
```

```
01:56:24.808: %LINEPROTO-5-UPDOWN: Line protocol on Interface Tunnel100, changed
              state to up
01:56:24.843: %OSPF-5-ADJCHG: Process 1, Nbr 2.2.2.2 on Tunnel100 from LOADING
              to FULL, Loading Done

! The Midchain syslog indicates the tunnel destination was learned through the tunnel
! itself. This is resolved by learning the tunnel destination through an interface
! other than the tunnel
01:56:34.829: %ADJ-5-PARENT: Midchain parent maintenance for IP midchain out of
              Tunnel100 - looped chain attempting to stack
! The following syslog indicates a recursive routing issue is occurring on the tunnel
01:56:39.808: %TUN-5-RECURDOWN: Tunnel100 temporarily disabled due to recursive
              routing
01:56:39.808: %LINEPROTO-5-UPDOWN: Line protocol on Interface Tunnel100, changed
              state to down
01:56:39.811: %OSPF-5-ADJCHG: Process 1, Nbr 2.2.2.2 on Tunnel100 from FULL to
              DOWN, Neighbor Down: Interface down or detached
01:57:44.813: %LINEPROTO-5-UPDOWN: Line protocol on Interface Tunnel100, changed
              state to up
01:57:44.849: %OSPF-5-ADJCHG: Process 1, Nbr 2.2.2.2 on Tunnel100 from LOADING to
              FULL, Loading Done
! This condition will cycle over and over until the recursive routing issue is
! resolved
01:57:54.834: %ADJ-5-PARENT: Midchain parent maintenance for IP midchain out of
              Tunnel100 - looped chain attempting to stack
01:57:59.813: %TUN-5-RECURDOWN: Tunnel100 temporarily disabled due to recursive
              routing
01:57:59.813: %LINEPROTO-5-UPDOWN: Line protocol on Interface Tunnel100, changed
state to down
01:57:59.818: %OSPF-5-ADJCHG: Process 1, Nbr 2.2.2.2 on Tunnel100 from FULL to
   DOWN, Neighbor Down: Interface down or detached
```

Recursive routing problems are remediated by preventing the tunnel endpoint address from being advertised across the tunnel network. For the issue shown in Example 16-6, removing the tunnel endpoint interfaces (Internet-facing interfaces) from OSPF would stabilize the topology.

IPsec Fundamentals

Key Topic

IPsec is a framework of open standards for creating highly secure virtual private networks (VPNs) using various protocols and technologies for secure communication across unsecure networks, such as the Internet. IPsec tunnels provide the security services listed in Table 16-3.

16

Key Topic

Table 16-3 IPsec Security Services

Security Service	Description	Methods Used
Peer authentication	Verifies the identity of the VPN peer through authentication.	■ Pre-Shared Key (PSK) ■ Digital certificates
Data confidentiality	Protects data from eavesdropping attacks through encryption algorithms. Changes plaintext into encrypted ciphertext.	■ Data Encryption Standard (DES) ■ Triple DES (3DES) ■ Advanced Encryption Standard (AES) The use of DES and 3DES is not recommended.
Data integrity	Prevents *man-in-the-middle (MitM)* attacks by ensuring that data has not been tampered with during its transit across an unsecure network.	Hash Message Authentication Code (HMAC) functions: ■ Message Digest 5 (MD5) algorithm ■ Secure Hash Algorithm (SHA-1) The use of MD5 is not recommended.
Replay detection	Prevents MitM attacks where an attacker captures VPN traffic and replays it back to a VPN peer with the intention of building an illegitimate VPN tunnel.	Every packet is marked with a unique sequence number. A VPN device keeps track of the sequence number and does not accept a packet with a sequence number it has already processed.

NOTE In Cisco IOS XE Release 17.11.1 and later, weak crypto algorithms such as RSA keys of less than 2048 bits, MD5 for authentication, DES, and 3DES for encryption are rejected by default due to their weak cryptographic properties. It is possible to disable this enforcement via configuration, but it is not recommended. More details can be found in Field Notice 72510.

IPsec uses two different packet headers to deliver the security services mentioned in Table 16-3:

- Authentication header
- Encapsulating Security Payload (ESP)

Key Topic

Authentication Header

The IP authentication header provides data integrity, peer authentication, and protection from hackers replaying packets (replay detection). The authentication header ensures that the original data packet (before encapsulation) has not been modified during transport on the public network. It creates a digital signature similar to a checksum to ensure that the packet has not been modified. AH is identified by the protocol number 51 in the preceding *Protocol* field in the IPv4 header or the *Next Header* field in the IPv6 header. The authentication header does not support encryption (data confidentiality) and *NAT traversal (NAT-T)*, and for this reason, its use is not recommended, unless authentication is all that is desired.

Key Topic

Encapsulating Security Payload

Encapsulating Security Payload (ESP) provides data confidentiality, authentication, and protection from hackers replaying packets. Typically, *payload* refers to the actual data minus any headers, but in the context of ESP, the payload is the portion of the original packet that is encapsulated within the IPsec headers. ESP ensures that the original payload (before encapsulation) maintains data confidentiality by encrypting the payload and adding a new set of headers during transport across a public network. ESP is identified by the protocol number 50 in the preceding *Protocol* field in the IPv4 header or the *Next Header* field in the IPv6 header. Unlike the authentication header, ESP does provide data confidentiality and supports NAT-T.

Traditional IPsec provides two modes of packet transport:

- **Tunnel mode:** Encrypts the entire original packet and adds a new set of IPsec headers. These new headers are used to route the packet and also provide overlay functions.
- **Transport mode:** Encrypts and authenticates only the packet payload. This mode does not provide overlay functions and routes based on the original IP headers.

16

Figure 16-3 shows an original packet, an IPsec packet in transport mode, and an IPsec packet in tunnel mode.

Key Topic

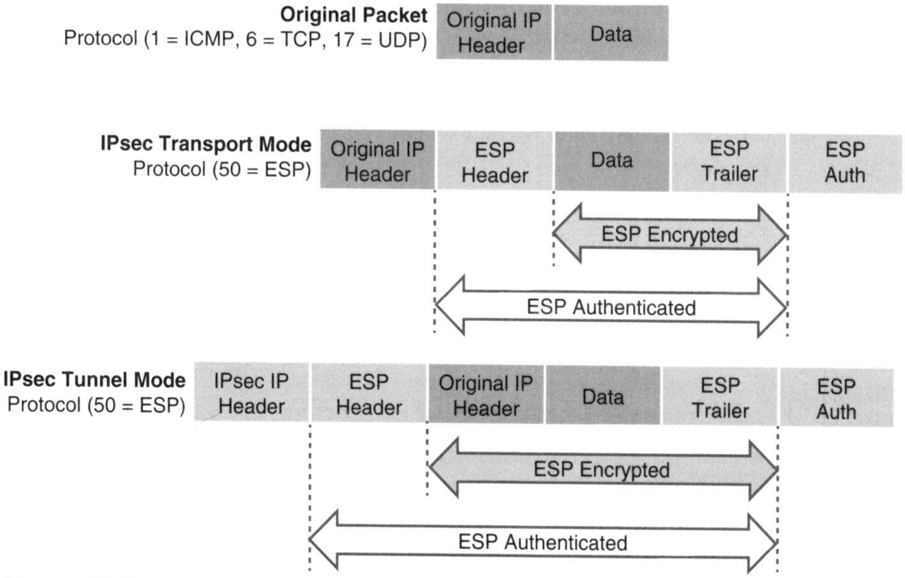

Figure 16-3 *IPsec Transport and Tunnel Encapsulation*

IPsec supports the following encryption, hashing, and keying methods to provide security services:

Key Topic

- **Data Encryption Standard (DES):** A 56-bit symmetric data encryption algorithm that can encrypt the data sent over a VPN. This algorithm is very weak and should be avoided.
- **Triple DES (3DES):** A data encryption algorithm that runs the DES algorithm three times with three different 56-bit keys. Using this algorithm is no longer recommended. The more advanced and more efficient AES should be used instead.
- **Advanced Encryption Standard (AES):** A symmetric encryption algorithm used for data encryption that was developed to replace DES and 3DES. AES supports key lengths of 128 bits, 192 bits, or 256 bits and is based on the Rijndael algorithm.
- **Message Digest 5 (MD5):** A one-way, 128-bit hash algorithm used for data authentication. Cisco devices use MD5 HMAC, which provides an additional level of protection against MitM attacks. Using this algorithm is no longer recommended, and SHA should be used instead.
- **Secure Hash Algorithm (SHA):** A one-way, 160-bit hash algorithm used for data authentication. Cisco devices use the SHA-1 HMAC, which provides additional protection against MitM attacks.
- **Diffie-Hellman (DH):** An asymmetric key exchange protocol that enables two peers to establish a shared secret key used by encryption algorithms such as AES over an unsecure communications channel. A DH group refers to the length of the key (modulus size) to use for a DH key exchange. For example, group 1 uses 768 bits, group 2 uses 1024, and group 5 uses 1536, where the larger the modulus, the more secure it is. The purpose of DH is to generate shared secret symmetric keys that are used by the two VPN peers for symmetrical algorithms, such as AES. The DH exchange itself is asymmetrical and CPU intensive, and the resulting shared secret keys that are generated are symmetrical. Cisco recommends avoiding DH groups 1, 2, and 5 and instead using DH groups 14 and higher.
- **RSA signatures:** A public-key (digital certificates) cryptographic system used to mutually authenticate the peers.
- **Pre-Shared Key:** A security mechanism in which a locally configured key is used as a credential to mutually authenticate the peers.

Key Topic

Transform Sets

A *transform set* is a combination of security protocols and algorithms. During the IPsec SA negotiation, the peers agree to use a particular transform set for protecting a particular data flow. When such a transform set is found, it is selected and applied to the IPsec SAs on both peers. Table 16-4 shows the allowed transform set combinations.

Table 16-4 Allowed Transform Set Combinations

Transform Type	Transform	Description
Authentication header transform (only one allowed)	ah-md5-hmac	Authentication header with the MD5 authentication algorithm (not recommended)
	ah-sha-hmac	Authentication header with the SHA authentication algorithm
	ah-sha256-hmac	Authentication header with the 256-bit SHA authentication algorithm
	ah-sha384-hmac	Authentication header with the 384-bit SHA authentication algorithm
	ah-sha512-hmac	Authentication header with the 512-bit SHA authentication algorithm
ESP encryption transform (only one allowed)	esp-aes	ESP with the 128-bit AES encryption algorithm
	esp-gcm esp-gmac	ESP-GCM—ESP with either a 128-bit (default) or a 256-bit authenticated encryption algorithm ESP-GMAC—ESP with either 128-bit (default) or a 256-bit authentication algorithm without encryption
	esp-aes 192	ESP with the 192-bit AES encryption algorithm
	esp-aes 256	ESP with the 256-bit AES encryption algorithm
	esp-des esp-3des	ESPs with 56-bit and 168-bit DES encryption (no longer recommended)
	esp-null	Null encryption algorithm
	esp-seal	ESP with the 160-bit SEAL encryption algorithm
ESP authentication transform (only one allowed)	esp-md5-hmac	ESP with the MD5 (HMAC variant) authentication algorithm (no longer recommended)
	esp-sha-hmac	ESP with the SHA (HMAC variant) authentication algorithm
IP compression transform	comp-lzs	IP compression with the Lempel-Ziv-Stac (LZS) algorithm

NOTE The authentication header and ESP algorithms cannot be specified on the same transform set in Cisco IOS XE releases.

Key Topic

Internet Key Exchange

Internet Key Exchange (IKE) is a protocol that performs authentication between two endpoints to establish security associations (SAs), also known as IKE tunnels. These security associations, or tunnels, are used to carry control plane and data plane traffic for IPsec. There are two versions of IKE: IKEv1 (specified in RFC 2409) and IKEv2 (specified in RFC 7296). IKEv2 was developed to overcome the limitations of IKEv1 and provides many improvements over IKEv1's implementation. For example, it supports EAP (certificate-based authentication), has anti-DoS capabilities, and needs fewer messages to establish an IPsec SA. Understanding IKEv1 is still important because some legacy infrastructures have not yet migrated to IKEv2 or have devices or features that don't support IKEv2.

Key Topic

IKEv1

Internet Security Association and Key Management Protocol (ISAKMP) is a framework for authentication and key exchange between two peers to establish, modify, and tear down SAs. It is designed to support many different kinds of key exchanges. ISAKMP uses UDP port 500 for communication between peers.

IKE is the implementation of ISAKMP using the Oakley and Skeme key exchange techniques. Oakley provides Perfect Forward Secrecy (PFS) for keys, identity protection, and authentication; Skeme provides anonymity, repudiability, and quick key refreshment. For Cisco platforms, IKE is analogous to ISAKMP, and the two terms are used interchangeably.

IKEv1 defines two phases of key negotiation for IKE and IPsec SA establishment:

- **Phase 1:** Establishes a bidirectional SA between two IKE peers, known as an ISAKMP SA. Because the SA is bidirectional, after it is established, either peer may initiate negotiations for phase 2.
- **Phase 2:** Establishes unidirectional IPsec SAs, leveraging the ISAKMP SA established in phase 1 for the negotiation.

Phase 1 negotiation can occur using main mode (MM) or aggressive mode (AM). The peer that initiates the SA negotiation process is known as the *initiator*, and the other peer is known as the *responder*.

Main mode consists of six message exchanges and tries to protect all information during the negotiation so that no information is exposed to eavesdropping:

- **MM1:** This is the first message that the initiator sends to a responder. One or multiple SA proposals are offered, and the responder needs to match one of them for this phase to succeed. The SA proposals include different combinations of the following:
  - **Hash algorithm:** MD5 or SHA
  - **Encryption algorithm:** DES (bad), 3DES (better but not recommended), or AES (best)
  - **Authentication method:** Pre-Shared Key or digital certificates
  - **Diffie-Hellman (DH) group:** Groups 1, 2, 5, and so on

- **Lifetime:** How long until this IKE Phase 1 tunnel should be torn down (default is 24 hours). This is the only parameter that does not have to exactly match with the other peer to be accepted. If the lifetime is different, the peers agree to use the smallest lifetime between them.

- **MM2:** This message is sent from the responder to the initiator with the SA proposal that it matched.
- **MM3:** In this message, the initiator starts the DH key exchange. This is based on the DH group the responder matches in the proposal.
- **MM4:** The responder sends its own key to the initiator. At this point, encryption keys have been shared, and encryption is established for the ISAKMP SA.
- **MM5:** The initiator starts authentication by sending the peer router its IP address.
- **MM6:** The responder sends back a similar packet and authenticates the session. At this point, the ISAKMP SA is established.

When main mode is used, the identities of the two IKE peers are hidden. Although this mode of operation is very secure, it takes longer than aggressive mode to complete the negotiation.

Aggressive mode consists of a three-message exchange and takes less time to negotiate keys between peers; however, it doesn't offer the same level of encryption security provided by main mode negotiation, and the identities of the two peers trying to establish a security association are exposed to eavesdropping. These are the three aggressive mode messages:

- **AM1:** In this message, the initiator sends all the information contained in MM1 through MM3 and MM5.
- **AM2:** This message sends all the same information contained in MM2, MM4, and MM6.
- **AM3:** This message sends the authentication that is contained in MM5.

Main mode is slower than aggressive mode, but main mode is more secure and more flexible because it can offer an IKE peer more security proposals than aggressive mode. Aggressive mode is less flexible and not as secure, but it is much faster.

Phase 2 uses the existing bidirectional IKE SA to securely exchange messages to establish one or more IPsec SAs between the two peers. Unlike the IKE SA, which is a single bidirectional SA, a single IPsec SA negotiation results in two unidirectional IPsec SAs, one on each peer. The method used to establish the IPsec SA is known as quick mode. Quick mode uses a three-message exchange:

- **QM1:** The initiator (which could be either peer) can start multiple IPsec SAs in a single exchange message. This message includes agreed-upon algorithms for encryption and integrity decided as part of phase 1, as well as what traffic is to be encrypted or secured.
- **QM2:** This message from the responder has matching IPsec parameters.

- **QM3:** After this message, there should be two unidirectional IPsec SAs between the two peers.

Perfect Forward Secrecy (PFS) is an additional function for phase 2 that is recommended but is optional because it requires additional DH exchanges that require additional CPU cycles. The goal of this function is to create greater resistance to crypto attacks and maintain the privacy of the IPsec tunnels by deriving session keys independently of any previous key. This way, a compromised key does not compromise future keys.

Based on the minimum number of messages that aggressive, main, and quick modes may produce for IPsec SAs to be established between two peers, the following can be derived:

- Main mode uses six messages, and quick mode uses three, for a total of nine messages.
- Aggressive mode uses three messages, and quick mode uses three, for a total of six messages.

Key Topic

IKEv2

IKEv2 is an evolution of IKEv1 that includes many changes and improvements that simplify it and make it more efficient. One of the major changes has to do with the way the SAs are established. In IKEv2, communications consist of request and response pairs called *exchanges* and sometimes just called *request/response pairs*.

The first exchange, IKE_SA_INIT, negotiates cryptographic algorithms, exchanges **nonces**, and performs a Diffie-Hellman exchange. This is the equivalent to IKEv1's first two pairs of messages MM1 to MM4 but done as a single request/response pair.

The second exchange, IKE_AUTH, authenticates the previous messages and exchanges identities and certificates. Then it establishes an IKE SA and a child SA (the IPsec SA). This is equivalent to IKEv1's MM5 to MM6 as well as QM1 and QM2 but done as a single request/response pair.

It takes a total of four messages to bring up the bidirectional IKE SA and the unidirectional IPsec SAs, as opposed to six with IKEv1 aggressive mode or nine with main mode.

If additional IPsec SAs are required in IKEv2, it uses just two messages (a request/response pair) with a CREATE_CHILD_SA exchange, whereas IKEv1 would require three messages with quick mode.

Since the IKEv2 SA exchanges are completely different from those of IKEv1, they are incompatible with each other.

Table 16-5 illustrates some of the major differences between IKEv1 and IKEv2.

Table 16-5 Major Differences Between IKEv1 and IKEv2

IKEv1	IKEv2
Exchange Modes	
Main mode	IKE Security Association Initialization (SA_INIT)
Aggressive mode	IKE_Auth
Quick mode	CREATE_CHILD_SA

IKEv1	IKEv2
Minimum Number of Messages Needed to Establish IPsec SAs	
Nine with main mode Six with aggressive mode	Four
Supported Authentication Methods	
Pre-Shared Key (PSK) Digital RSA Certificate (RSA-SIG) Public key Both peers must use the same authentication method.	Pre-Shared Key (PSK) Digital RSA Certificate (RSA-SIG) Elliptic Curve Digital Signature Certificate (ECDSA-SIG) Extensible Authentication Protocol (EAP) Asymmetric authentication is supported. Authentication method can be specified during the IKE_AUTH exchange.
Next-Generation Encryption (NGE)	
Not supported	AES-GCM (Galois/Counter Mode) mode SHA-256 SHA-384 SHA-512 HMAC-SHA-256 Elliptic Curve Diffie-Hellman (ECDH) ECDH-384 ECDSA-384
Attack Protection	
MitM protection Eavesdropping protection	MitM protection Eavesdropping protection Anti-DoS protection

NOTE For additional information on the differences between IKEv1 and IKEv2, consult RFC 7296.

Following are additional details about some of the new IKEv2 changes and improvements mentioned in Table 16-5:

- **Increased efficiency:** The exchanges are restructured to be lighter, so fewer exchanges and less bandwidth are required to establish SAs as compared to using IKEv1.
- **Elliptic Curve Digital Signature Algorithm (ECDSA-SIG):** This newer alternative to public keys is more efficient. It was introduced to IKEv1 late, as part of RFC 4754, and has seen little acceptance there, but it is widely deployed with IKEv2. For this reason, it is not included in Table 16-5 as an authentication method for IKEv1.
- **Extensible Authentication Protocol (EAP):** The addition of EAP made IKEv2 the perfect solution for remote-access VPNs.

- **Next-generation encryption (NGE):** Security threats as well as cryptography to counteract these threats are continuously evolving. Old cryptography algorithms and key sizes no longer provide adequate protection from modern security threats and should be replaced. Next-generation encryption (NGE) algorithms offer the best technologies for future-proof cryptography that meets the security and scalability requirements of the next two decades.
- **Asymmetric authentication:** IKEv2 removes the requirement to negotiate the authentication method and introduces the ability to specify the authentication method in the IKE_AUTH exchange. As a result, each peer is able to choose its method of authentication. This allows for asymmetric authentication to occur, so the peers can use different authentication methods.
- **Anti-DoS:** IKEv2 detects whether an IPsec router is under attack and prevents consumption of resources.

NOTE For more information on next-generation encryption, please visit https://sec.cloudapps.cisco.com/security/center/resources/next_generation_cryptography.

IPsec VPNs

As mentioned earlier in this chapter, VPNs allow private networks to communicate with each other across an untrusted network such as the Internet; they should communicate in a secure manner. This section describes the different VPN security solutions available.

Table 16-6 includes the currently available IPsec VPN security solutions, each of which has benefits and is customized to meet specific deployment requirements.

Key Topic

Table 16-6 Cisco IPsec VPN Solutions

Features and Benefits	Site-to-Site IPsec VPN	Cisco DMVPN	Cisco GET-VPN	FlexVPN	Remote-Access VPN
Product interoperability	Multivendor	Cisco only	Cisco only	Cisco only	Cisco only
Key exchange	IKEv1 and IKEv2	IKEv1 and IKEv2 (both optional)	IKEv1 and IKEv2	IKEv2 only	TLS/DTLS and IKEv2
Scale	Low	Thousands for hub-and-spoke; hundreds for partially meshed spoke-to-spoke connections	Thousands	Thousands	Thousands

Features and Benefits	Site-to-Site IPsec VPN	Cisco DMVPN	Cisco GET-VPN	FlexVPN	Remote-Access VPN
Topology	Hub-and-spoke; small-scale meshing as manageability allows	Hub-and spoke; on-demand spoke-to-spoke partial mesh; spoke-to-spoke connections automatically terminated when no traffic present	Hub-and-spoke; any-to-any	Hub-and-spoke; any-to-any, remote access	Remote access
Routing	Not supported	Supported	Supported	Supported	Not supported
QoS	Supported	Supported	Supported	Native support	Supported
Multicast	Not supported	Tunneled	Natively supported across MPLS and private IP networks	Tunneled	Not supported
Non-IP protocols	Not supported	Not supported	Not supported	Not supported	Not supported
Private IP addressing	Supported	Supported	Requires use of GRE or DMVPN with Cisco GET-VPN to support private addresses across the Internet	Supported	Supported
High availability	Stateless failover	Routing	Routing	Routing IKEv2-based dynamic route distribution and server clustering	Not supported
Encapsulation	Tunneled IPsec	Tunneled IPsec	Tunnel-less IPsec	Tunneled IPsec	Tunneled IPsec/TLS

16

Features and Benefits	Site-to-Site IPsec VPN	Cisco DMVPN	Cisco GET-VPN	FlexVPN	Remote-Access VPN
Transport network	Any	Any	Private WAN/ MPLS	Any	Any

Site-to-Site (LAN-to-LAN) IPsec VPNs

Site-to-site IPsec VPNs are the most versatile solution for site-to-site encryption because they allow for multivendor interoperability. However, they are very difficult to manage in large networks.

Cisco Dynamic Multipoint VPN (DMVPN)

Cisco Dynamic Multipoint VPN simplifies configuration for hub-and-spoke and spoke-to-spoke VPNs. It accomplishes this by combining multipoint GRE (mGRE) tunnels, IPsec, and Next Hop Resolution Protocol (NHRP).

Cisco Group Encrypted Transport VPN (GET VPN)

Cisco Group Encrypted Transport VPN was developed specifically for enterprises to build any-to-any tunnel-less VPNs (where the original IP header is used) across service provider MPLS networks or private WANs. It does this without affecting any of the existing MPLS private WAN network services (such as multicast and QoS). Moreover, encryption over private networks addresses regulatory-compliance guidelines such as those in the Health Insurance Portability and Accountability Act (HIPAA), Sarbanes-Oxley Act, the Payment Card Industry Data Security Standard (PCI DSS), and the Gramm-Leach-Bliley Act (GLBA).

Cisco FlexVPN

FlexVPN is Cisco's implementation of the IKEv2 standard, featuring a unified VPN solution that combines site-to-site, remote access, hub-and-spoke topologies and partial meshes (spoke-to-spoke direct). FlexVPN offers a simple but modular framework that extensively uses virtual access interfaces while remaining compatible with legacy VPN implementations using crypto maps.

Remote VPN Access

Remote VPN access allows remote users to VPN securely into a corporate network. It is supported on IOS XE with FlexVPN (IKEv2 only) and on ASA 5500-X and Cisco Secure Firewalls.

Site-to-Site IPsec Configuration

The GRE configuration example earlier in this chapter allowed for traffic between private sites to flow over the Internet. The problem with this solution is that GRE offers no encryption, authentication, or associated security services, so it is highly susceptible to attacks. One solution is to encrypt the traffic going over the GRE tunnel with IPsec. The following sections explore configuration and verification for the following site-to-site (also known as LAN-to-LAN) IPsec solutions:

- Site-to-site GRE over IPsec with Pre-Shared Key
- Site-to-site static virtual tunnel interfaces (VTIs) over IPsec with Pre-Shared Key

VTI over IPsec encapsulates IPv4 or IPv6 traffic without the need for an additional GRE header. GRE over IPsec encapsulates IPv4 or IPv6 in different ways, depending on whether the mode is transport or tunnel mode. In transport mode, the original packet is encapsulated within GRE, and only the GRE payload, not the GRE IP header, is encrypted by IPsec. In this mode, the GRE IP header is used for routing. In tunnel mode, the original packet is encapsulated in GRE, the entire GRE packet is encrypted by IPsec, and a new IPsec IP header is added. For this reason, GRE over IPsec in tunnel mode is commonly referred to as *IPsec over GRE*. In tunnel mode, routing is performed using the IPsec IP header. In both GRE over IPsec modes, the protocol number of the IP header is 50, indicating the next header is an ESP header. Figure 16-4 compares GRE over IPsec packet encapsulation in transport and tunnel mode and IPsec tunnel mode with a VTI.

Key Topic

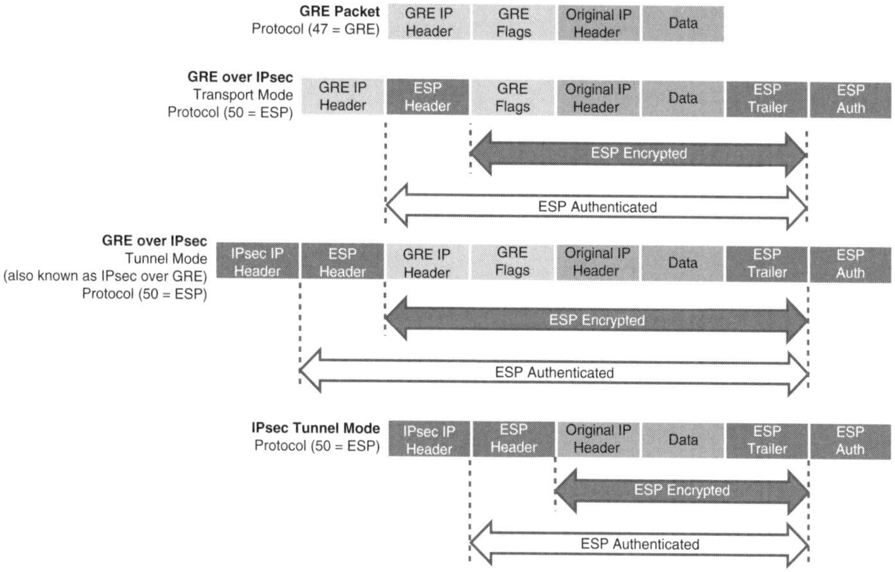

Figure 16-4 *GRE over IPsec Versus IPsec Tunnel Mode*

Key Topic

Site-to-Site GRE over IPsec

There are two different ways to encrypt traffic over a GRE tunnel:

- Using crypto maps
- Using tunnel IPsec profiles

Crypto maps should not be used for tunnel protection because they have many limitations that are resolved with IPsec profiles, including the following:

- Crypto maps cannot natively support the use of MPLS.
- Configuration can become overly complex.
- Crypto ACLs are commonly misconfigured.
- Crypto ACL entries can consume excessive amounts of TCAM space.

16

Even though crypto maps are no longer recommended for tunnels, they are still widely deployed and should be understood.

The steps to enable GRE over IPsec in tunnel or transport mode using crypto maps are as follows:

Key Topic

Step 1. Configure a crypto ACL to classify VPN traffic by using these commands:

ip access-list extended *acl_name*

permit gre host *tunnel-source IP* **host** *tunnel-destination IP*

This access list identifies traffic that needs to be protected by IPsec. It is used to match all traffic that passes through the GRE tunnel.

Step 2. Configure an ISAKMP policy for IKE SA by using the command **crypto isakmp policy** *priority*. Within the ISAKMP policy configuration mode, encryption, hash, authentication, and the DH group can be specified with the following commands:

encryption {**des** | **3des** | **aes** | **aes 192** | **aes 256**}

hash {**sha** | **sha256** | **sha384** | **md5**}

authentication {**rsa-sig** | **rsa-encr** | **pre-share**}

group {**1** | **2** | **5** | **14** | **15** | **16** | **19** | **20** | **24**}

The keyword *priority* uniquely identifies the IKE policy and assigns a priority to the policy, where 1 is the highest priority.

The DES and 3DES encryption algorithms are no longer recommended. DES is the default encryption used, so it is recommended to choose one of the AES encryption algorithms.

The MD5 hash is no longer recommended. The default is SHA.

Authentication allows for public keys (**rsa-encr**), digital certificates (**rsa-sig**), or PSK (**pre-share**) to be used.

The **group** command indicates the DH group, where 1 is the default. It is recommended to avoid using DH groups 1, 2, and 5 and instead use DH groups 14 and higher. The following DH groups are available:

- **1:** 768-bit DH (no longer recommended)
- **2:** 1024-bit DH (no longer recommended)
- **5:** 1536-bit DH (no longer recommended)
- **14:** The 2048-bit DH group
- **15:** The 3072-bit DH group
- **16:** The 4096-bit DH group
- **19:** The 256-bit ECDH group
- **20:** The 384-bit ECDH group
- **24:** The 2048-bit DH/DSA group

Step 3. Configure PSK by using the command **crypto isakmp key** *keystring* **address** *peer-address* [*mask*]. The *keystring* should match on both peers. For *peer-address* [*mask*], the value 0.0.0.0 0.0.0.0 can be used to allow a match against any peer.

Step 4. Create a transform set and enter transform set configuration mode by using the command **crypto ipsec transform-set** *transform-set-name transform1* [*transform2* [*transform3*]]. In transform set configuration mode, enter the command **mode** [**tunnel** | **transport**] to specify tunnel or transport modes. During the IPsec SA negotiation, the peers agree to use a particular transform set for protecting a particular data flow. **mode** indicates the GRE over IPsec encapsulation to be either tunnel or transport mode.

Step 5. Configure a crypto map and enter crypto map configuration mode by using the command **crypto map** *map-name seq-num* [**ipsec-isakmp**]. In crypto map configuration mode, use the following commands to specify the crypto ACL to be matched, the IPsec peer, and the transform sets to be negotiated:

```
match address acl-name
set peer {hostname | ip-address}
set transform-set transform-set-name1 [transform-set-name2...
transform-set-name6]
```

acl-name is the crypto ACL defined in step 1, which determines the traffic that should be protected by IPsec. The command **set peer** can be repeated for multiple remote peers. The command **set transform-set** specifies the transform sets to be negotiated. List multiple transform sets in priority order (highest priority first).

Step 6. Apply a crypto map to the outside physical interface (not the tunnel interface) by using the command **crypto map** *map-name*.

16

The steps to enable GRE over IPsec in tunnel or transport mode using IPsec profiles are as follows:

Key Topic

Step 1. Configure an ISAKMP policy for IKE SA by entering the command **crypto isakmp policy** *priority*. Within the ISAKMP policy configuration mode, encryption, hash, authentication, and the DH group can be specified with the following commands:

```
encryption {des | 3des | aes | aes 192 | aes 256}
hash {sha | sha256 | sha384 | md5}
authentication {rsa-sig | rsa-encr | pre-share}
group {1 | 2 | 5 | 14 | 15 | 16 | 19 | 20 | 24}
```

Step 2. Configure PSK by using the command **crypto isakmp key** *keystring* **address** *peer-address* [*mask*]. *keystring* should match on both peers.

Step 3. Create a transform set and enter transform set configuration mode by using the command **crypto ipsec transform-set** *transform-set-name transform1* [*transform2* [*transform3*]]. In the transform set configuration mode, enter the command **mode** [**tunnel** | **transport**] to specify tunnel or transport modes. During the IPsec SA negotiation, the peers agree to use a particular transform set for protecting a particular data flow. **mode** indicates the IPsec tunnel mode to be either tunnel or transport. To avoid double encapsulation (from GRE and IPsec), you should choose transport mode.

Step 4. Create an IPsec profile and enter IPsec profile configuration mode by entering the command **crypto ipsec profile** *ipsec-profile-name*. In IPsec profile configuration mode, specify the transform sets to be negotiated by using the command **set transform-set** *transform-set-name* [*transform-set-name2... transform-set-name6*]. List multiple transform sets in priority order (highest priority first).

Step 5. Apply the IPsec profile to a tunnel interface by using the command **tunnel protection ipsec profile** *profile-name*.

Example 16-7 shows a configuration example for a site-to-site IPsec tunnel using GRE over IPsec in transport mode with Pre-Shared Key. R1 is configured for GRE over IPsec in transport mode using crypto maps, and R2 is configured for GRE over IPsec in transport mode using IPsec profiles, using the configuration steps outlined here. For easier identification of the differences between the configuration options, the configuration portions that remain the same between the two are highlighted.

Example 16-7 *Configuring GRE over IPsec Site-to-Site Tunnel with Pre-Shared Key*

```
R1
crypto isakmp policy 10
 authentication pre-share
 hash sha256
 encryption aes
 group 14
!
crypto isakmp key CISCO123 address 100.64.2.2
!
crypto ipsec transform-set AES_SHA esp-aes esp-sha-hmac
 mode transport
!
ip access-list extended GRE_IPSEC_VPN
 10 permit gre host 100.64.1.1 host 100.64.2.2
!
crypto map VPN 10 ipsec-isakmp
 match address GRE_IPSEC_VPN
 set transform-set AES_SHA
 set peer 100.64.2.2
!
```

```
interface GigabitEthernet0/1
 ip address 100.64.1.1 255.255.255.252
 crypto map VPN
!
interface Tunnel100
 bandwidth 4000
 ip address 192.168.100.1 255.255.255.0
 ip mtu 1400
 tunnel source GigabitEthernet0/1
 tunnel destination 100.64.2.2

router ospf 1
 router-id 1.1.1.1
 network 10.1.1.1 0.0.0.0 area 1
 network 192.168.100.1 0.0.0.0 area 0
```

R2

```
crypto isakmp policy 10
 authentication pre-share
 hash sha256
 encryption aes
 group 14

crypto isakmp key CISCO123 address 100.64.1.1

crypto ipsec transform-set AES_SHA esp-aes esp-sha-hmac
 mode transport

crypto ipsec profile IPSEC_PROFILE
 set transform-set AES_SHA

interface GigabitEthernet0/1
 ip address 100.64.2.2 255.255.255.252

interface Tunnel100
 bandwidth 4000
 ip address 192.168.100.2 255.255.255.0
 ip mtu 1400
 tunnel source GigabitEthernet0/1
 tunnel destination 100.64.1.1
 tunnel protection ipsec profile IPSEC_PROFILE

router ospf 1
 router-id 2.2.2.2
 network 10.2.2.0 0.0.0.255 area 2
 network 192.168.100.2 0.0.0.0 area 0
```

16

Example 16-8 shows the commands to verify that the GRE IPsec tunnel between R1 and R2 is operational and demonstrates how crypto maps and IPsec profile configuration options are compatible with each other.

Example 16-8 *Verifying GRE over IPsec Site-to-Site Tunnel with Pre-Shared Key*

```
! The following command shows the tunnel type is GRE
R1# show interface tunnel100 | include Tunnel protocol
  Tunnel protocol/transport GRE/IP
R1#
```

```
! OSPF adjacency is established over the encrypted tunnel
R1# show ip ospf neighbor

Neighbor ID     Pri   State           Dead Time   Address         Interface
2.2.2.2           0   FULL/  -        00:00:38    192.168.100.2   Tunnel100
```

```
! OSPF routes from the IPsec peer are learned over tunnel 100
R1# show ip route ospf
! Output omitted for brevity
Gateway of last resort is 100.64.1.2 to network 0.0.0.0

      10.0.0.0/8 is variably subnetted, 3 subnets, 2 masks
O IA     10.2.2.0/24 [110/26] via 192.168.100.2, 00:03:30, Tunnel100
```

```
! The following output shows the ISAKMP SA status is active and in a QM_IDLE state.
 QM_IDLE means the SA remains authenticated with its peer and may be used for
subsequent quick mode exchanges for additional IPsec SAs.
R1# show crypto isakmp sa
IPv4 Crypto ISAKMP SA
dst             src             state          conn-id status
100.64.1.1      100.64.2.2      QM_IDLE           1008 ACTIVE
```

```
! The following command displays information about the IPsec SA
R1# show crypto ipsec sa
! Output omitted for brevity

! pkts encaps shows the number of outgoing packets that have been encapsulated
! pkts encrypt shows the number of outgoing packets that have been decrypted
! pkts decaps shows the number of incoming packets that have been decapsulated
! pkts decrypt shows the number of incoming packets that have been decrypted
    #pkts encaps: 40, #pkts encrypt: 40, #pkts digest: 40
    #pkts decaps: 38, #pkts decrypt: 38, #pkts verify: 38
..
! The following output shows there is an IPsec SA established with 100.64.2.2
```

```
 local crypto endpt.: 100.64.1.1, remote crypto endpt.: 100.64.2.2

! The following output shows the IPsec SA is active as well as the transform set and
the transport mode negotiated for both IPsec SAs
     inbound esp sas:
      spi: 0x1A945CC1(445930689)
       transform: esp-aes esp-sha-hmac ,
        in use settings ={Transport, }
..
        Status: ACTIVE(ACTIVE)
      outbound esp sas:
       spi: 0xDBE8D78F(3689469839)
        transform: esp-aes esp-sha-hmac ,
        in use settings ={Transport, }
..
        Status: ACTIVE(ACTIVE)
```

Key Topic

Site-to-Site VTI over IPsec

The steps to enable a VTI over IPsec are similar to those for GRE over IPsec configuration using IPsec profiles. The only difference is the addition of the command **tunnel mode ipsec** {**ipv4** | **ipv6**} under the tunnel interface to enable VTI on it and to change the packet transport mode to tunnel mode. To revert to GRE over IPsec, you use the command **tunnel mode gre** {**ip** | **ipv6**}.

Example 16-9 shows an example of the configuration changes that need to be made to the GRE over IPsec configuration to enable VTI over IPsec.

Example 16-9 *Configuring VTI over IPsec Site-to-Site Tunnel with Pre-Shared Key*

```
R1
! VTI uses IPsec profiles, therefore, the crypto map
! needs to be removed from interface GigabitEthernet0/1

interface GigabitEthernet0/1
no crypto map VPN

! Change transport mode to tunnel

crypto ipsec transform-set AES_SHA esp-aes esp-sha-hmac
 mode tunnel

! Configure IPsec profile

crypto ipsec profile IPSEC_PROFILE
 set transform-set AES_SHA
!
! Enable VTI on tunnel interface and apply IPsec profile
interface Tunnel100
 tunnel mode ipsec ipv4
```

16

```
 tunnel protection ipsec profile IPSEC_PROFILE
```

```
R2
! Change transport mode to tunnel
crypto ipsec transform-set AES_SHA esp-aes esp-sha-hmac
 mode tunnel

! Enable VTI on tunnel interface
interface Tunnel100
 tunnel mode ipsec ipv4
```

Example 16-10 shows the verification commands to make sure the VTI IPsec tunnel between R1 and R2 is operational.

Example 16-10 *Verifying VTI over IPsec Site-to-Site Tunnel with Pre-Shared Key*

```
! The following command shows the tunnel type is IPSEC
R1# show interface tunnel100 | include Tunnel protocol
  Tunnel protocol/transport IPSEC/IP
```

```
! OSPF adjacency is established over the encrypted tunnel
R1# show ip ospf neighbor

Neighbor ID     Pri   State           Dead Time   Address         Interface
2.2.2.2           0   FULL/  -        00:00:33    192.168.100.2   Tunnel100
```

```
! OSPF routes from the IPsec peer are learned over tunnel 100
R1# show ip route ospf
! Output omitted for brevity
Gateway of last resort is 100.64.1.2 to network 0.0.0.0

      10.0.0.0/8 is variably subnetted, 3 subnets, 2 masks
O IA     10.2.2.0/24 [110/26] via 192.168.100.2, 00:05:25, Tunnel100
```

```
! The following output shows the ISAKMP SA status is active and in a QM_IDLE state.
QM_IDLE means the SA remains authenticated with its peer and may be used for
subsequent quick mode exchanges for additional IPsec SAs.
R1# show crypto isakmp sa
IPv4 Crypto ISAKMP SA
dst             src             state          conn-id status
100.64.1.1      100.64.2.2      QM_IDLE           1010 ACTIVE
```

```
! The following command displays information about the IPsec SA
```

```
R1# show crypto ipsec sa
! Output omitted for brevity

! pkts encaps shows the number of outgoing packets that have been encapsulated
! pkts encrypt shows the number of outgoing packets that have been decrypted
! pkts decaps shows the number of incoming packets that have been decapsulated
! pkts decrypt shows the number of incoming packets that have been decrypted

  #pkts encaps: 47, #pkts encrypt: 47, #pkts digest: 47
   #pkts decaps: 46, #pkts decrypt: 46, #pkts verify: 46
..
! The following output shows there is an IPsec SA established with 100.64.2.2
 local crypto endpt.: 100.64.1.1, remote crypto endpt.: 100.64.2.2
..
..
! The following output shows the IPsec SA is active as well as the transform
set and the transport mode negotiated for both IPsec SAs
     inbound esp sas:
      spi: 0x8F599A4(150313380)
        transform: esp-aes esp-sha-hmac ,
        in use settings &#61;{Tunnel, }
..
        Status: ACTIVE(ACTIVE)
     outbound esp sas:
      spi: 0x249F3CA2(614415522)
        transform: esp-aes esp-sha-hmac ,
        in use settings &#61;{Tunnel, }
..
        Status: ACTIVE(ACTIVE)
```


Cisco Locator/ID Separation Protocol (LISP)

Key Topic

The rapid growth of the default-free zone (DFZ), also known as the Internet routing table, led to the development of the Cisco *Locator/ID Separation Protocol (LISP)*. LISP is a routing architecture and a data and control plane protocol that was created to address routing scalability problems on the Internet:

- **Aggregation issues:** Many routes on the Internet routing table are provider-independent routes that are non-aggregable, and this is part of the reason the Internet routing table is so large and still growing.
- **Traffic engineering:** A common practice for ingress traffic engineering into a site is to inject more specific routes into the Internet, which exacerbates the Internet routing table aggregation/scalability problems.
- **Multihoming:** Proper multihoming to the Internet requires a full Internet routing table (900,000+ IPv4 routes at the time of writing). If a small site requires multihoming, a powerful router is needed to be able to handle the full routing table (with large

memory, powerful CPUs, more TCAM, more power, cooling, and so on), which can be cost-prohibitive for deployment across small sites.

- **Routing instability:** Internet route instability (also known as *route churn*) causes intensive router CPU and memory consumption, which also requires powerful routers.

Key Topic

Even though LISP was created to address the routing scalability problems of the Internet, it is also being implemented in other types of environments, such as data centers, campus networks, branches, next-gen WANs, and service provider cores. In addition, it can also serve for applications or use cases such as mobility, network virtualization, Internet of Things (IoT), IPv4-to-IPv6 transition, traffic engineering, and Cisco's Software-Defined Access (SD-Access) solution.

Figure 16-5 is used as a reference in this section for the definitions of basic LISP terminology.

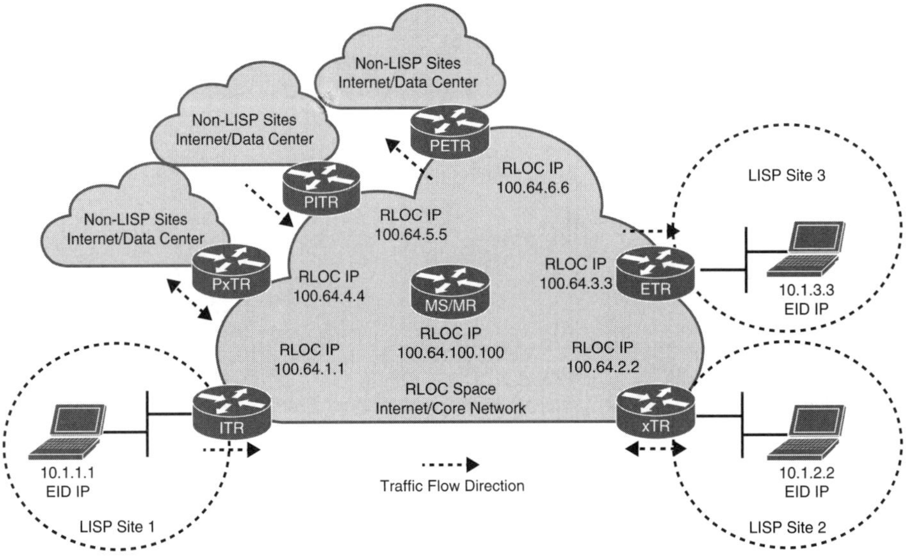

Figure 16-5 *LISP Architecture Reference Topology*

Following are the definitions for the LISP architecture components illustrated in Figure 16-5.

Key Topic

- **Endpoint identifier (EID):** An EID is the IP address of an endpoint within a LISP site. EIDs are the same IP addresses in use today on endpoints (IPv4 or IPv6), and they operate in the same way.
- **LISP site:** This is the name of a site where LISP routers and EIDs reside.
- **Ingress tunnel router (ITR):** ITRs are LISP routers that LISP-encapsulate IP packets coming from EIDs that are destined outside the LISP site.
- **Egress tunnel router (ETR):** ETRs are LISP routers that de-encapsulate LISP-encapsulated IP packets coming from sites outside the LISP site and destined to EIDs within the LISP site.
- **Tunnel router (xTR):** xTR refers to routers that perform ITR and ETR functions (which are most routers).

- **Proxy ITR (PITR):** PITRs are just like ITRs but for non-LISP sites that send traffic to EID destinations.
- **Proxy ETR (PETR):** PETRs act just like ETRs but for EIDs that send traffic to destinations at non-LISP sites.
- **Proxy xTR (PxTR):** PxTR refers to a router that performs PITR and PETR functions.
- **LISP router:** A LISP router is a router that performs the functions of any or all of the following: ITR, ETR, PITR, and/or PETR.
- **Routing locator (RLOC):** An RLOC is an IPv4 or IPv6 address of an ETR that is Internet facing or network core facing.
- **Map server (MS):** This network device (typically a router) learns EID-to-prefix mapping entries from an ETR and stores them in a local EID-to-RLOC mapping database.
- **Map resolver (MR):** This network device (typically a router) receives LISP-encapsulated map requests from an ITR and finds the appropriate ETR to answer those requests by consulting the map server.
- **Map server/map resolver (MS/MR):** When MS and the MR functions are implemented on the same device, the device is referred to as an MS/MR.

LISP Architecture and Protocols

Now that we've described the basic terminology, we explain the following three LISP main components:

- LISP routing architecture
- LISP control plane protocol
- LISP data plane protocol

Key Topic

LISP Routing Architecture

In traditional routing architectures, an endpoint IP address represents the endpoint's identity and location. If the location of the endpoint changes, its IP address also changes. LISP separates IP addresses into endpoint identifiers (EIDs) and routing locators (RLOCs). This way, endpoints can roam from site to site, and the only thing that changes is their RLOC; the EID remains the same.

Key Topic

LISP Control Plane

The control plane operates in a similar manner to the Domain Name System (DNS). Just as DNS can resolve a domain name into an IP address, LISP can resolve an EID into an RLOC by sending map requests to the MR, as illustrated in Figure 16-6. This makes it a very efficient and scalable on-demand routing protocol because it is based on a pull model, where only the routing information that is necessary is requested (as opposed to the push model of traditional routing protocols, such as BGP and OSPF, that push all the routes to the routers—including unnecessary ones).

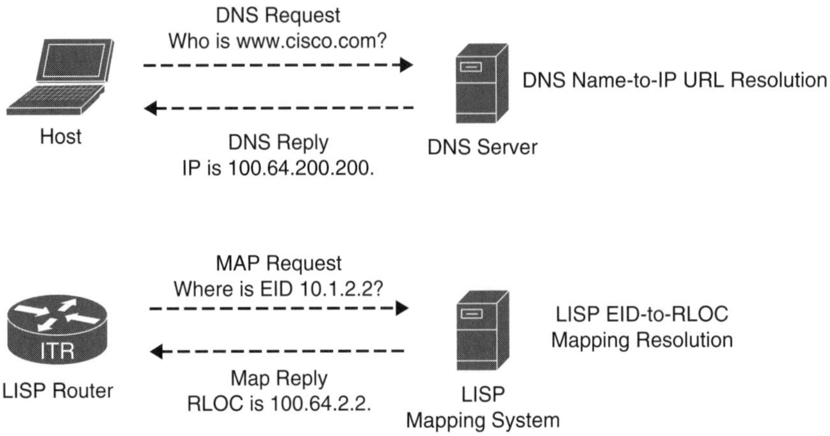

Figure 16-6 *LISP and DNS Comparison*

Key Topic

LISP Data Plane

ITRs LISP-encapsulate IP packets received from EIDs in an outer IP UDP header with source and destination addresses in the RLOC space; in other words, they perform IP-in-IP/UDP encapsulation. The original IP header and data are preserved; this is referred to as the *inner header*. Between the outer UDP header and the inner header, a LISP shim header is included to encode information necessary to enable forwarding plane functionality, such as network virtualization. Figure 16-7 illustrates the LISP packet frame format.

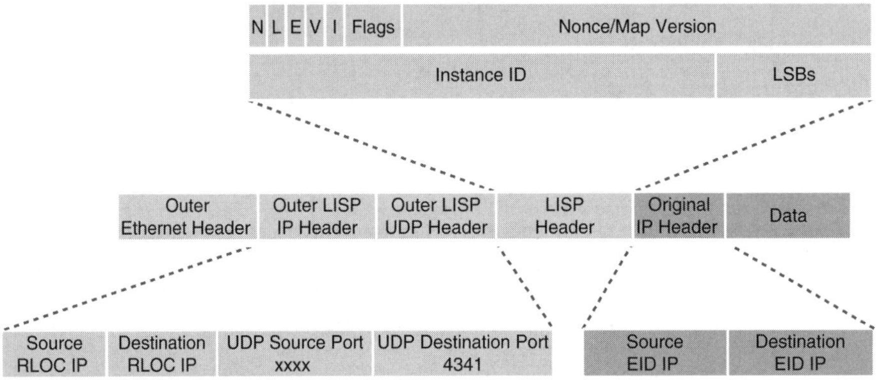

Figure 16-7 *LISP Packet Format*

The following are descriptions of some of most relevant header fields in Figure 16-7:

NOTE For details on the remaining header fields, see RFC 6830.

- **Outer LISP IP header:** This IP header is added by an ITR to encapsulate the EID IP addresses.
- **Outer LISP UDP header:** The UDP header contains a source port that is tactically selected by an ITR to prevent traffic from one LISP site to another site from taking

exactly the same path even if there are equal-cost multipath (ECMP) links to the destination; in other words, it improves load sharing by preventing polarization. The destination UDP port used by the LISP data plane is 4341.

- **Instance ID:** This field is a 24-bit value that is used to provide device- and path-level network virtualization. In other words, it enables VRF and VPNs for virtualization and segmentation much as VPN IDs do for MPLS networks. This is useful in preventing IP address duplication within a LISP site or just as a secure boundary between multiple organizations.
- **Original IP header:** This is the IP header as received by an EID.

Because EIDs and RLOCs can be either IPv4 or IPv6 addresses, the LISP data plane supports the following encapsulation combinations:

- IPv4 RLOCs encapsulating IPv4 EIDs
- IPv4 RLOCs encapsulating IPv6 EIDs
- IPv6 RLOCs encapsulating IPv4 EIDs
- IPv6 RLOCs encapsulating IPv6 EIDs

16

LISP Operation

This section describes the following LISP operational components:

- Map registration and map notify
- Map request and map reply
- LISP data path
- Proxy ETR
- Proxy ITR

Map Registration and Notification

When you're setting up LISP, the ETR routers need to be configured with the EID prefixes within the LISP site that will be registered with the MS. Any subnets attached to the ETR that are not configured as EID prefixes will be forwarded natively using traditional routing. Figure 16-8 illustrates this process.

The following steps describe the map registration process illustrated in Figure 16-8:

Key Topic

Step 1. The ETR sends a map register message to the MS to register its associated EID prefix 10.1.2.0/24. In addition to the EID prefix, the message includes the RLOC IP address 100.64.2.2 to be used by the MS when forwarding map requests (reformatted as encapsulated map requests) received through the mapping database system.

An ETR by default responds to map request messages, but in a map register message it may request that the MS answer map requests on its behalf by setting the proxy map reply flag (P-bit) in the message.

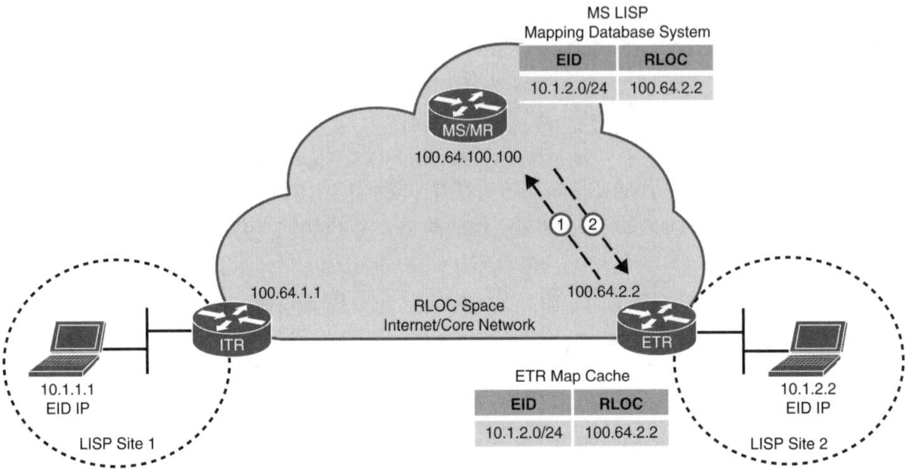

Figure 16-8 *Map Registration and Notification*

Step 2. The MS sends a map notify message to the ETR to confirm that the map register has been received and processed. A map notify message uses UDP port 4342 for both source and destination.

Map Request and Reply

When an endpoint in a LISP site is trying to communicate to an endpoint outside the LISP site, the ITR needs to perform a series of steps to be able to route the traffic appropriately. Figure 16-9 illustrates this process.

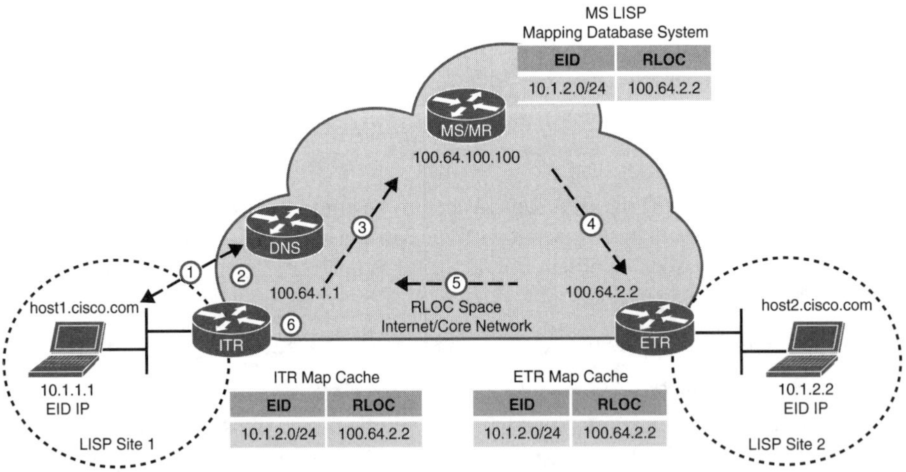

Figure 16-9 *Map Request and Reply*

Traditional routing is used within a LISP site; for example, an IGP such as OSPF can be configured. For this reason, when the endpoint in LISP Site 1 wants to communicate with the endpoint on LISP Site 2, the typical routing steps to achieve this are followed until the ITR is reached. When the ITR is reached, LISP comes into play. The following steps outline the map request and reply process illustrated in Figure 16-9:

Key Topic

Step 1. The endpoint in LISP Site 1 (host1) sends a DNS request to resolve the IP address of the endpoint in LISP Site 2 (host2.cisco.com). The DNS server replies with the IP address 10.1.2.2, which is the destination EID. host1 sends IP packets with destination IP 10.1.2.2 to its default gateway, which for this example is the ITR router. If host1 was not directly connected to the ITR, the IP packets would be forwarded through the LISP site as normal IP packets, using traditional routing, until they reached the ITR.

Step 2. The ITR receives the packets from host1 destined to 10.1.2.2. It performs an FIB lookup and evaluates the following forwarding rules:

- Did the packet match a default route because there was no route found for 10.1.2.2 in the routing table?
  - If yes, continue to the next step.
  - If no, forward the packet natively using the matched route.
- Is the source IP a registered EID prefix in the local map cache?
  - If yes, continue to the next step.
  - If no, forward the packet natively.

Step 3. The ITR sends an encapsulated map request to the MR for 10.1.2.2. A map request message uses the UDP destination port 4342, and the source port is chosen by the ITR.

Step 4. Because the MR and MS functionality is configured on the same device, the MS mapping database system forwards the map request to the authoritative (source of truth) ETR. If the MR and MS functions were on different devices, the MR would forward the encapsulated map request packet to the MS as received from the ITR, and the MS would then forward the map request packet to the ETR.

Step 5. The ETR sends to the ITR a map reply message that includes an EID-to-RLOC mapping 10.1.2.2 → 100.64.2.2. The map reply message uses the UDP source port 4342, and the destination port is the one chosen by the ITR in the map request message. An ETR may also request that the MS answer map requests on its behalf by setting the proxy map reply flag (P-bit) in the map register message.

Step 6. The ITR installs the EID-to-RLOC mapping in its local map cache and programs the FIB; it is now ready to forward LISP traffic.

LISP Data Path

After the ITR receives the EID-to-RLOC mapping from the ETR (or MS, if the ETR requested a proxy map reply), it is ready to send data from host1 to host2. Figure 16-10 illustrates the data path for a packet originating on host1 as it traverses the RLOC space and arrives at the destination.

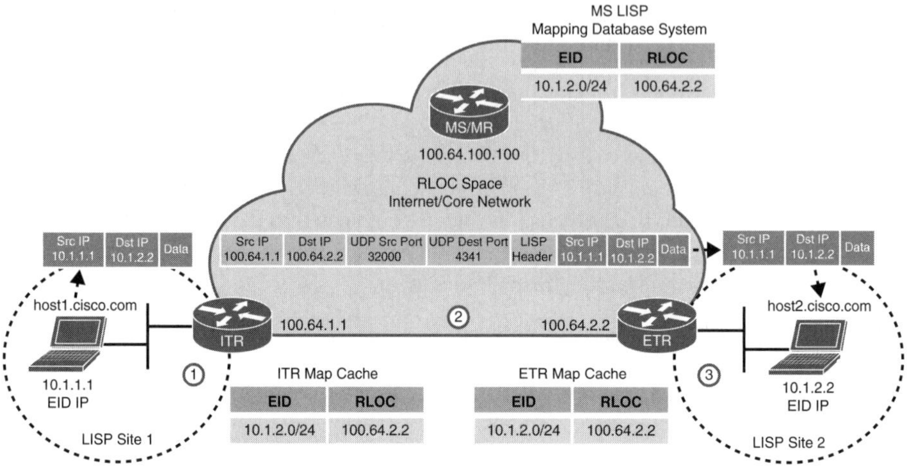

Figure 16-10 *LISP Data Path*

The following steps describe the encapsulation and de-encapsulation process illustrated in Figure 16-10:

Key Topic

Step 1. The ITR receives a packet from EID host1 (10.1.1.1) destined to host2 (10.1.2.2).

Step 2. The ITR performs an FIB lookup and finds a match. It encapsulates the EID packet and adds an outer header with the RLOC IP address from the ITR as the source IP address and the RLOC IP address of the ETR as the destination IP address. The packet is then forwarded using UDP destination port 4341 with a tactically selected source port in case ECMP load balancing is necessary.

Step 3. ETR receives the encapsulated packet and de-encapsulates it to forward it to host2.

Proxy ETR (PETR)

A *proxy ETR (PETR)* is a router connected to a non-LISP site (such as a data center or the Internet) that is used when a LISP site needs to communicate to a non-LISP site. Since the PETR is connected to non-LISP sites, a PETR does not register any EID addresses with the mapping database system. When an ITR sends a map request and the EID is not registered in the mapping database system, the mapping database system sends a negative map reply to the ITR. When the ITR receives a negative map reply, it forwards the LISP-encapsulated traffic to the PETR. For this to happen, the ITR must be configured to send traffic to the PETR's RLOC for any destinations for which a negative map reply is received.

When the mapping database system receives a map request for a non-LISP destination, it calculates the shortest prefix that matches the requested destination but that does not match any LISP EIDs. The calculated non-LISP prefix is included in the negative map reply so that the ITR can add this prefix to its map cache and FIB. From that point forward, the ITR can send traffic that matches that non-LISP prefix directly to the PETR.

Figure 16-11 illustrates the proxy ETR process.

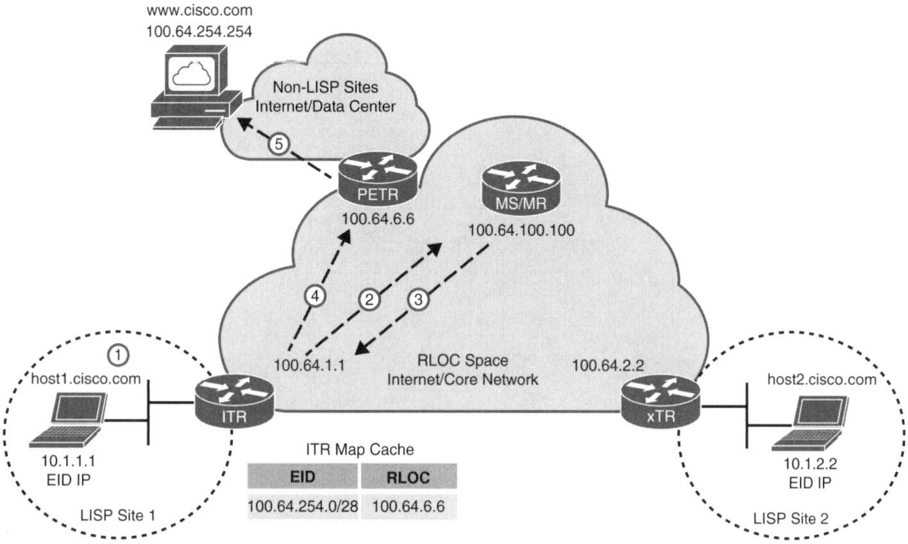

Figure 16-11 *Proxy ETR Process*

The following steps describe the proxy ETR process illustrated in Figure 16-11:

Key Topic

Step 1. host1 perform a DNS lookup for www.cisco.com. It gets a response from the DNS server with IP address 100.64.254.254 and starts forwarding packets to the ITR with the destination IP address 100.64.254.254.

Step 2. The ITR sends a map request to the MR for 100.64.254.254.

Step 3. The mapping database system responds with a negative map reply that includes a calculated non-LISP prefix for the ITR to add it to its mapping cache and FIB.

Step 4. The ITR can now start sending LISP-encapsulated packets to the PETR.

Step 5. The PETR de-encapsulates the traffic and sends it to www.cisco.com.

Proxy ITR (PITR)

PITRs receive traffic destined to LISP EIDs from non-LISP sites. PITRs behave in the same way as ITRs: They resolve the mapping for the destination EID and encapsulate and forward the traffic to the destination RLOC. PITRs send map request messages to the MR even when the source of the traffic is coming from a non-LISP site (that is, when the traffic is not originating on an EID). In this situation, an ITR behaves differently because an ITR checks whether the source is registered in the local map cache as an EID before sending a map request message to the MR. If the source isn't registered as an EID, the traffic is not eligible for LISP encapsulation, and traditional forwarding rules apply.

Figure 16-12 illustrates the proxy ITR process.

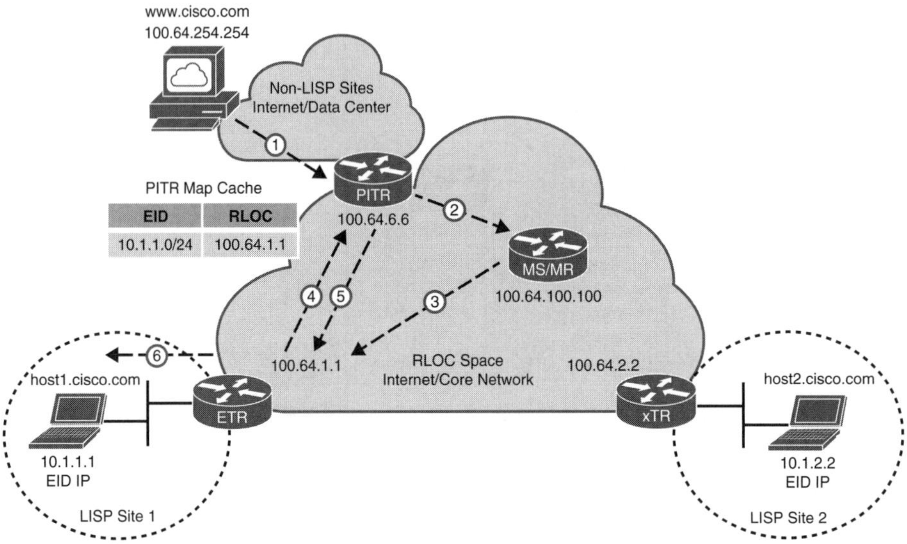

Figure 16-12 *Proxy ITR Process*

The following steps describe the proxy ITR process illustrated in Figure 16-12:

Step 1. Traffic from www.cisco.com is received by the PITR with the destination IP address 10.1.1.1 from host1.cisco.com.

Step 2. The PITR sends a map request to the MR for 10.1.1.1.

Step 3. The mapping database system forwards the map request to the ETR.

Step 4. The ETR sends a map reply to the PITR with the EID-to-RLOC mapping 10.1.1.1 → 100.64.1.1.

Step 5. The PITR LISP-encapsulates the packets and starts forwarding them to the ETR.

Step 6. The ETR receives the LISP-encapsulated packets, de-encapsulates them, and sends them to host1.

Virtual Extensible Local Area Network (VXLAN)

Server virtualization has placed increased demands on the legacy network infrastructure. A bare-metal server now has multiple virtual machines (VMs) and containers, each with its own MAC address. This has led to a number of problems with traditional Layer 2 networks, such as the following:

- The 12-bit VLAN ID yields 4000 VLANs, which are insufficient for server virtualization.
- Large MAC address tables are needed due to the hundreds of thousands of VMs and containers attached to the network.
- STP blocks links to avoid loops, and this results in a large number of disabled links, which is unacceptable.
- ECMP is not supported.
- Host mobility is difficult to implement.

Key Topic

VXLAN is an overlay data plane encapsulation scheme that was developed to address the various issues seen in traditional Layer 2 networks. It extends Layer 2 and Layer 3 overlay networks over a Layer 3 underlay network, using MAC-in-IP/UDP tunneling. Each overlay is termed a VXLAN **segment**.

The Internet Assigned Numbers Authority (IANA) assigned to VXLAN the UDP destination port 4789. There may be some older/prestandard implementations of VXLAN that are using UDP destination port 8472. The reason for this discrepancy is that when VXLAN was first implemented in Linux, the VXLAN UDP destination port had not yet been officially assigned, and Linux decided to use port 8472 because many vendors at the time were using UDP destination port 8472. Later, IANA assigned port 4789 for VXLAN, and to avoid breaking existing deployments, some Linux distributions decided to leave port 8472 as the default value. Be sure to check which is the right port to use when dealing with multiple vendor interoperability situations. Figure 16-13 illustrates the VXLAN packet format.

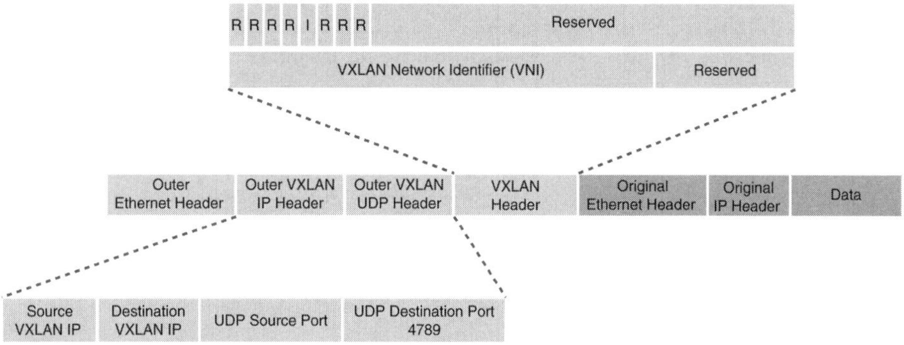

Figure 16-13 *VXLAN Packet Format*

Key Topic

Unlike the VLAN ID, which has only 12 bits and allows for 4000 VLANs, VXLAN has a 24-bit **VXLAN network identifier (VNI)**, which allows for up to 16 million VXLAN segments (more commonly known as *overlay networks*) to coexist within the same infrastructure.

The VNI is located in the VXLAN shim header that encapsulates the original inner MAC frame originated by an endpoint. The VNI is used to provide segmentation for Layer 2 and Layer 3 traffic.

Key Topic

To facilitate the discovery of VNIs over the underlay Layer 3 network, **virtual tunnel endpoints (VTEPs)** are used. VTEPs are entities that originate or terminate VXLAN tunnels. They map Layer 2 and Layer 3 packets to the VNI to be used in the overlay network. Each VTEP has two interfaces:

- **Local LAN interfaces:** These interfaces on the local LAN segment provide bridging between local hosts.
- **IP interface:** This is a core-facing network interface for VXLAN. The IP interface's IP address helps identify the VTEP in the network. It is also used for VXLAN traffic encapsulation and de-encapsulation.

16

Figure 16-14 illustrates the VXLAN VTEP with the IP interface and the local LAN interface.

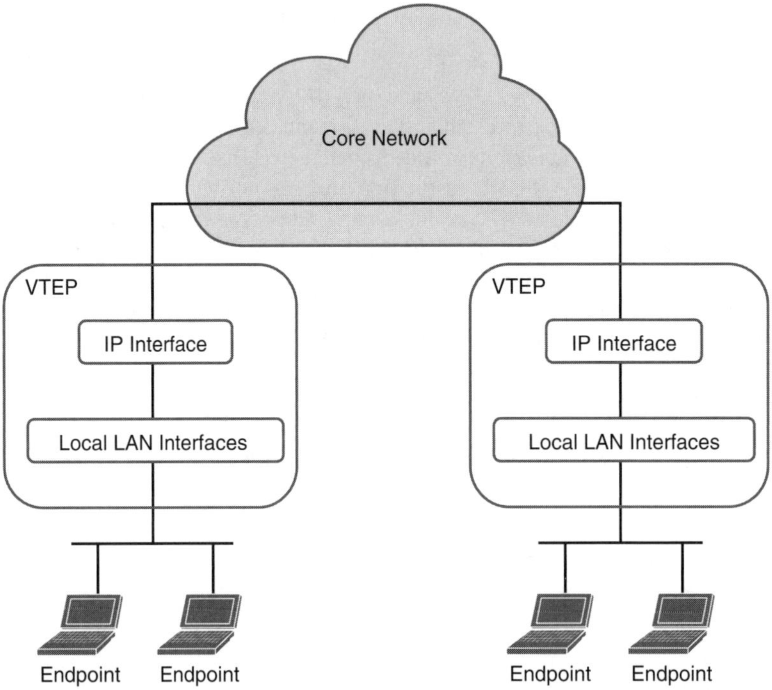

Figure 16-14 *VXLAN VTEP*

Devices that are not capable of supporting VXLAN and need to use traditional VLAN segmentation can be connected to VXLAN segments by using a VXLAN gateway. A VXLAN gateway is a VTEP device that combines a VXLAN segment and a classic VLAN segment into one common Layer 2 domain.

The VXLAN standard defines VXLAN as a data plane protocol, but it does not define a VXLAN control plane; it was left open to be used with any control plane. Currently four different VXLAN control and data planes are supported by Cisco devices:

Key Topic

- VXLAN with Multicast underlay
- VXLAN with static unicast VXLAN tunnels
- VXLAN with MP-BGP EVPN control plane
- VXLAN with LISP control plane

MP-BGP EVPN and Multicast are the most popular control planes used for data center and private cloud environments. For campus environments, VXLAN with a LISP control plane is the preferred choice.

Key Topic

Cisco Software-Defined Access (SD-Access) is an example of an implementation of VXLAN with the LISP control plane. An interesting fact is that the VXLAN specification originated from a Layer 2 LISP specification (draft-smith-lisp-layer2-00) that aimed to introduce Layer 2 segmentation support to LISP. The VXLAN specification introduced the term *VXLAN* in lieu of *Layer 2 LISP* and didn't port over some of the fields from the Layer 2 LISP specification into the VXLAN specification. The minor differences between the Layer 2 LISP specification and the VXLAN specification headers are illustrated in Figure 16-15. Fields that were not ported over from Layer 2 LISP into VXLAN were reserved for future use.

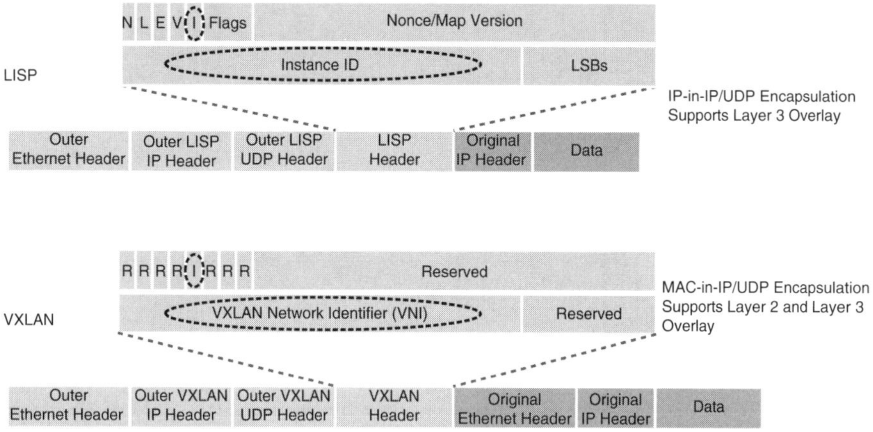

Figure 16-15 *LISP and VXLAN Packet Format Comparison*

As illustrated in Figure 16-15, LISP encapsulation is only capable of performing IP-in-IP/UDP encapsulation, which allows it to support Layer 3 overlays only, while VXLAN encapsulation is capable of encapsulating the original Ethernet header to perform MAC-in-IP encapsulation, which allows it to support Layer 2 and Layer 3 overlays.

Exam Preparation Tasks

You have a couple of choices for exam preparation: the exercises here, Chapter 30, "Final Preparation," and the exam simulation questions in the Pearson Test Prep Software Online.

Review All Key Topics

Review the most important topics in the chapter, noted with the Key Topic icon in the outer margin of the page. Table 16-7 lists these key topics and the page number on which each is found.

Key Topic

Table 16-7 Key Topics for Chapter 16

Key Topic Element	Description	Page
Paragraph	Generic Routing Encapsulation (GRE) definition	469
List	GRE configuration	471
Paragraph	IPsec definition	475
Table 16-3	IPsec Security Services	476
Section	Authentication Header	476
Section	Encapsulating Security Payload (ESP)	477
Figure 16-3	IPsec Tunnel and Transport Encapsulation	477

Key Topic Element	Description	Page
List	IPsec security services definitions	478
Section	Transform Sets	478
Section	Internet Key Exchange	480
Section	IKEv1	480
Section	IKEv2	482
Table 16-6	Cisco IPsec VPN Solutions	484
Figure 16-4	GRE over IPsec Versus IPsec Tunnel Mode	487
Section	Site-to-Site GRE over IPsec	487
List	GRE over IPsec with crypto maps	488
List	GRE over IPsec with IPsec profiles	493
Section	Site-to-Site VTI over IPsec	493
Paragraph	LISP definition	495
Paragraph	LISP applications	496
List	LISP architecture components	496
Section	LISP Routing Architecture	497
Section	LISP Control Plane	497
Section	LISP Data Plane	498
List	LISP map registration and notification	498
List	LISP map request and reply	501
List	LISP data path	502
List	PETR process	503
Paragraph	VXLAN definition	505
Paragraph	VNI definition	505
Paragraph	VTEP definition	506
List	VXLAN control plane	506
Paragraph	LISP and VXLAN packet format comparison	506

Complete Tables and Lists from Memory

Print a copy of Appendix B, "Memory Tables" (found on the companion website), or at least the section for this chapter, and complete the tables and lists from memory. Appendix C, "Memory Tables Answer Key," also on the companion website, includes completed tables and lists you can use to check your work.

Define Key Terms

Define the following key terms from this chapter and check your answers in the Glossary:

egress tunnel router (ETR), endpoint identifier (EID), ingress tunnel router (ITR), Internet Key Exchange (IKE), Internet Protocol Security (IPsec), Internet Security Association and Key Management Protocol (ISAKMP), LISP router, LISP site, map resolver (MR), map server (MS), map server/map resolver (MS/MR), nonce, overlay network, proxy ETR (PETR), proxy ITR (PITR), proxy xTR (PxTR), routing locator (RLOC), segment, segmentation, tunnel router (xTR), underlay network, virtual private network (VPN), virtual tunnel endpoint (VTEP), VXLAN network identifier (VNI)

Use the Command Reference to Check Your Memory

Table 16-8 lists the important commands from this chapter. To test your memory, cover the right side of the table with a piece of paper, read the description on the left side, and see how much of the command you can remember.

Table 16-8 Command Reference

Task	Command Syntax
Create a GRE tunnel interface	**interface tunnel** *tunnel-number*
Enable keepalives on a GRE tunnel interface	**keepalive** [*seconds* [*retries*]]
Create an ISAKMP policy	**crypto isakmp policy** *priority*
Create an IPsec transform set	**crypto ipsec transform-set** *transform-set-name transform1* [*transform2* [*transform3*]]
Create a crypto map for IPsec	**crypto map** *map-name seq-num* [**ipsec-isakmp**]
Apply a crypto map to an outside interface	**crypto map** *map-name*
Create an IPsec profile for tunnel interfaces	**crypto ipsec profile** *ipsec-profile-name*
Apply an IPsec profile to a tunnel interface	**tunnel protection** *ipsec profile profile-name*
Turn a GRE tunnel into a VTI tunnel	**tunnel mode ipsec** {**ipv4** | **ipv6**}
Turn a VTI tunnel into a GRE tunnel	**tunnel mode gre** {**ip** | **ipv6**}
Display information about ISAKMP SAs	**show crypto isakmp sa**
Display detailed information about IPsec SAs	**show crypto ipsec sa**

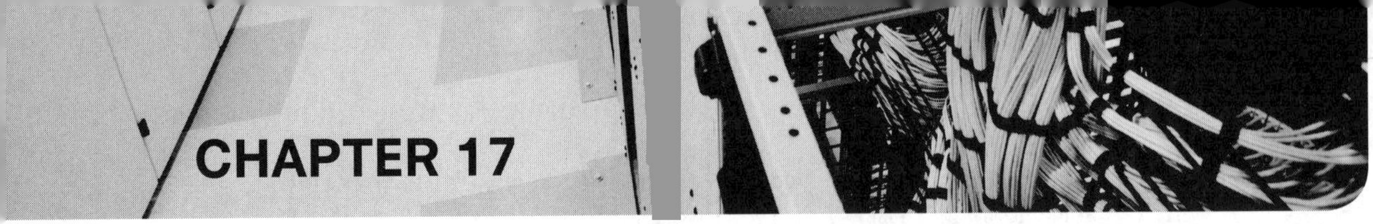

CHAPTER 17

Wireless Signals and Modulation

This chapter covers the following subjects:

- **Understanding Basic Wireless Theory:** This section covers the basic theory behind radio frequency (RF) signals, as well as measuring and comparing the power of RF signals.
- **Carrying Data Over an RF Signal:** This section provides an overview of basic methods and standards that are involved in carrying data wirelessly between devices and the network.

Wireless LANs must transmit a signal over radio frequencies to move data from one device to another. Transmitters and receivers can be fixed in consistent locations, or they can be free to move around. This chapter covers the basic theory behind wireless signals and the methods used to carry data wirelessly.

"Do I Know This Already?" Quiz

The "Do I Know This Already?" quiz enables you to assess whether you should read the entire chapter. If you miss no more than one of these self-assessment questions, you might want to move ahead to the "Exam Preparation Tasks" section. Table 17-1 lists the major headings in this chapter and the "Do I Know This Already?" quiz questions covering the material in those headings so you can assess your knowledge of these specific areas. The answers to the "Do I Know This Already?" quiz appear in Appendix A, "Answers to the 'Do I Know This Already?' Questions."

Table 17-1 "Do I Know This Already?" Foundation Topics Section-to-Question Mapping

Foundation Topics Section	Questions
Understanding Basic Wireless Theory	1–8
Carrying Data Over an RF Signal	9–10

1. Two transmitters are each operating with a transmit power level of 100 mW. When you compare the two absolute power levels, what is the difference in dB?

- **a.** 0 dB
- **b.** 20 dB
- **c.** 100 dB
- **d.** You can't compare power levels in dB.

2. A transmitter is configured to use a power level of 17 mW. One day it is reconfigured to transmit at a new power level of 34 mW. How much has the power level increased, in dB?
   a. 0 dB
   b. 2 dB
   c. 3 dB
   d. 17 dB
   e. None of these answers are correct; you need a calculator to figure this out.
3. Transmitter A has a power level of 1 mW, and transmitter B is 100 mW. Compare transmitter B to A using dB, and then identify the correct answer from the following choices.
   a. 0 dB
   b. 1 dB
   c. 10 dB
   d. 20 dB
   e. 100 dB
4. A transmitter normally uses an absolute power level of 100 mW. Through the course of needed changes, its power level is reduced to 40 mW. What is the power-level change in dB?
   a. 2.5 dB
   b. 4 dB
   c. –4 dB
   d. –40 dB
   e. None of these answers are correct; where is that calculator?
5. Consider a scenario with a transmitter and a receiver that are separated by some distance. The transmitter uses an absolute power level of 20 dBm. A cable connects the transmitter to its antenna. The receiver also has a cable connecting it to its antenna. Each cable has a loss of 2 dB. The transmitting and receiving antennas each have a gain of 5 dBi. What is the resulting EIRP?
   a. +20 dBm
   b. +23 dBm
   c. +26 dBm
   d. +34 dBm
   e. None of these answers are correct.
6. A receiver picks up an RF signal from a distant transmitter. Which one of the following represents the best signal quality received? Sample values are given in parentheses.
   a. Low SNR (10 dB), low RSSI (–75 dBm)
   b. High SNR (30 dB), low RSSI (–75 dBm)
   c. Low SNR (10 dB), high RSSI (–55 dBm)
   d. High SNR (30 dB), high RSSI (–55 dBm)

7. Which one of the following is the primary cause of free space path loss?
   a. Spreading
   b. Absorption
   c. Humidity levels
   d. Magnetic field decay
8. Which one of the following has the shortest effective range in free space, assuming that the same transmit power level is used for each?
   a. An 802.11g device
   b. An 802.11a device
   c. An 802.11b device
   d. None of these answers are correct.
9. QAM alters which of the following aspects of an RF signal? (Choose two.)
   a. Frequency
   b. Amplitude
   c. Phase
   d. Quadrature
10. Suppose that an 802.11a device moves away from a transmitter. As the signal strength decreases, which one of the following might the device or the transmitter do to improve the signal quality along the way?
    a. Aggregate more channels
    b. Use more radio chains
    c. Switch to a more complex modulation scheme
    d. Switch to a less complex modulation scheme

Foundation Topics

Understanding Basic Wireless Theory

To send data across a wired link, an electrical signal is applied at one end and is carried to the other end. The wire itself is continuous and conductive, so the signal can propagate rather easily. A wireless link has no physical strands of anything to carry the signal along.

How then can an electrical signal be sent across the air, or free space? Consider a simple analogy of two people standing far apart, and one person wants to signal something to the other. They are connected by a long and somewhat-loose rope; the rope represents free space. The sender at one end decides to lift his end of the rope high and hold it there so that the other end of the rope will also raise and notify the partner. After all, if the rope were a wire, he knows that he could apply a steady voltage at one end of the wire and it would appear at the other end. Figure 17-1 shows the end result; the rope falls back down after a tiny distance, and the receiver never notices a change at all.

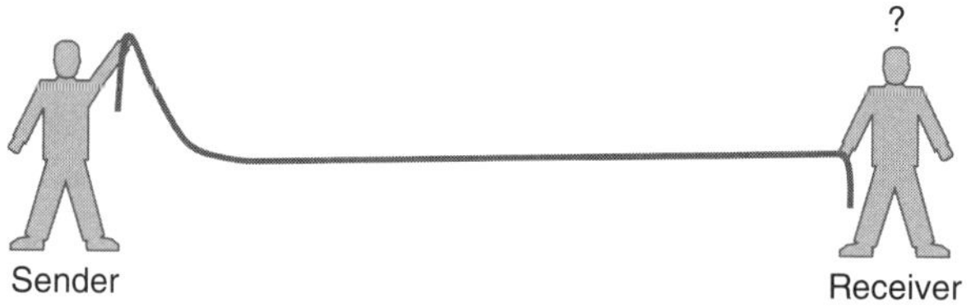

Figure 17-1 *Failed Attempt to Pass a Message Down a Rope*

The sender decides to try a different strategy. He cannot push the rope toward the receiver, but when he begins to wave it up and down in a steady, regular motion, a curious thing happens. A continuous wave pattern appears along the entire length of the rope, as shown in Figure 17-2. In fact, the waves (each representing one up and down cycle of the sender's arm) actually travel from the sender to the receiver.

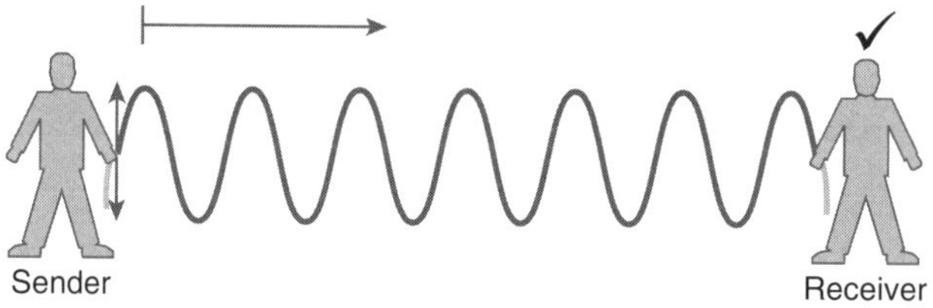

Figure 17-2 *Sending a Continuous Wave Down a Rope*

In free space, a similar principle occurs. The sender (a transmitter) can send an alternating current into a section of wire (an antenna), which sets up moving electric and magnetic fields that propagate out and away from the wire as traveling waves. The electric and magnetic fields travel along together and are always at right angles to each other, as shown in Figure 17-3. The signal must keep changing, or alternating, by cycling up and down, to keep the electric and magnetic fields cycling and pushing ever outward.

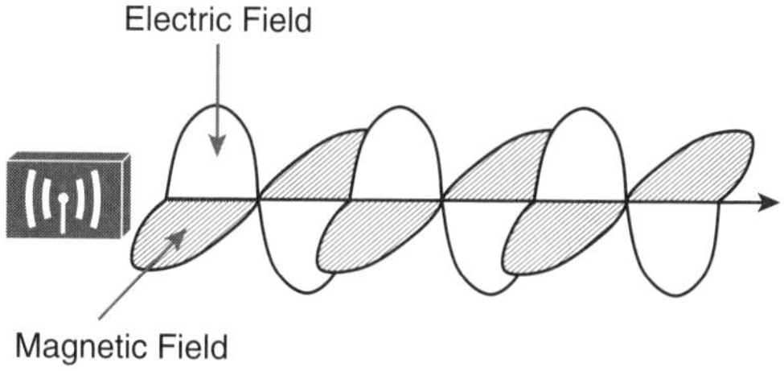

Figure 17-3 *Traveling Electric and Magnetic Waves*

Electromagnetic waves do not travel strictly in a straight line. Instead, they travel by expanding in *all* directions away from the antenna. To get a visual image, think of dropping a pebble into a pond when the surface is still. Where it drops in, the pebble sets the water's surface into a cyclic motion. The waves that result begin small and expand outward, only to be replaced by new waves. In free space, the electromagnetic waves expand outward in all three dimensions.

Figure 17-4 shows a simple idealistic antenna that is a single point, which is connected at the end of a wire. The waves produced from the tiny point antenna expand outward in a spherical shape. The waves will eventually reach the receiver, in addition to many other locations in other directions.

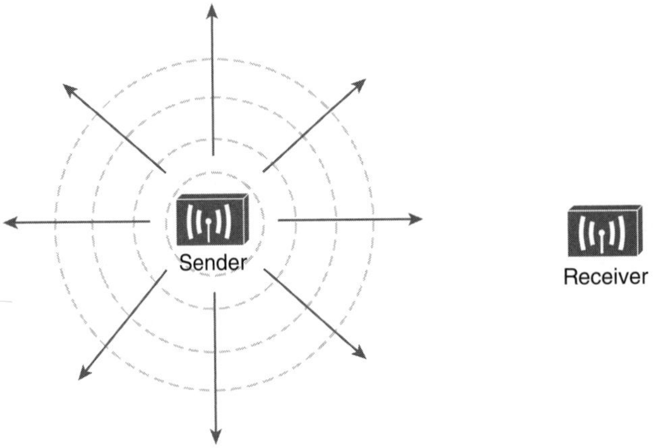

Figure 17-4 *Wave Propagation with an Idealistic Antenna*

> **NOTE** The idealistic antenna does not really exist but serves as a reference point to understand wave propagation. In the real world, antennas can be made in various shapes and forms that can limit the direction that the waves are sent. Chapter 18, "Wireless Infrastructure," covers antennas in more detail.

At the receiving end of a wireless link, the process is reversed. As the electromagnetic waves reach the receiver's antenna, they induce an electrical signal. If everything works right, the received signal will be a reasonable copy of the original transmitted signal.

Understanding Frequency

The waves involved in a wireless link can be measured and described in several ways. One fundamental property is the **frequency** of the wave, or the number of times the signal makes one complete up and down *cycle* in 1 second. Figure 17-5 shows how a cycle of a wave can be identified. A cycle can begin as the signal rises from the center line, falls through the center line, and rises again to meet the center line. A cycle can also be measured from the center of one peak to the center of the next peak. No matter where you start measuring a cycle, the signal must make a complete sequence back to its starting position where it is ready to repeat the same cyclic pattern again.

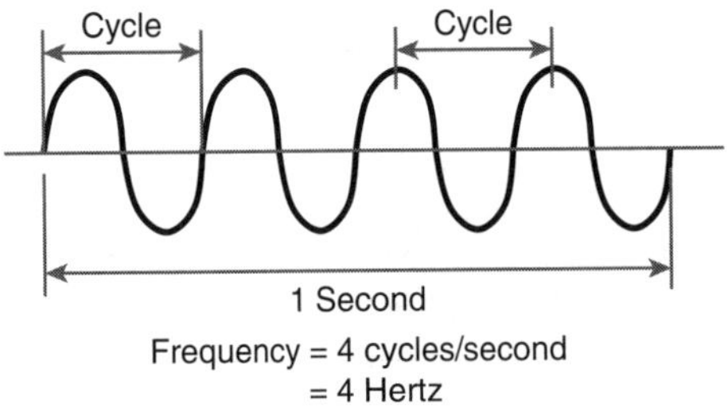

Figure 17-5 *Cycles Within a Wave*

Answers to the "Do I Know This Already?" quiz:

1 A **2** C **3** D **4** C **5** B **6** D **7** A **8** B **9** B, C **10** D

In Figure 17-5, suppose that 1 second has elapsed, as shown. During that 1 second, the signal progressed through four complete cycles. Therefore, its frequency is 4 cycles/second, or 4 hertz. A **hertz (Hz)** is the most commonly used frequency unit and is nothing other than one cycle per second.

Frequency can vary over a very wide range. As frequency increases by orders of magnitude, the numbers can become quite large. To keep things simple, the frequency unit name can be modified to denote an increasing number of zeros, as listed in Table 17-2.

Table 17-2 Frequency Unit Names

Unit	Abbreviation	Meaning
Hertz	Hz	Cycles per second
Kilohertz	kHz	1000 Hz
Megahertz	MHz	1,000,000 Hz
Gigahertz	GHz	1,000,000,000 Hz

Figure 17-6 shows a simple representation of the continuous frequency spectrum ranging from 0 Hz to 10^{22} (or 1 followed by 22 zeros) Hz. At the low end of the spectrum are frequencies that are too low to be heard by the human ear, followed by audible sounds. The highest range of frequencies contains light, followed by X, gamma, and cosmic rays.

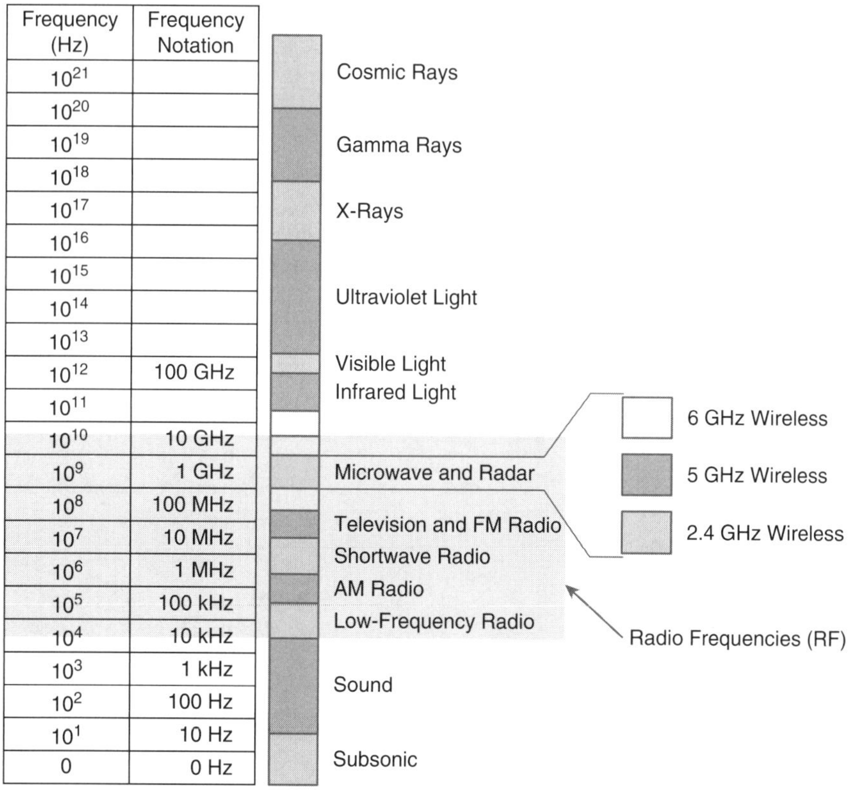

Figure 17-6 *Continuous Frequency Spectrum*

The frequency range from around 3 kHz to 300 GHz is commonly called **radio frequency (RF)**. It includes many different types of radio communication, such as low-frequency radio, AM radio, shortwave radio, television, FM radio, microwave, and radar. The microwave category also contains three main frequency ranges that are used for wireless LAN communication: 2.4, 5, and 6 GHz.

Because a range of frequencies might be used for the same purpose, it is customary to refer to the range as a **band** of frequencies. For example, the range from 530 kHz to around 1710 kHz is used by AM radio stations; therefore, it is commonly called the *AM band* or the *AM broadcast band.*

One of the three main frequency ranges used for wireless LAN communication lies between 2.400 and 2.4835 GHz. This is usually called the *2.4 GHz band*, even though it does not encompass the entire range between 2.4 and 2.5 GHz. It is much more convenient to refer to the band name instead of the specific range of frequencies included. The 2.4 GHz band is also known as one of the industrial, scientific, and medical (ISM) bands that is available for use without a license.

Another wireless LAN range is usually called the *5 GHz band* because it lies between 5.150 and 5.825 GHz. The 5 GHz band actually contains the following four separate and distinct bands, which are also known as Unlicensed National Information Infrastructure (U-NII) bands:

5.150 to 5.250 GHz	U-NII-1
5.250 to 5.350 GHz	U-NII-2A
5.470 to 5.725 GHz	U-NII-2C
5.725 to 5.825 GHz	U-NII-3

NOTE You might have noticed that most of the 5 GHz bands are contiguous except for a gap between 5.350 and 5.470 (also known as U-NII-2B). At the time of this writing, this gap exists and cannot be used for wireless LANs. However, some government agencies have moved to reclaim the frequencies and repurpose them for wireless LANs. Efforts are also underway to add 5.825 through 5.925 GHz (also known as U-NII-4).

The 6 GHz band lies between 5.925 and 7.125 GHz. It is broken up into four smaller bands, which are also part of the U-NII structure:

5.925 to 6.425 GHz	U-NII-5
6.425 to 6.525 GHz	U-NII-6
6.525 to 6.875 GHz	U-NII-7
6.875 to 7.125 GHz	U-NII-8

It is interesting that the 5 and 6 GHz bands can contain several smaller bands. Remember that the term *band* is simply a relative term that is used for convenience.

A frequency band contains a continuous range of frequencies. If two devices require a single frequency for a wireless link between them, which frequency can they use? Beyond that, how many unique frequencies can be used within a band?

To keep everything orderly and compatible, bands are usually divided into a number of distinct **channels**. Each channel is known by a channel number and is assigned to a specific frequency. As long as the channels are defined by a national or international standards body, they can be used consistently in all locations.

For example, Figure 17-7 shows the channel assignment for the 2.4 GHz band that is used for wireless LAN communication. The band contains 14 channels numbered 1 through 14, each assigned a specific frequency. First, notice how much easier it is to refer to channel numbers than the frequencies. Second, notice that the channels are spaced at regular intervals that are 0.005 GHz (or 5 MHz) apart, except for channel 14. The channel spacing is known as the channel separation or channel width.

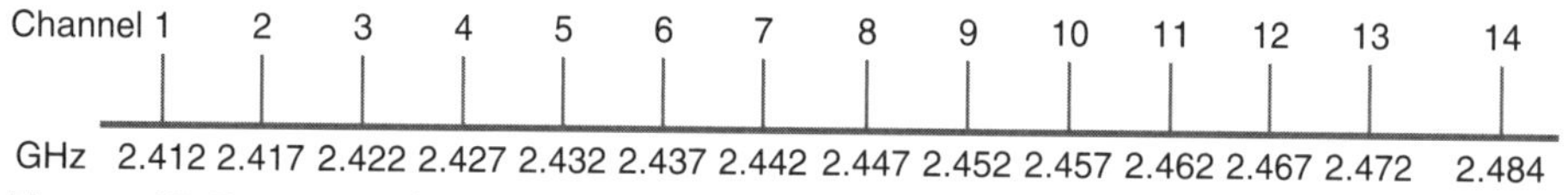

Figure 17-7 *Example of Channel Spacing in the 2.4 GHz Band*

If devices use a specific frequency for a wireless link, why do the channels need to be spaced apart at all? The reason lies with the practical limitations of RF signals, the electronics involved in transmitting and receiving the signals, and the overhead needed to add data to the signal effectively.

In practice, an RF signal is not infinitely narrow; instead, it spills above and below a center frequency to some extent, occupying neighboring frequencies, too. It is the center frequency that defines the channel location within the band. The actual frequency range needed for the transmitted signal is known as the signal **bandwidth**, as shown in Figure 17-8. As its name implies, bandwidth refers to the width of frequency space required within the band. For example, a signal with a 22 MHz bandwidth is bounded at 11 MHz above and below the center frequency. In wireless LANs, the signal bandwidth is defined as part of a standard. Even though the signal might extend farther above and below the center frequency than the bandwidth allows, wireless devices will use something called a *spectral mask* to ignore parts of the signal that fall outside the bandwidth boundaries.

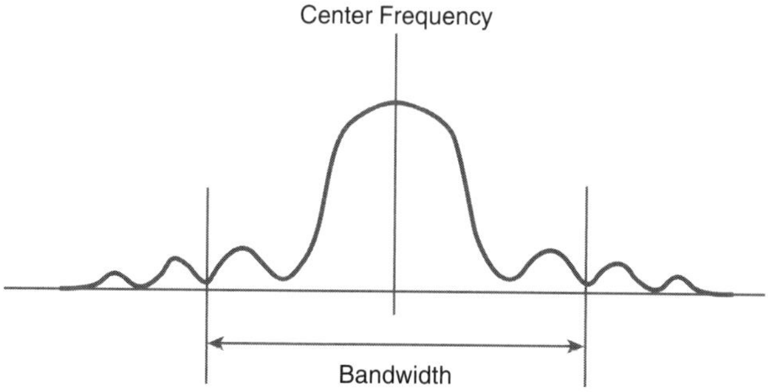

Figure 17-8 *Signal Bandwidth*

Ideally, the signal bandwidth should be less than the channel width so that a different signal could be transmitted on every possible channel, with no chance that two signals could overlap and interfere with each other. Figure 17-9 shows such a channel spacing, where the signals on adjacent channels do not overlap. A signal can exist on every possible channel without overlapping with others.

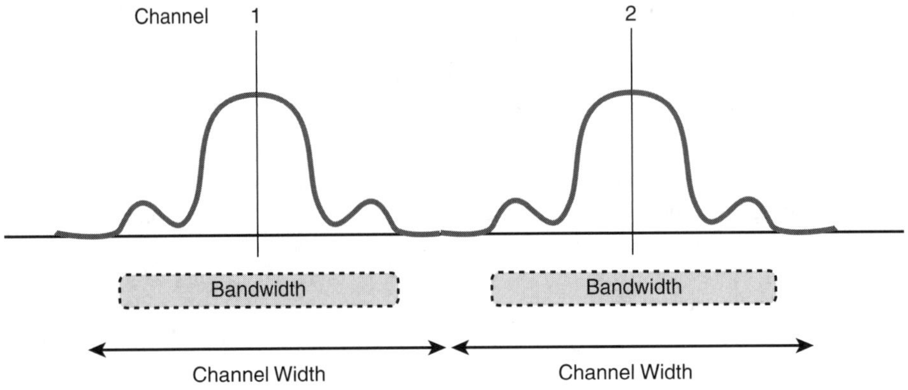

Figure 17-9 *Non-overlapping Channel Spacing*

However, you should not assume that signals centered on the standardized channel assignments will not overlap with each other. It is entirely possible that the channels in a band are narrower than the signal bandwidth, as shown in Figure 17-10. Notice how two signals have been centered on adjacent channel numbers 1 and 2, but they almost entirely overlap each other! The problem is that the signal bandwidth is slightly wider than four channels. In this case, signals centered on adjacent channels cannot possibly coexist without overlapping and interfering. Instead, the signals must be placed on more distant channels to prevent overlapping, thus limiting the number of channels that can be used in the band.

NOTE How can channels be numbered such that signals overlap? Sometimes the channels in a band are defined and numbered for a specific use. Later on, another technology might be developed to use the same band and channels, only the newer signals might require more bandwidth than the original channel numbering supported. Such is the case with the 2.4 GHz Wi-Fi band.

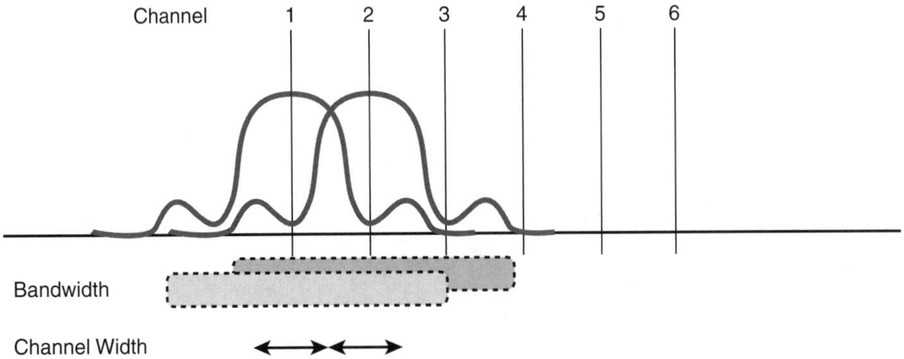

Figure 17-10 *Overlapping Channel Spacing*

The 2.4 GHz band is made up of channels that are 5 MHz wide with Wi-Fi signals that have a 22 MHz bandwidth. Adjacent channel numbers are not spaced far enough apart to be non-overlapping. However, in the 5 and 6 GHz bands, channels are non-overlapping because they are spaced every 20 MHz apart to support signals that are just about 20 MHz wide. That means every channel can be used without interfering with adjacent channels, maximizing the number of channels that are available for use.

Understanding Phase

RF signals are very dependent upon timing because they are always in motion. By their very nature, the signals are made up of electrical and magnetic forces that vary over time. The **phase** of a signal is a measure of shift in time relative to the start of a cycle. Phase is normally measured in degrees, where 0 degrees is at the start of a cycle, and one complete cycle equals 360 degrees. A point that is halfway along the cycle is at the 180-degree mark. Because an oscillating signal is cyclic, you can think of the phase traveling around a circle again and again.

When two identical signals are produced at exactly the same time, their cycles match up and they are said to be **in phase** with each other. If one signal is delayed from the other, the two signals are said to be **out of phase**. Figure 17-11 shows examples of both scenarios.

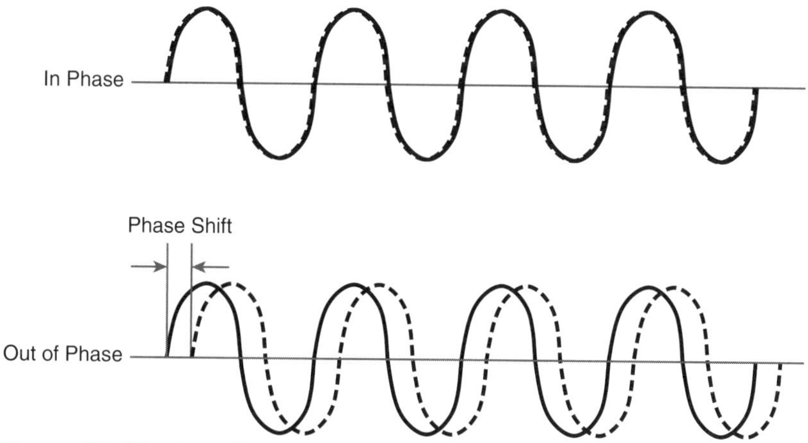

Figure 17-11 *Signals In and Out of Phase*

Phase becomes important as RF signals are received. Signals that are in phase tend to add together, whereas signals that are 180 degrees out of phase tend to cancel each other out.

Measuring Wavelength

RF signals are usually described by their frequency; however, it is difficult to get a feel for their physical size as they move through free space. The **wavelength** is a measure of the physical distance that a wave travels over one complete cycle. Wavelength is usually designated by the Greek symbol lambda (Λ). To get a feel for the dimensions of a wireless LAN signal, assuming that you could see it as it travels in front of you, a 2.4 GHz signal would have a wavelength of 4.92 inches, a 5 GHz signal would be 2.36 inches, and a 6 GHz signal would be 1.97 inches.

Figure 17-12 shows the wavelengths of three different waves. The waves are arranged in order of increasing frequency, from top to bottom. Regardless of the frequency, RF waves travel at a constant speed. In a vacuum, radio waves travel at exactly the speed of light; in air, the velocity is slightly less than the speed of light. Notice that the wavelength decreases as the frequency increases. As the wave cycles get smaller, they cover less distance. Wavelength becomes useful in the design and placement of antennas.

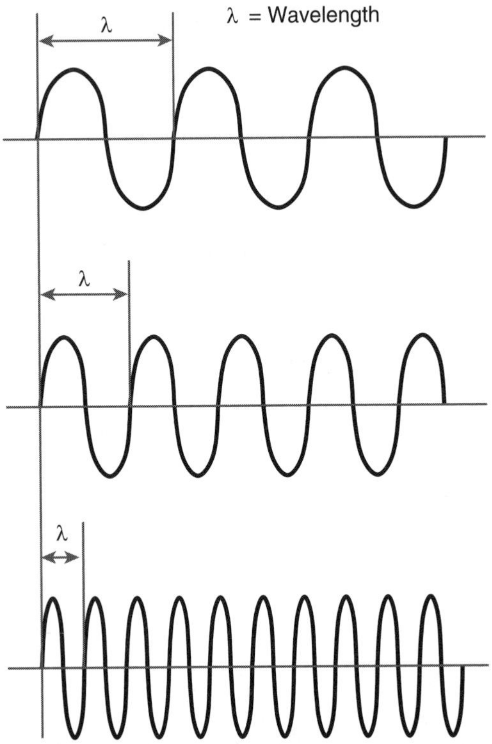

Figure 17-12 *Examples of Increasing Frequency and Decreasing Wavelength*

Understanding RF Power and dB

For an RF signal to be transmitted, propagated through free space, received, and understood with any certainty, it must be sent with enough strength or energy to make the journey. Think about Figure 17-1 again, where the two people are trying to signal each other with a rope. If the sender continuously moves his arm up and down a small distance, he will produce a wave in the rope. However, the wave will dampen out only a short distance away because of factors such as the weight of the rope, gravity, and so on. To move the wave all the way down the rope to reach the receiver, the sender must move his arm up and down with a much greater range of motion and with greater force or strength.

This strength can be measured as the **amplitude**, or the height from the top peak to the bottom peak of the signal's waveform, as shown in Figure 17-13.

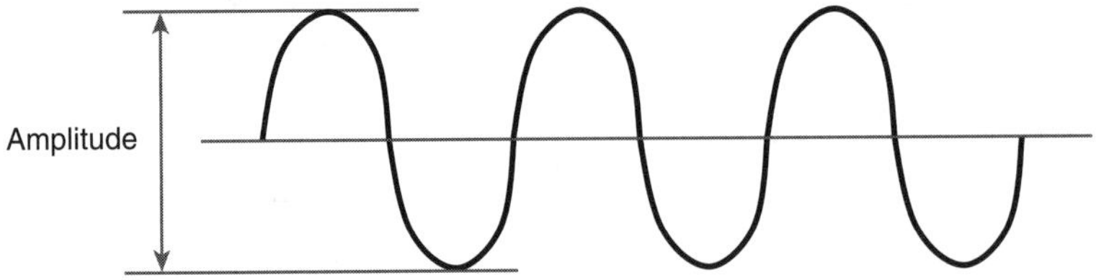

Figure 17-13 *Signal Amplitude*

The strength of an RF signal is usually measured by its power, in watts (W). For example, a typical AM radio station broadcasts at a power of 50,000 W; an FM radio station might use 16,000 W. In comparison, a wireless LAN transmitter usually has a signal strength between 0.1 W (100 mW) and 0.001 W (1 mW).

When power is measured in watts or milliwatts, it is considered to be an absolute power measurement. In other words, something has to measure exactly how much energy is present in the RF signal. This is fairly straightforward when the measurement is taken at the output of a transmitter because the transmit power level is usually known ahead of time.

Sometimes you might need to compare the power levels between two different transmitters. For example, suppose that device T1 is transmitting at 1 mW, while T2 is transmitting at 10 mW, as shown in Figure 17-14. Simple subtraction tells you that T2 is 9 mW stronger than T1. You might also notice that T2 is 10 times stronger than T1.

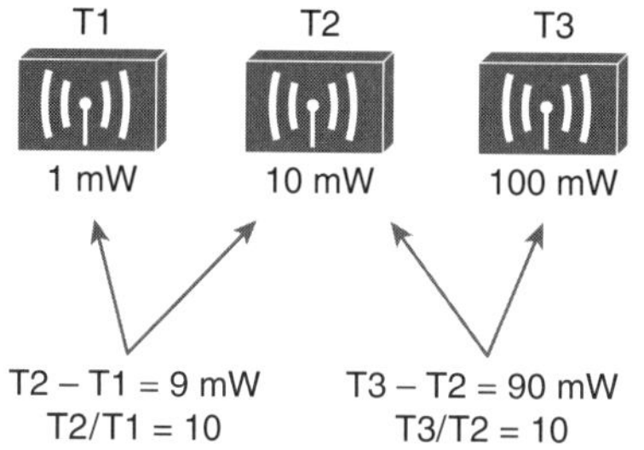

Figure 17-14 *Comparing Power Levels Between Transmitters*

Now compare transmitters T2 and T3, which use 10 mW and 100 mW, respectively. Using subtraction, T2 and T3 differ by 90 mW, but T3 is again 10 times stronger than T2. In each instance, subtraction yields a different result than division. Which method should you use?

Quantities like absolute power values can differ by orders of magnitude. A more surprising example is shown in Figure 17-15, where T4 is 0.00001 mW, and T5 is 10 mW—values you might encounter with wireless access points. Subtracting the two values gives their difference as 9.99999 mW. However, T5 is 1,000,000 times stronger than T4!

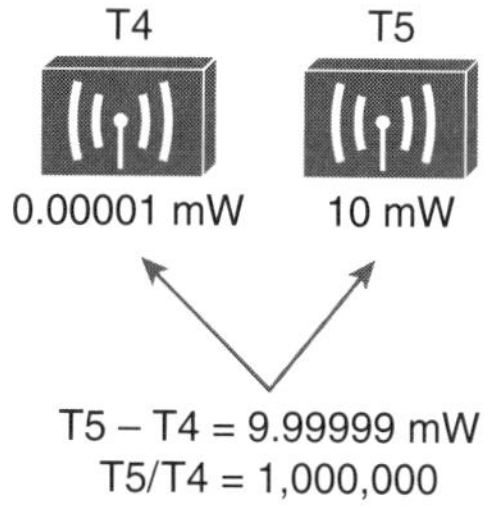

Figure 17-15 *Comparing Power Levels That Differ by Orders of Magnitude*

Because absolute power values can fall anywhere within a huge range, from a tiny decimal number to hundreds, thousands, or greater values, we need a way to transform the exponential range into a linear one. The logarithm function can be leveraged to do just that. In a nutshell, a logarithm takes values that are orders of magnitude apart (0.001, 0.01, 0.1, 1, 10, 100, and 1000, for example) and spaces them evenly within a reasonable range.

NOTE The base-10 logarithm function, denoted by log_{10}, computes how many times 10 can be multiplied by itself to equal a number. For example, $log_{10}(10)$ equals 1 because 10 is used only once to get the result of 10. The $log_{10}(100)$ equals 2 because 10 is multiplied twice (10 × 10) to reach the result of 100. Computing other log_{10} values is difficult, requiring the use of a calculator. The good news is that you will not need a calculator or a logarithm on the ENCOR 350-401 exam. Even so, try to suffer through the few equations in this chapter so that you get a better understanding of power comparisons and measurements.

Key Topic

The **decibel (dB)** is a handy function that uses logarithms to compare one absolute measurement to another. It was originally developed to compare sound intensity levels, but it applies directly to power levels too. After each power value has been converted to the same logarithmic scale, the two values can be subtracted to find the difference. The following equation is used to calculate a dB value, where P1 and P2 are the absolute power levels of two sources:

$$dB=10(log_{10}P2-log_{10}P1)$$

P2 represents the source of interest, and P1 is usually called the *reference* value or the source of comparison.

The difference between the two logarithmic functions can be rewritten as a single logarithm of P2 divided by P1, as follows:

$$dB = 10log_{10}\frac{P2}{P1}$$

Here, the *ratio* of the two absolute power values is computed first; then the result is converted onto a logarithmic scale.

Oddly enough, we end up with the same two methods to compare power levels with dB: a subtraction and a division. Thanks to the logarithm, both methods arrive at identical dB values. Be aware that the ratio or division form of the equation is the most commonly used in the wireless engineering world.

Important dB Laws to Remember

There are three cases where you can use mental math to make power-level comparisons using dB. By adding or subtracting fixed dB amounts, you can compare two power levels through multiplication or division. You should memorize the following three laws, which are based on dB changes of 0, 3, and 10, respectively:

Key Topic

- **Law of Zero:** A value of 0 dB means that the two absolute power values are equal.

  If the two power values are equal, the ratio inside the logarithm is 1, and the $log_{10}(1)$ is 0. This law is intuitive; if two power levels are the same, one is 0 dB greater than the other.

- **Law of 3s:** A value of 3 dB means that the power value of interest is double the reference value; a value of −3 dB means the power value of interest is half the reference.

When P2 is twice P1, the ratio is always 2. Therefore, $10\log_{10}(2) = 3$ dB.

When the ratio is 1/2, $10\log_{10}(1/2) = -3$ dB.

The Law of 3s is not very intuitive but is still easy to learn. Whenever a power level doubles, it increases by 3 dB. Whenever it is cut in half, it decreases by 3 dB.

- **Law of 10s:** A value of 10 dB means that the power value of interest is 10 times the reference value; a value of 10 dB means the power value of interest is 1/10 of the reference.

  When P2 is 10 times P1, the ratio is always 10. Therefore, $10\log_{10}(10) = 10$ dB.

  When P2 is one tenth of P1, then the ratio is 1/10 and $10\log_{10}(1/10) = -10$ dB.

  The Law of 10s is intuitive because multiplying or dividing by 10 adds or subtracts 10 dB, respectively.

Notice another handy rule of thumb: When absolute power values multiply, the dB value is positive and can be added. When the power values divide, the dB value is negative and can be subtracted. Table 17-3 summarizes the useful dB comparisons.

Table 17-3 Power Changes and Their Corresponding dB Values

Power Change	dB Value
=	0 dB
× 2	+3 dB
/ 2	–3 dB
× 10	+10 dB
/ 10	–10 dB

Try a few example problems to see whether you understand how to compare two power values using dB. In Figure 17-16, sources A, B, and C transmit at 4, 8, and 16 mW, respectively. Source B is double the value of A, so it must be 3 dB greater than A. Likewise, source C is double the value of B, so it must be 3 dB greater than B.

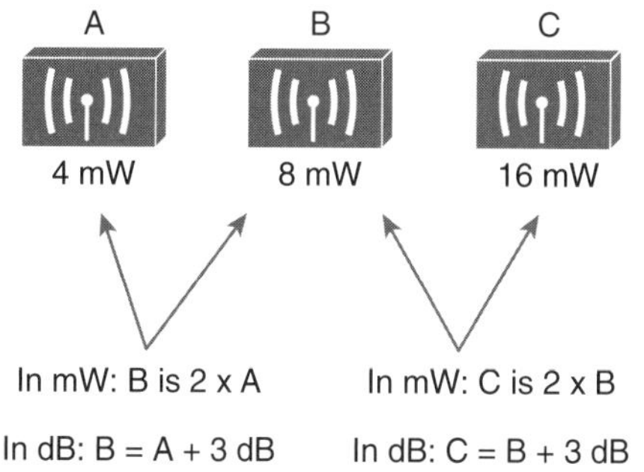

Figure 17-16 *Comparing Power Levels Using dB*

You can also compare sources A and C. To get from A to C, you have to double A, and then double it again. Each time you double a value, just add 3 dB. Therefore, C is 3 dB + 3 dB = 6 dB greater than A.

Next, try the more complicated example shown in Figure 17-17. Keep in mind that dB values can be added and subtracted in succession (in case several multiplication and division operations involving 2 and 10 are needed).

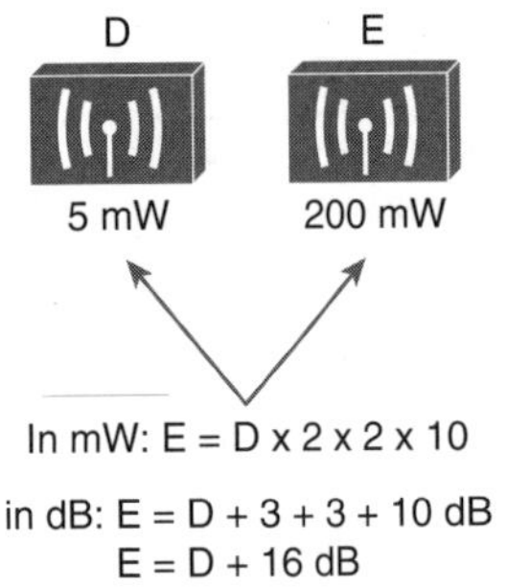

Figure 17-17 *Example of Computing dB with Simple Rules*

Sources D and E have power levels 5 and 200 mW. Try to figure out a way to go from 5 to 200 using only × 2 or × 10 operations. You can double 5 to get 10, then double 10 to get 20, and then multiply by 10 to reach 200 mW. Next, use the dB laws to replace the doubling and × 10 with the dB equivalents. The result is E = D + 3 + 3 + 10 or E = D + 16 dB.

You might also find other ways to reach the same result. For example, you can start with 5 mW, then multiply by 10 to get 50, then double 50 to get 100, then double 100 to reach 200 mW. This time the result is E = D + 10 + 3 + 3 or E = D + 16 dB.

Comparing Power Against a Reference: dBm

Beyond comparing two transmitting sources, a network engineer must be concerned about the RF signal propagating from a transmitter to a receiver. After all, transmitting a signal is meaningless unless someone can receive it and make use of that signal.

Figure 17-18 shows a simple scenario with a transmitter and a receiver. Nothing in the real world is ideal, so assume that something along the path of the signal will induce a net loss. At the receiver, the signal strength will be degraded by some amount. Suppose that you are able to measure the power level leaving the transmitter, which is 100 mW. At the receiver, you measure the power level of the arriving signal. It is an incredibly low 0.000031623 mW.

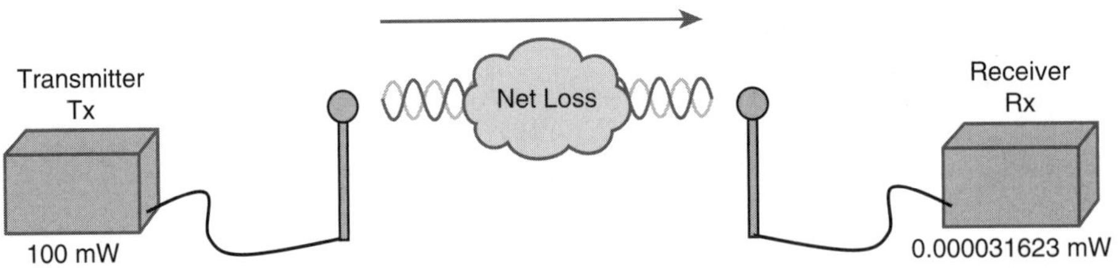

Figure 17-18 *Example of RF Signal Power Loss*

Wouldn't it be nice to quantify the net loss over the signal's path? After all, you might want to try several other transmit power levels or change something about the path between the transmitter and receiver. To design the signal path properly, you would like to make sure that the signal strength arriving at the receiver is at an optimum level.

You could leverage the handy dB formula to compare the received signal strength to the transmitted signal strength, as long as you can remember the formula and have a calculator nearby:

$$dB = 10\log_{10}\frac{0.000031623\,mW}{100\,mW} = -65\,dB$$

The net loss over the signal path turns out to be a decrease of 65 dB. Knowing that, you decide to try a different transmit power level to see what would happen at the receiver. It does not seem very straightforward to use the new transmit power to find the new signal strength at the receiver. That might require more formulas and more time at the calculator.

A better approach is to compare each absolute power along the signal path to one common reference value. Then, regardless of the absolute power values, you could just focus on the changes to the power values that are occurring at various stages along the signal path. In other words, you could convert every power level to a dB value and simply add them up along the path.

Recall that the dB formula puts the power level of interest on the top of the ratio, with a reference power level on the bottom. In wireless networks, the reference power level is usually 1 mW, so the units are designated by **dBm** (*dB-milliwatt*).

Returning to the scenario in Figure 17-18, the absolute power values at the transmitter and receiver can be converted to dBm, the results of which are shown in Figure 17-19. Notice that the dBm values can be added along the path: The transmitter dBm plus the net loss in dB equals the received signal in dBm.

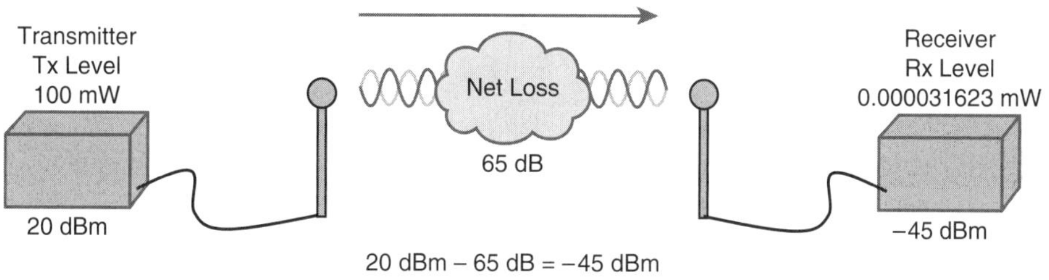

Figure 17-19 *Subtracting dB to Represent a Loss in Signal Strength*

Measuring Power Changes Along the Signal Path

Up to this point, this chapter has considered a transmitter and its antenna to be a single unit. That might seem like a logical assumption because many wireless access points have built-in antennas. In reality, a transmitter, its antenna, and the cable that connects them are all discrete components that not only propagate an RF signal but also affect its absolute power level.

When an antenna is connected to a transmitter, it provides some amount of gain to the resulting RF signal. This effectively increases the dB value of the signal above that of the transmitter alone. Chapter 18 explains this topic in greater detail; for now, just be aware that antennas provide positive gain.

By itself, an antenna does not generate any amount of absolute power. In other words, when an antenna is disconnected, no milliwatts of power are being pushed out of it. That makes it impossible to measure the antenna's gain in dBm. Instead, an antenna's gain is measured by comparing its performance with that of a reference antenna, then computing a value in dB.

Usually, the reference antenna is an **isotropic antenna**, so the gain is measured in **dBi** (*dB-isotropic*). An isotropic antenna does not actually exist because it is ideal in every way. Its size is a tiny point, and it radiates RF equally in every direction. No physical antenna can do that. The isotropic antenna's performance can be calculated according to RF formulas, making it a universal reference for any antenna.

Because of the physical qualities of the cable that connects an antenna to a transmitter, some signal loss always occurs. Cable vendors supply the loss in dB per foot or meter of cable length for each type of cable manufactured.

Once you know the complete combination of transmitter power level, the length of cable, and the antenna gain, you can figure out the actual power level that will be radiated from the antenna. This is known as the **effective isotropic radiated power (EIRP)**, measured in dBm.

Key Topic

EIRP is a very important parameter because it is regulated by government agencies in most countries. In those cases, a system cannot radiate signals higher than a maximum allowable EIRP. To find the EIRP of a system, simply add the transmitter power level to the antenna gain and subtract the cable loss, as illustrated in Figure 17-20.

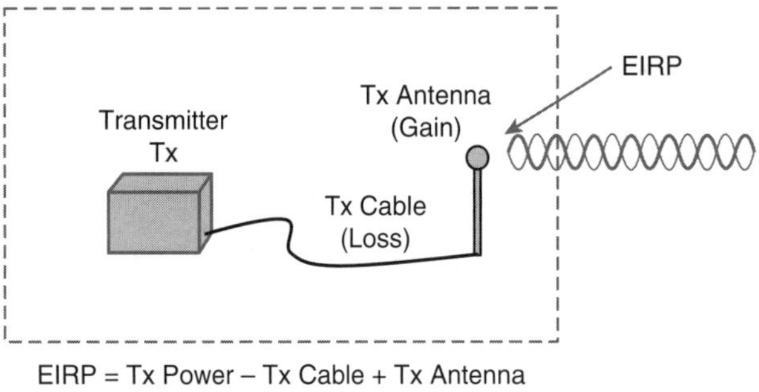

Figure 17-20 *Calculating EIRP*

Suppose a transmitter is configured for a power level of 10 dBm (10 mW). A cable with 5 dB loss connects the transmitter to an antenna with an 8 dBi gain. The resulting EIRP of the system is 10 dBm – 5 dB + 8 dBi, or 13 dBm.

You might notice that the EIRP is made up of decibel-milliwatt (dBm), dB relative to an isotropic antenna (dBi), and plain decibel (dB) values. Even though the units appear to be different, you can safely combine them for the purposes of calculating the EIRP. The only exception to this is when an antenna's gain is measured in **dBd** (*dB-dipole*). In that case, a dipole antenna has been used as the reference antenna, rather than an isotropic antenna. A dipole is a simple actual antenna, which has a gain of 2.14 dBi. If an antenna has its gain shown as dBd, you can add 2.14 dB to that value to get its gain in dBi units instead.

Power-level considerations do not have to stop with the EIRP. You should also be concerned with the complete path of a signal, to make sure that the transmitted signal has sufficient power so that it can effectively reach and be understood by a receiver. This is known as the **link budget**.

The dB values of gains and losses can be combined over any number of stages along a signal's path. Consider Figure 17-21, which shows every component of signal gain or loss along the path from transmitter to receiver.

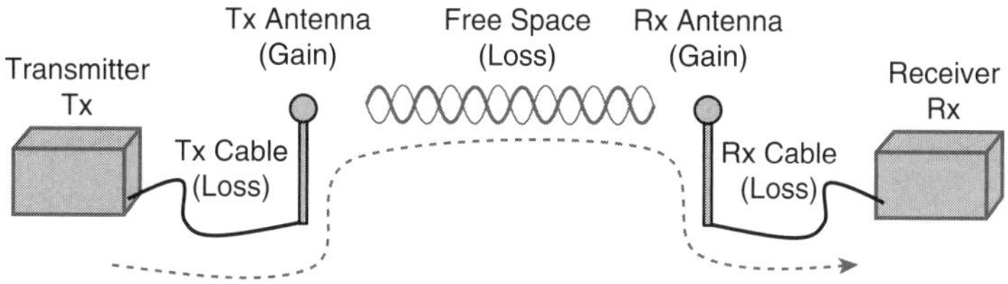

Rx Signal = Tx Power – Tx Cable + Tx Antenna – Free Space + Rx Antenna – Rx Cable

Figure 17-21 *Calculating Received Signal Strength Over the Path of an RF Signal*

At the receiving end, an antenna provides gain to increase the received signal power level. A cable connecting the antenna to the receiver also introduces some loss.

Figure 17-22 shows some sample dB values, as well as the resulting sum of the component parts across the entire signal path. The signal begins at 20 dBm at the transmitter, has an EIRP value of 22 dBm at the transmitting antenna (20 dBm – 2 dB + 4 dBi), and arrives at the receiver with a level of –45 dBm.

NOTE Notice that every signal gain or loss used in Figure 17-22 is given except for the 69 dB loss between the two antennas. In this case, the loss can be quantified based on the other values given. In reality, it can be calculated as a function of distance and frequency, as described in the next section. For perspective, you might see a 69 dB Wi-Fi loss over a distance of about 13 to 28 meters.

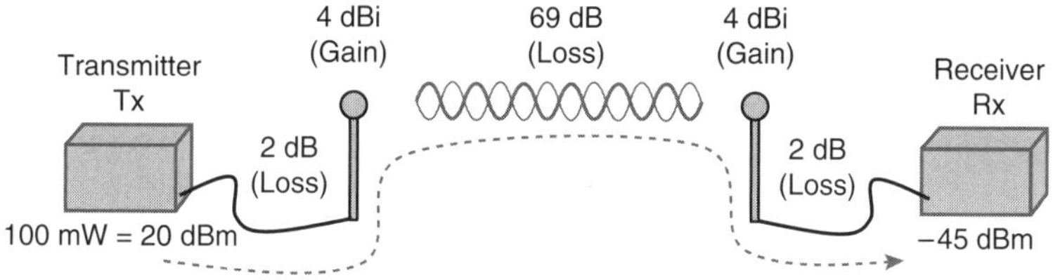

Rx Signal = 20 dBm – 2 dB + 4 dBi – 69 dB + 4 dBi – 2 dB = –45 dBm

Figure 17-22 *Example of Calculating Received Signal Strength*

If you always begin with the transmitter power expressed in dBm, it is a simple matter to add or subtract the dB components along the signal path to find the signal strength that arrives at the receiver.

Free Space Path Loss

Whenever an RF signal is transmitted from an antenna, its amplitude decreases as it travels through free space. Even if there are no obstacles in the path between the transmitter and receiver, the signal strength will weaken. This is known as *free space path loss*.

What is it about free space that causes an RF signal to be degraded? Is it the air or maybe the earth's magnetic field? No, even signals sent to and from spacecraft in the vacuum of outer space are degraded.

Recall that an RF signal propagates through free space as a wave, not as a ray or straight line. The wave has a three-dimensional curved shape that expands as it travels. It is this expansion or spreading that causes the signal strength to weaken.

Figure 17-23 shows a cutaway view of the free space loss principle. Suppose the antenna is a tiny point, such that the transmitted RF energy travels in every direction. The wave that is produced would take the form of a sphere; as the wave travels outward, the sphere increases in size. Therefore, the same amount of energy coming out of the tiny point is soon spread over an ever-expanding sphere in free space. The concentration of that energy gets weaker as the distance from the antenna increases.

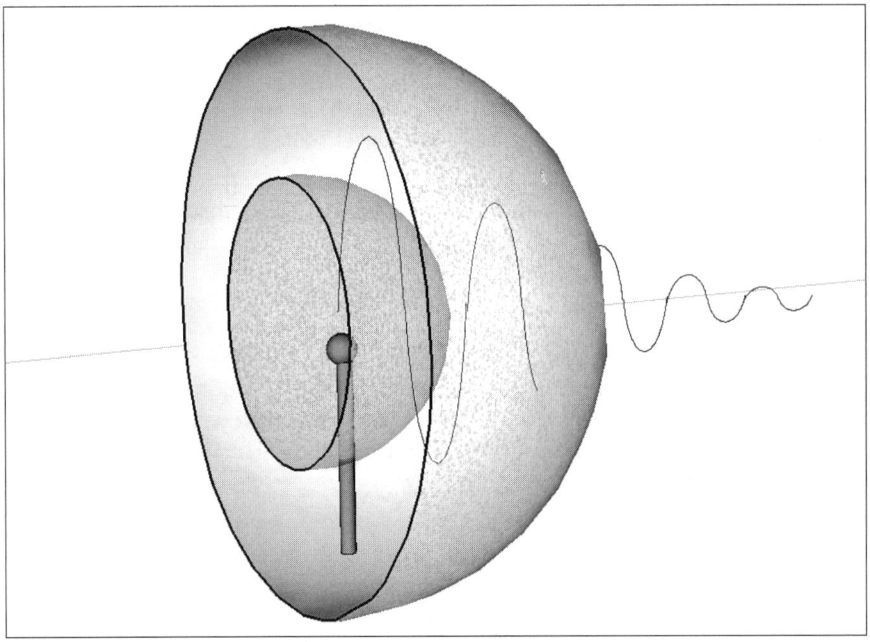

Figure 17-23 *Free Space Loss Due to Wave Spreading*

Even if you could devise an antenna that could focus the transmitted energy into a tight beam, the energy would still travel as a wave and would spread out over a distance. Regardless of the antenna used, the amount of signal strength loss through free space is consistent.

For reference, the free space path loss (FSPL) in dB can be calculated according to the following equation:

$$FSPL(dB) = 20\log_{10}(d) + 20\log_{10}(f) + 32.44$$

where *d* is the distance from the transmitter in kilometers and *f* is the frequency in megahertz. Do not worry, though: You will not have to know this equation for the ENCOR 350-401 exam. It is presented here to show two interesting facts:

Key Topic

- Free space path loss is an exponential function; the signal strength falls off quickly near the transmitter but more slowly farther away.
- The loss is a function of distance and frequency only.

With the formula, you can calculate the free space path loss for any given scenario, but you will not have to for the exam. Just be aware that the free space path loss is always an important component of the link budget, along with antenna gain and cable loss.

NOTE You might have noticed that the distance *d* is given in kilometers. In most indoor locations, wireless clients are usually less than 50 meters away from the access point they are using. Does that mean the free space path loss over a short indoor path is negligible? Not at all. Even at 1 meter away, the effects of free space cause a loss of around 46 dBm!

You should also be aware that the free space path loss is greater in the 5 GHz band than it is in the 2.4 GHz band. The loss is also greater in the 6 GHz band than in the 5 GHz band. In the equation, as the frequency increases, so does the loss in dB. This means that 2.4 GHz devices have a greater effective range than 5 GHz and 6 GHz devices, assuming an equal transmitted signal strength. Figure 17-24 shows the range difference, where both transmitters have an equal EIRP. The dashed circles show where the effective range ends, at the point where the signal strength of each transmitter is equal.

Key Topic

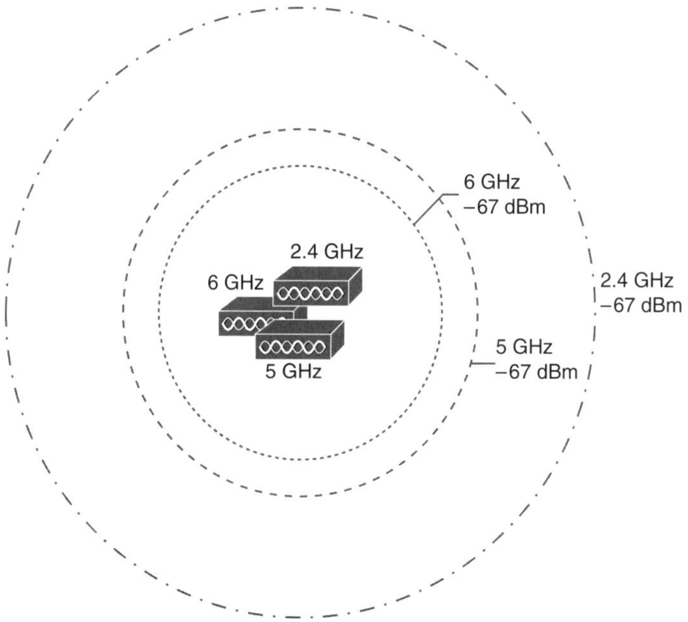

Figure 17-24 *Effective Range of 2.4 GHz, 5 GHz, and 6 GHz Transmitters*

NOTE To get a feel for the actual range difference between the different bands, an impromptu test was performed by carrying a test receiver away from co-located 2.4, 5, and 6 GHz transmitters until the received signal strength reached −67 dBm. On a 2.4 GHz channel, the range was measured to be 140 feet, whereas at 5 GHz it was reduced to 80 feet and at 6 GHz to 50 feet. While the free space path loss is the largest contributor to the difference, other factors like antenna size and receiver sensitivity that differ between the 2.4, 5, and 6 GHz radios have some effect too.

17

Understanding Power Levels at the Receiver

When you work with wireless LAN devices, the EIRP levels leaving the transmitter's antenna normally range from 100 mW down to 1 mW. This corresponds to the range +20 dBm down to 0 dBm.

At the receiver, the power levels are much, much less, ranging from 1 mW all the way down to tiny fractions of a milliwatt, approaching 0 mW. The corresponding range of received signal levels is from 0 dBm down to about –100 dBm. Even so, a receiver expects to find a signal on a predetermined frequency, with enough power to contain useful data.

Receivers usually measure a signal's power level according to the **received signal strength indicator (RSSI)** scale. The RSSI value is defined in the 802.11 standard as an internal 1-byte relative value ranging from 0 to 255, where 0 is the weakest and 255 is the strongest. As such, the value has no useful units and the range of RSSI values can vary between one hardware manufacturer and another. In reality, you will likely see RSSI values that are measured in dBm after they have been converted and scaled to correlate to actual dBm values. Be aware that the results are not standardized across all receiver manufacturers, so an RSSI value can vary from one receiver hardware to another.

Assuming that a transmitter is sending an RF signal with enough power to reach a receiver, what received signal strength value is good enough? Every receiver has a **sensitivity level**, or a threshold that divides intelligible, useful signals from unintelligible ones. As long as a signal is received with a power level that is greater than the sensitivity level, chances are that the data from the signal can be understood correctly. Figure 17-25 shows an example of how the signal strength at a receiver might change over time. The receiver's sensitivity level is –82 dBm.

Key Topic

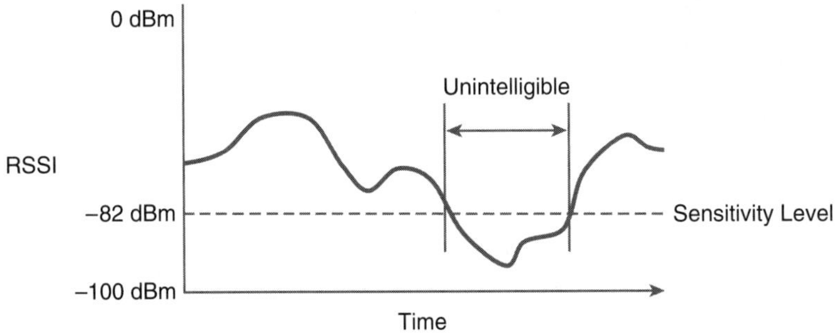

Figure 17-25 *Example of Receiver Sensitivity Level*

The RSSI value focuses on the expected signal alone, without regard to any other signals that may also be received. All other signals that are received on the same frequency as the one you are trying to receive are simply viewed as *noise*. The noise level, or the average signal strength of the noise, is called the **noise floor**.

It is easy to ignore noise as long as the noise floor is well below what you are trying to hear. For example, two people can effectively whisper in a library because there is very little competing noise. Those same two people would become very frustrated if they tried to whisper to each other in a crowded sports arena.

Similarly, with an RF signal, the signal strength must be greater than the noise floor by a decent amount so that it can be received and understood correctly. The difference between the signal and the noise is called the **signal-to-noise ratio (SNR)**, measured in dB. A higher SNR value is preferred.

Figure 17-26 shows the received signal strength of a signal compared with the noise floor that is received. The signal strength averages around –54 dBm. On the left side of the graph, the noise floor is –90 dBm. The resulting SNR is –54 dBm – (–90) dBm or 36 dB. Toward the right side of the graph, the noise floor gradually increases to –65 dBm, reducing the SNR to 11 dB. The signal is so close to the noise that it might not be usable.

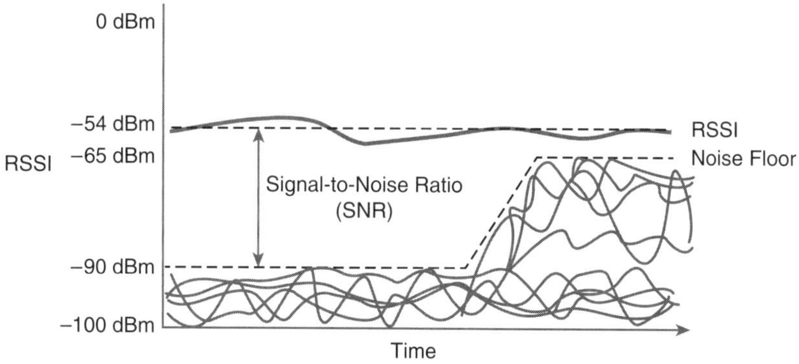

Figure 17-26 *Example of a Changing Noise Floor and SNR*

Carrying Data Over an RF Signal

Up to this point in the chapter, only the RF characteristics of wireless signals have been discussed. The RF signals presented have existed only as simple oscillations in the form of a sine wave. The frequency, amplitude, and phase have all been constant. The steady, predictable frequency is important because a receiver needs to tune to a known frequency to find the signal in the first place.

This basic RF signal is called a **carrier signal** because it is used to carry other useful information. With AM and FM radio signals, the carrier signal also transports audio signals. TV carrier signals have to carry both audio and video. Wireless LAN carrier signals must carry data.

To add data to the RF signal, the frequency of the original carrier signal must be preserved. Therefore, there must be some scheme of altering some characteristic of the carrier signal to distinguish a 0 bit from a 1 bit. Whatever scheme is used by the transmitter must also be used by the receiver so that the data bits can be correctly interpreted.

Figure 17-27 shows a carrier signal that has a constant frequency. The data bits 1001 are to be sent over the carrier signal, but how? One idea might be to simply use the value of each data bit to turn the carrier signal off or on. The Bad Idea 1 plot shows the resulting RF signal. A receiver might be able to notice when the signal is present and has an amplitude, thereby correctly interpreting 1 bits, but there is no signal to receive during 0 bits. If the signal becomes weak or is not available for some reason, the receiver will incorrectly think that a long string of 0 bits has been transmitted. A different twist might be to transmit only the upper half of the carrier signal during a 1 bit and the lower half during a 0 bit, as shown in the Bad Idea 2 plot. This time, a portion of the signal is always available for the receiver, but the signal becomes impractical to receive because important pieces of each cycle are missing. In addition, it is very difficult to transmit an RF signal with disjointed alternating cycles.

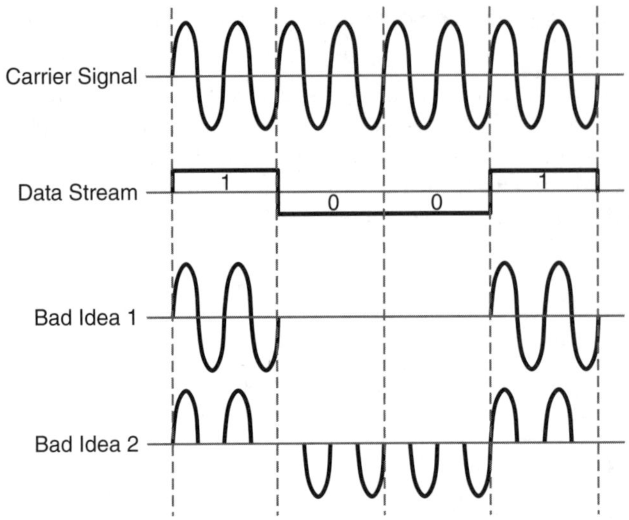

Figure 17-27 *Poor Attempts at Sending Data over an RF Signal*

Such naive approaches might not be successful, but they do have the right idea: to alter the carrier signal in a way that indicates the information to be carried. This is known as **modulation**, where the carrier signal is modulated or changed according to some other source. At the receiver, the process is reversed; **demodulation** interprets the added information based on changes in the carrier signal.

RF modulation schemes generally have the following goals:

- Carry data at a predefined rate
- Be reasonably immune to interference and noise
- Be practical to transmit and receive

Key Topic

Due to the physical properties of an RF signal, a modulation scheme can alter only the following attributes:

- Frequency, but only by varying slightly above or below the carrier frequency
- Phase
- Amplitude

The modulation techniques require some amount of bandwidth centered on the carrier frequency. This additional bandwidth is partly due to the rate of the data being carried and partly due to the overhead from encoding the data and manipulating the carrier signal. If the data has a relatively low bit rate, such as an audio signal carried over AM or FM radio, the modulation can be straightforward and requires little extra bandwidth. Such signals are called **narrowband** transmissions.

In contrast, wireless LANs must carry data at high bit rates, requiring more bandwidth for modulation. The end result is that the data being sent is spread out across a range of frequencies. This is known as **spread spectrum**. At the physical layer, modern wireless LANs can be broken down into the following two common spread-spectrum categories:

- **Direct sequence spread spectrum (DSSS):** Used in the 2.4 GHz band, where a small number of fixed, wide channels support complex phase modulation schemes and somewhat scalable data rates. Typically, the channels are wide enough to augment the data by spreading it out and making it more resilient to disruption.
- **Orthogonal Frequency Division Multiplexing (OFDM):** Used in the 2.4, 5, and 6 GHz bands, where a single 20 MHz channel contains data that is sent in *parallel* over multiple frequencies. Each channel is divided into many subcarriers (also called subchannels or tones); both phase and amplitude are modulated with **quadrature amplitude modulation (QAM)** to move the most data efficiently.

Maintaining AP–Client Compatibility

To provide wireless communication that works, an AP and any client device that associates with it must use wireless mechanisms that are compatible. The IEEE 802.11 standard defines these mechanisms in a standardized fashion. Through 802.11, RF signals, modulation, coding, bands, channels, and data rates all come together to provide a robust communication medium.

Since the original IEEE 802.11 standard was published in 1997, many amendments have been added to it. The amendments cover almost every conceivable aspect of wireless LAN communication, including quality of service (QoS), security, RF measurements, wireless management, more efficient mobility, and ever-increasing throughput.

By now, most of the amendments have been rolled up into the overall 802.11 standard and no longer stand alone. Even so, the amendments may live on and be recognized in the industry by their original task group names. For example, the 802.11b amendment was approved in 1999, was rolled up into 802.11 in 2007, but is still recognized by its name today. When you shop for wireless LAN devices, you will often find the 802.11a, b, g, and n amendments listed in the specifications. You might also see terms like *Wi-Fi* followed by a number, which indicates the generation number of the Wi-Fi Alliance's endorsement. The original 802.11 standard was termed *Wi-Fi 0* because it was the root generation.

Each step in the 802.11 evolution involves an amendment to the standard, defining things like modulation and coding schemes that are used to carry data over the air. For example, even the lowly (and legacy) 802.11b defined several types of modulation that each offered a specific data rate. Modulation and coding schemes are complex topics that are beyond the scope of the ENCOR 350-401 exam. However, you should understand the basic use cases for several of the most common 802.11 amendments. As you work through the remainder of this chapter, refer to Table 17-4 for a summary of common amendments to the 802.11 standard, along with the Wi-Fi generation, permitted bands, supported data rates, and channel width.

In the 2.4 GHz band, 802.11 has evolved through the progression of 802.11b and 802.11g, with a maximum data rate of 11 Mbps and 54 Mbps, respectively. Each of these amendments brought more complex modulation methods, resulting in increasing data rates. Notice that the maximum data rates for 802.11b and 802.11g are 11 Mbps and 54 Mbps, respectively, and both use a 22 MHz channel width. The 802.11a amendment brought similar capabilities to the 5 GHz band using a 20 MHz channel.

Key Topic

Table 17-4 A Summary of Common 802.11 Standard Amendments

Standard	2.4 GHz?	5 GHz?	Data Rates Supported	Channel Widths Supported
802.11b Wi-Fi 1	Yes	No	1, 2, 5.5, and 11 Mbps	22 MHz
802.11a Wi-Fi 2	No	Yes	6, 9, 12, 18, 24, 36, 48, and 54 Mbps	20 MHz
802.11g Wi-Fi 3	Yes	No	6, 9, 12, 18, 24, 36, 48, and 54 Mbps	22 MHz
802.11n Wi-Fi 4	Yes	Yes	Up to 150 Mbps* per spatial stream, up to 4 spatial streams	20 or 40 MHz
802.11ac Wi-Fi 5	No	Yes	Up to 866 Mbps per spatial stream, up to 4 spatial streams	20, 40, 80, or 160 MHz
802.11ax Wi-Fi 6	Yes*	Yes*	Up to 1.2 Gbps per spatial stream, up to 8 spatial streams	20, 40, 80, or 160 MHz

* 802.11ax is designed to work on any band from 1 to 7 GHz, provided that the band is approved for use.

The 802.11n amendment was published in 2009 in an effort to scale wireless LAN performance to a theoretical maximum of 600 Mbps. The amendment was unique because it defined a number of additional techniques known as *high throughput (HT)* that can be applied to either the 2.4 or 5 GHz band.

The 802.11ac amendment was introduced in 2013 and brought even higher data rates through more advanced modulation and coding schemes, wider channel widths, greater data aggregation during a transmission, and so on. 802.11ac is known as *very high throughput (VHT)* wireless and can be used only on the 5 GHz band. Notice that Table 17-4 lists the maximum data rate as 866 Mbps—but that can be reached only if every possible feature can be leveraged and RF conditions are favorable. Because there are so many combinations of modulation and efficiency parameters, 802.11ac offers around 320 different data rates!

The Wi-Fi standards up through 802.11ac have operated on the principle that only one device can claim air time to transmit to another device. Typically, that involves one AP transmitting a frame to one client device, or one client transmitting to one AP. Some exceptions are frames that an AP can broadcast to all clients in its basic service set (BSS) and frames that can be transmitted to multiple clients over multiple transmitters and antennas. Regardless, the focus is usually on very high throughput for the one device that can claim and use the air time. The 802.11ax amendment, also known as Wi-Fi 6 and *high efficiency (HE) wireless*, changes that focus by permitting multiple devices to transmit during the same window of air time. This becomes important in areas that have a high density of wireless devices, all competing for air time and throughput.

802.11ax leverages modulation and coding schemes that are even more complex and sensitive than 802.11ac, resulting in data rates that are roughly four times faster. Interference between neighboring BSSs can be avoided through better transmit power control and BSS marking or "coloring" methods. 802.11ax also uses OFDM Access (OFDMA) to schedule and control access to the wireless medium, with channel air time allocated as resource units that can be used for transmission by multiple devices simultaneously. 802.11ax is used in both Wi-Fi 6 (2.4 and 5 GHz bands only) and Wi-Fi 6E (6 GHz band only).

NOTE Although this section has summarized the 802.11 amendments for comparison, each one can be very complex to describe and understand. The main concept to remember is that an AP must support the same set of 802.11 amendments that is supported by the clients that will connect to it. For example, if some wireless clients support only 802.11n, whereas others support 802.11ac, you would be wise make sure the AP can support both standards and configure it to do so. Fortunately, most 802.11 amendments are backward compatible with previous ones that operate in the same band.

Using Multiple Radios to Scale Performance

Before 802.11n, wireless devices used a single transmitter and a single receiver. In other words, the components formed one radio, resulting in a single *radio chain*. This is also known as a single-in, single-out (SISO) system. One secret to the better performance of 802.11n, 802.11ac, and 802.11ax is the use of multiple radio components, forming multiple radio chains. For example, a device can have multiple antennas, multiple transmitters, and multiple receivers at its disposal. This is known as a multiple-input, multiple-output (MIMO) system.

17

Spatial Multiplexing

802.11n, 802.11ac, and 802.11ax devices are characterized according to the number of radio chains available. This is described in the form T×R, where *T* is the number of transmitters, and *R* is the number of receivers. A 2×2 MIMO device has two transmitters and two receivers, and a 2×3 device has two transmitters and three receivers. Figure 17-28 compares the traditional 1×1 SISO device with 2×2 and 2×3 MIMO devices.

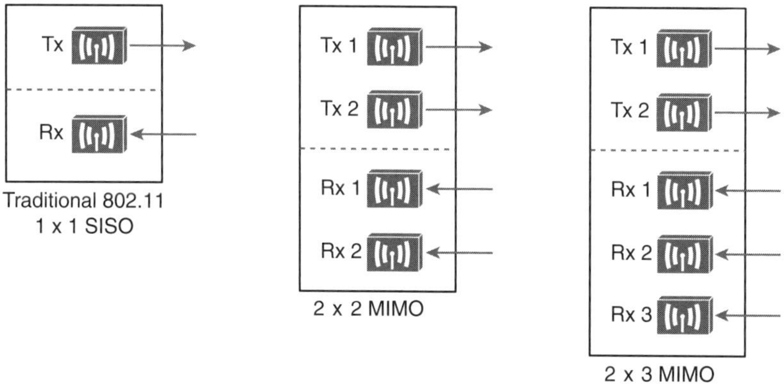

Figure 17-28 *Examples of SISO and MIMO Devices*

The multiple radio chains can be leveraged in a variety of ways. For example, extra radios can be used to improve received signal quality, to improve transmission to specific client locations, and to carry data to and from multiple clients simultaneously.

To increase data throughput, data can be multiplexed or distributed across two or more radio chains—all operating on the same channel but separated through spatial diversity. This is known as **spatial multiplexing**.

How can several radios transmit on the same channel without interfering with each other? The key is to try to keep each signal isolated or easily distinguished from the others. Each radio chain has its own antenna; if the antennas are spaced some distance apart, the signals arriving at the receiver's antennas (also appropriately spaced) will likely be out of phase with each other or at different amplitudes. This is especially true if the signals bounce off some objects along the way, making each antenna's signal travel over a slightly different path to reach the receiver.

In addition, data can be distributed across the transmitter's radio chains in a known fashion. In fact, several independent streams of data can be processed as **spatial streams** that are multiplexed over the radio chains. The receiver must be able to interpret the arriving signals and rebuild the original data streams by reversing the transmitter's multiplexing function.

Spatial multiplexing requires a good deal of digital signal processing on both the transmitting and receiving ends. This pays off by increasing the throughput over the channel; the more spatial streams that are available, the more data that can be sent over the channel.

The number of spatial streams that a device can support is usually designated by adding a colon and a number to the MIMO radio specification. For example, a 3×3:2 MIMO device would have three transmitters and three receivers, and it would support two unique spatial streams. Figure 17-29 shows spatial multiplexing between two 3×3:2 MIMO devices. A 3×3:3 device would be similar but would support three spatial streams.

NOTE Notice that a MIMO device can support a number of unique spatial streams that differs from the number of its transmitters or receivers. It might seem logical that each spatial stream is assigned to a transmitter/receiver, but that is not true. Spatial streams are processed so that they are distributed across multiple radio chains. The number of possible spatial streams depends on the processing capacity and the transmitter feature set of the device—not on the number of its radios.

Ideally, two devices should support an identical number of spatial streams to multiplex and demultiplex the data streams correctly. That is not always possible or even likely because having more spatial streams usually translates to greater cost. What happens when two devices have mismatched spatial stream support? They negotiate the wireless connection by informing each other of their capabilities. Then they can use the lowest number of spatial streams they have in common, but a transmitting device can leverage an additional spatial stream to repeat some information for increased redundancy.

Transmit Beamforming

Multiple radios provide a means to selectively improve transmissions. When a transmitter with a single radio chain sends an RF signal, any receivers that are present have an equal opportunity to receive and interpret the signal. In other words, the transmitter does nothing to prefer one receiver over another; each is at the mercy of its environment and surrounding conditions to receive at a decent SNR.

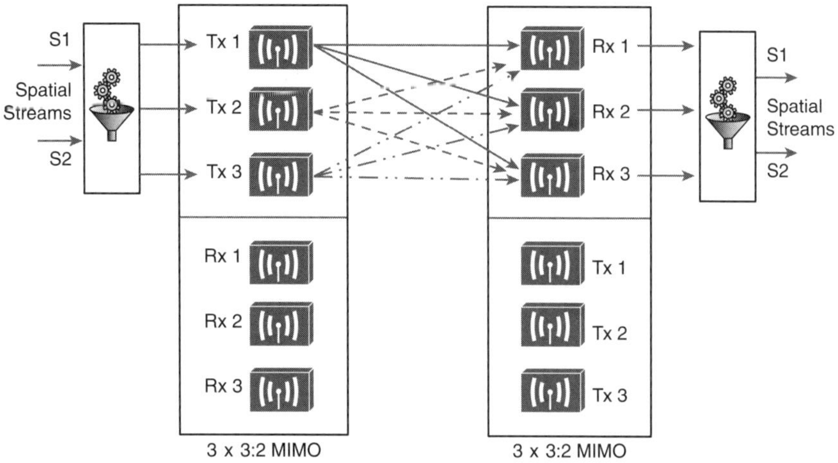

Figure 17-29 *Spatial Multiplexing Between Two 3×3:2 MIMO Devices*

The 802.11n, 802.11ac, and 802.11ax amendments offer a method to customize the transmitted signal to prefer one receiver over others. By leveraging MIMO, the same signal can be transmitted over multiple antennas to reach specific client locations more efficiently.

Usually multiple signals travel over slightly different paths to reach a receiver, so they can arrive delayed and out of phase with each other. This behavior is normally destructive, resulting in a lower SNR and a corrupted signal. With **transmit beamforming (TBF)**, the phase of the signal is altered as it is fed into each transmitting antenna so that the resulting signals will all arrive in phase at a specific receiver. This technique has a constructive effect, improving the signal quality and SNR.

Figure 17-30 shows a device on the left using transmit beamforming to target device B on the right. The phase of each copy of the transmitted signal is adjusted so that all three signals arrive at device B more or less in phase with each other. The same three signal copies also arrive at device A, which is not targeted by TBF. As a result, the signals arrive as is and are out of phase.

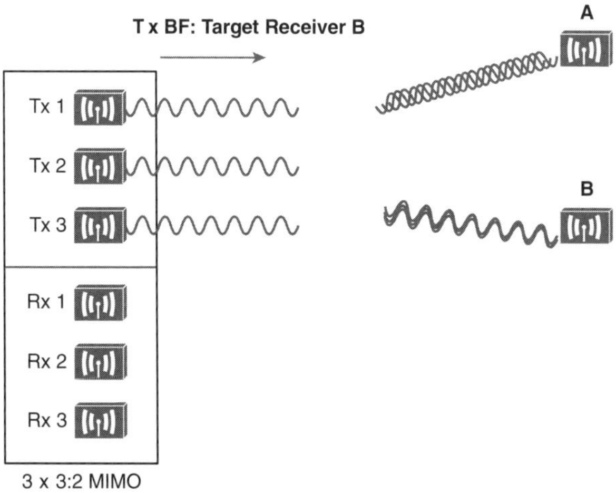

Figure 17-30 *Using Transmit Beamforming to Target a Specific Receiving Device*

The location and RF conditions can be unique for each receiver in an area. Therefore, transmit beamforming can use explicit feedback from the device at the far end, enabling the transmitter to make the appropriate adjustments to the transmitted signal phase. As TBF information is collected about each far-end device, a transmitter can keep a table of the devices and phase adjustments so that it can send focused transmissions to each one dynamically.

Maximal-Ratio Combining

When an RF signal is received on a device, it may look very little like the original transmitted signal. The signal may be degraded or distorted due to a variety of conditions. If that same signal can be transmitted over multiple antennas, as in the case of a MIMO device, then the receiving device can attempt to restore it to its original state.

The receiving device can use multiple antennas and radio chains to receive the multiple transmitted copies of the signal. One copy might be better than the others, or one copy might be better for a time, and then become worse than the others. In any event, **maximal-ratio combining (MRC)** can combine the copies to produce one signal that represents the best version at any given time. The end result is a reconstructed signal with an improved SNR and receiver sensitivity.

Maximizing the AP–Client Throughput

To pass data over an RF signal successfully, both a transmitter and receiver have to use the same modulation method. In addition, the pair should use the best data rate possible, given their current environment. If they are located in a noisy environment, where a low SNR or a low RSSI might result, a lower data rate might be preferable. If not, a higher data rate is better.

When wireless standards like 802.11n, 802.11ac, and 802.11ax offer many possible modulation methods and a vast number of different data rates, how do the transmitter and receiver select a common method to use? To complicate things, the transmitter, the receiver, or both might be mobile. As they move around, the SNR and RSSI conditions will likely change from one moment to the next. The most effective approach is to have the transmitter and receiver negotiate a modulation method (and the resulting data rate) dynamically, based on current RF conditions.

One simple solution to overcome free space path loss is to increase the transmitter's output power. Increasing the antenna gain can also boost the EIRP. Having a greater signal strength before the free space path loss occurs translates to a greater RSSI value at a distant receiver after the loss. This approach might work fine for an isolated transmitter but can cause interference problems when several transmitters are located in an area.

A more robust solution is to just cope with the effects of free space path loss and other detrimental conditions. Wireless devices are usually mobile and can move closer to or farther away from a transmitter at will. As a receiver gets closer to a transmitter, the RSSI increases. This, in turn, translates to an increased SNR. Remember that more complex modulation and coding schemes can be used to transport more data when the SNR is high. As a receiver gets farther away from a transmitter, the RSSI (and SNR) decreases. More basic modulation and coding schemes are needed there because of the increase in noise and the need to retransmit more data.

802.11 devices have a clever way to adjust their modulation and coding schemes based on the current RSSI and SNR conditions. If the conditions are favorable for good signal quality and higher data rates, a complex modulation and coding scheme (and a high data rate) is used. As the conditions deteriorate, less-complex schemes can be selected, resulting in a greater range but lower data rates. The scheme selection is commonly known as **dynamic rate shifting (DRS)**. As its name implies, it can be performed dynamically with no manual intervention.

NOTE Although DRS is inherently used in 802.11 devices, it is not defined in the 802.11 standard. Each manufacturer can have its own approach to DRS, so all devices don't necessarily select the same scheme at the same location. DRS is also known by many alternative names, such as *link adaptation*, *adaptive modulation and coding (AMC)*, and *rate adaptation*.

As a simple example, Figure 17-31 illustrates DRS operation on the 2.4 GHz band. Each concentric circle represents the range supported by a particular modulation and coding scheme. (You can ignore the cryptic names because they are beyond the scope of the ENCOR 350-401 exam.) The figure is somewhat simplistic because it assumes a consistent power level across all modulation types. Notice that the white circles denote OFDM modulation (802.11g), and the shaded circles contain DSSS modulation (802.11b). None of the 802.11n/ac/ax modulation types are shown, for simplicity. The data rates are arranged in order of increasing circle size or range from the transmitter.

Key Topic

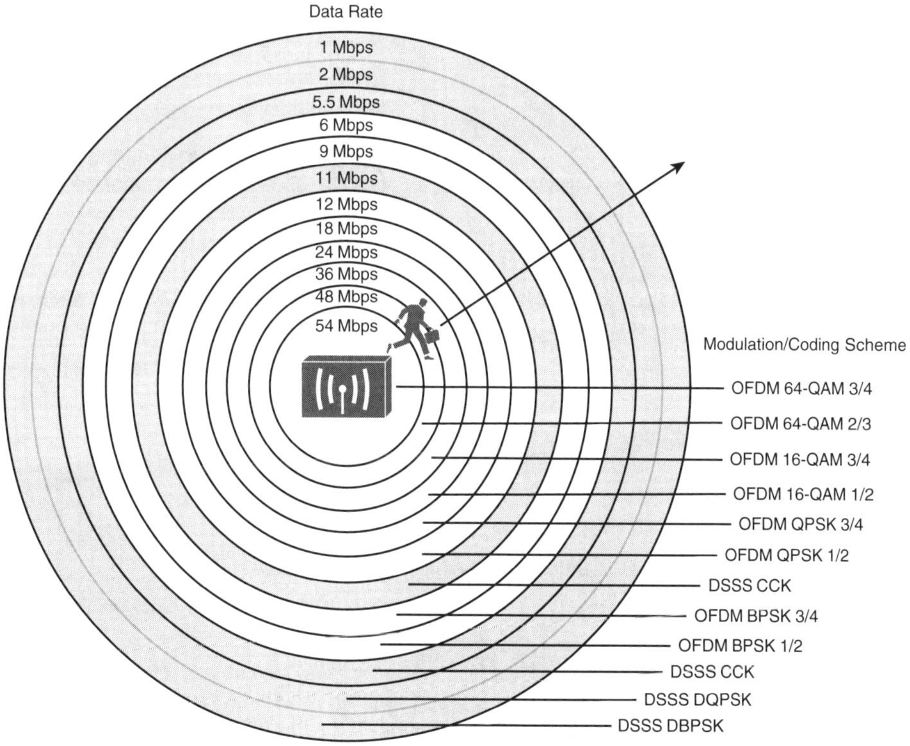

Figure 17-31 *Dynamic Rate Shifting as a Function of Range*

Suppose that a mobile user starts out near the transmitter, within the innermost circle, where the received signal is strong and SNR is high. Most likely, wireless transmissions will use the OFDM 64-QAM 3/4 modulation and coding scheme to achieve a data rate of 54 Mbps. As the user walks away from the transmitter, the RSSI and SNR fall by some amount. The new RF conditions will likely trigger a shift to a different and less complex modulation and coding scheme, resulting in a lower data rate.

In a nutshell, each move outward, into a larger concentric circle, causes a dynamic shift to a reduced data rate, in an effort to maintain the data integrity to the outer reaches of the transmitter's range. As the mobile user moves back toward the AP again, the data rates will likely shift higher and higher again.

The same scenario in the 5 GHz band would look very similar, except that every circle would use an OFDM modulation scheme and data rate corresponding to 802.11a, 802.11n, 802.11ac, or 802.11ax.

Exam Preparation Tasks

You have a couple of choices for exam preparation: the exercises here, Chapter 30, "Final Preparation," and the exam simulation questions in the Pearson Test Prep Software Online.

Review All Key Topics

Review the most important topics in this chapter, noted with the Key Topic icon in the outer margin of the page. Table 17-5 lists these key topics and the page number on which each is found.

Key Topic

Table 17-5 Key Topics for Chapter 17

Key Topic Element	Description	Page Number
Paragraph	dB definition	522
List	Important dB laws to remember	522
Paragraph	EIRP calculation	526
List	Free space path loss concepts	528
Figure 17-24	Effective Range of 2.4 GHz and 5 GHz Transmitters	529
Figure 17-25	Example of Receiver Sensitivity Level	530
List	Modulation scheme output	532
Table 17-4	A Summary of Common 802.11 Standard Amendments	534
Figure 17-31	Dynamic Rate Shifting as a Function of Range	539

Complete Tables and Lists from Memory

Print a copy of Appendix B, "Memory Tables" (found on the companion website), or at least the section for this chapter, and complete the tables and lists from memory. Appendix C, "Memory Tables Answer Key," also on the companion website, includes completed tables and lists you can use to check your work.

Define Key Terms

Define the following key terms from this chapter and check your answers in the Glossary:

amplitude, band, bandwidth, carrier signal, channel, dBd, dBi, dBm, decibel (dB), demodulation, direct sequence spread spectrum (DSSS), dynamic rate shifting (DRS), effective isotropic radiated power (EIRP), frequency, hertz (Hz), in phase, isotropic antenna, link budget, maximal-ratio combining (MRC), modulation, narrowband, noise floor, Orthogonal Frequency Division Multiplexing (OFDM), out of phase, phase, quadrature amplitude modulation (QAM), radio frequency (RF), received signal strength indicator (RSSI), sensitivity level, signal-to-noise ratio (SNR), spatial multiplexing, spatial stream, spread spectrum, transmit beamforming (TBF), wavelength

CHAPTER 18

Wireless Infrastructure

This chapter covers the following subjects:

- **Wireless Deployment Models:** This section describes autonomous, controller-based, controller-less, centralized, cloud-based, distributed, and remote branch wireless architectures. Modes of AP operation are also discussed.
- **Pairing Lightweight APs and WLCs:** This section explains the process that lightweight APs must go through to discover and bind to a wireless LAN controller.
- **Segmenting Wireless Configurations:** This section describes logical groupings you can use to configure parameters in a wireless network in a customized, granular fashion.
- **Leveraging Antennas for Wireless Coverage:** This section provides an overview of various antenna types and explains how each one alters the RF coverage over an area.

Chapter 17, "Wireless Signals and Modulation," described the mechanics of using wireless signals to send data over the air—work that is performed by a wireless AP or client device. This chapter takes a broader perspective and looks beyond a single AP to discuss the topologies that can be built with many APs.

The chapter also discusses the types of antennas you can connect to an AP to provide wireless coverage for various areas and purposes. Finally, this chapter discusses how lightweight APs discover and join with wireless LAN controllers in an enterprise network.

"Do I Know This Already?" Quiz

The "Do I Know This Already?" quiz enables you to assess whether you should read the entire chapter. If you miss no more than one of these self-assessment questions, you might want to move ahead to the "Exam Preparation Tasks" section. Table 18-1 lists the major headings in this chapter and the "Do I Know This Already?" quiz questions covering the material in those headings so you can assess your knowledge of these specific areas. The answers to the "Do I Know This Already?" quiz appear in Appendix A, "Answers to the 'Do I Know This Already?' Questions."

Table 18-1 "Do I Know This Already?" Foundation Topics Section-to-Question Mapping

Foundation Topics Section	Questions
Wireless Deployment Models	1–3
Pairing Lightweight APs and WLCs	4–8
Segmenting Wireless Configurations	9–10
Leveraging Antennas for Wireless Coverage	11–12

1. Suppose that a lightweight AP in default local mode is used to support wireless clients. Which one of the following paths would traffic usually take when passing from one wireless client to another?
   a. Through the AP only
   b. Through the AP and its controller
   c. Through the controller only
   d. None of these answers are correct. Traffic must go directly over the air.
2. A centralized wireless network is built with 1 WLC and 32 lightweight APs. Which one of the following best describes the resulting architecture?
   a. A direct Layer 2 path from the WLC to each of the 32 APs, all using the same IP subnet
   b. A direct Layer 3 path from the WLC to each of the 32 APs, all using the same IP subnet
   c. 32 CAPWAP tunnels daisy-chained between the APs, one CAPWAP tunnel to the WLC
   d. 32 CAPWAP tunnels—1 tunnel from the WLC to each AP, with no IP subnet restrictions
3. Which of the following unique features is true in an embedded wireless network architecture?
   a. An access layer switch can also function as an AP.
   b. All WLCs are converged into one device.
   c. Large groups of APs connect to a single access layer switch.
   d. An access layer switch can also function as a WLC.
4. Which one of the following comes first in a lightweight AP's state machine after it boots?
   a. Building a CAPWAP tunnel
   b. Discovering WLCs
   c. Downloading a configuration
   d. Joining a WLC
5. If a lightweight AP needs to download a new software image, how does it get the image?
   a. From a TFTP server
   b. From an FTP server
   c. From a WLC
   d. You must preconfigure it.
6. Which of the following is not a valid way that an AP can learn of WLCs that it might join?
   a. Primed entries
   b. List from a previously joined controller
   c. DHCP
   d. Subnet broadcast
   e. DNS
   f. Over-the-air neighbor message from another AP

7. If an AP tries every available method to discover a controller but fails to do so, what happens next?
   a. It broadcasts on every possible subnet.
   b. It tries to contact the default controller at 10.0.0.1.
   c. It reboots or starts discovering again.
   d. It uses IP redirect on the local router.
8. Which of the following is the most deterministic strategy you can use to push a specific AP to join a specific controller?
   a. Let the AP select the least-loaded controller.
   b. Use DHCP option 43.
   c. Specify the master controller.
   d. Specify the primary controller.
9. With an IOS XE controller, you can segment or customize an enterprise's wireless configuration with which one of following mechanisms?
   a. AP groups
   b. Profiles and tags
   c. WLANs and radios
   d. Locations and service policies
10. An IOS XE controller maps which one of the following sets of tags to each AP?
   a. Location, radio, security
   b. Domain, band, WLAN
   c. Site, RF, policy
   d. Customer, radio, WLAN
11. Which of the following antennas would probably have the greatest gain?
   a. Patch
   b. Dish
   c. Yagi
   d. Dipole
   e. Integrated
12. An omnidirectional antenna usually has which of the following characteristics? (Choose two.)
   a. Low gain
   b. Small beamwidth
   c. High gain
   d. Zero gain
   e. Large beamwidth

Foundation Topics

Wireless Deployment Models

Traditional APs operate autonomously, because they are self-sufficient and standalone. Cisco APs operate in a "lightweight" mode and require something bigger to complete their purpose. The following sections review the two and analyze the purpose and data paths that result. The lightweight mode is interesting because it can support several different network topologies, depending on where the companion **wireless LAN controllers (WLCs)** are located.

TIP You should be aware that Cisco has offered two WLC platforms. The most recent is based on hardware that runs the IOS XE operating system, while its predecessor was based on the AireOS operating system. From the AP's perspective, both platforms connect to it via CAPWAP tunnels, while IOS XE offers more scalability, higher performance, higher availability, and more seamless maintainability. While the CCNP and CCIE ENCOR exam blueprint stays platform agnostic, you may see scenarios from either platform on exam questions until AireOS products reach full end-of-life.

Autonomous Deployment

Autonomous APs are self-contained, each offering one or more fully functional, standalone basic service sets (BSSs). They are also a natural extension of a switched network, connecting wireless service set identifiers (SSIDs) to wired virtual LANs (VLANs) at the access layer. Figure 18-1 shows the basic architecture; even though only four APs are shown across the bottom, a typical enterprise network could consist of hundreds or thousands of APs.

Key Topic

18

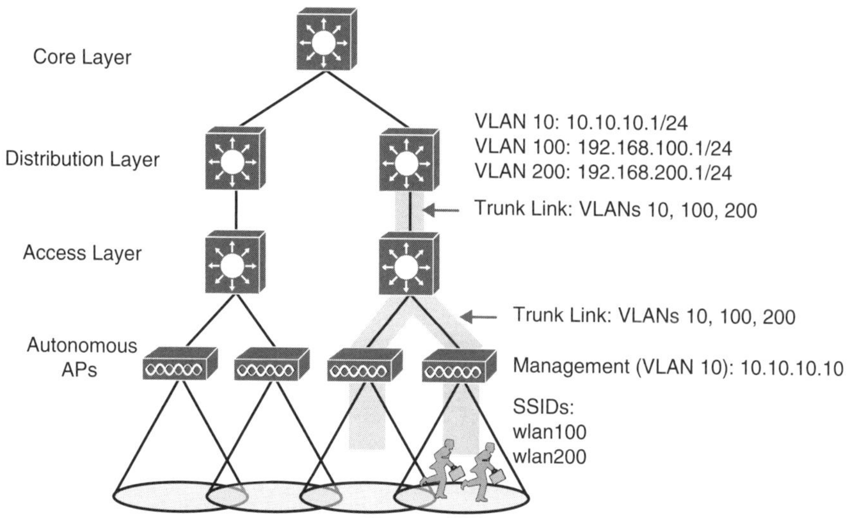

Figure 18-1 *Wireless Network Topology Using Autonomous APs*

Notice that the autonomous APs present two wireless LANs with SSIDs wlan100 and wlan200 to the wireless users. The APs also forward traffic between the wireless LANs and two wired VLANs 100 and 200. That means the wired VLANs must be trunked from the distribution layer, where routing occurs for each subnet, all the way down to the access layer switches where the VLANs touch each AP. The extent of a VLAN is shown in Figure 18-1 as a shaded area around the affected links.

An autonomous AP must also be configured with a management IP address (10.10.10.10 in Figure 18-1) to enable remote management. After all, you will want to configure SSIDs, VLANs, and many RF parameters like the channel and transmit power to be used. The management address is not normally part of any of the data VLANs, so a dedicated management VLAN (in this case, VLAN 10) must be added to the trunk links to reach the AP.

Because the data and management VLANs may need to reach every autonomous AP, the network configuration and efficiency can become cumbersome as the network scales. For example, you will likely want to offer the same SSID on many APs so that wireless clients can associate with that SSID in most any location or while roaming between any two APs. You might also want to extend the corresponding VLAN (and IP subnet) to each and every AP so that clients do not have to request a new IP address for each new association.

This process might seem straightforward until you have to add a new VLAN and configure every switch and AP in your network to carry and support it. Even worse, suppose your network has redundant links between the layers of switches. Spanning Tree Protocol (STP) running on each switch becomes a vital ingredient to prevent bridging loops from forming and corrupting the network. For these reasons, client roaming across autonomous APs is typically limited to the Layer 2 domain, or the extent of a single VLAN. As the wireless network expands, the infrastructure becomes more difficult to configure correctly and becomes less efficient.

A topology using autonomous APs does have one nice feature: a short and simple path for data to travel between the wireless and wired networks. Consider the two wireless users shown in Figure 18-2, which are associated to the same autonomous AP. One can reach the other through the AP, without having to pass up into the wired network. That should come as no great surprise if you remember that wireless users in a BSS must pass through an AP first. As the following sections reveal, this is not always the case with lightweight AP topologies.

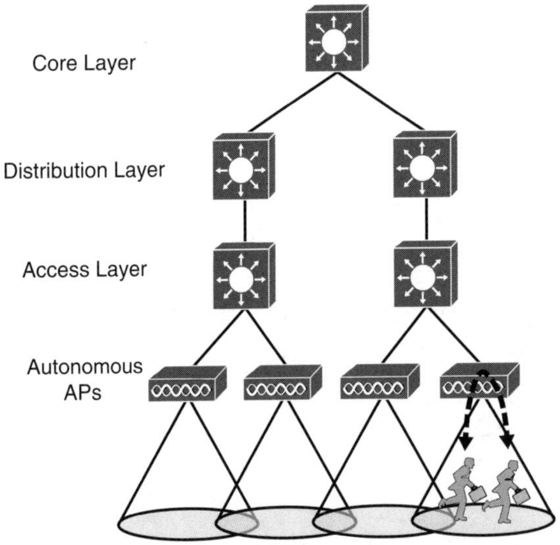

Figure 18-2 *Shortest Data Path Through an Autonomous AP Topology*

Answers to the "Do I Know This Already?" quiz:

1 B **2** D **3** D **4** B **5** C **6** F **7** C **8** D **9** B **10** C **11** B **12** A, E

Cisco AP Operation

As a "lightweight" device, a Cisco AP loses its self-sufficiency to provide a working BSS for wireless users. Instead, it has to join a WLC to become fully functional. This cooperation is known as a **split-MAC architecture**, where the AP handles most of the real-time 802.11 processes and the WLC performs the management functions.

An AP and a WLC are joined by a logical pair of **CAPWAP** tunnels that extends through the wired network infrastructure. Control and data traffic are transported across the tunnels. Many APs can join the same WLC, each with its own pair of CAPWAP tunnels. A wireless network can scale in this fashion, provided the WLC can support the maximum number of APs in use. Beyond that, additional WLCs would be needed.

From the WLC, you can configure a Cisco AP to operate in one of the following special-purpose modes:

Key Topic

- **Local:** The default lightweight mode that offers one or more functioning BSSs on a specific channel. In other words, an AP in **local mode** serves wireless clients. During times when it is not transmitting, the AP scans the other channels to measure the level of noise, measure interference, discover rogue devices, and match against intrusion detection system (IDS) events.
- **FlexConnect:** An AP at a remote site maintains a control CAPWAP tunnel to a central WLC while forwarding data normally, without a CAPWAP tunnel. If the remote site's WAN link goes down, taking the control CAPWAP tunnel down too, the AP can still switch traffic locally between an SSID and a connected VLAN.
- **Monitor:** The AP does not transmit at all, but its receiver is enabled to act as a dedicated sensor. The AP checks for IDS events, detects rogue access points, and determines the position of stations through location-based services.
- **Sniffer:** An AP dedicates its radios to receiving 802.11 traffic from other sources, much like a sniffer or packet capture device. The captured traffic is then forwarded to a PC running network analyzer software such as Wireshark, where it can be analyzed further.
- **Rogue detector:** An AP dedicates itself to detecting rogue devices by correlating MAC addresses heard on the wired network with those heard over the air. Rogue devices are those that appear on both networks.
- **Bridge:** An AP becomes a dedicated bridge (point-to-point or point-to-multipoint) between two networks. Two APs in bridge mode can be used to link two locations separated by a distance. Multiple APs in bridge mode can form an indoor or outdoor mesh network.
- **Flex+Bridge:** FlexConnect operation is enabled on a mesh AP.
- **SE-Connect:** The AP dedicates its radios to spectrum analysis on all wireless channels. You can remotely connect a PC running software such as MetaGeek Chanalyzer or Cisco Spectrum Expert to the AP to collect and analyze the spectrum analysis data to discover sources of interference.

NOTE Remember that a lightweight AP is normally in local mode when it is providing BSSs and allowing client devices to associate to wireless LANs. When an AP is configured to operate in one of the other modes, local mode (and the BSSs) is disabled.

Cisco Wireless Deployments

Several topologies can be built from a WLC and a collection of APs. These topologies differ according to where the WLC is located within the network. For example, a WLC can be placed in a central location, usually in a data center or near the network core, so that you can maximize the number of APs joined to it. This is known as a *centralized* wireless LAN deployment, as shown in Figure 18-3. This tends to follow the concept that most of the resources users need to reach are located in a central location, such as a data center or the Internet. Traffic to and from wireless users travels from the APs over CAPWAP tunnels that reach into the center of the network. A centralized WLC also provides a convenient place to enforce security policies that affect all wireless users.

Key Topic

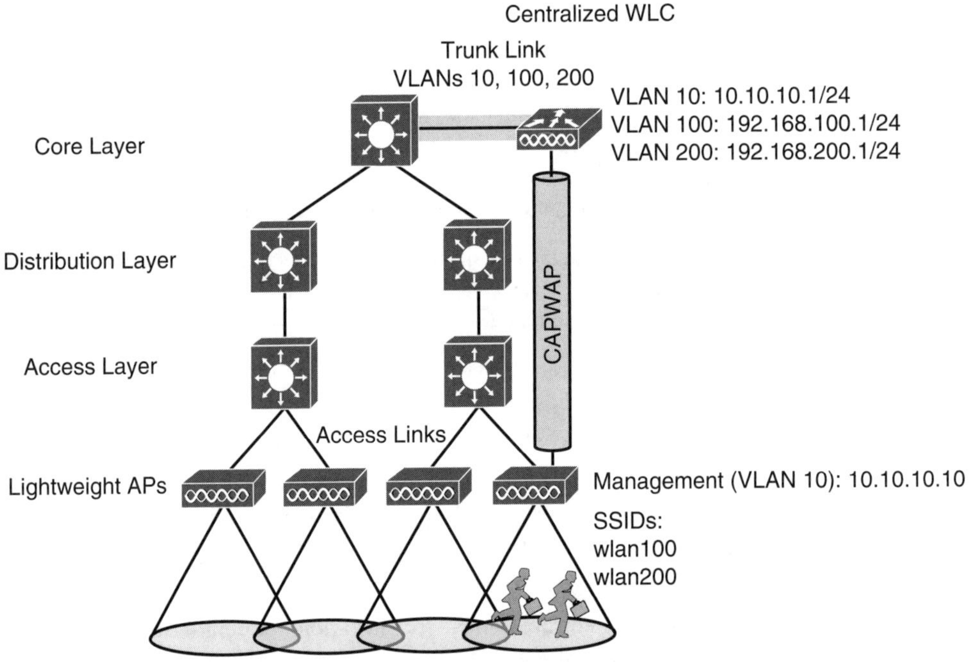

Figure 18-3 *WLC Location in a* **Centralized Wireless Deployment**

Figure 18-3 shows four APs joined to a single WLC, but your network might have more APs—many, many more. A large enterprise network might have thousands of APs in its access layer. Scalability then becomes an important factor in the centralized design. Each Cisco WLC model supports a maximum number of APs. If you have more APs than the maximum, you need to add more WLCs to the design, each located centrally. A typical centralized WLC meant for a large enterprise can support up to 6000 APs and up to 64,000 wireless clients.

Notice that the network infrastructure in Figure 18-3 has the same hierarchy as the autonomous topology in Figure 18-1. The only differences are that the APs are running in lightweight mode, and there is a WLC present high in the topology. Figure 18-3 shows one of the CAPWAP tunnels connecting one AP to the WLC, although each AP would also have its own tunnels to the controller. The Layer 3 boundary for each data VLAN is handled at or near the WLC, so the VLANs need only exist at that location, indicated by the shaded link. Each AP still has its own unique management IP address, but it connects to an access layer switch via an access link rather than a trunk link. Even if multiple VLANs and WLANs are involved, they are carried over the same CAPWAP tunnel to and from the AP. Therefore, the AP needs only a single IP address to terminate the tunnel.

The centralized architecture also affects wireless user mobility. For example, as a wireless user moves through the coverage areas of the four APs in Figure 18-3, that user might associate with many different APs in the access layer. Because all of the APs are joined to a single WLC, that WLC can easily maintain the user's connectivity to all other areas of the network as the user moves around.

Locating the WLC centrally also affects the path that wireless data must take. Recall that two wireless users associated with an autonomous AP can reach each other through the AP. In contrast, the path between two wireless users in a centralized network is shown in Figure 18-4. The traffic from one client must pass through the AP, where it is encapsulated in the CAPWAP tunnel, and then travel high up into the network to reach the WLC, where it is unencapsulated and examined. The process then reverses, and the traffic goes back down through the tunnel to reach the AP and back out into the air to the other client.

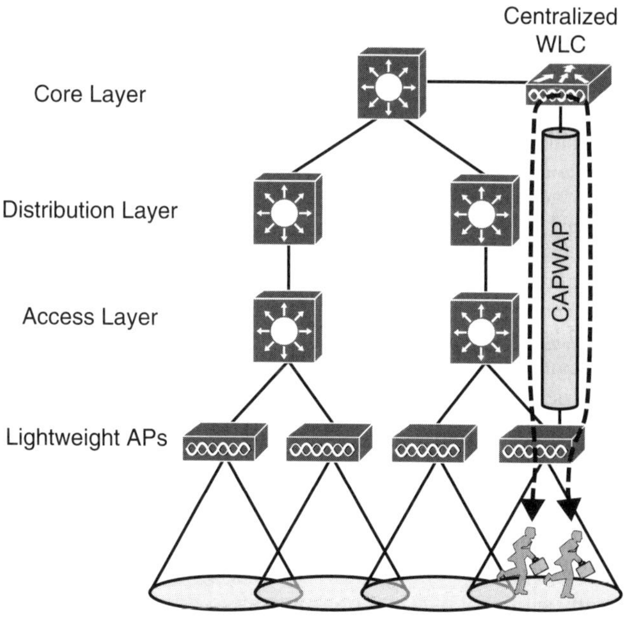

Figure 18-4 *Shortest Data Path Through a Centralized Wireless Deployment*

NOTE The length of the tunnel path can be a great concern for lightweight APs. The round-trip time (RTT) between an AP and a controller should be less than 100 ms so that wireless communication can be maintained in near real time. If the path has more latency than that, the APs may decide that the controller is not responding fast enough, so they may disconnect and find another, more responsive controller.

A centralized controller can also be located in a public cloud, remotely situated in relation to the enterprise, or in a private cloud within an enterprise data center. In either case, the controller deployment is called *cloud-based* rather than centralized. Figure 18-5 shows the public and private cloud controllers in relation to the enterprise they support.

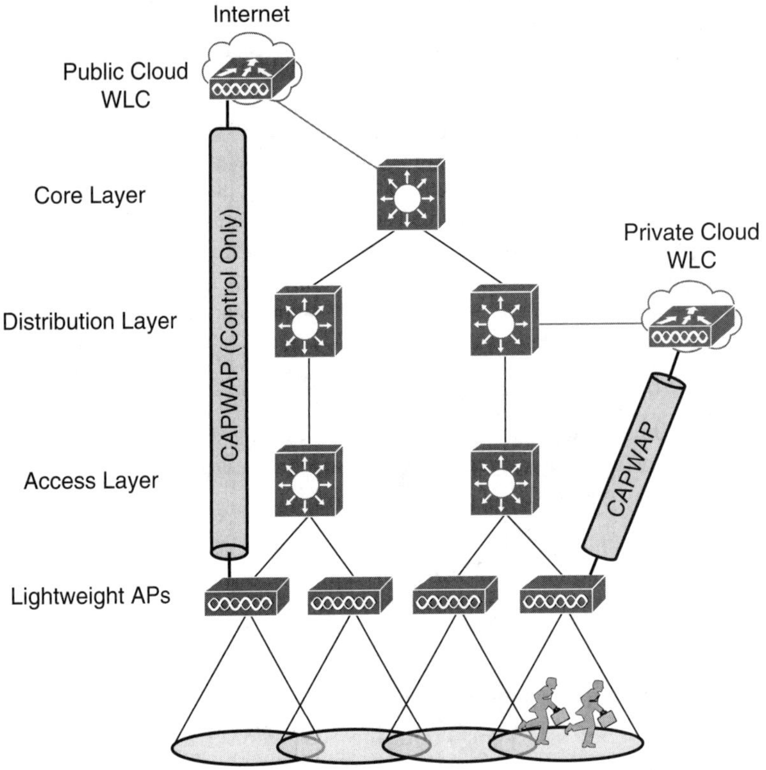

Figure 18-5 *WLC Location in a Cloud-Based Wireless Deployment*

In a public cloud deployment, the controller can be quite a distance from the APs that join to it. The APs maintain a CAPWAP control tunnel to the controller, but all wireless data passing through the APs must be locally switched in and out of the VLANs directly connected to the APs. Therefore, the APs must operate only in FlexConnect mode. Private cloud controllers are located within the enterprise, so the APs can operate in local or FlexConnect mode. Cloud-based controllers can typically support up to 6000 APs and up to 64,000 wireless clients.

Now imagine that a WLC can be located further down in the network hierarchy. Perhaps the network is made up of many remote sites or distributed locations. In that case, one large WLC might not be the best choice. Instead, smaller, appropriately sized WLCs can be placed at each site, forming a **distributed wireless deployment** as shown in Figure 18-6. Distributed controllers are commonly smaller standalone models that can support up to 250 APs and 5,000 wireless clients.

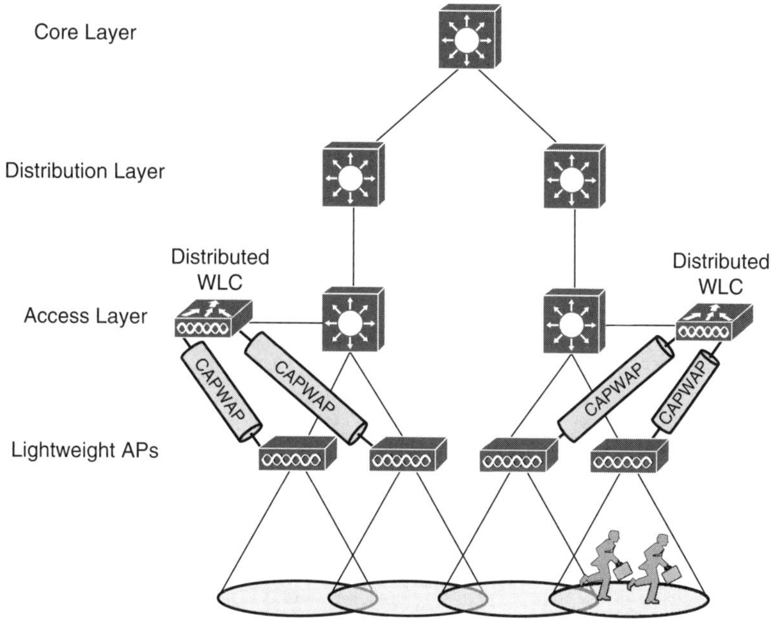

Figure 18-6 *WLC Location in a Distributed Wireless Deployment*

Notice that the centralized, cloud, and distributed deployments all involve standalone WLCs. As you might expect, those are all called *controller-based* deployments. At the smallest scale, distributed deployments can involve embedded wireless controllers (EWCs), which are regular APs that also run WLC software. Cisco describes this as a **controller-less deployment** because there is no discrete WLC involved; rather, the controller is embedded in an AP itself!

This deployment can be useful in small-scale environments, such as small, midsize, or multi-site branch locations, where you might not want to invest in dedicated WLCs at all. As Figure 18-7 illustrates, the AP that hosts the WLC forms a CAPWAP tunnel with the WLC, as do any other APs at the same location. EWC typically supports up to 100 APs and up to 2,000 wireless clients.

TIP Remember that when APs and WLCs are located in the same local network infrastructure, the CAPWAP tunnels can be easily maintained and latency minimized. In those cases, the APs operate in local mode, where both AP control and user data are tunneled to the WLC. In scenarios where the APs and their WLCs must be located remotely from each other, the APs should operate in FlexConnect mode.

Key Topic

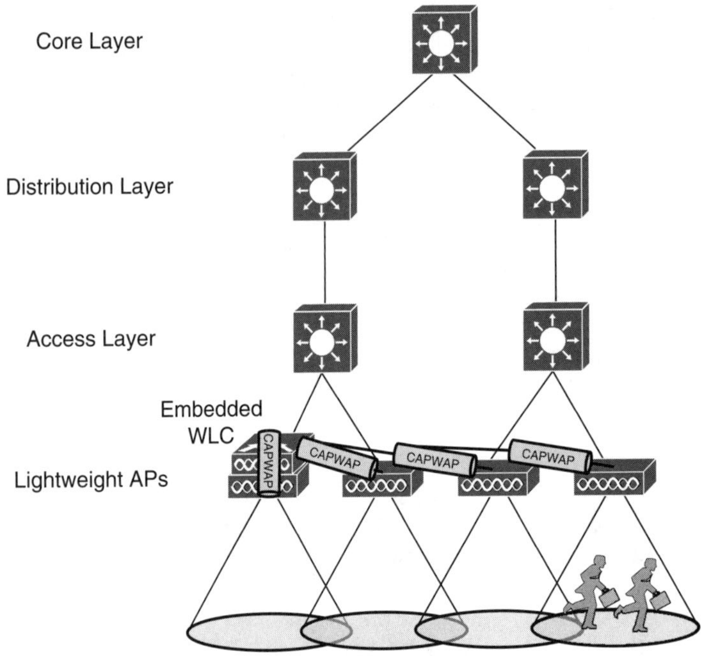

Figure 18-7 *WLC Location in a Controller-less Deployment Using EWC*

Pairing Lightweight APs and WLCs

A Cisco lightweight wireless AP needs to be paired with a WLC to function. Each AP must discover and bind itself with a controller before wireless clients can be supported.

Cisco **lightweight APs** are designed to be "touch free," so that you can simply unbox a new one and connect it to the wired network, without any need to configure it first. Naturally, you have to configure the switch port, where the AP connects, with the correct access VLAN, access mode, and inline power settings. From that point on, the AP can power up and use a variety of methods to find a viable WLC to join.

AP States

From the time it powers up until it offers a fully functional basic service set (BSS), a lightweight AP operates in a variety of states. Each of the possible states is well defined as part of the Control and Provisioning of Wireless Access Points (CAPWAP) specification, but they are simplified here for clarity. The AP enters the states in a specific order; the sequence of states is called a *state machine*. You should become familiar with the AP state machine so that you can understand how an AP forms a working relationship with a WLC. If an AP cannot form that relationship for some reason, your knowledge of the state machine can help you troubleshoot the problem.

NOTE CAPWAP is defined in RFC 5415 and in a few other RFCs. The terms used in the RFC differ somewhat from the ones that Cisco uses. For example, *access controller (AC)* refers to a WLC, whereas *wireless termination point (WTP)* refers to an AP.

The sequence of the most common states, as shown in Figure 18-8, is as follows:

Key Topic

1. **AP boots:** After an AP receives power, it boots on a small IOS image so that it can work through the remaining states and communicate over its network connection. The AP must also receive an IP address from either a Dynamic Host Configuration Protocol (DHCP) server or a static configuration so that it can communicate over the network.
2. **WLC discovery:** The AP goes through a series of steps to find one or more controllers that it might join. The steps are explained further in the next section.
3. **CAPWAP tunnel:** The AP attempts to build a CAPWAP tunnel with one or more controllers. The tunnel will provide a secure Datagram Transport Layer Security (DTLS) channel for subsequent AP-WLC control messages. The AP and WLC authenticate each other through an exchange of digital certificates.
4. **WLC join:** The AP selects a WLC from a list of candidates and then sends a CAPWAP Join Request message to it. The WLC replies with a CAPWAP Join Response message. The next section explains how an AP selects a WLC to join.
5. **Download image:** The WLC informs the AP of its software release. If the AP's own software is a different release, the AP downloads a matching image from the controller, reboots to apply the new image, and then returns to step 1. If the two are running identical releases, no download is needed.
6. **Download config:** The AP pulls configuration parameters down from the WLC and can update existing values with those sent from the controller. Settings include RF, service set identifier (SSID), security, and quality of service (QoS) parameters.
7. **Run state:** Once the AP is fully initialized, the WLC places it in the "run" state. The AP and WLC then begin providing a BSS and begin accepting wireless clients.
8. **Reset:** If an AP is reset by the WLC, it tears down existing client associations and any CAPWAP tunnels to WLCs. The AP then reboots and starts through the entire state machine again.

18

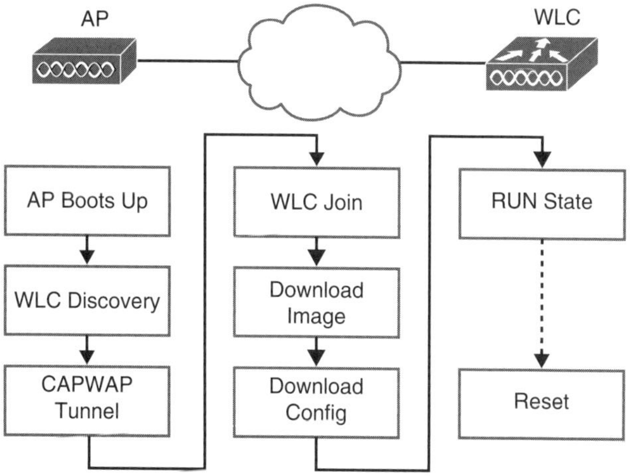

Figure 18-8 *State Machine of a Lightweight AP*

Be aware that you cannot control which software image release that a lightweight AP runs. Rather, the WLC that the AP joins determines the release, based on its own software version. Downloading a new image can take a considerable amount of time, especially if a large number of APs is waiting for the same download from one WLC. That might not matter when a newly installed AP is booting and downloading code because it does not yet have any wireless clients to support. However, if an existing, live AP happens to reboot or join a different controller, clients can be left hanging with no AP while the image downloads. Some careful planning with your controllers and their software releases will pay off later in terms of minimized downtime. Consider the following scenarios when an AP might need to download a different release:

- The AP joins a WLC but has a version mismatch.
- A code upgrade is performed on the WLC itself, requiring all associated APs to upgrade too.
- The WLC fails, causing all associated APs to be dropped and to join elsewhere.

If there is a chance that an AP could rehome from one WLC to another, you should make sure that both controllers are running the same code release. Otherwise, the AP move should happen under controlled circumstances, such as during a maintenance window. Fortunately, if you have downloaded a new code release to a controller but not yet rebooted it to run the new code, you can predownload the new release to the controller's APs. The APs will download the new image but will keep running the previous release. When it comes time to reboot the controller on the new image, the APs will already have the new image staged without having to take time to download it. The APs can reboot on their new image and join the controller after it has booted and become stable.

Discovering a WLC

An AP must be very diligent to discover any controllers that it can join—all without any preconfiguration on your part. To accomplish this feat, several methods of discovery are used. The goal of discovery is just to build a list of live candidate controllers that are available, using the following methods:

- Prior knowledge of WLCs
- DHCP and DNS information to suggest some controllers
- Broadcast on the local subnet to solicit controllers
- Plug-and-play with Cisco DNA Center

To discover a WLC, an AP sends a unicast CAPWAP Discovery Request to a controller's IP address over UDP port 5246 or a broadcast to the local subnet. If the controller exists and is working, it returns a CAPWAP Discovery Response to the AP. The sequence of discovery steps used is as follows:

Key Topic

Step 1. The AP broadcasts a CAPWAP Discovery Request on its local wired subnet. Any WLCs that also exist on the subnet answer with a CAPWAP Discovery Response.

NOTE If the AP and controllers lie on different subnets, you can configure the local router to relay any broadcast requests on UDP port 5246 to specific controller addresses. Use the following configuration commands:

- router(config) # **ip forward-protocol udp 5246**
- router(config) # **interface vlan** *vlan-number*
- router(config-int) # **ip helper-address WLC1-MGMT-ADDR**
- router(config-int) # **ip helper-address WLC2-MGMT-ADDR**

Step 2. An AP can be "primed" with up to three controllers—a primary, a secondary, and a tertiary. These are stored in nonvolatile memory so that the AP can remember them after a reboot or power failure. Otherwise, if an AP has previously joined with a controller, it should have stored up to 8 out of a list of 32 WLC addresses that it received from the last controller it joined. The AP attempts to contact as many controllers as possible to build a list of candidates.

Step 3. The DHCP server that supplies the AP with an IP address can also send DHCP option 43 to suggest a list of WLC addresses.

Step 4. The AP attempts to resolve the name CISCO-CAPWAP-CONTROLLER.*localdomain* with a DNS request (where *localdomain* is the domain name learned from DHCP). If the name resolves to an IP address, the AP attempts to contact a WLC at that address.

Step 5. If none of the steps have been successful, the AP resets itself and starts the discovery process all over again.

18

Selecting a WLC

When an AP has finished the discovery process, it should have built a list of live candidate controllers. Now it must begin a separate process to select one WLC and attempt to join it. Joining a WLC involves sending it a CAPWAP Join Request and waiting for it to return a CAPWAP Join Response. From that point on, the AP and WLC build a DTLS tunnel to secure their CAPWAP control messages.

The WLC selection process consists of the following three steps:

Step 1. If the AP has previously joined a controller and has been configured or "primed" with a primary, secondary, and tertiary controller, it tries to join those controllers in succession.

Step 2. If the AP does not know of any candidate controller, it tries to discover one. If a controller has been configured as a master controller, it responds to the AP's request.

Step 3. The AP attempts to join the least-loaded WLC, in an effort to load balance APs across a set of controllers. During the discovery phase, each controller reports its load—the ratio of the number of currently joined APs to the total AP capacity. The least-loaded WLC is the one with the lowest ratio.

If an AP discovers a controller but gets rejected when it tries to join it, what might be the reason? Every controller has a set maximum number of APs that it can support. This is defined by platform or by license. If the controller already has the maximum number of APs joined to it, it rejects any additional APs.

To provide some flexibility in supporting APs on an oversubscribed controller, where more APs are trying to join than a license allows, you can configure the APs with a priority value. All APs begin with a default priority of low. You can change the value to low, medium, high, or critical. A controller tries to accommodate as many higher-priority APs as possible. After a controller is full of APs, it rejects an AP with the lowest priority to make room for a new one that has a higher priority.

Maintaining WLC Availability

After an AP has discovered, selected, and joined a controller, it must stay joined to that controller to remain functional. Consider that a single controller might support as many as 1000 or even 6000 APs—enough to cover a very large building or an entire enterprise. If something ever causes the controller to fail, a large number of APs will also fail. In the worst case, where a single controller carries the enterprise, the entire wireless network will become unavailable, which might be catastrophic.

Fortunately, a Cisco AP can discover multiple controllers—not just the one that it chooses to join. If the joined controller becomes unavailable, the AP can simply select the next least-loaded controller and request to join it. That sounds simple, but it is not very deterministic. If a controller full of 1000 APs fails, all 1000 APs must detect the failure, discover other candidate controllers, and then select the least-loaded one to join. During that time, wireless clients can be left stranded with no connectivity. You might envision the controller failure as a commercial airline flight that has just been canceled; everyone who purchased a ticket suddenly joins a mad rush to find another flight out.

The most deterministic approach is to leverage the primary, secondary, and tertiary controller fields that every AP stores. If any of these fields are configured with a controller name or address, the AP knows which three controllers to try in sequence before resorting to a more generic search.

After an AP joins a controller, it sends *keepalive* (also called *heartbeat*) messages to the controller over the wired network at regular intervals. By default, keepalives are sent every 30 seconds. The controller is expected to answer each keepalive as evidence that it is still alive and working. If a keepalive is not answered, an AP escalates the test by sending four more keepalives at 3-second intervals. If the controller answers, all is well; if it does not answer, the AP presumes that the controller has failed. The AP then moves quickly to find a successor to join.

Using the default values, an AP can detect a controller failure in as little as 35 seconds. You can adjust the regular keepalive timer between 1 and 30 seconds and the escalated, or "fast," heartbeat timer between 1 and 10 seconds. When the minimum values are used, a failure can be detected after only 6 seconds.

To make the process much more efficient, WLCs also support high availability (HA) with stateful switchover (SSO) redundancy. SSO groups controllers into high availability pairs, where one controller takes on the active role and the other is in a hot standby mode. The APs need to know only the primary controller that is the active unit. Because each active controller has its own standby controller, there really is no need to configure a secondary or tertiary controller on the APs unless you need an additional layer of redundancy.

Each AP learns of the HA pair during a CAPWAP discovery phase and then builds a CAPWAP tunnel to the active controller. The active unit keeps CAPWAP tunnels, AP states, client states, configurations, and image files all in sync with the hot standby unit. The active controller also synchronizes the state of each associated client that is in the RUN state with the hot standby controller. If the active controller fails, the standby will already have the current state information for each AP and client, making the failover process transparent to the end users.

Segmenting Wireless Configurations

After APs discover a controller and join it, they must be configured with a variety of parameters so that they can support wireless clients in the enterprise. APs download their configuration from the controller so that they can be managed from a common source. The parameters that define AP operation fall into three general categories:

- Things that affect the AP controller and CAPWAP relationship and FlexConnect behavior on a per-site basis
- Things that define the RF operation on each wireless band
- Things that define each wireless LAN and security policies

Ideally, you should be able to configure the APs throughout an enterprise site in a granular fashion. For example, your enterprise might consist of many buildings. You might want the APs in one building to offer WLANs on only one band. Perhaps you want a group of APs to offer only a subset of the entire list of WLANs. In other buildings, you might need to support a different set of constraints.

When APs are joined to legacy Cisco AireOS WLCs, you have only a limited amount of customization because most AP parameters are configured on a global basis. You can group APs that are located in the same geographical areas into logical AP groups that share a common set of WLANs and RF parameters. To have granular control, you have to configure many granular AP groups and duplicate the same configuration changes to many groups. Each AP can be a member of only one AP group, so granular configuration becomes a challenge, especially if you need to support conflicting AP configurations within the same area. In addition, changes to an AP group often force the APs to reset their radios or reboot themselves to pick up the new configuration.

Cisco completely redesigned AP configuration in the IOS XE-based WLCs with an object-oriented approach. You can customize parameters that affect the categories of site-based CAPWAP operation, RF operation, and WLAN and security operation, independently and in a very granular manner. In fact, each of these three categories is applied to each AP in the network through configuration *profiles* and *tags*. You can define site, RF, and policy profiles that contain the desired customizations. Then each AP is tagged to identify which site, RF, and policy profiles it should use. This concept is illustrated in Figure 18-9, along with a list of the relevant parameters you can customize in each profile type.

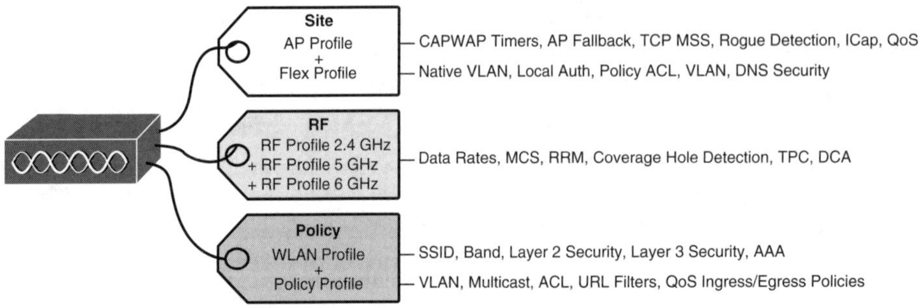

Figure 18-9 *AP Configuration with Profiles and Tags with an IOS XE Controller*

Notice that a site tag maps to two different profiles—an AP profile (sometimes called *AP join* profile) that is used when the AP is operating in local client-serving mode, and a Flex profile that is used for FlexConnect mode. Site tags use profiles that affect overall AP-controller CAPWAP and VLAN connectivity for APs located within a single site.

The RF tag maps to RF profiles that affect the radio operation on each frequency band that an AP supports. You can customize things like data rates and MCS, the dynamic transmit power and channel assignment algorithms, and coverage hole detection. You can tune each band independently because each has its own RF profile mapped by the RF tag.

The policy tag maps two different profiles—a WLAN profile that defines a list of SSIDs and WLAN security that an AP will offer, and a policy profile that defines how the AP will handle various types of traffic.

By default, all APs will be assigned the following three default tags:

- *default-site-tag*: Maps to default profiles named default-ap-profile and default-flex-profile
- *default-rf-tag*: Maps to the controller's global RF configuration
- *default-policy-tag*: Does not map to anything by default, because there is no default WLAN and SSID configuration for any network

Of course you could make all of your custom changes to the controller's default profiles, but that would affect all APs globally unless they have been assigned other non-default tags and profiles. Ideally, you should create your own set of custom profiles and tags to take full advantage of the granularity and to set the stage for future policy adjustments and custom tuning.

The customization process is simple:

Step 1. Configure AP and Flex profiles and map them to site tags.

Step 2. Configure RF profiles and map them to RF tags.

Step 3. Configure WLAN and policy profiles and map them to policy tags.

Step 4. Assign the appropriate site, RF, and policy tags to the APs.

To accomplish step 4, you can manually select APs, import a CSV file containing a list of APs, select by location, or use a regular expression to search for AP names. After you select the APs, you can select the tags to assign them.

Figure 18-10 illustrates the profile and tag concept further. Notice how the site, RF, and policy tags have been assigned to groups of APs and customized for each group. All of the APs belong to the same enterprise site or location, so they have all been assigned the site tag named Site-1. Two groups of APs share common RF and radio requirements, so they have been assigned the RF tag named RF-x, while another group is using the RF tag RF-y. All three groups of APs have unique WLAN and policy requirements, so each is using a different policy tag name that maps to unique WLAN and policy profiles. Remember that AP configuration isn't limited to just groups of APs; you can define profiles and tags that get mapped to a single AP if you want.

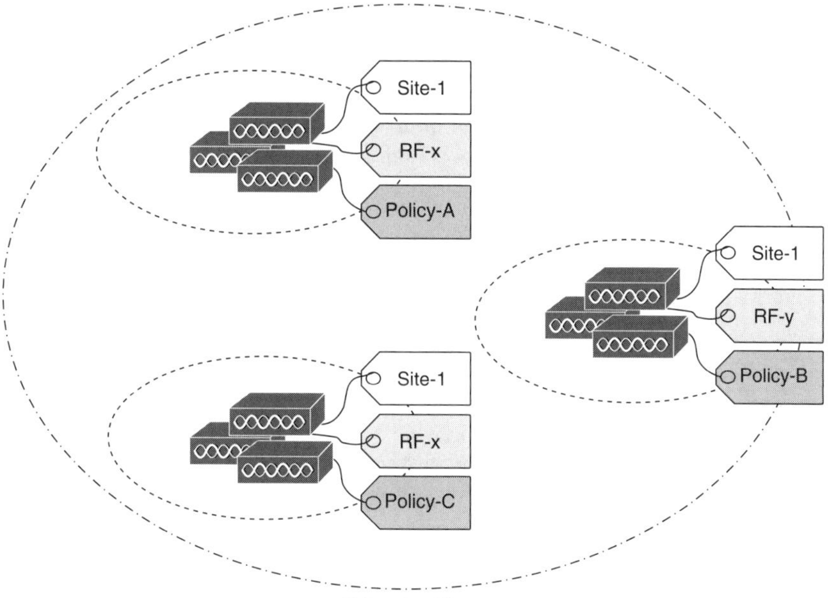

Figure 18-10 *An Example of Segmented AP Configuration with Profiles and Tags*

Leveraging Antennas for Wireless Coverage

The world of wireless LANs would be rather simple—too simple, in fact—if all antennas were created equal. To provide good wireless LAN coverage in a building, in an outdoor area, or between two locations, you might be faced with a number of variables. For example, an office space might be arranged as a group of open cubicles or as a strip of closed offices down a long hallway. You might have to cover a large open lobby, a large open classroom, a section of a crowded sports arena, an oblong portion of a hospital roof where helicopters land, a large expanse of an outdoor park, city streets where public safety vehicles travel, and so on.

In other words, one type of antenna cannot fit every application. Instead, antennas come in many sizes and shapes, each with its own gain value and intended purpose. The following sections describe antenna characteristics and considerations in more detail. As you work through them, you should also think about how a wireless network can support areas where many clients gather in close proximity to each other.

Client density is essentially the number of devices per AP. Where a single client is associated to an AP, it may take advantage of the full bandwidth available through the AP. No other device is present to contend for the airtime on the channel. The more active the clients are on the channel, the less airtime is available for any of them to use. The end results are poor performance and unsatisfactory user experience.

A good wireless design should provide RF coverage everywhere it is needed. It should also consider client density so that it can support the desired capacity through each AP. In other words, the design should provide an adequate number of APs such that the user population is distributed across the APs, giving more capacity to each. You can limit the number of clients served by an AP by selecting an antenna that has a more constrained coverage pattern where the clients are located.

Radiation Patterns

Recall from Chapter 17 that antenna gain is normally a comparison of one antenna against an isotropic antenna and is measured in dBi (decibel-isotropic). An isotropic antenna does not actually exist because it is ideal, perfect, and impossible to construct. It is also the simplest, most basic antenna possible, which makes it a good starting place for antenna theory.

An isotropic antenna is shaped like a tiny round point. When an alternating current is applied, an RF signal is produced, and the electromagnetic waves are radiated equally in all directions. The energy produced by the antenna takes the form of an ever-expanding sphere. If you were to move all around an isotropic antenna at a fixed distance, you would find that the signal strength is the same.

To describe the antenna's performance, you might draw a sphere with a diameter that is proportional to the signal strength, as shown in Figure 18-11. Most likely, you would draw the sphere on a logarithmic scale so that very large and very small numbers could be shown on the same linear plot. A plot that shows the relative signal strength around an antenna is known as the **radiation pattern**.

Key Topic

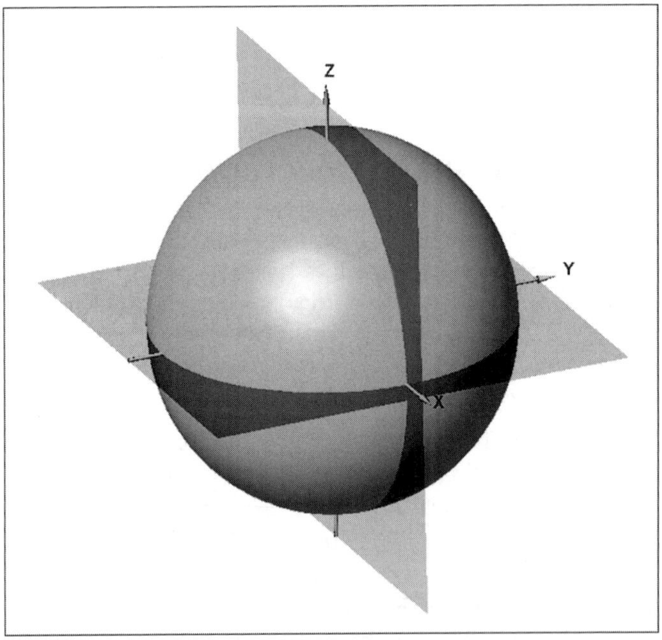

Figure 18-11 *Plotting the Radiation Pattern of an Isotropic Antenna*

It is rather difficult to show a three-dimensional plot or shape in a two-dimensional document, especially if the shape is complex or unusual. After all, most physical antennas are not ideal, so their radiation pattern is not a simple sphere. Instead, you could slice through the three-dimensional plot with two orthogonal planes and show the two outlines that are formed from the plot. In Figure 18-11, the sphere is cut by two planes. The XY plane, which lies flat along the horizon, is known as the **H plane**, or the *horizontal (azimuth) plane*, and it usually shows a top-down view of the radiation pattern through the center of the antenna. The XZ plane, which lies vertically along the elevation of the sphere, is known as the **E plane**, or *elevation plane*, and shows a side view of the same radiation pattern.

The outline of each plot can be recorded on a **polar plot**, as shown by the heavy dark lines in Figure 18-12. It might be hard to see the plots of an isotropic antenna because they are perfect circles that correspond with the outline of each circle shown.

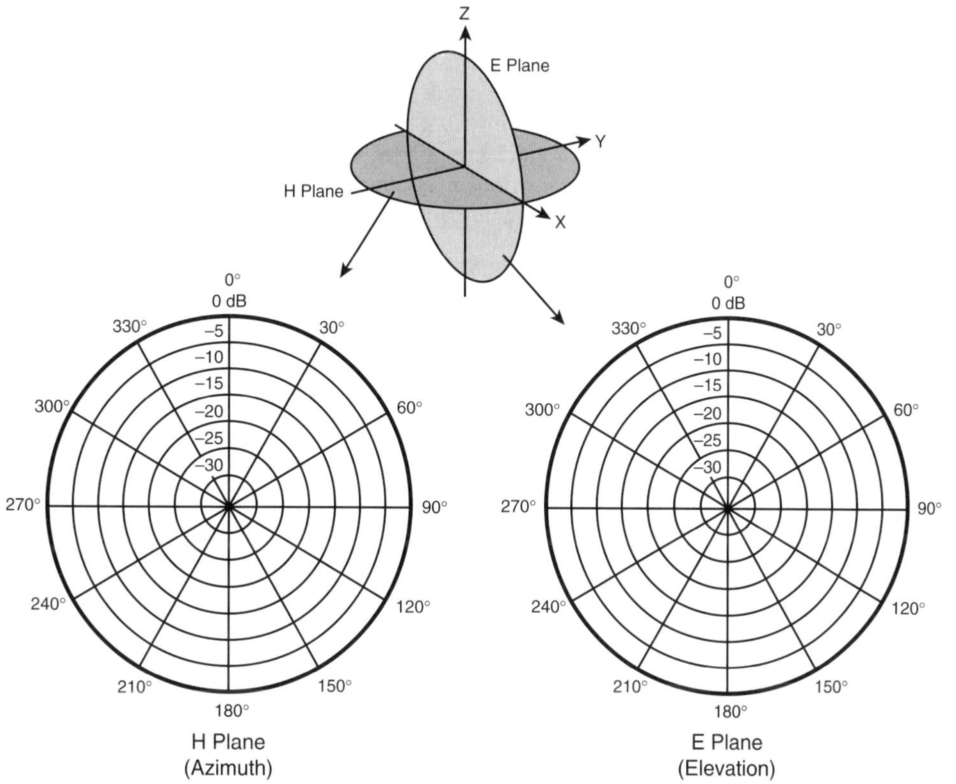

Figure 18-12 *Recording an Isotropic Antenna Pattern on E and H Polar Plots*

A polar plot contains concentric circles that represent relative changes in the signal strength, as measured at a constant distance from the antenna. The outermost circle usually represents the strongest signal strength, and the inner circles represent weaker signal strength. Although the circles are labeled with numbers like 0, –5, –10, –15, and so on, they do not necessarily represent any absolute dB values. Instead, they are measurements that are relative to the maximum value at the outside circle. If the maximum is shown at the outer ring, everything else will be less than the maximum and will lie further inward.

The circles are also divided into sectors so that a full sweep of 360 degrees can be plotted. This allows measurements to be taken at every angle around the antenna in the plane shown.

Antenna pattern plots can be a bit confusing to interpret. The E and H polar plots of the radiation pattern are presented here because most antenna manufacturers include them in their product literature. The antenna is always placed at the center of the polar plots, but you will not always be able to figure out how the antenna is oriented with respect to the E and H planes. Cisco usually includes a small picture of the antenna at the center of the plots as a handy reference.

As you decide to place APs in their actual locations, you might have to look at various antenna patterns and try to figure out whether the antenna is a good match for the environment you are trying to cover with an RF signal. You will need a good bit of imagination to merge the two plots into a 3D picture in your mind. As various antennas are described in this chapter, the plots, planes, and a 3D rendering are presented to help you get a feel for the thinking process.

Gain

Antennas are passive devices; they do not amplify a transmitter's signal with any circuitry or external power. Instead, they amplify or add gain to the signal by shaping the RF energy as it is propagated into free space. In other words, the **gain** of an antenna is a measure of how effectively it can focus RF energy in a certain direction.

Because an isotropic antenna radiates RF energy in all directions equally, it cannot focus the energy in any certain direction. Recall from Chapter 17 that the gain of an antenna in dBi is measured relative to an isotropic antenna. When an isotropic antenna is compared with itself, the result is a gain of 10log10(1), or 0 dBi.

Think of a zero gain antenna producing a perfect sphere. If the sphere is made of rubber, you could press on it in various locations and change its shape. As the sphere is deformed, it expands in other directions. Figure 18-13 shows some simple examples, along with some examples of gain values. As you work through this chapter and examine antennas on your own, notice that the gain is lower for omnidirectional antennas, which are made to cover a widespread area, and higher for directional antennas, which are built to cover more focused areas.

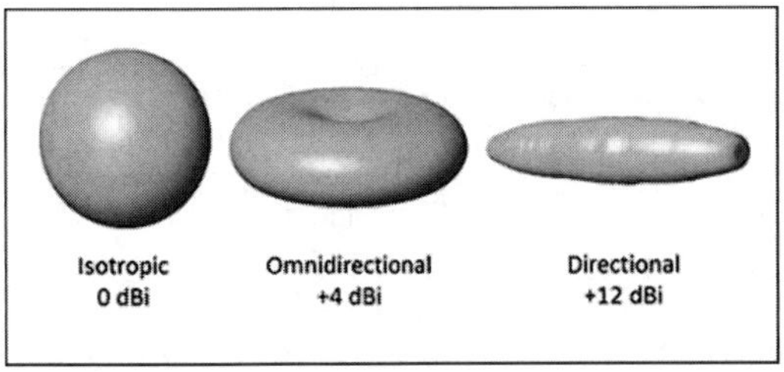

Figure 18-13 *Radiation Patterns for the Three Basic Antenna Types*

NOTE The gain is typically not indicated on either E or H plane radiation pattern plots. The only way to find an antenna's gain is to look at the manufacturer's specifications.

Beamwidth

The antenna gain can be an indicator of how focused an antenna's pattern might be, but it is really more suited for link budget calculations. Instead, many manufacturers list the **beamwidth** of an antenna as a measure of the antenna's focus. Beamwidth is normally listed in degrees for both the H and E planes.

The beamwidth is determined by finding the strongest point on the plot, which is usually somewhere on the outer circle. Next, the plot is followed in either direction until the value decreases by 3 dB, indicating the point where the signal is one-half the strongest power. A line is drawn from the center of the plot to intersect each 3 dB point, and then the angle between the two lines is measured. Figure 18-14 shows a simple example. The H plane has a beamwidth of 30 degrees, and the E plane has a beamwidth of 55 degrees.

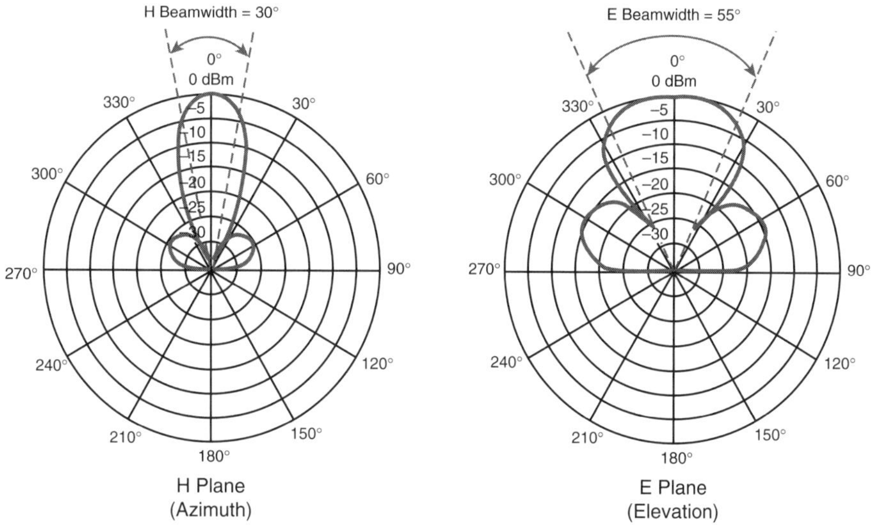

Figure 18-14 *Example of Antenna Beamwidth Measurement*

Polarization

When an alternating current is applied to an antenna, an electromagnetic wave is produced. In Chapter 17, you learned that the wave has two components: an electrical field wave and a magnetic field wave. The electrical portion of the wave will always leave the antenna in a certain orientation. For example, a simple length of wire that is pointing vertically will produce a wave that oscillates up and down in a vertical direction as it travels through free space. This is true of most Cisco antennas when they are mounted according to Cisco recommendations. Other types of antennas might be designed to produce waves that oscillate back and forth horizontally. Still others might produce waves that actually twist in a three-dimensional spiral motion through space.

The electrical field wave's orientation, with respect to the horizon, is called the antenna **polarization**. Antennas that produce vertical oscillation are vertically polarized; those that produce horizontal oscillation are horizontally polarized. (Keep in mind that there is always a magnetic field wave too, which is oriented at 90 degrees from the electrical field wave.) By itself, the antenna polarization is not of critical importance. However, the antenna polarization at the transmitter must be matched to the polarization at the receiver. If the polarization is mismatched, the received signal can be severely degraded.

Figure 18-15 illustrates antenna polarization. The transmitter and receiver along the top both use vertical polarization, so the received signal is optimized. The pair along the bottom is mismatched, causing the signal to be poorly received.

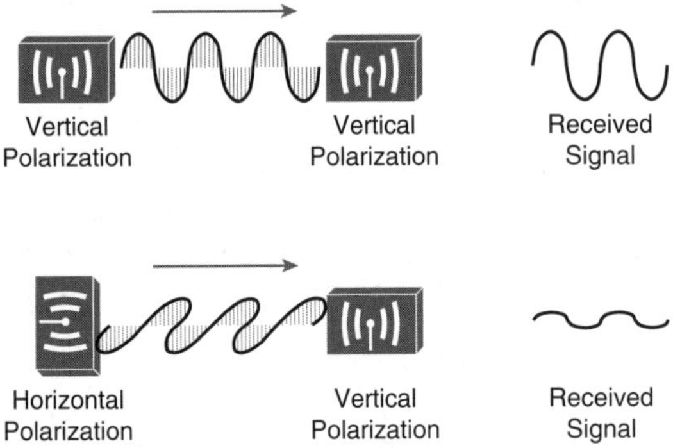

Figure 18-15 *Matching the Antenna Polarization Between Transmitter and Receiver*

> **NOTE** Even though Cisco antennas are designed to use vertical polarization, someone might mount an antenna in an unexpected orientation. For example, suppose you mount a transmitter with its antennas pointing upward. After you leave, someone knocks the antennas so that they are turned sideways. Not only does this change the radiation pattern you were expecting, it also changes the polarization.

Omnidirectional Antennas

There are two basic types of antennas, omnidirectional and directional, which are discussed in the following sections. An **omnidirectional antenna** is usually made in the shape of a thin cylinder. It tends to propagate a signal equally in all directions away from the cylinder but not along the cylinder's length. The result is a donut-shaped pattern that extends further in the H plane than in the E plane. This type of antenna is well suited for broad coverage of a large room or floor area, with the antenna located in the center. Because an omnidirectional antenna distributes the RF energy throughout a broad area, it has a relatively low gain.

A common type of omnidirectional antenna is the **dipole**, shown in the left portion of Figure 18-16. Some dipole models are articulated such that they can be folded up or down, depending on the mounting orientation, whereas others are rigid and fixed. As its name implies, the dipole has two separate wires that radiate an RF signal when an alternating current is applied across them, as shown in the right portion of Figure 18-16. Dipoles usually have a gain of around +2 to +5 dBi.

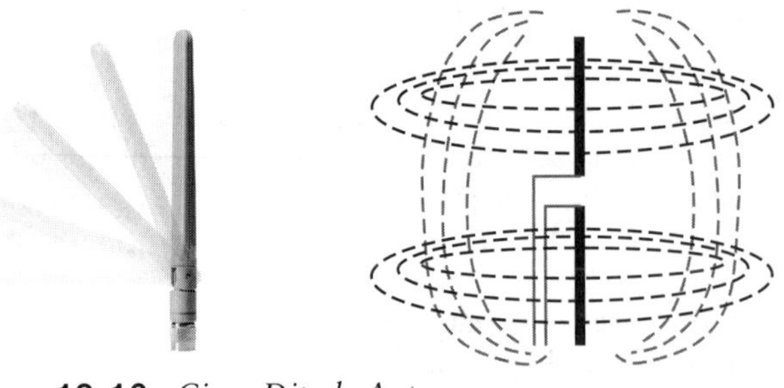

Figure 18-16 *Cisco Dipole Antenna*

The E and H plane radiation patterns for a typical dipole antenna are shown in Figure 18-17. In the E plane, think of the dipole lying on its side in the center of the plot; the H plane is looking down on the top of the dipole. Figure 18-18 takes the patterns a step further, showing how the two planes are superimposed and merged to reveal the three-dimensional radiation pattern.

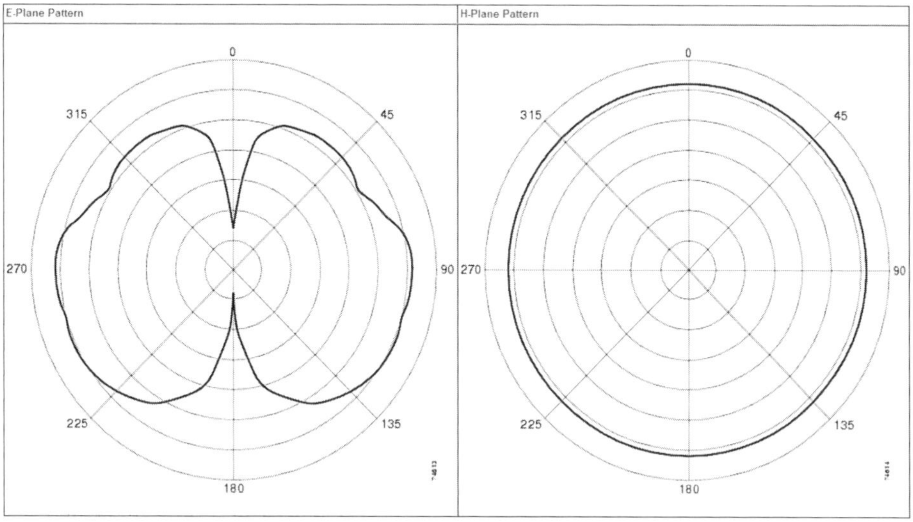

Figure 18-17 *E and H Radiation Patterns for a Typical Dipole Antenna*

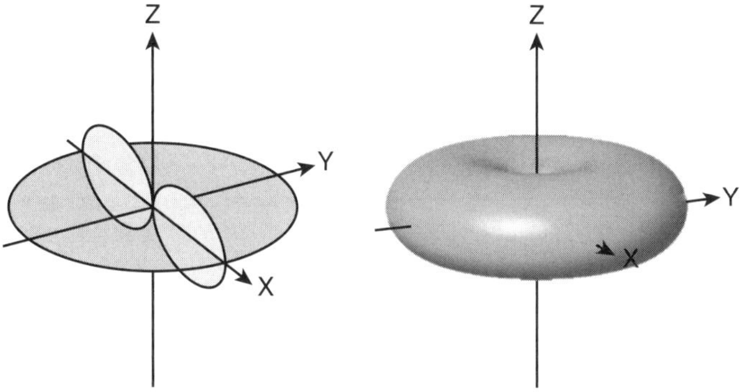

Figure 18-18 *Dipole Radiation Pattern in Three Dimensions*

To reduce the size of an omnidirectional antenna, many Cisco wireless access points (APs) have **integrated antennas** that are hidden inside the device's smooth case. For example, the AP shown in Figure 18-19 has six tiny antennas hidden inside it.

Integrated omnidirectional antennas typically have a gain of 2 dBi in the 2.4 GHz band and 5 dBi in the 5 GHz band. The E and H plane radiation patterns are shown in Figure 18-20. When the two planes are merged, the three-dimensional pattern still rather resembles a sphere.

Figure 18-19 *Cisco Wireless Access Point with Integrated Omnidirectional Antennas*

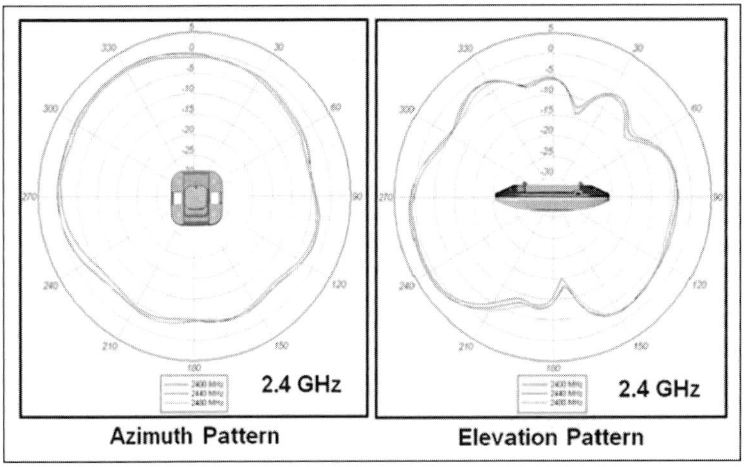

Figure 18-20 *E and H Radiation Patterns for a Typical Integrated Omnidirectional Antenna*

> **NOTE** What about wireless LAN adapters that are used in mobile devices like laptops and smartphones? Because the adapters are so small, their antennas must also be tiny. As a result, USB wireless adapters often have a gain of 0 dBi, while some smartphones even have a negative gain! This does not mean that the antennas do not radiate or receive signals. Instead, the antennas just have a lower performance compared with other, larger devices.

Directional Antennas

Directional antennas have a higher gain than omnidirectional antennas because they focus the RF energy in one general direction. Typical applications include elongated indoor areas, such as the rooms along a long hallway or the aisles in a warehouse. They can also be used to cover outdoor areas out away from a building or long distances between buildings. If they are mounted against a ceiling, pointing downward, they can cover a small floor area to reduce an AP's cell size.

Patch antennas have a flat rectangular shape, as shown in Figure 18-21, so that they can be mounted on a wall or ceiling.

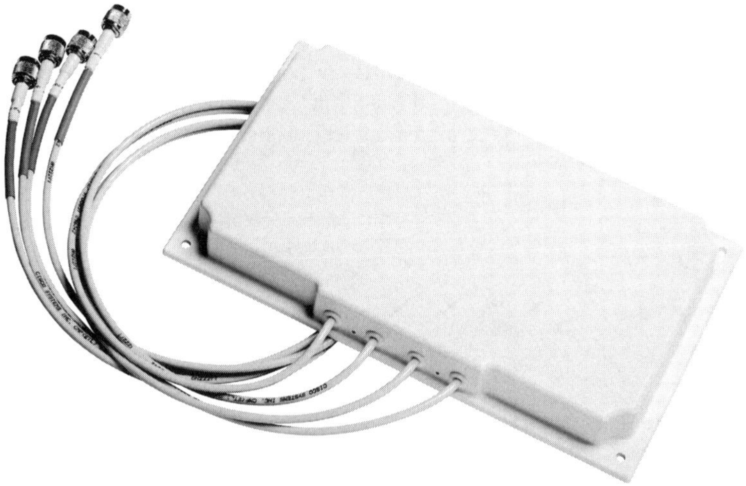

Figure 18-21 *Typical Cisco Patch Antenna*

Patch antennas produce a broad egg-shaped pattern that extends out away from the flat patch surface. The E and H radiation pattern plots are shown in Figure 18-22. When the planes are merged, as shown in Figure 18-23, you can see the somewhat broad directional pattern that results. Patch antennas have a typical gain of about 6 to 8 dBi in the 2.4 GHz band and 7 to 10 dBi at 5 GHz.

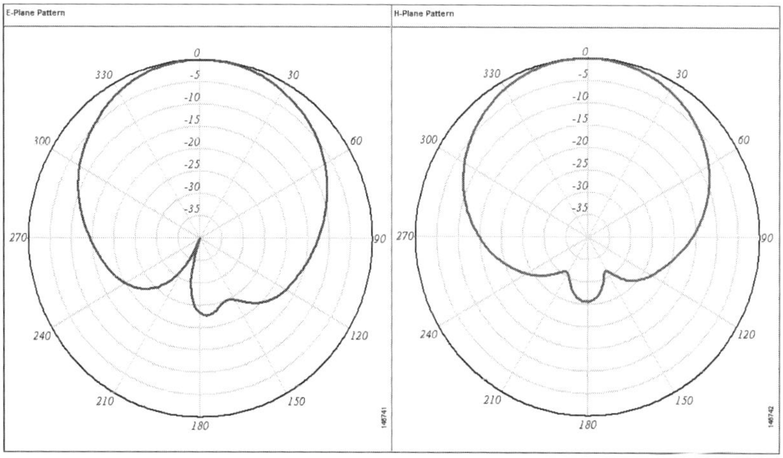

Figure 18-22 *E and H Radiation Patterns for a Typical Patch Antenna*

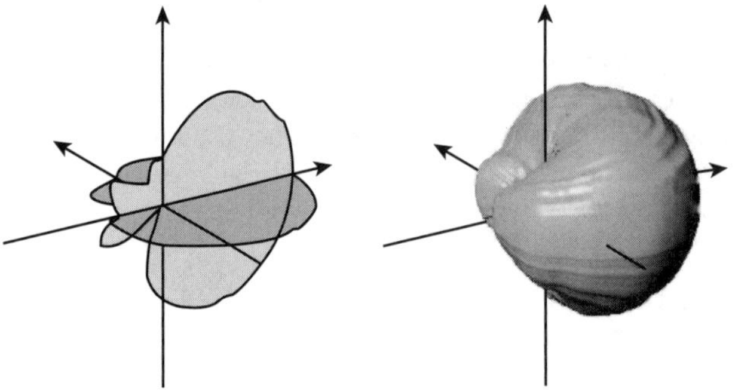

Figure 18-23 *Patch Antenna Radiation Pattern in Three Dimensions*

Figure 18-24 shows the Yagi–Uda antenna, named after its inventors, and more commonly known as the Yagi. Although its outer case is shaped like a thick cylinder, the antenna is actually made up of several parallel elements of increasing length.

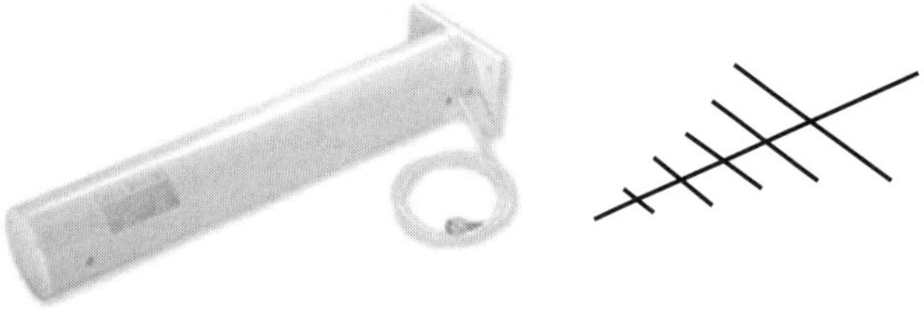

Figure 18-24 *Cisco Yagi Antenna*

Figure 18-25 shows the E and H radiation pattern plots. A Yagi produces a more focused egg-shaped pattern that extends out along the antenna's length, as shown in Figure 18-26. **Yagi antennas** have a gain of about 10 to 14 dBi.

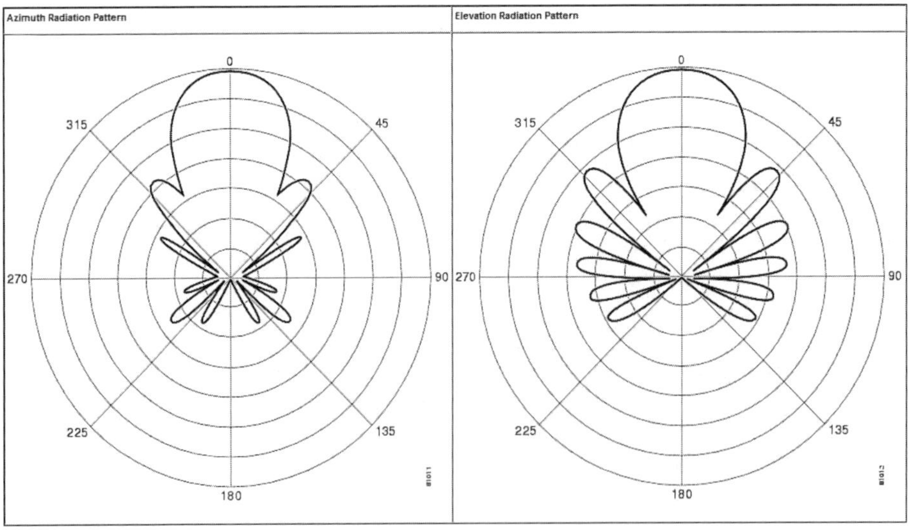

Figure 18-25 *E and H Radiation Patterns for a Typical Yagi Antenna*

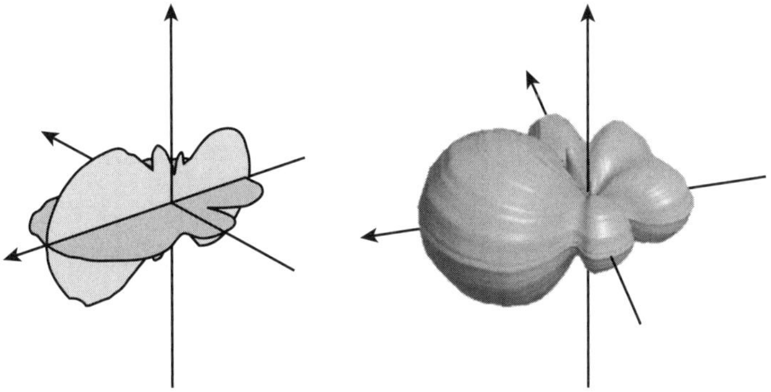

Figure 18-26 *Yagi Antenna Radiation Pattern in Three Dimensions*

In a line-of-sight wireless path, an RF signal must be propagated a long distance using a narrow beam. Highly directional antennas, such as a parabolic dish, are tailored for that use but focus the RF energy along one narrow elliptical pattern. Because the target is only one receiver location, the antenna does not have to cover any area outside of the line of sight.

Dish antennas, such as the one shown in Figure 18-27, use a parabolic dish to focus received signals onto an antenna mounted at the center. The parabolic shape is important because any waves arriving from the line of sight will be reflected onto the center antenna element that faces the dish. Transmitted waves are just the reverse: They are aimed at the dish and reflected such that they are propagated away from the dish along the line of sight.

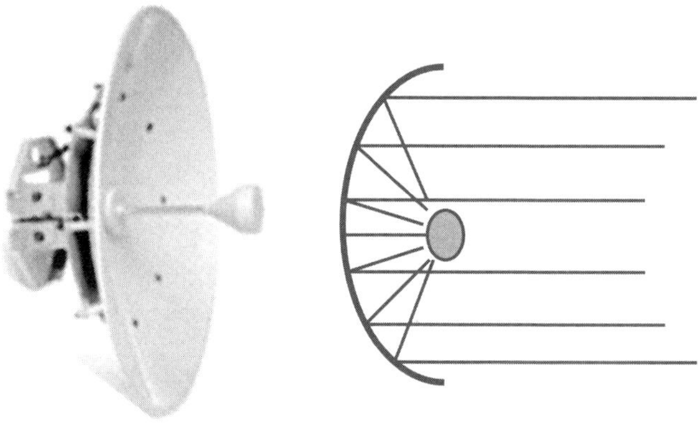

Figure 18-27 *Cisco* **Parabolic Dish Antenna**

Figure 18-28 shows the radiation patterns in the E and H planes, which are merged into three dimensions in Figure 18-29. Notice that the antenna's coverage pattern is long and narrow, extending out away from the dish. The focused pattern gives the antenna a gain of between 20 and 30 dBi—the highest gain of all the wireless LAN antennas.

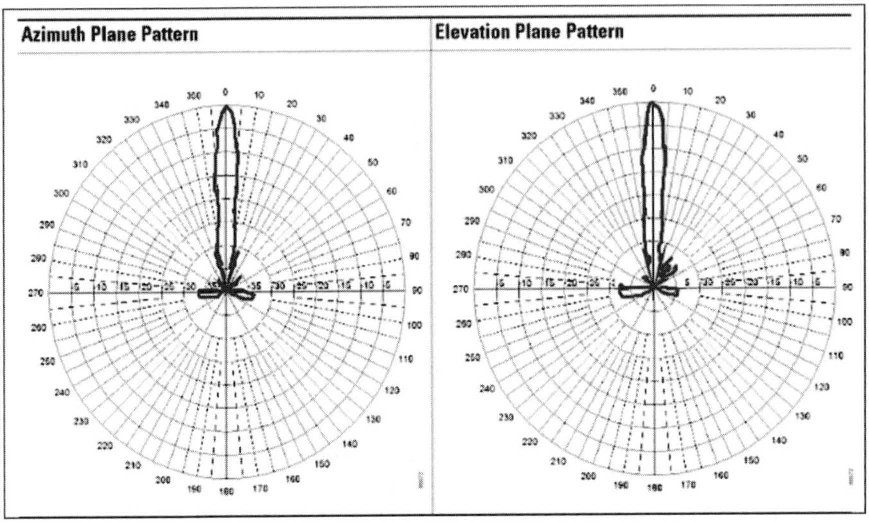

Figure 18-28 *E and H Radiation Patterns for a Parabolic Dish Antenna*

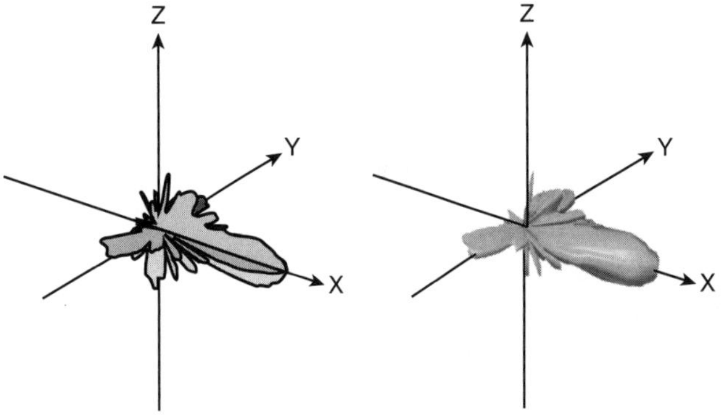

Figure 18-29 *Parabolic Dish Antenna Radiation Pattern in Three Dimensions*

Exam Preparation Tasks

You have a couple of choices for exam preparation: the exercises here, Chapter 30, "Final Preparation," and the exam simulation questions in the Pearson Test Prep Software Online.

Review All Key Topics

Review the most important topics in this chapter, noted with the Key Topic icon in the outer margin of the page. Table 18-2 lists these key topics and the page number on which each is found.

Key Topic

Table 18-2 Key Topics for Chapter 18

Key Topic Element	Description	Page Number
Figure 18-1	Wireless Network Topology Using Autonomous APs	545
List	Special-purpose modes	547

Key Topic Element	Description	Page Number
Figure 18-3	WLC Location in a Centralized Wireless Deployment	548
Figure 18-7	WLC Location in a Controller-less Deployment Using EWC	552
List	AP controller discovery states	553
List	AP controller discovery steps	554
Figure 18-11	Plotting the Radiation Pattern of an Isotropic Antenna	560

Complete Tables and Lists from Memory

There are no memory tables in this chapter.

Define Key Terms

Define the following key terms from this chapter and check your answers in the Glossary:

autonomous AP, beamwidth, CAPWAP, centralized wireless deployment, client density, dipole, directional antenna, E plane (elevation plane), controller-less deployment, gain, H plane (horizontal [azimuth] plane), integrated antenna, lightweight AP, local mode, distributed wireless deployment, omnidirectional antenna, parabolic dish antenna, patch antenna, polar plot, polarization, radiation pattern, split-MAC architecture, wireless LAN controller (WLC), Yagi antenna

CHAPTER 19

Understanding Wireless Roaming and Location Services

This chapter covers the following subjects:

- **Roaming Overview:** This section discusses client mobility from the AP and controller perspectives.
- **Intercontroller Roaming:** This section explains the mechanisms that allow wireless devices to roam from one AP/controller pair onto another.
- **Locating Devices in a Wireless Network:** This section explains how the components of a wireless network can be used to compute the physical location of wireless devices.

Wireless client devices are inherently mobile, so you should expect them to move around. This chapter discusses client mobility from the AP and controller perspectives. You should have a good understanding of client roaming so that you can design and configure your wireless network properly as it grows over time. In addition, you can leverage real-time location services to track client devices as they move around.

"Do I Know This Already?" Quiz

The "Do I Know This Already?" quiz enables you to assess whether you should read the entire chapter. If you miss no more than one of these self-assessment questions, you might want to move ahead to the "Exam Preparation Tasks" section. Table 19-1 lists the major headings in this chapter and the "Do I Know This Already?" quiz questions covering the material in those headings so you can assess your knowledge of these specific areas. The answers to the "Do I Know This Already?" quiz appear in Appendix A, "Answers to the 'Do I Know This Already?' Questions."

Table 19-1 "Do I Know This Already?" Foundation Topics Section-to-Question Mapping

Foundation Topics Section	Questions
Roaming Overview	1–2
Intercontroller Roaming	3–8
Locating Devices in a Wireless Network	9

1. When a client moves its association from one AP to another, it is actually leaving and joining which one of the following?
   a. SSID
   b. BSS
   c. ESS
   d. DS

2. Which one of the following makes the decision for a device to roam from one AP to another?
   a. The client device
   b. The original AP
   c. The candidate AP
   d. The wireless LAN controller
3. Ten lightweight APs are joined to a wireless LAN controller. If a client roams from one of the APs to another, which one of the following correctly describes the roam?
   a. Autonomous roaming
   b. Intercontroller roaming
   c. Intracontroller roaming
   d. Indirect roaming
4. Which of the following provides the most efficient means for roaming, as measured by the time to complete the roam?
   a. Layer 2 intercontroller roaming
   b. Layer 3 intercontroller roaming
   c. Intracontroller roaming
   d. All of these answers are correct; they all take equal amounts of time.
5. Which of the following is used to cache authentication key information to make roaming more efficient?
   a. PGP
   b. CCNA
   c. CCKM
   d. EoIP
6. In a Layer 2 roam, what mechanism is used to tunnel client data between the two controllers?
   a. GRE tunnel
   b. EoIP tunnel
   c. CAPWAP tunnel
   d. None of these answers are correct.
7. A client roams from controller A to controller B. If it undergoes a Layer 3 roam, which one of the following best describes the role of controller A?
   a. Foreign controller
   b. Host controller
   c. Master controller
   d. Anchor controller

8. A network consists of four controllers: A, B, C, and D. Mobility group 1 consists of controllers A and B, while mobility group 2 consists of controllers C and D; the mobility list on each controller contains both mobility group definitions. Which one of the following answers describes what happens when a client tries to roam between controllers B and C?
   a. Roaming is seamless and efficient.
   b. Roaming is not possible.
   c. Roaming is possible, but CCKM and key caching do not work.
   d. Only Layer 3 roaming is possible.
9. Which of the following parameters is useful for computing a client device's location with respect to an AP?
   a. BSS
   b. GPS
   c. RSS
   d. Channel

Foundation Topics

When a wireless client moves about, the expectations are simple: good, seamless coverage wherever the client goes. Clients know how to roam between access points (APs), but they are ignorant about the wireless network infrastructure. Even in a large network, roaming should be easy and quick, and it should not disrupt the client's service.

Cisco wireless networks offer several roaming strategies. From the perspective of a network professional, roaming configuration is straightforward. The inner workings can be complex, depending on the size of the wireless network, as measured by the number of APs and controllers. As you work through the sections in this chapter, you will review roaming fundamentals and then learn more about how the Cisco wireless controllers handle client roaming. You will also learn more about the network design aspects and functions that can be used to track and locate mobile client devices.

Roaming Overview

To understand how wireless roaming works, you should start simple. The following two sections discuss roaming between access points when no controller is present and when only one controller is present. More complex scenarios are covered later in the chapter.

Roaming Between Autonomous APs

Recall that a wireless client must associate and authenticate with an AP before it can use the AP's basic service set (BSS) to access the network. A client can also move from one BSS to another by roaming between APs. A client continuously evaluates the quality of its wireless connection, whether it is moving around or not. If the signal quality degrades, perhaps as the client moves away from the AP, the client will begin looking for a different AP that can offer a better signal. The process is usually quick and simple; the client actively scans channels and sends probe requests to discover candidate APs, and then the client selects one and tries to reassociate with it.

NOTE A client can send Association Request and Reassociation Request frames to an AP when it wants to join the BSS. Association Requests are used to form a new association, while Reassociation Requests are used to roam from one AP to another, preserving the client's original association status.

Figure 19-1 shows a simple scenario with two APs and one client. The client begins with an association to AP-1. Because the APs are running in autonomous mode, each one maintains a table of its associated clients. AP-1 has one client; AP-2 has none.

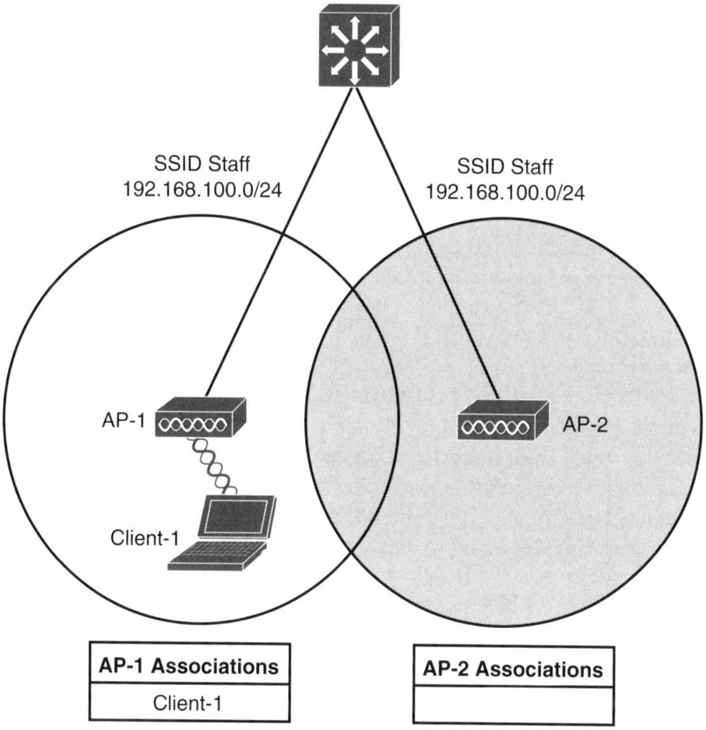

Figure 19-1 *Before Roaming Between Autonomous APs*

Suppose that the client then begins to move into AP-2's cell. Somewhere near the cell boundary, the client decides that the signal from AP-1 has degraded and it should look elsewhere for a stronger signal. The client decides to roam and reassociate with AP-2. Figure 19-2 shows the new scenario after the roam occurs. Notice that both APs have updated their list of associated clients to reflect Client 1's move from AP-1 to AP-2. If AP-1 still has any leftover wireless frames destined for the client after the roam, it forwards them to AP-2 over the wired infrastructure—simply because that is where the client's MAC address now resides.

Key Topic

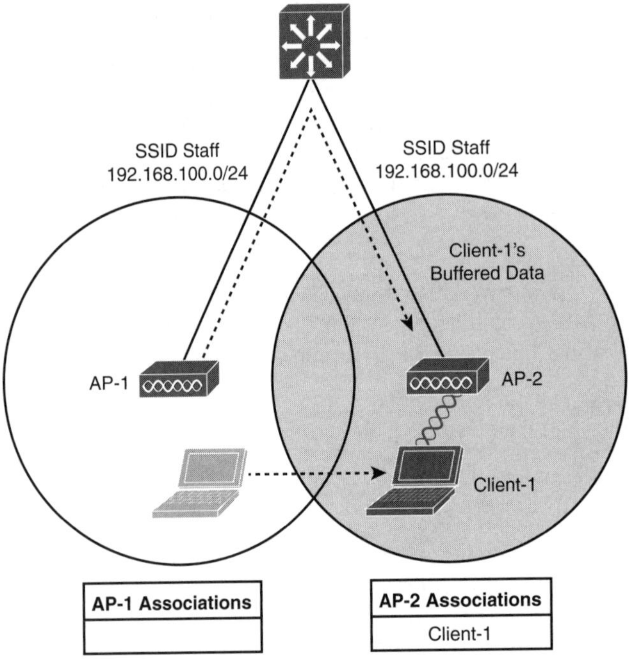

Figure 19-2 *After Roaming Between Autonomous APs*

Naturally, roaming is not limited to only two APs; instead, it occurs between any two APs as the client moves between them, at any given time. To cover a large area, you will probably install many APs in a pattern such that their cells overlap. Figure 19-3 shows a typical pattern. When a wireless client begins to move, it might move along an arbitrary path. Each time the client decides that the signal from one AP has degraded enough, it attempts to roam to a new, better signal belonging to a different AP and cell. The exact location of each roam depends on the client's roaming algorithm. To illustrate typical roaming activity, each roam in Figure 19-3 is marked with a dark ring.

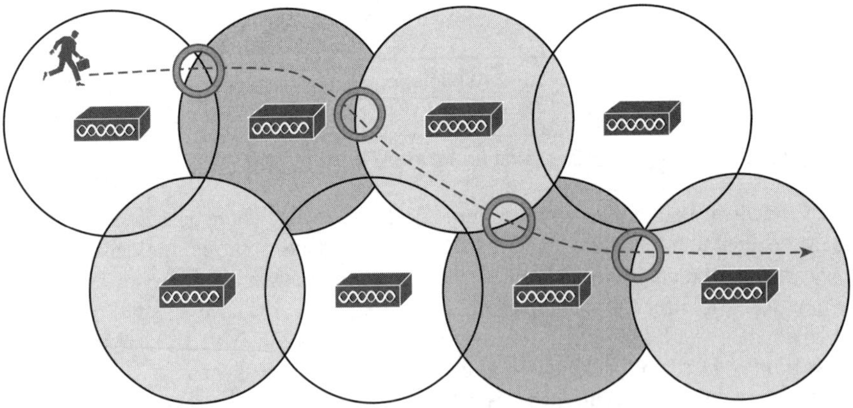

Figure 19-3 *Successive Roams of a Mobile Client*

Answers to the "Do I Know This Already?" quiz:

1 B **2** A **3** C **4** C **5** C **6** D **7** D **8** C **9** C

Intracontroller Roaming

In a Cisco wireless network, lightweight APs are bound to a wireless LAN controller through CAPWAP tunnels. The roaming process is similar to that of autonomous APs; clients must still reassociate to new APs as they move about. The only real difference is that the controller handles the roaming process, rather than the APs, because of the split-MAC architecture.

Figure 19-4 shows a two-AP scenario where both APs connect to a single controller. Client 1 is associated to AP-1, which has a Control and Provisioning of Wireless Access Points (CAPWAP) tunnel to controller WLC 1. The controller maintains a client database that contains detailed information about how to reach and support each client. For simplicity, Figure 19-4 shows the database as a list of the controller's APs, associated clients, and the wireless LAN (WLAN) being used. The actual database also contains client MAC and IP addresses, quality of service (QoS) parameters, and other information.

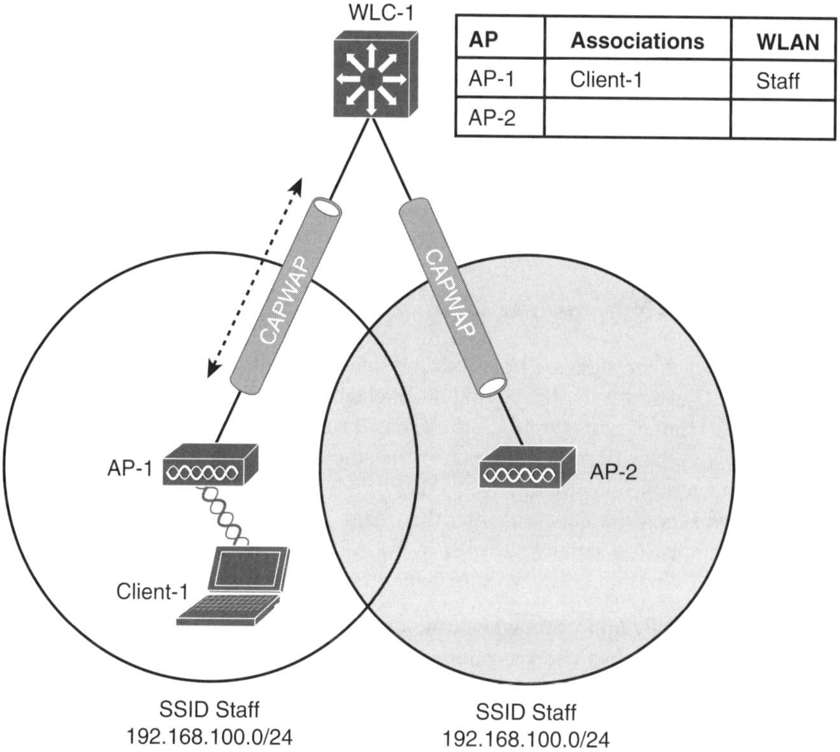

Figure 19-4 *Cisco Wireless Network Before an Intracontroller Roam*

When Client 1 starts moving, it eventually roams to AP-2, as shown in Figure 19-5. Not much has changed except that the controller has updated the client association from AP-1 to AP-2. Because both APs are bound to the same controller, the roam occurs entirely within the controller. This is known as **intracontroller roaming.**

Key Topic

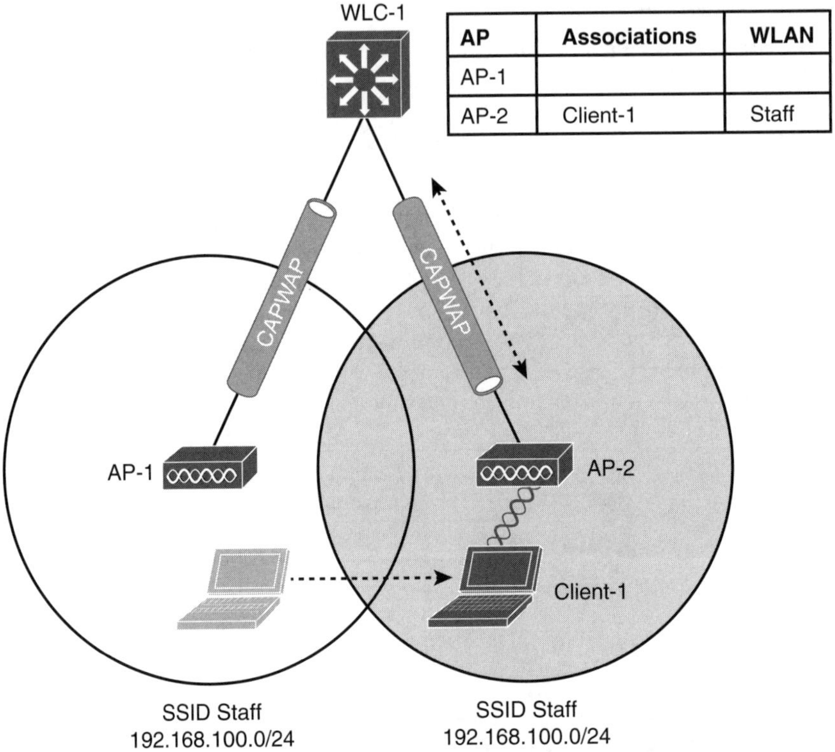

Figure 19-5 *Cisco Wireless Network After an Intracontroller Roam*

If both APs involved in a client roam are bound to the same controller, the roaming process is simple and efficient. The controller has to update its client association table so that it knows which CAPWAP tunnel to use to reach the client. Thanks to the simplicity, an intracontroller roam takes less than 10 ms to complete—the amount of processing time needed for the controller to switch the client entry from AP-1 to AP-2. From the client's perspective, an intracontroller roam is no different from any other roam. The client has no knowledge that the two APs are communicating with a controller over CAPWAP tunnels; it simply decides to roam between two APs based on its own signal analysis.

Efficient roaming is especially important when time-critical applications are being used over the wireless network. For example, wireless phones need a consistent connection so that the audio stream is not garbled or interrupted. When a roam occurs, there could be a brief time when the client is not fully associated with either AP. So long as that time is held to a minimum, the end user probably will not even notice that the roam occurred.

Along with the client reassociation, a couple other processes can occur:

- **DHCP:** The client may be programmed to renew the DHCP lease on its IP address or to request a new address.
- **Client authentication:** The controller might be configured to use an 802.1x method to authenticate each client on a WLAN.

To achieve efficient roaming, both of these processes should be streamlined as much as possible. For instance, if a client roams and tries to renew its IP address, it is essentially cut off from the network until the Dynamic Host Configuration Protocol (DHCP) server responds.

The client authentication process presents the biggest challenge because the dialog between a controller and a RADIUS server, in addition to the cryptographic keys that need to be generated and exchanged between the client and an AP or controller, can take a considerable amount of time to accomplish. Cisco controllers offer three techniques to minimize the time and effort spent on key exchanges during roams:

- **Cisco Centralized Key Management (CCKM):** One controller maintains a database of clients and keys on behalf of its APs and provides them to other controllers and their APs as needed during client roams. CCKM requires Cisco Compatible Extensions (CCX) support from clients.
- **Key caching:** Each client maintains a list of keys used with prior AP associations and presents them as it roams. The destination AP must be present in this list, which is limited to eight AP/key entries.
- **802.11r:** This 802.11 amendment addresses fast roaming or fast BSS transition; a client can cache a portion of the authentication server's key and present that to future APs as it roams. The client can also maintain its QoS parameters as it roams.

Each of the fast-roaming strategies requires help on the part of the wireless client. That means the client must have a supplicant or driver software that is compatible with fast roaming and can cache the necessary pieces of the authentication credentials.

Intercontroller Roaming

As a wireless network grows, one controller might not suffice. When two or more controllers support the APs in an enterprise, the APs can be distributed across them. As always, when clients become mobile, they roam from one AP to another—except they could also be roaming from one controller to another, depending on how neighboring APs are assigned to the controllers. As a network grows, AP roaming can scale too by organizing controllers into mobility groups. The following sections cover intercontroller roaming, mobility groups, and the mechanisms used to coordinate roaming.

19

Layer 2 Roaming

When a client roams from one AP to another and those APs lie on two different controllers, the client makes an intercontroller roam. Figure 19-6 shows a simple scenario prior to a roam. Controller WLC 1 has one association in its database—that of Client 1 on AP-1. Figure 19-7 shows the result of the client roaming to AP-2.

AP	Associations	WLAN	VLAN
AP-1	Client-1	Staff	100

AP	Associations	WLAN	VLAN
AP-2			

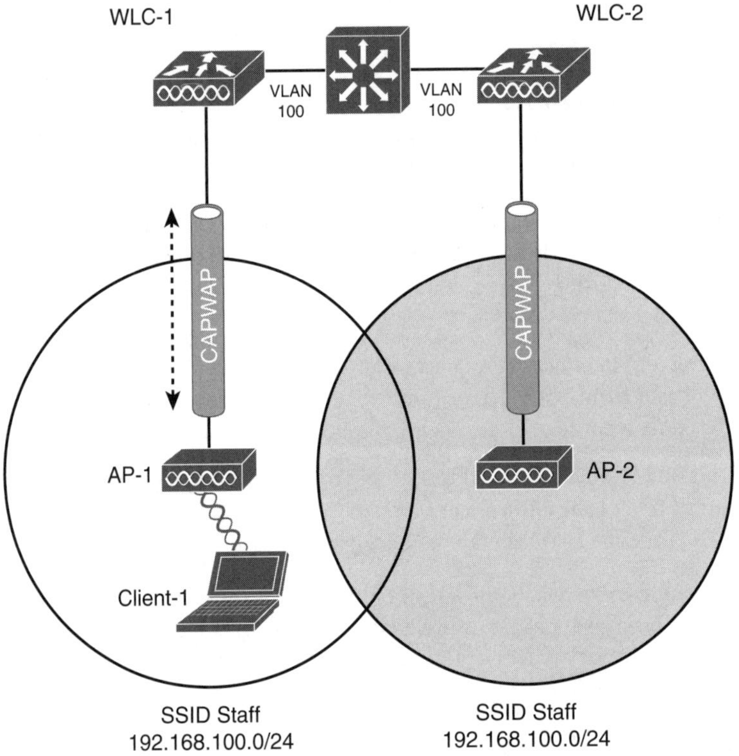

Figure 19-6 *Before an Intercontroller Roam*

The roam itself is fairly straightforward. When the client decides to roam and reassociate itself with AP-2, it actually moves from one controller to another, and the two controllers must coordinate the move. One subtle detail involves the client's IP address. Before the roam, Client 1 is associated with AP-1 and takes an IP address from the VLAN and subnet that are configured on the WLAN supplied by controller WLC 1. In Figure 19-6, WLAN Staff is bound to VLAN 100, so the client uses an address from the 192.168.100.0/24 subnet.

When the client roams to a different AP, it can try to continue using its existing IP address or work with a DHCP server to either renew or request an address. Figure 19-7 shows the client roaming to AP-2, where WLAN Staff is also bound to the same VLAN 100 and 192.168.100.0/24 subnet. Because the client has roamed between APs but stayed on the same VLAN and subnet, it has made a Layer 2 intercontroller roam. **Layer 2 roams** (commonly called local-to-local roams) are nice for two reasons: The client can keep its same IP address, and the roam is fast (usually less than 20 ms).

Key Topic

AP	Associations	WLAN	VLAN

AP	Associations	WLAN	VLAN
AP-2	Client-1	Staff	100

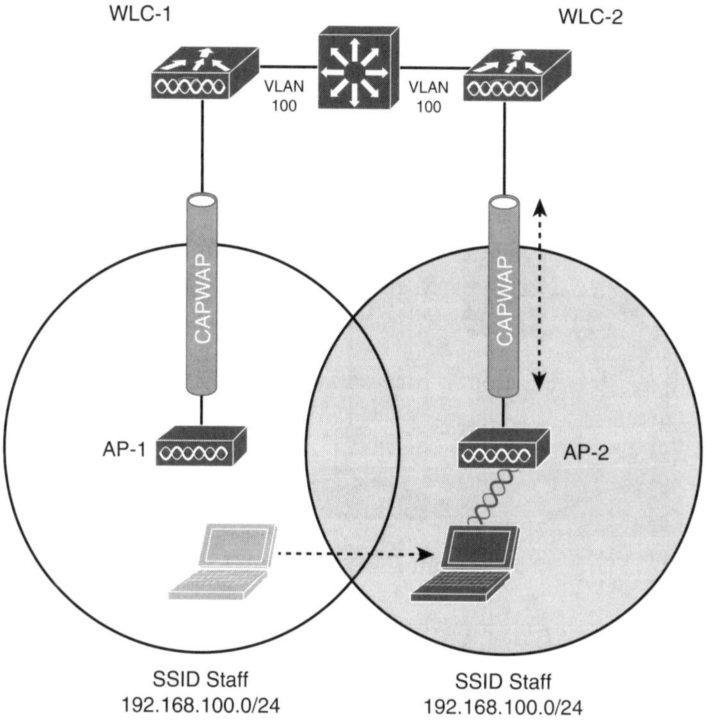

Figure 19-7 *After an Intercontroller Roam*

Layer 3 Roaming

What if a wireless network grows even more, such that the WLAN interfaces on each controller are assigned to different VLANs and subnets? Breaking up a large WLAN into individual subnets seems like a good idea from a scalability viewpoint. However, when a wireless client roams from one controller to another, it could easily end up on a different subnet from the original one.

Clients will not usually be able to detect that they have changed subnets. They will be aware of the AP roam but little else. Only clients that aggressively contact a DHCP server after each and every roam will continue to work properly. But to make roaming seamless and efficient, time-consuming processes such as DHCP should be avoided.

No worries—the Cisco wireless network has a clever trick up its sleeve. When a client initiates an intercontroller roam, the two controllers involved can compare the VLAN numbers that are assigned to their respective WLAN interfaces. If the VLAN IDs are the same, nothing special needs to happen; the client undergoes a Layer 2 intercontroller roam and can continue to use its original IP address on the new controller. If the two VLAN IDs differ, the controllers arrange a **Layer 3 roam** (also known as a local-to-foreign roam) that will allow the client to keep using its IP address.

Figure 19-8 illustrates a simple wireless network containing two APs and two controllers. Notice that the two APs offer different IP subnets in their BSSs: 192.168.100.0/24 and 192.168.200.0/24. The client is associated with AP-1 and is using IP address 192.168.100.199. On the surface, it looks like the client will roam into subnet 192.168.200.0/24 if it wanders into AP-2's cell and will lose connectivity if it tries to keep using its same IP address.

AP	Associations	WLAN	VLAN
AP-1	Client-1	Staff	100

AP	Associations	WLAN	VLAN
AP-2			

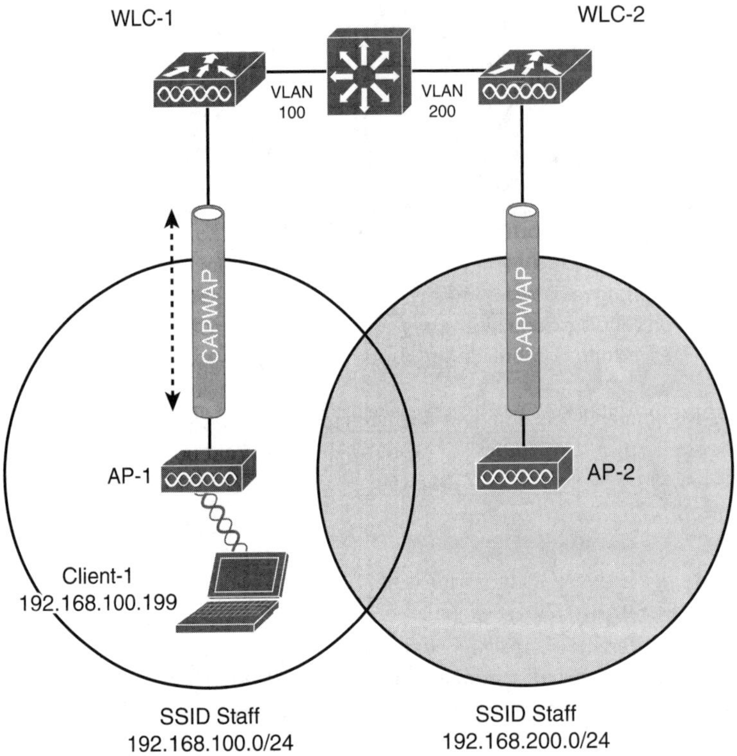

Figure 19-8 *Before a Layer 3 Intercontroller Roam*

A Layer 3 intercontroller roam consists of an extra tunnel that is built between the client's original controller and the controller it has roamed to. The tunnel carries data to and from the client as if it is still associated with the original controller and IP subnet. Figure 19-9 shows the results of a Layer 3 roam. The original controller (WLC 1) is called the **anchor controller**, and the controller with the roamed client is called the **foreign controller**. Think of the client being anchored to the original controller no matter where it roams later. When the client roams away from its anchor, it moves into foreign territory.

Key Topic

AP	Associations	WLAN	VLAN
WLC-2	Client-1 (Mobile)	Staff	100

AP	Associations	WLAN	VLAN
AP-2	Client-1	Staff	

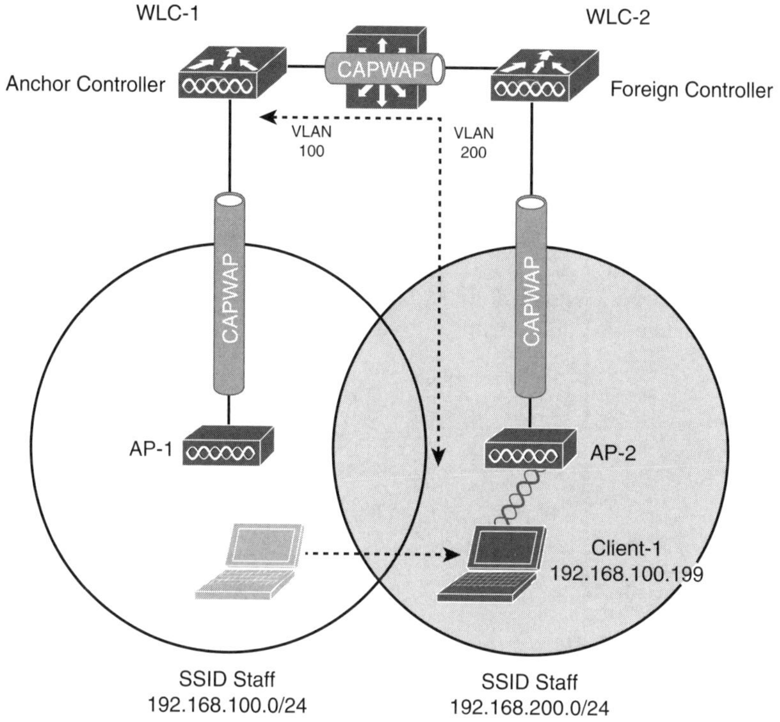

Figure 19-9 *After a Layer 3 Intercontroller Roam*

Recall that Cisco controllers use CAPWAP tunnels to connect with lightweight APs. CAPWAP tunnels are also built between controllers for Layer 3 roaming. The tunnel tethers the client to its original anchor controller (and original IP subnet), regardless of its location or how many controllers it roams through.

Anchor and foreign controllers are normally determined automatically. When a client first associates with an AP and a controller, that controller becomes its anchor controller. When the client roams to a different controller, that controller can take on the foreign role. Sometimes you might not want a client's first controller to be its anchor. For example, guest users should not be allowed to associate with just any controller in your network. Instead, you might want guests to be forced onto a specific controller that is situated behind a firewall or contained in a protected environment. You can configure one controller to be a static anchor for a WLAN so that other controllers will direct clients toward it through Layer 3 roaming tunnels.

Scaling Mobility with Mobility Groups

Cisco controllers can be organized into **mobility groups** to facilitate **intercontroller roaming**. Mobility groups become important as a wireless network scales, and there are more centralized controllers cooperating to provide coverage over a large area.

If two centralized controllers are configured to belong to the same mobility group, clients can roam quickly between them. Layer 2 and Layer 3 roaming are both supported, along with CCKM, key caching, and 802.11r credential caching. If two controllers are assigned to different mobility groups, clients can still roam between them, but the roam is not very efficient. Credentials are not cached and shared, so clients must go through a full authentication during the roam. A mobility group can contain up to 24 controllers.

Mobility groups have an implied hierarchy, as shown in Figure 19-10. Each controller maintains a mobility list that contains its own MAC address and the MAC addresses of other controllers. Each controller in the list is also assigned a mobility group name. In effect, the mobility list defines a **mobility domain** and gives a controller its view of the outside world; it knows of and trusts only the other controllers configured in the list. If two controllers are not listed in each other's mobility list, they are unknown to each other, and clients will not be able to roam between them. Clients will have to associate and authenticate from scratch. A mobility list can contain up to 72 different controller entries.

Key Topic

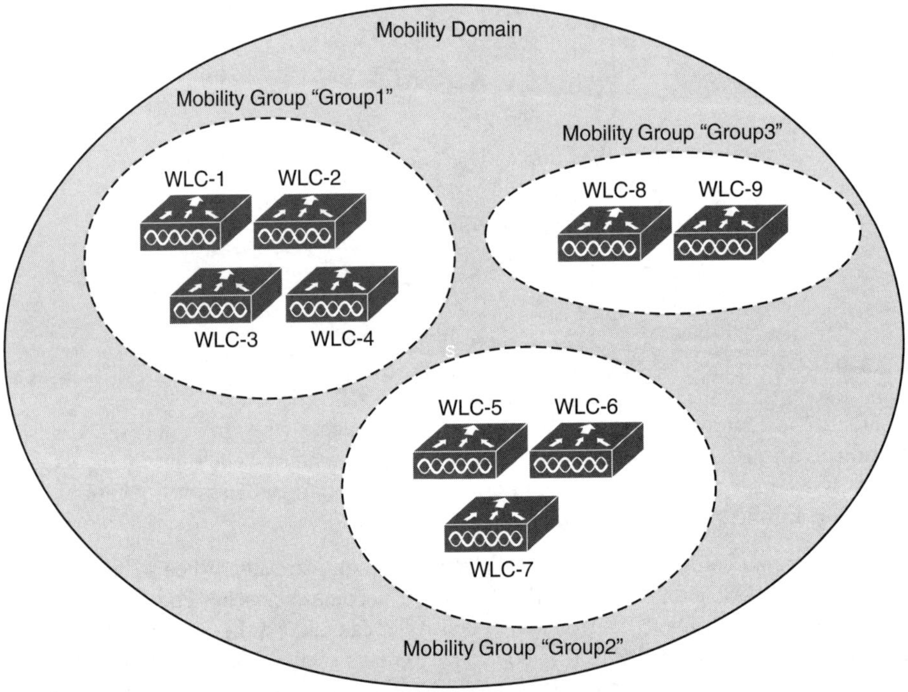

Figure 19-10 *Mobility Group Hierarchy*

Locating Devices in a Wireless Network

Wireless networks are usually designed to provide coverage and connectivity in all areas where client devices are expected to be located. For example, a hospital building will likely have seamless wireless coverage on all floors and in all areas where users might go. Usually, a user's exact location is irrelevant, as long as wireless coverage exists there. Locating a user or device is important in several use cases, and a wireless network can be leveraged to provide that information.

Device location can be an important part of tracking assets in a business. For instance, a large store might be interested in tracking potential customers as they walk around and shop The store might like to offer online advertising as customers enter various areas or walk near certain product displays. The same could be true of a museum that wants to present relevant online content as people move to each exhibit. A healthcare enterprise might want to track critical (and valuable) medical devices or patients as they move about the facility so that they can be quickly located. By tracking user locations, a large venue can provide wayfinding information on mobile devices to help people navigate through buildings.

Recall that before each wireless client can use the network, it must first be authenticated by and associated with an AP. At the most basic level, a client can then be located according to the AP to which it is currently joined. That may not be granular enough for every use case because one AP might cover a large area. In addition, a client device might not roam very aggressively, so it could well stay associated with one AP that is now far away, even though another AP with a better signal is very near.

To locate a device more accurately, an AP can use the **received signal strength (RSS)** of a client device as a measure of the distance between the two. Free space path loss causes an RF signal to be attenuated or diminished exponentially as a function of its frequency and the distance it travels. That means a client's distance from an AP can be computed from its received signal strength. If the distance is measured from a single AP only, it is difficult to determine where the client is situated in relation to the AP. In the case of an indoor AP with an omnidirectional antenna, the client could be located anywhere along a circular path of fixed distance because the received signal strength would be fairly consistent at all points on the circle. A better solution is to obtain the same measurement from three or more APs and then correlate the results and determine where they intersect. Figure 19-11 illustrates the difference in determining a client's location with a single and multiple APs.

Key Topic

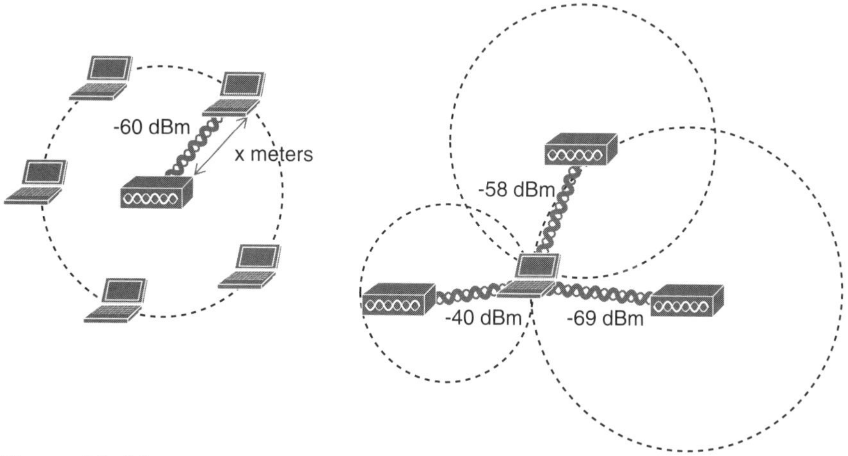

Figure 19-11 *Locating a Wireless Device with One AP (left) and Three APs (right)*

The components of a wireless network can be coupled with additional resources to provide real-time location services (RTLS). Cisco APs and WLCs can integrate with management platforms like DNA Center or Cisco Prime Infrastructure, along with location servers like Cisco Spaces, Cisco Mobility Services Engine (MSE), or Cisco Connected Mobile Experiences (CMX) to gather location information in real time and present that information in a relevant way.

Real-time location is not something inherent in a wireless network infrastructure. Through the familiar split-MAC architecture, the APs interface directly with the client devices at the lowest real-time layer, while the WLCs learn about the clients from the APs and handle normal data forwarding to and from them. The WLCs must keep a management platform like Cisco DNA Center or Cisco Prime Infrastructure informed as clients probe, join, and leave the network, and pass along wireless statistics such as each client's RSS value. The actual real-time location for each device must be computed on a separate location server platform.

The simple location example shown in Figure 19-11 is intuitive, but it is based on the assumption that the APs and client devices are located in open free space, with nothing but free space path loss to attenuate the client's RF signal. In a normal environment, the APs and clients exist in buildings where physical objects, such as walls, doors, windows, furniture, cubicles, and shelving, also exist and get in the way of the RF signals. Usually, the signals can pass through various materials but get attenuated along the way. That further complicates determining device location accurately.

The Cisco approach is to leverage **RF fingerprinting**, where each mapped area is influenced by an RF calibration template that more closely resembles the actual signal attenuation experienced by the APs and clients. The calibration applied to a map can be manually determined by walking through the area with a device and taking actual RF measurements. It can also be applied through a set of models that represents how the construction of a mapped area might affect signal propagation. Sample models include cubes and walled offices, drywalled offices, indoor high ceilings, and outdoor open spaces.

The most intuitive way to interpret location data is to view devices on a map that represents the building and floor where they are located. Figure 19-12 shows a sample map of one floor of a building from Cisco Spaces. The square icons represent AP locations, which were manually entered on the map. Cisco Spaces indicates device locations with small colored dots that are dynamically placed on the map at regular time intervals. Green dots represent wireless devices that have successfully associated with APs, and red dots represent devices that are not associated but are actively sending probe requests to find nearby APs.

Key Topic

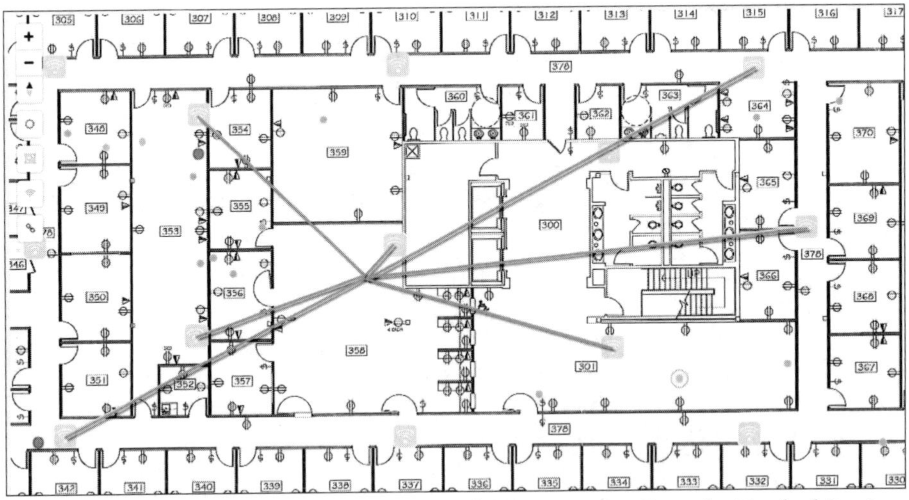

Figure 19-12 *A Sample Map Showing Real-Time Location Data for Tracked Devices*

One device has been selected in Figure 19-12, causing lines to be drawn to some of the APs that overheard the device. In this example, seven APs have recorded a current received signal strength measurement for the client, which is then used to derive an accurate location.

It might seem odd that so many different APs would be able to know about a device because it can associate and use only one AP at a time. In addition, the device and the AP where it is associated would communicate on only a single channel, while other APs would likely be using different channels. The secret is that wireless devices normally use 802.11 Probe Requests to discover any potential APs that might be nearby, either as a prelude to associating with an AP or in preparation for roaming to a different AP. A client will send Probe Requests on every possible channel and band that it is configured to support. Neighboring APs will receive the requests on their respective channels, all sourced by the same client MAC address.

The same real-time location service also supports wireless devices that might never actually associate with an AP. For example, you might be interested in locating or tracking a potential customer's smartphone as that person walks through a store. As long as Wi-Fi is enabled on the device, it will probably probe for available APs. RFID tags are another type of device that can be attached to objects so that they can be tracked and located. Some RFID tags can actively join a wireless network to exchange data, while others are meant to simply "wake up" periodically to send 802.11 Probe Requests or multicast frames to announce their presence.

Another interesting use case is locating rogue devices and sources of Wi-Fi interference. Rogue devices will likely probe the network and can be discovered and located. Interference sources, such as cordless phones, wireless video cameras, and other transmitters, might not be compatible with the 802.11 standard at all. Cisco APs can still detect the presence of interference with dedicated spectrum analysis and the Clean Air feature, and can determine the received signal strength on a channel. The location server can use this information to compute a probable location of the interference source and display it on a map.

Exam Preparation Tasks

19

You have a couple of choices for exam preparation: the exercises here, Chapter 30, "Final Preparation," and the exam simulation questions in the Pearson Test Prep Software Online.

Review All Key Topics

Review the most important topics in this chapter, noted with the Key Topic icon in the outer margin of the page. Table 19-2 lists these key topics and the page number on which each is found.

Key Topic

Table 19-2 Key Topics for Chapter 19

Key Topic Element	Description	Page Number
Figure 19-2	After Roaming Between Autonomous APs	576
Figure 19-5	Cisco Wireless Network After an Intracontroller Roam	578
Figure 19-7	After an Intercontroller Roam	581

Key Topic Element	Description	Page Number
Figure 19-9	After a Layer 3 Intercontroller Roam	583
Figure 19-10	Mobility Group Hierarchy	584
Figure 19-11	Locating a Wireless Device with One AP (left) and Three APs (right)	585
Figure 19-12	A Sample Map Showing Real-Time Location Data for Tracked Devices	586

Complete Tables and Lists from Memory

There are no memory tables in this chapter.

Define Key Terms

Define the following key terms from this chapter and check your answers in the Glossary:

anchor controller, foreign controller, intercontroller roaming, intracontroller roaming, Layer 2 roam, Layer 3 roam, mobility domain, mobility group, received signal strength (RSS), RF fingerprinting

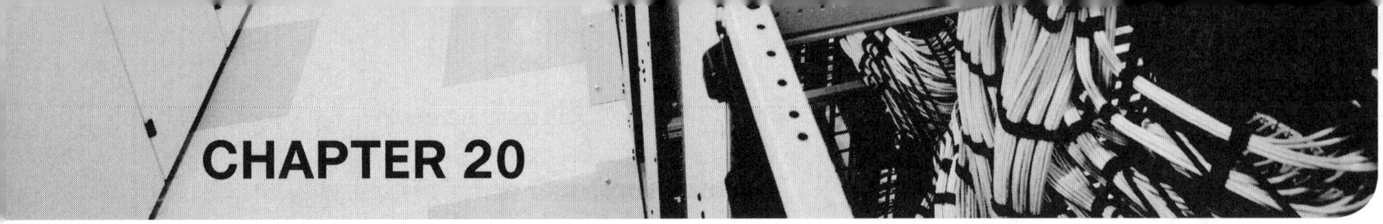

CHAPTER 20

Authenticating Wireless Clients

This chapter covers the following subjects:

- **Open Authentication:** This section covers authenticating wireless users using no credentials.
- **Authenticating with Pre-Shared Key:** This section covers authenticating clients with a static key that is shared prior to its use.
- **Authenticating with EAP:** This section covers authenticating clients with Extensible Authentication Protocol (EAP).
- **Authenticating with WebAuth:** This section covers authenticating clients through the use of a web page where credentials are entered.

You might remember from studying for the CCNA 200-301 exam that wireless networks can leverage many technologies and protocols to protect information that is sent over the air. For example, the WPA, WPA2, and WPA3 security suites can be used to protect data privacy and integrity. Beyond that, it is also important to identify the two endpoints (the AP and the client device) that use a wireless connection, as well as the end user. This chapter explores three different methods to authenticate wireless clients before they are granted access to a wireless network.

"Do I Know This Already?" Quiz

The "Do I Know This Already?" quiz enables you to assess whether you should read the entire chapter. If you miss no more than one of these self-assessment questions, you might want to move ahead to the "Exam Preparation Tasks" section. Table 20-1 lists the major headings in this chapter and the "Do I Know This Already?" quiz questions covering the material in those headings so you can assess your knowledge of these specific areas. The answers to the "Do I Know This Already?" quiz appear in Appendix A, "Answers to the 'Do I Know This Already?' Questions."

Table 20-1 "Do I Know This Already?" Foundation Topics Section-to-Question Mapping

Foundation Topics Section	Questions
Open Authentication	1–2
Authenticating with Pre-Shared Key	3–6
Authenticating with EAP	7–8
Authenticating with WebAuth	9–10

1. Open Authentication requires the use of which one of the following?
   a. 802.1x
   b. RADIUS
   c. HTTP/HTTPS
   d. Pre-Shared Key
   e. None of these answers are correct.
2. Open Authentication can be used in combination with which one of the following?
   a. PSK
   b. WebAuth
   c. EAP
   d. 802.1x
3. When PSK authentication is used on a WLAN, without the use of an ISE server, which of the following devices must be configured with the key string? (Choose two.)
   a. One wireless client (each with a unique key string)
   b. All wireless clients
   c. All APs and WLCs
   d. A RADIUS server
4. Which of the following authentication methods does WPA2 personal mode use?
   a. Open Authentication
   b. Pre-Shared Key
   c. EAP
   d. 802.1x
5. Which of the following WPA versions is considered to have the most secure personal mode?
   a. WPA
   b. WPA1
   c. WPA2
   d. WPA3
   e. The personal modes are all equivalent.
6. Pre-Shared Key is used in which of the following wireless security configurations? (Choose all that apply.)
   a. WPA personal mode
   b. WPA enterprise mode
   c. WPA2 personal mode
   d. WPA2 enterprise mode
   e. WPA3 personal mode
   f. WPA3 enterprise mode

7. The EAPOL four-way handshake is used to accomplish which one of the following tasks?
   a. Authenticating the end user
   b. Authenticating by RADIUS
   c. Exchanging encryption keys
   d. Joining an AP to a WLC
8. A Cisco WLC is configured for 802.1x authentication, using an external RADIUS server. The controller takes on which one of the following roles?
   a. Authentication server
   b. Supplicant
   c. Authenticator
   d. Adjudicator
9. When WPA2 enterprise mode is used on a WLAN, where is the supplicant role located?
   a. On the wireless client
   b. On the AP
   c. On the WLC
   d. On the RADIUS server
10. Suppose an enterprise offers a wireless network that guests can use but only after they read and accept an acceptable use policy document. Which one of the following methods can inherently handle this process?
    a. Open Authentication
    b. WPA3 personal
    c. WPA2 enterprise
    d. WebAuth

Foundation Topics

To join and use a wireless network, wireless clients must first discover a basic service set (BSS) and then request permission to associate with it. At that point, clients should be authenticated by some means before they can become functioning members of a wireless LAN. Why?

Suppose that your wireless network connects to corporate resources where confidential information can be accessed. In that case, only devices known to be trusted and expected should be given access. Guest users, if they are permitted at all, should be allowed to join a different guest WLAN where they can access nonconfidential or public resources. Rogue clients, which are not expected or welcomed, should not be permitted to associate at all. After all, they are not affiliated with the corporate network and are likely to be unknown devices that happen to be within range of your network.

To control access, wireless networks can authenticate the client devices before they are allowed to associate. Potential clients must identify themselves by presenting some form of credentials to the APs. Figure 20-1 shows the basic client authentication process.

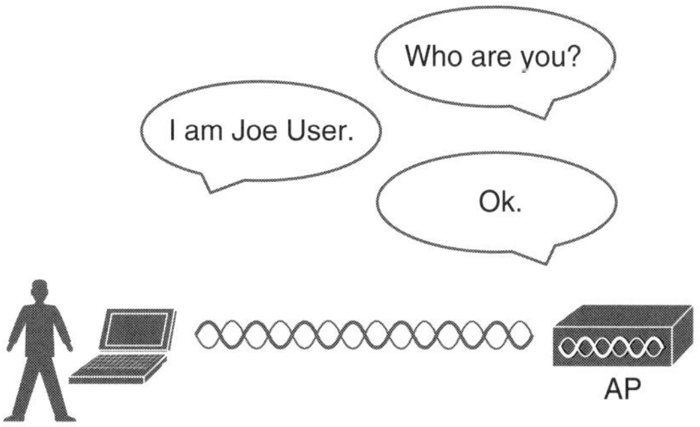

Figure 20-1 *Authenticating a Wireless Client*

Wireless authentication can take many forms. Some methods require only a static text string that is common across all trusted clients and APs. The text string is stored on the client device and presented directly to the AP when needed. What might happen if the device is stolen or lost? Most likely, any user who possesses the device would still be able to authenticate to the network. Other more stringent authentication methods require interaction with a corporate user database. In those cases, the end user must enter a valid username and password—something that would not be known to a thief or an imposter.

The sections that follow explain four types of client authentication you will likely encounter on the CCNP and CCIE Enterprise ENCOR exam and in common use. With each type, you will begin by creating a new WLAN on the wireless LAN controller, assigning a controller interface, and enabling the WLAN. Because wireless security is configured on a per-WLAN basis, all of the configuration tasks related to this chapter occur in the WLAN > Edit Security tab.

Open Authentication

Recall that a wireless client device must send 802.11 authentication request and association request frames to an AP when it asks to join a wireless network. The original 802.11 standard offered only two choices to authenticate a client: Open Authentication and WEP.

Open Authentication is true to its name; it offers open access to a WLAN. The only requirement is that a client must use an 802.11 authentication request before it attempts to associate with an AP. No other credentials are needed.

When would you want to use Open Authentication? After all, it does not sound very secure (and it is not). With no challenge, any 802.11 client may authenticate to access the network. That is, in fact, the whole purpose of Open Authentication—to validate that a client is a valid 802.11 device by authenticating the wireless hardware and the protocol. Authenticating the user's identity is handled as a true security process through other means.

20

You have probably seen a WLAN with Open Authentication when you have visited a public location. If any client screening is used at all, it comes in the form of Web Authentication (WebAuth), which is described in the "Authenticating with WebAuth" section of this chapter. A client can associate right away but must open a web browser to see and accept the terms for use and enter basic credentials. From that point, network access is opened up for the client.

To create a WLAN with Open Authentication on an IOS XE WLC, you can navigate to Configuration > Wireless Setup > WLAN Wizard. You can also create a WLAN directly by navigating to Configuration > Tags & Profiles > WLANs and selecting the **Add** button. Under the General tab, enter the SSID string, then select the **Security** tab to configure the WLAN security and user authentication parameters. Select **Layer 2** and then use the Layer 2 Security Mode drop-down menu to select None for Open Authentication, as shown in Figure 20-2. In this example, the WLAN is named guest, and the SSID is "Guest".

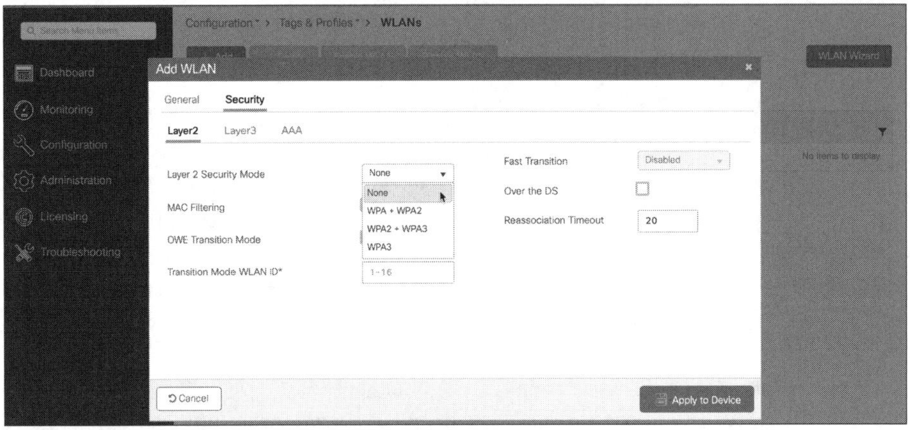

Figure 20-2 *Configuring Open Authentication for a WLAN*

When you are finished configuring the WLAN, click the **Apply to Device** button. Don't forget that you still have to configure a Policy profile to identify the appropriate VLAN number that the WLAN will map to and then apply the WLAN and Policy profiles to the APs.

You can verify the WLAN and its security settings from the list of WLANs shown under Configuration > Tags & Profiles > WLANs, as shown in Figure 20-3. The Security is shown as [open]. You can also verify that the WLAN status is enabled and active.

Figure 20-3 *Verifying Open Authentication from the List of WLANs*

Answers to the "Do I Know This Already?" quiz:

1 E **2** B **3** B, C **4** B **5** D **6** A, C, E **7** C **8** C **9** A **10** D

Authenticating with Pre-Shared Key

To secure wireless connections on a WLAN, you can leverage one of the **Wi-Fi Protected Access (WPA)** versions—WPA (also known as WPA1), **WPA2**, or **WPA3**. Each version is certified by the Wi-Fi Alliance so that wireless clients and APs using the same version are known to be compatible. The WPA versions also specify encryption and data integrity methods to protect data passing over the wireless connections.

Key Topic

All three WPA versions support two client authentication modes, pre-shared key (PSK) or **802.1x**, depending on the scale of the deployment. These are also known as **personal mode** and *enterprise mode*, respectively. With personal mode, a key string must be shared or configured on every client and AP before the clients can connect to the wireless network. The pre-shared key is normally kept confidential so that unauthorized users have no knowledge of it. The key string is never sent over the air. Instead, clients and APs work through a four-way handshake procedure that uses the pre-shared key string to construct and exchange encryption key material that can be openly exchanged. When that process is successful, the AP can authenticate the client, and the two can secure data frames that are sent over the air.

With WPA-Personal and WPA2-Personal modes, a malicious user can eavesdrop and capture the four-way handshake between a client and an AP. That user can then use a dictionary attack to automate the guessing of the pre-shared key. If the malicious user is successful, that user can then decrypt the wireless data or even join the network, posing as a legitimate user.

WPA3-Personal avoids such an attack by strengthening the key exchange between clients and APs through a method known as *Simultaneous Authentication of Equals (SAE)*. Rather than a client authenticating against a server or AP, the client and AP can initiate the authentication process equally and even simultaneously.

Even if a password or key is compromised, WPA3-Personal offers forward secrecy, which prevents attackers from being able to use a key to unencrypt data that has already been transmitted over the air.

> **TIP** The personal mode of any WPA version is usually easy to deploy in a small environment or with clients that are embedded in certain devices because a simple text key string is all that is needed to authenticate the clients. Be aware that every device using the WLAN must be configured with an identical pre-shared key, unless PSK with Identity Services Engine (ISE) is used. If you ever need to update or change the key, you must touch every device to do so. In addition, the pre-shared key should remain a well-kept secret; you should never divulge the pre-shared key to any unauthorized person. To maximize security, you should use the highest WPA version available on the WLCs, APs, and client devices in your network.

You can configure WPA2 or WPA3 personal mode and the pre-shared key in one step. Navigate to Configure > Tags & Profiles > WLANs and select **Add** or select an existing WLAN to edit. Make sure that the parameters on the General tab are set appropriately.

Next, select the **Security > Layer 2** tabs. In the Layer 2 Security Mode drop-down menu, select the appropriate WPA version for the WLAN. In Figure 20-4, WPA+WPA2 has been selected for the WLAN named "devices". Under WPA+WPA2 Parameters, the WPA version has been narrowed to only WPA2 by unchecking the box next to WPA Policy and checking both WPA2 Policy and WPA2 Encryption AES.

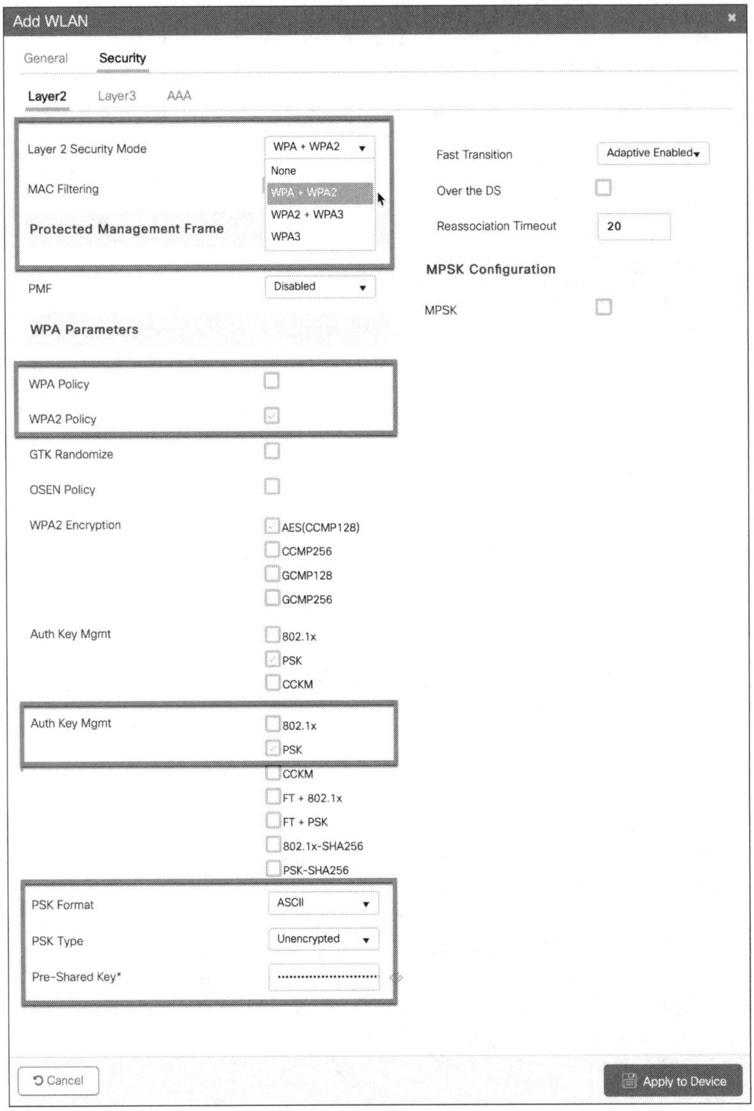

Figure 20-4 *Selecting the WPA2 Personal Security Suite for a WLAN*

For WPA2 personal mode, look under the Auth Key Mgmt section and check only the box next to PSK. You should then enter the pre-shared key string in the box next to Pre-Shared Key. In Figure 20-4, an ASCII text string has been entered. Be sure to click the **Apply to Device** button to apply the WLAN changes you have made.

TIP The controller allows you to enable both WPA and WPA2 check boxes. You should do that only if you have legacy clients that require WPA support and are mixed in with newer WPA2 clients. Be aware that the WLAN will only be as secure as the weakest security suite you configure on it. Ideally, you should use WPA2 or WPA3 with AES/CCMP and try to avoid any other hybrid mode. Hybrid modes such as WPA with AES and WPA2 with TKIP can cause compatibility issues; in addition, they have been deprecated.

You can verify the WLAN and its security settings from the list of WLANs under Configuration > Tags & Policies > WLANs, as shown in Figure 20-5. The Security column for the "devices" WLAN is shown as [WPA2][PSK][AES]. You can also verify that the WLAN status is enabled and active.

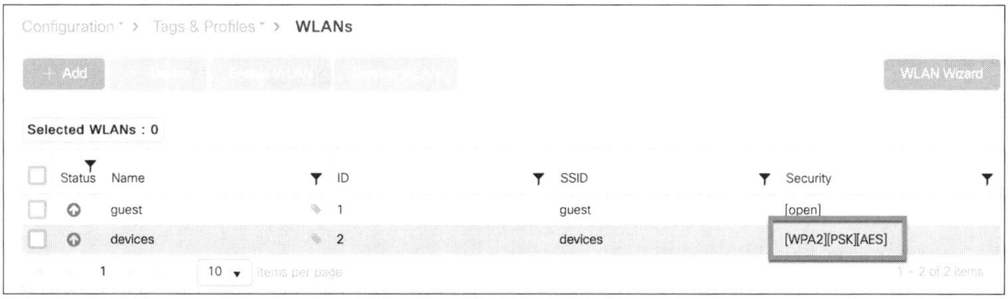

Figure 20-5 *Verifying PSK Authentication from the List of WLANs*

Authenticating with EAP

Client authentication generally involves some sort of challenge, a response, and then a decision to grant access. Behind the scenes, it can also involve an exchange of session or encryption keys, in addition to other parameters needed for client access. Each authentication method might have unique requirements as a unique way to pass information between the client and the AP.

Rather than build additional authentication methods into the 802.11 standard, **Extensible Authentication Protocol (EAP)** offers a more flexible and scalable authentication framework. As its name implies, EAP is extensible and does not consist of any one authentication method. Instead, EAP defines a set of common functions that actual authentication methods can use to authenticate users.

EAP has another interesting quality: It can integrate with the IEEE 802.1x port-based access control standard. When 802.1x is enabled, it limits access to a network medium until a client authenticates. This means that a wireless client might be able to associate with an AP but will not be able to pass data to any other part of the network until it successfully authenticates.

With Open Authentication and PSK authentication, wireless clients are authenticated locally at the AP without further intervention. The scenario changes with 802.1x; the client uses Open Authentication to associate with the AP, and then the actual client authentication process occurs at a dedicated authentication server. Figure 20-6 shows the three-party 802.1x arrangement, which consists of the following entities:

Key Topic

- **Supplicant:** The client device that is requesting access
- **Authenticator:** The network device that provides access to the network (usually a wireless LAN controller [WLC])
- **Authentication server (AS):** The device that takes user or client credentials and permits or denies network access based on a user database and policies (usually a **RADIUS server**)

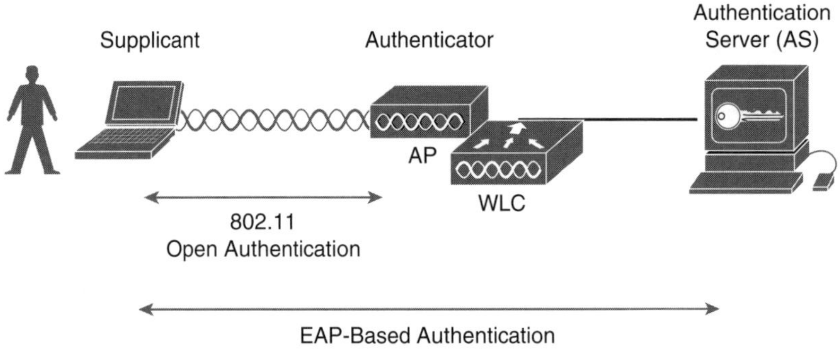

Figure 20-6 *802.1x Client Authentication Roles*

The controller becomes a middleman in the client authentication process, controlling user access with 802.1x and communicating with the authentication server using the EAP framework. For wired and wireless networks, this process uses EAP over LAN (EAPOL).

After the client is successfully authenticated, the over-the-air connection between the client and AP must be encrypted and protected. The two must build a set of encryption keys in a hierarchical fashion, beginning with a Pairwise Master Key (PMK) and a Groupwise Master Key (GMK) that get generated and distributed during the EAP authentication. Pairwise keys are used to protect unicast traffic across the air, whereas Groupwise keys are used to protect broadcast and multicast traffic.

> **NOTE** You might be wondering how WLANs using PSK are secured, because EAP is not used at all. In that case, the PSK itself is already known to both the client and the AP, so the PMK is derived from it.

Following that, the client and AP take part in a four-way EAPOL handshake to exchange the rest of the dynamic encryption key information. In a nutshell, the PMK is used to derive a Pairwise Transient Key (PTK), which is used to secure unicast traffic. The PTK is also used with the GMK to derive a Groupwise Transient Key (GTK) that is used to secure broadcast and multicast traffic.

Figure 20-7 illustrates the EAPOL handshake process. Notice the back-and-forth message exchange that begins with the AP and ends with the client, and also how the encryption keys are derived and installed along the way.

Key Topic

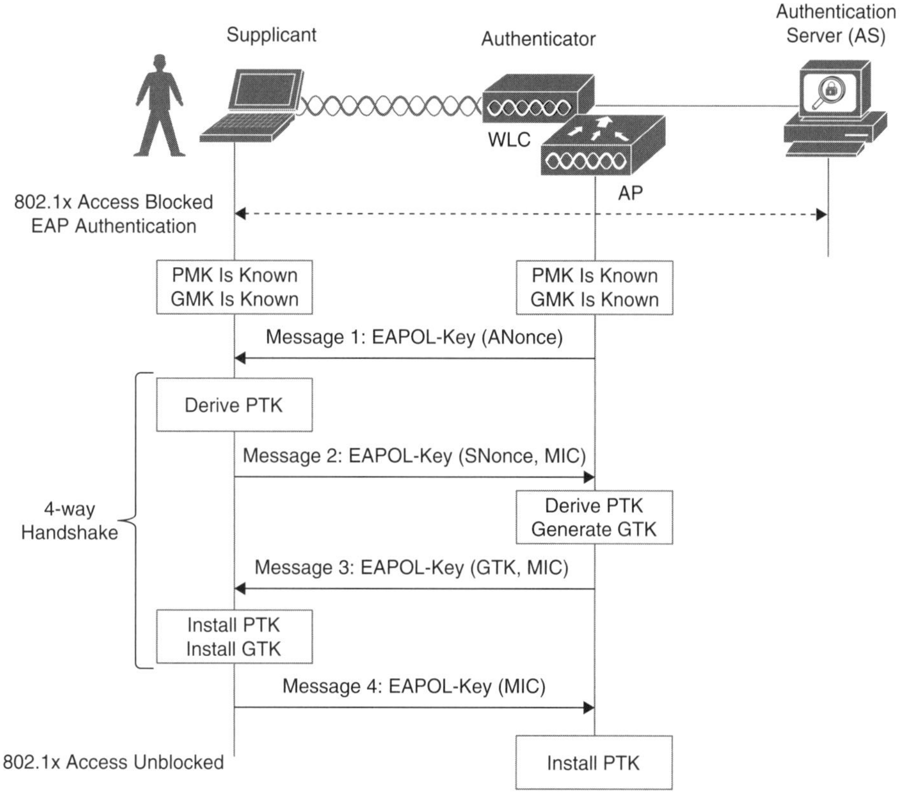

Figure 20-7 *Message Exchange During the Four-Way EAPOL Handshake*

The first two messages in the four-way handshake involve the AP and client exchanging enough information to derive a PTK. The last two messages involve exchanging the GTK that the AP generates and the client acknowledges. If all four messages are successful, the client's association can be protected and the 802.1x process unblocks wireless access for the client to use.

To use EAP-based authentication and 802.1x, you should leverage the enterprise modes of WPA, WPA2, and WPA3. (As always, you should use the highest WPA version that is supported on your WLCs, APs, and wireless clients.) The enterprise mode supports many EAP methods, such as LEAP, EAP-FAST, PEAP, EAP-TLS, EAP-TTLS, and EAP-SIM, but you do not have to configure any specific method on a WLC. Instead, specific EAP methods must be configured on the authentication server and supported on the wireless client devices. Remember that the WLC acts as the EAP middleman between the clients and the AS.

Cisco WLCs can use either external RADIUS servers located somewhere on the wired network or a local EAP server located on the WLC. The following sections discuss configuration tasks for each scenario.

20

Configuring EAP-Based Authentication with External RADIUS Servers

You should begin by configuring one or more external RADIUS servers on the controller. Navigate to Configuration > Security > AAA and select the **Servers/Groups** tab. Click the **Add** button to define a new server or select an existing server definition to edit.

In Figure 20-8, a new RADIUS server is being defined. Enter the server's name and IP address, along with the shared secret key that the controller will use to communicate with the server. Make sure that the RADIUS port number is correct; if it isn't, you can enter a different port number.

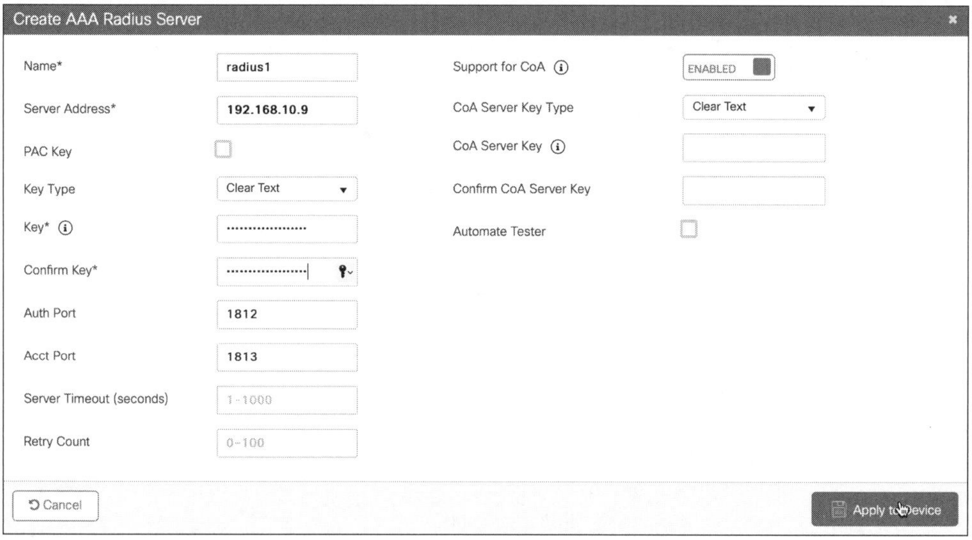

Figure 20-8 *Defining a RADIUS Server for WPA2 Enterprise Authentication*

Next, navigate to Configuration > Security > AAA and select the **AAA Method List** tab to define the order that various authentication and authorization methods will be used. You can select the "default" list or click the **Add** button to define a new one. In the Type drop-down menu, select **dot1x** to use external RADIUS servers. Then you define the order of server groups to use during authentication. Under Available Server Groups, select **radius** and select the **>** button to add radius to the Assigned Server Groups list. In Figure 20-9, a new method list named myRadius is being configured. Click the **Apply to Device** button to commit the change.

Next, you need to enable 802.1x authentication on the WLAN. Navigate to Configuration > Tags & Policies > WLANs and click **Add** to add a new WLAN. As an example, configure the WLAN security to use WPA2 Enterprise. Under the Layer 2 tab, select **WPA+WPA2** and make sure that WPA2 Policy is checked and WPA Policy is not. Beside WPA2 Encryption, check the box next to AES (CCMP128) to use the most robust encryption. Select **802.1x** under the Auth Key Mgmt section to enable the enterprise mode. Make sure that PSK is not checked so that personal mode will remain disabled. Figure 20-10 illustrates the settings that are needed on the WLAN named staff_eap.

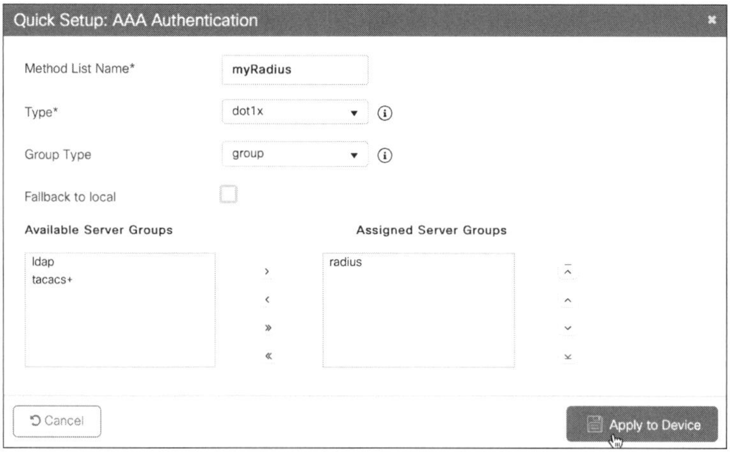

Figure 20-9 *Defining an AAA Authentication Group List*

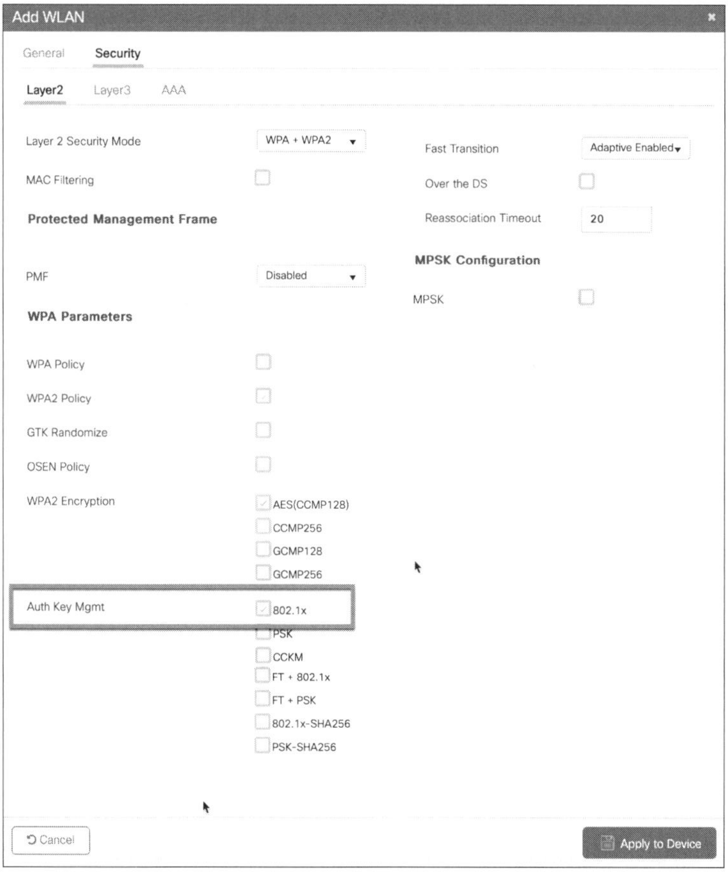

Figure 20-10 *Enabling WPA2 Enterprise Mode with 802.1x Authentication*

Next, you should select the **Security > AAA** tab and select the desired authentication group list in the Authentication List drop-down menu. In Figure 20-11, the group myRadius is selected. Click the **Apply to Device** button to apply the changes to the WLAN.

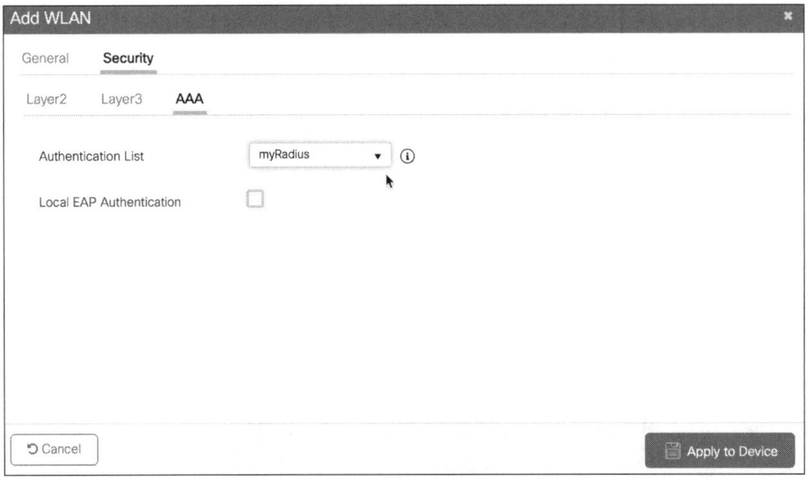

Figure 20-11 *Selecting the Authentication Group to Authenticate Clients in the WLAN*

> **TIP** As you worked through the WPA2 enterprise configuration, did you notice that you never saw an option to use a specific authentication method, like PEAP or EAP-TLS? The controller only has to know that 802.1x will be in use. The actual authentication methods are configured on the RADIUS server. The client's supplicant must also be configured to match what the server is using.

Verifying EAP-Based Authentication Configuration

You can verify the WLAN and its security settings from the list of WLANs by selecting **Configuration > Tags & Profiles > WLANs**, as shown in Figure 20-12. For EAP-based authentication, the Security column should display [802.1X], as the "staff_eap" WLAN shows. You can also verify that the WLAN status is enabled and active.

Figure 20-12 *Verifying EAP Authentication on a WLAN*

Authenticating with WebAuth

You might have noticed that none of the authentication methods described so far involve direct interaction with the end user. For example, Open Authentication requires nothing from the user or the device. PSK authentication involves a pre-shared key that is exchanged between the device and the AP. EAP-based authentication can present the end user with a prompt for credentials—but only if the EAP method supports it. Even so, the end user does not see any information about the network or its provider.

Web Authentication (WebAuth) is different because it presents the end user with content to read and interact with before granting access to the network. For example, it can present an acceptable use policy (AUP) that the user must accept before accessing the network. It can also prompt for user credentials, display information about the enterprise, and so on. Naturally, the user must open a web browser to see the WebAuth content. WebAuth can be used as an additional layer in concert with Open Authentication, PSK-based authentication, and EAP-based authentication.

Web Authentication can be handled locally on the WLC for smaller environments through Local Web Authentication (LWA). You can configure LWA in the following modes:

Key Topic

- LWA with an internal database on the WLC
- LWA with an external database on a RADIUS or LDAP server
- LWA with an external redirect after authentication
- LWA with an external splash page redirect, using an internal database on the WLC
- LWA with passthrough, requiring user acknowledgment

When there are many controllers providing Web Authentication, it makes sense to use LWA with an external database on a RADIUS server, such as ISE, and keep the user database centralized. The next logical progression is to move the Web Authentication page onto the central server too. This is called Central Web Authentication (CWA).

To configure WebAuth on a WLAN, first navigate to Configuration > Security > WebAuth and select the **Add** button to create a parameter map that contains the global and custom parameters that WebAuth will use. In Figure 20-13, a WebAuth parameter map named MyWebAuth has been created.

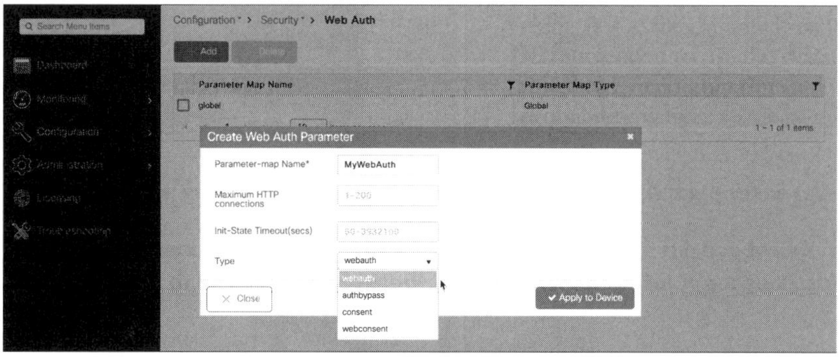

Figure 20-13 *Creating a WebAuth Parameter Map*

After selecting the **Apply to Device** button, you can select the newly created parameter map from the list and edit any of its parameters. In Figure 20-14, a WebAuth banner has been configured. You can also select the **Advanced** tab to define any WebAuth redirects and customized login success and failure pages.

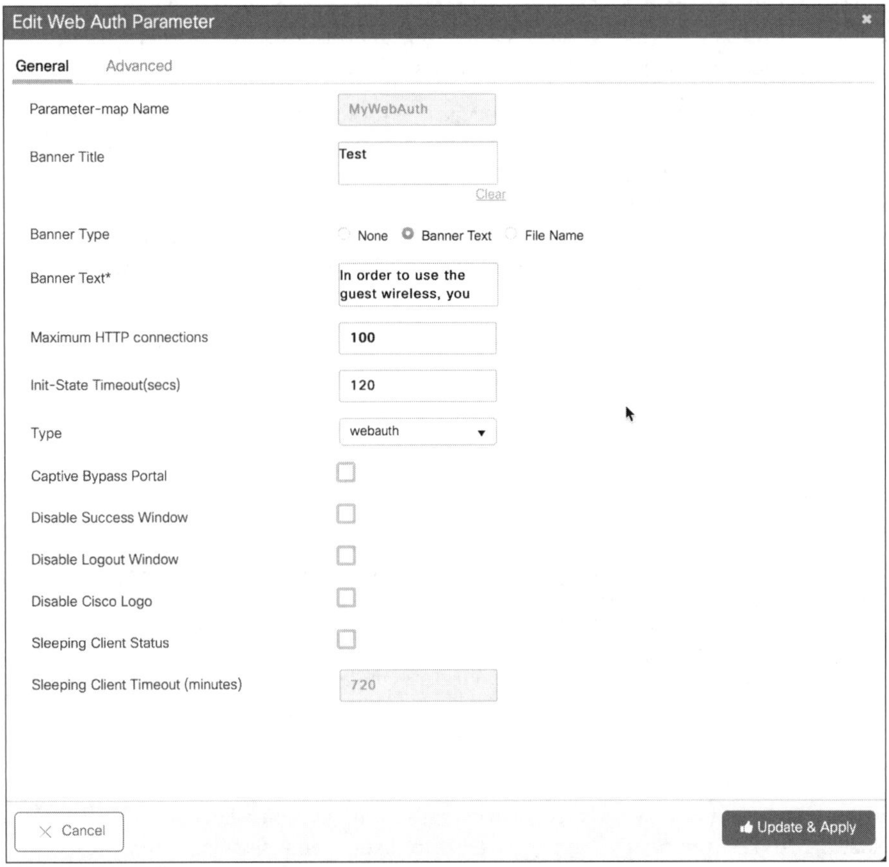

Figure 20-14 *Defining More WebAuth Parameters*

Next, navigate to Configuration > Security > AAA and define an authentication method list that WebAuth will use by selecting the **AAA Method List** tab. In this case, the method list Type must be set to "Login" to interact with the end user attempting to authenticate. In Figure 20-15, a method list named webauth has been created, with Type "login," and only radius added to the Assigned Server Groups.

Finally, configure WebAuth for a WLAN by navigating to Configuration > Tags & Profiles > WLANs. Name the WLAN and SSID in the General tab; then select the **Security** tab and define the Layer 2 parameters. Select the **Layer3** tab to configure the WebAuth operation, as shown in Figure 20-16. Select the appropriate WebAuth parameter map and authentication list too.

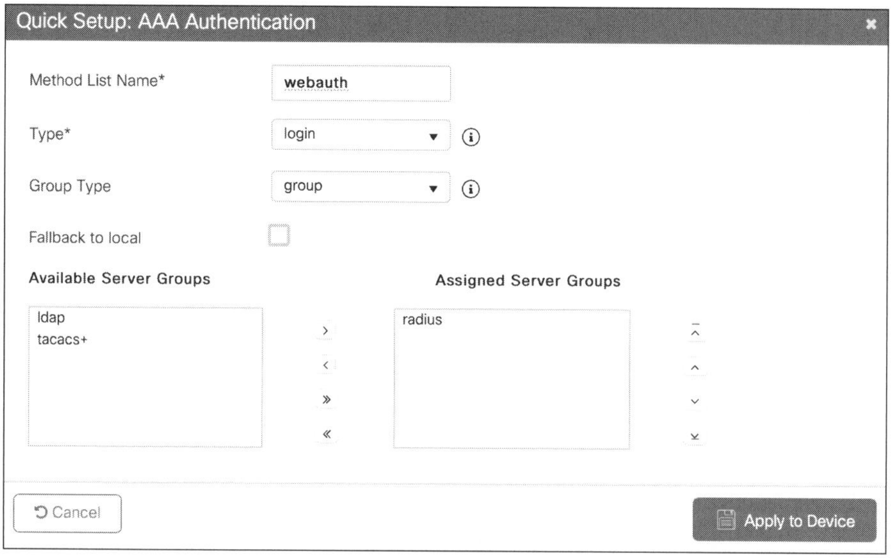

Figure 20-15 *Defining a Login Authentication Method List for WebAuth*

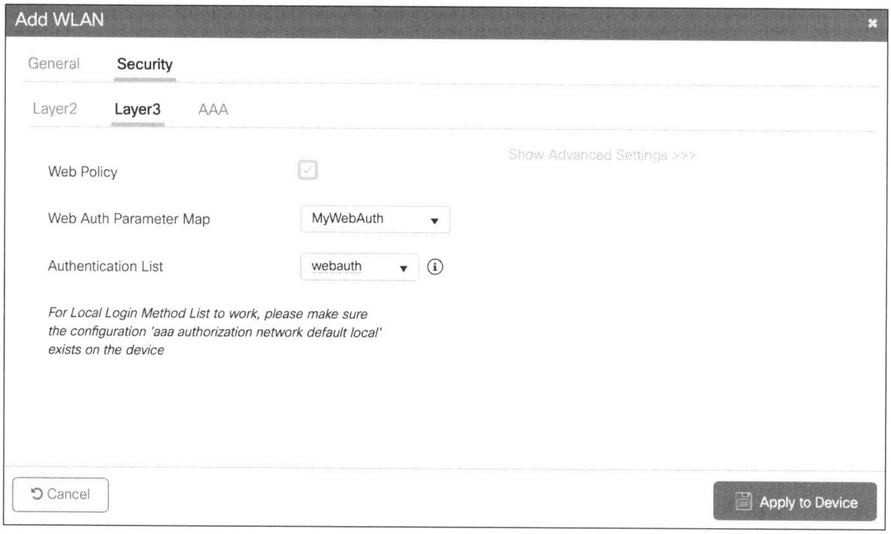

Figure 20-16 *Enabling WebAuth for WLAN Layer 3 Security*

Don't forget to complete the WLAN creation process by linking the WLAN profile to a policy profile via a policy tag and then apply the tag to some APs.

You can verify the WebAuth security settings from the list of WLANs by selecting **Configuration > Tags & Profiles > WLANs.** In Figure 20-17, the WLAN named Guest_webauth is shown with "[Web_Auth]" in the Security column.

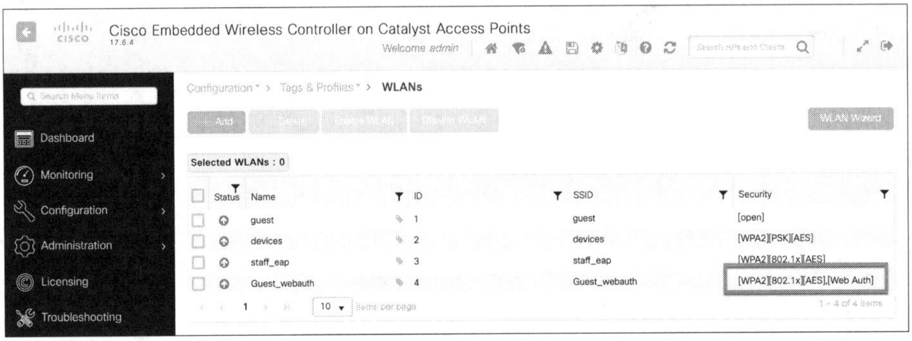

Figure 20-17 *Verifying WebAuth Authentication on a WLAN*

Exam Preparation Tasks

You have a couple of choices for exam preparation: the exercises here, Chapter 30, "Final Preparation," and the exam simulation questions in the Pearson Test Prep Software Online.

Review All Key Topics

Review the most important topics in this chapter, noted with the Key Topic icon in the outer margin of the page. Table 20-2 lists these key topics and the page number on which each is found.

Key Topic

Table 20-2 Key Topics for Chapter 20

Key Topic Element	Description	Page Number
Paragraph	WPA personal mode for PSK	595
List	802.1x roles	598
Figure 20-7	Message Exchange During the Four-Way EAPOL Handshake	599
List	WebAuth modes	603

Complete Tables and Lists from Memory

There are no memory tables in this chapter.

Define Key Terms

Define the following key terms from this chapter and check your answers in the Glossary:

802.1x, authentication server (AS), authenticator, Extensible Authentication Protocol (EAP), Open Authentication, personal mode, RADIUS server, supplicant, Wi-Fi Protected Access (WPA), WPA Version 2 (WPA2), WPA Version 3 (WPA3)

CHAPTER 21

Troubleshooting Wireless Connectivity

This chapter covers the following subjects:

- **Troubleshooting Client Connectivity from the WLC:** This section discusses how to use a wireless LAN controller as a troubleshooting tool to diagnose problems with wireless clients.
- **Troubleshooting Connectivity Problems at the AP:** This section discusses how to diagnose problems between a wireless LAN controller and an AP that might affect wireless client connectivity.

As a CCNP network professional, you will be expected to perform some basic troubleshooting work when wireless problems arise. The exam blueprint focuses on configuration of Cisco wireless LAN controllers (WLCs), as well as problems with wireless client connectivity. This chapter helps you get some perspective on wireless problems, develop a troubleshooting strategy, and become comfortable using the tools at your disposal.

"Do I Know This Already?" Quiz

The "Do I Know This Already?" quiz enables you to assess whether you should read the entire chapter. If you miss no more than one of these self-assessment questions, you might want to move ahead to the "Exam Preparation Tasks" section. Table 21-1 lists the major headings in this chapter and the "Do I Know This Already?" quiz questions covering the material in those headings so you can assess your knowledge of these specific areas. The answers to the "Do I Know This Already?" quiz appear in Appendix A, "Answers to the 'Do I Know This Already?' Questions."

Table 21-1 "Do I Know This Already?" Foundation Topics Section-to-Question Mapping

Foundation Topics Section	Questions
Troubleshooting Client Connectivity from the WLC	1–7
Troubleshooting Connectivity Problems at the AP	6–8

1. Which of the following is considered to be the best first step in troubleshooting a wireless problem?
   a. Reboot the wireless LAN controller.
   b. Gather more information to find the scope of the problem.
   c. Access the WLC and search for clients in the error logs.
   d. Access the WLC and look for alarms; if none are found, close the incident ticket.

2. To troubleshoot a single wireless client, which one of the following bits of information would be most helpful in finding the client device in a wireless LAN controller?
   a. The Ethernet MAC address of the client device
   b. The end user's name
   c. The wireless MAC address of the client device
   d. The name of the application having issues
3. Suppose an end user tried unsuccessfully to join a wireless network several minutes ago. The user is certain that she chose the correct SSID to join. Which one of the following things should you do to determine the root cause of her problem?
   a. Ask the user to reboot her device and keep trying to connect.
   b. Ask the user to move to a different floor in the building and try again.
   c. Disable the user's WLAN and SSID; then reenable it and ask her to try again.
   d. Run a Radioactive Trace on the user's MAC address and analyze the output.
4. Suppose that you have a large wireless network with several controllers, many APs, a RADIUS server, and a syslog server. A user has reported connectivity problems in a specific building location but has provided no details about the AP or controller he tried to join. Which one of the following is the most efficient troubleshooting method you can use to find information about the client?
   a. Go to the client's location and use your own computer to associate with the network and then find out which AP and controller you are using.
   b. Access each WLC and check the status of every AP that is joined to it.
   c. Search for the client's MAC address on each controller.
   d. Search for the client's MAC address on each AP.
5. Suppose that you have just received news that no users can connect with a newly installed AP. Which of the following bits of information would be important to verify when you search for the AP's name from the WLC? (Choose all that apply.)
   a. The AP has a valid IP address.
   b. The AP is found.
   c. The AP has valid channel numbers listed for the 2.4 and 5 GHz bands.
   d. The AP has a valid MAC address.
6. Suppose you search for an AP on a WLC and notice that the SNR is 5 on the 2.4 GHz band. Which of the following statements is correct?
   a. The SNR is at a very low level, which is good for wireless performance.
   b. The SNR is at a very high level, which is good for wireless performance.
   c. The SNR is at a very low level, which is bad for wireless performance.
   d. The SNR is at a very high level, which is bad for wireless performance.

7. Suppose you access a WLC and search for the name of a specific AP for which users have complained about problems. When you look at the 5 GHz information about the AP, you notice that it is using channel 60 and has 5 dBm transmit power, 6 clients, 45 dBm SNR level, and 85% channel utilization. Which of the following conclusions would be most accurate?
   a. The SNR is too high, which is causing poor performance.
   b. The SNR level is too low, which is causing poor performance.
   c. The channel utilization is too low, which is keeping clients from using the channel.
   d. The channel utilization is too high, which is keeping clients from using the channel.
8. Which one of the following describes the correct purpose of a Radioactive Trace?
   a. The WLC traces the roaming path of a user as that user traveled from AP to AP.
   b. The WLC collects event logs triggered by a specific MAC address for a period of time.
   c. The WLC performs a trace of its CPU activity and memory usage over time.
   d. The WLC traces the radio activity on each AP that is joined to it over time.

Foundation Topics

When one or more network users report that they are having problems, your first course of action should be to gather more information. Begin with a broad perspective and then ask pointed questions to narrow the scope of possible causes. You do not want to panic or waste time chasing irrelevant things. Instead, ask questions and try to notice patterns or similarities in the answers you receive.

For example, if you get reports from many people in the same area, perhaps an AP is misconfigured or malfunctioning. Reports from many areas or from a single service set identifier (SSID) may indicate problems with a controller configuration. However, if you receive a report of only one wireless user having problems, it might not make sense to spend time troubleshooting a controller, where many users are supported. Instead, you should focus on that one user's client device and its interaction with an AP.

As you prepare to troubleshoot a single wireless client, think about all the things a client needs to join and use the network. Figure 21-1 illustrates the following conditions that must be met for a successful association:

- The client is within RF range of an AP and asks to associate.
- The client authenticates.
- The client requests and receives an IP address.

Key Topic

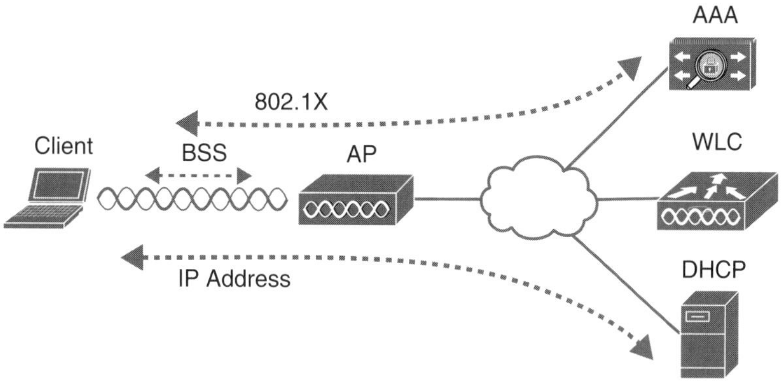

Figure 21-1 *Conditions for a Successful Wireless Association*

Try to gather information from the end user to see what the client is experiencing. "I cannot connect" or "The Wi-Fi is down" might actually mean that the user's device cannot associate, cannot get an IP address, or cannot authenticate. A closer inspection of the device might reveal more clues. Therefore, at a minimum, you need the wireless adapter MAC address from the client device, as well as its physical location. The end user might try to tell you about a specific AP that is in the room or within view. Record that information too, but remember that the *client device* selects which AP it wants to use—not the human user. The device may well be using a completely different AP.

The sections in this chapter start by focusing on a single client device and then broaden outward, where multiple clients might be affected.

Troubleshooting Client Connectivity from the WLC

Most of your time managing and monitoring a wireless network will be spent in the wireless LAN controller GUI. As a wireless client probes and attempts to associate with an AP, it is essentially communicating with the controller. You can access a wealth of troubleshooting information from the controller, as long as you know the client's MAC address.

Cisco WLCs based on IOS XE, such as the Catalyst 9800, have a GUI presentation where you can access monitoring, configuration, administration, licensing, and troubleshooting functions. When you open a browser to the WLC management address, you see the default screen that is shown in Figure 21-2. The default screen displays network summary dashboard information on the right portion and a menu of functions on the left.

If you know a specific wireless client's MAC address, you can enter it into the search bar at the top right of the screen. For example, in Figure 21-3, 38c9.86ed.476e is the target of the search. Because that MAC address is known to the controller, a "Client MAC Result" match is shown below the search bar, as displayed in Figure 21-4. You can select the client's MAC address to display detailed information about it.

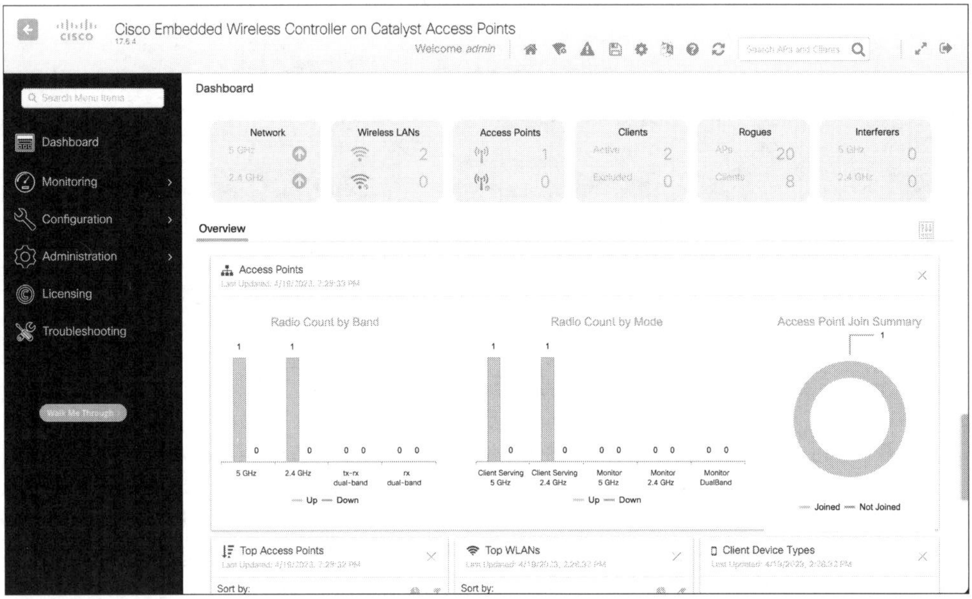

Figure 21-2 *The Initial Default WLC Display*

Figure 21-3 *Searching for a Client in the WLC GUI*

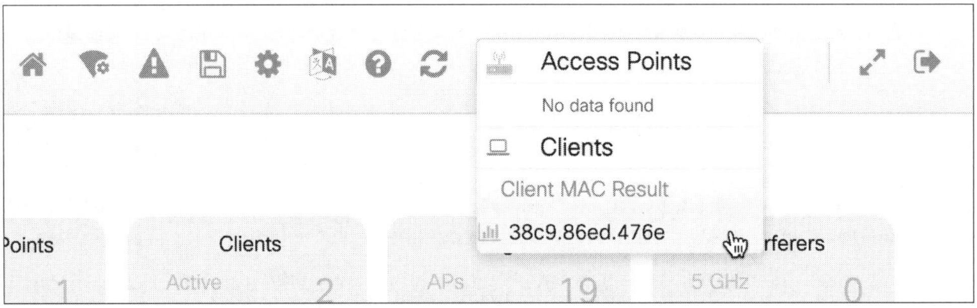

Figure 21-4 *A Client Search Shows One Match*

The resulting details about the client are displayed in the Client 360 View screen, shown in Figure 21-5. From this output, you can see many details about the client device listed in the left portion of the screen, and you can see connectivity and application information displayed on the right.

Answers to the "Do I Know This Already?" quiz:

1 B **2** C **3** D **4** C **5** A, B, C **6** C **7** D **8** B

Key Topic

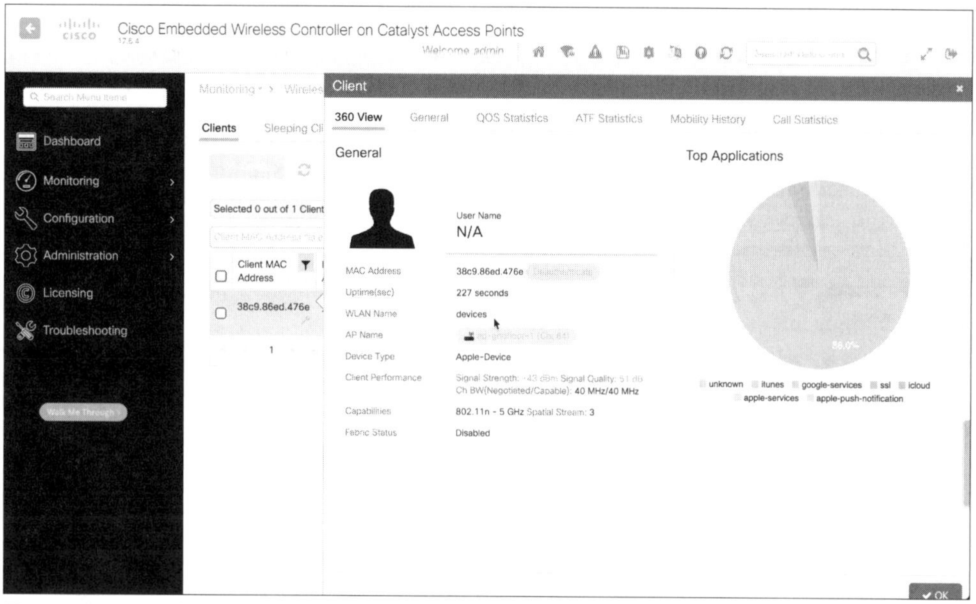

Figure 21-5 *Client 360 View Results*

Checking the Client's Association and Signal Status

In the 360 View screen, you can check the wireless client's username (if it is known), wireless MAC address, wireless connection uptime, and the WLAN name (SSID) used. In Figure 21-5, the username is not known because the client did not authenticate itself with a username. The client has associated and authenticated to the SSID named "devices". The WLC also displays the AP name where the client is associated, along with the channel. The signal strength at which each AP received the client is also shown, along with the signal quality (signal-to-noise ratio) and the channel width. You can also see the client device type (Apple-Device) and its wireless capabilities (802.11n with three spatial streams).

For troubleshooting purposes, you can find some important information next to Client Performance. In Figure 21-5, the client's signal has been received at −43 dBm, which is sufficiently strong. The signal quality, or signal-to-noise ratio (SNR), is 51 dB, which is very good. The client's current channel width is 40 MHz. Remember that the SNR measures how many decibels the signal is above the noise floor. The SNR can be a low value for lower data rates to be successfully used, but it must be greater to leverage higher data rates.

Suppose that the same client moves to a different location and then complains of poor performance. By searching for the client's MAC address on the WLC again, you see some new information. This time, the AP is receiving the client's signal strength at –75 dBm and the SNR at 18 dB—both rather low values, most likely causing the client to use a low data rate. It is safe to assume that the client has moved too far away from the AP where it is associated, causing the signal strength to become too low to support faster performance. This might indicate that you need to place a new AP in that area to boost the RF coverage. Or it could indicate a client device that is not roaming soon enough to a new AP with a stronger signal.

Checking the Client Properties

Under the **General > Client Properties** tab, as shown in Figure 21-6, you can verify the client's MAC address, IP address, policy profile in use on the AP, the WLAN/SSID being used, the AP's BSSID, client's connection uptime, and session timeout. Toward the bottom, you can verify the current transmit rate set or modulation and coding scheme (MCS) being used, along with many other parameters like QoS and the client's mobility or roaming activity.

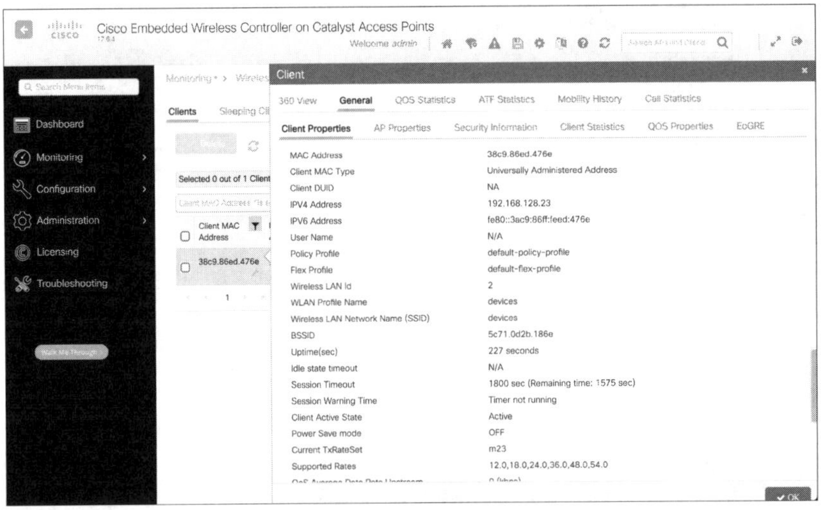

Figure 21-6 *Displaying the Client Properties*

Checking the AP Properties

By selecting the **General > AP Properties** tab, you can verify information about the client's AP, as shown in Figure 21-7. You can quickly learn the AP's wired MAC address and name, along with the client's current status (associated or not), the 802.11 protocol in use, and the current channel number.

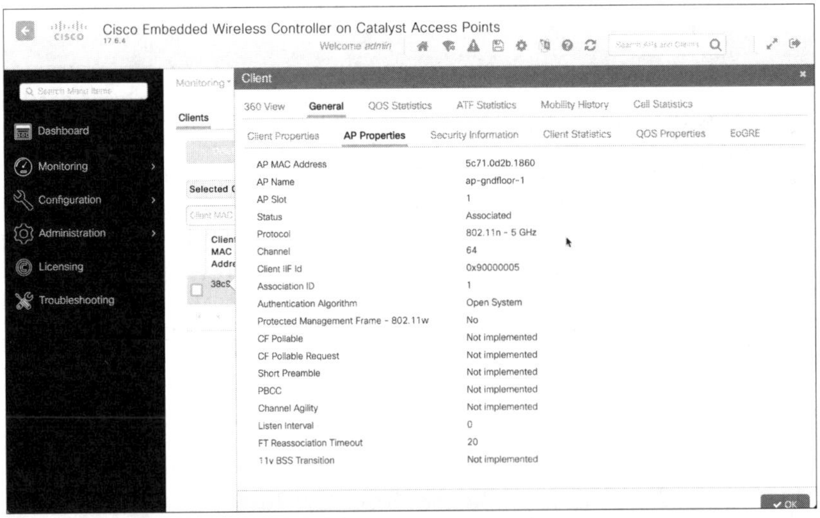

Figure 21-7 *Displaying the Client's AP Properties*

Checking the Client Security

Select the **General > Security Information** tab to display parameters related to the client's wireless security. In Figure 21-8, the client is using WPA2, CCMP (AES), pre-shared key, no EAP, and a 1800-second session timeout.

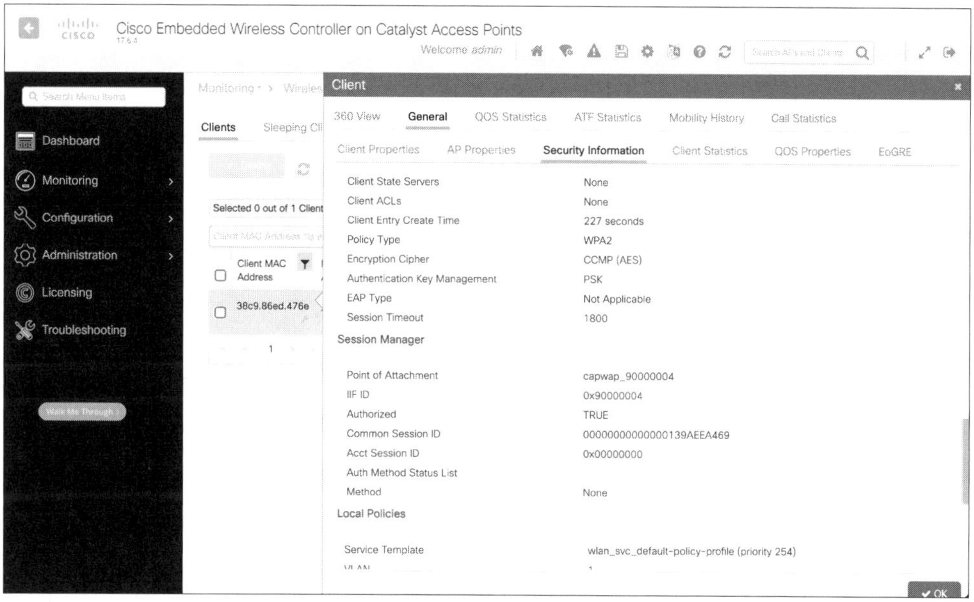

Figure 21-8 *Displaying the Client's Wireless Security Properties*

Troubleshooting the Client

Sometimes a wireless client might be having problems connecting or communicating, but the root cause won't be obvious. In that case, you can collect detailed Radioactive Trace troubleshooting information about the client from the WLC's perspective.

There are two ways to navigate there: Select the **Troubleshooting > Radioactive Trace** button on the main default WLC screen, or select the small wrench icon underneath the client's MAC address on the Monitoring > Wireless > Clients page, as shown in Figure 21-9.

Key Topic

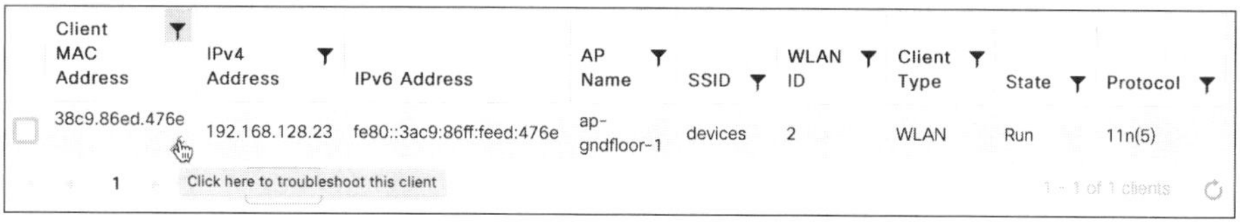

Figure 21-9 *Troubleshooting a Wireless Client*

Navigate to Troubleshooting > Radioactive Trace to access the troubleshooting controls, as shown in Figure 21-10. The client MAC address (38c9.86ed.476e) has already been populated. You can select the **Add** button to add more clients to the list so that troubleshooting information will be collected for them too.

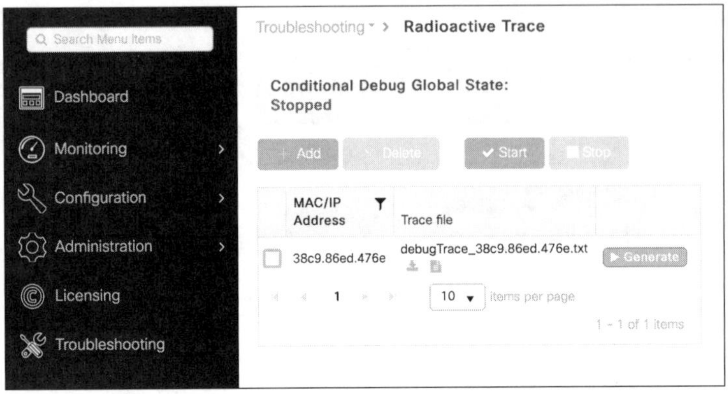

Figure 21-10 *Radioactive Trace Control Screen*

Select the **Start** button to begin collecting WLC logs involving the MAC addresses in the list. Let the Radioactive Trace run until you feel the client has had a chance to try to join the network again or experienced some event that needs further investigation. Select the **Stop** button to end the data collection; then select the green **Generate** button next to the client's MAC address to create a readable debug trace file. In a pop-up window, you will choose the time interval of logs to collect: the last 10 minutes, last 30 minutes, last one hour, or since the last WLC reboot. Check the Enable internal logs box to use the logs collected by the WLC.

After the debug trace file has been generated, two small blue icons will appear in the list next to the client's MAC address. You can select the icon with a downward arrow, as shown in Figure 21-11, to download the file to your local machine, or select the document icon to display the trace file contents in the bottom portion of the Radioactive Trace page.

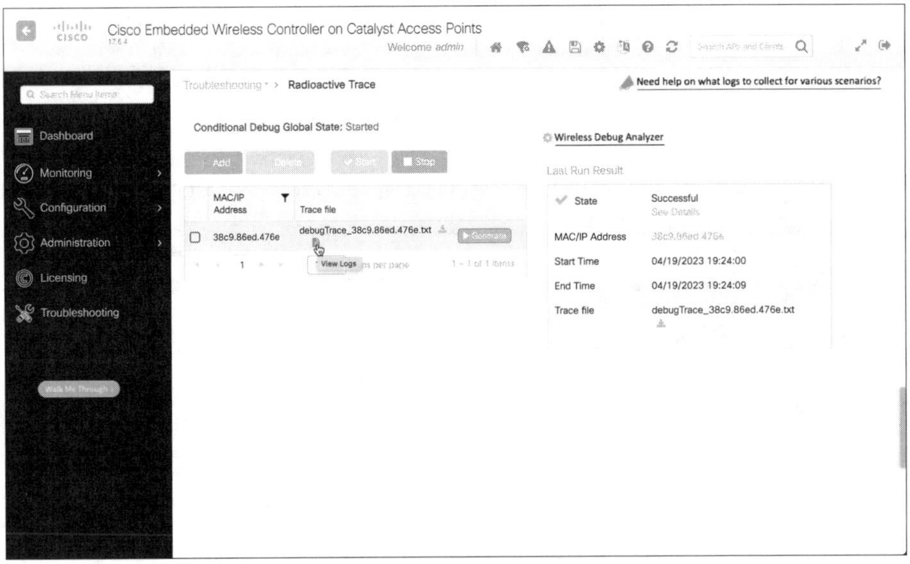

Figure 21-11 *Displaying a Radioactive Trace of a Client*

Troubleshooting Connectivity Problems at the AP

In cases where you get reports from multiple users who are all having problems in the same general area, you might need to focus your efforts on an AP. The problem could be as simple as a defective radio, where no clients are receiving a signal. In that case, you might have to go onsite to confirm that the transmitter is not working correctly.

Otherwise, the split-MAC architecture creates several different points where you can troubleshoot. Successfully operating the lightweight AP and providing a working BSS require the following:

- The AP must have connectivity to its access layer switch.
- The AP must have connectivity to its WLC, unless it is operating in FlexConnect mode.

First, verify the connectivity between an AP and a controller. Usually, you do this when a new AP is installed, to make sure it is able to discover and join a controller before clients arrive and try to use the wireless network. You can also do this at any time as a quick check of the AP's health.

The easiest approach is to simply look for the AP in the list of live APs that have joined the controller. Enter the AP's name in the search bar. If the search reveals a live AP that is joined to the controller, you can select it to display some basic AP statistics. Figure 21-12 shows the results from searching for "ap-gndfloor" in the AP's name. From this information, you can verify that AP "ap-gndfloor-1" is up (Admin status is a green checkmark) and joined to the controller. It is model C9115AXI-B, is running as an embedded wireless controller (EWC), and has a valid IP address.

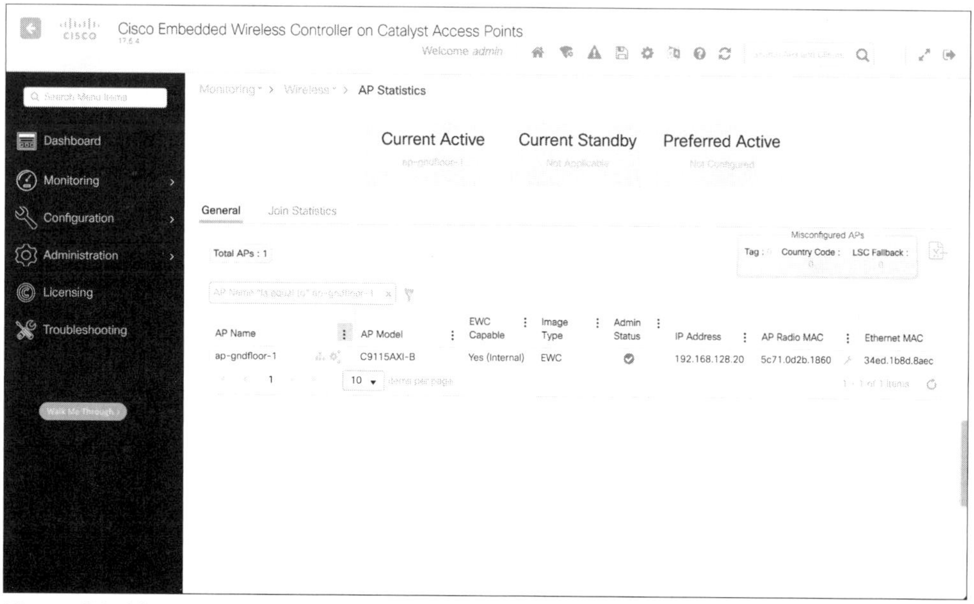

Figure 21-12 *AP Statistics After an AP Name Search*

You can select the **Join Statistics** tab to display some basic information about the last known events when the AP tried to join or leave the controller. In Figure 21-13, the AP's status is up, and there is no record of the reason it last rebooted. However, the AP did disconnect from the controller due to a tag being modified. That is usually expected behavior because a change in an AP's tag causes it to refresh its connection to the controller or cycle its radios or WLANs to commit changes to its operation.

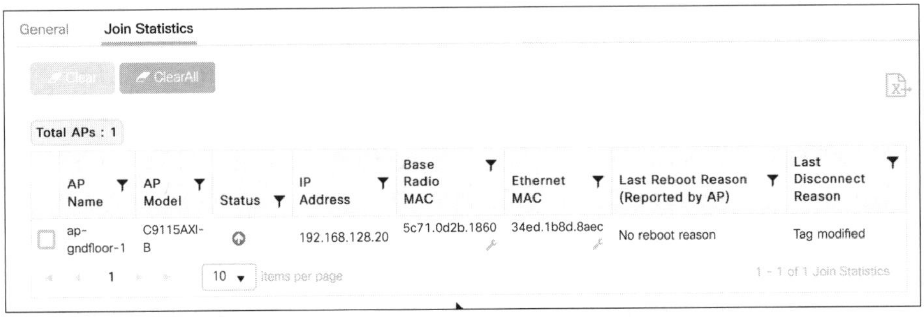

Figure 21-13 *Displaying AP Join Statistics*

To see more detailed information about the AP, select its name from the AP Name column of the AP Statistics page. The top portion of the 360 View tab displays the AP's location, IP address, model, serial number, PoE status, and country code. You can also determine if the AP is capable of using WPA3, the VLAN tag number, software version, and connection uptime, as shown in Figure 21-14.

Key Topic

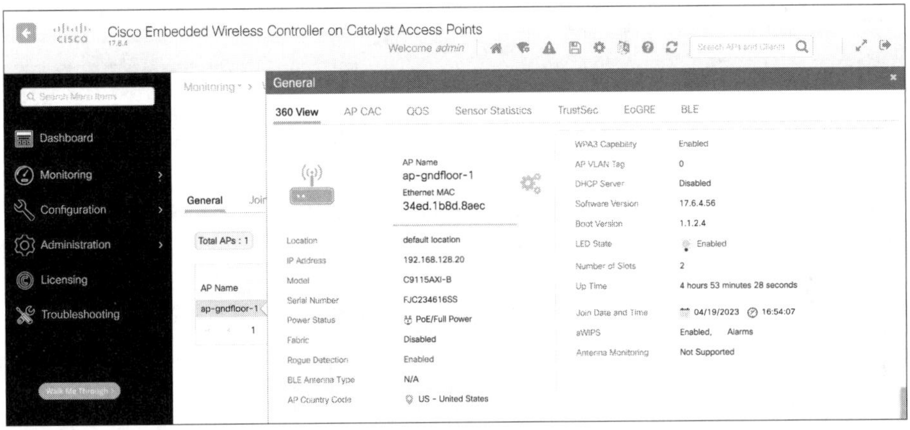

Figure 21-14 *Displaying the 360 View of an AP*

You can also scroll further down to display an operational summary of the AP's radios, as shown in Figure 21-15. From this information, you can verify that both of the AP's radios are enabled, the number of wireless clients currently connected to each, and which channel is being used. The transmit power level is shown, along with indicators of channel, transmit, and receive utilizations. If channel utilization values are high, you can assume that the channel is heavily used, probably slowing communication and making it difficult for wireless stations to have an opportunity to transmit.

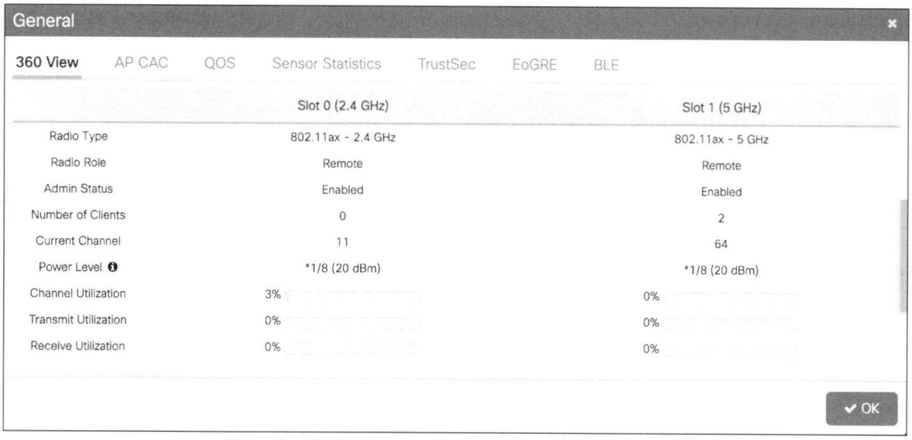

Figure 21-15 *Displaying the AP Radio Details in the 360 View*

Recall that each AP must be mapped to three tags, each mapping to one or more types of profiles. Sometimes you might have trouble remembering the profile and tag associations, especially if you have several of them configured to match unique requirements in various parts of your campus network. This information can be important when you're troubleshooting a problem that might be caused by unexpected or misconfigured profiles or tags.

Fortunately, the WLC offers a quick and easy way to view the entire profile and tag hierarchy that has been applied to an AP. You can display the AP's operational configuration by selecting the small hierarchy icon next to the AP's name, as shown in Figure 21-16.

Key Topic

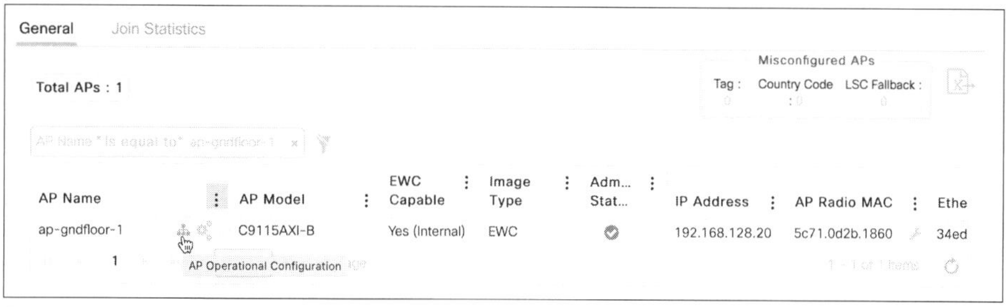

Figure 21-16 *Displaying AP Operational Configuration*

Figure 21-17 shows the corresponding configuration in hierarchical form. You can quickly verify that AP ap-gndfloor-1 is using the policy tag "my-policy-tag," the site tag "default-site-tag," and the RF tag "my-rf-tag."

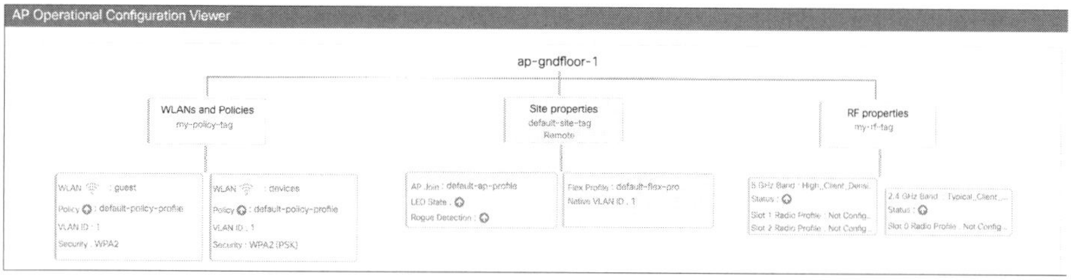

Figure 21-17 *Displaying a Hierarchical View of AP Configuration*

You can also see the individual profiles referenced by each tag and some basic operational information used by each profile.

Exam Preparation Tasks

You have a couple of choices for exam preparation: the exercises here, Chapter 30, "Final Preparation," and the exam simulation questions in the Pearson Test Prep Software Online.

Review All Key Topics

Review the most important topics in this chapter, noted with the Key Topic icon in the outer margin of the page. Table 21-2 lists these key topics and the page number on which each is found.

Key Topic

Table 21-2 Key Topics for Chapter 21

Key Topic Element	Description	Page Number
Figure 21-1	Conditions for a Successful Wireless Association	611
Figure 21-5	Client 360 View	613
Figure 21-9	Troubleshooting a Wireless Client	615
Figure 21-14	Displaying the 360 View of an AP	618
Figure 21-16	Displaying AP Operational Configuration	619

Complete Tables and Lists from Memory

There are no memory tables in this chapter.

Define Key Terms

There are no key terms in this chapter.

CHAPTER 22

Enterprise Network Architecture

This chapter covers the following subjects:

- **Hierarchical LAN Design Model:** This section describes the hierarchical network design, which improves performance, simplifies design, increases scalability, and reduces troubleshooting time.
- **High Availability Network Design:** This section describes high availability design guidelines as well as high availability technologies used as part of a network design to ensure business continuity.
- **Enterprise Network Architecture Options:** This section describes the different options available for deploying an enterprise campus architecture based on the hierarchical LAN design model.

Enterprise campus networks provide access to network services and resources to end users and endpoints spread over a single geographic location. Campus networks typically support many different kinds of endpoint connectivity for workers and guest users, such as laptops, PCs, mobile phones, IP phones, printers, and video conferencing systems.

A small campus network environment might span a single floor or a single building, while a larger campus network might span a large group of buildings spread over an extended geographic area. Large campus networks must have a core or backbone for interconnectivity to other networks, such as the campus end-user/endpoint access, the data center, the private cloud, the public cloud, the WAN, and the Internet edge. The largest enterprises might have multiple campus networks distributed worldwide, each providing both end-user access and core network connectivity.

An enterprise campus architecture is designed to meet the needs of organizations that range from a small single building or remote site to a large, multi-building location.

This chapter provides a high-level overview of the enterprise campus architectures that can be used to scale from a small environment (with just a few LAN switches) to a large campus-size network.

"Do I Know This Already?" Quiz

The "Do I Know This Already?" quiz enables you to assess whether you should read the entire chapter. If you miss no more than one of these self-assessment questions, you might want to move ahead to the "Exam Preparation Tasks" section. Table 22-1 lists the major headings in this chapter and the "Do I Know This Already?" quiz questions covering the material in those headings so you can assess your knowledge of these specific areas. The answers to the "Do I Know This Already?" quiz appear in Appendix A, "Answers to the 'Do I Know This Already?' Questions."

Table 22-1 "Do I Know This Already?" Foundation Topics Section-to-Question Mapping

Foundation Topics Section	Questions
Hierarchical LAN Design Model	1–3
High Availability Network Design	4–5
Enterprise Network Architecture Options	6–8

1. Which of the following best describe the hierarchical LAN design model? (Choose all that apply.)
   - a. It allows for easier troubleshooting.
   - b. It is highly scalable.
   - c. It provides a simplified design.
   - d. It offers improved performance.
   - e. It is the best design for modern data centers.
   - f. It allows for faster problem isolation.
2. The access layer is also commonly referred to as the _____.
   - a. endpoint layer
   - b. aggregation layer
   - c. end-user layer
   - d. network edge
3. What is the maximum number of distribution switches that can be deployed within a hierarchical LAN design building block?
   - a. Four
   - b. Two
   - c. Six
   - d. No limit
4. True or false: NSF can be enabled without enabling SSO.
   - a. True
   - b. False
5. Which of the following high availability technologies requires routing protocol extensions?
   - a. NSR
   - b. SSO/NSF
   - c. Graceful Restart (GR)
   - d. RNS
6. Which of the following enterprise network architectures is also known as the collapsed core?
   - a. Three-tier design
   - b. Simplified campus design
   - c. Two-tier design
   - d. Leaf–spine design

7. Which network blocks can provide access to cloud providers for end users? (Choose two.)
   a. WAN edge
   b. Internet edge
   c. Network services edge
   d. Data center
8. Which technologies are used to deploy a simplified campus design? (Choose all that apply.)
   a. Clustering technologies
   b. Stacking technologies
   c. Virtual Switching System (VSS)
   d. StackWise Virtual (SWV)
   e. Daisy-chaining

Foundation Topics

Hierarchical LAN Design Model

A hierarchical LAN design model divides the enterprise network architecture into modular layers. By breaking up the design into modular layers, you can have each layer to implement specific functions. These modular layers can be easily replicated throughout the network, which simplifies the network design and provides an easy way to scale the network as well as a consistent deployment method.

A hierarchical LAN design avoids the need for a flat and fully meshed network in which all nodes are interconnected. In fully meshed network architectures, network changes tend to affect a large number of systems. Hierarchical design provides fault containment by constraining the network changes to a subset of the network, which affects fewer systems and makes it easy to manage as well as improve resiliency. In a modular layer design, network components can be placed or taken out of service with little or no impact to the rest of the network; this facilitates troubleshooting, problem isolation, and network management.

The hierarchical LAN design divides networks or their modular blocks into the following three layers:

Key Topic

- **Access layer:** Gives endpoints and users direct access to the network.
- **Distribution layer:** Provides an aggregation point for the access layer and acts as a services and control boundary between the access layer and the core layer.
- **Core layer (also referred to as the backbone):** Provides connections between distribution layers for large environments.

Figure 22-1 illustrates a hierarchical LAN design using the three layers.

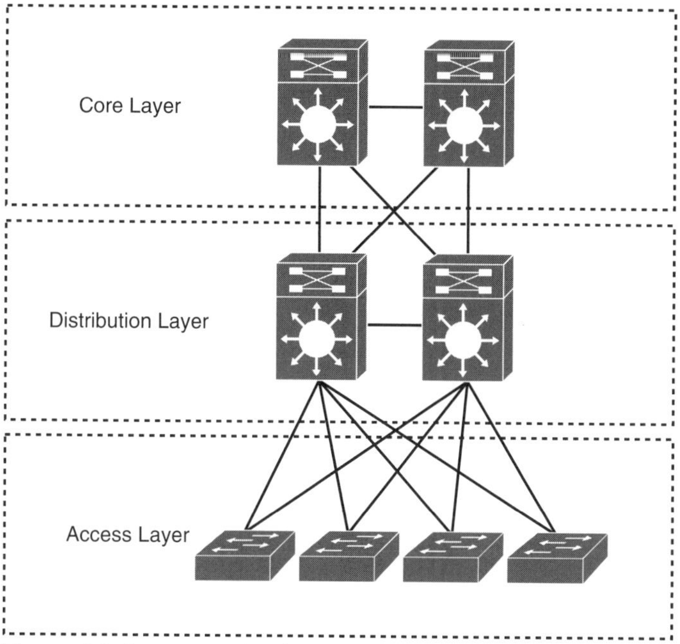

Figure 22-1 *Hierarchical LAN Design*

Each layer provides different functionalities and capabilities to the network. The number of layers needed depends on the characteristics of the network deployment site. As illustrated in Figure 22-2, a small campus in a single building might require only access and distribution layers, whereas a campus that spans multiple buildings will most likely require all three layers. Regardless of how many layers are implemented at a geographic location, the modularity of this design ensures that each layer will provide the same services and the same design methods.

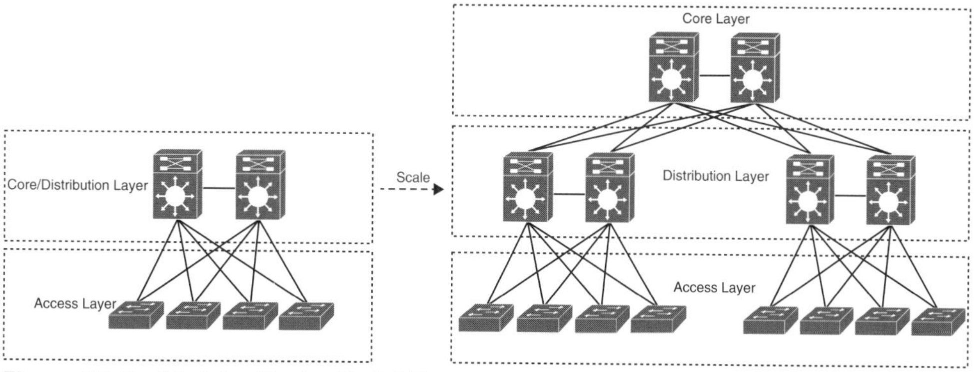

Figure 22-2 *Modular Design Scalability*

Key Topic

Access Layer

The *access layer*, also commonly referred as the *network edge*, is where end-user devices or endpoints connect to the network. It provides high-bandwidth device connectivity using wired and wireless access technologies such as Gigabit Ethernet and 802.11n, 802.11ac, and 802.11ax wireless. While endpoints in most cases will not use the full capacity of these connections for extended periods of time, the ability to burst up to these high bandwidths when required helps improve the quality of experience (QoE) and productivity of the end user.

Figure 22-3 illustrates the different types of endpoints that connect to the access layer, such as personal computers (PCs), IP phones, printers, wireless access points, personal telepresence devices, and IP video surveillance cameras. Wireless access points and IP phones are prime examples of devices that can be used to extend the access layer one more layer out from the access switch.

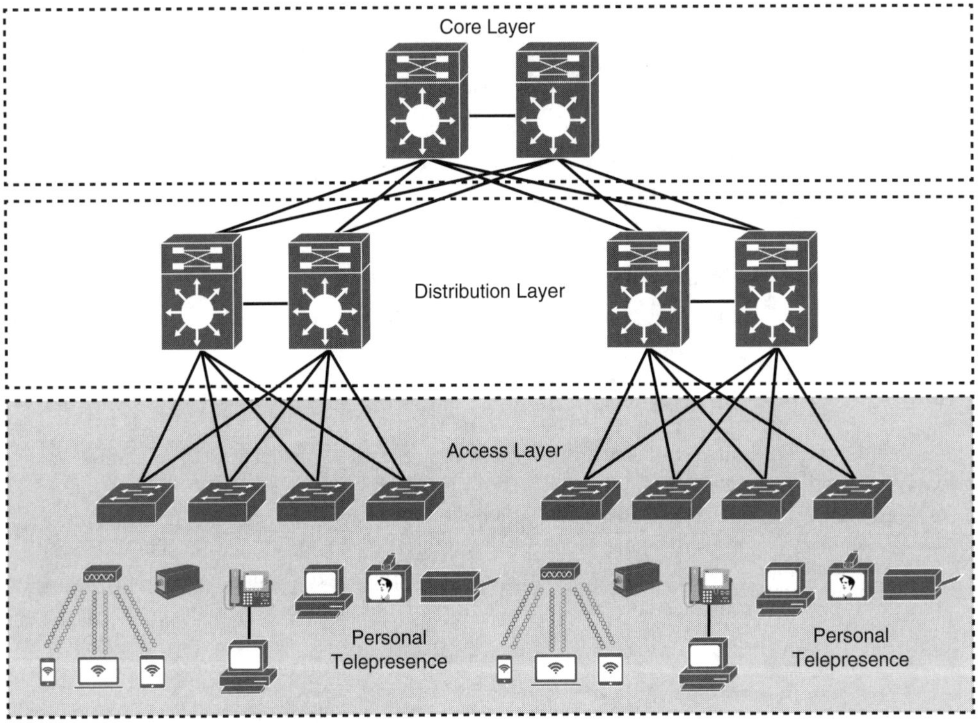

Figure 22-3 *Access Layer Connectivity*

The access layer can be segmented (for example, by using VLANs) so that different devices can be placed into different logical networks for performance, management, and security reasons. In the hierarchical LAN design, the access layer switches are not interconnected to each other. Communication between endpoints on different access layer switches occurs through the distribution layer.

Because the access layer is the connection point for endpoints, it plays a big role in ensuring that the network is protected from malicious attacks. This protection includes making sure the end users and endpoints connecting to the network are prevented from accessing services for which they are not authorized. Furthermore, the quality of service (QoS) trust boundary and QoS mechanisms are typically enabled on this layer to ensure that QoS is provided end-to-end to satisfy the end user's QoE.

Answers to the "Do I Know This Already?" quiz:

1 A, B, C, D, F **2** D **3** B **4** B **5** C **6** C **7** A, B **8** A, B, C, D

For business-critical endpoints that can connect to only a single access switch, it is recommended to use access switches with redundant supervisor engines to prevent service outages.

Key Topic

Distribution Layer

The primary function of the distribution layer is to aggregate access layer switches in a given building or campus. The distribution layer provides a boundary between the Layer 2 domain of the access layer and the core's Layer 3 domain. This boundary provides two key functions for the LAN: On the Layer 2 side, the distribution layer creates a boundary for Spanning Tree Protocol (STP), limiting propagation of Layer 2 faults, and on the Layer 3 side, the distribution layer provides a logical point to summarize IP routing information when it enters the core of the network. The summarization reduces IP routing tables for easier troubleshooting and reduces protocol overhead for faster recovery from failures.

Figure 22-4 illustrates the distribution layer. The distribution switches need to be deployed in pairs for redundancy. The distribution layer switch pairs should be interconnected to each other using either a Layer 2 or Layer 3 link.

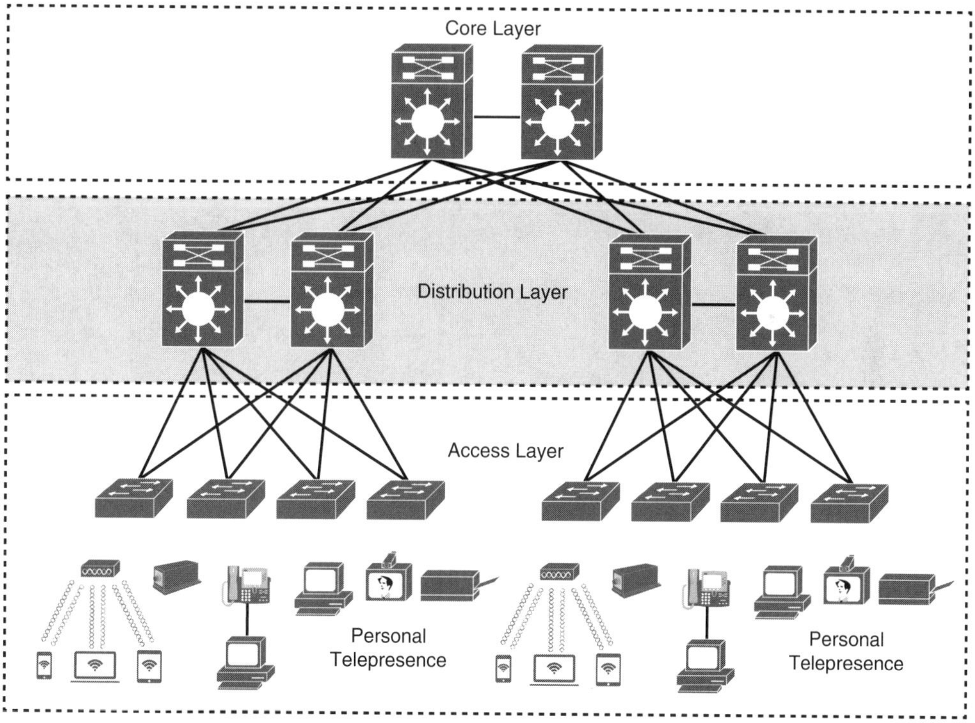

Figure 22-4 *Distribution Layer Connectivity*

In a large campus environment, multiple distribution layer switches are often required when access layer switches are located in multiple geographically dispersed buildings to reduce the number of fiber-optic runs (which are costly) between buildings. Distribution layer switches can be located in various buildings as illustrated in Figure 22-5.

22

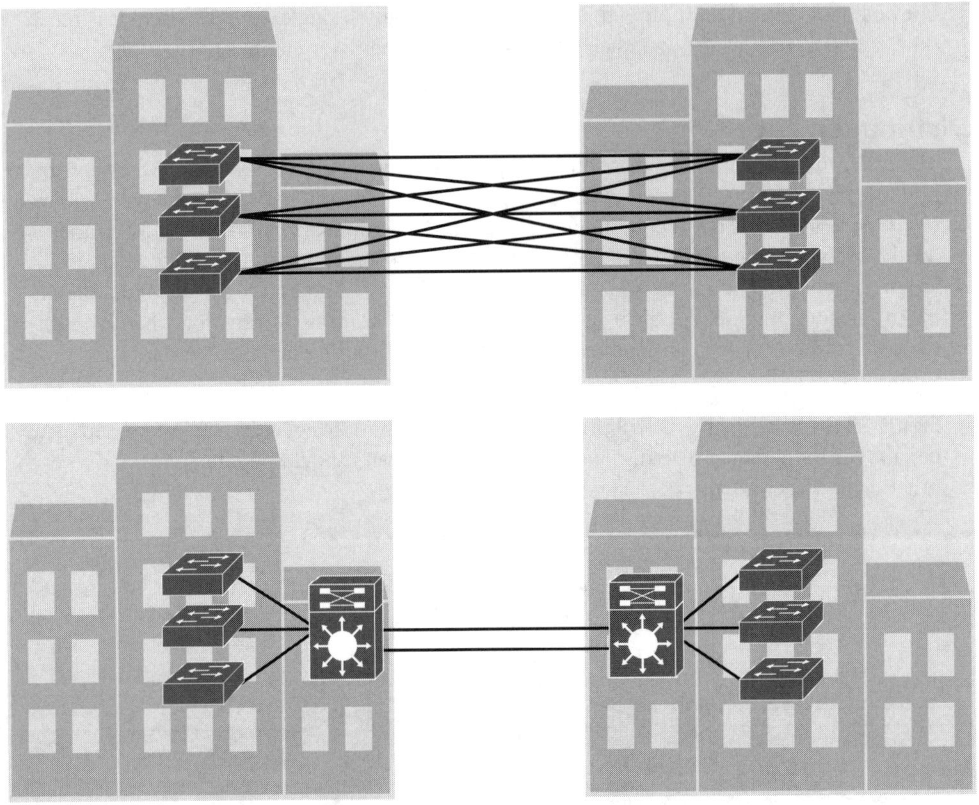

Figure 22-5 *Distribution Layer Reducing Fiber-Optic Runs*

Key Topic

Core Layer

As networks grow beyond three distribution layers in a single location, organizations should consider using a core layer to optimize the design. The core layer is the backbone and aggregation point for multiple networks and provides scalability, high availability, and fast convergence to the network.

The core can provide high-speed connectivity for large enterprises with multiple campus networks distributed worldwide, and it can also provide interconnectivity between the end-user/endpoint campus access layer and other **network blocks**, such as the data center, the private cloud, the public cloud, the WAN, the Internet edge, and network services, as discussed later in this chapter.

The core layer reduces the network complexity, from $N \times (N - 1)$ to N links for N distributions, as shown in Figure 22-6.

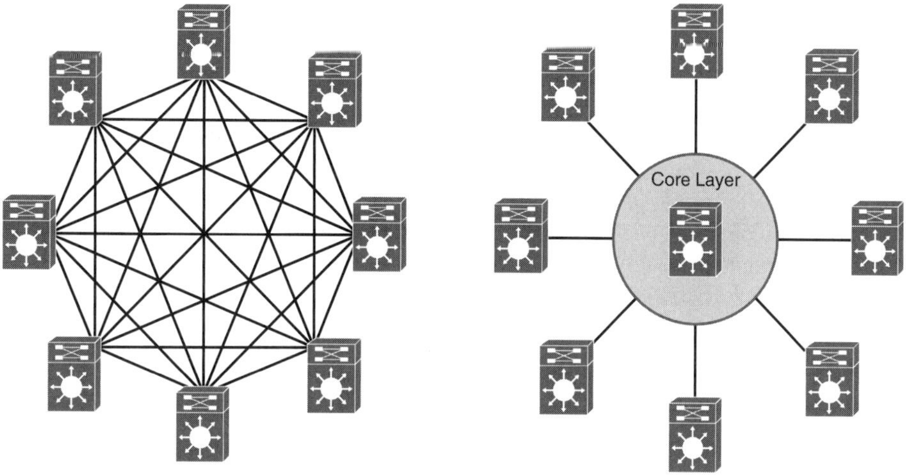

Figure 22-6 *Core Layer Reduces Large Network Complexity*

High Availability Network Design

In networking, high availability refers to a resilient network that can operate with continuous uptime without failure, for a given period of time, to ensure business continuity. High availability can be achieved by designing a network that takes into consideration network- and system-level components.

The following guidelines can be used in the network design for network-level high availability:

- Adding redundant devices and links at different layers of the network architecture
- Ensuring the design has no single points of failure and it is fault tolerant
- Simplifying the network design by using virtual network clustering technologies
- Implementing network monitoring systems to analyze all aspects of the network such as network capacity, faulty hardware, and security threats to prevent low network performance, network failures, and outages

The following guidelines can be used in the network design for system-level high availability:

- Using routers that support redundant hardware components such as redundant power supplies, redundant fans, redundant fan-trays, modular line cards, and dual route processor (RP) or supervisor engines
- Using routers that support hot-swappable and/or online insertion and removal (OIR) capable hardware components
- Enabling high availability technologies such as Stateful Switchover (SSO) and Nonstop Forwarding (NSF) with Graceful Restart (GR) or Nonstop Routing (NSR)
- Enabling protocols that can detect link failures such as BFD and UDLD
- Enabling first-hop redundancy (FHRP) protocols such as HSRP, VRRP, and GLBP

High Availability Technologies

In a router with redundant RPs (also known as supervisor engines in some Cisco platforms), one of the RPs is designated as "active" and the other one as "standby." The active RP handles the control plane, the routing table (RIB), and in centralized forwarding architectures (as described in Chapter 1), it also handles the Forwarding Information Base (FIB) and adjacency table. For this reason, an active RP failure can cause routing protocol adjacencies to go down, which can result in packet loss and network instability. To solve this problem, high availability technologies are used that allow the router to continue forwarding packets non-stop using the current Cisco Express Forwarding (CEF) entries in the FIB, versus dropping packets while waiting for the standby RP (new active RP) to re-establish routing protocol adjacencies and rebuild the routing table and the FIB.

The following are different combinations of high availability technologies that allow the network to continue forwarding traffic during an RP switchover:

Key Topic

- SSO and NSF
- SSO and NSF with GR
- SSO and NSF with NSR
- SSO and NSF with NSR and GR

Key Topic

SSO and NSF

SSO is an internal router redundancy feature that allows a router with redundant RPs to checkpoint (synchronize or mirror) the router configuration, line card operation, and Layer 2 protocol state information from the active RP to the standby RP. NSF is an internal Layer 3 data forwarding plane redundancy feature that checkpoints and frequently updates the FIB from the active to the standby RP.

During a switchover, the standby RP takes over as the new active RP. The new active RP uses the SSO-learned checkpoint information and keeps the interfaces on the router from flapping and the router and/or line cards from reloading; however, SSO doesn't checkpoint any Layer 3 control plane information about any neighbor router, and due to this, the existing routing protocol adjacencies go down and begin to re-establish. During this time, because the FIB was checkpointed by NSF, the data plane is not affected by the Layer 3 control plane going down, and traffic continues to be forwarded while the routing protocol adjacencies re-establish. After routing convergence is complete, the FIB is updated with new routing or topology information from the RIB if necessary.

Using SSO and NSF without GR or NSR has a downside. When the routing adjacencies go down during the RP switchover, the neighbor routers only see the routing adjacencies going down, which causes them to stop forwarding traffic to the failing router. To prevent this from happening, GR, NSR, or both need to be used with SSO and NSF.

NOTE NSF is not a configurable feature; it is enabled when SSO is enabled. This is the reason why SSO and NSF are typically referred to as SSO/NSF.

Key Topic

SSO/NSF with GR

GR is a standards-based feature defined in RFC 4724, and it is the only one that interacts with neighbor routers. GR is deployed with SSO/NSF to protect the Layer 3 forwarding plane during an RP switchover. For neighbor routers to continue forwarding traffic to the router undergoing an RP switchover, the neighbor routers need to support the GR routing protocol extensions. The GR extensions allow a neighbor router to be aware in advance that the router undergoing the RP switchover can continue to forward packets but may bring down its routing adjacency for a brief period of time.

There are three categories of GR routers:

Key Topic

- **SSO/NSF-capable router:** A router that has dual RPs and is configured to use SSO/NSF to preserve the FIB through an RP switchover. The routing protocol adjacencies are re-established upon completion of the RP switchover. An SSO/NSF-capable router is also GR-aware.
- **GR-aware router (also referred to as GR Helper, or the misnomer NSF-aware):** A neighbor router that supports GR routing protocol extensions and that continues to forward traffic to the SSO/NSF-capable router during the RP switchover by preserving the routes and adjacency state. A GR-aware router does not require dual RPs, and it doesn't need to be SSO/NSF capable.
- **GR-unaware router:** A neighbor router that doesn't support GR routing protocol extensions and is not GR-aware.

NSF (SSO/NSF) is the term initially used by Cisco to refer to Graceful Restart, which is still prevalent in Cisco documentation and the IOS XE command line. SSO/NSF is not a configurable feature; it is enabled by default when SSO is enabled. This means that any NSF command or keyword found in the documentation or the command line is referring to Graceful Restart. Another differentiator is that SSO/NSF is an internal capability, whereas Graceful Restart is an external capability that interacts with neighbor routers.

Key Topic

SSO/NSF with NSR

NSR is an internal Cisco router feature that does not use routing protocol extensions to signal neighbor routers that an RP switchover has taken place. Instead, the active RP is responsible for constantly checkpointing all relevant routing control plane information to the standby RP, including routing adjacency and TCP sockets. During an RP switchover, the new RP uses the "checkpoint" state information to maintain the current routing adjacencies and recalculate the routing table without having to alert the neighbor router that a switchover has occurred.

NSR's primary benefit over GR is that it is a completely self-contained "in box" high availability solution. There is no disruption to the routing protocol adjacencies, so the neighboring router does not need to be NSR-aware or GR-aware. It can be used in cases where the neighbor router is GR-unaware.

Key Topic

SSO/NSF with NSR and GR

A downside to NSR is that it increases the workload on the router due to the constant checkpointing of the routing and forwarding information to the standby RP. For scaled deployments, it is recommended to use GR for neighbor routers that are GR-aware and NSR for peers that are GR-unaware.

Enterprise Network Architecture Options

Multiple enterprise network architecture design options are available for deploying a campus network, depending on the size of the campus as well as the reliability, resiliency, availability, performance, security, and scalability required for it. Each possible option should be evaluated against business requirements. Because campus networks are modular, an enterprise network could have a mixture of all of these options deployed:

- Two-tier design (collapsed core)
- Three-tier design
- Layer 2 access layer (STP based)
- Layer 3 access layer (routed access)
- Simplified campus design
- Software-Defined Access (SD-Access)

Two-Tier Design (Collapsed Core)

Smaller campus networks may have multiple departments spread across multiple floors within a building. In these environments, a core layer may not be needed, and collapsing the core function into the distribution layer can be a cost-effective solution (because no core layer means no core layer devices) that requires no sacrifice of most of the benefits of the three-tier hierarchical model. Prior to selecting a two-tier collapsed core and distribution layers, future scale, expansion, and manageability factors need to be considered.

Figure 22-7 illustrates the two-tier design with the distribution layer acting as a collapsed core.

In Figure 22-7, the distribution/core layer provides connectivity to the WAN edge block, the Internet edge block, the network services block, and so on, and the same pair of core/distribution switches also provides LAN aggregation to the end-user access layer.

The WAN edge block is used to connect to remote data centers, remote branches, or other campus networks or for cloud connectivity to cloud providers such as the "big three" cloud service providers (Amazon Web Services, Microsoft Azure, and Google Cloud Platform) using dedicated interconnections.

The data center/server room block is where business-critical servers are placed to serve up websites, corporate email, business applications, storage, big data processing, backup services, e-commerce transactions, and so on.

The Internet edge block is used for regular Internet access, e-commerce, connection to remote branches, remote VPN access, and cloud provider connectivity that does not require dedicated interconnections.

The network services edge is where devices providing network services reside, such as the wireless LAN controllers (WLCs), Cisco Identity Services Engine (ISE), Cisco TelePresence Manager, and Cisco Unified Communications Manager (CUCM).

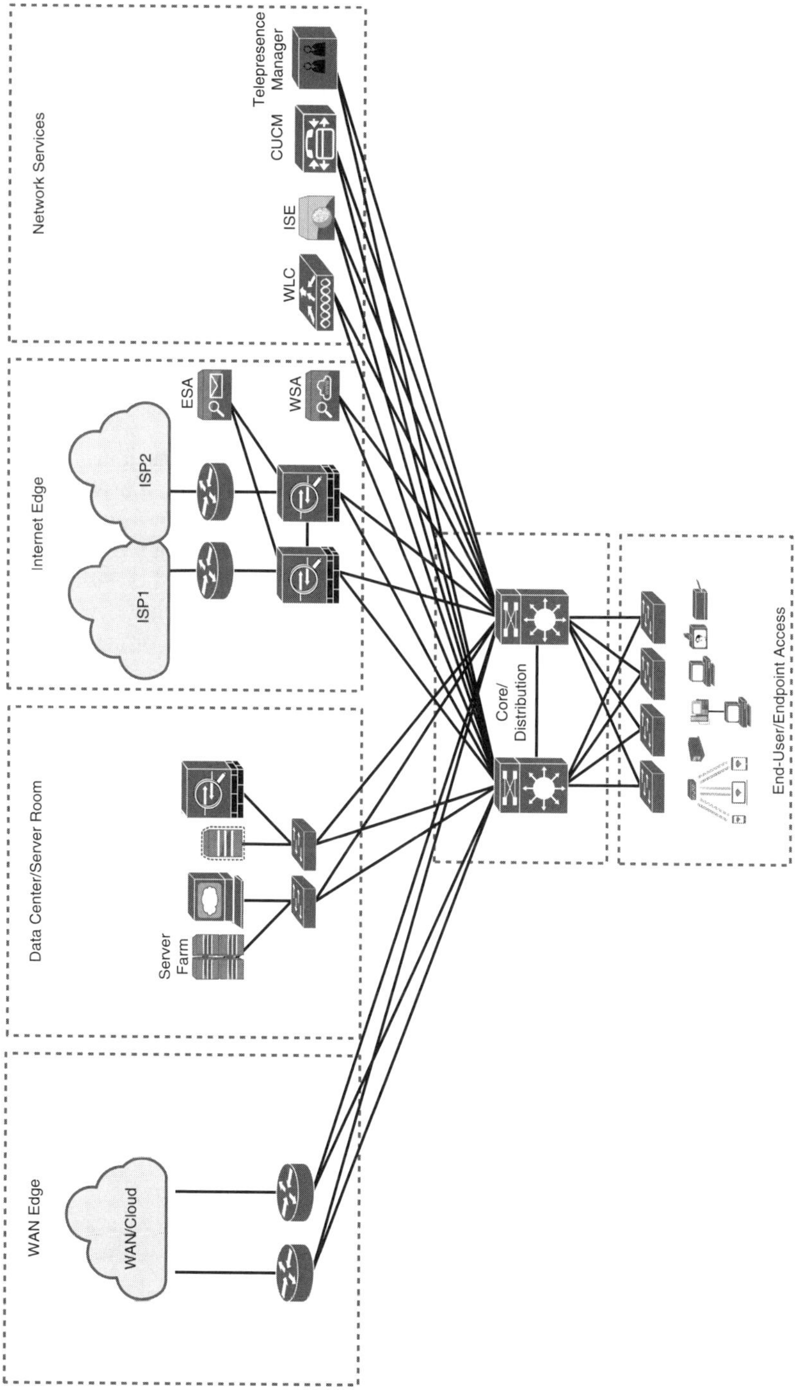

Figure 22-7 *Two-Tier/Collapsed Core Design*

Three-Tier Design

Three-tier designs separate the core and distribution layers and are recommended when more than two pairs of distribution switches are required. Multiple pairs of distribution switches are typically required for the following reasons:

- When implementing a network for a large enterprise campus composed of multiple buildings, where each building requires a dedicated distribution layer
- When the density of WAN routers, Internet edge devices, data center servers, and network services is growing to the point where they can affect network performance and throughput
- When geographic dispersion of the LAN access switches across many buildings in a larger campus facility would require more fiber-optic interconnects back to a single collapsed core

When multiple distribution layers need to be interconnected, it becomes necessary to use a core layer, as illustrated in Figure 22-8.

In Figure 22-8, the **building blocks** or **places in the network (PINs)** are each using the hierarchical design model, where each is deployed with a pair of distribution switches connected to the core block. The data center block is an exception because it is using the newer leaf–spine design, which is a common alternative to the three-tier design for modern data centers that have predominantly east–west traffic patterns between servers within the data center. The hierarchical LAN design is more appropriate for north–south traffic flows, such as endpoints communicating with the WAN edge, data center, Internet, or network services blocks.

Layer 2 Access Layer (STP Based)

Traditional LAN designs use a Layer 2 access layer and a Layer 3 distribution layer. The distribution layer is the Layer 3 IP gateway for access layer hosts. Whenever possible, it is recommended to restrict a VLAN to a single access layer switch to eliminate topology loops, which are common points of failure in LANs, even when STP is enabled in the network. Restricting a VLAN to a single switch provides a loop-free design, but at the cost of network flexibility because all hosts within a VLAN are restricted to a single access switch. Some organizations require that the same Layer 2 VLAN be extended to multiple access layer switches to accommodate an application or a service. The looped design causes STP to block links, which reduces the bandwidth from the rest of the network and can cause slower network convergence.

Figure 22-9 illustrates a loop-free topology where a VLAN is constrained to a single switch as well as a looped topology where a VLAN spans multiple access switches.

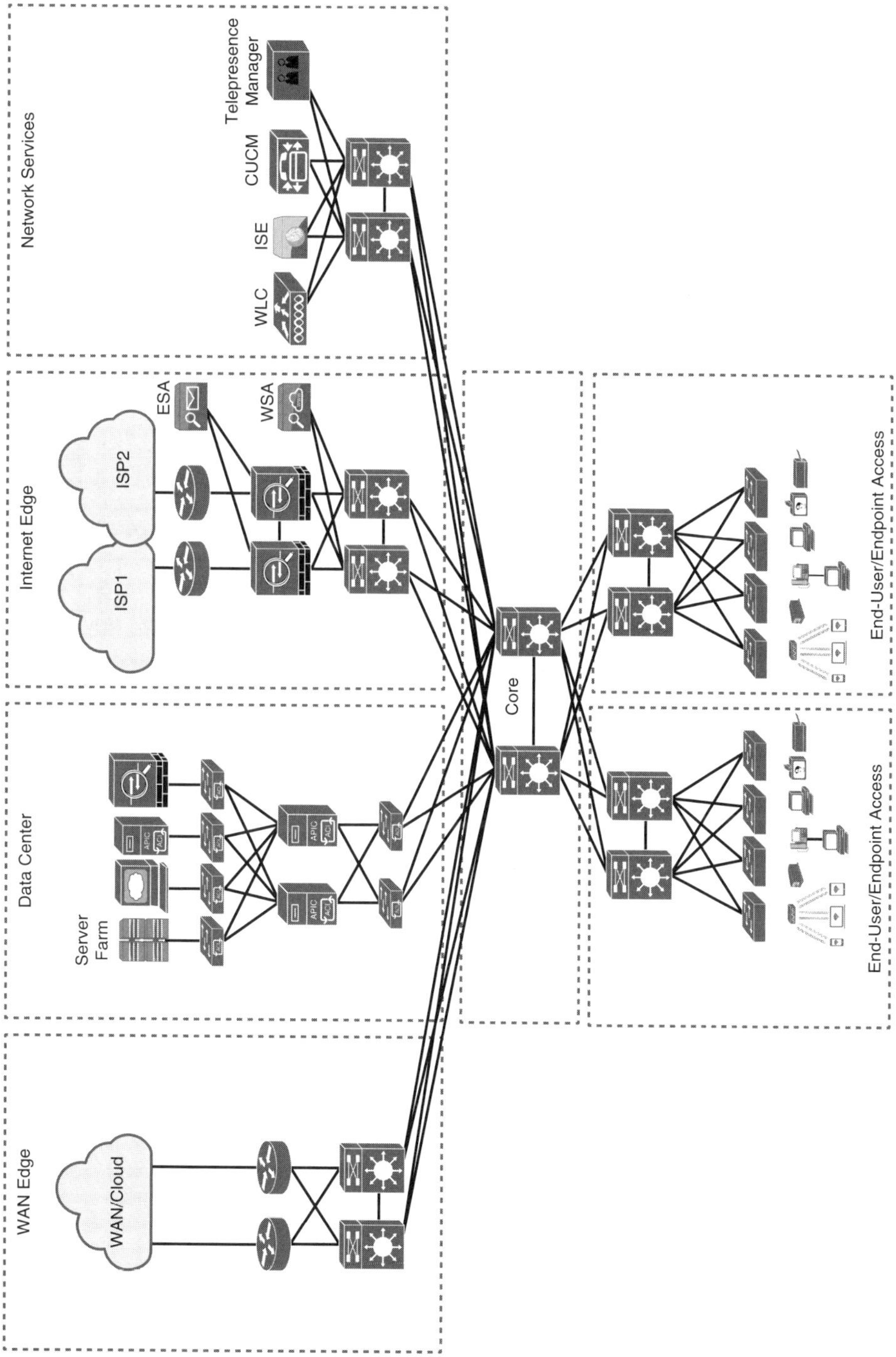

Figure 22-8 *Three-Tier Design*

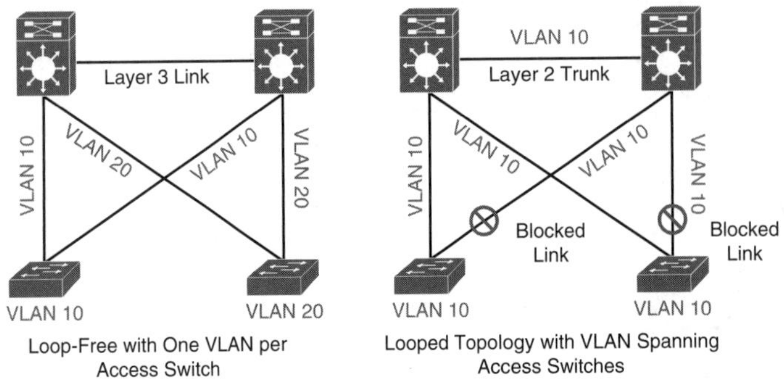

Figure 22-9 *Loop-Free Topology and Looped Topology*

To create a highly available IP gateway at the distribution layer, the distribution layer should have a pair of standalone switches configured with first-hop redundancy protocols (FHRPs) to provide hosts with a consistent MAC address and gateway IP address for each configured VLAN. *Hot Standby Router Protocol (HSRP)* and *Virtual Router Redundancy Protocol (VRRP)* are the most common first-hop redundancy protocols; a downside to these protocols is that they only allow hosts to send data out to the active first-hop redundancy protocol router through a single access uplink, which leaves one of the access layer-to-distribution layer uplinks unutilized. Manual configuration of the distribution layer is necessary to be able to load balance VLAN traffic across uplinks; this configuration involves making one of the distribution switches active for odd VLANs and the other active for even VLANs. *Gateway Load Balancing Protocol (GLBP)* provides greater uplink utilization for access layer-to-distribution layer traffic by load balancing the load from hosts across multiple uplinks; the downside is that it works only on loop-free topologies.

All these redundancy protocols require fine-tuning the default settings in order to allow for sub-second network convergence, which can impact switch CPU resources.

NOTE First-hop redundancy protocols are covered in detail in Chapter 15, "IP Services."

Layer 3 Access Layer (Routed Access)

Routed access is an alternative configuration in which Layer 3 is extended all the way to the access layer switches. In this design, access layer switches act as full Layer 3 routed nodes (providing both Layer 2 and Layer 3 switching), and the access-to-distribution Layer 2 uplink trunks are replaced with Layer 3 point-to-point routed links. Consequently, the Layer 2/Layer 3 demarcation point is moved from the distribution switch to the access switch, as illustrated in Figure 22-10.

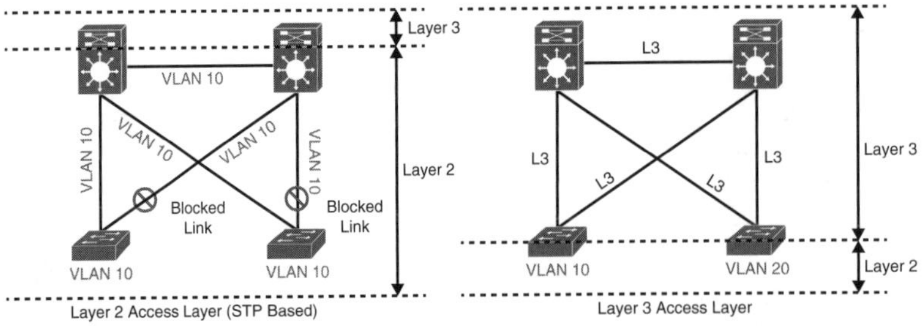

Figure 22-10 *Layer 2 Access Layer and Layer 3 Access Layer*

The routed access-to-distribution block design has a number of advantages over the Layer 2 access layer design:

- **No first-hop redundancy protocol required:** It eliminates the need for first-hop redundancy protocols such as HSRP and VRRP.
- **No STP required:** Because there are no Layer 2 links to block, this design eliminates the need for STP.
- **Increased uplink utilization:** Both uplinks from access to distribution can be used, increasing the effective bandwidth available to the end users and endpoints connected to the access layer switches.
- **Easier troubleshooting:** It offers common end-to-end troubleshooting tools (such as **ping** and **traceroute**).
- **Faster convergence:** It uses fast-converging routing protocols such as Enhanced Interior Gateway Routing Protocol (EIGRP) and Open Shortest Path First (OSPF).

While this is an excellent design for many environments, it has the same limitation as the Layer 2 access loop-free design: It does not support spanning VLANs across multiple access switches. In addition, it might not be the most cost-effective solution because access layer switches with Layer 3 routing capability might cost more than Layer 2 switches.

Simplified Campus Design

The simplified campus design relies on switch clustering technologies such as Virtual Switching System (VSS) and StackWise Virtual (SWV), in which two physical switches are clustered into a single logical switch, and StackWise, in which two or more switches (the maximum number depends on the platform) are stacked into a single logical switch, with a single management and control plane, which allows them to be logically managed as if it were a single physical switch.

The ability to deploy VSS, SWV, or StackWise depends on the platform. StackWise is supported on switches targeted for the access layer, whereas VSS and SWV are supported on switches that are targeted for the distribution and core layers; however, any of these technologies can be used for any layer as necessary.

VSS and SWV support EtherChannels that span across the two physical switches, referred to as *Multichassis EtherChannels (MEC)*, and StackWise supports EtherChannels that can span across all the switches in the stack, referred to as *cross-stack EtherChannels*. MEC and cross-stack EtherChannels allow devices to connect across all the physical switches using EtherChannel in the same way as if they were connecting to a single switch.

VSS, SWV, and StackWise, along with MEC and cross-stack EtherChannels, can be applied to any of the campus building blocks to simplify them even further. Using this design offers the following advantages:

- **Simplified design:** There are fewer boxes to manage, which reduces the amount of time spent on ongoing provisioning and maintenance.

- **No first-hop redundancy protocol required:** It eliminates the need for first-hop redundancy protocols such as HSRP and VRRP because the default IP gateway is on a single logical interface.
- **Reduced STP dependence:** Because EtherChannel is used, it eliminates the need for STP for a Layer 2 access design; however, STP is still required as a failsafe in case multiple access switches are interconnected.
- **Increased uplink utilization:** With EtherChannel, all uplinks from access to distribution can be used, increasing the effective bandwidth available to the end users and endpoints connected to the access layer switches.
- **Easier troubleshooting:** The topology of the network from the distribution layer to the access layer is logically a hub-and-spoke topology, which reduces the complexity of the design and troubleshooting.
- **Faster convergence:** With EtherChannel, all links are in a forwarding state, and this significantly optimizes the convergence time following a node or link failure event because EtherChannel provides fast sub-second failover between links in an uplink bundle.
- **Distributed VLANs:** With this design, VLANs can span multiple access switches without the need to block any links.
- **High Availability:** There is seamless traffic failover when one of the switches in the cluster fails by using interchassis SSO/NSF.

The simplified campus design is loop free, highly available, flexible, resilient, and easy to manage. Figure 22-11 illustrates how the network can be simplified by introducing VSS and SWV into the design.

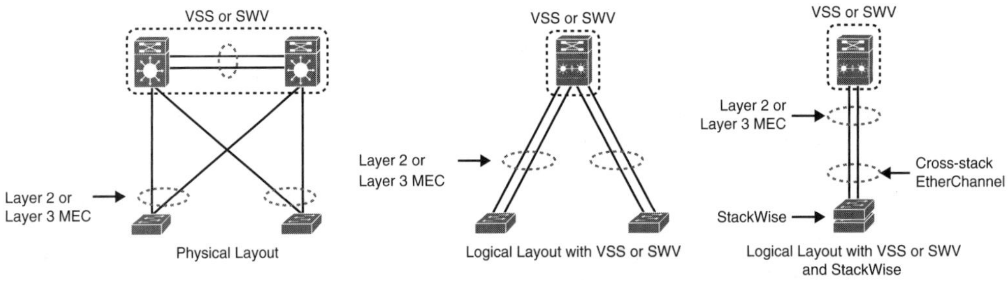

Figure 22-11 *Simplified Campus Design with VSS, SWV, and StackWise*

In addition, using this design approach across all the campus blocks (when possible) can provide an optimized architecture that is easy to manage, resilient, and more flexible, with higher aggregated uplink bandwidth capacity. Figure 22-12 illustrates what the end-to-end campus would look like with VSS and SWV used across the different building blocks and layers.

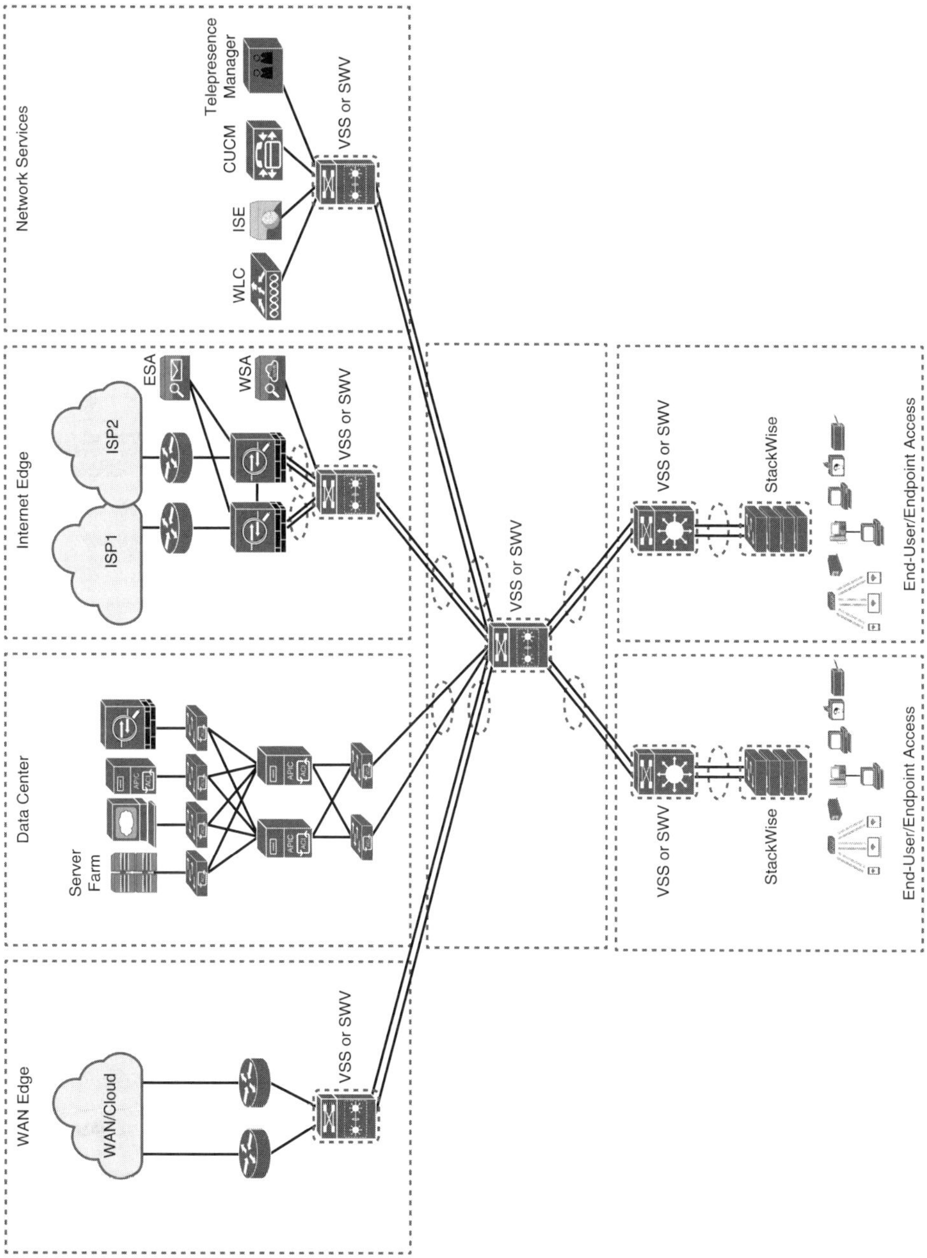

Figure 22-12 *Applying VSS, SWV, and StackWise in a Campus Network*

Software-Defined Access (SD-Access) Design

SD-Access, the industry's first intent-based networking solution for the enterprise, is built on the principles of the Cisco Digital Network Architecture (DNA). It is a combination of the campus fabric design and the Digital Network Architecture Center (Cisco DNA or DNAC). SD-Access adds fabric capabilities to the enterprise network through automation using SD-Access technology, and it provides automated end-to-end segmentation to separate user, device, and application traffic without requiring a network redesign. With its fabric capabilities, SD-Access provides services such as host mobility and enhanced security in addition to the normal switching and routing capabilities. SD-Access is covered in detail in Chapter 23, "Fabric Technologies."

Exam Preparation Tasks

You have a couple of choices for exam preparation: the exercises here, Chapter 30, "Final Preparation," and the exam simulation questions in the Pearson Test Prep Software Online.

Review All Key Topics

Review the most important topics in the chapter, noted with the Key Topic icon in the outer margin of the page. Table 22-2 lists these key topics and the page number on which each is found.

Key Topic

Table 22-2 Key Topics for Chapter 22

Key Topic Element	Description	Page
List	Hierarchical LAN design layers	624
Section	Access Layer	625
Section	Distribution Layer	627
Section	Core Layer	628
List	High availability technologies	630
Section	SSO and NSF	630
Section	SSO/NSF with GR	631
List	GR routers	631
Section	SSO/NSF with NSR	631
Section	SSO/NSF with NSR and GR	631

Complete Tables and Lists from Memory

Print a copy of Appendix B, "Memory Tables" (found on the companion website), or at least the section for this chapter, and complete the tables and lists from memory. Appendix C, "Memory Tables Answer Key," also on the companion website, includes completed tables and lists you can use to check your work.

Define Key Terms

Define the following key terms from this chapter and check your answers in the Glossary:

access layer, building block, core layer, distribution layer, network block, place in the network (PIN)

CHAPTER 23

Fabric Technologies

This chapter covers the following subjects:

- **Software-Defined Access (SD-Access):** This section defines the benefits of SD-Access over traditional campus networks as well as the components and features of the Cisco SD-Access solution, including the nodes, fabric control plane, and data plane.
- **Software-Defined WAN (SD-WAN):** This section defines the benefits of SD-WAN over traditional WANs as well as the components and features of the Cisco SD-WAN solution, including the orchestration plane, management plane, control plane, and data plane.

A fabric network is an **overlay network (virtual network [VN]**) built over an **underlay network** (physical network) using overlay tunneling technologies such as **VXLAN**. Fabric networks overcome shortcomings of traditional physical networks by enabling host mobility, network automation, network virtualization, and **segmentation**, and they are more manageable, flexible, secure (by means of encryption), and scalable than traditional networks. This chapter explores the following next-generation overlay fabric technologies:

- Software-Defined Access (SD-Access) for campus networks
- Software-Defined WAN (SD-WAN) for WAN networks

The Cisco SD-Access fabric is one of the main components of the Cisco Digital Network Architecture (Cisco DNA). Cisco DNA is the solution for the future of intent-based networking in Cisco enterprise networks. SD-Access provides policy-based network segmentation, host mobility for wired and wireless hosts, and enhanced security as well as other benefits in a fully automated fashion. Cisco SD-Access was designed for enterprise campus and branch network environments and not for other types of network environments, such as data center, service provider, and WAN environments.

Traditional WANs are typically designed using MPLS or other overlay solutions, such as Dynamic Multipoint Virtual Private Network (DMVPN) or Intelligent WAN (IWAN) to provide connectivity between different campus and branch sites. However, with the rise of Software as a Service (SaaS) cloud applications such as Microsoft Office 365 and Salesforce.com, and public Infrastructure as a Service (IaaS) cloud services from Amazon Web Services (AWS), Google Compute Engine (GCE), and Microsoft Azure, traffic patterns are changing so that the majority of enterprise traffic flows to public clouds and the Internet. Such changes are creating new requirements for security, application performance, cloud connectivity, WAN management, and operations that traditional WAN solutions were not designed to address. The Cisco SD-WAN fabric is a cloud-based WAN solution for enterprise and data center networks that was developed to address all the new WAN requirements.

This chapter defines the components, features, and functions of the Cisco SD-Access and Cisco SD-WAN solutions. Prior to reviewing this chapter, it is highly recommended to review Chapter 16, "Overlay Tunnels," and Chapter 25, "Secure Network Access Control." Chapter 16 describes overlay tunneling technologies such as IPsec, VXLAN, and LISP, and Chapter 25 describes Cisco TrustSec. Knowledge of these technologies is essential to understanding many of the concepts described in this chapter.

"Do I Know This Already?" Quiz

The "Do I Know This Already?" quiz enables you to assess whether you should read the entire chapter. If you miss no more than one of these self-assessment questions, you might want to move ahead to the "Exam Preparation Tasks" section. Table 23-1 lists the major headings in this chapter and the "Do I Know This Already?" quiz questions covering the material in those headings so you can assess your knowledge of these specific areas. The answers to the "Do I Know This Already?" quiz appear in Appendix A, "Answers to the 'Do I Know This Already?' Questions."

Table 23-1 "Do I Know This Already?" Foundation Topics Section-to-Question Mapping

Foundation Topics Section	Questions
Software-Defined Access (SD-Access)	1–6
Software-Defined WAN (SD-WAN)	7–11

1. What is the main reason SD-Access uses VXLAN data encapsulation instead of LISP data encapsulation?
   a. VXLAN supports IPv6.
   b. VXLAN supports Layer 2 networks.
   c. VXLAN has a much smaller header.
   d. VXLAN has a better ring to it.
2. True or false: The VXLAN header used for SD-Access is exactly the same as the original VXLAN header.
   a. True
   b. False
3. Which is the control plane used by SD-Access?
   a. LISP control plane
   b. EPVN MP-BGP
   c. Multicast
   d. VXLAN control plane
4. Which field was added to the VXLAN header to allow it to carry SGT tags?
   a. Group Policy ID
   b. Scalable Group ID
   c. Group Based Tag
   d. Group Based Policy

5. Which types of network environments was SD-Access designed for?
   a. Data center
   b. Internet
   c. Enterprise campus and branch
   d. Service provider
   e. WAN
   f. Private cloud
6. Which of the following components are part of the SD-Access fabric architecture? (Choose all that apply.)
   a. WLCs
   b. Cisco routers
   c. Cisco firewalls
   d. Cisco switches
   e. Access points
   f. Cisco ISE
   g. Cisco DNA Center
   h. Intrusion prevention systems
7. What are the mandatory components of the Cisco SD-WAN solution? (Choose four.)
   a. vManage network management system (NMS)
   b. vSmart controller
   c. SD-WAN routers
   d. vBond orchestrator
   e. vAnalytics
   f. Cisco ISE
   g. Cisco DNA Center
8. True or false: The vSmart controller establishes permanent and IPsec connections to all SD-WAN routers in the SD-WAN fabric.
   a. True
   b. False
9. True or false: SD-WAN only works over the Internet or MPLS networks.
   a. True
   b. False
10. Which of the following is the single pane of glass for the SD-WAN solution?
    a. DNA Center
    b. vBond
    c. vManage
    d. vSmart

11. What is the main function of the vBond orchestrator?

a. To authenticate the vManage NMS and the SD-WAN routers and orchestrate connectivity between them

b. To authenticate the vSmart controllers and the SD-WAN routers and orchestrate connectivity between them

c. To authenticate the vSmart controllers and the vManage NMS and orchestrate connectivity between them

Foundation Topics

Software-Defined Access (SD-Access)

There are many operational challenges in enterprise campus networks due to manual configuration of network devices. Manual network configuration changes are slow and lead to misconfigurations that cause service disruptions on the network, and the situation is exacerbated in a constantly changing environment where more users, endpoints, and applications are constantly being added. The constant growth in users and endpoints makes configuring user credentials and maintaining a consistent policy across the network very complex. If policies are inconsistent, there is an added complexity involved in maintaining separate policies between wired and wireless networks that leaves the network vulnerable to security breaches. As users move around the campus network, locating the users and troubleshooting issues also become more difficult. In other words, traditional campus networks do not address the existing campus network needs.

With SD-Access, an evolved campus network can be built that addresses the needs of existing campus networks by leveraging the following capabilities, features, and functionalities:

Key Topic

- **Network automation:** SD-Access replaces manual network device configurations with network device management through a single point of automation, orchestration, and management of network functions through the use of Cisco DNA Center. This simplifies network design and provisioning and allows for very fast, lower-risk deployment of network devices and services using best-practice configurations.

- **Network assurance and analytics:** SD-Access enables proactive prediction of network-related and security-related risks by using telemetry to improve the performance of the network, endpoints, and applications, including encrypted traffic.

- **Host mobility:** SD-Access provides host mobility for both wired and wireless clients.

- **Identity services:** *Cisco Identity Services Engine (ISE)* identifies users and devices connecting to the network and provides the contextual information required for users and devices to implement security policies for network access control and network segmentation.

- **Policy enforcement:** Traditional access control lists (ACLs) can be difficult to deploy, maintain, and scale because they rely on IP addresses and subnets. Creating access and application policies based on group-based policies using **Security Group Access**

Control Lists (SGACLs) provides a much simpler and more scalable form of policy enforcement based on identity instead of an IP address.

- **Secure segmentation:** With SD-Access, it is easier to **segment** the network to support guest, corporate, facilities, and IoT-enabled infrastructure.
- **Network virtualization:** SD-Access makes it possible to leverage a single physical infrastructure to support multiple virtual routing and forwarding (VRF) instances, referred to as *virtual networks (VNs)*, each with a distinct set of access policies.

What Is SD-Access?

SD-Access has two main components:

- Cisco Campus fabric solution
- Cisco DNA Center

The campus fabric is a Cisco-validated fabric overlay solution that includes all of the features and protocols (control plane, data plane, management plane, and policy plane) to operate the network infrastructure. When the campus fabric solution is managed using the command-line interface (CLI) or an **application programming interface (API)** using **Network Configuration Protocol (NETCONF)/YANG**, the solution is considered to be a campus fabric solution. When the campus fabric solution is managed via the Cisco DNA Center, the solution is considered to be SD-Access, as illustrated in Figure 23-1.

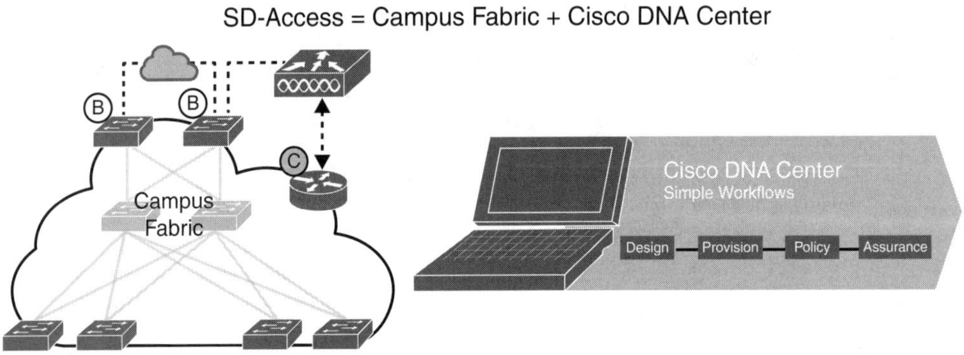

Figure 23-1 *SD-Access Solution*

SD-Access Architecture

Cisco SD-Access is based on existing hardware and software technologies. What makes Cisco SD-Access special is how these technologies are integrated and managed together. The Cisco SD-Access fabric architecture can be divided into four basic layers, as illustrated in Figure 23-2. The following sections focus on the relationships between these four layers.

Answers to the "Do I Know This Already?" quiz:

1 B **2** B **3** A **4** A **5** C **6** A, B, D, E, F, G **7** A, B, C, D **8** B **9** B **10** C **11** B

Key Topic

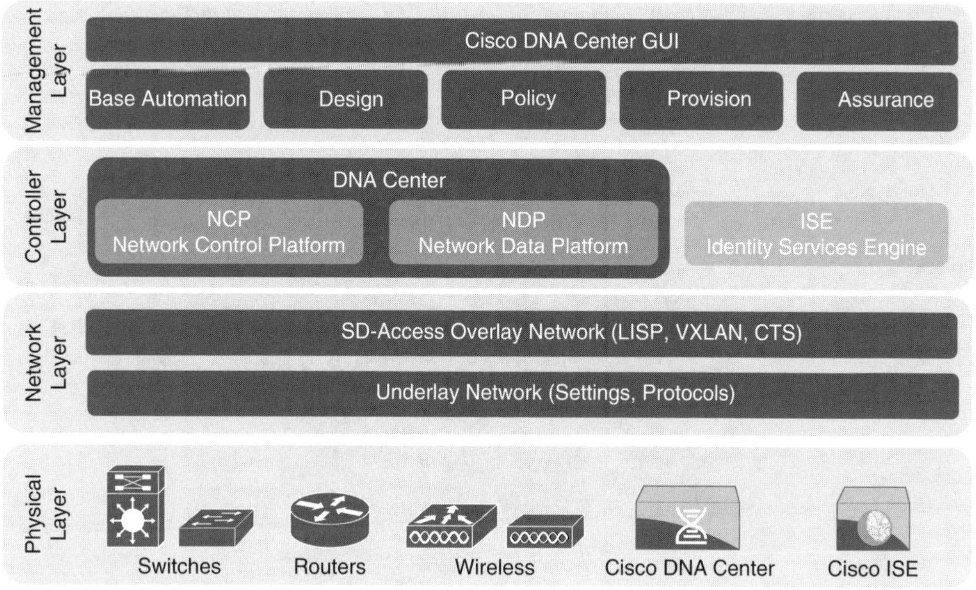

Figure 23-2 *Cisco SD-Access Architecture*

Physical Layer

While Cisco SD-Access is designed for user simplicity, abstraction, and virtual environments, everything runs on top of physical network devices—namely switches, routers, servers, wireless LAN controllers (WLCs), and wireless access points (APs). All Cisco network devices that actively participate in the SD-Access fabric must support all of the hardware application-specific integrated circuits (ASICs) and field-programmable gate arrays (FPGAs) and software requirements described in the "Network Layer" section later in this chapter. Cisco access layer switches that do not actively participate in the SD-Access fabric but that are part of it because of automation are referred to as *SD-Access extension nodes*. The following are the physical layer devices of the SD-Access fabric:

- **Cisco switches:** Switches provide wired (LAN) access to the fabric. Multiple types of Cisco Catalyst switches are supported, as well as Nexus switches.
- **Cisco routers:** Routers provide WAN and branch access to the fabric.
- **Cisco wireless:** Cisco WLCs and APs provide wireless (WLAN) access to the fabric.
- **Cisco controller appliances:** Cisco DNA Center and Cisco ISE are the two controller appliances required.

Network Layer

The network layer consists of the underlay network and the overlay network. These two sublayers work together to deliver data packets to and from the network devices participating in SD-Access. All this network layer information is made available to the controller layer.

The network underlay is the underlying physical layer, and its sole purpose is to transport data packets between network devices for the SD-Access fabric overlay.

The overlay network is a virtual (tunneled) network that virtually interconnects all of the network devices forming a fabric of interconnected nodes. It abstracts the inherent complexities and limitations of the underlay network.

Figure 23-3 shows a visual representation of the relationship between an overlay network and the network underlay.

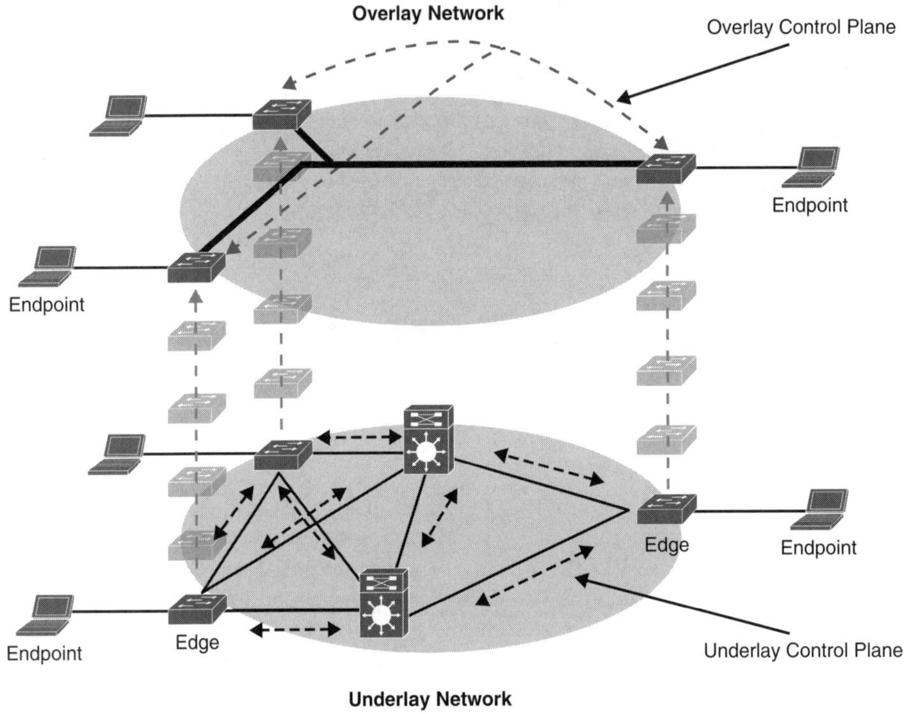

Figure 23-3 *Underlay and Overlay Networks*

Key Topic

Underlay Network

The underlay network for SD-Access should be configured to ensure performance, scalability, and high availability because any problems with the underlay can affect the operation of the fabric overlay. While it is possible to use a Layer 2 network underlay design running Spanning Tree Protocol (STP), it is not recommended. The recommended design for the network underlay is to use a Layer 3 routed access campus design using IS-IS as the IGP. IS-IS offers operational advantages such as neighbor establishment without IP dependencies, peering capability using loopback addresses, and agnostic treatment of IPv4, IPv6, and non-IP traffic.

Two models of underlay are supported:

Key Topic

- **Manual underlay:** This type of underlay network is configured and managed manually (such as with a CLI or an API) rather than through Cisco DNA Center. An advantage of the manual underlay is that it allows customization of the network to fit any special design requirements (such as changing the IGP to OSPF); in addition, it allows SD-Access to run on the top of a legacy (or third-party) IP-based network.

- **Automated underlay:** In a fully automated network underlay, all aspects of the underlay network are configured and managed by the Cisco DNA Center LAN Automation feature. The LAN Automation feature creates an IS-IS routed access campus design and uses the Cisco Network Plug and Play features to deploy both unicast and multicast routing configuration in the underlay to improve traffic delivery efficiency for SD-Access. An automated underlay eliminates misconfigurations and reduces the complexity of the network underlay. It also greatly simplifies and speeds the building of the network underlay. A downside to an automated underlay is that it does not allow manual customization for special design requirements.

Key Topic

Overlay Network (SD-Access Fabric)

The SD-Access fabric is the overlay network, and it provides policy-based network segmentation, host mobility for wired and wireless hosts, and enhanced security beyond the normal switching and routing capabilities of a traditional network.

In SD-Access, the fabric overlay is fully automated, regardless of the underlay network model used (manual or automated). It includes all necessary overlay control plane protocols and addressing, as well as all global configurations associated with operation of the SD-Access fabric.

> **NOTE** It is also possible to manually configure the overlay network without using DNA Center; however, when the overlay network is managed via the CLI or API using NETCONF/YANG, the solution is considered to be a campus fabric solution and not SD-Access.

As mentioned earlier, the Cisco SD-Access fabric is based on multiple existing technologies. The combination of these technologies and the automated management provided by Cisco DNA Center make Cisco SD-Access powerful and unique.

There are three basic planes of operation in the SD-Access fabric:

Key Topic

- Control plane, based on Locator/ID Separation Protocol (LISP)
- Data plane, based on Virtual Extensible LAN (VXLAN)
- Policy plane, based on Cisco TrustSec

Key Topic

SD-Access Control Plane

The SD-Access fabric control plane is based on *Locator/ID Separation Protocol (LISP)*. LISP is an IETF standard protocol defined in RFC 6830 that is based on a simple **endpoint identifier (EID)** to **routing locator (RLOC)** mapping system to separate the identity (endpoint IP address) from its current location (network edge/border router IP address).

LISP dramatically simplifies traditional routing environments by eliminating the need for each router to process every possible IP destination address and route. It does this by moving remote destination information to a centralized mapping database called the LISP **map server (MS)** (a control plane node in SD-Access), which allows each router to manage only its local routes and query the map system to locate destination EIDs.

This technology provides many advantages for Cisco SD-Access, such as smaller routing tables, dynamic host mobility for wired and wireless **endpoints**, address-agnostic mapping (IPv4, IPv6, and/or MAC), and built-in network segmentation through VRF instances.

In Cisco SD-Access, several enhancements to the original LISP specifications have been added, including distributed Anycast Gateway, VN Extranet, and Fabric Wireless, and more features are planned for the future.

Key Topic

SD-Access Fabric Data Plane

The tunneling technology used for the fabric data plane is based on Virtual Extensible LAN (VXLAN). VXLAN encapsulation is IP/UDP based, meaning that it can be forwarded by any IP-based network (legacy or third party) and creates the overlay network for the SD-Access fabric. Although LISP is the control plane for the SD-Access fabric, it does not use LISP data encapsulation for the data plane; instead, it uses VXLAN encapsulation because it is capable of encapsulating the original Ethernet header to perform MAC-in-IP encapsulation, while LISP does not. Using VXLAN allows the SD-Access fabric to support Layer 2 and Layer 3 virtual topologies (overlays) and the ability to operate over any IP-based network with built-in network segmentation (VRF instance/VN) and built-in group-based policy. The differences between the LISP and VXLAN packet formats are illustrated in Figure 23-4.

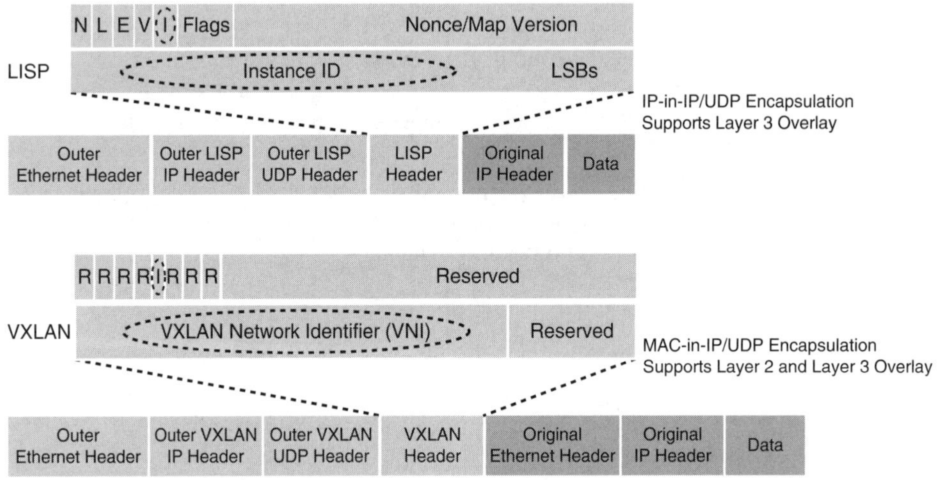

Figure 23-4 *LISP and VXLAN Packet Format Comparison*

The original VXLAN specification was enhanced for SD-Access to support Cisco TrustSec **Scalable Group Tags (SGTs)**. This was accomplished by adding new fields to the first 4 bytes of the VXLAN header in order to transport up to 64,000 SGT tags. The new VXLAN format is called **VXLAN Group Policy Option (VXLAN-GPO)**, and it is defined in the IETF draft draft-smith-vxlan-group-policy-05.

NOTE Cisco TrustSec Security Group Tags are referred to as Scalable Group Tags in Cisco SD-Access.

Figure 23-5 illustrates the VXLAN-GPO format compared to the original VXLAN format.

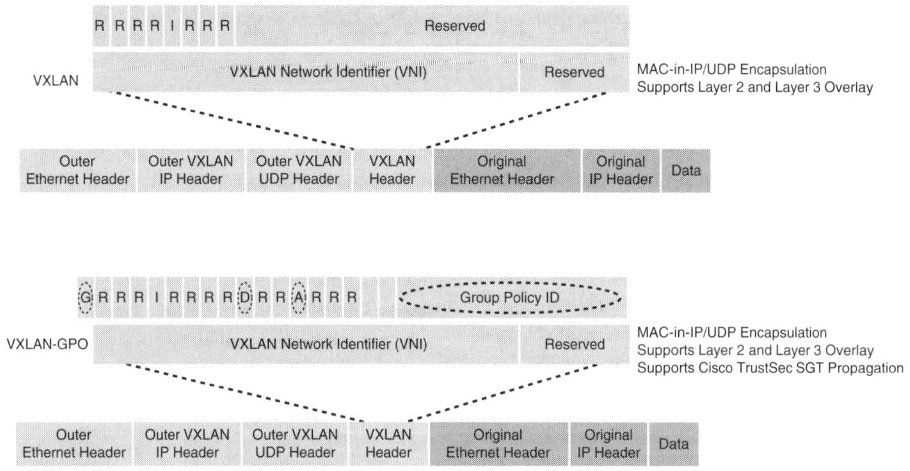

Figure 23-5 *VXLAN and VXLAN-GPO Packet Format Comparison*

The new fields in the VXLAN-GPO packet format include the following:

- **Group Policy ID:** 16-bit identifier that is used to carry the SGT tag.
- **Group Based Policy Extension Bit (G Bit):** 1-bit field that, when set to 1, indicates an SGT tag is being carried within the Group Policy ID field and set to 0 when it is not.
- **Don't Learn Bit (D Bit):** 1-bit field that, when set to 1, indicates that the egress **virtual tunnel endpoint (VTEP)** must not learn the source address of the encapsulated frame.
- **Policy Applied Bit (A Bit):** 1-bit field that is defined as the A bit only when the G bit field is set to 1. When the A bit is set to 1, it indicates that the group policy has already been applied to this packet, and further policies must not be applied by network devices. When it is set to 0, group policies must be applied by network devices, and they must set the A bit to 1 after the policy has been applied.

Key Topic

SD-Access Fabric Policy Plane

The fabric policy plane is based on **Cisco TrustSec**. Cisco TrustSec SGT tags are assigned to authenticated groups of users or end devices. Network policy (for example, ACLs, QoS) is then applied throughout the SD-Access fabric, based on the SGT tag instead of a network address (MAC, IPv4, or IPv6). This allows for the creation of network policies such as security, quality of service (QoS), policy-based routing (PBR), and network segmentation, based only on the SGT tag and not the network address (MAC, IPv4, or IPv6) of the user or endpoint.

TrustSec SGT tags provide several advantages for Cisco SD-Access, such as

- Support for both network-based segmentation using VNs (VRF instances) and group-based segmentation (policies)
- Network address-independent group-based policies based on SGT tags rather than MAC, IPv4, or IPv6 addresses, which reduces complexity

- Dynamic enforcement of group-based policies, regardless of location for both wired and wireless traffic
- Policy constructs over a legacy or third-party network using VXLAN
- Extended policy enforcement to external networks (such as cloud or data center networks) by transporting the tags to Cisco TrustSec-aware devices using SGT Exchange Protocol (SXP)

SD-Access Fabric Roles and Components

The operation of the SD-Access fabric requires multiple different device roles, each with a specific set of responsibilities. Each SD-Access-enabled network device must be configured for one (or more) of these roles. During the planning and design phase, it is important to understand the fabric roles and to select the most appropriate network devices for each role.

NOTE For more information on SD-Access design and deployment, please refer to the Cisco Validated Design (CVD) guides available at www.cisco.com/go/cvd.

There are five basic device roles in the fabric overlay:

- **Control plane node:** This node contains the settings, protocols, and mapping tables to provide the endpoint-to-location (EID-to-RLOC) mapping system for the fabric overlay.
- **Fabric border node:** This fabric device (for example, core layer device) connects external Layer 3 networks to the SDA fabric.
- **Fabric edge node:** This fabric device (for example, access or distribution layer device) connects wired endpoints to the SDA fabric.
- **Fabric WLAN controller (WLC):** This fabric device connects APs and wireless endpoints to the SDA fabric.
- **Intermediate nodes:** These intermediate routers or extended switches do not provide any sort of SD-Access fabric role other than underlay services.

Figure 23-6 illustrates the different SD-Access fabric design roles and how nodes in the fabric can play multiple roles. For example, the core layer routers in this figure are acting as fabric border nodes and control plane nodes.

Fabric Edge Nodes

A fabric edge node provides onboarding and mobility services for wired users and devices (including fabric-enabled WLCs and APs) connected to the fabric. It is a LISP **tunnel router (xTR)** that also provides the anycast gateway, endpoint authentication, and assignment to overlay **host pools** (static or DHCP), as well as group-based policy enforcement (for traffic to fabric endpoints).

A fabric edge first identifies and authenticates wired endpoints (through **802.1x**), in order to place them in a host pool (SVI and VRF instance) and scalable group (SGT assignment). It then registers the specific EID host address (that is, MAC, /32 IPv4, or /128 IPv6) with the control plane node.

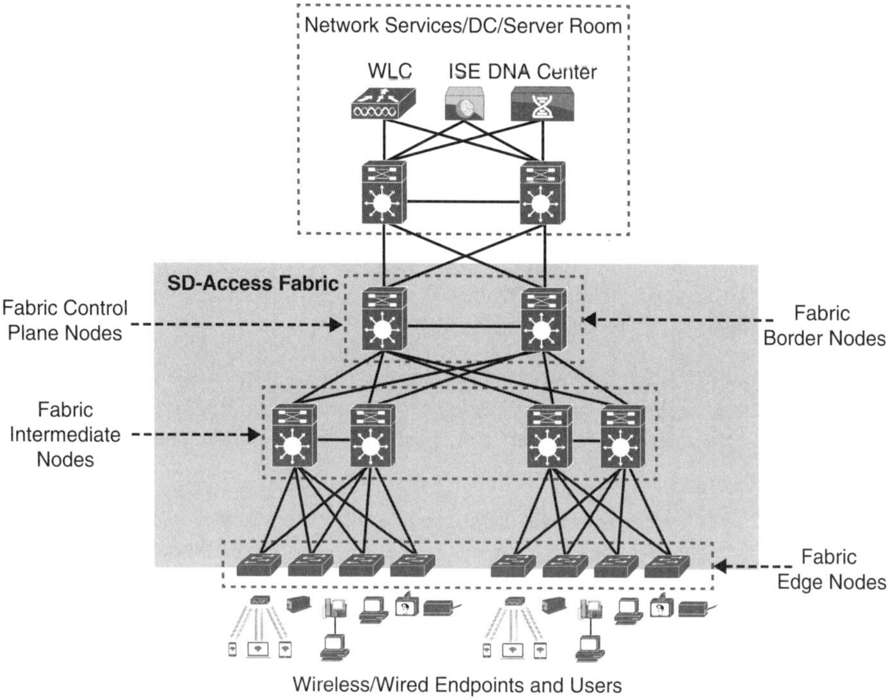

Figure 23-6 *SD-Access Fabric Roles*

A fabric edge provides a single Layer 3 anycast gateway (that is, the same SVI with the same IP address on all fabric edge nodes) for its connected endpoints and also performs the encapsulation and de-encapsulation of host traffic to and from its connected endpoints.

NOTE An edge node must be either a Cisco switch or router operating in the fabric overlay.

Key Topic

Fabric Control Plane Node

A fabric control plane node is a LISP map server/resolver (MS/MR) with enhanced functions for SD-Access, such as fabric wireless and SGT mapping. It maintains a simple host tracking database to map EIDs to RLOCs.

The control plane (host database) maps all EID locations to the current fabric edge or border node, and it is capable of multiple EID lookup types (IPv4, IPv6, or MAC).

The control plane receives registrations from fabric edge or border nodes for known EID prefixes from wired endpoints and from fabric mode WLCs for wireless clients. It also resolves lookup requests from fabric edge or border nodes to locate destination EIDs and updates fabric edge nodes and border nodes with wired and wireless client mobility and RLOC information.

NOTE Control plane devices must maintain all endpoint (host) mappings in a fabric. A device with sufficient hardware and software scale for the fabric must be selected for this function.

A control plane node must be either a Cisco switch or a router operating either inside or outside the SD-Access fabric.

Key Topic

Fabric Border Nodes

Fabric border nodes are LISP proxy tunnel routers (PxTRs) that connect external Layer 3 networks to the SD-Access fabric and translate reachability and policy information, such as VRF and SGT information, from one domain to another.

There are three types of border nodes:

Key Topic

- **Internal border (rest of company):** Connects only to the known areas of the organization (for example, WLC, firewall, data center).
- **Default border (outside):** Connects only to unknown areas outside the organization. This border node is configured with a default route to reach external unknown networks such as the Internet or the public cloud that are not known to the control plane nodes.
- **Internal + default border (anywhere):** Connects transit areas as well as known areas of the company. This is basically a border that combines internal and default border functionality into a single node.

Key Topic

Fabric Wireless Controller (WLC)

A fabric-enabled WLC connects APs and wireless endpoints to the SD-Access fabric. The WLC is external to the fabric and connects to the SD-Access fabric through an internal border node. A fabric WLC node provides onboarding and mobility services for wireless users and endpoints connected to the SD-Access fabric. A fabric WLC also performs PxTR registrations to the fabric control plane (on behalf of the fabric edges) and can be thought of as a fabric edge for wireless clients. The control plane node maps the host EID to the current fabric access point and fabric edge node location the access point is attached to.

In traditional wireless deployments, the WLC is typically centralized, and all control plane and data plane (wireless client data) traffic needs to be tunneled to the WLC through the Control and Provisioning of Wireless Access Points (CAPWAP) tunnel. In SD-Access, the wireless control plane remains centralized, but the data plane is distributed using VXLAN directly from the fabric-enabled APs. Figure 23-7 illustrates a traditional wireless deployment compared to an SD-Access wireless deployment.

Fabric APs establish a VXLAN tunnel to the fabric edge to transport wireless client data traffic through the VXLAN tunnel instead of the CAPWAP tunnel. For this to work, the AP must be directly connected to the fabric edge or a fabric extended node. Using a VXLAN tunnel to transport the wireless data traffic increases performance and scalability because the wireless client data traffic doesn't need to be tunneled to the WLC via CAPWAP, as in traditional wireless deployments because the routing decision is taken directly by the fabric edge. In addition, SGT- and VRF-based policies for wireless users on fabric SSIDs are applied at the fabric edge in the same way as for wired users. Wireless clients (SSIDs) use regular host pools for traffic and policy enforcement (the same as wired clients), and the fabric WLC registers client EIDs with the control plane node (as located on the edge).

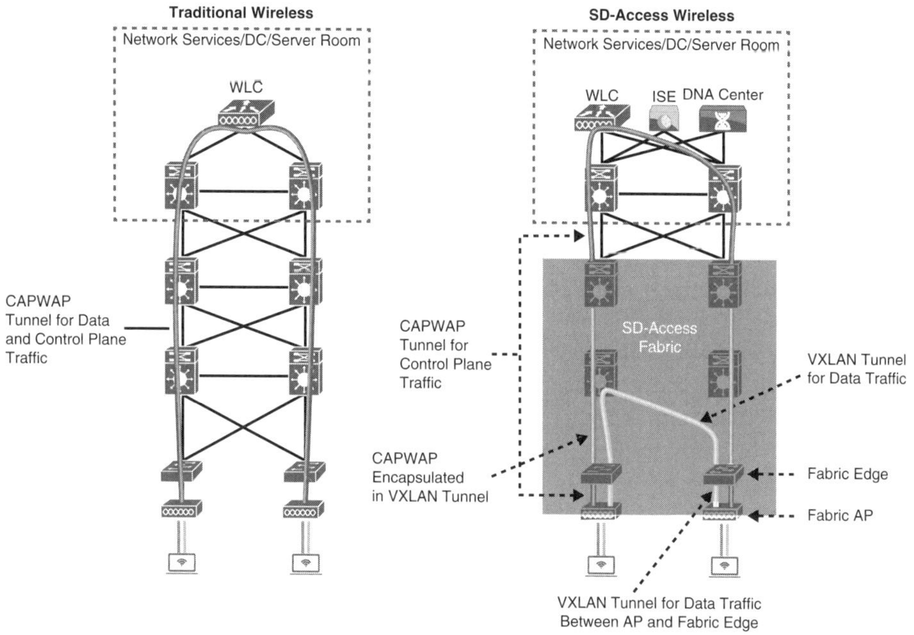

Figure 23-7 *Traditional Wireless and SD-Access Wireless Deployments*

SD-Access Fabric Concepts

Better understanding of the benefits and operation of Cisco SD-Access requires reviewing the following concepts related to how the multiple technologies that are used by the SD-Access solution operate and interact:

Key Topic

- **Virtual network (VN):** The VN provides virtualization at the device level, using VRF instances to create multiple Layer 3 routing tables. VRF instances provide segmentation across IP addresses, allowing for overlapped address space and traffic segmentation. In the control plane, LISP instance IDs are used to maintain separate VRF instances. In the data plane, edge nodes add a VXLAN VNID to the fabric encapsulation.
- **Host pool:** A host pool is a group of endpoints assigned to an IP pool subnet in the SDA-Access fabric. Fabric edge nodes have a Switched Virtual Interface (SVI) for each host pool to be used by endpoints and users as their default gateway. The SD-Access fabric uses EID mappings to advertise each host pool (per instance ID), which allows host-specific (/32, /128, or MAC) advertisement and mobility. Host pools can be assigned dynamically (using host authentication, such as 802.1x) and/or statically (per port).
- **Scalable group:** A scalable group is a group of endpoints with similar policies. The SD-Access policy plane assigns every endpoint (host) to a scalable group using TrustSec SGT tags. Assignment to a scalable group can be either static per fabric edge port or using dynamic authentication through AAA or RADIUS using Cisco ISE. The same scalable group is configured on all fabric edge and border nodes. Scalable groups can be defined in Cisco DNA Center and/or Cisco ISE and are advertised through

Cisco TrustSec. There is a direct one-to-one relationship between host pools and scalable groups. Therefore, the scalable groups operate within a VN by default. The fabric edge and border nodes include the SGT tag ID in each VXLAN header, which is carried across the fabric data plane. This keeps each scalable group separate and allows SGACL policy and enforcement.

- **Anycast gateway:** The anycast gateway provides a pervasive Layer 3 default gateway where the same SVI is provisioned on every edge node with the same SVI IP and MAC address. This allows an IP subnet to be stretched across the SD-Access fabric. For example, if the subnet 10.1.0.0/24 is provisioned on an SD-Access fabric, this subnet will be deployed across all of the edge nodes in the fabric, and an endpoint located in that subnet can be moved to any edge node within the fabric without a change to its IP address or default gateway. This essentially stretches these subnets across all of the edge nodes throughout the fabric, thereby simplifying the IP address assignment and allowing fewer but larger IP subnets to be deployed. In essence, the fabric behaves like a logical switch that spans multiple buildings, where an endpoint can be unplugged from one port and plugged into another port on a different building, and it will seem as if the endpoint is connecting to the same logical switch, where it can still reach the same SVI and other endpoints in the same VLAN.

Key Topic

Controller Layer

The controller layer provides all of the management subsystems for the management layer, and this is all provided by Cisco DNA Center and Cisco ISE. Figure 23-8 illustrates the different components that comprise the controller layer and how they interact with each other as well as with the campus fabric.

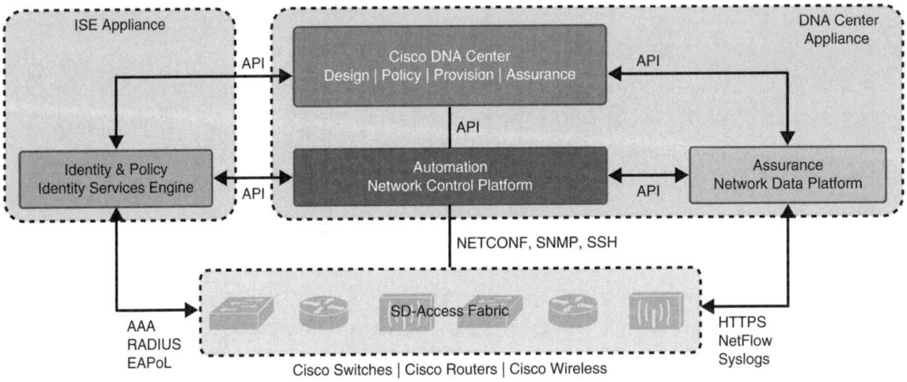

Figure 23-8 *SD-Access Main Components*

There are three main controller subsystems:

Key Topic

- **Cisco Network Control Platform (NCP):** This is a subsystem integrated directly into Cisco DNA Center that provides all the underlay and fabric automation and orchestration services for the physical and network layers. NCP configures and manages Cisco network devices using NETCONF/YANG, Simple Network Management Protocol (SNMP), SSH/Telnet, and so on and then provides network automation status and other information to the management layer.

- **Cisco Network Data Platform (NDP):** NDP is a data collection and analytics and assurance subsystem that is integrated directly into Cisco DNA Center. NDP analyzes and correlates various network events through multiple sources (such as NetFlow and Switched Port Analyzer [SPAN]) and identifies historical trends. It uses this information to provide contextual information to NCP and ISE, and it provides network operational status and other information to the management layer.
- **Cisco Identity Services Engine (ISE):** The basic role of ISE is to provide all the identity and policy services for the physical layer and network layer. ISE provides network access control (NAC) and identity services for dynamic endpoint-to-group mapping and policy definition in a variety of ways, including using 802.1x, **MAC Authentication Bypass (MAB)**, and **Web Authentication (WebAuth)**. ISE also collects and uses the contextual information shared from NDP and NCP (and other systems, such as Active Directory and AWS). ISE then places the profiled endpoints into the correct scalable group and host pool. It uses this information to provide information to NCP and NDP, so the user (management layer) can create and manage group-based policies. ISE is also responsible for programming group-based policies on the network devices.

Cisco ISE and the DNA Center (NCP and NDP) integrate with each other to share contextual information through APIs between themselves, and this contextual information is then provided to the user management layer:

- The NDP subsystem shares contextual analytics information with Cisco ISE and NCP subsystems and provides this information to the user (management layer).
- The NCP subsystem integrates directly with Cisco ISE and NDP subsystems to provide contextual automation information between them.
- Cisco ISE integrates directly with Cisco NCP and NDP subsystems (Cisco DNA Center) to provide contextual identity and policy information.

Key Topic

Management Layer

The Cisco DNA Center management layer is the user interface/user experience (UI/UX) layer, where all the information from the other layers is presented to the user in the form of a centralized management dashboard. It is the intent-based networking aspect of Cisco DNA.

A full understanding of the network layer (LISP, VXLAN, and Cisco TrustSec) or controller layer (Cisco NCP, NDP, and ISE) is not required to deploy the fabric in SD-Access. Nor is there a requirement to know how to configure each individual network device and feature to create the consistent end-to-end behavior offered by SD-Access.

The management layer abstracts all the complexities and dependencies of the other layers and provides the user with a simple set of GUI tools and workflows to easily manage and operate the entire Cisco DNA network (hence the name Cisco DNA Center).

Cisco DNA Center applications are designed for simplicity and are based on the primary workflows defined by Cisco DNA Center: design, policy, provision, and assurance.

Cisco DNA Design Workflow

The Cisco DNA design workflow provides all the tools needed to logically define the SD-Access fabric. The following are some of the Cisco DNA design tools:

- **Network Hierarchy:** Used to set up geolocation, building, and floorplan details and associate them with a unique site ID.
- **Network Settings:** Used to set up network servers (such as DNS, DHCP, and AAA), device credentials, IP management, and wireless settings.
- **Image Repository:** Used to manage the software images and/or maintenance updates, set version compliance, and download and deploy images.
- **Network Profiles:** Used to define LAN, WAN, and WLAN connection profiles (such as SSID) and apply them to one or more sites.

Figure 23-9 illustrates the DNA Center design workflow on the DNA Center dashboard.

Figure 23-9 *DNA Center Design Workflow*

Cisco DNA Policy Workflow

The Cisco DNA policy workflow provides all the tools to logically define Cisco DNA policies. The following are some of the Cisco DNA policy tools:

- **Dashboard:** Used to monitor all the VNs, scalable groups, policies, and recent changes.
- **Group-Based Access Control:** Used to create group-based access control policies, which are the same as SGACLs. Cisco DNA Center integrates with Cisco ISE to simplify the process of creating and maintaining SGACLs.

- **IP-Based Access Control:** Used to create IP-based access control policy to control the traffic going into and coming out of a Cisco device in the same way that an ACL does.
- **Application:** Used to configure QoS in the network through application policies.
- **Traffic Copy:** Used to configure Encapsulated Remote Switched Port Analyzer (ERSPAN) to copy the IP traffic flow between two entities to a specified remote destination for monitoring or troubleshooting purposes.
- **Virtual Network:** Used to set up the virtual networks (or use the default VN) and associate various scalable groups.

Figure 23-10 illustrates the DNA Center policy workflow on the DNA Center dashboard.

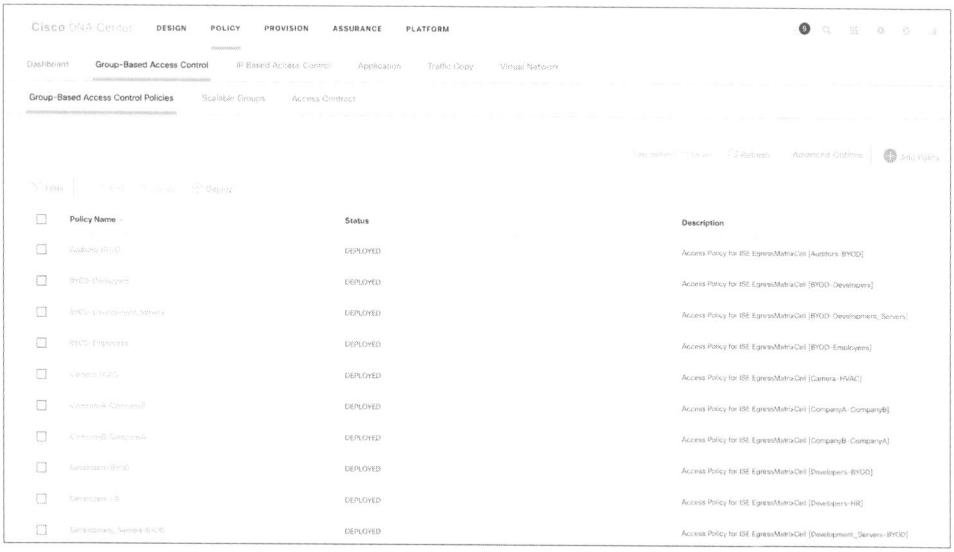

Figure 23-10 *DNA Center Policy Workflow*

Cisco DNA Provision Workflow

The Cisco DNA provision workflow provides all the tools to deploy the Cisco SD-Access fabric. The following are some of the Cisco DNA provision tools:

- **Devices:** Used to assign devices to a site ID, confirm or update the software version, and provision the network underlay configurations.
- **Fabrics:** Used to set up the fabric domains (or use the default LAN fabric).
- **Fabric Devices:** Used to add devices to the fabric domain and specify device roles (such as control plane, border, edge, and WLC).
- **Host Onboarding:** Used to define the host authentication type (static or dynamic) and assign host pools (wired and wireless) to various VNs.

Figure 23-11 illustrates the DNA Center provision workflow on the DNA Center dashboard.

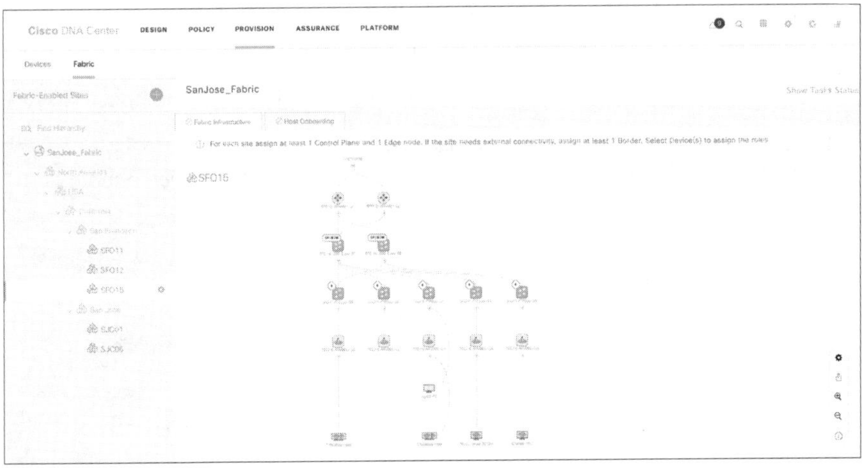

Figure 23-11 *DNA Center Provision Workflow*

Cisco DNA Assurance Workflow

The Cisco DNA assurance workflow provides all the tools to manage the SD-Access fabric. The following are some of the Cisco DNA assurance tools:

- **Dashboard:** Used to monitor the global health of all (fabric and non-fabric) devices and clients, with scores based on the status of various sites.
- **Client 360:** Used to monitor and resolve client-specific status and issues (such as onboarding and app experience), with links to connected devices.
- **Devices 360:** Used to monitor and resolve device-specific status and issues (such as resource usage and loss and latency), with links to connected clients.
- **Issues:** Used to monitor and resolve open issues (reactive) and/or developing trends (proactive) with clients and devices at various sites.

Figure 23-12 illustrates the DNA Center assurance workflow on the DNA Center dashboard.

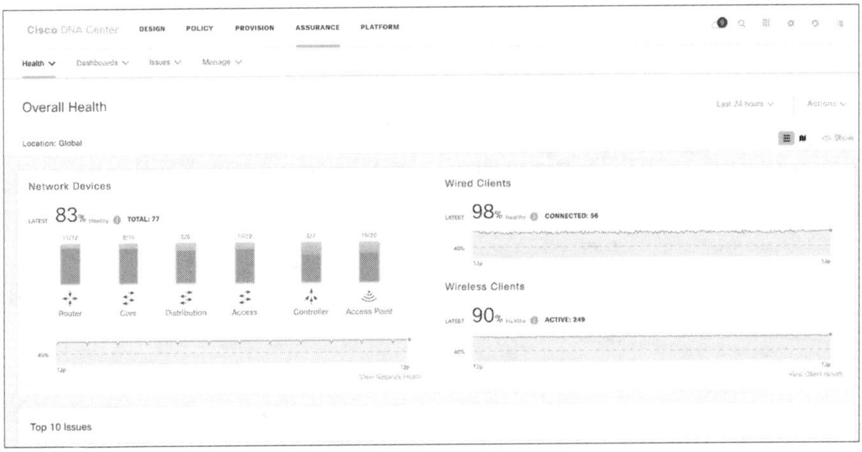

Figure 23-12 *DNA Center Assurance Workflow*

Software-Defined WAN (SD-WAN)

Managing enterprise networks is becoming more complex, with customers embracing a multicloud approach, applications moving to the cloud, mobile and IoT devices growing exponentially in the network, and the Internet edge moving to the branch. This digital transformation is powering the adoption of SD-WAN by customers looking to do the following:

- Centralize device configuration and network management.
- Lower costs and reduce risks with simple WAN automation and orchestration.
- Extend their enterprise networks (such as branch or on-premises) seamlessly into the public cloud.
- Provide optimal user experience for SaaS applications.
- Leverage a transport-independent WAN for lower cost and higher diversity. This means the underlay network can be any type of IP-based network, such as the Internet, MPLS, 3G/4G LTE, satellite, or dedicated circuits.
- Enhance application visibility and use that visibility to improve performance with intelligent path control to meet SLAs for business-critical and real-time applications.
- Provide end-to-end WAN traffic segmentation and encryption for protecting critical enterprise compute resources.

Cisco currently offers two SD-WAN solutions:

- **Cisco SD-WAN (based on Viptela):** This is the preferred solution for organizations that require an SD-WAN solution with cloud-based initiatives that provide granular segmentation, advanced routing, advanced security, and complex topologies while connecting to cloud instances.
- **Meraki SD-WAN:** This is the recommended solution for organizations that require unified threat management (UTM) solutions with SD-WAN functionality or that are existing Cisco Meraki customers looking to expand to SD-WAN. UTM is an all-in-one security solution delivered in a single appliance and typically includes the following security features: firewall, VPN, intrusion prevention, antivirus, antispam, and web content filtering.

The two SD-WAN solutions can achieve similar design goals, but this chapter covers only Cisco SD-WAN based on Viptela.

Cisco SD-WAN Architecture

Cisco SD-WAN (based on Viptela) is a cloud-delivered overlay WAN architecture that facilitates digital and cloud transformation for enterprises, and it addresses all the customer requirements mentioned earlier. Figure 23-13 illustrates the Cisco SD-WAN solution architecture.

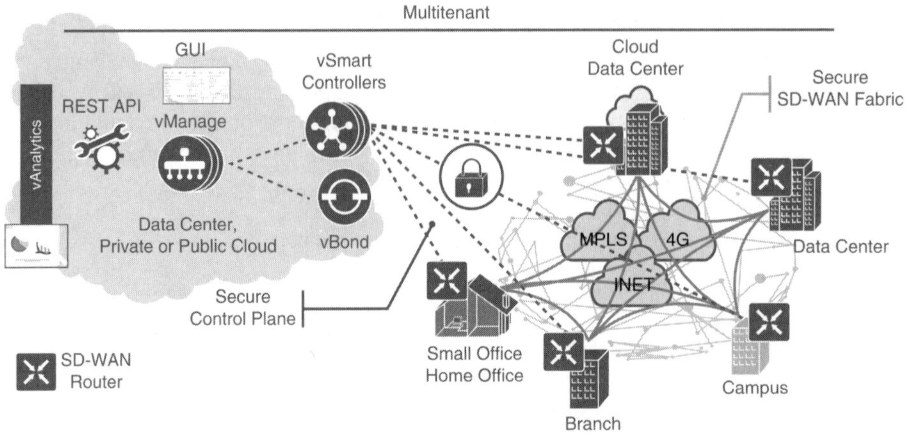

Figure 23-13 *SD-WAN Solution Architecture*

Figure 23-13 shows how SD-WAN can be used to provide secure connectivity to remote offices, branch offices, campus networks, data centers, and the cloud over any type of IP-based underlay transport network, such as the Internet, 3G/4G LTE, and MPLS. It also illustrates how some of the components to manage the SD-WAN fabric can be deployed on a data center, private cloud, or public cloud.

The Cisco SD-WAN solution has four main components and an optional analytics service:

Key Topic

- **SD-WAN edge devices:** These physical or virtual devices forward traffic across transports (that is, WAN circuits/media) between locations.
- **vManage Network Management System (NMS):** This SD-WAN controller persona provides a single pane of glass (GUI) for managing and monitoring the SD-WAN solution.
- **vSmart controller:** This SD-WAN controller persona is responsible for advertising routes and data policies to edge devices.
- **vBond orchestrator:** This SD-WAN controller persona authenticates and orchestrates connectivity between edge devices, vManage, and vSmart controllers.
- **vAnalytics:** This is an optional analytics and assurance service.

The vManage, vSmart, and vBond personas are independent and operate as separate devices or virtual machines. They can be hosted by Cisco, select Cisco partners, or under the control of customers in their own environments. Ensuring that edge devices can communicate with the three controller personas across all of the underlay circuits is an important design topic.

Key Topic

vBond Orchestrator

The vBond orchestrator is a virtualized vEdge running a dedicated function of the vBond persona. Devices can locate the vBond through specific IP addresses or fully qualified domain names (FQDNs). Using an FQDN is preferred because it allows for horizontal scaling of vBond devices and flexibility if a vBond ever needs to change its IP address.

The major components of the vBond orchestrator are

- **Authentication:** The vBond is responsible for authenticating every device in the fabric. As a device comes online, it must authenticate to the vBond, which determines the eligibility to join the SD-WAN fabric. Basic authentication of an SD-WAN router is done using certificates and RSA cryptography.
- **NAT detection:** The vBond can detect when devices are being placed behind NAT devices using Session Traversal Utilities for NAT (STUN) [RFC 5389] mechanisms. Placing a vBond behind a NAT device is not recommended but requires a 1:1 static NAT if it is placed behind a NAT device.
- **Load balancing:** The vBond provides load balancing of sessions to fabrics that have multiple vSmart or vManage controllers.

Every vBond has a permanent control plane connection over a **Datagram Transport Layer Security (DTLS)** tunnel with every vSmart controller. As edge devices authenticate with the vBond, they are directed to the appropriate vSmart and vManage device. NAT is detected, and then the edge device session is torn down. A session with vBond is formed across all edge device transports so that NAT detection can take place for every circuit.

Key Topic

vManage NMS

The vManage NMS is a single pane of glass network management system (NMS) GUI that is used to configure and manage the full SD-WAN solution. It contains all of the edge device configurations, controls software updates, and should be used for control and data plane policy creation. The vManage NMS also provides a method of configuring the SD-WAN fabric via APIs.

Key Topic

vSmart Controller

vSmart controllers uses DTLS tunnels with edge devices to establish Overlay Management Protocol (OMP) neighborships. OMP is a proprietary routing protocol similar to BGP that can advertise routes, next hops, keys, and policy information needed to establish and maintain the SD-WAN fabric.

The vSmart controller processes the OMP routes learned from the SD-WAN edge devices (or other vSmart controllers) and then advertises reachability information learned from these routes to the edge devices in the SD-WAN fabric.

vSmart controllers also implement all the control plane policies created on vManage, such as logical tunnel topologies (such as hub and spoke, regional, and partial mesh), service chaining, traffic engineering, and segmentation per VPN topology. For example, when a policy is created on vManage for an application (such as YouTube) that requires no more than 1% loss and 150 ms latency, that policy is downloaded to the vSmart controller. vSmart converts the policy into a format that all the edge devices in the fabric can understand and sends the data plane policy to the applicable edge devices without the need to log in to edge devices to configure the policy via a CLI.

Key Topic

Cisco SD-WAN Edge Devices

Cisco SD-WAN edge devices (that is, routers) deliver the essential WAN, security, and multicloud capabilities of the Cisco SD-WAN solution, and they are available as physical hardware, or in software with virtualized routers that sit at the perimeter of a site, such as a remote office, branch office, campus, data center, or cloud provider.

SD-WAN edge devices support standard router features, such as OSPF, EIGRP, BGP, ACLs, QoS, and routing policies, in addition to the SD-WAN overlay control and data plane functions. Each SD-WAN router automatically establishes a secure DTLS connection with the vSmart controller and forms an OMP neighborship over the tunnel to exchange routing information. It also establishes standard IPsec sessions with other SD-WAN routers in the fabric. SD-WAN routers have local intelligence to make site-local decisions regarding routing, high availability (HA), interfaces, ARP management, and ACLs. The vSmart controller provides remote site routes and the reachability information necessary to build the SD-WAN fabric.

NOTE The original Viptela hardware platforms running a dedicated Viptela OS are referred to as vEdge routers. vEdge router platforms are no longer available for purchase and are considered legacy platforms, because they do not provide some of the security features enabled on the Cisco IOS XE platforms.

The Cisco IOS XE platform devices are referred to as cEdge routers, and use a unified image with autonomous features starting with 17.2 version of software. vManage enables provisioning, configuration, and troubleshooting of cEdge and vEdge routers exactly the same way.

NOTE URL filtering and IPS are not supported on vEdge platforms and may not be present on some cEdge platforms because they operate outside of the operating system and process in IOS XE containers. Some platforms such as the ASR1K do not provide that capability.

vAnalytics

vAnalytics is an optional analytics and assurance service that has many advanced capabilities, including the following:

- Visibility into applications and infrastructure across the WAN
- Forecasting and what-if analysis
- Intelligent recommendations

These capabilities can bring many benefits to SD-WAN that are not possible without vAnalytics. For example, if a branch office is experiencing latency or loss on its MPLS link, vAnalytics detects this, and it compares that loss or latency with information on other organizations in the area that it is also monitoring to see if they are also having that same loss and latency in their circuits. If they are, vAnalytics can then report the issue with confidence to the SPs. vAnalytics can also help predict how much bandwidth is truly required for any location, and this capability is useful in deciding whether a circuit can be downgraded to a lower bandwidth to reduce costs.

Key Topic

Cisco SD-WAN Cloud OnRamp

Traditional enterprise WAN architectures are not designed for the cloud. As organizations adopt more SaaS applications such as Office 365 and public cloud infrastructures such as AWS and Microsoft Azure, the current network infrastructure poses major problems related to the level of complexity and end-user experience.

The Cisco SD-WAN solution includes a set of functionalities addressing optimal cloud SaaS application access and IaaS connectivity, called Cloud OnRamp (CoR). CoR delivers the best application quality of experience (QoE) for SaaS applications by continuously monitoring SaaS performance across diverse paths and selecting the best-performing path based on performance metrics (jitter, loss, and delay). In addition, it simplifies hybrid cloud and multicloud IaaS connectivity by extending the SD-WAN fabric to the public cloud while at the same time increasing high availability and scale.

SD-WAN Policy

The most powerful component of Cisco SD-WAN is the ability to push a unified policy across the fabric. The policy can modify the topology, influence traffic forwarding decisions, or be used to filter traffic. Configuring the SD-WAN policy on a vManage allows for changes in the network to be pushed out to thousands of devices in a matter of minutes.

Policies are further classified as

- **Local Policy:** Local policies are part of the configuration that is pushed to the edge device by the vManage. Local policies would include ACLs, QoS policies, and routing policies. Centralized policies would also include configuration of the on-device security stack.
- **Centralized Policy:** Centralized policies contain configuration changes to the vSmarts, where control plane functions are processed before OMP routes are advertised to edge devices. Data plane functionality is transmitted to edge devices' volatile memory for enforcement.

  Centralized policies can contain the following component policies:

  - **Topology:** A control plane policy to drop or modify routing behaviors by changing path metrics or even the next-hop.
  - **VPN Membership:** A control plane policy to control the advertisement of specific VPN prefixes to a specific site.
  - **Application-Aware Routing (AAR):** A data plane policy that enhances the forwarding of packets on an application-by-application basis, based on the characteristics of a tunnel.
  - **Traffic Data:** A data plane policy that can filter traffic on an application-by-application basis (or more general characteristics), modify traffic flows (change the next-hop, service-chaining, or even NAT), QoS functions, and/or implement packet loss protection mechanisms.

Application-Aware Routing

Application-aware routing (AAR) utilizes the *Bidirectional Forwarding Detection (BFD)* probes in the SD-WAN tunnels to track a tunnel's packet loss, latency, and jitter. BFD is a detection protocol originally designed to provide fast forwarding path failure detection times between two adjacent routers. For SD-WAN, it is leveraged to detect path liveliness (up/down) and to measure quality (loss/latency/jitter and IPsec tunnel MTU).

AAR provides the ability to consider factors in path selection outside of those used by standard routing protocols (such as interface bandwidth, interface delay, and hop count). An AAR policy can ensure that edge devices forward an application's traffic across a path that meets the needs defined for that application. AAR can be used to prefer one transport over another, but if the preferred transport exceeds the thresholds defined (packet loss, latency, and/or jitter) for that application, AAR will forward traffic across a different transport that meets its defined requirements.

AAR provides network engineers the capability to ensure their business-critical applications are taking the best available path when network brownouts or soft failures occur.

Cloud OnRamp for SaaS

SaaS applications reside mainly on the Internet, and to be able to achieve optimal SaaS application performance, the best-performing Internet exit point needs to be selected. In CoR SaaS, BFD is not used because there is no SD-WAN edge device on the SaaS side to form a BFD session with. When CoR for SaaS is configured for an SaaS application on vManage, the edge device at the remote site starts sending small HTTP probes to the SaaS application through both Internet circuits to measure latency and loss.

Figure 23-14 illustrates a remote site with dual Internet circuits from two different Internet service providers (ISP1 and ISP2). The remote site plans on forwarding SaaS applications directly out of both Internet circuits. A site that plans on forwarding SaaS traffic directly to the Internet is classified as a CoR DIA site.

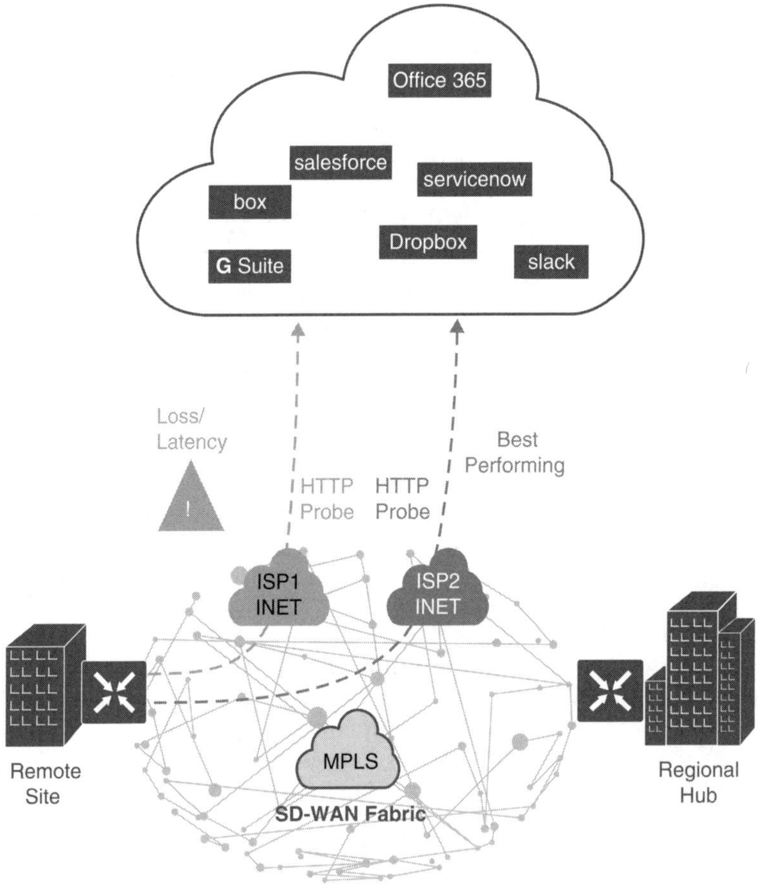

Figure 23-14 *Cloud OnRamp (CoR) for SaaS with Dual DIA*

NOTE CoR for SaaS does support load balancing across Internet circuits that are providing similar scores. The variations for packet loss and latency can be configured to increase or decrease the ability to load balance traffic at a site.

The quality of cloud SaaS application connection is quantified as a Viptela Quality of Experience (vQoE) score on a scale of 0 to 10, with 0 being the worst quality and 10 being the best. vQoE can be observed in the vManage GUI.

Based on the results, the ISP2 circuit is selected for that specific application. The remote site edge device will use the circuit with the highest QoE score for that application. The forwarding decision is made on an application-by-application basis. The process of probing continues, and if a change in performance characteristics of ISP2's Internet circuit occurs (for example, due to extreme latency), the remote site edge device makes a change to the circuit used.

Figure 23-15 illustrates another example of CoR for SaaS. In this case, the remote site has a single Internet circuit to ISP1 and an MPLS circuit providing connectivity to the regional hub.

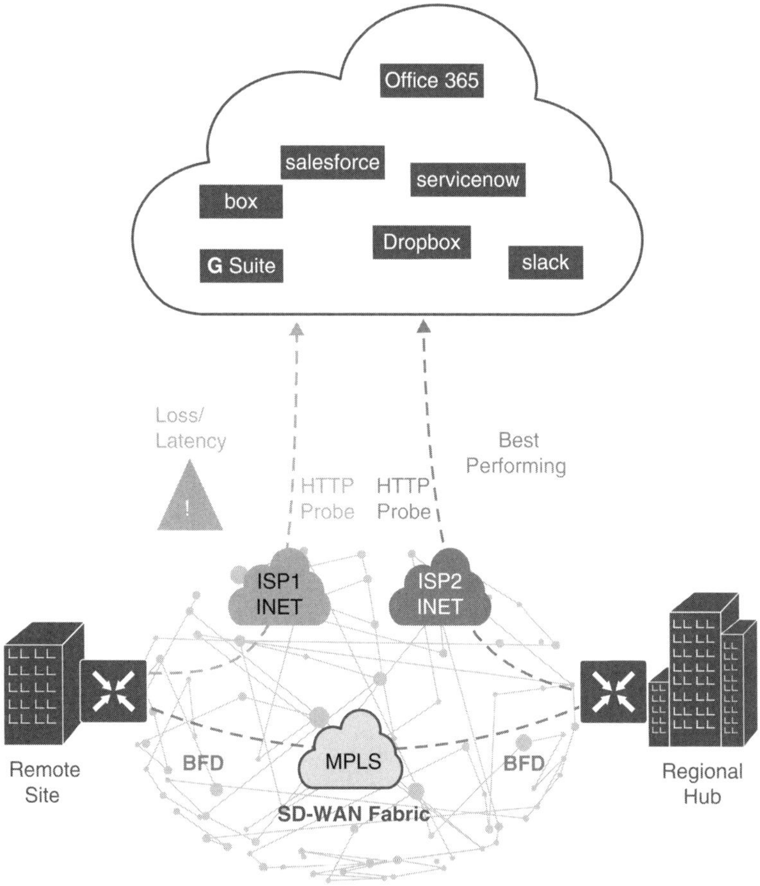

Figure 23-15 *Cloud OnRamp for SaaS DIA and Gateway*

Much as in the previous case, CoR for SaaS can be configured on the vManage and can become active on the remote site edge device. However, in this case, CoR for SaaS also gets enabled on the regional hub edge device and is designated as a gateway node. Quality probing service via HTTP toward the cloud SaaS application of interest starts on both the remote site SD-WAN and the regional hub SD-WAN.

The regional hub's edge device (gateway) reports its HTTP connection loss and latency characteristics to the remote site edge device in an Overlay Management Protocol (OMP) message exchange through the vSmart controllers. At this time, the remote site edge device can evaluate the performance characteristics of its local Internet circuit compared to the performance characteristics reported by the regional hub SD-WAN. It also takes into consideration the loss and latency incurred by traversing the SD-WAN fabric between the remote site and the hub site (calculated using BFD) and then makes an appropriate forwarding decision, sending application traffic down the best-performing path toward the cloud SaaS application of choice.

A third scenario for CoR for SaaS involves customers who use solely private transports (such as two different MPLS VPN providers). The remote site is classified as a client site. Client sites will identify which path between two different gateways is best for a specific application based on the QoE score. Traffic is then forwarded to the appropriate gateway site.

Cloud OnRamp for IaaS

Multicloud is now the new norm for enterprises. With multicloud, certain enterprise workloads remain within the boundaries of the private data centers, while others are hosted in the public cloud environments, such as AWS and Microsoft Azure. This approach provides enterprises the greatest flexibility in consuming compute infrastructure, as required.

With the Cisco SD-WAN solution, ubiquitous connectivity, zero-trust security, end-to-end segmentation, and application-aware QoS policies can be extended into the IaaS environments by using SD-WAN cloud routers, as illustrated in Figure 23-16. The transport-independent capability of the Cisco SD-WAN solution allows the use of a variety of connectivity methods by securely extending the SD-WAN fabric into the public cloud environment across any underlay transport network. These include the Internet, MPLS, 3G/4G LTE, satellite, and dedicated circuits such as AWS's DX and Microsoft Azure's ER.

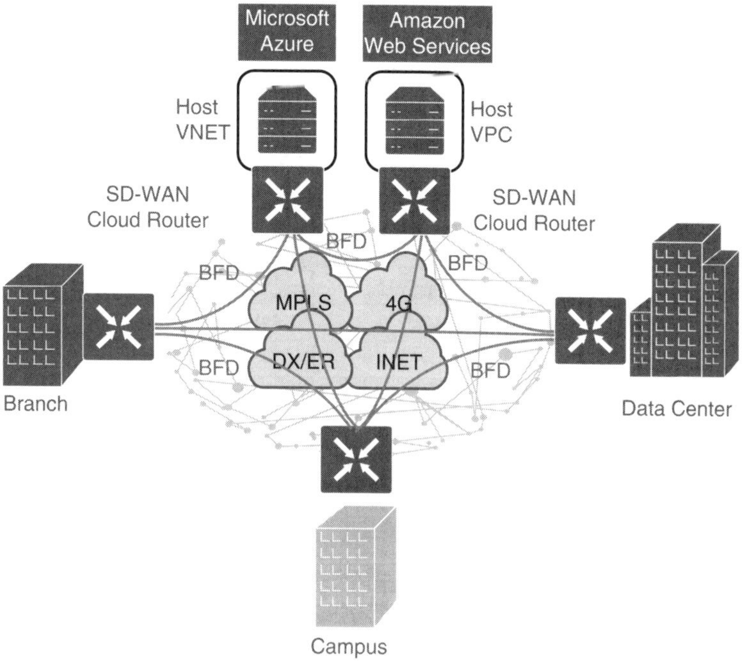

Figure 23-16 *Cloud OnRamp for IaaS*

Exam Preparation Tasks

You have a couple of choices for exam preparation: the exercises here, Chapter 30, "Final Preparation," and the exam simulation questions in the Pearson Test Prep Software Online.

Review All Key Topics

Review the most important topics in the chapter, noted with the Key Topic icon in the outer margin of the page. Table 23-2 lists these key topics and the page number on which each is found.

Key Topic

Table 23-2 Key Topics for Chapter 23

Key Topic Element	Description	Page
List	SD-Access capabilities, features, and functionalities	645
Figure 23-2	Cisco SD-Access Architecture	647
Section	Underlay Network	648
List	Types of underlay networks supported by SD-Access	648
Section	Overlay Network (SD-Access Fabric)	649
List	SD-Access basic planes of operation	649
Section	SD-Access Control Plane	649
Section	SD-Access Fabric Data Plane	650

Key Topic Element	Description	Page
Section	SD-Access Fabric Policy Plane	651
List	SD-Access fabric roles	652
Section	Fabric Edge Nodes	652
Section	Fabric Control Plane Node	653
Section	Fabric Border Nodes	654
List	Types of border nodes	654
Section	Fabric Wireless Controller (WLC)	654
List	SD-Access fabric concepts	655
Section	Controller Layer	656
List	SD-Access three main controller subsystems	656
Section	Management Layer	657
List	SD-WAN main components	662
Section	vBond Orchestrator	662
Section	vManage NMS	663
Section	vSmart Controller	663
Section	Cisco SD-WAN Edge Devices	663
Section	SD-WAN Cloud OnRamp	664

Complete Tables and Lists from Memory

Print a copy of Appendix B, "Memory Tables" (found on the companion website), or at least the section for this chapter, and complete the tables and lists from memory. Appendix C, "Memory Tables Answer Key," also on the companion website, includes completed tables and lists you can use to check your work.

Define Key Terms

Define the following key terms from this chapter and check your answers in the Glossary:

802.1x, application programming interface (API), Cisco TrustSec, Datagram Transport Layer Security (DTLS), endpoint, endpoint identifier (EID), host pool, MAC Authentication Bypass (MAB), map server (MS), Network Configuration Protocol (NETCONF)/YANG, overlay network, routing locator (RLOC), Security Group Access Control List (SGACL), Scalable Group Tag, segment, segmentation, tunnel router (xTR), underlay network, virtual network (VN), virtual tunnel endpoint (VTEP), VXLAN, VXLAN Group Policy Option (VXLAN-GPO), Web Authentication (WebAuth)

CHAPTER 24

Network Assurance

This chapter covers the following topics:

- **Network Diagnostic Tools:** This section covers the common use cases and operations of **ping**, **traceroute**, SNMP, and syslog.
- **Debugging:** This section describes the value of using debugging as a troubleshooting tool and provides basic configuration examples.
- **NetFlow and Flexible NetFlow:** This section examines the benefits and operations of NetFlow and Flexible NetFlow.
- **Switched Port Analyzer (SPAN) Technologies:** This section examines the benefits and operations of SPAN, RSPAN, and ERSPAN.
- **IP SLA:** This section covers IP SLA and the value of automated network probes and monitoring.
- **Cisco DNA Center Assurance:** This section provides a high-level overview of Cisco DNA Center Assurance and associated workflows for troubleshooting and diagnostics.

"Do I Know This Already?" Quiz

The "Do I Know This Already?" quiz enables you to assess whether you should read the entire chapter. If you miss no more than one of these self-assessment questions, you might want to move ahead to the "Exam Preparation Tasks" section. Table 24-1 lists the major headings in this chapter and the "Do I Know This Already?" quiz questions covering the material in those headings so you can assess your knowledge of these specific areas. The answers to the "Do I Know This Already?" quiz appear in Appendix A, "Answers to the 'Do I Know This Already?' Questions."

Table 24-1 "Do I Know This Already?" Foundation Topics Section-to-Question Mapping

Foundation Topics Section	Questions
Network Diagnostic Tools	1
Debugging	2
NetFlow and Flexible NetFlow	3–5
Switched Port Analyzer (SPAN) Technologies	6
IP SLA	7
Cisco DNA Center Assurance	8–10

1. True or false: The **traceroute** command tries 20 hops by default before quitting.
   a. True
   b. False
2. What are some reasons that debugging is used in OSPF? (Choose three.)
   a. Troubleshooting MTU issues
   b. Troubleshooting mismatched hello timers
   c. Viewing routing table entries
   d. Verifying BGP route imports
   e. Troubleshooting mismatched network masks
3. What is the latest version of NetFlow?
   a. Version 1
   b. Version 3
   c. Version 5
   d. Version 7
   e. Version 9
4. Which of the following allows for matching key fields?
   a. NetFlow
   b. Flexible NetFlow
   c. zFlow
   d. IPFIX
5. Which of the following are required to configure Flexible NetFlow? (Choose three.)
   a. Top talkers
   b. Flow exporter
   c. Flow record
   d. Flow sampler
   e. Flow monitor
6. What is ERSPAN for?
   a. Capturing packets from one port on a switch to another port on the same switch
   b. Capturing packets from one port on a switch to a port on another switch
   c. Capturing packets from one device and sending the capture across a Layer 3 routed link to another destination
   d. Capturing packets on one port and sending the capture to a VLAN
7. What is IP SLA used to monitor? (Choose four.)
   a. Delay
   b. Jitter
   c. Packet loss
   d. syslog messages
   e. SNMP traps
   f. Voice quality scores

8. Which are Cisco DNA Center components? (Choose three.)
   a. Assurance
   b. Design
   c. Plan
   d. Operate
   e. Provision
9. True or false: Cisco DNA Center Assurance can only manage routers and switches.
   a. True
   b. False
10. How does Cisco DNA Center Assurance simplify troubleshooting and diagnostics? (Choose two.)
    a. Using streaming telemetry to gain insight from devices
    b. Adding Plug and Play
    c. Simplifying provisioning for devices
    d. Using open APIs to integrate with other platforms to provide contextual information

Foundation Topics

Operating a network requires a specific set of skills. Those skills may include routing knowledge, troubleshooting techniques, and design experience. However, depth of skill sets can vary widely, based on years of experience and size and complexity of the networks that network operators are responsible for. For example, many small networks are very complex, and many very large networks are simple in design and complexity. Having a foundational skill set in key areas can help with the burden of operating and troubleshooting a network. Simply put, a network engineer who has experience with a technology will be more familiar with the technology in the event that the issue or challenge comes up again. This chapter covers some of the most common tools and techniques used to operate and troubleshoot a network. This chapter also covers some of the software-defined methods of managing, maintaining, and troubleshooting networks. Figure 24-1 shows the basic topology that is used to illustrate these technologies.

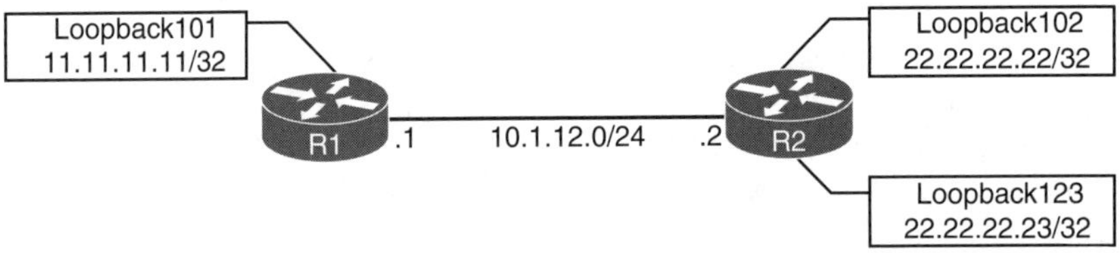

Figure 24-1 *Basic Topology*

Network Diagnostic Tools

Many network diagnostic tools are readily available. This section covers some of the most common tools available and provides use cases and examples of when to use them.

Key Topic

ping

ping is one of the most useful and underrated troubleshooting tools in any network. When you're following a troubleshooting flow or logic, it is critical to cover the basics first. For example, if a BGP peering adjacency is not coming up, it would make sense to check basic reachability between the two peers prior to doing any deep-dive BGP troubleshooting or debugging. Issues often lie in a lower level of the OSI model; physical layer issues, such as a cable being unplugged, can be found with a quick ping.

The following troubleshooting flow is a quick and basic way to check reachability and try to determine what the issue may be:

Step 1. Gather the facts. If you receive a trouble ticket saying that a remote location is down and cannot access the headquarters, it is important to know the IP address information for the remote site router or device. For example, using Figure 24-1, say that R2 is unable to reach the Loopback0 interface on R1. R2's IP address of its Ethernet0/0 is 10.1.12.2/24.

Step 2. Test reachability by using the **ping** command. Check to see whether the other end of the link is reachable by issuing the **ping 10.1.12.2** command at the command-line interface (CLI).

Step 3. Record the outcome of the **ping** command and move to the next troubleshooting step. If **ping** is successful, then the issue isn't likely related to basic reachability. If **ping** is unsuccessful, the next step could be checking something more advanced, such as interface issues, routing issues, access lists, or intermediate firewalls.

Example 24-1 illustrates a successful ping between R1 and R2. This example shows five 100-byte ICMP echo request packets sent to 10.1.12.2 with a 2-second timeout. The result is five exclamation points (!!!!!). This means that all five pings were successful within the default parameters, and ICMP echo reply packets were received from the destination. Each ping sent is represented by a single exclamation point (!) or period (.). This means that basic reachability has been verified. The success rate is the percentage of pings that were successful out of the total pings sent. The round-trip time is measured in a minimum/average/maximum manner. For example, if five ping packets were sent, and all five were successful, the success rate was 100%; in this case, the minimum/average/maximum were all 1 ms.

Example 24-1 *Successful ping Between R1 and R2*

```
R1# ping 10.1.12.2
Type escape sequence to abort.
Sending 5, 100-byte ICMP Echos to 10.1.12.2, timeout is 2 seconds:
!!!!!
Success rate is 100 percent (5/5), round-trip min/avg/max = 1/1/1 ms
```

It is important to illustrate what an unsuccessful ping looks like as well. Example 24-2 shows an unsuccessful ping to R2's Ethernet0/0 interface with an IP address of 10.1.12.2.

Example 24-2 *Unsuccessful ping Between R1 and R2*

```
R1# ping 10.1.12.2
Type escape sequence to abort.
Sending 5, 100-byte ICMP Echos to 10.1.12.2, timeout is 2 seconds:
.....
Success rate is 0 percent (0/5)
```

It is easy to count the number of pings when a low number of them is sent. The default is five. However, the parameters mentioned earlier for the **ping** command can be changed and manipulated to aid in troubleshooting. Example 24-3 shows some of the available options for the **ping** command on a Cisco device. These options can be seen by using the context-sensitive help (?) after the IP address that follows the **ping** command. This section specifically focuses on the **repeat**, **size**, and **source** options.

Example 24-3 ping 10.1.12.2 *Options*

```
R1# ping 10.1.12.2 ?
 data       specify data pattern
  df-bit    enable do not fragment bit in IP header
  repeat    specify repeat count
  size      specify datagram size
  source    specify source address or name
  timeout   specify timeout interval
  tos       specify type of service value
  validate  validate reply data
 <cr>
```

Suppose that while troubleshooting, a network operator wants to make a change to the network and validate that it resolved the issue at hand. A common way of doing this is to use the **repeat** option for the **ping** command. Many times, network operators want to run a continuous or a long ping to see when the destination is reachable. Example 24-4 shows a long ping set with a repeat of 100. In this case, the ping was not working, and then the destination became available—as shown by the 21 periods and the 79 exclamation points.

Example 24-4 ping 10.1.12.2 repeat 100 *Command*

```
R1# ping 10.1.12.2 repeat 100
Type escape sequence to abort.
Sending 100, 100-byte ICMP Echos to 10.1.12.2, timeout is 2 seconds:
.....................!!!!!!!!!!!!!!!!!!!!!!!!!!!!!!!!!!!!!!!!!!!!!!!!!!
!!!!!!!!!!!!!!!!!!!!!!!!!!!!!
Success rate is 79 percent (79/100), round-trip min/avg/max = 1/1/1 ms
```

Answers to the "Do I Know This Already?" quiz:

1 B **2** A, B, E **3** E **4** B **5** B, C, E **6** C **7** A, B, C, F **8** A, B, E **9** B **10** A, D

Another common use case for the **ping** command is to send different sizes of packets to a destination. An example might be to send 1500-byte packets with the DF bit set to make sure there are no MTU issues on the interfaces or to test different quality of service policies that restrict certain packet sizes. Example 24-5 shows a ping destined to R2's Ethernet0/0 interface with an IP address 10.1.12.2 and a packet size of 1500 bytes. The output shows that it was successful.

Example 24-5 ping 10.1.12.2 size 1500 *Command*

```
R1# ping 10.1.12.2 size 1500
Type escape sequence to abort.
Sending 5, 1500-byte ICMP Echos to 10.1.12.2, timeout is 2 seconds:
!!!!!
Success rate is 100 percent (5/5), round-trip min/avg/max = 1/1/1 ms
```

It is sometimes important to source pings from the appropriate interface when sending the pings to the destination. Otherwise, the source IP address used is the outgoing interface. In this topology, there is only one outgoing interface. However, if there were multiple outgoing interfaces, the router would check the routing table to determine the best interface to use for the source of the ping. If a network operator wanted to check a specific path—such as between the Loopback101 interface of R1 and the destination being R2's Loopback102 interface that has IP address 22.22.22.22—you could use the **source-interface** option of the **ping** command. Example 24-6 shows all the options covered thus far (**repeat**, **size**, and **source-interface**) in a single **ping** command. Multiple options can be used at the same time, as shown here, to simplify troubleshooting. Never underestimate the power of **ping**!

Example 24-6 ping *with Multiple Options*

```
R1# ping 22.22.22.22 source loopback 101 size 1500 repeat 10
Type escape sequence to abort.
Sending 10, 1500-byte ICMP Echos to 22.22.22.22, timeout is 2 seconds:
Packet sent with a source address of 11.11.11.11
!!!!!!!!!!
Success rate is 100 percent (10/10), round-trip min/avg/max = 1/1/1 ms
R1#
```

An extended ping can take advantage of the same options already discussed as well as some more detailed options for troubleshooting. These options are listed in Table 24-2.

Table 24-2 Extended ping Command Options

Option	Description
Protocol	IP, Novell, AppleTalk, CLNS, IPv6, and so on; the default is IP
Target IP address	Destination IP address of ping packets
Repeat Count	Number of ping packets sent; the default is 5 packets
Datagram Size	Size of the ping packet; the default is 100 bytes
Timeout in seconds	How long an echo reply response is waited for
Extended Commands	Yes or No to use extended commands; the default is No, but if Yes is used, more options become available

Option	Description
Source Address or Interface	IP address of the source interface or the interface name
Type of Service (ToS)	The Type of Service to be used for each probe; 0 is the default
Set DF bit in IP header	Sets the Do Not Fragment bit in the IP header; the default is No
Data Pattern	The data pattern used in the ping packets; the default is 0xABCD
Loose, Strict, Record, Timestamp, Verbose	The options set for the ping packets: ■ **Loose:** Specifies hops that ping packets should traverse ■ **Strict:** Same as Loose with the exception that packets can only traverse specified hops ■ **Record:** Displays IP addresses of first nine hops that the ping packets traverse ■ **Timestamp:** Displays the round-trip time to the destination for each ping ■ **Verbose:** Default option that is automatically selected with any and all other options

NOTE If Source Interface is used, the interface name must be spelled out and not abbreviated (for example, Ethernet0/0 rather than E0/0 or Eth0/0). Otherwise, you will receive the following error: "% Invalid source. Must use same-VRF IP address or full interface name without spaces (e.g. Serial0/1)."

Using the same topology shown in Figure 24-1, let's now look at an extended ping sent from R1's Loopback101 interface, destined to R2's Loopback123 interface. The following list provides the extended options that will be used:

- IP
- Repeat count of 1
- Datagram size of 1500 bytes
- Timeout of 1 second
- Source Interface of Loopback101
- Type of Service of 184
- Setting the DF bit in the IP Header
- Data pattern 0xABBA
- Timestamp and default of Verbose

Example 24-7 shows an extended ping using all these options and the output received from the tool at the command line. A repeat count of 1 is used in this example just to make the output more legible. Usually, this is 5 at the minimum or a higher number, depending on what is being diagnosed. Most common interface MTU settings are set at 1500 bytes. Setting the MTU in an extended ping and setting the DF bit in the IP header can help determine whether there are MTU settings in the path that are not set appropriately. A good example of when to use this is with tunneling. It is important to account for the overhead of the tunnel technology, which can vary based on the tunnel technology being used. Specifying a Type of Service of 184 in decimal translates to Expedited Forwarding (EF) or per-hop behavior (PHB). This behavior can be useful when testing real-time quality of service (QoS) policies in a network environment. However, some service providers do not honor pings or ICMP traffic marked with different PHB markings. Setting Data Patterns can help when troubleshooting framing errors, line coding, or clock signaling issues on serial interfaces. Service providers often ask network operators to send all 0s (0x0000) or all 1s (0xffff) during testing, depending on the issues they suspect. Finally, a timestamp is set in this example, in addition to the default Verbose output. This gives a clock timestamp of when the destination sent an echo reply message back to the source.

Example 24-7 *Extended ping with Multiple Options*

```
R1# ping
Protocol [ip]:
Target IP address: 22.22.22.23
Repeat count [5]: 1
Datagram size [100]: 1500
Timeout in seconds [2]: 1
Extended commands [n]: yes
Source address or interface: Loopback101
Type of service [0]: 184
Set DF bit in IP header? [no]: yes
Validate reply data? [no]:
Data pattern [0xABCD]: 0xABBA
Loose, Strict, Record, Timestamp, Verbose[none]: Timestamp
Number of timestamps [ 9 ]: 3
Loose, Strict, Record, Timestamp, Verbose[TV]:
Sweep range of sizes [n]:
Type escape sequence to abort.
Sending 1, 1500-byte ICMP Echos to 22.22.22.23, timeout is 1 seconds:
Packet sent with a source address of 11.11.11.11
Packet sent with the DF bit set
Packet has data pattern 0xABBA
Packet has IP options: Total option bytes= 16, padded length=16
 Timestamp: Type 0. Overflows: 0 length 16, ptr 5
  >>Current pointer<<
  Time= 16:00:00.000 PST (00000000)
```

```
  Time= 16:00:00.000 PST (00000000)
  Time= 16:00:00.000 PST (00000000)

 Reply to request 0 (1 ms). Received packet has options
 Total option bytes= 16, padded length=16
 Timestamp: Type 0. Overflows: 1 length 16, ptr 17
 Time=*08:18:41.697 PST (838005A1)
 Time=*08:18:41.698 PST (838005A2)
 Time=*08:18:41.698 PST (838005A2)
 >>Current pointer<<

Success rate is 100 percent (1/1), round-trip min/avg/max = 1/1/1 ms
```

ping and extended **ping** are very useful and powerful troubleshooting tools that you are likely to use daily. The information gained from using the **ping** command can help lead network operations staff to understand where an issue may exist within the network environment. More often than not, **ping** is used as a quick verification tool to confirm or narrow down the root cause of a network issue that is causing reachability problems.

Key Topic

traceroute

traceroute is another common troubleshooting tool. **traceroute** is often used to troubleshoot when trying to determine where traffic is failing as well as what path traffic takes throughout the network. **traceroute** shows the IP addresses or DNS names of the hops between the source and destination. It also shows how long it takes to reach the destination at each hop, measured in milliseconds. This tool is frequently used when more than one path is available to the destination or when there is more than one hop to the destination. Using the same topology shown in Figure 24-1, Example 24-8 shows a **traceroute** from R1 to R2's Loopback102 address of 22.22.22.22. Example 24-8 shows a successful **traceroute** from R1 to R2's Loopback102 interface. The output shows that the **traceroute** to 22.22.22.22 was sent to the next hop of 10.1.12.2 and was successful. Three probes were sent, and the second one timed out.

Example 24-8 *Basic* **traceroute** *to R2 Loopback102*

```
R1# traceroute 22.22.22.22
Type escape sequence to abort.
Tracing the route to 22.22.22.22
VRF info: (vrf in name/id, vrf out name/id)
  1 10.1.12.2 0 msec * 1 msec
```

Example 24-9 shows an unsuccessful **traceroute**. There are many reasons for unsuccessful **traceroutes**; however, one of the most common is a missing route or down interface. Example 24-9 illustrates a failed **traceroute** due to a missing route or mistyped destination. Notice that when a timeout has occurred, **traceroute** displays an asterisk. By default, **traceroute** tries up to 30 times/hops before completing.

Example 24-9 *Basic* traceroute *to a Nonexistent Route*

```
R1# traceroute 22.22.22.23
Type escape sequence to abort.
Tracing the route to 22.22.22.23
VRF info: (vrf in name/id, vrf out name/id)
  1 * * *
  2 * * *
  3 * * *
  4 * * *
  5 * * *
  6 * * *
  7 * * *
  8 * * *
  9 * * *
 10 * * *
 11 * * *
 12 * * *
 13 * * *
 14 * * *
 15 * * *
 16 * * *
 17 * * *
 18 * * *
 19 * * *
 20 * * *
 21 * * *
 22 * * *
 23 * * *
 24 * * *
 25 * * *
 26 * * *
 27 * * *
 28 * * *
 29 * * *
 30 * * *
```

Example 24-10 shows the R1 routing table. This output shows that R1 has a /32 host route to 22.22.22.22 using OSPF. However, there is no route for 22.22.22.23/32, which is why the traceroute is failing.

Example 24-10 *R1 Routing Table*

```
R1# show ip route
Codes: L - local, C - connected, S - static, R - RIP, M - mobile, B - BGP
       D - EIGRP, EX - EIGRP external, O - OSPF, IA - OSPF inter area
       N1 - OSPF NSSA external type 1, N2 - OSPF NSSA external type 2
```

```
       E1 - OSPF external type 1, E2 - OSPF external type 2
       i - IS-IS, su - IS-IS summary, L1 - IS-IS level-1, L2 - IS-IS level-2
       ia - IS-IS inter area, * - candidate default, U - per-user static route
       o - ODR, P - periodic downloaded static route, H - NHRP, l - LISP
       a - application route
       + - replicated route, % - next hop override

Gateway of last resort is not set

      10.0.0.0/8 is variably subnetted, 2 subnets, 2 masks
C        10.1.12.0/24 is directly connected, Ethernet0/0
L        10.1.12.1/32 is directly connected, Ethernet0/0
      11.0.0.0/32 is subnetted, 1 subnets
C        11.11.11.11 is directly connected, Loopback101
      22.0.0.0/32 is subnetted, 1 subnets
O IA     22.22.22.22 [110/11] via 10.1.12.2, 01:58:55, Ethernet0/0
```

Furthermore, if a less specific route is added to R1 that points to 22.0.0.0/8 or 22.0.0.0 255.0.0.0, the traceroute returns a "host unreachable" message. This is because there is a route to the next hop, R2 (10.1.12.2), but once the traceroute gets to R2, there is no interface or route to 22.22.22.23/32, and the traceroute fails. Example 24-11 shows this scenario.

Example 24-11 *Adding a Less Specific Route on R1*

```
R1# configure terminal
Enter configuration commands, one per line. End with CNTL/Z.
R1(config)# ip route 22.0.0.0 255.0.0.0 10.1.12.2
R1(config)# end
R1# traceroute 22.22.22.23
Type escape sequence to abort.
Tracing the route to 22.22.22.23
VRF info: (vrf in name/id, vrf out name/id)
 1 10.1.12.2 0 msec 0 msec 0 msec
 2 10.1.12.2 !H * !H
```

If a new loopback interface were added to R2 with the IP address 22.22.22.23 255.255.255.0, the traceroute would be successful. Example 24-12 shows the new Loopback123 interface configured on R2. Note that the response in Example 24-11 includes !H, which means R1 received an ICMP "destination host unreachable" message from R2. This is what happens when there is not a route present to the IP address.

Example 24-12 *Adding a Loopback123 Interface on R2*

```
R2# configure terminal
Enter configuration commands, one per line. End with CNTL/Z.
R2(config)# int loopback 123
R2(config-if)# ip add 22.22.22.23 255.255.255.255
R2(config-if)# end
```

Now that the new Loopback123 interface is configured on R2, it is important to circle back and rerun the traceroute from R1 to the 22.22.22.23 address to see if it is successful. Example 24-13 shows a successful traceroute from R1 to Loopback123 on R2.

Example 24-13 *Adding a Loopback123 Interface on R2*

```
R1# traceroute 22.22.22.23
Type escape sequence to abort.
Tracing the route to 22.22.22.23
VRF info: (vrf in name/id, vrf out name/id)
 1 10.1.12.2 0 msec * 0 msec
```


Another great benefit of **traceroute** is that it has options available, much like the **ping** command. These options can also be discovered by leveraging the context-sensitive help (?) from the command-line interface. Example 24-14 shows the list of available options to the **traceroute** command. This section focuses on the **port**, **source**, **timeout**, and **probe** options.

Example 24-14 *Available* **traceroute** *Options*

```
R1# traceroute 22.22.22.23 ?
 numeric display numeric address
 port    specify port number
 probe   specify number of probes per hop
 source  specify source address or name
 timeout specify time out
 ttl      specify minimum and maximum ttl
 <cr>
```

There are times when using some of the options available with **traceroute** may be useful (for example, if a network operator wants to change the port that the first probe is sent out on or source the traceroute from a different interface, such as a loopback interface). There are also times when there might be a reason to send a different number of probes per hop with different timeout timers rather than the default of three probes. As with the **ping** command, multiple **traceroute** options can be used at the same time. Example 24-15 shows the **traceroute** command being used on R1 to R2's Loopback123 interface with the **port**, **probe**, **source**, and **timeout** options all set.

Example 24-15 **traceroute** *to R2 Loopback123 with Options*

```
R1# traceroute 22.22.22.23 port 500 source loopback101 probe 5 timeout 10
Type escape sequence to abort.
Tracing the route to 22.22.22.23
VRF info: (vrf in name/id, vrf out name/id)
 1 10.1.12.2 1 msec * 0 msec * 0 msec
```

Much like the extended **ping** command covered earlier in this chapter, there is an extended **traceroute** command, and it has a number of detailed options available. Those options are listed in Table 24-3.

Table 24-3 Extended **traceroute** Command Options

Option	Description
Protocol	IP, Novell, AppleTalk, CLNS, IPv6, and so on; the default is IP
Target IP address	Destination IP address of ping packets
Numeric display	Shows only the numeric display rather than numeric and symbolic display
Timeout in Seconds	Time that is waited for a reply to a probe; the default is 3 seconds
Probe count	Number of probes sent at each hop; the default is 3
Source Address	IP address of the source interface
Minimum Time-to-live	TTL value of the first set of probes; can be used to hide topology information or known hops
Maximum Time-to-live	Maximum number of hops; the default is 30
Port number	Destination port number of probes; the default is 33434
Loose, Strict, Record, Timestamp, Verbose	The options set for the traceroute probes: ■ **Loose:** Specifies the hops that ping packets should traverse ■ **Strict:** Same as Loose with the exception that packets can traverse only specified hops ■ **Record:** Displays IP addresses of the first nine hops that the traceroute packets traverse ■ **Timestamp:** Displays the round-trip time to the destination for each ping ■ **Verbose:** Default option that is automatically selected with any and all other options

Using the same topology shown earlier in the chapter, in Figure 24-1, an extended traceroute will be sent from R1's Loopback101 interface destined to R2's Loopback123 interface. The following extended options will be used:

- IP
- Source Interface of Loopback101
- Timeout of 2 seconds
- Probe count of 1
- Port number 12345
- Timestamp and default of Verbose

Example 24-16 shows an extended **traceroute** using all these options and the output received from the tool at the command line. A probe count of 1 is used in this example just to make the output more legible. Usually, this is 3 by default, and it can be increased, depending on what is being diagnosed.

Example 24-16 *Extended* **traceroute** *to R2 Loopback123 with Options*

```
R1# traceroute
Protocol [ip]:
Target IP address: 22.22.22.23
Source address: 11.11.11.11
Numeric display [n]:
Timeout in seconds [3]: 2
Probe count [3]: 1
Minimum Time to Live [1]:
Maximum Time to Live [30]:
Port Number [33434]: 12345
Loose, Strict, Record, Timestamp, Verbose[none]: Timestamp
Number of timestamps [ 9 ]:
Loose, Strict, Record, Timestamp, Verbose[TV]:
Type escape sequence to abort.
Tracing the route to 22.22.22.23
VRF info: (vrf in name/id, vrf out name/id)
 1 10.1.12.2 1 msec
Received packet has options
Total option bytes= 40, padded length=40
 Timestamp: Type 0. Overflows: 0 length 40, ptr 13
 Time=*09:54:37.983 PST (83D7DB1F)
 Time=*09:54:37.983 PST (83D7DB1F)
 >>Current pointer<<
 Time= 16:00:00.000 PST (00000000)
 Time= 16:00:00.000 PST (00000000)
 Time= 16:00:00.000 PST (00000000)
 Time= 16:00:00.000 PST (00000000)
 Time= 16:00:00.000 PST (00000000)
 Time= 16:00:00.000 PST (00000000)
 Time= 16:00:00.000 PST (00000000)
```

Key Topic

Debugging

Debugging can be a powerful part of troubleshooting complex issues in a network. Debugging is also informational. This section provides some basic OSPF debugging examples and illustrates how to use debugging when trying to narrow down issues in a network.

One of the most common use cases for debugging is when there is a need to see things at a deeper level (such as when routing protocols are having adjacency issues). There is a normal flow that is taken from a troubleshooting perspective, depending on the routing protocol. However, there are times when these steps have been taken, and the issue is not evident. With OSPF, for example, when you're troubleshooting adjacency issues, it is very helpful to have debugging experience. Using the simple topology shown in Figure 24-2, in this section, debugging is used to fix a couple issues in the OSPF area 0.

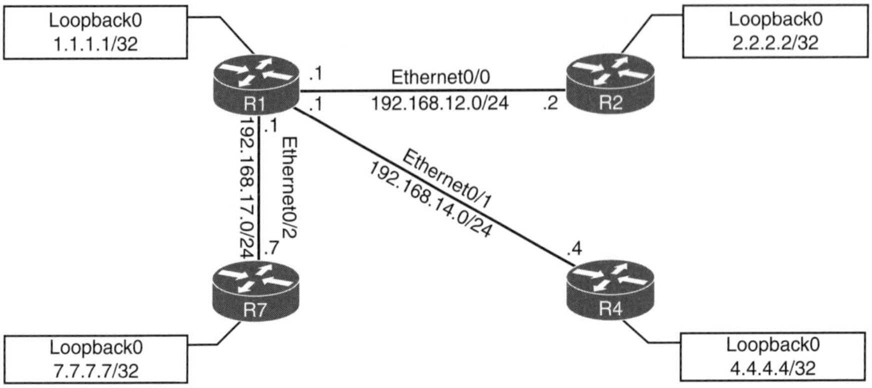

Figure 24-2 *Debugging Topology*

Some of the common OSPF adjacency issues can be resolved by using debugging. The following issues are covered in this section:

- MTU issues
- Incorrect interface types
- Improperly configured network mask

From the output of the **show ip ospf neighbor** command on R1 in Example 24-17, it can be seen that the neighbor adjacency to R4 is in the INIT state. If the command is run after a few seconds, the state changes to EXCHANGE but quickly cycles back to the INIT state when the command is run again.

Example 24-17 *Output of the* **show ip ospf neighbor** *Command*

```
R1# show ip ospf neighbor

Neighbor ID     Pri   State           Dead Time   Address         Interface
7.7.7.7           0   FULL/  -        00:00:31    192.168.17.7    Ethernet0/2
4.4.4.4           0   INIT/  -        00:00:37    192.168.14.4    Ethernet0/1
2.2.2.2           0   FULL/  -        00:00:33    192.168.12.2    Ethernet0/0
```

```
R1# show ip ospf neighbor

Neighbor ID     Pri   State           Dead Time   Address         Interface
7.7.7.7           0   FULL/  -        00:00:33    192.168.17.7    Ethernet0/2
4.4.4.4           0   EXCHANGE/  -    00:00:37    192.168.14.4    Ethernet0/1
2.2.2.2           0   FULL/  -        00:00:32    192.168.12.2    Ethernet0/0
```

```
R1# show ip ospf neighbor

Neighbor ID     Pri   State           Dead Time   Address         Interface
7.7.7.7           0   FULL/  -        00:00:31    192.168.17.7    Ethernet0/2
4.4.4.4           0   INIT/  -        00:00:38    192.168.14.4    Ethernet0/1
2.2.2.2           0   FULL/  -        00:00:39    192.168.12.2    Ethernet0/0
```

A typical approach to this line of troubleshooting is to log in to both devices and look at the logs or the running configuration. Although this approach may reveal the issue at hand, it may not be the most efficient way to troubleshoot. For example, a considerable amount of time is needed to log in to multiple devices and start combing through the configurations to see what may be missing or misconfigured. In the next example, debugging is used on R1 to try to determine what the issue is. Example 24-18 shows the output of the **debug ip ospf adj** command. This command is used to reveal messages that are exchanged during the OSPF adjacency process.

Example 24-18 *Output of the* **debug ip ospf adj** *Command on R1*

```
R1# debug ip ospf adj
OSPF adjacency debugging is on
R1#
19:20:42.559: OSPF-1 ADJ Et0/1: Rcv DBD from 4.4.4.4 seq 0x247A opt 0x52 flag 0x7
len 32 mtu 1400 state EXCHANGE
19:20:42.559: OSPF-1 ADJ Et0/1: Nbr 4.4.4.4 has smaller interface MTU
19:20:42.559: OSPF-1 ADJ Et0/1: Send DBD to 4.4.4.4 seq 0x247A opt 0x52 flag 0x2 len
152
R1# undebug all
All possible debugging has been turned off
```

With one **debug** command, it was easy to determine the root cause of the failed adjacency. The output of the **debug ip ospf adj** command in Example 24-18 clearly states that it received a Database Descriptor packet from the neighbor 4.4.4.4, and that the neighbor 4.4.4.4 has a smaller interface MTU of 1400. If the same **debug** command were run on R4, the output would be similar but show the reverse. Example 24-19 shows the output of the **debug ip ospf adj** command on R4 with the relevant fields highlighted.

Example 24-19 *Output of the* **debug ip ospf adj** *Command on R4*

```
R4# debug ip ospf adj
OSPF adjacency debugging is on
R4#
19:28:18.102: OSPF-1 ADJ Et0/1: Send DBD to 1.1.1.1 seq 0x235C opt 0x52 flag 0x7 len
32
19:28:18.102: OSPF-1 ADJ Et0/1: Retransmitting DBD to 1.1.1.1 [23]
19:28:18.102: OSPF-1 ADJ Et0/1: Rcv DBD from 1.1.1.1 seq 0x235C opt 0x52 flag 0x2
len 152 mtu 1500 state EXSTART
19:28:18.102: OSPF-1 ADJ Et0/1: Nbr 1.1.1.1 has larger interface MTU
R4# undebug all
All possible debugging has been turned off
```

The output of the **debug** command in Example 24-19 shows that R1 has an MTU size of 1500, which is larger than the locally configured MTU of 1400 on R4. This is a really quick way of troubleshooting this type of issue with adjacency formation.

The second issue to cover with adjacency formation is OSPF network type mismatch, which is a common reason for neighbor adjacency issues. Often this is simply a misconfiguration issue when setting up the network. When the **debug ip ospf hello** command is used on R1, everything appears to be normal: Hellos are sent to the multicast group 224.0.0.5 every 10 seconds. Example 24-20 shows the output of the **debug** command on R1.

Example 24-20 *Output of the* **debug ip ospf hello** *Command on R1*

```
R1# debug ip ospf hello
OSPF hello debugging is on
R1#
19:47:46.976: OSPF-1 HELLO Et0/0: Send hello to 224.0.0.5 area 0 from 192.168.12.1
19:47:47.431: OSPF-1 HELLO Et0/1: Send hello to 224.0.0.5 area 0 from 192.168.14.1
19:47:48.363: OSPF-1 HELLO Et0/2: Send hello to 224.0.0.5 area 0 from 192.168.17.1
19:47:50.582: OSPF-1 HELLO Et0/0: Rcv hello from 2.2.2.2 area 0 192.168.12.2
19:47:51.759: OSPF-1 HELLO Et0/2: Rcv hello from 7.7.7.7 area 0 192.168.17.7
19:47:56.923: OSPF-1 HELLO Et0/0: Send hello to 224.0.0.5 area 0 from 192.168.12.1
19:47:57.235: OSPF-1 HELLO Et0/1: Send hello to 224.0.0.5 area 0 from 192.168.14.1
19:47:58.159: OSPF-1 HELLO Et0/2: Send hello to 224.0.0.5 area 0 from 192.168.17.1
19:47:59.776: OSPF-1 HELLO Et0/0: Rcv hello from 2.2.2.2 area 0 192.168.12.2
19:48:01.622: OSPF-1 HELLO Et0/2: Rcv hello from 7.7.7.7 area 0 192.168.17.7
R1# undebug all
All possible debugging has been turned off
```

However, the situation is different if you issue the same **debug** command on R4. Example 24-21 shows the issue called out right in the **debug** output on R4. Based on the output, you can see that the hello parameters are mismatched. The output shows that R4 is receiving a dead interval of 40, while it has a configured dead interval of 120. You can also see that the hello interval R4 is receiving is 10, and the configured hello interval is 30. By default, the dead interval is 4 times the hello interval.

Example 24-21 *Output of the* **debug ip ospf hello** *Command on R4*

```
R4# debug ip ospf hello
OSPF hello debugging is on
R4#
19:45:45.127: OSPF-1 HELLO Et0/1: Rcv hello from 1.1.1.1 area 0 192.168.14.1
19:45:45.127: OSPF-1 HELLO Et0/1: Mismatched hello parameters from 192.168.14.1
19:45:45.127: OSPF-1 HELLO Et0/1: Dead R 40 C 120, Hello R 10 C 30
19:45:45.259: OSPF-1 HELLO Et0/3: Rcv hello from 7.7.7.7 area 0 192.168.47.7
19:45:48.298: OSPF-1 HELLO Et0/0: Send hello to 224.0.0.5 area 0 from 192.168.34.4
19:45:48.602: OSPF-1 HELLO Et0/0: Rcv hello from 3.3.3.3 area 0 192.168.34.3
R4# un all
All possible debugging has been turned off
```

Different network types have different hello intervals and dead intervals. Table 24-4 highlights the different hello and dead interval times based on the different OSPF network types.

Key Topic

Table 24-4 OSPF Network Types and Hello/Dead Intervals

Network Type	Hello Interval (in seconds)	Dead Interval (in seconds)
Broadcast	10	40
Non-broadcast	30	120
Point-to-point	10	40
Point-to-multipoint	30	120

The issue could be simply mismatched network types or mismatched hello or dead intervals. The **show ip ospf interface** command shows what the configured network types and hello and dead intervals are. Example 24-22 shows the output of this command on R4.

Example 24-22 *Output of the* **show ip ospf interface** *Command on R4*

```
R4# show ip ospf interface ethernet0/1
Ethernet0/1 is up, line protocol is up
  Internet Address 192.168.14.4/24, Area 0, Attached via Network Statement
  Process ID 1, Router ID 4.4.4.4, Network Type POINT_TO_MULTIPOINT, Cost: 10
  Topology-MTID    Cost    Disabled    Shutdown     Topology Name
        0           10        no          no           Base
  Transmit Delay is 1 sec, State POINT_TO_MULTIPOINT
  Timer intervals configured, Hello 30, Dead 120, Wait 120, Retransmit 5
    oob-resync timeout 120
    Hello due in 00:00:05
  Supports Link-local Signaling (LLS)
  Cisco NSF helper support enabled
  IETF NSF helper support enabled
  Index 2/2, flood queue length 0
  Next 0x0(0)/0x0(0)
  Last flood scan length is 1, maximum is 2
  Last flood scan time is 0 msec, maximum is 1 msec
  Neighbor Count is 0, Adjacent neighbor count is 0
  Suppress hello for 0 neighbor(s)
```

Simply changing the network type on R4 interface Ethernet0/1 back to the default of Broadcast fixes the adjacency issue in this case. The reason is that R1 is configured as Broadcast, and now the hello and dead intervals will match. Example 24-23 shows the **ip ospf network-type broadcast** command issued to change the network type to Broadcast on the Ethernet0/1 interface and the neighbor adjacency coming up. It is also verified with the **do show ip ospf neighbor** command.

Example 24-23 *Changing the Network Type on R4*

```
R4# configure terminal
Enter configuration commands, one per line.  End with CNTL/Z.
R4(config)# interface ethernet0/1
R4(config-if)# ip ospf network broadcast
R4(config-if)#
20:28:51.904: %OSPF-5-ADJCHG: Process 1, Nbr 1.1.1.1 on Ethernet0/1 from LOADING to
FULL, Loading Done
R4(config-if)# do show ip ospf neighbor

Neighbor ID     Pri   State           Dead Time   Address         Interface
7.7.7.7           0   FULL/  -        00:00:32    192.168.47.7    Ethernet0/3
1.1.1.1           1   FULL/BDR        00:00:39    192.168.14.1    Ethernet0/1
3.3.3.3           0   FULL/  -        00:00:33    192.168.34.3    Ethernet0/0
```

The final use case for using debugging to solve OSPF adjacency issues involves improper configuration of IP addresses and subnet masks on an OSPF interface. To troubleshoot this without having to look through running configurations or at a specific interface, you can use the same **debug ip ospf hello** command covered earlier in this section. Example 24-24 shows the output of running the **show ip ospf neighbor** command on R1. It indicates that there is no OSPF adjacency to R4 when there certainly should be one. The adjacency is stuck in INIT mode. In Example 24-24, the **debug ip ospf hello** command and the **debug ip ospf adj** command are enabled on R1 to see what is going on. The output shows a message that states, "No more immediate hello for nbr 4.4.4.4, which has been sent on this intf 2 times." This message indicates that something is wrong between R1 and R4.

Example 24-24 **show ip ospf neighbor, debug ip ospf hello,** *and* **debug ip ospf adj** *Commands on R1*

```
R1# show ip ospf neighbor

Neighbor ID     Pri   State           Dead Time   Address         Interface
7.7.7.7           0   FULL/  -        00:00:34    192.168.17.7    Ethernet0/2
4.4.4.4           0   INIT/  -        00:00:30    192.168.14.4    Ethernet0/1
2.2.2.2           0   FULL/  -        00:00:37    192.168.12.2    Ethernet0/0
R1#
R1# deb ip os hello
OSPF hello debugging is on
R1# deb ip ospf adj
OSPF adjacency debugging is on
20:55:02.465: OSPF-1 HELLO Et0/0: Send hello to 224.0.0.5 area 0 from 192.168.12.1
20:55:03.660: OSPF-1 HELLO Et0/0: Rcv hello from 2.2.2.2 area 0 192.168.12.2
20:55:04.867: OSPF-1 HELLO Et0/1: Send hello to 224.0.0.5 area 0 from 192.168.14.1
20:55:05.468: OSPF-1 HELLO Et0/1: Rcv hello from 4.4.4.4 area 0 192.168.14.4
```

```
20:55:05.468: OSPF-1 HELLO Et0/1: No more immediate hello for nbr 4.4.4.4, which has
been sent on this intf 2 times
20:55:06.051: OSPF-1 HELLO Et0/2: Send hello to 224.0.0.5 area 0 from 192.168.17.1
20:55:08.006: OSPF-1 HELLO Et0/2: Rcv hello from 7.7.7.7 area 0 192.168.17.7
R1#
R1# undebug all
All possible debugging has been turned off
```


Issuing the same **debug** commands on R4 provides the output shown in Example 24-25; the issue is mismatched hello parameters. R4 is receiving a network of 255.255.255.0, but it has a network mask of 255.255.255.248 locally configured. This causes an adjacency issue even though the hello and dead intervals are configured to match.

Example 24-25 **debug ip ospf hello** *and* **debug ip ospf adj** *Commands on R4*

```
R4# deb ip ospf hello
OSPF hello debugging is on
R4# deb ip ospf adj
OSPF adjacency debugging is on
21:05:50.863: OSPF-1 HELLO Et0/0: Rcv hello from 3.3.3.3 area 0 192.168.34.3
21:05:51.318: OSPF-1 HELLO Et0/1: Send hello to 224.0.0.5 area 0 from 192.168.14.4
21:05:51.859: OSPF-1 HELLO Et0/3: Send hello to 224.0.0.5 area 0 from 192.168.47.4
21:05:53.376: OSPF-1 HELLO Et0/0: Send hello to 224.0.0.5 area 0 from 192.168.34.4
21:05:56.906: OSPF-1 HELLO Et0/3: Rcv hello from 7.7.7.7 area 0 192.168.47.7
21:05:57.927: OSPF-1 HELLO Et0/1: Rcv hello from 1.1.1.1 area 0 192.168.14.1
21:05:57.927: OSPF-1 HELLO Et0/1: Mismatched hello parameters from 192.168.14.1
21:05:57.927: OSPF-1 HELLO Et0/1: Dead R 40 C 40, Hello R 10 C 10 Mask R
255.255.255.0 C 255.255.255.248
21:06:00.255: OSPF-1 HELLO Et0/0: Rcv hello from 3.3.3.3 area 0 192.168.34.3
21:06:00.814: OSPF-1 HELLO Et0/1: Send hello to 224.0.0.5 area 0 from 192.168.14.4
21:06:01.047: OSPF-1 HELLO Et0/3: Send hello to 224.0.0.5 area 0 from 192.168.47.4
R4# undebug all
All possible debugging has been turned off
```

To resolve this issue, the network mask on the Ethernet0/1 interface of R4 needs to be changed to match the one that R1 has configured and is sending to R4 through OSPF hellos. Example 24-26 shows the network mask being changed on the R4 Ethernet0/1 interface and the OSPF adjacency coming up. This is then verified with the **do show ip ospf neighbor** command.

Example 24-26 *Network Mask Change and* **show ip ospf neighbor** *on R4*

```
R4# configure terminal
Enter configuration commands, one per line. End with CNTL/Z.
R4(config)# interface ethernet0/1
R4(config-if)# ip address 192.168.14.4 255.255.255.0
R4(config-if)#
21:14:15.598: %OSPF-5-ADJCHG: Process 1, Nbr 1.1.1.1 on Ethernet0/1 from LOADING to
FULL, Loading Done
R4(config-if)# do show ip ospf neighbor

Neighbor ID     Pri   State           Dead Time   Address         Interface
1.1.1.1           1   FULL/BDR        00:00:38    192.168.14.1    Ethernet0/1
7.7.7.7           0   FULL/  -        00:00:37    192.168.47.7    Ethernet0/3
3.3.3.3           0   FULL/  -        00:00:30    192.168.34.3    Ethernet0/0
```

Conditional Debugging

As mentioned earlier in this chapter, debugging can be very informational. Sometimes, there is too much information, and it is important to know how to restrict the **debug** commands and limit the messages to what is appropriate for troubleshooting the issue at hand. Often, networking engineers or operators are intimidated by the sheer number of messages that can be seen while debugging. In the past, routers and switches didn't have as much memory and CPU as they do today, and running **debug** (especially running multiple **debug** commands simultaneously) could cause a network device to become unresponsive or crash, and it could even cause an outage.

Conditional debugging can be used to limit the scope of the messages that are being returned to the console or syslog server. A great example of this is the **debug ip packet** command. Issuing this command on a router that is in production could send back a tremendous number of messages. One way to alleviate this issue is to attach an access list to the **debug** command to limit the scope of messages to the source or destination specified within the access list. For example, say that you configure an access list that focuses on any traffic to or from the 192.168.14.0/24 network. This can be done using standard or extended access lists. The options for the **debug ip packet** command are as follows:

- **<1-199>:** Access list
- **<1300-2699>:** Access list with expanded range
- **detail:** More debugging detail

To showcase the power of conditional debugging, Example 24-27 uses a standard access list to limit the messages to the console and filter solely on traffic to and from the 192.168.14.0/24 subnet.

Example 24-27 *Conditional Debugging IP Packet for 192.168.14.0/24 on R4*

```
R4(config)# access-list 100 permit ip any 192.168.14.0 0.0.0.255
R4(config)# access-list 100 permit ip 192.168.14.0 0.0.0.255 any
R4# debug ip packet 100
IP packet debugging is on for access list 100
21:29:58.118: IP: s=192.168.14.1 (Ethernet0/1), d=224.0.0.2, len 62, rcvd 0
21:29:58.118: IP: s=192.168.14.1 (Ethernet0/1), d=224.0.0.2, len 62, input feature,
packet consumed, MCI Check(104), rtype 0, forus FALSE, sendself FALSE, mtu 0, fwdchk
FALSE
21:30:00.418: IP: s=192.168.14.4 (local), d=224.0.0.2 (Ethernet0/1), len 62, sending
broad/multicast
21:30:00.418: IP: s=192.168.14.4 (local), d=224.0.0.2 (Ethernet0/1), len 62, sending
full packet
21:30:01.964: IP: s=192.168.14.1 (Ethernet0/1), d=224.0.0.2, len 62, rcvd 0
21:30:01.964: IP: s=192.168.14.1 (Ethernet0/1), d=224.0.0.2, len 62, input feature,
packet consumed, MCI Check(104), rtype 0, forus FALSE, sendself FALSE, mtu 0, fwdchk
FALSE
21:30:02.327: IP: s=192.168.14.1 (Ethernet0/1), d=224.0.0.5, len 80, rcvd 0
21:30:02.327: IP: s=192.168.14.1 (Ethernet0/1), d=224.0.0.5, len 80, input feature,
packet consumed, MCI Check(104), rtype 0, forus FALSE, sendself FALSE, mtu 0, fwdchk
FALSE
21:30:03.263: IP: s=192.168.14.4 (local), d=224.0.0.5 (Ethernet0/1), len 80, sending
broad/multicast
21:30:03.263: IP: s=192.168.14.4 (local), d=224.0.0.5 (Ethernet0/1), len 80, sending
full packet
21:30:04.506: IP: s=192.168.14.4 (local), d=224.0.0.2 (Ethernet0/1), len 62, sending
broad/multicast
21:30:04.506: IP: s=192.168.14.4 (local), d=224.0.0.2 (Ethernet0/1), len 62, sending
full packet
R4# undebug all
All possible debugging has been turned off
```

Another common method of conditional debugging is to debug on a specific interface. This capability is extremely useful when trying to narrow down a packet flow between two hosts. Imagine that a network engineer is trying to debug a traffic flow between R1's Ethernet0/1 interface with source IP address 192.168.14.1/24 that is destined to R4's Loopback0 interface with IP address 4.4.4.4/32. One way to do this would certainly be to change the access list 100 to reflect these source and destination IP addresses. However, because the access list is looking for any traffic sourced or destined to the 192.168.14.0/24 network, this traffic flow would fall into matching that access list. Using conditional debugging on the Loopback0 interface of R4 would be a simple way of meeting these requirements. Example 24-28 shows the conditional debugging on R4. When that is in place, a ping on R1 sourced from the Ethernet0/1 interface matches the conditions set on R4.

Example 24-28 *Conditional Loopback0 Interface Debugging IP Packet for 192.168.14.0/24 on R4*

```
R4# debug interface Loopback0
Condition 1 set
R4# debug ip packet 100
IP packet debugging is on for access list 100
R4#
R4# show debug
Generic IP:
 IP packet debugging is on for access list 100
Condition 1: interface Lo0 (1 flags triggered)
        Flags: Lo0

21:39:59.033: IP: tableid=0, s=192.168.14.1 (Ethernet0/3), d=4.4.4.4 (Loopback0),
  routed via RIB
21:39:59.033: IP: s=192.168.14.1 (Ethernet0/3), d=4.4.4.4, len 100, stop process pak
   for forus packet
21:39:59.033: IP: tableid=0, s=192.168.14.1 (Ethernet0/3), d=4.4.4.4 (Loopback0),
  routed via RIB
21:39:59.033: IP: s=192.168.14.1 (Ethernet0/3), d=4.4.4.4, len 100, stop process pak
  for forus packet
21:39:59.033: IP: tableid=0, s=192.168.14.1 (Ethernet0/3), d=4.4.4.4 (Loopback0),
  routed via RIB
21:39:59.033: IP: s=192.168.14.1 (Ethernet0/3), d=4.4.4.4, len 100, stop process pak
  for forus packet
21:39:59.034: IP: tableid=0, s=192.168.14.1 (Ethernet0/3), d=4.4.4.4 (Loopback0),
  routed via RIB
21:39:59.034: IP: s=192.168.14.1 (Ethernet0/3), d=4.4.4.4, len 100, stop process pak
  for forus packet
21:39:59.034: IP: tableid=0, s=192.168.14.1 (Ethernet0/3), d=4.4.4.4 (Loopback0),
  routed via RIB
21:39:59.034: IP: s=192.168.14.1 (Ethernet0/3), d=4.4.4.4, len 100, stop process pak
  for forus packet
R4# undebug all
All possible debugging has been turned off
R4# undebug interface loopback0
This condition is the last interface condition set.
Removing all conditions may cause a flood of debugging
messages to result, unless specific debugging flags
are first removed.

Proceed with removal? [yes/no]: yes
Condition 1 has been removed
```

It is important to note that even if all debugging has been turned off using the **undebug all** command, the interface conditions set for Loopback0 on R4 remain. The way to remove this condition is to use the **undebug interface loopback0** command on R4. When this is executed, the user is asked to confirm whether to proceed with removing the condition. The conditions can be removed while live **debug** commands are still running, and the operating system wants to indicate that the user might receive a flood of debug messages when the condition is removed. Although many more debug operations are available, understanding the fundamental steps outlined here helps take the fear out of using this powerful diagnostic tool when troubleshooting issues that arise in the network environment.

NOTE When you're issuing debugging commands, it is best to practice within a test environment prior to using them in production. When you are comfortable with the outcomes, you can use these commands in production.

Key Topic

Simple Network Management Protocol (SNMP)

Network operations teams often have to rely on reactive alerting from network devices to be notified when something is happening—such as something failing or certain events happening on a device. The typical tool for this is **Simple Network Management Protocol (SNMP)**. SNMP can also be used to configure devices, although this use is less common. More often when network engineering teams need to configure devices, configuration management tools such as Cisco Prime Infrastructure are used.

This section focuses on SNMP from an alerting perspective and provides some configuration examples for enabling SNMP and some basic functionality of the protocol. SNMP sends unsolicited traps to an SNMP collector or network management system (NMS). These traps are in response to something that happened in the network. For example, traps may be generated for link status events, improper user authentication, and power supply failures. These events are defined in the SNMP Management Information Base (MIB). The MIB can be thought of as a repository of device parameters that can be used to trigger alerts. There are currently three versions of SNMP. Table 24-5 lists the versions and their differences.

Table 24-5 SNMP Version Comparison

Version	Level	Authentication	Encryption	Result
SNMPv1	noAuthNoPriv	Community string	No	Uses a community string match for authentication.
SNMPv2c	noAuthNoPriv	Community string	No	Uses a community string match for authentication.
SNMPv3	noAuthNoPriv	Username	No	Uses a username match for authentication.
SNMPv3	authNoPriv	Message Digest 5 (MD5) or Secure Hash Algorithm (SHA)	No	Provides authentication based on the HMAC-MD5 or HMAC-SHA algorithms.

Version	Level	Authentication	Encryption	Result
SNMPv3	authPriv (requires the cryptographic software image)	MD5 or SHA	Data Encryption Standard (DES) or Advanced Encryption Standard (AES)	Provides authentication based on the HMAC-MD5 or HMAC-SHA algorithms. Allows specifying the User-based Security Model (USM) with these encryption algorithms: DES 56-bit encryption in addition to authentication based on the CBC-DES (DES-56) standard. 3DES 168-bit encryption AES 128-bit, 192-bit, or 256-bit encryption

SNMPv3 provides the most security options and encryption capabilities. SNMPv3 uses usernames and SHA or MD5 for authentication, which makes SNMPv3 very secure compared to SNMPv1 or SNMPv2c. Using SNMPv3 is considered best practice in production. However, the examples in this section use SNMPv2c for simplicity's sake. SNMPv1 and SNMPv2c use access lists and a community password or string to control what SNMP managers can talk to the devices via SNMP. These community strings can be read-only (RO) or read/write (RW). As the names imply, read-only allows the polling of devices to get information from the device(s). Read/write allows pushing of information to a device or configuration of a device. It is critical to limit SNMP access to these devices by using access lists, as mentioned earlier in this section. Without access lists, there is a potential risk because the devices could be attacked by unauthorized users. SNMPv2c also has improved error handling and expanded error code information, which makes it a much better option than SNMPv1. By default, if no version is specified in configuration, SNMPv1 is used. However, to better show how SNMP works, this chapter focuses on SNMPv2c. SNMPv2c operations are listed in Table 24-6.

Table 24-6 SNMP Operations

Operation	Description
get-request	Retrieves a value from a specific variable
get-next-request	Retrieves a value from a variable within a table
get-bulk-request	Retrieves large blocks of data, such as multiple rows in a table, that would otherwise require the transmission of many small blocks of data
get-response	Replies to a get request, get next request, and set request sent by an NMS
set-request	Stores a value in a specific variable
trap	Sends an unsolicited message from an SNMP agent to an SNMP manager when some event has occurred

Figure 24-3 depicts the communications between an NMS and a network device.

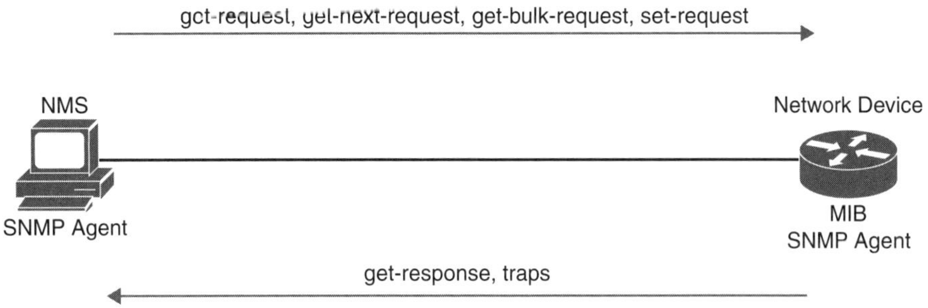

Figure 24-3 *SNMP Communication Between NMS Host and Network Device*

Now that the basic operations of SNMP have been listed, it is important to look at an MIB to understand some of the information or values that can be polled or send traps from SNMP. Example 24-29 shows some of the contents of the SNMPv2-MIB.my file. This file is publicly available on the Cisco website and shows what values can be polled in the MIB and to illustrate sending traps from SNMP.

NOTE To see a list of available Cisco MIBs, visit https://cfnng.cisco.com/mibs.

Example 24-29 *Partial Contents of SNMPv2-MIB.my*

```
-- the System group
--
-- a collection of objects common to all managed systems.

system   OBJECT IDENTIFIER ::= { mib-2 1 }

sysDescr OBJECT-TYPE
    SYNTAX      DisplayString (SIZE (0..255))
    MAX-ACCESS  read-only
    STATUS      current
    DESCRIPTION
            "A textual description of the entity.  This value should
            include the full name and version identification of
            the system's hardware type, software operating-system,
            and networking software."
    ::= { system 1 }

sysObjectID OBJECT-TYPE
    SYNTAX      OBJECT IDENTIFIER
    MAX-ACCESS  read-only
    STATUS      current
```

```
    DESCRIPTION
            "The vendor's authoritative identification of the
            network management subsystem contained in the entity.
            This value is allocated within the SMI enterprises
            subtree (1.3.6.1.4.1) and provides an easy and
            unambiguous means for determining 'what kind of box' is
            being managed.  For example, if vendor 'Flintstones,
            Inc.' was assigned the subtree 1.3.6.1.4.1.424242,
            it could assign the identifier 1.3.6.1.4.1.424242.1.1
            to its 'Fred Router'."
    ::= { system 2 }

sysUpTime OBJECT-TYPE
    SYNTAX      TimeTicks
    MAX-ACCESS  read-only
    STATUS      current
    DESCRIPTION
            "The time (in hundredths of a second) since the
            network management portion of the system was last
            re-initialized."
    ::= { system 3 }

sysContact OBJECT-TYPE
    SYNTAX      DisplayString (SIZE (0..255))
    MAX-ACCESS  read-write
    STATUS      current
    DESCRIPTION
            "The textual identification of the contact person for
            this managed node, together with information on how
            to contact this person.  If no contact information is
            known, the value is the zero-length string."
    ::= { system 4 }

sysName OBJECT-TYPE
    SYNTAX      DisplayString (SIZE (0..255))
    MAX-ACCESS  read-write
    STATUS      current
    DESCRIPTION
            "An administratively-assigned name for this managed
            node.  By convention, this is the node's fully-qualified
            domain name.  If the name is unknown, the value is
            the zero-length string."
    ::= { system 5 }
```

```
sysLocation OBJECT-TYPE
    SYNTAX      DisplayString (SIZE (0..255))
    MAX-ACCESS  read-write
    STATUS      current
    DESCRIPTION
            "The physical location of this node (e.g., 'telephone
            closet, 3rd floor').  If the location is unknown, the
            value is the zero-length string."
    ::= { system 6 }
```

The structure of this MIB file is well documented and human readable. This portion of the file was selected to illustrate some of the portions of the MIB used in the configuration examples in this chapter as well as make it easier to tie back what is configured on a device to what it corresponds to inside an MIB file. Although configuring an NMS is not covered in this chapter, the device side that points to an NMS is covered in this section. The following configuration steps are involved in setting up SNMP on a device to allow the device to be polled and send traps to an NMS:

- Define the SNMP host or the NMS to send traps to.
- Create an access list to restrict access via SNMP.
- Define the read-only community string.
- Define the read/write community string.
- Define the SNMP location.
- Define the SNMP contact.

These settings do not need to be configured in any particular order. However, it makes sense to configure the access list first and then the read-only and read/write strings. That way, when the device is accessible via SNMP, it is already locked down to only the allowed hosts within the access list. On R1, a standard access list is configured to permit access only from an NMS host on the 192.168.14.0/24 subnet. The host IP address is 192.168.14.100. After the access list is configured, the read-only and read/write community strings are configured and bound to that access list. Example 24-30 illustrates this on R1. It is important to try to use SNMP strings that are not easy to guess from a security perspective.

Example 24-30 *SNMP Access List on R1*

```
R1(config)# access-list 99 permit 192.168.14.100 0.0.0.0
R1(config)# snmp-server community READONLY ro 99
R1(config)# snmp-server community READWRITE rw 99
```

At this point, the device is configured to be polled from an NMS host with the IP address 192.168.14.100. If additional hosts need to be added, you simply add the new host IP addresses to the access list. It is also possible to permit the whole subnet. However, this is more of a security risk than specifying only the necessary hosts.

If a network operations team wants to send SNMP traps to an NMS, traps first must be enabled on the device. All available traps can be enabled by issuing the **snmp-server enable traps** command. However, this may enable unnecessary traps that have no significance to the network operations team. It might be more appropriate to be selective about which traps to enable. The traps that are available to be enabled are platform specific. A common approach to determining what traps are available is to look at the documentation for the device. It may be easier to simply issue the **snmp-server enable traps** command followed by **?** to leverage the context-sensitive help and determine what traps are available on the device. Example 24-31 shows a partial list of traps that are available on R1.

Example 24-31 *Available SNMP Traps on R1*

```
R1(config)# snmp-server enable traps ?
  aaa_server        Enable SNMP AAA Server traps
  atm                Enable SNMP atm traps
  bfd                Allow SNMP BFD traps
  bgp                Enable BGP traps
  bstun             Enable SNMP BSTUN traps
  bulkstat          Enable Data-Collection-MIB Collection notifications
  ccme               Enable SNMP ccme traps
  cef                Enable SNMP CEF traps
  cnpd               Enable NBAR Protocol Discovery traps
  config             Enable SNMP config traps
  config-copy       Enable SNMP config-copy traps
  config-ctid       Enable SNMP config-ctid traps
  cpu               Allow cpu related traps
  dial              Enable SNMP dial control traps
  diameter          Allow Diameter related traps
  dlsw              Enable SNMP dlsw traps
  dnis              Enable SNMP DNIS traps
  ds1               Enable SNMP DS1 traps
  dsp               Enable SNMP dsp traps
  eigrp             Enable SNMP EIGRP traps
  entity            Enable SNMP entity traps
  entity-ext        Enable SNMP entity extension traps
 --More--
```

A significant number of traps can be enabled to send to an NMS. For the purpose of this section, the **config** trap will be enabled. To configure this trap, the **snmp-server enable traps config** command must be issued. Example 24-32 shows this command being used on R1 to enable the **config** trap to be sent to the NMS host at 192.168.14.100.

Example 24-32 *Enabling SNMP Config Traps on R1*

```
R1(config)# snmp-server enable traps config
R1(config)# snmp-server host 192.168.14.100 traps READONLY
```

syslog

Devices can generate a tremendous amount of useful information, including messages sent to the console, to the logging buffer, and to off-box **syslog** collectors. In fact, all three can be sent the same or different message types. This section briefly covers these options and provides a use case for each one. By default, all syslog messages are sent to the console. (This is how the **debug** commands from earlier in this chapter are displayed on the console port.) However, this can be adjusted, as can what messages are sent to the logging buffer or off-box syslog collector. It is critical to note that prior to configuring any device to send log information, the date and time of the clock *must* be properly configured for accurate time. If it is not, the time stamps on all the logging messages will not reflect the appropriate and accurate time, which will make troubleshooting much more difficult because you will not be able to correlate issues with the logs by using the time stamps generated. Ensuring that NTP is configured properly helps with this issue.

Messages that are generated have specific severity levels associated with them, but these levels can be changed. The default severity level of each message type is listed in Table 24-7.

> **NOTE** NTP is not covered in this chapter.

Table 24-7 Syslog Message Severity Levels

Level Keyword	Level	Description	syslog Definition
emergencies	0	System unstable	LOG_EMERG
alerts	1	Immediate action needed	LOG_ALERT
critical	2	Critical conditions	LOG_CRIT
errors	3	Error conditions	LOG_ERR
warnings	4	Warning conditions	LOG_WARNING
notifications	5	Normal but significant conditions	LOG_NOTICE
informational	6	Informational messages only	LOG_INFO
debugging	7	Debugging messages	LOG_DEBUG

These messages can be used to provide valuable information to the network operations staff, or they can be so overwhelming that they make it difficult to sift through to find or pinpoint an issue. It is important to note that having syslog configured doesn't mean that an issue will be found. It still takes the proper skill to be able to look at the messages and determine the root cause of the issue. However, syslog is helpful in guiding you toward the issue at hand.

The logging buffer is the first area to focus on. On R1, you can enable logging to the buffer as follows:

1. Enable logging to the buffer.
2. Set the severity level of syslog messages to send to the buffer.
3. Set the logging buffer to a larger size.

The **logging buffered ?** command is issued from the global configuration mode to see the available options. Example 24-33 shows the list of available options. It is important to note that you can configure the severity level by simply specifying the level with a number from 0 to 7 or the name of the severity (listed next to the severity level number). The default size of the logging buffer is 4096 bytes. This size can get overwritten quite quickly. It is good practice to expand the buffer size so that you can capture more logging information.

Example 24-33 *Logging the Buffer Severity Level on R1*

```
R1(config)# logging buffered ?
  <0-7>              Logging severity level
  <4096-2147483647>  Logging buffer size
  alerts             Immediate action needed           (severity=1)
  critical           Critical conditions               (severity=2)
  debugging          Debugging messages                (severity=7)
  discriminator      Establish MD-Buffer association
  emergencies        System is unusable                (severity=0)
  errors             Error conditions                  (severity=3)
  filtered           Enable filtered logging
  informational      Informational messages            (severity=6)
  notifications      Normal but significant conditions (severity=5)
  warnings           Warning conditions                (severity=4)
  xml                Enable logging in XML to XML logging buffer
  <cr>
```

Debugging or severity 7 is the level that will be configured in this example; with this configuration, any debugging can be sent to the logging buffer instead of the console, which makes working on a device and troubleshooting less daunting because the debugging doesn't interfere with the console output—that is, as long as the debugging level is not set on the console as well. In Example 24-34, the logging is configured to debugging level 7, and it is set to 100000 bytes. The **do show logging** command is then run to confirm the changes. Notice the syslog message that shows the logging size was changed.

Example 24-34 *Configuring the Logging Buffer Size and Severity Level on R1*

```
R1(config)# logging buffer 100000
R1(config)# logging buffer debugging
R1(config)# do show logging
Syslog logging: enabled (0 messages dropped, 4 messages rate-limited, 0 flushes,
  0 overruns, xml disabled, filtering disabled)

No Active Message Discriminator.



No Inactive Message Discriminator.
```

```
    Console logging: disabled
    Monitor logging: level debugging, 0 messages logged, xml disabled,
                     filtering disabled
    Buffer logging:  level debugging, 1 messages logged, xml disabled,
                    filtering disabled
    Exception Logging: size (4096 bytes)
    Count and timestamp logging messages: disabled
    Persistent logging: disabled

No active filter modules.

    Trap logging: level informational, 108 message lines logged
        Logging Source-Interface:       VRF Name:

Log Buffer (100000 bytes):

*Jul 10 19:41:05.793: %SYS-5-LOG_CONFIG_CHANGE: Buffer logging: level debugging, xml
   disabled, filtering disabled, size (100000)
```

Now that the logging buffer has been configured for a severity level of debugging, it is good to show what happens when a **debug** command is used and stored in the buffer. Example 24-35 shows how to disable console logging and run **debug ip ospf hello** followed by the **show logging** command to reveal the debugging output on R1.

Example 24-35 *Using the Logging Buffer on R1 for Debugging*

```
R1(config)# no logging console
R1(config)# end
R1# debug ip ospf hello
OSPF hello debugging is on
R1# show logging
Syslog logging: enabled (0 messages dropped, 4 messages rate-limited, 0 flushes,
  0 overruns, xml disabled, filtering disabled)

No Active Message Discriminator.



No Inactive Message Discriminator.



    Console logging: disabled
    Monitor logging: level debugging, 0 messages logged, xml disabled,
                     filtering disabled
    Buffer logging:  level debugging, 11 messages logged, xml disabled,
                    filtering disabled
```

```
    Exception Logging: size (4096 bytes)
    Count and timestamp logging messages: disabled
    Persistent logging: disabled

No active filter modules.

    Trap logging: level informational, 109 message lines logged
        Logging Source-Interface:       VRF Name:

Log Buffer (100000 bytes):

*Jul 10 19:41:05.793: %SYS-5-LOG_CONFIG_CHANGE: Buffer logging: level debugging,
  xml disabled, filtering disabled, size (100000)
*Jul 10 19:51:05.335: %SYS-5-CONFIG_I: Configured from console by console
*Jul 10 19:51:28.110: OSPF-1 HELLO Et0/0: Send hello to 224.0.0.5 area 0 from
  192.168.12.1
*Jul 10 19:51:30.923: OSPF-1 HELLO Et0/2: Send hello to 224.0.0.5 area 0 from
  192.168.17.1
*Jul 10 19:51:31.259: OSPF-1 HELLO Et0/2: Rcv hello from 7.7.7.7 area 0 192.168.17.7
*Jul 10 19:51:32.990: OSPF-1 HELLO Et0/0: Rcv hello from 2.2.2.2 area 0 192.168.12.2
*Jul 10 19:51:33.026: OSPF-1 HELLO Et0/1: Rcv hello from 4.4.4.4 area 0 192.168.14.4
*Jul 10 19:51:36.231: OSPF-1 HELLO Et0/1: Send hello to 224.0.0.5 area 0 from
  192.168.14.1
*Jul 10 19:51:37.376: OSPF-1 HELLO Et0/0: Send hello to 224.0.0.5 area 0 from
  192.168.12.1
*Jul 10 19:51:40.219: OSPF-1 HELLO Et0/2: Send hello to 224.0.0.5 area 0 from
  192.168.17.1
*Jul 10 19:51:40.706: OSPF-1 HELLO Et0/2: Rcv hello from 7.7.7.7 area 0 192.168.17.7
R1# undebug all
All possible debugging has been turned off
```

If a network operations team wanted to send these same logs to an off-box collector, that could be configured as well. By default, these messages are sent to the logging host through UDP port 514, but this can be changed if necessary. Configuring logging to a host is similar to configuring logging on the console or buffer. In this case, it is configured by using the following steps:

1. Enable logging to host 192.168.14.100.
2. Set the severity level of syslog messages to send to the host.

Example 24-36 shows the basic configuration for sending syslog messages to a collector or host from R1.

Example 24-36 *Sending Logging to a Host on R1 for Debugging*

```
R1(config)# logging host 192.168.14.100
R1(config)# logging trap 7
R1(config)# do show logging
Syslog logging: enabled (0 messages dropped, 4 messages rate-limited, 0 flushes,
  0 overruns, xml disabled, filtering disabled)

No Active Message Discriminator.



No Inactive Message Discriminator.



    Console logging: disabled
    Monitor logging: level debugging, 0 messages logged, xml disabled,
                     filtering disabled
    Buffer logging:  level debugging, 22 messages logged, xml disabled,
                    filtering disabled
    Exception Logging: size (4096 bytes)
    Count and timestamp logging messages: disabled
    Persistent logging: disabled

No active filter modules.

    Trap logging: level debugging, 112 message lines logged
        Logging to 192.168.14.100  (udp port 514, audit disabled,
              link up),
              1 message lines logged,
              0 message lines rate-limited,
              0 message lines dropped-by-MD,
              xml disabled, sequence number disabled
              filtering disabled
```

The power of using syslog is evident even in these basic examples. It can be used to notify of power supply failures, CPU spikes, and a variety of other things. It is important not to underestimate the level of granularity and detail that can be achieved by setting up proper notification policies in a network. This section provides a high-level discussion on the topic, but it is easy to go extremely deep on the subject. It is ultimately up to the network operations team to determine how deep is appropriate to meet the business's needs. Many options are available, such as multiple logging destinations and ways to systematically set up different levels of logging. It all depends on what the network operations team feels is appropriate for their environment.

Key Topic

NetFlow and Flexible NetFlow

Gathering statistics about a network during its operations is not only useful but important. Gathering statistical information on traffic flows is necessary for a number of reasons. Some businesses, such as service providers, use it for customer billing. Other businesses use it to determine whether traffic is optimally flowing through the network. Some use it for troubleshooting if the network is not performing correctly. **NetFlow** is versatile and provides a wealth of information without much configuration burden. That being said, NetFlow has two components that must be configured: *NetFlow Data Capture* and *NetFlow Data Export*. NetFlow Data Capture captures the traffic statistics. NetFlow Data Export exports the statistical data to a NetFlow collector, such as Cisco DNA Center or Cisco Prime Infrastructure. Examples of each of these are provided in this section.

There are a couple things to note from a design perspective prior to enabling NetFlow. First, NetFlow consumes memory resources. The traffic statistics are captured in the memory cache. The default size of the cache is platform specific and should be investigated prior to enabling NetFlow. This is especially the case with older platforms that potentially have lower memory resources available.

NetFlow captures traffic on ingress and egress—that is, traffic that is coming into the devices as well as traffic that is leaving them. Table 24-8 lists the different types of ingress and egress traffic collected with NetFlow Version 9 on a Cisco IOS-XE device.

Table 24-8 NetFlow Ingress and Egress Collected Traffic Types

Ingress	Egress
IP to IP packets	NetFlow accounting for all IP traffic packets
IP to Multiprotocol Label Switching (MPLS) packets	MPLS to IP packets
Frame Relay terminated packets	
ATM terminated packets	

NetFlow collects traffic based on flows. A *flow* is a unidirectional traffic stream that contains a combination of the following key fields:

- Source IP address
- Destination IP address
- Source port number
- Destination port number
- Layer 3 protocol type
- Type of service (ToS)
- Input logical interface

The following example shows how to enable NetFlow on a device. (If the desired intention is not to export the NetFlow data to a collector, that step can be skipped.) This example covers configuring R1's Ethernet0/1 interface for NetFlow Data Capture and exporting the data to the 192.168.14.100 collector. The steps are rather simple. Example 24-37 illustrates the process of configuring NetFlow Data Capture and NetFlow Data Export on R1.

Example 24-37 *Configuring NetFlow and NetFlow Data Export on R1*

```
R1# configure terminal
Enter configuration commands, one per line. End with CNTL/Z.
R1(config)# ip flow-export version 9
R1(config)# ip flow-export destination 192.168.14.100 9999
R1(config)# interface Ethernet0/1
R1(config-if)# ip flow ingress
R1(config-if)# ip flow egress
R1(config-if)# end
R1#
```

To verify that NetFlow and NetFlow Data Export were configured properly, you can run a few commands from the command-line interface. The first is **show ip flow interface**, which shows the interfaces that are configured for NetFlow. The second is the **show ip flow export** command, which shows the destination for the NetFlow data to be exported to as well as statistics on the export, including any errors that may arise. Finally, the **show ip cache flow** command shows the traffic flows that NetFlow is capturing. Example 24-38 shows the output of these three commands.

Example 24-38 *Verifying NetFlow and NetFlow Data Export Configuration on R1*

```
R1# show ip flow interface
Ethernet0/1
  ip flow ingress
  ip flow egress
R1#
R1# show ip flow export
Flow export v9 is enabled for main cache
  Export source and destination details :
  VRF ID : Default
    Destination(1)  192.168.14.100 (9999)
  Version 9 flow records
  0 flows exported in 0 udp datagrams
  0 flows failed due to lack of export packet
  0 export packets were sent up to process level
  0 export packets were dropped due to no fib
  0 export packets were dropped due to adjacency issues
  0 export packets were dropped due to fragmentation failures
  0 export packets were dropped due to encapsulation fixup failures
R1# show ip cache flow
```

```
IP packet size distribution (6 total packets):
   1-32   64   96  128  160  192  224  256  288  320  352  384  416  448  480
   .000 .666 .333 .000 .000 .000 .000 .000 .000 .000 .000 .000 .000 .000 .000

    512  544  576 1024 1536 2048 2560 3072 3584 4096 4608
   .000 .000 .000 .000 .000 .000 .000 .000 .000 .000 .000

IP Flow Switching Cache, 278544 bytes
  2 active, 4094 inactive, 2 added
  29 ager polls, 0 flow alloc failures
  Active flows timeout in 30 minutes
  Inactive flows timeout in 15 seconds
IP Sub Flow Cache, 34056 bytes
  2 active, 1022 inactive, 2 added, 2 added to flow
  0 alloc failures, 0 force free
  1 chunk, 1 chunk added
  last clearing of statistics never
Protocol         Total    Flows   Packets Bytes  Packets Active(Sec) Idle(Sec)
--------         Flows     /Sec     /Flow  /Pkt     /Sec     /Flow     /Flow

SrcIf         SrcIPaddress    DstIf          DstIPaddress    Pr SrcP DstP  Pkts
Et0/1         192.168.14.4    Null           224.0.0.5       59 0000 0000     2

SrcIf         SrcIPaddress    DstIf          DstIPaddress    Pr SrcP DstP  Pkts
Et0/1         192.168.14.4    Null           224.0.0.2       11 0286 0286     4
```

Another great option for NetFlow is being able to configure the top specified number of talkers on the network. A useful and quick configuration allows you to gain a great snapshot of what is going on in a device from a flow perspective. This view can be enabled by issuing the global configuration mode command **ip flow-top-talkers** and configuring the **top** command for the number of talkers (1–200) and the **sort-by** command to sort by bytes or packets, depending on the use case. Example 24-39 shows the configuration steps on R1 and the associated verification steps.

Example 24-39 *Configuring and Verifying the Top Talkers on R1*

```
R1# configure terminal
Enter configuration commands, one per line. End with CNTL/Z.
R1(config)# ip flow-top-talkers
R1(config-flow-top-talkers)# top 10
R1(config-flow-top-talkers)# sort-by bytes
R1(config-flow-top-talkers)# end
R1#
R1# show ip flow top-talkers
```

```
SrcIf        SrcIPaddress    DstIf         DstIPaddress    Pr SrcP DstP Bytes
Et0/1        192.168.14.4    Null          224.0.0.2       11 0286 0286  9610
Et0/1        192.168.14.4    Null          224.0.0.5       59 0000 0000  5820
2 of 10 top talkers shown. 2 of 2 flows matched.
```


Flexible NetFlow was created to aid in more complex traffic analysis configuration than is possible with traditional NetFlow. Flexible NetFlow allows for the use and reuse of configuration components. Table 24-9 lists the components that make Flexible NetFlow powerful. Flexible NetFlow allows for the use of multiple flow monitors on the same traffic at the same time. This means that multiple different flow policies can be applied to the same traffic as it flows through a device. If two different departments have a reason to analyze the traffic, they can both do so by using different parameters in each flow monitor.

Table 24-9 Flexible NetFlow Components

Component Name	Description
Flow Records	Combination of key and non-key fields. There are predefined and user-defined records.
Flow Monitors	Applied to the interface to perform network traffic monitoring.
Flow Exporters	Exports NetFlow Version 9 data from the Flow Monitor cache to a remote host or NetFlow collector.
Flow Samplers	Samples partial NetFlow data rather than analyzing all NetFlow data.

There are trade-offs in using sampled NetFlow data. The biggest one is that there is a reduced load on the device in terms of memory and CPU. However, by sampling NetFlow data only at specific intervals, something could be missed because the accuracy goes down with sampling compared to when gathering all data. Depending on the use case and the environment, however, sampling may be perfectly acceptable. It all depends on the business and its priorities.

Security has been a huge driver in the adoption of Flexible NetFlow due to its ability to track all parts of the IP header as well as the packet and normalize it into flows. Flexible NetFlow can dynamically create individual caches for each type of flow. In addition, Flexible NetFlow can filter ingress traffic destined to a single destination. These factors make Flexible NetFlow a powerful security asset.

You can use the **collect** and **match** commands to create a customized flow record. To create a custom flow record, certain key and non-key fields must be matched so that the flow record is usable. The **match** command is used to select key fields, and the **collect** command is used to select non-key fields. Table 24-10 shows a list of the key and non-key fields that can be used to mimic the original NetFlow capabilities when building a custom flow record.

Table 24-10 Flow Record Key and Non-Key Fields

Field	Key or Non-Key Field	Definition
IP ToS	Key	Value in the type of service (ToS) field
IP protocol	Key	Value in the IP protocol field
IP source address	Key	IP source address
IP destination address	Key	IP destination address
Transport source port	Key	Value of the transport layer source port field
Transport destination port	Key	Value of the transport layer destination port field
Interface input	Key	Interface on which the traffic is received
Flow sampler ID	Key	ID number of the flow sampler (if flow sampling is enabled)
IP source AS	Non-key	Source autonomous system number
IP destination AS	Non-key	Destination autonomous system number
IP next-hop address	Non-key	IP address of the next hop
IP source mask	Non-key	Mask for the IP source address
IP destination mask	Non-key	Mask for the IP destination address
TCP flags	Non-key	Value in the TCP flag field
Interface output	Non-key	Interface on which the traffic is transmitted
Counter bytes	Non-key	Number of bytes seen in the flow
Counter packets	Non-key	Number of packets seen in the flow
Time stamp system uptime first	Non-key	System uptime (time, in milliseconds, since this device was first booted) when the first packet was switched
Time stamp system uptime last	Non-key	System uptime (time, in milliseconds, since this device was first booted) when the last packet was switched

Configuring flow records is an important step in enabling Flexible NetFlow because the flow record defines what type of traffic will be analyzed or monitored. There are predefined flow records, and you can also create custom flow records. Custom flow records can have hundreds of different combinations to meet the exact needs of the business. Configuring a custom flow record involves the following steps:

1. Define the flow record name.
2. Set a useful description of the flow record.
3. Set match criteria for key fields.
4. Define non-key fields to be collected.

Although many of the predefined flow records that are available may be suitable for many use cases, there are too many of them to cover here. Having the ability to build a custom flow record for a specific and unique use case makes it extremely powerful. Example 24-40 shows a custom flow record called CUSTOM1 being defined on R4. This example uses the **match** command to match the IPv4 destination address and the **collect** command to gather the byte and packet counts. To verify the flow record configuration, you can use the command **show flow record CUSTOM1.** To see all flow records configured, including predefined flow records, you can use the **show flow record command** by itself. The **show run flow record** command also shows the running configuration of the custom flow records that were created.

Example 24-40 *Configuring and Verifying the Custom Flow Record on R4*

```
R4# configure terminal
Enter configuration commands, one per line.  End with CNTL/Z.
R4(config)# flow record CUSTOM1
R4(config-flow-record)# description Custom Flow Record for IPv4 Traffic
R4(config-flow-record)# match ipv4 destination address
R4(config-flow-record)# collect counter bytes
R4(config-flow-record)# collect counter packets
R4(config-flow-record)# exit
R4(config)#
R4(config)# do show flow record CUSTOM1
flow record CUSTOM1:
  Description:        Custom Flow Record for IPv4 Traffic
  No. of users:       0
  Total field space:  12 bytes
  Fields:
    match ipv4 destination address
    collect counter bytes
    collect counter packets

R4(config)#
R4(config)# do show running-config flow record
Current configuration:
!
flow record CUSTOM1
  description Custom Flow Record for IPv4 Traffic
  match ipv4 destination address
  collect counter bytes
  collect counter packets
```

Now that a custom flow record has been configured, the flow exporter can be created. There are a few important steps to complete when building a flow exporter:

1. Define the flow exporter name.
2. Set a useful description of the flow exporter.

3. Specify the destination of the flow exporter to be used.
4. Specify NetFlow version to export.
5. Specify the UDP port.

In this instance, the exporter that will be created will point to the 192.168.14.100 host that has been used in other examples in this chapter. This step in the process exports flow data from the device to a NetFlow collector or management platform such as Cisco DNA Center or Cisco Prime Infrastructure. Example 24-41 illustrates the configuration of the flow exporter as well as how to verify the configuration on R4.

Example 24-41 *Configuring and Verifying the Custom Flow Exporter on R4*

```
R4# configure terminal
Enter configuration commands, one per line. End with CNTL/Z.
R4(config)# flow exporter CUSTOM1
R4(config-flow-exporter)# description EXPORT-TO-NETFLOW-COLLECTOR
R4(config-flow-exporter)# destination 192.168.14.100
R4(config-flow-exporter)# export-protocol netflow-v9
R4(config-flow-exporter)# transport UDP 9999
R4(config-flow-exporter)# exit
R4(config)# exit
R4# sh run flow exporter
Current configuration:
!
flow exporter CUSTOM1
  description EXPORT-TO-NETFLOW-COLLECTOR
  destination 192.168.14.100
  transport udp 9999
!
R4# show flow exporter CUSTOM1
Flow Exporter CUSTOM1:
  Description:              EXPORT-TO-NETFLOW-COLLECTOR
  Export protocol:          NetFlow Version 9
  Transport Configuration:
    Destination IP address: 192.168.14.100
    Source IP address:      192.168.14.4
    Transport Protocol:     UDP
    Destination Port:       9999
    Source Port:             50192
    DSCP:                      0x0
    TTL:                       255
    Output Features:        Not Used
```

Now that a custom flow exporter called CUSTOM1 has been configured, the flow monitor must be created. Each flow monitor requires a flow record to be assigned to it. Each flow monitor has its own cache, and the flow record provides the layout and how to carve up the cache for the defined traffic defined in the flow record. The flow monitor can use the predefined flow records or custom flow records. For the purpose of this section, the CUSTOM1 flow record is used to illustrate the configuration steps. To configure a flow monitor, the following high-level steps must be taken:

1. Define the flow monitor name.
2. Set a useful description of the flow monitor.
3. Specify the flow record to be used.
4. Specify a cache timeout of 60 for active connections.
5. Assign the exporter to the monitor.

Configuring a flow monitor is a straightforward task. The cache timeout tells the device to export the cache to the collector every 60 seconds. It is important when creating a flow monitor for the description of the flow monitor to be useful and to map back to the flow record. Similarly, when you're configuring QoS, it is nice to have the descriptions self-document the intent of what the policy is doing. This information helps when configuring the flow monitor and when using context-sensitive help, because the description that is configured shows in the output. Example 24-42 shows this as well as the configuration and verification for the flow monitor called CUSTOM1.

Example 24-42 *Configuring and Verifying the Custom Flow Monitor on R4*

```
R4(config)# flow monitor CUSTOM1
R4(config-flow-monitor)# description Uses Custom Flow Record CUSTOM1 for IPv4$
R4(config-flow-monitor)# record ?
  CUSTOM1            Custom Flow Record for IPv4 Traffic
  netflow            Traditional NetFlow collection schemes
  netflow-original   Traditional IPv4 input NetFlow with origin ASs
R4(config-flow-monitor)# record CUSTOM1
R4(config-flow-monitor)# cache timeout active 60
R4(config-flow-monitor)# end
R4# show run flow monitor CUSTOM1
Current configuration:
!
flow monitor CUSTOM1
  description Uses Custom Flow Record CUSTOM1 for IPv4 Traffic
  cache timeout active 60
  record CUSTOM1
!
R4# show flow monitor CUSTOM1
Flow Monitor CUSTOM1:
  Description:        Uses Custom Flow Record CUSTOM1 for IPv4 Traffic
```

```
  Flow Record:        CUSTOM1
  Cache:
    Type:                   normal
    Status:                 not allocated
    Size:                   4096 entries / 0 bytes
    Inactive Timeout:       15 secs
    Active Timeout:         60 secs
    Update Timeout:         1800 secs
    Synchronized Timeout: 600 secs
```

The next step is to map the flow exporter CUSTOM1 to the flow monitor CUSTOM1. You need to essentially map the two together so the traffic that is being collected by the flow record can be exported to the NetFlow collector at 192.168.14.100. Example 24-43 shows the process and verification for adding the flow exporter CUSTOM1 to the flow monitor CUSTOM1 on R4. The output illustrates the need for clear and detailed descriptions throughout the process.

Example 24-43 *Configuring and Verifying the Flow Exporter Mapping to the Flow Monitor on R4*

```
R4# configure terminal
Enter configuration commands, one per line. End with CNTL/Z.
R4(config)# flow monitor CUSTOM1
R4(config-flow-monitor)# exporter ?
 CUSTOM1 EXPORT-TO-NETFLOW-COLLECTOR
R4(config-flow-monitor)# exporter CUSTOM1
R4(config-flow-monitor)# end
R4# show run flow monitor
Current configuration:
!
flow monitor CUSTOM1
  description Uses Custom Flow Record CUSTOM1 for IPv4 Traffic
  exporter CUSTOM1
  cache timeout active 60
  record CUSTOM1
!
R4# show flow monitor CUSTOM1
Flow Monitor CUSTOM1:
 Description: Uses Custom Flow Record CUSTOM1 for IPv4 Traffic
 Flow Record: CUSTOM1
 Flow Exporter: CUSTOM1 (inactive)
 Cache:
    Type:                   normal
    Status:                 not allocated
```

```
Size:                   4096 entries / 0 bytes
Inactive Timeout:       15 secs
Active Timeout:         60 secs
Update Timeout:         1800 secs
Synchronized Timeout: 600 secs
```

The final step necessary in enabling Flexible NetFlow is to apply the flow monitor to the interfaces. This step turns on the collection of NetFlow statistics, and it can be enabled for ingress or egress or both. This scenario highlights the ingress option, using the **ip flow monitor CUSTOM1 input** command on the desired interfaces. Example 24-44 illustrates the process as well as how to verify that Flexible NetFlow is working by issuing the **show ip flow monitor CUSTOM1 cache** command.

Example 24-44 *Configuring and Verifying the Flow Monitor Interface Commands on R4*

```
R4(config)# interface ethernet0/1
R4(config-if)# ip flow monitor ?
 CUSTOM1       Uses Custom Flow Record CUSTOM1 for IPv4 Traffic
R4(config-if)# ip flow monitor CUSTOM1 input
R4(config-if)# interface ethernet0/2
R4(config-if)# ip flow monitor CUSTOM1 input
R4(config-if)# end
R4# show flow monitor CUSTOM1 cache
  Cache type:                               Normal
  Cache size:                                 4096
  Current entries:                               3
  High Watermark:                                3

  Flows added:                                   8
  Flows aged:                                    5
    - Active timeout      (    60 secs)          5
    - Inactive timeout    (    15 secs)          0
    - Event aged                                 0
    - Watermark aged                             0
    - Emergency aged                             0

IPV4 DST ADDR          bytes          pkts
==============  =========  =========
224.0.0.5                560             7
224.0.0.2                372             6
4.4.4.4                  674            11
```

The modularity of Flexible NetFlow makes the tool much more scalable and powerful than traditional NetFlow. Having the ability to export to multiple destinations or collectors as well as having the capability of using the tool for security forensics to identify DoS attacks and worm propagation is tremendous. Although quite a few steps are involved in enabling Flexible NetFlow, the process is easily replicable, so network engineers can easily create traffic analysis to meet the individual needs of the business or multiple departments within the same organization.

Switched Port Analyzer (SPAN) Technologies

The famous saying about "three sides to every story" holds true when troubleshooting network-based issues, where there are the perspectives of the local device, the remote device, and what is transmitted on the wire. Regardless of whether one device is a router, a firewall, a load balancer, or a computer, there are often tools that allow for troubleshooting processes locally on the device. Understanding what was transmitted on the wire can help pinpoint problems.

Gaining the perspective of what happens on the wire can be more complicated. When the problem appears to be a Layer 2 issue, there are a few options:

- Insert a splitter between the devices. Splitters are generally applicable to optical connections because they split the light across a prism. The original source stays intact, and a second stream can be sent to a traffic analyzer.
- Configure the network device to mirror the packets at the data plane level to an additional destination. The destination can be a local port or a remote port that is connected to a traffic analyzer.
- Insert a switch between the two devices and then configure the switch to mirror the transient traffic to a traffic analyzer.

Catalyst switches provide the Switched Port Analyzer (**SPAN**), which makes it possible to capture packets using the second two options in the preceding list by using the following techniques:

- **Local Switched Port Analyzer:** You can capture local network traffic on a switch and send a copy of the network traffic to a local port attached to some sort of traffic analyzer.
- **Remote Switched Port Analyzer (RSPAN):** You can capture network traffic on a remote switch and send a copy of the network traffic to the local switch through Layer 2 (switching) toward a local port attached to some sort of traffic analyzer.
- **Encapsulated Remote Switched Port Analyzer (ERSPAN):** You can capture network traffic on a remote device and send the traffic to the local system through Layer 3 (routing) toward a local port attached to some sort of traffic analyzer.

Figure 24-4 shows a sample topology with four computers (PC-A, PC-B, PC-C, and PC-D) spread across three switches and a traffic analyzer connected to SW1. PC-A, PC-B, and PC-C are all connected to VLAN 123 on the 10.123.1.0/24 network, and PC-D is connected to

VLAN 34, which is on the 10.34.1.0/24 network. This topology is used to demonstrate the concepts of SPAN, RSPAN, and ERSPAN.

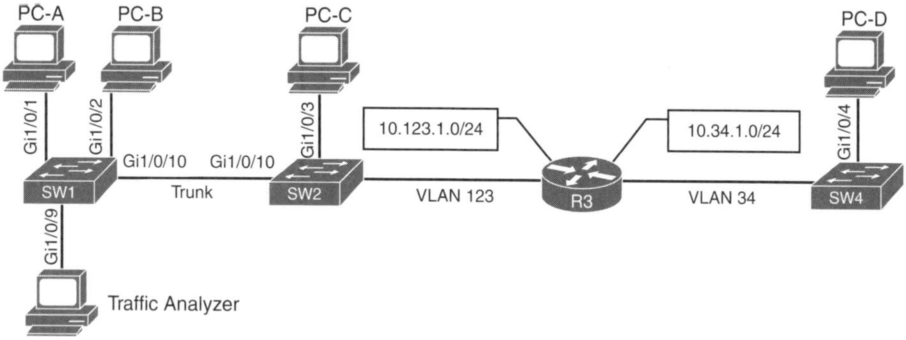

Figure 24-4 *Sample Topology for Packet Captures*

Local SPAN

A local SPAN session is the most basic form of packet capture because all the configuration occurs on a single switch. The destination of the mirrored traffic can be one or more local ports. The source of the packet capture can be only one of the following:

- One or more specific switch ports
- A port channel (also known as an EtherChannel)
- A VLAN (To be more explicit, this is the traffic received by the switch for all the hosts associated with the VLAN specified. This does not include an SVI interface.)

Also consider the following:

- Most switches support at least two SPAN sessions, but newer hardware can support more than two sessions.
- The source port can be reused between two different SPAN sessions.
- Source ports can be switched or routed ports.
- The destination cannot be reused between two different SPAN sessions.
- It is possible to saturate the destination port if the source ports are receiving more data than the destination port can transmit. In other words, if the source ports are 10Gigabit ports and the destination port is just Gigabit, it is possible that packet loss will occur on the destination port.

Key Topic

Specifying the Source Ports

The source ports are defined with the global configuration command **monitor session** *session-id* **source** {**interface** *interface-id* | **vlan** *vlan-id*} [**rx** | **tx** | **both**]. The SPAN *session-id* allows for the switch to correlate the source ports to specific destination ports. One or more interfaces or VLANs can be entered by using either a comma (for delimiting multiple interfaces) or a hyphen (for setting a range). Another option is to repeat the command with a different value and let the system update the source range accordingly.

The direction of the traffic can be specified as part of the configuration. With the optional **rx** keyword, you capture only traffic received on that source; with the optional **tx** keyword, you capture traffic sent by that source; and with the **both** keyword, you capture all traffic. By default, traffic is captured for both.

You can specify a trunk port as a source port to capture traffic for all VLANs that traverse that port. This might provide too much data and add noise to the traffic analysis tool. The VLANs can be filtered on the capture with the command **monitor session** *session-id* **filter vlan** *vlan-range*.

Specifying the Destination Ports

The destination port is specified with the global configuration command:

```
monitor session session-id destination interface interface-id [encapsulation
{dot1q [ingress {dot1q vlan vlan-id | untagged vlan vlan-id | vlan vlan-id}]
| replicate [ingress {dot1q vlan vlan-id | untagged vlan vlan-id}] | ingress
{dot1q vlan vlan-id | untagged vlan vlan-id | vlan vlan-id}]
```

As you can see, there are a lot of different nested options. The main options involve the choice between **encapsulation** and **ingress** (which is the last optional selection in the command).

A SPAN session normally copies the packets without including any 802.1Q VLAN tags or Layer 2 protocols, like Spanning Tree Protocol (STP) bridge protocol data units (BPDUs), CDP, VTP, DTP, Port Aggregation Protocol (PAgP), or Link Aggregation Control Protocol (LACP). Using the **encapsulation replicate** keywords includes that information. The full global configuration command is:

```
monitor session session-id destination interface interface-id [encapsulation
  replicate]
```

Normally, the SPAN destination port only receives traffic and drops ingress traffic. However, in some scenarios, connectivity to the traffic analyzer might be required. For example, if the traffic analyzer is a Windows PC and is accessed using RDP, the port must be able to send and receive traffic for the Windows PC in addition to the traffic from the SPAN session. Situations like this require the following global configuration command:

```
monitor session session-id destination interface interface-id ingress {dot1q vlan
  vlan-id | untagged vlan vlan-id}
```

Selecting the **dot1q** keyword requires the packets to be encapsulated with the specified VLAN ID. Selecting the **untagged** keyword accepts incoming packets and associates them to the specified VLAN ID.

These commands might seem confusing, but the following section illustrates a couple scenarios (using Figure 24-4) and provides the associated configurations to help clarify the commands.

NOTE STP is disabled on the destination port to prevent extra BPDUs from being included in the network analysis. Great care should be taken to prevent a forwarding loop on this port.

Local SPAN Configuration Examples

Example 24-45 shows how to monitor both PC-A's and PC-B's communication on SW1 and send it toward the local traffic analyzer.

Example 24-45 *Enabling a SPAN Session on SW1*

```
SW1(config)# monitor session 1 source interface gi1/0/1 - 2
SW1(config)# monitor session 1 destination interface gi1/0/9
```

The session information can be viewed with the command **show monitor session** {*session-id* [**detail**] | **local** [**detail**]}. A specific SPAN session can be viewed, or the output can be restricted to the local SPAN session, as shown in Example 24-46.

Example 24-46 *Verifying the Configured SPAN Session*

```
SW1# show monitor session local
Session 1
---------
Type                      : Local Session
Source Ports              :
    Both                    : Gi1/0/1-2
Destination Ports         : Gi1/0/9
    Encapsulation           : Native
          Ingress           : Disabled
```

The next example illustrates monitoring the trunk port Gi1/0/10 and provides the output to PC-B for PC-A and PC-B communication on SW1 and sending it toward the local traffic analyzer. The source port is a trunk port, and it is important to restrict traffic to VLAN 123 and capture Layer 2 QoS markings.

Example 24-47 shows the commands that are entered on SW1 and then shows the configuration verified by examining the SPAN session.

Example 24-47 *Configuring and Verifying SPAN for the SW1 Gi1/0/10 Source*

```
SW1(config)# monitor session 1 source interface gi1/0/10
! Some of the following command keywords were shortened for autocomplete
! so they all appear on the same line.
SW1(config)# monitor session 1 destination interface Gi1/0/9 encapsulation replicate
SW1(config)# monitor session 1 filter vlan 123
```

```
SW1# show monitor session 1
Session 1
---------
```

```
Type                        : Local Session
Source Ports                :
    Both                    : Gi1/0/10
Destination Ports           : Gi1/0/9
    Encapsulation           : Replicate
          Ingress           : Disabled
Filter VLANs                : 123
```

In the last scenario, the switch is configured to monitor PC-A's traffic, and it uses an already installed network traffic analysis tool on PC-B. When the switch is configured, PC-B can be accessed remotely to view the network traffic by using RDP. Example 24-48 lists the commands that are entered on SW1 to capture the ingress traffic and shows the configuration being verified.

Example 24-48 *Configuring and Verifying SPAN for the SW1 Gi1/0/1 Source*

```
SW1(config)# monitor session 1 source interface gi1/0/1
! Some of the following command keywords were shortened for autocomplete
! so they all appear on the same line.
SW1(config)# monitor session 1 destination interface gi1/0/2 ingress untagged vlan
123
```

```
SW1# show monitor session 1
Session 1
---------
Type                         : Local Session
Source Ports                 :
    Both                     : Gi1/0/1
Destination Ports            : Gi1/0/2
    Encapsulation            : Native
          Ingress            : Enabled, default VLAN = 123
    Ingress encap            : Untagged
```

Remote SPAN (RSPAN)

In large environments, it might be not be possible to move a network analyzer to other parts of the network. The **RSPAN** function allows the source ports to be located on one switch and the destination port on a different switch. The mirror traffic is placed on a special VLAN called the RSPAN VLAN, which is designated for SPAN traffic only.

A switch with the RSPAN VLAN operates differently from a typical switch:

- MAC addresses are not learned on ports associated with the RSPAN VLAN. This ensures that the switch does not try to use the port associated with the RSPAN VLAN to transmit data to the end host, which in turn ensures that the normal forwarding path is maintained.

- Traffic is flooded out all the ports associated with the RSPAN VLAN. The RSPAN VLAN should not be associated with ports that are not trunk ports between the source and destination switches.

The configuration for RSPAN is straightforward: A VLAN is created and then identified as an RSPAN VLAN with the command **remote-span.** The VLAN needs to be the same on all switches for that RSPAN session. Example 24-49 shows the RSPAN VLAN being created on SW1 and SW2.

Example 24-49 *Creating the RSPAN VLAN*

```
SW1(config)# vlan 99
SW1(config-vlan)# name RSPAN_VLAN
SW1(config-vlan)# remote-span
```

```
SW2(config)# vlan 99
SW2(config-vlan)# name RSPAN_VLAN
SW2(config-vlan)# remote-span
```

On the source port switch, the source ports are selected just as explained earlier for local SPAN. However, the destination is the RSPAN VLAN, which is set with the command **monitor session** *session-id* **destination remote vlan** *rspanvlan-id*. While the *session-id* is locally significant, keeping it the same on both the source and destination switches prevents confusion.

Example 24-50 shows the configuration of RSPAN on the source switch, SW2. Traffic from PC-C is sent to SW1 for analysis.

Example 24-50 *Configuring a Source RSPAN Switch*

```
SW2(config)# monitor session 1 source interface gi1/0/3
SW2(config)# monitor session 1 destination remote vlan 99
```

On the destination port switch, the destination ports are selected just as explained earlier for local SPAN. However, the source is the RSPAN VLAN, and this is set with the command **monitor session** *session-id* **source remote vlan** *rspanvlan-id*. While the *session-id* is locally significant, keeping it the same on both the source and destination switches prevents confusion.

Example 24-51 shows the configuration of RSPAN on the destination switch, SW1. The traffic is sent to the traffic analyzer for analysis.

Example 24-51 *Configuring a Destination RSPAN Switch*

```
SW1(config)# monitor session 1 source remote vlan 99
SW1(config)# monitor session 1 destination interface gi1/0/9
```

Example 24-52 verifies the configuration of RSPAN on both SW1 and SW2.

Example 24-52 *Verifying the RSPAN Settings*

```
SW1# show monitor session 1
Session 1
---------
Type                     : Remote Destination Session
Source RSPAN VLAN        : 99
Destination Ports        : Gi1/0/9
    Encapsulation        : Native
          Ingress        : Disabled
```

```
SW2# show monitor session remote
Session 1
---------
Type                       : Remote Source Session
Source Ports             :
    Both                   : Gi1/0/3
Dest RSPAN VLAN          : 99
```

Just as with a local SPAN session, traffic is duplicated with an RSPAN. This is significant in that additional traffic must traverse the trunk link and could starve out normal network traffic. Because a trunk link is used to carry the RSPAN VLAN, STP operates on the RSPAN VLAN, and STP BPDUs cannot be filtered because filtering could introduce a forwarding loop.

Key Topic

Encapsulated Remote SPAN (ERSPAN)

In large environments, it might not be possible to move a network analyzer to other parts of the network. **ERSPAN** provides the ability to monitor traffic in one area of the network and route the SPAN traffic to a traffic analyzer in another area of the network through Layer 3 routing. Think of a large-scale WAN with multiple remote sites and being able to do packet captures from anywhere that has IP connectivity. That is a powerful use case for ERSPAN. The configuration commands are similar in nature to those for SPAN and RSPAN. However, because the traffic is routed to another portion of the network, some additional configuration settings must take place to enable this capability.

Specifying the Source Ports

A source and destination must be configured. To configure a source, you issue the following command: **monitor session** *span-session-number* **type erspan-source.** This command defines the session number as well as the session type, **erspan-source**. Equally important as configuring the session is setting a useful description to document the purpose of the ERSPAN session. You can use the **description** *description* command for this purpose.

After the initial session is created, the source must be defined in the session. You accomplish this by issuing the **source** { **interface** *type number* | **vlan** *vlan-ID* } [, | - | *both* | *rx* | *tx*] command. As mentioned earlier in this chapter, if the source is a trunk port, it is important to filter based on the specific VLAN to be used as a source. You can do this using the **filter** { **ip** { *standard-access-list* | *expanded-access-list* | *acl-name* } | **ipv6** { **access-group** *acl-name* } | **vlan** *vlan-ID* } command. This example does not use a trunk link as a source interface.

When all these settings have been configured, the session must be enabled with the **no shutdown** command to ensure that the session is active.

Specifying the Destination

When the source has been configured, it is necessary to configure the destination of the ERSPAN session. To enter the destination subconfiguration mode, you use the **destination** command. The rest of the commands will be issued in the destination subconfiguration mode to specify the destination of the ERSPAN session as well as any parameters associated with the configuration of the destination.

The next step is to identify the IP address of the destination for the ERSPAN session. Because this is a Layer 3 SPAN session, this IP address is where the traffic will be sent to be analyzed. The command to configure this action is simply **ip address** *ip-address*. Much like the source session, the destination session must have a unique identifier. This is configured with the **erspan-id** *erspan-ID* command. After this is configured, the source IP address or origin of the ERSPAN traffic must be specified. You achieve this by issuing the **origin ip address** *ip-address* command.

The final step is to assign a ToS or TTL to the ERSPAN traffic. You do this with the **erspan** { **tos** *tos-value* | **ttl** *ttl-value* } command from global configuration mode. This example shows the **ttl** option being set. Example 24-53 illustrates this whole process. In addition, to verify the configured sessions, the **show monitor session erspan-source session** is issued on SW4.

Example 24-53 *Configuring ERSPAN on SW1*

```
SW4# configure terminal
SW4(config)# monitor session 1 type erspan-source
SW4(config-mon-erspan-src)# description SOURCE-PC-D-TRAFFIC
SW4(config-mon-erspan-src)# source interface GigabitEthernet 1/0/4 rx
SW4(config-mon-erspan-src)# filter vlan 34
SW4(config-mon-erspan-src)# no shutdown
SW4(config-mon-erspan-src)# destination
SW4(config-mon-erspan-src-dst)# ip address 10.123.1.100
SW4(config-mon-erspan-src-dst)# erspan-id 2
SW4(config-mon-erspan-src-dst)# origin ip address 10.34.1.4
SW4(config-mon-erspan-src)# exit
SW4(config)# erspan ttl 32
SW4(config)# end
SW4#
SW4# show monitor session erspan-source session

Type : ERSPAN Source Session
Status : Admin Enabled
Source Ports :
RX Only : Gi1/0/4
Destination IP Address : 10.123.1.100
Destination ERSPAN ID : 2
Origin IP Address : 10.34.1.4
IPv6 Flow Label : None
```

Key Topic

IP SLA

IP SLA is a tool built into Cisco IOS software that allows for the continuous monitoring of various aspects of the network. The different types of probes that can be configured to monitor traffic within a network environment include the following:

- Delay (both round-trip and one-way)
- Jitter (directional)
- Packet loss (directional)
- Packet sequencing (packet ordering)
- Path (per hop)
- Connectivity (directional)
- Server or website download time
- Voice quality scores

IP SLA has proven to be a useful tool because it provides a variety of flexible monitoring options. Typically, any SLA received from a service provider only monitors or guarantees the traffic as it flows across the service provider's network. This doesn't provide an end-to-end SLA—or visibility, for that matter. However, IP SLA is a robust tool that can help with troubleshooting. Figure 24-5 shows this scenario and illustrates why IP SLA provides more visibility than a typical service provider SLA.

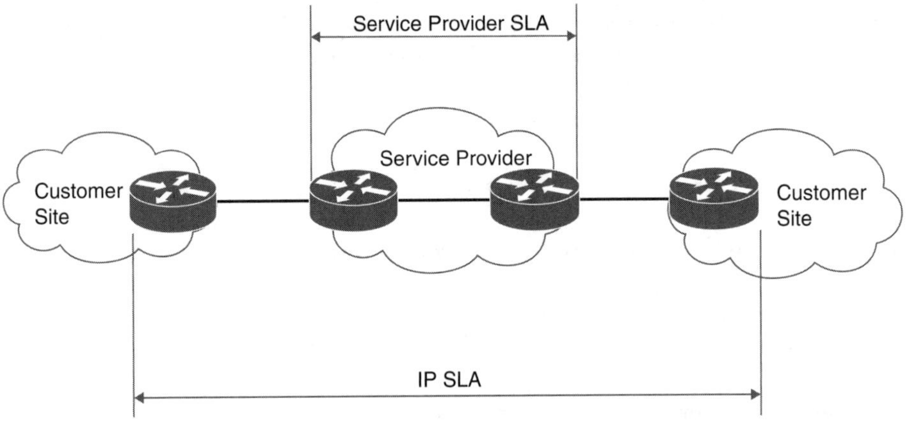

Figure 24-5 *IP SLA and Typical Service Provider SLA*

Although many different options and probes are available for IP SLA, this section focuses only on the ICMP echo and HTTP operations of IP SLA. The ICMP echo operation can functionally be thought of as testing reachability by leveraging ICMP echo and echo replies or pings. Figure 24-6 illustrates how the ICMP echo operation works in IP SLA.

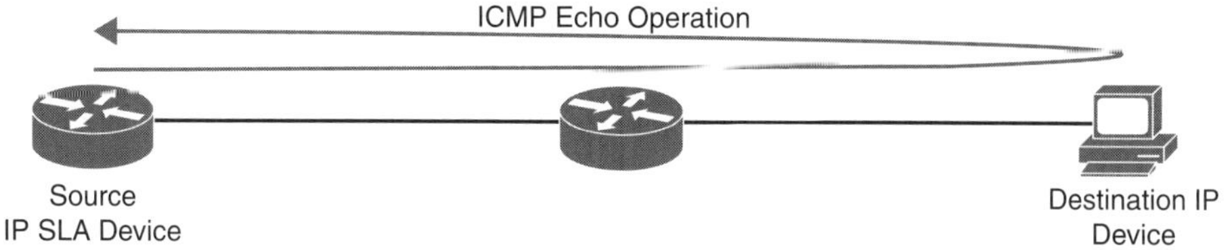

Figure 24-6 *IP SLA Echo Operation*

To configure any IP SLA operation, the **ip sla** *operation-number* command must be used to enter IP SLA configuration mode, where *operation-number* is the configuration for the individual IP SLA probe. This is necessary because there can be multiple IP SLA instances configured on a single device, all doing different operations or verification tasks. Once in IP SLA configuration mode, the command **icmp-echo** {*destination-ip-address* | *destination-hostname*} [**source-ip** {*ip-address* | *hostname*} | **source-interface** *interface-name*] is used to configure the destination IP address of the device or host to be monitored.

The next step is to specify how often the ICMP echo operation should run. You accomplish this by issuing the **frequency** *seconds* command. Note that many additional optional parameters are available for configuring IP SLA. This section focuses only on the basic setup and scheduling of IP SLA ICMP echo operations. Example 24-54 shows the process covered so far on R1.

Example 24-54 *Configuring IP SLA ICMP Echo Operation on R1*

```
R1(config)# ip sla 1
R1(config-ip-sla)# icmp-echo 192.168.14.100 source-interface Loopback0
R1(config-ip-sla-echo)# frequency 300
```

When the IP SLA configuration is complete, an important step is to schedule and activate the IP SLA operation that has been configured. This is where the **ip sla schedule** *operation-number* [**life** {**forever** | *seconds*}] [**start-time** {[*hh:mm:ss*] [*month day* | *day month*] | **pending** | **now** | **after** *hh:mm:ss*}] [**ageout** *seconds*] [**recurring**] command comes into play.

When the IP SLA operation is scheduled, it can be verified with the **show ip sla configuration** command. Example 24-55 illustrates the configuration steps to schedule the IP SLA 1 operation with a start time of now and a lifetime of forever. This example also shows the verification that it is running and configured properly.

Example 24-55 *Scheduling IP SLA 1 on R1*

```
R1(config)# ip sla schedule 1 life forever start-time now
R1(config)# do show ip sla configuration 1
IP SLAs Infrastructure Engine-III
Entry number: 1
Owner:
Tag:
```

```
Operation timeout (milliseconds): 5000
Type of operation to perform: icmp-echo
Target address/Source interface: 192.168.14.100/Loopback0
Type Of Service parameter: 0x0
Request size (ARR data portion): 28
Verify data: No
Vrf Name:
Schedule:
   Operation frequency (seconds): 300  (not considered if randomly scheduled)
   Next Scheduled Start Time: Start Time already passed
   Group Scheduled : FALSE
   Randomly Scheduled : FALSE
   Life (seconds): Forever
   Entry Ageout (seconds): never
   Recurring (Starting Everyday): FALSE
   Status of entry (SNMP RowStatus): Active
Threshold (milliseconds): 5000
Distribution Statistics:
   Number of statistic hours kept: 2
   Number of statistic distribution buckets kept: 1
   Statistic distribution interval (milliseconds): 20
Enhanced History:
History Statistics:
   Number of history Lives kept: 0
   Number of history Buckets kept: 15
   History Filter Type: None
```

Another common use case for IP SLA is to monitor HTTP destinations for operation. This can be done by using the HTTP GET operation of IP SLA. To configure this type of monitor, as mentioned earlier, you must use the **ip sla** *operation-number* command to enter IP SLA configuration mode. When the operation number is specified, the next step is to configure the HTTP GET probe by issuing the command **http** {**get** | **raw**} *url* [**name-server** *ip-address*] [**version** *version-number*] [**source-ip** {*ip-address* | *hostname*}] [**source-port** *port-number*] [**cache** {**enable** | **disable**}] [**proxy** *proxy-url*].

When the probe is configured, as with any other IP SLA operation, this operation needs to be scheduled by using the command **ip sla schedule** *operation-number* [**life** {**forever** | *seconds*}] [**start-time** {[*hh:mm:ss*] [*month day* | *day month*] | **pending** | **now** | **after** *hh:mm:ss*}] [**ageout** *seconds*] [**recurring**]. Example 24-56 highlights these steps on R1.

Example 24-56 *Configuring the IP SLA HTTP GET Operation on R1*

```
R1(config)# ip sla 2
R1(config-ip-sla)# http get http://192.168.14.100
R1(config-ip-sla-http)# frequency 90
```

```
R1(config-ip-sla-http)# end
R1# configure terminal
Enter configuration commands, one per line. End with CNTL/Z.
R1(config)# ip sla schedule 2 start-time now life forever
R1(config)# end
```

```
R1# show ip sla configuration 2
IP SLAs Infrastructure Engine-III
Entry number: 2
Type of operation to perform: http
Target address/Source address: 192.168.14.100/0.0.0.0
Target port/Source port: 80/0
Type Of Service parameters: 0x0
Vrf Name:
HTTP Operation: get
HTTP Server Version: 1.0
URL: http://192.168.14.100
Proxy:
Raw String(s):
Cache Control: enable
Owner:
Tag:
Operation timeout (milliseconds): 60000
Schedule:
   Operation frequency (seconds): 90  (not considered if randomly scheduled)
   Next Scheduled Start Time: Start Time already passed
   Group Scheduled : FALSE
   Randomly Scheduled : FALSE
   Life (seconds): Forever
   Entry Ageout (seconds): never
   Recurring (Starting Everyday): FALSE
   Status of entry (SNMP RowStatus): Active
Threshold (milliseconds): 5000
Distribution Statistics:
   Number of statistic hours kept: 2
   Number of statistic distribution buckets kept: 1
   Statistic distribution interval (milliseconds): 20
History Statistics:
   Number of history Lives kept: 0
   Number of history Buckets kept: 15
   History Filter Type: None
```

When IP SLA is set up and running appropriately, it can be monitored using the CISCO-RTTMON-MIB file with SNMP, and traps can be sent to an NMS via syslog. Documentation for this configuration can be found on the Cisco website.

NOTE There are many other things that IP SLA can help with, including tracking reachability, monitoring interface states, and manipulating routing based on IP SLA operations. These advanced topics can be found on www.cisco.com.

Key Topic

Cisco DNA Center Assurance

Networks have grown very complex. The influx of mobile devices strains network resources and the network operations staff. Security has become one of the most important pieces of the network, and users expect a better experience. Customers demand a simple way to manage Day 0–2 operations and require a scalable and simple approach to running the network. Cisco DNA Center Assurance provides a tool for handling the most relevant customer requirements. Traditionally, multiple management tools were required to meet the needs of the business in terms of managing, operating, and troubleshooting the network. This all changes with Cisco DNA Center Assurance. From a high level, Cisco DNA Center Assurance offers some of the following capabilities (as well as many more):

- Cisco SD-Access fabric configuration
- Software image management (SWIM)
- Simplified provisioning for devices
- Wireless network management
- Simplified security policies
- Configuration templates
- Third-party integration
- Network assurance
- Plug and Play

This section covers some of the workflows that Cisco DNA Center Assurance is designed to help businesses with. Typically, when an issue arises in the network, a helpdesk ticket is created. However, by the time the network operations team gets the ticket assigned, the issue is either resolved on its own, or the information provided in the ticket to assist with troubleshooting the issue is stale or out of date. Another typical scenario is that users say things like "last Tuesday at 3 p.m. I wasn't able to get on the wireless network." In a traditional network, if someone says she had an issue last week, there isn't much that can be done about it. However, Cisco DNA Center Assurance has *Network Time Travel*, and it is as cool as it sounds. Network Time Travel acts as a digital video recorder (DVR) for the network. But rather than recording television and enabling the user to play back shows at a later time, Network Time Travel records what is going on in the environment using streaming telemetry and can play back something that happened in the past. It also can show how the network is performing now as well as use things such as sensors to provide predictive analytics on how the network will perform in the future. Figure 24-7 shows the main Cisco DNA Center page that is shown upon logging in to the software.

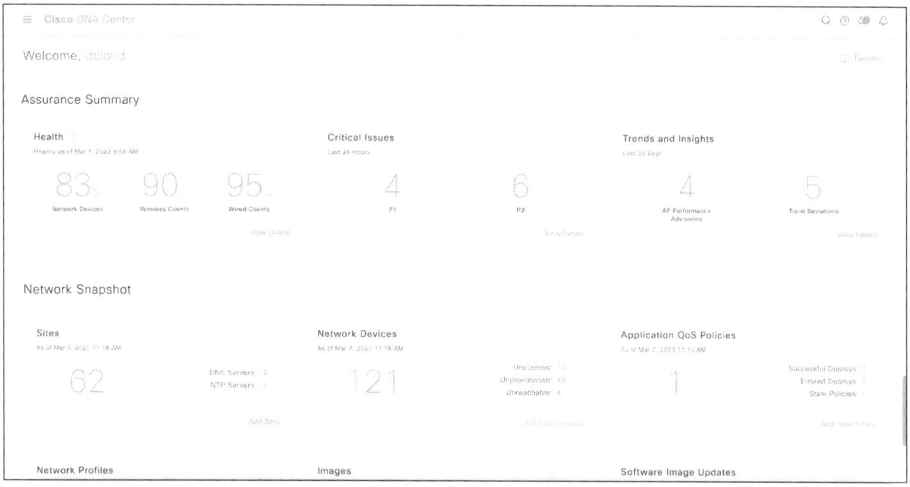

Figure 24-7 *Cisco DNA Center Main Page*

Cisco DNA Assurance is part of Cisco DNA Center. Assurance takes 30+ years of Cisco Technical Assistance Center (TAC) experience and puts it into a tool that uses machine learning to diagnose issues within a network. In addition to finding and diagnosing the issues, Assurance gives guided remediation steps to fix the issue. The Assurance tab is shown in Figure 24-8. Notice that it provides an overview of how the network is performing from an overall health perspective to a client perspective. It includes both wired and wireless clients. It also shows the top issues that are impacting the network. The health scores for each section enable you to see how the network is performing at quick glance.

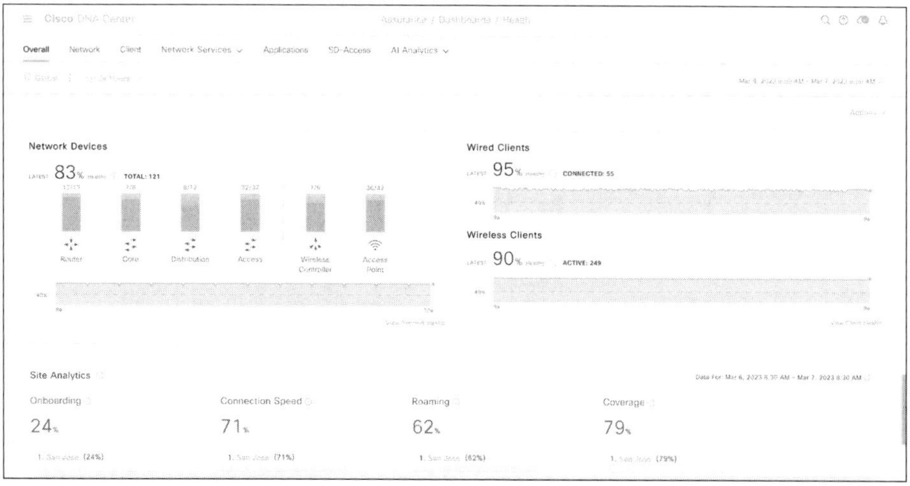

Figure 24-8 *Cisco DNA Center Assurance Page*

If a user walks up and has an issue, the typical approach is to ask the user's IP address or MAC address so that the network operations staff can jump from device to device, issuing multiple **show** commands to try to track down where the user is connected, as well as what issue might be causing the poor user experience. With Assurance, if a user walks up or a helpdesk ticket comes in, a simple search of the user's name yields all the information necessary. Cisco DNA Center integrates with many other tools, such as Active Directory, Identity Services Engine (ISE), ServiceNow, and Infoblox. This is possible because of the open APIs and SDKs available for Cisco DNA Center. Because of the integration with Active Directory and ISE, all the context of the user is searchable in Cisco DNA Center.

Say that a user named Grace has a problem. To search for Grace, you click the magnifying glass in the top-right corner and type her name in the search box. Because Cisco DNA Center is integrated with AD, all names populate as the search term is being typed. As you type Grace's name, all users whose names start with *G* come up, then all users whose names start with *Gr*, and so on. Figure 24-9 shows the search box and Grace Smith as the matching user. It also shows all the devices on the network associated with Grace Smith—in this case, a PC, an iPad, and an iPhone.

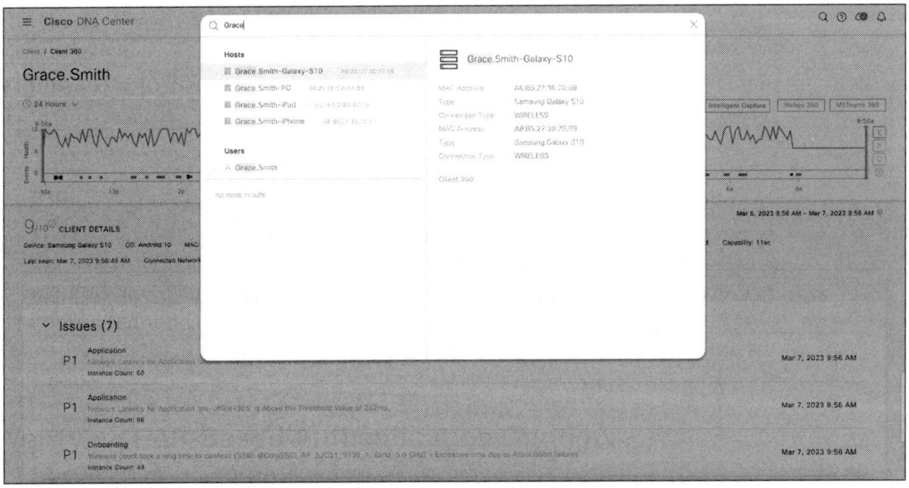

Figure 24-9 *Cisco DNA Center Assurance Search Page*

From this view, you can do many different things. You can click the user's name to see details related to that specific user. You can click each device to see specifics about that device in the Client 360 view. Figure 24-10 shows the entire Client 360 view for the user Grace Smith. Notice that all three of Grace's devices can be seen in this view, along with color-coded health scores for the devices.

The amount of information that this screen provides is tremendous. Just for the selected iPad, you can see that the following pieces of information have been gathered automatically:

- Device type
- OS version

- MAC address
- IPv4 address
- VLAN ID
- Connectivity status
- When the device was last seen on the network
- What device it is connected to
- Wireless SSID
- Last known location

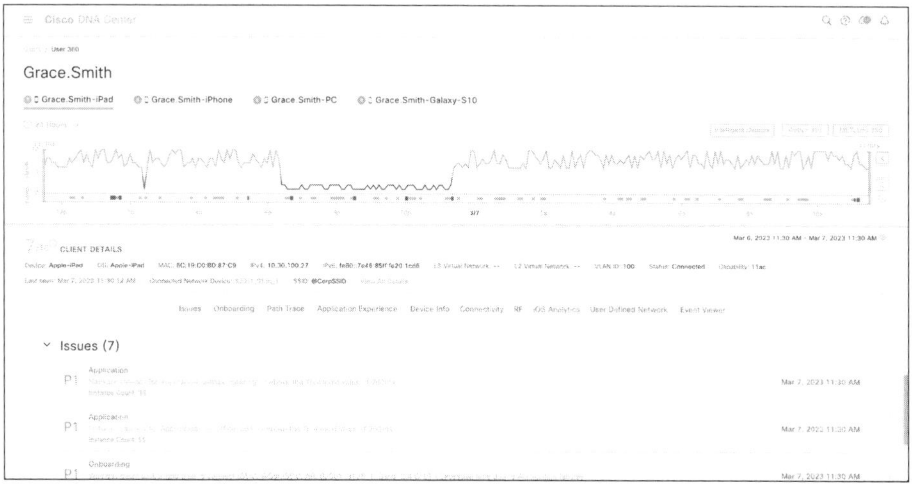

Figure 24-10 *Cisco DNA Center Assurance Client 360 Page*

Remember that all you have to do to get this information is search for Grace's name.

The timeline in the Client 360 view shows issues that have impacted Grace. This is also a Network Time Travel capability. Since Assurance records the telemetry, it is possible to search back in time to see exactly what has affected Grace. The issues listed correlate to the timeline. The issue list changes based on the timeline and what time period is being investigated. Hovering over different times on the timeline allows you to see all the different issues that happened at various specific points in time. At first glance, it is easy to see some application latency issues are impacting Grace's user experience.

Earlier in this chapter, you saw **traceroute** and **ping** used as troubleshooting tools when something is not working properly in the network environment. Assurance has a tool called **Path Trace**; the Run New Path Trace button is just underneath the issues listed on the Client 360 view. Path Trace is a visual traceroute and diagnostic tool that can be run periodically or continuously, with a specific refresh interval. Figure 24-11 shows a path trace being set up for Grace's iPad to John's PC, which are both wirelessly connected to the network. This path trace is set to refresh every 30 seconds.

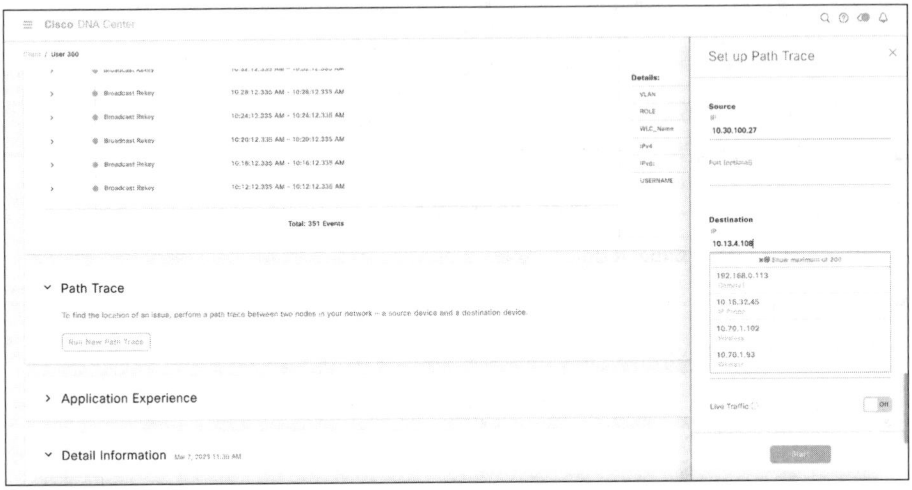

Figure 24-11 *Cisco DNA Center Assurance Client 360 Path Trace*

The path trace output shows a topology view of the traceroute, and in this instance, Path Trace has also detected that there is an access control list (ACL) blocking the traffic from Grace's iPad to John's PC (see Figure 24-12).

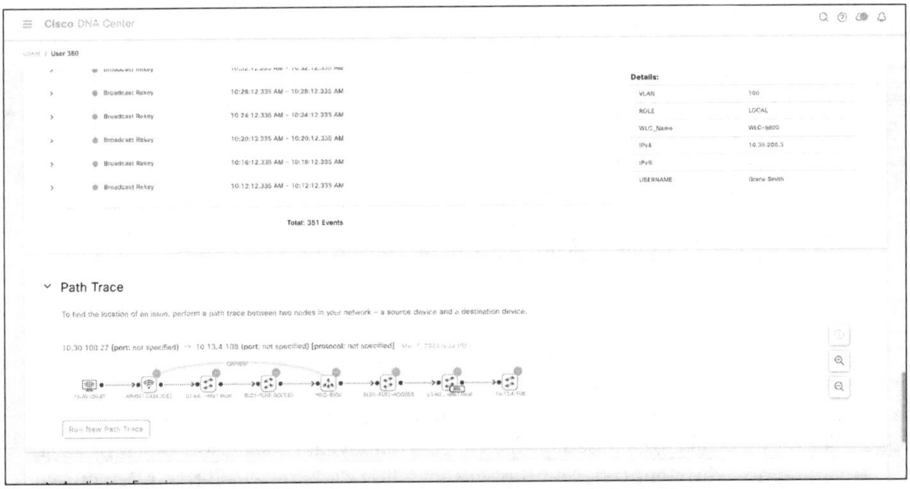

Figure 24-12 *Cisco DNA Center Assurance Client 360 Path Trace Output*

By hovering over the ACL entry, the following information can be seen:

- The ACL's name
- The interface the ACL is applied to
- The direction (ingress or egress)
- The ACL result (permit or deny)

Figure 24-13 shows the access list information found in this example.

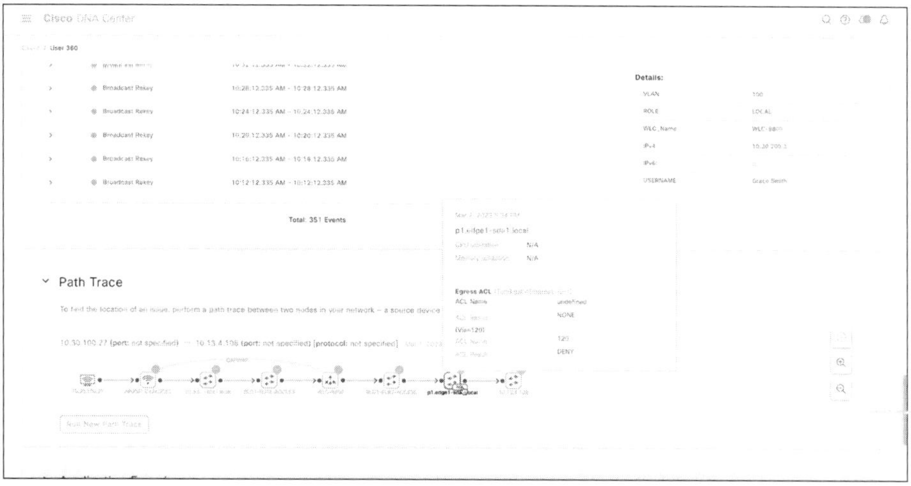

Figure 24-13 *Cisco DNA Center Assurance Client 360 Path Trace ACL Information*

By clicking on one of the issues listed under Grace's Client 360 view, such as the P1 Onboarding issue, a user can investigate the root cause of the issue. Figure 24-14 shows the issues that are impacting Grace.

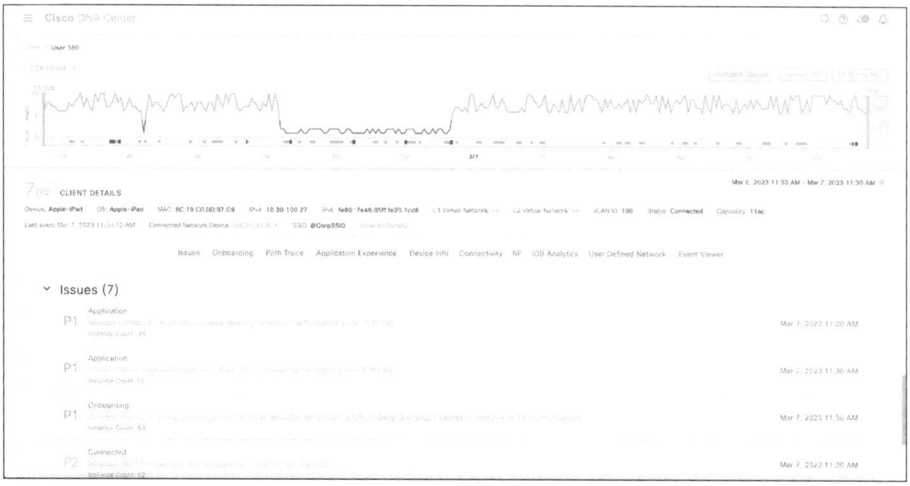

Figure 24-14 *Cisco DNA Center Assurance Client 360 Issues*

Figure 24-15 shows a large amount of useful information. The Impact of Last Occurrence states that this issue is impacting one building and seven wireless clients. There is also a detailed description of what is actually happening, along with suggested remediation steps to fix the issue. A user can click the arrows to see options such as average client onboarding times and impacted clients along with names, MAC address information, and the access points they are connected to. Although Cisco DNA Assurance can provide a wealth of information and details, this section shows only the high-level workflow used to diagnose and troubleshoot issues.

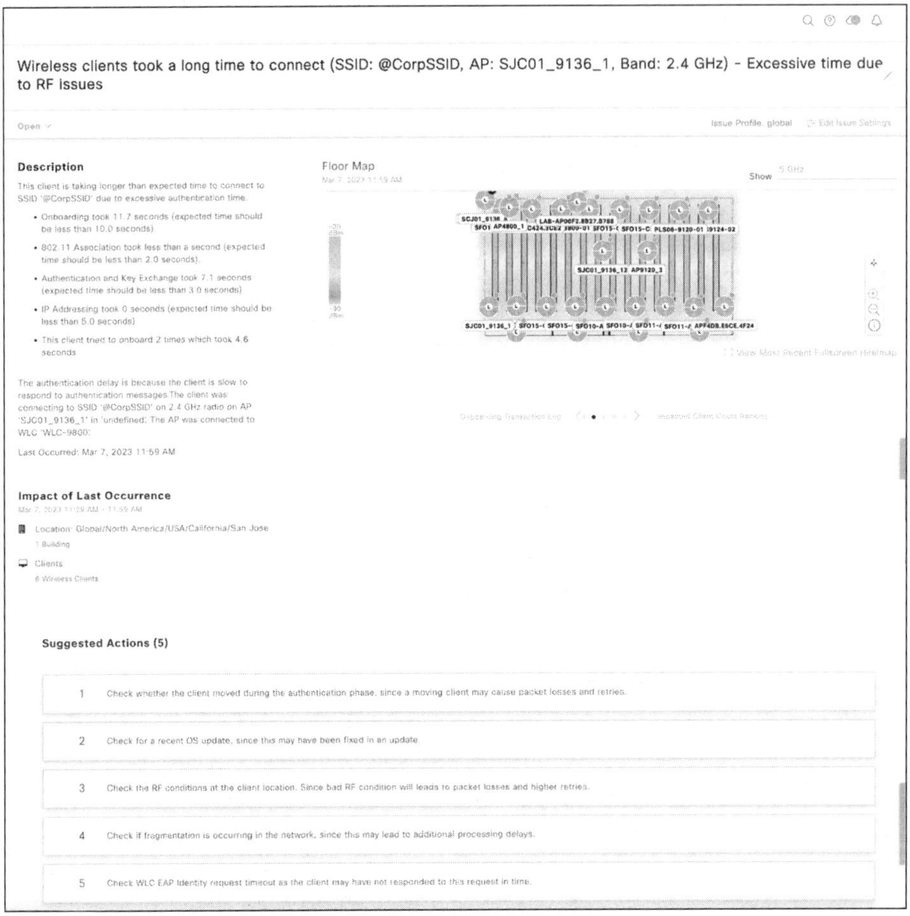

Figure 24-15 *Cisco DNA Center Assurance Client 360 Root Cause and Guided Remediation Steps*

Remember the traditional flow that network operations teams use to troubleshoot—logging in to multiple devices and trying to track down the root cause of an issue using **traceroute**, **ping**, and **show**? In less than the time it takes those teams to log in to a single device and issue all those commands, you can use Cisco DNA Center Assurance to quickly see the root cause of an issue and how to fix it. Thanks to open APIs and integration with helpdesk ticketing platforms such as ServiceNow, you can have all of the issues, impacted locations, path trace information, and remediation steps automatically added to helpdesk tickets so when the network operations staff gets a ticket, they already know what the issue is and how to fix it—without having to chase down the issue by using **show** commands on multiple devices in the network environment.

Exam Preparation Tasks

You have a couple of choices for exam preparation: the exercises here, Chapter 30, "Final Preparation," and the exam simulation questions in the Pearson Test Prep Software Online.

Review All Key Topics

Review the most important topics in the chapter, noted with the Key Topic icon in the outer margin of the page. Table 24-11 lists these key topics and the page number on which each is found.

Key Topic

Table 24-11 Key Topics for Chapter 24

Key Topic Element	Description	Page
Section	**ping**	675
Section	**traceroute**	680
Section	Debugging	685
Table 24-4	OSPF Network Types and Hello/Dead Intervals	689
Section	Simple Network Management Protocol (SNMP)	695
Section	NetFlow and Flexible NetFlow	706
Section	Specifying the Source Ports	717
Section	Encapsulated Remote SPAN (ERSPAN)	722
Section	IP SLA	724
Section	Cisco DNA Center Assurance	728

Complete Tables and Lists from Memory

There are no memory tables in this chapter.

Define Key Terms

Define the following key terms from this chapter, and check your answers in the Glossary:

ERSPAN, IP SLA, NetFlow, Path Trace, RSPAN, Simple Network Management Protocol (SNMP), SPAN, syslog

CHAPTER 25

Secure Network Access Control

This chapter covers the following subjects:

- **Network Security Design for Threat Defense:** This section describes a Cisco security framework to protect networks from evolving cybersecurity threats.
- **Next-Generation Endpoint Security:** This section describes security components such as Cisco Advanced Malware Protection (AMP), Cisco Secure Endpoint, Cisco Secure Client, Cisco Secure Firewall, Cisco Secure Web Appliance, and Cisco Secure Email that are part of the Cisco Secure portfolio to protect endpoints from threats and attacks.
- **Network Access Control (NAC):** This section describes technologies such as 802.1x, Web Authentication (WebAuth), MAC Authentication Bypass (MAB), TrustSec, and MACsec to enforce network access control.

In campus networks, endpoints such as mobile devices and laptops are extremely vulnerable to security threats such as malware and ransomware, and they can become infected through various means, such as phishing, smishing, malicious websites, and infected applications. For this reason, a solid network security design is necessary to protect the endpoints from these types of security threats, and to enforce endpoint network access control, by validating the identities of end users, to determine who and what they are allowed to access in the network before they are granted access. This chapter describes the components of network security design for a campus environment that are used to protect, detect, and remediate security threats and attacks.

"Do I Know This Already?" Quiz

The "Do I Know This Already?" quiz enables you to assess whether you should read the entire chapter. If you miss no more than one of these self-assessment questions, you might want to move ahead to the "Exam Preparation Tasks" section. Table 25-1 lists the major headings in this chapter and the "Do I Know This Already?" quiz questions covering the material in those headings so you can assess your knowledge of these specific areas. The answers to the "Do I Know This Already?" quiz appear in Appendix A, "Answers to the 'Do I Know This Already?' Questions."

Table 25-1 "Do I Know This Already?" Foundation Topics Section-to-Question Mapping

Foundation Topics Section	Questions
Network Security Design for Threat Defense	1–3
Next-Generation Endpoint Security	4–7
Network Access Control (NAC)	8–10

1. The Cisco Secure Architectural Framework is known as ______.
   a. Cisco SEAF
   b. Cisco Secure Malware Analytics
   c. Cisco SAFE
   d. Cisco Validated Designs
2. Which of the following are Cisco SAFE's PINs in the network? (Choose all that apply.)
   a. Internet
   b. Data center
   c. Branch office
   d. Edge
   e. Campus
   f. Cloud
   g. WAN
3. Cisco SAFE includes which of the following secure domains? (Choose all that apply.)
   a. Threat defense
   b. Segmentation
   c. Segregation
   d. Compliance
4. Which of the following is the Cisco threat intelligence organization?
   a. Cisco Secure Network Analytics
   b. Cisco Secure Malware Analytics
   c. Cisco Talos
   d. Cisco Threat Research, Analysis, and Communications (TRAC) team
5. What is Cisco Secure Malware Analytics?
   a. The Cisco threat intelligence organization
   b. The Cisco sandbox malware analysis solution
   c. The Cisco security framework
   d. An aggregator of network telemetry data
6. Which of the following relies on NetFlow data for security analysis?
   a. Cisco Secure Web Appliance
   b. Cisco Secure Network Analytics
   c. Cisco Talos
   d. Cisco Secure Malware Analytics
7. True or false: Without Cisco ISE, it would not be possible to implement pxGrid.
   a. True
   b. False

8. Which of the following EAP methods supports EAP chaining?
   a. EAP-TTLS
   b. EAP-FAST
   c. EAP-GTC
   d. PEAP
9. True or false: SGT tags extend all the way down to the endpoints.
   a. True
   b. False
10. Which of the following phases are defined by Cisco TrustSec? (Choose all that apply.)
    a. Classification
    b. Enforcement
    c. Distribution
    d. Aggregation
    e. Propagation

Foundation Topics

Network Security Design for Threat Defense

Key Topic

Evolving cybersecurity threats such as phishing, smishing, malware, ransomware, and web-based exploits are very common. There is no single product in the industry that can successfully secure organizations from all these threats. To address this issue, Cisco created a Secure Architectural Framework (SAFE) that helps design secure solutions for the following places in the network (PINs):

- **Branch:** Branches are typically less secure than the campus and data center PINs because the potentially large number of branches makes it cost-prohibitive to try to apply on them all the security controls found in campus and data center PINs. Branch locations are therefore prime targets for security breaches. It is important to ensure that vital security capabilities are included in the design while keeping it cost-effective. Top threats on branch PINs include endpoint malware (point-of-sale [POS] malware), wireless infrastructure exploits such as the use of rogue APs for man-in-the-middle (MitM) and/or denial-of-service (DoS) attacks, unauthorized/malicious client activity, and exploitation of trust.

- **Campus:** Campuses contain a large number of users, including employees, contractors, guests, and partners. Campuses are easy targets for phishing, web-based exploits, unauthorized network access, malware propagation, and botnet infestations.

- **Data center:** Data centers contain an organization's most critical information assets and intellectual capital, and they are therefore the primary goal of all targeted threats. Data centers typically contain hundreds or thousands of servers, which makes it very difficult to create and manage proper security rules to control network access. Typical threats seen in data centers are data extraction, malware propagation, unauthorized network access (application compromise), botnet infestation (scrumping), data loss, privilege escalation, and reconnaissance.

- **Edge:** The edge is the primary ingress and egress point for traffic to and from the Internet, and for this reason, it is the highest-risk PIN and the most important for e-commerce. Typical threats seen on the edge include web server vulnerabilities, distributed denial-of-service (DDoS) attacks, data loss, and MitM attacks.
- **Cloud:** Security in the cloud is dictated by service-level agreements (SLAs) with the cloud service provider and requires independent certification audits and risk assessments. The primary threats are web server vulnerabilities, loss of access, data loss, malware, and MitM attacks.
- **Wide area network (WAN):** The WAN connects the PINs together. In a large organization with hundreds of branches, managing security on the WAN is very challenging. Typical threats seen in WANs are malware propagation, unauthorized network access, WAN sniffing, and MitM attacks.

NOTE **Cisco SAFE** focuses on the integration of security services within each of the PINs. For information on the underlying networking design and infrastructure, see the Cisco Validated Design (CVD) guides, which provide detailed networking design and implementation guidance. CVDs can be found at www.cisco.com/go/cvd.

Cisco SAFE also defines secure domains, which are operational areas used to protect the different PINs. The following security concepts are used to evaluate each PIN:

- **Management:** Management of devices and systems using centralized services is critical for consistent policy deployment, workflow change management, and keeping systems patched. Management coordinates policies, objects, and alerting.
- **Security intelligence:** Security intelligence provides detection of emerging malware and cyber threats. It enables an infrastructure to enforce policy dynamically, because reputations are augmented by the context of new threats. This enables accurate and timely security protection.
- **Compliance:** Examples of compliance include PCI DSS 3.0 and HIPAA.
- **Segmentation:** Segmentation involves establishing boundaries for both data and users. Traditional manual segmentation uses a combination of network addressing, VLANs, and ACLs for policy enforcement. Advanced segmentation using Cisco TrustSec software-defined segmentation reduces operational challenges by leveraging identity-aware infrastructure to enforce policies in an automated and scalable manner.
- **Threat defense:** It is important to have visibility into the most dangerous cyber threats. Threat defense provides this visibility through network traffic telemetry, file reputation, and contextual information (such as device types, locations, users, identities, roles, privilege levels, login status, posture status, and so on). It enables assessment of the nature and the potential risk of suspicious activity so that the correct next steps for cyber threats can be taken.

- **Secure services:** These technologies include access control, virtual private networks (VPNs), and encryption. They include protection for insecure services (such as applications, collaboration, and wireless).

The SAFE key, shown in Figure 25-1, illustrates the PINs and security domains.

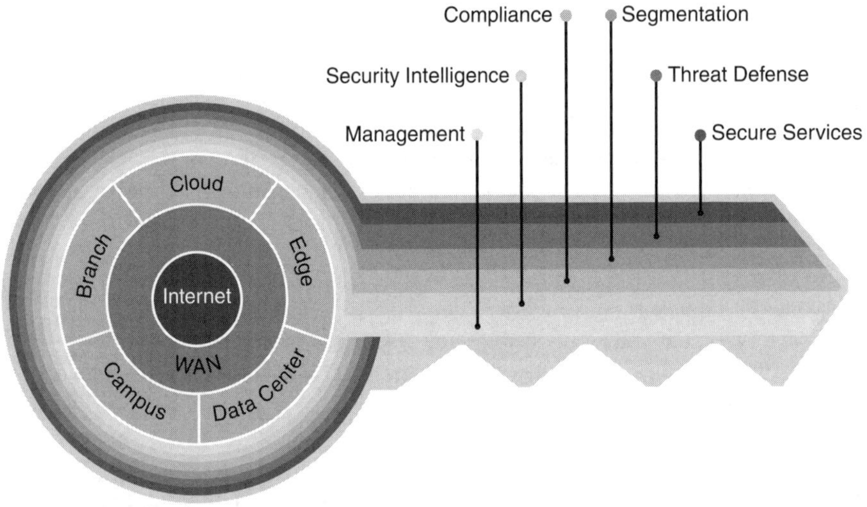

Figure 25-1 *The Key to Cisco SAFE*

The Cisco SAFE framework is designed to be modular. PINs that do not exist in a network can be removed.

Implementing the Cisco SAFE framework in an organization provides advanced threat defense protection that spans the full attack continuum before, during, and after an attack for all the PINs:

Key Topic

- **Before:** In this phase, full knowledge of all the assets that need to be protected is required, and the types of threats that could target these assets need to be identified. This phase involves establishing policies and implementing prevention to reduce risk. Cisco solutions for this phase include Cisco Secure Firewalls, network access control, and identity services.
- **During:** This phase defines the abilities and actions that are required when an attack gets through. Threat analysis and incident response are some of the typical activities associated with this phase. For this phase, organizations can leverage next-generation intrusion prevention systems, next-generation firewalls, malware protection, and email and web security solutions that make it possible to detect, block, and defend against attacks that have penetrated the network and are in progress.
- **After:** This phase defines the ability to detect, contain, and remediate an attack. After a successful attack, any lessons learned need to be incorporated into the existing

---

Answers to the "Do I Know This Already?" quiz:

1 C **2** B through G **3** A, B, D **4** C **5** B **6** B **7** A **8** B **9** B **10** A, B, E

security solution. Organizations can leverage Cisco Advanced Malware Protection, next-generation firewalls, and malicious network behavior analysis using Cisco Secure Network Analytics to quickly and effectively scope, contain, and remediate an attack to minimize damage.

Next-Generation Endpoint Security

As mentioned in the introduction to this chapter, *endpoints* are easy targets for evolving threats, they are ubiquitous, and they come in many different forms, such as mobile devices, laptops, tablets, IP phones, personal computers (PCs), and Internet of Things (IoT) devices. Thanks to the ubiquity of bring-your-own-device (BYOD) policies, any of them can be connected to a corporate network. Organizations have used antivirus products to protect endpoints against malware for decades, and while these products have done a good job, they can't keep up with the rapidly evolving threat landscape. Attackers have become very skilled at developing malware that can evade detection. When the effectiveness of a specific type of malware declines, attackers create new variants. Their approach is very dynamic and continuously changes at a pace that static point-in-time (for example, antivirus) tools can't cope with. Solutions to overcome these dynamic threats require a thorough understanding of how these attacks work and the evasion techniques that allow them to infiltrate networks.

To be able to detect the rapidly evolving threats, organizations should design their networks using a security framework such as that provided by Cisco SAFE. The following sections describe the most critical components needed to implement the Cisco SAFE framework for a campus environment (or *PIN*, in Cisco SAFE terminology).

Key Topic

Cisco Talos

Cisco Talos is the Cisco threat intelligence organization, an elite team of security experts who are supported by sophisticated security systems to create threat intelligence that detects, analyzes, and protects against both known and emerging threats for Cisco products.

Cisco Talos was created from the combination of three security research teams:

- IronPort Security Applications (SecApps)
- The Sourcefire Vulnerability Research Team (VRT)
- The Cisco Threat Research, Analysis, and Communications (TRAC) team

Talos tracks threats across endpoints, networks, cloud environments, the web, and email to provide a comprehensive understanding of cyber threats, their root causes, and scopes of outbreaks. Every day Talos receives and analyzes nearly 16 billion web requests, 600 billion emails, and 1.5 million unique malware samples. Talos also receives valuable intelligence that no other cybersecurity research team can match through the following intelligence feeds:

- Advanced Microsoft and industry disclosures
- The Advanced Malware Protection (AMP) community
- ClamAV, Snort, Immunet, SpamCop, SenderBase, Cisco Secure Malware Analytics, and Talos user communities
- Honeypots

- The Sourcefire Awareness, Education, Guidance, and Intelligence Sharing (AEGIS) program
- Private and public threat feeds
- Dynamic analysis

All this data is used to create comprehensive threat intelligence that is fed into a wide range of security products and solutions to provide protection against an extensive range of threats.

Key Topic

Cisco Secure Malware Analytics (Threat Grid)

Cisco Secure Malware Analytics, formerly Threat Grid, is a solution that can perform static file analysis (for example, checking filenames, MD5 checksums, file types, and so on) as well as dynamic file analysis (also known as behavioral analysis) by running the files in a controlled and monitored sandbox environment to observe and analyze the behavior against millions of samples and billions of malware artifacts to determine whether it is malware or not. Behavioral analysis is combined with threat intelligence feeds from Talos as well as with existing security technologies to protect against known and unknown attacks. If Malware Analytics identifies a file as malware, it begins to understand what it is doing or attempting to do, the scope of the threat it poses, and how to defend against it. Malware typically includes code to detect whether it is being analyzed in a virtual sandbox environment, and if the malware detects that it is being executed in a sandbox, it won't run, rendering the analysis useless. However, Malware Analytics evades being detected by malware by not having the typical instrumentation.

It is also possible to upload suspicious files into a sandbox environment called Glovebox to safely interact with them and observe malware behavior directly.

Malware Analytics is available as an appliance and in the cloud, and it is also integrated into existing Cisco Secure products and third-party solutions.

NOTE Automatic submission of suspicious files and samples is available for products and solutions integrated with Malware Analytics. When automatic submission is not available, files can also be uploaded manually into Malware Analytics for analysis.

Key Topic

Cisco Advanced Malware Protection (AMP)

Cisco Advanced Malware Protection (AMP), also referred to as Malware Defense, is a malware analysis and protection solution that goes beyond point-in-time detection. Using targeted, context-aware malware, attackers have the resources, persistence, time, and expertise to compromise any network relying solely on point-in-time detection mechanisms. Point-in-time detection is completely blind to the scope and depth of a breach after it happens.

Cisco AMP provides comprehensive protection for organizations across the full attack continuum:

- **Before:** Global threat intelligence from Cisco Talos and Cisco Secure Malware Analytics feeds into AMP to protect against known and new emerging threats.
- **During:** File reputation to determine whether a file is clean or malicious as well as sandboxing is used to identify threats during an attack.

- **After:** Cisco AMP provides retrospection, indicators of compromise (IoCs), breach detection, tracking, analysis, and surgical remediation after an attack, when advanced malware has slipped past other defenses.

The architecture of AMP can be broken down into the following components:

Key Topic

- AMP Cloud (private or public)
- AMP connectors
  - Cisco Secure Endpoint, formerly FireAMP or AMP for Endpoints—supported on Microsoft Windows, macOS X, Google Android, Apple iOS, and Linux
  - Cisco Secure Email, formerly AMP for Email or Email Security Appliance (ESA)
  - Cisco Secure Web Appliance, formerly AMP for Web or Web Security Appliance (WSA)
  - **AMP for Networks**—supported on Cisco Secure Firewall appliances and Cisco AMP dedicated appliances
  - AMP for Meraki MX
- Threat intelligence from Cisco Talos and Cisco Secure Malware Analytics

NOTE The Cisco Secure Endpoint on Apple iOS is known as the Cisco Security Connector (CSC). The CSC incorporates Cisco Secure Endpoint and Cisco Umbrella.

Figure 25-2 illustrates how all the AMP components come together to form the AMP/Malware Defense architecture.

The most important component of the AMP architecture is AMP Cloud, which contains the database of files and their reputations (malware, clean, unknown, and custom), also referred to as *file dispositions*. The file disposition in the AMP Cloud can change based on data received from Talos or Malware Analytics.

If an AMP connector uploads a sample file to AMP Cloud and the file's reputation is deemed to be malicious, it is stored in the cloud and reported to AMP connectors that see the same file. If the file is unknown, it is sent to Malware Analytics, where its behavior is analyzed in a secure sandbox environment.

AMP Cloud performs decision making in real time, evolving constantly based on the data that is received. AMP Cloud can identify malware on files that were previously deemed to be clean.

Unlike traditional antivirus or malware protection software that uses a local database of signatures to match malicious software or a bad file, AMP connectors remain lightweight by instead sending a hash to the cloud and allowing the cloud to make the intelligent decisions and return a verdict (about reputation or file disposition) of clean, malicious, or unknown.

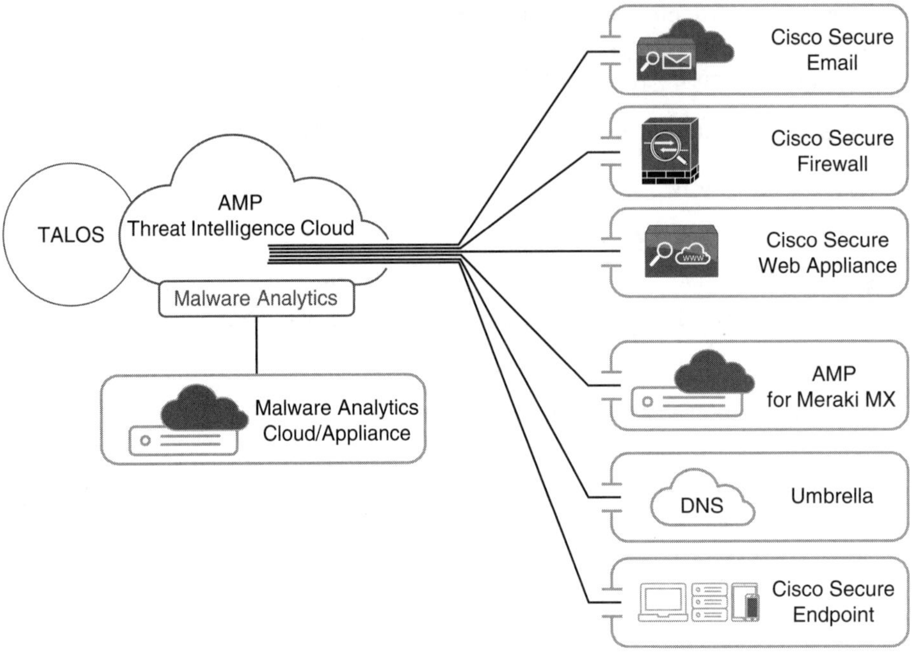

Figure 25-2 *AMP/Malware Defense Architecture*

Key Topic

Cisco Secure Client (AnyConnect)

The **Cisco Secure Client**, formerly Cisco AnyConnect Secure Mobility Client, is a modular endpoint software product that is not only a VPN client that provides VPN access through Transport Layer Security (TLS)/Secure Sockets Layer (SSL) and IPsec IKEv2, but also offers enhanced security through various built-in modules, such as a VPN Posture (HostScan) module and an ISE Posture module. These modules enable Cisco Secure Client to assess an endpoint's compliance for antivirus, antispyware, and firewall software installed on the host, for example. If an endpoint is found to be noncompliant, network access can be restricted until the endpoint is in compliance.

Cisco Secure Client also includes web security through Cisco Cloud Web Security, network visibility into endpoint flows within Cisco Secure Network Analytics, and roaming protection with Cisco Umbrella—even while the Secure Client is not connected to the corporate network through a VPN. Secure Client is supported across a broad set of platforms, including Windows, macOS, iOS, Linux, Android, Windows Phone/Mobile, BlackBerry, and ChromeOS.

NOTE TLS/SSL is often used to indicate that either protocol is being discussed. The SSL protocol has been deprecated by the IETF in favor of the more secure TLS protocol, so TLS/SSL can be interpreted as referring to TLS only.

Key Topic

Cisco Umbrella

Cisco Umbrella, formerly OpenDNS, provides the first line of defense against threats on the Internet by blocking requests to malicious Internet destinations (domains, IPs, URLs) using the Domain Name System (DNS) before an IP connection is established or a file is downloaded. It is 100% cloud delivered, with no hardware to install or software to maintain.

The Umbrella global network includes over 40 data centers around the world using Anycast DNS, which allows it to guarantee 100% uptime. Thanks to its Anycast DNS infrastructure, it doesn't matter where each site is physically located; DNS traffic is routed to the closest location. Security intelligence is gathered from an average of 500 billion daily DNS requests from more than 90 million users. All this data is fed in real time into Umbrella's massive graph database, where statistical and machine learning models are continuously run against it. This information is also constantly analyzed by the Umbrella security researchers and supplemented with intelligence from Cisco Talos.

Setting up Umbrella in the corporate network is as easy as changing the DHCP configuration on all Internet gateways (that is, routers, access points) so that all devices, including guest devices, forward their DNS traffic to Umbrella's global network.

For devices such as laptops that are off the corporate network, if they are using the Cisco Secure Client, there is an option to enable a roaming security module, which allows for all DNS requests to be sent to Umbrella's global network even when the VPN is turned off, and it does this without requiring an additional agent. Another option is to deploy the Umbrella roaming client, which tags, encrypts, and forwards DNS queries bound for the Internet to the Umbrella global network so per-device security policies can be enforced everywhere without latency or complexity.

Figure 25-3 illustrates Cisco Umbrella blocking a phishing website.

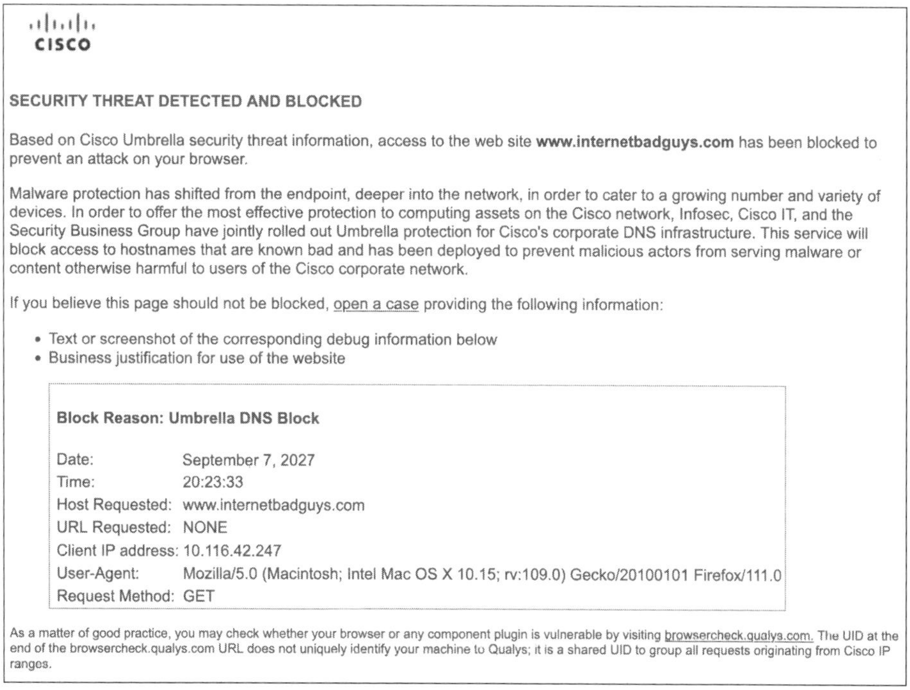

SECURITY THREAT DETECTED AND BLOCKED

Based on Cisco Umbrella security threat information, access to the web site **www.internetbadguys.com** has been blocked to prevent an attack on your browser.

Malware protection has shifted from the endpoint, deeper into the network, in order to cater to a growing number and variety of devices. In order to offer the most effective protection to computing assets on the Cisco network, Infosec, Cisco IT, and the Security Business Group have jointly rolled out Umbrella protection for Cisco's corporate DNS infrastructure. This service will block access to hostnames that are known bad and has been deployed to prevent malicious actors from serving malware or content otherwise harmful to users of the Cisco corporate network.

If you believe this page should not be blocked, open a case providing the following information:

- Text or screenshot of the corresponding debug information below
- Business justification for use of the website

Block Reason: Umbrella DNS Block

Date:	September 7, 2027
Time:	20:23:33
Host Requested:	www.internetbadguys.com
URL Requested:	NONE
Client IP address:	10.116.42.247
User-Agent:	Mozilla/5.0 (Macintosh; Intel Mac OS X 10.15; rv:109.0) Gecko/20100101 Firefox/111.0
Request Method:	GET

As a matter of good practice, you may check whether your browser or any component plugin is vulnerable by visiting browsercheck.qualys.com. The UID at the end of the browsercheck.qualys.com URL does not uniquely identify your machine to Qualys; it is a shared UID to group all requests originating from Cisco IP ranges.

Figure 25-3 *Cisco Umbrella Blocking a Phishing Website*

Key Topic

Cisco Secure Web Appliance (WSA)

The **Cisco Secure Web Appliance** is an all-in-one web gateway that includes a wide variety of protections that can block hidden malware from both suspicious and legitimate websites. It leverages real-time threat intelligence from the AMP Threat Intelligence Cloud that allows it to stay one step ahead of the evolving threat landscape to prevent the latest exploits from infiltrating the network. It also provides multiple layers of malware defense and vital data loss prevention (DLP) capabilities across the full attack continuum, as illustrated in Figure 25-4.

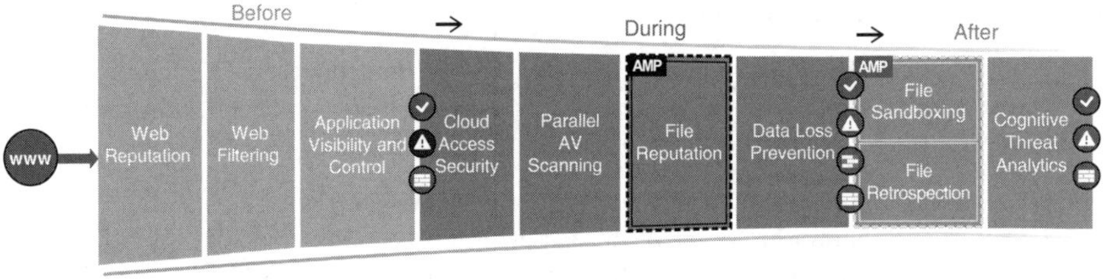

Figure 25-4 *Secure Web Appliance Capabilities Across the Attack Continuum*

The following sections describe the Secure Web Appliance involvement across the attack continuum before, during, and after an attack.

Before an Attack

Before an attack, the Secure Web Appliance actively detects and blocks potential threats before they happen by applying web reputation filters and URL filtering and by controlling web application usage:

- **Web reputation filters:** The Cisco Secure Web Appliance detects and correlates threats in real time by leveraging Cisco Talos. To discover where threats are hiding, Cisco Talos constantly refreshes web reputation filtering information every three to five minutes, adding intelligence to and receiving intelligence from the Cisco Secure Web Appliance and other network security devices. Web reputation filtering prevents client devices from accessing dangerous websites containing malware or phishing links. The Cisco Secure Web Appliance analyzes and categorizes unknown URLs and blocks those that fall below a defined security threshold. When a web request is made, web reputation filters analyze more than 200 different web traffic and network-related parameters to determine the level of risk associated with a website. After it checks the domain owner, the server where the site is hosted, the time the site was created, and the type of site, the site is assigned a reputation score, which ranges from –10 to +10, instead of the binary good or bad categorizations of most malware detection applications. Based on that reputation score and selected security policies, the site is blocked, allowed, or delivered with a warning.

- **Web filtering:** Traditional URL filtering is combined with real-time dynamic content analysis. This process is used to shut down access to websites known to host malware with specific policies for URL filtering, which checks against a list of known websites from the Cisco URL filtering database of more than 50 million blocked sites. Inappropriate content is accurately identified in real time for 90% of unknown URLs using the Dynamic Content Analysis (DCA) engine. The DCA engine scans text, scores the text for relevancy, calculates model document proximity, and returns the closest category match. Every three to five minutes, Cisco Talos updates the URL filtering database with information from multiple vectors: firewalls, IPS, the web, email, and VPNs.

- **Cisco Application Visibility and Control (AVC):** Cisco AVC identifies and classifies the most relevant and widely used web and mobile applications (such as Facebook) and more than 150,000 micro-applications (such as Facebook Messenger) to provide administrators with the most granular control over application and usage behavior. For example, AVC can be configured to permit users to access Facebook or YouTube while blocking users from activities such as clicking the "Like" button or viewing certain videos or YouTube channels.

During an Attack

During an attack, the Secure Web Appliance uses security intelligence from cloud access security broker (CASB) providers, Talos, and AMP for Networks to identify and block zero-day threats that managed to infiltrate the network:

- **Cloud access security:** The Cisco Secure Web Appliance can protect against hidden threats in cloud apps by partnering with leading CASB providers (such as Cisco CloudLock) to monitor cloud app usage in real time to help combat evolving threats through intelligent protection powered by data science.
- **Parallel antivirus (AV) scanning:** The Cisco Secure Web Appliance enhances malware defense coverage with multiple anti-malware scanning engines running in parallel on a single appliance while maintaining high processing speeds and preventing traffic bottlenecks.
- **Layer 4 traffic monitoring:** The Cisco Secure Web Appliance scans all traffic, ports, and protocols to detect and block spyware "phone-home" communications with an integrated Layer 4 traffic monitor. Based on this scanning, it identifies infected clients to help stop malware that attempts to bypass classic web security solutions.
- **File reputation and analysis with Cisco AMP:** With the Secure Web Appliance, files are assessed using the latest threat information from Cisco Talos, which, as mentioned before, is updated every three to five minutes. The Cisco Secure Web Appliance captures a fingerprint of each file as it traverses the gateway and sends it to AMP Cloud for a reputation verdict checked against zero-day exploits.
- **Data loss prevention (DLP):** The Cisco Secure Web Appliance uses Internet Content Adaptation Protocol (ICAP) to integrate with DLP solutions from leading third-party DLP vendors. When all outbound traffic is directed to the third-party DLP appliance, content is allowed or blocked based on the third-party rules and policies. Deep content inspection can be enabled for regulatory compliance and intellectual property protection. Powerful engines inspect outbound traffic and analyze it for content markers, such as confidential files, credit card numbers, customer personal data, and so on

and prevent this data from being uploaded into cloud file-sharing services such as Box, iCloud, and Dropbox.

After an Attack

After an attack, the Cisco Secure Web Appliance inspects the network continuously for instances of undetected malware and breaches. After an initial detection, using Cisco AMP retrospection capabilities, the Cisco Secure Web Appliance continues to scan files over an extended period of time, using the latest detection capabilities and collective threat intelligence from Talos and Malware Analytics. Alerts are sent when a file disposition changes (that is, is unknown to malware) to provide awareness and visibility into malware that evades initial defenses.

Global Threat Analytics (GTA), formerly Cognitive Threat Analytics (CTA), analyzes web traffic, endpoint data from Cisco Secure Endpoint, and network data from Cisco Secure Network Analytics. It then uses machine learning to identify malicious activity before it can exfiltrate sensitive data.

The Secure Web Appliance can be deployed in the cloud, as a virtual appliance, on-premises, or in a hybrid arrangement. All features are available across any deployment option.

Key Topic

Cisco Secure Email (ESA)

For business organizations, email is the most important business communication tool, and at the same time, it is one of the top attack vectors for security breaches. **Cisco Secure Email** enables users to communicate securely via email and helps organizations combat email security threats with a multilayered approach across the attack continuum.

Cisco Secure Email includes the following advanced threat protection capabilities that allow it to detect, block, and remediate threats across the attack continuum:

- **Global threat intelligence:** It leverages real-time threat intelligence from Cisco Talos and Cisco Secure Malware Analytics.
- **Reputation filtering:** Cisco Secure Email blocks unwanted email with reputation filtering, which is based on threat intelligence from Talos.
- **Spam protection:** Cisco Secure Email uses the Cisco Context Adaptive Scanning Engine (CASE) to block spam emails; it delivers a spam catch rate greater than 99%, with a false-positive rate of less than 1 in 1 million.
- **Forged email detection:** Forged email detection protects high-value targets such as executives against business email compromise (BEC) attacks.
- **Cisco Advanced Phishing Protection (CAPP):** CAPP combines Cisco Talos threat intelligence with local email intelligence and advanced machine learning techniques to model trusted email behavior on the Internet, within organizations, and between individuals. It uses this intelligence to stop identity deception–based attacks such as fraudulent senders, social engineering, and BEC attacks.
- **Cisco Domain Protection (CDP):** CDP for external email helps prevent phishing emails from being sent using a customer domain.

- **Malware defense:** Cisco Secure Email protects against malware.
- **Graymail detection and Safe Unsubscribe:** Cisco Secure Email detects and classifies graymail for an administrator to take action on it if necessary. Graymail consists of marketing, social networking, and bulk messages (that is, mailing list emails). This type of email typically comes with an unsubscribe link, which may be used for phishing. Safe Unsubscribe protects against this type of phishing technique.
- **URL-related protection and control:** Cisco Secure Email protects against malicious URLs with URL filtering and scanning of URLs in attachments and shortened URLs.
- **Outbreak filters:** Outbreak filters defend against emerging threats and blended attacks by leveraging security intelligence information from Cisco Talos. Outbreak filters can rewrite URLs included in suspicious email messages. When clicked, the new rewritten URLs redirect the email recipient to the Secure Web Appliance. The website content is then actively scanned, and outbreak filters display a block screen to the user if the site contains malware.
- **Web interaction tracking:** Cisco Secure Email generates reports that track the end users who click on URLs that have been rewritten by the outbreak filters. The reports include the following information:
  - Top users who clicked on malicious URLs
  - The top malicious URLs clicked by end users
  - Date and time, rewrite reason, and action taken on the URLs
- **Data security for sensitive content in outgoing emails:** Confidential outbound messages that match one of the more than 100 expert policies included with Cisco Secure Email are automatically protected by encryption, footers and disclaimers, blind carbon copies (BCCs), notifications, and quarantining.

Cisco Secure Email is available as a hardware appliance or as a cloud offering called Cisco Secure Email Threat Defense.

Key Topic

Cisco Secure IPS (FirePOWER NGIPS)

A system that passively monitors and analyzes network traffic for potential network intrusion attacks and logs the intrusion attack data for security analysis is known as an *intrusion detection system (IDS)*. A system that provides IDS functions and also automatically blocks intrusion attacks is known as an *intrusion prevention system (IPS)*.

A next-generation IPS (NGIPS), according to Gartner, Inc., should include IPS functionality as well as the following capabilities:

Key Topic

- Real-time contextual awareness
- Advanced threat protection
- Intelligent security automation
- Unparalleled performance and scalability
- Application visibility and control (AVC) and URL filtering

With the acquisition of Sourcefire in 2013, Cisco added to its portfolio the FirePOWER NGIPS, which is now called Cisco Secure IPS. Cisco Secure IPS exceeds the NGIPS requirements defined by Gartner. Following are some of the most important capabilities included with Cisco Secure IPS:

- **Real-time contextual awareness:** Discovers and provides contextual information such as applications, users, endpoints, operating systems, vulnerabilities, services, processes, network behaviors, files, and threats.
- **Advanced threat protection and remediation:** Rapidly detects, blocks, contains, and remediates advanced threats through integrated AMP for Networks and Secure Malware Analytics sandboxing solutions.
- **Intelligent security automation:** Automatically correlates threat events, contextual information, and network vulnerability data to perform the following:
  - Optimizing defenses by automating protection policy updates
  - Quickly identifying users affected by a client-side attack
  - Receiving alerts when a host violates a configuration policy
  - Detecting the spread of malware by baselining normal network traffic and detecting network anomalies
  - Detecting and tagging hosts that might potentially be compromised by malicious means (exploit kit, malware, command-and-control) with an IoC
- **Unparalleled performance and scalability:** Purpose-built Cisco Secure Firewall and Cisco Secure Firewall ASA appliances incorporate a low-latency, single-pass design for unprecedented performance and scalability.
- **AVC:** Reduces threats through application detection of more than 4000 commercial applications, with support for custom applications.
- **URL filtering:** Provides access control to more than 80 categories of websites and covers more than 280 million individual URLs.

In addition, following are some of the capabilities available in the Cisco Secure IPS that exceed the requirements for the definition of NGIPS:

- **Centralized management:** Centralized management by the Cisco Secure Firewall Management Center (FMC), formerly Firepower Management Center, which is a single pane of glass for event collection and policy management.
- **Global threat intelligence from the Cisco Talos:** Integration with Cisco Talos for up-to-the-minute IPS signature updates as well as URL filtering information to blocklist connections to or from IP addresses, URLs, and/or domain names.
- **Snort IPS detection engine:** The detection engine is Snort, the world's most powerful open-source IPS engine.

- **Third-party and open-source ecosystem:** Open API for integration with third-party products.
- **Integration with Cisco ISE:** The FMC can use Cisco ISE to apply remediation on compromised hosts:
  - **Quarantine:** Limits or blocks an endpoint's access to the network
  - **Unquarantine:** Removes the quarantine
  - **Shutdown:** Shuts down the port that a compromised endpoint is attached to

Key Topic

Cisco Secure Firewall (NGFW)

A *firewall* is a network security device that monitors incoming and outgoing network traffic and allows or blocks traffic by performing simple packet filtering and stateful inspection based on ports and protocols. A firewall essentially establishes a barrier between trusted internal networks and untrusted outside networks such as the Internet.

In addition to providing standard firewall functionality, a **next-generation firewall (NGFW)** can block threats such as advanced malware and application-layer attacks. According to Gartner, Inc.'s definition, an NGFW firewall must include

Key Topic

- Standard firewall capabilities such as stateful inspection
- An integrated IPS
- Application-level inspection (to block malicious or risky apps)
- The ability to leverage external security intelligence to address evolving security threats

Cisco integrated ASA software with the Cisco Secure IPS services software, and the combination of the two far exceeds the NGFW definition set by Gartner. This integration gave birth to the Cisco Firepower NGFW (now called Cisco Secure Firewall), which is the industry's first fully integrated, threat-focused NGFW with unified management.

Cisco Secure Firewall is available in the following form factors:

- Cisco Secure Firewall Appliances
- Cisco Secure Industrial Security Appliance (ISA)
- Cisco Secure Firewall Threat Defense Virtual
- Cisco Secure Firewall Cloud Native
- Cisco Secure Web Application Firewall (WAF) and bot protection
- All ASA 5500-X appliances (except 5585-X)

The Cisco Secure Firewalls support the following software:

- **ASA software image:** Turns the appliance into a standard legacy firewall with no Cisco Secure IPS services. It is supported on all Cisco Secure Firewall and ASA appliances.

- **ASA software image with Cisco Secure IPS software image (FirePOWER NGIPS):** Runs two software images in the same appliance, with each one requiring different management applications. Cisco Secure IPS (NGIPS) enables the ASA to be a NGFW. This type of configuration is supported only on 5500-X appliances (except the 5585-X).
- **Firepower Threat Defense (FTD) software image:** Merges the ASA software image and the Cisco Secure IPS image into a single unified image. Supported on all Cisco Secure Firewall and ASA 5500-X appliances (except the 5585-X).

> **NOTE** In Cisco's documentation, FirePOWER (uppercase) refers to the Cisco Secure IPS (NGIPS) services software or the NGIPS services ASA module, while Firepower (lowercase) refers to the Cisco Secure Firewall or the FTD unified image.

FTD is also supported on the following platforms:

- ISR modules
- Cisco Secure Firewall Threat Defense Virtual and Cloud Native appliances, supported in VMware, KVM, Amazon Web Services (AWS), Google Cloud Platform (GCP), Cisco HyperFlex, Nutanix, OpenStack, Alibaba Cloud, and Microsoft Azure environments

The following management options are available for Cisco Secure Firewalls:

- For FTD or Cisco Secure IPS Services software:
  - Cisco SecureX
  - Cisco Secure Firewall Management Center (FMC), formerly Firepower Management Center
  - Cisco Secure Firewall Device Manager (FDM), formerly Firepower Device Manager, for small appliances
- For ASA software:
  - The command-line interface (CLI)
  - Cisco Security Manager (CSM)
  - Cisco Secure Firewall Adaptive Security Device Manager (ASDM)
  - Cisco Defense Orchestrator

> **NOTE** FTD or Cisco Secure IPS Services software CLI configuration is not supported. CLI is available only for initial setup and troubleshooting purposes.

Cisco Secure Firewall Management Center (FMC)

The Cisco FMC is a centralized management platform that aggregates and correlates threat events, contextual information, and network device performance data. It can be used to monitor information that Cisco Secure Firewall devices are reporting to each other and examine the overall activity occurring in the network.

The FMC performs event and policy management for the following Cisco Secure Firewall security solutions:

- Cisco Secure Firewall (physical) and Cisco Firewall Threat Defense (virtual)
- Cisco FTD for ISR
- Cisco ASA with FirePOWER Services

Key Topic

Cisco Secure Network Analytics (Stealthwatch Enterprise)

Cisco Secure Network Analytics, formerly *Stealthwatch Enterprise,* is a collector and aggregator of network telemetry data that performs network security analysis and monitoring to automatically detect threats that manage to infiltrate a network, as well as the ones that originate from within a network. Using advanced security analytics, Cisco Secure Network Analytics can quickly and with high confidence detect threats such as command-and-control (C&C) attacks, ransomware, DDoS attacks, illicit cryptomining, unknown malware, and inside threats. It is an agentless solution that brings threat visibility that can be scaled into the cloud (when used in combination with Cisco Secure Cloud Analytics), across the network, to branch locations, in the data center, and down to the endpoints, and it can detect malware in encrypted traffic and ensure policy compliance without decryption.

Key Topic

At the core of Cisco Secure Network Analytics are the following components:

- **Cisco Secure Network Analytics Manager, formerly Stealthwatch Management Console (SMC):** The Network Analytics Manager is the control center for Cisco Secure Network Analytics. It aggregates, organizes, and presents analysis from up to 25 Flow Collectors, Cisco ISE, and other sources. It offers a powerful yet simple-to-use web console that provides graphical representations of network traffic, identity information, customized summary reports, and integrated security and network intelligence for comprehensive analysis. The Network Analytics Manager is available as a hardware appliance or a virtual machine.
- **Cisco Secure Network Analytics Flow Collectors:** The Flow Collectors collect and analyze enterprise telemetry data such as NetFlow, IP Flow Information Export (IPFIX), and other types of flow data from routers, switches, firewalls, endpoints, and other network devices. The Flow Collectors can also collect telemetry from proxy data sources, which can be analyzed by Global Threat Analytics, formerly Cognitive Threat Analytics. It can also pinpoint malicious patterns in encrypted traffic using Encrypted Traffic Analytics (ETA), without having to decrypt it, to identify threats and accelerate response. Flow Collectors are available as hardware appliances and as virtual machines.
- **Cisco Secure Network Analytics Flow Rate License:** The Flow Rate License is required for the collection, management, and analysis of flow telemetry data and

aggregates flows at the Network Analytics Manager as well as to define the volume of flows that can be collected.

Optional but recommended components include the following:

- **Cisco Secure Network Analytics Flow Sensors:** Produce telemetry data for segments of the networking infrastructure that can't generate NetFlow data and also provide visibility into the application layer data. They are available as hardware appliances and as virtual machines.
- **Cisco Secure Network Analytics UDP (User Datagram Protocol) Director:** Receives essential network and security UDP data streams from multiple locations and then forwards them in a single UDP data stream to one or more destinations. For example, instead of having every router in the network configured with multiple NetFlow exports for multiple destinations such as Flow Collectors, LiveAction, Arbor, and so on, every router could be configured with a single NetFlow export and send the data to the UDP Director. The UDP Director takes the data and replicates the NetFlow data from all routers to the multiple destinations in a single stream of data. It is available as a hardware appliance or a virtual machine.
- **Cisco Telemetry Broker:** Just like the UDP Director can take UDP data streams from multiple inputs and replicate them to multiple destinations, the Telemetry Broker can ingest telemetry data (for example, AWS VPC Flow Logs) from multiple inputs, filter unneeded data, and transform it into a format (for example, IPFIX) that can be understood by the telemetry consumer of choice, such as Cisco Secure Network Analytics and Splunk.
- **Cisco Secure Network Analytics Data Store:** Used for centralized flow data and network telemetry storage instead of a distributed model across multiple Flow Collectors. The centralized model offers greater storage capacity, greater flow rate, and increased resiliency versus the distributed model. The Data Store is composed of a minimum of three Data Node appliances.
- **Cisco Secure Network Analytics Threat Feed License:** Enables a feed of threat intelligence from Cisco Talos.
- **Cisco Secure Network Analytics Endpoint License:** Extends visibility into endpoints.
- **Cisco Secure Cloud Analytics:** Can be used in combination with Cisco Secure Network Analytics to extend visibility into Amazon Web Services (AWS), Google Cloud Platform (GCP), and Microsoft Azure cloud infrastructures.

Cisco Secure Network Analytics offers the following benefits:

- Real-time threat detection
- Incident response and forensics
- Network segmentation

- Network performance and capacity planning
- Ability to satisfy regulatory requirements

Key Topic

Cisco Secure Cloud Analytics (Stealthwatch Cloud)

Cisco Secure Cloud Analytics, formerly Stealthwatch Cloud, provides the visibility and continuous threat detection required to secure the on-premises, hybrid, and multicloud environments. It can accurately detect threats in real time, regardless of whether an attack is taking place on the network, in the cloud, or across both environments. Cisco Secure Cloud Analytics is a cloud-based Software-as-a-Service (SaaS) solution. It detects malware, ransomware, data exfiltration, network vulnerabilities, and role changes that indicate compromise.

Cisco Secure Cloud Analytics supports two deployment models:

Key Topic

- Cisco Secure Cloud Analytics Public Cloud Monitoring, formerly Stealthwatch Cloud Public Cloud Monitoring
- Cisco Secure Network Analytics SaaS, formerly Stealthwatch Cloud Private Network Monitoring

Cisco Secure Cloud Analytics Public Cloud Monitoring

Public Cloud Monitoring provides visibility and threat detection in AWS, GCP, and Microsoft Azure cloud infrastructures. It is an SaaS-based solution that can be deployed easily and quickly.

Public Cloud Monitoring can be deployed without software agents, instead relying on native sources of telemetry such as its virtual private cloud (VPC) flow logs. Cisco Secure Cloud Analytics models all IP traffic inside VPCs, between VPCs, or to external IP addresses generated by an organization's resources and functions. Cisco Secure Cloud Analytics is also integrated with additional AWS services such as Cloud Trail, Amazon CloudWatch, AWS Config, Inspector, Identity and Access Management (IAM), Lambda, and more.

Public Cloud Monitoring can be used in combination with Cisco Secure Network Analytics or Cisco Secure Network Analytics SaaS to provide visibility and threat detection across the entire network, from the private network and branch offices to the public cloud.

Cisco Secure Network Analytics SaaS

Network Analytics SaaS provides visibility and threat detection for the on-premises network, delivered from a cloud-based SaaS solution. It is a perfect solution for organizations that want better awareness and security in their on-premises environments while reducing capital expenditure and operational overhead.

A lightweight virtual appliance needs to be installed in a virtual machine or server that can consume a variety of native sources of telemetry data or extract metadata from network packet flow. The collected metadata is encrypted and sent to the Cisco Secure Cloud Analytics platform for analysis.

NOTE Cisco Secure Cloud Analytics consumes metadata only. The actual packet payloads are never retained or transferred outside the network.

Key Topic

Cisco Identity Services Engine (ISE)

Cisco Identity Services Engine (ISE) is a security policy management platform that provides highly secure network access control (NAC) to users and devices across wired, wireless, and VPN connections. It allows for visibility into what is happening in the network, such as who is connected (endpoints, users, and devices), which applications are installed and running on endpoints (for posture assessment), and much more.

Some of the most important features, benefits, services, and integrations supported by Cisco ISE include the following:

- **Streamlined network visibility:** Through a simple web-based interface, ISE stores a detailed attribute history of all the devices, endpoints, and users (guests, employees, and contractors) on the network.
- **Cisco Digital Network Architecture (DNA) Center integration:** Cisco DNA Center is the Cisco intent-based network controller and analytics platform. It makes it easy to design, provision, and apply policy across the network. Through its integration with Cisco ISE, it can apply TrustSec software-defined segmentation through SGT tags and Security Group Access Control Lists (SGACLs).
- **Centralized secure network access control:** Cisco ISE supports the RADIUS protocol, required to enable 802.1x/EAP, MAB, and local and centralized WebAuth for consistent access control into wired, wireless, and VPN networks.
- **Centralized device access control:** Cisco ISE supports the TACACS+ protocol, which is required for AAA device access control services (covered in Chapter 26, "Network Device Access Control and Infrastructure Security").
- **Cisco TrustSec:** Cisco ISE implements Cisco TrustSec policy for software-defined secure segmentation through SGT tags, SGACLs, and SXP.
- **Guest lifecycle management:** It can be used to create customizable guest user web portals for WebAuth that can be branded with a company logo.
- **Streamlined device onboarding:** Cisco ISE automates 802.1x supplicant provisioning and certificate enrollment. It also integrates with mobile device management (MDM)/enterprise mobility management (EMM) vendors for mobile device compliance and enrollment.
- **Internal certificate authority:** Cisco ISE can act as an internal certificate authority.
- **Device profiling:** It automatically detects, classifies, and associates endpoints that connect to the network to endpoint-specific authorization policies based on device type.

- **Endpoint posture service:** Cisco ISE performs powerful posture audits on endpoints to make sure they are compliant. For example, it can check for the latest OS patch, see if the endpoint firewall is enabled, make sure anti-malware packages have the latest definitions, look for disk encryption, see a mobile PIN lock, determine rooted or jailbroken phone status, and much more. Devices that are not compliant can be remediated (prevented from accessing the network, applications, or services) until they become compliant. It also provides hardware inventory of every single device and endpoint connected to the network for full network visibility.
- **Active Directory support:** Cisco ISE supports integration with Microsoft Active Directory 2012, 2012R2, 2016, and 2019.
- **Cisco Platform Exchange Grid (pxGrid):** Cisco ISE shares contextual information using a single API between different Cisco platforms as well as more than 50 technology partners. pxGrid is an Internet Engineering Task Force (IETF) framework that makes it possible to automatically and quickly identify, contain, mitigate, and remediate security threats across the entire network. Cisco ISE is the central pxGrid controller (also referred to as pxGrid server), and all Cisco and third-party security platforms (referred to as *pxGrid nodes*) interface with it to publish, subscribe to, and query contextual information. There are two versions of pxGrid:
    - **pxGrid 1.0:** Released with ISE 1.3 and based on Extensible Messaging and Presence Protocol (XMPP). Starting with ISE Release 3.1, all pxGrid connections must be based on pxGrid 2.0.
    - **pxGrid 2.0:** Uses WebSocket and the REST API over Simple Text Oriented Message Protocol (STOMP) 1.2.

Example 25-1 shows the type of contextual information Cisco ISE can share with devices integrated with it through pxGrid.

Example 25-1 *Contextual Information from Cisco ISE Session Directory*

```
Session={ip=[192.168.1.2]
Audit Session Id=0A000001000000120001C0AC
UserName=dewey.hyde@corelab.com
ADUserDNSDomain=corelab.com
ADUserNetBIOSName=corelab,
ADUserResolvedIdentities=dewey.hyde@corelab.com
ADUserResolvedDNs=CN=Dewey Hyde
CN=Users
DC=corelab
DC=com
MacAddresses=[00:0C:C1:31:54:69]
State=STARTED
ANCstatus=ANC_Quarantine
SecurityGroup=Quarantined_Systems
```

```
EndpointProfile=VMWare-Device
NAS IP=192.168.1.1
NAS Port=GigabitEthernet0/0/1
RADIUSAVPairs=[ Acct-Session-Id=0000002F]
Posture Status=null
Posture Timestamp=
LastUpdateTime=Sat Aug 21 11:49:50 CST 2019
Session attributeName=Authorization_Profiles
Session attributeValue=Quarantined_Systems
Providers=[None]
EndpointCheckResult=none
IdentitySourceFirstPort=0
IdentitySourcePortStart=0
```

Network Access Control (NAC)

This section describes multiple network access control (NAC) technologies, such as 802.1x, MAC Authentication Bypass (MAB), and Web Authentication (WebAuth), as well as next-generation NAC technologies such as TrustSec and MACsec.

802.1x

Key Topic

IEEE **802.1x** (referred to as Dot1x) is a standard for port-based network access control (PNAC) that provides an authentication mechanism for local area networks (LANs) and wireless local area networks (WLANs).

802.1x comprises the following components:

Key Topic

- **Extensible Authentication Protocol (EAP):** This message format and framework defined by RFC 4187 provides an encapsulated transport for authentication parameters.
- **EAP method (also referred to as EAP type):** Different authentication methods can be used with EAP.
- **EAP over LAN (EAPoL):** This Layer 2 encapsulation protocol is defined by 802.1x for the transport of EAP messages over IEEE 802 wired and wireless networks.
- **RADIUS protocol:** This is the AAA protocol used by EAP.

802.1x network devices have the following roles:

Key Topic

- **Supplicant:** Software on the endpoint communicates and provides identity credentials through EAPoL with the authenticator. Common 802.1x supplicants include Windows and macOS native supplicants as well as Cisco Secure Client. All these supplicants support 802.1x machine and user authentication.

- **Authenticator:** A network access device (NAD) such as a switch or wireless LAN controller (WLC) controls access to the network based on the authentication status of the user or endpoint. The authenticator acts as the liaison, taking Layer 2 EAP-encapsulated packets from the supplicant and encapsulating them into RADIUS packets for delivery to the authentication server.
- **Authentication server:** A RADIUS server performs authentication of the client. The authentication server validates the identity of the endpoint and provides the authenticator with an authorization result, such as accept or deny.

The 802.1x roles and components are illustrated in Figure 25-5.

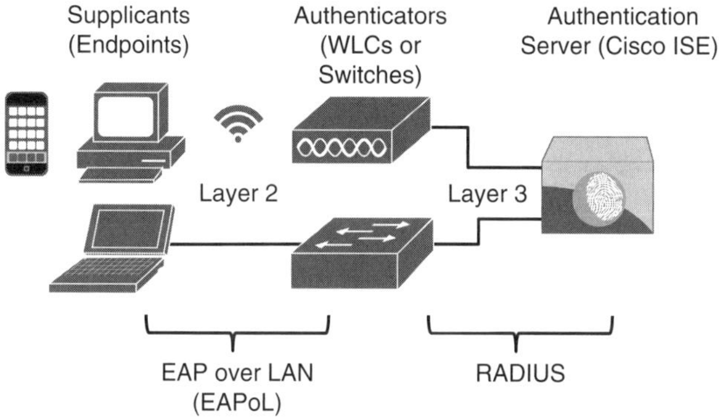

Figure 25-5 *802.1x Roles and Components*

The EAP identity exchange and authentication occur between the supplicant and the authentication server. The authenticator has no idea what EAP type is in use; it simply takes the EAPoL encapsulated frame from the supplicant and encapsulates it within the RADIUS packet sent to the authentication server and then opens up the port if the authentication server directs it to. Therefore, the EAP authentication is completely transparent to the authenticator.

Figure 25-6 illustrates the process flow of a successful 802.1x authentication.

Figure 25-6 illustrates the following steps:

Step 1. When the authenticator notices a port coming up, it starts the authentication process by sending periodic EAP-request/identify frames. The supplicant can also initiate the authentication process by sending an EAPoL-start message to the authenticator.

Step 2. The authenticator relays EAP messages between the supplicant and the authentication server, copying the EAP message in the EAPoL frame to an AV-pair inside a RADIUS packet and vice versa until an EAP method is selected. Authentication then takes place using the selected EAP method.

Step 3. If authentication is successful, the authentication server returns a RADIUS access-accept message with an encapsulated EAP-success message as well as an authorization option such as a downloadable ACL (dACL). When this is done, the authenticator opens the port.

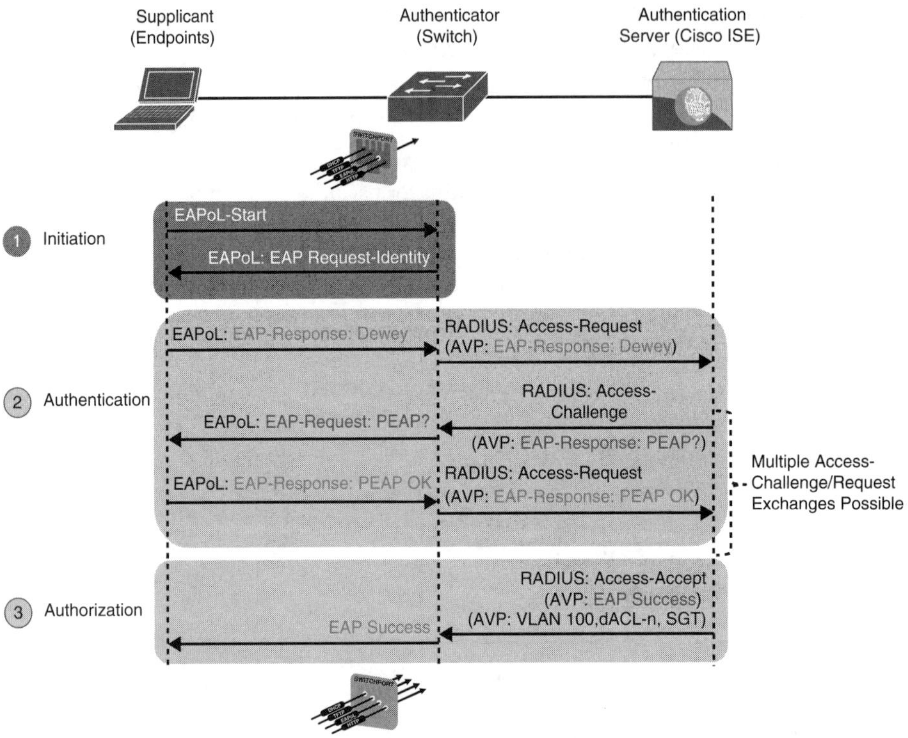

Figure 25-6 *Successful 802.1x Authentication Process Flow*

EAP Methods

Many different EAP authentication methods are available, most of them based on Transport Layer Security (TLS). Which one to choose depends on the security requirements and the EAP methods supported by the supplicants and the authentication server.

The following are the most commonly used EAP methods, which are described in this section:

Key Topic

- EAP challenge-based authentication method
  - Extensible Authentication Protocol-Message Digest 5 (EAP-MD5)
- EAP TLS authentication method
  - Extensible Authentication Protocol-Transport Layer Security (EAP-TLS)
- EAP tunneled TLS authentication methods
  - Extensible Authentication Protocol Flexible Authentication via Secure Tunneling (EAP-FAST)
  - Extensible Authentication Protocol Tunneled Transport Layer Security (EAP-TTLS)
  - Protected Extensible Authentication Protocol (PEAP)

- EAP inner authentication methods
  - EAP Generic Token Card (EAP-GTC)
  - EAP Microsoft Challenge Handshake Authentication Protocol Version 2 (EAP-MSCHAPv2)
  - EAP TLS

EAP inner authentication methods are tunneled within PEAP, EAP-FAST, and EAP-TTLS, which are also known as *outer* or *tunneled TLS authentication methods*. Tunneled TLS authentication methods establish a TLS outer tunnel between the supplicant and the authentication server; after the encrypted tunnel is established, client authentication credentials are negotiated using one of the EAP inner methods within the TLS outer tunnel. This tunneling authentication method is similar to the way an HTTPS session is established between a web browser and a secure website (such as a bank's website). The HTTPS TLS tunnel is formed after the web browser validates the authenticity of the website's certificate (one-way trust), and when the TLS tunnel is established, the user can enter the login credentials on the website through the secure TLS tunnel.

Following is a description of each of the EAP authentication methods:

- **EAP-MD5:** Uses the MD5 message-digest algorithm to hide the credentials in a hash. The hash is sent to the authentication server, where it is compared to a local hash to validate the accuracy of the credentials. EAP-MD5 does not have a mechanism for mutual authentication; in other words, the authentication server validates the supplicant, but the supplicant does not validate the authentication server to see if it is trustworthy. This lack of mutual authentication makes it a poor choice as an authentication method.
- **EAP-TLS:** Uses the TLS Public Key Infrastructure (PKI) certificate authentication mechanism to provide mutual authentication of supplicant to authentication server and authentication server to supplicant. With EAP-TLS, both the supplicant and the authentication server must be assigned a digital certificate signed by a certificate authority (CA) that they both trust. Because the supplicant also requires a certificate, this is the most secure authentication method; however, it is also the most difficult to deploy due to the administrative burden of having to install a certificate on the supplicant side.
- **PEAP:** In PEAP, only the authentication server requires a certificate, which reduces the administrative burden of implementing EAP. PEAP forms an encrypted TLS tunnel between the supplicant and the authentication server. After the tunnel has been established, PEAP uses one of the following EAP authentication inner methods to authenticate the supplicant through the outer PEAP TLS tunnel:
  - **EAP-MSCHAPv2 (PEAPv0):** Using this inner method, the client's credentials are sent to the server encrypted within an MSCHAPv2 session. This is the most common inner method, because it allows for simple transmission of username and

password, or even computer name and computer password, to the RADIUS server, which can then authenticate them using Microsoft's Active Directory.

- **EAP-GTC (PEAPv1):** This inner method was created by Cisco as an alternative to MSCHAPv2 to allow generic authentications to virtually any identity store, including OTP token servers, LDAP, NetIQ eDirectory, and more.
- **EAP-TLS:** This is the most secure EAP authentication since it is essentially a TLS tunnel within another TLS tunnel. It is rarely used due to its deployment complexity because it requires certificates to be installed on the supplicants.
- **EAP-FAST:** EAP-FAST, which is similar to PEAP, was developed by Cisco Systems as an alternative to PEAP to allow for faster re-authentications and support for faster wireless roaming. Just like PEAP, EAP-FAST forms a TLS outer tunnel and then transmits the client authentication credentials within that outer TLS tunnel. A major difference between FAST and PEAP is FAST's ability to re-authenticate faster by using protected access credentials (PACs). A PAC is similar to a secure cookie, stored locally on the host as "proof" of a successful authentication. EAP-FAST also supports EAP chaining, which is explained later in this chapter.
- **EAP-TTLS:** EAP-TTLS is similar in functionality to PEAP but is not as widely supported as PEAP. One major difference between them is that PEAP only supports EAP inner authentication methods, while EAP-TTLS can support additional inner methods such as legacy Password Authentication Protocol (PAP), Challenge Handshake Authentication Protocol (CHAP), and Microsoft Challenge Handshake Authentication Protocol (MS-CHAP).

Key Topic

EAP Chaining

EAP-FAST includes the option of EAP chaining, which supports machine and user authentication inside a single outer TLS tunnel. It enables machine and user authentication to be combined into a single overall authentication result. This allows the assignment of greater privileges or posture assessments to users who connect to the network using corporate-managed devices.

Key Topic

MAC Authentication Bypass (MAB)

MAC Authentication Bypass (MAB) is an access control technique that enables port-based access control using the MAC address of an endpoint, and it is typically used as a fallback mechanism to 802.1x. A MAB-enabled port can be dynamically enabled or disabled based on the MAC address of the endpoint that connects to it.

Figure 25-7 illustrates the process flow of a successful MAB authentication.

The steps outlined in Figure 25-7 are as follows:

Step 1. The switch initiates authentication by sending an EAPoL identity request message to the endpoint every 30 seconds by default. After three timeouts (a period of 90 seconds by default), the switch determines that the endpoint does not have a supplicant and proceeds to authenticate it via MAB.

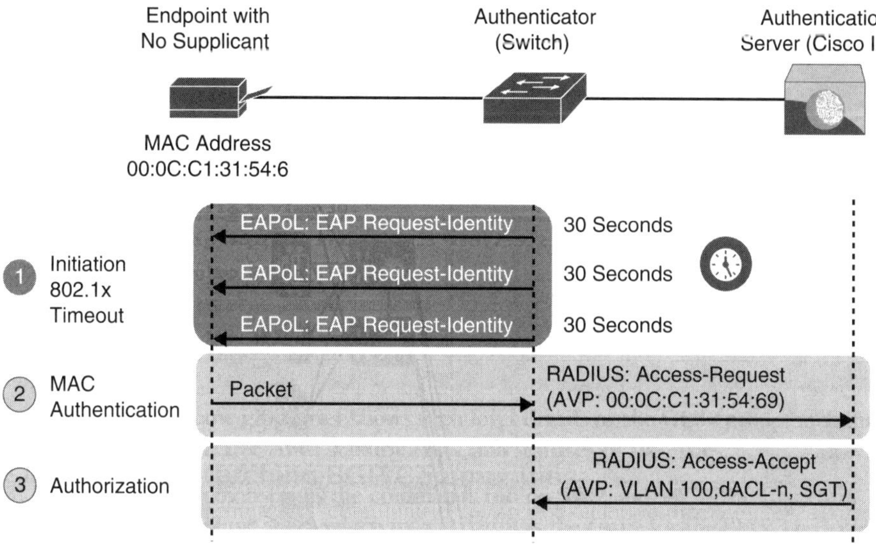

Figure 25-7 *Successful MAB Authentication Process Flow*

Step 2. The switch begins MAB by opening the port to accept a single packet from which it will learn the source MAC address of the endpoint. Packets sent before the port has fallen back to MAB (that is, during the IEEE 802.1x timeout phase) are discarded immediately and cannot be used to learn the MAC address.

After the switch learns the source MAC address, it discards the packet. It crafts a RADIUS access-request message using the endpoint's MAC address as the identity. The RADIUS server receives the RADIUS access-request message and performs MAC authentication.

Step 3. The RADIUS server determines whether the device should be granted access to the network and, if so, what level of access to provide. The RADIUS server sends the RADIUS response (access-accept) to the authenticator, allowing the endpoint to access the network. It can also include authorization options such as dACLs, dVLANs, and SGT tags.

NOTE If 802.1x is not enabled, the sequence is the same except that MAB authentication starts immediately after linkup instead of waiting for IEEE 802.1x to time out.

MAC addresses are easily spoofed, which means any endpoint can be configured to use a MAC address other than the burned-in address. For this reason, MAB authenticated endpoints should be given very restricted access and should only be allowed to communicate to the networks and services that the endpoints are required to speak to. If the authenticator is a Cisco switch, then many authorization options can be applied as part of the authorization result from the authentication server, including the following:

- Downloadable ACLs (dACLs)
- Dynamic VLAN assignment (dVLAN)
- Security Group Tags (SGT) tags

Key Topic

Web Authentication (WebAuth)

In an organization, endpoints that try to connect to the network might not have 802.1x supplicants and might not know the MAC address to perform MAB. These endpoints can be employees and contractors with misconfigured 802.1x settings that require access to the corporate network or visitors and guests that need access to the Internet. For these cases, **Web Authentication (WebAuth)** can be used. WebAuth, like MAB, can be used as a fallback authentication mechanism for 802.1x. If both MAB and WebAuth are configured as fallbacks for 802.1x, when 802.1x times out, a switch first attempts to authenticate through MAB, and if it fails, the switch attempts to authenticate with WebAuth.

With WebAuth, endpoints are presented with a web portal requesting a username and password. The username and password that are submitted through the web portal are sent from the switch (or wireless controller, firewall, and so on) to the RADIUS server in a standard RADIUS access-request packet. In a similar way to what occurs with MAB, the switch sends the request on behalf of the endpoint to the RADIUS server because the endpoint is not authenticating directly to the switch. Unlike MAB, WebAuth is only for users and not devices because it requires a web browser and manual username and password entry.

There are two types of WebAuth:

Key Topic

- Local Web Authentication
- Centralized Web Authentication with Cisco ISE

Local Web Authentication

Local Web Authentication (LWA) is the first form of Web Authentication that was created. For this type of WebAuth, the switch (or wireless controller) redirects web traffic (HTTP and/or HTTPS) to a locally hosted web portal running in the switch where an end user can enter a username and a password.

When the login credentials are submitted through the web portal, the switch sends a RADIUS access-request message along with the login credentials to the RADIUS server. It is important to remember that when the switch sends the login credentials on behalf of the user, it is considered to be LWA.

On Cisco switches, the LWA web portals are not customizable. Some organizations require that the web portals be customized to match their corporate branding. For those companies, LWA is not an acceptable solution.

In addition, with Cisco switches, there is no native support for advanced services such as acceptable use policy (AUP) acceptance pages (for example, a popup requesting acceptance of terms and conditions before access is allowed), password changing capabilities, device registration, and self-registration. For those advanced capabilities, a centralized web portal is required.

LWA does not support VLAN assignment; it supports only ACL assignment. It also doesn't support the change of authorization (CoA) feature to apply new policies; therefore, access policies cannot be changed based on posture or profiling state, and even administrative changes cannot be made as a result of malware to quarantine the endpoint.

> **NOTE** Cisco switches and a variety of third-party 802.1x-compliant switches have the option to assign a guest VLAN to endpoints that don't have an 802.1x supplicant. Many production deployments of 802.1x still use this legacy option to provide wired guests access to the Internet; however, it is important to note that guest VLAN and LWA are mutually exclusive.

Central Web Authentication with Cisco ISE

Cisco created Centralized Web Authentication (CWA) to overcome LWA's deficiencies. CWA supports CoA for posture profiling as well as dACL and VLAN authorization options. CWA also supports all the advanced services, such as client provisioning, posture assessments, acceptable use policies, password changing, self-registration, and device registration.

Just like LWA, CWA is only for endpoints that have a web browser, where the user can manually enter a username and a password. With CWA, WebAuth and guest VLAN functions remain mutually exclusive.

Authentication for CWA is different from authentication for LWA. The following steps detail how CWA authentication takes place:

Step 1. The endpoint entering the network does not have a configured supplicant or the supplicant is misconfigured.

Step 2. The switch performs MAB, sending the RADIUS access-request to Cisco ISE (the authentication server).

Step 3. The authentication server (ISE) sends the RADIUS result, including a URL redirection, to the centralized portal on the ISE server itself.

Step 4. The endpoint is assigned an IP address, DNS server, and default gateway using DHCP.

Step 5. The end user opens a browser and enters credentials into the centralized web portal. Unlike with LWA, the credentials are stored in ISE and are tied together with the MAB coming from the switch.

Step 6. ISE sends a re-authentication change of authorization (CoA-reauth) to the switch.

Step 7. The switch sends a new MAB request with the same session ID to ISE. ISE sends the final authorization result to the switch for the end user, including an authorization option such as a downloadable ACL (dACL).

Enhanced Flexible Authentication (FlexAuth)

By default, a Cisco switch configured with 802.1x, MAB, and WebAuth always attempts 802.1x authentication first, followed by MAB, and finally WebAuth. If an endpoint that does not support 802.1x tries to connect to the network, it needs to wait for a considerable amount of time before WebAuth is offered as an authentication option. Enhanced FlexAuth (also referred to as *Access Session Manager*) addresses this problem by allowing multiple authentication methods concurrently (for example, 802.1x and MAB) so that endpoints can be authenticated and brought online more quickly. Enhanced FlexAuth is a key component of the Cisco Identity-Based Networking Services (IBNS) 2.0 integrated solution, which offers authentication, access control, and user policy enforcement.

Cisco Identity-Based Networking Services (IBNS) 2.0

Cisco IBNS 2.0 is an integrated solution that offers authentication, access control, and user policy enforcement with a common end-to-end access policy that applies to both wired and wireless networks. It is a combination of the following existing features and products:

- Enhanced FlexAuth (Access Session Manager)
- Cisco Common Classification Policy Language (C3PL)
- Cisco ISE

Key Topic

Cisco TrustSec

Cisco TrustSec is a next-generation access control enforcement solution developed by Cisco to address the growing operational challenges of traditional network segmentation using VLANs and maintaining firewall rules and ACLs by using Security Group Tags (SGT) tags.

TrustSec uses SGT tags to perform ingress tagging and egress filtering to enforce access control policy. Cisco ISE assigns the SGT tags to users or devices that are successfully authenticated and authorized through 802.1x, MAB, or WebAuth. The SGT tag assignment is delivered to the authenticator as an authorization option (in the same way as a dACL). After the SGT tag is assigned, an access enforcement policy (allow or drop) based on the SGT tag can be applied at any egress point of the TrustSec network.

NOTE SGT tags are referred to as *scalable group tags* in Cisco Software-Defined Access (SD-Access).

SGT tags represent the context of the user, device, use case, or function. This means SGT tags are often named after particular roles or business use cases. For example, a corporate user with a Mac that successfully authenticates via 802.1x using EAP chaining could be assigned an SGT by ISE named Mac_Corporate. If the Mac is not compliant with posture requirements because it is not owned by the corporation, then it can be assigned an SGT named Mac_Guest.

NOTE Endpoints are not aware of the SGT tag. The SGT tag is only known and applied in the network infrastructure.

Figure 25-8 illustrates a list of default SGT tags on Cisco ISE. Notice that the SGT tags all have business-relevant names and descriptions. The SGT name is available on ISE and network devices to create security group policies; what is actually inserted into a Layer 2 frame SGT tag is a numeric value like the ones shown in the SGT column in decimal and hexadecimal notation.

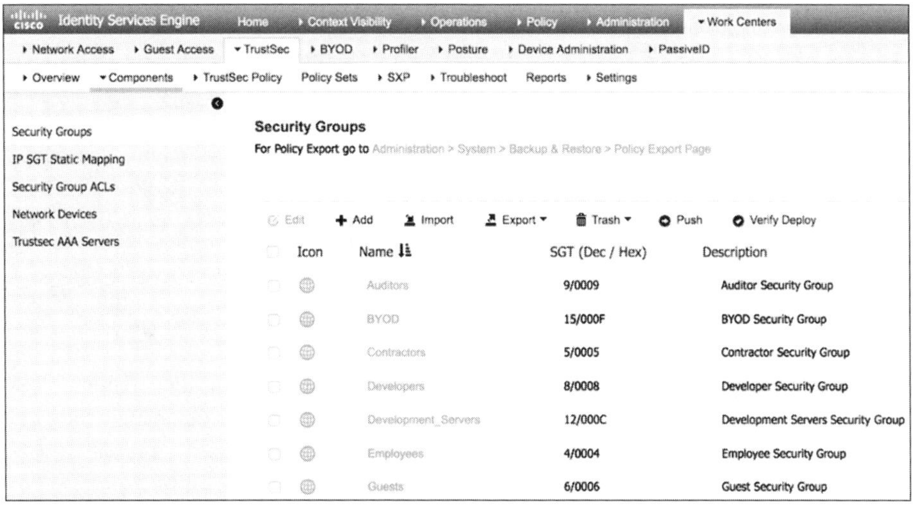

Figure 25-8 *Default SGT Tags in Cisco ISE*

TrustSec configuration occurs in three phases:

- Ingress classification
- Propagation
- Egress enforcement

Ingress Classification

Ingress classification is the process of assigning SGT tags to users, endpoints, or other resources as they ingress the TrustSec network, and it can happen in one of two ways:

- **Dynamic assignment:** The SGT is assigned dynamically and can be downloaded as an authorization option from ISE when authenticating using 802.1x, MAB, or WebAuth.
- **Static assignment:** In environments such as a data center that do not require 802.1x, MAB, or WebAuth authentication, dynamic SGT assignment is not possible. In these cases, SGT tags can be statically mapped on SGT-capable network devices. Static assignment on a device can be one of the following:
  - IP to SGT tag
  - Subnet to SGT tag

- VLAN to SGT tag
- Layer 2 interface to SGT tag
- Layer 3 logical interface to SGT tag
- Port to SGT tag
- Port profile to SGT tag

As an alternative to assigning an SGT tag to a port, Cisco ISE added the ability to centrally configure a database of IP addresses and their corresponding SGT tags. Network devices that are SGT capable can download the list from Cisco ISE.

Propagation

Propagation is the process of communicating the mappings to the TrustSec network devices that will enforce security group policy based on SGT tags.

Key Topic

There are two methods available for propagating an SGT tag: inline tagging (also referred to as *native tagging*) and the Cisco-created protocol SGT Exchange Protocol (SXP):

- **Inline tagging:** With inline tagging, a switch inserts the SGT tag inside a frame to allow upstream devices to read and apply policy. Native tagging is completely independent of any Layer 3 protocol (IPv4 or IPv6), so the frame or packet can preserve the SGT tag throughout the network infrastructure (routers, switches, firewalls, and so on) until it reaches the egress point. The downside to native tagging is that it is supported only by Cisco network devices with ASIC support for TrustSec. If a tagged frame is received by a device that does not support native tagging in hardware, the frame is dropped. Figure 25-9 illustrates a Layer 2 frame with a 16-bit SGT value.

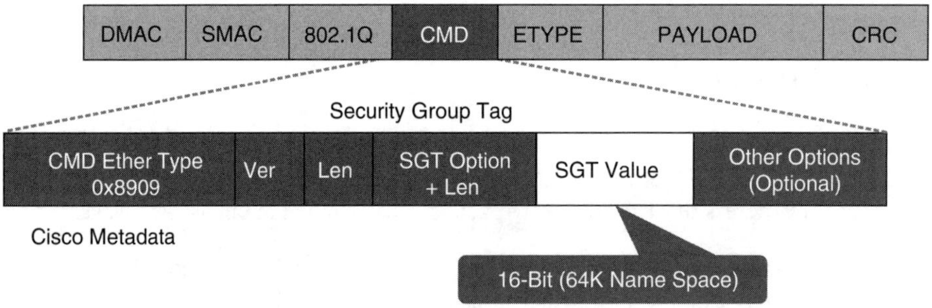

Figure 25-9 *Layer 2 Ethernet Frame with an SGT Tag*

- **SXP propagation:** SXP is a TCP-based peer-to-peer protocol used for network devices that do not support SGT inline tagging in hardware. Using SXP, IP-to-SGT mappings can be communicated between non-inline tagging switches and other network devices. Non-inline tagging switches also have an SGT mapping database to check packets against and enforce policy. The SXP peer that sends IP-to-SGT bindings is called a *speaker*. The IP-to-SGT binding receiver is called a *listener*. SXP connections can be single-hop or multi-hop, as shown in Figure 25-10.

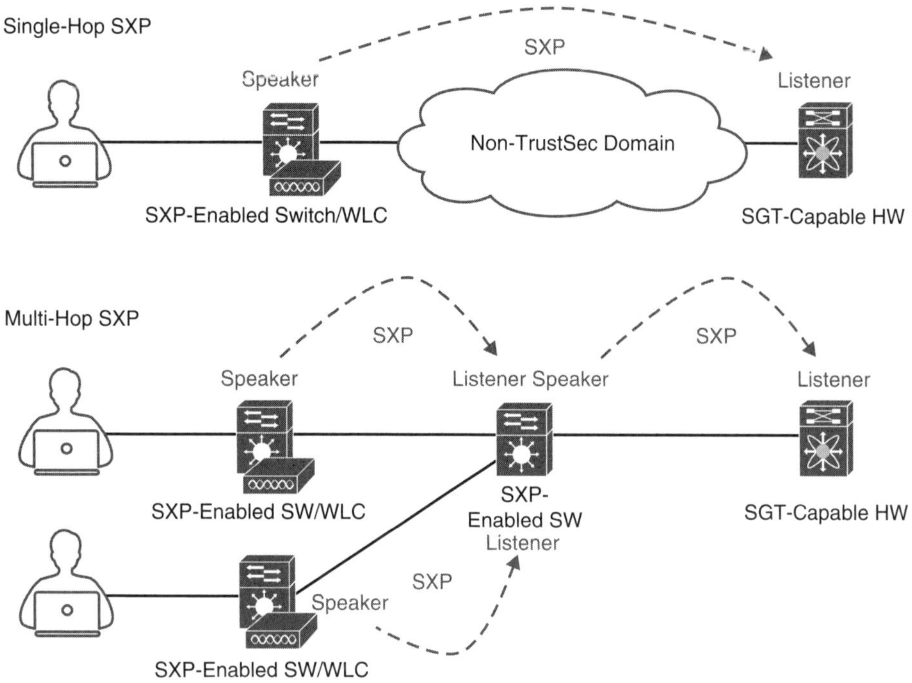

Figure 25-10 *Single-Hop and Multi-Hop SXP Connections*

Figure 25-11 shows an example of one access switch that supports native tagging. The packets get tagged on the uplink port and through the infrastructure. It also shows a switch that is not capable of inline tagging and that uses SXP to update the upstream switch. In both cases, the upstream switch continues to tag the traffic throughout the infrastructure.

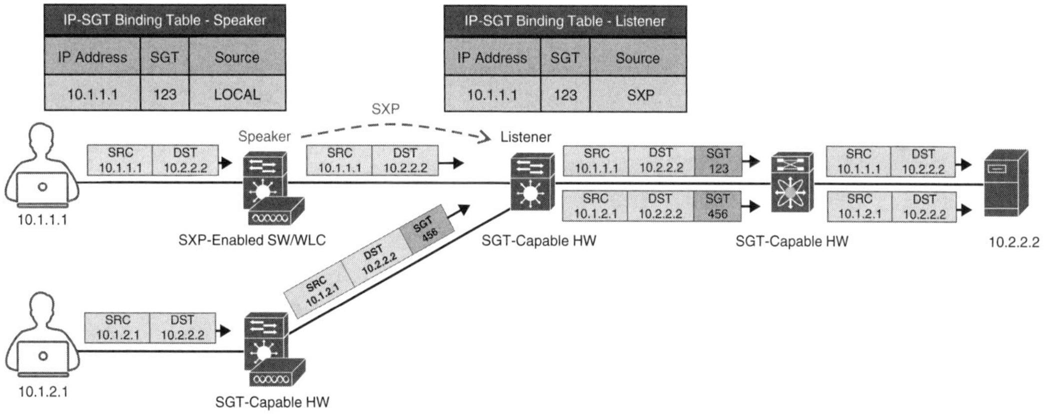

Figure 25-11 *Inline Tagging and SXP Propagation*

Figure 25-12 illustrates an example where a user authenticates to ISE via 802.1x. The user is connected to a switch that does not support inline tagging or SXP. This means an SGT-to-IP binding cannot be assigned to the user on the switch. The solution is for ISE to assign an SGT to the user by sending a mapping through SXP to an upstream device that supports TrustSec.

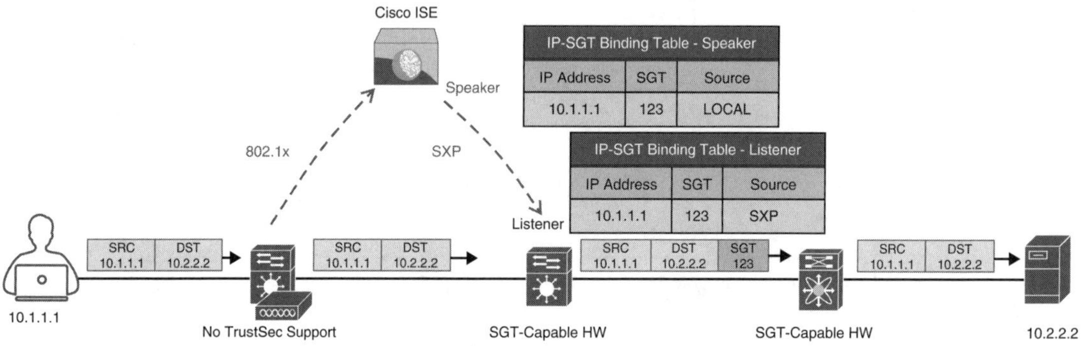

Figure 25-12 *SXP Peering Between Cisco ISE and TrustSec-Capable Devices*

> **NOTE** Cisco ISE also supports assigning the SGT mapping information to an upstream device through pxGrid.

Egress Enforcement

After the SGT tags have been assigned (classification) and are being transmitted across the network (propagation), policies can be enforced at the egress point of the TrustSec network.

There are multiple ways to enforce traffic based on the SGT tag, and they can be divided into two major types:

Key Topic

- **Security Group ACL (SGACL):** Provides enforcement on routers and switches. Access lists provide filtering based on source and destination SGT tags.
- **Security Group Firewall (SGFW):** Provides enforcement on Cisco Secure Firewalls. It requires tag-based rules to be defined locally on the firewall.

Figure 25-13 illustrates how an SGACL is blocking access to traffic with an SGT value of 123.

Figure 25-14 illustrates an SGACL egress policy production matrix from Cisco ISE that allows the defined SGACL enforcements to be visualized. The left column represents the source SGT tags, and the top row represents the destination SGT tags. The ACL enforced is the cell within the matrix where the source and destination SGT tags meet, and the direction is always from source SGT to destination SGT. For example, the matrix shows that developers (left column) are allowed to communicate to development servers using a permit IP ACL, while all other source SGT tags are denied with a deny IP ACL. Permit IP is the equivalent of permitting all, and deny IP is the equivalent of denying all.

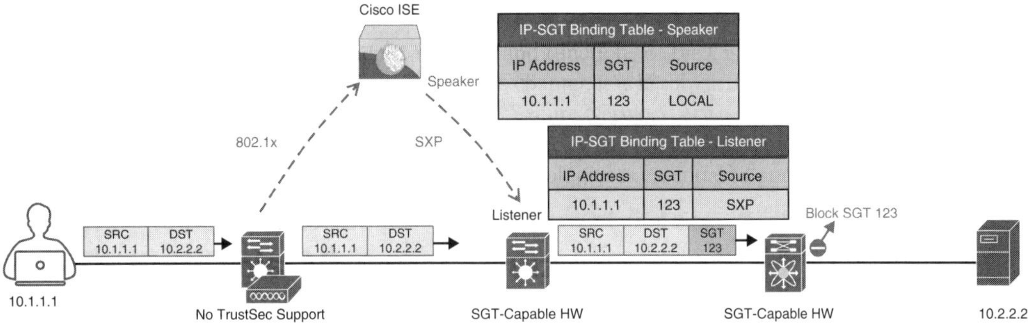

Figure 25-13 *TrustSec Enforcement with SGACL*

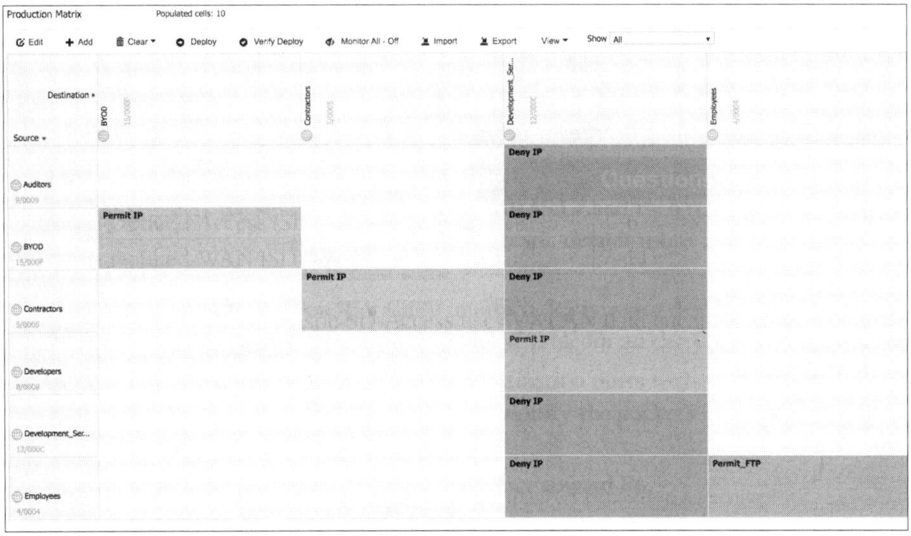

Figure 25-14 *SGACL Production Matrix View*

In addition to permit all and deny all SGACLs, more granular SGACLs are supported. Figure 25-14 also shows that employees trying to communicate with other employees will have a Permit_FTP ACL applied on egress. Figure 25-15 shows the SGACL Permit_FTP configuration on Cisco ISE, which is only allowing FTP traffic (TCP port 21) and denying all other traffic.

SGACL policies can be used to provide TrustSec software-defined segmentation capabilities to wired, wireless, and VPN networks, all centrally managed through ISE, as an alternative method to the traditional VLAN-based segmentation.

Figure 25-16 illustrates an example of TrustSec software-defined segmentation where only developers have access to the development servers, and any other employee trying to access them is blocked. Notice that traffic is blocked on egress and not on ingress. This example also illustrates that FTP is the only protocol allowed between employees (even within the same VLAN), while any other type of traffic is blocked. For the employees connected to the same switch, the switch is acting as the ingress and egress point.

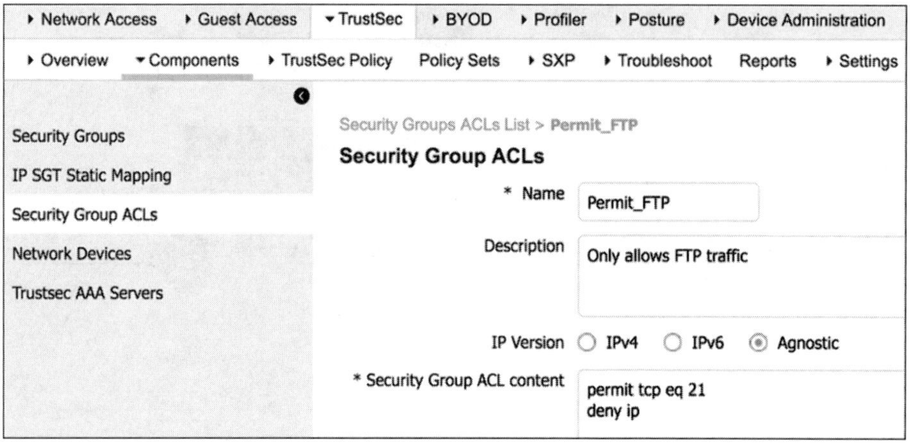

Figure 25-15 *Permit FTP SGACL Contents*

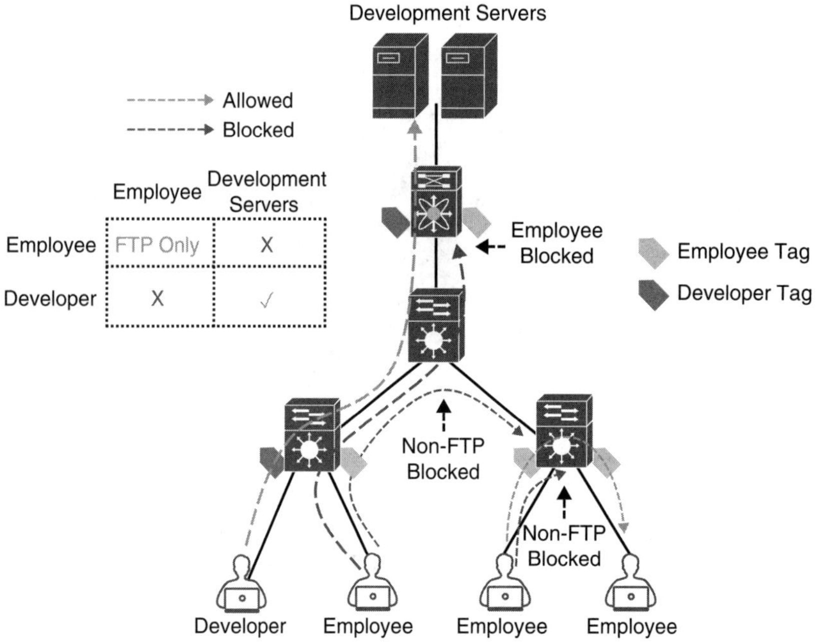

Figure 25-16 *TrustSec Software-Defined Segmentation*

Key Topic

MACsec

MACsec is an IEEE 802.1AE standards-based Layer 2 hop-by-hop encryption method; this means the traffic is encrypted only on the wire between two MACsec peers and is unencrypted as it is processed internally within the switch. This allows the switch to look into the inner packets for things like SGT tags to perform packet enforcement or QoS prioritization. MACsec also leverages onboard ASICs to perform the encryption and decryption rather than having to offload to a crypto engine, as with IPsec.

MACsec is based on the Ethernet frame format; however, an additional 16-byte MACsec Security Tag field (802.1AE header) and a 16-byte Integrity Check Value (ICV) field are added. This means that all devices in the flow of the MACsec communications must support MACsec for these fields to be used and to secure the traffic. MACsec provides authentication using Galois Message Authentication Code (GMAC) or authenticated encryption using Galois/Counter Mode Advanced Encryption Standard (AES-GCM).

Figure 25-17 illustrates the MACsec frame format and how it encrypts the TrustSec SGT tag.

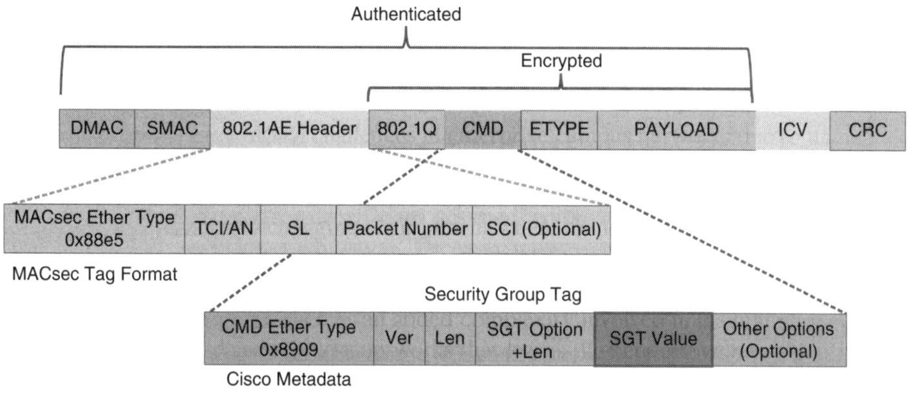

Figure 25-17 *MACsec Ethernet Frame with SGT*

NOTE Check the documentation to verify your software release supports SGT encapsulation in MACsec.

The MACsec Security Tag fields are as follows:

- **MACsec EtherType (first two octets):** Set to 0x88e5, designating the frame as a MACsec frame
- **TCI/AN (third octet):** Tag Control Information/Association Number field, designating the version number if confidentiality or integrity is used on its own
- **SL (fourth octet):** Short Length field, designating the length of the encrypted data
- **Packet Number (octets 5–8):** The packet number for replay protection and building of the initialization vector
- **SCI (octets 9–16):** Secure Channel Identifier, for classifying the connection to the virtual port

Two MACsec keying mechanisms are available:

Key Topic

- **Security Association Protocol (SAP):** This is a proprietary Cisco keying protocol used between Cisco switches.

- **MACsec Key Agreement (MKA) protocol:** MKA provides the required session keys and manages the required encryption keys. The 802.1AE encryption with MKA is supported between endpoints and the switch as well as between switches.

Key Topic

Downlink MACsec

Downlink MACsec is the term used to describe the encrypted link between an endpoint and a switch. The encryption between the endpoint and the switch is handled by the MKA keying protocol. This requires a MACsec-capable switch and a MACsec-capable supplicant on the endpoint (such as Cisco Secure Client). The encryption on the endpoint may be handled in hardware (if the endpoint possesses the correct hardware) or in software, using the main CPU for encryption and decryption.

The Cisco switch has the ability to force encryption, make encryption optional, or force non-encryption; this setting may be configured manually per port (which is not very common) or dynamically as an authorization option from Cisco ISE (which is much more common). If ISE returns an encryption policy with the authorization result, the policy issued by ISE overrides anything set using the switch CLI.

Key Topic

Uplink MACsec

Uplink MACsec is the term for encrypting a link between switches with 802.1AE. By default, uplink MACsec uses Cisco proprietary SAP encryption. The encryption is the same AES-GCM-128 encryption used with both uplink and downlink MACsec.

Uplink MACsec may be achieved manually or dynamically. Dynamic MACsec requires 802.1x authentication between the switches.

Exam Preparation Tasks

You have a couple of choices for exam preparation: the exercises here, Chapter 30, "Final Preparation," and the exam simulation questions in the Pearson Test Prep Software Online.

Review All Key Topics

Review the most important topics in the chapter, noted with the Key Topic icon in the outer margin of the page. Table 25-2 lists these key topics and the page number on which each is found.

Key Topic

Table 25-2 Key Topics for Chapter 25

Key Topic Element	Description	Page
Paragraph	Cisco SAFE places in the network (PINs)	738
List	Cisco SAFE Full attack continuum	740
Section	Cisco Talos	741
Section	Cisco Secure Malware Analytics (Threat Grid)	742
Section	Cisco Advanced Malware Protection (AMP)	742
List	Cisco AMP components	743

Key Topic Element	Description	Page
Section	Cisco Secure Client (AnyConnect)	744
Section	Cisco Umbrella	744
Section	Cisco Secure Web Appliance (WSA)	746
Section	Cisco Secure Email (ESA)	748
Section	Cisco Secure IPS (FirePOWER NGIPS)	749
List	Next-generation IPS (NGIPS) capabilities	749
Section	Cisco Secure Firewall (NGFW)	751
List	NGFW firewall capabilities	751
Section	Cisco Secure Network Analytics (Stealthwatch Enterprise)	753
List	Cisco Secure Network Analytics components	753
Section	Cisco Secure Cloud Analytics (Stealthwatch Cloud)	755
List	Cisco Secure Network Analytics offerings	755
Section	Cisco Identity Services Engine (ISE)	756
Section	802.1x	758
List	802.1x components	758
List	802.1x roles	758
List	EAP methods	760
Section	EAP Chaining	762
Section	MAC Authentication Bypass (MAB)	762
Section	Web Authentication (WebAuth)	764
List	WebAuth types	764
Section	Cisco TrustSec	766
List	Cisco TrustSec phases	767
Paragraph	Cisco TrustSec SGT propagation methods	768
List	Cisco TrustSec SGT types of enforcement	770
Section	MACsec	772
List	MACsec keying mechanisms	773
Section	Downlink MACsec	774
Section	Uplink MACsec	774

Complete Tables and Lists from Memory

Print a copy of Appendix B, "Memory Tables" (found on the companion website), or at least the section for this chapter, and complete the tables and lists from memory. Appendix C, "Memory Tables Answer Key," also on the companion website, includes completed tables and lists you can use to check your work.

Define Key Terms

Define the following key terms from this chapter and check your answers in the Glossary:

802.1x, Cisco Advanced Malware Protection (AMP), AMP for Networks, Cisco Secure Client, Cisco Secure Email, Cisco Secure Firewall, Cisco Identity Services Engine (ISE), Cisco SAFE, Cisco Secure Network Analytics, Cisco Talos, Cisco Secure Malware Analytics, Cisco TrustSec, Cisco Secure Web Appliance, endpoint, Extensible Authentication Protocol (EAP), MAC Authentication Bypass (MAB), MACsec, next-generation firewall (NGFW), Web Authentication (WebAuth), Firepower Threat Defense (FTD) software image

CHAPTER 26

Network Device Access Control and Infrastructure Security

This chapter covers the following subjects:

- **Access Control Lists (ACLs):** This section explains how to configure and verify ACLs to secure the network infrastructure.
- **Terminal Lines and Password Protection:** This section explains how to configure and verify local network device access control through local usernames and passwords for authentication and how to configure and verify role-based access control (RBAC) through privilege levels.
- **Authentication, Authorization, and Accounting (AAA):** This section explains how to configure and verify network device access control on IOS XE through an AAA TACACS+ server.
- **Zone-Based Firewall (ZBFW):** This section explains how to configure and verify stateful firewall functionality on IOS XE routers.
- **Control Plane Policing (CoPP):** This section explains how to configure and verify CoPP, which is used to protect the route processor (RP) or CPU of a router.
- **Device Hardening:** This section provides additional configuration tips for hardening the security of IOS XE routers.

This chapter focuses on how to configure and verify network device access control through local authentication and authorization as well as through AAA. It also explains how to configure and verify router security features such as ACLs, CoPP, and ZBFW that are used to provide device and infrastructure security.

"Do I Know This Already?" Quiz

The "Do I Know This Already?" quiz enables you to assess whether you should read the entire chapter. If you miss no more than one of these self-assessment questions, you might want to move ahead to the "Exam Preparation Tasks" section. Table 26-1 lists the major headings in this chapter and the "Do I Know This Already?" quiz questions covering the material in those headings so you can assess your knowledge of these specific areas. The answers to the "Do I Know This Already?" quiz appear in Appendix A, "Answers to the 'Do I Know This Already?' Questions."

Table 26-1 "Do I Know This Already?" Foundation Topics Section-to-Question Mapping

Foundation Topics Section	Questions
Access Control Lists (ACLs)	1
Terminal Lines and Password Protection	2–6
Authentication, Authorization, and Accounting (AAA)	7–9
Zone-Based Firewall (ZBFW)	10–11
Control Plane Policing (CoPP)	12–13
Device Hardening	14

1. Which command is used to apply an ACL to an interface?
   a. **ip access-group** {*access-list-number* | *name*} {**in**|**out**}
   b. **ip access-class** {*access-list-number* | *name*} {**in**|**out**}
   c. **ip access-list** {*access-list-number* | *name*} {**in**|**out**}
2. Which of the following password types is the weakest?
   a. Type 5
   b. Type 7
   c. Type 8
   d. Type 9
3. What type of encryption does the command **service password encryption** provide?
   a. Type 0
   b. Type 5
   c. Type 7
4. What is the difference between the line configuration command **login** and the line configuration command **login local**? (Choose two.)
   a. The **login** command is used to enable line password authentication.
   b. The **login** command is used to enable username-based authentication.
   c. The **login local** command is used to enable line and username-based authentication.
   d. The **login local** command is used to enable username-based authentication.
5. Which of these commands are available to a user logged in with privilege level 0? (Choose all that apply.)
   a. disable
   b. enable
   c. show
   d. configure terminal
   e. exit
   f. logout

6. Which of the following options can be used to only allow inbound SSH access to the vty lines of a router? (Choose two.)
   a. **line vty 0 4 transport output ssh**
   b. **line vty 0 4 transport input all**
   c. **line vty 0 4 transport input ssh**
   d. **ip access-list extended SSH permit tcp any any eq 22 line vty 0 4 access-class SSH in**
7. True or false: The command **aaa authorization exec default group ISE-TACACS+ if-authenticated** enables authorization for all terminal lines on the router, including the console line.
   a. True
   b. False
8. Which of the following AAA functions can help log the commands executed by a user on a network device?
   a. AAA next-generation logging
   b. Authorization
   c. Accounting
   d. Auditing
9. What is the protocol of choice for network device access control?
   a. RADIUS
   b. SSHv2
   c. Telnet
   d. TACACS+
10. Which of the following options describe ZBFW? (Choose two.)
    a. Provides high security with stateless inspection functionality
    b. Provides stateful firewall functionality
    c. Is a network interface module
    d. Is an integrated IOS XE solution
    e. Is a security appliance similar to an ASA 5500-X
11. What are the two system-built zones for ZBFW? (Choose two.)
    a. Inside zone
    b. Twilight zone
    c. System zone
    d. Outside zone
    e. Self zone
    f. Default zone
12. Which of the following features was developed specifically to protect the CPU of a router?
    a. ZBFW
    b. AAA
    c. CoPP
    d. ACLs

13. True or false: CoPP supports input and output policies to control inbound and outbound traffic.

   a. True

   b. False

14. Which of the following are features that can be disabled to improve the overall security posture of a router? (Choose two)

   a. CoPP

   b. CDP

   c. ZBFW

   d. LLDP

   e. LDP

Foundation Topics

Key Topic

Access Control Lists (ACLs)

Access control lists (also known as *ACLs* or *access lists*) are sequential lists of access control entries (ACEs) that perform permit or deny packet classification, based on predefined conditional matching statements. Packet classification starts at the top (lowest sequence) and proceeds down (higher sequence) until a matching pattern is identified. When a match is found, the appropriate action (permit or deny) is taken, and processing stops. At the end of every ACL is an implicit deny ACE, which denies all packets that did not match earlier in the ACL.

NOTE Access lists applied on Layer 3 interfaces are sometimes referred to as *router ACLs (RACLs)*.

ACLs can be used to provide packet classification for a variety of features, such as quality of service (QoS), Network Address Translation (NAT), or network identification within routing protocols. This section explores their primary use, which is to provide basic traffic filtering functionality.

While many different kinds of ACLs can be used for packet filtering, only the following types are covered in this chapter:

Key Topic

- **Numbered standard ACLs:** These ACLs define packets based solely on the source network, and they use the numbered entries 1–99 and 1300–1999.
- **Numbered extended ACLs:** These ACLs define packets based on source, destination, protocol, port, or a combination of other packet attributes, and they use the numbered entries 100–199 and 2000–2699.
- **Named ACLs:** These ACLs allow standard and extended ACLs to be given names instead of numbers and are generally preferred because the name can be correlated to the functionality of the ACL.

- **Port ACLs (PACLs):** These ACLs can use standard, extended, named, and named extended MAC ACLs to filter traffic on Layer 2 switch ports.
- **VLAN ACLs (VACLs):** These ACLs can use standard, extended, named, and named extended MAC ACLs to filter traffic on VLANs.

ACLs use wildcard masks instead of subnet masks to classify packets that are being evaluated. For example, to match all packets with the IP address 192.168.1.0 and the subnet mask 255.255.255.0, an ACL would use an inverted subnet mask, better known as a *wildcard mask*, of 0.0.0.255 to match the first three octets exactly, while all the bits of the last octet could be any value between 0 and 255.

All that is required to convert a subnet mask into a wildcard mask is to subtract the subnet mask from 255.255.255.255. The following shows a subnet mask 255.255.128.0 being converted into a wildcard mask by subtracting it from 255.255.255.255. The end result is a 0.0.127.255 wildcard mask.

	255	255	255	255	
–	255	255	128	0	Subnet Mask
	0	0	127	255	Wildcard Mask

Key Topic

ACLs have no effect until they are applied to an interface. Therefore, the next step after creating an ACL is to apply it to an interface. In addition to the interface, you have to specify the direction (in or out) in which the ACL needs to be applied. Cisco routers allow only one inbound ACL and one outbound ACL per interface.

ACLs can also be used for various other services in addition to applying to interfaces, such as route maps, class maps, NAT, SNMP, virtual terminal (vty) lines, or traffic-classification techniques.

Numbered Standard ACLs

The process for defining a numbered standard ACL for IOS XE devices is as follows:

Step 1. Define the ACL by using the command **access-list** *acl-number* { **deny** | **permit** } *source* [*source-wildcard*] [**log**]. The ACL number can be 1–99 or 1300–1999.

Step 2. Apply the ACL to an interface by using the command **ip access-group** {*acl-number*} {**in**|**out**} under interface configuration mode.

The keywords **any** and **host** can be used as abbreviations for *source* [*source-wildcard*]. Using the keyword **any** is the equivalent to specifying 0.0.0.0 255.255.255.255, which matches all packets. For example, **access-list 1 permit 0.0.0.0 255.255.255.255** is equivalent to **access-list 1 permit any**.

The keyword **host** is used to match a specific host. It is the equivalent to having specified a host IP address followed by a wildcard mask of 0.0.0.0. For example, **access-list 1 permit 192.168.1.1 0.0.0.0** is equivalent to **access-list 1 permit host 192.168.1.1**.

Answers to the "Do I Know This Already?" quiz:

1 A **2** B **3** C **4** A, D **5** A, B, E, F **6** C, D **7** B **8** C **9** D **10** B, D **11** E, F **12** C **13** A **14** B, D

The *source* and *source-wildcard* reflect a matching pattern for the network prefix that is being matched. Table 26-2 provides sample ACE entries from within the ACL configuration mode and specifies the networks that would match with a standard ACL.

Table 26-2 Standard ACL-to-Network Entries

ACE Entry	Networks
permit any	Permits all networks
permit 172.16.0.0 0.0.255.255	Permits all networks in the 172.16.0.0/16 range
permit host 192.168.1.1	Permits only the 192.168.1.1/32 network

Example 26-1 demonstrates how a numbered standard ACL is created and applied to an interface to deny traffic from the 172.16.0.0/24 subnet and from host 192.168.1.1/32 while allowing all other traffic coming into interface Gi0/1. Notice that the last ACE in the ACL explicitly permits all traffic (**permit any**). If this ACE is not included, all traffic will be dropped because of the implicit deny (**deny any**) at the end of every ACL.

Example 26-1 *Creating and Applying a Numbered Standard ACL*

```
R1(config)# access-list 1 deny 172.16.0.0 0.0.255.255
R1(config)# access-list 1 deny host 192.168.1.1
R1(config)# access-list 1 permit any
R1(config)# interface GigabitEthernet0/1
R1(config-if)# ip access-group 1 in
```

Numbered Extended ACLs

The process for defining a numbered extended ACL is as follows:

Step 1. Define the ACL by using the command **access-list** *acl-number* {**deny**|**permit**} *protocol source source-wildcard destination destination-wildcard* [*protocol-options*] [**log** | **log-input**]. The ACL number can be 100–199 or 2000–2699.

Step 2. Apply the ACL to an interface by using the command **ip access-group** {*acl-number*} {**in**|**out**} under interface configuration mode.

As with standard ACLs, *source source-wildcard* and *destination destination-wildcard* can be defined to match a single host with the **host** keyword or match any subnet with the **any** keyword.

The *protocol-options* keyword differs based on the protocol specified in the ACE. For example, when TCP or UDP protocols are defined, **eq**, **lt**, and **gt** (equal to, less than, and greater than) keywords become available to specify ports to be matched as well as more granular options, such as SYN and ACK.

Example 26-2 demonstrates how a numbered extended ACL is created and applied to an interface to block all **Telnet** and ICMP traffic as well as deny all IP traffic from host 10.1.2.2 to host 10.1.2.1. Notice how Telnet's TCP port 23 is being matched with the **eq** keyword.

Example 26-2 *Creating and Applying Numbered Extended ACLs*

```
R1(config)# access-list 100 deny tcp any any eq 23
R1(config)# access-list 100 deny icmp any any
R1(config)# access-list 100 deny ip host 10.1.2.2 host 10.1.2.1
R1(config)# access-list 100 permit ip any any
R1(config)# interface GigabitEthernet0/1
R1(config-if)# ip access-group 100 in
```

Named ACLs

Named ACLs allow for ACLs to be named, which makes administering ACLs much easier as long as proper ACL naming conventions are followed. They function in the same way as standard and extended ACLs; the only difference is in the CLI syntax used to create them. To create and apply a named ACL, follow these steps:

Step 1. Define the ACL by using the command **ip access-list standard|extended** {*acl-number* | *acl-name*}. Entering this command places the CLI in ACL configuration mode.

Step 2. Configure the specific ACE in ACL configuration mode by using the command [*sequence*] {**permit** | **deny**} *source source-wildcard*.

Step 3. Apply the ACL to an interface by using the command **ip access-group** { *acl-number* | *acl-name* } {**in**|**out**} under interface configuration mode.

Notice in step 1 that the CLI for named ACLs starts with **ip** instead of just **access-list** and that the **standard** and **extended** ACL keywords need to be explicitly defined.

Example 26-3 shows how named standard and extended ACLs are created and applied to an interface. The numbered ACLs in Examples 26-1 and 26-2 are included as a reference for easy comparison to named ACLs.

Example 26-3 *Standard and Extended Named ACLs*

```
Named Standard ACL

R1(config)# ip access-list standard STANDARD_ACL
R1(config-std-nacl)# deny 172.16.0.0 0.0.255.255
R1(config-std-nacl)# deny host 192.168.1.1
R1(config-ext-nacl)# permit any
R1(config-ext-nacl)# exit
R1(config)# interface GigabitEthernet0/1
R1(config-if)# ip access-group STANDARD_ACL in

Numbered Standard ACL
R1(config)# access-list 1 deny 172.16.0.0 0.0.255.255
R1(config)# access-list 1 deny host 192.168.1.1
R1(config)# access-list 1 permit any
```

```
R1(config)# interface GigabitEthernet0/1
R1(config-if)# ip access-group 1 in
```

```
Named Extended ACL

R1(config)# ip access-list extended EXTENDED_ACL
R1(config-ext-nacl)# deny tcp any any eq 23
R1(config-ext-nacl)# deny icmp any any
R1(config-ext-nacl)# deny ip host 10.1.2.2 host 10.1.2.1
R1(config-ext-nacl)# permit ip any any
R1(config-ext-nacl)# exit
R1(config)# interface GigabitEthernet0/1
R1(config-if)# ip access-group EXTENDED_ACL in

Numbered Extended ACL

R1(config)# access-list 100 deny tcp any any eq 23
R1(config)# access-list 100 deny icmp any any
R1(config)# access-list 100 deny ip host 10.1.2.2 host 10.1.2.1
R1(config)# access-list 100 permit ip any any
R1(config)# interface GigabitEthernet0/1
R1(config-if)# ip access-group 100 in
```


Port ACLs (PACLs) and VLAN ACLs (VACLs)

Layer 2 Cisco switches support access lists that can be applied on Layer 2 ports as well as VLANs. Access lists applied on Layer 2 ports are called *port access control lists (PACLs)*, and access lists applied to VLANs are called *VLAN access control lists (VACLs)*.

PACLs

The CLI syntax for configuring PACLs that are used to filter Layer 3 traffic is the same as the syntax for RACLs on any IOS XE router; the only difference is that PACLs also support Layer 2 MAC address-based filtering, which uses different CLI syntax. PACLs can be standard, extended, or named IPv4 ACLs for Layer 3, and they can be named MAC address ACLs for Layer 2.

PACLs have a few restrictions that vary from platform to platform. The following are some of the most common restrictions:

- PACLs only support filtering incoming traffic on an interface (no outbound filtering support).
- PACLs cannot filter Layer 2 control packets, such as CDP, VTP, DTP, PAgP, UDLD, and STP.
- PACLs are supported only in hardware.

- PACLs do not support ACLs to filter IPv6, ARP, or Multiprotocol Label Switching (MPLS) traffic.

An IPv4 PACL is applied to an interface with the **ip access-group** *access-list* **in** command. Example 26-4 shows a PACL applied to a Layer 2 interface Gi0/1 to block RDP, Telnet traffic, and host 10.1.2.2 access to host 10.1.2.1.

Example 26-4 *Applying a PACL*

```
R1(config)# ip access-list extended PACL
R1(config-ext-nacl)# deny tcp any any eq 23
R1(config-ext-nacl)# deny icmp any any
R1(config-ext-nacl)# deny ip host 10.1.2.2 host 10.1.2.1
R1(config-ext-nacl)# permit ip any any
R1(config-ext-nacl)# exit
R1(config)# interface GigabitEthernet0/1
R1(config-if)# switchport
R1(config-if)# ip access-group PACL in
```

VACLs

VACLs can filter traffic that is bridged within a VLAN or that is routed into or out of a VLAN. To create and apply a VACL, follow these steps:

Step 1. Define a VLAN access map by using the command **vlan access-map** *name sequence*. A VLAN access map consists of one or more VLAN access map sequences where each VLAN access map sequence is composed of one match and one action statement.

Step 2. Configure the match statement by using the command **match** { **ip address** { *acl-number* | *acl-name* } | **mac address** *acl-name* }. The match statement supports standard, extended, or named IPv4 ACLs as well as named MAC address ACLs as the matching criteria.

Step 3. Configure the action statement by using the command **action forward|drop** [**log**]. The action statement specifies the action to be taken when a match occurs, which could be to forward or to drop traffic. Only dropped traffic can be logged using the **log** keyword.

Step 4. Apply the VACL by using the command **vlan filter** *vlan-access-map-name vlan-list*. *vlan-list* can be a single VLAN, a range of VLANs (such as 5–30), or a comma-separated list of multiple VLANs (such as 1,2–4,6).

Example 26-5 shows a VLAN access map applied to VLAN 20 to drop ICMP and Telnet traffic and allow other traffic. Notice that the named ACLs, ICMP and TELNET, only include ACEs with a **permit** statement. The reason is that the ACLs are used as matching criteria only by the VLAN access maps, while the VLAN access maps are configured with the action to drop the matched traffic.

Example 26-5 *Creating and Applying a VACL*

```
SW1(config)# ip access-list extended ICMP
SW1(config-ext-nacl)# permit icmp any any
SW1(config-ext-nacl)# exit

SW1(config)# ip access-list extended TELNET
SW1(config-ext-nacl)# permit tcp any any eq 23
SW1(config-ext-nacl)# exit

SW1(config)# ip access-list extended OTHER
SW1(config-ext-nacl)# permit ip any any
SW1(config-ext-nacl)# exit

SW1(config)# vlan access-map VACL_20 10
SW1(config-access-map)# match ip address ICMP
SW1(config-access-map)# action drop
SW1(config-access-map)# exit

SW1(config)# vlan access-map VACL_20 20
SW1(config-access-map)# match ip address TELNET
SW1(config-access-map)# action drop log
SW1(config-access-map)# exit

SW1(config)# vlan access-map VACL_20 30
SW1(config-access-map)# match ip address OTHER
SW1(config-access-map)# action forward

SW1(config)# vlan filter VACL_20 vlan-list 20
```


PACL, VACL, and RACL Interaction

When a PACL, a VACL, and an RACL are all configured in the same VLAN, the ACLs are applied in a specific order, depending on whether the incoming traffic needs to be bridged or routed:

Bridged traffic processing order (within the same VLAN):

1. Inbound PACL on the switch port (for example, VLAN 10)
2. Inbound VACL on the VLAN (for example, VLAN 10)
3. Outbound VACL on the VLAN (for example, VLAN 10)

Routed traffic processing order (across VLANs):

1. Inbound PACL on the switch port (for example, VLAN 10)
2. Inbound VACL on the VLAN (for example, VLAN 10)
3. Inbound ACL on the SVI (for example, SVI 10)

4. Outbound ACL on the SVI (for example, SVI 20)
5. Outbound VACL on the VLAN (for example, VLAN 20)

NOTE As mentioned earlier, outbound PACLs are not supported.

Downloadable ACLs (dACLs) are another form of PACL that can be assigned dynamically by a RADIUS authentication server, such as Cisco ISE. After successful network access authentication, if a PACL is configured on a switch port and a dACL is assigned by Cisco ISE on the same switch port, the dACL overwrites the PACL.

Terminal Lines and Password Protection

Password protection to control or restrict access to the CLI to protect the router from unauthorized remote access and unauthorized local access is the most common type of security that needs to be implemented.

There are three basic methods to gain access to the CLI of an IOS XE device:

Key Topic

- **Console port (cty) line:** On any IOS XE device, this line appears in configuration as **line con 0** and in the output of the command **show line** as **cty**. The console port is mainly used for local system access using a console terminal.
- **Auxiliary port (aux) line:** This line appears in the configuration as **line aux 0**. The aux port is mainly used for remote access into the device through a modem.
- **Virtual terminal (vty) lines:** These lines are displayed by default in the configuration as **line vty 0 4**. They are used solely for remote Telnet and SSH connections. They are virtual because they are logical lines with no physical interface associated with them.

Example 26-6 shows what the default configuration looks like for the cty, aux, and vty lines on an IOS XE device.

Example 26-6 *vty, cty, and aux Lines in the Running Configuration*

```
R1# show running-config | section line
Building configuration...

line con 0
line aux 0
line vty 0 4
!
End
```

Each of these types of terminal lines should be password protected. There are three ways to add password protection to the lines:

Key Topic

- **Using a password configured directly on the line:** Not recommended
- **Using username-based authentication:** Recommended as a fallback

- **Using an AAA server:** Highly recommended and covered later in this chapter, in the section "Authentication, Authorization, and Accounting (AAA)"

Key Topic

Password Types

The following five password types are available in Cisco IOS XE; they are mentioned in the order of evolution:

- **Type 0 passwords:** These passwords are the most insecure because they are not encrypted or hashed, and they are visible in the device configuration in plaintext. The command **enable password** is an example of a command that uses a type 0 password. Type 0 passwords are not recommended to be used.
- **Type 7 passwords:** These passwords use a Cisco proprietary Vigenere cypher encryption algorithm, which is a very weak encryption algorithm. There are multiple online password utilities available that can decrypt type 7 encrypted passwords in less than a second. Type 7 encryption is enabled by the command **service password-encryption** for commands that use type 0 passwords, such as the **enable password**, **username password**, and **line password** commands. Type 7 passwords are not recommended to be used.
- **Type 5 passwords:** These passwords use the MD5 hashing algorithm with password salting. This makes them much stronger than type 0 or type 7 passwords, but they are also very easy to crack. The command **enable secret** is an example of a command that uses a type 5 password. Type 5 passwords are not recommended to be used.
- **Type 8 passwords:** These passwords use the Password-Based Key Derivation Function 2 (PBKDF2) with a SHA-256 hashed secret and password salting. They are considered to be uncrackable and recommended to be used.
- **Type 9 passwords:** These passwords use the scrypt hashing algorithm and password salting. Just like type 8 passwords, they are considered to be uncrackable, and Cisco recommends that they be used.

Type 4 passwords are available in a limited number of Cisco IOS XE releases based on the Cisco IOS XE 15 code base. They were not mentioned in the preceding list because they should never be used due to a security flaw in the implementation (security advisory cisco-sa-20130318-type4). Type 4 passwords were deprecated, and type 8 and 9 password hashing was introduced. Types 8 and 9 are the recommended password types to use, where type 9 is recommended by Cisco.

Password Encryption

The **service password-encryption** command in global configuration mode is used to encrypt type 0 passwords in the configuration (for example, BGP passwords) or over a plaintext session such as Telnet in an effort to prevent unauthorized users from viewing the password. For example, if someone executed the command **show running-configuration** during a Telnet session, a protocol analyzer would be able to display the password. However, if the command **service password-encryption** were used, the password would be encrypted even during the same plaintext Telnet session.

Passwords configured prior to configuring the command **service password-encryption** are not encrypted and must be reentered into the configuration.

Password encryption is applied to all type 0 passwords, including authentication key passwords; cty, aux, and vty line passwords; and BGP neighbor passwords. The command **service password-encryption** is primarily useful for keeping unauthorized individuals from viewing a password in a configuration file. Unfortunately, the command **service password-encryption** encrypts passwords with type 7 encryption, which is easily reversible. Using plaintext password authentication should be avoided if a more secure option exists, such as using username-based authentication instead of passwords, as discussed in the next section.

Username and Password Authentication

The previous section discusses how to create encrypted or hashed passwords that can be used to authenticate a user; however, user identification can best be achieved with a combination of a username and a password. Username accounts can be used for several applications, such as console, aux, and vty lines.

To establish a username and password login authentication system, you can create usernames on a device for all device users or groups. Usernames configured from global configuration mode are stored in the device's configuration. The login accounts created can be assigned different **privilege levels** and passwords. (Privilege levels are discussed in more detail later in the chapter.)

There are three different ways to configure a username on IOS XE:

Key Topic

- Using the command **username** {*username*} **password** {*password*} configures a plaintext password (type 0).
- Using the command **username** {*username*} **secret** {*password*} provides type 5 hashing.
- Using the command **username** {*username*} **algorithm-type** {**md5** | **sha256** | **scrypt**} **secret** {*password*} provides type 5, type 8, or type 9 hashing, respectively.

Of the three username commands, the command **username** {*username*} **algorithm-type** {**md5** | **sha256** | **scrypt**} **secret** {*password*} is the recommended one because it allows for the highest level of password hashing (type 8 and type 9). If type 8 or type 9 password types are not supported, a software upgrade is recommended.

Configuring Line Local Password Authentication

To enable password authentication on a line, the following two commands are required under line configuration mode:

- **password** *password* to configure the password
- **login** to enable password checking at login

In Example 26-7, a password is configured for all users attempting to connect to the cty, vty, and aux lines.

Example 26-7 *vty, cty, and aux Lines with Password-Based Authentication*

```
R1# show running-config | section line
Building configuration...

line con 0
password My.C0n5ole.P@s5
login
line aux 0
password My.AuX.P@s5
login
line vty 0 4
password My.vTy.P@s5
login
!
end
```


Notice that the passwords are shown in plaintext (type 0). They can be encrypted with type 7 encryption using the command **service password-encryption**; however, type 7 passwords are easy to decrypt. For this reason, it is not recommended to use line local password authentication.

Verifying Line Local Password Authentication

Example 26-8 shows an example in which the console line password is being tested. All that is required to test the password is to log off the console and log back in again using the configured console password.

NOTE When you're performing this test, an alternate connection into the router, such as a Telnet connection, should be established just in case there is a problem logging back in to the router using the console.

Example 26-8 *Console Password Test*

```
R1# exit


Router con0 is now available


Press RETURN to get started.


User Access Verification
Password:

! Password entered here is not displayed by the router



Router>
```

Configuring Line Local Username and Password Authentication

To enable username and password authentication, the following two commands are required:

- The command **username** in global configuration mode (using one of the options shown in the "Username and Password Authentication" section, earlier in this chapter)
- The command **login local** under line configuration mode to enable username-based authentication at login

NOTE Username-based authentication for the aux and cty lines is only supported in combination with AAA for some IOS XE releases. This topic is covered later in this chapter, in the section "Configuring AAA for Network Device Access Control."

Example 26-9 shows three usernames configured with password types 0, 5, and 9. Notice that the type 0 user password is shown in plaintext, while type 5 and type 9 user passwords are hashed.

Example 26-9 *Local Username-Based Authentication for a vty Line*

```
R1# show running-config
Building configuration...
!
! Output Omitted for Brevity

username type0 password 0 weak

username type5 secret 5 $1$b1Ju$kZbBS1Pyh4QzwXyZ1kSZ2/

username type9 secret 9 $9$vFpMf8elb4RVV8$seZ/bDAx1uV4yH75Z/
nwUuegLJDVCc4UXOAE83JgsOc
!
! Output Omitted for Brevity

line con 0
 login local

line aux 0
 login local

line vty 0 4
 login local
!
end
```

Verifying Line Local Username and Password Authentication

Example 26-10 shows user type5 establishing a Telnet session from R2 into R1 using username-based authentication.

Example 26-10 *Verifying Local Username-Based Authentication for vty Lines*

```
! Telnet session initiated from R2 into R1

R2# telnet 10.1.12.1
Trying 10.1.12.1 ... Open



User Access Verification



Username: type5
Password:

! Password entered is not displayed by the router


R1>
```


Privilege Levels and Role-Based Access Control (RBAC)

The Cisco IOS XE CLI by default includes three privilege levels, each of which defines what commands are available to a user:

Key Topic

- **Privilege level 0:** Includes the **disable**, **enable**, **exit**, **help**, and **logout** commands.
- **Privilege level 1:** Also known as User EXEC mode. The command prompt in this mode includes a greater-than sign (R1>). From this mode it is not possible to make configuration changes; in other words, the command **configure terminal** is not available.
- **Privilege level 15:** Also known as Privileged EXEC mode. This is the highest privilege level, where all CLI commands are available. The command prompt in this mode includes a hash sign (R1#).

Additional privilege levels ranging from 2 to 14 can also be configured to provide customized access control. The global configuration command **privilege** {*mode*} **level** {*level*}{*command string*} is used to change or set a privilege level for a command to any of these levels. For example, to allow a group of users to configure only specific interface configuration commands while not allowing them access to additional configuration options, a custom privilege level can be created to allow only specific interface configuration commands and share the login information for that level with the group of users.

Example 26-11 shows a configuration where the user noc is created along with the type 9 (scrypt) secret password cisco123. Notice that the privilege level is also configured to level 5 as part of the **username** command. In this particular case, a user logging in to the router using the username and password noc and cisco123 would be placed into privilege level 5 and would be allowed to go into any interface on the router and shut it down, unshut it, and configure an IP address on it, which are the only commands allowed under privilege level 5 in interface configuration mode.

Example 26-11 *Configuring a Username with Privilege Level*

```
R1(config)# username noc privilege 5 algorithm-type scrypt secret cisco123
R1(config)# privilege exec level 5 configure terminal
R1(config)# privilege configure level 5 interface
R1(config)# privilege interface level 5 shutdown
R1(config)# privilege interface level 5 no shutdown
R1(config)# privilege interface level 5 ip address
```

Verifying Privilege Levels

When you set the privilege level for a command with multiple keywords, the commands starting with the first keyword also have the specified access level. For example, if you set the **no shutdown** command to level 5, as shown in Example 26-11, the **no** command and **no shutdown** command are automatically set to privilege level 5, unless you set them individually to different levels. This is necessary because you can't execute the **no shutdown** command unless you have access to the **no** command. Example 26-12 shows what the configuration shown in Example 26-11 would look like in the running configuration. It also shows a quick test to verify that the only commands allowed for privilege level 5 users are those specified by the **privilege level** command.

Example 26-12 *Verifying Privilege Levels*

```
R1# show running configuration

! Output Omitted for Brevity

username noc privilege 5 secret 9
$9$OvP8u.A0x8dSq8$tF9qrYHnW31826rUGJaKzt6sLxqCEcK0rBZTpeitGa2

privilege interface level 5 shutdown
privilege interface level 5 ip address
privilege interface level 5 ip
privilege interface level 5 no shutdown
privilege interface level 5 no ip address
privilege interface level 5 no ip
privilege interface level 5 no
privilege configure level 5 interface
privilege exec level 5 configure terminal
privilege exec level 5 configure

! Output Omitted for Brevity

R1# telnet 1.2.3.4
Trying 1.2.3.4 ... Open

User Access Verification
Username: noc
```

```
Password: cisco123

R1# show privilege
Current privilege level is 5
R1#
R1# configure terminal
Enter configuration commands, one per line. End with CNTL/Z.
R1(config)# interface gigabitEthernet 0/1
R1(config-if)# ?

Interface configuration commands:
  default   Set a command to its defaults
  exit      Exit from interface configuration mode
  help      Description of the interactive help system
  ip        Interface Internet Protocol config commands
  no        Negate a command or set its defaults
  shutdown  Shutdown the selected interface

R1 (config-if)# ip ?
Interface IP configuration subcommands:
  address  Set the IP address of an interface

R1(config-if)# ip address 10.1.1.1 255.255.255.0
R1(config-if)# no ?
  ip        Interface Internet Protocol config commands
  shutdown  Shutdown the selected interface

R1(config-if)# no shutdown
R1(config-if)#
*Apr 27 18:14:23.749: %LINK-3-UPDOWN: Interface GigabitEthernet0/1, changed state to
up
*Apr 27 18:14:24.750: %LINEPROTO-5-UPDOWN: Line protocol on Interface GigabitEthernet
0/1,
  changed state to up
R1(config-if)#
R1(config-if)# shutdown
R1(config-if)# end
*Apr 27 18:14:38.336: %LINK-5-CHANGED: Interface GigabitEthernet0/1, changed state
  to administratively down
*Apr 27 18:14:39.336: %LINEPROTO-5-UPDOWN: Line protocol on Interface
GigabitEthernet0/1,
  changed state to down
R1#
*Apr 27 18:14:40.043: %SYS-5-CONFIG_I: Configured from console by noc on vty0
  (1.2.3.4)
R1#
```

While using local authentication and privilege levels on the device provides adequate security, it can be cumbersome to manage on every device, and inconsistent configuration across the network is very likely. To simplify device access control and maintain consistency, a more scalable and preferred approach is to use the **authentication, authorization, and accounting (AAA)** framework. This can be accomplished by using an AAA server such as the Cisco Identity Services Engine (ISE).

With AAA, network devices can use the Terminal Access Controller Access-Control System Plus (TACACS+) protocol to authenticate users, authorize commands, and provide accounting information.

Because the configuration is centralized on the AAA servers, access control policies are applied consistently across the whole network; however, it is still recommended to use local authentication as a fallback mechanism in case the AAA servers become unavailable.

Controlling Access to vty Lines with ACLs

Access to the vty lines of an IOS XE device can be further secured by applying inbound ACLs on them, allowing access only from a restricted set of IP addresses. Outbound vty connections from an IOS XE device can also be controlled by applying outbound ACLs to vtys.

A best practice is to only allow IP addresses that are part of an internal or trusted network to access the vty lines. Extreme care is necessary when allowing IP addresses from external or public networks such as the Internet.

To apply a standard or an extended access list to a vty line, use the command **access-class** {*access-list-number*|*access-list-name*} {**in**|**out**} under line configuration mode. The **in** keyword applies an inbound ACL, and the **out** keyword applies an outbound ACL.

Verifying Access to vty Lines with ACLs

Example 26-13 demonstrates R1 using Telnet to get into R2 before and after applying an ACL to R2's vty line. R1 is configured with IP address 10.12.1.1 and R2 with 10.12.1.2. The ACL being applied to R2's vty line is meant to block vty access into it from R1.

Example 26-13 *Verifying Access to vty Lines with ACLs*

```
! Prior to applying an ACL to R2's vty line, R1 is allowed to telnet into R2

R1# telnet 10.12.1.2
Trying 10.12.1.2... Open

User Access Verification

Username: noc
Password:

R2#
R2# exit
```

```
[Connection to 10.12.1.2 closed by foreign host]

! Access list to deny R1's IP address is created and applied to the vty lines 0 to 4

R2# configure terminal
Enter configuration commands, one per line. End with CNTL/Z.
R2(config)# access-list 1 deny 10.12.1.1
R2(config)# access-list 1 permit any
R2 (config)# line vty 0 4
R2(config-line)# access-class 1 in
R2(config-line)# end
R2#
R2# show running-config | section line vty
line vty 0 4
 access-class 1 in
 login local
R2#
*Apr 27 19:49:45.599: %SYS-5-CONFIG_I: Configured from console by console

! After applying an ACL to R2's vty line, R1 is not allowed to telnet into R2

R1# telnet 10.12.1.2
Trying 10.12.1.2 ...
% Connection refused by remote host

R1#
```

26

Controlling Access to vty Lines Using Transport Input

Another way to further control what types of protocols are allowed to access the vty lines is to use the command **transport input** {**all** | **none** | **telnet** | **ssh**} under line configuration mode. Table 26-3 includes a description for each of the **transport input** command keywords.

Table 26-3 Transport Input Command Keyword Description

Keyword	Description
all	Allows Telnet and SSH
none	Blocks Telnet and SSH
telnet	Allows Telnet only
ssh	Allows SSH only
telnet ssh	Allows Telnet and SSH

Example 26-14 shows the vty lines from 0 to 4 configured with different **transport input** command keywords. Keep in mind that vty lines are evaluated from the top (vty 0) onward, and each vty line accepts only one user.

Example 26-14 *vty Lines with Different* **transport input** *Keywords*

```
line vty 0
 login local
 transport input all
line vty 1
 login local
 transport input none
line vty 2
 login local
 transport input telnet
line vty 3
 login local
 transport input ssh
line vty 4
 login local
 transport input telnet ssh
```

NOTE The AUX port should be provisioned with the **transport input none** command to block reverse Telnet into the AUX port.

Verifying Access to vty Lines Using Transport Input

Example 26-15 demonstrates how Telnet sessions are assigned to different vty lines on R1. R1 is configured based on the configuration shown in Example 26-14, which only allows Telnet sessions on vty 0 (**input all**), vty 2 (**input telnet**), and vty 4 (**input telnet ssh**).

Example 26-15 *Verifying Access to vty Lines*

```
! An asterisk to the left of the row indicates the line is in use
! The output below shows a user is connected into the console (cty)

R1# show line
   Tty Typ     Tx/Rx    A Modem  Roty AccO AccI   Uses   Noise  Overruns   Int
*    0 CTY              -   -     -    -    -        0       0     0/0       -
     1 AUX   9600/9600  -   -     -    -    -        0       0     0/0       -
   578 VTY              -   -     -    -    -        1       0     0/0       -
   579 VTY              -   -     -    -    -        0       0     0/0       -
   580 VTY              -   -     -    -    -        0       0     0/0       -
   581 VTY              -   -     -    -    -        0       0     0/0       -
   582 VTY              -   -     -    -    -        0       0     0/0       -
R1#

! Telnet connection from R2 into R1 is established
```

```
R2# telnet 10.1.12.1
Trying 10.1.12.1 ... Open

User Access Verification
Username: noc
Password:
R1>

! The asterisk in the output of show line on R1 indicates the first vty 0 is now
in use.
! vty 0 is mapped to vty 578 automatically.

R1# show line
   Tty Typ     Tx/Rx     A Modem  Roty AccO AccI   Uses   Noise  Overruns   Int
*    0 CTY               -    -      -    -    -      0       0     0/0       -
     1 AUX   9600/9600   -    -      -    -    -      0       0     0/0       -
*  578 VTY               -    -      -    -    -      2       0     0/0       -
   579 VTY               -    -      -    -    -      0       0     0/0       -
   580 VTY               -    -      -    -    -      0       0     0/0       -
   581 VTY               -    -      -    -    -      0       0     0/0       -
   582 VTY               -    -      -    -    -      0       0     0/0       -
R1#

! Telnet connection from R3 into R1 is established

R3# telnet 10.1.13.1
Trying 10.1.13.1 ... Open

User Access Verification
Username: noc
Password:
R1>

! The output of show line on R1 indicates the vty 0 and vty 2 are now in use
! vty 2 is mapped to vty 580

R1# show line
   Tty Typ     Tx/Rx     A Modem  Roty AccO AccI   Uses   Noise  Overruns   Int
*      0 CTY             -    -      -    -    -      0       0     0/0       -
       1 AUX   9600/9600 -    -      -    -    -      0       0     0/0       -
*    578 VTY             -    -      -    -    -      2       0     0/0       -
     579 VTY             -    -      -    -    -      0       0     0/0       -
*    580 VTY             -    -      -    -    -      1       0     0/0       -
     581 VTY             -    -      -    -    -      0       0     0/0       -
     582 VTY             -    -      -    -    -      0       0     0/0       -
```

26

```
R1#
! Telnet connection from R4 into R1 is established

R4# telnet 10.1.14.1
Trying 10.1.14.1 ... Open

User Access Verification
Username: noc
Password:
R1>

! The output of show line on R1 indicates the vty 0, vty 2 and vty 4 are now in use
! vty 4 is mapped to vty 582. This leaves no more vty lines available for telnet

R1# show line
   Tty Typ     Tx/Rx     A Modem  Roty AccO AccI   Uses   Noise  Overruns   Int
*    0 CTY               -   -     -    -    -      0       0      0/0       -
     1 AUX   9600/9600   -   -     -    -    -      0       0      0/0       -
*  578 VTY               -   -     -    -    -      2       0      0/0       -
   579 VTY               -   -     -    -    -      0       0      0/0       -
*  580 VTY               -   -     -    -    -      1       0      0/0       -
   581 VTY               -   -     -    -    -      0       0      0/0       -
*  582 VTY               -   -     -    -    -      1       0      0/0       -

R1#

! Trying to telnet into R1 from R5 will fail since there are no more vtys
available for telnet

R5# telnet 10.1.15.1
Trying 10.1.15.1 ...
% Connection refused by remote host

R5#
```

Enabling SSH vty Access

Telnet is the most popular yet most insecure protocol used to access IOS XE devices for administrative purposes. Telnet session packets are sent in plaintext, and this makes it very easy to sniff and capture session information. A more reliable and secure method for device administration is to use the **Secure Shell (SSH)** protocol.

SSH, which provides secure encryption and strong authentication, is available in two versions:

Key Topic

- **SSH Version 1 (SSHv1):** This is an improvement over using plaintext Telnet, but some fundamental flaws exist in its implementation, so it should be avoided in favor of SSHv2.
- **SSH Version 2 (SSHv2):** This is a complete rework and stronger version of SSH that is not compatible with SSHv1. SSHv2 has many benefits and closes a security hole that is found in SSH version 1. SSH version 2 is certified under the National Institute of Standards and Technology (NIST) Federal Information Processing Standards (FIPS) 140-1 and 140-2 U.S. cryptographic standards and should be used where feasible.

The steps needed to configure SSH on an IOS XE device are as follows:

Step 1. Configure a hostname other than Router by using the command **hostname** {*hostname name*}.

Step 2. Configure a domain name by using the command **ip domain-name** {*domain-name*}.

Step 3. Generate crypto keys by using the command **crypto key generate rsa**. When entering this command, you are prompted to enter a modulus length. The longer the modulus, the stronger the security. However, a longer modulus takes longer to generate. The modulus length needs to be at least 768 bits for SSHv2.

NOTE Starting with Cisco IOS XE Release 17.11.1 and later, weak crypto algorithms such as RSA keys of less than 2048 bits are rejected by default due to their weak cryptographic properties. It is possible to disable this enforcement via configuration, but it is not recommended. More details can be found in Field Notice 72510.

Example 26-16 demonstrates SSH being configured on R1.

Example 26-16 *Configuring vty Access Using SSH*

```
R1(config)# hostname R1
R1(config)# username cisco secret cisco
R1(config)# ip domain-name cisco.com
R1(config)# crypto key generate rsa
The name for the keys will be: R1.cisco.com
Choose the size of the key modulus in the range of 360 to 4096 for your
 General Purpose Keys. Choosing a key modulus greater than 512 may take
 a few minutes.

How many bits in the modulus [512]: 768
% Generating 768 bit RSA keys, keys will be non-exportable...
[OK] (elapsed time was 1 seconds)
```

```
R1(config)#
*May 8 20:44:48.319: %SSH-5-ENABLED: SSH 1.99 has been enabled
R1(config)#
R1(config)# line vty 0 4
R1(config-line)# login local
R1(config-line)# end
R1#
```

SSH 1.99, shown in the log message in Example 26-16, indicates that SSHv1 and SSHv2 are enabled. To force the IOS XE SSH server to disable SSHv1 and accept only SSHv2 connections, enter the command **ip ssh version 2** under global configuration mode.

Auxiliary Port

Some devices have an auxiliary (aux) port available for remote administration through a dialup modem connection. In most cases, the aux port should be disabled by using the command **no exec** under line aux 0.

EXEC Timeout

The default idle timeout value for an EXEC session is 10 minutes. The command **exec-timeout** {*minutes*}{*seconds*} under line configuration mode can be used to change the default idle timeout value.

Example 26-17 shows a configuration in which the **exec-timeout** for the console line is configured to time out after 5 minutes of inactivity and 2 minutes and 30 seconds for the vty lines.

Example 26-17 *Configuring EXEC Timeout*

```
line con 0
 exec-timeout 5 0
line vty 0 4
 exec-timeout 2 30
```

NOTE The commands **exec-timeout 0 0** and **no exec-timeout** disable the EXEC timeout. Although using them is useful for lab environments, it is not recommended for production environments.

Absolute Timeout

The command **absolute-timeout** {*minutes*} under line configuration mode terminates an EXEC session after the specified timeout period has expired, even if the connection is being used at the time of termination. It is recommended to use it in combination with the command **logout-warning** {*seconds*} under line configuration mode to display a "line termination" warning to users about an impending forced timeout.

Example 26-18 shows the commands **absolute-timeout** and **logout-warning** configured on the vty lines.

Example 26-18 *Configuring Absolute Timeout*

```
line vty 4
 exec-timeout 2 0
 absolute-timeout 10
 logout-warning 20
```

Authentication, Authorization, and Accounting (AAA)

AAA is an architectural framework for enabling a set of three independent security functions:

Key Topic

- **Authentication:** Enables a user to be identified and verified prior to being granted access to a network device and/or network services.
- **Authorization:** Defines the access privileges and restrictions to be enforced for an authenticated user.
- **Accounting:** Provides the ability to track and log user access, including user identities, start and stop times, executed commands (that is, CLI commands), and so on. In other words, it maintains a security log of events.

AAA requires a protocol designed to carry authentication requests and responses, including authorization results and accounting logs. Many AAA protocols are available, but the two most popular ones are **Remote Authentication Dial-In User Service (RADIUS)** and **Terminal Access Controller Access-Control System Plus (TACACS+)**.

AAA is commonly used in the networking industry for the following two use cases:

Key Topic

- **Network device access control:** As described earlier in this chapter, Cisco IOS XE provides local features for simple device access control, such as local username-based authentication and line password authentication. However, these features do not provide the same degree of access control and scalability that is possible with AAA. For this reason, AAA is the recommended method for access control. TACACS+ is the protocol of choice for network device access control.
- **Secure network access control:** AAA can be used to obtain the identity of a device or user before that device or user is allowed to access the network. RADIUS is the preferred protocol for secure network access. Secure network access control is covered in Chapter 25, "Secure Network Access Control."

The following sections explain why TACACS+ is preferred for network access control while RADIUS is preferred for secure network access.

TACACS+

Cisco developed TACACS+ and released it as an open standard in the early 1990s. Although TACACS+ is mainly used for AAA device access control, it is possible to use it for some types of AAA network access.

The TACACS+ protocol uses Transmission Control Protocol (TCP) port 49 for communication between the TACACS+ clients and the TACACS+ server.

Figure 26-1 shows an end user who can access a Cisco switch using Telnet, SSH, or the console. The Cisco switch is acting as a TACACS+ client that communicates with the TACACS+ server using the TACACS+ protocol.

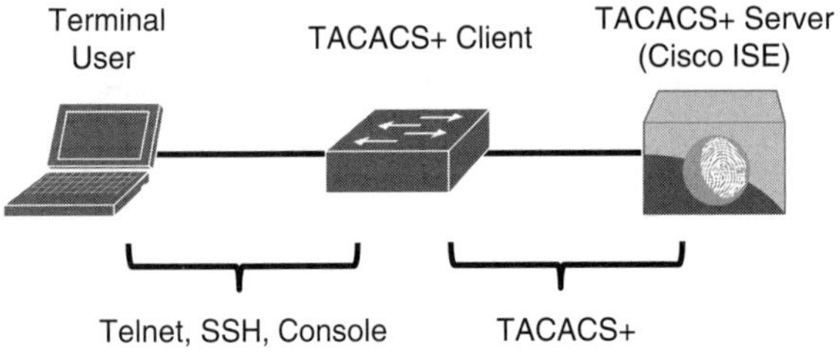

Figure 26-1 *TACACS+ Client/Server Communication*

Key Topic

One of the key differentiators of TACACS+ is its capability to separate authentication, authorization, and accounting into independent functions. This is why TACACS+ is so commonly used for device administration instead of RADIUS, even though RADIUS is capable of providing network device access control.

RADIUS

Key Topic

RADIUS is an IETF standard AAA protocol. As with TACACS+, it follows a client/server model, where the client initiates the requests to the server. RADIUS is the AAA protocol of choice for secure network access. The reason for this is that RADIUS is the AAA transport protocol for Extensible Authentication Protocol (EAP), while TACACS+ does not support this functionality. EAP is used for secure network access (wired and wireless) and is covered in Chapters 20, "Authenticating Wireless Clients," and 23, "Fabric Technologies."

Another major difference between TACACS+ and RADIUS is that RADIUS needs to return all authorization parameters in a single reply, while TACACS+ can request authorization parameters separately and multiple times throughout a session.

For example, a network device, such as a Cisco switch or router, can request a TACACS+ server to individually authorize every command that a user tries to execute after logging in to the device. In contrast, RADIUS would require those commands to be sent in the initial authentication response, and because there could be thousands of CLI command combinations, a large authorization result list could trigger memory exhaustion on the network device. This is the main reason TACACS+ is preferred for network device access control. However, if all that is required is AAA authentication without authorization, then either RADIUS or TACACS+ can be used.

Table 26-4 provides a summary comparison of RADIUS and TACACS+.

Table 26-4 RADIUS and TACACS+ Comparison

Component	RADIUS	TACACS+
Protocol and port(s) used	Cisco's implementation: ■ UDP: port 1645 (authentication and authorization) ■ UDP: port 1646 (accounting) Industry standard: ■ UDP: port 1812 (authentication and authorization) ■ UDP: port 1813 (accounting)	TCP: port 49
Encryption	■ Encrypts only the password field ■ Supports EAP for 802.1x authentication	■ Encrypts the entire payload ■ Does not support EAP
Authentication and authorization	■ Combines authentication and authorization ■ Cannot be used to authorize which CLI commands can be executed individually	■ Separates authentication and authorization ■ Can be used for CLI command authorization
Accounting	Does not support network device CLI command accounting	Supports network device CLI command accounting
Primary use	Secure network access	Network device access control

For many years, the Cisco Secure Access Control Server (ACS) was the AAA server of choice for organizations that required TACACS+ for device administration and RADIUS for secure network access. However, starting with ISE 2.0, ISE has taken over as Cisco's AAA server for both RADIUS and TACACS+.

Configuring AAA for Network Device Access Control

As previously mentioned, TACACS+ was designed for device access control by authenticating and authorizing users into network devices. There are two parts to configuring TACACS+:

- The configuration of the device itself
- The configuration of the TACACS+ AAA server (for example, Cisco ISE)

The following steps are for configuring an IOS XE device with TACACS+ for device access control. Configuration for the TACACS+ server is not included here because it is beyond the scope of this book:

Step 1. Create a local user with full privilege for fallback or to avoid being locked out after enabling AAA by using the command

```
username {username} privilege 15 algorithm-type {md5 | sha256 |
scrypt} secret {password}
```

Step 2. Enable AAA functions on the IOS XE device by using the command **aaa new-model.**

Step 3. Add a TACACS+ server using one of these methods, depending on the IOS XE version:

- To add a TACACS+ server on IOS XE versions prior to 16.12.2, use the command

```
tacacs-server host { hostname | host-ip-address } key key-string
```

- To add a TACACS+ server on IOS XE versions 16.12.2 and later, use the following commands:

```
tacacs server name
address ipv4 { hostname | host-ip-address }
key key-string
```

Step 4. Create an AAA group by using the following commands:

```
aaa group server tacacs+ group-name
server name server-name
```

These commands create an AAA group that includes the TACACS+ servers that are added to the group with the **server name** command.

Multiple server names can be added, and the order in which the servers are added to the group dictates the failover order, from top to bottom (that is, the first one added is the highest priority).

Step 5. Enable AAA login authentication by using the command

```
aaa authentication login { default | custom-list-name } method1 [
method2 . . . ]
```

Method lists enable login authentication. The **default** keyword applies the method lists that follow (*method1* [*method2* . . .) to all lines (cty, tty, aux, and so on). The *custom list-name* CLI assigns a custom name for the method lists that follow it. This allows different types of lines to use different login authentication methods. To apply a custom list to a line, use the command **login authentication** *custom-list-name* under line configuration mode.

Method lists are applied sequentially from left to right. For example, in the command **aaa authentication login default group ISE-TACACS+ local enable**, the ISE-TACACS+ server group is used for authentication because it's the first method listed, and if the TACACS+ servers become unavailable or are unavailable, local username-based authentication is used because it is the second method from left to right. If no usernames are defined in the configuration, then the **enable** password, which is third in line, would be the last resort to log in; if there is no **enable** password configured, the user is effectively locked out.

Step 6. Enable AAA authorization for EXEC by using the command

```
aaa authorization exec { default | custom-list-name } method1
[ method2 . . . ]
```

This command enables EXEC shell authorization for all lines except the console line.

Step 7. Enable AAA authorization for the console by using the command

aaa authorization console

Authorization for the console is disabled by default to prevent unexperienced users from locking themselves out.

Step 8. Enable AAA command authorization by using the command

aaa authorization commands {*privilege level*} { **default** | *custom-list-name* } *method1* [*method2* . . .]

This command authorizes all commands with the AAA server before executing them. Command authorization is applied on a per-privilege-level basis, so it is necessary to configure a command authorization method list for every privilege level that requires command authorization. Command authorization is commonly configured for levels 0, 1, and 15 only. The other levels, 2 through 14, are useful only for local authorization with the **privilege level** command. See Example 26-19 for a sample configuration.

Step 9. Enable command authorization in global configuration mode (and all global configuration submodes) by using the command

aaa authorization config-commands

Step 10. Enable login accounting by using the command

aaa accounting exec { **default** | *custom-list-name* } {**start-stop** | **stop-only** | **wait-start**} *method1* [*method2* . . .]

It is common to use the keyword *start-stop* for AAA accounting. It causes accounting to start as soon as a session starts and stop as soon as the session ends.

Step 11. Enable command accounting by using the command

aaa accounting commands {*privilege level*} { **default** | *custom-list-name* } {**start-stop** | **stop-only** | **wait-start**} *method1* [*method2* . . .]

Just as with authorization, command accounting is applied per privilege level, so it is necessary to configure a command accounting method list for every privilege level that requires command accounting.

NOTE When all the AAA servers become unreachable, the AAA client falls back to one of the local methods for authentication (local, enable, or line), but AAA command authorization might still be trying to reach the AAA server to authorize the commands. This prevents a user from being able to execute any more commands because that user isn't authorized to use other commands. For this reason, it is recommended to include the *if-authenticated* method at the end of every single authorization command to allow all commands to be authorized as long as the user has successfully authenticated locally.

The *if-authenticated* method and the none method are mutually exclusive because the none method disables authorization.

26

Example 26-19 shows a common AAA IOS XE configuration for device access control.

Example 26-19 *Common AAA Configuration for Device Access Control*

```
aaa new-model

tacacs server ISE-PRIMARY
 address 10.10.10.1
 key my.S3cR3t.k3y

tacacs server ISE-SECONDARY
 address 20.20.20.1
 key my.S3cR3t.k3y

aaa group server tacacs+ ISE-TACACS+
 server name ise-primary
 server name ise-secondary

aaa authentication login default group ISE-TACACS+ local
aaa authentication login CONSOLE-CUSTOM-AUTHENTICATION-LIST local line enable
aaa authentication enable default group ISE-TACACS+ enable
aaa authorization exec default group ISE-TACACS+ if-authenticated
aaa authorization exec CONSOLE-CUSTOM-EXEC-AUTHORIZATION-LIST none
aaa authorization commands 0 CONSOLE-CUSTOM-COMMAND-AUTHORIZATION-LIST none
aaa authorization commands 1 CONSOLE-CUSTOM-COMMAND-AUTHORIZATION-LIST none
aaa authorization commands 15 CONSOLE-CUSTOM-COMMAND-AUTHORIZATION-LIST none
aaa authorization commands 0 default group ISE-TACACS+ if-authenticated
aaa authorization commands 1 default group ISE-TACACS+ if-authenticated
aaa authorization commands 15 default group ISE-TACACS+ if-authenticated
aaa authorization console
aaa authorization config-commands
aaa accounting exec default start-stop group ISE-TACACS+
aaa accounting commands 0 default start-stop group ISE-TACACS+
aaa accounting commands 1 default start-stop group ISE-TACACS+
aaa accounting commands 15 default start-stop group ISE-TACACS+
line con 0
  authorization commands 0 CONSOLE-CUSTOM-COMMAND-AUTHORIZATION-LIST
  authorization commands 1 CONSOLE-CUSTOM-COMMAND-AUTHORIZATION-LIST
  authorization commands 15 CONSOLE-CUSTOM-COMMAND-AUTHORIZATION-LIST
  authorization exec CONSOLE-CUSTOM-EXEC-AUTHORIZATION-LIST
  privilege level 15
  login authentication CONSOLE-CUSTOM-AUTHENTICATION-LIST

line vty 0 4
<uses default method-lists for AAA>
```

Apart from the IOS XE configuration, the AAA server also needs to be configured with the AAA client information (hostname, IP address, and key), the login credentials for the users, and the commands the users are authorized to execute on the device.

Verifying AAA Configuration

Example 26-20 demonstrates SSH sessions being initiated from R2 into R1, using the netadmin and netops accounts. The netadmin account was configured in the AAA server with privilege 15, and netops was configured with privilege 1. The netadmin account has access to the full set of commands, while netops is very limited.

Example 26-20 *Verifying AAA Configuration*

```
! Establish SSH session from R2 into R1 using netadmin account
R2# ssh netadmin@10.12.1.1
Password:
R1# show privilege
Current privilege level is 15
R1#
R1# configure terminal
R1(config)#

! Establish SSH session from R2 into R1 using netops account

R2# ssh netops@10.12.1.1
Password:
R1> show privilege
Current privilege level is 1
R1> show version
Cisco IOS Software, IOSv Software (VIOS-ADVENTERPRISEK9-M), Version 15.6(3)M2,
RELEASE SOFTWARE (fc2)
! Output Omitted for Brevity

R1> show running-config
Command authorization failed.

R1> enable
Command authorization failed.
```


Zone-Based Firewall (ZBFW)

ACLs control access based on protocol, source IP address, destination IP address, and ports. Unfortunately, they are stateless and do not inspect a packet's payload to detect whether attackers are using a port that they have found open. Stateful firewalls are capable of looking into Layers 4 through 7 of a network packet to verify the state of the transmission. A stateful firewall can detect whether a port is being piggybacked and can mitigate DDoS intrusions.

Key Topic

Cisco **Zone-Based Firewall (ZBFW)** is the latest integrated stateful firewall technology included in IOS XE. ZBFW reduces the need for a firewall at a branch site to provide stateful network security.

ZBFW uses a flexible and straightforward approach to providing security by establishing security zones. Router interfaces are assigned to a specific zone, which can maintain a one-to-one or many-to-one relationship. A zone establishes a security border on the network and defines acceptable traffic that is allowed to pass between zones. By default, interfaces in the same security zone can communicate freely with each other, but interfaces in different zones cannot communicate with each other without passing the configured policy.

Figure 26-2 illustrates the concept of ZBFW and the association of interfaces to a security zone.

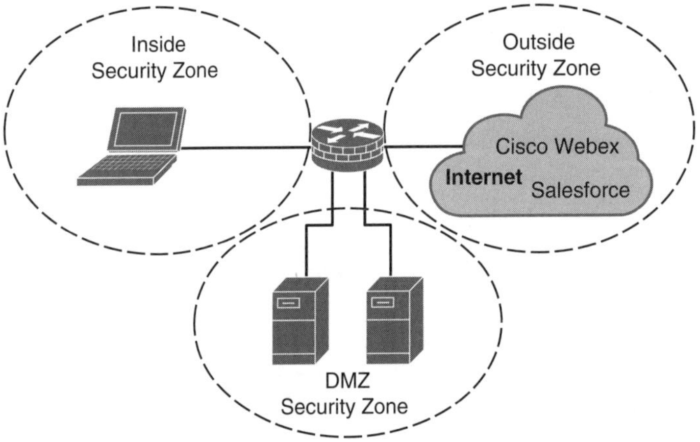

Figure 26-2 *Zone-Based Firewall and Security Zones*

Key Topic

Within the ZBFW architecture, there are two system-built zones: self and default.

The Self Zone

The self zone is a system-level zone and includes all the routers' IP addresses. By default, traffic to and from this zone is permitted to support management (for example, SSH protocol, SNMP) and control plane (for example, EIGRP, BGP) functions.

After a policy is applied to the self zone and another security zone, interzone communication must be explicitly defined.

Key Topic

The Default Zone

The default zone is a system-level zone, and any interface that is not a member of another security zone is placed in this zone automatically.

When an interface that is not in a security zone sends traffic to an interface that is in a security zone, the traffic is dropped. Most network engineers assume that a policy cannot be configured to permit these traffic flows, but it can, if you enable the default zone. Upon initialization of this zone, any interface not associated with a security zone is placed in this zone. When the unassigned interfaces are in the default zone, a policy map can be created between the two security zones.

ZBFW Configuration

This section explains the process for configuring a ZBFW outside zone on an Internet-facing router interface. ZBFW is configured in five steps:

Step 1. Configure the security zones by using the command **zone security** *zone-name*. A zone needs to be created for the outside zone (the Internet). The self zone is defined automatically. Example 26-21 demonstrates the configuration of a security zone.

Example 26-21 *Defining the Outside Security Zone*

```
Zone security OUTSIDE
 description OUTSIDE Zone used for Internet Interface
```


Step 2. Define the inspection class map. The class map for inspection defines a method for classification of traffic. The class map is configured using the command **class-map type inspect [match-all | match-any]** *class-name*. The **match-all** keyword requires that network traffic match all the conditions listed in the class map to qualify (Boolean AND), whereas **match-any** requires that network traffic match only one of the conditions in the class map to qualify (Boolean OR). If neither keyword is specified, the **match-all** function is selected. Example 26-22 shows a sample configuration of inspection class maps and their associated ACLs.

Example 26-22 *Inspecting the Class Map Configuration*

```
ip access-list extended ACL-IPSEC
 permit udp any any eq non500-isakmp
 permit udp any any eq isakmp
ip access-list extended ACL-PING-AND-TRACEROUTE
 permit icmp any any echo
 permit icmp any any echo-reply
 permit icmp any any ttl-exceeded
 permit icmp any any port-unreachable
 permit udp any any range 33434 33463 ttl eq 1
ip access-list extended ACL-ESP
 permit esp any any
ip access-list extended ACL-DHCP-IN
 permit udp any eq bootps any eq bootpc
ip access-list extended ACL-GRE
 permit gre any any
!
class-map type inspect match-any CLASS-OUTSIDE-TO-SELF-INSPECT
 match access-group name ACL-IPSEC
 match access-group name ACL-PING-AND-TRACEROUTE
class-map type inspect match-any CLASS-OUTSIDE-TO-SELF-PASS
 match access-group name ACL-ESP
 match access-group name ACL-DHCP-IN
 match access-group name ACL-GRE
```

The configuration of inspect class maps can be verified with the command **show class-map type inspect** [*class-name*], as shown in Example 26-23.

Example 26-23 *Verifying the Inspect Class Map Configuration*

```
R1# show class-map type inspect
 Class Map type inspect match-any CLASS-OUTSIDE-TO-SELF-PASS (id 2)
   Match access-group name ACL-ESP
   Match access-group name ACL-DHCP-IN
   Match access-group name ACL-GRE

 Class Map type inspect match-any CLASS-OUTSIDE-TO-SELF-INSPECT (id 1)
   Match access-group name ACL-IPSEC
   Match access-group name ACL-PING-AND-TRACEROUTE
```

Step 3. Define the inspection policy map, which applies firewall policy actions to the class maps defined in the policy map. The policy map is then associated with a zone pair.

The inspection policy map is defined with the command **policy-map type inspect** *policy-name*. After the policy map is defined, the various class maps are defined with the command **class type inspect** *class-name*. Under the class map, the firewall action is defined with these commands:

- **drop [log]:** This default action silently discards packets that match the class map. The **log** keyword adds syslog information that includes source and destination information (IP address, port, and protocol).
- **pass [log]:** This action makes the router forward packets from the source zone to the destination zone. Packets are forwarded in only one direction. A policy must be applied for traffic to be forwarded in the opposite direction. The **pass** action is useful for protocols like IPsec, Encapsulating Security Payload (ESP), and other inherently secure protocols with predictable behavior. The optional **log** keyword adds syslog information that includes the source and destination information.
- **inspect:** The **inspect** action offers state-based traffic control. The router maintains connection/session information and permits return traffic from the destination zone without the need to specify it in a second policy.

The inspect policy map has an implicit class default that uses a default drop action. This provides the same implicit "deny all" as an ACL. Adding it to the configuration may simplify troubleshooting for junior network engineers.

Example 26-24 demonstrates the configuration of the inspect policy map. Notice that in the class-default class, the **drop** command does not include the **log** keyword because of the potential to fill up the syslog.

Example 26-24 *Configuring the Inspection Policy Map*

```
policy-map type inspect POLICY-OUTSIDE-TO-SELF
 class type inspect CLASS-OUTSIDE-TO-SELF-INSPECT
  inspect
 class type inspect CLASS-OUTSIDE-TO-SELF-PASS
  pass
 class class-default
  drop
```

The inspection policy map can be verified with the command **show policy-map type inspect** [*policy-name*], as shown in Example 26-25.

Example 26-25 *Verifying the Inspection Policy Map*

```
R1# show policy-map type inspect
 Policy Map type inspect POLICY-OUTSIDE-TO-SELF
  Class CLASS-OUTSIDE-TO-SELF-INSPECT
    Inspect
  Class CLASS-OUTSIDE-TO-SELF-PASS
    Pass
  Class class-default
    Drop
```


Step 4. Apply a policy map to a traffic flow source to a destination by using the command **zone-pair security** *zone-pair-name* **source** *source-zone-name* **destination** *destination-zone-name*. The inspection policy map is then applied to the zone pair with the command **service-policy type inspect** *policy-name*. Traffic is statefully inspected between the source and destination, and return traffic is allowed. Example 26-26 defines the zone pairs and associates the policy map with the zone pair.

Example 26-26 *Configuring the ZBFW Zone Pair*

```
zone-pair security OUTSIDE-TO-SELF source OUTSIDE destination self
 service-policy type inspect POLICY-OUTSIDE-TO-SELF
```

NOTE The order of the zone pair is significant; the first zone indicates the source zone, and the second zone indicates the destination zone. A second zone pair needs to be created with bidirectional traffic patterns when the **pass** action is selected.

Step 5. Apply the security zones to the appropriate interfaces. An interface is assigned to the appropriate zone by entering the interface configuration submode with the command **interface** *interface-id* and associating the interface to the correct zone with the command **zone-member security** *zone-name*, as defined in step 1.

Example 26-27 demonstrates the outside security zone being associated with the Internet-facing interface GigabitEthernet 0/2.

Example 26-27 *Applying the Security Zone to the Interface*

```
interface GigabitEthernet 0/2
 zone-member security OUTSIDE
```

Now that the outside-to-self policy has been fully defined, traffic statistics can be viewed with the command **show policy-map type inspect zone-pair** [*zone-pair-name*]. Example 26-28 demonstrates the verification of the configured ZBFW policy.

Example 26-28 *Verifying the Outside-to-Self Policy*

```
R1# show policy-map type inspect zone-pair

policy exists on zp OUTSIDE-TO-SELF
  Zone-pair: OUTSIDE-TO-SELF

  Service-policy inspect : POLICY-OUTSIDE-TO-SELF

    Class-map: CLASS-OUTSIDE-TO-SELF-INSPECT (match-any)
      Match: access-group name ACL-IPSEC
        2 packets, 208 bytes
        30 second rate 0 bps
      Match: access-group name ACL-PING-AND-TRACEROUTE
        0 packets, 0 bytes
        30 second rate 0 bps

   Inspect
        Packet inspection statistics [process switch:fast switch]
        udp packets: [4:8]

        Session creations since subsystem startup or last reset 2
        Current session counts (estab/half-open/terminating) [0:0:0]
        Maxever session counts (estab/half-open/terminating) [2:1:0]
        Last session created 00:03:39
        Last statistic reset never
        Last session creation rate 0
        Maxever session creation rate 2
        Last half-open session total 0
        TCP reassembly statistics
        received 0 packets out-of-order; dropped 0
        peak memory usage 0 KB; current usage: 0 KB
        peak queue length 0
```

```
    Class-map: CLASS-OUTSIDE-TO-SELF-PASS (match-any)
      Match: access-group name ACL-ESP
        186 packets, 22552 bytes
        30 second rate 0 bps
      Match: access-group name ACL-DHCP-IN
        1 packets, 308 bytes
        30 second rate 0 bps
      Match: access-group name ACL-GRE
        0 packets, 0 bytes
        30 second rate 0 bps
      Pass
        187 packets, 22860 bytes

    Class-map: class-default (match-any)
      Match: any
      Drop
        30 packets, 720 bytes
```


NOTE Making the class maps more explicit and thereby adding more of the explicit class maps to the policy map provides more visibility to the metrics.

Even though the ACLs are not used for blocking traffic, the counters do increase as packets match the ACL entries for the inspect class maps, as demonstrated in Example 26-29.

Example 26-29 *ACL Counters from the Inspect Class Maps*

```
R1# show ip access
Extended IP access list ACL-DHCP-IN
  10 permit udp any eq bootps any eq bootpc (1 match)
Extended IP access list ACL-ESP
  10 permit esp any any (170 matches)
Extended IP access list ACL-GRE
  10 permit gre any any
Extended IP access list ACL-IPSEC
  10 permit udp any any eq non500-isakmp
  20 permit udp any any eq isakmp (2 matches)
Extended IP access list ACL-PING-AND-TRACEROUTE
  10 permit icmp any any echo
  20 permit icmp any any echo-reply
  30 permit icmp any any ttl-exceeded
  40 permit icmp any any port-unreachable
  50 permit udp any any range 33434 33463 ttl eq 1
```

Verifying ZBFW

After the outside-to-self policy has been defined, it is time to verify connectivity to the Internet, as shown in Example 26-30. Notice here that a simple ping from R1 to one of Google's Public DNS IP addresses 8.8.8.8 is failing.

Example 26-30 *Verifying Outside Connectivity*

```
R1# ping 8.8.8.8
Type escape sequence to abort.
Sending 5, 100-byte ICMP Echos to 8.8.8.8, timeout is 2 seconds:
.....
Success rate is 0 percent (0/5)
```

The reason for the packet failure is that the router needs to allow locally originated packets with a self-to-outside policy. Example 26-31 demonstrates the configuration for the self-to-outside policy. ACL-IPSEC and ACL-ESP are reused from the outside-to-self policy.

Example 26-31 *Configuring the Self-to-Outside Policy*

```
ip access-list extended ACL-DHCP-OUT
permit udp any eq bootpc any eq bootps
!
ip access-list extended ACL-ICMP
permit icmp any any
!
class-map type inspect match-any CLASS-SELF-TO-OUTSIDE-INSPECT
 match access-group name ACL-IPSEC
 match access-group name ACL-ICMP

class-map type inspect match-any CLASS-SELF-TO-OUTSIDE-PASS
 match access-group name ACL-ESP
 match access-group name ACL-DHCP-OUT
!
policy-map type inspect POLICY-SELF-TO-OUTSIDE
 class type inspect CLASS-SELF-TO-OUTSIDE-INSPECT
 inspect
class type inspect CLASS-SELF-TO-OUTSIDE-PASS
 pass
class class-default
 drop log
!
zone-pair security SELF-TO-OUTSIDE source self destination OUTSIDE
 service-policy type inspect POLICY-SELF-TO-OUTSIDE
```

Now that the second policy has been configured, R1 can successfully ping 8.8.8.8, as shown in Example 26-32.

Example 26-32 *Successful ping Test Between R1 and Google's Public DNS 8.8.8.8*

```
R31-Spoke# ping 8.8.8.8
Sending 5, 100-byte ICMP Echos to 8.8.8.8, timeout is 2 seconds:
!!!!!
Success rate is 100 percent (5/5), round-trip min/avg/max = 1/1/1 ms
```

Key Topic

Control Plane Policing (CoPP)

A **control plane policing (CoPP)** policy is a QoS policy that is applied to traffic to or sourced by the router's control plane CPU. CoPP policies are used to limit known traffic to a given rate while protecting the CPU from unexpected extreme rates of traffic that could impact the stability of the router.

Typical CoPP implementations use only an input policy that allows traffic to the control plane to be policed to a desired rate. In a properly planned CoPP policy, network traffic is placed into various classes, based on the type of traffic (management, routing protocols, or known IP addresses). The CoPP policy is then implemented to limit traffic to the control plane CPU to a specific rate for each class.

When a rate is defined for a CoPP policy, the rate for a class may not be known without further investigation. The QoS **police** command uses **conform**, **exceed**, and **violate** actions, which can be configured to transmit or drop traffic. By choosing to transmit traffic that exceeds the policed rate and monitoring CoPP, you can adjust the policy over time to meet day-to-day requirements.

Understanding what is needed to define a traffic class can be achieved from protocol documentation or by performing network protocol analysis. You can use the Cisco Embedded Packet Capture (EPC) feature for this purpose because it allows you to capture network traffic and export it to a PCAP file to identify the necessary traffic classes.

Configuring ACLs for CoPP

After the network traffic has been identified, ACLs can be built for matching in a class map.

Example 26-33 demonstrates a list of ACLs matching traffic identified by EPC and network documentation. Notice that these ACLs do not restrict access and are open, allowing anyone to send traffic matching the protocols. For some types of external network traffic (such as BGP), the external network address can change and is better managed from a ZBFW perspective. A majority of these protocols are accessed only using controlled internal prefixes, minimizing the intrusion surface. Management protocols are an area that can easily be controlled by using a few jump boxes for direct access and limiting SNMP and other management protocols to a specific range of addresses residing in the NOC.

Example 26-33 *Configuring an Access List for CoPP*

```
ip access-list extended ACL-CoPP-ICMP
 permit icmp any any echo-reply
 permit icmp any any ttl-exceeded
 permit icmp any any unreachable
 permit icmp any any echo
```

26

```
 permit udp any any range 33434 33463 ttl eq 1
!
ip access-list extended ACL-CoPP-IPsec
 permit esp any any
 permit gre any any
 permit udp any eq isakmp any eq isakmp
 permit udp any any eq non500-isakmp
 permit udp any eq non500-isakmp any
!
ip access-list extended ACL-CoPP-Initialize
 permit udp any eq bootps any eq bootpc
!
ip access-list extended ACL-CoPP-Management
 permit udp any eq ntp any
 permit udp any any eq snmp
 permit tcp any any eq 22
 permit tcp any eq 22 any established
!
ip access-list extended ACL-CoPP-Routing
 permit tcp any eq bgp any established
 permit eigrp any host 224.0.0.10
 permit ospf any host 224.0.0.5
 permit ospf any host 224.0.0.6
 permit pim any host 224.0.0.13
 permit igmp any any
```

NOTE The ACL-CoPP-Routing ACL in Example 26-33 does not classify unicast routing protocol packets such as unicast PIM, unicast OSPF, and unicast EIGRP.

Configuring Class Maps for CoPP

The class configuration for CoPP uses the ACLs to match known protocols being used and is demonstrated in Example 26-34.

Example 26-34 *Class Configuration for CoPP*

```
class-map match-all CLASS-CoPP-IPsec
 match access-group name ACL-CoPP-IPsec
class-map match-all CLASS-CoPP-Routing
 match access-group name ACL-CoPP-Routing
class-map match-all CLASS-CoPP-Initialize
 match access-group name ACL-CoPP-Initialize
class-map match-all CLASS-CoPP-Management
 match access-group name ACL-CoPP-Management
class-map match-all CLASS-CoPP-ICMP
 match access-group name ACL-CoPP-ICMP
```

Configuring the Policy Map for CoPP

The policy map for how the classes operate shows how to police traffic to a given rate in order to minimize any ability to overload the router. However, finding the correct rate without impacting network stability is not a simple task. To guarantee that CoPP does not introduce issues, the **violate** action is set to **transmit** for all the vital classes until a baseline for normal traffic flows is established. Over time, the rate can be adjusted. Other traffic, such as ICMP and DHCP traffic, is set to **drop** because it should have low packet rates.

In the policy map, the class default exists and contains any unknown traffic. Under normal conditions, nothing should exist within the class default, but allowing a minimal amount of traffic within this class and monitoring the policy permits discovery of new or unknown traffic that would have otherwise been denied. Example 26-35 shows the CoPP policy.

Example 26-35 *Policy Configuration for CoPP*

```
policy-map POLICY-CoPP
class CLASS-CoPP-ICMP
  police 8000 conform-action transmit  exceed-action transmit
         violate-action drop
 class CLASS-CoPP-IPsec
  police 64000 conform-action transmit  exceed-action transmit
         violate-action transmit
 class CLASS-CoPP-Initialize
  police 8000 conform-action transmit  exceed-action transmit
         violate-action drop
 class CLASS-CoPP-Management
  police 32000 conform-action transmit  exceed-action transmit
         violate-action transmit
 class CLASS-CoPP-Routing
  police 64000 conform-action transmit  exceed-action transmit
         violate-action transmit
 class class-default
  police 8000 conform-action transmit  exceed-action transmit
         violate-action drop
```

NOTE Keep in mind that the policy needs to be tweaked based on the routing protocols in use in the network.

Applying the CoPP Policy Map

The CoPP policy map needs to be applied to the control plane with the command **service-policy** {**input**|**output**} *policy-name* under control plane configuration mode, as demonstrated in Example 26-36.

Example 26-36 *Applying the Policy for CoPP*

```
control-plane
 service-policy input POLICY-CoPP
```

Verifying the CoPP Policy

After the policy map has been applied to the control plane, it needs to be verified. In Example 26-37, traffic matching CLASS-CoPP-Routing has exceeded the configured rate. In addition, the default class sees traffic. To identify what is happening, EPC could be used again to tweak the policies, if necessary. This time, the access lists can be reversed from **permit** to **deny** as the filter to gather unexpected traffic.

Example 26-37 *Verifying the Policy for CoPP*

```
R1# show policy-map control-plane input
Control Plane

  Service-policy input: POLICY-CoPP

    Class-map: CLASS-CoPP-ICMP (match-all)
      154 packets, 8912 bytes
      5 minute offered rate 0000 bps, drop rate 0000 bps
      Match: access-group name ACL-CoPP-ICMP
      police:
          cir 8000 bps, bc 1500 bytes, be 1500 bytes
        conformed 154 packets, 8912 bytes; actions:
          transmit
        exceeded 0 packets, 0 bytes; actions:
          transmit
        violated 0 packets, 0 bytes; actions:
          drop
        conformed 0000 bps, exceeded 0000 bps, violated 0000 bps

    Class-map: CLASS-CoPP-IPsec (match-all)
      0 packets, 0 bytes
      5 minute offered rate 0000 bps, drop rate 0000 bps
      Match: access-group name ACL-CoPP-IPsec
      police:
          cir 64000 bps, bc 2000 bytes, be 2000 bytes
        conformed 0 packets, 0 bytes; actions:
          transmit
        exceeded 0 packets, 0 bytes; actions:
          transmit
        violated 0 packets, 0 bytes; actions:
          transmit
        conformed 0000 bps, exceeded 0000 bps, violated 0000 bps
```

```
Class-map: CLASS-CoPP-Initialize (match-all)
  0 packets, 0 bytes
  5 minute offered rate 0000 bps, drop rate 0000 bp

  Match: access-group name ACL-CoPP-Initialize
  police:
      cir 8000 bps, bc 1500 bytes, be 1500 bytes
    conformed 0 packets, 0 bytes; actions:
      transmit
    exceeded 0 packets, 0 bytes; actions:
      transmit
    violated 0 packets, 0 bytes; actions:
      drop
    conformed 0000 bps, exceeded 0000 bps, violated 0000 bps

Class-map: CLASS-CoPP-Management (match-all)
  0 packets, 0 bytes
  5 minute offered rate 0000 bps, drop rate 0000 bps
  Match: access-group name ACL-CoPP-Management
  police:
      cir 32000 bps, bc 1500 bytes, be 1500 bytes
    conformed 0 packets, 0 bytes; actions:
      transmit
    exceeded 0 packets, 0 bytes; actions:
      transmit
    violated 0 packets, 0 bytes; actions:
      transmit
    conformed 0000 bps, exceeded 0000 bps, violated 0000 bps

Class-map: CLASS-CoPP-Routing (match-all)
  92 packets, 123557 bytes
  5 minute offered rate 4000 bps, drop rate 0000 bps
  Match: access-group name ACL-CoPP-Routing
  police:
      cir 64000 bps, bc 2000 bytes, be 2000 bytes
    conformed 5 packets, 3236 bytes; actions:
      transmit
    exceeded 1 packets, 1383 bytes; actions:
      transmit
    violated 86 packets, 118938 bytes; actions:
      transmit
    conformed 1000 bps, exceeded 1000 bps, violated 4000 bps
Class-map: class-default (match-any)
```

26

```
    56 packets, 20464 bytes
    5 minute offered rate 1000 bps, drop rate 0000 bps
    Match: any
    police:
        cir 8000 bps, bc 1500 bytes, be 1500 bytes
      conformed 5 packets, 2061 bytes; actions:
        transmit
      exceeded 0 packets, 0 bytes; actions:
        transmit
      violated 0 packets, 0 bytes; actions:
        drop
      conformed 0000 bps, exceeded 0000 bps, violated 0000 bps
```

NOTE Some Cisco platforms, such as the Catalyst 9000 series, have a default CoPP policy that typically does not require modification. If a default CoPP policy needs to be modified, please consult the Cisco documentation for restrictions, caveats, and configuration details specific to your platform.

Device Hardening

In addition to all the features discussed in this chapter for providing device access control and protection, such as AAA, CoPP, and ZBFW on the routers, disabling unused services and features improves the overall security posture by minimizing the amount of information exposed externally. In addition, hardening a router reduces the amount of router CPU and memory utilization that would be required to process these unnecessary packets.

This section provides a list of additional commands that can be used to harden a router. All interface-specific commands are applied only to the interface connected to the public network. Consider the following device hardening measures:

- **Disable topology discovery tools:** Tools such as Cisco Discovery Protocol (CDP) and Link Layer Discovery Protocol (LLDP) can provide unnecessary information to routers outside your control. The services can be disabled with the interface parameter commands **no cdp enable**, **no lldp transmit**, and **no lldp receive**.
- **Enable keepalives for TCP sessions:** The commands **service tcp-keepalive-in** and **service tcp-keepalive-out** ensure that devices send TCP keepalives for inbound/outbound TCP sessions. This ensures that the device on the remote end of the connection is still accessible and that half-open or orphaned connections are removed from the local device.
- **Disable IP redirect services:** An ICMP redirect is used to inform a device of a better path to the destination network. An IOS XE device sends an ICMP redirect if it detects network traffic hairpinning on it. This behavior is disabled with the interface parameter command **no ip redirects**.
- **Disable proxy Address Resolution Protocol (ARP):** Proxy ARP is a technique that a router uses to answer ARP requests intended for a different router. The router fakes

its identity and sends out an ARP response for the router that is responsible for that network. A man-in-the-middle intrusion enables a host on the network with a spoofed MAC address of the router and allows traffic to be sent to the hacker. Disabling proxy ARP on the interface is recommended and accomplished with the command **no ip proxy-arp**.

- **Disable service configuration:** Cisco devices support automatic configuration from remote devices through TFTP and other methods. This service should be disabled with the command **no service config**.
- **Disable the Maintenance Operation Protocol (MOP) service:** The MOP service is not needed and should be disabled globally with the command **no mop enabled** and with the interface parameter command **no mop enabled**.
- **Disable the packet assembler/disassembler (PAD) service:** The PAD service is used for X.25 and is not needed. It can be disabled with the command **no service pad**.

Exam Preparation Tasks

You have a couple of choices for exam preparation: the exercises here, Chapter 30, "Final Preparation," and the exam simulation questions in the Pearson Test Prep Software Online.

Review All Key Topics

Review the most important topics in the chapter, noted with the Key Topic icon in the outer margin of the page. Table 26-5 lists these key topics and the page number on which each is found.

Key Topic

Table 26-5 Key Topics for Chapter 26

Key Topic Element	Description	Page
Section	Access Control Lists (ACLs)	781
List	ACL categories	781
Paragraph	Applying ACL to an interface	782
List	CLI access methods	788
List	Line password protection options	788
Section	Password Types	789
List	Local username configuration options	790
List	Privilege levels	793
List	SSH versions	801
List	Authentication, authorization, and accounting (AAA)	803
List	AAA primary use cases	803
Paragraph	TACACS+ key differentiator	804
Paragraph	RADIUS key differentiators	804
Paragraph	Zone-Based Firewall (ZBFW)	810
Paragraph	ZBFW default zones	810
Section	Control Plane Policing (CoPP)	817

Complete Tables and Lists from Memory

Print a copy of Appendix B, "Memory Tables" (found on the companion website), or at least the section for this chapter, and complete the tables and lists from memory. Appendix C, "Memory Tables Answer Key," also on the companion website, includes completed tables and lists you can use to check your work.

Define Key Terms

Define the following key terms from this chapter and check your answers in the Glossary:

access control list (ACL), authentication, authorization, and accounting (AAA), control plane policing (CoPP), privilege level, Remote Authentication Dial-In User Service (RADIUS), Secure Shell (SSH), Telnet, Terminal Access Controller Access-Control System Plus (TACACS+), Zone-Based Firewall (ZBFW)

Use the Command Reference to Check Your Memory

Table 26-6 lists the important commands from this chapter. To test your memory, cover the right side of the table with a piece of paper, read the description on the left side, and see how much of the command you can remember.

Table 26-6 Command Reference

Task	Command Syntax
Apply an ACL to an interface	**ip access-group** {*access-list-number* | *name*} {**in**|**out**}
Apply an ACL to a vty line	**access-class** {*access-list-number*|*access- list-name*} {**in**|**out**}
Encrypt type 0 passwords in the configuration	**service password-encryption**
Create a username with a type 8 and type 9 password option	**username** {*username*} **algorithm-type** {**md5** | **sha256** | **scrypt**} **secret** {*password*}
Enable username and password authentication on vty lines	**login local**
Change command privilege levels	**privilege** {*mode*} **level** {*level*}{*command string*}
Allow only SSH for a vty line without using an ACL	**transport input ssh**
Enable SSHv2 on a router	**hostname** {*hostname name*} **ip domain-name** {*domain-name*} **crypto key generate rsa**
Disconnect terminal line users that are idle	**exec-timeout** {*minutes*} {*seconds*}
Enable AAA	**aaa new-model**
Enable AAA authorization for the console line	**aaa authorization console**
AAA fallback authorization method that authorizes commands if a user is successfully authenticated	**if-authenticated**

Task	Command Syntax
Enable AAA authorization for config commands	**aaa authorization config-commands**
Apply a ZBFW security zone to an interface	**zone-member security** *zone-name*
Apply an inspection policy map to a zone pair	**service-policy type inspect** *policy-name*
Apply a CoPP policy map to the control plane (two commands)	**control plane** **service-policy** {**input**|**output**} *policy-name*

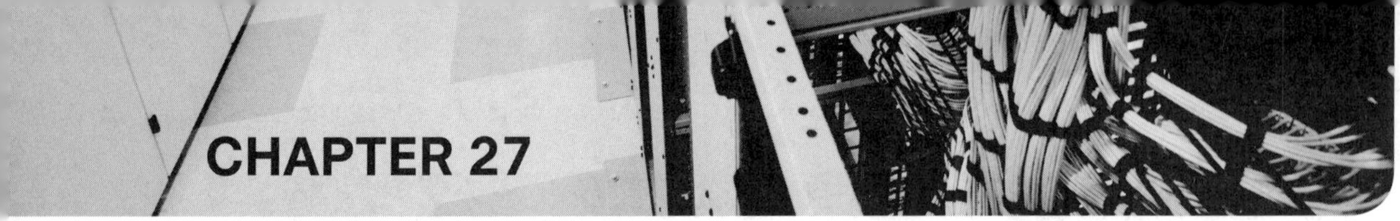

CHAPTER 27

Virtualization

This chapter covers the following subjects:

Server Virtualization: This section describes server virtualization technologies such as virtual machines, containers, and virtual switching.

Network Functions Virtualization: This section describes the NFV architecture and its application to an enterprise network.

Server virtualization is the process of using software to create multiple independent virtual servers (virtual machines) or multiple independent containerized operating systems (containers) on a physical x86 server. Network functions virtualization (NFV) is the process of virtualizing specific network functions, such as a firewall function, into a virtual machine (VM) so that they can be run in common x86 hardware instead of a dedicated appliance. This chapter describes server virtualization and NFV and the benefits they bring to an enterprise network.

NOTE Virtualization using containers is also known as containerization.

"Do I Know This Already?" Quiz

The "Do I Know This Already?" quiz allows you to assess whether you should read the entire chapter. If you miss no more than one of these self-assessment questions, you might want to move ahead to the "Exam Preparation Tasks" section. Table 27-1 lists the major headings in this chapter and the "Do I Know This Already?" quiz questions covering the material in those headings so you can assess your knowledge of these specific areas. The answers to the "Do I Know This Already?" quiz appear in Appendix A, "Answers to the 'Do I Know This Already?' Quiz Questions."

Table 27-1 "Do I Know This Already?" Foundation Topics Section-to-Question Mapping

Foundation Topics Section	Questions
Server Virtualization	1–6
Network Functions Virtualization	7–12

1. What is a virtual machine?

a. A software emulation of a virtual server with an operating system

b. A software emulation of a physical server with an operating system

c. A software emulation of a physical server without an operating system

d. A software emulation of a virtual server with or without an operating system

2. What is a container?
   a. A lightweight virtual machine
   b. A software emulation of a physical server without an operating system
   c. An application with its dependencies packaged inside a tarball
   d. An isolated environment where containerized applications run
3. Which of the following are container engines? (Choose all that apply.)
   a. rkt
   b. Docker
   c. vSphere hypervisor
   d. LXD
4. What is a virtual switch (vSwitch)?
   a. A software version of a physical multilayer switch
   b. A software version of a physical Layer 2 switch
   c. A software version of a physical switch with advanced routing capabilities
   d. A cluster of switches forming a virtual switching system (VSS)
5. True or false: Only a single vSwitch is supported within a virtualized server.
   a. True
   b. False
6. True or false: Containers do not need vSwitches to communicate with each other or with the outside world.
   a. True
   b. False
7. Which of the following is the virtual or software version of a network function and typically runs on a hypervisor as a VM?
   a. VNF
   b. NFV
   c. NFVI
   d. NFVIS
8. Which of the following is an architectural framework created by ETSI that defines standards to decouple network functions from proprietary hardware-based appliances and have them run in software on standard x86 servers?
   a. VNF
   b. NFV
   c. NFVI
   d. NFVIS

9. Connecting VNFs together to provide an NFV service or solution is known as _____.

   a. daisy chaining
   b. bridging
   c. switching
   d. service chaining
   e. linking

10. Which of the following is the I/O technology that uses VFs and PFs?

   a. OVS
   b. OVS-DPDK
   c. SR-IOV
   d. PCI passthrough

11. Which platform plays the role of the orchestrator in Cisco's Enterprise NFV solution?

   a. APIC-EM
   b. Cisco DNA Center
   c. Cisco Enterprise Service Automation (ESA)
   d. APIC Controller

12. True or false: NFVIS is based on a standard version of Linux packaged with additional functions for virtualization, VNF lifecycle management, monitoring, device programmability, and hardware acceleration.

   a. True
   b. False

Foundation Topics

Server Virtualization

Key Topic

One of the main drivers behind server virtualization was that server hardware resources were being underutilized; physical servers were typically each running a single operating system with a single application and using only about 10% to 25% of the CPU resources. VMs and containers increase the overall efficiency and cost-effectiveness of a server by maximizing the use of the available resources.

> **NOTE** Physical servers running a single operating system and dedicated to a single user are referred to as *bare-metal servers.*

Virtual Machines

Key Topic

A *virtual machine (VM)* is a software emulation of a physical server with an operating system. From an application's point of view, the VM provides the look and feel of a real physical server, including all its components, such as CPU, memory, and network interface cards (NICs). The virtualization software that creates VMs and performs the hardware abstraction that allows multiple VMs to run concurrently is known as a *hypervisor*. VMware vSphere, Microsoft Hyper-V, Citrix XenServer, and Red Hat Kernel-based Virtual Machine (KVM) are the most popular hypervisors in the server virtualization market. Figure 27-1 provides a side-by-side comparison of a bare-metal server and a server running virtualization software.

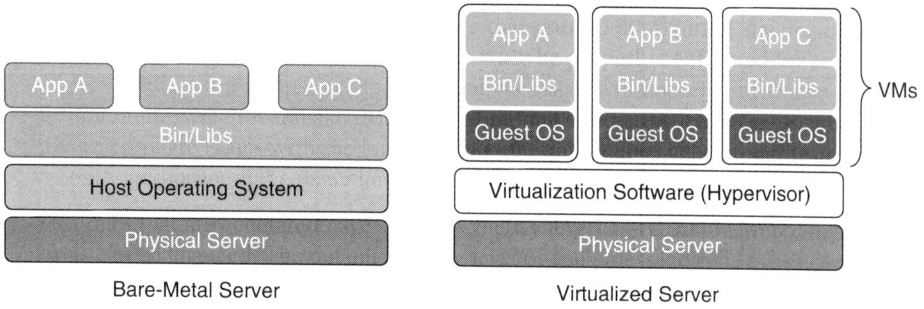

Figure 27-1 *Bare-Metal Server and Virtualized Server*

There are two types of hypervisors, as illustrated in Figure 27-2:

27

Key Topic

- **Type 1:** This type of hypervisor runs directly on the system hardware. It is commonly referred to as "bare metal" or "native."
- **Type 2:** This type of hypervisor (for example, VMware Fusion) requires a host OS to run. This is the type of hypervisor that is typically used by client devices.

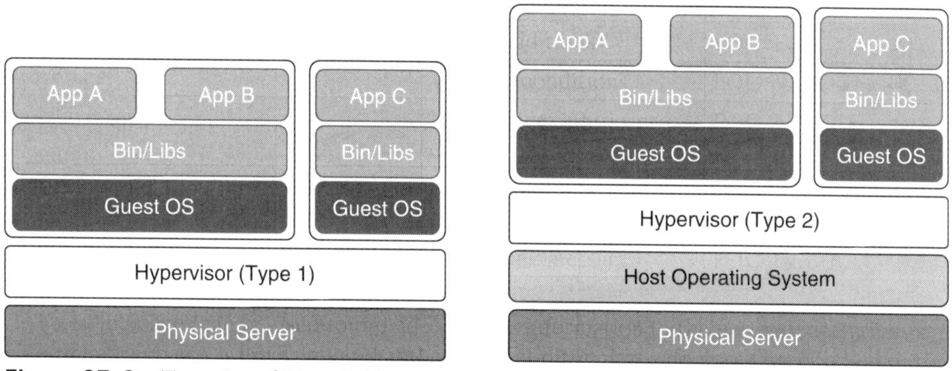

Figure 27-2 *Type 1 and Type 2 Hypervisors*

One key capability of VMs is that they can be migrated from one server to another while preserving transactional integrity during movement. This can enable many advantages; for example, if a physical server needs to be upgraded (for example, a memory upgrade), the VMs can be migrated to other servers with no downtime. Another advantage is that it provides high availability; for example, if a server fails, the VMs can be spun up on other servers in the network, as illustrated in Figure 27-3.

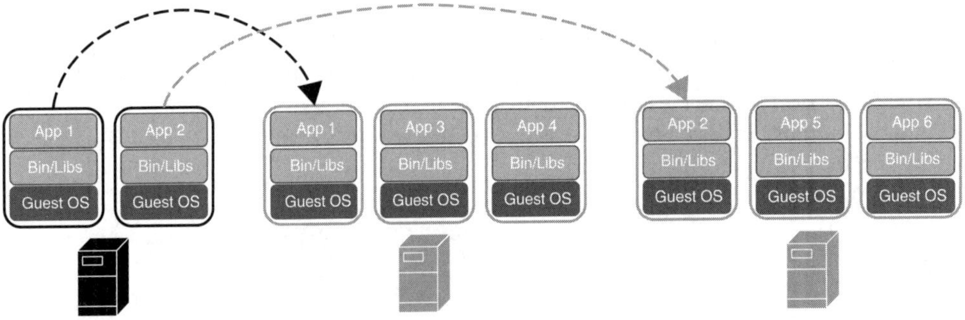

Figure 27-3 *VM Migration*

Containers

Key Topic

A *container* is an isolated environment where containerized applications run. It contains the application, along with the dependencies that the application needs to run. Even though they have these and many other similarities to VMs, containers are not the same as VMs, and they should not be referred to as "lightweight VMs."

Figure 27-4 shows a side-by-side comparison of VMs and containers. Notice that each VM requires an OS and that containers all share the same OS while remaining isolated from each other.

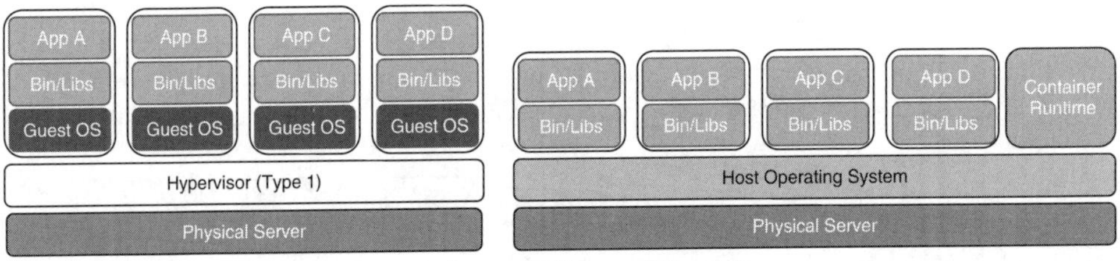

Figure 27-4 *Side-by-Side Comparison of VMs and Containers*

A VM includes a guest OS, which typically comes with a large number of components (including executables, libraries, and dependencies) that are really not required for the application to run; it's up to the developer to strip any unwanted services or components from it to make it as lightweight as possible. Remember that a VM is basically a virtualized physical server, which means it includes all the components of a physical server but in a virtual fashion.

Containers, on the other hand, share the underlying resources of the host operating system and do not include a guest OS, as VMs do; containers are therefore lightweight (small in size). The application, along with the specific dependencies (binary files and libraries) that it needs to run, are included within the container. Containers originate from container images. A *container image* is a file created by a container engine that includes the application code along with its dependencies. Container images become containers when they are run by the container engine. Because a container image contains everything the application code within it needs to run, it is extremally portable (easy to move/migrate). Container images eliminate some typical problems, such as applications working on one machine but not another and applications failing to run because the necessary libraries are not part of the operating system and need to be downloaded to make it run.

Answers to the "Do I Know This Already?" quiz:

1 B **2** D **3** A, B, D **4** B **5** B **6** B **7** A **8** B **9** D **10** C **11** B **12** A

A container does not try to virtualize a physical server as a VM does; instead, the abstraction is the application or the components that make up the application.

Here is one more example to help clarify the difference between VMs and containers: When a VM starts, the OS needs to load first, and once it's operational, the application in the VM can then start and run. This whole process usually takes minutes. When a container starts, it leverages the kernel of the host OS, which is already running, and it typically takes a few seconds to start.

Many container engines to create, run, and manage containers are available. The most popular container engine is the Docker engine. Here's a list of some of the other container engine options available:

- rkt (pronounced "rocket")
- Open Container Initiative
- LXD (pronounced "lexdi"), from Canonical Ltd.
- Linux-VServer
- Windows Containers

Virtual Switching

Key Topic

A *virtual switch (vSwitch)* is a software-based Layer 2 switch that operates like a physical Ethernet switch. A vSwitch enables VMs to communicate with each other within a virtualized server and with external physical networks through the physical network interface cards (pNICs). Multiple vSwitches can be created under a virtualized server, but network traffic cannot flow directly from one vSwitch to another vSwitch within the same host, and the vSwitches cannot share the same pNIC.

The most popular vSwitches include the following:

- Open vSwitch (OVS)
- VMware's vSphere Standard Switch (VSS), the vSphere Distributed Switch (VDS), and the NSX vSwitch
- Microsoft Hyper-V Virtual Switch
- Libvirt Virtual Network Switch

Figure 27-5 illustrates a virtualized server with three vSwitches connected to the virtual network interface cards (vNICs) of the VMs as well as the pNICs. vSwitch1 and vSwitch3 are linked to pNIC 1 and pNIC 3, respectively, to access the physical network, whereas vSwitch2 is not linked to any pNICs. Since network traffic cannot flow from one vSwitch to another, network traffic from VM1 destined to the external network, or VM0, needs to flow through the virtual next-generation firewall (NGFWv).

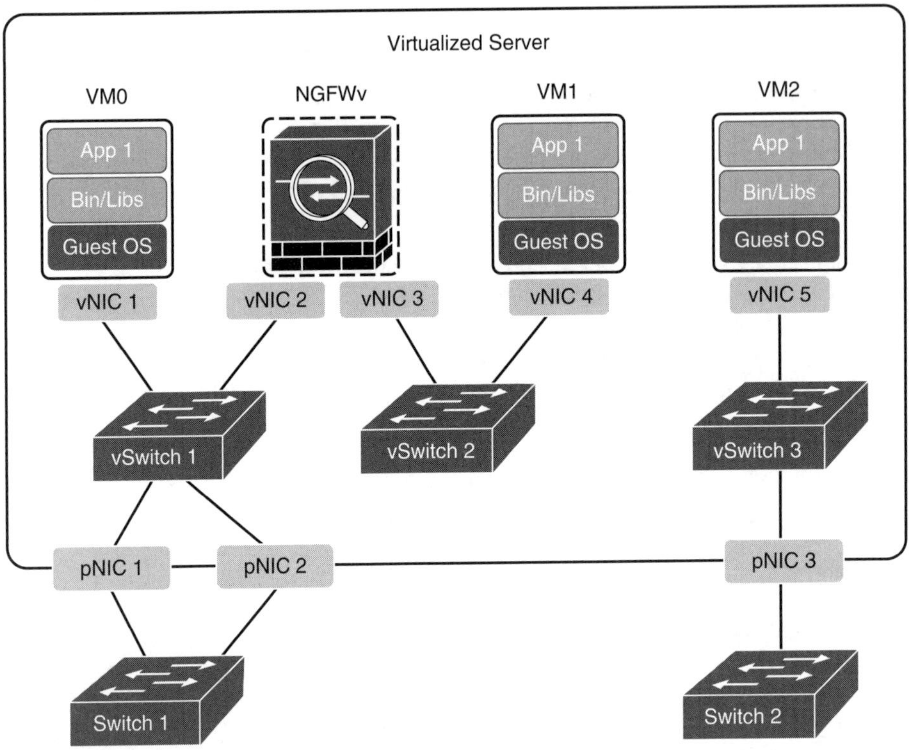

Figure 27-5 *Virtualized Server with vSwitches*

One of the downsides of standard vSwitches is that every vSwitch that is part of a cluster of virtualized servers needs to be configured individually in every virtual host. This problem is solved by using distributed virtual switching, a feature that aggregates vSwitches together from a cluster of virtualized servers and treats them as a single distributed virtual switch. These are some of the benefits of distributed switching:

- Centralized management of vSwitch configuration for multiple hosts in a cluster, which simplifies administration
- Migration of networking statistics and policies with virtual machines during a live VM migration
- Configuration consistency across all the hosts that are part of the distributed switch

Like VMs, containers rely on vSwitches (also known as virtual bridges) for communication within a node (server) or the outside world. Docker, for example, by default creates a virtual bridge called Docker0, and it is assigned the default subnet block 172.17.0.0/16. This default subnet can be customized, and user-defined custom bridges can also be used.

Figure 27-6 illustrates how every container created by Docker is assigned a virtual Ethernet interface (veth) on Docker0. The veth interface appears to the container as eth0. The eth0 interface is assigned an IP address from the bridge's subnet block. As more containers are created by Docker within the node, they are each assigned an eth0 interface and an IP address from the same private address space. All containers can then communicate with each other only if they are within the same node. Containers in other nodes are not reachable by default, and this can be managed using routing at the OS level or by using an overlay network.

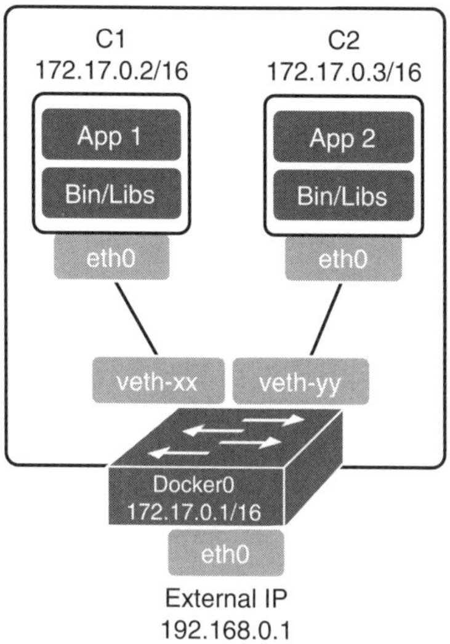

Figure 27-6 *Container Bridging*

If Docker is installed on another node using the default configuration, it ends up with the same IP addressing as the first node, and this needs to be resolved on a node-by-node basis. A better way to manage and scale containers and the networking connectivity between them within and across nodes is to use a container orchestrator such as Kubernetes.

Network Functions Virtualization

Key Topic

Network functions virtualization (NFV) is an architectural framework created by the European Telecommunications Standards Institute (ETSI) that defines standards to decouple network functions from proprietary hardware-based appliances and have them run in software on standard x86 servers. It also defines how to manage and orchestrate the network functions. *Network function (NF)* refers to the function performed by a physical appliance, such as a firewall or a router function.

Some of the benefits of NFV are similar to the benefits of server virtualization and cloud environments:

- Reduced capital expenditure (capex) and operational expenditure (opex) through reduced equipment costs and efficiencies in space, power, and cooling
- Faster time to market (TTM) because VMs and containers are easier to deploy than hardware
- Improved return on investment (ROI) from new services
- Ability to scale up/out and down/in capacity on demand (elasticity)
- Openness to the virtual appliance market and pure software networking vendors
- Opportunities to test and deploy new innovative services virtually and with lower risk

Figure 27-7 illustrates the ETSI NFV architectural framework.

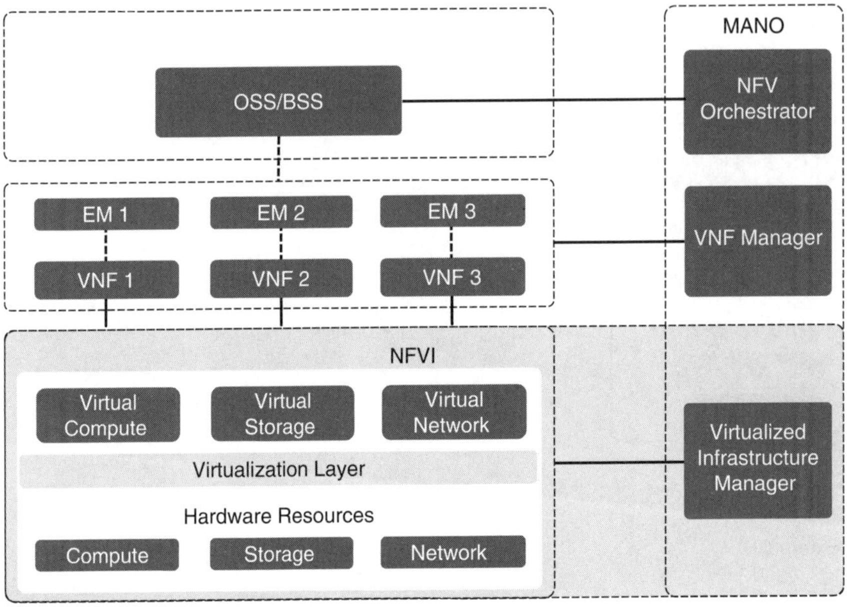

Figure 27-7 *ETSI NFV Architectural Framework*

NFV Infrastructure

NFV infrastructure (NFVI) is all the hardware and software components that comprise the platform environment in which virtual network functions (VNFs) are deployed.

Virtual Network Functions

A *virtual network function (VNF)*, as its name implies, is the virtual or software version of an NF, and it typically runs on a hypervisor as a VM. VNFs are commonly used for Layer 4 through Layer 7 functions, such as those provided by load balancers (LBs) and application delivery controllers (ADCs), firewalls, intrusion detection systems (IDSs), and WAN optimization appliances. However, they are not limited to Layer 4 through Layer 7 functions; they can also perform lower-level Layer 2 and Layer 3 functions, such as those provided by routers and switches.

Some examples of Cisco VNFs include the following:

- Cisco Catalyst 8000V
- Cisco Secure Firewall ASA Virtual
- Cisco Secure Firewall Threat Defense Virtual

Virtualized Infrastructure Manager

The NFVI *Virtualized Infrastructure Manager (VIM)* is responsible for managing and controlling the NFVI hardware resources (compute, storage, and network) and the virtualized resources. It is also responsible for the collection of performance measurements and fault information. In addition, it performs lifecycle management (setup, maintenance, and teardown) of all NFVI resources as well as VNF service chaining. *Service chaining* refers to connecting two or more VNFs in a chain to provide an NFV service or solution. Figure 27-8 illustrates the "physical" and the logical view of VNFs connected in a service chain. External Switch 1 provides connectivity to the external network and connects the virtual load balancer to the virtual firewall; vSwitch 1 connects the virtual firewall to the virtual WAN optimization VNF; pNIC 4 connects the virtual WAN optimization VNF to the virtual router; and the virtual router connects to the external network via External Switch 2.

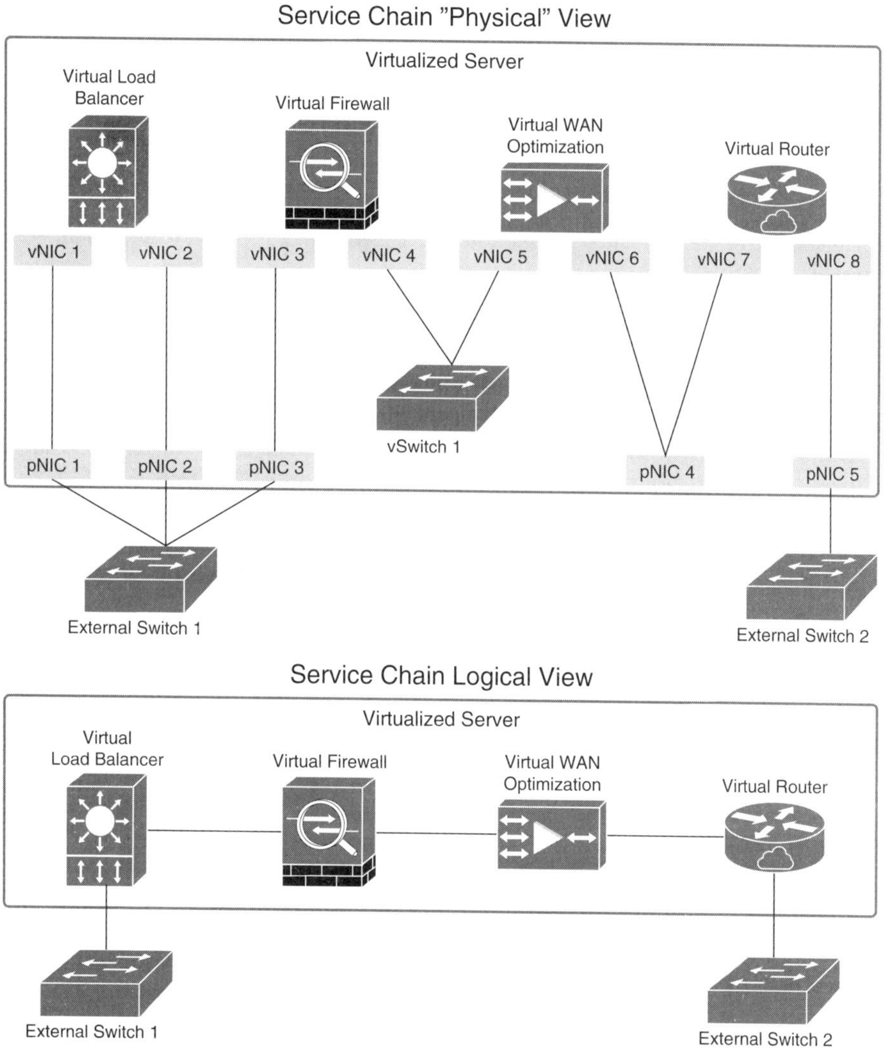

Figure 27-8 *Service Chaining*

Element Managers

Element managers (EMs), also known as *element management systems (EMSs)*, are responsible for the functional management of VNFs; in other words, they perform fault, configuration, accounting, performance, and security (FCAPS) functions for VNFs. A single EM can manage one or multiple VNFs, and an EM can also be a VNF.

Management and Orchestration

The NFV orchestrator is responsible for creating, maintaining, and tearing down VNF network services. If multiple VNFs are part of a network service, the NFV orchestrator enables the creation of an end-to-end network service over multiple VNFs. The VNF manager manages the lifecycle of one or multiple VNFs as well as FCAPS for the virtual components of a VNF. The NFV orchestrator and VNF manager together are known as NFV *management and orchestration (MANO)*.

Operations Support System (OSS)/Business Support System (BSS)

OSS is a platform typically operated by service providers (SPs) and large enterprise networks to support all their network systems and services. The OSS can assist them in maintaining network inventory, provisioning new services, configuring network devices, and resolving network issues. For SPs, OSS typically operates in tandem with BSS to improve the overall customer experience. BSS is a combination of product management, customer management, revenue management (billing), and order management systems that are used to run the SP's business operations.

VNF Performance

In NFV solutions, the data traffic has two different patterns: north–south and east–west. North–south traffic comes into the hosting server through a physical NIC (pNIC) and is sent to a VNF; then it is sent from the VNF back out to the physical wire through the pNIC. East–west traffic comes into the hosting server through a pNIC and is sent to a VNF. From there, it could be sent to another VNF (service chained) and possibly service chained to more VNFs and then sent back out to the physical wire through a pNIC. There can also be combinations of the two, where a VNF uses a north–south traffic pattern for user data and an east–west traffic pattern to send traffic to a VNF that is just collecting statistics or that is just being used for logs or storage. These patterns and the purpose of the VNFs are important to understand when deciding which technology to use to switch traffic between VNFs as well as to the outside world. Picking the right technologies will ensure that the VNFs achieve optimal throughput and performance. The most popular technologies to achieve optimal VNF performance and throughput are described in this section, but before describing them, it is important to understand the following terminology:

- **Input/output (I/O):** The communication between a computing system (such as a server) and the outside world. Input is the data received by the computing system, and output is the data sent from it.
- **I/O device:** A peripheral device such as a mouse, keyboard, monitor, or network interface card (NIC).
- **Interrupt request (IRQ):** A hardware signal sent to the CPU by an I/O device (such as a NIC) to notify the CPU when it has data to transfer. When the CPU receives the interrupt (IRQ), it saves its current state, temporarily stops what it's doing, and runs an interrupt handler routine associated to the device. The interrupt handler determines the cause of the interrupt, performs the necessary processing, performs a CPU state restore, and issues a return-from-interrupt instruction to return control to the CPU so

that it can resume what it was doing before the interrupt. Each I/O device that generates IRQs has an associated interrupt handler that is part of the device's driver.

- **Device driver:** A computer program that controls an I/O device and allows the CPU to communicate with the I/O device. A NIC is an example of an I/O device that requires a driver to operate and interface with the CPU.
- **Direct memory access (DMA):** A memory access method that allows an I/O device to send or receive data directly to or from the main memory, bypassing the CPU, to speed up overall computer operations.
- **Kernel and user space:** The core part of an operating system (OS) and a memory area where applications and their associated libraries reside. The kernel ("core" in German) is a program that is the central (core) part of an OS. It directly manages the computer hardware components, such as RAM and CPU, and provides system services to applications that need to access any hardware components, including NICs and internal storage. Because it is the core of an OS, the kernel is executed in a protected area of the main memory (kernel space) to prevent other processes from affecting it. Non-kernel processes are executed in a memory area called the user space, which is where applications and their associated libraries reside.

Figure 27-9 illustrates an operating system's kernel and user space as well as typical I/O devices that interface with the operating system.

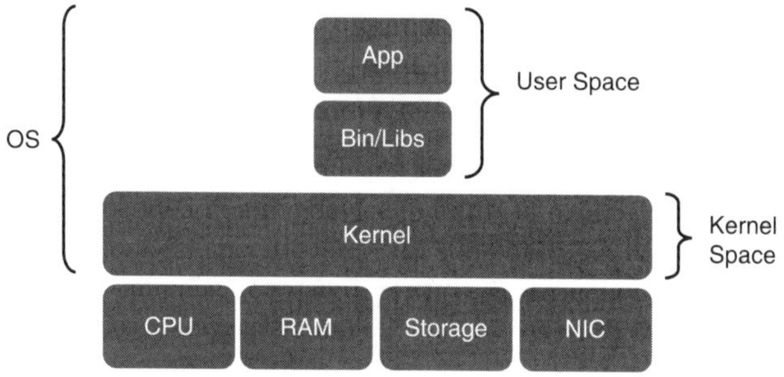

Figure 27-9 *Operating System Kernel and User Space*

In non-virtualized environments, data traffic is received by a pNIC and then sent through the kernel space to an application in the user space. In a virtual environment, there are pNICs and virtual NICs (vNICs) and a hypervisor with a virtual switch in between them. The hypervisor and the virtual switch are responsible for taking the data from the pNIC and sending it to the vNIC of the VM/VNF and finally to the application. The addition of the virtual layer introduces additional packet processing and virtualization overhead, which creates bottlenecks and reduces I/O packet throughput.

The packet flow for a virtualized system with an Open vSwitch (OVS) architecture is illustrated in Figure 27-10.

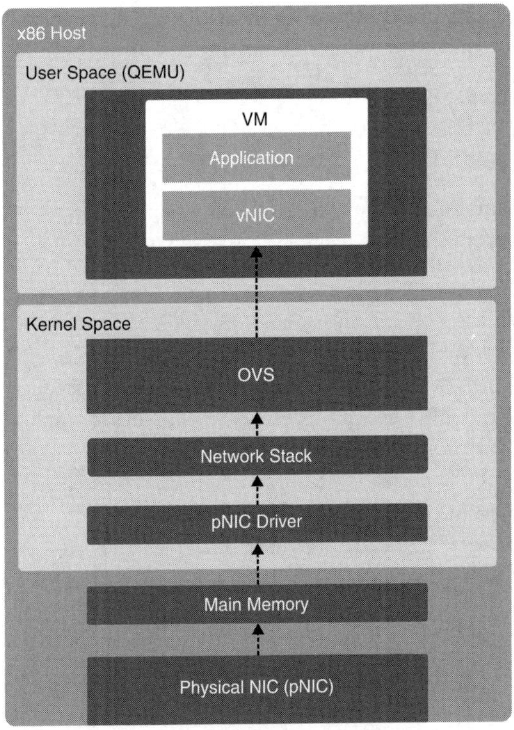

Figure 27-10 *x86 Host with OVS*

The high-level packet flow steps for packets received by the pNIC and delivered to the application in the VM are as follows:

Step 1. Data traffic is received by the pNIC and placed into an Rx queue (ring buffers) within the pNIC.

Step 2. The pNIC sends the packet and a packet descriptor to the main memory buffer through DMA. The packet descriptor includes only the memory location and size of the packet.

Step 3. The pNIC sends an IRQ to the CPU.

Step 4. The CPU transfers control to the pNIC driver, which services the IRQ, receives the packet, and moves it into the network stack, where it eventually arrives in a socket and is placed into a socket receive buffer.

Step 5. The packet data is copied from the socket receive buffer to the OVS virtual switch.

Step 6. OVS processes the packet and forwards it to the VM. This entails switching the packet between the kernel and user space, which is expensive in terms of CPU cycles.

Step 7. The packet arrives at the virtual NIC (vNIC) of the VM and is placed into an Rx queue.

Step 8. The vNIC sends the packet and a packet descriptor to the virtual memory buffer through DMA.

Step 9. The vNIC sends an IRQ to the vCPU.

Step 10. The vCPU transfers control to the vNIC driver, which services the IRQ, receives the packet, and moves it into the network stack, where it eventually arrives in a socket and is placed into a socket receive buffer.

Step 11. The packet data is copied and sent to the application in the VM.

Every packet received needs to go through the same process, which requires the CPU to be continuously interrupted. The number of interrupts increases when using high-speed NICs (for example, 40 Gbps) and the packet size is small because more packets need to be processed per second. Interrupts add a lot of overhead because any activity the CPU is doing must be stopped, the state must be saved, the interrupt must be processed, and the original process must be restored so that it can resume what it was doing before the interrupt.

To avoid all the overhead and increase packet throughput, multiple I/O technologies have been developed. The most prevalent of these technologies are the following:

- OVS Data Plane Development Kit (OVS-DPDK)
- PCI passthrough
- Single-root I/O virtualization (SR-IOV)

NOTE To be able to implement these I/O technologies, physical NICs that support them are required.

OVS-DPDK

Key Topic

To overcome the performance impact on throughput due to interrupts, OVS was enhanced with the Data Plane Development Kit (DPDK) libraries. OVS with DPDK operates entirely in user space. The DPDK Poll Mode Driver (PMD) in OVS polls for data that comes into the pNIC and processes it, bypassing the network stack and the need to send an interrupt to the CPU when a packet is received—in other words, bypassing the kernel entirely. To be able to do this, DPDK PMD requires one or more CPU cores dedicated to polling and handling the incoming data. Once the packet is in OVS, it's already in user space, and it can then be switched directly to the appropriate VNF, resulting in huge performance benefits. Figure 27-11 illustrates an x86 host with a standard OVS compared to an x86 host with an OVS with DPDK.

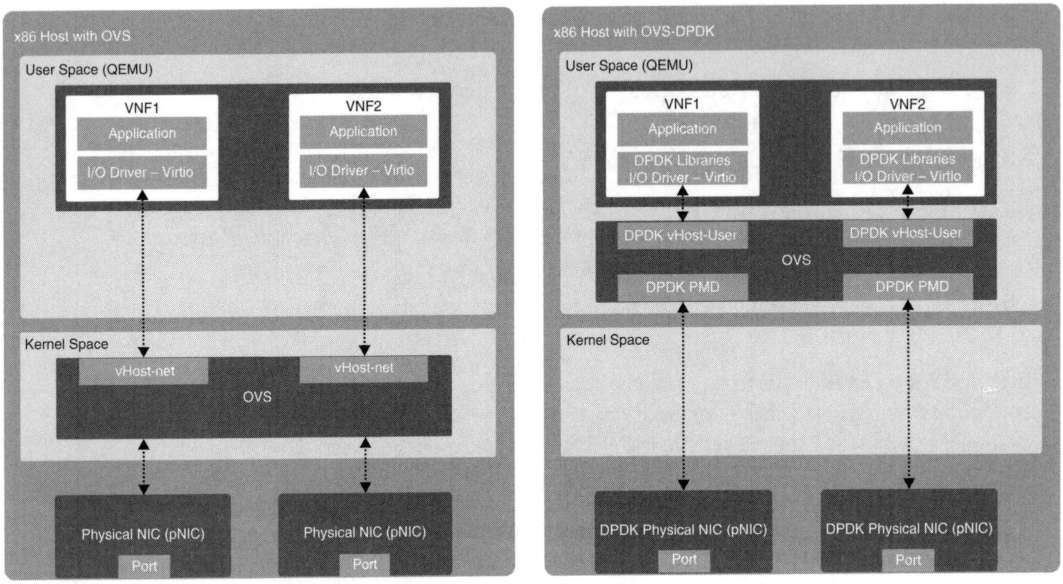

Figure 27-11 *Standard OVS and OVS-DPDK*

PCI Passthrough

Key Topic

PCI passthrough allows VNFs to have direct access to physical PCI devices, which appear and behave as if they were physically attached to the VNF. This technology can be used to map a pNIC to a single VNF, and from the VNF's perspective, it appears as if it is directly connected to the pNIC.

PCI passthrough offers many performance advantages:

- Exclusive one-to-one mapping
- Bypassed hypervisor
- Direct access to I/O resources
- Reduced CPU utilization
- Reduced system latency
- Increased I/O throughput

The downside to PCI passthrough is that the entire pNIC is dedicated to a single VNF and cannot be used by other VNFs, so the number of VNFs that can use this technology is limited by the number of pNICs available in the system. Figure 27-12 illustrates an x86 host with a standard OVS and an x86 host with PCI passthrough.

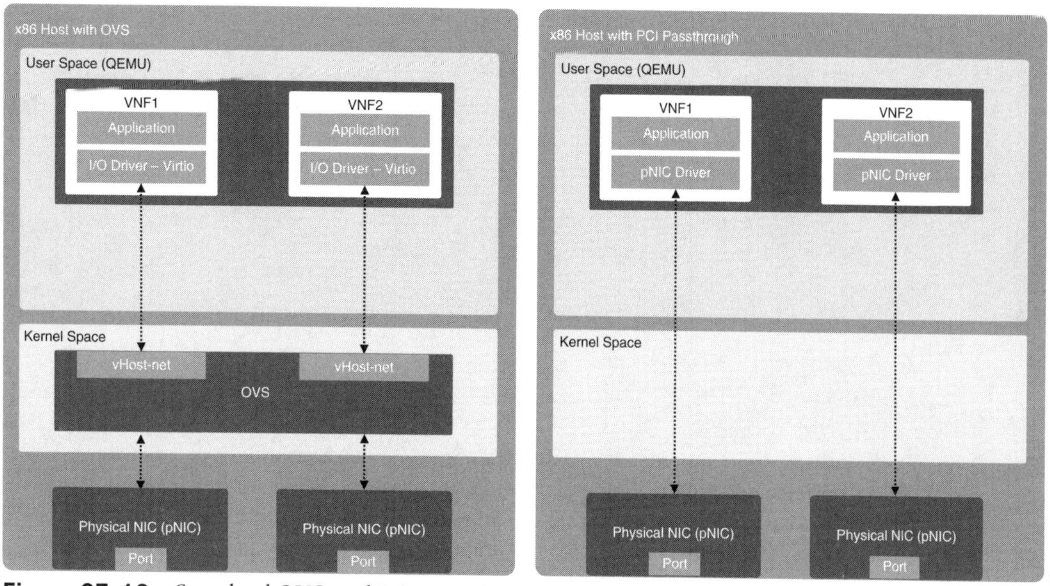

Figure 27-12 *Standard OVS and PCI Passthrough*

SR-IOV

Key Topic

SR-IOV is an enhancement to PCI passthrough that allows multiple VNFs to share the same pNIC. SR-IOV emulates multiple PCIe devices on a single PCIe device (such as a pNIC). In SR-IOV, the emulated PCIe devices are called *virtual functions (VFs)*, and the physical PCIe devices are called *physical functions (PFs)*. The VNFs have direct access to the VFs, using PCI passthrough technology.

An SR-IOV-enabled pNIC supports two different modes for switching traffic between VNFs:

- **Virtual Ethernet Bridge (VEB):** Traffic between VNFs attached to the same pNIC is hardware switched directly by the pNIC.
- **Virtual Ethernet Port Aggregator (VEPA):** Traffic between VNFs attached to the same pNIC is switched by an external switch.

Figure 27-13 illustrates an x86 host with a standard OVS compared to an x86 host with SR-IOV.

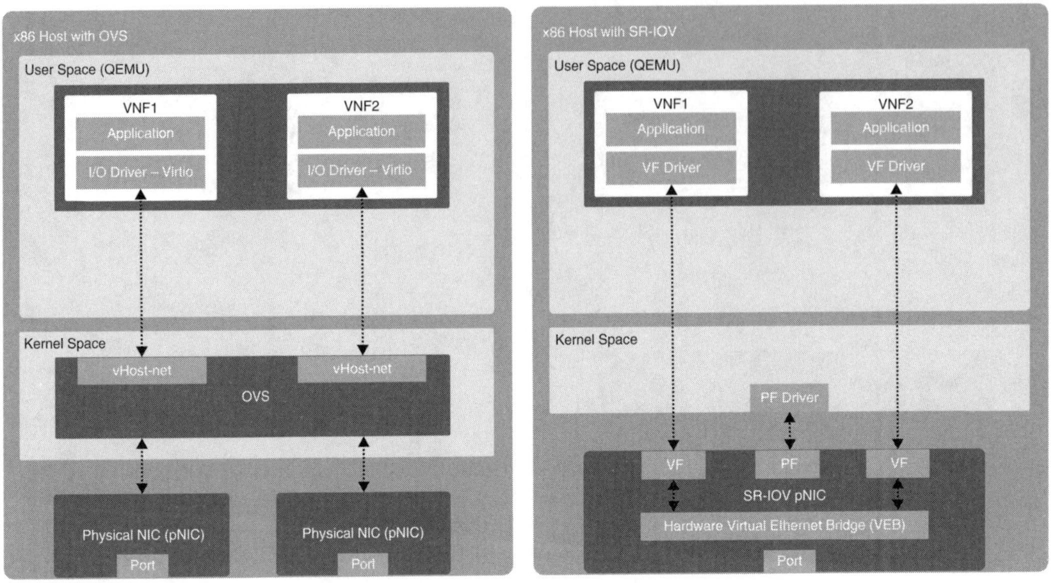

Figure 27-13 *Standard OVS and SR-IOV*

Cisco Enterprise Network Functions Virtualization (ENFV)

Enterprise branch offices often require multiple physical networking devices to perform network functions such as WAN acceleration, firewall protection, wireless LAN controller, intrusion prevention, collaboration services, and routing and switching. Sometimes these physical devices are deployed with redundancy, further increasing the number of devices installed and operated in the branch. An enterprise typically has multiple branches, and needing to manage so many different devices can create many challenges.

Key Topic

The Cisco ENFV solution is a Cisco solution based on the ETSI NFV architectural framework. It reduces the operational complexity of enterprise branch environments by running the required networking functions as virtual networking functions (VNFs) on standard x86-based hosts. In other words, it replaces physical firewalls, routers, WLC, load balancers, and so on with virtual devices running in a single x86 platform. The Cisco ENFV solution provides the following benefits:

- Reduces the number of physical devices to be managed at the branch, resulting in efficiencies in space, power, maintenance, and cooling
- Reduces the need for truck rolls and technician site visits to perform hardware installations or upgrades
- Offers operational simplicity that allows it to roll out new services, critical updates, VNFs, and branch locations in minutes
- Centralizes management through Cisco DNA Center, which greatly simplifies designing, provisioning, updating, managing, and troubleshooting network services and VNFs
- Enhances network operations flexibility by taking full advantage of virtualization techniques such as virtual machine moves, snapshots, and upgrades

- Supports Cisco SD-WAN cEdge and vEdge virtual router onboarding
- Supports third-party VNFs

Cisco ENFV Solution Architecture

Key Topic

Cisco ENFV delivers a virtualized solution for network and application services for branch offices. It consists of four main components that are based on the ETSI NFV architectural framework:

- **Management and Orchestration (MANO):** Cisco DNA Center provides the VNF management and NFV orchestration capabilities. It allows for easy automation of the deployment of virtualized network services, consisting of multiple VNFs.
- **VNFs:** VNFs provide the desired virtual networking functions.
- **Network Functions Virtualization Infrastructure Software (NFVIS):** An operating system that provides virtualization capabilities and facilitates the deployment and operation of VNFs and hardware components.
- **Hardware resources:** x86-based compute resources that provide the CPU, memory, and storage required to deploy and operate VNFs and run applications.

Figure 27-14 illustrates the main components of Cisco's Enterprise NFV solution.

> **NOTE** Managed service providers (MSPs) have the option of adding an OSS/BSS component using the Cisco Network Service Orchestrator (NSO) or Cisco Managed Services Accelerator (MSX).

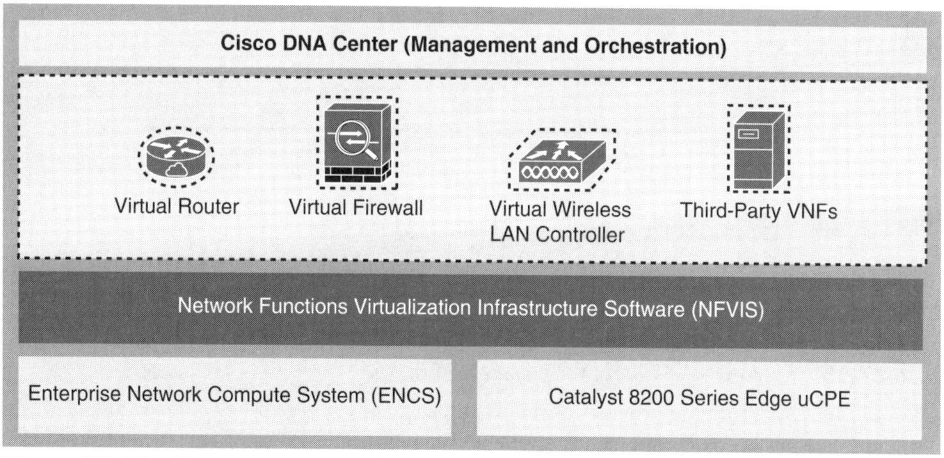

Figure 27-14 *Enterprise NFV Solution Main Components*

Management and Orchestration

Key Topic

Cisco DNA Center provides the MANO functionality to the Cisco Enterprise NFV solution. It includes a centralized dashboard and tools to design, provision, manage, and monitor all branch sites across the enterprise. Two of the main functions of DNA Center are to roll out new branch locations or deploy new VNFs and virtualized services.

Cisco DNA Center provides centralized policies, which enables consistent network policies across the enterprise branch offices. Centralized policies are created by building network profiles. Multiple network profiles can be created, each with specific design requirements and virtual services. Once they are created, branch sites are then assigned to network profiles that match the branch requirements. Network profiles include information such as the following:

- Configuration for LAN and WAN virtual interfaces
- Services or VNFs to be used, such as a firewall or WAN optimizer, and their requirements, such as service chaining parameters, CPU, and memory requirements
- Device configuration required for the VNFs, which can be customized by using custom configuration templates created through a template editor tool

Figure 27-15 shows the Cisco DNA Center Add Services window, where services or VNFs can be added and services can be service chained to each other using multiple interface types, such as LAN, management, and services interface.

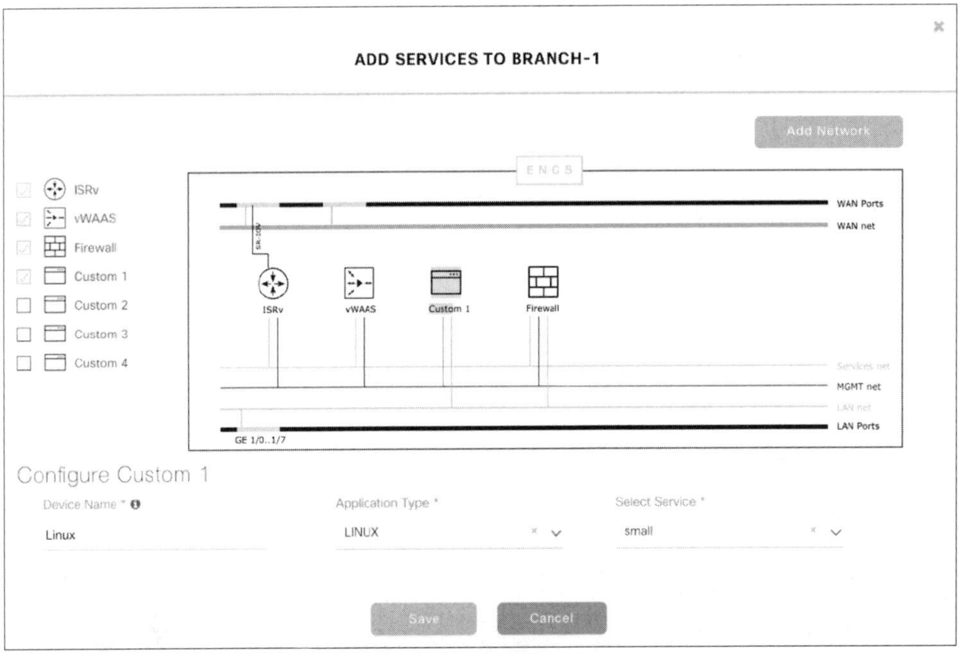

Figure 27-15 *Cisco DNA Center Add Services Window*

Plug and Play provisioning provides a way to automatically and remotely provision and onboard new network devices. When a new ENFV platform is brought up for the first time, it can use Plug and Play to register with DNA Center. Then DNA Center matches the site to the network profile assigned for the site and then provisions and onboards the device automatically.

Key Topic

Virtual Network Functions and Applications

The Cisco Enterprise NFV solution provides an environment for the virtualization of both network functions and applications in the enterprise branch. Both Cisco and third-party VNFs can be onboarded onto the solution. Applications running in a Linux server or Windows server environment can also be instantiated on top of NFVIS (discussed later in this chapter) and can be supported by DNA Center.

Cisco-supported VNFs include the following:

- Cisco Catalyst 8000V Edge for Viptela SD-WAN and virtual routing
- Cisco vEdge SD-WAN Cloud Router for Viptela SD-WAN
- Cisco Secure Firewall ASA Virtual for a virtual firewall
- Cisco Secure Firewall Threat Defense Virtual for integrated firewall and intrusion detection and prevention
- Cisco virtual Wide Area Application Services (vWAAS) for virtualized WAN optimization
- Cisco Catalyst 9800-CL Cloud Wireless Controller for virtualized wireless LAN controllers
- ThousandEyes
- Meraki vMX

VNFs from the following third-party vendors are supported:

- Microsoft Windows Server
- Linux Server
- Accedian
- AVI Networks
- Check Point
- Citrix
- CTERA
- F5
- Fortinet
- InfoVista
- NETSCOUT
- Palo Alto Networks
- Riverbed Technology

Key Topic

Network Function Virtualization Infrastructure Software (NFVIS)

NFVIS is based on standard Linux packaged with additional functions for virtualization, VNF lifecycle management, monitoring, device programmability, and hardware acceleration. The components and functionality delivered by NFVIS are illustrated in Figure 27-16:

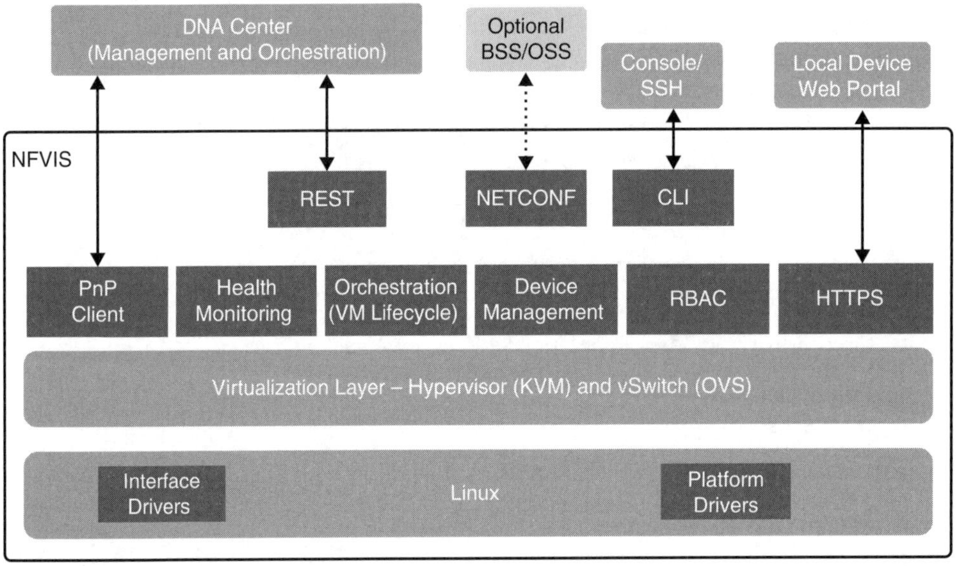

Figure 27-16 *NFVIS Components*

- **Linux:** Linux drives the underlying hardware platforms (for example, ENCS, Cisco UCS servers, or x86 enhanced network devices) and hosts the virtualization layer for VNFs, virtual switching API interfaces, interface drivers, platform drivers, and management.
- **Hypervisor:** The hypervisor for virtualization is based on Kernel-based Virtual Machine (KVM) and includes Quick Emulator (QEMU), Libvirt, and other associated processes.
- **Virtual switch (vSwitch):** The vSwitch is Open vSwitch (OVS), and it enables communication between different VNFs (service chaining) and to the outside world.
- **VM lifecycle management:** NFVIS provides the VIM functionality as specified in the NFV architectural framework through the NFVIS embedded Elastic Services Controller (ESC) Lite. ESC-Lite supports dynamic bringup of VNFs—creating and deleting VNFs and adding CPU cores, memory, and storage. It also includes built-in VNF monitoring capability that allows for auto restart of VNFs when they are down and sending alarms (SNMP or syslogs).

- **Plug and Play client:** This client automates the bringing up of any NFVIS-based host. The Plug and Play client communicates with a Plug and Play server running in Cisco DNA Center and is provisioned with the right host configuration. It also enables a true zero-touch deployment model (that is, no human intervention) and allows for quick and error-free deployment of network services.
- **Orchestration:** REST, CLI, HTTPS, and NETCONF/YANG communication models are supported for orchestration and management.
- **HTTPS web server:** The web server can enable connectivity into NFVIS through HTTPS to a local device's web portal. From this portal, it is possible to upload VNF packages, implement full lifecycle management, turn services up and down, connect to VNF consoles, and monitor critical parameters, without the need for complex commands.
- **Device management:** Tools are packaged into NFVIS to support device management, including a resource manager to get information on the number of CPU cores allocated to VMs and the CPU cores that are already used by the VMs.
- **Role-based access control (RBAC):** Users accessing the platform are authenticated using RBAC.

x86 Hosting Platforms

Cisco Enterprise NFVIS is supported on the following Cisco x86 hosting platforms:

- Cisco Enterprise Network Compute System (ENCS)
- Cisco Catalyst 8200 Series Edge uCPE

Which platform to choose depends on the requirements and features needed, such as voice over IP (VoIP), requirements for non-Ethernet-based interfaces (such as T1 or DSL), 4G-LTE, I/O technologies supported (for example, SR-IOV), and the number of CPU cores needed to support the existing service requirements (VNFs and services) as well as future requirements.

Exam Preparation Tasks

You have a couple of choices for exam preparation: the exercises here, Chapter 30, "Final Preparation," and the exam simulation questions in the Pearson Test Prep Software Online.

Review All Key Topics

Review the most important topics in the chapter, noted with the Key Topic icon in the outer margin of the page. Table 27-2 lists these key topics and the page number on which each is found.

Key Topic

Table 27-2 Key Topics for Chapter 27

Key Topic Element	Description	Page
Section	Server Virtualization	828
Paragraph	Virtual machine definition	828
List	Hypervisor types	829
Paragraph	Container definition	830
Paragraph	Virtual switch definition	831
Paragraph	NFV definition	833
Paragraph	OVS-DPDK definition	839
Paragraph	PCI passthrough definition	840
Paragraph	SR-IOV definition	841
Paragraph	Enterprise NFV definition	842
List	Enterprise NFV architecture	843
Paragraph	Enterprise NFV MANO definition	843
Section	Virtual Network Functions and Applications	845
Section	Network Function Virtualization Infrastructure Software (NFVIS)	846

Complete Tables and Lists from Memory

Print a copy of Appendix B, "Memory Tables" (found on the companion website), or at least the section for this chapter, and complete the tables and lists from memory. Appendix C, "Memory Tables Answer Key," also on the companion website, includes completed tables and lists you can use to check your work.

Define Key Terms

Define the following key terms from this chapter and check your answers in the Glossary:

container, container image, hypervisor, network function (NF), network functions virtualization (NFV), NFV infrastructure (NFVI), service chaining, virtual machine (VM), virtual network function (VNF), virtual switch (vSwitch)

CHAPTER 28

Foundational Network Programmability Concepts

This chapter covers the following subjects:

Command-Line Interface (CLI): This section provides an overview of the pros and cons of managing devices with the traditional command-line interface approach.

Application Programming Interface (API): This section describes what APIs are, the different types of APIs, and how they are used.

Data Models and Supporting Protocols: This section describes some of the most common data models and associated tools.

Cisco DevNet: This section provides a high-level overview of the various Cisco DevNet components and learning labs.

GitHub: This section illustrates different use cases for version control and the power of community code sharing.

Basic Python Components and Scripts: This section illustrates the components of Python scripts and how to interpret them.

This chapter discusses some of the ways that networks have been traditionally managed. It also focuses on some of the most common network programmability concepts and programmatic methods of management.

"Do I Know This Already?" Quiz

The "Do I Know This Already?" quiz allows you to assess whether you should read the entire chapter. If you miss no more than one of these self-assessment questions, you might want to move ahead to the "Exam Preparation Tasks" section. Table 28-1 lists the major headings in this chapter and the "Do I Know This Already?" quiz questions covering the material in those headings so you can assess your knowledge of these specific areas. The answers to the "Do I Know This Already?" quiz appear in Appendix A, "Answers to the 'Do I Know This Already?' Quiz Questions."

Table 28-1 "Do I Know This Already?" Foundation Topics Section-to-Question Mapping

Foundation Topics Section	Questions
Command-Line Interface (CLI)	13
Application Programming Interface (API)	2–6, 10
Cisco DevNet	11
GitHub	12
Data Models and Supporting Protocols	14
Basic Python Components and Scripts	1, 7–9

1. True or false: Python is considered one of the most difficult programming languages to learn and adopt.
   a. True
   b. False
2. To authenticate with Cisco's DNA Center, which type of HTTP request method must be used?
   a. PUT
   b. PATCH
   c. GET
   d. POST
   e. HEAD
3. What does CRUD stand for?
   a. CREATE, RESTORE, UPDATE, DELETE
   b. CREATE, READ, UPDATE, DELETE
   c. CREATE, RETRIEVE, UPDATE, DELETE
   d. CREATE, RECEIVE, UPLOAD, DOWNLOAD
   e. CREATE, RECEIVE, UPLOAD, DELETE
4. When using the Cisco vManage Authentication API, what is the Headers Content-Type that is used?
   a. MD5
   b. X-Auth-Token
   c. SSH
   d. x-www-form-urlencoded
   e. JSON
5. Which of the following is in JSON data format?
   a.
```
{
  "user": "root",
  "father": "Jason",
  "mother": "Jamie",
  "friend": "Luke"
}
```
   b.
```
<users>
      <user>
        <name>root</name>
      </user>
      <user>
        <name>Jason</name>
      </user>
```

```
        <user>
          <name>Jamie</name>
        </user>
        <user>
          <name>Luke</name>
        </user>
      </users>
```

c.

```
root
Jason
Jamie
Luke
```

d.

```
[users[root|Jason|Jamie|Luke]]
```

6. What is the HTTP status code for Unauthorized?

- **a.** 201
- **b.** 400
- **c.** 401
- **d.** 403
- **e.** 404

7. In Python, why would you use three quotation marks in a row? (Choose two.)

- **a.** To begin a multiple-line string
- **b.** To start a function
- **c.** To represent a logical OR
- **d.** To end a multiple-line string
- **e.** To call a reusable line of code

8. Which of the following is a Python dictionary?

a.

```
dnac = {
    "host": "sandboxdnac.cisco.com",
    "port": 443,
    "username": "devnetuser",
    "password": "Cisco123!"
}
```

b.

```
[users[root|Jason|Jamie|Luke]]
```

c.

```
def dnac_login(host, username, password):
    url = "https://{}/api/system/v1/auth/token".
          format(host)
```

```
    response = requests.request("POST", url,
                    auth=HTTPBasicAuth(username, password),
                    headers=headers, verify=False)
    return response.json()["Token"]
```

d.

```
print(dnac_devices)
```

9. Which of the following are Python functions? (Choose two.)

a.

```
dnac = {
    "host": "sandboxdnac.cisco.com",
    "port": 443,
    "username": "devnetuser",
    "password": "Cisco123!"
}
```

b.

```
[users[root|Jason|Jamie|Luke]]
```

c.

```
def dnac_login(host, username, password):
    url = "https://{}/api/system/v1/auth/token".
          format(host)
    response = requests.request("POST", url,
                    auth=HTTPBasicAuth(username, password),
                    headers=headers, verify=False)
    return response.json()["Token"]
```

d.

```
print(dnac_devices)
```

10. When using the Cisco DNA Center Token API, what authentication method is used?

a. MD5

b. X-Auth-Token

c. SSH

d. Basic authentication

e. JSON

11. What is the DevNet Documentation page used for?

a. To ask questions

b. To exchange code

c. To access learning labs

d. To access API information

e. To get news on local DevNet events

28

12. When using GitHub, what is the purpose of a repository? (Choose three.)

- **a.** Provides a place to store a developer's code
- **b.** Provides a place to store music and photos
- **c.** Gives the option to share a developer's code with other users
- **d.** Provides documentation on code examples
- **e.** Offers a sandbox to test custom code

13. Why is using the command-line interface (CLI) to configure a large number of devices considered difficult to scale? (Choose two.)

- **a.** The CLI is prone to human error and misconfiguration.
- **b.** The CLI is quick and efficient for configuring many devices simultaneously.
- **c.** Telnet access to the CLI is best practice.
- **d.** The command line is used on a device-by-device basis.
- **e.** Using APIs is considered a legacy method of configuration.

14. Which of the following are part of the YANG model? (Choose two.)

- **a.** Type
- **b.** Leaf
- **c.** Container
- **d.** String
- **e.** Method

Foundation Topics

Command-Line Interface

There are many different ways to connect to and manage a network. The most commonly used method for the past 30 years has been by using the *command-line interface (CLI)*. However, like almost everything else, the CLI has pros and cons. Perhaps one of the most glaring and biggest flaws with using CLI to manage a network is misconfiguration. Businesses often have frequent changes in their network environments, and some of those changes can be extremely complex. When businesses have increased complexity in their networks, the cost of something failing can be very high due to the increased time it takes to troubleshoot the issues in a complex network.

Failure in a network, however, doesn't necessarily mean software or a hardware component is to blame. A majority of network outages are caused by human beings. Many outages occur because of misconfigurations due to lack of network understanding. While not all outages or failures can be avoided, there are tools that can assist in reducing the number of outages that are caused by human error due to misconfigurations in the CLI (see Chapter 29, "Introduction to Automation Tools"). Table 28-2 shows a brief list of common pros and cons associated with using the CLI.

Table 28-2 CLI PROs and CONs

PROs	CONs
Well known and documented	Difficult to scale
Commonly used method	Large number of commands
Commands can be scripted	Must know IOS command syntax

PROs	CONs
Syntax help available on each command	Executing commands can be slow
Connection to CLI can be encrypted (using SSH)	Not intuitive
	Can execute only one command at time
	CLI and commands can change between software versions and platforms
	Using the CLI can pose a security threat if using Telnet (plaintext)

Of course there are programmatic ways of accomplishing the same configurations that are possible with the CLI, as discussed in the following sections.

Application Programming Interface

Another very popular method of communicating with and configuring a network is through the use of **application programming interfaces (APIs)**. APIs are mechanisms used to communicate with applications and other software. They are also used to communicate with various components of the network through software. It is possible to use APIs to configure or monitor specific components of a network. There are multiple different types of APIs. However, the focus of this chapter is on two of the most common APIs: the Northbound and Southbound APIs. The following sections explain the differences between the two through the lens of network automation. Figure 28-1 illustrates the basic operations of Northbound and Southbound APIs.

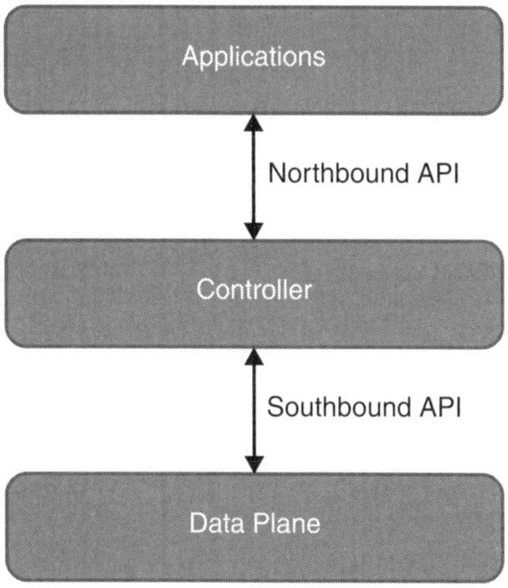

Figure 28-1 *Basic API Operations*

Northbound API

Northbound APIs are often used to communicate from a network controller to its management software. For example, Cisco DNA Center has a software graphical user interface (GUI) that is used to manage the network controller. Typically, when a network operator logs into a controller to manage the network, the information that is being passed from the management software is leveraging a Northbound REST-based API. Best practices suggest that the traffic should be encrypted using TLS between the software and the controller. Most types of APIs have the ability to use encryption to secure the data in flight.

NOTE REST APIs are covered later in this chapter.

Southbound API

If a network operator makes a change to a switch's configuration in the management software of the controller, those changes are then pushed down to the individual devices by using a Southbound API. These devices can be routers, switches, or even wireless access points. APIs interact with the components of a network through the use of a programmatic interface.

Representational State Transfer (REST) APIs

An API that uses REST is often referred to a RESTful API. RESTful APIs use HTTP methods to gather and manipulate data. Because there is a defined structure for how HTTP works, it offers a consistent way to interact with APIs from multiple vendors. REST uses different HTTP functions to interact with the data. Table 28-3 lists some of the most common HTTP functions and their associated use cases.

Key Topic

Table 28-3 HTTP Functions and Use Cases

HTTP Function	Action	Use Case
GET	Requests data from a destination	Viewing a website
POST	Submits data to a specific destination	Submitting login credentials
PUT	Replaces data in a specific destination	Updating an NTP server
PATCH	Appends data to a specific destination	Adding an NTP server
DELETE	Removes data from a specific destination	Removing an NTP server

HTTP functions are similar to the functions that most applications or databases use to store or alter data—whether the data is stored in a database or within the application. These functions are called "CRUD" functions. CRUD is an acronym that stands for CREATE, READ, UPDATE, and DELETE. For example, in a SQL database, the CRUD functions are used to interact with or manipulate the data stored in the database. Table 28-4 lists the CRUD functions and their associated actions and use cases.

Key Topic

Table 28-4 CRUD Functions and Use Cases

CRUD Function	Action	Use Case
CREATE	Inserts data in a database or application	Updating a customer's home address in a database
READ	Retrieves data from a database or application	Pulling up a customer's home address from a database
UPDATE	Modifies or replaces data in a database or application	Changing a street address stored in a database
DELETE	Removes data from a database or application	Removing a customer from a database

Answers to the "Do I Know This Already?" quiz:

1 B **2** D **3** B **4** D **5** A **6** C **7** A, D **8** A **9** C, D **10** D **11** A, D **12** A, C, D **13** A, D **14** B, C

API Tools and Resources

Whether you're trying to learn how APIs interact with applications or controllers, need to test code and outcomes, or want to become a full-time developer, one of the most important pieces of interacting with any software using APIs is testing. Testing code helps ensure that developers are accomplishing the outcome that was intended when executing the code. This section covers some tools and resources related to using APIs and REST functions. This information will help you hone development skills in order to become a more efficient network engineer with coding skills.

Introduction to Postman

Earlier, this chapter mentioned being able interact with a software controller using RESTful APIs. It also discussed being able to test code to see if the desired outcomes are accomplished when executing the code. Keep in mind that APIs are software interfaces into an application or a controller. Many APIs require authentication. This means that such an API is considered just like any other device to which a user needs to authenticate to gain access to utilize the APIs. A developer who is authenticated has access to making changes using the API, which can impact that application. This means if a REST API call is used to delete data, that data will be removed from the application or controller just as if a user logged into the device via the CLI and deleted it. It is best practice to use a test lab or the Cisco DevNet sandbox while learning or practicing any of these concepts to avoid accidental impact to a production or lab environment.

NOTE Cisco DevNet is covered later in this chapter.

Postman is an application that makes it possible to interact with APIs using a console-based approach. Postman allows for the use of various data types and formats to interact with REST-based APIs. Figure 28-2 shows the main Postman application dashboard.

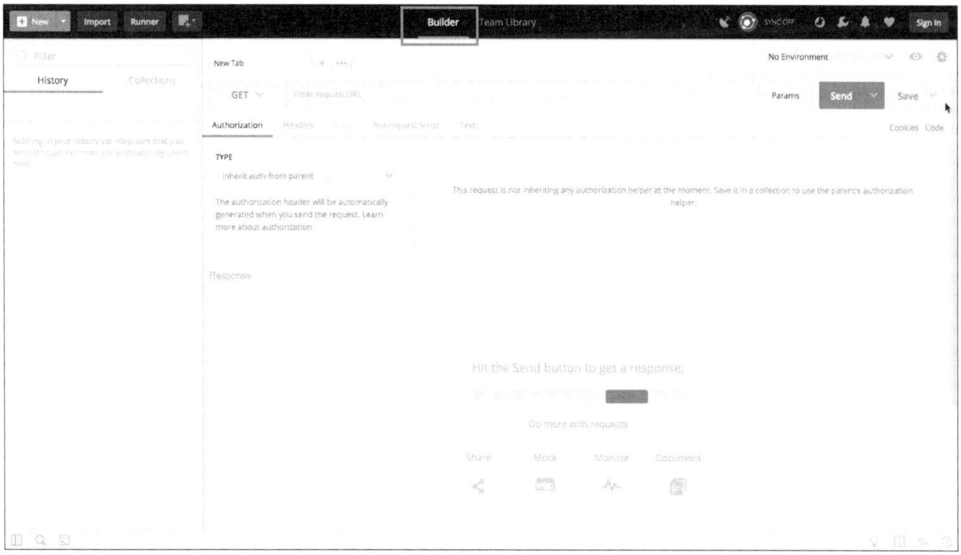

Figure 28-2 *Postman Dashboard*

NOTE The screenshots of Postman used at the time of this writing may differ from the currently available version.

The Postman application has various sections that you can interact with. The focus here is on using the Builder portion of the dashboard. The following sections are the ones that require the most focus and attention:

- History
- Collections
- New Tab
- URL bar

The History tab shows a list of all the recent API calls made using Postman. Users have the option to clear their entire history at any time if they want to remove the complete list of API calls that have been made. This is done by clicking the Clear All link at the top of the Collection window (see Figure 28-3). Users also have the ability to remove individual API calls from the history list by simply hovering the mouse over an API call and clicking the trash can icon in the submenu that pops up.

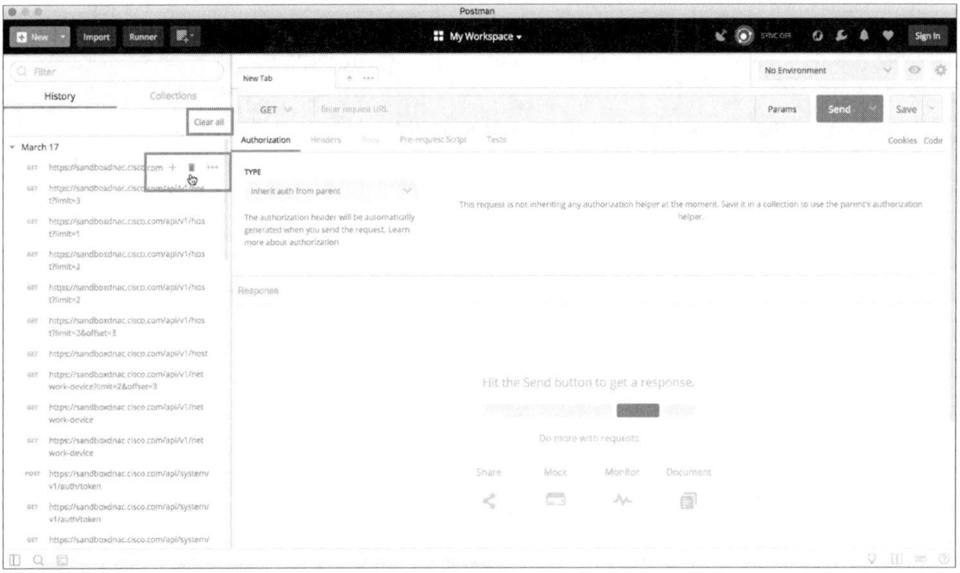

Figure 28-3 *Clearing the Postman API History*

API calls can be stored in groups, called *collections*, that are specific to a structure that fits the user's needs. Collections can follow any naming convention and appear as a folder hierarchy. For example, it's possible to have a collection called DNA-C to store all the Cisco DNA Center API calls. Saving API calls to a collection helps during testing phases as the API calls can easily be found and sorted. It is also possible to select a collection to be a favorite by clicking the star icon to the right of the collection name. Figure 28-4 shows a collection called DNA-C that is selected as a favorite.

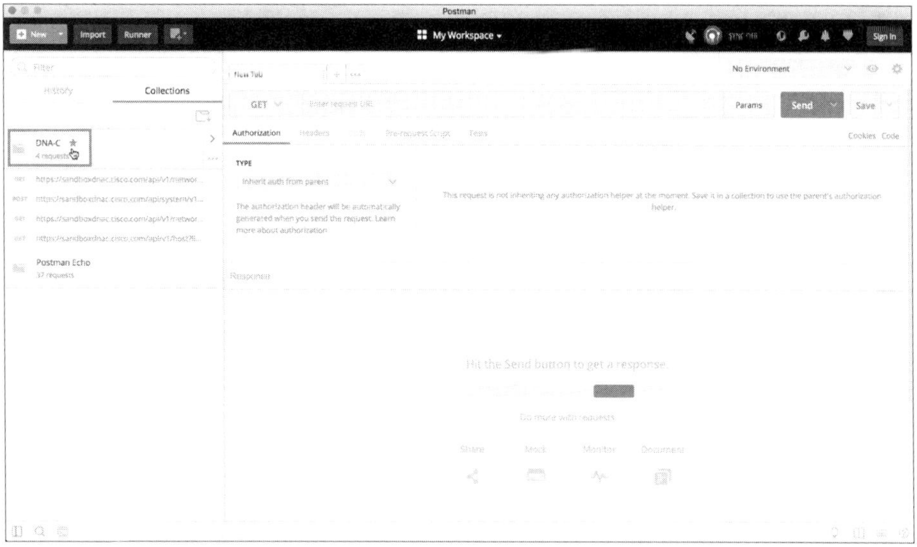

Figure 28-4 *A Favorite Postman Collection*

Tabs provide another very convenient way to work with various API calls. Each tab can have its own API call and parameters that are completely independent of any other tab. For example, a user can have one tab open with API calls interacting with the Cisco DNA Center controller and another tab open that is interacting with a completely different platform, such as a Cisco Nexus switch. Each tab has its own URL bar to be able to use a specific API. Remember that an API call using REST is very much like an HTTP transaction. Each API call in a RESTful API maps to an individual URL for a particular function. This means every configuration change or poll to retrieve data a user makes in a REST API has a unique URL—whether it is a GET, POST, PUT, PATCH, or DELETE function. Figures 28-5 and 28-6 show two different tabs using unique URLs for different API calls.

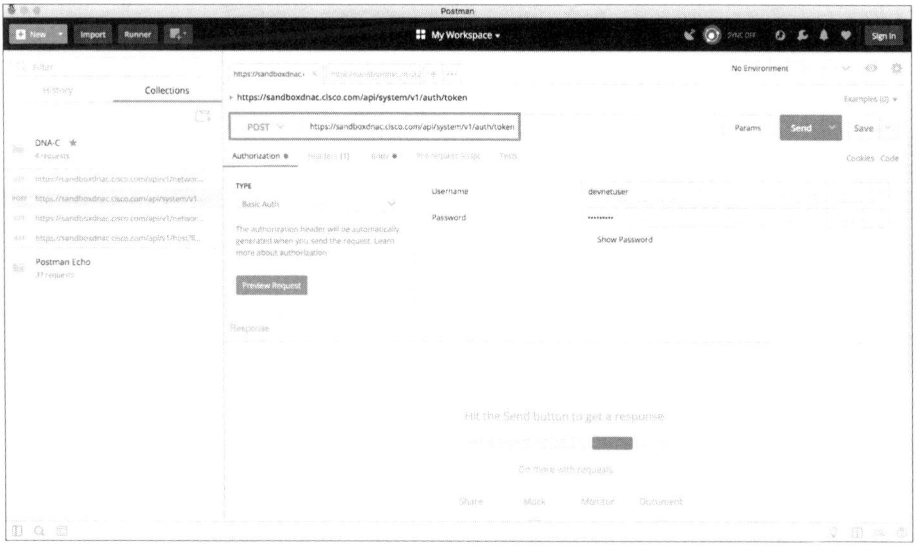

Figure 28-5 *Postman URL Bar with Cisco DNA Center Token API Call*

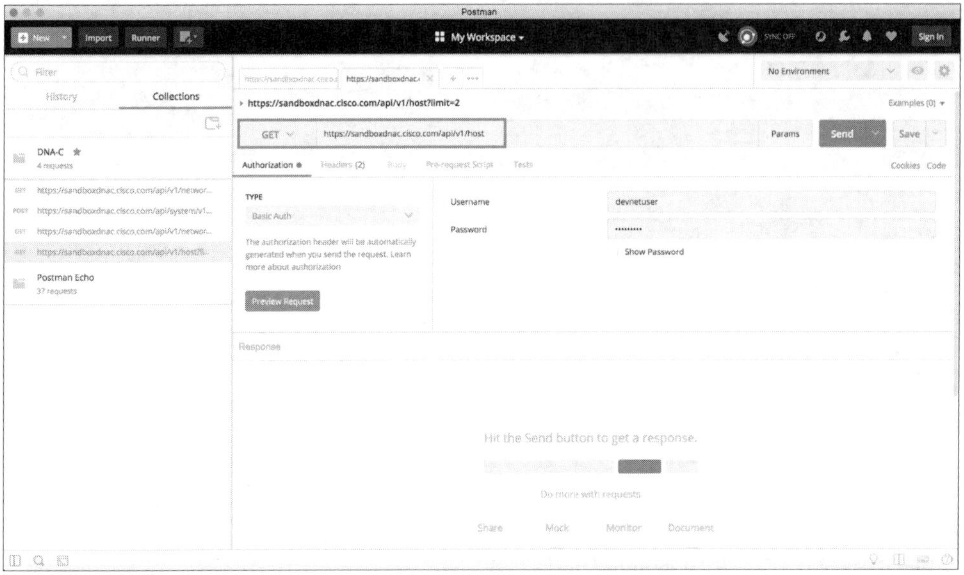

Figure 28-6 *Postman URL Bar with Cisco DNA Center Host API Call*

Data Formats (XML and JSON)

Now that the Postman dashboard has been shown, it's time to discuss two of the most common data formats that are used with APIs. The first one is called **Extensible Markup Language (XML)**. This format may look familiar, as it is the same format that is commonly used when constructing web services. XML is a tag-based language, and a tag must begin with a < symbol and end with a > symbol. For example, a start tag named interface would be represented as <interface>. Another XML rule is that a section that is started must also be ended. So, if a start tag is called <interface>, the section needs to be closed by using an accompanying end tag. The end tag must be the same as the string of the start tag preceded by /. For example, the end tag for <interface> would be </interface>. Inside the start tag and end tag, you can use different code and parameters. Example 28-1 shows a snippet of XML output with both start and end tags as well as some configuration parameters.

Example 28-1 *XML Code Snippet*

```
<users>
   <user>
     <name>root</name>
   </user>
   <user>
     <name>Jason</name>
   </user>
   <user>
     <name>Jamie</name>
   </user>
   <user>
     <name>Luke</name>
   </user>
 </users>
```

Notice that each section of Example 28-1 has a start tag and an end tag. The data is structured so that it contains a section called "users," and within that section are four individual users:

- root
- Jason
- Jamie
- Luke

Before and after each username is the start tag <user> and the end tag </user>. The output also contains the start tag <name> and the end tag </name>. These tags are used for each user's name. If it is necessary to create another section to add another user, you can simply follow the same logic as used in the previous example and build out more XML code.

Remember that one of the key features of XML is that it is readable by both humans and applications. Indentation of XML sections is part of what makes it so readable. For instance, if indentation isn't used, it is harder to read and follow the sections in XML output. Although indentation is not required, it is certainly a recommended best practice from a legibility perspective. Example 28-2 shows an XML snippet listing available interfaces on a device. In this case, the XML code snippet has no indentation, so you can see how much less readable this snippet is than the one in Example 28-1.

Example 28-2 *XML Code Snippet Without Indentation*

```
<interfaces>
<interface>
<name>GigabitEthernet1</name>
</interface>
<interface>
<name>GigabitEthernet11</name>
</interface>
<interface>
<name>Loopback100</name>
</interface>
<interface>
<name>Loopback101</name>
</interface>
</interfaces>
```

The second data format that is important to cover is called **JavaScript Object Notation (JSON)**. Although JSON has not been around as long as XML, it is taking the industry by storm, and some say that it will soon replace XML. The reason this data format is gaining popularity is that it can be argued that JSON is much easier to work with than XML. It is simple to read and create, and the way the data is structured is much cleaner. JSON stores all its information in key/value pairs. As with XML, JSON is easier to read if the data is indented. However, even without indentation, JSON is extremely easy to read. As the name suggests, JSON uses objects for its format. Each JSON object starts with a { and ends with a }. (These are commonly referred to as curly braces.) Example 28-3 shows how JSON can be used to represent the same username example shown for XML in Example 28-1. You can see that it has four separate key/value pairs, one for each user's name.

Example 28-3 *JSON Code Snippet*

```
{
  "user": "root",
  "father": "Jason",
  "mother": "Jamie",
  "friend": "Luke"
}
```

In this JSON code snippet, you can see that the first key is user, and the value for that key is a unique username, root.

Now that the XML and JSON data formats have been explained, it is important to circle back to actually using the REST API and the associated responses and outcomes of doing so. First, we need to look at the HTTP response status codes. Most Internet users have experienced the dreaded "404 Not Found" error when navigating to a website. However, many users don't know what this error actually means. Table 28-5 lists the most common HTTP status codes as well as the reasons users may receive each one.

Key Topic

Table 28-5 HTTP Status Codes

HTTP Status Code	Result	Common Reason for Response Code
200	OK	Using GET or POST to exchange data with an API
201	Created	Creating resources by using a REST API call
400	Bad Request	Request failed due to client-side issue
401	Unauthorized	Client not authenticated to access site or API call
403	Forbidden	Access not granted based on supplied credentials
404	Not Found	Page at HTTP URL location does not exist or is hidden

Cisco DNA Center APIs

The Cisco DNA Center controller expects all incoming data from the REST API to be in JSON format. It is also important to note that the HTTP POST function is used to send the credentials to the Cisco DNA Center controller. Cisco DNA Center uses basic authentication to pass a username and password to the Cisco DNA Center Token API to authenticate users. This API is used to authenticate a user to the Cisco DNA Center controller to make additional API calls. Just as users do when logging in to a device via the CLI, if secured properly, they should be prompted for login credentials. The same method applies to using an API to authenticate to software. The key steps necessary to successfully set up the API call in Postman are as follows (see Figure 28-7):

Key Topic

Step 1. In the URL bar, enter **https://sandboxdnac.cisco.com/api/system/v1/auth/token** to target the Token API.

Step 2. Select the HTTP POST operation from the dropdown box.

Step 3. Under the Authorization tab, ensure that the type is set to Basic Auth.

Step 4. Enter **devnetuser** as the username and **Cisco123!** as the password.

Step 5. Select the Headers tab and enter **Content-Type** as the key.

Step 6. Select application/json as the value.

Step 7. Click the Send button to pass the credentials to the Cisco DNA Center controller via the Token API.

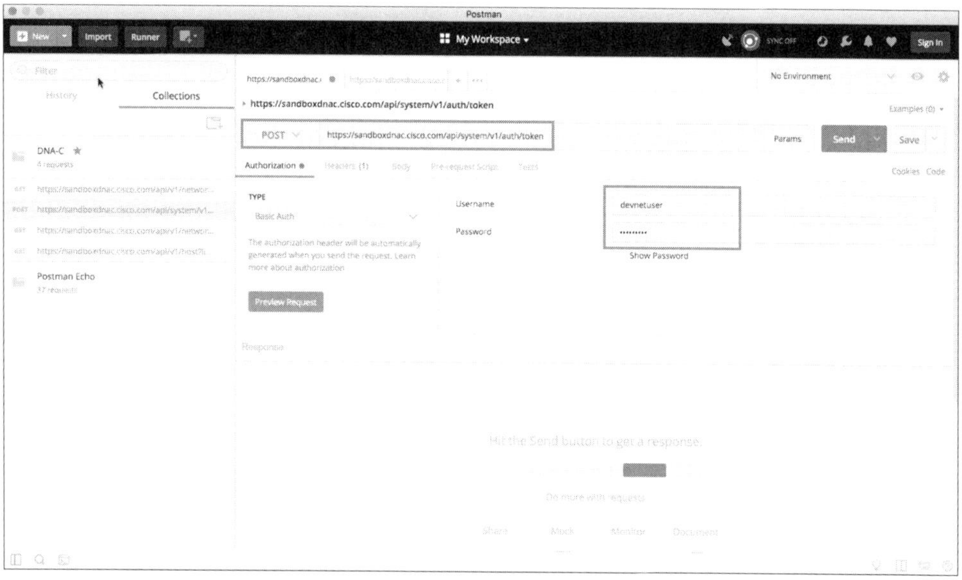

Figure 28-7 *Setting Up Postman to Authenticate with the Cisco DNA Center Controller*

You need a token for any future API calls to the Cisco DNA Center controller. When you are successfully authenticated to the Cisco DNA Center controller, you receive a token that contains a string that looks similar to the following:


```
"eyJ0eXAiOiJKV1QiLCJhbGciOiJIUzI1NiJ9.eyJzdWIiOiI1YTU4Y2QzN2UwNWJiYTAwOGVmNjJiOT
IiLCJhdXRoU291cmNlIjoiaW50ZXJuYWwiLCJ0ZW5hbnROYW1lIjoiVE5UMCIsInJvbGVzIjpbIjVhMz
E1MTYwOTA5MGZiYTY5OGIyZjViNyJdLCJ0ZW5hbnRJZCI6IjVhMzE1MTlkZTA1YmJhMDA4ZWY2
MWYwYSIsImV4cCI6MTUyMTQ5NzI2NCwidXNlcm5hbWUiOiJkZXZuZXR1c2VyIn0.tgAJfLc1OaUwa
JCX6lzfjPG7Om2x97oiTIozUpAzomM"
```


Think of it as a hash that is generated from the supplied login credentials. The token changes every time an authentication is made to the Cisco DNA Center controller. It is important to remember that when you are authenticated, the token you receive is usable only for the current authenticated session to the controller. If another user authenticates via the Token API, he or she will receive a unique token to be able to utilize the API based on his or her login credentials. Figure 28-8 shows the response from Cisco DNA Center after you issue the POST operation to the Token API.

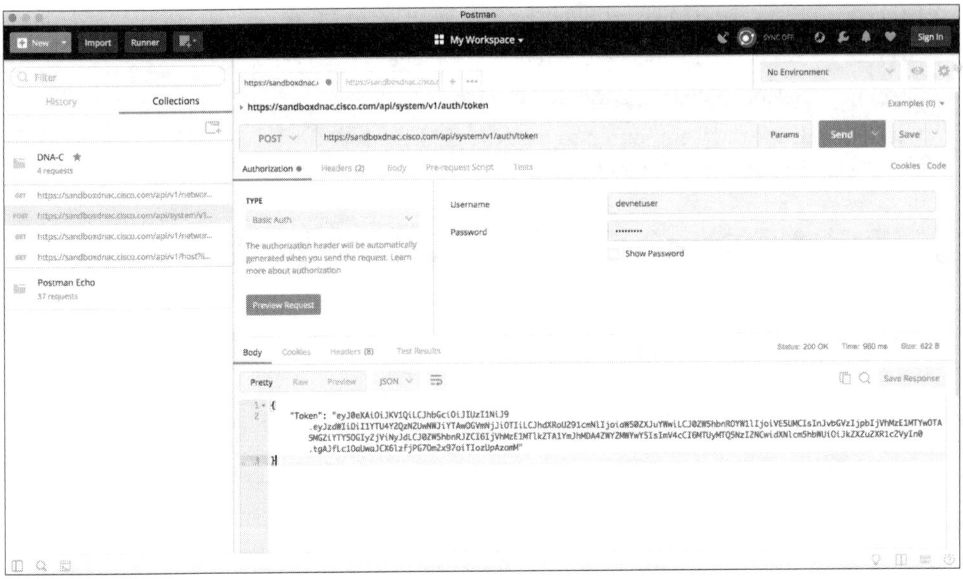

Figure 28-8 *Cisco DNA Center POST Operation*

You can see in the top right of the screen shown in Figure 28-8 that the received HTTP status code from the Cisco DNA Center controller is 200 OK. Based on the list in Table 28-5, you can tell that the HTTP status code 200 means that the API call completed successfully. In addition, you can see how long it took to process the HTTP POST request: 980 ms.

Now we can take a look at some of the other available API calls. The first API call that is covered in this section is the Network Device API, which allows users to retrieve a list of devices that are currently in inventory that are being managed by the Cisco DNA Center controller. You need to prepare Postman to use the token that was generated when you successfully authenticated to the controller by following these steps (see Figure 28-9):

Key Topic

Step 1. Copy the token you received earlier and click a new tab in Postman.

Step 2. In the URL bar enter **https://sandboxdnac.cisco.com/api/v1/network-device** to target the Network Device API.

Step 3. Select the HTTP GET operation from the dropdown box.

Step 4. Select the Headers tab and enter **Content-Type** as the key.

Step 5. Select application/json as the value.

Step 6. Add another key and enter **X-Auth-Token.**

Step 7. Paste the token in as the value.

Step 8. Click Send to pass the token to the Cisco DNA Center controller and perform an HTTP GET to retrieve a device inventory list using the Network Device API.

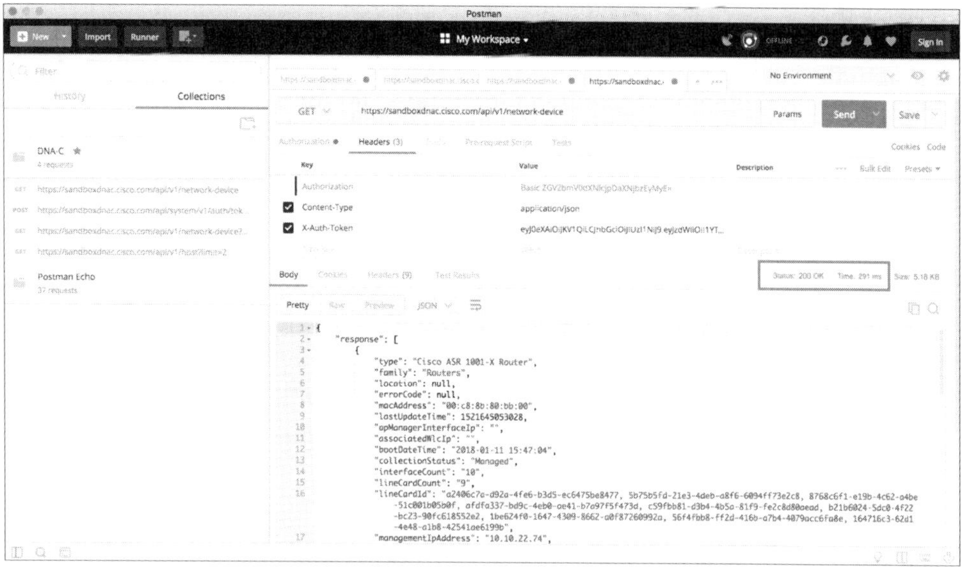

Figure 28-9 *Postman Setup for Retrieving the Network Device Inventory with an API Call*

> **NOTE** The token you receive will be different from the one shown in this book. Remember that a token is unique to each authenticated user.

Based on the response received from the Cisco DNA Center controller, you can see the HTTP status code 200 OK, and you can also see that a device inventory was received, in JSON format. Example 28-4 shows a list of devices in the inventory that were pulled using the Network Device API.

Example 28-4 *Device Inventory Pulled Using a Network Device API Call in Postman*

```
{
    "response": [
        {
            "type": "Cisco ASR 1001-X Router",
            "family": "Routers",
            "location": null,
            "errorCode": null,
            "macAddress": "00:c8:8b:80:bb:00",
            "lastUpdateTime": 1521645053028,
            "apManagerInterfaceIp": "",
            "associatedWlcIp": "",
            "bootDateTime": "2018-01-11 15:47:04",
            "collectionStatus": "Managed",
            "interfaceCount": "10",
            "lineCardCount": "9",
```

```
            "lineCardId": "a2406c7a-d92a-4fe6-b3d5-ec6475be8477,
5b75b5fd-21e3-4deb-a8f6-6094ff73e2c8, 8768c6f1-e19b-4c62-a4be-51c001b05b0f,
afdfa337-bd9c-4eb0-ae41-b7a97f5f473d, c59fbb81-d3b4-4b5a-81f9-fe2c8d80aead,
b21b6024-5dc0-4f22-bc23-90fc618552e2, 1be624f0-1647-4309-8662-a0f87260992a,
56f4fbb8-ff2d-416b-a7b4-4079acc6fa8e, 164716c3-62d1-4e48-a1b8-42541ae6199b",
            "managementIpAddress": "10.10.22.74",
            "memorySize": "3956371104",
            "platformId": "ASR1001-X",
            "reachabilityFailureReason": "",
            "reachabilityStatus": "Reachable",
            "series": "Cisco ASR 1000 Series Aggregation Services Routers",
            "snmpContact": "",
            "snmpLocation": "",
            "tunnelUdpPort": null,
            "waasDeviceMode": null,
            "locationName": null,
            "role": "BORDER ROUTER",
            "hostname": "asr1001-x.abc.inc",
            "upTime": "68 days, 23:23:31.43",
            "inventoryStatusDetail": "<status><general code=\"SUCCESS\"/></status>",
            "softwareVersion": "16.6.1",
            "roleSource": "AUTO",
            "softwareType": "IOS-XE",
            "collectionInterval": "Global Default",
            "lastUpdated": "2018-03-21 15:10:53",
            "tagCount": "0",
            "errorDescription": null,
            "serialNumber": "FXS1932Q1SE",
            "instanceUuid": "d5bbb4a9-a14d-4347-9546-89286e9f30d4",
            "id": "d5bbb4a9-a14d-4347-9546-89286e9f30d4"
        },
Output Snipped for brevity
```

By now you should see how powerful APIs can be. Within a few moments, users are able to gather a tremendous amount of information about the devices currently being managed by the Cisco DNA Center controller. In the time it takes someone to log in to a device using the CLI and issue all the relevant **show** commands to gather data, an API call can be used to gather that data for the entire network. APIs give network engineers time to do other things!

When using APIs, it is common to manipulate data by using filters and offsets. Say that a user wants to leverage the Network Device API to gather information on only the second device in the inventory. This is where the API documentation becomes so valuable. Most APIs have documentation that explains what they can be used to accomplish.

Key Topic

In Postman, it is possible to modify the Network Device API URL and add **?limit=1** to the end of the URL to show only a single device in the inventory. It is also possible to add the **&offset=2** command to the end of the URL to state that only the second device in the inventory should be shown. These query parameters are part of the API and can be invoked using a client like Postman as well. Although it may sound confusing, the **limit** keyword simply states that a user only wants to retrieve one record from the inventory; the **offset** command states that the user wants that one record to be the second record in the inventory. Figure 28-10 shows how to adjust the Network Device API URL in Postman to show information on only the second device in the inventory.

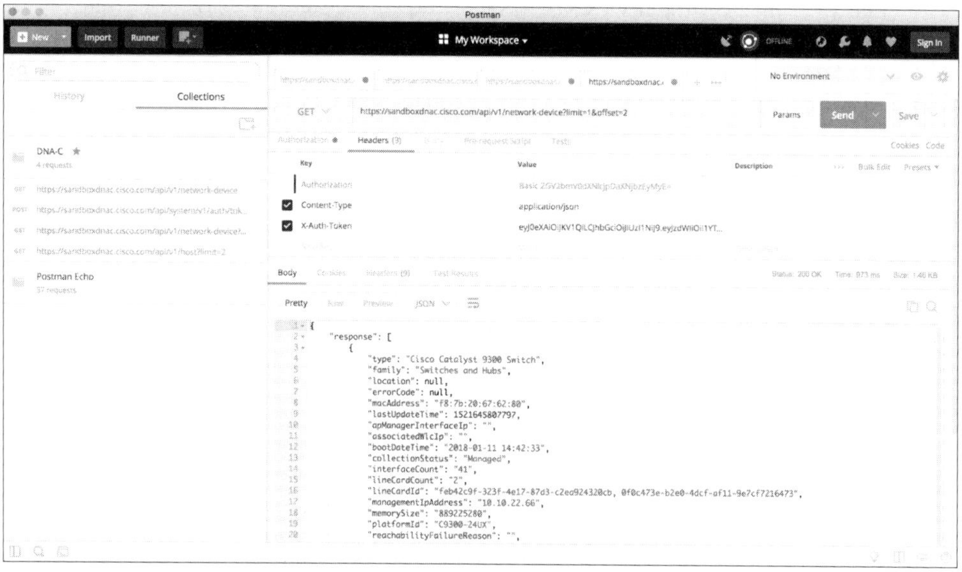

Figure 28-10 *Filtered Output of the Network Device API*

You can see from the response that the second device is consistent with the output that was shown in the initial Network Device API call (refer to Example 28-4). This device is a Cisco Catalyst 9300 switch with the MAC address f8:7b:20:67:62:80.

Cisco vManage APIs

This section discusses the various APIs available in the Cisco SD-WAN (specifically, the vManage controller). This section provides some examples of how to interact with APIs programmatically by using Postman. Leveraging Cisco SD-WAN APIs is a bit different from using the Cisco DNA Center APIs, but the two processes are quite similar. As when using a Cisco DNA Center API, with a Cisco SD-WAN API you need to provide login credentials to the API in order to be able to utilize the API calls. Some key pieces of information are necessary to successfully set up the API call in Postman:

- The URL bar must have the API call to target the Authentication API.
- The HTTP POST operation is used to send the username and password to Cisco vManage.
- The Headers Content-Type key must be application/x-www-form-urlencoded.
- The body must contain keys with the j_username devnetuser and thej_password Cisco123!.

The steps for connecting to APIs are different for Cisco SD-WAN than for Cisco DNA Center. Detailed steps for setting up the Postman environment for Cisco SD-WAN are available at https://developer.cisco.com/sdwan/. The Cisco DNA Center Postman environment setup steps are available at https://developer.cisco.com/learning/tracks/dnacenter-programmability/.

To set up a Postman environment, you can simply download steps into Postman from DevNet by going to https://developer.cisco.com/sdwan/. By doing so, you can quickly set up an environment that contains all the necessary authentication details and practice with the APIs without having to spend much time getting familiar with the details of Postman. Figure 28-11 shows the Postman environment set up for the Cisco SD-WAN API calls—specifically, the Authentication API.

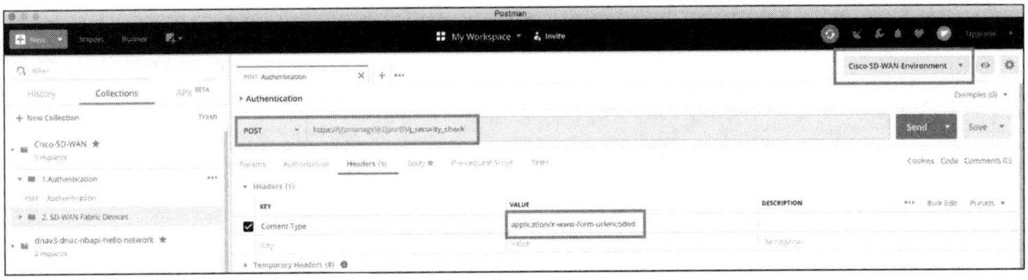

Figure 28-11 *Cisco vManage Authentication API Setup for Postman*

When the Postman environment is all set up and you click the Send button, the credentials are passed to vManage using the Authentication API (see Figure 28-12). The response you receive delivers something called a *Java session ID*, which is displayed as JSESSIONID. This is similar to the Cisco DNA Center token you worked with earlier in this chapter. This session ID is passed to vManage for all future API calls for this user. The HTTP status code 200 OK indicates a successful POST to vManage with the proper credentials.

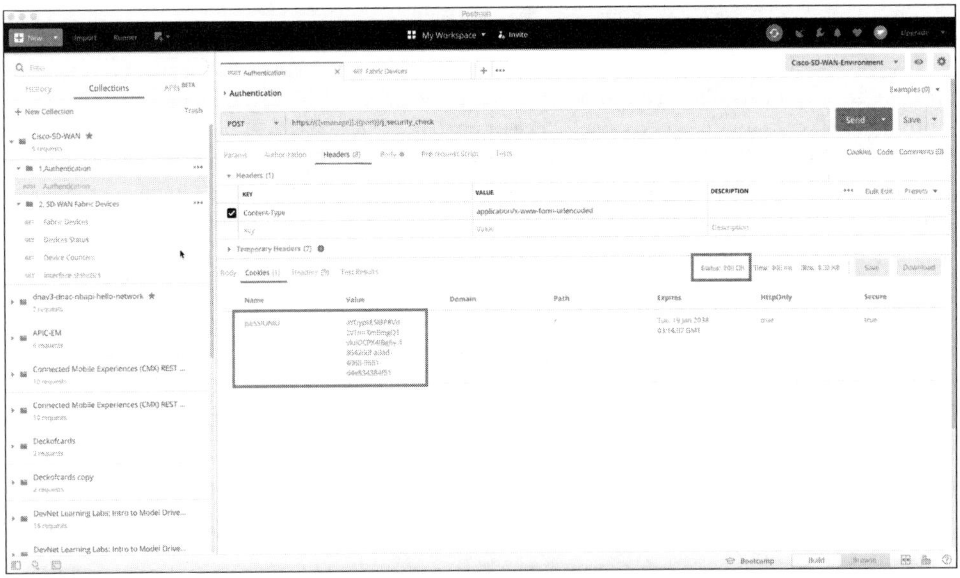

Figure 28-12 *Successful HTTP POST to Cisco vManage Authentication API*

Now let's look at another API call that collects an inventory of fabric devices within Cisco vManage. Using the HTTP GET operation, this API collects the requested information and displays it in Postman. In Figure 28-13 you can see a lot from Cisco vManage's response. You can see the URL for this API in the URL bar, and you can also see the HTTP GET request. You can also see that the response is in JSON format, which makes the data easy to read and consume.

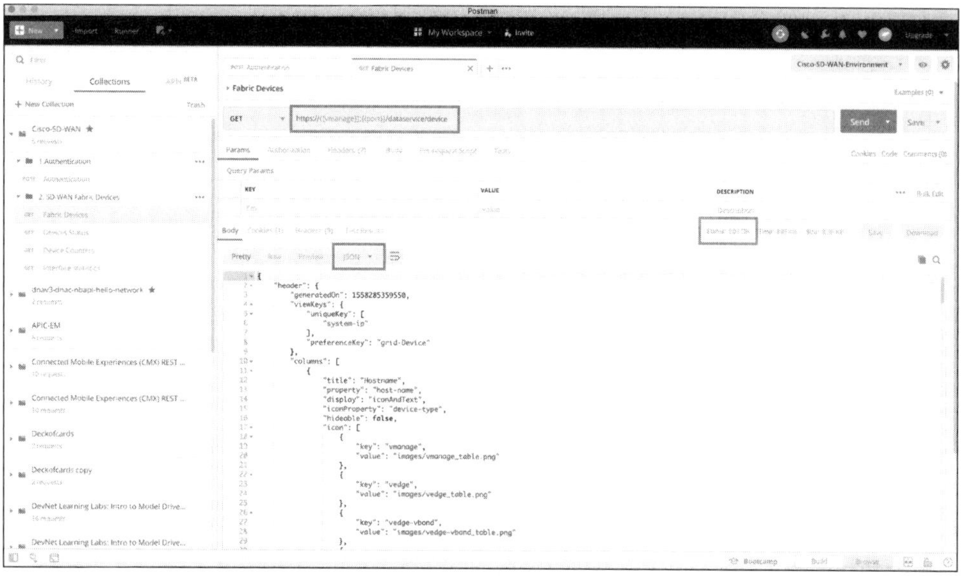

Figure 28-13 *Successful HTTP GET to the Cisco vManage Fabric Device API*

If you scroll down in the response, you can see a list of devices under the "data" key received from the API call. This list contains a series of information about each fabric device within Cisco vManage. Some of the information you can see in Figure 28-14 is as follows:

- Device ID
- System IP
- Host name
- Reachability
- Status
- Device type
- Site ID

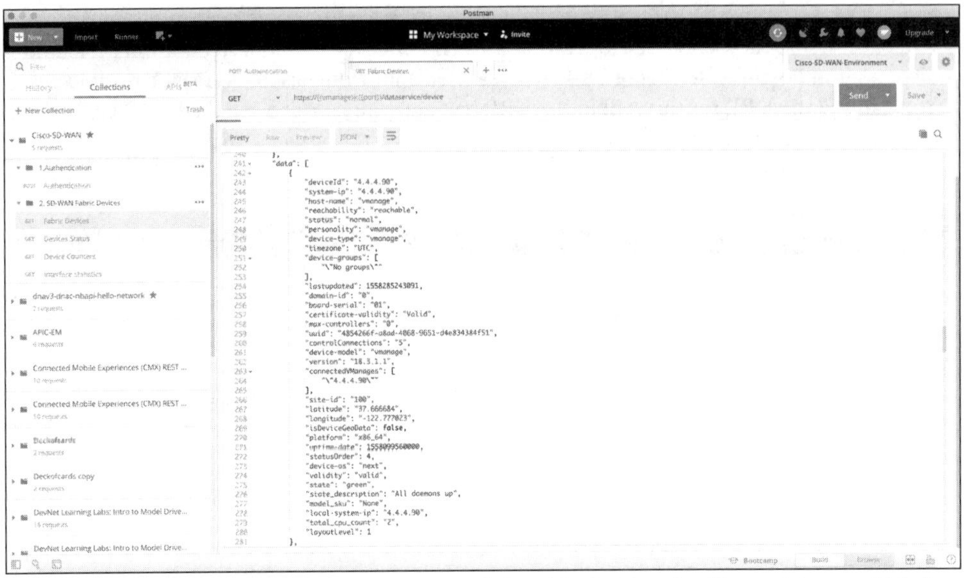

Figure 28-14 *Data Received with a Successful HTTP GET to the Cisco vManage Fabric Device API*

As you can see, a single API call has the power to gather a significant amount of information. How the data is used is up to the person making the API calls and collecting the data. All the tools, processes, and APIs can be leveraged to provide tremendous value to the business—from visibility into the environment to building relevant use cases to be consumed by the business or its customers.

Data Models and Supporting Protocols

This section provides a high-level overview of some of the most common data models and tools and how they are leveraged in a programmatic approach:

- Yet Another Next Generation (**YANG**) modeling language
- Network Configuration Protocol (NETCONF)
- RESTCONF

YANG Data Models

SNMP is widely used for fault handling and monitoring. However, it is not often used for configuration changes. CLI scripting is used more often than other methods. YANG data models are an alternative to SNMP MIBs and are becoming the standard for data definition languages. YANG, which is defined in RFC 6020, uses data models. Data models are used to describe whatever can be configured on a device, everything that can be monitored on a device, and all the administrative actions that can be executed on a device, such as resetting counters or rebooting the device. This includes all the notifications that the device is capable of generating. All these variables can be represented within a YANG model. Data models are very powerful in that they create a uniform way to describe data, which can be beneficial across vendors' platforms. Data models allow network operators to configure, monitor, and interact with network devices holistically across the entire enterprise environment.

YANG models use a tree structure. Within that structure, the models are similar in format to XML and are constructed in modules. These modules are hierarchical in nature and contain all the different data and types that make up a YANG device model. YANG models make a clear distinction between configuration data and state information. The tree structure represents how to reach a specific element of the model, and the elements can be either configurable or not configurable.

Every element has a defined type. For example, an interface can be configured to be on or off. However, the operational interface state cannot be changed; for example, if the options are only up or down, it is either up or down, and nothing else is possible. Example 28-5 illustrates a simple YANG module taken from RFC 6020.

Example 28-5 *YANG Model Example*

```
container food {
  choice snack {
      case sports-arena {
          leaf pretzel {
              type empty;
          }
          leaf popcorn {
              type empty;
          }
      }
      case late-night {
          leaf chocolate {
              type enumeration {
                  enum dark;
                  enum milk;
                  enum first-available;
              }
          }
      }
  }
}
```

The output in Example 28-5 can be read as follows: There is food. Of that food, there is a choice of snacks. The snack choices are pretzels and popcorn. If it is late at night, the snack choices are two different types of chocolate. A choice must be made to have milk chocolate or dark chocolate, and if the consumer is in a hurry and does not want to wait, the consumer can have the first available chocolate, whether it is milk chocolate or dark chocolate. Example 28-6 shows a more network-oriented example that uses the same structure.

Example 28-6 *Network-Oriented YANG Model*

```
list interface {
    key "name";

    leaf name {
        type string;
    }
    leaf speed {
        type enumeration {
            enum 10m;
            enum 100m;
            enum auto;
        }
    }
    leaf observed-speed {
        type uint32;
        config false;
    }
}
```

The YANG model in Example 28-6 can be read as follows: There is a list of interfaces. Of the available interfaces, there is a specific interface that has three configurable speeds. Those speeds are 10 Mbps, 100 Mbps, and auto, as listed in the leaf named speed. The leaf named observed-speed cannot be configured due to the **config false** command. This is because as the leaf is named, the speeds in this leaf are what was auto-detected (observed); hence, it is not a configurable leaf. This is because it represents the auto-detected value on the interface, not a configurable value.

NETCONF

NETCONF, defined in RFC 4741 and RFC 6241, is an IETF standard protocol that uses the YANG data models to communicate with the various devices on the network. NETCONF runs over SSH, TLS, and (although not common), Simple Object Access Protocol (SOAP). Some of the key differences between SNMP and NETCONF are listed in Table 28-6. One of the most important differences is that SNMP can't distinguish between configuration data and operational data, but NETCONF can. Another key differentiator is that NETCONF uses paths to describe resources, whereas SNMP uses object identifiers (OIDs). A NETCONF path can be similar to interfaces/interface/eth0, which is much more descriptive than what you would expect from SNMP. The following is a list of some of the common use cases for NETCONF:

- Collecting the status of specific fields
- Changing the configuration of specific fields
- Taking administrative actions
- Sending event notifications
- Backing up and restoring configurations
- Testing configurations before finalizing the transaction

Table 28-6 Differences Between SNMP and NETCONF

Feature	SNMP	NETCONF
Resources	OIDs	Paths
Data models	Defined in MIBs	YANG core models
Data modeling language	SMI	YANG
Management operations	SNMP	NETCONF
Encoding	BER	either XML or JSON
Transport stack	UDP	SSH/TCP

Transactions are all or nothing. There is no order of operations or sequencing within a transaction. This means there is no part of the configuration that is done first; the configuration is deployed all at the same time. Transactions are processed in the same order every time on every device. Transactions, when deployed, run in a parallel state and do not have any impact on each other. Parallel transactions touching different areas of the configuration on a device do not overwrite or interfere with each other. They also do not impact each other if the same transaction is run against multiple devices.

Example 28-7 provides an example of a NETCONF element from RFC 4741. This NETCONF output can be read as follows: There is an XML list of users named users. In that list, there are individual users named Dave, Rafael, and Dirk.

Example 28-7 *NETCONF Element Example*

```
<rpc-reply message-id="101"
        xmlns="urn:ietf:params:xml:ns:netconf:base:1.0">
     <data>
       <top xmlns="http://example.com/schema/1.2/config">
         <users>
           <user>
             <name>Dave</name>
           </user>
           <user>
             <name>Rafael</name>
           </user>
           <user>
             <name>Dirk</name>
           </user>
         </users>
       </top>
     </data>
   </rpc-reply>
```

An alternative way of looking at this type of NETCONF output is to simply look at it as though it were a shopping list. Example 28-8 provides an example of the shopping list concept. It can be read as follows: There is a group called beverages. Of these beverages, there are soft drinks and tea. The available soft drinks are cola and root beer. Of the available tea, there is sweetened or unsweetened.

Example 28-8 *Shopping List Example*

```
Beverages
    Soft Drinks
        Cola
        Root Beer
    Tea
        Sweetened
        Unsweetened
```

Figure 28-15 illustrates how NETCONF uses YANG data models to interact with network devices and then talk back to management applications. The dotted lines show the devices talking back directly to the management applications, and the solid lines illustrate the NETCONF protocol talking between the management applications and the devices.

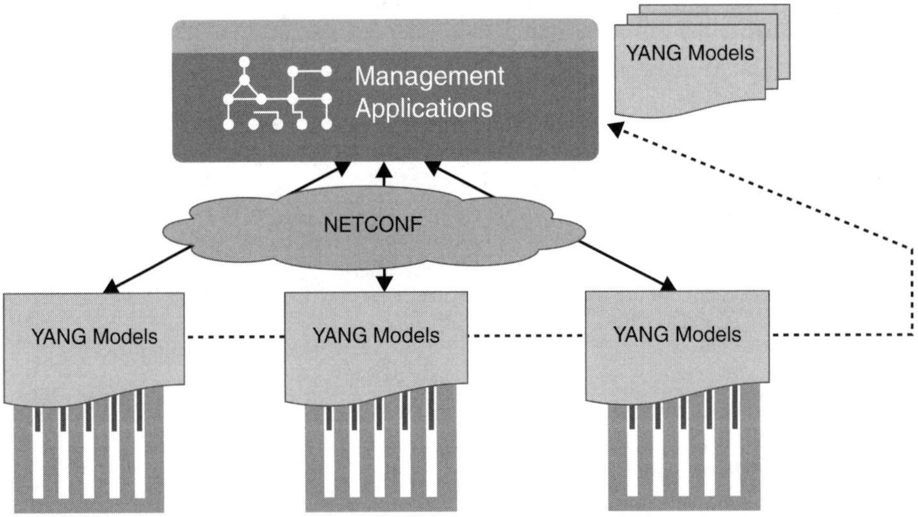

Figure 28-15 *NETCONF/YANG Interfacing with Management Applications*

NETCONF exchanges information called *capabilities* when the TCP connection has been made. Capabilities tell the client what the device it's connected to can do. Furthermore, other information can be gathered by using the common NETCONF operations shown in Table 28-7.

Table 28-7 NETCONF Operations

NETCONF Operation	Description
<get>	Requests running configuration and state information of the device
<get-config>	Requests some or all of the configuration from a datastore
<edit-config>	Edits a configuration datastore by using CRUD operations
<copy-config>	Copies the configuration to another datastore
<delete-config>	Deletes the configuration

Information and configurations are stored in datastores. Datastores can be manipulated by using the NETCONF operations listing in Table 28-7. NETCONF uses Remote Procedure Call (RPC) messages in XML format to send the information between hosts.

Now that we've looked at the basics of NETCONF and XML, let's examine some actual examples of a NETCONF RPC message. Example 28-9 shows an example of an OSPF NETCONF RPC message that provides the OSPF routing configuration of an IOS XE device.

Example 28-9 *NETCONF OSPF Configuration Example*

```
<rpc-reply message-id="urn:uuid:0e2c04cf-9119-4e6a-8c05-238ee7f25208"
xmlns="urn:ietf:params:xml:ns:netconf:base:1.0" xmlns:nc="urn:ietf:params:
xml:ns:netconf:base:1.0">
  <data>
    <native xmlns="http://cisco.com/ns/yang/ned/ios">
      <router>
        <ospf>
          <id>100</id>
          <redistribute>
            <connected>
              <redist-options>
                <subnets/>
              </redist-options>
            </connected>
          </redistribute>
          <network>
            <ip>10.10.0.0</ip>
            <mask>0.0.255.255</mask>
            <area>0</area>
          </network>
          <network>
            <ip>20.20.0.0</ip>
            <mask>0.0.255.255</mask>
            <area>0</area>
          </network>
          <network>
            <ip>100.100.0.0</ip>
            <mask>0.0.255.255</mask>
            <area>0</area>
          </network>
        </ospf>
      </router>
    </native>
  </data>
</rpc-reply>
```

28

The same OSPF router configuration that would be seen in the command-line interface of a Cisco router can be seen using NETCONF. The data is just structured in XML format rather than what users are accustomed to seeing in the CLI. It is easy to read the output in these examples because of how legible XML is. Example 28-10 saves the configuration of a Cisco network device by leveraging NETCONF.

Example 28-10 *NETCONF Save Config Example*

```
<?xml version="1.0" encoding="utf-8"?>
<rpc xmlns="urn:ietf:params:xml:ns:netconf:base:1.0" message-id="">
  <cisco-ia:save-config xmlns:cisco-ia="http://cisco.com/yang/cisco-ia"/>
</rpc>
```

RESTCONF

RESTCONF, defined in RFC 8040, is used to programmatically interface with data defined in YANG models while also using the datastore concepts defined in NETCONF. There is a common misconception that RESTCONF is meant to replace NETCONF, but this is not the case. Both are very common methods used for programmability and data manipulation. In fact, RESTCONF uses the same YANG models as NETCONF and Cisco IOS XE. The goal of RESTCONF is to provide a RESTful API experience while still leveraging the device abstraction capabilities provided by NETCONF. RESTCONF supports the following HTTP methods and CRUD operations:

- GET
- POST
- PUT
- DELETE
- OPTIONS

The RESTCONF requests and responses can use either JSON or XML structured data formats. Example 28-11 shows a brief example of a RESTCONF GET request on a Cisco router to retrieve the logging severity level that is configured. This example uses JSON instead of XML. Notice the HTTP status 200, which indicates that the request was successful.

Example 28-11 *RESTCONF GET Logging Severity Example*

```
RESTCONF GET

------------------------

URL: https://10.85.116.59:443/restconf/data/Cisco-IOS-XE-native:native/logging/
monitor/severity

Headers: {'Accept-Encoding': 'gzip, deflate',  'Accept': 'application/
yang-data+json, application/yang-data.errors+json'}
```

```
Body:

RESTCONF RESPONSE

----------------------------

200

{

  "Cisco-IOS-XE-native:severity": "critical"

}
```

Cisco DevNet

The examples and tools discussed in this chapter are all available for use and practice at Cisco **DevNet** (http://developer.cisco.com). Network operators who are looking to enhance or increase their skills with APIs, coding, Python, or even controller concepts can find a wealth of help at DevNet. At DevNet it is easy to find learning labs and content to help solidify current knowledge in network programmability. Whether you're just getting started or are a seasoned programming professional, DevNet is the place to be! This section provides a high-level overview of DevNet, including the different sections of DevNet and some of the labs and content that are available. Figure 28-16 shows the DevNet main page.

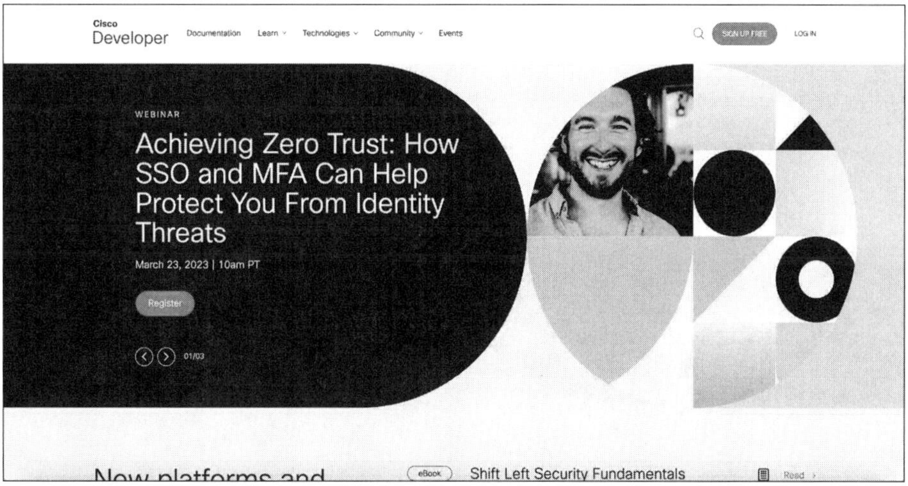

Figure 28-16 *DevNet Main Page*

Across the top of the main page are a few menu options:

- Documentation
- Learn
- Technologies

- Community
- Events

Documentation

The Documentation page is a single place to get information on API documentation for a variety of solutions such as Cisco DNA Center, Cisco SD-WAN, IoT, Collaboration, and more. These API references include information on how to programmatically interact with these solutions. This is a great place to start when learning how to interact with devices and software-defined controllers.

Learn

The Learn page is where you can navigate the different offerings that DevNet has available. Under this tab are subsections for guided learning tracks, which guide you through various technologies and the associated API labs. Some of the labs you interact with are Programming the Cisco Digital Network Architecture (DNA), ACI Programmability, Getting Started with Cisco WebEx Teams APIs, and Introduction to DevNet. When you choose a learning lab and start a module, the website tracks all your progress so you can go away and come back and continue where you left off. This is helpful for continuing your education over the course of multiple days or weeks.

Technologies

The Technologies page allows you to pick relevant content based on the technology you want to study and dive directly into the associated labs and training for that technology. Figure 28-17 illustrates some of the networking content that is currently available.

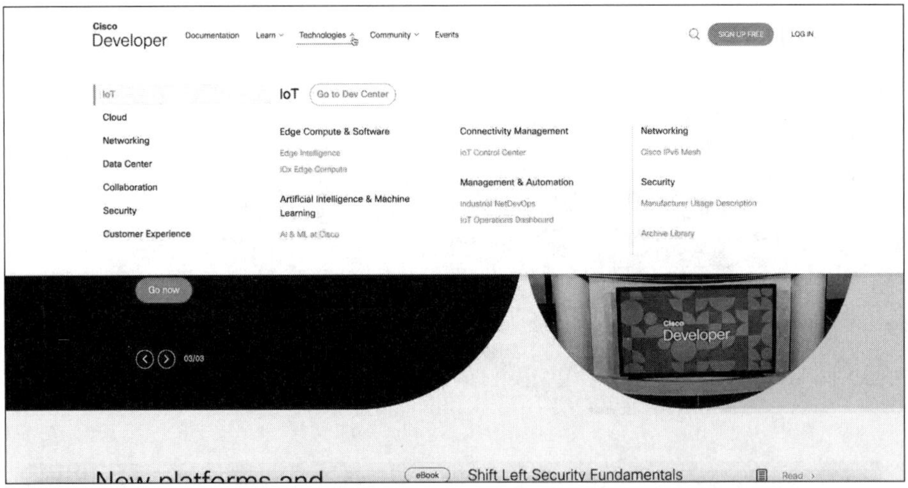

Figure 28-17 *DevNet Technologies Page*

> **NOTE** Available labs may differ from what is shown in this chapter. Please visit http://developer.cisco.com to see the latest content available and to interact with the latest learning labs and sandbox environments.

Community

Perhaps one of the most important sections of DevNet is the Community page. This is where users have access to many different people at various stages of learning. DevNet ambassadors and evangelists are available to help at various stages of your learning journey. The Community page puts the latest events and news at your fingertips. This is also the place to read blogs, sign up for developer forums, and follow DevNet on all major social media platforms. This is a safe zone for asking questions, simple or complex. The DevNet Community page is the place to start for all things Cisco and network programmability. Figure 28-18 shows some of the available options for users on the Community page.

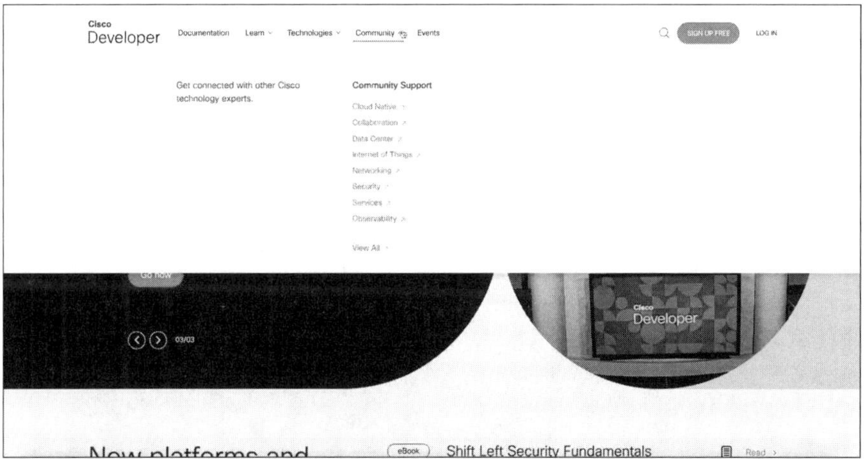

Figure 28-18 *DevNet Community Page*

Events

The DevNet Events page, shown in Figure 28-19, provides a list of all events that have happened in the past and that will be happening in the future. This is where a user can find the upcoming DevNet Express events as well as conferences where DevNet will be presenting. Bookmark this page if you plan on attending any live events.

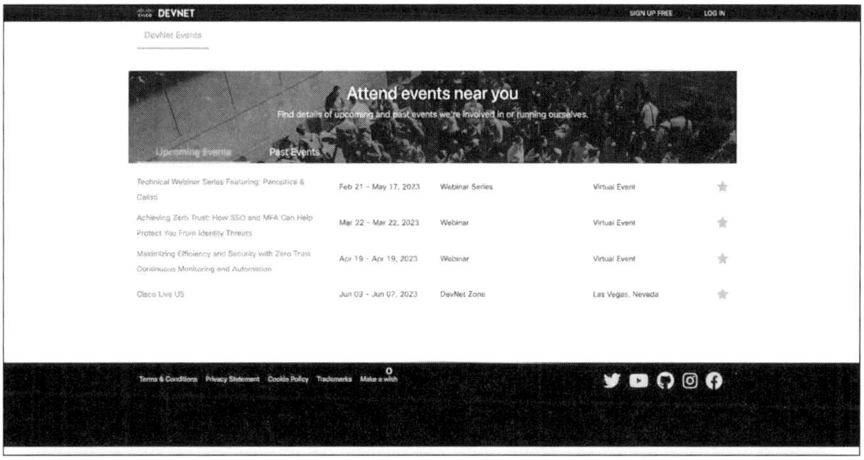

Figure 28-19 *DevNet Events Page*

GitHub

One of the most efficient and commonly adopted ways of using version control is by using GitHub. *GitHub* is a hosted web-based repository for code. It has capabilities for bug tracking and task management as well. Using GitHub is one of the easiest ways to track changes in your files, collaborate with other developers, and share code with the online community. It is a great place to look for code to get started on programmability. Often times, other engineers or developers are trying to accomplish similar tasks and have already created and tested the code necessary to do so. One of the most powerful features of using GitHub is the ability to rate and provide feedback on other developers' code. Peer review is encouraged in the coding community. Figure 28-20 shows the main GitHub web page that appears after you log in.

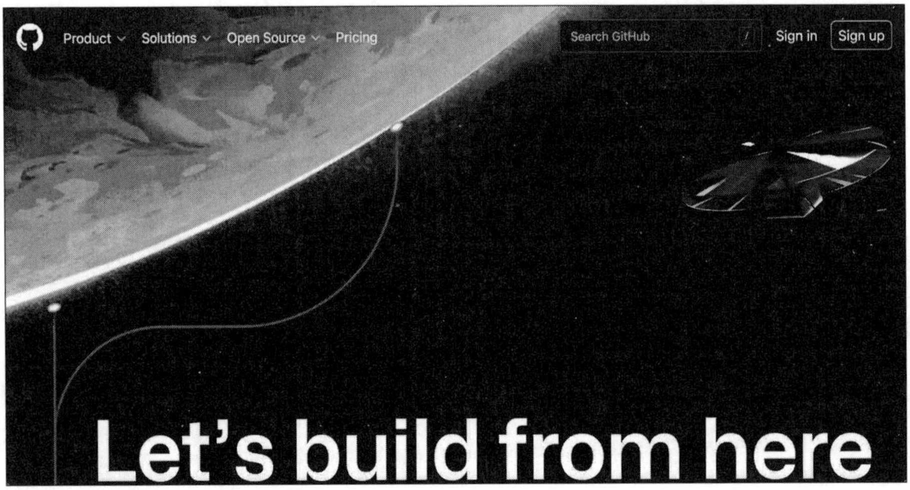

Figure 28-20 *GitHub Main Web Page*

GitHub provides a guide that steps through how to create a repository, start a branch, add comments, and open a pull request. You can also just start a GitHub project when you are more familiar with the GitHub tool and its associated processes.

Projects are repositories that contain code files. GitHub provides a single pane to create, edit, and share code files. Figure 28-21 shows a repository called ENCORE that contains three files:

- ENCORE.txt
- JSON_Example.txt
- README.md

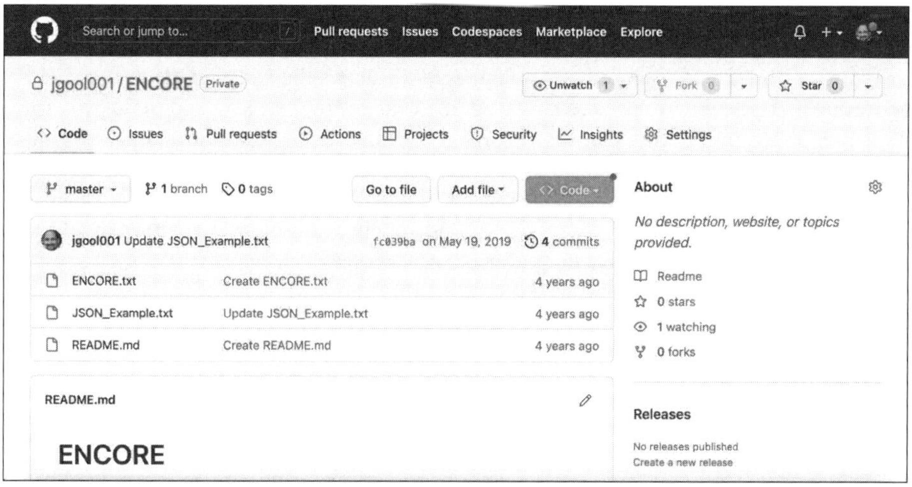

Figure 28-21 *GitHub ENCORE Repository*

GitHub also gives a great summary of commit logs, so when you save a change in one of your files or create a new file, GitHub shows details about it on the main repository page (refer to Figure 28-21). If you drill down into one of the files in the repository, you can see how easy it is to edit and save code. If you drill down into JSON_Example.txt, for example, GitHub shows its contents and how to edit the file in the repository. If you click the filename JSON_Example.txt, you can see that the file has seven lines of code and it is 77 bytes in size. Figure 28-22 shows the contents of the JSON_Example.txt file and the options available with the file.

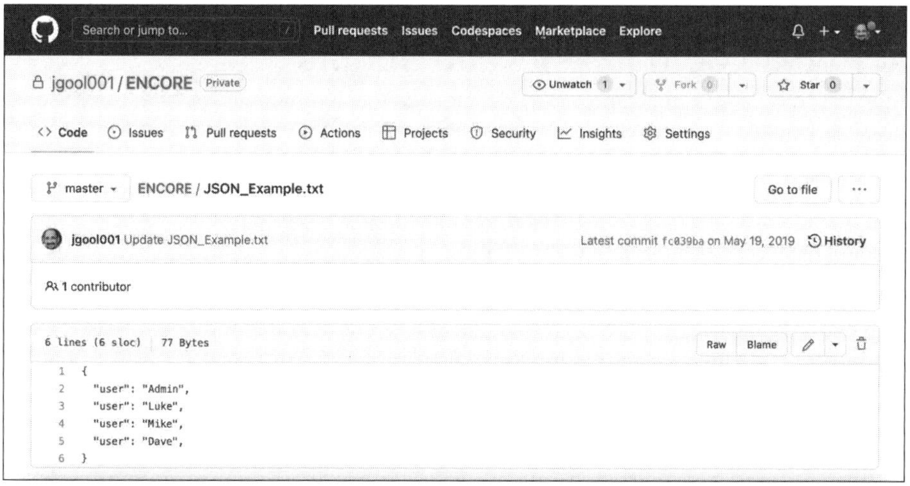

Figure 28-22 *JSON_Example.txt Contents*

The pencil allows you to go into editing mode and alter the file contents. This editor is very similar to any text editor. You can simply type into the editor or copy and paste code from other files directly into it. The example in Figure 28-23 shows the addition of another user, named Zuul. If the code were to be committed, the changes in the file would be saved with the new user added to the file. Now that the file is available in the repository, other GitHub users and developers can contribute to this code or add and delete lines of code based on the code that was originally created. For example, if a user has some code to add a new user via JSON syntax, someone could use that code and simply modify the usernames or add to the code to enhance it. This is the true power of sharing code.

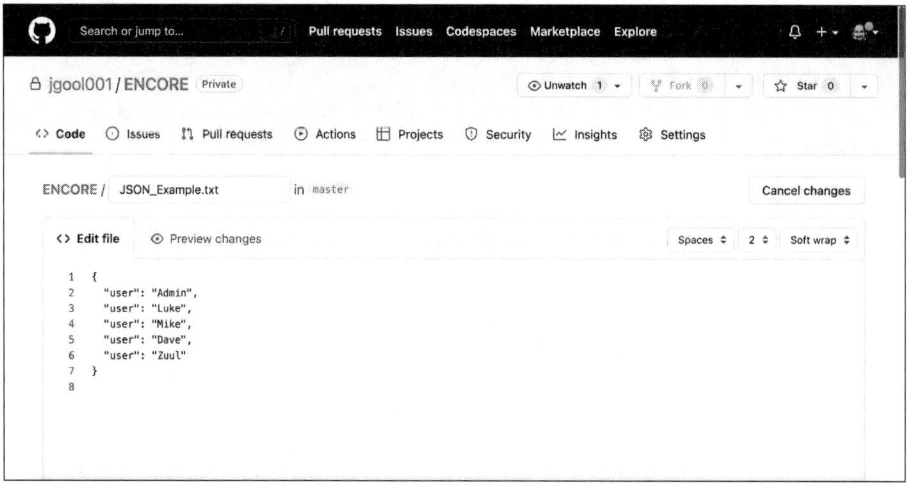

Figure 28-23 *Editing the JSON_Example.txt Contents*

Basic Python Components and Scripts

Python has by a longshot become one of the most common programming languages in terms of network programmability. Learning to use programming languages can be daunting. Python is one of the easier languages to get started with and interpret. Although this section does not cover how to create or write complex programs or scripts in Python, it does teach some of the fundamental skills necessary to be able to interpret Python scripts. When you understand the basics of interpreting what a Python script is designed to do, it will be easier to understand and leverage other scripts that are available.

GitHub has some amazing Python scripts available for download that come with very detailed instructions and documentation. Everything covered in this section is taken from publicly available GitHub scripts. This section leverages the new knowledge you have gained in this chapter about APIs, HTTP operations, DevNet, and GitHub. Example 28-12 shows a Python script that sets up the environment to log in to the Cisco DNA Center sandbox. This script uses the same credentials used with the Token API earlier in this chapter.

NOTE The scripts covered in this section are available at https://github.com/.

Example 28-12 *Env_Lab.py*

```
"""Set the Environment Information Needed to Access Your Lab!

The provided sample code in this repository will reference this file to get the
information needed to connect to your lab backend.  You provide this info here
once and the scripts in this repository will access it as needed by the lab.


Copyright (c) 2018 Cisco and/or its affiliates.

Permission is hereby granted, free of charge, to any person obtaining a copy
of this software and associated documentation files (the "Software"), to deal
in the Software without restriction, including without limitation the rights
to use, copy, modify, merge, publish, distribute, sublicense, and/or sell
copies of the Software, and to permit persons to whom the Software is
furnished to do so, subject to the following conditions:

The above copyright notice and this permission notice shall be included in all
copies or substantial portions of the Software.

THE SOFTWARE IS PROVIDED "AS IS", WITHOUT WARRANTY OF ANY KIND, EXPRESS OR
IMPLIED, INCLUDING BUT NOT LIMITED TO THE WARRANTIES OF MERCHANTABILITY,
FITNESS FOR A PARTICULAR PURPOSE AND NONINFRINGEMENT. IN NO EVENT SHALL THE
AUTHORS OR COPYRIGHT HOLDERS BE LIABLE FOR ANY CLAIM, DAMAGES OR OTHER
LIABILITY, WHETHER IN AN ACTION OF CONTRACT, TORT OR OTHERWISE, ARISING FROM,
OUT OF OR IN CONNECTION WITH THE SOFTWARE OR THE USE OR OTHER DEALINGS IN THE
SOFTWARE.
"""



# User Input

# Please select the lab environment that you will be using today
#     sandbox - Cisco DevNet Always-On / Reserved Sandboxes
#     express - Cisco DevNet Express Lab Backend
#     custom  - Your Own "Custom" Lab Backend
ENVIRONMENT_IN_USE = "sandbox"

# Set the 'Environment Variables' based on the lab environment in use
if ENVIRONMENT_IN_USE == "sandbox":
    dnac = {
        "host": "sandboxdnac.cisco.com",
        "port": 443,
        "username": "devnetuser",
        "password": "Cisco123!"
    }
```

28

The Env_Lab.py python script starts with three quotation marks. These three quotation marks begin and end a multiple-line string. A *string* is simply one or more alphanumeric characters. A string can comprise many numbers or letters, depending on the Python version in use. In the case of this script, the creator used a multiple-line string to put additional overall comments into the script. This is not mandatory, but you can see that comments are helpful. The # character indicates a comment in the Python script file. Such comments usually describe the intent of an action within the code. Comments often appear right above the action they describe. Some scripts have a comment for each action, and some are not documented very well, if at all. The comments in this Env_Lab.py script indicate that there are three available options for selecting the lab environment to use:

- **Sandbox:** The line in this Python script that says ENVIRONMENT IN USE= "sandbox" corresponds to the selection of the sandbox type of lab environments available through DevNet. In this instance, "sandbox" refers to the always-on and reserved sandboxes that can be accessed through http://developer.cisco.com.
- **Express:** This is the back end that is used for the DevNet Express Events that are held globally at various locations and Cisco office locations, as mentioned earlier in this chapter.
- **Custom:** This is used in the event that there is already a Cisco DNA Center installed either in a lab or another facility, and it needs to be accessed using this script.

This chapter uses the sandbox lab environment for all examples and explanations.

As you can see in the Python script in Example 28-12, a few variables are used to target the DevNet Cisco DNA Center sandbox specifically. Table 28-8 describes these variables.

Table 28-8 Python Variables for Cisco DNA Center Sandbox in Env_Lab.py

Variable	Value	Description
host	**sandboxdnac.cisco.com**	Cisco DNA Center sandbox URL
port	**443**	TCP port to access URL securely (HTTPS)
username	**devnetuser**	Username to log in to Cisco DNA Center sandbox (via API or GUI)
password	**Cisco123!**	Password to log in to Cisco DNA Center sandbox (via API or GUI)

The variables shown in Table 28-8 should look familiar as they are similar to the JSON data format that was discussed earlier in this chapter. Remember that JSON uses key/value pairs and is extremely easy to read and interpret. In Example 28-13, you can see the key/value pair "username": "devnetuser". The structure used to hold all the key/value pairs in this script is called a *dictionary*. In this particular Python script, the dictionary is named dnac. The dictionary named dnac contains multiple key/value pairs, and it starts and ends with curly braces ({}).

Example 28-13 *Dictionary Used in Env_Lab.py*

```
dnac = {
    "host": "sandboxdnac.cisco.com",
    "port": 443,
    "username": "devnetuser",
    "password": "Cisco123!"
}
```

Dictionaries can be written in multiple different ways. Whereas Example 28-13 shows a multiple-line dictionary that is easily readable, Example 28-14 shows the same dictionary written as a single line.

Example 28-14 *Single-Line Example of the Dictionary Used in Env_Lab.py*

```
    dnac = {"host": "sandboxdnac.cisco.com", "port": 443, "username": "devnetuser",
"password": "Cisco123!"}
```

Notice that the line ENVIRONMENT_IN_USE = “sandbox” is used in this script. Following that line in the script is a line that states if ENVIRONMENT_IN_USE == “sandbox”: This is called a *condition*. A logical *if* question is asked, and depending on the answer, an action happens. In this example, the developer called out to use the sandbox option with the line of code ENVIRONMENT_IN_USE = “sandbox” and then used a condition to say that if the environment in use is sandbox, call a dictionary named dnac to provide the sandbox details that are listed in key/value pairs. Example 28-15 shows the two relevant lines of code to illustrate this.

Example 28-15 *Condition Example Used in Env_Lab.py*

```
ENVIRONMENT_IN_USE = "sandbox"

# Set the 'Environment Variables' based on the lab environment in use
if ENVIRONMENT_IN_USE == "sandbox":
```

Now let’s look at a script that showcases much of the API information that was covered in this chapter and also builds on all the basic Python information that has just been provided. Example 28-16 shows a Python script called get_dnac_devices.py.

Example 28-16 *The Full get_dnac_devices.py Script*

```
#! /usr/bin/env python3

from env_lab import dnac
import json
import requests
import urllib3
from requests.auth import HTTPBasicAuth
from prettytable import PrettyTable
```

```
dnac_devices = PrettyTable(['Hostname','Platform Id','Software Type','Software
Version','Up Time' ])
dnac_devices.padding_width = 1

# Silence the insecure warning due to SSL Certificate
urllib3.disable_warnings(urllib3.exceptions.InsecureRequestWarning)

headers = {
              'content-type': "application/json",
              'x-auth-token': ""
          }


def dnac_login(host, username, password):
    url = "https://{}/api/system/v1/auth/token".format(host)
    response = requests.request("POST", url, auth=HTTPBasicAuth(username, password),
                                headers=headers, verify=False)
    return response.json()["Token"]


def network_device_list(dnac, token):
    url = "https://{}/api/v1/network-device".format(dnac['host'])
    headers["x-auth-token"] = token
    response = requests.get(url, headers=headers, verify=False)
    data = response.json()
    for item in data['response']:
    dnac_devices.add_row([item["hostname"],item["platformId"],item["softwareType"],
    item["soft.   wareVersion"],item["upTime"]])


login = dnac_login(dnac["host"], dnac["username"], dnac["password"])
network_device_list(dnac, login)

print(dnac_devices)
```

It might seem like there is a lot going on in the get_dnac_device.py script. However, many of the details have already been explained in the chapter. This section ties together all the components discussed previously and expands on how they work together by breaking the script into five sections, with explanations.

The first section of code tells the Python interpreter what modules this particular script will use. Think of a module as a collection of actions and instructions. To better explain the contents in this script, comments are inserted throughout the script to help document each section. Example 28-17 shows the first section of the get_dnac_devices.py with comments that explain what's going on.

Example 28-17 *Explanation of the First Section of get_dnac_devices.py*

```
# Specifies which version of Python will be used
#! /usr/bin/env python3

# Calls "dnac" dictionary from the env_lab.py script covered earlier
from env_lab import dnac

# Imports JSON module so Python can understand the data format that contains key/
value pairs
import json

# Imports requests module which handles HTTP headers and form data
import requests

# Imports urllib3 module which is an HTTP client
import urllib3

# Imports HTTPBasicAuth method from the requests.auth module for authentication to
Cisco DNA Center
from requests.auth import HTTPBasicAuth

# Imports prettytable components from PrettyTable module to structure return data
from Cisco DNA Center in table format
from prettytable import PrettyTable
```


Modules help Python understand what it is capable of. For example, if a developer tried to do an HTTP GET request without having the Requests modules imported, it would be difficult for Python to understand how to interpret the HTTP call. Although there are other ways of doing HTTP calls from Python, the Requests modules greatly simplify this process.

Example 28-18 shows the second section of the get_dnac_devices.py script along with explanatory comments.

Example 28-18 *Explanation of the Second Section of get_dnac_devices.py*

```
# Puts return data from Cisco DNA Center Network Device API call into easily read-
able table with column names Hostname, Platform Id, Software Type, Software Version
and Up Time.
dnac_devices = PrettyTable(['Hostname','Platform Id','Software Type','Software
Version','Up Time' ])
dnac_devices.padding_width = 1

# Silences the insecure warning due to SSL Certificate
urllib3.disable_warnings(urllib3.exceptions.InsecureRequestWarning)

# Sends specific HTTP headers to Cisco DNA Center when issuing HTTP GET to the Net-
work Devices API
```

```
headers = {
              'content-type': "application/json",
              'x-auth-token': ""
          }
```

Functions are blocks of code that are built to perform specific actions. Functions are very structured in nature and can often be reused later on within a Python script. Some functions are built into Python and do not have to be created. A great example of this is the print function, which can be used to print data to a terminal screen. You can see the print function at the end of the get_dnac_devices.py script. Remember that in order to execute any API calls to Cisco DNA Center, you must be authenticated using the Token API. Example 28-19 shows the use of the Token API within a Python script. (Recall that you saw this API used with Postman earlier in the chapter.)

Example 28-19 *Explanation of the Third Section of get_dnac_devices.py*

```
# This function does an HTTP POST of the username devnetuser and the password of
Cisco123! to the Token API located at https://sandboxdnac.cisco.com/api/system/v1/
auth/token and uses the values built in the JSON key-value pairs from the Env_Lab.
py. The JSON response from the API called is stored as the Token that will be used
for future API calls for this authenticated user.

def dnac_login(host, username, password):
    url = "https://{}/api/system/v1/auth/token".format(host)
    response = requests.request("POST", url, auth=HTTPBasicAuth(username, password),
                                headers=headers, verify=False)
    return response.json()["token"]
```

NOTE The API URL in this example is exactly the same one used earlier in this chapter.

This section of the script shown in Example 28-20 ties the Token API to the Network Device API call to retrieve the information from Cisco DNA Center. The line that says headers ["x-auth-token"] = token is mapping the JSON response from the previous example, which is the token, into the header called x-auth-token. In addition, the URL for the API has changed to network_device, and the response is sending a requests.get to that URL. This is exactly the same example used with Postman earlier in this chapter.

Example 28-20 *Explanation of the Fourth Section of get_dnac_devices.py*

```
def network_device_list(dnac, token):
    url = "https://{}/api/v1/network-device".format(dnac['host'])
    headers["x-auth-token"] = token
    response = requests.get(url, headers=headers, verify=False)
    data = response.json()
    for item in data['response']:
        dnac_devices.add_row([item["hostname"],item["platformId"],item["softwareType
"],item["softwareVersion"],item["upTime"]])
```

The final section of get_dnac_devices.py shows code that ties the dnac dictionary that is in the Env_Lab.py script to the dnac_login function covered earlier. In addition, the print function takes the response received from the response.get that was sent to the Network Device API and puts it into the table format that was specified earlier in the script with the name dnac_devices. Example 28-21 shows the final lines of code in the script.

Example 28-21 *Explanation of the Fifth Section of get_dnac_devices.py*

```
login = dnac_login(dnac["host"], dnac["username"], dnac["password"])
network_device_list(dnac, login)

print(dnac_devices)
```

The Python script examples in this chapter make it easy to see the power and easy-to-use nature of Python. You practice with the examples in this chapter to increase your experience with Python and API structures. The tools mentioned in this chapter, including Postman and Python, are readily available on the Internet for free. These tools, examples, and much more can be studied in depth at http://developer.cisco.com.

The tools covered in this chapter are available online and are very useful in terms of building skill and expertise. Go to DevNet to practice with any of the technologies covered in this chapter. It is often said of programmability that you can start small, but you should just start! A great way to practice is by using a sandbox environment and just building code and running it to see what can be accomplished. You are only limited by your imagination and coding skills! Remember to have fun and keep in mind that programmability is a journey, not a destination. Separating your learning into small, manageable chunks will make it easier to get better with practice and time.

Exam Preparation Tasks

You have a couple of choices for exam preparation: the exercises here, Chapter 30, "Final Preparation," and the exam simulation questions in the Pearson Test Prep Software Online.

Review All Key Topics

Review the most important topics in the chapter, noted with the Key Topic icon in the outer margin of the page. Table 28-9 lists these key topics and the page number on which each is found.

Key Topic

Table 28-9 Key Topics for Chapter 28

Key Topic Element	Description	Page
Table 28-3	HTTP Functions and Use Cases	856
Table 28-4	CRUD Functions and Use Cases	856
Table 28-5	HTTP Status Codes	862
List	Steps to authenticate to Cisco DNA Center using a POST operation and basic authentication	862
List	Steps to leverage the Network Device API to retrieve a device inventory from Cisco DNA Center	864
Paragraph	Using the offset and limit filters with the Network Device API when gathering device inventory	866

Complete Tables and Lists from Memory

Print a copy of Appendix B, "Memory Tables" (found on the companion website), or at least the section for this chapter, and complete the tables and lists from memory. Appendix C, "Memory Tables Answer Key," also on the companion website, includes completed tables and lists you can use to check your work.

Define Key Terms

Define the following key terms from this chapter and check your answers in the Glossary:

application programming interface (API), command-line interface (CLI), DevNet, Extensible Markup Language (XML), JavaScript Object Notation (JSON), NETCONF, Python, RESTCONF, YANG

References in This Chapter

RFC 4741, *NETCONF Configuration Protocol*, R. Enns. https://tools.ietf.org/html/rfc4741, December 2006.

RFC 6020, *YANG—A Data Modeling Language for the Network Configuration Protocol (NETCONF)*, M. Bjorklund. https://tools.ietf.org/html/rfc6020, October 2010.

RFC 6241, *Network Configuration Protocol (NETCONF)*, R. Enns, M. Bjorklund, J. Schoenwaelder, A. Bierman. https://tools.ietf.org/html/rfc6241, June 2011.

RFC 8040, *RESTCONF*, A. Bierman, M. Bjorklund, and K. Watsen. https://tools.ietf.org/html/rfc8040, January 2017.

CHAPTER 29

Introduction to Automation Tools

This chapter covers the following subjects:

Embedded Event Manager (EEM): This section illustrates common use cases and operations of the on-box EEM automation tool as well as the Tcl scripting engine.

Agent-Based Automation Tools: This section examines the benefits and operations of the various agent-based automation tools.

Agentless Automation Tools: This section examines the benefits and operations of the various agentless automation tools.

This chapter is intended to provide a high-level overview of some of the most common configuration management and automation tools that are available. This chapter also discusses some on-box tools and describes some common programmatic methods of management.

"Do I Know This Already?" Quiz

The "Do I Know This Already?" quiz allows you to assess whether you should read the entire chapter. If you miss no more than one of these self-assessment questions, you might want to move ahead to the "Exam Preparation Tasks" section. Table 29-1 lists the major headings in this chapter and the "Do I Know This Already?" quiz questions covering the material in those headings so you can assess your knowledge of these specific areas. The answers to the "Do I Know This Already?" quiz appear in Appendix A, "Answers to the 'Do I Know This Already?' Quiz Questions."

Table 29-1 "Do I Know This Already?" Foundation Topics Section-to-Question Mapping

Foundations Topics Section	Questions
Embedded Event Manager (EEM)	1
Agent-Based vs. Agentless Management Tools	11
Agentless Automation Tools	2
Ansible	3, 5, 8–10
SaltStack (Agent and Server Mode)	4
Chef	6
Puppet	7

1. True or false: Configuring network components by using the CLI is considered the fastest approach when dealing with a large number of devices.
   a. True
   b. False

2. Which of these tools are agentless in operation? (Choose three.)
   a. Ansible
   b. Puppet Bolt
   c. SaltStack
   d. Chef
   e. Salt SSH
3. Which of the following are features of Ansible? (Choose two.)
   a. Manifests
   b. Modules
   c. Playbooks
   d. Tasks
   e. Recipes
4. What configuration management software is built on Python? (Choose two.)
   a. Ansible
   b. Chef
   c. Puppet
   d. SaltStack
5. Which of the following is a YAML example?
   a.

```
{
  "user": "root",
  "user": "Jason",
  "user": "Jamie",
  "user": "Luke"
}
```

   b.

```
# HR Employee record
Employee1:
    Name: John Dough
    Title: Developer
    Nickname: Mr. DBug
```

   c.

```
root
Jason
Jamie
Luke
```

   d.

```
[users[root|Jason|Jamie|Luke]]
```

6. What is the language associated with Chef?
   a. Python
   b. C++

- **c.** Ruby
- **d.** Q-Basic
- **e.** Tcl

7. What are some of the benefits of Puppet Forge and GitHub? (Choose all that apply.)

- **a.** Keeping track of various versions of code
- **b.** Knowing which developers are involved with code revisions
- **c.** Collaborating with other developers and sharing code
- **d.** Increasing the speed in working on software projects
- **e.** Accessing a real-time telemetry software database
- **f.** Automatically blocking malicious code

8. What are the PPDIOO lifecycle components?

- **a.** Prepare, Plan, Design, Implement, Observe, Optimize
- **b.** Prepare, Plan, Design, Implement, Operate, Optimize
- **c.** Prepare, Plan, Design, Implement, Operate, Optimize
- **d.** Plan, Prepare, Design, Implement, Observe, Optimize
- **e.** Prepare, Plan, Design, Integrate, Observe, Optimize

9. Ansible uses the TAML syntax, which starts with three dashes (---), in the creation of playbook files.

- **a.** True
- **b.** False

10. What is the proper command to execute a playbook using Ansible?

- **a.** **ansible-playbook ConfigureInterface.yaml**
- **b.** **ansible ConfigureInterface.yaml**
- **c.** **play ansible-book ConfigureInterface.yaml**
- **d.** **play ansible-book ConfigureInterface.taml**

11. What tools are agentless in operation? (Choose three.)

- **a.** Ansible
- **b.** Puppet Bolt
- **c.** SaltStack
- **d.** Chef
- **e.** Salt SSH

Foundation Topics

Embedded Event Manager

Key Topic

Embedded Event Manager (EEM) is a very flexible and powerful Cisco IOS tool. EEM allows engineers to build software applets that can automate many tasks. EEM also derives some of its power from the fact that it enables you to build custom scripts using **Tcl**. Scripts can automatically execute, based on the output of an action or an event on a device. One of the main benefits of EEM is that it is all contained within the local device. There is no need to rely on an external scripting engine or monitoring device in most cases. Figure 29-1 illustrates some of the EEM event detectors and how they interact with the IOS subsystem.

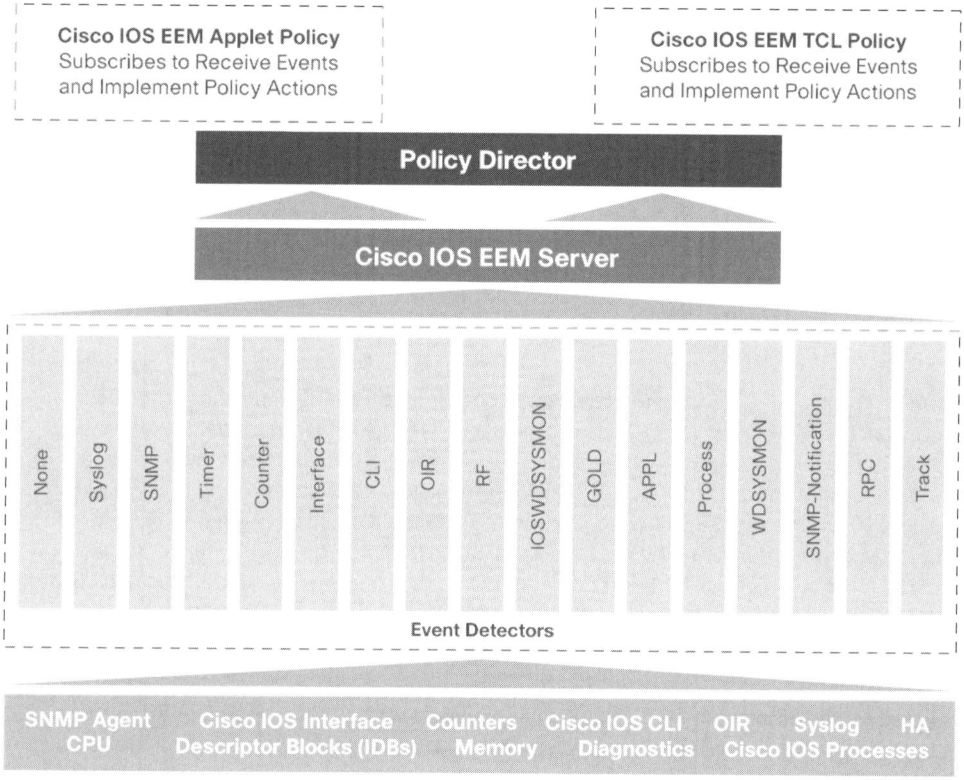

Figure 29-1 *EEM Event Detectors*

EEM Applets

EEM applets are composed of multiple building blocks. This chapter focuses on two of the primary building blocks that make up EEM applets: *events* and *actions*.

EEM applets use a similar logic to the *if-then* statements used in some of the common programming languages (for instance, *if* an event happens, *then* an action is taken). The following example illustrates a very common EEM applet that is monitoring syslog messages on a router.

Example 29-1 shows an applet that is looking for a specific syslog message, stating that the Loopback0 interface went down. The specific syslog message is matched using regular expressions. This is a very powerful and granular way of matching patterns. If this specific syslog pattern is matched (an event) at least once, then the following actions will be taken:

1. The Loopback0 interface will be shut down and brought back up (because of **shutdown** and **no shutdown**).
2. The router will generate a syslog message that says, "I've fallen, and I can't get up!"
3. An email message that includes the output of the **show interface loopback0** command will be sent to the network administrator.

Example 29-1 *Syslog Applet Example*

```
event manager applet LOOP0
 event syslog pattern "Interface Loopback0.* down" period 1
 action 1.0 cli command "enable"
 action 2.0 cli command "config terminal"
 action 3.0 cli command "interface loopback0"
 action 4.0 cli command "shutdown"
 action 5.0 cli command "no shutdown"
 action 5.5 cli command "show interface loopback0"
 action 6.0 syslog msg "I've fallen, and I can't get up!"
 action 7.0 mail server 10.0.0.25 to neteng@yourcompany.com
  from no-reply@yourcompany.com subject "Loopback0 Issues!"
  body "The Loopback0 interface was bounced. Please monitor
  accordingly. "$_cli_result"
```

NOTE Remember to include the **enable** and **configure terminal** commands at the beginning of actions within an applet. This is necessary as the applet assumes the user is in exec mode, not privileged exec or config mode. In addition, if AAA command authorization is being used, it is important to include the **event manager session cli username** *username* command. Otherwise, the CLI commands in the applet will fail. It is also good practice to use decimal labels similar to 1.0, 2.0, and so forth when building applets. This makes it possible to insert new actions between other actions in the future. For example, you could insert a 1.5 action between the 1.0 and 2.0 actions. Remember that labels are parsed as strings, which means 10.0 would come after 1.0, not 9.0.

Based on the output from the **debug event manager action cli** command, you can see the actions taking place when the applet is running. Example 29-2 shows the applet being engaged when a user issues the **shutdown** command on the Loopback0 interface. It also shows that an error occurred when trying to connect to the SMTP server to send the email to the administrator. This is because the SMTP server being used for this test is not configured. Notice that because the **$_cli_result** keyword was used in the configuration, the output will include the output of any CLI commands that were issued in the applet. In this case, the output of the **show interface loopback0** command will be included in the debugging and in the email message.

Example 29-2 *Debugging Output of an Event Manager Action*

```
Switch#
Switch# configure terminal
Enter configuration commands, one per line.  End with CNTL/Z.
Switch(config)# interface loopback0
Switch(config-if)# shutdown
Switch(config-if)#
```

Answers to the "Do I Know This Already?" quiz:

1 B **2** A, B, E **3** C, D **4** A, D **5** B **6** C **7** A, B, C, D **8** B **9** B **10** A **11** B, C

```
17:21:59.214: %LINK-5-CHANGED: Interface Loopback0, changed state to administratively
  down
17:21:59.217: %HA_EM-6-LOG: LOOP0 : DEBUG(cli_lib) : : CTL : cli_open called.
17:21:59.221: %HA_EM-6-LOG: LOOP0 : DEBUG(cli_lib) : : OUT : Switch>
17:21:59.221: %HA_EM-6-LOG: LOOP0 : DEBUG(cli_lib) : : IN  : Switch>enable
17:21:59.231: %HA_EM-6-LOG: LOOP0 : DEBUG(cli_lib) : : OUT : Switch#
17:21:59.231: %HA_EM-6-LOG: LOOP0 : DEBUG(cli_lib) : : IN  : Switch#show
  interface loopback0
17:21:59.252: %HA_EM-6-LOG: LOOP0 : DEBUG(cli_lib) : : OUT : Loopback0 is
  administratively down, line protocol is down
17:21:59.252: %HA_EM-6-LOG: LOOP0 : DEBUG(cli_lib) : : OUT :   Hardware is Loopback
17:21:59.252: %HA_EM-6-LOG: LOOP0 : DEBUG(cli_lib) : : OUT :   MTU 1514 bytes,
  BW 8000000 Kbit/sec, DLY 5000 usec,
17:21:59.252: %HA_EM-6-LOG: LOOP0 : DEBUG(cli_lib) : : OUT :      reliability
  255/255, txload 1/255, rxload 1/255
17:21:59.252: %HA_EM-6-LOG: LOOP0 : DEBUG(cli_lib) : : OUT :   Encapsulation
  LOOPBACK, loopback not set
17:21:59.252: %HA_EM-6-LOG: LOOP0 : DEBUG(cli_lib) : : OUT :   Keepalive set
  (10 sec)
17:21:59.252: %HA_EM-6-LOG: LOOP0 : DEBUG(cli_lib) : : OUT :   Last input never,
  output never, output hang never
17:21:59.252: %HA_EM-6-LOG: LOOP0 : DEBUG(cli_lib) : : OUT :   Last clearing of
  "show interface" counters never
17:21:59.252: %HA_EM-6-LOG: LOOP0 : DEBUG(cli_lib) : : OUT :   Input queue:
  0/75/0/0 (size/max/drops/flushes); Total output drops: 0
17:21:59.252: %HA_EM-6-LOG: LOOP0 : DEBUG(cli_lib) : : OUT :   Queueing strategy:
  fifo
17:21:59.252: %HA_EM-6-LOG: LOOP0 : DEBUG(cli_lib) : : OUT :   Output queue:
  0/0 (size/max)
17:21:59.252: %HA_EM-6-LOG: LOOP0 : DEBUG(cli_lib) : : OUT :   5 minute input rate
  0 bits/sec, 0 packets/sec
17:21:59.252: %HA_EM-6-LOG: LOOP0 : DEBUG(cli_lib) : : OUT :   5 minute output rate
  0 bits/sec, 0 packets/sec
17:21:59.252: %HA_EM-6-LOG: LOOP0 : DEBUG(cli_lib) : : OUT :      0 packets input,
  0 bytes, 0 no buffer
17:21:59.252: %HA_EM-6-LOG: LOOP0 : DEBUG(cli_lib) : : OUT :      Received 0
  broadcasts (0 IP multicasts)
17:21:59.252: %HA_EM-6-LOG: LOOP0 : DEBUG(cli_lib) : : OUT :      0 runts, 0 giants,
  0 throttles
17:21:59.252: %HA_EM-6-LOG: LOOP0 : DEBUG(cli_lib) : : OUT :      0 input errors,
  0 CRC, 0 frame, 0 overrun, 0 ignored, 0 abort
17:21:59.252: %HA_EM-6-LOG: LOOP0 : DEBUG(cli_lib) : : OUT :      0 packets output,
  0 bytes, 0 underruns
17:21:59.252: %HA_EM-6-LOG: LOOP0 : DEBUG(cli_lib) : : OUT :      0 output errors,
  0 collisions, 0 interface resets
17:21:59.252: %HA_EM-6-LOG: LOOP0 : DEBUG(cli_lib) : : OUT :      0 unknown protocol
  drops
17:21:59.252: %HA_EM-6-LOG: LOOP0 : DEBUG(cli_lib) : : CTL : 20+ lines read from
  cli, debug output truncated
17:21:59.252: %HA_EM-6-LOG: LOOP0 : DEBUG(cli_lib) : : IN  : Switch#config terminal
17:21:59.266: %HA_EM-6-LOG: LOOP0 : DEBUG(cli_lib) : : OUT : Enter configuration
  commands, one per line.  End with CNTL/Z.
17:21:59.266: %HA_EM-6-LOG: LOOP0 : DEBUG(cli_lib) : : OUT : Switch(config)#
```

29

```
17:21:59.266: %HA_EM-6-LOG: LOOP0 : DEBUG(cli_lib) : : IN  : Switch(config)#interface
  loopback0
17:21:59.277: %HA_EM-6-LOG: LOOP0 : DEBUG(cli_lib) : : OUT : Switch(config-if)#
17:21:59.277: %HA_EM-6-LOG: LOOP0 : DEBUG(cli_lib) : : IN  : Switch(config-if)
  #shutdown
17:21:59.287: %HA_EM-6-LOG: LOOP0 : DEBUG(cli_lib) : : OUT : Switch(config-if)#
17:21:59.287: %HA_EM-6-LOG: LOOP0 : DEBUG(cli_lib) : : IN  : Switch(config-if)#no
  shutdown
17:21:59.298: %HA_EM-6-LOG: LOOP0 : DEBUG(cli_lib) : : OUT : Switch(config-if)#
17:21:59.298: %HA_EM-6-LOG: LOOP0: I've fallen and I can't get up!
17:22:01.293: %LINK-3-UPDOWN: Interface Loopback0, changed state to up
17:22:11.314: %HA_EM-3-FMPD_SMTP: Error occurred when sending mail to SMTP server.
  10.0.0.25 : error in connecting to SMTP server
17:22:11.314: %HA_EM-3-FMPD_ERROR: Error executing applet LOOP0 statement 7.0
17:22:11.314: %HA_EM-6-LOG: LOOP0 : DEBUG(cli_lib) : : CTL : cli_close called.
```

NOTE For troubleshooting purposes, using the **debug event manager all** command shows all the output for the configured actions while the applet is being executed. For instance, it shows the same output as shown above but includes more details on all the other actions. To specifically troubleshoot the mail configuration and related error messages in an EEM applet, the **debug event manager action mail** command is most useful as it filters out all the other debugging messages that are unnecessary when you're trying to troubleshoot the mail configuration. This allows a user to focus specifically on SMTP errors, as shown in the previous example.

Another very useful aspect of EEM applets is that CLI patterns can be matched as an event. This means that when certain commands are entered into the router using the CLI, they can trigger an EEM event within an applet. Then the configured actions can take place as a result of the CLI pattern being matched. Example 29-3 uses another common EEM applet to match the CLI pattern "*write mem.*". When the applet is triggered, the following actions are invoked:

1. The router generates a syslog message that says "Configuration File Changed! TFTP backup successful."
2. The startup-config file is copied to a TFTP server.

Example 29-3 *WR MEM Applet*

```
event manager environment filename Router.cfg
event manager environment tftpserver tftp://10.1.200.29/
event manager applet BACKUP-CONFIG
 event cli pattern "write mem.*" sync yes
 action 1.0 cli command "enable"
 action 2.0 cli command "configure terminal"
 action 3.0 cli command "file prompt quiet"
 action 4.0 cli command "end"
 action 5.0 cli command "copy start $tftpserver$filename"
 action 6.0 cli command "configure terminal"
```

```
action 7.0 cli command "no file prompt quiet"
action 8.0 syslog priority informational msg "Configuration File Changed!
  TFTP backup successful."
```

NOTE The **file prompt quiet** command disables the IOS confirmation mechanism that asks to confirm a user's actions.

NOTE The priority and facility of the syslog messages can be changed to fit any environment's alerting structure. For example, informational is used in Example 29-3.

As shown in the previous examples, there are multiple ways to call out specific EEM environment values. The first example illustrates that it's possible for a user to use a single line to configure the mail environment and send messages with CLI output results. Using the EEM environment variables shown in the second example, users can statically set different settings that can be called on from multiple actions instead of calling them out individually on a single line. Although it is possible to create custom names and values that are arbitrary and can be set to anything, it is good practice to use common and descriptive variables. Table 29-2 lists some of the email variables most commonly used in EEM.

Table 29-2 Common EEM Email Variables

EEM Variable	Description	Example
_email_server	SMTP server IP address or DNS name	**10.0.0.25** or **MAILSVR01**
_email_to	Email address to send email to	**neteng@yourcompany.com**
_email_from	Email address of sending party	**no-reply@yourcompany.com**
_email_cc	Email address of additional email receivers	**helpdesk@yourcompany.com**

29

EEM and Tcl Scripts

Using an EEM applet to call Tcl scripts is another very powerful aspect of EEM. This chapter has covered multiple ways to use EEM applets. You have already seen multiple ways of executing actions, based on the automatic detection of specific events while they are happening. In this section, the focus is on how to call a Tcl script from an EEM applet.

Example 29-4 shows how to manually execute an EEM applet that, in turn, executes a Tcl script that is locally stored in the device's flash memory. It is important to understand that there are many different ways to use EEM and that manually triggered applets are also very useful tools. Example 29-4 shows an EEM script configured with the **event none** command, which means there is no automatic event that the applet is monitoring, and this applet runs only when it is triggered manually. To manually run an EEM applet, the **event manager run** *applet-name* command must be used, as illustrated in the second part of the output.

Example 29-4 *Manually Execute EEM Applet*

```
event manager applet Ping
 event none
 action 1.0 cli command "enable"
 action 1.1 cli command "tclsh flash:/ping.tcl"
```

```
Router# event manager run Ping
Router#
19:32:16.564: %HA_EM-6-LOG: Ping : DEBUG(cli_lib) : : CTL : cli_open called.
19:32:16.564: %HA_EM-6-LOG: Ping : DEBUG(cli_lib) : : OUT : Router>
19:32:16.568: %HA_EM-6-LOG: Ping : DEBUG(cli_lib) : : IN  : Router>enable
19:32:16.578: %HA_EM-6-LOG: Ping : DEBUG(cli_lib) : : OUT : Router#
19:32:16.578: %HA_EM-6-LOG: Ping : DEBUG(cli_lib) : : IN  : Router#tclsh
  flash:/ping.tcl
19:32:16.711: %HA_EM-6-LOG: Ping : DEBUG(cli_lib) : : OUT : Type escape sequence
  to abort.
19:32:16.711: %HA_EM-6-LOG: Ping : DEBUG(cli_lib) : : OUT : Sending 5, 100-byte
  ICMP Echos to 192.168.0.2, timeout is 2 seconds:
19:32:16.711: %HA_EM-6-LOG: Ping : DEBUG(cli_lib) : : OUT : !!!!!
19:32:16.711: %HA_EM-6-LOG: Ping : DEBUG(cli_lib) : : OUT : Success rate is
  100 percent (5/5), round-trip min/avg/max = 1/1/4 ms
19:32:16.711: %HA_EM-6-LOG: Ping : DEBUG(cli_lib) : : OUT : Type escape sequence
  to abort.
19:32:16.711: %HA_EM-6-LOG: Ping : DEBUG(cli_lib) : : OUT : Sending 5, 100-byte
  ICMP Echos to 192.168.0.3, timeout is 2 seconds:
19:32:16.711: %HA_EM-6-LOG: Ping : DEBUG(cli_lib) : : OUT : !!!!!
19:32:16.711: %HA_EM-6-LOG: Ping : DEBUG(cli_lib) : : OUT : Success rate is
  100 percent (5/5), round-trip min/avg/max = 1/1/1 ms
19:32:16.711: %HA_EM-6-LOG: Ping : DEBUG(cli_lib) : : OUT : Type escape sequence
  to abort.
19:32:16.711: %HA_EM-6-LOG: Ping : DEBUG(cli_lib) : : OUT : Sending 5, 100-byte
  ICMP Echos to 192.168.0.4, timeout is 2 seconds:
19:32:16.711: %HA_EM-6-LOG: Ping : DEBUG(cli_lib) : : OUT : !!!!!
19:32:16.711: %HA_EM-6-LOG: Ping : DEBUG(cli_lib) : : OUT : Success rate is
  100 percent (5/5), round-trip min/avg/max = 1/1/3 ms
19:32:16.711: %HA_EM-6-LOG: Ping : DEBUG(cli_lib) : : OUT : Type escape sequence
  to abort.
19:32:16.711: %HA_EM-6-LOG: Ping : DEBUG(cli_lib) : : OUT : Sending 5, 100-byte
  ICMP Echos to 192.168.0.5, timeout is 2 seconds:
19:32:16.711: %HA_EM-6-LOG: Ping : DEBUG(cli_lib) : : OUT : !!!!!
19:32:16.711: %HA_EM-6-LOG: Ping : DEBUG(cli_lib) : : OUT : Success rate is
  100 percent (5/5), round-trip min/avg/max = 1/1/4 ms
19:32:16.711: %HA_EM-6-LOG: Ping : DEBUG(cli_lib) : : OUT : Type escape sequence
  to abort.
19:32:16.711: %HA_EM-6-LOG: Ping : DEBUG(cli_lib) : : OUT : Sending 5, 100-byte
  ICMP Echos to 192.168.0.6, timeout is 2 seconds:
19:32:16.711: %HA_EM-6-LOG: Ping : DEBUG(cli_lib) : : OUT : !!!!!
19:32:16.711: %HA_EM-6-LOG: Ping : DEBUG(cli_lib) : : OUT : Success rate is
  100 percent (5/5), round-trip min/avg/max = 1/1/1 ms
19:32:16.711: %HA_EM-6-LOG: Ping : DEBUG(cli_lib) : : CTL : 20+ lines read from cli,
  debug output truncated
19:32:16.711: %HA_EM-6-LOG: Ping : DEBUG(cli_lib) : : CTL : cli_close called.
```

For reference, Example 29-5 displays a snippet for the exact content of the ping.tcl script used in the manually triggered EEM applet in Example 29-4. To see the contents of a Tcl script that resides in flash memory, issue the **more** command followed by the file location and filename. The **more** command can be used to view all other text-based files stored in the local flash memory as well.

Example 29-5 *ping.tcl Script Contents*

```
Router# more flash:ping.tcl
foreach address {
192.168.0.2
192.168.0.3
192.168.0.4
192.168.0.5
192.168.0.6
} { ping $address}
```

EEM Summary

There are many ways to use EEM. From applets to scripting, the possible use cases can only be limited by an engineer's imagination. EEM provides on-box monitoring of various different components based on a series of events. Once an event is detected, an action can take place. This helps make network monitoring more proactive rather than reactive and can also reduce the load on the network and improve efficiency from the monitoring system because the devices can simply report when there is something wrong instead of continually asking the devices if there is anything wrong.

NOTE For information on EEM and its robust features, visit http://www.cisco.com/c/en/us/products/ios-nx-os-software/ios-embedded-event-manager-eem/index.html.

Many steps must be taken when onboarding new devices into a network environment. Often, these steps are very time-consuming and repetitive. This section compares the high-level differences between agent-based and agentless automation and configuration management tools. Understanding how the various tools work can greatly help network operators pinpoint the value that each tool can bring to the table. There is a considerable amount of overlap in the tasks or steps various tools can automate. Some tools take similar approaches. However, there are times when the use of multiple tools from different software vendors is appropriate.

Much of the value in using automation and configuration management tools is in moving more quickly than is possible with manual configuration. In addition, automation helps ensure that the level of risk due to human error is significantly reduced through the use of proven and tested automation methods. A network operations team configuring 1000 devices manually by logging into each device individually is likely to introduce misconfigurations—and the process will be very time-consuming. The following are some of the most common and repetitive configurations for which network operators leverage automation tools to increase speed and consistency:

- Device name/IP address
- Quality of service
- Access list entries
- Usernames/passwords
- SNMP settings
- Compliance

Agent-Based Automation Tools

This section covers a number of agent-based tools as well as some of the key concepts to help network operators decide which tool best suits their environment and business use cases.

Key Topic

Puppet

Puppet is a robust configuration management and automation tool. Cisco supports the use of Puppet on a variety of devices, such as Catalyst switches, Nexus switches, and the Cisco Unified Computing System (UCS) server platform. Puppet works with many different vendors and is one of the more commonly used tools for automation. Puppet can be used during the entire lifecycle of a device, including initial deployment, configuration management, and repurposing and removing devices in a network.

Puppet uses the concept of a *puppet server* to communicate with devices that have the *puppet agent* (client) installed locally on the device. Changes and automation tasks are executed within the *puppet console* and then shared between the puppet server and puppet agents. These changes or automation tasks are stored in the *puppet database* (PuppetDB), which can be located on the same puppet server or on a separate box. This allows the tasks to be saved so they can be pushed out to the puppet agents at a later time.

To help you better understand how Puppet functions, Figure 29-2 illustrates the basic communications path between the puppet server and the puppet agents as well as the high-level architecture. The solid lines show the primary communications path, and the dotted lines indicate high availability (which is optional). With high availability, in the event that the server is unreachable, communications can go over the backup path to the server replica, which is a backup server.

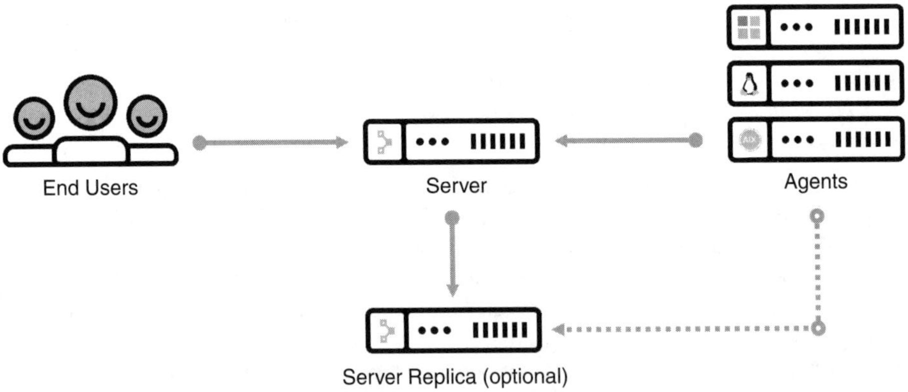

Figure 29-2 *High-Level Puppet Architecture and Basic Puppet Communications Path*

Puppet allows for the management and configuration of multiple device types at the same time. From a basic operation perspective, puppet agents communicate to the puppet server by using different TCP connections. Each TCP port uniquely represents a communications path from an agent running on a device or node. Puppet also has the capability to periodically verify the configuration on devices. This can be set to any frequency that the network operations team deems necessary. Then, if a configuration is changed, it can be alerted on as well as automatically put back to the previous configuration. This helps an organization standardize its device configurations while simultaneously enforcing a specific set of parameters that may be critical to the devices.

There are three different installation types with Puppet. Table 29-3 describes the scale differences between the different installation options.

Table 29-3 Puppet Installation Modes

Installation Type	Scale
Monolithic	Up to 4000 nodes
Monolithic with compile servers	4000 to 20,000 nodes
Monolithic with compile servers and standalone PE-PostgreSQL	More than 20,000 nodes

The typical and recommended type of deployment is a monolithic installation, which supports up to 4000 nodes. However, with regard to deployment use cases, it is helpful to understand that Puppet can scale to very large environments. In these cases, some best practices such as high availability and centralized management may be considered important. Although the architecture is very similar, within large-scale deployments, operations staff may need a *server of servers (SoS)* to manage the distributed puppet servers and their associated databases; having an SoS greatly simplifies the management of the environments. In addition, large deployments need compile servers, which are simply load-balanced Puppet servers that help scale the number of agents that can be managed. Figure 29-3 shows a typical large-scale enterprise deployment model of Puppet and its associated components.

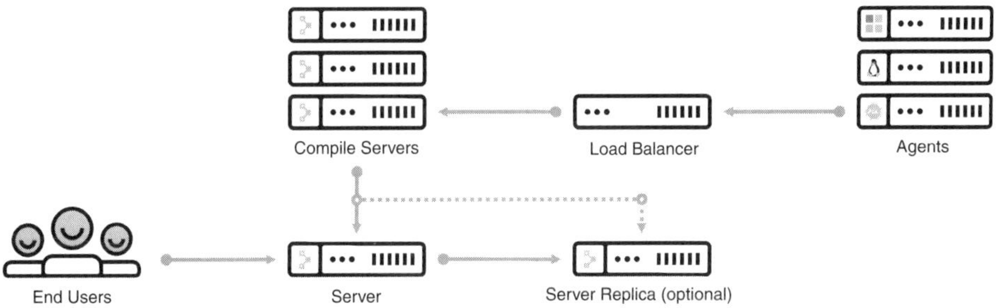

Figure 29-3 *Large-Scale Puppet Enterprise Deployment*

Let's now explore the structure of Puppet. Puppet **modules** allow for the configuration of practically anything that can be configured manually. Modules contain the following components:

- Manifests
- Templates
- Files

Manifests are the code that configures the clients or nodes running the puppet agent. These manifests are pushed to the devices using SSL and require certificates to be installed to ensure the security of the communications between the puppet server and the puppet agents.

Puppet has many modules available for many different vendors and device types. The focus in this chapter is on a module called cisco_ios, which contains multiple manifests and leverages SSH to connect to devices. Each of these manifests is used to modify the running configuration on Cisco Catalyst devices in some fashion. Manifests can be saved as individual files and have a file extension .pp. Example 29-6 shows an example of a manifest file, named NTP_Server.pp, that configures a Network Time Protocol (NTP) server on a Cisco Catalyst device.

Example 29-6 *Puppet NTP_Server.pp Manifest*

```
ntp_server { '1.2.3.4':
  ensure => 'present',
  key => 94,
  prefer => true,
  minpoll => 4,
  maxpoll => 14,
  source_interface => 'Vlan 42',
}
```

This example shows that the NTP server IP address is configured as 1.2.3.4, and it uses VLAN 42 as the source interface. The line ensure => 'present' means that the NTP server configuration should be present in the running configuration of the Catalyst IOS device on which the manifest is running. Remember that Puppet can periodically run to ensure that there is a specific configuration present. The NTP_Server.pp manifest can be run periodically to check for an NTP server configuration.

Puppet leverages a domain-specific language (DSL) as its "programming language." It is largely based on the Ruby language, which makes it quite simple for network operators to build custom manifests to accomplish their specific configuration tasks without having to be software developers. Example 29-7 shows a manifest file called MOTD.pp that is used to configure a message-of-the-day (MOTD) banner on Catalyst IOS devices.

Example 29-7 *Puppet MOTD.pp Manifest*

```
banner { 'default':
  motd => 'Violators will be prosecuted',
}
```

All the modules and manifests used in this chapter can be found on the Puppet Forge website, https://forge.puppet.com. Puppet Forge is a community where puppet modules, manifests, and code can be shared. There is no cost to Puppet Forge, and it is a great place to get started with Puppet. Although this chapter does not discuss installation processes, procedures, or system requirements, you can find that information at Puppet Forge, along with code examples and specifics on how to design and install a Puppet environment from scratch. Many of the same modules, manifests, and code can also be found on www.github.com by searching for Puppet.

Key Topic

Chef

Chef is an open-source configuration management tool that is designed to automate configurations and operations of a network and server environment. Chef is written in Ruby and Erlang, but when it comes to actually writing code within Chef, Ruby is the language used.

Configuration management tools function in two different types of models: push and pull. Push models push configuration from a centralized tool or management server, while pull models check in with the server to see if there is any change in the configuration, and if there is, the remote devices pull the updated configuration files down to the end device.

Chef is similar to Puppet in several ways:

- Both have free open source versions available.
- Both have paid enterprise versions available.
- Both manage code that needs to be updated and stored.
- Both manage devices or nodes to be configured.
- Both leverage a pull model.
- Both function as a client/server model.

However, Chef's structure, terminology, and core components are different from those of Puppet. Figure 29-4 illustrates the high-level architecture of Chef and the basic communications path between the various areas within the Chef environment. Although this chapter doesn't cover every component shown in this architecture, it is important to understand some of the elements that are available.

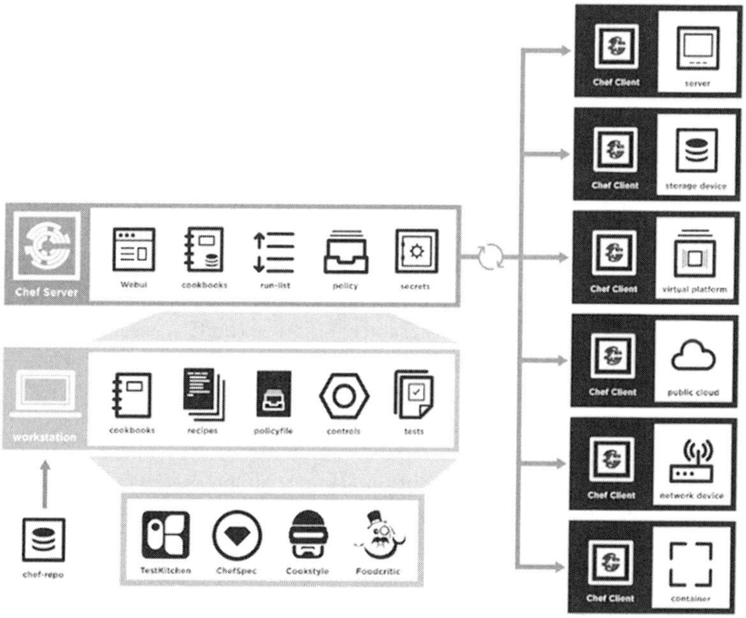

Figure 29-4 *High-Level Chef Architecture*

You can see from Figure 29-4 that Chef leverages a similar client/server functionality to Puppet. Although the core concepts of Puppet and Chef are similar, the terminology differs. Whereas Puppet has modules and manifests, Chef has **cookbooks** and **recipes**. Table 29-4 compares the components of Chef and Puppet and provides a brief description of each component.

Table 29-4 Puppet and Chef Comparison

Chef Components	Puppet Components	Description
Chef server	Puppet server	Server functions
Chef client	Puppet agent	Client/agent functions
Cookbook	Module	Collection of code or files
Recipe	Manifest	Code being deployed to make configuration changes
Workstation	Puppet console	Where users interact with configuration management tool and create code

Code is created on the Chef workstation. This code is stored in a file called a recipe. As mentioned previously, recipes in Chef are analogous to manifests in Puppet. Once a recipe is created on the workstation, it must be uploaded to the Chef server in order to be used in the environment. **knife** is the name of the command-line tool used to upload cookbooks to the Chef server. The command to execute an upload is **knife upload** *cookbookname*. The Chef server can be hosted locally on the workstation, hosted remotely on a server, or hosted in the cloud. In addition, all the components can be within the same enterprise network.

There are four types of Chef server deployments:

- **Chef Solo:** The Chef server is hosted locally on the workstation.
- **Chef Client and Server:** This is a typical Chef deployment with distributed components.
- **Hosted Chef:** The Chef server is hosted in the cloud.
- **Private Chef:** All Chef components are within the same enterprise network.

Like the puppet server, the Chef server sits in between the workstation and the nodes. All cookbooks are stored on the Chef server, and in addition to the cookbooks, the server holds all the tools necessary to transfer the node configurations to the Chef clients. *OHAI*, a service that is installed on the nodes, is used to collect the current state of a node to send the information back to the Chef server through the Chef client service. The Chef server then checks to see if there is any new configuration that needs to be on the node by comparing the information from the OHAI service to the cookbook or recipe. The Chef client service that runs on the nodes is responsible for all communications to the Chef server. When a node needs a recipe, the Chef client service handles the communication back to the Chef server to signify the node's need for the updated configuration or recipe. Because the nodes can be unique or identical, the recipes can be the same or different for each node. Example 29-8 shows a recipe file constructed in Ruby; recipe files have the filename extension .rb. You can see that the file is very simple to read and interpret.

Example 29-8 *Chef demo_install.rb Recipe*

```
#
# Cookbook Name:: cisco-cookbook
# Recipe:: demo_install
#
# Copyright (c) 2014-2017 Cisco and/or its affiliates.
```

```
#
# Licensed under the Apache License, Version 2.0 (the "License");
# you may not use this file except in compliance with the License.
# You may obtain a copy of the License at
#
#     http://www.apache.org/licenses/LICENSE-2.0
#
# Unless required by applicable law or agreed to in writing, software
# distributed under the License is distributed on an "AS IS" BASIS,
# WITHOUT WARRANTIES OR CONDITIONS OF ANY KIND, either express or implied.
# See the License for the specific language governing permissions and
# limitations under the License.

# In our recipes, due to the number of different parameters, we prefer to align
# the arguments in a single column rather than following rubocop's style.

Chef::Log.info('Demo cisco_command_config provider')

cisco_command_config 'loop42' do
  action :update
  command '
    interface loopback42
      description Peering for AS 42
      ip address 192.168.1.42/24
  '
end

cisco_command_config 'system-switchport-default' do
  command 'no system default switchport'
end

cisco_command_config 'feature_bgp' do
  command ' feature bgp'
end

cisco_command_config 'router_bgp_42' do
  action :update
  command '
    router bgp 42
      router-id 192.168.1.42
      address-family ipv4 unicast
        network 1.0.0.0/8
        redistribute static route-map bgp-statics
      neighbor 10.1.1.1
```

29

```
        remote-as 99
  '
end

cisco_command_config 'route42' do
  action :update
  command ' ip route 10.42.42.42/32 Null0 '
end

# The following tests 'no' commands that do not
# nvgen when enabled.
# We need to first configure the port-channel interface
# so that it exists before applying the 'no' commands.

cisco_command_config 'port-channel55-setup' do
  action :update
  command '
    feature bfd
    interface port-channel55
  '
end

cisco_command_config 'port-channel55' do
  action :update
  command '
    interface port-channel55
      no switchport
      no bfd echo
      no ip redirects
  '
End
```

NOTE All recipes and cookbook examples used in this chapter are available at http://www.github.com.

With Chef, the *kitchen* is a place where all recipes and cookbooks can automatically be executed and tested prior to hitting any production nodes. This is analogous to large companies in the food industry that use test kitchens to make food recipes that will not interfere with other recipes in their production environment. The kitchen allows for not only testing within the enterprise environment but also across many cloud providers and virtualization technologies. The kitchen also supports many of the common testing frameworks that are used by the Ruby community:

- Bash Automated Testing System (BATS)
- Minitest

- RSpec
- Serverspec

Puppet and Chef are often seen as interchangeable because they are very similar. However, which one you use ultimately depends on the skillset and adoption processes of your network operations.

Key Topic

SaltStack (Agent and Server Mode)

SaltStack is another configuration management tool, in the same category as Chef and Puppet. Of course, SaltStack has its own unique terminology and architecture. SaltStack is built on Python, and it has a Python interface so a user can program directly to SaltStack by using Python code. However, most of the instructions or states that get sent out to the nodes are written in YAML or a DSL. These are called *Salt formulas*. Formulas can be modified but are designed to work out of the box. Another key difference from Puppet and Chef is SaltStack's overall architecture. SaltStack uses the concept of *systems*, which are divided into various categories. For example, whereas the Puppet architecture has a puppet server and puppet agents, SaltStack has *masters** and *minions*.

NOTE *Use of this term is ONLY in association with the official terminology used in industry specifications and/or standards, and in no way diminishes Pearson's commitment to promoting diversity, equity, and inclusion, and challenging, countering and/or combating bias and stereotyping in the global population of the learners we serve.

SaltStack can run remote commands to systems in a parallel fashion, which allows for very fast performance. By default, SaltStack leverages a distributed messaging platform called 0MQ (ZeroMQ) for fast, reliable messaging throughout the networking stack. SaltStack is an event-driven technology that has components called *reactors* and *beacons*. A reactor lives on the master and listens for any type of changes in the node or device that differ from the desired state or configuration. These changes include the following:

29

- Command-line configuration
- Disk/memory/processor utilization
- Status of services

Beacons live on minions. (The minions are similar to the Puppet agents running on nodes.) If a configuration changes on a node, a beacon notifies the reactor on the master. This process, called the *remote execution system*, helps determine whether the configuration is in the appropriate state on the minions. These actions are called *jobs*, and the executed jobs can be stored in an external database for future review or reuse.

Another notable difference between Puppet and SaltStack is that instead of using modules and manifests to control state and send configuration changes, SaltStack uses **pillars** and **grains**. SaltStack grains are run on the minions to gather system information to report back to the master. This information is typically gathered by the *salt-minion* daemon. (This is analogous to Chef's use of the OHAI service.) Grains can provide specifics to the master (on request) about the host, such as uptime for example. Pillars, on the other hand, store data that a minion can retrieve from the master. Pillars can also have certain minions assigned to them, and other minions that are not assigned to a specific pillar would not have access to that data. This means data can be stored for a specific node or set of nodes inside a pillar, and it is completely separate from any other node that is not assigned to this particular pillar. Confidential or sensitive information that needs to be shared with only specific minions can be secured in this way.

In terms of overall scale and management, SaltStack, much like Puppet and Chef, can scale to a very large number of devices. Like Puppet and Chef, SaltStack also has an enterprise version and a GUI; this GUI, called *SynDic*, makes it possible to leverage the master of masters. Although this section focuses more on the command line delivery of SaltStack, it is important to understand that this tool, like the others, offers some very similar features. Figure 29-5 shows the overall architecture of SaltStack and its associated components. Again, although the components in this architecture are not all covered in this chapter, it is important to understand some of the elements that are available.

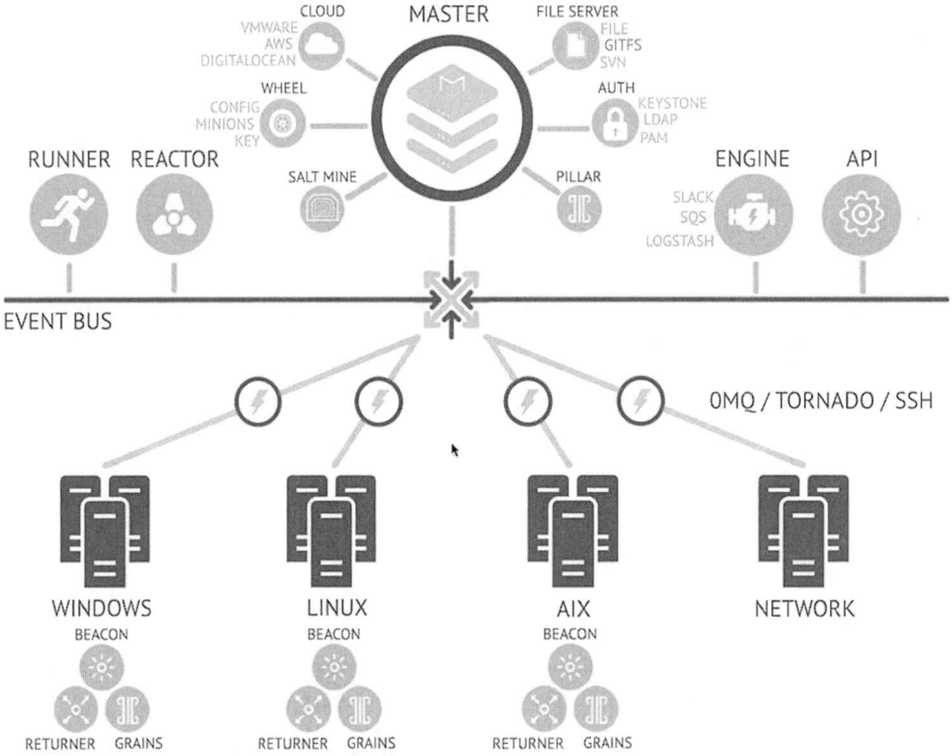

Figure 29-5 *High-Level SaltStack Architecture*

Like Puppet, SaltStack has its own DSL. The SaltStack command structure contains *targets*, *commands*, and *arguments*. The target is the desired system that the command should run. It is possible to target the system by using the MinionID of a minion. It is also very common to target all systems with the asterisk (*), which is a wildcard indicating all systems that are currently managed by SaltStack. Another possibility is to use a combination of the two; for example, Minion* would grab any system that has a MinionID that starts with the word *Minion*. This is called *globbing*. The command structure uses the *module.function* syntax followed by the argument. An argument provides detail to the module and function that is being called on in the command. Figure 29-6 shows the correct SaltStack syntax as well as the power of running a command called **cmd.run** that executes the ad hoc Linux CLI command **ls -l /etc** across all SaltStack managed nodes and returning the output of the command to the master.

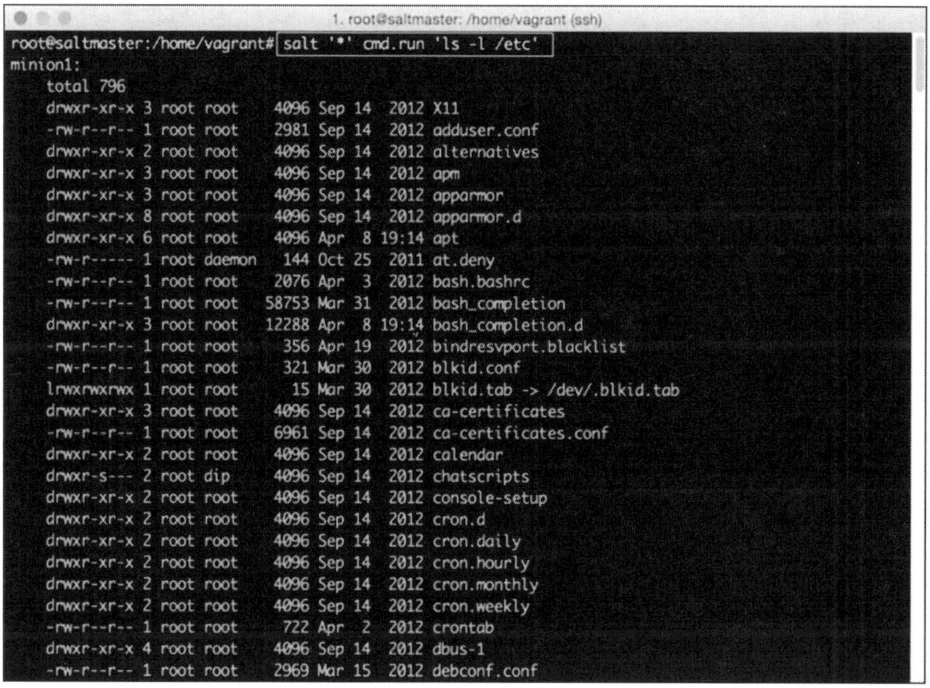

Figure 29-6 *SaltStack CLI Command* **cmd.run ls -l /etc**

Imagine that a network operations team is looking to deploy a new feature on the network and needs a list of all the IP addresses on all the Linux servers in the environment. The team could use **cmd.run** to achieve this. However, other commands and modules are specifically designed for such use cases. Rather than having to write up all the ad hoc commands necessary to get the desired outputs from all the nodes, the team could leverage something like the **network.interfaces** command to gather much more data from the disparate systems, such as the MAC address, interface names, state, and IPv4 and IPv6 addresses assigned to those interfaces. Figure 29-7 provides an example of output on a Linux host showing this specific use case.

SaltStack can provide some immediate benefits, especially for operations teams that are used to working in the command-line environment on network and server nodes. A team can easily tie the power of Python scripts into SaltStack to create a very powerful combination. Other tools use Python as well, but which one to use ultimately comes down to what the operations staff is most comfortable with.

29

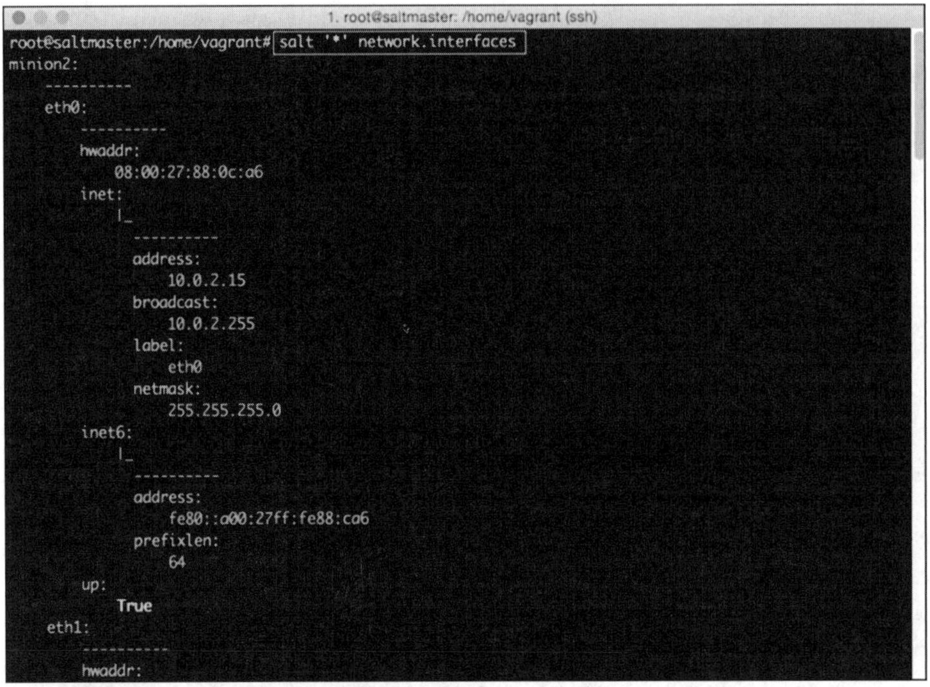

1. root@saltmaster: /home/vagrant (ssh)
root@saltmaster:/home/vagrant# salt '*' network.interfaces
minion2:
----
eth0:
----
hwaddr:
08:00:27:88:0c:a6
inet:
|_
----
address:
10.0.2.15
broadcast:
10.0.2.255
label:
eth0
netmask:
255.255.255.0
inet6:
|_
----
address:
fe80::a00:27ff:fe88:ca6
prefixlen:
64
up:
True
eth1:
----
hwaddr:

Figure 29-7 *SaltStack CLI Command* **network.interfaces**

Agentless Automation Tools

This section covers a variety of agentless tools as well as some of the key concepts to help network operators decide which tool best suits their environment and business use cases.

Key Topic

Ansible

Ansible is an automation tool that is capable of automating cloud provisioning, deployment of applications, and configuration management. Ansible has been around for quite some time and was catapulted further into the mainstream when RedHat purchased the company in 2015. Ansible has grown very popular due to its simplicity and the fact that it is open source. Ansible was created with the following concepts in mind:

- Consistent
- Secure
- Highly reliable
- Minimal learning curve

Unlike the automation tools covered in the previous section of this chapter, Ansible is an agentless tool. This means that no software or agent needs to be installed on the client machines that are to be managed. Some consider this to be a major advantage of using Ansible compared to using other products. Ansible communicates using SSH for a majority of devices, and it can support Windows Remote Management (WinRM) and other transport methods to the clients it manages. In addition, Ansible doesn't need an administrative account on the client. It can use built-in authorization escalation such as **sudo** when it needs to raise the level of administrative control.

Ansible sends all requests from a control station, which could be a laptop or a server sitting in a data center. The control station is the computer used to run Ansible and issue changes and send requests to the remote hosts. Figure 29-8 illustrates the Ansible workflow.

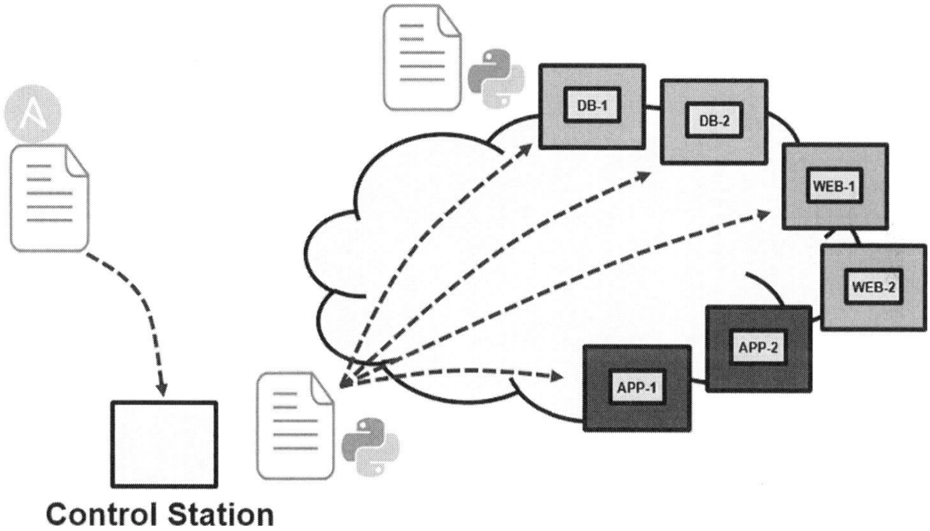

Figure 29-8 *Ansible Workflow*

Administrators, developers, and IT managers like to use Ansible because it allows for easy ramp-up for users who aim to create new projects, and it sets the stage for long-term automation initiatives and processes to further benefit the business. Automation, by nature, reduces the risk of human error by automatically duplicating known best practices that have been thoroughly tested in an environment. However, automation can be dangerous if it duplicates a bad process or an erroneous configuration. (This applies to any tool, not just Ansible.) When preparing to automate a task or set of tasks, it is important to start with the desired outcome of the automation, and then it's possible to move on to creating a plan to achieve the outcome. A methodology commonly used or this process is the PPDIOO (Prepare, Plan, Design, Implement, Operate, Optimize) lifecycle, shown in Figure 29-9.

Ansible uses **playbooks** to deploy configuration changes or retrieve information from hosts within a network. An Ansible playbook is a structured set of instructions—much like the playbooks football players use to make different plays on the field during a game. An Ansible playbook contains multiple plays, and each **play** contains the tasks that each player must accomplish in order for the particular play to be successful. Table 29-5 describes the components used in Ansible and provides some commonly used examples of them.

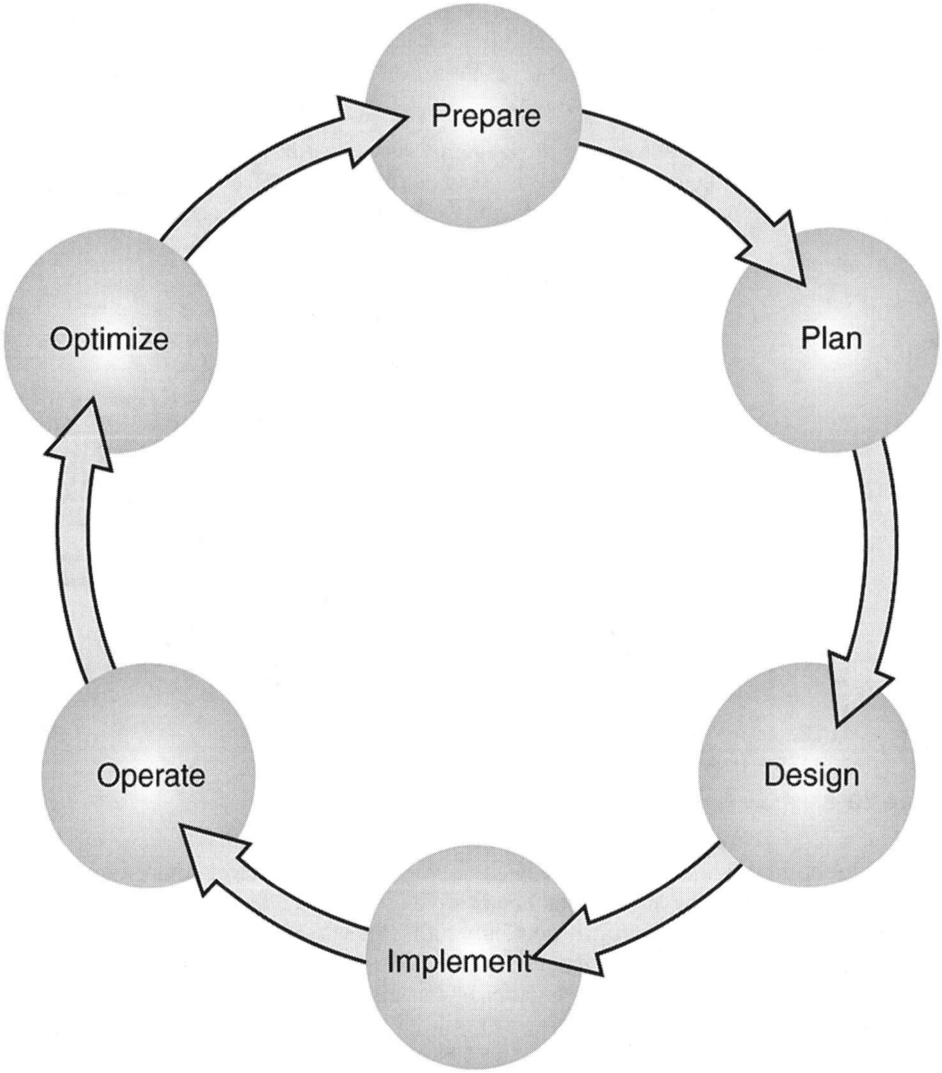

Figure 29-9 *The PPDIOO Lifecycle*

Table 29-5 Ansible Playbook Structure and Examples

Components	Description	Use Case
Playbook	A set of plays for remote systems	Enforcing configuration and/or deployment steps
Play	A set of tasks applied to a single host or a group of hosts	Grouping a set of hosts to apply policy or configuration to them
Task	A call to an Ansible module	Logging in to a device to issue a **show** command to retrieve output

Ansible playbooks are written using YAML (Yet Another Markup Language). Ansible YAML files usually begin with a series of three dashes (---) and end with a series of three periods (...). Although this structure is optional, it is common. YAML files also contain lists and dictionaries. Example 29-9 shows a YAML file that contains a list of musical genres.

Example 29-9 *YAML List Example*

```
---
# List of music genres
Music:
       - Metal
       - Rock
       - Rap
       - Country
...
```

YAML lists are very easy to read and consume. As you can see in Example 29-9, it is possible to add comments in YAML by beginning lines with a pound sign (#). As mentioned earlier, a YAML file often begins with --- and ends with ...; in addition, as you can see in Example 29-9, each line of a list can start with a dash and a space (-), and indentation makes the YAML file readable.

YAML uses dictionaries that are similar to JSON dictionaries as they also use key/value pairs. Remember from Chapter 28, "Foundational Network Programmability Concepts," that a JSON key/value pair appears as "key": "value"; a YAML key/value pair is similar but does not need the quotation marks—key: value. Example 29-10 shows a YAML dictionary containing an employee record.

Example 29-10 *YAML Dictionary Example*

```
---
# HR Employee record
Employee1:
    Name: John Dough
    Title: Developer
    Nickname: Mr. DBug
```

Lists and dictionaries can be used together in YAML. Example 29-11 shows a dictionary with a list in a single YAML file.

Example 29-11 *YAML Dictionary and List Example*

```
---
# HR Employee records
-   Employee1:
    Name: John Dough
    Title: Developer
    Nickname: Mr. DBug
    Skills:
      - Python
```

```
        - YAML
        - JSON
-   Employee2:
     Name: Jane Dough
     Title: Network Architect
     Nickname: Lay DBug
     Skills:
        - CLI
        - Security
        - Automation
```

YAML Lint is a free online tool you can use to check the format of YAML files to make sure they have valid syntax. Simply go to www.yamllint.com and paste the contents of a YAML file into the interpreter and click Go. Lint alerts you if there is an error in the file. Figure 29-10 shows the YAML dictionary and list file from Example 29-11 in Lint, with the formatting cleaned up and the comment removed.

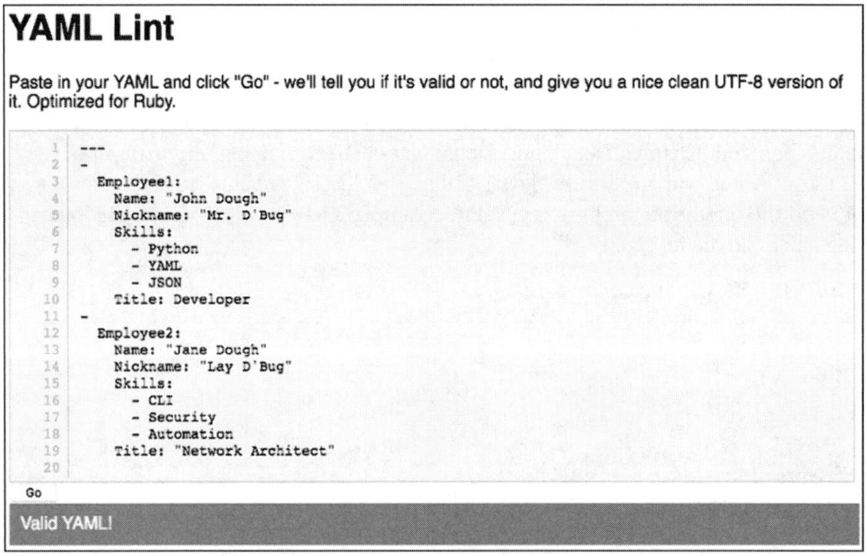

Figure 29-10 *YAML Lint Example*

Ansible has a CLI tool that can be used to run playbooks or ad hoc CLI commands on targeted hosts. This tool has very specific commands that you need to use to enable automation. Table 29-6 shows the most common Ansible CLI commands and associated use cases.

Table 29-6 Ansible CLI Commands

CLI Command	Use Case
ansible	Runs modules against targeted hosts
ansible-playbook	Runs playbooks
ansible-docs	Provides documentation on syntax and parameters in the CLI
ansible-pull	Changes Ansible clients from the default push model to the pull model
ansible-vault	Encrypts YAML files that contain sensitive data

Ansible uses an inventory file to keep track of the hosts it manages. The inventory can be a named group of hosts or a simple list of individual hosts. A host can belong to multiple groups and can be represented by either an IP address or a resolvable DNS name. Example 29-12 shows the contents of a host inventory file with the host 192.168.10.1 in two different groups.

Example 29-12 *Ansible Host Inventory File*

```
[routers]
192.168.10.1
192.168.20.1

[switches]
192.168.10.25
192.168.10.26

[primary-gateway]
192.168.10.1
```

Now let's look at some examples of Ansible playbooks used to accomplish common tasks. Imagine using a playbook to deploy interface configuration on a device without having to manually configure it. You might take this idea a step further and use a playbook to configure an interface and deploy an EIGRP routing process. Example 29-13 shows the contents of an Ansible playbook called ConfigureInterface.yaml, which you can use to configure the GigabitEthernet2 interface on a CSR 1000V router. By leveraging the *ios_config* Ansible module, this playbook adds the following configuration to the GigabitEthernet2 interface on the CSR1KV-1 router:

```
description Configured by ANSIBLE!!!
ip address 10.1.1.1
subnet mask 255.255.255.0
no shutdown
```


Example 29-13 *Ansible ConfigureInterface.yaml Playbook*

```
---
- hosts: CSR1KV-1

  gather_facts: false
  connection: local

  tasks:
   - name: Configure GigabitEthernet2 Interface
     ios_config:
       lines:
         - description Configured by ANSIBLE!!!
         - ip address 10.1.1.1 255.255.255.0
```

```
          - no shutdown
        parents: interface GigabitEthernet2

        host: "{{ ansible_host }}"
        username: cisco
        password: testtest
```

To execute this playbook, the **ansible-playbook** command is used to call the specific playbook YAML file (ConfigureInterface.yaml). Figure 29-11 shows the output from calling the playbook from the Linux shell. The important things to note in the output are the PLAY, TASK, and PLAY RECAP sections, which list the name of the play and each individual task that gets executed in each play. The PLAY RECAP section shows the status of the playbook that is executed. The output in Figure 29-11 shows that one play, named CSR1KV-1, was launched, followed by a task called Configure GigabitEthernet2 Interface. Based on the status ok=1, you know the change was successful; the changed=1 status means that a single change was made on the CSR1KV-1 router.

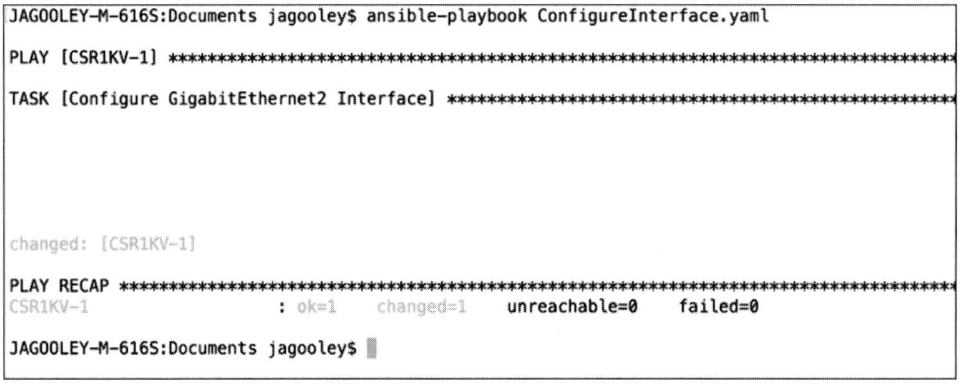

Figure 29-11 *Executing the ConfigureInterface.yaml Playbook*

Building out a playbook can greatly simplify configuration tasks. Example 29-14 shows an alternative version of the ConfigureInterface.yaml playbook named EIGRP_Configuration_Example.yaml, with EIGRP added, along with the ability to save the configuration by issuing a "write memory." These tasks are accomplished by leveraging the ios_command module in Ansible. This playbook adds the following configuration to the CSR1KV-1 router:

- On GigabitEthernet2:

  ```
  description Configured by ANSIBLE!!!
  ip address 10.1.1.1
  subnet mask 255.255.255.0
  no shutdown
  ```

- On GigabitEthernet3:

  ```
  description Configured by ANSIBLE!!!
  no ip address
  shutdown
  ```

- Global configuration:

```
router eigrp 100
eigrp router-id 1.1.1.1
no auto-summary
network 10.1.1.0 0.0.0.255
```

- Save configuration:

```
write memory
```

Example 29-14 *Ansible EIGRP_Configuration_Example.yaml Playbook*

```
---
- hosts: CSR1KV-1

  gather_facts: false
  connection: local

  tasks:
   - name: Configure GigabitEthernet2 Interface
     ios_config:
       lines:
         - description Configured by ANSIBLE!!!
         - ip address 10.1.1.1 255.255.255.0
         - no shutdown
       parents: interface GigabitEthernet2

       host: "{{ ansible_host }}"
       username: cisco
       password: testtest

   - name: CONFIG Gig3
     ios_config:
       lines:
         - description Configured By ANSIBLE!!!
         - no ip address
         - shutdown
       parents: interface GigabitEthernet3

       host: "{{ ansible_host }}"
       username: cisco
       password: testtest

   - name: CONFIG EIGRP 100
     ios_config:
       lines:
         - router eigrp 100
```

29

```
          - eigrp router-id 1.1.1.1
          - no auto-summary
          - network 10.1.1.0 0.0.0.255

        host: "{{ ansible_host }}"
        username: cisco
        password: testtest

    - name: WR MEM
      ios_command:
        commands:
          - write memory

        host: "{{ ansible_host }}"
        username: cisco
        password: testtest
```

When the playbook is run, the output shows the tasks as they are completed and the status of each one. Based on the output shown in Figure 29-12, you can see that tasks with the following names are completed and return the status *changed*:

- Configure GigabitEthernet 2 Interface
- CONFIG Gig3
- CONFIG EIGRP 100

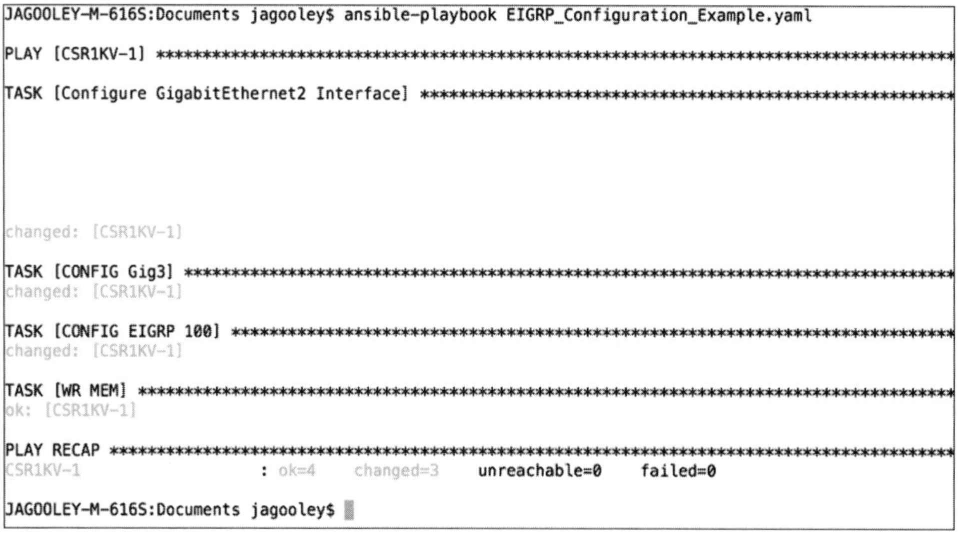

```
JAGOOLEY-M-616S:Documents jagooley$ ansible-playbook EIGRP_Configuration_Example.yaml

PLAY [CSR1KV-1] ****************************************************************

TASK [Configure GigabitEthernet2 Interface] ************************************




changed: [CSR1KV-1]

TASK [CONFIG Gig3] *************************************************************
changed: [CSR1KV-1]

TASK [CONFIG EIGRP 100] ********************************************************
changed: [CSR1KV-1]

TASK [WR MEM] ******************************************************************
ok: [CSR1KV-1]

PLAY RECAP *********************************************************************
CSR1KV-1                   : ok=4    changed=3    unreachable=0    failed=0

JAGOOLEY-M-616S:Documents jagooley$
```

Figure 29-12 *Executing the EIGRP_Configuration_Example.yaml Playbook*

Furthermore, the WR MEM task completes, which is evident from the status ok: [CSR1KV-1]. At the bottom of the output, notice the PLAY RECAP section, which has the status ok=4 and changed=3. This means that out of the four tasks, three actually modified the router and made configuration changes, and one task saved the configuration after it was modified.

Now that the EIGRP_Configuration_Example.yaml playbook has been run against CSR1KV-1, you need to verify the configuration to make sure it was correctly applied. Example 29-15 shows the relevant sections of the startup configuration from CSR1KV-1 to verify the tasks that were applied to the router.

Example 29-15 *Relevant startup-config Post Playbook*

```
!
interface GigabitEthernet1
 ip address 172.16.38.101 255.255.255.0
 negotiation auto
 no mop enabled
 no mop sysid
!
interface GigabitEthernet2
 description Configured by ANSIBLE!!!
 ip address 10.1.1.1 255.255.255.0
 negotiation auto
!
interface GigabitEthernet3
 description Configured By ANSIBLE!!!
 no ip address
 shutdown
 negotiation auto
!
router eigrp 100
 network 10.1.1.0 0.0.0.255
 eigrp router-id 1.1.1.1
!
```


The last task in the playbook is to issue the **write memory** command, and you can verify that it happened by issuing the **show startup-config** command with some filters to see the relevant configuration on the CSR1KV-1 router. Figure 29-13 shows the output from the **show startup-config | se GigabithEthernet2|net3|router eigrp 100** command.

```
CSR1KV-1#show startup-config | se GigabitEthernet2|net3|router eigrp 100
interface GigabitEthernet2
 description Configured by ANSIBLE!!!
 ip address 10.1.1.1 255.255.255.0
 negotiation auto
interface GigabitEthernet3
 description Configured By ANSIBLE!!!
 no ip address
 shutdown
 negotiation auto
router eigrp 100
 network 10.1.1.0 0.0.0.255
 eigrp router-id 1.1.1.1
CSR1KV-1#
```

Figure 29-13 *Verifying the EIGRP_Configuration_Example.yaml Playbook on CSR1KV-1*

Puppet Bolt

Puppet Bolt allows you to leverage the power of Puppet without having to install a puppet server or puppet agents on devices or nodes. Much like Ansible, Puppet Bolt connects to devices by using SSH or WinRM connections. Puppet Bolt is an open source tool that is based on the Ruby language and can be installed as a single package.

In Puppet Bolt, tasks can be used for pushing configuration and for managing services, such as starting and stopping services and deploying applications. Tasks are sharable. For example, users can visit Puppet Forge to find and share tasks with others in the community. Tasks are really good for solving problems that don't fit in the traditional model of client/server or puppet server and puppet agent. As mentioned earlier in this chapter, Puppet is used to ensure configuration on devices and can periodically validate that the change or specific value is indeed configured. Puppet Bolt allows you to execute a change or configuration immediately and then validate it. There are two ways to use Puppet Bolt:

- **Orchestrator-driven tasks:** Orchestrator-driven tasks can leverage the Puppet architecture to use services to connect to devices. This design is meant for large-scale environments.
- **Standalone tasks:** Standalone tasks are for connecting directly to devices or nodes to execute tasks and do not require any Puppet environment or components to be set up in order to realize the benefits and value of Puppet Bolt.

Individual commands can be run from the command line by using the command **bolt command run** *command name* followed by the list of devices to run the command against. In addition to manually running the commands, you can construct scripts that contain multiple commands. You can construct these scripts in Python, Ruby, or any other scripting language that the devices can interpret. After a script is built, you can execute it from the command line against the remote devices that need to be configured, using the command **bolt script run** *script name* followed by the list of devices to run the script against. Figure 29-14 shows a list of some of the available commands for Puppet Bolt.

NOTE The Puppet Bolt command line is not the Cisco command line; rather, it can be in a Linux, OS-X Terminal, or Windows operating system. Puppet Enterprise allows for the use of a GUI to execute tasks.

```
Usage: bolt <subcommand> <action> [options]

Available subcommands:
    bolt command run <command>       Run a command remotely
    bolt script run <script>         Upload a local script and run it remotely
    bolt task run <task> [params]    Run a Puppet task
    bolt plan run <plan> [params]    Run a Puppet task plan
    bolt file upload <src> <dest>    Upload a local file

where [options] are:
    -n, --nodes NODES                Node(s) to connect to in URI format [protocol://]host[:port]
                                     Eg. --nodes bolt.puppet.com
                                     Eg. --nodes localhost,ssh://nix.com:2222,winrm://windows.puppet.com

                                     * NODES can either be comma-separated, '@<file>' to read
                                     * nodes from a file, or '-' to read from stdin
                                     * Windows nodes must specify protocol with winrm://
                                     * protocol is `ssh` by default, may be `ssh` or `winrm`
                                     * port is `22` by default for SSH, `5985` for winrm (Optional)
    -u, --user USER                  User to authenticate as (Optional)
    -p, --password [PASSWORD]        Password to authenticate with (Optional).
                                     Omit the value to prompt for the password.
        --private-key KEY            Private ssh key to authenticate with (Optional)
    -c, --concurrency CONCURRENCY    Maximum number of simultaneous connections (Optional, defaults to 100)
        --modulepath MODULES         List of directories containing modules, separated by :
        --params PARAMETERS          Parameters to a task or plan
        --format FORMAT              Output format to use: human or json
    -k, --insecure                   Whether to connect insecurely
        --transport TRANSPORT        Specify a default transport: ssh, winrm, pcp
        --run-as USER                User to run as using privilege escalation
        --sudo [PROGRAM]             Program to execute for privilege escalation. Currently only sudo is supported.
        --sudo-password [PASSWORD]   Password for privilege escalation
        --[no-]tty                   Request a pseudo TTY on nodes that support it
    -h, --help                       Display help
        --verbose                    Display verbose logging
        --debug                      Display debug logging
        --version                    Display the version
```

Figure 29-14 *The Puppet Bolt Command Line*

Puppet Bolt copies the script into a temporary directory on the remote device, executes the script, captures the results, and removes the script from the remote system as if it were never copied there. This is a really clean way of executing remote commands without leaving residual scripts or files on the remote devices.

Much as in the Cisco DNA Center and Cisco vManage APIs, Puppet Bolt tasks use an API to retrieve data between Puppet Bolt and the remote device. This provides a structure for the data that Puppet Bolt expects to see. Tasks are part of the Puppet modules and use the naming structure *modulename::taskfilename*. Tasks can be called from the command line much like commands and scripts. You use the command **bolt task run** *modulename::taskfilename* to invoke these tasks from the command line. The *modulename::taskfilename* naming structure allows the tasks to be shared with other users on Puppet Forge. A task is commonly accompanied by a metadata file that is in JSON format. A JSON metadata file contains information about a task, how to run the task, and any comments about how the file is written. Often, the metadata file is named the same as the task script but with a JSON extension. This is a standard way of sharing documentation about what a script can do and how it is structured. You can see this documentation by running the command **bolt task show** *modulename::taskfilename* at the command line.

Key Topic

SaltStack SSH (Server-Only Mode)

SaltStack offers an agentless option called Salt SSH that allows users to run Salt commands without having to install a minion on the remote device or node. This is similar in concept to Puppet Bolt. The main requirements to use Salt SSH are that the remote system must have SSH enabled and Python installed.

Salt SSH connects to a remote system and installs a lightweight version of SaltStack in a temporary directory and can then optionally delete the temporary directory and all files upon completion, leaving the remote system clean. These temporary directories can be left on the remote systems along with any necessary files to run Salt SSH. This way, the files do not have to be reinstalled to the remote device, which can be useful when time is a consideration. This is often useful on devices that are using Salt SSH more frequently than other devices in the environment.

Another benefit of using Salt SSH is that it can work in conjunction with the master/minion environment, or it can be used completely agentless across the environment. By default, Salt SSH uses roster files to store connection information for any host that doesn't have a minion installed. Example 29-16 shows the content structure of this file. It is easy to interpret the roster file and many other files associated with Salt SSH because they are constructed in human-readable form.

Example 29-16 *Salt SSH Roster File*

```
managed:
        host: 192.168.10.1
        user: admin
```

One of the major design considerations when using Salt SSH is that it is considerably slower than the 0MQ distributed messaging library. However, Salt SSH is still often considered faster than logging in to the system to execute the commands.

By automating daily configuration tasks, users can gain some of the following benefits:

- Increased agility
- Reduced opex
- Streamlined management
- Reduced human error

Comparing Tools

Many organizations face lean IT problems and high turnover, and network engineers are being asked to do more with less. Utilizing some of the tools covered in this chapter can help alleviate some of the pressure put on IT staff by offloading some of the more tedious, time-consuming, and repetitious tasks. A network operator can then focus more on critical mission responsibilities such as network design and growth planning. As mentioned earlier in this chapter, a majority of these tools function very similarly to one another. Table 29-7 provides a high-level comparison of the tools covered in this chapter.

Key Topic

Table 29-7 High-Level Configuration Management and Automation Tool Comparison

Factor	Puppet	Chef	Ansible	SaltStack
Architecture	Puppet servers and puppet agents	Chef server and Chef clients	Control station and remote hosts	Salt master and minions
Language	Puppet DSL	Ruby DSL	YAML	YAML
Terminology	Modules and manifests	Cookbooks and recipes	Playbooks and plays	Pillars and grains

Factor	Puppet	Chef	Ansible	SaltStack
Support for large-scale deployments	Yes	Yes	Yes	Yes
Agentless version	Puppet Bolt	N/A	Yes	Salt SSH

The most important factors in choosing a tool are how the tools are used and the skills of the operations staff who are adopting them. For instance, if a team is very fluent in Ruby, it may make sense to look at Chef. On the other hand, if the team is very confident at the command line, Ansible or SaltStack might be a good fit. The best tool for the job depends on the customer, and choosing one requires a thorough understanding of the differences between the tools and solid knowledge of what the operations team is comfortable with and that will play to their strengths.

Exam Preparation Tasks

You have a couple of choices for exam preparation: the exercises here, Chapter 30, "Final Preparation," and the exam simulation questions in the Pearson Test Prep Software Online.

Review All Key Topics

Review the most important topics in the chapter, noted with the Key Topic icon in the outer margin of the page. Table 29-8 lists these key topics and the page number on which each is found.

Key Topic

Table 29-8 Key Topics for Chapter 29

Key Topic Element	Description	Page
Paragraph	EEM applets and configuration	894
Section	Puppet	902
Section	Chef	904
Section	SaltStack (agent and server mode)	909
Section	Ansible	912
Section	Puppet Bolt	922
Section	SaltStack SSH (server-only mode)	923
Table 29-7	High-Level Configuration Management and Automation Tool Comparison	924

Complete Tables and Lists from Memory

There are no memory tables in this chapter.

Define Key Terms

Define the following key terms from this chapter and check your answers in the Glossary:

cookbooks, Embedded Event Manager (EEM), grain, manifest, module, pillar, play, playbook, recipe, Tcl

CHAPTER 30

Final Preparation

The first 29 chapters of this book cover the technologies, protocols, design concepts, and considerations required to be prepared to pass the 350-401 CCNP and CCIE Enterprise Core ENCOR exam. Although these chapters supply the detailed information, most people need more preparation than simply reading the first 29 chapters of this book. This chapter describes a set of tools and a study plan to help you complete your preparation for the exam.

This short chapter has two main sections. The first section lists exam preparation tools that you might find useful at this point in the study process. The second section provides a suggested study plan for you to follow now that you have completed all the earlier chapters in this book.

Getting Ready

Here are some important tips to keep in mind to ensure that you are ready for this rewarding exam:

- **Build and use a study tracker:** Consider using the exam objectives shown in this chapter to build a study tracker for yourself. Such a tracker can help ensure that you have not missed anything and that you are confident for your exam. As a matter of fact, this book offers a sample Study Planner as a website supplement.
- **Think about your time budget for questions on the exam:** When you do the math, you will see that, on average, you have one minute per question. While this does not sound like a lot of time, keep in mind that many of the questions will be very straightforward, and you will take 15 to 30 seconds on those. This leaves you extra time for other questions on the exam.
- **Watch the clock:** Check in on the time remaining periodically as you are taking the exam. You might even find that you can slow down pretty dramatically if you have built up a nice block of extra time.
- **Get some earplugs:** The testing center might provide earplugs but get some just in case and bring them along. There might be other test takers in the center with you, and you do not want to be distracted by their screams. I personally have no issue blocking out the sounds around me, so I never worry about this, but I know it is an issue for some.
- **Plan your travel time:** Give yourself extra time to find the center and get checked in. Be sure to arrive early. As you test more at a particular center, you can certainly start cutting it closer time-wise.

- **Get rest:** Most students report that getting plenty of rest the night before the exam boosts their success. All-night cram sessions are not typically successful.
- **Bring in valuables but get ready to lock them up:** The testing center will take your phone, your smartwatch, your wallet, and other such items and will provide a secure place for them.
- **Take notes:** You will be given note-taking implements and should not be afraid to use them. I always jot down any questions I struggle with on the exam. I then memorize them at the end of the test by reading my notes over and over again. I always make sure I have a pen and paper in the car, and I write down the issues in my car just after the exam. When I get home—with a pass or fail—I research those items!

Tools for Final Preparation

This section lists some information about the available tools and how to access the tools.

Pearson Test Prep Practice Test Software and Questions on the Website

Register this book to get access to the Pearson Test Prep practice test software (software that displays and grades a set of exam-realistic, multiple-choice questions). Using the Pearson Test Prep practice test software, you can either study by going through the questions in Study Mode or take a simulated (timed) CCNP and CCIE Enterprise Core exam.

The Pearson Test Prep practice test software comes with two full practice exams. These practice tests are available to you either online or as an offline Windows application. To access the practice exams that were developed with this book, please see the instructions in the card inserted in the sleeve in the back of the book. This card includes a unique access code that enables you to activate your exams in the Pearson Test Prep practice test software.

Accessing the Pearson Test Prep Software Online

The online version of this software can be used on any device with a browser and connectivity to the Internet including desktop machines, tablets, and smartphones. To start using your practice exams online, simply follow these steps:

Step 1. Go to http://www.PearsonTestPrep.com.

Step 2. Select Pearson IT Certification as your product group.

Step 3. Enter your email and password for your account. If you don't have an account on PearsonITCertification.com or CiscoPress.com, you need to establish one by going to PearsonITCertification.com/join.

Step 4. In the My Products tab, click the Activate New Product button.

Step 5. Enter the access code printed on the insert card in the back of your book to activate your product. The product will now be listed in your My Products page.

Step 6. Click the Exams button to launch the exam settings screen and start your exam.

Accessing the Pearson Test Prep Software Offline

If you wish to study offline, you can download and install the Windows version of the Pearson Test Prep practice test software. You can find a download link for this software on the book's companion website, or you can just enter this link in your browser:

http://www.pearsonitcertification.com/content/downloads/pcpt/engine.zip

To access the book's companion website and the software, simply follow these steps:

Step 1. Register your book by going to PearsonITCertification.com/register and entering the ISBN: **9780138216764**.

Step 2. Respond to the challenge questions.

Step 3. Go to your account page and select the Registered Products tab.

Step 4. Click the Access Bonus Content link under the product listing.

Step 5. Click the Install Pearson Test Prep Desktop Version link in the Practice Exams section of the page to download the software.

Step 6. When the software finishes downloading, unzip all the files on your computer.

Step 7. Double-click the application file to start the installation, and follow the onscreen instructions to complete the registration.

Step 8. When the installation is complete, launch the application and click the Activate Exam button on the My Products tab.

Step 9. Click the Activate a Product button in the Activate Product Wizard.

Step 10. Enter the unique access code found on the card in the sleeve in the back of your book and click the Activate button.

Step 11. Click Next, and then click the Finish button to download the exam data to your application.

Step 12. You can now start using the practice exams by selecting the product and clicking the Open Exam button to open the exam settings screen.

Note that the offline and online versions sync together, so saved exams and grade results recorded on one version will also be available to you on the other.

Customizing Your Exams

When you are in the exam settings screen, you can choose to take exams in one of three modes:

- Study Mode
- Practice Exam Mode
- Flash Card Mode

Study Mode enables you to fully customize your exams and review answers as you are taking the exam. This is typically the mode you use first to assess your knowledge and identify information gaps. Practice Exam Mode locks certain customization options to present a realistic exam experience. Use this mode when you are preparing to test your exam readiness. Flash Card Mode strips out the answers and presents you with only the question stem.

This mode is great for late-stage preparation, when you really want to challenge yourself to provide answers without the benefit of seeing multiple-choice options. This mode does not provide the detailed score reports that the other two modes provide, so it is not the best mode for helping you identify knowledge gaps.

In addition to these three modes, you will be able to select the source of your questions. You can choose to take exams that cover all the chapters, or you can narrow your selection to just a single chapter or the chapters that make up specific parts in the book. All chapters are selected by default. If you want to narrow your focus to individual chapters, simply deselect all the chapters and then select only those on which you wish to focus in the Objectives area.

You can also select the exam banks on which to focus. Each exam bank comes complete with a full exam of questions that cover topics in every chapter. You can have the test engine serve up exams from all banks or just from one individual bank by selecting the desired banks in the exam bank area.

There are several other customizations you can make to your exam from the exam settings screen, such as the time allowed to take the exam, the number of questions served up, whether to randomize questions and answers, whether to show the number of correct answers for multiple-answer questions, and whether to serve up only specific types of questions. You can also create custom test banks by selecting only questions that you have marked or questions on which you have added notes.

Updating Your Exams

If you are using the online version of the Pearson Test Prep practice test software, you should always have access to the latest version of the software as well as the exam data. If you are using the Windows desktop version, every time you launch the software, it will check to see if there are any updates to your exam data and automatically download any changes made since the last time you used the software. This requires that you are connected to the Internet at the time you launch the software.

Sometimes, due to a number of factors, the exam data might not fully download when you activate your exam. If you find that figures or exhibits are missing, you might need to manually update your exams.

To update a particular exam you have already activated and downloaded, simply select the Tools tab and click the Update Products button. Again, this is only an issue with the desktop Windows application.

If you wish to check for updates to the Windows desktop version of the Pearson Test Prep exam engine software, simply select the Tools tab and click the Update Application button. Doing so allows you to ensure that you are running the latest version of the software engine.

Premium Edition

In addition to the free practice exam provided on the website, you can purchase additional exams with expanded functionality directly from Pearson IT Certification. The Premium Edition of this title contains an additional two full practice exams and an eBook (in both PDF and ePub format). In addition, the Premium Edition title has remediation for each question to the specific part of the eBook that relates to that question.

Because you have purchased the print version of this title, you can purchase the Premium Edition at a deep discount. There is a coupon code in the book sleeve that contains a one-time-use code and instructions for where you can purchase the Premium Edition.

To view the Premium Edition product page, go to www.informit.com/title/9780138216931.

Chapter-Ending Review Tools

Chapters 1 through 29 each have several features in the "Exam Preparation Tasks" section at the end of the chapter. You might have already worked through these in each chapter. It can also be useful to use these tools again as you make your final preparations for the exam.

Suggested Plan for Final Review/Study

This section lists a suggested study plan from the point at which you finish reading through Chapter 29, until you take the 350-401 CCNP and CCIE Enterprise Core ENCOR exam. You can ignore this plan, use it as is, or just take suggestions from it.

The plan involves two steps:

Step 1. **Review key topics and "Do I Know This Already?" (DIKTA?) questions:** You can use the table that lists the key topics in each chapter or just flip the pages, looking for key topics. Also, reviewing the DIKTA? questions from the beginning of the chapter can be helpful for review.

Step 2. **Use the Pearson Test Prep practice test engine to practice:** The Pearson Test Prep practice test engine enables you to study using a bank of unique exam-realistic questions available only with this book.

Summary

The tools and suggestions listed in this chapter have been designed with one goal in mind: to help you develop the skills required to pass the 350-401 CCNP and CCIE Enterprise Core ENCOR exam. This book has been developed from the beginning to not just tell you the facts but to also help you learn how to apply the facts. No matter what your experience level leading up to when you take the exam, it is our hope that the broad range of preparation tools, and even the structure of the book, will help you pass the exam with ease. We hope you do well on the exam.

CHAPTER 31

ENCOR 350-401 Exam Updates

The Purpose of This Chapter

For all the other chapters, the content should remain unchanged throughout this edition of the book. Instead, this chapter will change over time, with an updated online PDF posted so that you can see the latest version of the chapter even after you purchase this book.

Why do we need a chapter that updates over time? For two reasons:

1. To add more technical content to the book before it is time to replace the current book edition with the next edition. This chapter will include additional technology content and possibly additional PDFs containing more content.
2. To communicate details about the next version of the exam, to tell you about our publishing plans for that edition, and to help you understand what that means to you.

After the initial publication of this book, Cisco Press will provide supplemental updates as digital downloads for minor exam updates. If an exam has major changes or accumulates enough minor changes, we will then announce a new edition. We will do our best to provide any updates to you free of charge before we release a new edition. However, if the updates are significant enough in between editions, we may release the updates as a low-priced standalone eBook.

If we do produce a free updated version of this chapter, you can access it on the book's companion website. Simply go to the companion website page and go to the "Exam Updates Chapter" section of that page.

If you have not yet accessed the companion website, follow this process:

Step 1. Browse to www.ciscopress.com/register.

Step 2. Enter the print book ISBN (even if you are using an eBook): **9780138216764**.

Step 3. After registering the book, go to your account page and select the **Registered Products** tab.

Step 4. Click on the **Access Bonus Content** link to access the companion website. Select the **Exam Updates Chapter** link or scroll down to that section to check for updates.

The following two sections give more detail about the primary purposes of the chapter. Any technical content or exam update details follow later in the chapter.

About Possible Exam Updates

Cisco introduced CCNA and CCNP in 1998. For the first 25 years of those certification tracks, Cisco updated the exams on average every 3–4 years. However, Cisco did not pre-announce the exam changes, so exam changes felt very sudden. Usually, a new exam would be announced, with new exam topics, giving you 3–6 months before your only option was to take the new exam. As a result, you could be studying with no idea about Cisco's plans, and the next day, you had a 3–6-month timeline to either pass the old exam or pivot to prepare for the new exam.

Thankfully, Cisco changed its exam release approach in 2023. Called the Cisco Certification Roadmap (https://cisco.com/go/certroadmap), the new plan includes these features:

1. Cisco considers changes to all exam tracks (CCNA, CCNP Enterprise, CCNP Security, and so on) annually.
2. Cisco uses a predefined annual schedule for each track, so even before any announcements, you know the timing of possible changes to the exam you are studying for.
3. The schedule moves in a quarterly sequence:
    a. Privately review the exam to consider what to change.
    b. Publicly announce if an exam is changing, and if so, announce details like exam topics and release date.
    c. Release the new exam.
4. Exam changes might not occur each year. If changes occur, Cisco characterizes them as minor (less than 20% change) or major (more than 20% change).

The specific dates for a given certification track can be confusing because Cisco organizes the work by fiscal year quarters. Figure 31-1 spells out the quarters with a sample 2024 fiscal year. The fiscal year begins in August, so, for example, the first quarter (Q1) of fiscal year (FY) 2024 begins in August 2023.

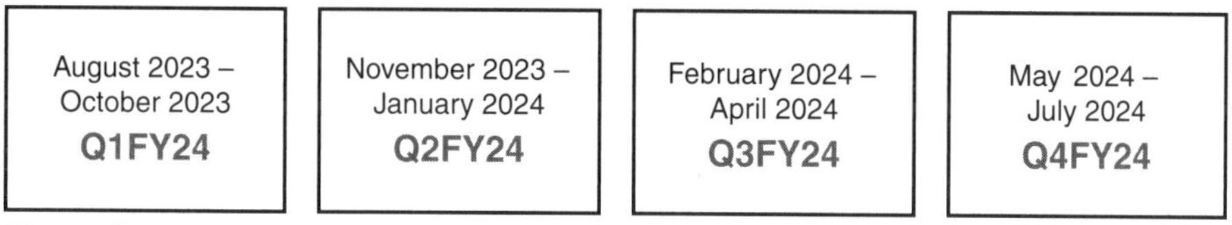

Figure 31-1 *Cisco Fiscal Year and Months Example (FY2024)*

Focus more on the sequence of the quarters to understand the plan. Over time, Cisco may make no changes in some years and minor changes in others.

Impact on You and Your Study Plan

Cisco's new policy helps you plan, but it also means that the exam might change before you pass the current exam. That impacts you, affecting how we deliver this book to you. This chapter gives us a way to communicate in detail about those changes as they occur. But you should watch other spaces also.

For those other information sources to watch, bookmark and check these sites for news. In particular:

- **Cisco:** Check the Certification Roadmap page: https://cisco.com/go/certroadmap. Make sure to sign up for automatic notifications from Cisco on that page.

- **Publisher:** View information about new certification products, offers, discounts, and free downloads related to the more frequent exam updates: https://www.ciscopress.com/newcert
- **Cisco Learning Network:** Subscribe to the CCNA Community at cs.co/9780138216764. We expect ongoing discussions about exam changes over time. If you have questions, search for "roadmap" in the CCNA community, and if you do not find an answer, ask a new one!

As changes arise, we will update this chapter with more details about exam and book content. At that point, we will publish an updated version of this chapter, listing our content plans. Those details will likely include the following:

- Content removed, so if you plan to take the new exam version, you can ignore those when studying.
- New content planned per new exam topics, so you know what's coming.

The remainder of the chapter shows the new content that may change over time.

News About the Next Exam Release

This statement was last updated on May 15, 2023, before the publication of the *CCNP and CCIE Enterprise Core ENCOR 350-401 Official Cert Guide*.

This version of this chapter has no news to share about the next exam release.

At the most recent version of this chapter, the 350-401 ENCOR: Implementing Cisco Enterprise Network Core Technologies exam version number was Version 1.1.

Updated Technical Content

The current version of this chapter has no additional technical content.

APPENDIX A

Answers to the "Do I Know This Already?" Questions

Chapter 1

1. D. The switch uses the destination MAC address to identify the port out of which the packet should be forwarded.
2. B. A switch uses the MAC address table to limit the Layer 2 communication between only the two devices communicating with each other.
3. B. The destination IP address is used to locate the longest matching route and the outbound interface out which it should be forwarded.
4. D. Broadcast domains do not cross Layer 3 boundaries. Splitting a Layer 2 topology into multiple subnets and joining them with a router reduces the size of a broadcast domain.
5. B. The CAM is high-speed memory that contains the MAC address table.
6. D. A distributed architecture uses dedicated components for building the routing table, adjacency table, and forwarding engines. This allows for the forwarding decisions to be made closer to the packet's egress and is more scalable.
7. B and D. CEF is composed of the adjacency table and the Forwarding Information Base.

Chapter 2

1. B. There are two BPDU types: the configuration BPDU and topology change notification BPDU.
2. B. The switch with the lowest bridge priority is elected as the root bridge. In the event of a tie, the bridge MAC address is used to elect a root bridge.
3. C. The original 802.1D specification set the value of 4 for a 1 Gbps interface.
4. B. All of the ports on a root bridge are assigned the designated port role (forwarding).
5. D. The default 802.1D specification places a switch port in the listening state for 15 seconds.
6. D. Upon receipt of a TCN BPDU, a switch sets the age for all MAC addresses to 15 seconds. Non-active/older entries are flushed from the MAC address table.
7. A and B. The blocking and listening states have been combined into the discarding state of RSTP.
8. B. False. STP has five port states, and RSTP has three port states: Discarding, Learning, and Forwarding.

9. B. False. RSTP allows for traffic to flow between switches that have synchronized with each other, while other parts of the Layer 2 topology converge. It is essential to understand that there is a potential for packet loss on any network that has not fully converged.

Chapter 3

1. D. A switch's STP priority increments in values of 4096. The priority is actually added to the VLAN number as part of the advertisement. The VLAN identifier is 12 bits, which is a decimal value of 4096.
2. B. False. The advertising path cost includes the calculate path cost but does not include the path cost of the interface from which the BPDU is being advertised.
3. A. True. As part of the STP algorithm, when two links exist between two switches, on the upstream switch, the port with the lower port priority is preferred.
4. D. BPDU guard generates a syslog message and places the port into an err-disabled state upon receipt of a BPDU. No traffic is forwarded until the port is recovered.
5. B. Root guard ensures that the designated port does not transition into a root port when a superior BPDU is received. In scenarios like this, the port is placed in a root inconsistent state for any VLANs that received a superior BPDU.
6. B. Unidirectional Link Detection (UDLD) solves the problem when a cable sends traffic in only one direction.

Chapter 4

1. A and B. MST enables traffic load balancing for specific VLANs through assignment of VLANs to specific instances that might have different topologies. MST also reduces the amount of CPU and memory processing as multiple VLANs are associated with an MST instance.
2. C. VLANs are associated with MST instances, and an instance defines the Layer 2 forwarding topology for the VLANs that are associated with it.
3. A. The original 802.1D specification accounted for one topology for all the VLANs, and Common Spanning Tree (CST) uses one topology for building a loop-free topology.
4. B. False. MST uses an internal spanning tree (IST) to advertise itself and other MST instances for building the topology. The local switch configuration associates VLANs with the MST instances.
5. B. False. The MST configuration is relevant to the entire MST region and should be the same for all switches in the region.
6. A. True. The MST topology can be tuned by setting priority, port cost, and port priority for each MST instance.
7. A and C. MST can interact with PVST+/RSTP environments by acting as a root bridge for all VLANs or ensuring that the PVST+/RSTP environment is the root bridge for all VLANs. MST cannot be a root bridge for some VLANs and then let the PVST+/RSTP environment be the root bridge for other VLANs.

Chapter 5

1. C. A switch can operate with the VTP roles client, server, transparent, and off.
2. B. False. The VTP summary includes the VTP version, domain, configuration revision, and timestamp.
3. B. False. There can be multiple VTP servers in a VTP domain. They process updates from other VTP servers just as with a client.
4. B. If the switch has a higher revision number than the current VTP domain, when a VLAN is deleted, it can send an update to the VTP server and remove that VLAN from all switches in the VTP domain.
5. B. False. Dynamic auto requires the other side to initiate a request in order for a trunk link to form.
6. C. The command **switchport nonegotiate** disables DTP on a port.
7. B. False. PAgP is a Cisco proprietary link bundling protocol.
8. A, B, and C. An EtherChannel bundle allows for a virtual port channel that acts as a Layer 2 (access or trunk) or Layer 3 routed interface.
9. A and B. An EtherChannel bundle provides increased bandwidth between devices and does not generate a topology change with the addition/removal of member links.
10. C. Desirable. If one device is configured with PAgP auto, the other device must be configured with desirable to form an EtherChannel bundle.
11. B. False. Only LACP allows you to set the maximum number of member links in an EtherChannel bundle.

Chapter 6

1. E. BGP is the only Exterior Gateway Protocol listed here.
2. A, B, C, and D. RIP, EIGRP, OSPF, and IS-IS are all classified as Interior Gateway Protocols.
3. E. BGP is a path vector routing protocol that selects the best path based on path attributes such as MED, local preference, and AS_PATH length.
4. A. Distance vector protocols, such as RIP, use only hop count to select the best path.
5. D. Link-state routing protocols use the interface cost as the metric for shortest path first (SPF) calculations.
6. C. The Cisco CEF sorts all network prefixes from shortest match to longest match for programming of the FIB. The path with the longest match is more explicit than a generic path.
7. B. When two different routing protocols attempt to install the same route into the RIB, the route with the lowest AD is installed into the RIB.
8. C. Equal-cost multipath is the installation of multiple paths (that are deemed the best path) into the RIB when they come from the same routing protocol.
9. C. Ethernet links should not use a directly attached static route, and a link failure could result in the resolution of the next-hop IP address resolving to an unintentional

link. The fully specified static route ensures that the next hop is resolvable using only the specified interface.

10. D. VRFs support multiprotocol (IPv4 and IPv6) addressing.

Chapter 7

1. B. EIGRP uses protocol number 88.
2. C. EIGRP uses the hello, request, reply, update, and query packet types.
3. A. An EIGRP successor is the next-hop router for the successor route (which is the loop-free route with the lowest path metric).
4. A, B, C, and E. The EIGRP topology table contains the destination network prefix, path attributes (hop count, minimum path bandwidth, and total path delay), and a list of nearby EIGRP neighbors.
5. B and D. EIGRP uses the multicast IP address 224.0.0.10 or MAC address 01:005E:00:00:0A when feasible.
6. C. The interface delay can be modified to change the EIGRP path calculations without modifying the path calculation of OSPF.
7. C. EIGRP uses a reference bandwidth of 10 Gbps with the default metrics.
8. B. EIGRP uses a default hello timer of 5 seconds for high-speed interfaces.
9. A. EIGRP considers stable paths to be passive.
10. C. EIGRP sends out a query packet with the delay set to infinity to indicate that a route has gone active.
11. B. False. Summarization of prefixes occurs as traffic is advertised out an interface with summarization configured.

Chapter 8

1. C. OSPF uses protocol number 89.
2. C. OSPFv2 uses five packet types for communication: hello, database description, link state request, link state update, and link state acknowledgment.
3. A and D. OSPF uses the multicast IP address 224.0.0.5 or the MAC address 01:00:5e:00:00:05 for the AllSPFRouters group.
4. B. False. OSPF can also be enabled with the interface parameter command **ip ospf** *process-id* **area** *area-id*.
5. B. False. The OSPF process ID is locally significant and is not required to match for neighbor adjacency.
6. B. False. An OSPF advertised default route always appears as an external route.
7. B. False. Serial point-to-point links are automatically set as an OSPF point-to-point network type, which does not have a designated router.
8. A. IOS XE uses a reference bandwidth of 100 Mbps for dynamic metric assignment to an interface.
9. A. Setting the interface priority to 0 removes the interface from the DR election process.
10. C. The loopback address is classified as an OSPF loopback interface type, which is always advertised as a /32 address, regardless of the subnet mask.

Chapter 9

1. B. False. A router needs to have an interface in Area 0 so that it can be an ABR.
2. B. False. An OSPF router contains copies of the LSDBs only for the areas it participates in.
3. D. OSPF uses six OSPF LSA types for routing IPv4 packets (Types 1, 2, 3, 4, 5, and 7). Additional LSAs exist for IPv6 and MPLS.
4. D. LSAs are deemed invalid when they reach 3600 seconds and are purged from the LSDB.
5. C. A router LSA (type 1) is associated with each OSPF-enabled interface.
6. B. False. Network LSAs (type 2) are not advertised outside the originating area. They are used with router LSAs (type 1) to build the summary LSA (type 3).
7. B. Type 3 LSAs received from a nonbackbone area only insert into the LSDB for the source area. ABRs do not create type 3 LSAs for the other areas.
8. B. False. OSPF prefers intra-area routes over inter-area routes as the first logic check. In the event that both paths use the same type, the total path metric is used.
9. A. True. While the number of network prefixes might remain the same, the numbers of type 1 and type 2 LSAs are reduced.
10. C. OSPF summarization occurs at the area level and is configured under the OSPF process.

Chapter 10

1. C. OSPFv3 uses five packet types for communication: hello, database description, link-state request, link-state update, and link-state acknowledgment. These packet types have exactly the same names and functions as the same packet types in OSPFv2.
2. F. OSPFv3 uses link-local addresses for a majority of communication, but it uses the destination IPv6 address (FF02::5) for hello packets and link-state updates.
3. C. Enabling OSPFv3 requires the interface configuration command **ospfv3** *process-id* **ipv6 area** *area-id*.
4. B. False. Without an IPv4 address, the router ID is set to 0.0.0.0, and it needs to be statically set to form a neighborship with another OSPFv3 router.
5. B. False. OSPFv3 requires an IPv6 link-local address to establish neighborship to exchange IPv6 or IPv4 routes.

Chapter 11

1. A and C. ASNs 64,512–65,534 are private ASNs within the 16-bit ASN range, and 4,200,000,000–4,294,967,294 are private ASNs within the extended 32-bit range.
2. A. Well-known mandatory attributes must be recognized by all BGP implementations and included with every prefix advertisement.
3. B. False. BGP neighbors are statically defined. There is a feature that supports dynamic discovery by one peer (though it is beyond the scope of this book), but the other router must still statically configure the remote BGP peer.

4. B. False. BGP supports multi-hop neighbor adjacency.
5. B. False. The IPv4 address family is automatically initialized by default on IOS-based devices.
6. B. The command **show bgp** *afi safi* **neighbors** displays all the neighbors, their capabilities, session timers, and other useful troubleshooting information.
7. C. BGP uses three tables (Adj-RIB-In, Loc-RIB, and Adj-RIB-Out) for storing BGP prefixes.
8. B. False. BGP advertises only the path that the local router deems is the best path.
9. B. The command **aggregate-address** *network subnet-mask* **summary-only** creates a BGP aggregate and suppresses the component routes.
10. A. True. The IPv6 address family does not exist by default on IOS-based devices.

Chapter 12

1. A, B, and D. Transit routing for enterprises is generally acceptable only for data centers connecting to MPLS networks.
2. A. True. IGPs use the destination field to select the smallest prefix length, whereas BGP uses it to match the subnet mask for a route.
3. B and C. Please see Figure 12-6 for an explanation.
4. D. Please see Table 12-6 for an explanation.
5. C. All routes are accepted and processed.
6. A. Because the route does not match the prefix list, sequence 10 does not apply, and the route moves on to sequence 20, which sets the metric to 200. It is implied that the route proceeds because it was modified.
7. A. True. A distribute list and a prefix list cannot be used at the same time for a neighbor. All other filtering techniques can be combined.
8. D. The other communities are common global communities.
9. B. Local preference is the second selection criterion for the BGP best path.
10. B. False. For MED to be used, the routes must come from the same AS.

Chapter 13

1. E. Multicast uses the one-to-many transmission method, where one server sends multicast traffic to a group of receivers.
2. B and C. Multicast relies on Internet Group Management Protocol (IGMP) for its operation in Layer 2 networks and Protocol Independent Multicast (PIM) for its operation in Layer 3 networks. It is routing protocol independent and can work with static RPs.
3. A and D. 239.0.0.0/8 (239.0.0.0 to 239.255.255.255) is the IANA IP multicast address range assigned to the administratively scoped block.
4. C. The first 24 bits of a multicast MAC address always start with 01:00:5E. The low-order bit of the first byte is the individual/group bit (I/G) bit, also known as the unicast/multicast bit, and when it is set to 1, it indicates that the frame is a multicast frame and the 25th bit is always 0.

5. A and B. When a receiver wants to receive a multicast stream, it sends an unsolicited membership report, commonly referred to as an IGMP join, to the local router for the group it wants to join.
6. C. IGMPv3 supports all IGMPv2's IGMP message types and is backward compatible with it. The differences between the two are that IGMPv3 added new fields to the IGMP membership query and introduced a new IGMP message type called a Version 3 membership report to support source filtering.
7. B. IGMPv3 is backward compatible with IGMPv2. To receive traffic from all sources, which is the behavior of IGMPv2, a receiver uses exclude mode membership with an empty exclude list.
8. C. IGMP snooping, defined in RFC 4541, examines IGMP joins sent by receivers and maintains a table of interfaces to IGMP joins. When a switch receives a multicast frame destined for a multicast group, it forwards the packet only out the ports where IGMP joins were received for that specific multicast group. This prevents multicast traffic from flooding in a Layer 2 network.
9. B and C. A source tree is a multicast distribution tree where the source is the root of the tree, and branches form a distribution tree through the network all the way down to the receivers. When this tree is built, it uses the shortest path through the network from the source to the leaves of the tree; for this reason, it is also referred to as a *shortest path tree*. A shared tree is a multicast distribution tree where the root of the shared tree is not the source but a router designated as the rendezvous point (RP). For this reason, shared trees are also referred to as RP trees (RPTs).
10. B. The last-hop router (LHR) is a router that is directly attached to the receivers. It is responsible for sending PIM joins upstream toward the RP or to the source after an SPT switchover.
11. B. When there is an active source attached to the FHR, the FHR encapsulates the multicast data from the source in a special PIM-SM message called the register message and unicasts that data to the RP by using a unidirectional PIM tunnel. When the RP receives the register message, it decapsulates the multicast data packet inside the register message, and if there is no active shared tree because there are no interested receivers, the RP sends a register stop message to the FHR, instructing it to stop sending the register messages.
12. C. Auto-RP is a Cisco proprietary mechanism that automates the distribution of group-to-RP mappings in a PIM network.
13. B. PIM-DM does not use RPs. When PIM is configured in sparse mode, it is mandatory to choose one or more routers to operate as rendezvous points (RPs).

Chapter 14

1. B, C, and E. The leading causes of quality of service issues are lack of bandwidth, latency and jitter, and packet loss.
2. A, C, D, and F. Network latency can be broken down into propagation delay, serialization delay, processing delay, and delay variation.
3. B. Best effort, IntServ, and DiffServ are the three QoS implementation models.

4. A. IntServ uses Resource Reservation Protocol (RSVP) to reserve resources throughout a network for a specific application and to provide call admission control (CAC) to guarantee that no other IP traffic can use the reserved bandwidth.

5. C. DiffServ is the most popular and most widely deployed QoS model. It was designed to address the limitations of the best effort and IntServ.

6. D. The command **class-map [match-any | match-all]** *class-map-name* is used to configure the class map that is then applied as a traffic class under the policy map with the command **class** *class-map-name*. The command **class [match-any | match-all]** *class-map-name* does not exist.

7. D. The command **service-policy [input|output]** *policy-map-name* is used to apply policy maps to interfaces in an inbound and/or outbound direction. The command **service-policy** *policy-map-name* is used to apply a child policy map inside a parent policy map. The commands **policy-map [input|output]** *policy-map-name* and **policy-map [inbound|outbound]** *policy-map-name* do not exist.

8. B. Packet classification should take place at the network edge, as close to the source of the traffic as possible, in an effort to provide an end-to-end QoS experience.

9. B. The IPv4 ToS field and the IPV6 traffic class field were redefined as an 8-bit Differentiated Services (DiffServ) field. The DiffServ field is composed of a 6-bit Differentiated Services Code Point (DSCP) field that allows for classification of up to 64 values (0 to 63) and a 2-bit Explicit Congestion Notification (ECN) field.

10. B and C. The commands **set ip dscp** and **set dscp** can be used to mark classified traffic. The command **mark ip dscp** does not exist.

11. A. Policers drop or re-mark incoming or outgoing traffic that goes beyond a desired traffic rate.

12. A and C. The Committed Time Interval (Tc) is the time interval in milliseconds (ms) over which the Committed Burst (Bc) is sent. Tc can be calculated with the formula Tc = (Bc [bits] / CIR [bps]) × 1000. For single-rate three-color markers/policers (srTCMs) and two-rate three-color markers/policers (trTCMs), Tc can also refer to the Bc Bucket Token Count (Tc), which is the number of tokens in the Bc bucket.

13. A and D. CBWFQ and LLQ provide real-time, delay-sensitive traffic bandwidth and delay guarantees while not starving other types of traffic.

14. A. WRED provides congestion avoidance by selectively dropping packets before the queue buffers are full. Packet drops can be manipulated by traffic weights denoted by either IP Precedence (IPP) or DSCP. Packets with lower IPP values are dropped more aggressively than are those with higher IPP values; for example, IPP 3 would be dropped more aggressively than IPP 5 or DSCP, and AFx3 would be dropped more aggressively than AFx2, and AFx2 would be dropped more aggressively than AFx1.

15. B and D. The command **priority level** {**1** | **2**} **percent** *police-rate-in-percentage* [*burst-in-bytes*] enables multilevel strict priority with the policing rate calculated as a percentage of the interface bandwidth or the shaping rate in a hierarchical policy. With this type of policer, policing is in effect only during times of congestion. This means that if there is enough free bandwidth available, classified traffic can go over the configured policing percentage.

Chapter 15

1. B. NTP uses the stratum to measure the number of hops a device is from a time source to provide a sense of time accuracy.
2. B. False. An NTP client can be configured with multiple NTP servers but can synchronize its time with only one active NTP server. Only during failure does the NTP client use a different NTP server.
3. B. False. PTPv2 is not backward-compatible with PTP.
4. A and D. A first-hop redundancy protocol creates a virtual IP address for a default gateway, and this address can be used by computers or devices that only have a static default route.
5. B and C. HSPR and GLBP are Cisco proprietary FHRPs.
6. A. The HSRP VIP gateway instance is defined with the command **standby** *instance-id* **ip** *vip-address*.
7. D. Gateway Load Balancing Protocol provides load-balancing support to multiple AVFs.
8. D. The command **show ip nat translations** displays the active translation table on a NAT device.
9. A. The router would be using a form of inside NAT, and the 10.1.1.1 IP address is the inside local IP address; the IP address that a server on the Internet would use for return traffic is the inside global address.
10. D. The default NAT timeout is 24 hours.

Chapter 16

1. C and D. When you are configuring a tunnel interface, the default mode is GRE, so there is no need to specify the tunnel mode with the command **tunnel mode gre {ip | ipv6}**.The command is useful when the tunnel mode is changed to another type (such as IPsec) and there is a need to change the tunnel mode back to GRE.

   The **keepalive** command is also optional. It is used to make sure the other end of the tunnel is operational. This command does not need to be configured on both ends of the tunnel in order to work.
2. A. GRE was originally created to provide transport for non-routable legacy protocols such as Internetwork Packet Exchange (IPX) across an IP network, and it is now more commonly used as an overlay for IPv4 and IPv6.
3. B. The tunnel source interface or source IP address should not be advertised into a GRE tunnel because it would cause recursive routing issues.
4. A and C. Traditional IPsec provides two modes of packet transport: tunnel mode and transport mode.
5. A and B. DES and 3DES are weak encryption protocols that are no longer recommended for use.
6. C. The message exchange method used to establish an IPsec SA for IKEv1 is known as quick mode. Main mode and aggressive mode are IKEv1 methods used to establish IKE SAs. For IKEv2, IKE_Auth creates an IPsec SA. If additional IPsec SAs are needed, a CREATE_CHILD_SA exchange is used to establish them.

A

7. A and D. LISP separates IP addresses into endpoint identifiers (EIDs) and routing locators (RLOCs).

8. A. The destination UDP port used by the LISP data plane is 4341. UDP port 4342 is used for LISP's control plane messages.

9. B. An ETR may also request that the MS answer map requests on its behalf by setting the proxy map reply flag (P-bit) in the map register message.

10. B. The IANA's assigned VXLAN UDP destination port is 4789, while for Linux it is port 8472. The reason for this discrepancy is that when VXLAN was first implemented in Linux, the VXLAN UDP destination port had not yet been officially assigned, and Linux decided to use port 8472 because many vendors at the time were using that value.

11. B. The VXLAN specification defines VXLAN as a data plane protocol, but it does not define a VXLAN control plane, which was left open to be used with any control plane.

Chapter 17

1. A. When the two power levels are the same, the result is 0 dB. As long as you remember the first handy 0 dB fact, you will find exam questions like this easy. If not, you will need to remember that dB = 10log 10 (100 mW / 100 mW) = 10log 10 (1) = 0 dB.

2. C. At first glance, 17 mW and 34 mW might seem like odd numbers to work with. Notice that if you double 17, you get 34. The second handy dB fact says that doubling a power level will increase the dB value by 3.

3. D. Start with transmitter A's level of 1 mW and try to figure out some simple operations that can be used to get to transmitter B's level of 100 mW. Remember the handy dB facts, which use multiplication by 2 and 10. In this case, 1 mW × 10 = 10mW × 10 = 100 mW. Each multiplication by 10 adds 10 dB, so the end result is 10 + 10 = 20 dB. Notice that transmitter B is being compared to A (the reference level), which is 1 mW. You could also state the end result in dB-milliwatt (dBm).

4. C. This question involves a *reduction* in the power level, so the dB value must be negative. Try to find a simple way to start with 100 and get to 40 by multiplying or dividing by 2 or 10. In this case, 100 / 10 = 10; 10 × 2 = 20; 20 × 2 = 40. Dividing by 10 reduced the dB value by 10 dB; then multiplying by 2 increased the total by + 3 dB; multiplying again by 2 increased the total by +3 more dB. In other words, dB = 10 + 3 + 3 = 4 dB.

5. B. Remember that the EIRP involves radiated power, and that is calculated using only the transmitter components. The EIRP is the sum of the transmitter power level (+20 dBm), the cable loss (2 dB), and the antenna gain (+5 dBi). Therefore, the EIRP is +23 dBm.

6. D. A high SNR is best, where the received signal strength is more elevated above the noise floor. A 30 dBm SNR separates the signal from the noise more than a 10 dBm SNR does. Likewise, a higher RSSI value means that the signal strength alone is higher. When RSSI values are presented in dBm, remember that 0 dBm is high, while 100 dBm is very low.

7. A. Energy traveling in an electromagnetic wave spreads in three dimensions, weakening the signal strength over a distance.
8. B. The 802.11b and g devices operate at 2.4 GHz, which is less affected by free space loss than the 802.11a device, at 5 GHz.
9. B and C. Both 16-QAM and 64-QAM alter the amplitude and phase of a signal.
10. D. When you switch to a less-complex modulation scheme, more of the data stream can be repeated to overcome worsening RF conditions. This can be done automatically through DRS.

Chapter 18

1. B. An AP transports client traffic through a tunnel back to a wireless LAN controller. Therefore, client-to-client traffic typically passes through both the AP, the controller, and back through the AP.
2. D. Because the network is built with a WLC and APs, CAPWAP tunnels are required. One CAPWAP tunnel connects each AP to the WLC, for a total of 32 tunnels. CAPWAP encapsulates wireless traffic inside an additional IP header, so the tunnel packets are routable across a Layer 3 network. That means the APs and WLC can reside on any IP subnet as long as the subnets are reachable. There are no restrictions for the APs and WLC to live on the same Layer 2 VLAN or Layer 3 IP subnet.
3. D. In an embedded design, an access layer switch also functions as a WLC so that all user access (wired and wireless) converges in a single layer.
4. B. An AP discovers all possible WLCs before attempting to build a CAPWAP tunnel or join a controller.
5. C. After an AP boots, it compares its own software image to that of the controller it has joined. If the images differ, the AP downloads a new image from the controller.
6. F. An AP can learn controller addresses by using any of the listed methods except for an over-the-air neighbor message. APs do send neighbor messages over the air, but they are used to discover neighboring APs—not potential WLCs to join.
7. C. If an AP cannot find a viable controller, it reboots and tries the discovery process over again.
8. D. If the primary controller responds to an AP's discovery methods, the AP will always try to join it first, ahead of any other controller. Configuring an AP with a primary controller is the most specific method because it points the AP to a predetermined controller. Other methods are possible, but they can yield ambiguous results that could send an AP to one of several possible controllers.
9. B. By configuring profiles and tags, you can map customized properties to specific APs.
10. C. IOS-XE controllers map site tags, RF tags, and policy tags to each AP.
11. B.
12. A and E. An omnidirectional antenna is usually used to cover a large area. Therefore, it has a large beamwidth. Because it covers a large area, its gain is usually small.

Chapter 19

1. B. The client must associate with a BSS offered by an AP.
2. A. The client device is in complete control of the roaming decision, based on its own roaming algorithm. It uses active scanning and probing to discover other candidate APs that it might roam to.
3. C. Because a single controller is involved, the roam occurs in an intracontroller fashion. Even though the client thinks it is associating with APs, the associations actually occur at the controller, thanks to the split-MAC architecture.
4. C. Intracontroller roaming is the most efficient because the reassociation and client authentication occur within a single controller.
5. C. Cisco Centralized Key Management (CCKM) is used to cache key information between a client and an AP. The cached information is then used as a quick check when a client roams to a different AP.
6. D. In a Layer 2 roam, the client's IP subnet does not change as it moves between controllers. Therefore, there is no need to tunnel the client data between the controllers; instead, the client simply gets handed off to the new controller.
7. D. The anchor controller, where the client starts, maintains the client's state and builds a tunnel to the foreign controller, to which the client has now roamed.
8. C. Controllers A and B are listed in each other's mobility list, so they are known to each other. However, they are configured with different mobility group names. Clients may roam between the two controllers, but CCKM and PKC information will not be exchanged.
9. C. The client's received signal strength (RSS) can be used to calculate an approximate distance from the AP based on the free space path loss attenuation.

Chapter 20

1. E. Open Authentication requires no other mechanism. The wireless client must simply send an 802.11 authentication request to the AP.
2. B. Open Authentication cannot be used with authentication methods based on PSK, EAP, or 802.1x, because they are mutually exclusive. It can be used with WebAuth to allow wireless clients to easily connect and view or authenticate through a web page.
3. B and C. The same key must be configured on all client devices that will need to connect to the WLAN. In addition, the key must be configured on all APs and WLCs where the WLAN will exist. These keys are not normally unique to each wireless client unless the identity PSK feature is used in conjunction with ISE. PSK-based authentication does not require a RADIUS server.
4. B. The WPA, WPA2, and WPA3 personal modes all use Pre-Shared Key authentication.
5. D. Each successive WPA version is considered to be more secure than its predecessor. Therefore, WPA3 is the most secure due to its new and more complex features.
6. A, C, and E. The personal modes of all WPA versions use Pre-Shared Key authentication.
7. C. The EAPOL four-way handshake is used to exchange encryption key material between a wireless client and an AP.

8. C. A controller becomes an authenticator in the 802.1x process.
9. A. The supplicant is located on the wireless client. The WLC becomes the authenticator, and the RADIUS server is the authentication server (AS).
10. D. WebAuth authentication can display policies and require interaction from the end user, provided that the user opens a web browser after attempting to connect to the WLAN. WebAuth can integrate with the other authentication methods, but it is the only one that can display the policy and receive the users' acceptance.

Chapter 21

1. B. The first course of action should always be to gather as much information as possible so that you can reduce the scope of the problem. Then you can investigate the few potential causes that remain.
2. C. The wireless MAC address is always an important parameter because you can enter it into the search bar of a WLC to find the client device.
3. D. The status Online means that the client has passed through each phase and policy that the WLC required and has successfully joined the wireless network.
4. C. The status Online means that the client has successfully joined the network. The other states occur earlier in the connection sequence.
5. A, B, and C. The client has not yet passed the Authentication stage, so it must have failed to authenticate itself correctly. If the WLAN uses WPA2-Personal, then the client's pre-shared key could be incorrect.
6. C. An SNR value of 5 is extremely low. Ideally, you would want to see a high signal level and a low noise level, which would yield a high SNR.
7. D. From the information given, you can verify that the AP is operating on a valid 5GHz channel number and has a valid transmit power level. The SNR value of 45 dBm is high, which is good. The number of clients seems low, which might indicate that the channel utilization should be low too. However, the channel utilization is very high, which would impede stations from being able to transmit efficiently on the channel.
8. B. A radioactive trace on an IOS-XE controller is used to collect event logs that are triggered by a specific MAC address while the trace is running.

Chapter 22

1. A, B, C, D, and F. The benefits of a hierarchical LAN design include the following:
   - It allows for easier troubleshooting and management.
   - It is highly scalable.
   - It provides a simplified design.
   - It offers improved performance.
   - It allows for faster problem isolation.
   - It provides cost-effective redundancy.

The best design for modern data centers with east-west traffic patterns is a leaf-spine architecture.

2. D. The access layer, also commonly referred as the network edge, is where end-user devices and endpoints connect to the network.
3. B. In a hierarchical LAN design, distribution layer switches are deployed in pairs within building blocks or places in the network (PINs).
4. B. NSF is not a configurable feature; it is enabled when SSO is enabled. This is the reason why SSO and NSF are typically referred to as SSO/NSF.
5. C. Graceful Restart (GR) uses routing protocol extensions to notify a BGP neighbor router that the router undergoing the RP switchover can continue to forward packets, but may bring down its routing adjacency for a brief period of time.
6. C. Small campus networks that don't require an independent core can collapse the core function into the distribution layer. This is known as a two-tier, or collapsed core, design.
7. A and B. The WAN edge can provide dedicated interconnections to cloud providers, and the Internet edge can provide cloud provider connectivity not requiring dedicated interconnections.
8. A, B, C, and D. A simplified campus design relies on switch clustering such as virtual switching systems (VSSs) and stacking technologies such as StackWise, in which multiple physical switches act as a single logical switch.

Chapter 23

1. B. Although LISP is the control plane for the SD-Access fabric, it does not use LISP data encapsulation for the data plane; instead, it uses VXLAN encapsulation because it is capable of encapsulating the original Ethernet header, and this allows SD-Access to support Layer 2 and Layer 3 overlays.
2. B. The original VXLAN specification was enhanced for SD-Access to support Cisco TrustSec Scalable Group Tags (SGTs). This was accomplished by adding new fields to the first 4 bytes of the VXLAN header in order to transport up to 64,000 SGTs. The new VXLAN format is called *VXLAN Group Policy Option (GPO)*, and it is defined in the IETF draft draft-smith-vxlan-group-policy-05.
3. A. The SD-Access fabric control plane is based on Locator/ID Separation Protocol (LISP).
4. A. The VXLAN-GPO specification includes a 16-bit identifier that is used to carry the SGT tag called the Group Policy ID.
5. C. Cisco SD-Access was designed for enterprise campus and branch network environments and not for other types of network environments, such as data center, service provider, and WAN environments.
6. A, B, D, E, F, and G. The SD-Access architecture includes the following components:
   - **Cisco switches:** Provide wired (LAN) access to the fabric. Multiple types of Cisco Catalyst switches are supported, including NX-OS.
   - **Cisco routers:** Provide WAN and branch access to the fabric. Multiple types of Cisco ASR 1000, ISR, and CSR routers, including the CSRv and ISRv cloud routers, are supported.

- **Cisco wireless:** Cisco WLCs and APs provide wireless (WLAN) access to the fabric.
- **Cisco controller appliances:** There are only two types of appliances to consider: Cisco DNA Center and Cisco ISE. Cisco ISE supports both VM and physical appliance deployment models.

7. A, B, C, and D. The Cisco SD-WAN solution is composed of four mandatory components and an optional analytics service:
   - vManage network management system (NMS)
   - vSmart controller
   - SD-WAN routers
   - vBond orchestrator
   - *vAnalytics (optional)*
8. B. The vSmart controller establishes permanent and secure Datagram Transport Layer Security (DTLS) connections to all SD-WAN routers in the SD-WAN fabric and runs a proprietary routing protocol called Overlay Management Protocol (OMP) over each of the DTLS tunnels.
9. B. SD-WAN is transport agnostic and can use any type of IP-based underlay transport networks, such as the Internet, satellite, dedicated circuits, 3G/4G LTE, and MPLS.
10. C. vManage is the single pane of glass for the SD-WAN solution.
11. B. The main function of the vBond orchestrator is to authenticate the vSmart controllers and the SD-WAN routers and orchestrate connectivity between them.

Chapter 24

1. B. The default number of attempted hops for **traceroute** is 30 hops.
2. A, B, and E. MTU, hello timers, and network masks have to match for OSPF neighbor adjacencies to form.
3. E. The latest version of NetFlow is Version 9.
4. B. Flexible NetFlow allows for matching on key fields and collecting non-key fields.
5. B, C, and E. Flexible NetFlow requires a flow record, a flow monitor, and a flow exporter. A flow sampler is optional.
6. C. ERSPAN is used to send captures to an analyzer across a Layer 3 routed link.
7. A, B, C, and F. IP SLA can be used to monitor many different things related to monitoring traffic. SNMP and syslog are used to send IP SLA traps and messages.
8. A, B, and E. Cisco DNA Center currently has Design, Policy, Provision, Assurance, and Platform components.
9. B. Cisco DNA Center also manages wireless components.
10. A and D. Cisco DNA Center Assurance gathers streaming telemetry from devices and uses open API to integrate with Cisco Identity Services Engine (ISE) to provide user/group context. Plug and Play and simplified provisioning are not related to troubleshooting or diagnostics.

Chapter 25

1. C. Cisco SAFE is the Cisco security architectural framework.
2. B through G. Cisco SAFE places in the network (PINs) are data center, branch office, edge, campus, cloud, and WAN.
3. A, B, and D. Cisco SAFE secure domains include management, security intelligence, compliance, segmentation, threat defense, and secure services.
4. C. Talos is the Cisco threat intelligence organization.
5. B. Cisco Secure Malware Analytics (formerly Threat Grid) is a solution that performs static and dynamic file analysis by testing files in a sandbox environment.
6. B. Cisco Secure Network Analytics (formerly Cisco Stealthwatch) relies on telemetry data from NetFlow, IPFIX, and other sources for security analysis.
7. A. pxGrid requires a pxGrid controller, and Cisco ISE is the only platform that can perform this role.
8. B. Cisco EAP-FAST is the only EAP method that can perform simultaneous machine and user authentication, also known as EAP chaining.
9. B. This is false because endpoints are completely unaware of SGT tags. Only the networking infrastructure can be aware of SGT tags.
10. A, B, and E. TrustSec configuration is divided into three different phases to make it simple to understand and implement: classification, enforcement, and propagation.

Chapter 26

1. A. ACLs are applied to interfaces with the command **ip access-group** {*access-list-number* | *name*} {**in**|**out**}.
2. B. Type 7 passwords use a Cisco proprietary Vigenere cypher encryption algorithm that is very weak and can be easily decrypted using multiple online password decryption utilities.
3. C. The command **service password encryption** encrypts plaintext passwords in the configuration and Telnet sessions with type 7 password encryption.
4. A and D. The **login** command is used to enable line password authentication, and the **login local** command is used to enable username-based authentication.
5. A, B, E, and F. Privilege level 0 makes available the **disable**, **enable**, **exit**, **help**, and **logout** commands.
6. C and D. Using the command **transport input ssh** and applying an ACL to the line that only allows port 22 are valid options to allow only SSH traffic into the line. The other two options are not valid because the command **transport output ssh** does not affect inbound connections, and the command **transport input all** allows all inbound SSH and Telnet sessions.
7. B. This is false because AAA authorization for the console is disabled by default to prevent inexperienced users from locking themselves out. Authorization for the console is enabled with the command **aaa authorization console**.

8. C. Accounting provides the ability to track and log user access, including user identities, start and stop times, executed commands (that is, CLI commands), and so on. In other words, it maintains a security log of events.
9. D. TACACS+ is preferred for device access control because it can individually authorize every command that a user tries to execute after logging in to a device. In contrast, RADIUS requires those commands to be sent in the initial authentication response, and because there could be thousands of CLI command combinations, a large authorization result list could trigger memory exhaustion on the network device.
10. B and D. ZBFW is an integrated IOS solution that provides router stateful firewall functionality.
11. E and F. Within the ZBFW architecture, there are two system-built zones: self and default.
12. C. Control plane policing (CoPP) was created with the sole purpose of protecting the CPU or control plane of a router.
13. A. CoPP supports inbound and outbound policies; however, outbound policies are not commonly used.
14. B and D. Cisco Discovery Protocol (CDP) and Link Layer Discovery Protocol (LLDP) can provide unnecessary information to routers outside of the organization and should be disabled where applicable.

Chapter 27

1. B. A virtual machine is a software emulation of a virtual server with an operating system.
2. D. A container is an isolated environment where containerized applications run. It contains the application, along with the dependencies that the application needs to run. It is created by a container engine running a container image.
3. A, B, and D. Rkt, Docker, and LXD are container engines. The vSphere hypervisor is a hypervisor that enables the creation of VMs.
4. B. A virtual switch (vSwitch) is a software-based Layer 2 switch that operates like a physical Ethernet switch and enables VMs to communicate with each other within a virtualized server and with external physical networks through the physical network interface cards (pNICs).
5. B. Multiple vSwitches can be created under a virtualized server, but network traffic cannot flow directly from one vSwitch to another vSwitch within the same host, and they cannot share the same pNIC.
6. B. Containers, just like VMs, rely on vSwitches (also known as virtual bridges) for communication within a node (server) or the outside world.
7. A. A virtual network function (VNF) is the virtual or software version of a physical network function (NF) such as a firewall, and it typically runs on a hypervisor as a VM.
8. B. Network functions virtualization (NFV) is an architectural framework created by the European Telecommunications Standards Institute (ETSI) that defines standards

to decouple network functions from proprietary hardware-based appliances and have them run in software on standard x86 servers. It also defines how to manage and orchestrate the network functions.

9. D. Service chaining refers to chaining VNFs together to provide an NFV service or solution.
10. C. In SR-IOV, the emulated PCIe devices are called *virtual functions (VFs)*, and the physical PCIe devices are called *physical functions (PFs)*.
11. B. Cisco DNA Center provides the VNF management and NFV orchestration capabilities. It allows for easy automation of the deployment of virtualized network services, consisting of multiple VNFs. APIC-EM and ESA are no longer part of the Enterprise NFV solution.
12. A. NFVIS is based on standard Linux packaged with additional functions for virtualization, VNF lifecycle management, monitoring, device programmability, and hardware acceleration.

Chapter 28

1. B. Python is one of the easier programming languages to learn and adopt.
2. D. To authenticate to the Cisco DNA Center controller, a POST operation must be used. The reason is that the login credentials need to be sent to the controller to be verified.
3. B. CRUD stands for CREATE, READ, UPDATE, and DELETE. These are the common actions associated with the manipulation of data. For example, a database uses these actions.
4. D. Cisco vManage uses the Headers Content-Type x-www-form-urlencoded. X-Auth-Token is for Cisco DNA Center.
5. A. A JSON data format is built from key/value pairs. For example, "father": "Jason" is a key/value pair, where father is the key, and Jason is the value.
6. C. The HTTP status code 401 means Unauthorized—referring to incorrect login credentials or not having valid authentication to a destination. The following table lists more HTTP status codes.

HTTP Status Code	Result	Common Reason for This Code
200	OK	Using GET or POST to exchange data with an API
201	Created	Creating resources using a REST API call
400	Bad Request	Request failed due to client-side issue
401	Unauthorized	Client not authenticated to access site or API call
403	Forbidden	Access not granted based on supplied credentials
404	Not Found	Page at HTTP URL location does not exist or is hidden

7. A and D. Python uses quotation marks in a row to begin and end a multiple-line string, such as for a long comment.
8. A. Python uses curly braces ({}) as one way to signify a dictionary.

9. C and D. Functions can be defined or can already exist within Python. print is a default function, whereas dnac_login is a custom-created function.
10. D. Cisco DNA Center uses basic authentication for the initial authentication method. The Headers Content-Type X-Auth-Token is used to send the token back to Cisco DNA Center for future API calls. JSON is the data format of the requests and responses.
11. D. To access API information.
12. A, C, and D. GitHub is a place to store and share code with other developers as well as provide documentation for that code.
13. A and D. The CLI is difficult to scale when configuring multiple devices at the same time. The reason is that the CLI is designed for configuration of a single device on a device-by-device basis. Although scripting can help with some of the burden, it is not the best method for scaling. Consistency in configuration from device to device also becomes more difficult to manage as a network grows.
14. B and C. Leaf and Container are parts of a YANG model. A container can hold multiple leafs.

Chapter 29

1. B. Configuring a large number of devices by using the CLI is not only time-consuming but also leads to an increase in human error, ultimately putting the business at risk.
2. A, B, and E. Ansible, Puppet Bolt, and Salt SSH all are agentless tools.
3. C and D. Ansible uses playbooks, plays, and tasks.
4. A and D. Ansible and SaltStack are built on Python and can leverage Python to programmatically interact with the tool.
5. B. This is a YAML structure. A YAML file can also begin with three dashes (---).
6. C. Chef uses Ruby DSL for its cookbooks.
7. A, B, C, and D. Puppet Forge and GitHub can help with many different aspects of software delivery, including code revisions, associated developers, sharing of code, and becoming more agile in the development process.
8. B. PPDIOO consists of six components: Prepare, Plan, Design, Implement, Operate, and Optimize. Figure 29-9 provides more information.
9. B. Ansible uses Yet Another Markup Language (YAML) for the creation of playbook files. TAML doesn't exist.
10. A. **ansible-playbook** *FileName*.**yaml** is the correct command to execute a playbook. Playbooks are built from Yet Another Markup Language (YAML) files. TAML files do not exist.
11. B and C. Chef and SaltStack are agent-based tools.

GLOSSARY

802.1p An IEEE specification that defines the use of the 3-bit Priority Code Point (PCP) field to provide different classes of service. The PCP field is contained within the TCI field, which is part of the 802.1Q header.

802.1Q An IEEE specification that defines two 2-byte fields, Tag Protocol Identifier (TPID) and Tag Control Information (TCI), that are inserted within an Ethernet frame.

802.1x An IEEE standard for port-based network access control (PNAC) that provides an authentication mechanism for local area networks (LANs) and wireless LANs (WLANs).

A

access control list (ACL) A mechanism that provides packet classification for quality of service (QoS), routing protocols, and basic firewall functionality.

access layer The network layer that gives endpoints and users direct access to the network.

access port A switch port that is configured for only one specific VLAN and generally connects end-user devices.

address family A major classification of type of network protocol, such as IPv4, IPv6, or VPNv4.

Address Resolution Protocol (ARP) A protocol that resolves a MAC address to a specific IP address.

administrative distance A rating of trustworthiness for a route. Generally, it is associated with the routing process that installs the route into the RIB.

AMP for Networks AMP running on Cisco Secure Firewall appliances and dedicated Cisco AMP appliances for network malware defense.

amplitude The height from the top peak to the bottom peak of a signal's waveform; also known as the peak-to-peak amplitude.

anchor controller The original controller a client was associated with before a Layer 3 intercontroller roam. An anchor controller can also be used for tunneling clients on a guest WLAN or with a static anchor. Traffic is tunneled from the client's current controller (the foreign controller) back to the anchor.

application programming interface (API) A set of functions and procedures used for configuring or monitoring computer systems, network devices, or applications that involves programmatically interacting through software. It can be used for connecting to individual devices or multiple devices simultaneously.

area border router (ABR) A router that connects an OSPF area to Area 0 (that is, the backbone area).

AS_Path A BGP attribute used to track the autonomous systems a network has been advertised through as a loop-prevention mechanism.

AS path access control list (ACL) An ACL based on regex for identifying BGP routes based on the AS path and used for direct filtering or conditional matching in a route map.

atomic aggregate A BGP path attribute which indicates that a prefix has been summarized, and not all of the path information from component routes was included in the aggregate.

authentication, authorization, and accounting (AAA) An architectural framework that enables secure network access control for users and devices.

authentication server (AS) An 802.1x entity that authenticates users or clients based on their credentials, as matched against a user database. In a wireless network, a RADIUS server is an AS.

authenticator An 802.1x entity that exists as a network device that provides access to the network. In a wireless network, a WLC acts as an authenticator.

autonomous AP A wireless AP operating in a standalone mode, such that it can provide a fully functional BSS and connect to the DS.

autonomous system (AS) A set of routers running the same routing protocol under a single realm of control and authority.

B

backbone area The OSPF Area 0, which connects to all other OSPF areas. The backbone area is the only area that should provide connectivity between all other OSPF areas.

backup designated router (BDR) A backup pseudonode that maintains the network segment's state to replace the DR in the event of its failure.

band A contiguous range of frequencies.

bandwidth The range of frequencies used by a single channel or a single RF signal.

beamwidth A measure of the angle of a radiation pattern in both the E and H planes, where the signal strength is 3 dB below the maximum value.

BGP community A well-known BGP attribute that allows for identification of routes for later actions such as identification of source or route filtering/modification.

BGP multihoming A method of providing redundancy and optimal routing that involves adding multiple links to external autonomous systems.

BPDU filter An STP feature that filters BPDUs from being advertised/received across the configured port.

BPDU guard An STP feature that places a port into an ErrDisabled state if a BPDU is received on a portfast-enabled port.

bridge protocol data unit (BPDU) A network packet that is used to identify a hierarchy and notify of changes in the topology.

broadcast domain A portion of a network where a single broadcast can be advertised or received.

building block A distinct place in the network (PIN) such as the campus end-user/endpoint block, the WAN edge block, the Internet edge block, or the network services block. The components of each building block are the access layer, the distribution layer, and/or the core (backbone) layer. Also known as a network block or a place in the network (PIN).

C

CAPWAP A standards-based tunneling protocol that defines communication between a lightweight AP and a wireless LAN controller.

carrier signal The basic, steady RF signal that is used to carry other useful information.

centralized WLC deployment See *unified WLC deployment*.

channel An arbitrary index that points to a specific frequency within a band.

Cisco Advanced Malware Protection (AMP) A Cisco malware analysis and protection solution that goes beyond point-in-time detection and provides comprehensive protection for organizations across the full attack continuum: before, during, and after an attack.

Cisco Express Forwarding (CEF) A method of forwarding packets in hardware through the use of the FIB and adjacency tables. CEF is much faster than process switching.

Cisco Identity Services Engine (ISE) A Cisco security policy management platform that provides highly secure network access control to users and devices across wired, wireless, and VPN connections. It allows for visibility into what is happening in the network, such as who is connected (endpoints, users, and devices), which applications are installed and running on endpoints (for posture assessment), and much more.

Cisco SAFE A framework that helps design secure solutions for the campus, data center, cloud, WAN, branch, and edge.

Cisco Secure Client A VPN client that is an 802.1x supplicant that can perform posture validations and that provides web security, network visibility into endpoint flows within Cisco Secure Network Analytics, and roaming protection with Cisco Umbrella.

Cisco Secure Email A Cisco solution that enables users to communicate securely via email and helps organizations combat email security threats with a multilayered approach across the attack continuum.

Cisco Secure Firewall A next-generation firewall (NGFW) with legacy firewall capabilities such as stateful inspection as well as integrated intrusion prevention, application-level inspection, and techniques to address evolving security threats, such as advanced malware and application-layer attacks.

Cisco Secure Malware Analytics A malware sandbox solution.

Cisco Secure Network Analytics A Cisco collector and aggregator of network telemetry data (NetFlow data) that performs network security analysis and monitoring to automatically detect threats that manage to infiltrate a network as well as threats that originate within a network.

Cisco Secure Web Appliance An all-in-one web gateway that includes a wide variety of protections that can block advanced threats from both suspicious and legitimate websites.

Cisco Talos The Cisco threat intelligence organization.

Cisco TrustSec A next-generation access control enforcement solution developed by Cisco that performs network enforcement by using Security Group Tags (SGTs) instead of IP addresses and ports. In SD-Access, Cisco TrustSec Security Group Tags are referred to as Scalable Group Tags.

Cisco Umbrella A Cisco solution that blocks requests to malicious Internet destinations (domains, IP addresses, URLs) using Domain Name System (DNS).

Client density The relative number of client devices served by an AP and its antenna, as determined by the antenna's RF coverage pattern.

collision domain A set of devices in a network that can transmit data packets that can collide with other packets sent by other devices (that is, devices that can detect traffic from other devices using CSMA/CD).

command-line interface (CLI) A text-based user interface for configuring network devices individually by inputting configuration commands.

Common Spanning Tree (CST) A single spanning-tree instance for the entire network, as defined in the 802.1D standard.

configuration BPDU The BPDU that is responsible for switches electing a root bridge and communicating the root path cost so that a hierarchy can be built.

container An isolated environment where containerized applications run. It contains the application along with the dependencies that the application needs to run. It is created by a container engine running a container image.

container image A file created by a container engine that includes application code along with its dependencies. Container images become containers when they are run by a container engine.

content addressable memory (CAM) A high-performance table used to correlate MAC addresses to switch interfaces that they are attached to.

control plane policing (CoPP) A policy applied to the control plane of a router to protect the CPU from high rates of traffic that could impact router stability.

cookbook A Chef container that holds recipes.

core layer The network layer, also known as the backbone, that provides high-speed connectivity between distribution layers in large environments.

D

Datagram Transport Layer Security (DTLS) A communications protocol designed to provide authentication, data integrity, and confidentiality for communications between two applications, over a datagram transport protocol such as User Datagram Protocol (UDP). DTLS is based on TLS, and it includes enhancements such as sequence numbers and retransmission capability to compensate for the unreliable nature of UDP. DTLS is defined in IETF RFC 4347.

dBd dB-dipole, the gain of an antenna, measured in dB, as compared to a simple dipole antenna.

dBi dB-isotropic, the gain of an antenna, measured in dB, as compared to an isotropic reference antenna.

dBm dB-milliwatt, the power level of a signal measured in dB, as compared to a reference signal power of 1 milliwatt.

dead interval The amount of time required for a hello packet to be received for the neighbor to be deemed healthy. Upon receipt, the value resets and decrements toward zero.

decibel (dB) A logarithmic function that compares one absolute measurement to another.

demodulation The receiver's process of interpreting changes in the carrier signal to recover the original information being sent.

designated port (DP) A network port that receives and forwards BPDUs to other downstream switches.

designated router (DR) (Context of OSPF) A pseudonode to manage the adjacency state with other routers on the broadcast network segment.

designated router (DR) (Context of PIM) A PIM-SM router that is elected in a LAN segment when multiple PIM-SM routers exist to prevent the sending of duplicate multicast traffic into the LAN or the RP.

DevNet A single place to go to enhance or increase skills with APIs, coding, Python, and even controller concepts.

Differentiated Services (DiffServ) A field that uses the same 8 bits of the IP header that were previously used for the ToS and IPv6 Traffic Class fields. This allows it to be backward compatible with IP Precedence. The DiffServ field is composed of a 6-bit Differentiated Services Code Point (DSCP) field that allows for classification of up to 64 values (0 to 63) and a 2-bit Explicit Congestion Notification (ECN) field.

Differentiated Services Code Point (DSCP) A 6-bit field within the DiffServ field that allows for classification of up to 64 values (0 to 63).

dipole An omnidirectional antenna composed of two wire segments.

direct sequence spread spectrum (DSSS) A wireless LAN method in which a transmitter uses a single fixed, wide channel to send data.

directional antenna A type of antenna that propagates an RF signal in a narrow range of directions.

directly attached static route A static route that defines only the outbound interface for the next-hop device.

discontiguous network An OSPF network where Area 0 is not contiguous and generally results in routes not being advertised pervasively through the OSPF routing domain.

distance vector routing protocol A routing protocol that selects the best path based on next hop and hop count.

distribute list A list used for filtering routes with an ACL for a specific BGP neighbor.

distribution layer The network layer that provides an aggregation point for the access layer and acts as a services and control boundary between the access layer and the core layer.

downstream Away from the source of a tree and toward the receivers.

downstream interface An interface that is used to forward multicast traffic down the tree, also known as the outgoing interface (OIF).

dynamic rate shifting (DRS) A mechanism used by an 802.11 device to change the modulation coding scheme (MCS) according to dynamic RF signal conditions.

Dynamic Trunking Protocol (DTP) A protocol that allows for the dynamic negotiation of trunk ports.

E

E plane The "elevation" plane, which passes through an antenna that shows a side view of the radiation pattern.

eBGP session A BGP session maintained with BGP peers from a different autonomous system.

effective isotropic radiated power (EIRP) The resulting signal power level, measured in dBm, of the combination of a transmitter, cable, and an antenna, as measured at the antenna.

egress tunnel router (ETR) A router that de-encapsulates LISP-encapsulated IP packets coming from other sites and destined to EIDs within a LISP site.

Embedded Event Manager (EEM) An on-box automation tool that allows scripts to automatically execute, based on the output of an action or an event on a device.

embedded WLC deployment A wireless network design that places a WLC in the access layer, co-located with a LAN switch stack, near the APs it controls.

endpoint A device that connects to a network, such as a laptop, tablet, IP phone, personal computer (PC), or Internet of Things (IoT) device.

endpoint identifier (EID) The IP address of an endpoint within a LISP site.

enhanced distance vector routing protocol A routing protocol that selects the best path based on next hop, hop count, and other metrics, such as bandwidth and delay.

equal-cost multipathing The installation of multiple best paths from the same routing protocol with the same metric that allows for load-balancing of traffic across the paths.

ERSPAN Encapsulated Remote Switched Port Analyzer, a tool for capturing network traffic on a remote device and sending the traffic to the local system via Layer 3 (routing) toward a local port that would be attached to some sort of traffic analyzer.

EtherChannel bundle A logical interface that consists of physical member links to increase a link's bandwidth while preventing forwarding loops.

Extensible Authentication Protocol (EAP) A standardized authentication framework defined by RFC 4187 that provides encapsulated transport for authentication parameters.

Extensible Markup Language (XML) A human-readable data format that is commonly used with web services.

F

feasibility condition A condition under which, for a route to be considered a backup route, the reported distance received for that route must be less than the feasible distance calculated locally. This logic guarantees a loop-free path.

feasibility successor A route that satisfies the feasibility condition and is maintained as a backup route.

feasible distance The metric value for the lowest-metric path to reach a destination.

Firepower Threat Defense (FTD) software image A single unified image in which the ASA software image and the Cisco Secure IPS image are merged. It is supported on all Cisco Secure Firewall and ASA 5500-X appliances (except the 5585-X).

first-hop redundancy protocol A protocol that creates a virtual IP address on a router or a multilayer device to ensure continuous access to a gateway when there are redundant devices.

first-hop router (FHR) A router that is directly attached to the source, also known as the root router. It is responsible for sending register messages to the RP.

floating static route A static route with an elevated AD so that it is used only as a backup in the event that a routing protocol fails or a lower-AD static route is removed from the RIB.

foreign controller The current controller that a client is associated with after a Layer 3 intercontroller roam. Traffic is tunneled from the foreign controller back to an anchor controller so that the client retains connectivity to its original VLAN and subnet.

forward delay The amount of time that a port stays in a listening and learning state.

Forwarding Information Base (FIB) The hardware programming of a forwarding table. The FIB uses the RIB for programming.

frequency The number of times a signal makes one complete up and down cycle in 1 second.

fully specified static route A static route that specifies the next-hop IP address and the outbound interface.

G

gain A measure of how effectively an antenna can focus RF energy in a certain direction.

GitHub An efficient and commonly adopted way of using version control for code and sharing code repositories.

grain In SaltStack, code that runs on nodes to gather system information and report back to the master.

H

H plane The "azimuth" plane, which passes through an antenna that shows a top-down view of the radiation pattern.

hello interval The frequency at which hello packets are advertised out an interface.

hello packets Packets that are sent out at periodic intervals to detect neighbors for establishing adjacency and ensuring that neighbors are still available.

hello time The time interval for which a BPDU is advertised out of a port.

hello timer The amount of time between the advertisement of hello packets and when they are sent out an interface.

hertz (Hz) A unit of frequency equaling one cycle per second.

host pool The IP subnet, SVI, and VRF information assigned to a group of hosts that share the same policies.

hypervisor Virtualization software that creates VMs and performs the hardware abstraction that allows multiple VMs to run concurrently.

I

iBGP session A BGP session maintained with BGP peers from the same autonomous system.

IGMP snooping A mechanism to prevent multicast flooding on a Layer 2 switch.

in phase The condition when the cycles of two identical signals are in sync with each other.

incoming interface (IIF) The only type of interface that can accept multicast traffic coming from the source. It is the same as the RPF interface.

ingress tunnel router (ITR) A router that LISP-encapsulates IP packets coming from EIDs that are destined outside the LISP site.

inside global The public IP address that represents one or more inside local IP addresses to the outside.

inside local The actual private IP address assigned to a device on the inside network(s).

integrated antenna A very small omnidirectional antenna that is set inside a device's outer case.

inter-area route An OSPF route learned from an ABR from another area. These routes are built based on type 3 LSAs.

intercontroller roaming Client roaming that occurs between two APs that are joined to two different controllers.

interface priority The reference value for an interface to determine preference for being elected as the designated router.

internal spanning tree (IST) The first MSTI in the MST protocol. The IST is responsible for building a CST across all VLANs, regardless of their VLAN membership. The IST contains advertisements for other MSTIs in its BPDUs.

Internet Group Management Protocol (IGMP) The protocol used by receivers to join multicast groups and start receiving traffic from those groups.

Internet Key Exchange (IKE) A protocol that performs authentication between two endpoints to establish security associations (SAs), also known as IKE tunnels. IKE is the implementation of ISAKMP using the Oakley and Skeme key exchange techniques.

Internet Protocol Security (IPsec) A framework of open standards for creating highly secure VPNs using various protocols and technologies for secure communication across unsecure networks such as the Internet.

Internet Security Association and Key Management Protocol (ISAKMP) A framework for authentication and key exchange between two peers to establish, modify, and tear down SAs that is designed to support many different kinds of key exchanges. ISAKMP uses UDP port 500 to communicate between peers.

intra-area route An OSPF route learned from a router within the same area. These routes are built based on type 1 and type 2 LSAs.

intracontroller roaming Client roaming that occurs between two APs joined to the same controller.

IP SLA An on-box diagnostic tool that executes probes to monitor network devices and application performance.

isotropic antenna An ideal, theoretical antenna that radiates RF equally in every direction.

J

JavaScript Object Notation (JSON) Notation used to store data in key/value pairs that is said to be easier to work with and read than XML.

K

K values Values that EIGRP uses to calculate the best path.

L

LACP interface priority An attribute assigned to a switch port on an LACP primary switch to identify which member links are used when there is a maximum link.

LACP system priority An attribute in an LACP packet that provides priority to one switch over another to control which links are used when there is a maximum link.

last-hop router (LHR) A router that is directly attached to the receivers, also known as a leaf router. It is responsible for sending PIM joins upstream toward the RP or to the source after an SPT switchover.

Layer 2 forwarding The forwarding of packets based on the packets' destination Layer 2 addresses, such as MAC addresses.

Layer 2 roam An intercontroller roam where the WLANs of the two controllers are configured for the same Layer 2 VLAN ID; also known as a local-to-local roam.

Layer 3 forwarding The forwarding of packets based on the packets' destination IP addresses.

Layer 3 roam An intercontroller roam where the WLANs of the two controllers are configured for different VLAN IDs; also known as a local-to-foreign roam. To support the roaming client, a tunnel is built between the controllers so that client data can pass between the client's current controller and its original controller.

lightweight AP A wireless AP that performs real-time 802.11 functions to interface with wireless clients, while relying on a wireless LAN controller to handle all management functions.

link budget The cumulative sum of gains and losses measured in dB over the complete RF signal path; a transmitter's power level must overcome the link budget so that the signal can reach a receiver effectively.

link-state routing protocol A routing protocol that contains a complete view of the topology, where every router can calculate the best path based on its copy of the topology.

LISP router A router that performs the functions of any or all of the following: ITR, ETR, PITR, and/or PETR.

LISP site A site where LISP routers and EIDs reside.

load-balancing hash An algorithm for balancing network traffic across member links.

Loc-RIB table The main BGP table that contains all the active BGP prefixes and path attributes that is used to select the best path and install routes into the RIB.

local bridge identifier A combination of the advertising switch's bridge system MAC, the system ID extension, and the system priority of the local bridge.

local mode The default mode of a Cisco lightweight AP that offers one or more functioning BSSs on a specific channel.

Locator/ID Separation Protocol (LISP) A routing architecture and data and control plane protocol that was created to address routing scalability problems on large networks.

M

MAC address table A table on a switch that identifies the switch port and VLAN with which a MAC address is associated for Layer 2 forwarding.

MAC Authentication Bypass (MAB) A network access control technique that enables port-based access control using the MAC address of an endpoint and is typically used as a fallback mechanism to 802.1x.

MACsec An IEEE 802.1AE standards-based Layer 2 link encryption technology used by TrustSec to encrypt Secure Group Tag (SGT) frames on Layer 2 links between switches and between switches and endpoints.

manifest In Puppet, the code to be executed that is contained within modules.

map resolver (MR) A network device (typically a router) that receives LISP-encapsulated map requests from an ITR and finds the appropriate ETR to answer those requests by consulting the map server. If requested by the ETR, the MS can reply on behalf of the ETR.

map server (MS) A network device (typically a router) that learns EID-to-prefix mapping entries from an ETR and stores them in a local EID-to-RLOC mapping database.

map server/map resolver (MS/MR) A device that performs MS and MR functions. The MS function learns EID-to-prefix mapping entries from an ETR and stores them in a local EID-to-RLOC mapping database. The MR function receives LISP-encapsulated map requests from an ITR and finds the appropriate ETR to answer those requests by consulting the mapping server. If requested by the ETR, the MS can reply on behalf of the ETR.

Max Age The timer that controls the maximum length of time that passes before a bridge port saves its BPDU information.

maximal-ratio combining (MRC) An 802.11n technique that combines multiple copies of a signal, received over multiple antennas, to reconstruct the original signal.

member links The physical links used to build a logical EtherChannel bundle.

mobility domain A logical grouping of all mobility groups within an enterprise.

Mobility Express WLC deployment A wireless network design that places a WLC co-located with a lightweight AP.

mobility group A logical grouping of one or more MCs between which efficient roaming is expected.

modulation The transmitter's process of altering the carrier signal according to some other information source.

module A Puppet container that holds manifests.

MST instance (MSTI) A single spanning-tree instance for a specified set of VLANs in the MST protocol.

MST region A collection of MSTIs that operate in the same MST domain.

MST region boundary Any switch port that connects to another switch in a different MST region or that connects to a traditional 802.1D or 802.1W STP instance.

Multicast Forwarding Information Base (MFIB) A forwarding table that derives information from the MRIB to program multicast forwarding information in hardware for faster forwarding.

Multicast Routing Information Base (MRIB) A topology table that is also known as the multicast route table (mroute), which derives from the unicast routing table and PIM.

multicast state The traffic forwarding state that is used by a router to forward multicast traffic. The multicast state is composed of the entries found in the mroute table (S, G, IIF, OIF, and so on).

N

narrowband RF signals that use a very narrow range of frequencies.

native VLAN A VLAN that correlates to any untagged network traffic on a trunk port.

NETCONF A protocol defined by the IETF for installing, manipulating, and deleting the configuration of network devices.

NetFlow A Cisco network protocol for exporting flow information generated from network devices in order to analyze traffic statistics.

Network Address Translation (NAT) The systematic modification of source and/or destination IP headers on a packet from one IP address to another.

network block See *building block.*

Network Configuration Protocol (NETCONF)/YANG An IETF standard protocol that uses the YANG data models to communicate with the various devices on the network. NETCONF runs over SSH, TLS, or Simple Object Access Protocol (SOAP).

network function (NF) The function performed by a physical appliance, such as a firewall function or a router function.

network functions virtualization (NFV) An architectural framework created by the European Telecommunications Standards Institute (ETSI) that defines standards to decouple network functions from proprietary hardware-based appliances and have them run in software on standard x86 servers.

network LSA A type 2 LSA that advertises the routers connected to the DR pseudonode. Type 2 LSAs remain within the OSPF area of origination.

NFV infrastructure (NFVI) All the hardware and software components that comprise the platform environment in which virtual network functions (VNFs) are deployed.

noise floor The average power level of noise measured at a specific frequency.

nonce A random or pseudo-random number issued in an authentication protocol that can be used just once to prevent replay attacks.

NTP client A device that queries a time server by using Network Time Protocol so that it can synchronize its time to the server.

NTP peer A device that queries another peer device using Network Time Protocol so that the two devices can synchronize and adjust their time to each other.

NTP server A device that provides time to clients that query it with Network Time Protocol.

O

omnidirectional antenna A type of antenna that propagates an RF signal in a broad range of directions in order to cover a large area.

Open Authentication An 802.11 authentication method that requires clients to associate with an AP without providing any credentials at all.

optional non-transitive A BGP path attribute that might be recognized by a BGP implementation that is not advertised between autonomous systems.

optional transitive A BGP path attribute that might be recognized by a BGP implementation that is advertised between autonomous systems.

Orthogonal Frequency Division Multiplexing (OFDM) A data transmission method that sends data bits in parallel over multiple frequencies within a single 20 MHz wide channel. Each frequency represents a single subcarrier.

out of phase The condition when the cycles of one signal are shifted in time in relation to another signal.

outgoing interface (OIF) An interface that is used to forward multicast traffic down the tree, also known as the downstream interface.

outgoing interface list (OIL) A group of OIFs that are forwarding multicast traffic to the same group.

outside global The public IP address assigned to a host on the outside network by the owner of the host. This IP address must be reachable by the outside network.

outside local The IP address of an outside host as it appears to the inside network. The IP address does not have to be reachable by the outside but is considered private and must be reachable by the inside network.

overlay network A logical or virtual network built over a physical transport network referred to as an underlay network.

P

parabolic dish antenna A highly directional antenna that uses a passive dish shaped like a parabola to focus an RF signal into a tight beam.

passive interface An interface that has been enabled with a routing protocol to advertise its associated interfaces into its RIB but that does not establish neighborship with other routers associated to that interface.

patch antenna A directional antenna that has a planar surface and is usually mounted on a wall or column.

Path Trace A visual troubleshooting tool in Cisco DNA Center Assurance that is used to trace a route and display the path throughout the network between wired or wireless hosts.

path vector routing protocol A routing protocol that selects the best path based on path attributes.

per-hop behavior (PHB) The QoS action applied to a packet (expediting, delaying, or dropping) on a hop-by-hop basis, based on its DSCP value.

personal mode Pre-Shared Key authentication as applied to WPA, WPA2, or WPA3.

phase A measure of shift in time relative to the start of a cycle; ranges between 0 and 360 degrees.

pillar A SaltStack value store that stores information that a minion can access from the master.

place in the network (PIN) See *building block*.

play In Ansible, the code to be executed that is contained within playbooks.

playbook An Ansible container that holds plays.

polar plot A round graph that is divided into 360 degrees around an antenna and into concentric circles that represent decreasing dB values. The antenna is always placed at the center of the plot.

polarization The orientation (horizontal, vertical, circular, and so on) of a propagating wave with respect to the ground.

policy-based routing Conditional forwarding of packets based on packet characteristics besides the destination IP address; for example, routing by protocol type (ICMP, TCP, UDP, and so on) or routing by source IP address, destination IP address, or both.

pooled NAT A dynamic one-to-one mapping of a local IP address to a global IP address. The global IP address is temporarily assigned to a local IP address. After a certain amount of idle NAT time, the global IP address is returned to the pool.

Port Address Translation (PAT) A dynamic many-to-one mapping of a global IP address to many local IP addresses. The NAT device keeps track of the global IP address-to-local IP address mappings using multiple different port numbers.

precision time protocol A mechanism to provide clock synchronization for networked measurement and control systems.

prefix length The number of leading binary bits in the subnet mask that are in the on position.

prefix list A method of selecting routes based on binary patterns, specifically the high-order bit pattern, high-order bit count, and an optional prefix length parameter.

privilege level A Cisco IOS CLI designation of what commands are available to a user.

process switching The process of forwarding traffic by software and processing by the general CPU. It is typically slower than hardware switching.

Protocol Independent Multicast (PIM) A multicast routing protocol that routes multicast traffic between network segments. PIM can use any of the unicast routing protocols to identify the path between the source and receivers.

proxy ETR (PETR) An ETR but for LISP sites that sends traffic to destinations at non-LISP sites.

proxy ITR (PITR) An ITR but for a non-LISP site that sends traffic to EID destinations at LISP sites.

proxy xTR (PxTR) A router that performs proxy ITR (PITR) and proxy ETR (PETR) functions.

PVST simulation check The process of ensuring that the MST region is the STP root bridge for all the VLANs or none of the VLANs. If the MST region is a partial STP root bridge, the port is shut down.

Python A commonly used programming language that is easy to interpret and use. It is often used to manage network devices and for software scripting.

Q

quadrature amplitude modulation (QAM) A modulation method that combines QPSK phase shifting with multiple amplitude levels to produce a greater number of unique changes to the carrier signal. The number preceding the QAM name designates how many carrier signal changes are possible.

R

radiation pattern A plot that shows the relative signal strength in dBm at every angle around an antenna.

radio frequency (RF) The portion of the frequency spectrum between 3 kHz and 300 GHz.

RADIUS server An authentication server used with 802.1x to authenticate wireless clients.

received signal strength (RSS) The signal strength level in dBm that an AP receives from a wireless device.

received signal strength indicator (RSSI) The relative measure of signal strength (0 to 255), as seen by the receiver.

recipe In Chef, the code to be executed that is contained within cookbooks.

recursive static route A static route that specifies the next-hop IP address and requires the router to recursively locate the outbound interface for the next-hop device.

regular expressions (regex) Search patterns that use special key characters for parsing and matching.

Remote Authentication Dial-In User Service (RADIUS) An AAA protocol that is primarily used to enable network access control (secure access to network resources).

rendezvous point (RP) A single common root placed at a chosen point of a shared distribution tree. In other words, it is the root of a shared distribution tree known as a rendezvous point tree (RPT).

rendezvous point tree (RPT) Also known as a shared tree, a multicast distribution tree where the root of the shared tree is not the source but a router designated as the rendezvous point (RP).

reported distance The distance reported by a router to reach a prefix. The reported distance value is the feasible distance for the advertising router.

RESTCONF An IETF draft that describes how to map a YANG specification to a RESTful interface.

Reverse Path Forwarding (RPF) interface The interface with the lowest-cost path (based on administrative distance [AD] and metric) to the IP address of the source (SPT) or the RP.

RF fingerprinting A method used to accurately determine wireless device location by applying a calibration model to the location algorithm so that the RSS values measured also reflect the actual environment.

root bridge The topmost switch in an STP topology. The root bridge is responsible for controlling STP timers, creating configuration BPDUs, and processing topology change BPDUs. All ports on a root bridge are designated ports that are in a forwarding state.

root bridge identifier A combination of the root bridge system MAC address, system ID extension, and system priority of the root bridge.

root guard An STP feature that places a port into an ErrDisabled state if a superior BPDU is received on the configured port.

root path cost The cost for a specific path toward the root switch.

root port The most preferred switch port that connects a switch to the root bridge. Often this is the switch port with the lowest root path cost.

route map A feature used in BGP (and other IGP components) that allows for filtering or modification of routes using a variety of conditional matching.

router ID (RID) A 32-bit number that uniquely identifies the router in a routing domain.

router LSA A type 1 LSA that is a fundamental building block representing an OSPF-enabled interface. Type 1 LSAs remain within the OSPF area of origination.

Routing Information Base (RIB) The software database of all the routes, next-hop IP addresses, and attached interfaces. Also known as a routing table.

routing locator (RLOC) An IPv4 or IPv6 address of an ETR that is Internet facing or network core facing.

RPF neighbor The PIM neighbor on the RPF interface.

RSPAN Remote Switched Port Analyzer, a tool for capturing network traffic on a remote switch and sending a copy of the network traffic to the local switch via Layer 2 (switching) toward a local port that would be attached to some sort of traffic analyzer.

S

Scalable Group Tag (SGT) A technology that is used to perform ingress tagging and egress filtering to enforce access control policy. The SGT tag assignment is delivered to the authenticator as an authorization option. After the SGT tag is assigned, an access enforcement policy based on the SGT tag can be applied at any egress point of the TrustSec network. In SD-Access, Cisco TrustSec Security Group Tags are referred to as Scalable Group Tags.

Secure Shell (SSH) A secure network communication protocol that provides secure encryption and strong authentication.

Security Group Access Control List (SGACL) A technology that provides filtering based on source and destination SGT tags.

segment An overlay network.

segmentation A process that enables a single network infrastructure to support multiple Layer 2 or Layer 3 overlay networks.

sensitivity level The RSSI threshold (in dBm) that divides unintelligible RF signals from useful ones.

service chaining Chaining VNFs together to provide an NFV service or solution.

shortest path tree (SPT) A router's view of the topology to reach all destinations in the topology, where the router is the top of the tree, and all of the destinations are the branches of the tree. In the context of multicast, the SPT provides a multicast distribution tree where the source is the root of the tree and branches form a distribution tree through the network all the way down to the receivers. When this tree is built, it uses the shortest path through the network from the source to the leaves of the tree.

signal-to-noise ratio (SNR) A measure of received signal quality, calculated as the difference between the signal's RSSI and the noise floor. A higher SNR is preferred.

Simple Network Management Protocol (SNMP) A protocol that can send alerts when something fails on a device as well as when certain events happen on a device (for example, power supply failure).

SPAN Switched Port Analyzer, a tool for capturing local network traffic on a switch and sending a copy of the network traffic to a local port that would be attached to some sort of traffic analyzer.

spatial multiplexing Distributing streams of data across multiple radio chains with spatial diversity.

spatial stream An independent stream of data that is sent over a radio chain through free space. One spatial stream is separate from others due to the unique path it travels through space.

split-MAC architecture A wireless AP strategy based on the idea that normal AP functions are split or divided between a wireless LAN controller and lightweight APs.

spread spectrum RF signals that spread the information being sent over a wide range of frequencies.

static NAT A static one-to-one mapping of a local IP address to a global IP address.

static null route A static route that specifies the virtual null interface as the next hop as a method of isolating traffic or preventing routing loops.

STP loop guard An STP feature that prevents a configured alternative or root port from becoming a designated port toward a downstream switch.

STP portfast An STP feature that places a switch port directly into a forwarding state and disables TCN generation for a change in link state.

stratum A level that makes it possible to identify the accuracy of the time clock source, where the lower the stratum number, the more accurate the time is considered.

successor The first next-hop router for the successor route.

successor route The route with the lowest path metric to reach a destination.

summarization A method of reducing a routing table by advertising a less specific network prefix in lieu of multiple more specific network prefixes.

summary LSA A type 3 LSA that contains the routes learned from another area. Type 3 LSAs are generated on ABRs.

supplicant An 802.1x entity that exists as software on a client device and serves to request network access.

syslog Logging of messages that can be sent to a collector server or displayed on the console or stored in the logging buffer on the local device.

system ID extension A 12-bit value that indicates the VLAN that the BPDU correlates to.

system priority A 4-bit value that indicates the preference for a switch to be root bridge.

T

Tcl A scripting language that can be run on Cisco IOS devices to automate tasks such as **ping** scripts.

Telnet An insecure network communication protocol that communicates using plaintext and is not recommended for use in production environments.

Terminal Access Controller Access-Control System Plus (TACACS+) An AAA protocol that is primarily used to enable device access control (secure access to network devices).

ternary content addressable memory (TCAM) A high-performance table or tables that can evaluate packet forwarding decisions based on policies or access lists.

topology change notification (TCN) A BPDU that is advertised toward the root bridge to notify the root of a topology change on a downstream switch.

topology table A table used by EIGRP that maintains all network prefixes, advertising EIGRP neighbors for prefixes and path metrics for calculating the best path.

transit routing The act of allowing traffic to flow from one external autonomous system through your autonomous system to reach a different external autonomous system.

transmit beamforming (TBF) A method of transmitting a signal over multiple antennas, each having the signal phase carefully crafted, so that the multiple copies are all in phase at a targeted receiver.

trunk port A switch port that is configured for multiple VLANs and generally connects a switch to other switches or to other network devices, such as firewalls or routers.

tunnel router (xTR) A router that performs ingress tunnel router (ITR) and egress tunnel router (ETR) functions (which is most routers).

Type of Service (ToS) An 8-bit field where only the first 3 bits, referred to as IP Precedence (IPP), are used for marking, and the rest of the bits are unused. IPP values range from 0 to 7 and allow the traffic to be partitioned into up to six usable classes of service; IPP 6 and 7 are reserved for internal network use.

U

underlay network The traditional physical networking infrastructure that uses an IGP or a BGP.

unequal-cost load balancing The installation of multiple paths that include backup paths from the same routing protocol. Load balancing across the interface uses a traffic load in a ratio to the interface's route metrics.

Unidirectional Link Detection (UDLD) A protocol that provides bidirectional monitoring of fiber-optic cables.

unified WLC deployment A wireless network design that places a WLC centrally within a network topology.

upstream Toward the source of a tree, which could be the actual source with a source-based tree or the RP with a shared tree. A PIM join travels upstream toward the source.

upstream interface The interface toward the source of the tree. Also known as the RPF interface or the incoming interface (IIF).

V

variance value The feasible distance (FD) for a route multiplied by the EIGRP variance multiplier. Any feasible successor's FD with a metric below the EIGRP variance value is installed into the RIB.

virtual local area network (VLAN) A logical segmentation of switch ports based on the broadcast domain.

virtual machine (VM) A software emulation of a physical server with an operating system.

virtual network (VN) Virtualization at the device level, using virtual routing and forwarding (VRF) instances to create multiple Layer 3 routing tables.

virtual network function (VNF) The virtual version of an NF, typically run on a hypervisor as a VM (for example, a virtual firewall such as the Cisco Secure Firewall Threat Defense Virtual or a virtual router such as the Cisco Catalyst 8000V).

virtual private network (VPN) An overlay network that allows private networks to communicate with each other across an untrusted underlay network such as the Internet.

virtual switch (vSwitch) A software-based Layer 2 switch that operates like a physical Ethernet switch and enables VMs to communicate with each other within a virtualized server and with external physical networks using physical network interface cards (pNICs).

virtual tunnel endpoint (VTEP) An entity that originates or terminates a VXLAN tunnel. It maps Layer 2 and Layer 3 packets to the VNI to be used in the overlay network.

VLAN Trunking Protocol (VTP) A protocol that enables the provisioning of VLANs on switches.

VXLAN An overlay data plane encapsulation scheme that was developed to address the various issues seen in traditional Layer 2 networks. It does this by extending Layer 2 and Layer 3 overlay networks over a Layer 3 underlay network, using MAC-in-IP/UDP tunneling. Each overlay is termed a *VXLAN segment*.

VXLAN Group Policy Option (GPO) An enhancement to the VXLAN header that adds new fields to the first 4 bytes of the VXLAN header in order to support and carry up to 64,000 SGT tags.

VXLAN network identifier (VNI) A 24-bit field in the VXLAN header that enables up to 16 million Layer 2 and/or Layer 3 VXLAN segments to coexist within the same infrastructure.

W–X

wavelength The physical distance that a wave travels over one complete cycle.

Web Authentication (WebAuth) A network access control technique that enables access control by presenting a guest web portal requesting a username and password. It is typically used as a fallback mechanism to 802.1x and MAB.

well-known discretionary A BGP path attribute recognized by all BGP implementations that may or may not be advertised to other peers.

well-known mandatory A BGP path attribute recognized by all BGP implementations that must be advertised to other peers.

wide metrics A new method of advertising and identifying interface speeds and delay to account for higher-bandwidth interfaces (20 Gbps and higher).

Wi-Fi Protected Access (WPA) A Wi-Fi Alliance standard that requires Pre-Shared Key or 802.1x authentication, TKIP, and dynamic encryption key management; based on portions of 802.11i before its ratification.

wireless LAN controller (WLC) A device that controls and manages multiple lightweight APs.

WPA Version 2 (WPA2) A Wi-Fi Alliance standard that requires Pre-Shared Key or 802.1x authentication, TKIP or CCMP, and dynamic encryption key management; based on the complete 802.11i standard after its ratification.

WPA Version 3 (WPA3) The third version of a Wi-Fi Alliance standard, introduced in 2018, that requires Pre-Shared Key or 802.1x authentication, GCMP, SAE, and forward secrecy.

Y

Yagi antenna A directional antenna made up of several parallel wire segments that tend to amplify an RF signal to each other.

YANG Model A model that represents anything that can be configured or monitored, as well as all administrative actions that can be taken on a device.

Z

Zone Based Firewall (ZBFW) An IOS integrated stateful firewall.

Index

Numbers

A

B

C

D

E

F

J

K

L

M

N

O

P

Q

R

S

T

U

V

W

X-Y

Z

Companion Website and Pearson Test Prep Access Code

Access interactive study tools on this book's companion website, including practice test software, review exercises, a Key Term flash card application, a study planner, and more!

To access the companion website, simply follow these steps:

1. Go to **www.ciscopress.com/register.**
2. Enter the **print book ISBN:** 9780138216764.
3. Answer the security question to validate your purchase.
4. Go to your account page.
5. Click on the **Registered Products** tab.
6. Under the book listing, click on the **Access Bonus Content** link.

When you register your book, your Pearson Test Prep practice test access code will automatically be populated in your account under the Registered Products tab. You will need this code to access the practice test that comes with this book. You can redeem the code at **PearsonTestPrep.com.** Simply choose Pearson IT Certification as your product group and log in to the site with the same credentials you used to register your book. Click the **Activate New Product** button and enter the access code. More detailed instructions on how to redeem your access code for both the online and desktop versions can be found on the companion website.

If you have any issues accessing the companion website or obtaining your Pearson Test Prep practice test access code, you can contact our support team by going to **pearsonitp.echelp.org.**